MURROW:

His Life and Times

MURROW

His Life and Times

A. M. SPERBER

MICHAEL JOSEPH
LONDON

First published in Great Britain by Michael Joseph Ltd
27 Wrights Lane, London W8
1987

British Library Cataloguing in Publication Data
Sperber, A.M.
  Murrow : his life and times.
  1. Murrow, Edward   2. Broadcasters – United States
  – Biography
  791.44'092'4   PN1990.72.M/

  ISBN 0 7181 2809 5

Printed in Great Britain by
Butler & Tanner Ltd, Frome and London

The author and the publisher wish to thank Mrs. Edward R. Murrow and the
Murrow Estate for permission to quote from letters, and from correspondence
and broadcast manuscripts in the Murrow Collection, Tufts University, The
Fletcher School of Law and Diplomacy. Grateful acknowledgment is made to the
BBC Written Archives Centre, Caversham Park, Reading, for permission to quote
from BBC records. For permission to quote from private collections the author is
grateful to the following: David Halberstam, Harold R. Isaacs, Marvin Kalb,
Supreme Court Justice Lewis F. Powell, Jr., Wilmott Ragsdale, David
Schoenbrun, William L. Shirer, Chester S. Williams, and to Charles Kuralt, for
permission to excerpt from his talk, "Edward R. Murrow."

Acknowledgment is gratefully made to the following authors and publishers, for
permission to reprint from their work:

Edward Bliss, Jr., "Remembering Edward Murrow," *Saturday Review*, May 31,
1975.

"CBS: Of the People, By the People, for the People," Copyright © 1935, CBS,
Inc. All rights reserved. Originally broadcast over the CBS Radio Network.

Harry Castlemann and Walter J. Podrazik, *Watching TV: Four Decades of
American Television*, Copyright © 1981, McGraw-Hill Book Company.

Sinclair Lewis, abridged from *Elmer Gantry*, Harcurt Brace Jovanovich, Inc.

R. Franklin Smith: *Edward R. Murrow:* The War Years, copyright © 1978, New
Issues Press of Western Michigan University.

Theodore H. White, Excerpted from *The Making of The President*, 1972,
Copyright © 1973, Theodore H. White. Reprinted with the permission of
Atheneum Publishers, Inc.

FOR FRED AND LISA SPERBER
with gratitude

CONTENTS

FOREWORD

More than 1,300 people attended the Murrow funeral. Outside the church, on Madison Avenue, hundreds crowded the sidewalk, on the lookout for media stars. Inside, a celebrity-studded audience sat packed together in the Spanish Gothic gloom, an illustrated Who's Who of government and the press. Toward the front, not far from the family, were RCA Chairman David Sarnoff and William Paley of CBS; nearby were Averell Harriman, Robert Lovett, Adlai Stevenson. Carl Rowan, Murrow's successor as Director of the United States Information Agency, had come down as the representative for President Lyndon B. Johnson. Broadcasting celebrities sat stiffly, uncaring of their images, out of context. Robert Trout had the look of a man in a catatonic state. Walter and Betsy Cronkite were grim, the anchorman's avuncular features twisted into a glum mask, the old competition between him and Murrow momentarily set aside. A lineup of top correspondents—the ones known in the past as the Murrow boys, some still with CBS—formed an honor guard.

There was a brief service, a few words from the Reverend Arthur Kinsolving, but no speeches, then the recessional. The crowd broke up, moved toward the doors. Robert Kennedy stepped over to Janet Murrow. They talked for a few minutes, mostly about their time together in Washington and the Kennedy days. The Senator shook his head. "I wish Ed would have spoken more in the NSC." Then they followed the others out onto Madison Avenue.

The events of those weeks notwithstanding—marines in Santo Domingo, ground troops in Vietnam—the press still made room for one of its own: on page 1 of The New York *Times*; in headlines across the country; tributes in the editorial columns, some from the very papers that had tried repeatedly, in Murrow's lifetime, to drive him off the air. Write-ups and photos filled the center sections: the pioneer in radio and TV, shaper of the media, founding father of the CBS news team; the great American reporter, who had capped a brilliant broadcasting career with a second career in government and a cabinet seat in John Kennedy's Camelot.

Yet the attention was more than the press lauding its own, more than the expected splash over the passing of a news celebrity, even one long since out of the limelight. For a moment, it seemed, the clock had stopped. It was the end of an era, flashed in the banner headlines of the Scripps-Howard chain: ED MURROW IS DEAD, the passing of an age in which, for thirty years, he had played out his role.

Memorial programs went out over the networks, recalling the famous Murrow broadcasts—from the London rooftops in World War II; the 1954 telecast against Senator McCarthy; the controversial documentaries of the latter fifties. The New York *Times* saluted his "singular style and authority on the air," his "knack" for being "one jump ahead of the news, to plunge into the hot issue before it really got hot," his use of TV as a primary news source, rather than following on the heels of the print medium. Newsmen by now well into middle age recalled the colleague who had nurtured the careers of a list of names that read like an honor role of broadcasting. On the evening Cronkite program, Eric Sevareid's voice had tears in it: "He was a shooting star. . . ." *De mortuis nil nisi bonum.* "Good night, sweet prince." CBS ran an hourlong documentary with an epilogue by Murrow's longtime friend and former employer, William S. Paley, retracing Murrow's career while skirting the issues that had led to his embittered departure from broadcasting, four-and-a-half years prior to his death at fifty-seven of lung cancer.

In Washington there were tributes from the floors of both houses of Congress: George McGovern; Jack Javits; Scoop Jackson, speaking for Washington State, the broadcaster's boyhood home. Robert Kennedy quoted Shakespeare; Mike Mansfield, a personal friend, read in a halting voice, "Good night . . . and good luck . . . and thanks."

From the White House a Presidential statement took note of the occasion: ". . . We have all lost a friend." It raised a smile among those who knew the intense hatred that had flared at times between Ed Murrow and Lyndon Johnson. Cabled messages came in from governments in the West and the Third World. Consular officials in India wrote of small people—shopkeepers, laborers, clerical workers—stopping by to pay condolences. In England, Murrow's second home, the BBC ran special programs; the Queen had knighted him in the weeks just before his death.

In the sudden sweep of nostalgia—a moment of relief in a time of upheaval, assassinations, ghettos erupting, rumblings of hot summers to come—few voices sounded a dissonant note. Yet controversy, ever-present in Murrow's life, was hardly absent at his death. The *National Review* dubbed him "the father of a dangerous art form"; a Hearst paper noted "his drive to self-destruction." The TV critic for the *Saturday Review*, a former CBS producer and veteran of the blacklist, brought up the stories, never wholly denied or confirmed, of Murrow's troubles with his employers. In an article entitled "Murrow's Lost Fight," he recalled the broadcaster's address to his colleagues, back in 1958—the speech which, more than anything, had effectively ended his broadcasting career—urging TV to serve society, warning the industry that "if we go on as we are, then history will take its revenge . . . ."

> Then television and those who finance it, those who look at it and those who work at it, may see a totally different picture too late.

Who was this man?

The public persona was readily identifiable. Jack Gould, in The New York *Times*, called him the "man who put a spine in broadcasting," who extended almost single-handedly the perimeters of broadcast freedom. "There is not a major commentator on any network who will not agree that whatever he is privileged to say today in no small part is due to Mr. Murrow." Theodore White, in 1972:

> Murrow bequeathed a sense of conscience and importance with which neither management nor government might interfere. . . . And at CBS, a huge corporation more vulnerable than most to government pressure and Washington reprisal, he . . . left behind a tradition that the reporting of news . . . was to be what its correspondents and producers wanted it to be, not what management sought to make it. . . . It was as inconceivable for [Paley and Stanton] to lift the telephone and tell a Cronkite or a Sevareid what to say as, for example, the Elector of Saxony to tell Johann Sebastian Bach how to compose his music. . . .

Yet the man behind the Murrow legend was elusive—a fact apparent to anyone plumbing the recollections of those who knew him or thought they did: "A great man—in a class by himself" . . . "eye always on the main chance—an opportunist" . . . "he'd give you the shirt off his back— people took advantage of him" . . . "always measuring things in terms of his advantage—you'd never ask Ed Murrow to do anything for you" . . . "when he came into a room, the conversation *died*" . . . "a man who smiled a lot and joked a lot" . . . "that great self-confidence" . . . "suffering from some great disappointment—I felt sorry for him."

Ed Murrow kept no diaries, made few confidences. Like every human being, he was a composite of different personalities, drives, characteristics. He was a distinct American type, the product of an older social order, preindustrial, Calvinistic, with heavy overtones of guilt, a stern morality, and a sense of right and wrong that owed more to the Bible— "doing the right thing"—than to any set political doctrine. He came of the Anglo-Celtic stock that first settled the inland frontier, those historian Bernard De Voto called "the tall, gaunt, powerful, sallow, saturnine men," his basic values those of a society reflected in the pages of Hawthorne and Fenimore Cooper. If Murrow in his broadcasting career understood the American public, therefore, it was because he was of it—sometimes leading, sometimes merely reflecting, typical at all times of that public in its most, and occasionally less, admirable moments.

Those same origins, however, were a source of the contradictions that made a continuing battleground of his life and career: the skeptic versus the enthusiast; the olympian versus the activist; the loner versus the team player; the "man's man" shaped largely by women. And above all were the conflicts raised by what psychologists have noted as a basic dichotomy in the American Protestant tradition: the drive to do right versus the drive to do well. Yet Murrow succeeded in making those contradictions work for him, as a creative force in his profession; as writer and editor; as chronicler of his age and sometime mover; as a man repeatedly handed a situation for which no precedent existed, who created that precedent and on departing left the operation a going concern.

Quincy Howe, writing to Janet Murrow after the broadcaster's death, observed that the person with several talents often has a harder time of it than the person with only one talent: "Ed . . . was a perfectionist, in other words an artist, and his genius lay in the way he organized, channeled and eventually exhausted and expended all that was in him. Nobody can say where this spark comes from. Whenever and wherever it appears, it is a kind of miracle. . . ."

In his fifty-seven years Ed Murrow was to contend, on screen and off, with both the dichotomies in his nature and the questions raised by an era that saw the witch-hunts, the birth of the arms race, and worldwide military commitments:

How does a responsible broadcaster function in an industry caught between government licensing and the marketplace? Where does individual responsibility assert itself? How does one react when society no longer supports the just, when the absolutes of one age become the gray areas of another? When does going along turn into acquiescence? Can one, in fact, remain within the system and stay effective?

In a career spanning the years from the New Deal to Tonkin, in the watershed years of World War II and after, Murrow faced these and other questions—the moral choices confronting all those at the top levels of government and communications.

PROLOGUE

"I Have No Hope Whatever . . ."

"Dear Ed: A straight lead is the quickest way into a hard news story, and this is our story. . . ."

That was what had started it off—the invitation to Chicago. But those sending it out hadn't really expected him to accept. Murrow was the busiest man in broadcasting—TV documentaries; radio news, live, five nights a week; his Friday night *Person to Person* consistently in the top ten. He was a network unto himself, said *Time* magazine; the king of broadcast news.

Still, they had tried, writing to his office at CBS, New York City, in the spring of 1958. Would he address the upcoming meeting of the Radio-Television News Directors Association (RTNDA) at the Sheraton-Blackstone Wednesday evening, October 15, any subject of his choice? "Like yourself, the officers and directors of RTNDA have as their goals raising the sights and standards of broadcast news everywhere." The signature at the bottom was that of Bill Garry, news chief for CBS in Chicago and a regional vice-president of the RTNDA.

It was a long shot. Murrow had been cutting back on his personal appearances. Besides, he got hundreds of such requests, and he usually turned them down—once he got around to answering.

The answer, however, came within two weeks. Garry spotted the envelope in his in box at WBBM, recognized the unmistakable thick cream-colored letterhead marked simply "Edward R. Murrow/ 485 Madison Avenue/ New York 22." No company logo, just name and address elegantly embossed. Even the Chairman of the Board of CBS didn't use anything like it. But then, William Paley didn't earn as much as Ed Murrow—not in salary anyway. A story had once made the rounds that the Chairman, asked the reason at a stockholders' meeting, had reputedly smiled, with the faintest suggestion of a shrug, and said, "I guess he's worth more."

They were known to be extremely close, friends since the 1930s, wartime comrades-in-arms. Murrow was a pillar of the network—he had once been a company vice-president—unmoved by the fanciest outside offers, bound to CBS by ties of friendship and long-term contracts.

Garry was therefore unprepared for Murrow's response that April: Yes, he would love to try his hand at a piece for them: "Somebody ought to make a speech on one of those occasions which would outrage all of our employers. The only trouble is I don't know where the hell I will be on October 15th. . . . What is your deadline?"

William Small, News Director at WHAS in Louisville and program chairman for the convention, accepted on behalf of the surprised RTNDA leadership: delighted with his answer; never mind the deadline; they'd wait until mid-September if they had to.

As it turned out, they didn't have to. By late August Murrow had given them the go-ahead, his tone oddly combative: "This may do neither of us any good. . . ." He also told Small that he intended to write out the speech—another departure from standard practice; most RTNDA addresses were strictly informal, off the cuff. He intended, he said, to have the text distributed.

The directors restrained their curiosity, asked no questions. Confirming arrangements, Small assured Murrow they were looking forward to those words which would outrage their employers. Said Small later: "It didn't matter. We were just glad to have him."

The afternoon of October 15, he arrived at O'Hare with his news writer, Edward Bliss, Jr., and the text for the evening newscast. WBBM, the CBS-owned station in Chicago, sent a car around. The RTNDA had looked to the overnight accommodations for both men at the convention hotel.

They were driven first to the station, where Murrow did the nightly radio news, then on to the Blackstone for the reception already in progress. Small remembered Murrow as he appeared that day: tall—that always came as a shock to those who didn't know him; weary; a little older than he seemed on the screen; his smile, like his hands, faintly yellowed with flecks of nicotine from the ever-present cigarettes.

In a separate folder he carried the speech: twenty-one pages, double-spaced. Transcripts had begun going out to the major news media that morning, with release time set at 9:00 P.M. Copies had also gone to the CBS management. Throughout the months of work he had shown the original to no one—not even his partner and coproducer, Fred Friendly, his alter ego according to some, his *bête noire* in the eyes of others. Instead, everything had been carefully, quietly set up: the AP alerted, along with selected TV columnists; the *Reporter* magazine arranging for reprints; additional copies supplied for distribution by the RTNDA.

At the Blackstone he caught the tail end of the reception, everyone crowding around for a chance at the celebrity guest of honor, Leslie Atlass, formerly owner, now manager of WBBM, dancing attendance. Murrow was smiling but tense.

At seven-thirty they went in to dinner. He took his place on the dais, an RTNDA official on one side; on the other, Atlass, representing CBS. Mayor Richard Daley welcomed the newsmen to Chicago.

By nine, the formalities out of the way, Murrow rose to address the capacity audience crowding the Mayfair Room to the edges. It was a working session—the big bash, awards, black ties, was to come on Friday night—and they were working press, a small group in those days, run by and for local news directors across the country. The networks played a minor role.

He got the usual big hand as he stood before them, the establishment personified—gray suit, narrow lapels, the corporate uniform of the 1950s; hardly the picture of a rebel.

"This might just do nobody any good. . . ."

Down at the ballroom level Ed Bliss watched the men at his table exchange blank looks. What kind of opening was *that*?

"At the end of this discourse a few people may accuse this reporter of fouling his own comfortable nest, and your organization may be accused of having given hospitality to heretical and even dangerous thoughts. But . . . it is my desire, if not my duty, to try to talk to you journeymen with some candor about what is happening to radio and television. . . ."

"Candor" was, if anything, an understatement, as for the next twenty minutes the nation's highest-paid newsman, the friend of William Paley and David Sarnoff, early supporter of Dwight Eisenhower, golfing partner of U.S. senators and FCC commissioners, ripped away at the government, the administration, the broadcasting industry, and specifically those who paid his salary: "Our history will be what we make it. And if there are any historians about fifty or a hundred years from now, and there should be preserved the kinescopes for one week of all three networks, they will find there . . . evidence of decadence, escapism and insulation from the realities of the world in which we live. . . ." The audience mood had gone from quizzical to one of rapt attention.

> If there were to be a competition in indifference . . . then Nero and his fiddle, Chamberlain and his umbrella could not find a place on an early afternoon sustaining show. If Hollywood were to run out of Indians, the program schedules would be mangled. . . . Then some courageous soul with a small budget might be able to do a documentary telling what, in fact, we have done—and are still doing—to the Indians in this country. But that would be unpleasant. . . .

He hauled off against the FCC for rubber-stamping license renewals and abdicating its responsibilities under the Communications Act. The station owners, pledged to operate in the public interest, had "welshed" on their promises: "The money-making machine somehow blunts their memories." Leslie Atlass, sitting at Murrow's elbow, stared stonily into space, his face expressionless.

He scored the networks for "timidity":

> When my employer, CBS, . . . did an interview with Nikita Khrushchev, the President uttered a few ill-chosen uninformed words on the subject and the network practically apologized. . . .
>
> Likewise when John Foster Dulles, by personal decree, banned American journalists from going to Communist China . . . the networks entered only a mild protest. . . . Can it be that this national industry is content to leave its viewers in ignorance of the cataclysmic changes that are occurring in a nation of six hundred million people?
>
> Their spokesmen say, 'We are young; we have not developed the traditions . . . of the older media.' If they but knew it, they are building those traditions, creating those precedents every day. Each time they yield to a voice from Washington. . . .

Then he got to the nitty-gritty and, in doing so, broke the first taboo of broadcasting: "Sometimes there is a clash between the public interest and the corporate interest. . . . Upon occasion economic and editorial judgment are in conflict. . . ." With that he had placed himself beyond the pale. Statesmanlike speeches in broadcasting circles could be just about anything—government pressure, sponsor pressure, the difficulties of being a license-dependent business—anything but the bottom line.

He took a breath and dived in:

> One of the basic troubles with radio and television news is that both instruments have grown up as an incompatible combination of show business, advertising and news. Each of the three is a rather bizarre and demanding profession. And when you get all three under one roof, the dust never settles.
>
> The top management of the networks, with a few notable exceptions, has been trained in advertising, research, or show business. But by the nature of the corporate structure, they also make the final and crucial decisions having to do with news and public affairs. Frequently they have neither the time nor the competence to do this. . . .

This time it was the audience that drew breath, fascinated. Bill Small, watching Murrow from the dais, could detect no anger or rancor in his voice. What he heard were rather the accents of despair: "Let us have a little competition, not only in selling soap, cigarettes and automobiles. . . . Just once in a while let us exalt the importance of ideas. . . . Surely we shall pay . . . I mean the word *survive* literally . . ." And, repeatedly, "the money-making machine."

To the news director, the man at the rostrum, so conspicuously a beneficiary of the medium he now denounced with all the fervor of his puritan background, seemed a confessor still a little in love with his sins, a man in conflict not only with his industry but with himself, turning on what he had helped build up. "Potentially we have in this country a free enterprise system. . . . But to achieve its promise it must be both free and enterprising.

"There is no suggestion here that networks or individual stations should operate as philanthropies. But I can find nothing in the Bill of Rights or the Communications Act which says that they must increase their net profits each year, lest the Republic collapse."

Richard Salant, assistant to CBS President Frank Stanton and himself a company vice-president, was in the CBS boardroom when the speech came in, copies passed around among the assembled top management. Murrow had been sending transcripts upstairs for the last two days ("Here is a draft of what I am saying . . ."), directed to everyone in the hierarchy—except the company president and the chairman of the board.

Salant watched the speech go from hand to hand, the decibel level rising abruptly, the effect like that of Pearl Harbor night at the White House: "Ingrate! . . . Fouling his nest! . . . Biting the hand that feeds him! . . ." Said Salant later: "They were flabbergasted. The reactions were *so* strong—great surprise, anger. It was kind of like the child you've nurtured turning on you."

Down on the seventeenth floor, Sig Mickelson, President of CBS News, appeared in the doorway of the newsroom to announce the speech was to be given full play wherever possible.

Earlier in the day Stanton—cool, trim, perfectly in control—had withdrawn to his office to draft the company reply. On 17, CBS Press Information rushed out a release: "TO CITY AND TV EDITORS: IN RESPONSE TO INQUIRIES ON A TALK SCHEDULED TO BE MADE BY EDWARD R. MURROW. . . ."

Down the corridor, news writers were already at work sandwiching the details—first Murrow, then the rebuttal ("What he has to say does not, of course, reflect the views of CBS management . . .") into the 11:00 P.M. newscast, beating out the AP wire, with repeats slated for midnight, 1:00 A.M., and the early hours.

Nine-thirty in Chicago, Murrow was finishing up.

It may be that the present system . . . can survive. Perhaps the money-making machine has some kind of built-in perpetual motion, but I do not think so. . . . We are currently wealthy, fat, comfortable and complacent. . . . Our mass media reflect this. But unless we get up off our fat surpluses and recognize that television . . . is being used to distract, delude, amuse and insulate us, then television and those who finance it, those who look at it and those who work at it, may see a totally different picture too late. . . .

I began by saying that our history will be what we make it. If we go on as we are, then history will take its revenge, and retribution will not limp in catching up with us. . . .

There were a few seconds of silence, then roaring acclamation. Newsmen crowded around Murrow's place on the dais. An adman from Young & Rubicam nodded agreement. Bill Garry saw a colleague, a man known never to sit still for more than a few minutes at a time, turn to him, "It could have been longer, and he could have gone into more detail."

Bill Small and his wife guided Murrow to the elevator past scores of well-wishers waiting to shake his hand. There were no misgivings. "We felt it was a good, tough speech," said Small later, "that he said what needed saying."

Out in the corridor Murrow's face was momentarily dark as he muttered, "Dirty, rotten sonuvabitch!" Only one of those present caught it. Back in the ballroom someone he thought of as a friend had supposedly turned his back. " . . . coward . . ." A mistaken impression perhaps, perhaps not; it had been a long, tense evening.

Upstairs, they relaxed, Murrow back on his high—"I need a drink!" Glasses were passed around. No one referred to the speech, least of all Atlass. They engaged in small talk, shoptalk—anything but the events of the last two hours. Atlass, never careful with his language, indulged in a foul expression. Mrs. Small took offense; Murrow stepped in angrily. The speech, an unseen presence, hung over the suite.

In fact, it was a bombshell, both inside and outside the industry. TV, already undergoing investigation that fall for the quiz show scandals, had been exposed, denounced by one of its superstars. Murrow's challenge was picked up in TV columns, on the news pages, sometimes on the front pages across the country. In Chicago the RTNDA was inundated with requests for copies. The *Reporter*, which had carried the address *in toto*, received more than 2,000 requests for offprints in the first few days alone. Excerpts ran in publications as diverse as the *Times* of London, *Reader's Digest*, and the *New Republic*. The Los Angeles *Times'* television columnist devoted three days to the address, which otherwise got curt handling in the Southern California press.

The University of Chicago wanted offprints for the faculty. So did journalism schools and political science departments across the country. Bill Garry begged for more transcripts; not a single negative reaction, he reported: "My own reaction is that the thoughts expressed by you in Chicago will be quoted for months . . . to come; the most positive reactions will be reserved for the future."

The speech was praised by Walter Reuther and John Kenneth Galbraith, damned by Henry Luce; analyzed, discussed, kudoed, and condemned—as was Murrow himself, to a degree unrivaled since the time four years before, when he had taken on Joe McCarthy. This time, however, he was a general without an army.

The Chicago address, and the issue it raised, had indeed been given full play—in the print media; not, barring the brief news items of the first night, on network television.

The reason was obvious. As a *New Republic* reader commented, "Here is a man who has the ear of the industry; they can't simply shrug him off as a harmless crank."

What really stung Madison Avenue, in other words, was not merely the criticism; it was also the source. "Paley was furious about that speech," said Salant, "just furious. As he had a right to be. Ed had been part of management but chose to go outside. When somebody—not just staff, talent, but part of management—does that, it's seen as a breach of faith."

Not that there were wholesale or even noticeable reproaches on Murrow's return to New York. Not from Paley, who had withdrawn, or from anyone in the hierarchy. Murrow's social life with the CBS people seemed to continue as always. But a curtain of silence had been drawn over the events in Chicago. In the past, of course, management had often kept its silence after a controversial broadcast—he was used to that—but it seemed a bit odd to his partner, Fred Friendly, even eerie. "Nobody," Friendly recalled, "said anything to him or asked him about it—like 'Why did you do it?' Nothing was ever said about that speech. As if it had never happened."

Despite the usual praise from the usual liberal cheering section, there were signs, on and off, that things were getting rough. An anonymous viewer was thanked fervently: "In a sometimes lonely battle . . . it is most encouraging to receive letters such as [yours]." Thanking a CBS colleague for his "kind words," Murrow confided, "Your sentiments are not universally shared in this shop." The RTNDA was back in touch. It was running out of transcripts. Any chance of getting more from CBS? Murrow referred the group to the *Reporter*: "I doubt that CBS would be eager to supply copies."

Election night, November 4, he was for the first time in his TV career missing from the commentator's desk, replaced by Eric Sevareid. Instead, he had been put to work on the catwalk, reporting regional returns.

That winter a friend lunching with him at the Century Club found him more than usually nervous, with a pinched look about the eyes. They talked about the speech. Congratulations were offered; Murrow acknowledged: Oh, yes, he had really worked on that talk, sweated blood over every word. He looked sideways at his companion—"Didn't make me very popular with my company."

On top of the professional rupture had come a personal one. The twenty-two-year friendship that had been a broadcasting legend, between the CBS Chairman of the Board and the man once described as his conscience, had suffered a body blow. From then on, said one observer, there was that tear between Murrow and Paley: "The closeness was gone. It was 'we' and 'they.'"

In the aftershock one question kept coming up, posed alike by columnists, co-workers, and close friends enclosing notes in envelopes marked "personal": Just what the hell had he expected to accomplish?

There was, it turned out, no easy answer. "It may be a futile effort," he told a listener, "but it has to be done."

To Lester Markel at the *Times*: "I have not detected any indication that it has had any effect as far as the industry is concerned, but it did stir up a little talk."

"I have no hope whatever," he wrote a Washington friend late in the year, "that my words will produce any change in this industry, which seems determined to destroy itself. . . .

"This could be the most exciting and fruitful method of communication yet devised, but it is in the hands of timid and avaricious men and the public appears to be incredibly apathetic."

Weeks later, however, he was raising the issue again, this time on public television, appearing with Louis Lyons of the Nieman Foundation on WGBH's *The Press and the People*. CBS had just announced that Edward R. Murrow was going off on a year's sabbatical, amid rumors speculating on the reasons for his departure and his chances of coming back. Parrying the question of a TV columnist—had he any further comment on his Chicago speech?—he replied, "I will neither add nor detract one word."

At one point, back in October, a Chicago journalist had come right out and asked Murrow exactly why he had "lashed out at the hand that feeds him."

He sat back and grinned, for the first time in days.

"I've always been on the side of the heretics against those who burned them," he replied, "because the heretics so often proved right in the long run. Dead—but right!"

I

The Heretics

They were southern Quakers: abolitionists in a slaveholding state; pacifists in the war-torn 1860s; Union supporters in Confederate territory; Republicans in a sea of Democrats. Throughout their history the Murrows had always gone against the tide—from post-Reconstruction days, when Joshua Murrow waited for the night riders, Winchester in hand, back to antebellum times when his father, Andrew, conducted escaped blacks across the Ohio and closed his door to the census taker.

Like their neighbors in Guilford County, they were known as contrary people, marching to their own music, always a shade different—right from the day John Murrow had come down to Greensboro, North Carolina back in 1820, with his half-Indian wife and a passel of red-headed children.

They were from eastern Virginia, his people from Lunenburg Parish up Richmond way, she, the daughter of a Quaker missionary and a Cherokee woman. As Quakers, however, they were traveling at the wrong time and in the wrong direction.

The North Carolina Yearly Meeting, once a lodestone for Quaker settlers, had been losing members steadily, pressured by a cotton-dependent, slaveholding society that didn't take kindly to the abolitionist doctrine of the Society of Friends. The one-time emigration to central Carolina had gone into reverse, John and Lucindy Murrow moving in just as others were getting out.

Their stay in Guilford, however, was pathetically brief. Settling around the little county capital of Greensboro, they joined the New Garden Monthly Meeting, opened a remount station and tavern along the stage line to Hillsboro, then died four years later within a month of each other, leaving seven orphans, a house and lot in town, and a load of debts.

The courts looked after the debts; the younger children were parceled out among the neighbors. Joshua Stanley, a local Quaker merchant with no children of his own, took in four-year-old Andy Murrow.

Guilford County, though roughhewn, was pleasant enough in those years, midway between the mountains and the sea, in the heart of the plateau country known as the Piedmont: rolling plains; fields of wheat, corn, cotton, and tobacco; small, swift rivers; broad-backed ridges; wild flowers not found elsewhere; forests of oak, pine, hickory, walnut, maple, and persimmon. It was a middling county, mid-state, in the middle South.

It was also a hotbed of abolitionism, thanks to a sizable—and vocal—Quaker minority. Joshua Stanley, who had taken in Andrew Murrow, was a mover in the New Garden Monthly Meeting, a focus of antislavery sentiment and local base of operations for the covert network of escape routes known as the Underground Railroad. The Stanley house was a so-called station, concealing blacks on their way north, Andrew Murrow growing up there in embattled years that saw the position of his foster family and the southern Friends grow increasingly untenable.

As a young man he became a conductor, guiding parties of fugitives northwest from central Carolina, through the mountains of Virginia and Kentucky, and over the Ohio River, crossing to free soil at Covington, and points west.

The fugitives walked by night; he went by day, alerting stations all along the route, his cover a huge, false-bottomed wagon loaded with cornmeal and pottery, ostensibly for sale in Cincinatti or Evansville (the settlers liked their cornmeal ground Southern style).

They rendezvoused just before the river, the wagon's seatboard raised, the passengers slipping down into a crawlspace, and concealment. Agents were on the lookout all along the Ohio, a by-product of the Fugitive Slave Acts, which made Andrew Murrow liable, if caught, to a federal charge.

At the ferry the federal marshals poked around among the cornmeal, Andy Murrow keeping up a pleasant conversation as he sat on top of the hatchway. By the eve of the Civil War he had made numerous such trips into Ohio and Indiana.

His upbringing was one reason; his background, possibly another. Andy Murrow, one-quarter Cherokee, had been eighteen when his mother's people were uprooted under the removal order that sent the southern tribes on a death march into the wastes of Oklahoma. There was nothing romantic about being part Indian in those days and the family's later political involvement may have arisen from its opposition not only to slavery but to the party of Andrew Jackson.

In any case, the Murrows would always be acutely conscious of their mixed blood. When Andy married Miriam Hodgin of the neighboring Center Meeting, she was disowned by the congregation, a not uncommon practice. "Marrying out of unity" they called it. The Friends, however enlightened on questions of slavery, were less so on matters of member-ship. Besides, the Hodgins were old family, of good English stock. After appropriate apologies Miriam was taken back into the fold, Andrew, as a "birthright Quaker," invited to follow her. He refused point-blank. The young couple were joined in a civil bond, without the blessings of the Center Meeting.

Their children were to become pillars of the meeting, but Andrew never forgot. He never did join up, always aware of a difference, fond of relating an incident from his travels in western Carolina: He and a friend had stopped at a mountain cabin for the night, paying the mountaineers for a meal and a place to sleep. An old woman stirred up the pot; the men moved to the fire and warmed themselves. Andy Murrow drew a hand through his strong hair and chuckled: "Will, I'm part Indian," then went on at some length on how you could always tell about the Indian blood, by the hair, etc. Perhaps at too much length. The old woman finally hooted.

"You furriners may call that Indian blood downcountry; we call it nigger blood up here."

(It was an awareness perpetuated long after the thin Cherokee strain had worn to a trickle. A century later, a CBS colleague of Ed Murrow would remember the time a group of them shared a washroom, scrubbing up after work. It was after the summer, everyone with a tan, Murrow's body, visible through a shirt open to the waist, burnt absolutely black. The newsman did a double take: "You got a lot of Indian in you." Murrow just smiled. "That's what they call it in North Carolina.")

By 1860 the War Between the States was imminent. The Murrows were staunchly Union—Republicans from the outset, Andy an organizer of the first Republican club in Guilford, an avid free-soiler and county-level supporter of Abraham Lincoln; founder of the family love affair with politics in general and the Republican Party in particular.

(It got to be a local legend. The story goes that a merchant in heavily Democratic Greensboro was once teasing a Murrow descendant in the 1920s, about his adherence to the GOP. Just why in tarnation was he a Republican? Tradition, he was told; they had always been Republicans. His granddaddy was a Republican; *ergo* he was one, too. And what, the merchant shot back, if his granddaddy had been a sonuvabitch?

(The grandson of Andrew Murrow thought that one over a bit. "Well," he answered finally, "I guess that'd make me a Democrat.")

When the break came, North Carolina was the last state to secede— pro-Union until asked for troops to fight the Confederacy, referring to itself ever after as "the state forced out of the Union." Guilford, never a large slaveholding or landholding area, had always been divided on the big issues, the divisions ripping down the center of entire families. In Guilford and neighboring Randolph, the stream of departing Quakers had become a torrent, families packing up and selling out. The frightened

Murrow children wept and pleaded with their father to pull up stakes, but Andrew was immovable, stubborn to the last: They were not leaving North Carolina.

Like the others who stayed, they had the worst of both sides: part of a suspect community, its sympathies with the North, yet sharing the privations of the South, its young men conscripted by the Home Guard in a deadly house-to-house search, imprisoned and tortured when they refused to fight.

Andy Murrow, overage and tapped for Home Guard service, stuffed dirt down the barrel of his rifle, attended the meetings, and made a mental note of those homes targeted for the next day. Later that night he would send out the two older boys—Josh, ten, and John, twelve— under cover of darkness to warn the families.

Miriam Murrow, facing food shortages and closed schools, lined up her brood every night and held class by the fire, their textbooks those basic possessions of old-time farm families: the Bible, Webster's "Blue-backed Speller," and two plays by Shakespeare. Ten-year-old Joshua, the future grandfather of Ed Murrow, not only got to know the Bible from lid to lid but could later recite, letter-perfect, entire scenes from *Hamlet* and *Macbeth*.

Nor were they spared, despite their pacifism, the tragedy common to many families in those years. The eldest son, sent to Indiana for schooling, had enlisted with a local Union regiment when the war broke out. Captured in battle, Will Murrow was sent to the Confederate prison camp at Andersonville, sprung in 1865, rotten with TB, and died five years later. He was twenty-five years old.

The surviving sons and daughters came of age just as Reconstruction was ending—thoroughgoing individualists, clannish yet independent-minded; intellectually agile people with a gift of ready repartee, a sense of social commitment, and the unparalleled command of the English language that had been nurtured in Miriam Murrow's night school.

There were seven of them, three women, four men. But it was the third son, Joshua Stanley, named for the old abolitionist, who was the family star.

A nephew later recalled him vividly: tall, reserved—"solemn but full of wit"—unlike his extroverted father, though with the same easy knack of making friends. He was a quiet man, charismatic, a presence. Said those who remembered, "There was just *something* about him."

In the 1870s he married Kelly Coltrane's daughter Roella, a dark-haired, good-natured woman whose family had known the particular trauma of wartime Guilford: One brother had fought for the Union; another for the Confederacy. Their household was small enough: a boy, Roscoe; a girl, Gracey; the nephew, Edgar, a brother's son brought over for rearing following his mother's death of childbed fever; and a flock of hired boys to whom Joshua Murrow was surrogate father.

A full-time farmer and part-time politician, he had learned his practical civics at age ten, running through the darkened countryside in wartime on the late-night errands the discovery of which would have meant a firing squad for Andrew Murrow. He had been fourteen when the long, slow trains crept into Greensboro bearing Confederate wounded and dying from the fighting below Richmond; fifteen when the elder brother, in his Union blues, came home gray-faced from Andersonville; approached maturity when Reconstruction Era violence ripped the state from end to end.

The Ku Klux Klan avoided southern Guilford. But in neighboring Alamance County a wave of terror finally had the Reconstruction governor sending in the state militia, only to be impeached for his trouble.

By 1876 Reconstruction had run its course, the wartime leadership again in control of the statehouse, local bodies stripped of their power to tax or register voters, the progressive west subjected to the domination of the conservative east. Such was the climate in which Joshua S. Murrow, Republican, entered politics.

The two-party system, though lopsided, was still viable in the Old North State, Republican sentiments still deep-rooted. The result was a native party organization and genuine political alternative, more progressive than the national party,[1] including blacks and whites, making Guilford a swing county even in the years of the backlash. As for the Murrows, party politics were more than ever their lifeblood, the household staples including, after the Bible, the Kansas City *Star*, and the Winston *Union-Republican*. Joshua even named his son in honor of the national party leader, Senator Roscoe Conkling of New York.

Taking the stump for the GOP, Josh Murrow became a familiar face and voice on the county debating circuit, testing his mettle before the crowds gathered at the local groceries and boardinghouses—Dave Coble's store or at the widow Summers'[2]—political shows playing one- or two-a-day in the townships, the 1880s rural equivalent of radio, TV, movies, theater, and revival meeting, all rolled into one. Afterward the party faithful, Republicans and Democrats alike, would converge on Roella Murrow's front yard, in buggies or on horseback, for the postdebate dinner.

Josh Murrow, for all his essential earnestness, loved every minute of it—the exhilaration of public contact, the give-and-take of open debate, no holds barred. He was an adept swayer of crowds, a deft performer, and a canny reader of the public mood.

In 1886, at age thirty-five, he ran for the State Senate on a platform of equal rights before the law, power to the local governments, restrictions on the use of convict labor, and legislation "as will protect the laboring classes of the country . . . secure to them just compensation for their work and protect them from the wrongful encroachments of monopolies or money power."[3]

He entered as a dark horse, ran an outsider's campaign, his slogan "Give the Lawyers a Rest," and soon made his mark. "J. S. Murrow," wrote the Republican Greensboro *North State*, "will have a walk over. . . .He has gained a fine reputation in this canvass for readiness of debate, mastery of public affairs and fine delivery."

> The boys from the country occasionally compare very well with Chapel Hill graduates and lawyers of long experience at the bar. It is no small thing for a self made young man and a farmer to take the field with such a man as Col. Morehead and have the people say, "He is all Morehead wants to handle."[4]

The opposition sensed a comer, the Democratic Party organ lamenting only that "unfortunately for Josh, he is on the wrong side. Indeed, it is a mystery to us how a man possessing Murrow's calibre can be a Republican."[5]

He won in a three-way squeaker, capitalizing on a split in the Democratic ranks and beating out two patricians. The Republicans were jubilant, sensing a rising star, a candidate in the Abe Lincoln mold. The party, confident of having a winner, was ready to capitalize on it:

> The legislative ticket went through with a whoop, and in the ruins we find Col. Morehead, defeated by a young farmer, Josh S. Murrow . . . a young man of good attainments and enlarged views on political affairs. . . . Boys, this shows what the Republican Party will do for young men. It is the place for youth who have not the prestige of family name. . . . [6]

In early 1887, he went to the high-domed State Capitol at Raleigh for the biennial session of the General Assembly, sitting from January to April at his mahogany desk alongside forty-nine other legislators, while the overhead gas fixtures lit up the gray Carolina winter.

It was an exercise in frustration, the Senate rubber-stamping bills favorable to a few, legislating for the powerless local bodies while the South slid downhill, attempts to grapple with the issues of the day all beaten back by a leadership hanging on to its majority by waving the bogey of Reconstruction at white voters every two years.

Senator Murrow, sitting for the twenty-fourth District, supported attempts at railroad regulation, generally following the line expected from a Guilford County liberal: money for schools, roads, ferries; the deletion of "whites only" clauses from Senate bills; opposition to the sale of guns, the farming out of convict labor, and intelligence gathering on workers attending union meetings.[7] On the other hand, he was all for railroad consolidation and tax breaks for new industries. The Murrows never were and never would be radicals.

Family legend also had him mediating a voting coalition setting up the agricultural school that was to become the state university: a school, at the start, for poor white boys. The swing vote—so goes the story—lay with the remaining blacks still in office. The Lieutenant Governor therefore approached Josh Murrow, known to have some pull with the "colored." What had he to offer? asked the Senator from Guilford.

"Trade."

The Charter went through. The blacks had to wait two more sessions but in 1891, the legislature finally chartered the North Carolina Agricultural and Mechanical—later Technical—College for the Colored Race, which as North Carolina A&T became one of the top black schools in the country.

Otherwise, Joshua Murrow found little gratification in the circumscribed duties of a freshman senator. He served on no standing committees, introduced little significant legislation. Around him he saw his colleagues spend their days voting down reforms, debating tax money for local jails, passing on city charters and private bills while the economy stagnated. Urged to run again in 1888, he declined. Instead, he took a second job with the Post Office, left active politics, spent the rest of his life farming and sorting mail in the mailcar shuttling between Greensboro and Wilmington.

Politics were rotten, he told his children, and the most ignorant people in the world were found in North Carolina. But essentially, he left because he couldn't afford to stay. Crop prices were down, the economy in ruins thanks to the war, cash scarce; the Murrow lands wouldn't bring in more than a few dollars an acre. They had become land-poor. And politics, then as later, was no place for a poor man.

As Josh Murrow left politics, North Carolina prepared for the twentieth century, for capital pouring in from both North and South, for development—an age, however, that saw the state's large farming class, once the backbone of the economy, losing out steadily in power and prestige to the townsfolk and the new caste of railroad officials, bankers, millowners, and tobacco tycoons.

In the 1890s a fusion ticket of Republicans and Populists briefly gained control of the state in a four-year attempt at reform. Guilford County gave its support, Joshua Murrow attending the conventions as a private citizen, unable to resist the heady wine of public life in a heady time. But it was doomed from the start—the prelude, instead, to a fiery backlash that would end by sending history into reverse gear, disenfranchising the blacks and effectively ending the two-party system in North Carolina.

Racism had always been a powerful factor in local politics. "This is a White Man's country," thundered the Greensboro Patriot, "and White men (and not with black hearts) must rule it."[8] By 1898, the stage was set, the Democrats, marching under the banner of "White Supremacy," launching a massive drive to recapture the statehouse, the issue, so-called "Negro rule." Josh Murrow, riding the mail train, saw his home state once again erupt in violence. In racially troubled Wilmington, armed whites moved against the newly prosperous black community, leaving numberless dead. The authorities and the press called it a race riot.

The young Murrows saw their father return from the Wilmington run carrying a Winchester rifle—the dreaded repeating weapon. He held it out to them. *"This* is what they're using to kill colored folks in Wilmington!"

He took it all over Guilford, trying to get people to listen. Only Roscoe, age nineteen, didn't seem to understand, seeing only the wonderful rifle and firing it off, round after round.

But the weapon probably also meant protection in case of night riders: the first time the family had ever seen Josh Murrow with a gun.

The climate grew unpleasant. Edgar Murrow, reared with the children of former slaves, was taunted at school with cries of "nigger lover!" In Salisbury, to the south, seven blacks were dragged from a local jail and hanged by the neck from a railroad bridge. An ancient black preacher, visiting the Murrow house, discussed the lynching with Joshua. Edgar watched the two men going over the events in low, despairing tones, their heads bent forward in conversation—one gray, the other graying rapidly.

Joshua Murrow was still capable of indignation, but he was wearing out physically, his health eroded by the 200-mile-a-day railway postal stint, seven days a week, turning more and more to his work in his frustration, sinking every spare dollar into his beloved farm. When, in 1899, the victorious Democrats proposed a constitutional amendment depriving blacks of the right to vote, he denounced it bitterly. Said cousin Edgar Murrow, "He was up in arms; he blasted them on every occasion he could."

But politically he was muzzled, a civil servant now, unable to mount the soapbox and take part in the public debate.

In 1900, Guilford joined the majority of counties in voting to disenfranchise the black citizens of North Carolina, locking in place the pattern of white one-party rule that persisted for well over half a century. Josh Murrow, exiled in his mail car, watched as the incoming vote wiped out the efforts of thirty-five years, watched the independent farmers grow poorer and more powerless vis-à-vis the corporate barons of the New South. He still attended party meetings *pro forma*, but Tarheel Republicanism as he had known it was dead or dying. The Republicans themselves were reading black members out of the party; there was no real place for the Joshua Murrows.

In 1913 Roscoe, his only son, emigrated to the Pacific Northwest with his wife and children; he came back for a brief summer's stay, left, and never returned. Joshua died four years later in 1917, just before his sixty-sixth birthday; the doctors called it a kidney malfunction. To the family, aware of those years of working the double shift, standing on his feet in

8

the bumping, rattling mail car, it was more as though he had worked himself to death.

The *Patriot*, in a brief obituary, described him simply as "a prominent local citizen and longtime resident of Southern Guilford." In the same issue, front-page headlines announced the first official tallies on Allied losses in the great European war that was about to suck in the United States.

He was buried at Center Meeting, near his parents and a grandson who had died in infancy; a large gray stone bore the epitaph "A POSTAL CLERK FOR THIRTY YEARS." Roella Murrow lived to the age of ninety-one; she never saw her son again.

Of Joshua, the grandsons would retain only a vague recollection of a taciturn, unapproachable figure, always hard at work, rarely available. Ed Murrow never really knew the solemn, austere man who had been his father's father.

II

"Egg"

The year of Ed Murrow's birth—1908—the bands were playing in Greensboro, the city filled with parades, oratory, races, and sporting events and as a special attraction, the New York All-Star Quartet playing selections from Verdi, Wagner, Handel, and Gounod. All of which had nothing to do with the birth of Edward R. Murrow, but rather the fact that Greensboro was celebrating its centennial.

The facts of the future broadcaster's birth were quite another matter. Sent to fetch the doctor the night of April 25, cousin Edgar Murrow had gotten lost in the dark, turning in circles as he tried to find the house where, he had been told, the doctor was delivering another baby. In desperation he finally knocked at a farmhouse door: Did anyone there know the way to the McCullough house? A nurse appeared at the second-story window: "You're *at* the McCullough house." Dr. Tyson, it turned out, was just finishing up.

He found the doctor in the kitchen, halfway through pulling off his boots. Wearily, Thomas Tyson told the boy to hitch up the mare, and he'd be right with him.

They made their way back in the early-morning hours, the doc in his buggy, Edgar on horseback, arriving to find the baby already delivered by his grandmothers and audible from far off: "Edward R. was broadcasting."[1]

He had been born Egbert Roscoe, the last of four sons born to Roscoe and Ethel, the son and daughter-in-law of Joshua Murrow. Their first child had come along in 1901, the year following their marriage. The baby, named for its father, did not survive; Roscoe Murrow, Jr., died within hours of his birth. In time there were three more children, all boys, but evidently the parents never spoke of their firstborn again. It was seven years before they would give the name to another child; so it was that Egbert—later Edward—Roscoe Murrow carried the name not only of his father but of his dead infant brother.

He was a little character from the start, the runt of the litter, in the family mold—bright, self-assertive, an individual. Possibly it was also a matter of survival, of holding his own in competition with two intelligent, attractive older brothers. That at least was how the three small boys, all born within a four-year span, were remembered by the family: Lacey Van Buren, already darkly handsome, a likable boy and a born leader; Dewey Joshua, blue-eyed and fair-haired like his mother, with the solemn, grave manner of the grandfather whose name he carried; and Egbert Roscoe— "the loud-voiced 'un"—quick-tempered, undersize, overweight, trying to keep up with the others on short, stumpy legs.

Accordingly, he had the inevitable mishaps—one of those active children who never walk when they can run, never reach when they can jump—living down constantly the disadvantages of being the smallest, the burden of a name that he hated, and a resonant, oddly mature speaking voice that set him apart from the others and subjected him to ridicule. Said their uncle, reminiscing: "His brothers, they'd *laugh* about it. Egg, they called him—he didn't like the name, but that's what they called him; that was his nickname. They was *laughin'*. . . . They was older, you know, and they'd pick at him—oh, you could hear him for miles."

All three had been born on the old Hodgin place, the roomy 1750s farmhouse that had been in the family since the time of Great-Grandmother Miriam. Out in back was the little river, running all through the Murrow property, called Polecat Creek—a raging torrent in winter, good for fishing in summer. The woods to either side abounded in deer, otter, wild turkey, and all kinds of small game. There was a sense of history all around, the old clapboard Center Meeting House just a few steps from the property, the windows of the farmhouse looking out on one side toward the cemetery where Andrew Murrow's generation lay buried.

Unlike the earlier generations, however, the younger Murrow household was a matriarchy. Roscoe had grown to be a big, easygoing man, a good man with the cheerful disposition and physical prowess of his grandfather but without the intellectual agility of either Joshua or Andrew or, for that matter, of the family in general. It was Ethel Lamb Murrow— small, slight, fair-haired—who set her stamp upon the household, a hard-working, hard-driven woman.

She had to be. The Lambs were former English Quakers, an old and well-established Guilford family who had turned to Methodism in the years before the war. Captain Lamb, Ethel's father, had been an officer in the Confederate Army, and seen action in most of the big battles. But for George Van Buren Lamb the clock had stopped in 1865.

Those who knew him later remembered a big man—blond, handsome, gifted, intelligent, and living in a fantasy world. He had never gotten over his years in the Gentlemen's Army, the days of the gallant Lost

Cause, or his exploits as a dashing officer. Mercurial, subject to wide mood swings, he was alternately charming and brutal: a gifted reader and a spellbinding speaker—Edgar remembered taking the path to the Lamb house every Sunday, through woods of oak and pine, just to hear the Captain talk ("He would *charm* you, just reading an ordinary item out of the newspaper")—yet brutal when he hit the bottle, beating his wife and children in drunken rages.

Said his Murrow relations: "The war ruined him."

It was the mother who held things together. Isabelle Coble Lamb, of Palatinate German stock, was the family mainstay and breadwinner, selling books and home-made carpets to keep the family going and saving enough, in time, to buy seventy acres of farmland from Joshua Murrow.

Ethel, reared in the shadow of Van Lamb's instability, was her mother's daughter—"a wheelhorse of work"—with a horror of idleness and a compulsiveness about staying busy that she passed on to her youngest son. A sufferer from asthma, her health often uncertain, with a touch of her father's flair for the dramatic and an understandable streak of pessimism that made her foresee disaster at every turn, she was nevertheless a woman of iron self-control, with a straitlaced personal sense of morality matching that of the Murrows. Her favorite dictum, "It's better to wear out than rust out," determined a way of life not only for herself but for the next generation.

Ambitious, intelligent, she completed high school and enrolled in town at the State Normal and Industrial School for Girls, later the Woman's College of the University of North Carolina at Greensboro. She never finished, returning, instead, to teach at the two-teacher school near the Center Meeting House before marrying Roscoe in March of 1900, a man younger than she, less educated, the only son of Joshua Murrow.

Ethel Lamb, Belle Coble, Roella Coltrane, Miriam Hodgin—they all followed the family pattern of strong women, the earliest prototypes of those who were to be a formative influence on Ed Murrow's life.

At her marriage Ethel had joined the Society of Friends, taking on the habits and the plain dress of the Quaker women. The traditional ways of doing things, therefore, were kept up in her home—prayers before meal-time; Bible reading aloud every night; meeting on Sunday; prayer meeting on Wednesday. It was also, like the older Murrow household, governed by rigorous discipline, with one essential difference: Joshua Murrow had maintained order through the force of his personality, rarely resorting to corporal punishment. Ethel, on the other hand, applied the switch liberally—a dim echo of her own childhood, perhaps, but more in keeping with the practice of the time and a quick way of establishing discipline in a household dominated by four males.

For the rest, Ed Murrow would recall a pleasant rural Carolina early childhood: his mother singing old English ballads; Grandpa Van holding the children spellbound with stories of the War Between the States.[2] They knew little of their father's family.[3]

All three boys were still quite small when, in 1913, Roscoe moved his family out to the state of Washington. Joshua was bitterly opposed, but in the end it was the younger Murrows' decision.

There were many reasons for the move, not all of them completely clear. Roscoe's stint with the army, during the Spanish-American War, was a factor. He never left the continental United States, but evidently the travel experience was enough to set off a deep-seated restlessness that his sons were eventually to share. His cousin Edgar later claimed he had spent time at Vancouver Barracks in Washington and come back with the Northwest in his blood. Then, too, the move must be seen in the context of a tide of emigration—Southern families fleeing a depressed sector of the country, drawn to the last frontier by hopes of a better life. Belle Coble's brothers, gone out years before, were doing well on their own farms, extolling the virtues of the Pacific Northwest in letter after letter. The Cobles told Cousin Ethel that she'd do better in the mild climate of Puget Sound than in old Guilford, whose exotic plants and flowering trees, however pleasing to the eye, made spring and fall a torment to those suffering from asthma.

In addition, Roscoe, a hardworking man who had never shared his father's passion for the land, was not making ends meet, with farm prices continuing their downward spiral. The Quakers of those times would not raise tobacco; Roscoe's corn and wheat, competing with Western crops, didn't bring in enough, no matter how much the family pitched in.

For all five Murrows, parents and children, the ground base of their existence was hard work, striving for a living when there was none to be made, even the youngest making himself useful. Ed Murrow later said he couldn't remember a time when he wasn't working, and certainly his earliest impressions included those of hard times, his father out in the fields, walking behind the mule team, from morning to night.

Their financial situation, therefore, as well as the father's restlessness, the mother's health, possibly Roscoe's desire to be out from under his own father's shadow, the hope for a better life—all these combined to make Roscoe and Ethel leave the land that the Murrows had hung onto for two generations in the face of war, social upheaval and economic hardship.

They boarded the train at the old open-air station in Greensboro, essentially unchanged since the time the Confederate supply trains had gone through, now crowded in by the commercial buildings of an expanding city. Outside of the crop money, they took very little with them—two baskets of food; several suitcases of clothing, secured with rope, the modest paraphernalia of those who seldom traveled. The rest—the mule team, equipment, household effects—had been auctioned off; for years afterward Edgar would run into people whose parents had come away with an item from Roscoe Murrow's sale. In time, he himself bought out Roscoe's acreage.

The children were eager, excited, nothing more; the family had long since moved from the house on Polecat Creek, and one home was as good as another. Almost forty-four years later, however, a controversial *See it Now* documentary would be severely criticized for dwelling, in a lengthy sequence, on the auction of a family farm, the sale of household effects, of a cradle—a common enough occurrence in the Midwest of the 1950s, yet also reflecting, perhaps, the recollections of a small boy who had seen the family goods go under the hammer.

They sat up on the train six days and nights,[4] living off their packed fried chicken, broke the journey at Kansas City, then continued westward—the tall, dark, rawboned farmer; the small woman in her gray Quaker shawl; the two serious older boys; and a chunky, obstreperous five-year-old with a quick smile, a quick temper, and a voice like a foghorn on Puget Sound.

Skagit County was a long, narrow strip of land in the northwest corner of Washington State—100 miles across, 24 miles deep, the Cascade Mountains at one end, at the other, the Rosario Strait leading from Puget Sound toward the Pacific. Over a million acres of farmland and forest; fertile river valleys; mineral deposits; mountain stands of fir, cedar, hemlock, and larch; mountain streams that carried the timber wealth down to salt water, to be floated to the mills all along the sound; the second-largest producer of lumber in the state of Washington.

The town of Blanchard—the Cobles' home and the Murrows' last stop—was at the westernmost end of the county, at the mouth of the Samish River, flowing down from Canada, some thirty miles to the north and emptying into Puget Sound. It was typical of the little settlements dotting the shoreline, rising along the path of the railroad, its very name derived from a company official. A local guidebook of the time gave the following description:

> *Blanchard*: Population about 300. Located on the Great Northern Railway, 12 mi. so. of Bellingham, at outer edge of Samish flats. Lumbering, shingle manufacturing, farming. Climate mild and equable, resembling North Carolina and Georgia, with less variations. Principal products: hay and oats, also fruits, hops, vegetables, dairy products due to rich pasturage.[5]

To arrivals from the East, it seemed almost a frontier town—muddy streets, wooden sidewalks, picket fences; earth dikes along the water, forever being shored up; huge piles of stumps, which were burned periodically; and the smoke of forest fires.[6] The town itself consisted of a cluster of frame houses, a two-room school, a general store, a mill, and

a Methodist church. On the hill overlooking Blanchard was the campsite
of the Samish Bay Logging Company, sending down timber for the mill
on the bay, starting the cycle that marked the factory town. Those for-
tunates who farmed, like the Cobles, lived on three sides of the settlement, behind earth dikes, raising the small crops and dairy cows that
earned them the name of stump ranchers.

It was a boom town, but Roscoe Murrow, at first, wasn't making it. He
tried one job after another; nothing seemed to work. The crop money
ran out. With a housing shortage and no grubstake, the family had pitched
a tent on a bald spot on the cousins' property, where salt water crept up
on three sides every time the tide came in. They were proud, not wanting
handouts. The brothers, when grown, would remember silent mealtimes
in the tent, three children downing their food in the consciousness that
their parents were going hungry. Even in later, better times in the Murrow household, what you left over was what you began your next meal
with.[7] And even before the onset of his chain smoking, Murrow grown
to adulthood would have trouble eating.

The mother kept them going. "She kept us together," Ed Murrow said
once to a friend. "We'd have gone *down* without her."

In his years of celebrityhood, the newsman would indulge in fake nostalgia images of poverty: his father as sharecropper; a few acres of poor
cotton land. It was a veil for the remembered reality of those early days
in Washington, never spoken of outside the family, the time when they
had skirted the very edges of starvation.[8]

The Murrows, emigrating when they did, had stepped into an exploi-
tative situation. By 1913 the dream of the Northwest had soured, much
of the county and state given over to federal reserve land, railroad rights,
and lumber syndicates—squeezing out those come looking for land and
offering instead wage labor. Skagit County for all its natural wealth was
a supplier of raw commodities, its main cash crop—timber—controlled
by corporate absentee owners,[9] its underpaid work force caught in an
eternal pinch between low wages and the need to pay for finished goods.

Roscoe Murrow, finding his feet at last, liked the railroad, working his
way up to the position of engineer on the logging locomotive hauling the
timber down from Blanchard Mountain. The family moved from their
tent into the frame house that was to be their home for the next twelve
years. But life would always be spare: money for necessities—even a car—
but none for amenities. That was true of the community in general. They
were for the most part the working poor—no luxuries, but they had roofs
over their heads, clothes on their backs, steady employment; they didn't
go hungry and considered themselves fortunate.

Ethel Murrow soon established herself in the community—the one
everyone turned to in an emergency, a no-nonsense type whose personality kept the others in line. The Blanchard school board, of which she
was treasurer, soon learned to finish its meetings by 3:00, when school

was out. Everyone knew Mrs. Murrow had to be home for the children; all were anxious to avoid, if possible, the sight of Ethel looking at her watch, snapping her bag shut, and marching out in silent judgment on any group that couldn't wind up its business by 3:00 P.M.[10]

Her sons, accordingly, were goal-oriented, working for the farmers and the sawmill while attending school, making top grades.

At home, the boys had to read aloud from the Bible, a chapter every night. It hardly encouraged piety; they generally spent more time arguing, well out of earshot of the parents, that it was the other's turn. Yet the sessions continued the oral tradition so strong in both families: a first encounter with formal speech, in the strong, rhythmic measures of the King James Version of the Bible, the bedrock of Ed Murrow's career as a public speaker—and to some extent, of his philosophy—fostering a lifelong love of the English language and a total commitment, almost biblical in its intensity, to the power of the Word.

The underside of that picture, however—one often endemic to strongly religious households—was a sense of guilt, an awareness of sin and the need for atonement, a dark view of the human condition that owed more, perhaps, to Ethel's harsh upbringing and rural Methodism than the gentler teachings of the Society of Friends. "Withhold not correction from the child. . . . Thou shalt beat him with the rod, and shalt deliver his soul from hell." (Proverbs 23:13–14).

(The youngest son soon found a way of avoiding the worst of a whipping. Said brother Dewey: "He found that if he yelled loud enough, she'd ease up a bit.")

Underlying formal piety, however, was the strong social conscience brought from southern Guilford—the uncompromising sense of right and wrong; of the right to disagree, basic to both Quaker doctrine and American liberalism, and of individual responsibility: the feeling of a direct connection between one's actions and what happened in the world.

In the general extolling of Ethel Murrow, her husband was often overlooked. Roscoe, described by one daughter-in-law as "a golden-natured man,"[11] was proud of his enterprising, intelligent wife and seemed content to live in her shadow. His wants were few and simple; he was honest, liked his work, loved his family. His sons, in turn, respected not only his physical strength but also his unpretentious workingman's common sense.

The mother figure, however, was predominant, the tie between Ethel and her sons uncommonly close—and sometimes complicated. When, in the 1920s, Lacey Murrow was ready to graduate from Washington State, the first in his family to get a college education, he sent for his mother. Then something happened. As a family friend told the story, Ethel, her suitcase packed, was waiting for the eastbound stage when news came of an accident in the woods: a neighbor badly injured, his wife distracted, the solution—go get Mrs. Murrow. Instead of taking the stage, therefore, Ethel accompanied the dying man and his wife to the hospital, saw them through to the end, handled arrangements for the widow, and, in the midst of it, wired Lacey that she wasn't coming.

On receiving the telegram, her eldest son—a class officer and honor cadet who had worked his way through college hefting wheat sacks and cutting brush on the state highways—walked out on his graduation. Lacey Murrow, in the black anger that could make the Murrow men their own worst enemies, hurt and disappointed that no one would be there, packed his belongings, bought a ticket to where he had a job lined up, and departed, leaving only a forwarding address.[12]

Vis-à-vis the outside world, the brothers observed an unmistakable masculine soldarity, the newest generation of Murrow boys in unwitting echo of Joshua and his brothers: a pattern of fraternal relationships that Ed Murrow was to duplicate throughout his life.

Between their chores, the Murrow boys went fishing. They rode the log rafts in the bay and speared salmon; dug for clams in secluded coves and hunted in forests of evergreen. In that happy setting, Egbert Murrow seemed the quintessential happy kid—the hell raiser of the family, quick to bounce back from minor disasters (including possibly a broken nose; he developed the only aquiline profile in the family). An "outgoing, open, optimistic youngster"; such was brother Dewey's recollection.

Clouding the image of the Tom Sawyer boyhood, however, were the traits often characterizing the youngest sons of strong-willed mothers. One was a slight tendency to asthma, an indication in itself of the pulmonary weakness that was also probably inherited from Ethel. The other lay in the periodic outbursts—the family called them moody streaks— marking the onset of depression; they were sudden, inexplicable, probably frightening; the earliest indication of the black moods that beset him all his life. It was not a matter of the usual childhood tantrums. "The world," said Dewey later, by way of explanation, "just became a dreary-looking place to him."[13]

The adult managed to turn it inward. The small boy, however, struck out in anger and frustration at whatever was closest—generally, two bigger brothers, who weren't about to stand for it; a hardworking family hadn't the time to cope with moody streaks. By necessity, he learned to cope alone—a first sign that life was not easy and a source, perhaps, of the iron self-discipline and the quintessential loneliness that were to characterize the adult: one who would keep to himself, never asking for and indeed discouraging help in times of stress, even from those closest to him.

On April 6, 1917, the United States entered the Great War. Fewer than four weeks before, Grandpa Murrow had died in Greensboro. Down in Everett, forty miles south of Blanchard, organizers for the Industrial Workers of the World were being tried for conspiracy following a shootout with local police. In the Samish Valley, local boys were enlisting and

Liberty bond rallies organized, with down-home entertainment that included nine-year-old Egbert Murrow, up on a soapbox, singing, "Gee-ap Maw, gee-ap Paw, gee-ap Mule with the haw-hee-haw." Orders went up for local timber, lumber prices soared; wages stayed down.

Elsewhere, Washington's labor troubles, long brewing, were coming to a head amid strikes and countering violence as the radical IWW, bringing the message of socialism and an eight-hour day to Washington's migrant labor force, fought the lumber companies, the mine operators, local vigilantes, and the U.S. Department of Justice.

To Ed Murrow, the IWW would always have the aura of the great lost cause, a soft-focus memory of stalwart men and great songs and failed native radicalism. By the time he entered the logging labor force, the back of the movement had been broken. And while he alternately claimed or denied membership in later years—his lifelong favorite song would be "Joe Hill"—no one could ever prove he had or hadn't carried the red card.

There was no mistaking, however, where Roscoe Murrow stood—as his youngest son found out one day when they were together, working. Singing came as naturally to the Murrows as breathing, and the boy let out, as they worked, with a rousing Wobbly number.

Roscow Murrow reared up, all 200 pounds of him, to his full six feet, the good nature gone out of his lean face, his eyes narrowed to slits, the long jaw set.

"Sing one of those songs again in my presence," he told his son, "and I'll break your back!"[14]

In Blanchard itself, the movement hadn't much impact beyond the echoes of the violence elsewhere. There was no union hall, the great interurban trolley system linking the Skagit towns with the turbulent population centers to the south not yet completed.

It was a town largely of mill hands, the loggers a different breed—itinerants, figures of awe to the Murrow children, fiercely independent men who'd go off if they didn't like the look in a boss's eye. To the people of the Samish Flats, the IWW was somehow linked up with the hoboes who jumped the train at the edge of town at haying or harvest time; the "I-Won't-Works," they called them.

Local reactions to Everett and the chain of violent events that followed were therefore mixed. Some were indignant; others blamed the union—just a bunch of hell raisers, things were okay, why the fuss—the same ones, the Murrows noted, who were hot and heavy in their eagerness to praise the hell raisers once concessions had been wrung from the lumber companies.

As industrial warfare racked the state, Roscoe and Ethel may have sensed an echo of the turmoil that had overshadowed their youth. Skeptical, their sense of justice offended, they were people who were of comfort to neither side—neither models of proletarian class consciousness nor partisans of Weyerhauser, Bloedel-Donovan, or the Samish Bay Logging Company, which was eventually to fire Roscoe for insubordination.

For their children it meant growing up in an atmosphere heavy with whispered accounts, as adults talked among themselves of bloody encounters that saw lawmen and vigilantes on one side, blue-collar people on the other. Egbert Murrow was eight years old when deputies opened fire on union organizers in Everett, leaving seven dead and forty-eight wounded. He was nine when the U.S. Government began raiding union halls across the state, charged the IWW with sabotage of the war effort, and sent the army in to replace the strikers. He was eleven when in Centralia, down in Lewis County, a union man was castrated and hanged by the neck from a railroad bridge, and at the start of his teens when, following the Bolshevik Revolution, U.S. Attorney General A. Mitchell Palmer, his eye on the presidency, brought the power of the Justice Department down on radicals and dissidents with nationwide raids, trials, and deportations—marking the nation's first "red scare" and anticipating the anti-Communist hysteria of the late 1940s and 1950s.

For Ed Murrow, therefore, the so-called Palmer raids were not something learned from a history book or a newspaper. Though not directly experienced, they were part of the climate in which he grew up, a sharp memory that would grow even sharper in the era of Tom Clark, Joe McCarthy, and Herbert Brownell.

That same climate, moreover, helped shape the teenager who, emerging from childhood, was showing an interest in issues, a love of argument, an adeptness at debate that recalled his paternal grandfather and the mores of Guilford County.

At fourteen he had shot up—a tall, suddenly serious boy, thin for his height, taking on the good looks and big proportions of his mother's family: a dark copy of the younger Van Buren Lamb, though sounding increasingly like Joshua Murrow. Indeed, Edgar Murrow was always to feel that he could hear in his younger cousin's voice the accents of his adoptive father. There was also a faintly exotic cast to his dark coloring, quite unlike that of the Scottish Coltranes, which among the eastern Murrows stirred tribal memories of the half-Indian Lucindy Hubbard. It helped set him apart further; the high school yearbook would later carry a reference to "a darkie"—a distinctive presence among classmates who were largely of English, German, and Scandinavian descent.

Summers he worked in the logging camp; winters he attended high school in the nearby town of Edison: two separate worlds, two educations.

By 1922, young men like the Murrow brothers were spared the lice, dawn-to-dusk hours, and rotting food of the old days. But working in the camps still meant learning how to live with death and danger—huge trees, crashing in the wrong direction; sparks from a saw that could ignite whole stands of timber within minutes. The men worked themselves recklessly, knowing they came second to the lumber; boys working as whistle punks, signaling the stages of the felling operation, knew it too.

Dewey Murrow, age thirteen, his first day on the job, had seen a steel cable suddenly snap, strike, and kill a workman. As the others stooped to pick up the body, the superintendent stopped them: "Let 'im lie. When 'e's stiff, you can carry 'im easier."[15]

At such times a youngster had to learn to keep his lunch down, his mind on his work, and his trust in his own reflexes.

Yet in the fall the young workman made the switch back, apparently without difficulty, to student—star debater; high school athlete; student body officer; the regulation "bright boy" of any high school environment.

Actually, he was fortunate in finding Edison High. The small union high school serving a largely blue-collar district knew what it had to work with, its five-member faculty dedicated to the needs of the pupils, most of whom would never have a chance at a higher education. It had the top debating team in the region, the top basketball team, a chorus, an orchestra, student-faculty outings, and a firm sense of mission in the community, its guidelines, as laid down by the strong-minded superintendent, faintly Etonian: "Service . . . fair play . . . to embody in the classroom and playfield the idea that there is more at stake than personal aggrandizement or glory. . . ."[16]

College, as Murrow himself acknowledged, would be crucial to his development. But the eighty-pupil school in the farming town of Edison— in particular the efforts of Ruth Lawson, the English teacher, debating coach, and sometime principal—helped lay the groundwork.

At Edison the sons and daughters of the farmers and mill hands were encouraged to think for themselves, guided into an awareness of the world beyond Puget Sound, the Edison debating team, accordingly, well known for its high level of expertise on the high school circuit. Egbert Murrow, as its star, probably got his earliest political education traveling through the Pacific counties, arguing the issues of the day, working in partnership with the two young women who were his teammates, the three of them coordinating efforts, later sharing the sweetness of victory ("That girl thought the Philippine question was so simple, didn't she?".)[17]

Like many super-achievers, he functioned at more than one level: He played championship basketball, sang in the glee club and in school musicals, played in the school orchestra, was cheerleader and student officer, and, though working summers and part time, still managed to graduate at the head of his class. But it was in one special capacity that he was immortalized, so to speak, in the class poem for 1924:

And Egbert is due for his special praise
For doesn't he his opponents' hair raise

When in debate he meets them face to face
And of their thoughts there's not left one trace.

From early on, he knew the glow of being part of a winning combination, whether in championship basketball or championship debate, the sometime loner balanced off by the team player—welcoming challenges, anticipating success. (Also developing the knack of getting to the power source: in the "will" drafted by his graduating class, he left not only his "gift of elocution," but his method for "getting an in with the teachers.")[18]

Nor had he any problems, managing the tightrope act of success vis-à-vis popularity, playing many roles, even as a teenager, his different personalities caught and preserved in high school photos: Egbert Murrow, ebullient, as cheerleader; somber in the group portrait of the student government; smiling sunnily with his debating teammates or in the first row of the glee club; sitting macho position, arms folded, legs akimbo, in the blue-and-white underwear of the Edison Sparkies, the county basketball trophy perched between two bony knees. For all the occasional moods, therefore, the composite picture for those years would be one of optimism—the cheerful grin of the class star and school star, the kid who thought the world was his oyster, who expected to be liked and was liked in return.

The school yearbook, doing the ritual "forty years from today" prediction, saw his future not as a politician—that was left to the girl heading the student body—but as a professor of sociology at the University of Washington, returning to his high school alma mater to speak on "social reform." The date given was May 2, 1965.

Yet there were times when the model boy suddenly turned maverick, the unpredictability inherent in both the Murrows and the Lambs surfacing. The school calendar for October 31, 1924, recorded: "The Junior class is the scene of a rebellion, an uprising, a mutiny, when Egbert and Bill vehemently declare themselves NOT JUNIORS!" The incident was later described, when tempers had cooled, by the class Longfellow: "Trouble was threatening . . ./led on by rebels."

Hotly the battle was waged, lasting the whole term.
Radicals left in anger; others stood firm. . . .[19]

It is not known exactly what made the young Murrow walk out and disrupt the school year—his first, though hardly last, brush with authority. In college a run-in with faculty was to cost him his chance at entering Phi Beta Kappa, though he had the marks (the key he carried resulted from an honorary membership bestowed in later years).[20]

The class of 1925 left Edison High amid the backlash following Teapot Dome and the slowly unfolding revelations of corruption in the administration of the late Warren Harding—the highest-reaching political scandal in the federal government until Watergate. In his message to the departing students, Superintendent Stanley Brode inveighed against "the moral callousness of men in public and business life.

"Until our officials, businessmen and the public at large, are willing to put character before pleasure or monetary profit, we can expect more oil scandals, more crooked officials, more hijacking. . . ."[21]

But for the boys and girls graduating in May of that year the note was definitely upbeat, of its time, their class motto "Impossible is Un-American." Egbert Murrow, as valedictorian, addressed his classmates, parents, teachers, and the student body. He was also Vice-President of the Student Association, of his graduating class, and was designated in the Edison poll as the boy who had done the most for the school. The all-round scholar and athlete had his class picture captioned with the lines from Shakespeare's *Love's Labour's Lost*, "A man in the world's new fashion planted/ that hath a mint of phrases in his brain."

In the world outside Edison, however, he was just another local kid with college ambitions and no money. Joshua's estate had settled $1,000 on Roscoe and $500 apiece for the three grandchildren. For reasons undisclosed, the grandsons' money would be tied up for almost thirty years.[22]

In the summer of 1925, therefore, Egbert Murrow, top student, athlete, and debater, became temporarily a dropout. Dewey had gotten a small scholarship when he was valedictorian, but no such funds came Egbert's way. Upward mobility did not come easily in the Samish Valley.

There never seemed to be any doubt that the Murrow brothers would go to college. As one son recalled, it always seemed a foregone conclusion. Certainly there was encouragement at school, but a good deal of the credit must undoubtedly go to their mother, ambitious for all three, determined that her children would not disappear into the logging camps.

Supposedly her youngest son wanted to go to school back East—specifically, the socially prestigious University of Virginia, rather a tall order for a blue-collar boy from Puget Sound, albeit one already displaying a taste for the finer things of life. Very possibly, too, it was the one thing that hadn't been done by Lacey and Dewey.

In the meantime, there wasn't enough to fund a year at Washington State, let alone at Virginia. The solution: work in the woods and save up.

Murrow's feelings about his dropout year were to remain divided. There was romanticism, of course—back to nature, the great outdoors, the value of honest work among honest workingmen—and indeed, the work answered a need in his nature that was as deeply rooted as the drive to get an education. Yet there was always an underlying element of resentment, surfacing at odd moments: random comments on dropping out to pay for "a half-baked education"; a nagging awareness that some had it easier than others, a sense of being of the underclasses; tirades before friends about how tough he had it. A quarter century later, during the Korean War, he was to launch a savage attack on the college deferment system for its implied judgment on those who couldn't afford a higher education, using the poor as cannon fodder. For a young person in 1925, above all, there was the sense of time lost in his single-minded effort to break out of the poverty cycle.

That same summer he received a further lesson on the ways of life in a one-industry town. In an incident later recorded by Alexander Kendrick in his biography of Edward R. Murrow, Roscoe Murrow came home one day with the news that he had knocked down his superintendent. It was the end of his job with the Samish Bay Logging Company and the end of the family's life in Blanchard. The youngest son was the only one of the three still at home and presumably a witness to the mother's panic: "What will become of us and the boys?"[23] If Ed Murrow later had a different view of the world from that of his colleagues, an intense, admittedly pro-union bias, a strong need for security, a need to know where the next paycheck was coming from—even in his palmiest days—there was good reason.

A similar opening was found in a logging camp on the Olympic Peninsula, but for the parents, no longer young, it meant pulling up stakes, leaving their neighbors, their Coble relations, again cutting ties to the community. Ethel Murrow swallowed her panic and faced down another of the moves that had brought her from independent landholding to a rented home in a northwestern village and, finally, to a tiny company house in a logging settlement deep in the Olympic rain forest.

Clallam County was at the very top of the peninsula, facing west toward the Pacific and north toward Canada, and included the spectacular terrain of what would become Olympic National Park. The Murrows' new home was at the western end, in Beaver Camp—high up in the mountains, at the tip of a small lake, one road leading to the nearby town of Forks, another leading four miles down to the Pacific Ocean and an Indian reservation. It was run as part of a massive logging operation by the Bloedel-Donovan Lumber Mills.

The summer of 1925, the mills provided employment not only to Roscoe Murrow but to his youngest son—at seventeen, still more of a big boy than a man, grown a trifle too fast to his full six-foot-two-inch height, popular with men, shy with women of his own age, inept at dancing, earning extra money baby-sitting during his evenings off at Beaver Camp.

He started as an axman on a logging crew, clearing tracts on the western slope of the Olympic forests. It was grueling work, a far cry from the logging operations of later times, carried out in virgin timberland—which meant no roads or access trails, rivers that had to be forded, long, hard days in the bush. The men worked in teams, the competition intense. Young Murrow, doing a man's work, didn't mind it; he loved it, as he would always love physical labor as an outlet for his nervous energy. It was also a world free of pretensions. To many in the middle class, particularly following the labor wars, the loggers were the timberbeasts—distant figures in sweat-stiffened work shirts, coarse "tin pants" that kept off the heavy rain, immense corked boots, working in all kinds of weather, living in a society of their own, emerging only on pay day. But they were hardworking men, taciturn, no-nonsense, quick to see through a false front, contemptuous of anyone who wasn't ready to back up words with action, endowed with the commonsense quality that Ed Murrow respected in his father—a supermasculine world, ruled by the "man's man" ethos, easily prompting a young man's desire for acceptance.

Finally, there was the setting, the snowcapped mountains of the Olympic Range—glaciers; mountain meadows; vast unbroken stretches of virgin forest that were among the last of their kind in the United States. To Murrow, particularly amid the pressures of later years, "the woods" became a symbol, the memory of a rough sort of Eden and a counterpoise to that of wartime London. (He also acquired, he later said, an "extensive vocabulary of profanity,"[24] the ability to make coffee in a lard pail, and a long-standing revulsion against the outdoor barbecue.)

He was well liked—regarded as good-natured, a strong worker, and was soon moved up to compass man, or surveyor's assistant. Mapping out areas marked for felling, he learned the skills in reading the terrain that would prove useful to the combat correspondent.[25]

He had long since dropped the hated name of Egbert. At school he was Blow; at home, Southern style, he was either Son, Sonny, or Brother. In the camp he called himself Ed. It had a good, masculine ring to it, was more suitable for a logger. He also said at one point that he hadn't wanted to have to fight every lumberjack on the West Coast.

But he was more than ready, when the time came, to turn in his boots and tin pants. The summer of 1926, expense money saved up—plus a little financial help from Lacey—he sat down in Beaver Camp with his application for Washington State College; no University of Virginia, not even the University of Washington. There was no getting away from Lacey and Dewey. At the bottom, in the blank space opposite the question "When does the applicant intend to begin classes?" he scrawled, "At once!"

Pullman in the 1920s was a thriving grain center in the southeastern corner of Washington State, six miles from the Idaho border. It was the county seat, set in the wheatlands of the high plateau and site of the agricultural land-grant school, part of the two-tier system governing higher education in the state: the middle class attended the University of Washington in Seattle; those farther down or farther east, the cow college at Pullman.

To the freshman from the lumber country, however, the pleasant, tree-shaded campus, with its redbrick buildings and large fraternity houses, was a step up and a vital one at that. To stretch his logging money, he took a job, that first winter, as janitor/houseboy for a sorority house—washing dishes, stoking the furnace, taking out the garbage—with sleeping quarters in the basement. One of his lasting recollections would be that of himself at age eighteen, lying on his cot at night, listening to the girls upstairs talk about their love lives—informative but no revelations; they stopped the minute they got around to sex.[26]

Uncertain about his future, he first enrolled as a major in business administration, drawing Bs and Cs in a welter of economics courses. Then Ida Lou Anderson entered his life.

She liked men who combined strength and tenderness, she said once, men with a stoic nature, as she put it, toughened and sweetened by experience.[27]

Her likes and loves, however, were to be vicarious because Ida Lou Anderson, a great teacher, had been left deformed and crippled by a childhood case of polio.

She was a speech instructor, twenty-six when Ed Murrow first took her classes and the youngest member of the faculty. Her course was simply called "Interpretation," with various levels of advancement. Ed Murrow took them all. She became for him, as for others in her classes, a major influence—so much so, and so publicly, that Joe McCarthy, fighting Murrow years later, was tempted to attack her memory.

Remarkable by any standards, she was later recalled by one of her students as "cruelly dwarfed, twisted and hunched. . . . But to [us] she was a fount, a flaming spirit."[28] Students entering her classes in the hope of easy grades found themselves working as never before. In a time of rote education she didn't lecture, use a textbook, or give formal examinations, treating the country boys and girls instead as individuals; setting them in competition not with each other, but with themselves.

Her method, a student remembered, was that of assigning prose and poetry—first for intensive study, extracting everything that could be extracted from the printed page, then reading it before the class as she listened, eyes burning, in a corner chair at the back of the room, following up with a searching, provocative critique. The purpose was to "motivate a student to find *all* the meaning. The author's intent and thought. In mood, in sound, in beauty. And project that to the rest of the class."

In Ed Murrow the extraordinary teacher found an extraordinary student.

Perhaps it was inevitable that the grandson of Joshua Murrow and Van Buren Lamb would become a speech major. But Ida Lou Anderson, herself a former Southerner, was also part of an intensely moral tradition that the boy from Guilford County felt right at home with, drawn to her not only for her technical competence—she was also a broadcasting coach and critic, adviser to the college radio station—but for what she was:

She "believed nothing and reverenced all." . . . [She was] a tolerant skeptic with all the tenacity of her Tennessee ancestors—a great teacher and a great student of those she taught. . . . The margin between mediocrity and mastery of the spoken word was measured in terms of her confidence, example and inspiration. She demanded not so much excellence as integrity. She could recognize not only ability, but humility, and she was inclined to place more value upon the latter. . . .[29]

Ed Murrow, accordingly, became her star pupil, disciple, and devoted friend. She in turn introduced him to the world of the classics, to poetry, and encouraged his love of music. Under her influence he became a voracious reader, soaking up what he could, like a sponge, in every possible area, the beginnings of a lifelong curiosity about the world.

The relationship was hardly one-sided, the age differential not all that acute. An intellectual and emotional bond was forged, lasting to the end of Anderson's life, a chaste but intense relationship in which she was at once mother, mistress, and mentor; she called him her masterpiece. (Not unnaturally, there was also a certain amount of jealousy vis-à-vis the favored pupil. A classmate and fellow speech major later wrote to Murrow that while he had liked him personally in those days, "Miss Anderson so often held you up as an example that there were times I wished you'd get laryngitis.") In his early years as a broadcaster, Murrow would continue to solicit her advice while she, her health finally failing, would spend the last months of her short life, blind and bedridden, listening by the radio, waiting for his voice to come in from London.

Ida Lou Anderson brought to its epitome a pattern laid down early and sustained through Ed Murrow's formative years—that of intellectual role models provided to a large extent by women. The male figures of his boyhood had been almost exclusively the workers and providers—lumberjacks, railroad men, farmers—home and school representing the feminine element, a pattern continuing into college. His development, therefore, the unfolding of his personality, was to proceed on two distinct levels, not always reconcilable—the blue-collar world, with its masculine camaraderie, and the world of the mind, female-dominated both in his earliest years and throughout the time of his formal education.

(He also enrolled in a radio broadcasting course, reputedly the first to be offered as part of a college curriculum. Its teacher, Maynard Lee Daggy, a well-known author and expert on public speaking, would sometimes be cited, along with Anderson, as an influence on Murrow, but the personal element was lacking from the outset; Professor Daggy thought the young man conceited and a bit too smooth.)[30]

Outside the classroom, he followed the success pattern of his high school years. His time served as janitor, he pledged to Kappa Sigma, his brothers' fraternity—the best on campus—moving into the big house on California Street and fitting in without a hitch. Kappa Sigs would later recall the brother known as "Tall Timber," pitching curve balls in front of 500 California Street, or graciously sharing dinner on the floor with the miserable initiates during "rough week."

He learned to dress, to move with a certain distinction, that sense of extra dimension evoked at the time by the novelist Sinclair Lewis in his just-published *Elmer Gantry*, describing another up-and-coming small-town boy:

> [He] had fastidiousness, a natural elegance. All the items of his wardrobe. . .were ready made. . .but on him they were graceful. . . .You felt that he would belong to any set in the world which he sufficiently admired. There was a romantic flair to his upturned overcoat collar . . .and his thoroughly commonplace ties hinted of clubs and regiments.[31]

He continued as star debater, representing WSC in the Pacific Forensic League competition. He joined the campus theater, playing leads, recalled by colleagues later as an exceptionally good actor—a memory that was to plague his career; no other journalist would be so held to account for having acted while in college. But it was in debating, arguing issues up and down the West Coast, and dealing in campus matters, that he found his greatest satisfaction, a political animal in the family tradition.

He made class president, was top ROTC cadet, an able campus politician—friendly to all though choosing real friends with care, and for life. Strikingly handsome by now, a gallant escort to Ida Lou Anderson, he seldom dated; lent his stellar presence to school dances, then stood aside, unable to dance; was popular, sought after, yet drew back from the battle of the sexes.

No one seemed to notice; it was easily precluded by the image of the campus leader and serious young man who hefted wheat sacks part time at the railyards and worked the logging camps in summertime to keep the college money coming in.

Not surprisingly, perhaps, his marks outside of Speech were not exceptional, his interests always elsewhere. (Including, at one point, basketball: Westerman Whillock, a friend of Lacey Murrow's, would recall his playing for WSC the night the team came through Boise—a big event; WSC was "one of the four powerhouses of the Northwest." Lacey's younger brother opened the game—"a scrawny, gangling kid"—hard-driving, workmanlike. The visitors won hands down, changed, and without a break, drove off to Pocatello. Whillock wondered how they did it.)[32]

By his senior year, Ed Murrow was president of the student government, an ROTC colonel and head of the Pacific Student Presidents Association, his full-page picture leading off the senior yearbook for the class of 1930. He had finally put the name "Egbert" behind him (though not yet legally. Whitman County records would disclose no petition for a change of name. It probably wasn't until 1944, with the filing of a delayed birth certificate—like many country boys, he hadn't had one to begin with—that the official "Edward" would be confirmed under law.)

He was "Ed Murrow" in the yearbook, "Ed Roscoe Murrow" in the records of his ROTC unit, which drilled faithfully every morning. Two years of duty was compulsory but he'd stayed with it, commanded now himself, captained Scabbard and Blade, the honorary military society. The school magazine, *Chinook*, showed the student officers standing at attention, dashing in the polished boots and high, stiff collars of their World War I uniforms, looking like figures out of the Hemingway novels so popular among their generation.

The atmosphere in which they trained was quite another matter. As Teapot Dome had shattered illusions about politics at the top, so had the aftermath of the war that was to have made the world safe for democracy. As a generation, the students shared the disenchantment of the post-Wilson era, the sense of postwar disillusion as much a part of their outlook as the more traditional values that saw honor and virtue in military service.

It is likely, therefore, that to the boys doing their morning drill, military service meant marching, camping, weaponry, discipline, all the manly stuff—playing soldier; but that war itself was not a reality. If the young people thought about it at all, in that final year of the 1920s, it was generally with revulsion and a determination never again to participate in another European conflict 6,000 miles away.

Perhaps in consequence, the students had chosen for their college play Channing Pollock's controversial antiwar drama, *The Enemy*, the sensation of the 1925 Broadway season—everything took a little longer, getting out to Washington—and a near miss for the Pulitzer Prize. Ed Murrow played the male lead.

It was an earnest play, full of good, round speeches, in keeping with the earnestness of both players and audience: "We must refute the teachings of centuries . . . that rage and murder are brave and glorious . . . and learn to be ashamed of a dishonest fatherland as we are of a dishonest father!" The students were right up there with the heroine, screaming above the roll of the drums: "Not *my* baby. *He* won't answer your trumpets. . . . We're through—*all of us!*"[33] (The original actress was reportedly cashing in, playing the scene two-a-day in vaudeville houses across the country.)

It was six years before the Nye committee hearings into World War I profits stacked up by the armaments industry, but the public backlash was already building; said the young yearbook editors, sagely: "The production left the audience with the conviction that the real enemy is commercialized hate."[34] (Parenthetically, it was Ed Murrow, ROTC officer, who stunned the audience with his portrayal of the doomed, neurotic antiwar protagonist.)

Late fall and winter of 1929 brought news of the crash on Wall Street, but the panic in New York hadn't much meaning to the young people in the small towns and cities of the Northwest, the ripple effect not yet felt. In Pullman, Ed Murrow was getting ready to attend the midwinter meeting of the National Student Federation of America, a loosely organized group representing the student governments of 300 to 400 member colleges across the country. The convention was to be held at Stanford University, the agenda ranging from campus problems to programs plugging "the furtherance of an enduring peace." The WSC delegate would be chairing two of the discussion groups.

Christmas week, instead of going home, he got his papers in order, packed his bags, and bought two coach seats to Palo Alto—one for himself, the other for the second WSC delegate. In the closing days of 1929 they boarded the train and headed for California, Murrow for a major change in his life.

Harry Chandler, publisher of the Los Angeles *Times*, was a Republican conservative with a sharp nose for politics, a passing interest in international affairs, and a low opinion of college students. Possibly he was also a betting man, because that winter $30,000 was at stake for the NSFA, with Chandler holding the purse strings.

The story has it that Chandler's portrait was being painted by the artist Winifred Rieber, wife of a UCLA dean, fund raiser, and part-time den mother to the NSFA; she had also lost a son in the Great War. Finding Chandler forced to sit and at her mercy, she sold him on her pet idea, at least as far as giving it a hearing—that contact between countries promoted peace and understanding, so why not begin with the leaders of tomorrow, i.e., the international program of the NSFA? Chandler, from either conviction or exhaustion, finally agreed to host a dinner to raise the money—provided the kids came up with a suitably impressive program and leadership at their upcoming meeting. Mrs. Rieber assured him they would; she also, she later said, threatened to paint donkey's ears on the portrait and sell it elsewhere if he didn't come across.

The plenary sessions of the Fifth Annual Congress of the National Student Federation of America began on January 1, 1930. In the campus auditorium at Palo Alto, 159 delegates from 109 colleges and universities met—a pretty good showing, considering the time and distance involved in the thirties, not to mention the state of everyone's finances. Speakers addressed the students; Judge Jackson H. Ralston of the American Civil Liberties Union on international law; George Creel, Wilson's wartime propaganda chief, on "The Power of Opinion"; Ray Lyman Wilbur, President of Stanford, now Hoover's Secretary of the Interior, spoke over a radio hookup. Resolutions were offered; votes taken; brief speeches made for or against.

It was in support of one such resolution that Ed Murrow took the floor, accusing his fellow students of sticking their heads in the sand, of being provincial, concerned overly with "fraternities, football and fun," and calling for a broadening of student interest in national and world affairs. In the audience a UCLA senior named Chester Williams, active in the federation's inner circle, watched the six-foot-two delegate from Washington State College speaking in a deep, obviously trained voice and thought: *Harry Chandler*. It seemed like the answer to a prayer.

It was not by any means a first impression. Williams and Murrow had met at an intercollegiate debating match in Southern California, Murrow preceded by his reputation as a West Coast debater. Williams' debating partner on that occasion had been a fellow undergraduate named Ralph Bunche. They had met again at a gathering of local student presidents at the University of Washington in Seattle. Williams would recall being impressed, "but that time we weren't thinking of a president to be elected at Stanford."[35]

The short speech had taken the convention by storm. More importantly, it impressed the power group, the executive committee, quickly sold on the idea of Murrow for president—with the result that the genuinely surprised delegate from Washington State found himself approached by the kingmakers, ready to put him up as candidate. He was not, of course, from a first-line school, but that was no problem. Had he thought of running? No. Wouldn't he like to run? Well—no, not really.

The traditional picture of Murrow is that of a man who instantly recognized opportunity. But not on this occasion. In fact, he was uncertain about the whole thing, and for good reason: the job was unpaid. His predecessors in office had been undergraduates, operating out of dormitory rooms; he had no money, no plans for after graduation, was dubious about tying himself up for a year. He needed a job, not a title; a salary, not an unpaid position.[36]

On the other hand, there were organizational inducements: the Chandler offer, an international debating program, a weekly radio series over the Columbia Broadcasting System—and, no doubt, the opportunity to wield power, get some action, among his peers. Besides, they assured him, he could always be defeated.

For whatever reason, he finally said yes. The executive committee put up another candidate to make him feel comfortable—the boy was firmly pledged to withdraw, which he did on the second ballot; but there was no need. The candidate from Washington State won overwhelmingly, becoming for the year 1930–31 president of the nation's largest and most influential secular student organization.

He was graduated with his class on June 2, 1930, a B.A. in Speech and a second lieutenant in the inactive reserve. Beyond the campus, Washington State, like the rest of the country, was reeling in the backwash of Black Thursday: businesses folding; the mills and canneries closing down; mines curtailing operations; ships idle at the dockside in the coastal cities. For the students leaving school, things had changed too quickly; their expectations had been blasted, the dream gone sour, the children of permanent prosperity become the children of the Depression. The graduating class reflected the dichotomy of the time: the Jazz Age plunged into depression; the student cadets marching in parade, Ed Murrow in the lead, yet fearing nothing so much as another war.

Few, under the circumstances, paid attention to the bad news from abroad: the spread of the Depression; financial chaos in Central Europe; new masses of unemployed ready to listen to anyone promising a way out; hard times sharpening old national differences; intensified conflict in Asia.

Europe and Asia were a long way off; besides, this was the peace generation. America had had a bellyful the last time around, and times were hard enough at home. If the rest of the world went to war, it would have to do so without the class of 1930.

In the meantime, Ed Murrow was on his way to New York and the central office of the NSFA. It was two weeks after graduation. He had a one-way train ticket in his pocket, forty dollars in cash, and two pieces of matched luggage. No job yet, but friends were finding him a place to stay for a while. After that, summer in Europe and an international students' meeting; he hoped to work his way over. He was twenty-two.

III

New York

1.

He later recalled the old man as he first saw him, seated at the far end of the tower office, behind the massive desk cluttered with the artifacts of a lifetime in the news business. He was frail-looking, the heavy head and shrunken shoulders outlined against the tall windows looking out over Forty-third Street, wisps of thin white hair creating an aureole of light in the late-autumn sun: Adolph Ochs at seventy-two, publisher and patriarch of The New York *Times*.

The visitor sat on the edge of one of the straight-backed chairs reserved for guests or at least callers of lesser importance, impressed with the appurtenances of power: the twenty-foot ceiling; oil paintings; the endless Oriental carpet; the large double doors leading to the assembly area where the *Times* staff gathered on state occasions.

He had gotten an appointment just by calling and, now that he was in the presence, wasted no time. Quietly and methodically the visitor outlined his plans for the upcoming student convention at the Atlanta Biltmore—hardly an earthshaking event, generally grist for the education desk. Except that the meeting was to be racially integrated and this was 1930 and he was explaining, with perfect logic, exactly how he intended to run, without incident, a five-day integrated convention at a major hotel in the Deep South—with, if Mr. Ochs was agreeable, the help of The New York *Times*.

They wanted sympathetic coverage, of course, but not just a rewrite of their press releases. Specifically he needed a reporter there—preferably someone from the Deep South, someone understanding and, most important of all, a damn good newspaperman. Ochs, who knew something of prejudice as the son of German-Jewish immigrants, fell in with the plan. The young man went back to his basement office, where he reported the results to the volunteer staff. They were jubilant. He smiled wryly. "Well . . . we'll see."

By the fall of 1930, Ed Murrow was fairly well established in New York City. By contrast, his arrival there, in the early summer, had been unpromising. Martha Biehle of the NSFA inner circle wrote a quick letter to her New York friend Mary Marvin Breckinridge, part of their network and past officer, seeking help for the new incumbent:

> He seems to have picked up his belongings and will hunt for some kind of a job while here.
> He is a boy who has worked his way through school and cannot afford any extra expenses. I am therefore very eager to find some place for him to stay for a few weeks while he is trying to locate something to maintain himself here. If we can find some family who will be willing to give Ed room and breakfast for about two weeks, it will mean a great deal to him and will make the little money that he has go so much further. Can you suggest a family who have a home in N.Y.C.? . . . Ed is a very charming boy who would be very pleasant company I think. . . .

The problem was settled by the time he arrived on a sweltering Wednesday afternoon. New York in 1930 was hardly the end of the rainbow: Depression-ridden; breadlines; shantytowns in Central Park. "See it while you can," newcomers were told, "because there's going to be a revolution."

His destination was on lower Madison Avenue, at the end of a row of crumbling redbrick town houses, once elegant, now given over to organizations of modest means. Around the corner, past the peeling columns of the fake Greek portico, he found the side entrance, the office two or three steps down—a long, low room shared with two other youth groups and running the length of the basement. Inside there was a jumble of old desks, rattan furniture, volunteers working the typewriters, telephone, and mimeograph. Posters of faraway places lined the bare walls. The telephone listing proclaimed, rather grandiosely: "NSFA, Foreign Relations Office."

The group had begun five years before, the offshoot of an intercollegiate conference at Princeton, students from the forty-eight states gathered to hear Norman Thomas, Clarence Darrow, and Henry Stimson debate the question of U.S. entry into the World Court. Formation of the federation followed, the first of its kind, its aims set forth in terms that were properly earnest, if a little vague—"understanding among the students of the world"; development of a student opinion on the big issues; no more war. To that end the office on Thirty-sixth Street sponsored open-forum discussions on the American campuses, polled the membership on matters of controversy, brought foreign debating teams to the United States. At the same time they ran a student news service, operated cheap tours to Europe, and were just beginning a dialogue with student groups in China, Japan, and Latin America.

They were the great American student center: nonradical and—at the time of Murrow's accession—totally apolitical.

They also sent delegates to the yearly student congresses held in Europe by the Conférence Internationale des Étudiants. The first group had gone off in 1926. In the summer of 1930, it was the turn of Ed Murrow, barely two weeks out of the Northwest.

In the backyard of an Italian speakeasy he had a quick briefing from Biehle and also Chet Williams, in from California, both battle-scarred veterans of the often stormy CIE meetings in Europe. Murrow, who had never been beyond the West Coast, showed an instinctive grasp of what was needed. "I remember it was like trying to explain a mathematical problem to Einstein," Williams recalled. "But Ed listened as if his life depended upon what we were telling him."

July 4, he was on a boat headed for England, one of several group leaders shepherding the NSFA delegation across northern Europe in exchange for expenses and a third-class ticket on the Holland-America Line. (The delegates also included a new friend and erstwhile booster from Stanford—Lewis F. Powell, later of the U.S. Supreme Court, then a studious prelaw from Washington and Lee whom Murrow promptly nicknamed "Judge.")

At Brussels, the CIE was sufficiently impressed with the young American to offer him the presidency.

Murrow, for his part, was less impressed with the CIE, watching the national delegations at one another's throats over the boundaries drawn at Versailles and Trianon. Two weeks at a CIE congress, it was said, was usually enough to deflate undue hopes about "understanding among students."

The fifty-eight Americans were part of an English-speaking contingent, often voting together; the British student union had been instrumental in getting the NSFA on its feet. Yet Murrow, at twenty-two, was no Anglophile. The young man transported directly from an American backwater into the middle of Europe's postwar problems had come with secondhand knowledge and no language skills—more pro-German than pro-Ally, his views reflective of the prevailing wisdom on American campuses: Versailles as an injustice; Germany as victim; the postwar boundaries a violation of ethnic rights; the defeated nations dealt the short end of the stick. He supported the Deutsche Studentenschaft despite its bid to represent the ethnic Germans of the Sudetenland and Austria, and he refused the CIE's presidency offer when equal status was denied to the German delegation.

At the personal level, it was the most stimulating time he had ever known. In meeting rooms and student cafés, Ed Murrow found himself plunged into the mainstream of European student life, with its clash of cultures and opinions: Slavic delegates from successor states; black-shirted Italian Fascist youth; young French disciples of Romain Rolland; Germans with paper editions of Karl Kraus.

They were older, more sophisticated then he, politically active, many with outright party affiliations. Some were the functionaries of ministries back home. It was Murrow's first contact with students as a class and as a political force.

The mix left him uneasy. The NSFA leader who had called for more student participation in his own country shrank from the overtly partisan activism of his older European contemporaries. Yet the influence of the Europeans held over: Four years later, when the NSFA was torn by the question of joining with the student Left to form the American Youth Congress, Murrow, by then on the NSFA board, would throw his weight to those in favor of entry. "People like Ed brought in the connection with the Left," said an NSFA friend of the time, a serious-minded young Marxist named Joseph Cadden. "He quickly came to our side in favor of bringing politics into the organization."

He spent eight weeks abroad that summer, swinging through England, Holland, France, and Germany, developing contacts that would ripen into important sources, sometimes close friendships: Ivison Macadam, his British counterpart at Brussels, later head of the Royal Institute for International Affairs; young socialists and centrists; Dr. Fritz Beck of Munich University, head of international programs, father figure to visiting Americans and youth leaders of the Catholic Center party.

In Depression-ridden Berlin, he saw Adolf Hitler electioneering, thought him rather ludicrous at first—he knew no German—then watched, riveted, as in only ten minutes the little brown-clad man had the crowd in the palm of his hand. The upcoming German elections were about to transform his party from a small splinter group into the second-largest bloc in the Reichstag.

And England? It had been his first and last stop, but Murrow, perhaps determinedly, remained unimpressed with the mother country. England, he told a BBC audience years later, seemed to him "a sort of museum piece. . . . small. . . . complacent, not important.

"I thought your streets narrow and mean; your tailors overadvertised; your climate unbearable, your class-consciousness offensive. . . . Your young men seemed without vigor or purpose. I admired your history, doubted your future and suspected the historians had merely agreed upon a myth. . . ."

Returning to New York, he found a place to live, got the federation's agreement to a weekly stipend, and turned to domestic matters, including—just two weeks after his arrival—his first venture into network radio.

The Columbia Broadcasting System was just over two years old, a small growing cluster of stations, its operations centering largely on the key station and prime outlet, WABC in New York.[1] Months before, under the leadership of its aggressive young president—William Paley was then not yet thirty—the company had vacated its quarters in the Paramount Building to take a lease on one of the new office towers going up among the old mansions of midtown Madison Avenue. Number 485 stood alone at the corner of Fifty-second Street, a spanking new, multi-tiered beige brick giant, dwarfing the flower-bordered town houses across the way.

In 1929, the company had agreed to provide airtime for the NSFA, mostly in the afternoon. It was a fair exchange: Daytime radio, dead air waiting to be filled, brought in little or no revenue. The young people helped fill it; more than that, they lined up as speakers public figures who appeared at no cost whatever, lending prestige and a note of gravity to a new and still-suspect medium.

They took themselves seriously and so, apparently, did the network. *The University of the Air* went out over thirty stations. On September 15, 1930, at three-thirty in the afternoon, Edward Murrow made his debut over the Columbia Broadcasting System as host to one Robert L. Kelly, Executive Secretary of the Association of American Colleges, speaking on the earnest topic, "Looking Forward with Students."

Their CBS contact was an Anglo-American named Fred Willis, a former adman fond of regaling the students with stories of how, jobless in the Depression and weighing a return to England, he had invested one last nickel in a telephoned request for an interview, and come away as assistant to William Paley. He was attractive, ambitious, new to radio, and out to prove himself. Never mind the education officials, he told Murrow and Williams; he wanted names—big names, radio exclusives that would add luster to the network. The boys in turn spun visions before his eyes of world figures virtually lining up for the CBS microphone.

That they succeeded was due partly to Murrow's powers of persuasion, partly to the help of the European student unions, but mostly to the readiness of world leaders to address the young. There were remote pickups from London of Mahatma Gandhi and Prime Minister Ramsay MacDonald, from Berlin, the aged President Paul von Hindenburg. Transatlantic broadcasting was still a novelty, and Murrow, at twenty-two, was already learning something of the excitement, frustration, and expense of arranging an overseas hookup.

In New York, they lined up Albert Einstein and the Indian poet Rabindranath Tagore, both on first-time visits to the United States. Murrow decided he liked the program and by 1931 was in overall charge, selecting speakers, appearing often as host and interlocutor on a wide variety of topics, from women's rights to the world struggle for markets.

From the start, he was attuned to the possibilities of the new medium. But the real power was still with the print press. He knew it, and he acted on it. Under its new president, the student federation moved out of the travel category of the metropolitan dailies into the news columns. Suddenly The New York *Times* was carrying the results of NSFA polls on disarmament, military training, the League of Nations, its young president scoring in print the "political apathy and smug complacency" of academia. He took his opinions on the road, working the college lecture circuit, speaking on "Provincialism on the American Campus" or "Mass Production in the College Factory." The NSFA flyer showed an amiable collegian with a large-toothed grin and brilliantined hair, the heading proclaiming in bold-faced type: THE SPOKESMAN FOR AMERICAN STUDENTS.

The point of his travels had at times less of consciousness raising than fund raising. Harry Chandler had reneged on Mrs. Rieber's deal, dues-paying membership was at an all-time low. But Murrow was magnetic, capable of rallying the troops to the cause, knowing instinctively how to get others, in the words of one associate, to "help him paint the fence and think it a privilege."

In New York, he teamed up with Chet Williams, now Executive Secretary of the NSFA, to rent a walk-up over on Thirty-eighth Street, where a few high-stooped brownstones-turned-rooming houses survived between the storefronts.

Their shared home was three flights up—a high-ceilinged cavern of a room, dimmed from its former elegance: bare floors; high, bare windows facing the street; the usual furnished-room appointments; wallpaper faded to a uniform brown; electric hot plate and cupboard in the bathroom; no telephone. One of the young women in the office had donated a radio. When temperatures began plunging, the newcomer faced with his first Northeastern winter also took lessons in cheap insulation—convincing him, he later said, of the true superiority of the print medium:

> Do you know what a triple layer of newspaper will do if you wrap it around you or under your coat—or if you spread it between the mattress and the springs? There's warmth and real protection there (and *no* radio or television station can make this claim!).[2]

By Depression standards their salaries, though modest, were more than adequate and, when pooled, left them comparatively well-off. But there wasn't much spare change. When they weren't taking in a blue plate special somewhere, Murrow, a tolerable short-order cook, concocted dinner over the hot plate, the apartment permeated by the smell of fried fish from the bathroom. (And admittedly, the kitchen-lavatory setup had its drawbacks. Williams would recall Murrow on one occasion, proudly

CHAPTER III

displaying the technique of flipping a fried egg, a demo by the master;
the egg went up, over, and into the toilet.)

Otherwise, they shared the chores, with allowances made for the fact
that one of the roommates was partly disabled. A polio victim, Chet
Williams had fought his way back from childhood paralysis that had left
his body with a degree of overall impairment. "I was somewhat limited,"
he recalled later, "especially on the steps. But Ed was very perceptive
in recognizing that anyone handicapped likes to do it on their own and
not to be constantly helped gratuitously. . . . In any case, he always
treated me as a normal person, to be helped when I *asked* for help."

Evenings were often spent at the Nippon Club, where the Japanese
consul general, an old-line liberal, held informal bull sessions to sound
out American attitudes on outstanding questions between Washington
and Tokyo. Williams was to recall his roommate on those nights: hunched
over, a careful listener (and already a chain smoker), laying out his arguments vis-à-vis Japanese claims on Manchuria.

At twenty-two he was already showing traces of a deep-lying skepticism,
possibly engendered by his hard upbringing. "We were both optimists,
but Ed had a tendency to be much more critical and less hopeful about
how things would turn out."[3] A supporter of peace movements, he was
doubtful of their chances, placed little hope in either the League of
Nations or the Kellogg-Briand Pact of two years before, which had presumably guaranteed peace to his generation.

Nor was he particularly attracted to domestic politics, drawn neither
to the major parties, which had so miserably failed, nor to the radicalism
drawing so many of the young. He was a man of the center, pro-estab-
lishment, like the organization he headed. But there was nothing in his
attitude inimical either to communism per se or to the Soviet Union.
Indeed, the crash and its aftermath had given Marxism a wider credibility;
the Depression did seem to be doing what the Communists said would
happen all along. If he and his friends weren't converts, therefore, they
did maintain an open, even well-disposed curiosity, seeing the enemy in
Rome and, lately, Berlin but not in Moscow.

The mimeo machines hummed all through the fall in the basement
office on Thirty-sixth Street. In the outer room Williams and a staff of
eleven kept the programs going. Murrow, in a separate alcove, caught
up on backlog and saw foreign visitors. They worked long hours and
weekends, trading cracks at closing time with the stenographer's husband,
a young reporter for the *Daily Worker*, the newspaper of the American
Communist Party, who, stopping by for his wife, would tease the young
men about their conservatism.

Most of the volunteers, like most of the past officers, were women—
bright, active WASPs from Ivy League colleges who had helped found the
organization and still formed the working nucleus. Murrow, taking office,

found himself dealing with the kind of women he had never known before: independent-minded; financially secure; educated at the choicest schools of the Northeast. The liberated women of the postwar period, riding the crest of what seemed like a new momentum. Student leaders in their own right, they had no compunctions about dealing with their male colleagues on an equal footing. Murrow would wind up marrying one of them.

The women liked him, and the men, too. He was easy to get along with, uncontentious. Male friends regarded him as a good group politician—charming, even jovial, a middling poker player and an expert crapshooter. Joe Cadden remembered his "great capacity to laugh," offset on occasion by sudden retreats into gloomy silence.

Still, except as colleagues, women played almost no role in his life. The NSFA women were chums, fellow workers. If they met outside the office, it was usually they who did the inviting, with Williams and the others along, a group affair with well-disposed parents picking up the tab. The fact was, Murrow dated little or not at all, his roommate later recalling nothing of the usual masculine exchanges between two young men sharing quarters.

"Actually," said Williams, "I cannot remember he dated except for organizational purposes, and he never did talk about sex life or refer to women in terms of sex objects. No one ever heard him talk about conquests or indulge in the usual fraternity stuff. His good looks and chivalrous behavior attracted women, but I never heard *them* talk about that aspect of his relationship. . . . Whether he had a girlfriend who was close, I never knew. . . ."

"He was tall and good-looking," said Mary Marvin Breckinridge, another NSFA regular, "attractive. He was never especially a beau, but we were always nice friends. He had poise and confidence and courtesy, never seemed like a country bumpkin."

"I think he was scared of gals," said a third friend; "he was not easy with them. No womanizer. He had a lot of personal charm—warm, not ebullient. But it needed motivation."[4]

Even so, Chet Williams hardly expected the storm that broke over his head the day he agreed to a double date for himself and Murrow without first clearing it. It was nothing special: His friend had a friend, and could he bring a friend? "Oh, I'm sure Ed won't mind," he answered innocently.

Ed minded. Very much. In a sudden, icy fury that caught the other completely off-balance, Murrow turned on his roommate—what made him presume, he'd pick his own girls, thank you, and so on. Williams had never seen him so upset; their first and only serious conflict. "My fault," he decided. It was a while before they were back on speaking terms, and for a few days the atmosphere in the walk-up was glacial.

The sights from the train windows, in the early winter of 1930, were not particularly heartening, the Depression tightening its grip. Ed Murrow, crossing the country in preparation for the year-end student congress, moved through a landscape of hobo jungles, families fleeing dust and foreclosure, clashes between farmers and the National Guard—images that drove home the realities of the Depression and formed his earliest political consciousness.

"Ed felt the world something fierce," a friend remembered. "He brooded; he felt what people were going through—the poverty all around; I remember the foreclosures were taking place in the Farm Belt."[5]

By contrast the tidy campuses seemed a little unreal, and in a year's time he was to shock a New York audience by labeling the college system "a method for prolonging infancy."

In the meantime, he was learning about continental America, traveling for days, sometimes weeks on end by bus and rail through the isolated small towns of the South and Midwest, folding his long basketball player's frame across two seats at night. He wore a cross in his lapel; divinity students rode at half fare.

As it turned out, it was a practical education in the diversities of American life—the sheer distances; the regional concerns; the attitudes of those beyond the population centers—and invaluable, in the long run, to the broadcaster interpreting events to a nationwide mass audience.

He was also traveling with a hidden agenda.

The NSFA was almost entirely white, black colleges represented by a purely token enrollment. Yet its constitution specifically stipulated representative meetings "irrespective of race." Murrow and Williams, sparked that year by YW-YMCA plans for an integrated meeting at Detroit, decided on a small-scale "affirmative action" of their own.[6]

The months on the road, therefore, were also a time of undercover planning, of arrangements which to the post-sixties generation would seem almost bizarre in view of their modest ends—i.e., the simple seating of blacks and whites in the same room. Murrow was out, moreover, to reform not the South but his own organizaton, with its Middle American base.

To that purpose he made the rounds of as many black colleges as he could reach, actively recruiting membership, sounding out student officers on his idea. Some said yes; others, no. In the end a few more declared themselves ready to go along, the token enrollment just a little less token.

At certain white Southern women's colleges, he met with campus leaders—student body officials, newspaper editors—recruiting volunteers for what he called the flying squadron, ostensibly to serve as ushers, their real purpose kept under wraps. "The women will carry the day," he told his roommate on returning, "if anyone can."

In Atlanta, he finalized arrangements with the Biltmore, the contract carefully drawn up to specify the seating of *all delegates*, affixed to it, a list of participating colleges and a copy of the NSFA constitution. Heading the list was Atlanta University, a black school, one of the three host colleges (the other two were Agnes Scott and the Georgia Institute of Technology). There was an awful lot of fine print. The management gave it a brief once-over, as Murrow suspected they would, and signed without further questions.

Finally, he met with Adolph Ochs. By early winter they were ready to move.

The last week of December, the executive committee met behind closed doors at the NSFA suite in the Atlanta Biltmore. Earlier that day, at Murrow's invitation, the presidents of the host colleges had come to lunch—Dr. John Hope of Atlanta University was light enough to "pass" the Biltmore portals unimpeded—Murrow reasoning correctly that recalcitrant committee members were unlikely to object to an open convention in the black educator's presence.

They discussed the arrangements: entertainment; delegate housing in the holiday-emptied dorms. Then came the question, What about the final banquet and dance?

A pall descended on the room. Throats were cleared. Tactful queries: Could not Atlanta U perhaps make separate arrangements for its delegates—just to spare them embarrassment, of course? Dr. Hope said he'd ask the student council; did they want him to do that? More silences, more carefully worded suggestions as Murrow and Hope sat quietly, watching the others squirm.

Finally, Murrow broke the tension: Could they put off further discussion until he'd talked with the hotel management? The relief in the room was palpable. Murrow laughed quietly and turned to the President of Atlanta University: "Dr. Hope, we won't ask you to rescue us before we really find ourselves in trouble."

Later in the day, the guests departed, he threw his cards on the table: *Did the committee wish him to press for full execution of the contract with the hotel?* The dam broke. The fight went on for several hours. Murrow waited while the others argued themselves hoarse; then, once passions were spent, suggested again that they await reactions to the opening session. Again, there were no demurrals. Said one member who was present: "He'd have been a great labor negotiator."

Then, in a change of pace, he told the committee that he regarded it his duty to uphold the constitution. Anyone who didn't like it was, of course, free to offer an amendment, but it would have to be submitted to the member colleges.

He was completely in control, well into high gear now that the plan was launched, though far from sanguine. No amount of contractual arm twisting, he told his lieutenant, was going to get the black delegates served in the ballroom. As for the opening session, a single hothead, challenging the seating arrangements, could make the whole thing blow up in their faces.

* * *

Monday afternoon, December 29, 1930, the Sixth Annual Congress of the NSFA opened in the ballroom of the Atlanta Biltmore—some 300 delegates from more than 150 colleges and universities, the largest and most eagerly attended convention in the short history of the federation. The Atlanta papers were full of its presence, the student president and his officers smiling away in the front sections of the *Journal* and the *Constitution*.

Murrow, gaveling the meeting to order, opened on a note of levity, with Will Rogers' words to the business community for 1931: "Please on New Year's don't predict prosperity. Don't predict anything. Just say 'I pass.' Good times are coming but if you guys say it, it's liable to crab it."

As laughter washed over the convention hall, a delegate bolted from his seat. "Where's the telegraph office? I've got to wire my college that I'm leaving this convention."

Signals went out, and the flying squadron moved into action. The delegate found his path blocked by a human barrier of resolutely soft-voiced Southern women, anxious to help: Why, whatever was the trouble?

The young man, halted in his tracks, was by now reduced to embarrassment, his adrenaline dissipated, mumbling something about college rules forbidding him to attend meetings where "Negroes" were admitted on an equal footing with whites.

Then, like the payoff in a one-two punch, The New York *Times* reporter came ambling up. Ochs had outdone himself. His man had turned out to be from Alabama—fatherly, understanding, responsive to Murrow's pre-convention briefing.

Gently but firmly, he drew the boy aside and in a quiet Birmingham drawl asked, Did he really want to bolt and make him write a story that would make them all look like monkeys in the pages of that Yankee paper he worked for? The delegate, chastened, returned to his seat.

With that, the fight moved underground, lasting all week beneath the surface of receptions, student workshops, sightseeing, and debates over the Hawley-Smoot Tariff. In committee a Southern white faction rammed through an amendment authorizing exclusion of members "for just cause"— a transparent attempt to impose a racial ban. By midweek the opposition had drafted a countering resolution specifically rejecting race as a bar to membership. In the regional meetings the issue had begun heating up, with a possible split looming ahead, solid North versus solid South. Murrow, lining up support among his contacts, advised the Northeastern delegation to stay out of the debate.

New Year's Eve, cold and wet, ushered in the second year of the Depression. Atlantans that week read of New York Governor Franklin Roosevelt, inaugurated for his second term, deploring the growing concentration of governmental power. The broadcasting industry reported a boom despite the economic slump, radio factories projecting record sales for 1931. The NSFA had gotten nowhere near the electronic medium this time, beyond a radio address by Norman Thomas over a CBS hookup. While Ed Murrow gaveled his group through its paces, the big news on the radio page was Otis Skinner launching the *RCA Hour,* Bobby Jones signed for a series of golf talks, and the closing of the popular Sunday series of Ernestine Schumann-Heink.

That Wednesday night at the Biltmore, two ballrooms had been cleared for the annual New Year's Eve gala, the visiting white students mingling with Atlanta society. Murrow, as NSFA head, put in an appearance, following a day of intensive lobbying among the delegates. The two opposing measures would be coming up before the full session on Thursday evening, with an all-out floor fight threatening the closing day.

In the meantime, the students were enjoying themselves, the dancers moving back and forth between the dining room and the Georgian Room, two orchestras playing, the tables, as described by a local society reporter, "softly illuminated by glowing candles and artistic lamps with table decorations of mixed flowers whose warm colors pleasingly contrasted with the brilliant greens and vivid reds of the decorations of the rooms."[7]

Friday morning, they opened the final session. On the dais, Nellie Tayloe Ross, former Governor of Wyoming, Vice-Chairman of the Democratic National Committee, called on the students to assert their leadership: "If you have views . . . dare to voice them. Dare to stand alone." She, too, had had a private briefing.

Finally, the convention got to the matter listed as "unfinished business." The resolution came up, a motion made to table it, that motion in turn challenged. When the vote was taken, the entire congress, by a wide margin, had gone on record specifically instructing the executive committee "not to discriminate against any applicant for membership because of race or color." Murrow had succeeded in putting together a coalition of Southern, Western, and Midwestern votes, isolating the diehards to the point where only a handful of delegates were ready to go on record in support of a racial ban. The Atlanta *Constitution* and, of course, The New York *Times* carried the results, a last service of their resident reporter: STUDENTS REJECT BAN FOR RACE OR COLOR/NATIONAL FEDERATION OF ATLANTA [*sic*] VOTES DOWN OBJECTIONS BY SOUTH. . . .

As the congress ended, Ed Murrow was reelected NSFA president for 1931, by unanimous acclaim.

On one point, the federation had to face 1930 realities. The contract on seating all the delegates said nothing about serving them dinner. On the matter of the final banquet, the law was with the management. Civil disobedience was unthought-of; separate but equal arrangements with Atlanta U. were unthinkable. They ate together—at the Biltmore—in a manner of speaking, the flying squadron members passing their plates to the black delegates. However it might have seemed in later times, in

1930 it was outsmarting the opposition. Later they learned that the Y interracial conference, meeting in the North, had been evicted and forced to move to another hotel.

(It was hardly the millennium either. Several years later at an NSFA dinner in Washington, D.C., a group of whites forced black delegates off the dance floor; the leadership after an emergency all-night session reaffirmed the antidiscrimination clause of the constitution. They all had a way to go.)

Nevertheless, the 1930 Atlanta congress remained a vivid memory for those who were there. Sometime in the late fifties, Chester S. Williams, dining at the Atlanta Biltmore, found himself the object of close scrutiny by the black maître d'. Hadn't they met somewhere before? Williams drew a blank; he didn't recollect eating in the ballroom. How long had the gentleman been with the hotel? More than thirty-five years. Then it dawned. Did he perhaps know of Edward R. Murrow?

The elderly maître d' beamed and grasped his hand: "I know now. You are Mr. Williams, and you were here way back when Mr. Murrow opened the front door of the Atlanta Biltmore for the first time to Negro students. Do I remember! I'll never forget. . . ."[8]

In December, 1931, Ed Murrow stood before the NSFA convention in Toledo as outgoing president and honorary director for the coming spring. Outside, financial panic was spreading, the new senior class graduating into chronic unemployment. Overseas events were also casting their shadow: economic chaos in Europe; Japanese troops in Manchuria; fascism on the rise. Murrow, attending a CIE meeting in Bucharest, had had his first glimpse of the green-shirted Iron Guard. Returning, he reported national hatreds "rife," sharpened by depressed economic conditions. By contrast, U.S. college polls were revealing overwhelming student support for arms reduction, and the Toledo congress had voted against ROTC. Under Murrow's leadership, his own support of ROTC notwithstanding, the NSFA had arranged for special campus screenings of the antiwar film *All Quiet on the Western Front*.

Yet within two years a *Times* report would note a growing conservatism within the NSFA, a backing off from controversy, student activism already preempted by those farther to the left.

Murrow, taking his leave in the winter of 1931, departed with a last swipe at the "provincialism" of American students. The new leadership had his agreement to chair the spring campaign, but in essence he had already moved on, the result of an offer made in the closing months of the year—his first real job, and one that would draw him, at twenty-three, closer to the center of the events heating up in Europe.

2.

At sixty-seven, Stephen Pierce Duggan, founder and Director of the Institute of International Education, still cut an imposing figure: handsome, charismatic, with a small white beard and searching blue eyes; a riveting public speaker and communicator who had been among the earliest commentators on network radio.

In 1931, casting around for a replacement for his longtime assistant at the institute, he decided on Ed Murrow.

They had met in 1930, Duggan a mainstay of the NSFA—his elder daughter had been among the founders—the two organizations, the federation and the institute, cooperating informally on student programs. As Murrow's term ended, Duggan, impressed with the younger man's ability, had offered to put up his name for the opening. Ed, restless with city life, wasn't sure he wanted it.

He said as much to his ex-roommate when they lunched one day in late 1931. Their Thirty-eighth Street household had split up that January—Williams into married life uptown, Murrow to a shared bachelor apartment in Greenwich Village.

They discussed the offer. Said Williams later: "He told me that he was giving it some consideration, though he didn't know what he was going to do. Then, in his usual open manner he said, 'Why don't you apply, too?' And so we both did. And—he got it."

He had also found his father figure. A sought-after lecturer and consultant, Stephen Duggan had traveled extensively, studied educational systems around the world, advised the Soviet government on the administration of its workers' colleges. In 1931 he was four years retired as professor emeritus from the College of the City of New York, where he had been a founder of the departments of political science, education, and adult education. His farewell dinner had been a glittering civic occasion, with tributes from such as Walter Lippmann, Franklin Roosevelt, and Carrie Chapman Catt.

Duggan was a reformer, a passionate believer in human betterment, noblesse oblige, the duty of the educated to change the world. Opening the first NSFA conference in 1926, he had called upon the students to "shoulder the burden"—i.e., enter politics—and upon the colleges to confront "the serious problems of the political, social and economic organization of society."

Inevitably the twenty-three-year-old Murrow and the sixty-seven-year-old Duggan were drawn to each other, working in tandem, Murrow as surrogate son.

Founded in 1919 with backing from the Carnegie Endowment for International Peace, the IIE was a pioneer in international educational exchange, later becoming administering body for the Fulbright program with its own glass and steel palace opposite the United Nations. In 1931, however, it was a shoestring operation, more ideals than money, operating out of a set of rooms atop a narrow loft building on New York's West Side—some 2,000 square feet of crowded space accommodating the founder-director, his assistant, several women officers, and a handful of overworked stenographers.

"A sort of unofficial educational embassy" Murrow called it, with informal ties to the State Department: the focal point of exchanges in programs and ideas between the United States and Europe, Asia, Latin America, and the Middle East.

Much of his new job was routine: supervising the student exchanges; corresponding with bureaus abroad; evaluating project proposals; drafting reports; making recommendations for increases or cuts in operating expenditures. From early on he showed a capacity for turning out a large, steady volume of work, a highly organized mind, able to function simultaneously at different levels yet capable of focusing on each with apparently single-minded concentration: the perfect *apparatchik*, disdainful of anyone who couldn't quite measure up as an administrator.

Underlying the daily routine, however—and of greater impact on his future—was his unofficial role as backup to a politically acute boss with a finger in every pie.

Stephen Duggan was a man of causes: against Fascism, and the Japanese military presence in China; for academic freedom, and openings to the Soviet Union; an active opponent of U.S. policy in the Caribbean and South America, and an outspoken critic of the Platt Amendment. He was a high-profile figure in peace movement circles—Channing Pollock, playwright of *The Enemy*, wouldn't consider a Broadway opening without Professor Duggan in the audience.

He broadcast for CBS, sat on the Council on Foreign Relations and the editorial board of its influential house organ, *Foreign Affairs*. An early backer of Franklin Roosevelt, he was a welcome guest in Albany and at the Roosevelt town house in Manhattan—a man whose opinions were said to carry considerable weight with the Governor and who in New Deal days would round off a Washington trip with visits to the President and Secretary of State Cordell Hull.

Where Duggan went, his assistant followed. At a time when many of his contemporaries were drawn to radicalism, young Murrow, at twenty-four, was catapulted into the school-tie world of old and exclusive club-rooms, venerable advisers, informal dinner meetings at the Century or the Town Hall clubs—the interlocking circles of academics, foundations, university trustees, Wall Street lawyers, and financial figures that would later be lumped together under the heading of the "Eastern Establishment."

Entering as "Edw. R. Murrow of the staff," he would become, in time, the youngest member by some thirty years to be elected to the Council on Foreign Relations.

At the office, he followed up on the professor's initiatives and his often controversial public positions, working closely with League of Nations officials and a network of public interest groups, chief among them the prestigious Institute of Pacific Relations, then about to acquire the services of a capable young Sinologist named Owen Lattimore.

Following Duggan's lead, Murrow also joined the American-Russian Institute, organized in the twenties by American intellectuals such as John Dewey and George Counts of Columbia University: domestically anti-Communist, pro-Soviet at the water's edge. Its stated objective: "to promote international peace through the fostering of friendship between the USSR and the USA."

They called themselves nonpolitical, pushed for U.S. recognition of the Soviet regime, planned a program of cultural exchange, and arranged Town Hall lectures by Maurice Hindus, Julien Bryan, and Anna Louise Strong. Murrow, as assistant to the director, arranged the meetings and handled the details.

"He was excited about it—loved his work at the institute," said Stephen, Jr., the younger of the two Duggan sons, who became a close friend when the professor began bringing his assistant up for a home-cooked meal. "Ed used to come to dinner or lunch—Mother was alive at the time. Though the closest connection, the one he revered, was my father. He just had a great influence on him. . . ."

The Duggans were Irish-American, warm, gregarious, open-mannered. For Murrow, not yet twenty-five, with no roots in the city, their apartment on East Sixty-fifth Street provided a home and family: Sarah Duggan, warm and motherly, the younger daughter Sally; the brothers Stephen, Jr., studying law at Columbia, and Laurence, in from Washington, shy, bespectacled, quietly brilliant, one of the youngest career officers at the State Department and, like his father, a stubborn critic of U.S. policy in Latin America.

To Ed Murrow, the Duggans were the golden people, aware—"You couldn't be brought up in our house without being reminded of social issues; that's particularly what attracted Ed to my father"[1]—successful, engaged in good works, and basking in the anticipated glow of Roosevelt's imminent election.

The summer of 1932, Ed Murrow returned to Europe—no longer as a student leader making the grand tour of youth hostels, bunk beds, and cold showers but as Stephen Duggan's second-in-command, with introductions to IIE contacts across the Continent. His job: to evaluate candidates for lectureships in America and, along the way, to assess the budgetary problems of the financially strapped IIE operations overseas.

In England, Ivison Macadam of NSFA days proved helpful in tracking down the celebrated ("Will you please inform Dr. Duggan that Proff. [sic] Toynbee has left London but is to be at Williamstown?").[2] In Germany he touched base with old friends like Fritz Beck, and made a few new ones, all deeply concerned at the drift of events in their country.

Doors opened for him everywhere; IIE lectureships meant American money in a Depression-ridden world. He sat in countless aulas, visited ministries, consulted with the top minds of Europe, tore across the Continent, armed with a thick packet of instructions. The institute wanted names in history, economics, political science, something equal to the seriousness of the times. Try for André Siegfied, also Professor Keynes, though his fees were said to be on the steep side. Discourage J. Middleton Murry—"Not important enough to spend much time on."[3] Suggested lecture topics: Japan and Russia in Manchuria; what an overturn in Germany would mean to the USSR; the situation in Chile, etc., etc. Find an outstanding economist, IIE contacts would advise. Persuade the Czechs to send their education minister to the United States for a year: "If you should see President Masaryk, you might drop a word to him. . . ."

All in all, an awesome assignment the first time out, but he did the job his elders had come to expect of him—meticulously, methodically, representing the institute, evaluating speakers for the home office, concerned not so much with slickness as basic competence and the ability to communicate: *"Knows his subject thoroughly . . . not a very colorful individual but his lectures will be unique"; ". . . pleasing personality but more than a little conceited and is interested primarily in the prestige and money"; ". . . good voice, pleasing personality, an excellent sense of humor and apparently knows his subject thoroughly. . . ."* The assessments went back to New York for further disposition, all basic training for the man who would eventually be hiring a generation of communicators on the air.

Then, suddenly, he was stopped short, halted for the first time in his life by forces beyond his control.

He had always tended to the dramatic, even in student days and particularly on the matter of his health, raising fine hands to a fine forehead—implying he was just about at the end of his *rope*, hadn't had a good night's sleep in he didn't know *when*—indicating delicately to anyone within hearing distance that he was literally on the verge of collapse. Friends smiled, saw it as theatrics, a self-awarded badge of honor in the traditon of the compulsive worrier, and told him he had a disaster complex. True, he did work long hours, seemed able to forgo sleep for long periods of time. But his complaints seemed a little unreal, coming from an energetic six-footer and outdoorsman who otherwise gave every indication of robust good health.

Ironically, the early symptoms went unheeded, hidden, the insidiousness of pulmonary trouble that was probably inherited, developing unsuspectedly—until July 1932.

England had begun the dizzying marathon of conferences, trains, small planes, budget meetings by day, memorandum writing at night. In between he reported back to New York on the political situation: nationalism sharply up in Britain; "absolutely nothing" expected from the disarmament conference at Ottawa, an American exchange student in Germany badly beaten at a National Socialist demonstration—any word from the Berlin office?

July 3, he had departed early for France, where he was booked solid for the week, the one break a projected trip to Caen as guest of the local university's 500-year celebration. Dr. Krans, Director of the Paris office, had made arrangements. "We are going there tomorrow morning," Murrow wrote home excitedly.

The morning of July 8, he tried to get up and couldn't. A doctor was called in, poked around, pronounced it a "serious cold," and said Caen was out of the question, as was the rest of his Paris schedule. It was several days before he was back on his feet, though by the time worried inquiries arrived from New York, he had already caught the train to Berlin.

Somehow he completed the assignment with stopovers in Prague, Vienna, and Brno, arriving in Geneva in a state of near-exhaustion. "The return voyage," he wrote home, "will be more than welcome."

It was a warning—the first of many—that he could not drive himself as he wished to, of something in his physical makeup, his nervous energy notwithstanding, that would simply not stand up to long-term stress without serious repercussions.

Back in New York, he returned to the routine—special projects; dinner meetings with the IIE trustees, rubbing shoulders with the likes of inventor Leo Baekeland and the elder Henry Morgenthau. He was the bright young man of the organization, personable, mixing easily in higher circles, a natty dresser, fond of good clothes, well cut—a little too well, some thought, the shoulders just a bit wide, the waist a trifle narrow, stopping just short of dandyism.

His superiors saw him as a capable junior executive, on the way up. To his contemporaries he was a lonely young man, with no family and few real friends. Especially on Saturday night.

"New York was a big city for Ed," the younger Duggan recalled. "He was a country boy, unsophisticated, trying to be sophisticated, trying to be big time, though he was growing fast."

Weekends, they would meet over a cheap meal and talk politics, Duggan glad for a chance to emerge from his law books at Columbia. "We were both raw and in the formative stages. I didn't have any money and he didn't have any money. I worked hard, never saw anybody, was anxious for company. He was as lonely as I was.

"Ed did not have the easy way with him . . . a tremendously shy fellow. The fact that he gave up a Saturday night to have dinner with me . . .

49

He didn't know girls. There were other things a young guy could do in the Big Apple than meet a poor struggling law student even though he was the son of your boss."

Janet Huntington Brewster was a senior at Mount Holyoke—pretty, with the fair-haired, all-American type of good looks, president of the student body. Christmas, 1932, she was on her way to the NSFA convention at New Orleans. She had boarded the train at Springfield, Massachusetts. Ed Murrow got on in North Carolina, bound for the same convention. They knew each other from earlier meetings but had never really talked.

It was a long train ride. By the time they arrived in New Orleans, the NSFA agenda had taken on decidedly secondary importance.

The Brewsters were from Middletown, Connecticut, New Englanders with a lineage extending directly back to Elder Brewster of the *Mayflower* and with roots in the soil of the Yankee hill communities. Charles Brewster had been the first of his family to leave the hills, settling in the sheltered valley of the Connecticut River and marrying the daughter of a Swedish immigrant. Janet, the elder of their two children, was strictly reared, quietly charming, a topflight student who in the Depression had decided to opt for graduate work in economics.

Temperamentally, Ed Murrow and Janet Brewster were polar opposites: She was quiet to the point of serenity; he, emotional. Yet they both shared traces of shyness and a determination born of a puritanical upbringing and, in Janet Brewster's case, parental protectiveness following a close call with childhood pneumonia and rheumatic fever. The doctors had said at first she wouldn't live, then that she'd never live a normal life. She had proved them wrong, faced down efforts to wrap her in cotton wool, and gone on to become a campus leader.[4]

Active and committed in public, they both were reserved in private. He was ill-adept at small talk, ill-equipped by upbringing or inclination for the demands of social life in the East. She was open, direct, with a love of excitement underneath the quiet, and a leavening humor alternately roguish or faintly touched with irony. Between them was set off something that enabled the young man to transcend the usual constraints that beset him in his relationships with women. The convention over, he began pouring out his innermost feelings in daily letters back to South Hadley or the Brewster home in Middletown.

The courtship was mostly by mail and strictly private. Even so, curiosity ran high at Mount Holyoke as the handsome young Assistant Director of the IIE, up from New York on business for the institute, hung around the pleasant tree-shaded campus at South Hadley when there seemed no visible reason for his staying on. "It's on account of *you*," Brewster's friends told her excitedly. She played it cool. "Really? . . . That's nice."

But tongues kept wagging, the one question posed constantly: Was he good enough for Janet?

Like other young couples, they made plans for the future: homeowning (they hoped); family life in suburbia. Two nearly simultaneous occurrences, however, were already changing the outline of their conventional projections—both, as it happened, carried in the *New York Times* of Sunday, March 5, 1933.

Both Ed Murrow and Janet Brewster had cast their first votes for Franklin Roosevelt, Murrow by default. "We had our fingers crossed about him," said a friend of that time, "felt he was a kind of mama's boy with a silver spoon in his mouth, so how would he know about things?"

He still had his fingers crossed as the new President, that March, said the only thing Americans had to fear was fear itself and declared his intention of asking Congress for war powers, if necessary, to deal with the economic crisis. The banner headlines covering the inaugural almost obscured another, smaller item on page 1, with a Berlin dateline: VICTORY FOR HITLER IS EXPECTED TODAY . . . ELECTION TRIUMPH FOR REGIME INEVITABLE. . . .

Less than three years had gone by since Ed Murrow first saw the Brownshirts campaigning, a splinter group trying to improve on its poor showing in the Reichstag. By the spring of 1933, they were the government of Germany, Hitler appointed Chancellor, the Reichstag itself an abandoned, fire-gutted shell, the Nazi Party in complete control. Massive dismissals of the "racially" and politically unacceptable had begun, focusing largely on Germany's Jewish minority.

As the purges swept through the faculties of the venerable German universities, the repercussions were felt on both sides of the Atlantic, appeals pouring into the IIE. What happened in the following months and years changed the face of the Western intellectual community; it also changed Stephen Duggan's assistant, at twenty-six, from a pleasantly busy junior executive into a dedicated antifascist.

Early anti-Hitler momentum had come from anthropologist Franz Boas, onetime mentor of Margaret Mead, organizing help on the Columbia campus. From London, nuclear physicist Leo Szilard wrote of the formation of an academic rescue group spearheaded by William Beveridge, later architect of Britain's wartime economy, Nobel scientist Ernest Rutherford, and Harold Laski of the London School of Economics, its aim to create positions for scholars dismissed on political or religious grounds.

That May, as student mobs in Berlin, fired by the creed of Nordic purity, incinerated 20,000 "subversive" books—Einstein, Gide, Upton Sinclair, et al.—at the doorstep of the Friedrich-Wilhelm University, twenty-one U.S. college and university heads, under the leadership of Stephen Duggan, formed the Emergency Committee in Aid of Displaced German Scholars; its Assistant Secretary was Edward R. Murrow.

Within weeks the Emergency Committee, with Murrow as its writer, had fired the opening salvo—"An ancient university tradition is now challenged in Germany"—calling upon the American academic community to welcome the ousted scholars "irrespective of race, religion and political opinion." They were cautious, however, sensitive to possible charges of interference:

> Every people has the right to live under the form of government it selects for itself. It is not for foreigners to object because they do not like it. But it is reasonable to deplore an action anywhere that may be absolutely destructive of gains in human progress that have been made only at great sacrifice. . . . It is everywhere incumbent upon university faculties . . . to be alive to the dangers which threaten them and by a declaration of faith to range themselves on the side of freedom of speech and freedom of teaching.

The program was modest: small stipends to be provided for academic refugees from funds outside the universities, one-half to be put up by the Carnegie or Rockefeller Foundations, the rest raised by the Emergency Committee from private sources to avoid even the appearance of siphoning off faculty funds while American scholars went jobless. It was a stopgap measure, a kind of visiting professor program, attendant on the cooling of revolutionary fervor in Germany. Or so they hoped.

In the meantime, the schools in effect were paid for taking scholars, some of them Nobel laureates, at bargain-basement rates. The procedures were cumbersome. Scholars had to be requested specifically, from an approved list. Their courses were highly advanced, often noncompetitive. Even then, the committee had to walk a fine line, cognizant of the realities of the Depression and the prejudices of the time.

Some schools, invited to join the general committee, had refused outright. A. Lawrence Lowell of Harvard went it one better with an explicit declaration against creating places on the faculty—either for émigrés or in protest against the Nazi policies—a policy confirmed the following year by his successor, James Bryant Conant.

The overall response, however, was warm and—more important—nationwide. The committee as finally set up included such names as Robert Hutchins of the University of Chicago; Robert A. Millikan, who had been Einstein's host at the California Institute of Technology; Karl Compton of MIT; Mary Woolley of Mount Holyoke; Ray Lyman Wilbur of Stanford; mathematician Oswald Veblen; astronomer Harlow Shapley of Harvard, later a prominent target of Joe McCarthy. The chair was taken by Livingston Farrand, President of Cornell University. All were listed by name, not institution, again to avoid controversy.

From that time on, Edward Murrow's life was synonymous with the work of the Emergency Committee. "We brought 91 of the best minds out of Europe," he later wrote of that early experience, which at the height of his broadcasting career he still referred to as "the most richly rewarding of anything I have ever undertaken."

Technically he was a volunteer, on loan from the institute. A small executive group of which he was part coordinated the job hunting and money raising. But much of the burden fell on the Assistant Secretary, already carrying a fulltime work load for the IIE. For the next two years the efforts of the Emergency Committee, both national and international, funneled through Murrow's paper-strewn office at 2 West Forty-fifth Street and the room down the hall where his assistant, Betty Drury, coped with day-to-day matters, crowded in by rows of filing cabinets filling up too quickly with the dossiers that streamed in daily from London, Paris, and Geneva.

With characteristic self-debunking, Murrow afterward described his role as that of "the youngster who did the donkey work." Only when the committee papers were unsealed some forty years later was the full extent of his participation revealed—one that carried through on a policy as well as a day-to-day level, involving contacts with the U.S. and foreign governments, the League of Nations, and the international network of rescue groups.

It was in the midst of this time that the cigarette smoking begun in college turned compulsive—the result of pressure and the need for a physical outlet of some kind, something to do with his hands, to make up for the total absence, for the first time in his life, of physical activity.

In the meantime he worked around the clock—compiling and clearing lists, data, and qualifications on those dismissed; cross-checking new information coming out of Europe; making the linkup between the U.S. colleges and the scholars; handling finances, from yearly budgets to the box office take on a benefit. He wrote appeals, articles, and reports; carried on an endless correspondence with the Academic Assistance Council, the committee's British counterpart in London; interviewed numberless applicants; and sifted anxiously through published and unpublished material on the drift of public opinion in Europe and America.

Concurrently, wearing his other hat as Assistant Director of the IIE, he was gathering and analyzing information from within the Reich, using the best possible sources—i.e., the exchange students: "An increasing number of requests for information makes it necessary that we try to give accurate and unbiased answers to all questions. . . . An analysis of the replies to this letter will be made and published but your indival comments will be treated as strictly confidential."[5]

What emerged was a comprehensive view of the rise of the new order in Central Europe—names; statistics; governmental moves; grass-roots observations. An ad hoc news-gathering effort, with Murrow at the center, making him in those months one of the best-informed men in New York.

"All 'Marxists' as well as Jews generally have been 'purged,' " read one report, "universities and colleges are going to be cleaned up (*gesäubert*)

53

and made instruments for educating the young along strictly nationalistic—Hitleristic—lines. . . ."

Einstein has long ago left the country. . . . His bank account has been confiscated. Newspaper cartoons represent him as buzzard, monkey, etc. . . . Former political opponents of the Nazis are concentrated in prison camps and shot if they try to escape. . . . The masses are to get their information only through channels absolutely under government control. . . .

All noted the decrees further tightening the screws on German Jewry: economic boycott; *Studentenschaft* posters on university walls screaming out their message in heavy Gothic type: "The Jew can only think Jewish; if he writes in German, he lies;" "The German who writes German but thinks un-German is a traitor. . . ."

"The head of a foreign language school," wrote an American from Heidelberg, "sat down at my table. . . . With burning eyes he promised me the exquisite pleasure of witnessing the greatest pogrom ever accomplished.

"You cannot imagine, he [said], how these people feel towards the Jews, the hate all these young men feel—der Hass! Hass!! Hass!!! It was a nightmare hymn. . . ."

"Universal military service is to be re-established on the old scale" a correspondent reported. "Teachers suspected of not being in sympathy have no place in the New Germany. It is perhaps well to ask what sort of instruction children . . . will get under the new regime. The answer is the most intense form of nationalistic propaganda designed to breed the desire to die for the Fatherland and for Adolf Hitler. . . . The foregoing sounds crazy. I know it. But in describing a madhouse. . . .

For the influence of the mob is very strong. Only one who has often been in the mob yelling—Heil Hitler and singing Deutschland Über Alles or the Nazi song . . . can appreciate the full force of what is officially termed a nationalistic reawakening but which often appears to me to be an emotional orgy bordering on insanity. . . .

"I cannot refrain from expressing my admiration," wrote one student sarcastically, "for the skill of the present Reichs chancellor. . . . His ability to stage vast national-militaristic displays. . . . His skillful use of the support of the Junkers and big industrialists to get financial aid. . . ."

A Leipzig music student had "acquired a deep affection for Germany in these three semesters. . . . It is because of this that I see a great danger for Germany in the present developments. . . ."

A tiny minority sympathized with the Nazi Party: If Americans would only understand that this was a revolution, if Americans would only look at the facts of the case, see the thing in perspective, "then one will marvel at the orderly fashion in which changes are carried out rather than shed tears at the individual cases."

The overriding tone of the replies, however, remained one of concern and even raw fear. "I came to Germany," wrote a boy from North Carolina, "somewhat uncertain as to whether the United States did the clever thing in entering the World War. There was even some question in my mind if we came in on the right side. Personal reacquaintance with the reawakened Prussianism has dispelled both these doubts. If defeated Prussianism can stage the shows I saw in Berlin. . . ."

> The German nation did not so much make the revolution of 1918 as permit it. Hitler recognized all this, drew the logical conclusions and went to work. His success proves that he was right. . . .
> That the corollary of all this is another European war, as soon as the distribution of power becomes favorable to those now desirous of revenge is self-evident.

In the meantime, the fifteenth-floor office at West Forty-fifth Street was swamped, just one more stop in the constellation of assistance groups dotting the canyons of Depression New York. Their constituency was tiny, elitist, sharply defined. Yet inevitably they drew the homeless and aimless: ". . . a very old man . . . sent up to us . . . who was a private tutor. . . . He said he had to sleep at a different place every night. . . . I called Miss Hahn at the Joint Clearing Bureau who said he should be sent up. If we could get a clear statement, we would know where to refer these people. . . ."[6]

The American Friends Service Committee sent up distress signals continually: Could the Emergency Committee help place an educator; a civil servant; Mr. Ernst Reuter, formerly lord mayor of Magdeburg—"we are at a loss to know what to suggest."[7] Murrow himself saw people at all hours, in between reports, meetings, and digesting the exhaustive forms that were the committee questionnaire. ("Have you been officially dismissed?"; "For what period longer will the means at your disposal last?"; "How well do you speak English?"; "How many dependents?"; "Would you go to tropical countries? The Far East? USSR? South America?")

To the émigrés, the thin, chain-smoking young man was at once a power figure and a father figure, the keeper of the keys and an anchor for those lost in their new environment, his personal intervention sought in a stream of requests—a scholar unable to meet expenses; an historian whose grant had run out; an anthropologist nervous about applying for a fellowship: "He turns to you as the one person who understands him. . . ."[8]

They kept a low profile, attended no rallies. They were educators, they insisted—respectable; correct; nonpartisan. "The Committee has refrained from associating itself with protests of either a political or economic nature."[9] Yet their very existence was a statement, lining them up solidly in the antifascist camp.

As the committee's representative, Murrow kept up a dialogue with the other groups. He clipped copies of the *Nation* and the *New Republic*, following up anxiously on the latest propaganda initiatives from Berlin: Ivy Lee, once John D. Rockefeller's image brightener, now an adviser to the German government, heading up all-expenses-paid junkets for Americans designed to "correct" attitudes toward the New Germany; the public relations firm of Carl Byoir Associates, over on Fortieth Street, newly on retainer from Berlin, reportedly to promote tourism in the Reich.

But even on the side of the angels there were, it seemed, no absolutes. In one of those ironic twists of fate, the institute itself was coming in for criticism, with Murrow, wearing his other hat as Assistant Director, in the hot seat.

The German exchange students going home in mid-1933 had been the last of the Weimar crop. Ever since, there had been unsettling rumors of new criteria set by the Nazi Party, reports of exchange fellows approached by the German Foreign Office with requests to carry on propaganda in the United States.

In a hurried letter, Murrow had put the matter squarely before Adolf Morsbach, director of the *Austauschdienst,* the exchange office in Berlin: Was it true that students were to undergo ideological screening, that a questionnaire was being circulated among prospective candidates concerning "political affiliation, racial background and similar matters?"

"Rumors such as these," he wrote Berlin, "have given rise to the fear . . . that German exchange students may in the future engage in anti-Semitic propaganda while in this country. This problem of anti-Semitism is sufficiently acute in our institutions for this to be a matter of grave concern." Attempts at agitation, he advised, would result in immediate withdrawal of the fellowships. "I cannot emphasize too strongly the necessity of warning students arriving this fall against actions or words that may be interpreted as an attempt to arouse or augment racial animosities in this country."

Morsbach, in reply, assured "Lieber Freund Murrow" that no such thing was planned; the boys and girls were not to propagandize, but rather to show by their truly exemplary behavior the mettle of the youth of the New Germany. He sidestepped the screening issue. Twelve months later, he would be sent to a concentration camp.

That winter, the complaints began coming in—from the Midwest, above all, where official propaganda efforts were being aimed at the large German-American communities. Murrow, inquiring among his contacts, got mostly evasions—yes, they had heard things, very worrisome, nothing concrete to go on, of course—and passed the buck back to the Assistant Director. A dean of graduate studies at St. Louis wrote of "confirmed fears . . . real trouble in the offing," then asked that the matter be kept quiet.

"Regardless of whether you get complaints . . . or not," a New School professor informed him, "propaganda does go on, and is being complained of by individuals, if not by spokesmen of institutions, who do not want to trouble muddy waters. . . ."

When a clear-cut case came to light—an exchange fellow caught in "extracurricular activities of a questionable nature"—Murrow fell on it almost with relief. The young man, a personal friend from Germany, had been bragging that the IIE would see him through.

Murrow reacted with fury: "Dr. von Simson certainly has no reason to believe that this Institute will 'see him through.' . . . With your permission, I should like to address a letter to [him] informing him that his action makes him liable to deportation and that in the event of such action . . . he can count on no assistance from us.

"If, in your opinion, formal action withdrawing von Simson's fellowship is desirable, I shall cable Professor Duggan to that effect."[10]

The only answer seemed to be: close down the program. He took a straw poll among participating colleges and came up with no result. Some, genuinely concerned, were considering a break in relations; others thought the whole matter irrelevant—e.g., the president of a women's college answered Murrow's query about a specific exchange student to the effect that Miss X was, of course, a convinced Hitlerite—otherwise, she wouldn't be here, would she?—but was in all other respects a really charming person.

"So far," Murrow told a friend, "there is little indication that they desire to discontinue the existing arrangements." In fact, several schools uninterested in cultural relations under the Weimar Republic now seemed anxious to open academic ties to the New Germany; among them was the Fletcher School of Law and Diplomacy, a main-line supplier of personnel to the State Department.

Nor did the thought get much support from Murrow's chief. For Stephen Duggan, his distaste for Hitler notwithstanding, the idea of termination struck at the roots of the IIE, an admission that not all things could be solved through dialogue between reasonable men and women of education.

But Duggan was off on a ten-month tour of Europe, and it was his young assistant who was taking the flak, answering inquiries with replies that were no replies, sending thick reports to Duggan, promising decisive action once the professor was in Berlin, stating publicly that the IIE had no control over selection methods while agonizing privately over their posture: "I am very conscious of our responsibility in this matter. . . ."[11]

At the same time, the IIE was taking its lumps from the right, accused of being anti-German. In Berlin the *Austauschdienst* was upset: "It is a well-known fact here that . . . Professor Duggan has taken a very definite stand against the New Germany. . . . One has heard that he signed a great number of resolutions and protests which was [sic] directed against the Hitler Government. . . . It cannot be denied that this lack of good will from your side adds to the unfriendly feeling against the Institute."[12] (Duggan, off in Europe, was delighted, assured friends he intended to continue his editorials: "They know where I stand.")

The controversy, however, continued. Advisers suggested a statement to clear the air, assure the public that the IIE was keeping the program, as they put it, "free from political contamination."

At the institute, they knew better. Not much point in making the statement, read an internal memo; "We know there is 'political contamination.' "

It was never resolved. The exchange program, and the debate, continued over Duggan's increased misgivings and the silence of the trustees into September 1939, ending only when the German armies were five days into Poland.

As for Duggan's assistant, it was a first encounter, in the midst of fighting the good fight, with the gray areas of ambiguity—that and a first awareness of the drawbacks involved in being an organization man.

Nor was it the only controversy of those months. Another problem was brewing in the background, this one largely of Murrow's making—less noticeable at the time but one which, unlike the German problem, was to haunt his career.

In December, 1932, he had opened negotiations with the Soviet authorities to set up summer courses for visiting Americans in Moscow. The timing seemed right—Roosevelt elected, American recognition of the Soviet Union imminent. Cultural relations between the United States and the USSR, Murrow told a colleague excitedly, were going to assume a new importance. Duggan gave him his head; the IIE had been running summer seminars abroad for years, all of them successful. Also, it fitted in with the institute's new function as a clearinghouse for contacts opening up in the wake of the thaw.

There followed nine months of development—meetings with Intourist officials, proposals by Murrow to the proper quarters in Moscow: He wanted courses in sociology, Soviet literature, agriculture, economics, brushups in elementary Russian for anyone who needed it—all at the highest scholarly level, of course, nonpolitical, with good sound American professors monitoring the students. The function of the Russians, he told Moscow earnestly, was to be "purely intellectual."

Then, suddenly, the deal was off. The Soviets, he was told, had their own plans and their own man: a certain Professor Sollins, experienced in Soviet affairs, head of a cultural exchange office known as the Anglo-American Institute. If the IIE still wanted to cooperate, fine.

In fact, the new director seemed eager to work with them. His professor's credentials would turn out to be bogus, the "Anglo-American Institute" funded by Intourist and consisting of one employee: I. V. Sollins. But that was later.

They tried to set up safeguards with a blue-ribbon American advisory council. Duggan traveled to Moscow to lay the ground rules. But as the months went by, they saw control gradually slipping out of their hands. Writing Duggan in Europe, Murrow urged that they either regain control by 1935 or forget the whole thing. In the meantime, the 1934 summer session went forward, over his increased misgivings.

Three people were closest to him through those troubled months of 1934, as he ran the IIE virtually alone, in Duggan's absence. One was his closest associate on the executive board of the Emergency Committee: Alfred Einstein Cohn, a New York cardiologist and researcher at the Rockefeller Institute, an intimate of Stephen Duggan and Felix Frankfurter of Harvard, a world traveler and inveterate supporter of international causes who had taught medicine in Peking and seen the worst of World War I as an army doctor in France.

The second was a dark, intense young Austrian Quaker named Walter Kotschnig, General Secretary of the International Student Service, a Geneva-based student relief organization, now assisting young people driven out of Germany. Kotschnig became a confidant and comrade-in-arms, Cohn, another surrogate father.

But above all, there was Janet Brewster.

Their long-distance romance had prospered, and in mid-1933 he had asked her to be his wife. The announcement was put off until the following year; Depression economics didn't allow for quick marriages. For all their closeness, the proposal when it came, took her by surprise; the footloose, lanky young man whose work always came first just hadn't seemed the marrying kind.

What made Janet Huntington Brewster different from the other, admittedly attractive women activists he had known in the student world? She had, of course, the right credentials, was the proper sort of prospective wife for a superachiever on his way up. But so were the upper-class girls of the NSFA who had treated him longingly to dinner or the family box at the opera.

On the surface, the differences could not have been greater. She was a Connecticut Yankee of Anglo-Swedish stock, practical, serene. He was a Celtic Southerner, self-made, moody, explosive. He was blue-collar, she was middle-class: Charles Brewster sold Studebakers and Pierce-Arrows in his Middletown showroom; his wife was a pillar of the Episcopal Church, friends with Bishop Acheson, whose brilliant son Dean had just joined the Roosevelt Administration.

Yet underneath they had a good deal in common, both very much of the new generation, committed—Janet herself worked on behalf of the International Student Service—with a shared vision of the world and a shared desire for change, the offspring of rock-ribbed Republican families who had cast their lot with the New Deal.

CHAPTER III

He was ambitious, a doer. She had enterprise, an uncompromising honesty, and an IQ level which, they both suspected, surpassed his. She stood five feet four inches, diminutive beside her big, mercurial fiancé, with the look still of the very young girl about her. A steadying, quietly determined presence in conservative, figure-concealing clothes: short, fair hair, waved in the fashion of the time, and lazy-lidded blue eyes that seemed to appraise the world with an amused, if kindly, tolerance.

But there was a romantic side as well to Janet Brewster, an often concealed desire to go on the stage, for in fact she was a gifted actress. To her fiancé, up from New York one day to watch her play the lead in summer stock, she was perhaps a little *too* good. He'd even been afraid, he told her sometime later, that she'd opt for the stage rather than for married life with him. No danger of that, but that romantic streak was probably what drew her to this good-looking young man from somewhere out West, whom she knew only slightly.

The Brewsters weren't thrilled. It was not, of course, the money. Charles Brewster's showroom had never recovered from the crash, while the unwanted suitor was obviously doing very well. He was just not their sort: too strange, too New York. Jenny Brewster shook her head: This young man from the wicked city, tall . . . No good would come of it. It was Janet Brewster herself who stood firm in the face of parental disapproval.

In the meantime, she exchanged her dream of a graduate degree for an education certificate and a job in Middletown teaching high school English. Weekends when he could, he would give up golfing with campus bigwigs to be with her. Occasionally she came down to New York, weathering the shock of her first look at the "shambles" of his Greenwich Village apartment. Murrow and his roommate hadn't bothered to clean up; the young lady stopped cold at the threshold, gaping at the dirt—"I was just a nice girl from Connecticut. I'd never seen a place where two men lived."

They set the date for October 27, 1934.

He had warned her from the outset of his black moods, his sudden depressions; he wanted her to know, he said. And there was something else. His manner was so intense that she started getting edgy. The institute, he began, thought he was twenty-eight. Well, it wasn't true. He paused. "I'm . . . twenty-six."

She tried not to laugh.

"I am to be married in the fall," Murrow wrote Kotschnig, "probably the last of October. As you may suspect the victim is your friend Janet Brewster."

Summer 1934 began in a glow. Murrow put off his plans to attend the experts' committee meetings in London in favor of weekends in Connecticut. The first boatloads of exchange students were departing for the capitals of Europe. In Berlin, the committee representatives thought things were quieting down.

July 1, the glow was dispelled in a burst of headlines, six columns wide, elbowing aside Joseph Kennedy's appointment to the Securities and Exchange Commission: HITLER CRUSHES REVOLT BY NAZI RADICALS . . . BERLIN IN AN IRON GRIP . . . GOERING POLICE NET CATCHES LEADERS . . . KILLINGS FOLLOW RAIDS ON HOMES . . . HITLER FLIES TO MUNICH. . . .

Hitler had turned on his own storm troopers, whose calls for a "second revolution" were embarrassing him with his allies of the Old Right; no one knowledgeable believed the insurrection charges. The AP story described Berlin aswarm with police and armored detachments, excited crowds surging along Unter den Linden like bloodhounds on the scent. The Berlin–Paris phone lines had been cut, France accused of complicity in the "plot." Whitehall worried openly at the prospect of an alliance between Hitler and the old German military-industrial machine, which, unlike the raw, street Nazis, had the means and competence to prepare Germany for a revanchist war.

At the IIE in New York, anxious queries were pouring in from the families of American exchange students. Murrow had delayed the sailings to Germany. Privately, he worried about his German friends as the Nazi dragnet showed signs of spreading beyond the Brownshirt radicals to the Catholic center.

Thursday morning, July 7, he opened The New York *Times* for a quick rundown: new killings; photos of those who had moved up in the party shake-up. Just to the right of the sharp features of Deputy Leader Rudolf Hess was a column with a Munich dateline: 4 FOES OF PUTSCH SLAIN. Hitler was paying off old scores for 1923 and the beer hall fiasco. Then, just below was EDUCATOR AMONG VICTIMS: "Others reported dead are Fritz Beck, Director of the German Academic Foreign Bureau. . . ."

Since Murrow's NSFA days Dr. Beck had typified the best of the old Germany, a stubborn opponent of Nazi policies. "It is nothing short of a miracle," he had written before his death, "that I am still able to continue . . . in spite of the fact that I have not gone over to the powers that now rule. May God Almighty . . . cause the victorious cross of Christ to shine forth with its saving powers over Europe and our poor Germany, lest another war sweep Central Europe into annihilation and ashes."

The body, riddled with bullets, had been found in a clump of woods. Another NSFA contact, a Catholic Youth Association leader, had disappeared en route to a conference in Berlin. Eleven days later the anxious young wife was told that her husband had been "shot while attempting to escape" and that the ashes would be sent to her by parcel post.

"I am sick over the whole thing," Murrow wrote Kotschnig, "and cannot see how people of normal intelligence can long continue to work with those barbarians."

There was more to come. In Berlin Adolf Morsbach, director of the Berlin office, had fallen. July 10, fifty Americans arriving under the auspices of Ivy Lee's goodwill program began asking questions when the distinguished Dr. Morsbach failed to turn up on the reception committee as promised. All answers were evasive. Persistent inquiries finally revealed that he had been arrested and sent to Dachau.

The American press had a field day: "The object of the tour is aimed to correct what are characterized here as false notions regarding Nazi rule....The party of about fifty representatives...brought here at considerable expense...seems likely to go home harboring some doubts as to the universality of the blessings conferred by Nazism."[13]

In the last days, the Berlin director had been a worried, much chastened man, trying to fend off a complete Party take-over. Released after weeks of interrogation, he was dead within twenty-four months.

"As long as you had Morsbach," wrote Kotschnig from Geneva, "you had a fair chance of getting rather decent people. Now that the terror has become worse . . ."

The summer was getting to be a nightmare. In Moscow, their students had arrived to utter confusion: the faculty unformed, living conditions inadequate. A critical remark at the opening reception, made by an American resident of Moscow and picked up by the New York *Herald Tribune*, was reported back home as an attack on American institutions. In the meantime, I. V. Sollins was going around Moscow bragging that he had used the IIE as a front. Murrow, making inquiries in New York, found local Intourist officials totally unresponsive.

A *modus operandi* was finally arrived at, classes and dorms set up— largely through Duggan's intervention, the goodwill of the Soviet educators, and Intourist/Moscow, which had no liking for Sollins either. The seminar went forward as planned, the institute keeping its fingers crossed and preparing for a confrontation in the fall.

But it was the Emergency Committee that continued to hold center stage for Murrow. They were out of funds again, the waiting lists endless, renewals a constant worry. At the Union Theological Seminary the money had run out for Paul Tillich, who had wanted no part of Hitler's new order; Murrow promised to help: "We should do everything possible to provide for his continuation. . . ."

He did; Tillich stayed on. But for a young person reared to believe in the traditional values, there was a growing sense of disillusion, watching the great minds of the age knocking at the doors of the Western community, hats in hand.

Nor was the League of much help. A commission had been set up in late 1933, presumably to deal with the new flow of refugees; its appointed High Commissioner was James G. McDonald, head of the Foreign Policy Association, later U.S. Ambassador to the state of Israel. Murrow had sat in on meetings with McDonald, drawing up managerial charts, furiously determined to centralize efforts on behalf of academics and to get his own man in as assistant to the High Commissioner.

The commission, however, seemed unable to deal with the situation or the reluctant Western governments. "Even now," Kotschnig wrote from Europe, "it makes me sick to think of the refugee children I saw in the slums of Paris. . . . It is the question of permits of work. What good is the right of asylum if . . . people are forbidden to make their living honestly?"

With a pessimism that was becoming habitual, Murrow foresaw the imminent demise of the commission and felt the League would soon wash its hands of the problem.

In mid-1934 the Emergency Committee issued its first report. Murrow in his opening statement compared the present intellectual migration with the expulsion of the Jews from Spain in 1492, the Huguenots' forced exit from France, and the migration of the Greek scholars to Italy after the fall of Byzantium. Meanwhile, the committee was bringing over the pride of the great mathematics department of the University of Göttingen; legal scholars from Berlin and Breslau; pioneers in nuclear physics, such as Nobel physicist James Franck, later a member of the atomic establishment and protester against the building of the H-bomb; mathematicians Richard Courant, Emmy Noether, and Otto Szasz; art historian Erwin Panofsky; political scientist Karl Loewenstein, an old Munich contact of Murrow's, on his way to Yale. From Princeton Albert Einstein kept up a constant stream of recommendations and advice couched in his courteous, old-fashioned German, opening invariably with "Sehr geehrter Herr Murrow. . . ."

Thomas Mann arrived in midsummer, a voluntary exile, meeting with Murrow to discuss a lecture tour. Matters were arranged satisfactorily despite a momentary gaffe vis-à-vis the novelist's publisher, Alfred A. Knopf, when the young Assistant Secretary confused Thomas Mann with his brother Heinrich.

Names such as Herbert Marcuse and Martin Buber were eventually to join the roster. But underwriting remained a grueling nickel-and-dime job, without the spiritual support that hindsight would lend to the humanity and practical benefits of the venture, as the new migration seeded university departments across the country, brought about a quantum leap ahead in the sciences, and left a permanent imprint on intellectual life, the arts, and the military.

Arthur Hays Sulzberger, son-in-law of Adolph Ochs, proved a valuable ally, in terms of both discreet New York *Times* coverage and funding. In fact, most of the private money raised came from Jewish sources, although fully half the scholars, in the final count, would be, as Murrow later described them, "pure Aryans even under Hitler's definition. . . . men who like their Jewish colleagues refused to bend."[14]

Yet the liberal community in that early period generally held aloof from what was seen as a "Jewish" operation,[15] despite the goodwill of isolated individuals such as Oswald Garrison Villard or Bruce Bliven of the *New Republic*. The foundations were at once a source of help and irritation, doling out grants by the spoonful, oblivious of urgency, everything done by the book. To the officials, the well-groomed, dark-haired young WASP from the institute seemed the ideal contact man—cool yet amiable, a complete pro; his reports were concise, facts and figures in place, with no time wasted. They were after scholars, not refugees, and hoped there wouldn't be too many.

Murrow, in turn, picked up quickly on the ground rules: when to press a point and when not to; when to try again and when to drop the matter—his first lessons in dealing with institutional power. Also never, never to blow his cool. That he did elsewhere. "I find it quite impossible to become irritated with the individuals who are actually doing the job," he told Kotschnig.

"But I confess that I do gnash my teeth occasionally about this whole business of intrigue and manipulation in the process of educating people who have no desire to be educated. . . ."

Given the odds—of the 6,000 applying to the committee over its lifetime, only 335 would make it—the near misses outran the successes, and for Murrow, the former weighed more heavily than the latter: "the decision was an unfavorable one"; "keenly regret the disappointment"; "the project has failed"; "sorry not to seem more helpful but wish to give my honest opinion. . . ."

"I am sure that you must often feel that we over here are too 'hard boiled' about this whole business," he wrote to Walter Adams, his English counterpart at the Academic Assistance Council in London. "I assure you that this is not the case. . . ."

European friends tried to entice him over, promising him he wouldn't be "killed with meetings." He declined: "I need a rest and Europe is no place to get it."

Neither, for that matter, was New York. On top of his other duties, he had joined an umbrella commission coordinating the activities of the various relief agencies, all the while penning appeals that simmered with scorn for Hitler's new order ("the philosophy of lower middle class obscurantism . . . this wretched new orientation . . . compounded of half-truth, error, shallowness, and ill-considered prejudice"). At the same time he was organizing for the International Student Service, now the League's official arm for assistance to the young, making his pitch at fund-raising teas in New York and Boston, handing out the pledge cards, following up on every one- and five-dollar contribution with single-minded determination.

On one occasion a Boston contributor, puzzled at the unexplained return of his check, queried the local ISS representative, the query duly forwarded to Murrow's office in New York. There must have been a wrong address, a secretary replied, "because I cannot imagine this Institute, particularly its Assistant Director, returning a cent belonging to it or any of its 'ramifications.' "

Eventually something had to give way. Murrow's temper, never even, was growing shorter under the pressure, icy anger one day, conciliation the next ("I am no longer interested in attempting to secure funds . . ."; "Walter—as I read this it seems a bit abrupt! It was dictated late at night and today I feel better . . ."). The English-based chairman of the ISS wrote in, chiding the rich Americans for coming up with too little, and set off an explosion that resounded back to Kotschnig's office in Geneva.

"Of all the supercilious, tactless communications that I have ever read from an egotistical Englishman, he is the worst! . . . I am having [someone else] handle all the correspondence with him, because if I wrote him a letter it would be simply to tell him to go to hell. . . ."

Relations with the London-based Academic Assistance Council (AAC), touchy in its present early stages, were getting even touchier, hampered by slow mails, marked by American fears of their British colleagues possibly skimming the academic cream, and by Murrow's perceptible streak of a deep-rooted native Anglophobia.

Cohn tried to allay his mistrust: "I fear that if I write enthusiastically . . . you will conclude that I have slipped my moorings and have been captured by the perfidious British. . . . Be assured that I haven't gone over to the enemy—merely admired him for his obvious virtues. . . . Are you getting any rest?"

From Geneva, Duggan had written, concerned, urging Murrow to take time out, a leave of absence, perhaps, go visit his folks in Washington: "You have been carrying a big load and must not risk a breakdown."

But he was too much into it by now, living his public role nearly twenty-four hours a day, proprietary about what he had come to refer to as "my Committee."[15] In international councils he was regarded not only as one of the best-informed members but as one of those emotionally closest to the problem. When, therefore, the spring meetings abroad seemed to give the English group ultimate authority, he hit the ceiling, calling the committee into session, cabling London ("UNSATISFACTORY"), firing off furious questions.

Duggan, in Europe, made the appropriate soothing noises: The boy was overworked, hadn't had a vacation in three years. It was in any case a tempest in a teapot, a breakdown in transatlantic communications, the English anxious to clear up any misunderstandings.

"You must disabuse yourself," wrote their London man, "of the idea that the AAC is trying to 'put something over' either on us or the other committees. . . ."

Murrow was duly, diplomatically apologetic: "I understand perfectly. . . . I was doubtless at fault. . . . I do hope that no misunderstanding may be allowed to affect the cordial relations and cooperation between this Committee and the people in London. . . ."

Things proceeded more smoothly after that. Nonetheless, Duggan, meeting with Kotschnig that summer, while praising his assistant, confirmed his intention—nay, his determination—to send Murrow "on a long holiday" immediately following his return to the United States.

His assistant was skeptical. Too many things were happening, he told friends—an understatement. The Brownshirt purges in Germany had touched off new emigration. A civil war in Austria between socialists and the right-wing regime of Engelbert Dollfuss had just ended in a Dollfuss victory and left working-class Vienna a scarred battleground. Kotschnig, just then thanking Murrow for some personal assistance—"without you my family would probably be starving by now"—was bitter about his native country: "If I should become Chancellor of Austria, I shall see to it that you are made President of the Republic, or whatever that country calls itself at present. You would certainly have less to do in that position."

To Murrow, Austria seemed a kind of small, semifascist Ruritania, a political sideshow. But weeks later Dollfuss himself would be murdered in an attempted Nazi coup, while four years hence a further shift of the political winds in Austria would extend Nazi domination into southern Europe, and change the direction of Murrow's life.

In the meantime, he followed developments elsewhere. The new French labor laws—were they good or bad for their people? There was the upcoming plebiscite in the Saar, certain to set off further emigration if Germany won, as seemed likely, and mounting tensions in Spain—how many émigrés if civil war broke out? The upcoming India Act, the hot issue of Palestine, political unrest in Chile, in Iran—all were monitored, all assessed in terms of committee needs: What was the political climate, the overall sentiments of governments and local populations—i.e., what would newcomers be up against?

He sifted and evaluated, acquiring a sense of global interdependence—history seen in terms of shifting demographic patterns and national power plays, a thoroughgoing, firsthand education in realpolitik at a time when most reporters of his age were still covering the courthouse.

Sunday, October 28, 1934, the *Press* of Middletown, Connecticut, carried a brief lead item in the column headed *"News Notes and Social Events"*:

> Miss Janet Huntington Brewster, daughter of Mr. and Mrs. Charles Brewster of Mt. Vernon Street, was married to Mr. Edward R. Murrow, son of Mr. and Mrs. R. C. Murrow of Beaver, Washington at 4 o'clock Saturday afternoon at the home of her parents. Dr. Frank F. German, rector of the Church of the Holy Trinity, performed the ceremony. . . . Both the bride and groom were unattended. . . .

The affair was simple, the one festive note being Janet's gown of ivory lace, complemented by a spray of brown orchids. A small group of friends and family—her family—were on hand; the elder Murrows, though invited, hadn't come. Following the reception, the bride and groom got into a car and headed south, first stop North Carolina; he had a two-month leave of absence.

In Guilford County, the clan turned out for the newlyweds. There was a seemingly endless stream of relations: Uncle Edgar and Aunt Hazel; Grandma Roella, the widow of Joshua Murrow, now almost eighty-one; the various nieces, nephews, grandchildren, and great-grandchildren of Andrew Murrow and Van Buren Lamb.

They regarded each other across the culture gap—the Murrow women in their Sears dresses and the young guest from New England, Janet, trying hard to match up names and faces, aware of their innocently appraising glances and herself as the center of attention.

She was welcomed into the family—"They were terribly nice"—with one exception: the matriarch Roella Murrow, grown fat and formidable in her high age, making no secret of her displeasure with her grandson for marrying a Yankee.

They motored south, Murrow, the complete reporter, sending Duggan ecstatic reports on the effectiveness of the New Deal—"a living reality," he said. He'd talked with ten to fifteen people a day—farmers; service station operators; country storekeepers. The Tennessee Valley Authority area was seeing "a political revolution," everyone convinced this was a government "concerned primarily with the welfare of the working class"; they liked what they'd seen of this administration.

Duggan relayed the report to his good friend FDR ("My assistant director, Mr. Edward Murrow . . ."), to be noted personally by the President.

They honeymooned in Mexico, then swung north again, headed for Washington State and Murrow's parents, plus a detour to Pullman for a visit with Ida Lou Anderson. They'd been invited to take dinner with her at her sister's. It was an uncomfortable evening. Ida Lou was obviously in love with Ed; and just as obviously resented his having gotten married.

The coastal hills of western Washington were a relief.

"Greetings and salutations from the Far West!" he wrote Kotschnig from Olympia. "This trip is making me a confirmed nationalist and at this moment I have no desire to have anything to do with all of you warring Europeans."

But he couldn't escape himself: "The only thing that is disturbing my peace of mind is whether or not negotiations are doing satisfactorily with reference to the placement of the younger German art scholars. . . . I have no word concerning the matter from the office. . . ."

In the final analysis, even his honeymoon would not be free of the Emergency Committee. There were stops at colleges along the way so that Murrow could gauge current attitudes toward refugee professors. He had also left his parents' address with the New York office for the forwarding of material to be used in anti-Nazi speeches he was scheduled to deliver on the West Coast.

The idyll, therefore, was in effect already drawing to a close when Ed and Janet Murrow pulled up in front of the small company house at Beaver Camp in late November.

They were welcomed once again, and there was more scrutiny for the bride. Ethel Murrow approved, in her restrained way: acceptance without warmth. She would always be possessive about her youngest son. Roscoe, on the other hand, was openly delighted: "Ed, you got better than you deserve."[16]

Waiting was a stack of mail—questions, case reports, minutes, financial statements, the bulging 1934 report of the Joint Distribution Committee—sent on with some trepidation by Betty Drury: "it seems a crime to send along so much solid reading matter." There were also confidential memorandums, League papers, statements from McDonald, more reports from London, new lists of grants to date: "You and Mrs. Murrow must be having a wonderful trip around these United States!"

Far from resenting the flood of material, Murrow was delighted. It was first-class, he answered, "ample ammunition" for his appearances in California. Everything was read over, letters answered from a string of hotel rooms between Olympia and Berkeley. In San Francisco he was appalled at the lack of information getting through to the West Coast.

By early January they were back in New York, taking up residence in a high-rise on Manhattan's East Side. No more shared furnished rooms for the Assistant Director of the IIE, now raised to $5,000 a year, a good bit in the Depression. The Art Deco building rose among the tenements of Third Avenue, cheek by jowl with the elevated train that crashed uptown every few minutes.

At the institute, Murrow returned to a brimming desk and the usual crises.

"We are living, or rather Janet is living at 210 East 68th Street," he wrote a friend that month. "I seem to be living at the office most of the time." They had been married ten weeks.

In the meantime, the Nazis were reportedly furious at the adverse publicity generated by the Emergency Committee. Joseph Goebbels' minister of education had cracked down on one of their affiliates under the League—the *Notgemeinschaft*, or Emergency Society of German Scientists abroad, an émigré group often acting as go-between for those left behind, and a reliable source of information on developments in the Reich.

Perhaps too reliable. From Adams, Murrow had suddenly gotten wind of a notice circulated by "one of the new Nazi rectors"—"The *Notgemeinschaft* demands particularly careful observation. . . ."

The Herr Minister therefore orders that professors make a note of any approaches on the part of the *Notgemeinschaft* . . . or representatives

68

of this organization, not to answer, but instead to turn over all such communications immediately to the Ministry. . . .

"I thought you would want to know about this," said Adams in the covering note. It was the first indication that the game could get rough.

On the domestic front, Murrow, writing England, noted "a rather amazing increase in the general feeling of 'anti-foreignism' in . . . this country." At the IIE, warnings were coming in from the educational journals, telling of articles newly submitted, protesting not only the newly arrived foreign scholars but those who were longtime residents of the United States. "So far," he told Kotschnig, "these articles have not been published, but that doesn't help the situation very much."

He was also getting to be an expert on visa problems, countering the hostility of American consular officials abroad, gathering employment statistics in the committee's defense, driving to Washington to consult on work permits, now threatening to become a source of controversy. "A very discouraging business," he wrote to Geneva.

It is not unlikely that this whole matter of refugees will be thrown into the political ring in Washington. Several groups both in and out of the Democratic Party, are gunning for the Secretary of Labor [Frances Perkins].

Miss Perkins has not yet published the immigration figures which she is required to do by law. I am going to Washington for a few days . . . and shall write again if . . . there will be further developments in this matter. Will you please treat the above information as entirely confidential?[17]

The country, feeling the economic pinch, was wrapping itself increasingly in a mantle of isolationism which would lead by midsummer to the Neutrality Act—a neutrality which, to the IIE, had nothing peaceful about it. Duggan, speaking for the institute, had branded the new congressional military appropriations bill as oversized and therefore "wholly unjustified in terms of national defense. . . . Moreover, the Chairman of the Committee on Military Affairs of the House emphasized the fact that there was much unrest in the United States and that therefore we needed internal as well as external defense. This has a sinister tone for me."

Father Charles Coughlin was shrilling over the radio; the Ku Klux Klan was winning new recruits; the Hearst newspaper chain, reversing a seventeen-year policy of friendship for the Soviet Union, had embarked on an anti-Communist crusade with overtones of its publisher's newfound admiration for Hitler and Mussolini.

Older members of the institute were bemoaning Rooseveltian radicalism. Murrow laughed it off ("Every indication seems to be that the Roosevelt administration is moving more to the right all the while"). However:

A tremendous mistake is being made, in my opinion, by the majority of Americans in ignoring that strange individual, Huey P. Long. His

"Share the Wealth Clubs" are increasing in number every day. . . .
Long has mastered the techniques of effective radio broadcasting to a
greater extent even than Roosevelt. He has a rather unique ability to
talk economics and to illustrate his point by quotations both from the
Bible and from the agreement of the Pilgrim Fathers. He is unquestionably a dangerous demagogue and if the economic pressures do not
lift, I think we can expect a tremendous increase in his power and
influence during the next few years.[18]

Murrow's true wrath, however, was reserved for "the so-called liberals
in this country—"

They have no effective leadership, nor do they have a very strong
conviction that the principles for which they stand are applicable to
the present situation. So far as the universities are concerned, I am
quite convinced that if we were faced with a situation similar to that
in Germany our scholars would not defend themselves with any more
vigor nor with any more success. . . .

The committee's two-year mandate was running out, with no sign of
renewal. Foundation requirements had stiffened further. A campus contact reported rising resentment among mathematicians against the newcomers. Some colleges were imposing qualifications, requesting "Aryan"
scholars or "preferably Aryan and Protestant." One school, inquiring about
an economist, requested "the assurance that the man's thinking has not
been, or will not soon be classified as communistic."

Adams had once described himself and Murrow as a couple of Micaw-
bers, always hoping something would turn up.

"I think that even Micawber's optimism might have wavered," Murrow
wrote that spring, "had he been in our business."

And always, there was the underlying fear of stirring up a hornet's nest.
A New York *Times* article listing the participants in the program had
omitted Harvard, thereby setting off loud denials from a spokesman for
President Conant: The omission was unjustified; Harvard had four émigrés
on the faculty; it did "not wish to defend itself against the Emergency
Committee."

Murrow quickly confirmed that the four named were neither commit-
tee-sponsored scholars nor on assistance from the university administration. In a stinging letter to Cambridge, the twenty-six-year-old Assistant
Secretary reminded the distinguished educator of his explicit refusal to
join in the program.

Eventually, it was papered over; Harvard itself became a beneficiary.
But it had been a bruising encounter, one they could have done without.

In those months Harold Laski, visiting New York, left the Emergency
Committee a check for $100. Under Laski's leadership a number of En-
glish faculties, though sorely pressed, had voted themselves a three percent pay cut to create places for their distressed colleagues.

Murrow almost fell over himself with gratitude: "I often wish that the realization of what this whole situation means might penetrate the campus-conscious indifference of American scholars to the same extent which it has in England. Two years of rather intimate association with the whole matter have left me with very few illusions. . . ."

And again to Adams:

> The thing that really concerns me over here is the general indifference of the university world and the smug complacency in the face of what has happened to Germany.
>
> There is a tendency to consider the matter as a Jewish problem and a failure to realise [*sic*] that it represents a threat to academic freedom in this country as well as in England. Part of this attitude undoubtedly has its roots in a latent anti-Semitism which in my judgment is increasing very rapidly. . . . I hope that we may have time to discuss the larger implications of this whole business. . . .

The ISS in Geneva, setting up a conference, asked about the chances of obtaining an honorary American chairman. No problem, he replied: "Americans are pretty swell at acting in honorary capacities so far as the whole refugee situation is concerned."

The bitterness was taking over. There were too many breaks in the dike, too many calls for help. "Sometimes I feel so tired," wrote a European colleague, "that I don't know whether I want to weep or simply chuck the whole business. It's really only people like yourself who keep me in the work."

Therefore, the newspaper attack, coming as it did, hit hard even though the primary target was not the committee, but the good, gray IIE. William Randolph Hearst, deciding he liked Hitler better than Stalin, had launched his 180-degree turn on his old socialist sympathies, with a nationwide anti-Communist offensive including, among its targets, the Moscow summer school. (Not coincidentally, perhaps, the attack would focus on an advisor to the summer session—George Counts of Columbia University, who had had the temerity to criticize the Hearst empire.)

On February 18, 1935, the front page of the Hearst-owned New York *American,* in a special insert running beneath the latest on alleged kidnapper Bruno Hauptmann, denounced the summer school as a tool of the Soviet conspiracy (MOSCOW-LINKED PROFESSORS IN DRIVE ON U.S. SCHOOLS). Inside, a six-column story, with facsimile copies of the 1934 summer session pamphlet, spread across the page, spinning out charges of treason, listing the advisory council under a bold-faced head: LINKED TO MOSCOW/AMERICAN "ADVISORS" TO COMMUNIST PROPAGANDA SCHOOL. In the story, catchwords, sprinkled throughout the text in capital letters, drove home the message: "SOVIET AGENCY . . . PROMINENT SOVIET LEADERS . . . PROPAGANDA SCHOOL . . . COMMUNIST PROPAGANDISTS . . ."

Similar stories were appearing on Hearst front pages around the country, including Pittsburgh, headquarters for Carnegie, the lifeblood of the IIE.

Pittsburgh was disturbed; others raised questions. Ironically the attack had come after a winter of confrontation and plain talk between the advisory council and the Russians which had left the Americans in clear control of their program. Eighteen years later the Pittsburgh "exposé" would find its way into the files of Joseph R. McCarthy.

"The current red-baiting campaign," Murrow wrote a friend, "and general attitude of anti-foreignism is not a very healthful atmosphere in which to cooperate. . . ." He was wearing out, once again skirting the edges of exhaustion. "I have not been as discouraged in five years as I am now. . . . The situation is at least 50% worse. . . . If my correspondence of late seems to be a little curt and discourteous, please do not mind. I have time only to dictate letters and memoranda after office hours."

This time, however, there was a new factor in the equation—a young wife at home, his bride of less than half a year. His married friend Kotschnig tried to be reassuring: "Tell her that Elined has stood by me in my work for more than ten years and that Janet therefore should not give up hope."

It was not, of course, all grimness. Janet, as expected, had fallen in with his life-style, the young couple now drawn into the cosmopolitan world of the old intellectual elite. They visited, entertained in pleasant evenings with the Reinhold Niebuhrs, the Paul Tillichs, Karl Loewenstein, the Alfred Cohns—friendships that would survive the vicissitudes of the years to come. Janet held ISS fund raisers at home. Ed acted as guide to Judah Magnes, Chancellor of the Hebrew University, speaking in New York on Arab-Jewish cooperation. He drove out to Princeton to discuss problems with Einstein.

Undeniably, too, the situation was easing; the committee's life had been extended at the eleventh hour. "I think none of our people will really be out on the street," Murrow informed a colleague. In fact, its funding would soon double, the committee's activities expanding in response to German expansion in Europe, becoming a semiofficial body eventually, with ties to the State Department, no longer fighting a lonely battle in the dark.

But something was changing—not at the committee, where he had always been his own man, but at the IIE, the domain of Stephen P. Duggan.

For most of 1934, it was Murrow who had run the institute—efficiently, deferentially, careful to keep the chief informed during his peregrinations among the world's great. They were a team. In March, the committee's executive group had voted "wide discretion" not only to Duggan as its secretary, but to Murrow as well.

That spring, small memos started appearing, signed "SPD," questioning actions taken—not often, but enough: Who sent this? Who sent that? Had there been others? Murrow tried to be accommodating.

Matters finally peaked when a European query on a work program, addressed to Murrow and forwarded to Duggan, came back with an angry scrawl across the top: *"Such a letter should be directed to me. This is a matter of policy not administration."*

The younger man summoned up what he could of his dignity ("I should like to point out that this letter was not written at my request"), laid down the facts of the case, put the usual options—i.e., what was the boss's pleasure? The copy for his personal file, however, went back into the drawer a little worse for the wear, the top torn and crumpled, then carefully smoothed out as if in afterthought.

An appropriate disclaimer went back to Europe, one carbon copy to Dr. Duggan: "Inasmuch as your letter involves a question of policy with which I am not competent to deal. . . ."

He had known for some time that he would always be the assistant. They were still father and son; no grudges. But like most sons, he had outgrown his subordinate role, changed from the green youngster taken aboard in the winter of 1931. The message was clear: The institute was a one-man show. For Murrow, at twenty-seven, it was time to move on.

There had been no lack of job offers in the past, some lucrative. Always he had elected to stay with the institute and a job he loved despite— perhaps because of—its difficulties. The foundations eyed him with interest, seeing a good head for administration, executive timber. In the end, it was again the unforeseen factor, the imponderable that determined his next move.

Over the years his contacts with the Columbia Broadcasting System, close in NSFA days, had dropped off. A radio talk or two, then nothing. There never seemed enough time. Once in a while at educational meetings he would come across Fred Willis, William Paley's personable young assistant. It was finally Stephen Duggan who, launching a commentary series over network radio, got him back into a working relationship with CBS.

The professor had first broadcast on foreign affairs back in 1930, on the then two-year-old Columbia Broadcasting System. In late 1934, with world jitters rising, he was invited for a twenty-five week return engagement over the American School of the Air—Columbia's educational network, with a nationwide hookup—Friday afternoons, fifty dollars a broadcast. It was the prevailing *modus operandi*. The networks were young; their news departments, embryonic. Presentation of news in depth was largely a matter for outsiders—people like Raymond Gram Swing of the *Nation*, also broadcasting over the *School of the Air*—though a middle-aged ex-newspaperman, Hans von Kaltenborn, formerly of the Brooklyn *Eagle*, now came in to broadcast regularly, as an employee of CBS.

Last Week Abroad was billed as "an objective and analytical commentary concerning foreign news of the week . . . with particular reference to possible influence on American policy." Though aired in daytime hours over a school network, the series easily found an audience eager to understand what was going on, appealing not only to special interest groups— young Joseph Lash of the Student League for Industrial Democracy asked for a special mailing—but to the general public.

The Duggan talks were frankly lectures, delivered by a great lecturer. At the same time they offered something new, at least on radio: a dispassionate exploration of areas of public controversy, dealing more with issues than with personalities, couched in a popular idiom and aimed at a middlebrow audience. It was a contrast with the open partisanship and theatricality of the popular prime-time commentators of the day and an early precursor of the type of news analysis that would come to be associated specifically with CBS.

There was, however, another element that would be passed along: one of a subtle, guarded advocacy, coupled with an awareness that the quiet, informed, "objective" voice was often the best persuader—in Duggan's case, persuading an insular country to look outward. "Our national welfare," he had told the CBS management in late 1934, "is inextricably bound with that of the other countries of the world. We cannot live to ourselves alone."

Murrow's interest in the broadcasts was acute from the start. As Duggan's second-in-command, he sifted regularly through the confidential reports from their sources around the world. Fridays, at the studio, he listened in, a familiar figure to the engineers—chain-smoking, head down, eyes fixed on the floor, a human photographic plate absorbing attitudes that would go a long way toward shaping his own: "The policy of the Open Door in China is not based on altruism; we were concerned with our own interests. . . . The Americans are a lawless people. . . . The Cubans must work out their own solution in their own way without direct or indirect interference [from] the United States . . . our adventures in Nicaragua . . . Russia's entrance into the League . . . will strengthen the forces of peace . . . The policy of isolation . . . will eventually result in our being more embroiled in foreign wars than if we were in the League. . . . The problem of our neutrality in war is one of the major issues. It ought not to be left for solution to the time when war breaks out and passions are so aroused as to prevent a sane solution. . . ."

The listener response delighted CBS. "Widespread interest," Willis reported, and could they do it again?

For Murrow the net results went a good deal farther.

Much of the backup work involved in setting up the series had been his responsibility, and Willis was impressed. As it happened, the young man who went under the title of Assistant to the President needed more time for corporate—i.e., Mr. Paley's—matters, less for programming. As it happened, too, a new position was opening up: Director of **Talks to** Coordinate Broadcasts on Current Issues, or, in short, **Director of Talks**. It also involved responsibility for educational programming. **Murrow was** experienced in both. He was affable, efficient, knowledgeable **in political** matters, a good manager—able with equal ease to negotiate **a fee, figure** printing costs for publicity posters, or discuss the latest **changes in the** British cabinet.

Murrow for his part liked his CBS contacts and what **seemed to be an** oasis of public service in the brash world of commercial radio. **The network** had just issued new rulings, curbs on advertising, more **time for broad-** casting in the public interest—all of it ideal, seemingly, for the young man from the nonprofit world.

The new Talks position was part of that policy. "Fred had enormous respect for Ed's ability," said a mutual friend later, "and thought he was perfect for the job." He was not, admittedly, the first in line: Raymond Swing had applied for the post, gotten it, then withdrew on learning that broadcasting wasn't part of the deal. Nor was Murrow himself any too eager, cagey as always about changing his life-style or the source of a paycheck—the innate caution born of early hardship that would always be part of his emotional makeup.

Besides, there was the Depression. "Freddy Willis had quite a time persuading Ed," a friend recalled. "At the institute he had security, a job for a lifetime if he wanted it. He loved his work. In radio, you didn't know. . . ."

June 25, 1935, Ed and Janet Murrow boarded the *Statendam*, sailing from Hoboken to Plymouth, England. It was her first trip to Europe, his first since before the Hitler take-over—a working vacation, paid for out of the hoarded pennies of the Emergency Committee and the IIE. Not sufficient, therefore, to cover wives. In a separate arrangement with the Holland-America Line they signed on as shipboard social directors in exchange for her ticket. The long Atlantic swells thereupon reduced the team to one, Ed with his cast-iron stomach running the bingo nights alone, his bride seasick and chagrined in the cabin.

From the outset, there was no doubt about what kind of trip it was going to be. The cables had begun arriving before they landed—from the Secretary-General of the High Commission, from others in London, all anxious to see him. At once.

London was a nine-day marathon of meetings and interviews. Evenings and odd afternoons, they could still be newlywed tourists. English associates opened their homes; to Janet the people and places were new and exciting. For Ed, it would be largely a grand tour of committee rooms, closed-door sessions, urgent, often desperate consultations.

In Paris, at the American University Union, he answered a stream of communiqués arriving from New York at the rate of two and three a day, full of case-load questions. A friend had inquired after an opening with a relief organization; what did Murrow know about it? Murrow knew nothing about it: "You might also tell him that any position connected with refugees would turn out to be a nightmare!"

At the Cité, they enjoyed the hospitality of Dr. Krans, the Paris director, who had been filling in Duggan and Murrow on the rising Fascist Right in France. For a time it had looked as though Moscow might be added to their itinerary. But two days before the Murrows' arrival in Paris, Duggan's representative in Moscow, fresh from inspecting the dormitories newly readied for the summer school, was called to the office of Intourist and there told that the seminar had been canceled. Students could accept either substitute tours of the Soviet Union or refunds. Subsequent inquiries revealed that none of the proposed faculty had ever been appointed.

At the American Embassy, Ambassador William Bullitt assured the IIE man that there had been no official pressure from the American government. Nor did he think that "unofficial pressure" had been brought to bear. It was six months since the Hearst attack.

The institute was stunned. Krans, querying Murrow, found him as puzzled as the rest. It was the end of the program. In 1948, an attempt at its revival died in the cold war atmosphere.

"It looks as though the Moscow affair will not require my presence," Murrow wrote from Holland, where they attended an ISS conference— a stopover which, he told the office, had left him a little more time for relaxation than the weeks in London and Paris. "To Germany on Sunday to see how the Nazis will greet a friend of the refugees!"

Berlin was, as expected, bristling with uniforms. The Nuremberg Laws were only weeks away. Friends from the old days were dead or exiled; contacts with those left, disheartening. Making his calls, he found that while Education Ministry officials welcomed, even courted, the Assistant Director of the IIE—"I make every effort not to be 'coordinated' during my visit," he told Adams—his Emergency Committee credentials led to a distinct chilliness in other respects. Efforts to obtain information on government decrees ran up against a wall of silence. "Take care of yourself in Berlin," Adams warned him. Murrow committed nothing to paper but, once over the border in Switzerland, asked the Englishman urgently for a meeting on their return trip through London. "I am very anxious to talk to you about my visit to Germany."

There was a good deal, in fact, that he had not told Janet, which she had nevertheless sensed. How else explain, she later said, those phone calls in the hotel room, followed by his sudden, unexplained departures; his meetings on street corners, furtive and in twilight, with people whom she didn't know and whose identities were kept from her? It took no great guess that contacts were being made, that she was being kept out of it for her own protection.

Passing through Paris, he fell ill again—briefly, nothing serious, just the by now familiar malaise. August 31, they sailed home. "I hope you will take care of yourself," Krans wrote worriedly, "and . . . contrive to have a little rest on your return." Cohn, from Paris, urged "an additional holiday when you arrive in New York.

"Need I enlarge on this topic? There are difficult times ahead for which your best imaginative qualities are wanted."

All through the summer, there had been no indication that Murrow contemplated any immediate changes. In letter after letter he discussed committee plans, made projections, detailed new programs, new methods. To Cohn in a last note from England, he expressed his satisfaction at hammering out "a very workable arrangement with Adams concerning the continuation of our cooperation. . . . By the time you arrive in New York, I shall hope to have cleared away most of the papers on my desk and we can then discuss our own plans for the coming year."

In New York, however, Fred Willis was back in the picture, and so was CBS. The job was definitely open. Did he want it or didn't he? And if he did, wouldn't he have a talk with Mr. Klauber, the Executive Vice-President, who ran the network for Mr. Paley.

At first, he hesitated, undecided between the commercial world and the dead-end job that he loved and in some ways needed. But he was also young, married, and ambitious. Columbia offered upward mobility, the chance to learn something new. And he was never one to stand still.

He was also tired—rubbed raw by the strain of the past four years, alert to the attractions of a field that seemed to promise regular hours, time for a home life, where he could put the troubles of the world, the constant crises behind him. Something less gut-wrenching than his present employment. Like radio.

The second week of September, he returned to the usual backlog on West Forty-fifth Street: reports, decisions pending, a questionnaire for posting to the Americans returned from Moscow, and stacks of carbons. At the bottom, a copy dated June 27, two days after his departure for England: the institute's answer to the European correspondent whose query to Murrow, back in the spring, had unexpectedly raised the professor's hackles. Up to now, he hadn't seen Duggan's reply: "Mr. Murrow turned over to me your letter of May 24th . . . because that was a matter of policy and not of administration which I must decide for myself."

Underneath, in the professor's hand: "Copy to EM."

That Friday, a note came through from Betty Drury: They had run out of committee letterheads, and she was re-ordering. So far his name hadn't been listed along with Duggan's, as was the case for the IIE. Didn't he want it included this time?

Across the memo he slashed a wide "No," then penciled in: "Better order after. . . ."

He stopped. Drew a long stroke—"after next meeting. There may be changes."

Thirteen days later, there was a new Director of Talks at CBS.

IV

860 On Your Dial

Helen Sioussat stormed out the front doors of Phillips Lord, producers and packagers for the broadcast industry. She had had it with packaging radio programs, managing insane schedules, spending days, nights, and weekends chained to a desk. She wanted out—the Blue Network, the Red Network, Radio City and NBC, or Mutual Broadcasting, anywhere. Just out.

Crossing Madison Avenue, she saw the glass and bronze doors of 485. NBC could wait, she figured.

Personnel was most receptive: Why, yes, the Director of Talks had an opening; he was swamped, needed an assistant—matter of fact, he needed five assistants! Before she could say anything, the officer had picked up the phone: Mr. Murrow had a luncheon appointment but would see her. Trapped again.

Upstairs, a pleasant young secretary led her to the Director's office. As she stepped inside, her jaw dropped. "I had never seen such a handsome man in my life," she said later. "I just stood and looked at him." Then she sat and looked at him while Murrow went on, obliviously, earnestly, about the requirements of the job. She answered a few perfunctory questions. Finally, he looked at his watch: He was terribly sorry, but he was expected at the Astor—some clubwomen types, always poking holes in radio; one didn't dare not show up. Did she mind talking further in the taxi?

In the elevator he suddenly turned to her—"What do you do evenings?" She stiffened. "I go to *concerts*, I go to the *opera*, I—"

He shook his head impatiently. "No, no, I didn't mean *that*. I mean reading. What kinds of newspapers do you read, magazines? Very important to the job, you know."

She relaxed, honor intact; he was all business. Underneath she thought, *Darn*.

He talked all the way across town as the taxi careened at breakneck speed toward Times Square. At the Astor, he paid the driver and told the young woman to let him know if she wanted the job. "But you don't even know my qualifications—" She found herself addressing an open cab door, swinging idly in the city sunlight, aware of a gruff voice from the front seat: "Hey, lady, you gettin' in or out?"[1]

He had been with CBS some nine months by that time, assured, the perfect radio man. His beginnings, however, had been anything but quiet. Within three weeks of his arrival, in fact, he had managed to get the network embroiled in an international controversy that splashed onto the front page of The New York *Times*.

Perhaps it was inevitable, the result of a lengthy list of duties that came with the job: political programming, education, and overseeing overseas broadcasting in a time when foreign crises seemed to be multiplying geometrically—Japanese troops pouring southward from Manchuria; a right-wing coup in Greece; Italian troops in Ethiopia.

In New York, Columbia's newest official coped with a maddening situation, holding down the domestic side of his job while keeping an eye on events abroad with virtually no overseas staff—one man, London-based, ran around obtaining spokespersons—with primitive transatlantic facilities, and a fragmented, inefficient patchwork system of international broadcasting, dependent on a single overseas circuit from Great Britain.

Adding to the pressures of the new job—and unknown to anyone at CBS—was the fact that pending his replacement, he was still Assistant Secretary of the Emergency Committee.

"The radio business is fascinating," he told Kotschnig that October, "but between that, the Institute, and the Committee, I am losing my hair rapidly. Nobody has the slightest understanding of what is going on in this whole Ethiopian business. . . ."

The "Ethiopian business" had broken on October 2, as Benito Mussolini's army rolled across the Eritrean border into the highlands of East Africa. In New York Murrow had gotten on the phone with London and Geneva, where the League, in heated session, debated sanctions against Italy. The idea was to mount broadcasts by both sides from Geneva— first the Ethiopian delegation, then the Italians. Simple, right?

Not necessarily.

The problem wasn't the technology—a cumbersome matter of setting up a feed from Geneva, beamed to London, then relayed across the Atlantic for pickup by the RCA shortwave receiving station at Riverhead, Long Island. However clumsy it might seem in the age of communications satellites, in 1935 it was high technology. In Geneva, Edgar Ansel Mowrer, Paris correspondent for the Chicago *Daily News*, was lined up to interview the official spokesmen. It all seemed fairly straightforward.

Wednesday night, October 9, with the war a week old, Beirond Tecle Hawariate, chief Ethiopian delegate, speaking over the Geneva–London–New York hookup, presented the case for the government of Haile Selassie.

The following night, the Italians were scheduled to go on. In Geneva Ed Mowrer waited at the microphone with Baron Pompeo Aloisi, head of the Italian delegation. In New York it was almost 6:15 P.M., the usual program pre-empted. With minutes to spare, the telephones began ringing in the Geneva studio. London was calling; the message—no broadcast. The British Post Office, which controlled the London–New York circuit, had refused to relay the talk, citing League sanctions voted against Italy that day.

In New York, RCA informed the near-frantic Columbia officials that nothing was coming through. The program originally scheduled went on while Murrow, boiling, shot off a query to London. The following day he held in his hand a cabled reply from the British delegation: In view of the imposition of Article XVI of the League Covenant, "it was thought neither proper nor desirable to extend British facilities to an Italian speaker."

Friday morning it was front-page news, part of the larger story of nations at war, running under banner headlines: "51 NATIONS VOTE SANCTIONS AGAINST ITALY. BRITAIN CUTS OFF BROADCAST BY ITALIANS."[2] Radio had arrived—explosively, permanently—as a factor in international politics.

The Italians eventually got their broadcast—via the on-again, off-again Rome transmitter, which permitted direct beaming to the United States. From a studio at the RAI *palazzo* in Rome, Baron Aloisi appealed to the American public for "justice." In New York Murrow, facing the press, cited the company policy of presenting speakers on both sides of controversial issues; he was cool, unruffled, the perfect company spokesman.

Privately he was incensed. His own sympathies were strongly pro-Ethiopian, yet he was furious at what seemed like unilateral interference with an American broadcast—*his* broadcast. "At the moment," he wrote Kotschnig, "I am anti-British." Kotschnig, replying from Geneva, commiserated regarding "British righteousness. . . . I thought at the time that [they] had made a mistake." None of which, they agreed, improved the Italians' case.

In diplomatic circles, the so-called Aloisi affair died down quickly—an empty gesture like the sanctions themselves, watered down in committee by Samuel Hoare of Britain and France's Pierre Laval, future prime minister of the Vichy regime, leaving the worst of both worlds: continuation of the war in Africa; no end to the flow of munitions; Italy lined up solidly in the German camp. The end of the Stresa front of World War I and the beginning of the Rome-Berlin Axis.

CHAPTER IV

For those working in communications, however, the Aloisi affair had raised disturbing questions with no clear-cut answers—questions of control of the airwaves, the vulnerability of news sources, and whether one country, controlling a radio circuit, had a right to impose its policy on another. Back in Washington, the Federal Communications Commission had already forced reluctant AT&T officials into closing a deal with the French government for a new circuit between Paris and a receiving station in Lawrenceville, New Jersey. The license was being rushed through, but new problems were appearing every day, spurred by an explosive new technology, still in its infancy, the rules constantly rewritten, communications law almost nonexistent.

In the midst of it, Ed Murrow, age twenty-seven (the company thought he was thirty-two), was getting a firsthand glimpse from the very center of the vortex, his first weeks on the job.

He hadn't arrived with any fanfare. In fact, no one had even bothered to tell the tiny news staff. Robert Trout, the young news announcer, field reporter, and general man of all work, had simply come in as usual one Monday morning, gotten off the elevator at 17—"and there was a strange fella in a very small cubicle." The new Director of Talks, he was told. Director of Talks?

Puzzled, he went to see Paul White, Director of Special Events, heretofore in charge of all news operations. What had happened? White was deliberately casual: Oh, he just wasn't going to be responsible for these special things anymore; if there were talks in the studio or out in the field, they would come under Ed.

Trout was still uneasy. Where did that leave him, White? Was he losing out on anything?

"Paul *professed* to say no," he recalled later. "It was great—he was glad to get rid of all this and have somebody like Murrow in there, taking care of these things while he could concentrate on the exciting events that he liked to do better.

"That's as much as he would tell *me*, and I had to take it that it was true, that Paul didn't mind. *Whether* it was true or not, I'll never know."

Murrow, emerging from the protective cocoon of the institute into the corporate world, found himself in a new kind of situation, one in which he was no longer the head boy or the bright young man brought along by surrogate fathers. CBS meant, for the first time, raw competition, in the person of Paul White—six years his senior, a five-year veteran of radio news, and, for the last two, Director of Special Events for the network.

Everything about Paul White was larger than life—a beefy, overwhelming presence, a former newspaperman in *The Front Page* tradition, hard-drinking, as exuberant as Murrow was understated, with the center-parted, lacquered-down look of an oversize Dink Stover and the shoulders of a seasoned linebacker. He was large of gesture, loud of laugh, startlingly well read; addicted to word games, practical joking, and impromptu "pomes" on his battered Royal:

> *A gent I know whose life is superfluidity*
> *took a job in C.B.S. Continuity.*
> *One night after too much Scotch paregoric,*
> *He turned in a script just too prehistoric.*
> *He was fired and said, as he read his doxology . . .*
> *"I thought they would like my Paley-ontology."*

Kansas-born and trained in the tradition of William Allen White (who was evidently no relation), Paul Welrose White had come up via the classic route of high school cub reporter, a veteran editor by the time he graduated college, and a graduate of the Columbia School of Journalism. By the time he joined CBS in 1930, he had a six-year record as editor and ace reporter for the then-small United Press, covering big trials, strikes, and transatlantic flights, in the course of which his by-line had become one of the best known in the country.

Two years later he had faced down his old bosses when the wire agencies, bowing to newspaper pressure, began withholding their services from radio. With the backing of Edward Klauber, Executive Vice-President of CBS, White had then organized the first network news staff—600 correspondents and stringers across the country, feeding regular news reports in sponsored time periods. A few months of that, and the agencies came to terms; the Columbia News Service was disbanded—a promising trial run, proving that radio could do its own news gathering, independent of the traditional sources of print.

Brilliant in his job, White could be merciless when he sensed vulnerability in others—and he sensed it in the new Director of Talks.

From the start, there was a kind of electricity between Paul White and Ed Murrow. They were young, ambitious, vying for their places on the corporate ladder in a situation where the lines of authority were blurred. Theoretically, White had the seniority, was higher up in the hierarchy; in fact, they were autonomous of each other, both reporting to Klauber, who ran CBS as right-hand man to William Paley.

There seemed nothing to object to in the new Director of Talks. He was easy to know, likable, cooperative, a friendly man who never talked politics or spoke much of his former job; supposedly it had had something to do with education. For White, however, the new kid on the block was just a touch too self-contained, too smooth-edged, too pretty.

"This guy could model for an Arrow collar ad," had been the first reaction of White's assistant, J. G. ("Jap") Gude, as the new employee was brought around.

Said Gude: "I realized later that he really *was* an Arrow collar man. In that day of soft, button-down-shirt informality, Ed was the only man I ever knew who actually wore collarless shirts and starched collars—a little *too* well dressed. Without calling him vain, I think he was quite aware of his rather romantic good looks."

So was Paul White, who, quickly sensing the strain of straitlaced hick beneath the Arrow collar, would breeze mornings into Murrow's cubicle on a wave of high-decibel heartiness, trying repeatedly to rattle the other's surface quiet: *"Boy! You're a good-lookin' feller!"*

Since the Director of Talks had no defenses, only openings, the needling kept up, preferably in the presence of Murrow's assistant ("Say, Ed, I know this cute little piece, how about letting me fix you up?"/"I'm not interested; you *know* I'm a married man"). Helen Sioussat would then sit between them, an uncomfortable witness, listening to the replying chortle, watching the two men confront each other like motionless combatants, matched in size if not girth: White waiting, eyes atwinkle with unconcealed glee, Murrow glaring at his tormentor, fighting visibly with the urge to rush out from behind the desk and start punching.

At other times they would be chummy over drinks or poker, everything forgotten.

The truth was, they worked well together. Murrow respected White as a newsman; White noted just as quickly that the "educator" had awfully good contacts in Europe and America, knew what he was talking about, and was a generally useful fellow to have about the office. He found his niche, the starched collar notwithstanding, a congenial companion and a reliable source of cigarettes. Colleagues running low found they could save themselves a trip to the lobby by bumming a pack from Murrow; he stocked them by the carton.

Yet with White, there would always be a certain competitive edge. As late as World War II—the two men 3,000 miles apart, the pillars of a great news department—when Murrow's real date of birth was finally revealed, White was heard to mumble a low, barely audible "I *thought* there was something . . . immature."

The company Ed Murrow had joined in late 1935 had grown considerably beyond the struggling network that carried the first efforts of the NSFA. By the mid-thirties, the Columbia Broadcasting System was of nationwide importance, a web of telephone lines connecting almost 100 master control rooms across the country—ninety-seven stations in all, more than either the Red or Blue networks of NBC, surging ahead in net profits and dollar volume of sales, with a flourishing business outlook and a lively schedule of pioneering programs in sustaining—i.e., unsponsored—time periods.

For that growth, three men had been largely responsible: William Paley, the company's young president; Paul Kesten, heading network promotion; and Ed Klauber, the chief executive officer, a former city editor of The New York *Times*, who had first sensed radio's potential as a medium for public information as well as for entertainment and advertising, who had hired Paul White in 1930 and Ed Murrow five years later, and who would soon give the green light for the building of a formal news operation.

> He was a great editor, always insisting that it had to be *right*, before it was written. He was sparing with praise and penetrating with his criticism. . . . If there be standards of integrity, responsibility and restraint in American radio news, Ed Klauber, more than any other man, is responsible for them.

Thus Murrow at the height of his career, describing the man who had brought him into broadcasting, the successor, as role model, to Stephen Duggan.

However, there was nothing particularly fatherly about Edward Klauber, a nerveless topflight administrator who ran CBS without a hitch and without a smile. In contrast with encounters with the benevolent Duggan, Murrow now found dilemmas tossed back in his lap with a sharp-edged "That's *your* problem" as the Executive Vice-President swiveled back in his red leather armchair, gazing coldly from behind a fortress of a desk through the narrow spectacles that made him a cross between an old-time city editor and a Prussian drillmaster—a heavyset, bearlike man who took the world seriously and whose forbidding manner masked a basic shyness.

He was also a Rooseveltian liberal, a believer whose concept of broadcasting struck a responsive chord in the young Director of Talks. Klauber gave Murrow full leeway and backed him up in times of controversy. (Their relationship, however, always retained something of its original flavor. In the 1950s, when Klauber, fatally ill, asked Murrow to speak at his funeral, the younger man, jarred by the sudden request, laughed nervously. Well . . . what did he want him to say? Ed Klauber swiveled back in the red armchair, fixed him with a cold, myopic gaze, and said, "That's *your* problem.")

Balancing Klauber was Paul Kesten, the company promotional genius: slight, articulate, fast-thinking, as dynamic in his area as Klauber was in his. Kesten had started the company into market research and attracted the attention of the Madison Avenue agencies; he kept the image bright but solvent, the dollars and affiliates coming in, the other half of a two-sided rivalry over who was to be closest to William Paley.

"The two men were totally different," said Frank Stanton, later President of CBS, then a bright young member of Kesten's staff, brought in to measure audience listening habits and draw up statistics for the advertisers. "They were apart philosophically, stylistically, and perhaps even emotionally. . . . Ed came out of journalism; Paul came out of advertising, retailing. Paul was fast; Ed was deliberate. . . . Their working relationship

85

was productive, but I would characterize it as strained when it came to anything else but the nuts and bolts of running the company . . . just two different, totally different people."

"Klauber was sound and direct and earnest," said Adrian Murphy, another early staffer who was Kesten's assistant in those days.

> Klauber was a dragon in the company but a sincere guy, a dedicated newsman. Murrow was his man; they were compatible in their earnestness, their seriousness.
> Kesten didn't care about that as long as he could win. He was *so* facile, so brilliant. . . . Everyone was terrified of him; I wasn't and Stanton wasn't, but that was because we played his game.

To the troops on the lower floors—"those of us," said Stanton, "who saw the things that were going on in the executive suite"—it was something of a joke, remarks replete about being careful not to stick your head out the door on 20, the implication being that someone might take a potshot. But they considered it, on the whole, none of their business; tensions were inevitable in a company, the ultimate impact of the Klauber-Kesten rivalry still some time off.

While on 17, Murrow and the others felt themselves concerned only peripherally or not at all. They were Klauber's people, and Klauber, backed by Paley—infighting or no infighting—ran CBS.

To a generation familiar with the worldwide operations of CBS News, the Columbia setup of 1935 would seem almost laughable—a handful of people, five or six at the most, including White, Murrow, Jap Gude, formerly of the New York *Telegram*, now doing publicity and news editing, an assistant or two, and Bob Trout as the voice on the air.

CBS had its star commentators, but these were essentially freewheelers, with their own staffs and, often, their own sources: Boake Carter, the network's prime-time news attraction, a disembodied voice coming in from Philadelphia, closer to his Philco sponsor than to the CBS office in New York; or Hans von Kaltenborn, not yet a celebrity and a more familiar face at 485—stocky, autocratic, with a fringe of gray-white hair, master of the ad lib, developing his topics like a lecturer, joining the news team for conventions and election nights.

For the rest, it was up to the little staff in the corner of 17—hardworking, improvising as they went along, a hard-driven, close-knit group working together, relaxing together around the bar downstairs or at a former speakeasy several doors away, where the genial proprietor could fix a meal or float a loan (anyone sent off on assignment after the CBS cashier had closed could usually cadge a small advance from Joseph).

Like radio itself, informational programming had grown up haphazardly, network functions dealing with public affairs simply thrown together—"a mishmash," as one denizen described it: Publicity; Special Events, which handled everything from the brief three-a-day newscasts to election night returns to man-in-the-street interviews to coverage of the visiting Italian air flotilla; and Talks, presenting speakers, discussions, just about anything not specifically fast-breaking hard news, running afoul inevitably, at times, of Special Events.

It was a hybrid—partly a spin-off of the talks programming of the BBC and partly pragmatic, instituted in a burst of goodwill following the defeat, in 1934, of efforts by public-interest groups to gain access to channels on the existing broadcast band. Instead, the Communications Act as finally written by Congress simply obliged the industry licensees, who had so successfully lobbied against the idea, to operate in the "public interest, convenience and necessity," direct access traded for a vague commitment to public service within the existing framework.

Just how vague, Murrow discovered in the process of clearing time for his speakers, the magic phrases unspecific about just how many hours were to serve the "public interest, convenience and necessity" or what to do if an affiliate refused to carry a broadcast since talks made no money.

A twentieth floor that took its commitments seriously ensured that slots would be available, an outlet guaranteed in WABC, Columbia's New York key station, operating in those days at 860 kilocycles from a relatively low-wattage transmitter in New Jersey.[3] For the rest, Murrow and Siousset would haggle with the station managers for time, and particularly for prime time. (Generally an evening slot meant the time had been written off—Representative Emanuel Celler of Brooklyn, for example, paired with the star-studded opening of NBC's Hollywood studios. Under the circumstances, management was only too glad to let Murrow have the time opposite for Manny Celler speaking on U.S. attitudes toward Mexico.)

Nor were the prominent necessarily beating down the doors to get on the air. Radio was new, brash, the poor man's medium.

Some, however, were picking up quickly on the unique power of the airwaves, on radio's potential as a national public forum—the start of the trend that would turn the disdain of 1935 into a demand for airtime reaching near-avalanche proportions. Murrow scheduled speakers on the order of Cordell Hull, Secretary of State, speaking on foreign policy, Senator William Borah on inflation. Former New York Governor Al Smith accused the Roosevelt administration of socialism, followed by Norman Thomas objecting that Roosevelt wasn't carrying out socialism "unless he carried it out on a stretcher." Floyd B. Olson, the populist Governor of Minnesota, called for a radical third party and a new economic order to replace the old ("The game is fixed; the dice are loaded").

Earl Browder, Secretary of the Communist Party, spoke as the CP's next presidential nominee—the first time a radio chain granted free time to a Communist spokesman. The CP was registered in thirty-nine states, Murrow explained easily to reporters, therefore qualified under the fairness doctrine—as pickets massed downstairs. By the time it was over, six New England stations had dropped the talk, Hearst editorials across the

CHAPTER IV

country had denounced the network, and Congressman John McClellan of Arkansas had accused CBS of treason, thereby starting a shouting match on the floor of the House of Representatives.

(Presumably for his own safety, necessity and convenience, Browder had spoken not from 485, where the picketers were, but from the older CBS studios on West Fifty-seventh Street, atop Steinway Hall. Al Smith, menaced by the more obstreperous followers of Father Coughlin, had had to be led out a back door.)

Perhaps inevitably for a small company, the Director of Talks was also responsible for education and religion, separate units which pretty much ran themselves: both the Columbia School of the Air and the Church of the Air, the latter providing time to religious groups on a rotating basis, eliminating thereby the sale of airtime to electronic preachers.

He also began a quarterly digest of radio talks and, for the uninitiated, wrote an instructional pamphlet on radio speaking and writing. He increased the amount of time given the student movement and, with Bob Trout as "announcer" (applied in those days to any staffer speaking on the air), broadcast the proceedings of the American Youth Congress, a function that was to be viewed with a jaundiced eye by the dossier compilers of the early fifties.

Through it all, he was first and foremost "the educator"; it was part of his job, part of his aura. William Paley, meeting with the new Director of Talks, had the impression of an efficient administrator—"very attractive, very responsible," he recalled later—knowledgeable in world affairs (so much so, Paley was to write, that he got off a memo to Klauber recommending Murrow to head CBS's international broadcasting, should the occasion arise), but whose job record, to all appearances, seemed pristinely academic. He'd worked for an international organization, dealt with student exchange, done a good job of it. Said Paley: "I knew about that in a general way, and I have a recollection that our idea of how he conducted that job was very favorable, and...had a lot to do with getting the assignment here. But I never had a discussion with him about it."

Nor did anyone else. To colleagues and superiors alike, he was the man from the IIE—whatever that was—a pipe-smoking professorial type, a pleasant transplant from the groves of academe. The image pleased him. Quite possibly, too, it provided protective coloration since the Director of Talks, particularly in his early months at CBS, was in effect living in two worlds.

The news of Murrow's departure from the IIE had sent a minor shock wave through nonprofit circles, particularly those involved in rescue operations. "It must be a great loss to you," Joseph Chamberlain of the National Coordinating Committee wrote to Duggan, "but he also leaves a great void in the refugee work. Could you let [us] know who is taking his place and . . . to . . . whom we shall send our academic cases?"

The answer, for some months, was: to Murrow as usual. Pending his replacement, there was no one else to do the job, and a steady stream of communications started up between Madison Avenue and West Forty-fifth Street. He tried to keep the two worlds apart, meeting with foundations on his own time, following up on thorny cases, negotiating a salary, finding a job for the murdered Fritz Beck's nephew, escaped from Germany and arrived in New York with nothing but the clothes on his back.

Replies would be dictated in off hours at committee headquarters, the typed copies sent to his office for the signature that still read "E. R. Murrow, Assistant Secretary" and returned by Western Union messenger. Drury, anxious to spare a dime, had offered to run them up herself, but there were limits. Murrow commented, "Surely we ain't that hard up!" The committee was also moving, touching off further headaches regarding rent, billing, furnishing—and what should they do with the stock closet?

At one point he begged her to stop, send nothing more, hold it at the institute—"The atmosphere here is not conducive to reflection about Refugee problems!"

Even after his replacement at the year's end, indeed up to his departure for London, he continued active as part of the committee's inner circle, involved in long-range planning and the problems multiplying in the wake of the Nuremberg Laws; coping directly with the crises which, to his colleagues in the newsroom, were only items on the ticker (and possessing, often, better inside information than they).

At work he was guarded, taciturn by nature about himself—"extremely articulate, but not the sort of fella to confide," Bob Trout recalled. They didn't even know if he voted.

There was nothing covert about it; his name was listed openly on the committee letterhead. But it was another world, sensitivities running high in both Ed Klauber's office and in 1930s radio in general—CBS was, after all, government-licensed—on anything even hinting at nonobjectivity, a taking of sides at a time when the ink was barely dry on the first Neutrality Act. Paley, asked in later years, would not commit himself on the matter, didn't know what company rules and regulations were as to "extracurricular work," but if it conflicted with duties, something probably would have been said about it, he couldn't say; those were different times; he was no longer living them.

Only in the newsroom, where isolationist sentiments ran high, did Trout, a minority of one, sense an ally: "Ed was not talkative, of course. Nothing really was said about it. We were all supposed to be very neutral about politics, which we always were. But I think that we both felt exactly the same way. . . ."

The upshot was to create a strange situation, a virtual set of identities underlying Murrow's existence in his early years with CBS: the committed, cosmopolitan participant in the action of the time; the dispassionate broadcast executive, dispensing airtime with an even hand; the Director

89

of Talks and presumed "educator," who knew more about what was happening abroad than the newsmen who worked with him.

As things stood, Special Events reflected the concerns of a still-isolated country, its chief a superb craftsman—geared to domestic reporting and, in those years, something of an isolationist, whose expertise in foreign affairs was as yet largely confined to the news wires, a situation that would change but that in the immediate future was to cause strains between CBS in New York and CBS abroad.

In the meantime, Murrow lived his role—he was not about to tell trained journalists how to do their job—with only an occasional cry of frustration sent up to friends, well out of earshot of 485: "Nobody has the slightest understanding of what is going on. . . ."

The year 1936 was one of banner headlines: the death of George V; the collapse of Ethiopia; civil war in Spain; German troops in the once-demilitarized Rhineland, in defiance of Versailles.

But to the broadcasting industry 1936 was, above all, a year of politics: elections, unprecedented spending of party moneys, and a scramble for airtime, arraying on one side the Congress and the Republican National Committee, on the other, the networks and the first broadcasting President, who played the medium with the deftness of a pro.

The FDR-radio connection had actually predated the New Deal, going back to the time when Governor Roosevelt had first gone on the air and NBC was the only game in town. NBC President Merlin Aylesworth, completing fireside chat arrangements with his old friend and FDR lieutenant Louis Howe, could casually toss in his regards to the Chief and the gang with the easy assurance of an insider. When the Hyde Park radios were down to a sputter, NBC technicians put them in order. NBC had two networks, the Red and the Blue, two Washington stations, the common channels for network lobbying and general point of contact with the administration.

In 1935 Bill Paley, out to narrow the edge, requested an audience. Stephen Early, then assistant secretary in charge of press relations, urged that the President see him: "He is friendly, so is Columbia. Confidentially, I understand that he desires to tell the President something of Columbia's political policy, plus a willingness to be of service during the campaign."[4]

More often, though, personal contacts were kept up through the local station—in CBS's case WJSV and specifically the office of Station Manager Harry Butcher, Vice-President, CBS, later wartime aide to Dwight David Eisenhower, but in 1936, warm personal friend to both presidential secretaries.

The connection was a two-way street, mutually beneficial. For radio—not quite respectable, a parvenu in communications—it meant reflected power and prestige; for Roosevelt, with some four-fifths of the print press against him, an open line to the public. For those handling it, an old-boy connection subject ever so gently to the expert guidance of Steve Early, the veteran journalist and ex-newsreel executive who had revolutionized White House–press relations, raised the ante for both news access and news management while virtually creating the role of the presidential press secretary. There were advance itineraries for presidential junkets, schedules of requested radio talks along the way, sent out in confidence to Butcher and his counterparts, everything spelled out—the stops, dates, regional time, and number of minutes, whether local or on a regional or national hookup: a totally professional job.[5]

Nonpolitical trips, the White House called them. Campaign trips, countered the Republicans—while remaining discreetly silent about out-spending the Democrats in a media blitz, backed by a record party war chest, and aimed specifically at New Deal programs.

As for the young people at CBS—most, except for Klauber, still in their thirties—they were whole-heartedly for Roosevelt; for the New Deal, against the Liberty Lobby; for the people, progress, and the working man. In 1935, at Paul White's suggestion, CBS had mounted a two-hour special marking the second anniversary of the New Deal, produced by White, with help from WJSV. Billed as a two-year review of the three branches of government, it was pure political theater, an impression reinforced by the prevalent custom of dramatization, the result: a hybrid that left the radio documentary of those days a cross between soap opera and *The March of Time*:

> ANNC'R: March 4th, 1933!
> *Woman*: Why Henry . . . What are you doing in the kitchen at seven in the morning?
> *Man*: (far from cheerful) Couldn't sleep . . . The whole country's going to the dogs. . . . How do we know what Mr. Roosevelt's going to do?
> *Woman*: We'll have to be patient—and—and have faith—faith in ourselves . . . in our President . . . in our country . . . just think—today down in Washington (FADE). . . .
> BIZ: FADE IN: SOUND OF CROWD MURMUR. . . .
> *Man*: It's almost time, isn't it?
> *2nd Man*: Yes . . . Got our camera set?—Roosevelt will start his inauguration speech in a minute. . . .
> *Man*: I've got a feeling that we're making history in Washington today.
> ANNC'R: In quick succession the National Recovery Act . . . became law. . . .The New Deal had been launched!—*The country was marching forward to the future!* CUE
> MUSIC: MARCHING ALONG TOGETHER . . . UP . . . HOLD . . .[6]

A rough draft had gone to Early, requesting "comments and suggestions."

Small wonder, therefore, that the anti–New Deal opposition regarded radio, especially CBS, as enemy territory, or that Talks and political programming in general would develop in an atmosphere of confrontation.

Murrow had been at CBS only four months when, in January 1936, FDR caused an uproar by delivering the annual message to Congress in person—an unprecedented move—before a joint session at night, with microphones open for a national hookup, the State of the Union address turned into a prime-time broadcast, in a presidential election year.

Campaigning, the Republicans called it, and demanded equivalent reply time. NBC and Mutual complied; CBS, defiant, said time would be forthcoming at the network's discretion and *it* would decide if a president was or was not speaking as a candidate.

The matter had been handled at the highest level. But when, in the following year, partisans took to the air over the so-called Supreme Court packing plan, Talks was directly on the line, Murrow keeping close score as speakers lined up for and against.

But he couldn't control reluctant affiliates—or keep local engineers from cutting off a politician going into overtime. Burton Wheeler of Montana, leader of the Senate opposition to the plan, thought he was speaking over a nationwide hookup; he wasn't. Even worse, Eastern engineers lopped off the last ten minutes.

Wheeler's roars of displeasure found a powerful echo among anti-administration forces on the Senate Judiciary Committee, charging White House manipulation of the networks in the Supreme Court battle and threatening an investigation.

Murrow, replying for CBS, defended the network's record, complete with score card—seventeen speakers for the plan so far, seventeen against; the Senator had spoken twice, had been offered facilities for a third time—the facts and figures as usual in hand.

In the background, more worrisome to the industry, was legislation pending in the lower house, extending the equal time provision of the Communications Act—which mandated equal time for candidates—to equal time not only for candidates, but issues. The hullabaloo over the Wheeler affair now threatened to dislodge the bill from committee and rush it into law on a tidal wave of congressional resentment.

Nothing came of it in the end. The Wheeler affair died down—a highwater mark, however, in the ongoing struggle for control of the medium, and in the midst of it, the CBS Director of Talks—learning the hard way about communications law and regulation, the paradox of media power and media vulnerability, and the never-ending tug-of-war between the broadcasters, the President, and the Congress, all claiming to be "for the people," who presumably owned the airwaves.

The New York *Times* of late May, 1936, billed the upcoming political conventions as "the biggest show on the air," and they were.

Convention broadcasting went back to 1924, when no networks existed, when a hookup of some twenty independent stations carried the nomination of Calvin Coolidge. They had been cut-and-dried affairs for the most part—vote tallies, party speeches, with here and there a glint of human drama, enough to alert broadcasters, politicians, and the public to the possibilities of convention coverage.

By 1936, however, the networks were entering the political scene bigger, richer, securer, the broadcast conventions a display of what radio could do—from the seven-and-a-half miles of wire strung along the floor of Cleveland's Public Auditorium, scene of the Republican Convention, to the sixty-eight microphones scattered throughout the hall to the 224 stations lined up by the three networks, from Bangor, Maine, to Honolulu. NBC had brought in big-time newspaper names—Walter Lippmann, Dorothy Thompson—to supplement house celebrities such as Lowell Thomas and Graham McNamee. Gabriel Heatter was announced for Mutual.

The watchword was technology. NBC reporters carried miniaturized microwave transmitters, minibroadcasting stations flashing words picked up to a master control center for relay to the network. CBS, not to be topped, added a built-in camera plus flash attachment, guaranteed to photograph the delegate in the act of speaking, with complimentary copies "for the folks back home."

The first week of June, the CBS team arrived in Cleveland—a small, lean group compared to the star-studded NBC contingent, Paul White at its head and including Trout, Gude, Kaltenborn, Percy Winner of the Havas news agency, and Washington columnist Mabelle Jennings, billed as "the only feminine member of the CBS political convention staff."

White had also asked Murrow along; Ed had good contacts.

It was a scene that would be familiar to succeeding generations of convention broadcasters: the teeming hall wired in those days for sound; the network booths seemingly hovering above the crowds. CBS was at one end, NBC and Mutual directly opposite, accessible on presentation of a pass reading "RADIO EMPLOYEE" and stamped with the unsmiling features of William McKinley.

Murrow's job consisted largely of corralling politicians for extended commentary at the makeshift studios set up in a nearby hotel. Otherwise, there were the usual features and fillers—discussions; appearances by party notables; sidewalk interviews billed by the network as "a radio symposium of pre-convention opinion." He had wanted Raymond Swing for the nightly sum-up, had tried repeatedly, in fact, to secure the veteran journalist a regular spot in New York only to be frozen in his tracks by a sharp reprimand from Klauber, who objected to Swing's radio voice.

He also found his patience tried repeatedly by H. V. Kaltenborn, who handled commentary for the network from the speaker's platform—a top newsman and mainstay of the team but inclined to be high-handed vis-à-vis his younger colleagues; admired, respected, and a thorough irritant.

In the meantime, the press played up the new medium: the sleek, efficient broadcast centers—air-cooled, comfortable, so different from the scruffy newspaper offices, where the roars from the hall could be muted by the turn of a dial—and its practitioners, acolytes of the new art. The radio editor of a local paper, interviewing Murrow for his readers, described the CBS Director of Talks as "a dark-haired slim young man of No. 1 personality.

"I discover he has no intention of turning 'instructor' for the Elephant word hurlers. . . . However, if some of the old school speakers inquire— well, he might be a valuable assistant. . . ."

In fact, radio was changing the traditional mode of American politics, convention main events now pegged to the evening hours in a bid for prime-time audiences, politicians rated by the way they came across on the air. Republican nominee Alf Landon sounded disastrously like Herbert Hoover; William Borah made it all too clear that he was reading copy. Stirring orators were suddenly corny; seasoned urban politicians, caricatures of the party hack.

Yet party leaders, far from resenting the medium in their midst, welcomed it, courted it, saw the microphone as an extension of their power, and tailored their speeches to the clock, one of their fears, that of a possible voter backlash over the pre-empting of *Amos 'n Andy*.

Two weeks later, the CBS team repeated the whole thing at Philadelphia, where to no one's surprise the Democratic incumbent was nominated by acclamation. They were veterans by now, the job fairly routine. As a favor to Paul White, Boake Carter, Columbia's star commentator, stopped in briefly: dapper, gracious, bestowing his presence much like a rich relation.

(But the conventions couldn't pass without at least one dig at Murrow. Sioussat, in New York, got a phone call from White in Cleveland. It seemed there was a big sale of men's ties at some New York store and could she buy some for him and Ed, they'd pay her later. "I don't know your tastes," she protested. Oh, no problem, they had the same tastes: the louder, the better.

(Returned to 485, Murrow blinked at the riot of color on his desk: weren't these ties for Paul? "Oh no, they're yours." But he wore *very conservative* ties, he protested; hadn't she noticed? "Why no," she answered miserably, "I never really looked."

(Murrow was as upset as she'd ever seen him—that his own assistant couldn't even tell what kind of *ties* he wore. . . .

(He paid the bill, though.)

The radio campaign included acceptance speeches from the smaller conventions, from the Trotskyites on the left to the Coughlin-backed Union Party on the right, ending with Earl Browder's nomination by the CP, carried by both NBC and CBS, as the band alternated "John Brown's Body" and the "Internationale."

Election night at 485 was a studio extravaganza—a huge chart, serviced by two pages in earphones, listing incoming totals state by state; a platform for the anchorman and commentators; a line of desks and teletypes with the latest bulletins; and an invited audience to observe the whole thing.

Murrow, however, was at Hyde Park, dispatched there to cover Presidential reactions—Trout was needed back at CBS—armed with a microphone, engineer, sound equipment, and a recommendation from Harry Butcher as "a peach of a fellow." Mrs. Roosevelt served the young man scrambled eggs.

That January in Washington—the inauguration had been moved up from March—Murrow watched from a reserved section as the reelected incumbent, flanked by microphones, told his generation that it had a rendezvous with destiny.

Murrow's own destiny, in the opening of 1937, seemed firmly set behind a desk, a rising executive in a rising company, good prospects, a good address, a lovely wife. The twentieth floor had its eye on him; Paley heard good things about him. The way seemed open for a swift, smooth rise up the corporate ladder.

Inevitably his friendships were being drawn more and more from within the company, notably with the personable assistant treasurer, James Seward, a soft-spoken Marylander of courtly manners and subtle sensibilities. He had also made the acquaintance, in passing, of a contemporary who had joined CBS the same week, met when an old NSFA buddy visiting New York brought to lunch a former colleague—now also with CBS, he said—and introduced Frank Stanton, a Ph.D. psychologist from Ohio State. The slight, reserved young man with a shock of strawberry blond hair, brought east by Paul Kesten to measure audience reactions with a view to better sales information, was toiling downstairs at the third desk in the three-man research department. They went to lunch together. Murrow and the out-of-town visitor happily rehashed days in the student movement, Stanton sitting diffidently silent; he had never been with the NSFA.

In general, however, Murrow was known in the company, popular with Kesten's no less than Klauber's people: a good conversationalist, charming yet reticent enough to take the curse off it; outgoing yet with a perceptible strain of shyness (some said, inferiority complex), who automatically attracted and intrigued people without seeming to work at it. Who was at the same time a smooth-running component of the company machinery—"totally cooperative," Adrian Murphy recalled, a man who got you what you needed, when you needed it, and without a whole lot of questions.

Outside, the Murrows were the ideal, upwardly mobile young couple, their world bounded by the golden rectangle of midtown Manhattan, a striking pair, friends remembered—Ed with his cinematic good looks; Janet pretty, fashionable, inevitable little hat set among the fair curls, patent-leather shoes, introduced invariably by her towering husband as "my child bride."

He was the star; she provided the setting. He sang at parties; she accompanied, presiding deftly over their social life, chatelaine of the small but comfortably elegant Sixty-eighth Street apartment, coolly ignoring the Third Avenue el that made its presence felt at jangling intervals when it almost seemed to crash in one bedroom window and out the other. Murrow couldn't stand it.

She was learning, however, to live with his hypersensitivities, less evident on the job—the emotional outbursts and wide mood swings, the depressions and sudden silences he had warned her about; as a New Englander she did not find silence a problem. But the young husband also had a fearsome temper, easily touched off, his storming increasing in inverse proportion to her quiet. Enraged, he accused her of sulking.

The "child bride" set her jaw, blue-eyed gaze fixed levelly somewhere in the middle distance, and answered in low, measured tones: "I'm not sulking. I'm . . . holding . . . my . . . *temper!*" He learned to control himself. It was a good thing they didn't both have a temper, she said afterward, or they'd have killed each other.

Storms aside, it was the good life, the American dream come true for the logging engineer's son from western Washington, with every prospect for its continuation, maybe even a corporate vice-presidency at the top.

Only once, after an office Christmas party, had there been an indication that things might turn out otherwise.

He had been fascinated with broadcasting ever since 1930, developing his interest now in long-running dialogues with Bob Trout, so fluent over the air, so much at ease. He asked, "How do you *do* that . . . just taking that microphone . . ." Easy enough, said Trout; he was shy, terrified of live audiences. That thing was like a telephone; you just talked to someone without facing him; nothing could be easier. Murrow didn't understand; *he couldn't; he knew*—he'd given lectures, needed an audience, needed that reaction, that interplay between himself and the public.

But he had obviously made up his mind to try.

The party had been in the afternoon, with, of course, the usual imbibing—Trout hardly at all, Murrow just enough to keep up. Then, as Christmas Eve approached, the floor gradually emptied, leaving Trout to read the late-night newscast and Murrow, waiting until everyone else had gone home, trying to convince the other that he had had too much to drink.

"I'm perfectly all right, Ed!"

"No, no, I don't want you to get into trouble; you better let me do this for you."

Said Trout later, "It finally got to the point where he practically ordered me, and after all, he was my boss." They sat down at the desk, Trout watching.

Murrow read it through perfectly, from end to end, without a fluff.

Afterward they got cold feet. "He had had no business doing it, and I had no business letting him do it, except he was my superior." What if there was an inquiry? But it was Christmas Eve, and no one was paying any attention. "As far as I know, nobody ever mentioned it; it went out into the void. . . ."

In fact, the change coming up for Ed as well as Janet Murrow would be from an altogether different direction.

Overseas radio, for all Murrow's efforts, had been in the main a novelty act, fifteen minutes of voices from abroad at noon Sundays, introduced by the chirped "Hello, America" of Cesar Saerchinger, the CBS European Director and representative in London. Murrow, as Director of Talks, scheduled and cleared weekly or biweekly commentaries from London or Paris by distinguished editorial writers, some of them contacts from IIE days; scheduled live debates from the League of Nations and talks by world figures lined up by Saerchinger, from Bernard Shaw to Haile Selassie, from Benito Mussolini to Leon Trotsky to John Maynard Keynes.

Basically it was still exotica, cutting through the shortwave crackle, its primary attraction the sheer idea of sound transmitted from other lands, other cultures; a CBS promo for a broadcast from a Soviet collective farm promised listeners "translated interviews with peasants, sounds of farm machinery, and the bleating of livestock."

There had been glimpses of other worlds, other possibilities; the Aloisi affair had hinted at the potential power of international broadcasting. Then in mid-1936, Kaltenborn, covering the Spanish Civil War at his own expense, broadcast the sounds of battle from a mobile transmitter with a French engineer, conveying the realities of the struggle and riveting public attention.

But it was an event of an altogether different nature which, surfacing late that year, first harnessed the facilities of network radio—both NBC and CBS—to produce sustained coverage of a foreign crisis and in its course cracked the managerial façade of Columbia's Director of Talks.

It began with a small item in the Chicago *Daily News* to the effect that a Mrs. E. A. Simpson had filed for divorce against Mr. Simpson, in the Suffolk town of Ipswich. It was a newsbreak of magnum proportions, blowing the cover on the ongoing relationship between the King of England and a soon twice-divorced American socialite. For weeks on end the Western world was to hang on to every development on what was becoming the hottest story on two continents—albeit suppressed at first in Britain—snowballing by December into a threatened constitutional crisis at the heart of the British Empire.

Considering the elements, it was bound to dominate the press; but radio, carrying the voices of English commentators directly from London, found itself uniquely equipped to convey the flavor and full impact in up-to-the-minute reports that could be flashed nationwide over the networks, beating out the newspapers and wire agencies—a breakthrough for over-seas broadcasting, though reported by European surrogates.

At CBS, it was Murrow who had first pointed out the significance, at the earliest stages, of what was happening. Paul White was away, off in South America for the network. Murrow went to White's news editor, Jap Gude. This was a constitutional issue, he said, not just royal soap opera; it needed covering. Gude agreed.

"There was nothing about it on the BBC," he later recalled, "no news about it in England. . . . Ed and I thought, *What the hell, why should there be any restrictions here?* So I went up to Klauber, as I was sure White would have done and said, 'This is a hell of a story.' "

Klauber agreed and teamed them up with Freddy Willis, who, ac-cording to Gude, "didn't know very much about news, but he knew the English, and Ed had so many contacts in other places. . . ." Together, the men made up a troika, working around the clock, with Murrow on the phone day and night with Saerchinger, lining up English broadcasters, instructing Saerchinger to watch the situation closely, breaking into the network at all hours with news flashes in what The New York *Times* would call "a steady tattoo between London and New York."[7]

"Ed was really more useful than I was," said Gude. "There were people that he was able to get to broadcast. We were in a bit of a sticky wicket; the BBC was very uncooperative; they didn't control the wires, but we had to use their facilities. At first they refused. Then we used it, don't know how. Of course, after a while the story broke in England, and once *we* went, everything broke. It was like taking your finger out of the dike."

Working with Murrow in the newsroom, Gude became suddenly aware of another personality emerging: "I saw what a good grasp of the news he had. He knew England and various parts of Europe. He knew the British system of government—what it meant for a king to abdicate. It was the first time I really got to know Ed. . . ."

They arranged thirty-nine broadcasts, covering every aspect of the crisis, offering with NBC, over a ten-day period, more expert commentary and analysis than those available to listeners in Britain.

The crowning touch, for CBS, came in what would be the closing hours of the crisis, December 11, 1936. Saerchinger, in London, was keeping close tabs on the situation. At 485 Madison, Murrow and Herbert Ro-senthal, second-in-command of the program department, haunted the control rooms of the studios in which on-air programs were originating, alive to the possibility of a news flash. Jerry Maulsby, an operations supervisor, watched the two men prowling from room to room, waiting tensely.[8]

They were in a small talks studio off master control, up on the twenty-third floor, when Saerchinger suddenly came in on the London–New York circuit, demanding air—immediately. Murrow interrupted a Heinz program, and Saerchinger made the announcement, direct from the House of Commons, before even the MPs had had a chance to hear the news that Edward VIII had abdicated.

It was a first-magnitude scoop, beating out all competition in both radio and the press, though the New York *Herald Tribune*, in a shrewd guess, had headlined a daring forecast Thursday night. No matter, CBS was awash in self-congratulations, Murrow a minor celebrity on 17, everyone high and bubbly and tired. Said Gude: "It was a bit of journalistic history."

Later that day Murrow and Willis sat in Helen Sioussat's office, listening to the voice of the former Edward VIII, cutting through the shortwave crackle, throwing it all over for "the woman I love." Willis, English to the core, had been deeply perturbed throughout the crisis. Murrow, for his part, had little use for royalty, less for the former king.

The speech ended, the two men just sat awhile. Then Sioussat watched them both stand up—very straight—turn, and walk slowly out of the room, back to their offices. "Ed looked like he was going to cry any moment."

Nevertheless, NBC's coverage had been better, both before and during the crisis—in part because of the energies of Fred Bate, Saerchinger's NBC rival in London, in part because of an able, articulate youngster named Alistair Cooke, film critic for BBC Talks, who had lived in America and moonlighted for NBC in a weekly broadcast series to the States. When the abdication story first broke in England, Bate, stranded in New York, had ordered Cooke, over the transatlantic telephone, to get to the BBC and broadcast over the one circuit available a quarter hour before CBS had its booking. Cooke had done just that, appearing up to five or six times a day, broadcasting something like a quarter of a million words in the ten-day period that followed, graphic proof that overseas broadcasting was turning into overseas reporting, and placing a sudden premium on youth and swiftness.

Saerchinger, forty-eight, wanted to go home, a hardworking newspaperman and pioneer who had established Columbia's first London office, who had scored notable beats for radio, including its most recent, a writer on music whose first love had been the cultural scene. But in 1937, Cesar Saerchinger's Europe was dying, the times calling for another kind of representation—younger, more politically oriented, capable of building up the operations of CBS abroad in preparation for the war Ed Klauber knew was coming.

In late February, the telephone rang in the Murrows' hotel room in New Orleans, where they were attending a meeting of the National Education Association. The operator had a call from New York City on the line. Janet sat and watched, then heard her husband say, "I do have a wife and I'd like to talk it over with her." He promised to call back. Then he told her that Klauber had asked him to take the job in London, as European Director for CBS.

99

They sat up all night talking, knowing they would go in any case, both with the definite feeling "that there would be a war and that Ed would be setting up the broadcasting of news events." Whatever happened, they decided, it would be interesting.

Then, in a temporary switch, came the letdown. Back at 485, the prospect of leaving headquarters seemed abruptly less alluring. London was a long way off, far from the center of the action; company scuttlebutt had it that he was being exiled, had lost out to White—all rumor but enough to make him seem, in those last days, less than enthusiastic.

Trout, watching Murrow glumly clear out his desk, couldn't understand. Who in his right mind wouldn't want to go to Europe?

The answer, in the upshot, was no one—Murrow included. Upstairs, management was pleased: Paley considered the posting important, knew exactly whom he wanted to fill Saerchinger's shoes. As for Klauber, it was a brilliant move, setting up, in effect, the framework for the development and nurturing of the wartime CBS news team, with White as managing editor, Murrow as foreign bureau head, Klauber as editor in chief.

The company threw a farewell luncheon. Murrow made his good-byes, stopping along the way in Jim Seward's office, among others. Seward, aware of the raise that came with the new position, asked if he shouldn't open a savings account for him, perhaps deposit some of the money. Murrow, never one to hold on to a dollar, told him without hesitation to hold out the amount of the raise. Seward did so, eventually looking after all of Murrow's financial and contractual affairs with CBS's blessing, a valued adviser and friend.[9]

There was just one more stop: at the Emergency Committee, which he had served steadily and devotedly since the rise of Hitler. Now he had to resign, noting, in a letter to Duggan, "the satisfaction and pleasure that I have derived from my association with you and the other members . . . in the work which will continue to pay many dividends for years to come. The privilege of being associated . . . with such a group as composed the Committee has given me many things that cannot be taken away even by a large American corporation."

Only the packing remained. Outside, the Third Avenue el crashed by in bone-rattling accompaniment. Janet Murrow finally saw her husband pause, knee-deep in debris, straighten up, and glare out the window.

"It's a good thing we're going to Europe. Any more of *that* and I'd have gone out of my mind."

V

Anschluss

CBS, Europe was three rooms in London, opposite the BBC—two secretaries and an office boy, the large inner room reserved for the Director. A minimal setup, broadcasting arrangements made through British facilities, studios and circuit rented by the hour. Ed Murrow's new domain.

Across the way was Broadcasting House, a great white wedge of masonry, raised five years before in the first flush of Art Deco, a multilevel monster bristling with flagpoles and metal towers, looming high above the Adam and Regency town houses that made the area one of the most elegant in London. A joke at the BBC had it that an early official, an admiral, had deliberately planned the building to look like a battleship.

In its shadow Ed Murrow settled easily into his new job, the process eased considerably by Katherine ("Kay") Campbell, Saerchinger's efficient young secretary who had stayed on: a tiny figure with blond curls, spectacles, and a softness of manner that disarmed opposition, adept equally at running the office or clearing BBC facilities, the indispensable backup.

At first it was a time of looking around, assessment: a courtesy call on Sir John Reith, the forbidding, Bible-conscious six-foot-seven Director-General of the BBC, whose bristling brows went up when the newcomer announced his intention of scheduling broadcasts from pubs and talks with cockneys, in addition to the eminent who made up the main diet of broadcasts from Britain.

For American audiences, who knew little of travel and less of foreign countries, overseas meant England and France, possibly Germany. It seemed only natural: power was concentrated in the West and London was its capital, center of the power structure that ruled both the industrialized and the colonial worlds.

This was the London that Ed and Janet Murrow had come to, in the Indian summer of the British Empire, seemingly embodied in the endless columns of foreign regiments marching in the coronation procession of King George VI, under the cold, drippy skies of May 1937.

CBS of course was broadcasting, but the Murrows that day were observers, the coverage handled by Saerchinger, easing the new man into his job, and by White and Trout, arrived on an earlier boat. The Murrows' only real concern turned out to be the common one of tourists in the overcrowded city, bumped from their hotel room by others who had reserved it for the coronation.

The crossing itself had been a pleasant one, unlike their shoestring passage of two years back—strictly first-class, old friends like Harold Laski, Mary Marvin Breckinridge of NSFA days, now a successful photojournalist, plus the elder Breckinridges, who in 1930 had put up Ed Murrow, just in from Washington State with forty dollars in his pocket.

At Waterloo Station, there had been a welcoming committee of one, thoughtfully provided by the BBC, a tall, well-spoken young man with an upper-middle-class inflection who introduced himself as Richard Marriott of the Foreign Department: Welcome to England. Was everything all right? Indeed, yes. A bit of handshaking; then the American couple whisked themselves into a taxi; they seemed to know where they were going.[1]

At the outset, they had taken over the Saerchingers' furnished flat in Queen Anne Street, a small, charming apartment for small, charming people. The Saerchingers were five feet two, and Murrow soon began to feel like an awkward giant bumping around among doll furniture. They finally replaced the bed after he kept crashing his head against the headboard. Eventually they took a larger flat, with their own furniture from New York, at 84 Hallam Street, some four blocks from Broadcasting House.

He had come to London with the priority of cutting into the traditional lead abroad of the National Broadcasting Company, the domain of Fred Bate—a handsome, graying expatriate American, a personal friend of the former Prince of Wales, with access to the best circles.

On the Continent, the NBC lead was reinforced by a system of contracts dating from the twenties, ensuring an exclusive relationship with the state radios, notably Germany and Austria, including first rejection rights for broadcasts originating in the Reich. There was also a misapprehension prevailing that "National" somehow denoted the U.S. government, a state radio system like theirs, with Columbia a two-bit outsider—an impression NBC did nothing to correct.

On the contrary, they'd done everything possible to encourage it, on the lookout for any development likely to threaten the status quo. And the new CBS appointment was just such a development.

Long before his arrival in London, Murrow had been the subject of urgent internal memos at NBC, his assumption of the job viewed as proof of "increased CBS competition." The NBC foreign office, accordingly, scrambled to checkmate his every move, a ploy in which the key player would be less the gentlemanly Bate than NBC's representative on the Continent, Max Jordan—a wire agency veteran, formerly of INS, otherwise known as the Ubiquitous Max, German-educated, American-trained, resourceful, competitive, an aggressive newshound. Knowing Murrow would be kept in London for the coronation, Jordan had started making the rounds of the European capitals, tying knots, as he went, in every state radio relationship from Stockholm to Budapest.[2]

Murrow, obviously, couldn't be in two places at once. CBS needed what NBC had: a second warm body in Europe, preferably a crack journalist, knowledgeable about the Continent. That summer Murrow found one.

William Lawrence Shirer was of German-American stock, Chicago-born, reared in Cedar Rapids, part of the generation that, like Hemingway and Fitzgerald, had cast off the isolationism of the Middle West, working the classic route to Europe by cattle boat, settling in Paris to write, but drawn irresistibly to journalism; onetime Central European bureau chief for the Chicago *Tribune*—the youngest ever; by age thirty, a veteran reporter with a string of datelines from India and Afghanistan to the major capitals of the West; by age thirty-four, unemployed. The Depression had hit the news business like any other, and in August 1937 Shirer's wire agency job in Berlin had folded.

In his wartime classic, *Berlin Diary*, Shirer was to describe the telegram materializing the day he got his notice, signed "Murrow, Columbia Broadcasting," sending him to a dinner appointment at the Hotel Adlon and a job offer as continental representative for CBS.

They made an unlikely couple: Shirer, shorter and stocky, a news veteran, hair already wearing thin, the classic picture of the rumpled reporter, peering at the world through thick, metal-rimmed glasses; Murrow, tall and thin, with his Savile Row look, knifelike crease in the trousers, not a hair out of place. Indeed, Shirer's first impression, as he watched the younger man make his way toward him through the lobby, had not been a happy one: *Just what you'd expect from radio*, he figured. Thus the unlikely beginning of a partnership that became one of the legends of broadcasting.

It almost didn't come off, though. True, the job involved arranging broadcasts, not making them, but New York needed an audition all the same. A trial broadcast was made in early September. 485 got back to Murrow: no deal; Shirer's flat, Midwestern tones weren't broadcast quality.

Murrow, coming home that night, couldn't get over management's thinking: For heaven's sake, Paul was a newspaperman himself; he should know better! Said Janet Murrow: "He was appalled." Arguments followed that week via the transatlantic phone, Murrow arguing that he was hiring reporters, not announcers, and did they want a great reporter or a pretty voice? New York backed down.

Shirer, on tenterhooks for the past eight days, was considering a low-paying New York *Times* job when Murrow called. It was okay; he was hired.

And New York?

"They think you're terrific."[3]

Shirer's reactions at the outset had been par for the course. To the press corps of 1937, radio was an overfunded upstart, as Murrow discovered when his application to the correspondents' association in London met with a flat rebuff. Yes, the bylaws opened membership to newspapers, news agencies, and "other press organizations," but that didn't include radio. "I wasn't even allowed to attend the meetings," he recalled later, "much less become a member."

It was a tough circle to crack, the hardworking, close-knit world of the overseas press corps, heirs to a decades-old print tradition. They were the cream of the Western news media, veterans of datelines in Addis Ababa, Kabul, Delhi, and Madrid, the last bloom of the postwar golden age of the foreign correspondent. And this radio *arriviste* automatically expected to sit in council with the heirs of Richard Harding Davis? A circle glittering at various times with names like John Gunther, Vincent Sheean, H. R. Knickerbocker, the brothers Paul Scott and Edgar Ansel Mowrer? He had to be kidding.

In seven years he would become president of the association. In 1937 he swallowed the rebuff and concentrated on cracking the NBC monopoly in Central Europe. In Italy, Shirer's language skills came in handy, as did contacts with an old wire agency buddy. Frank Gervasi, Rome bureau chief for INS, had an inside track at the Vatican—hitherto closed to CBS—through a combination of ingenuity and lavish backing from Hearst. The agency man, who sometimes broadcast for CBS, knew all the tricks: whom to contact; how much to pay for what kind of information; how much to shell out for a legible copy of the Vatican newsletter; and whom to wine and dine in the Piazza Navona—contacts gladly shared with an old agency buddy and an organization so small it could hardly be called competition.

By the following spring, those contacts widened, Shirer would be broadcasting directly from Rome on Hitler's reception by Mussolini, microphones open from atop the royal stables just opposite the Quirinal Palace, and just minutes short of the Führer's arrival.

But in those first months, for Murrow as for Shirer, there was no reporting. In fact, their contracts specifically excluded broadcasting—a clause which caused both men, informed as they were, some irritation. When necessary, newspaper reporters, paid a flat fee, did the talking on the air. Murrow and Shirer were the arrangers—at best anonymous voices, doing the introductions—living out of suitcases, setting up broadcasts anywhere from Amsterdam to Athens, seeing to it that they reached New

York on schedule from points of origin where schedules mattered little or not at all. Murrow, with a smattering of French and German, a few words of Italian, found his fieldwork in America of little use as he learned to deal with the state-controlled radios of more than a dozen European countries, familiarizing himself with a complex infrastructure—what there was of it—of transmitters and telephone lines, broadcasting convention rulings, and variations in language, time zones, currencies, broadcasting personnel, and broadcasting practices.

In London, relations with the competition, contentious professionally, were cordial personally, despite pressure from Paul White on one side and NBC news chief A. A. Schechter on the other. It was hard, everyone agreed, to dislike Fred Bate, and he and Murrow became the best of friends, even though the NBC man, backed by a larger organization, showed a positive genius for tying up the wire on the Continent when CBS wanted it—a situation sometimes resolved only by a call from Columbia, New York, to the proper government official, threatening mayhem or an international incident if CBS's request was not honored.

The content, however, was anything but earthshaking, despite the interjection of serious reporting and commentary. The network wanted pleasant peacetime entertainment of the people-to-people variety, spiced by the live broadcasts from pubs and street corners—a novelty for the Depression audiences back home—which had so raised the massive eyebrows of Sir John. Mix-ups abounded, complicated further by the vicissitudes of cables. When Princess Juliana of the Netherlands became a mother, CBS planned a fifteen-minute spot about the new heir to the House of Orange. For reasons of scheduling, New York changed its mind. The decision made to drop it, a cabled order went back to London: "KILL JULIANA'S BABY." That afternoon Helen Sioussat found two FBI men at her door.

But all in all, it was a time that Murrow would remember as leisurely, civilized, the calm before the storm, the closing of an elegant age for those with money in their pockets and, for Ed and Janet Murrow, a time of travel and meetings in beautiful places, of separations bridged by endless messages from the young husband in letters that rarely paused for punctuation:

> *Hotel Beau Rivage*
> *Geneve*
> *Sat.* A.M.

Dearest "Guppy"

Broadcast went off *ok*. . . . Beautiful flight coming out. Have swell room facing lake—just cool enough last night to sleep well. How I wish you were here—we must try to spend some time here after Nice.

Have just had big breakfast. About two quarts of biggest strawberries in the world! Am now off to see people at "Palais des Nations."

I love you pretty much!

> Hyman Kaplan[4]

Hotel Beau Rivage, June 19th

Dearest Beppo—

Have I ever told you about Geneva? Well, it's raining—all day I've been seeing stuffy people. . . . [I saw] some new Swans on the lake—they have black necks (not bottoms).

There's a strange atmosphere of un-reality about this place—looked in on the I.L.O.[5] Conference this A.M. reminded me of puppets—what they say and do really doesn't matter a damn. . . . Have had three drinks so far—two of them sherry!

I'm lonesome for you—strange how I've gotten used to your being about—Never used to be lonesome for anyone—Soon you'll be getting to be as indispensable as a razor!

Everyone here thinks the Blum govt. will last a long while. There are evidences of fascism in Switzerland. The atmosphere is hardly care-free. I'll probably be back Friday P.M.

All my love—

John Hyman Calvin Murrow

Bournemouth
Saturday—

Darling—

No plane today—slept till noon and went for long walk along the Front this P.M.—nice sun and soft breeze—was very lonesome for you. Somehow doesn't seem right to have even one day to play or do nothing without you to share it. Each time I'm away from you the sense of how much I love you and depend on you deepens. Some day we shall have that long vacation *and* the baby—saw a nice one. . . . Plane now promised for tomorrow but I doubt it. . . . Wish you had come with me. Why we no think of that? . . .

Have nice rest—sleep well—I shall be back soon—all my love

Ed

London
Wednesday

Darling—

Where are you? On Saturday night and again Sunday night I tried to call you from Paris—each time was told that you were un-known at the Continentale in Nice. Have you received my letters & cards? . . .

Have just wired you I can't come to Nice—Paley is coming back. . . . I must be in Paris Aug 10th . . . and can definitely be in Geneva on the P.M. of the eleventh. Then we'll either go to Rome & Turin or drive slowly to Salzburg.

I'm lonesome as hell. But there's plenty of work to do here now. . . . Do you have any money? Don't forget to have the car greased!

Love, Ed

Aug. 6th

Janet Darling—

What ho! It's really hot in London. I've been wandering about this town at night like a lost soul in Hades—all alone—lonesome for my cook. Never before have I missed you so much.

. . . leave for Paris on 8:00 plane Monday A.M. . . . Have made reservations at Beau Rivage in Geneva. . . .

How I long to arrive in Geneva—if the plane is slow in landing I shall jump out. . . .

The more I think of it the smarter I think it is that you should see something of Europe while you can. Later on even if we don't have any money we'll have a few memories. What a swell time we'll have in Salzburg & Vienna. I'm trying to arrange a program from Budapest immediately after. . . . If it comes off we'll swim in the pool at the St. Gellert! . . .

You are the nicest girl I've ever known—Three years ago it seemed impossible that I could love anyone more than I did you but I do and it's still you! I think part of it's because you're such an honest and decent sort of person and I'm not—part of it is that you're a hussy! I'm lonesome for you! Someday perhaps we shall go back to the West Coast for a while. I wonder if we'd like it? Something tells me we've an interesting few years ahead of us. Sometime I'll have a real row with New York and then we'll do something else. I hope you don't mind having a husband who's a bit mad—it must be the Irish ancestry way back somewhere!

Drive carefully over the hill to Geneva—how I'd love to be with you—after seeing you drive in Mexico I'm sure you can drive any mountain road. Ha!

It seems ages since you left and I want to see you so much. If Air France wants to aim for the field in Geneva and fish tail in for a fast landing it will be all right with me!

All my love
Ed

Shirer would later describe him as uncomfortable on the Continent, but New York friends such as Helen Sioussat, meeting him in Paris, thought he seemed younger, more relaxed—delighting in the city and the small, frail old women who sold flowers by the curb, taking friends to the little restaurants on Shirer's list or to the nightclub run by Brick Top, the black American entertainer, a favorite of Cole Porter and the smart set.

He had also taken by now to wrinkling his forehead in a deliberate attempt to make himself look older. Protests from women friends ("such a nice, smooth forehead!") would bring on a growl: "I don't *want* a nice, smooth forehead. I think a lot!"

Dorothy Paley, wife of the CBS President, was impressed with him as she passed through London on a visit, a spirited, articulate New Dealer, friend to Walter Kotschnig and Alfred Cohn, and a onetime member of the board for ISS.

She spoke the language; Murrow, so reticent with most CBS people, suddenly opened up on his concerns, with no holds or hesitations. "I think he felt," she said afterward, "that there was a kindred spirit."

She became a consistent backer.

Though they had met casually in New York, the first London impression would be what she remembered: a large head topped by the ubiquitous gray hat; beneath, a "very longish, thinnish face . . . extremely handsome"; a man liked universally yet somehow guarded, except, she soon noted, when in the company of platonic women friends, the NSFA situation all over again:

> Men, of course, were attracted to him, he was such a *male* man. But I always had the feeling Ed was more comfortable with women. It's a curious thing: Ed, I think, thought of himself as a rather unsophisticated person. And he felt oftentimes with men that he was competing with a kind of sophistication which he didn't possess. . . .
>
> I don't think men knew him. I don't think they really knew Ed at all.

They would talk by the hour, belaboring U.S. policy on Spain—the Neutrality Act had just been broadened and amended specifically, it seemed, to preclude aid to the Republic—both critical of Roosevelt for what they felt to be a lack of leadership, Dorothy Paley insisting FDR had misread the public mood, Murrow less certain that Roosevelt, following another tack, could carry the country with him.

There were kindred spirits, too, in the liaison unit at Broadcasting House known as the Foreign Department—a small group for the most part, including Dick Marriott, by now a close friend, the young Felix Greene, and Cecilia Reeves, an outspoken employee alerted early to Murrow's arrival by mutual friends in ISS.

They were young, skeptical, referred to with a smile as the Warmongers: concerned about the spread of Fascism on the Continent; less insular than their elders in the hierarchy; less sanguine about the future, Chamberlain, and Baldwin; openly restive with BBC policies that preached objectivity while denying the microphone to critics of the Foreign Office.

To the young dissenters, therefore, Ed Murrow—scheduling heretics like Winston Churchill and later Anthony Eden, if only for American audiences—had seemed like a breath of fresh air. After Cesar Saerchinger, who had thought Dollfuss a sweet little man; after pleasant Fred Bate, friend of the Duke of Windsor and the status quo, the new CBS man was something different—sharing their skepticism; energetic; innovative; requesting ever more facilities, which were gladly provided.

Reserved by U.S. standards, he seemed free and easy to his English colleagues, very American. Marriott remembered stopping by at the Murrow flat for dinner one night. Murrow, checking his watch, suddenly remarked that he still had time for a bath before mealtime. Before Marriott knew it, they were continuing the conversation in the bathroom, the Englishman perched, a little stupefied, uncomfortably by the tub while his host soaped himself, happily, obliviously, discussing the problems of broadcasting.

In midyear, 1937, the Japanese attacked Peking. In Spain, the fascist insurgents were advancing, supported by German and Italian arms, Mussolini sending troops to fight for Franco while the German Condor Legion bombed Guernica off the map. In America, the broadened Neutrality Act, loopholes and all, starved the Spanish Republic and kept vital raw materials headed for Japan and Italy.

That October at Chicago, Roosevelt, testing the waters, warned that neutrality alone might not ensure America against the "contagion" of escalating world violence, hinting thereby at a possible major shift in U.S. policy. There had been a little byplay in London when recorded excerpts, broadcast over the BBC Home Service, prompted an unexpectedly furious letter from Ed Murrow to Harry Butcher in Washington. The recordings, reaching a maximum audience, had been "pretty terrible," made from an obviously poor overseas transmission. "Then the BBC . . . made an effort to increase the volume, which resulted in the President sounding like a sissified Kaltenborn!" Would he please tell Early or whoever it was who gave permission for rebroadcasting of the Presidential voice? There was a sharp reaction from the White House, with due apologies from the BBC. Naturally the CBS man also tried for a leg up over the competition. Perhaps he and "someone from the Embassy" could audit prospective recordings in the future: "It would increase our standing with the B.B.C. considerably and . . . prevent a repetition of last night's fiasco"[6]; the offer evidently was not taken up.

That fall, Murrow addressed the prestigious Royal Institute of International Affairs, where his old NSFA friend Ivison Macadam was director; the topic: "International Aspects of Broadcasting." Outside, a new crisis was bubbling up, not in Spain this time but in Central Europe—Germany, its position consolidated in the Rhineland, renewing pressure on Austria in a heightened replay of 1934, radio mobilized on all sides in a rising propaganda barrage.

On a Tuesday evening in late November at Chatham House, introduced by John Coatman, head of news for the BBC, Ed Murrow rose to accept the applause of a high-powered audience that included figures from the worlds of diplomacy and broadcasting.

He was twenty-nine, the representative of a major network, well regarded at all levels of the BBC, symbol of the Anglo-American amity prevailing at Broadcasting House and a favorite of Coatman, who had once observed that the English personnel would cheerfully show up at three in the morning if the Americans needed it. (In four months they would be doing so routinely.)

Intended as a comment on the contemporary scene, the talk was in effect a first-time formulation of Edward Murrow's views on broadcasting, now crystallized as he stood before the select group, in the graceful London house that had been the home of William Pitt: "If these comments of mine are considered to be rude or discourteous . . . I hope you will put it down to a desire to be both honest and brief."

He began disarmingly, observing that most broadcasters were "cautious" and "circumspect": "We enjoy a tremendous asset in talking to you in your own homes, because then we are able to answer all the questions that no one but a fool would ask in the first place, and to leave unanswered most of the questions in which intelligent men and women must be interested. . . ."

With that he began posing questions and answers of his own, sounding the themes that were to dominate his life as a communicator—"the failure of broadcasting to accept its responsibilities, to seek for truth wherever it might be found and to disseminate that truth as widely as possible"— firm in his belief that the content, not the medium, was the message.

> I think we are all prepared to . . . marvel at the technical excellence of present-day broadcasting. But I am convinced that most of its achievements to date must be credited to the engineers and technicians rather than those responsible for programme [sic] content. Broadcasting . . . has not been properly related to the social, political and economic structure that it inevitably reflects. There has been too much blind acceptance of the broadcasters' statements of policy and principle.
>
> I would suggest that the only way to judge broadcasting, national or international, is by what issues forth from your receiving set.

People, he said, had grown suspicious of these modern inventions. The printing press was to have set them free, but "we forgot that the ability to read does not carry with it the ability to understand." The transatlantic cable, instead of cementing international goodwill, carried hasty reports on international chaos.

He cited the propaganda war now escalating over European shortwave, Dr. Goebbels' transmitters in the lead: "Listen to the so-called news. Hear the Italians, Russians, Germans and Spaniards broadcasting in every language save their own. . . .

"New and more powerful stations are being erected in order that nation may hurl invective at nation. . . . Radio crosses boundaries and fortunately or unfortunately there is no one there to inspect the contents of its luggage." Propaganda itself he called "a legacy of the World War, and since lying is an attribute of war, it is quite natural that that word . . . should play a very considerable part in this war that is going on in the air today." Still he pointed out, "There does not exist in my opinion such a thing as a broadcasting system without propaganda. We may make propaganda on behalf of the right to have monarchy or the status quo, or we may make propaganda on behalf of more tangible things such as cigarettes, soap or automobiles. In this last field of propaganda, I must maintain with all humility that Americans are without equal. . . ."

Yet he was ready to take his chances with the latter. "Individuals and I suppose nations may suffer from smoking too many cigarettes or from buying too many motor cars that they can ill-afford, but those troubles are hardly to be classed with the suffering resulting from the acceptance of an ideal or political objective." Of the former, he listed a few techniques "familiar in America"—e.g., name-calling ("Communist, outside agitator, economic royalist")—or card-stacking, defined as "under-emphasis or the complete elimination of unfavorable material," warning his audience—in a conviction relevant in 1937, even more so in the postwar years—that "the extent to which the broadcaster is meeting his responsibilities must be judged not only by what is broadcast but . . . [by] what he does *not* broadcast."

With that he got to the heart of the matter—the mission of the reporter and of broadcasting, as he saw it, to hold "an honest mirror" to events in the world, to report without fear or favor. "If there exists a vital difference of opinion, let us say on British foreign policy," he continued, "we propose to reflect that difference of opinion. If the reaction of the British press towards a particular move of the United States . . . is critical, we propose to reflect that too."

He was still speaking as producer, not reporter, but the elements were lined up (had been so, in fact, since the time when, as Director of Talks, he had written guidelines for speakers over CBS)—the need to be concrete, specific, avoiding the abstract, the talking down; the emphasis on the everyday and the familiar.

Overseas broadcasting, he charged, had become too conscious of its dignity, speakers sounding like unofficial ambassadors; the voice of a cabby or a fisherman might, he suggested, do more to sway American public opinion than "a learned discourse" by a scholar.

Above all, it was the raw power of broadcasting that concerned him. That, and the seeming inability of the people in charge—"those interested in safeguarding democracy"—to grasp, as did the men in Berlin, this overriding fact:

> I happen to have handled all the political broadcasting [for CBS] in connection with the last Presidential campaign in America.
>
> I saw the power of [the] medium demonstrated at first-hand. I saw it cut through a paper barrage laid down against one candidate by eighty-five per cent of the nation's Press. Few people, even those intimately connected with broadcasting, appreciate the potential power of this medium in both national and international affairs.

Yet radio executives, he complained, knew little about their audiences or the effect on the individual listener of a given broadcast; educational institutions, those responsible for the young, often seemed complacent, uninterested.

> Parents' and Citizens' committees concern themselves actively with . . . the qualifications of their teachers. But they remain strangely indifferent concerning those who direct the affairs of broadcasting. They seldom ask, as they should, who makes these decisions, and what is his or her competence to do so.
>
> Some day broadcasting may be asking these people to risk their lives as a result of one of the situations in the world today. Certainly broadcasters have an obligation to keep us informed of those fundamental problems and conflicts which are determining national policy. . . . If we deny this thesis, then we refuse to accept the first principle of a democratic society.

The next few years, he concluded, would undoubtedly see great technological improvements—existing problems simplified, mobility increased, equipment now in use made obsolete.

> But the problem is not a technical one. There must be a greater definition of objective and an increasing sense of responsibility on the part of the broadcasters of the democracies. And above all we must eliminate that unconscious major premise which causes us to believe that it is unwise or unsafe to provide our listeners with the information they desire.
>
> The only alternative is to attempt to justify broadcasting because it entertains, but that is just like justifying newspapers because they carry funny pictures and cartoons. . . .

Broadcasting, properly used, he said on that evening in November, 1937, might be "a real aid in keeping the light of Western civilization burning." But he voiced a warning, articulated repeatedly in the course of his remaining twenty-eight years: The medium had "enormous power . . . but it has no character, no conscience of its own. It reflects the hatreds, the jealousies and ambitions of those men and governments that control it. It can become a powerful force for mutual understanding between nations, but not until we have made it so."

He was speaking off the record. Meetings were closed, institute rules ritually enjoining members from the attribution of remarks. Chances are Murrow's comments never reached New York, where, even in the expansive atmosphere of 1937, they might have grated.

In the lively question-and-answer period that followed, one member had posed a skeptical query. This whole matter of "truth"—wasn't one of the difficulties of broadcasting inherent in the presentation of "facts," few of them colorless, open to interpretation by whoever appeared on the air? And was one not, therefore, brought back to the classic question put to a colonial administrator nearly 2,000 years ago—namely: What is truth?

Murrow, in rejoinder, declined to answer a question which, as he said, had gone unanswered for 2,000 years. So far as broadcasting went, the answer would be to strike a balance between differing viewpoints, differing speakers and to let the listener decide: "truth" as composite.

As for truth in the abstract, he preferred to turn on its head the biblical injunction of St. John—i.e., "Ye shall know the truth"—believing rather that truth, once accepted as such, had very often enslaved man and that doubt had often set him free.

The West seemed to be holding its breath that autumn. In Spain, the Loyalist government, under pressure, had moved its seat to Barcelona. To the east, the unequal struggle heightened between Berlin and Vienna—at stake, control of Austria and the mountain roads leading to southeastern Europe. In London, life proceeded as usual. The Murrows went about their business, saw visitors from America, among them a couple referred by friends, the husband a newspaperman just three years Murrow's junior, fresh out of Minneapolis—a big, long-faced young man with massive shoulders, and a big-boned healthy young woman, Midwesterners who introduced themselves as Eric and Lois Sevareid. He was, he said, originally from North Dakota. They were on their way to the Continent and spoke of possibly bicycling through Europe.

The two couples spent the evening talking, and watching the antiwar drama, *Journey's End*, via a strange glass rectangle set into a wired box— little green figures on a little green screen. The box was from the BBC. "That's television," said Murrow. "That's the future, my friend."

Also passing through was Davidson Taylor of CBS programming—sensitive, talented, returning from a vacation in Germany and profoundly disturbed, he told Murrow, at what he had seen: troop maneuvers, men advancing, firing, hitting the dirt; worker battalions marching off to Nuremberg, keeping perfect step, shovels slung over their shoulders—*just like guns*, Taylor thought.

"There's going to be a war, isn't there?"

Murrow's answer was a little weary: "Yes, there's going to be a war.

"But it won't do you any good to talk about it when you get back," he added, "because nobody will believe you."

In the meantime, they had narrowly skirted tragedy at home.

Janet Murrow had only meant to set the electric heater aright. It listed a little; otherwise, nothing seemed amiss.

She had extended her hand. A sudden charge of white-hot energy spun out in an arc and sent her flying toward the doorway.

Their young maid, Betty, stood there, mouth open. A second later there was contact, the two women slammed about the room by the current. Miraculously, the charge failed to find grounding.

Murrow rushed in. The smell of burned meat hung in the air; Janet Murrow stood bemused, staring at a blackened hand.

Dazedly, for days afterward, she watched it deteriorate. A Harley Street physician finally operated, but only after a family friend had warned her to see a doctor about the hand or be prepared to lose it.

That February of 1938, public attention focused eastward again as the unequal diplomatic struggle between Berlin and Vienna sped toward its climax, to a rising tattoo of German ultimatums, rushed meetings, threats of invasion.

Almost four years had gone by since the aborted Nazi coup; three since Hitler disavowed all interest in the *Anschluss*, or annexation of Austria; two since the forced bilateral treaty giving the Nazis a foothold in the smaller state. But Mussolini, this time, was secretly in Hitler's pocket.

Frank Gervasi, the INS bureau chief in Rome and CBS's contact, up in chilly late-winter Venice, had seen the Austrian representatives alone and forlorn on the deserted piazza, two black figures outlined against the gray: Kurt von Schuschnigg, successor to Dollfuss, and an aide, down to seek help from the noncommittal Duce.

The reporter tried approaching, only to be warned off by uniformed *carbonari*. Retreating, he felt like asking the chancellor, who sat huddled, looking out toward the empty lagoon, "How does it feel to be betrayed by your ally?"

In the midst of it all, the American network rivalry continued unimpeded, CBS, meaning Murrow and Shirer, still trying to crack Germany and dead-ending every time. The Austrian crisis was moving toward the boiling point, but Murrow, in Berlin, was fighting for the right to cover the maiden voyage of yet another dirigible, though clearly more was at stake than a going-away party for a zeppelin.

NBC as usual had the exclusive. Murrow, in a surprise move, demanded an audience with Goebbels. Now.

Max Jordan, alerted from the inside, began pulling strings. The CBS man was promptly informed that the minister was unavailable. Very well; Murrow, Shirer, and their Berlin representative, Claire Trask, asked to see his second-in-command for broadcasting.

In a crackling three-hour session, Murrow insisted point-blank on equal treatment for Columbia, that the NBC exclusive contract, moreover, be canceled, that CBS be allowed in on the zeppelin broadcasts, also on the new Richard Strauss premiere in Munich—in fact, on all major nonpolitical events coming out of Germany. *Non*political, he specified; anyone with a mike and a phone line could pick up a Party rally.

In response, the smiling Nazi officials assured him that the Rundfunk had no desire whatever to discontinue its very pleasant and satisfactory relationship with NBC. Germany was, of course, interested in seeing its programs disseminated as widely as possible in America—there was Mutual, too, after all—but its friends at NBC were naturally entitled to first choice, and if they should wish to let Columbia share in the programming, why, that was entirely up to NBC.

Murrow, glaring, asked again to see Goebbels—a tactical error, as Hitler's minister of public enlightenment had specifically deputized the Party man who, no longer smiling, assured him it would be of no use.

A gleeful Max Jordan chortled back to John Royal at Rockefeller Center that "a major attack . . . the worst and most determined so far, has been repulsed." But obviously, he added, Columbia would try to step up their programming from Germany, and he therefore urged that NBC, accordingly, not endanger its position with the German broadcasters.[7]

It was March 5, 1938. Nazis were rioting in the Austrian cities, demanding Anschluss. Hitler was beating the drum in the name of self-determination for those Germans beyond the borders of the Reich.

The press association wires sizzled with hourly bulletins, read off in studios in New York. Otherwise, it was business as usual for the networks. March 10, despite rumblings of the Wehrmacht massed at the borders, of a last-ditch plebiscite on independence called by the desperate home government, neither CBS nor NBC had anyone in place at the epicenter. Max Jordan was on a slow train from Basel to Vienna. Shirer had moved his base to Vienna, but CBS had ordered him to Yugoslavia that week to arrange a fifteen-minute children's concert for the *School of the Air*, with Murrow similarly held up in Warsaw, both men thinking unkind thoughts about New York's priorities and awaiting the explosion.

It came soon enough. Murrow, returning to his Warsaw hotel room the night of March 11, found a stack of telephone messages marked "Urgent." In a surprisingly short time he had the Vienna operator on the line, then the voice of Shirer, returned that day to the Austrian capital.

"The opposing team has just crossed the goal line."

"Are you sure?"

Shirer's answer was pure *Front Page*. "I'm paid to be sure."

The German Army had marched into Austria.

Shirer filled in the rest of the details: the resignation of Schuschnigg; his replacement by the Nazi appointee Arthur Seyss-Inquart; the plebiscite called off; ecstatic Nazi mobs rampaging, unimpeded, through the streets.

He had tried to do a broadcast—not a chance of getting a newspaperman to do so—but couldn't. The Austrian state radio building was bristling with German uniforms, local radio officials guarded by SS men clutching revolvers. All broadcasting had been routed over Berlin, the wire in the hands of the Wehrmacht. After hours of arguing, the CBS man had been shown the door by determined youths with bayonets. End of argument.

Now, at three-thirty in the morning, he and Murrow discussed their next move, the events of those hectic hours recounted afterward in *Berlin Diary*: how he had called Murrow in Warsaw; how Murrow directed him to London to broadcast his report, with Murrow coming in to take his place and await the lifting of the German ban.

By 7:00 A.M. Shirer was at the airport. German tanks were rolling toward the capital, Hitler at last report on his way south to proclaim the Anschluss. German warplanes covered the airfield at Aspern, the few flights cleared to London jammed with refugees, most of them Jewish. Finally Shirer took a plane to Berlin, there changed to a Dutch plane bound for London, and at eleven-thirty that night sat before a BBC microphone to broadcast to America his eyewitness account of the crisis.

Broadcasts from Vienna, however, would prove infinitely more complicated. Even without the Nazis, there was the matter of NBC's contract with Ravag, the Austrian state radio. Max Jordan, arriving in Vienna, had started broadcasting, courtesy of NBC's favored position, the lines running over Berlin miraculously cleared up.

With a full-blown emergency on hand, Paley himself called the head of Ravag, a personal friend, last seen by Shirer as a prisoner in his own building. The call, though going through, proved useless. He was no longer in control, the official babbled; "other people" were there, sitting right in his office—"Please, please understand." Paley, who had called from a sickbed, held the phone, speechless, as the sound of uncontrolled weeping came out of the receiver.

In the meantime, something had to be done. The press was covering the crisis in full. NBC was carrying the story in eyewitness accounts, albeit censored ones, and CBS wasn't. How to top them once, as must inevitably happen, CBS got access to the microphone?

Someone came up with the idea of broadcasting a series of reactions from the different capitals, different points of origin, all on one show— London, Paris, Berlin, Rome, Vienna—the prototype of the radio, later TV news roundup. Paley remembered it as his idea, born in the anxious hours following the phone call to Vienna, while he talked with Klauber about doing "something special." Trout remembered it as evolving in the course of a hastily convened meeting, an idea that made sense both journalistically and from the point of view of economics: "We said, 'Why not put 'em *all* on, on Sunday night and put 'em all on together—use up the whole half hour instead of breaking into other programs and switching just to *one!*' "[8]

But it was new, cumbersome to set up, a technique rarely tried, never ventured in a newscast or on such short notice. Klauber, asked to sound out the engineering department, had called at first to say it was impossible.

Unacceptable, Paley told him; ask again.

Half an hour later he was back: "They've found a way."[9]

* * *

Sunday morning, March 13, Murrow arrived in Vienna. Hard as it was to get out of the city, it had been almost impossible to get in. In Warsaw all Vienna-bound flights were canceled. Finally he, too, had hopped a plane to Berlin, chartered another to Vienna, and at Aspern, with no taxis available, made the last lap into town by trolley car.

By early evening he was again on the telephone with Shirer. At five that afternoon—late morning in New York—Paul White had called the London office. Columbia wanted a half-hour news roundup for that night—reactions from the major European capitals: his own report from London, preferably with an MP in tow; "Ed Murrow, of course, from Vienna"; American newspaper correspondents from Paris, Rome, Berlin.

The broadcast was slated for 8:00 P.M. eastern standard time—1:00 A.M. in London, 2:00 A.M. in Vienna. They would be telephoned the exact timing and cues for each capital. They would, of course, have to line up correspondents, write their own reports, and coordinate all technical details on broadcasting arrangements that would normally take months of preparation. They had eight hours in which to do it: eight hours to arrange facilities in five countries, negotiate in four languages, account for time differences, and line up, from cities separated by hundreds of miles and more, reports timed to the exact second, ready to begin on cue.

It was also Sunday evening. People were out of town, some stations nearly closed down for the night, officials off on holiday, part of Central Europe in a state of turmoil.

But White had only one question: "Can you do it?"

Did they have a choice? Shirer said yes, without much conviction, and called Murrow in Vienna.

As they talked, everything fell into place. Murrow had always carried his office in his head, and now the year of roaming the Continent paid off unexpected dividends. On the telephone he outlined to Shirer the technical requirements for each report: a powerful shortwave transmitter to carry the signal to New York; telephone lines to be rented to the nearest available transmitter in case none was close by; those cities with access to a transmitting station and those without—London and Berlin, yes; Paris, no; Rome, yes, but probably not available. In addition, New York would have to know which transmitters were to be used and what their wavelengths would be.

He spelled it all out, knowing that Kay Campbell would be on the extension, taking notes, ready to put in orders for landlines, circuits to New York, studio time at the BBC, her fluent French and German invaluable in the arrangements Shirer was having to make in an unfamiliar setting.

As the hours went by, chief engineers in five countries were mobilized, newspaper colleagues lined up: Ed Mowrer in Paris; Pierre Huss of INS in Berlin; and Frank Gervasi in Rome, covering the question: What would

Austria's traditional protector do? The newsman guessed it would be nothing—no Italian tanks in the Brenner Pass this time, meaning a free hand for Hitler. In the meantime, he was having trouble persuading RAI officials to let him have the studio in the late-night hours, imperiling the Rome report.[10]

In Vienna, Murrow sat by the phone, handling arrangements with RRG, Berlin, while dealing with what was left of the leadership at Ravag.

Coming in from the airport, he had gotten off the trolley to find the city in an uproar, the uncertainty of the past days turned into a lemminglike rush to join the winning side—crowds frenzied; paving blocks torn from their beds, sailing into shopwindows; the old waltz capital hung with swastikas, a nightmare of noise and flushed, distorted faces.

By the early hours of Monday morning the city had grown quieter. In New York it was Sunday evening, following a day of headlines and news bulletins. In Paris and Berlin respectively, arrangements were going through for Mowrer and Huss, while in Rome Gervasi's arguments continued as airtime approached and the RAI director threw up his hands: The studio would be no problem, but the *signor* must understand; they simply could not arrange use of the transmitter on such short notice.

Cursing silently, the newsman had called Shirer, who told him to try for a feed over Geneva; if that didn't work, phone the story in to London and he'd read it over the air.

Sunday night, March 12, at 8:00 P.M. eastern standard time, CBS listeners heard the familiar voice of Bob Trout announcing cancellation of the program *St. Louis Blues* to make way for a special broadcast with reports directly from Europe. In London and on the Continent, it was already March 13.

First there were the wire agency bulletins: Hitler on his way to Vienna, troop movements in France, and talk of reinforcing ties with the Soviet Union, Labourites and a few Communists demonstrating before the German Embassy in London, shouting, "Hitler is pushing Europe into war."

Then, as the engineers in master control prepared to bring in the overseas broadcast signal, the frantic hours of dialing, talking, cabling, writing, and running suddenly made sense, the pattern emerging. The correspondents, scattered across the map of Europe, moved into position like figures on a chessboard.

At Trout's cue, Shirer began, comparing the hysteria of the Vienna he had left to the "tame" demonstrations seen in London and wondering if Czechoslovakia, with its ethnic German minority, would be next in Hitler's calls for German self-determination. Shirer's guest, Labour MP Ellen Wilkinson, summed up the British reaction as "interested curiosity," nothing more, while noting a switch in political reactions: Labourites and Socialists in general, pro-German in the twenties, now marching on the embassy, while the British Right, anxious to accommodate the new order, had become dovish in outlook.

Radio was not only giving the news but examining events as they occurred, with a speed and immediacy unmatched by any other medium.

From Paris, Ed Mowrer reminded the audience that France had suffered two German invasions in the last seventy years. Now, watching Hitler's army spilling over the German border, the French people had "felt an electric shock. . . .

"Even the slowest peasant realized that the 1918 peace had collapsed." Nevertheless, he thought the French government would write off Austria.

From Berlin, Pierre Huss reported the Reich capital quiet, no victory parades; to the average German citizen, he said, this was a purely German affair.

There had been worries about how much of the program would get through, even warnings to the audience about communications channels available "at this late hour." But once begun, there was no letup, the signal continuing to travel from Europe to the Riverhead receiver, through the underground telephone lines to Madison Avenue and master control, and from there to the network—the birth of a major news medium.

Finally, the engineers switched to Vienna and to a young, assured voice, the pitch at times uneven, yet with a quality uniquely its own, pausing now and then to fit the copy to the time period allotted:

> This is Edward Murrow speaking from Vienna. It's now nearly 2:30 in the morning and Herr Hitler has not yet arrived. No one seems to know just when he will get here, but most people expect him sometime after 10:00 o'clock tomorrow morning. . . .

The Warsaw he had left was calm, he said. The cafés were full, the government leaders as remote from the crisis as the hansom cabdrivers muffled up in their furs on the street corners. Poland seemed unlikely to protest. But Vienna had changed.

> They lift the right arm a little higher here than in Berlin and the 'Heil Hitler' is said a little more loudly. . . . Young storm troopers are riding about the streets, riding about in trucks and vehicles of all sorts, singing and tossing oranges out to the crowd. Nearly every principal building has its armed guard, including the one from which I am speaking. . . .

It was as much as he could get past the censor at his elbow, but it conveyed a vivid picture, the first of more than 5,000 broadcasts he was to make in the coming years.

There was a second switchback from New York to London so that Shirer could read the Rome report, phoned in by Gervasi minutes before airtime when Geneva, too, had failed.

The roundup closed with a statement from Washington, Senator Lewis Schwellenbach of the Senate Foreign Relations Committee, concluding:

"If the rest of the world wants to involve itself in its brawl, that is *its* business!" Then it was eight-thirty; finished, right on cue.

In New York and throughout the country, the program's effect was electric. White immediately requested another news roundup for later that night, and Murrow and Shirer obliged—that night, the next day, and into the following Tuesday. They had brought it off. Three of the five reporters had been newspaper journalists, but the technique was pure radio.

Up on the twentieth floor, the gravity of the reports was offset by the heady knowledge that a good deal had changed in the last half hour. From her vantage point in Talks, Helen Sioussat watched Paul White rushing back and forth between 20 and 17, to discuss the new situation and the roles of the two overseas men. Shirer was, of course, an experienced correspondent. But in Murrow, radio had found one of its own—a penetrating, graphic reporter with a trained voice of unusual quality and intensity. Within the broadcasting hierarchy it seemed like a variation on the show business success story, from obscurity to stardom. "The people in the production department were so happy for him," Sioussat remembered.

But Madison and Fifty-second were a long way, in a more than physical sense, from the turbulent streets of Vienna. For Murrow, it was a week without sleep—sleep for which there was not time at first and which, once there was time, simply wouldn't come.

Elsewhere in the city Tess Shirer, the correspondent's young Austrian wife, was lying with her newborn infant in a maternity hospital after a delivery that had nearly cost her her life. Murrow, his duties put temporarily on hold, stopped in daily, telephoning a worried Shirer in London with constant updates on his family.

The leisurely, civilized life was over; it was back to 1933 and the Emergency Committee, no surrogates this time to filter the events, the horror stories come to life as Viennese mobs turned on the city's Jewish minority in a wave of violence and sadism that would shock even longtime foreign residents—shops smashed, homes looted, the occupants, men and women, dragged off to clean army latrines or scrub independence slogans from the sidewalks on their hands and knees, to the jeers of SS guards and grinning spectators. Killings, mass arrests, and suicides had begun their upward curve, the streets echoing to shots and screams as the young American walked home nightly from the studio past scenes that Josh Murrow might have found familiar.

Seeking respite in a quiet café one evening, he had just ordered a drink when the doors flew open to a street gang dragging a man inside[11]— Murrow guessed he was Jewish—beating and kicking their victim while the patrons smiled or roared approval. He watched, paralyzed, then paid his tab and stumbled out into the cold March street, fighting the urge to throw up.

At Ravag, he tried to slip what he could past the Nazi censor, who picked over his script at the studio door and sat guard as he talked. "Please don't think that everyone was out to greet Herr Hitler today. There is tragedy as well as rejoicing in this city tonight." The Führer had arrived, the roars of welcome in the inner city rattling windows in the suburbs.

The next day, March 15, Hitler, speaking from a balcony, proclaimed the absorption of Austria into the Reich, to the cheers of the crowds below. In the studio Murrow reported "no halfway measures about this cheering. It's either wholehearted . . . or complete silence." It was over. He ended that night with a final statement from the Nazi authorities, then, unable to contain himself, blurted out an unscripted "Tell that to the marines!"

The censor looked up sharply, but it had gone out over the air. Murrow left the studio hurriedly, aware that he had been skating on thin ice.

Shirer, returning from London that Friday, found him waiting at the airport, a mass of exposed, frayed nerve endings. They went for supper to Shirer's small apartment in the Ploesslgasse, next door to the Rothschild mansion, now being looted by the SS, steel-helmeted guards with bayonets barring every doorway on the street. A silver-laden commandant allowed Shirer and his guest upstairs to the apartment with an armed guard and a warning that no one was allowed to leave.

At dinner Murrow couldn't stay seated, eating a mouthful, then pacing up and down . . . over to the window . . . back to his chair. Shirer watched him. He'd been through it—the years in India, riots, protests, human bestiality—though he hadn't been prepared for it in civilized Vienna. Neither, obviously, had Murrow. Well, Ed had always been a nervous guy. He'd learn.[12]

Murrow suddenly stopped at the window. "Look what they're doing down there!" Next door, the loot was being carried away, a steady stream of metal snaking from basement to curb, a metallic river of reflected light under street lamps that cast their glow alike on gold and silver, bayonets and steel helmets.

Thirty-five years later, Shirer could still remember the scene, his younger colleague standing motionless as if transfixed, eyes wide and staring: "He'd never seen anything like that before." Later in the street, having given their guard the slip, they sought a café to talk further. Shirer chose one, only to be urged away nervously by Murrow. Why? Well, he'd been there the other night and a Jewish-looking fellow at the bar had suddenly taken a razor from his pocket and slashed his own throat. It was all he would say.

Early Sunday morning, Cecilia Reeves of the BBC Foreign Department was called to Broadcasting House to ready studio facilities for Ed Murrow, just back from Vienna. He came in at 3:00 A.M., directly from the plane, looking rather shattered, she thought, and terribly fatigued.

They got to work, Reeves on the telephone line—"Would you put me through to New York, please?"—the circuits opened, the cue given, and Murrow finished the story of the Anschluss, uncensored:

It was called a bloodless conquest and in some ways it was—

But I'd like to be able to forget the haunted look on the faces of those long lines of people outside the banks and travel offices. People trying to get away. I'd like to forget the tired futile look of the Austrian army officers, and the thud of hobnail boots and the crash of light tanks in the early hours of the morning in the Ringstrasse. . . . I'd like to forget the sound of the smashing glass as the Jewish shop streets were raided; the hoots and jeers at those forced to scrub the sidewalk. . . .

When it was finished, he turned to Reeves. Was she very tired? He hadn't slept since he came back from Vienna, he told her. "If you're not very tired, I'd love to have a chance to talk."

Reeves, who had sat riveted throughout the broadcast, was anxious for news of friends. Together they walked back in the dark to Murrow's flat near the BBC. Janet Murrow was sleeping quietly in the back.

He poured drinks, and they talked, or rather he talked, the traumas of the past week tumbling out as she sat and listened. "We knew plenty of the persecution of the Jews," she later recalled, "but this was the first time in Vienna. . . . I still have a picture of the horror . . . this sort of hideous picture, and of the agony with which he told it."

Austria had ceased to exist, the mountain roads to Southeastern Europe and the Balkans, under Nazi control; the map of Europe changed overnight, with almost no Western response. Shirer, from London, had ventured that Czechoslovakia would be next. Murrow, describing the Austrian take-over, wondered aloud "when similar things may happen again."

In the meantime, he had become a reporter. CBS wanted more "radio talks." From Shirer, too. On top of their usual duties, of course. After two-and-a-half years away, Murrow was back in the trenches. In midcrisis he had found his profession, or more specifically perhaps, it had found him.

But something else had changed, colleagues noted, barely perceptible in the low-keyed American: a certain projection, faint but constant, of concern and tension; that, and the worry lines which, suddenly appearing, streaked his forehead with three deep grooves before the year was out— a strange birthday present, welcoming him to his thirtieth year.

VI

The Steamroller

1.

"I won't say anything about Vienna," he wrote Chet Williams that spring, "since I am not too reasonable about it, and it's the sort of thing you can't write [about] except at great length. . . .

"The one thing that worried me was the possibility of not doing an honest job from there. I am finding it more and more difficult to suppress my personal convictions."

The letter had gone out on March 28. That same day, a quiet gym teacher named Konrad Henlein, leader of the Nazi-funded Sudeten German party, sat in conference with Hitler over demands to be made on the Beneš government in Prague—demands deliberately designed to be unacceptable.

The airwaves were heating up again, Hitler turning on Czechoslovakia as predicted, the immediate focus, the Sudetenland—industrialized, mineral-rich, a natural mountain barrier—where a German-speaking population, turned into an ethnic minority by Versailles,[1] marched increasingly to a Nazi drumbeat. But the Czech republic, tied by treaty to the West and the Soviet Union, was no isolated Austria, the prospect now raised of a military confrontation between the powers, should the Germans invade.

On the air in March, Shirer had wondered: Would France and Britain go to war to back the Czechs? By early summer Neville Chamberlain had answered with an off-the-record no—unless the Sudetenland was ceded—while the *Times* of London urged the Czechs to do so for their own good.

"The Old Lady simply won't learn," Shirer entered in his diary.[2] He had met at Lausanne that June with Murrow and Dick Marriott, in from London, disheartened at the power of what they called "the appeasement crowd," all three men aware of a fact known to every military man in

Europe—that German control of the Sudeten highlands would leave the Czechs defenseless while placing the huge Skoda armaments works in Hitler's grasp.

Following the Anschluss, Murrow had suggested regular broadcasts from Prague; New York had turned it down. However, Shirer would be in and out of the Czech capital as the crisis grew.

For both men, life had changed radically. Murrow was now director-reporter, making rounds, meeting with sources, telephoning, writing, and broadcasting (though not yet on a daily basis)—while still scheduling speakers and maintaining total responsibility for the direction and day-to-day functioning of the CBS European office, a function that had suddenly acquired tremendous news significance. Shirer, now Geneva-based, had become their roving reporter and general man-of-all-crises, on the spot in Prague, Berlin, wherever necessary. They were two young people covering a continent in turmoil, their only backup their stamina, imagination, and professionalism, in recognition of which the prestigious Head-liners Club back home had presented them with the Silver Plaque for their reporting of the Anschluss.

In the meantime in Prague, Shirer scheduled President Beneš—booked over the Berlin transmitter, fading mysteriously in spots—then covered the British-inspired mission of Lord Runciman, sent ostensibly to mediate, actually to pressure. "The whole mission . . . smells," Shirer noted privately,[3] as Czech engineers began testing a new transmitter with the help of CBS technicians in New York, both sides working against time.

In eastern France, Murrow broadcast from the Maginot Line, deep within the earth, on French preparedness—the first reporter to do so—brought off through a daring personal approach to Premier Édouard Daladier. The story gave him a feeling of unreality—"these long miles of white corridors twelve stories underground; the unknown thousands of men spending their lives down here . . . waiting. . . ."

> As we drove up here a man pointed out to me a delightful little chateau in a clump of woods. "My grandfather was killed there in 1870," he said.

The broadcast and others like it called attention increasingly to the quality of CBS's coverage, irritating the opposition at Radio City. A spokesman for NBC, soft-pedaling the crisis in those months, protested that the Maginot report could only alienate the Germans. Had *they* thought of broadcasting from the Maginot Line? a reporter asked. "No, but . . ."

Yet there were moments, in the grimness, of unwitting comedy. Murrow also broadcast that spring from Paris with Fred Bate from atop a hangar at Le Bourget, both networks covering together the Paris-Moscow segment of Howard Hughes's historic flight around the world—an event accorded all the eager interest later given space shots.

The problem was, there was no takeoff, the big Lockheed undergoing minor open-ended repair work behind closed doors. The two reporters were reduced to a virtual vaudeville act as they took turns filling dead air with nonstop platitudes—"*Mechanics are running in and out of the hangar. . . . I think he is coming out—any minute now. . . the air is full of expectancy. . . .*"[4]—expatiating endlessly about the beautiful weather, the interest of the French people, and the hangar door that was about to open, while colleagues in the New York newsrooms doubled over.

After almost an hour, CBS took time out for a commercial break. Two minutes later, NBC audiences heard Fred Bate yell, "There she goes! She has taken off!"[5]

At CBS there was not a dry eye in the house. Murrow was back on the closed-circuit "cue" channel with New York, embarrassed, the flawless ad-libber of the Maginot report aware that he had made a complete fool of himself. White, recovering, laid it on—"You really limped through *that* one!"—enjoying, savoring the moment until a cry of frustration penetrated the shortwave crackle, loud and clear:

"*Hell, Paul, I'm no Bob Trout!*"

That summer, the Czech crisis snowballed into its final weeks amid top-level meetings, diplomatic notes, protests, and pressures. Offstage, Western leaders were ignoring the advice of their own military, secret appeals from the German general staff to take a stand against Hitler falling on deaf ears, ignoring, too, Russia's repeated offers to enter into military consultations with the West.

As tensions rose, Murrow and Shirer combed Europe's major cities, lining up journalists ready to broadcast to America at a moment's notice. By early September everything was in place as the countdown began.

Monday, September 12, at 2:15 P.M. eastern standard time, Columbia's regular programming was interrupted—"to bring our listeners the world-awaited talk on Germany's foreign policy to be delivered by Adolf Hitler. . . . We take you now to Nuremberg."

At the Nuremberg stadium, it was 8:15 in the evening, the last, climactic day of the Nazi *Parteitag*, Hitler stepping into the glare of torches and floodlights, calling for "justice" and threatening war, to the loud *Sieg heils* of half a million followers.

At seven-thirty that evening, CBS held its first news roundup on the crisis, with reports from Edward Murrow in London, William Shirer in Prague, and newspapermen in Berlin and Paris.

The bulletins were pouring in: Nazis rioting in the Sudetenland; France to mobilize two million reservists; gas masks distributed in England; German-speaking refugees, mostly non-Nazis, fleeing the Sudetenland to Prague; Chamberlain to fly to Berchtesgaden to meet with Hitler and head off a war.

In London, Murrow was working around the clock, setting in motion

CHAPTER VI

the apparatus pieced together over the past months, preparing his own broadcasts while arranging the reports fed to CBS master control at all hours of the day and night. At 485 Madison announcers were pulled off their duties in other departments to beef up the tiny news staff, reading agency copy in shifts, the center of operations, the small studio where Hans von Kaltenborn presided as analyst and anchorman.

It had been Paul White's idea to have a single broadcaster in New York hold everything together, from the briefest news flashes to the major roundups. One account has it that Trout, for reasons of his own, turned it down, so the job had gone to the sixty-year-old Kaltenborn, his 1936 successes somewhat faded, moving in on the assignment as if born to it—translating from the German; dissecting key statements; analyzing events as they occurred, calling in the correspondents; leading round table discussions linking the European capitals with New York.[6]

As for Murrow, at the other end in London, he had become two men: the anonymous network director, feeding broadcasts to New York, and the rising radio reporter. From Studio 9 Kaltenborn would throw out the cue, "Calling Edward Murrow, come in Ed Murrow," and a voice grown increasingly familiar to the public would cut through the shortwave static: "Hello America, this is London calling," the standard opening from overseas.

The pace helped keep his mind on his work, in the face of developments rolling steadily downhill. Chamberlain, returning from Berchtesgaden with Hitler's demands, was in conference with Daladier, discussing the cession of the Sudetenland, with a four-power guarantee of what was left.

From Prague, Shirer declared that the Czechs would not "lie down and trust their fate" even to the West. "What would a new . . . guarantee be worth, they ask, the first moment a big country wanted to break it?"[7]

Two nights later, Murrow was on the phone from London: Britain and France had agreed to pressure Czechoslovakia into turning over the Sudetenland, with a cosmetic ten-day interval before the Wehrmacht moved in. Chamberlain was bringing the proposal to Hitler at Godesberg, and CBS wanted Shirer there to cover it.

The newsman was incredulous. It was crazy, didn't make sense. The Czechs would never accept dismemberment; they'd fight alone if they had to.

"Maybe so. I hope you're right."

But on Wednesday, the twenty-first, news bulletins announced that Czechoslovakia, now completely isolated, had agreed to the conditions.

That evening one of Murrow's guests, maverick Labourite D. N. Pritt, speaking out against the background of his party's silence, stated that the British government, choosing between shame and war, had "almost certainly chosen both," charging the government, moreover, with "a tremendous betrayal . . . carried out behind the back of the British public.

126

"Our British press has been more severely censored than in any period of its history. Our people probably know less than even the German public of what Hitler said to Chamberlain. . . ."

It was a sore point. All through the crisis, and before it, dissenting voices had been kept off the BBC, and therefore off the air; Pritt himself was a case in point. Background information on the controversy was almost nonexistent; few "topical talks" were scheduled—"as the situation was a delicate one," according to BBC house personnel, "and the Foreign Office preferred that there should be no comment on it."[8]

Americans, beaming to the United States, could, of course, program as they liked, and when Murrow carried a talk by Anthony Eden, who had quit as Foreign Secretary in protest over Chamberlain's appeasement policies, the switchboard at Langham Place was jammed with calls from English shortwave listeners, asking how to tune in.

For the larger English public, however, there were simply the hard news bulletins that the BBC was best at—troop movements; shuttle diplomacy moves; the who, what, when, where, how, though not the why; addresses by leaders on all sides, by members of the Chamberlain government; broadcast prayers for peace; air-raid precautions; what to do with a gas mask.[9] No context, little or no discussion of what was at stake, the overriding message being that Europe was on the brink of the unthinkable because of "people of whom we know nothing"—the phrase was Chamberlain's—and that the PM was doing his best to avoid it.

"There was a terrible fear," Cecilia Reeves recalled, "a real panic fear; I never saw this again during the war."

In contrast were the stage-managed arrivals and departures of Chamberlain himself—well-wishing crowds; the readied plane; microphones open; the Prime Minister among his people, a civilized, fatherly figure speaking to the newsreel and early television cameras,[10] the seeming last voice of reason in a world gone mad, speaking quietly of peace and Herr Hitler's earnest intentions.

It was a lesson in media management, repudiated by the wartime BBC, never forgotten by the American guest, the fears expressed at Chatham House come to life.

In the meantime, Jan Masaryk, Czech ambassador in London, son of the founder of Czechoslovakia and an American-born mother, spoke to CBS late-night listeners, vowing somehow to resist, "in full confidence that this time England and France will not forsake us."

But at Godesberg a smiling Hitler raised the ante, rejecting the concessions wrung from the Czechs, sending the aged Chamberlain back to London in a state of shock.

"There aren't any experts on European affairs anymore," said Murrow at 1:45 in the morning. "Things are moving too fast . . . and one man's guess is as good as another's."

Saturday, September 24, the West faced a new ultimatum: unconditional and immediate German occupation of the Sudetenland, the target date, October 1—one week away.

Czechoslovakia had mobilized. France had reportedly a million men under arms; Germany, a million and a half. Roosevelt was cabling to Hitler, in a desperate plea for peace, making it clear, however, that America would remain an onlooker. For Murrow it answered the question put repeatedly to him in the past days: What did America think, what would America do, and if war came, how long before America came in?

In New York the two big networks were now running neck and neck, providing fulltime coverage. At Columbia Bob Trout, reading off the text of the presidential cable, was at his post with Paul White and the others. Kaltenborn was living in Studio 9, taking his meals on a tray, his naps on an army cot, and his morning shave within reach of the microphone.

Next door, the news tickers went mad, agency reports and bulletins unrolling hourly from the machines like so much paper toweling. Cots lined the corridors, hot coffee and sandwiches set out for the hollow-eyed announcers working the news-reading shifts. To one staff member the seventeenth floor, with its gaunt, unshaved faces, looked like a cross between *The Front Page* and a convalescent home.

At CBS in London, Murrow and Campbell, on the phone with White on one hand, with Shirer and their stringers on the other, organized the European end, setting up transmissions that would total 35 from London alone—with Murrow as reporter or interviewer on all of them—and assisting in another 151 from the Continent,[11] the Murrow-Shirer effort supplemented by the expertise of newspaper veterans in every capital. American radio coverage, growing through the crisis though still borrowing talent, was in fact outstripping other services; Raymond Swing, in Prague for Mutual, found that while BBC bulletins were the best in Europe, Americans were getting more and better in-depth information via shortwave, through the networks, than those living virtually next door to the crisis.[12]

Wednesday, September 28, war seemed certain. Hitler stood by his ultimatum. From London, Murrow reported the mobilization of the British fleet, trenches dug in London parks, trucks roaring by in the night, loaded with sandbags and gas masks.

He had made his report at 1:00 that afternoon, London time. At 2:35 P.M. in Westminster, MPs gathered to hear the Prime Minister's report on the situation, in what a New York announcer described as "the most momentous session in twenty years." A microphone had been installed—not for broadcasting, but to relay the speech to the Lords' Library and the Commons Gallery, where the Queen Mother sat listening.

In New York it was still Wednesday morning. Then, at ten-thirty eastern standard time, a news flash went out over the airwaves to the effect that Chancellor Hitler had just invited Chamberlain, Daladier, and Mussolini to Munich "for the purpose of settling the Sudetenland problem."

There was no mention of the Soviet Union or, for that matter, Czechoslovakia.

Over in London, Chamberlain had been handed the message part way through his report. As the stunned Czech ambassador looked down from the gallery, the Commons burst into wild cheering. Further bulletins reported a wave of buying on the stock market and a rallying of the British pound. That night Ambassador Masaryk was informed that his country was not to be allowed at the bargaining table; Hitler wouldn't stand for it.

The whole strange day was logged by the news media. At CBS, Murrow had started it off with the early-morning report. Then came hours of presiding over the broadcasts of others: Bill Shirer in Berlin; correspondents Thomas Grandin in Paris and Vincent Sheean in Prague; the British commentators at the House of Commons; the interpolation of a speech by Daladier. Murrow introduced the Archbishop of Canterbury with a prayer for peace—it pre-empted the Kentucky Derby—ending his day at 6:00 A.M., London time, with final summaries from Paris and Prague. By that time it was the morning of September 29—six-and-a-half hours before the scheduled meeting of the four powers at the Führerhaus in Munich.

The accord came after midnight, ceding the Sudetenland to Germany while the Czech delegation waited in the next room. Murrow, in mid-broadcast, picked up the first official word of the agreement from a Munich radio station and flashed the news to America.[13]

"The German Führer got what he wanted," Shirer noted from Munich, "only he has to wait a little longer for it . . . ten days. His waiting ten short days has saved Europe from a world war. To Americans it must seem a strange thing, but there it is. . . ."

In New York, Kaltenborn called the agreement "a complete victory for Hitler," noting, however, "one great Power . . . that has been excluded from any contact with the conference . . . and yet it is a Power whose might cannot be wished out of the world, it is a Power that will become more cynical because of what has happened at Munich—Soviet Russia."

Back in London, Murrow ended his broadcast with a final statement from Prague: "At this critical juncture the Czech government is placing the interest of civilization and world peace before the distress of its own peoples and is resolved to make sacrifices which never in history were expected from an undefeated state. . . ."

It was over. He was exhausted, depressed, unable to go home. Instead, he went to the Czech Embassy, where Jan Masaryk, a personal friend and favorite of American newsmen, sat alone. He had been waiting all day, he told Murrow, for a call from the British Foreign Office; no one had called.

They sat in a night-long death watch, recollected by Murrow years later, following Masaryk's own death:

> He knew it meant war, knew that his country and its people were doomed, but there was no bitterness in the man, nor was there resignation or defeat. . . .
>
> As I rose to leave, the gray dawn pressed against the windows. Jan pointed to a big picture of Hitler and Mussolini that stood on the mantel and he said: "Don't worry, Ed. There will be dark days and many men will die, but there is a God and He will not let two such men rule Europe."

Next day, Murrow watched the jubilant crowds thronging Whitehall and Downing Street. The news of Munich had hit with the force of a bombshell, setting off a mood of near-euphoria. Cecilia Reeves, seeking respite at a play, heard of it when the shouting of the newsboys penetrated the theater. She watched the man in front of her turn to his wife—"It's peace"—and, unable to contain herself, fetched the surprised citizen a large kick under the seat.

Late that afternoon the Warmongers, seated before a TV screen at Broadcasting House, watched in helpless anger as Chamberlain, alighting at Heston Aerodrome, proclaimed "peace in our time." The PM's return was being televised, albeit on a modest basis. As members of the Liaison unit, they had been assigned to viewing the event as "a broadcast in which foreigners might be interested."

The gas-tight doors at Broadcasting House, put up during the crisis, were taken down. In the chapel studio, the BBC Director of Religion was to conduct a special service of thanksgiving and prayer. In Parliament, Winston Churchill, calling the agreement "a total, unmitigated defeat," was shouted down by outraged MPs.

Among the small group of BBC dissenters there was no thanksgiving, only "general shame and misery," as one recalled, shared in by Murrow.[14] Professionally he kept a lid on his feelings, always the disciple of Ed Klauber, telling listeners of the crowds lined up to greet the Prime Minister, the bells ringing out a welcome, London papers speculating on his chances of a knighthood or the Nobel Peace Prize. The average Englishman, he said, was relieved and grateful: "Men who predicted the crisis and the lines it would follow . . . did not entirely share that optimism and relief."

For him, the marathon was over, though not the questions it had raised—questions that had haunted his mind as he had sat at five that morning in the studio, surveying the wreckage of the past eighteen days:

> Is this the end of the crisis or have we really witnessed the realignment of the forces in Europe? The dismemberment of Czechoslovakia, the isolation of Russia, the domination of Middle Europe by a totalitarian

state. Is it a prelude to a trial of strength between contradictory economic and political philosophies?

In the meantime, questions concerning the media were being raised in the backwash of Munich. At the BBC, John Coatman, former Home Service news chief, who had heard Murrow at Chatham House the year before and admired the American, charged the corporation, in a confidential in-house memorandum, with "a conspiracy of silence." The British public, he contended, had been kept in "ignorance" throughout the crisis, only officials permitted to speak out. The outcome, he went on, might have been different had the public "been in possession of essential knowledge which was denied to them. . . ."

His country's position was now "infinitely more dangerous," he charged, and in words echoing Murrow's Chatham House address, he pleaded for "a new responsibility," a determination to let the people know "just what is happening."[15]

Broadcasting House was in fact about to undergo a metamorphosis, with Murrow's growth a part of that development—one that would make the wartime BBC in many ways his spiritual home. But the questions raised in his mind in September, 1938 seemed to confirm both his innate wariness of a broadcasting monopoly, however admirable, and his tolerance, for all its faults, of the flawed, raucous, yet theoretically diverse system of American commercial broadcasting.

Meanwhile, he was on his way to stardom, and so was radio news. In the eighteen days between September 12 and September 30, millions of people had reached automatically for their dials at all hours, turning to radio as a primary news source for instant firsthand information from Europe. Between 100 and 200 overseas reports had been shortwaved to the United States by each of the two big networks, the edge going to CBS for its analysis, number of broadcasts, and depth of coverage. Kaltenborn's eighteen-day marathon of analysis and anchoring had made him a national celebrity.

But at the workaday level, another force was emerging: the radio correspondent, uniting in one person the functions of news gatherer, writer, and broadcaster, neither a commentator nor a news reader, but a staff reporter—a figure new to communications.

"He has more influence upon America's reaction to foreign news than a shipful of newspapermen," said writer Robert Landry that winter, describing Murrow for readers of *Scribner's* magazine (*"Edward R. Murrow/ Scribner's Examines: a radio foreign correspondent . . . his technique, rivals and influence on American opinion . . . his tactics in Columbia's battle abroad with NBC"*). For the first time, print attention was focusing not on commentators but on network reporters and on Murrow in particular, both as bureau head and as prototype of the new breed: a power in his own right; a newsman who could address a nationwide audience directly—no editors, no rewriters, no headlines shoved over his copy—beating the newspapers by hours, reaching millions otherwise dependent for their foreign news on provincial papers, a rising national figure with direct access to the vast American public that was beyond the reach of the great metropolitan dailies.

Beyond that, Landry found himself intrigued by Columbia's European Director—pleasant, self-contained, so oddly young by comparison with the fortyish Bate or the leathery newspaper veteran John Steele of Mutual—who had suddenly been catapulted, back home, to overnight fame ("To quote *Variety*, 'his name was figuratively up in lights for the first time,' " wrote Landry).

Yet despite the easy manner, the fund of funny stories, the man himself remained elusive, noncommittal on all but professional matters, wrapping his privacy around him like a protective covering. Landry, questioning associates and former co-workers, came up with nothing colorful, no personal anecdotes, no legends; colleagues, when asked, "never seem to have heard about him doing anything flamboyant, picturesque or silly."[16]

Munich, as anticipated, brought no peace. The Wehrmacht had in fact moved immediately into the Sudetenland, in open violation of even the ten-day grace period. German cannon now pointed downhill at the Bohemian plain, Slovakia, and farther south to the oilfields of Rumania, a potential fascist sphere of influence. Shirer, granted permission finally to enter the ceded Sudeten territory, was told by Paul White to stow it. People were tired, White said, and just wanted to forget the whole thing.

But Munich jitters lingered on, bursting forth four weeks later in a sudden mass blurring of fantasy and reality, triggered off by radio. The Sunday before Halloween, American listeners, flipping their dials to CBS at eight-thirty, came upon news flashes of alien invasion, statements by government officials, on-the-spot reports by newscasters, all familiar to a traumatized public—except that the invasion reports were coming from New Jersey.

It would be remembered as Orson Welles's "panic broadcast," the Mercury Theater production of H.G. Wells's *The War of the Worlds*, news techniques used to hype up an old sci-fi chestnut, loaded with dead giveaways at the orders of Davidson Taylor, network supervisor for the show, after he had found the earlier drafts "altogether too realistic."[17]

No use. By eight forty-five, there was panic nationwide: bus terminals mobbed, switchboards jammed with hysterical calls—America was being invaded by creatures from Mars. They had heard it on the radio.

By nine, 485 Madison was swarming with police and press, the switchboard lit up, amid rumblings of lawsuits and FCC investigations; Paul White, at the typewriter, knocked out reassurances to be read over the air, to the effect that the United States was not—repeat *not*—being invaded by men from Mars. Next morning, Ed Klauber summoned in his shaking executives. "I think we've learned something from all this, and that is *not* to simulate news."

All the devices familiar to the public, plus a few more, had been thrown into *The War of the Worlds*. But what sounded especially convincing was the nameless "reporter" broadcasting from a rooftop, staunch and steady-nerved in his description of the Martian attack on New York. It was all acting and sound effects, but many listeners still recovering from three weeks of brinkmanship, who had learned to trust radio, heard one thing only: the controlled tones of a CBS correspondent reporting the death of a city, his broadcast trailing off into ominous silence.[18]

That winter, the Murrows were back in New York, Murrow for consultations with Klauber and White on the building of a news staff, preparing for what now seemed inevitable. Elsewhere at 485, he made friends with Columbia's latest boy genius, Norman Corwin, whose verse radio play, *The Plot to Overthrow Christmas*, was the greatest thing, he told the author, since W. S. Gilbert.

He traveled in the Midwest, addressing the local Council on Foreign Relations in Chicago, fulsomely introduced by a thirty-eight-year-old lawyer named Adlai Stevenson. Back in New York, the young Murrows found themselves minor celebrities, squired out on New Year's Eve by Paley's brother-in-law Isaac Levy; Paley himself was on for the following Monday.

"Then as soon as . . . a few bigwigs have had their say," Janet wrote her family, "Ed is to perform and we're to depart." When they returned, finally, to England, it would be with Klauber's authorization to begin hiring. And with a last-minute memento from 17, delivered to the stateroom just before sailing time—a massive bag of coal with a note requesting the bearer to carry the coals to Newcastle, signed "Paul White." Murrow's dazed request that the coal be removed was promptly rejected. Sorry, the order was for delivery only.

But both Ed and Janet Murrow had been anxious to leave, restive during those last days in New York as 1939 dawned, cold and wet and heavy with a sense of final deadlines. "If they're going to have some kind of organizational upset in February Ed's got to get over there to lay the ground," Janet wrote home. "You can't jump into a thing like that cold. . . ."

For the Paris spot Murrow had hired Thomas Grandin, who had served them in the Munich crisis, bringing the European staff to three—overworked, fleshed out by print journalists subject to yanking at any time by their editors. Murrow often had to jump in at a moment's notice, earning him the title of General Understudy to the Fourth Estate.

Get yourself a really good assistant, Klauber told him. But how to find the right one? "I don't know whether Ed's going to do it or not," Janet Murrow wrote her family; "however I think he's a fool if he doesn't."

In fact, it was growing increasingly clear that the day of the one-man show was over. In February the Murrows met in Paris with Shirer and Grandin, then broke off the meeting a day later as news of the Pope's death sent Shirer off to Rome, probably indefinitely, pending the election of a new pontiff.

Back in London Murrow, still covering all bases, arranged a broadcast with six women MP's, with one of the six, Ellen Wilkinson, due back at the apartment afterward for a bite to eat. "I hope she doesn't stay long," Janet noted, "because Ed is so tired and we have to be up at seven. Ed leaves for Switzerland at 8."

Six days later there was a call from Kay Campbell, saying he had come down with influenza on his arrival in Switzerland and had run a fever of 104, now happily broken. She'd have called earlier, but he had made her promise not to tell.

Janet Murrow called Switzerland; he was pretty weak, he said, but otherwise all right and she was *not* to come. He had two good doctors and a good nurse, and anyway, they said he could travel in a few days. She put the receiver down, preparing in her mind for what would be needed on his arrival and torn, not for the last time, about whether she was doing the right thing in staying put.

She was waiting with the car when he came off the plane four days later, shaken by a long, rough trip bucking headwinds but walking, to her great relief, under his own steam; she'd half expected him to be wheeled out. But he betrayed his weakness when he allowed her to drive.

The days that followed, moreover, showed that he had by no means recovered, attempts to work followed by setbacks and retreats to bed, followed by a premature return to the routine, simply because he had to.

Bill Shirer came to London. The two friends sat up talking until all hours while Janet Murrow fidgeted like a nanny. She didn't begrudge the company—Bill's presence did Ed a world of good—but didn't Ed *realize?* Something much more fundamental, more disturbing, was emerging in the pattern of her husband's life-style: that of wearing himself out, then using doctors as palliatives. "Sometimes I get very discouraged," she wrote home, "and see in his disregard of the simple essentials of health only a resulting long life of dragging around, never being fit. . . ."

At the back of her mind lay another, even more nagging question: What was to become of them when war came, with no allowances for illness, no time left for those slow, recuperative walks in the sun?

March 28, 1939, the Spanish Republic fell to the fascists. The war had cost a million-and-a-half lives.

March 15, the German Army had moved into Prague. The West's guarantees had not been enough to save what was left of Czechoslovakia.

Events were rushing toward a final flashpoint as Hitler demanded the old Hanseatic port of Danzig, separated from the Reich by Versailles, along with the Corridor and parts of western Poland. The Chamberlain government, recovering from the Prague take-over, warned that Britain would support Poland in case of attack.

The drumbeat was accelerating, Hitler declaring as his sole interest the self-determination of the East Germans while telling his generals that Poland would have to go and he hoped some *Schweinhund* wouldn't head it off again with a peace proposal.[19]

In early April, Italy invaded Albania, aiming at Greece.

It was no longer a question of if but of when. In New York, Ed Klauber called in Adrian Murphy, whose duties included office design, and handed him a slip detailing what Paul White and the others would need in the forthcoming reconstruction of the newsroom. The job had to be done by July 15, "so everyone will have practice using it by the time the war starts."[20]

Four weeks later, Germany and Italy announced the so-called Pact of Steel. British and French guarantees had gone to Greece and Yugoslavia.

That July, Paul White flew to London via the new Atlantic Clipper service, for a meeting with Murrow, Shirer, and Grandin. He returned to 485 with a detailed account on how they would cover the war. The plans went up to 20 with a one-line P.S.: "I don't think they'll work either."

In London the News Director's visit had exacerbated the continuing tensions between White and Murrow. Janet Murrow had complained home about game playing by New York, showing most recently in the rejection of Ed's broadcast ideas, followed by a sudden change of mind, the onus falling on Murrow when it proved too late to make arrangements. Luckily, she said, Ed had hung on to his cables and would, she hoped, use them if and when, regarding Mr. White! Paul and Sue White both had shown up that July, unwelcome guests. Unwillingly, Janet cleared drawers and cupboards in the apartment, which Paul had requested of his ol' buddy while they themselved took a brief, much-needed vacation. Ed arranged to broadcast en route. Departing Friday, they heard from Kay Campbell before the weekend was out, that White had written Klauber that Murrow was "resting in the country" and that he, White, was taking care of the office in his absence.

"The nerve of the man!" Janet Murrow exploded. "He'd no more know *what* to do than Adam. Miss Campbell does all the work. . . ."

H. V. Kaltenborn came through, with instructions for Murrow to set up appointments for Chamberlain, Churchill, and other notables—"over the week-end!!! Who does he think he is. . . ."

After forty-eight hours, she wrote home, Kaltenborn had evidently sized up everything in England to the point of broadcasting "fifteen minutes of definite statements and promises to the American public. It makes us both sick. . . . But the American public likes prophecies [and] we have to be nice to him and arrange for him to meet all of the big bugs because we had orders. . . . Mr. K. is after all working for someone who buys time from Columbia."

Personally, Murrow was convinced of the imminence of another Munich, though the point, Janet Murrow wrote her family, "is that no one— and I mean no one—knows what is going to happen."

August 21, a cloudless day: the Murrows were sitting with Hans von Kaltenborn in the garden of a cottage they had taken near Reading, enjoying the flowers and the end of a two-day rain, when the news came in of the Hitler-Stalin pact, assuring Germany of a one-front war. Chamberlain, foot-dragging on cooperation with the USSR, had ended by isolating Britain and France.

So much for the flowers. They packed up and returned to a stunned London. Kaltenborn was due in Berlin in two days. Murrow had already seen about the "really good assistant" urged on him by Klauber.

Actually, it was the Paris spot he was thinking of when, in mid-August, he had contacted Eric Sevareid, the newspaperman who had come through London in 1937, now making a name for himself on the English-language Paris *Herald*. Sevareid, by his later account, was moonlighting for the United Press and considering an agency offer when Murrow's call came through, offering him the Columbia job. He didn't know much about Sevareid's experience, he said, but he liked the way he wrote, and he liked his ideas.[21]

New York, however, didn't like his voice, and the Shirer battle began all over again. The new man wouldn't do, they said; content—fine, voice— awful. Murrow repeated that he was hiring reporters, not announcers, that content and credibility were more important than vocal sheen. They came out of the fight with Sevareid on the payroll.

Sevareid, now in, reported to London with wife and worldly goods. A joint broadcast was set up with Kaltenborn—a total shambles, it turned out, when the veteran commentator talked his way through most of the time period, nearly squeezing out his younger, inexperienced colleague.

The broadcast ended, they filed out in silence—Murrow in the lead, then a sheepish Kaltenborn, and the miserable Sevareid. The European Director stalked on ahead, his face black with fury. Sevareid watched a pencil, held tightly in his grip, snap in two.[22] But nothing was said, then or later.

With hostilities imminent, they needed more warm bodies. Bill Henry, a newspaperman working for CBS on special assignment, came through London and was talked into staying.

In Paris, Grandin had his hands full; two days after his arrival in London, Eric Sevareid was dispatched back to France, leaving Janet Murrow to see about room, board, and a French visa for Lois Sevareid.

On the Continent, Larry LeSueur, an upstate New Yorker on a month's leave from UP, caught a Channel steamer bound for England. Months earlier he had asked Murrow for a job; check back, came the answer, if anything happened to indicate the outbreak of war. Accordingly, the Hitler-Stalin pact had set the tourists rushing for the boats, and he had come back to Britain amid a complement of nuns and English chorus girls.

Arriving to find all slots filled at CBS, he cashed in his return ticket to New York and waited.

In the meantime, 485 was having its bizarre moments. Paul White, deciding a lighter tone was called for, wanted a change of pace from Murrow and Shirer: a cabaret roundup; call it *Europe Dances*. The horrified correspondents protested, but New York insisted. Shirer pictured himself outside a nightclub in Hamburg's St. Pauli district, engineer and equipment in tow, with Armaggedon approaching. He contacted Murrow: "I can't stand it." Neither could the other man: "I'll tell them the hell with it."[23]

The summer ended in a flurry of shuttling diplomats, hurried meetings, last-minute appeals, nonstop broadcasting, Britain's repeat of support to Poland mixed in with appeals to continue negotiations. At the Danzig border Shirer looked at the German guns and tank traps and thought of the Sudetenland. At Führer headquarters the German foreign minister, asked by Mussolini's son-in-law, what was it they really wanted—was it Danzig, was it the Corridor?—answered simply, "We want war!"[24]

In London, air raid precaution signs were up again; trenches opened in the parks. The night of August 31, Murrow read to American audiences the evacuation instructions issued to the parents of London: "If you have a child of school age, and wish to have him evacuated . . . send him to school tomorrow, Friday, with hand luggage containing the child's gas mask, a face cloth, a toothbrush, a packet of food for the day. . . ."

In Berlin, the Polish Ambassador, urged on by the anxious governments in London and Paris, had been at the Foreign Ministry in the Wilhelmstrasse, keeping negotiations alive. Returning to the embassy, he found the phone gone dead, the lines cut between Berlin and Warsaw.

Friday, September 1, dawned clear and cloudless. In her Lucerne hotel room, Marvin Breckinridge was awake when the knock came at her door announcing room service. She was going to cover the Lucerne Music Festival for *Town & Country*, then possibly stop on the way back in London and see her friends Ed and Janet Murrow if her luck held.

The door opened, the ancient waiter shuffled in with the breakfast tray. Outside, Lake Lucerne was blue-green, unruffled beneath a perfect sky. The old man laid out the silver, great tears silently streaming down his cheeks.

"They have gone into Poland."

2.

S. W. ("Pat") Smithers, of BBC public relations and a former newspaperman, had been ordered to report to the newsroom at Broadcasting House the moment Britain seemed likely to enter the war.

The morning of Sunday, September 3, with Western governments still teetering undecidedly, he had caught the train in from the suburbs, hopping a bus from Victoria Station headed northward toward the BBC. As they turned into Bond Street, an old cockney climbed aboard: "It's war, mates. 'E just said so on the wireless." No one responded. The double-decker continued up Bond Street. Minutes later the first sirens went off.

Figuring he was close enough, Smithers jumped off and began to run the last quarter mile, passing as he did so his fellow Londoners, calmly window-shopping, contemptuous of both the sirens and the running figure. Embarrassed, he slowed to a walk, still out of breath as he made his way past the bronze doors of Broadcasting House and into the lobby, where Ed Murrow, whom he knew, was standing around with a few senior people.

The American came over, took his arm: "What's it like out there, Pat?"

Smithers recounted his story. Murrow, with a nod, headed back upstairs to the newsroom. "Thanks, you've just given me my lead."[1]

Broadcasting House had changed overnight: sandbags materialized out of nowhere; the gas-tight doors back up again; guards at the entrances. Security plans long in preparation had become stark reality—the once-elegant BBC with its black-tie announcers stripped down now to wartime essentials, most of its divisions scattered to unnamed locations elsewhere, leaving Broadcasting House, as the London nerve center, devoted almost entirely to news.

Upstairs on the fifth floor, a suddenly expanded news department waited for instructions, some twenty people milling about, many, like Smithers, called in from other sections for their journalistic experience. At length a wiry, graying figure in soft slippers padded into the newsroom, unfastened shirt cuffs flapping loosely about his wrists: R. T. Clark, Home Service News Editor for the BBC.[2] He climbed onto a rickety chair, clapped his hands somewhat diffidently for silence.

"Well, brothers, now that war's come, your job is to tell the truth. And if you aren't sure it is the truth, don't use it." It was the only directive they were to receive.

Out of the corner of his eye, Smithers could make out Ed Murrow, his broadcast finished, standing quietly at the back of the room, his gaze fixed on R. T. Clark: the beginning of a close and fruitful relationship between the rising American reporter and the veteran Scottish news chief.

That morning had ended sixty hours of waiting, of trying to read the confusing signals out of Downing Street and the Élysée, as German divisions plunged deeper into Poland and Warsaw buckled and burned. Murrow, broadcasting nearly twenty-four hours after the initial incursion, had reported British and French pledges to Poland not yet "operative," a British ultimatum for withdrawal gone out with no time limit, an expected radio speech by the Prime Minister not forthcoming.

Like his counterparts in Paris and Berlin, he had been broadcasting virtually around the clock, feeding the latest on the European cliff-hanger to the newsroom in New York, where veteran journalist Elmer Davis, (formerly of The New York *Times*) now news analyst for CBS, was watching the tickers. Ed Klauber, down from 20, was spending all day in the newsroom, in direct control. Trout, holding it all together at the microphone, wasn't sure if he was more unnerved by the onset of war or by the presence of the steely-eyed Klauber, sitting at his elbow.

From London, Murrow reported rumblings of military differences between the Allies, despite repeated public assurances, he said, of "complete solidarity": the English privately unprepared; the French privately unwilling. "This isn't simply a matter of declaring war. Decisions must be taken. . . . How, for instance, are Britain and France to bring help to the Poles? Are they to take the initiative in the bombing of women and children? Well, this situation could not have come as a surprise to His Majesty's Government. . . ."

The only bombing in progress, however, was the bombing of Polish cities, while the Chamberlain government, treading water, faced a backlash in the Commons as an opposition Labour leader, rising in a house two-thirds Conservative, was met with a shout from the majority benches to "Speak for England!"

"The Prime Minister was almost apologetic. He's a politician; he sensed the temper of the House and of the country."

A growing body of opinion in the American press had begun predicting, or at least suspecting, another Munich, with Murrow among the holdouts, sensing a swing in the British mood, insisting that this time "the rank and file . . . the little man in the bowler hat, the clerks, the bus drivers and all the others" would have to be reckoned with.

In the last days of August, he had been almost the only American correspondent to place due emphasis on the Conservative party organization's report to the Prime Minister—understated, overshadowed by the dramatic announcements from the diplomatic front. The party regulars were simply informing the PM that having duly taken samplings of public opinion, they were supporting him in his policy of "firmness." An unspoken warning, as Murrow read it, that any other course would in effect leave Chamberlain a man without a party. "From the moment Ed Murrow put that on the air," wrote Elmer Davis later, "some of us were convinced that there would be war."

Sunday, September 3, at 2:00 A.M., American broadcasters in London lined up for the microphone at the BBC's underground studio. The German invasion had been under way for forty-eight hours, unimpeded, appeals for withdrawal unanswered, no action by the Allies. One by one the correspondents predicted another sellout. Murrow was on last. "Some people have told me tonight that they believe a big deal is being cooked up which will make Munich and the betrayal of Czechoslovakia look like a pleasant tea party. I find it difficult to accept this thesis. . . . To Britishers, their pledged word is important, and I should be very much surprised to see any government which betrayed that pledge remain long in office." The country, he contended, was in no mood for a temporary solution:

> And that's why I believe that Britain in the end of the day will stand where she is pledged to stand, by the side of Poland. . . .
>
> The British during the past few weeks have done everything possible in order to set the record straight. When historians come to sum up the last six months of Europe's existence, when they come to write the story of the origins of the war, or of the collapse of democracy, they will have many documents from which to work. . . .
>
> Don't think for a moment that these people here aren't conscious of what's going on. . . . They're a patient people, and they're perhaps prepared to wait until tomorrow for the definite word. . . . If it is peace, with the price being paid by Poland, this government will have to deal with the passion it has aroused during the past few weeks. . . .

The final decision, he felt, based on the evidence so far, would be to fight. "But those of us who've watched this story unroll at close range have lost the ability to be surprised."

A copy of the text was filed with Cecilia Reeves, rushed into duty that night as censor. "Am I right on this?" he asked as he gave her the script. "I've got to be right!"

He was grim as death about it. Earlier, there had been a long-distance confrontation with H. V. Kaltenborn in New York, still predicting a sellout, analyzing the incoming reports as usual, and a Murrow report in particular, as confirmation that another Munich was imminent. To Murrow, no fan of the procedure to begin with, it was not only useless but worse, a twisting of his words. Said a colleague: "Ed was furious."

Within an hour he was back on the air, with comments from the British press. First, though, he had something to say: "I should like to recapitulate a few things said from here on an earlier broadcast. . . ."

Friends in the newsroom recognized the controlled anger in the disembodied voice coming out of the loudspeaker, going over the earlier report, step by step, like a laundry list: *First . . . second . . . third . . . I also said . . . I reported those things. . . .*

Hans Kaltenborn in Studio 9 listened, speechless, as the voice continued:

Greensboro, 1908 or 1909. (Courtesy of Janet Murrow)

Blanchard, Washington. Miss Crawshaw's class; front row, second from right: Egbert Murrow. (Courtesy of the Murrow Collection)

The Murrow brothers,
left to right: Ed, Lacey,
Dewey. (Courtesy of
Janet Murrow)

Washington State College, sophomore
year. (Courtesy of the Murrow
Collection)

In front of the Kappa
Sigma House, WSC.

Janet Huntington
Brewster.

NSFA officers: with Lewis F. Powell (right). (Courtesy of Janet Murrow)

Edward and Janet Murrow, 1937. (Courtesy of Janet Murrow.
Photo by Mme. Yevonde, London)

At home in London: 84 Hallam Street. (Courtesy of Janet Murrow)

1938, after Munich, left to right: Murrow, Paul White, Maurice Hindus, Robert Trout, H. V. Kaltenborn. (Courtesy of CBS)

At the end of that broadcast you were told that my remarks might have created the impression that appeasement was in the air. . . .

I have said my say concerning appeasement. . . . I have also given you such facts as are available in London tonight. I have an old-fashioned belief that Americans like to make up their own minds on the basis of all available information. The conclusions you draw are your own affair. I have no desire to influence them and shall leave such efforts to those who have more confidence in their own judgment than I have in mine.

Kaltenborn sat in silence. Trout, sitting by his side, watched as a patch of red formed on the older man's neck, creeping slowly upward past the fringe of white hair until the bald head and face turned slowly, apoplectically scarlet. Murrow's voice was the only sound in the room: "I suggest that it is hardly time to become impatient over the delayed outbreak of a war which may spread over the world like a dark stain of death and destruction. We shall have the answer soon enough. . . ."

At six minutes past noon that Sunday, the deadline having run out on a final appeal for withdrawal, the Prime Minister announced that Great Britain was now in a state of war with Germany. France followed six hours later. The Polish invasion had become a European war.

At first American radio coverage was truncated. The sinking that first day of the British liner *Athenia*, with a loss of British and American lives, had stirred up memories of the *Lusitania* and a storm back home over American neutrality. For a time NBC and Mutual stopped all broadcasts from the Continent; CBS plowed on alone. Shirer, listening to Murrow over a monitor in Berlin—they could no longer speak over the telephone—thought Ed sounded dead tired, then realized he himself probably sounded the same.

In the meantime, London awaited the bombs. In the travel agency windows near Broadcasting House, the tour posters had come down, the offices themselves mobbed by American vacationers trying frantically to book passage west, Ed and Janet Murrow's apartment jammed with friends from the States, anxious about getting home.

Others were staying—including Marvin Breckinridge, in from Lucerne, who, after one glance at the families lined up six deep before the American Express office, opted for a job with the Black Star Agency in Fleet Street. Murrow knew her credits as a journalist and documentarian whose work had taken her into the hills of Kentucky, filming the Frontier Nursing Service, riding the lonely mountain trails, equipment in saddlebags, with the nurses and midwives who cared for the women of Appalachia. The result had been the thirty-five-millimeter classic, *The Forgotten Frontier*.

And what, Murrow asked over dinner, was she doing now? Well, there was this piece coming up on evacuated slum kids in country villages, how they were adjusting, that sort of thing. How about a broadcast about it?

Fine. It came off, with just one word of advice: "Keep your voice low."

Soon afterward he was on the phone. Could she do a piece on the women now running the centers coordinating London fire-fighting, as the men were mobilized, find out how war had changed these women's lives, how they felt about their work?

She obliged, and soon thereafter joined the payroll as the first woman staff correspondent for CBS and therefore a rarity in radio news, generally a closed shop to female journalists on anything other than a one-shot or stringer basis. The broadcast industry alleged a public prejudice against the female voice—particularly in so important a function—but Murrow kept up the encouragement: Her stuff was good; it was "first rate—I am pleased, New York is pleased, and so far as I know the listeners are pleased. If they aren't, to hell with them!"[3]

She would always remember, in later years, his brief instructions. CBS laid down no set policy for its reporters, he said. Give the *human* side of the news; be neutral; be honest; talk like yourself.

Slowly the picture was filling out for European coverage—Shirer now holding down Berlin; Sevareid and Grandin in Paris; Breckinridge in Amsterdam and Paris but more often the roving reporter. For Rome, he hired a new man, Cecil Brown, and as London backup, LeSueur who'd been waiting for the opening, marking time on the slender proceeds of his return ticket home.

In the meantime, the British capital, awaiting the bombs, had become a wartime city: sandbagged buildings; barrage balloons adding strange shapes to the skyline; the nightly blackout, with the "All's well" of an air-raid warden booming through the dark streets like a watchman in the time of Dickens—all described in nightly broadcasts, painted in clear, concise word pictures for American listeners. Security measures were beginning to make inroads on a rigidly stratified society, and Murrow, watching it happen, couldn't conceal a certain relish as he wove the image, for his audiences, of "the man with a fine car, good clothes, and perhaps an unearned income" caught between a waitress and a laborer as sirens at midday sent him scurrying to shelter underground.

But no bombs fell on London that winter, or on Paris. In the east Poland, attacked from two sides (September 17 the Soviets had invaded), was being crushed like an egg, unaided by its allies. In the west Allied planes dropped leaflets on the Rhineland. Despite a British naval blockade, despite isolated incidents, the byword seemed to be that of reported German broadcasts to the French—i.e., "We won't if you won't"—an uneasy lull setting in between the armies, the Allies in effect permitting Hitler a one-front war until it was their turn.

Reporters knew it couldn't last. In R. T. Clark's office off the BBC newsroom, Murrow watched the graying veteran, a lifelong student of Clausewitz and longtime opponent of the Nazis, project the invasion of

France, map in hand: Forget the Maginot Line, a white elephant, out-dated. Bypass and encirclement, that was how they'd do it, just as in World War I: "Yes, brothers, I'd bet on the Schlieffen plan all over again. They'll sidetrack those bloody forts, they'll come in across *here*, and they'll come down *there*."

Meanwhile, on a smaller scale, Murrow found himself fighting a different kind of war, one with long-range implications for the broadcasting of overseas news.

The onset of hostilities had brought the imposition of military censorship, the total freedom of prewar days ended as the rules changed abruptly: no more ad-libbing before the microphone, no more ad-libbed on-the-spot reports, travel itself restricted. They wanted prepared scripts only, read off in the studio, and checked beforehand by the liaison people of the BBC, acting now as censors but also smoothing the increasingly difficult path for American broadcasters through a growing web of wartime restrictions. Restrictions applying as much to Ed Murrow as to anyone else.

Personally he was admired and respected, his access to sources at all levels already something of a legend among colleagues; American reporters, suspect in appeasement days, were now being sought out as the ones who had been right, who moreover had the ear of the American public. But as bureau chief for a relatively new and misunderstood news medium, he found every step becoming a battle, up against the tradition-bound thinking of a military bureaucracy that now held the keys to coverage—a bureaucracy accustomed to dealing with the print press but with no understanding, seemingly, of radio.

In late September, 1939, place had been made for only two broadcast correspondents among the fifty accompanying the British Expeditionary Force (BEF) to France, sending a shock of dismay through the BBC Liaison Unit and its American charges: Why only two slots when there were three networks? The authorities remained adamant: two allocations, take it or leave it. Murrow, Bate, and Steele—now increasingly pooling their efforts—finally worked out a scheme for dividing two by three, settling the matter among themselves after their respective home offices had come up in a deadlock.

Yet they remained humble petitioners, the Liaison Unit pleading constantly on their behalf with the service ministries—the RAF was the most open; the venerable Navy, controlling censorship, the most rigid—spelling out the very basics. There were three American networks. They broadcast news to America. Every night. To some 50 million people. Broadcasting *counted* in this war; American opinion counted. But circuits to America were expensive, had to be kept open, fed with material, and to do this, they needed stories, stories they could check out; they needed access, mobility. All the assumptions later taken for granted had to be explained to a class-ridden service distrustful of journalists in general and

Americans in particular, which regarded radio as a toy and its reporters as something less than second-class citizens.

Adding to the broadcasters' woes was the time-honored insistence on protocol, a clinging to the established procedures of formal applications to the proper people in the proper time and place. Some officials positively exuded kindness: Delighted to help the Americans, now here's the chap they should *really* see, they'd have to write first, of course, with outstanding matters possibly settled by appointment over lunch or dinner at the club.

In the meantime, the Germans, highly conscious of the power of the medium, were flying radio correspondents to the Polish front, with a great show, if not always the substance, of providing technical facilities, despite a censorship far exceeding that of the English. In London, S. J. de Lotbinière, tireless head of the American Liaison Unit, in contact with Murrow on one hand, beating down ministry doors on the other—"the moment has come when radio reporters have got to take their place alongside newspaper correspondents"—found himself talking to deaf ears, official replies cool and distant.[4]

Instead, new rulings from the Ministry of Information (MOI) were decreeing long, elaborate applications on a case-by-case basis, with appropriate copies to appropriate quarters plus appropriate covering letter indicating applicant was fully conversant with the rules—practically guaranteeing that a story would be old news by the time the networks got to it if, in fact, they got to it at all.

"The worst has happened," De Lotbinière told Murrow as the rulings were handed down. "I suppose the only thing is to follow it up. . . . I am persisting, and no doubt you are too. . . ."[5]

He was indeed persisting, their bellwether in the battle for access; where Murrow got in, they figured, the other Americans would follow.

But progress was proving maddeningly slow, decisions inching through joint military committees—four weeks before Murrow could join a mass "home front" tour visiting aviation training centers; six weeks before completion of the paper work enabling his man Bill Henry to follow the British Expeditionary Force to France.

On the surface, the CBS London reports continued as always: the status of the war; the political situation; the haunting essays on London in the blackout, the comforting glow of a cigarette in the dark. But so did the underlying skirmishes with the ministries, heightened now by an overriding sense of time running out. De Lotbinière wrote of trying to arrange a meeting with an MOI official, trying to circumvent the stringent rulings: "He very kindly said he would see me tomorrow afternoon at 5 o'clock. Alas for democracy!"[6]

October 14, the country was shaken as the battleship *Royal Oak* went down in a daring German submarine attack on the naval base at Scapa Flow in the Orkneys, torpedoed at anchor, nearly 800 aboard. With conflicting reports coming in, Murrow, Bate, and Steele declared themselves ready to go at a moment's notice. The Admiralty vetoed the idea.

At one point, in desperation, they appealed to Winston Churchill, back in government as First Lord of the Admiralty, requesting his personal intervention to help open doors for Murrow, Bate, and Steele—"Three intelligent and eager men whose job it is to broadcast daily to the United States. . . ."[7]

A chilly reply came back from a private secretary to the effect that "certain naval facilities" had already been arranged and suggesting pointedly that proper channels be used in the future.

In the meantime, Poland had fallen, partitioned between Germany and the Soviet Union. In November the Soviets invaded Finland. Ships were going down in the North Atlantic. The BEF sat in northern France, the French Army in its bunkers on the Maginot Line, the western front in a state of stasis, with rumors flying about what might happen in the spring.

In the nervous lull, reporters pursued whatever stories could be cleared, though Murrow, as Columbia's representative, always seemed to want more. Along with military sites, he wanted to see the internment camps where refugees from Hitler's Germany had been rounded up as enemy aliens ("They have been living just one jump ahead of the concentration camp and now . . .");[8] he wanted to broadcast from an air-raid shelter, go out with the mine sweepers. Through the New York office, he helped work out a hookup with Shirer in Berlin, the two correspondents in a broadcast discussion linking the two belligerent capitals via New York City. "The things Ed would dream up," said Shirer in later years, "that never occurred to me!"

He was, in fact, putting in time on all fronts, even with the dearth of hard news—deploying his reporters, dealing on policy matters with New York on one hand and the Information Ministry on the other; all the while making his own daily reporter's rounds of ministries and embassies, checking with private sources, sitting in on key parliamentary debates, and, of course, writing and delivering the newscasts, which in times of crisis were demanded up to four or five times a night.

He also kept a discreet watch on the performance of his European staff. Breckinridge, broadcasting from Holland one night, had felt a sudden tickle rising in her throat. Somehow she managed to suppress it, first to the end of the sentence, then to the end of the broadcast. Next day Murrow was on the telephone from London: "If you feel like coughing, go ahead and cough!"

The amazing thing in retrospect would be his continuing ability, given the work load, to deliver the tight, meticulous, handcrafted reports that not only informed about the day-to-day news but depicted a world in transition, the reporter as sociologist. Neville Chamberlain was not only wartime Prime Minister but a man "fighting the war on two fronts—against Hitlerism and against changes in the social and economic structure of Britain." The home front was no piece of wartime exotica but a real place, where wages were being outstripped by the cost of living, where Labour MPs in Parliament questioned government policies toward India, where businesses were folding, school systems disrupted.

He spoke in the first person singular, the prevailing custom at the time in radio, an individual talking to other individuals, crafting audio vignettes: "The council chambers of Fulham Town Hall look like a courtroom. Five elderly men sit behind a bench. . . . Down on the floor all alone looking up at the five men is a boy. He is twenty years and seven months old. He is small and wiry, with sandy hair, an Irishman if there ever was one."

In a few sentences, he wove a small drama. Why didn't the witness want to fight? Because it was murder; war settled nothing; four cousins had been killed fighting in the Irish troubles, and nothing was settled.

"The boy is given plenty of time. . . . There is a whispered conversation on the bench, and the judge tells him that he will be registered as a conscientious objecter and need not go to war. And up in the gallery an elderly lady leans back in her chair and relaxes. . . ."

In a December dawn, aboard an ancient trawler, he talked with a crew out on mine-sweeping patrol:

> The men in those ships are small. They are of all ages and voices. Some of them come from the rocky coast of Scotland, others from the quiet, dark waters on the coast of Essex. . . . All of them were fishermen in peacetime and their job now is to fish for mines. . . .
> It was rough and wet out there today, and I wasn't particularly sorry when we saw the white cliffs of England, looking like a dirty white sheet hanging from the edge of a green roof, just before dusk. . . . Those fishermen sailors do it every day and many nights. All for about sixty cents a day, plus family allowance. . . .

Afterward the skipper brewed tea—"said he hoped to tie up his boat somewhere north of the border again. The deck hand looked foward to taking care of [his] cabbage patch. . . . I wonder how many men on both sides of this war, both on the sea and beneath it, would rather be doing something else."

Paul White, listening in New York, was fervently wishing that Murrow, too, had been doing something else, not much relishing the thought of their European Director, who couldn't swim, fishing for mines in the English Channel.

January 1940, the Murrows left England for neutral territory—Ed to Holland and a meeting with Bill Shirer, in from Berlin, Janet to Switzerland to stay with Shirer's wife, Tess, look up old friends, and sound out local attitudes on the war.

On the seventeenth, Ed Murrow arrived in Amsterdam, ostensibly for a joint broadcast with Shirer. In actuality it was a holiday, both men enjoying good food, bright lights, no air-raid alerts—all the benefits of neutrality. If the Netherlands kept strictly out of it, their Dutch contacts told them, Hitler would have no excuse to march in. The law was accordingly laid down regarding anything said over the airwaves, and the two guest commentators, broadcasting from the Dutch station at Hilversum, were to find themselves carefully censored.

Meanwhile, they lived it up, buoyant with a sudden release of tension; "a wonderful time," Shirer recalled. They shopped in the well-stocked stores and skated the canals with Marvin Breckinridge, who had made the Amsterdam arrangements.

To Marvin, it was like watching the reunion of two old college friends, the closeness obvious. "They trusted each other," she remembered.

The broadcast, though censored, went off without a hitch, sending all three—Murrow, Shirer, and Breckinridge—back to Amsterdam on a wave of elation at one in the morning. "It was a beautiful night," she recalled later, "it was snowing and the lights were on and we had chocolate and we had coffee; for me, it wasn't so surprising, but for both of *them*, the lights and everything. . . ."

Under a street lamp they stopped and had a snowball fight. Shirer, no match for the star pitcher of Edison High, lost his hat and his glasses. Finally, the three of them limped back to the Carlton, their laughter trailing through the quiet streets.

The last morning, it was back to reality. Shirer wanted a fortnight's leave to visit his wife and daughter in Switzerland. Murrow said fine, asked Breckinridge to cover in Berlin, and caught the 1:32 to Paris for a small broadcaster's conference, a brief meeting with Sevareid and Grandin, and, finally, a return to London.

Or so he thought.

The Paris conference was full of familiar faces, among them Fred Bate, the BBC correspondent Richard Dimbleby, Cecilia Reeves. It was bitter cold. At Le Bourget a fresh fall of snow delayed the Paris-London flights. The radio people, trying to return, hung around the airport, shivering in the damp chill, then gave up and returned to their hotels. Reeves would remember feeling "sick as a dog" and listening to Murrow coughing heavily as they sloshed together through the snow.

He was still in Paris the next day, the beginning of a week of growing illness, hoping every day to get home; but the weather had settled in for the duration, no planes flying. He took to his bed at the hotel, with visitors trooping in and out of his room, making rest impossible. Someone had gotten hold of a doctor—an ineffectual hack who seemed content to look on in a state of utter perplexity.

Several times he had dragged himself to Le Bourget, hoping to get to London. The airport still closed down, he taxied back to the Ritz and back to bed, somewhat the worse for the excursion.

There was concern in the Paris bureau: Shouldn't someone contact his wife? And where?

"I'm worried," Sevareid told Reeves,[9] and reserved a room—just in case—at the American Hospital at Neuilly, on the outskirts of Paris.

Janet Murrow thought she'd stay a few more days in Switzerland. It had been such a chore, traveling through wartime red tape to get there, and the sunshine was so beautiful. Oddly, though, she hadn't heard from Ed despite numerous cables sent to London. She cabled again, saying she was staying on a bit.

Answers suddenly arrived—from Campbell in London, from the Sevareids: Ed was at the American Hospital in Paris. Nothing to worry about. Just a little flu, a little fatigue; he'd be fine.

It didn't sound too bad at first, and obviously he was in good hands. She made arrangements to get out of neutral Switzerland, her concern growing in proportion to the continuing reassurances from London that he'd be fine, just fine.

In Paris, she arrived at a scene that filled her with anger. He wasn't fine at all, was, in fact, "frightfully ill," she later recalled; the diagnosis, a severe strep infection and what seemed like pneumonia. Why hadn't they told her? Asking, she pieced the story together, ending in the day Fred Bate had stopped in at Murrow's room, taken one look, and rushed Ed to the American Hospital before he blacked out. As an old *Parisien* he knew the doctors. "Thank goodness Fred was there," said Janet Murrow later.

Murrow's white corpuscle count was alarmingly down. They had a drug to knock out the germ, they told her, but it would probably lower the corpuscle count even further; it was all a question of what happened first and how long it would take to happen.

The drug was administered. Ed began burning up, his resistance almost nonexistent. Then gradually the drug took hold, the tide turned, and he grew cooler to the touch. All he needed now was rest, the doctors said.

The arguments started up. She suggested going to the mountains; he didn't want hotel food. No problem, they'd take a chalet, she'd cook. He didn't want a long train trip; he wanted to go back to London. *And go right back to work*, she thought, and made a mental note to have the doctor throw a good scare into him. Otherwise, how could he hope to make it through the spring?

The attending physician was, in fact, already urging a long stay in the south of France. Impossible, said Murrow; he had to get back to London. "In that case," replied the physician, "I refuse to take responsibility."

But Murrow, in that way of his, was already trivializing the whole thing—real men didn't get sick—joking with friends about how he had awakened after three days in a barred and padded room, the only one available ("And when I came to . . ."), just another anecdote to share with the boys.

Janet had been staying with the Sevareids on the Rue Casimir-Perrier, waiting for him to recover sufficiently to travel. Together, much against her wishes, they returned to the fogs and coal smoke of midwinter London.

Back at 14 Langham Place, he tried to get back into the routine and couldn't. The Russians had broken the Finnish defense line. He got himself to the studio, broadcast, and almost had a relapse. She argued, raged inwardly, furious in her concern and frustration: "He is the most *difficult* patient. He calls me stubborn. He's not only stubborn, but stupid—when it comes to his health. He is behaving now though. . . ."

But he had to give in—if not to the doctor, his wife, or his friends, then to a pair of unsteady lungs that wouldn't be dictated to. The Murrows headed for the Devonshire coast, an enforced convalescence, and a Victorian monstrosity of a hotel, where they read or walked by the sea, and where the over-sixty clientele avoided the strange young couple who spoke American and didn't dress for dinner. Just as well, she wrote home, "because Ed just isn't up to having to be nice to people."

Just before leaving, however, they had had a lesson about business as usual when, coming home one night, they found the apartment burglarized. The door showed no sign of forced entry, nor did the lock; Janet suspected a woman briefly in her employ.

It was a professional job, no vandalism. His cuff-link box was gone; so was her jewel case with the two good pieces he had given her, both insured. But gone, too, she wrote her mother, were the childhood mementos that could not be replaced: "the little chain bracelet Aunt Jane gave me . . . and the moonstone ring . . . plus other things less valuable and endeared to my heart. . . ." Gone, too, was the feeling of security she had had, lost in thoughts of strangers padding about among their few possessions.

In March, Murrow came back to the job, amid indications of change approaching with the coming of spring: Finland surrendered, the Atlantic war stepped up, while from off the coast of Norway came signs that the quiet in the West was nearly over.

At the same time his own problems and those of radio were escalating, the cause, a deadening compound of military censorship and bureaucratic indifference—indifference that was knocking askew all efforts at balanced programming.

In early January Murrow, prior to his trip, had arranged a double feature: Shirer in Berlin interviewing Ernest Udet, the German air chief, former ace pilot and architect of the Luftwaffe, and himself in London with Udet's British counterpart. The British Air Ministry first agreed, then found the broadcast date "inconvenient." Udet, who had once barnstormed in the U.S., went on alone and charmed his audience, the next day's morning papers in America headlining the interview.

In early March on NBC, Admiral Erich Raeder, commander in chief of the German fleet, speaking from Berlin, explained smoothly why *all* shipping—neutral as well as Allied, unarmed as well as armed—had to be attacked. In London attempts to arrange a broadcast reply—Murrow, Bate, and Steele immediately offered air time, indeed the whole of their networks, for a statement—met with stonewalling from the Admiralty. After five days one official, breaking with the rest, agreed to speak, then canceled out because of illness. Glumly the three Americans and their BBC allies agreed it was too late to do anything further.[10]

In the north the German supply ship *Altmark*, carrying imprisoned British seamen illegally through neutral Norwegian waters, had been captured there by a British destroyer—likewise illegally—amid escalating accusations on both sides of neutrality violated. Breckinridge, rushed to the scene for CBS, got an interview from the German captain, silence from the English.

Britons aware of what was going on, were nearly frantic. The MOI, trying to mediate for the Americans, understood but lacked the power. At Broadcasting House a red-headed Englishman named Roger Eckersley, a friend of Murrow's, who had inherited from de Lotbinière the thankless job of running interference, complained of "knocking at the Ministerial doors, begging for facilities, whereas . . . the reverse should be the case."[11] It was, in fact, the Englishman Eckersley who would be among the unsung heroes of the upcoming communications battle—whose efforts, in concert with those of Murrow, would open the way to the landmark broadcasts that were to swing American public opinion toward Britain.

That spring, however, he was making no more headway than his predecessor, despite constant urging that the Germans had been quick to seize the opportunity, that "the powers that be . . . have [not] sufficiently realized what part broadcasting can play in a war and that we cannot afford to rest on old tradition. . . .

"My Americans are constantly rubbing this in to me and they get disheartened—pro-Ally as they are—when they fail to secure what they know is most wanted."[12]

But the old tradition continued even when that April, German land, sea, and air forces invaded Denmark and Norway, ending arguments over neutrality, raising the specter of enemy bases facing the British coast, and propelling British troops north to aid the Norwegians.

In Parliament, Murrow watched from the gallery as tempers flew and galvanized MPs asked how the Germans could effect a landing when Britain claimed control of the sea. "The debate was brief. . . . But there were many indications that Parliament expects prompt and decisive action. If it should be said of Norway, as it was of Finland, that Allied help was too little and too late, there would be changes in the political leadership of this country."

The future, it seemed to him, rested in "the rather pudgy hands of Winston Churchill," but so far the First Sea Lord showed no sign of withdrawing from the cabinet.

As the debate heightened, Murrow and the others had asked for a microphone to be installed on the premises. Not, of course, in the Chamber itself—that was out of the question—but somewhere, anywhere in the building, an unused room perhaps, permitting a rapid relay to America of the fast-moving events that might well determine the outcome of the war.

After a week's delay, the Speaker refused permission: If the Commons did it for the Americans, they'd have to do it for "other representatives of the Foreign Press." Besides, they hadn't the space.[13]

In the meantime, an anxious country, eager for word of the fighting, was being flooded by contradictory reports, some of doubtful origin, many unduly optimistic, threatening to undermine the credibility of the British news media. The press and radio were "helpless," Murrow reported over CBS. "They begged the Admiralty and the War Office for confirmation or denial and got neither. Departmental and personal jealousies have not been entirely eliminated. There is no indication that the Ministry of Information has established any effective degree of control over the issuance of news or denials. The fighting services still have the whip hand."[14]

Strong language, but he was speaking from personal experience, his own position as newsman having taken a decided turn for the worse.

The growing signs of resentment had been unmistakable that spring, even before Norway: resentment at an America now permitted to sell armaments—the Neutrality Law had been relaxed to cash-and-carry only—expanding its plants, yet comfortably out of the fighting. Murrow reported rising bitterness over American advice from the sidelines, over the defeatist statements of American Ambassador Joseph Kennedy—father of the future President, supporter of Munich and the pro-appeasement circles that regarded Hitler as a bulwark against Bolshevism. Pointed comments were making the rounds in London—"Protect us from a German victory and an American peace"—indicating coming friction between London and Washington, a trend Murrow called "impossible to ignore . . . when the signposts are so clearly marked."

Just how clearly, he was to discover for himself, as the first casualties began returning from the Norwegian front. April 12, survivors of the British destroyer *Gurkha*, sunk in the bitter fighting off Narvik, were set ashore in Scotland, the first eyewitnesses to a fierce, confused, and underreported war. The Admiralty, asked for on-the-spot facilities, clamped the lid down: no interviews.

Next day Ed Murrow, visibly annoyed, stalked into the BBC studio, brandishing a banner-headlined *Daily Mail*, featuring a full account—interviews, details, the works. *Why* hadn't they been allowed at the *Gurkha* story?

The Admiralty response was glacial: No one had authorized it, the press had done it on the sly. In any case, authorization for future broadcast interviews could accommodate only the BBC, in which case the Americans would be "unfortunate." Besides—

> As very little impression seemed to be made on the United States by the invasion of Denmark and Norway . . . a survivor from the *Gurkha* was just a waste of time, and in fact the granting of any facilities to the Americans was just a waste of time.[15]

It was a shocker. If that was going to be the Admiralty's attitude, a BBC official noted, then it was indeed unfortunate. The message seemed clear: "that unless and until the Americans join us in the war, so long shall they not have facilities!"[16]

Elsewhere, the prestigious *New Statesman* complained that the U.S. expected Britain to run a box-office war for the benefit of American correspondents. For Murrow, it all seemed indicative of a change of atmosphere, of a country grown grimmer, tougher, decidedly less tolerant as disaster followed disaster.

The news on his side of the Atlantic had grown "completely prostituted," he wrote a friend in the States. "I haven't got the guts to quit and go home, and I haven't even the energy to argue with myself about it any more. I have come to realize in the last few months just how few friends I have, and how little it matters to me what happens to most of them. I hope that life goes well for you in America, and that your nostrils are not assailed by the odour of death and decay that permeates the atmosphere over here. . . ."[17]

Norway fell the first week of May, most Allied troops evacuated, King Haakon fled to England. Isolated pockets of resistance would hold out until late May, when most of Western Europe would be fighting for its life. "Reports reaching London from Switzerland," Murrow told his audience, "say that the Swiss are unable to understand why the Allies failed to anticipate lightning retaliation by the Germans. . . . [They] seem to feel that the Allies will continue to be caught unawares by swift German moves until they come to appreciate and anticipate the dynamic character of national socialism."

Jefferson Patterson of the American Embassy in Berlin was driving a bright red Ford westward on his way to Amsterdam and Miss Breckinridge. They'd become engaged following her Berlin assignment, she calling Murrow in London with the news, holding the receiver as an exuberant "Wheeee!" came exploding out of the earpiece.

At the German-Dutch border, he was stopped by a swastikaed official: Yes, he could continue across, though not in the car. Arms were piled up by the highway; all road signs had been taken down—a dead giveaway.

In Amsterdam it was a beautiful day. The young people took a taxi to the tulip fields, the Dutch all around them on bicycles, enjoying the Sunday and the fine May weather. Patterson, fresh from Germany, looked around at the smiling faces, the picnic baskets, then turned, perplexed, to his fiancée: "I can't understand why they're all having such a good *time*. This is when the invasion is supposed to be."[18]

At 5:00 A.M. the following Friday, German armored columns rolled across the border where, five days before, Jeff Patterson had parked his Ford. It was May 10, 1940, the invasion of the West, the blitzkrieg, complete with paratroops and dive bombers striking deep into the Low Countries, the classic invasion route into northern France.

Britain, caught midway through a cabinet crisis, was in a state of shock. Press offices in London, Paris, and New York were inundated by calls, telegrams, and agency tapes, broadcasters back to emergency schedules. Murrow, roused from sleep in the early morning, told his audience numbly that history had been made too fast: "First in the early hours this morning came the news of the British unopposed landing in Iceland. Then the news of Hitler's triple invasion came rolling into London, climaxed by the German air bombing of five nations. British mechanized troops rattled across the frontier into Belgium. . . ."

At Westminster, he watched the MPs turn on Neville Chamberlain and, in a broadcast few would forget who heard it that day, later brought the scene to life—the Prime Minister, white with anger, defying the jeering opposition; old David Lloyd George rising to throw down the challenge; the cry "L. G. is up!" running through the lounges, absent members rushing back into the House through both doors—"as though the little gray-haired, wide-shouldered Welshman were a magnet to draw them back to their seats"; Lloyd George, on his feet, charging that Hitler had beaten the Prime Minister in peace and in war, that the government failed to realize the danger, that Britain's promises to neutrals were now considered worthless:

> He traced the history of Czechoslovakia, Spain, Poland and Norway, and he whipped off his gold-rimmed spectacles to pour scorn and condemnation upon the government front bench facing him ten feet away. . . . He ended by saying that the Prime Minister could make his greatest contribution to victory by handing in his seals of office. In other words, resigning.

Winston Churchill, by unanimous vote, was the new Prime Minister. "The historians will have to devote more than a footnote to this remarkable man. . . ."

> He enters office with the tremendous advantage of being the man who was right. He also has the advantage of being the best broadcaster in this country. Mr. Churchill can inspire confidence. And he can preach

a doctrine of hate that is acceptable to the majority of this country. That may be useful during these next few months. . . ."

In the meantime, the British watched in disbelief as the blitzkrieg sliced through northern Europe, a new kind of mechanized warfare spreading a corridor of destruction as flamethrowers cremated garrisons, villages were leveled in minutes, and Stukas blasted the crowded center of Rotterdam midway through surrender talks.

Holland had fallen in four days; Belgium, in eighteen. By May 20 the Germans had reached the Somme, trapping Allied forces in the north and forcing them back toward the Channel. Six days later at Dunkirk, despite steady pounding from the Luftwaffe, the British began evacuating what was left of their forces.

With the war at Britain's doorstep, Janet Murrow begged her parents repeatedly not to be frantic, to understand why she was not coming home. True, Americans were being advised to leave: Ed had left the decision up to her. But no one here was panicking, and the truth was, Ed had never fully recovered from the attack—she hadn't told his family he wasn't very strong yet—and without her policing he'd be up until all hours and forget to eat. Even now she wondered how he could survive another English winter.

They'd come through it, she assured them. And if they didn't—well, it couldn't be helped: "We decided a year ago that the only thing to do was to live dangerously and not run away from things. There's no way to get home now that doesn't cost a fortune and I couldn't leave Ed over here. He's really not well and I worry more about his not being able to stand the strain of the work—rather than being hit by a splinter."

With the collapse of the front, the correspondents came stumbling back to London amid a flood tide of refugees and fleeing armies, reduced to finding their own way out. LeSueur had made it over on a troopship, but Grandin, bringing his Rumanian wife to a U.S.-bound ship, had hopped aboard on being told she wouldn't be admitted without him. In a chaotic France, Sevareid was still broadcasting and trying to get his wife and newborn twin sons home as the French government prepared to abandon Paris.

At 1:00 A.M. at Hallam Street, Janet Murrow woke to the sound of two sets of footsteps at the front door and her husband's voice: "What would you like to eat? Some scrambled eggs?" In the corridor she saw Dick Marriott, mud-splattered, dark circles under his eyes, with a story of sleeping at roadsides, part of the crawling mass of humanity fleeing Paris, before talking his way aboard a British army transport plane.

In the Commons, unlimited emergency powers had been voted to Churchill's new Conservative-Labour coalition. A quiet revolution, Murrow called it on radio, led by Labour leader Clement Attlee: control over all persons, all property, an excess profits tax of 100 percent, industry to be run for the public and not for private profit.

"During most of the postwar period this country has been ruled by . . . an oligarchy which has believed in its right to rule. Whether they ruled well or ill is not at this moment important. . . . Had the old government recognized the lateness of the hour, these new powers might not have been necessary. But this country is now united and it is important that a lifelong Socialist introduced that revolutionary bill today."

Gun shops were being raided by Scotland Yard, the national mood grown bitter, "not only against the Germans, but against the men of this country who failed to realize the nature of the German threat, who failed to prepare to meet it. . . ." On the south coast, Murrow watched crowds of men and women, once friendly toward incoming German POWs, greet captured airmen with shouts of "Shoot the murdering swine!"

The so-called Miracle of Dunkirk in early June raised spirits momentarily with its epic feat of 300,000 troops removed from the beach, under enemy fire, by the Navy and a civilian flotilla of anything that would float—an incredible rescue operation, though pointing up the hard fact, Murrow told listeners, that the British Expeditionary Force had been undertrained, underequipped, and that responsibility rested "squarely" upon the old leadership: "They purchased a few months of normal living and normal working, while assuring the country that . . . time was on the side of the Allies. But they bought that quiet and complacency in an expensive market."

The afternoon of June 4, he watched Churchill in the Commons, praising the operation and warning that wars were not won by evacuations. "Nearly a thousand guns had been lost. All transport and all armored vehicles with the northern armies. . . . A colossal military disaster had occurred, and another blow must be expected almost immediately."

Then, like others packed into the galleries and benches of the airless neo-Gothic chamber, he had caught the sense of something else—an audience riveted, and a possible turning point in history:

> Mr. Churchill believed that these islands could be successfully defended, could ride out the storm of war and outlive the menace of tyranny. If necessary, for years. If necessary, alone.
>
> There was a prophetic quality about that speech. "We shall go on to the end," he said. "We shall fight in France; we shall fight on the seas and oceans; we shall fight on the beaches, in the fields, in the streets and in the hills; we shall never surrender. . . ."

Across the Channel, the French cabinet was fleeing toward Bordeaux; Sevareid and Edmund Taylor, a newspaper colleague commandeered for CBS, joined the stream of refugees following the government, broadcasting wherever they could on the collapse of France. June 14, German troops entered Paris, a shocked British and American public staring, incredulous, at the press photos of the Wehrmacht goose-stepping down the Champs-Élysées. France, surrendering, was out of the war. Italy, which had attacked from the south, was in it. From across twenty miles of water, Britain faced a hostile continent.

For Americans in England now, if ever, was the time to get the story to the public. But for those in radio, old attitudes and new orders were threatening to make it impossible. As Britain stood alone, united and determined, Murrow and his colleagues suddenly found themselves class- ified as aliens in a pre-invasion atmosphere, fighting impending restric- tions on their freedom to report, in a country that was fighting for its life.

VII

Trial by Fire

1.

The problems had begun in late May 1940, as the Germans overran the old port of Antwerp, controlling strategic waterways to the Channel, described by Napoleon more than a century before as a gun aimed at England's heart.

That same day in London, Frank Darvall, second-in-command at the American Division, MOI, had bad news for Ed Murrow and Roger Eckersley: The request for press passes, freeing American broadcasters from the new restrictions on aliens, had "not gone as well as we had hoped."[1] The Home Secretary had no power to grant exemptions. Sorry, but that was the situation.

Dropped into the middle of a breaking story, it was a bombshell, making the Americans' earlier troubles pale by comparison.

At the crux was their standing as neutrals and the new Prohibited Areas Order, restricting movement in those countries now shaping up as Britain's next line of defense—regions that were now broken down into a kaleidoscope of separate jurisdictions, all clearance power, all exemptions, each valid only within a given district, placed in the hands of local chief constables.

American journalists—and the same applied, of course, to broadcasters—wishing to "motor" in a restricted area, or be out of doors between 8:00 P.M. and 6:00 A.M., would have to proceed there by rail "or public conveyance" and, once there, apply for a permit. The ministry would of course intercede for known reporters with the local constable, to ensure that their applications would be "sympathetically considered."

Plainly stated, it meant endless delays and red tape while one tried to cover a story that was changing from hour to hour; that, and the at least theoretical prospect—should London itself come under attack—of becoming suddenly subject to curfew, unable to drive a car, ride a bicycle, or, for that matter, get to the BBC.

Murrow, Steele, and Bate were stunned; Eckersley was frantic. Was this a way to treat our friends?

May 21, as the French and British armies retreated toward the Channel, American Liaison in London took up the cudgel once again in a desperate appeal to the government, playing the one card likely to get a positive reaction from the controlling powers: that the broadcasts to America were, if nothing else, in the Allies' best interests.

> These relays are listened to by a mass of sentimental, friendly people eager for news, and subconsciously at all events, glad of Allied success and anxious for them to win the war. . . . Broadcasting can play an enormously important part. . . . I am convinced (and this view is largely influenced by the specialized knowledge of the American representatives in this country) that this . . . is a sure way of enlisting American sympathy and support.[2]

Even then, the wheels ground slowly, small concessions wrung piecemeal out of an entrenched bureaucracy, the perimeters of the possible widened inches at a time—never quickly enough to keep pace with the blitzkrieg, Murrow and his colleagues always one step away, it seemed, from the story they really wanted to cover.

By early June, the broadcaster was at last able to drive south on his own, visiting airfields, talking to pilots back from Dunkirk. He was outfitted finally with the various pieces of paper necessary to travel over a checkerboard of restricted counties, past checkpoints guarded by sentries with fixed bayonets. His request to set up live remotes, however, got a quick no; the military might need the lines, and besides, the Post Office, controlling the wires, "would not look kindly on it."[3] A BBC offer to put a recording unit at Murrow's disposal was turned down by New York— no recorded broadcasts allowed.

In the north and midlands, the first air raids were hitting factories and military targets. A single bomb hit the outskirts of London. In the south, Channel shipping was coming under attack.

Mid-month, the first bombs fell on Cambridge; Murrow and Bate applied for permission to see the damage. The Air Ministry and the MOI gave the trip their blessing, everything set until suddenly Eckersley remembered: The MOI passes, valid for travel, wouldn't get them past the police cordons at the site. Hours of shuttling between the two ministries brought sympathy but not the necessary passes. That was, alas, a matter for the Ministry of Home Security. They canceled the trip and went back to square one; another day shot.[4]

Two weeks later, as the RAF engaged the Luftwaffe over southeastern England, Murrow was back on the telephone: Could they view the coastal defenses—admittedly poor, thanks to Dunkirk, and, by that time, no great secret.

The routine request, however, seemed strangely difficult to satisfy. The War Office wanted something on paper; a letter was sent around immediately. Then came two days of telephoning as Murrow and Bate waited, the proper person never available, persistent queries finally turning up someone's assistant on a Friday evening, saying the trip was off.[5]

The broadcasters, on the point of going, were more depressed than angry. "[They] are very anxious to do everything in their power," Eckersley noted unhappily, "and this kind of thing throws them back and makes them feel they are checked at every turn."[6]

Darvall, at the Information Ministry, exploded:

> I cannot see why letting . . . American broadcasters, whose material will be censored . . . and who are all well known to us . . . and are wholly reliable and friendly, see something of our South Coast defences, involves more than a telephone call, followed by a post card if necessary. . . .
>
> Could the War Office be reminded of the immense importance of meeting this type of request quickly and fully? We and they ought to be begging the American radio chains to carry material about our preparedness, not resisting their efforts to do so.[7]

Somewhat testily, the War Office offered other facilities, claiming insufficient time to "accommodate Mr. Murrow and Mr. Bate"; besides, they preferred accredited war correspondents—which the broadcasters were not—in that the former could be more closely controlled. If the broadcasters insisted, the War Office suggested an interview with General H.R.L.G. Alexander; "Possibly a talk of this nature will be of greater benefit than touring defences."[8]

In the meantime, it was learned that the Germans, on direct order from Dr. Goebbels, were rushing neutral reporters to southern France in the wake of the British attack on the French fleet at Oran, to keep it from falling into German hands—survivors straggling in from North Africa, telling correspondents of being bombed and machine-gunned by the RAF. A painful episode, with Berlin the only winner.[9]

"I only wish," sighed Darvall in London, "our officials were as quick to provide broadcasting opportunities. . . .

"I shall almost be prepared to become a target for a German bomb on the day when we have succeeded in galvanizing [them] . . . . It is difficult enough nowadays to persuade them to allow correspondents to travel by bus at their own expense fifteen minutes to see something. . . ."[10]

All the more frustrating was the fact that it was not a matter of on-the-spot broadcasting but the right of access with pad and pencil, the time-honored tools of print journalism. The press itself, though beset by wartime censorship, was encountering fewer obstructions, the ministries accustomed to dealing with the print media, whether British or American, familiar by tradition with their special needs in times of crisis.

"The Royal Air Force early on understood that the ball game was up to them," one correspondent recalled. "The Army would tell you everything, of what little they had. . . . The Royal Navy just didn't want you to know how badly off they were."[11]

In the end it was not the hard-pressed armed services or the persistence alone of Murrow and Bate, the BBC, or the MOI that forced the issue, but the post-Dunkirk atmosphere itself, imparting an overriding sense of urgency, at decision-making levels, to the question of radio coverage and American opinion.

By the time the Battle of Britain was joined, Murrow and his colleagues would have police passes from Scotland Yard, guaranteeing mobility in London, plus the promise of quick clearance in the regions, from the Ministry of Home Security. Still, it was not until late summer, with the air war at its height, that procedures would be finalized, simplifying and expediting everything, even seeing to the provision, on short notice, of precious cans of gasoline.

With the exodus from Paris, a new journalistic constellation had formed that summer in London. "Never before, I think," Janet Murrow wrote home, "has there been such a concentration of journalists in such a small area. Already they're ready to tear each other's eyes out!"

One star, however, was soon stringing for CBS—the celebrated newsman, Vincent "Jimmy" Sheean, a Midwestern socialist with radical opinions and a taste for high living, who became Murrow's boon companion and debating partner in all-night shouting matches over politics, at 84 Hallam.

"They have the most terrific battles," Janet grumbled to her mother, "but there's always a deadly fascination about an argument to Ed—and believe me it's all argument when those two get together. Perhaps Jimmy doesn't need the sleep but Ed does. . . . And then Ed wonders why he's so tired all the time."

Putting her foot down finally one night, she sat up into the dawn, a silently reproving presence, until Sheean beat a retreat at 6:00 A.M. "As if the world weren't full enough of battles without their little squabbles," she fumed afterward. "I was so disgusted . . . I wanted to give them both a good hiding."

Elsewhere, the modest CBS forces had regrouped. Sevareid, escaped from France on an overloaded freighter, was now ensconced in a one-room flat across the street from the Murrows, LeSueur, just a little farther away near Marble Arch; both men stopped in twice a week for meals.

Janet Murrow had begun broadcasting, spelling the little staff with "home front" pieces.

But Breckinridge, marrying a U.S. diplomat, had had to resign; regulations, they explained to her at the Paris embassy. Janet, responding to her letters, packed and forwarded the clothes she had left behind in London. Marvin had ruffled feathers at 485 in any case, reproved by a management that thought her broadcast on the fleeing refugees "too sensational."

"Really sickening," Janet Murrow commented. "New York cries for more sensational stuff. . . . Then when you can truthfully do a heart-rending piece they get all scared because the listeners in America might get all upset!"

By late summer the front line of the war had shifted to Dover, lodestone for the news media, facing the Continent across the narrow strait: beaches empty of vacationers; the harbor clogged with wrecked shipping; shells lobbed in from German gun emplacements on the French coast that was clearly visible in the bright sunlight, just twenty-two miles away.

Murrow, driving down from London with Jimmy Sheean, or with Ed Beattie of UP and Drew Middleton of AP, usually headed for Shakespeare Cliff—gun site, gathering place, and arena for the war being waged hundreds of feet up for control of the skies, as the Luftwaffe tried to shatter England's air defenses, the prelude to invasion. Spitfires and Messerschmitts fighting it out in a windless, cloudless sky, with an audience below. Said Middleton later: "You could lie on your back, with glasses, and look up and there was the whole goddamn air battle!"

They all were regulars at the cliff, the club sharing Britain's Finest Hour and including among others, Bill Stoneman and Helen Kirkpatrick of the Chicago *Daily News* and Ben Robertson of the militantly antifascist *PM* of New York. Those not overnighting at the local Grand Hotel, now emptied for the armed services, would drive at dusk to London to file their stories.

"We all worked hard," said Middleton of that time, "but Ed worked harder than anybody else." He was to recall Murrow in those days as "jovial." Others recalled mood swings, times of animation, when he gave small lessons in radio speaking during quiet intervals, alternating with gloom and discouragement.

Like many, Murrow had found himself disquieted by the new mechanical, faceless warfare, the sense of remoteness as they watched on Shakespeare Cliff—above them, the killing; behind them, the serene English countryside.

"There is something unreal about this air war," he told his audience. "Much of it you can't see. . . . Even when the Germans come down to dive-bomb. . . . You just see a bomber slanting down toward his target;

three or four little things that look like marbles fall out, and it seems to take a long time for those bombs to hit the ground." Repeatedly he would speak of that sense of strangeness, of driving at midday through emptied village streets in the south of England, the population taking cover, the air quiet and heavy, as though before a thunderstorm.

In late August, bombs fell on London's outskirts, the spillover, apparently, of attacks on strategic targets. But there was no way of ascertaining as Murrow, producing innumerable passes, failed to get past the military guards, his damage report therefore confined, he explained carefully that night, to civilian areas—"the working class districts, cheap, flimsy houses jammed one against the other.

"One tenant had constructed a sort of lean-to and in it he had a bathroom. That pitiful little bathroom had been sheared away from the house as though by a giant meat cleaver. . . . One of [the houses] appeared to have been jabbed with a huge, blunt stick. It was just dust and rubble, a pile about ten feet high. . . ."

He found himself drawn to "the little people who live in those little houses, who have no uniforms and get no decoration for bravery."

As yet, however, German strategy seemed unchanged: Clear the skies; hit at military targets. The base at Biggin Hill, site of prewar radar development, was taking pounding after pounding. Murrow, driving up, had come in time to see a women's detachment in air force blue marching briskly back into the still-smouldering buildings. "Some of them were probably frightened, but every head was up. . . . I was told that three members of the Women's Auxiliary Air Force were killed in a raid there this morning."

It was Sunday, August 18. Five days later, Luftwaffe bombers, heading for targets outside London, strayed in heavy flak and jettisoned their cargo in the heart of the city—a fatal mistake and the first link in an unforeseen chain of events.

The following night, August 24, the Luftwaffe switched tactics, escalating the air war—1,000 planes in the sky, outnumbering the British, hitting not only at oil dumps and factories but at the vital sector stations, the communications centers of the RAF, seven close by London. It was a now-or-never attempt at supremacy, smashing at the heart of Britain's air defenses at the very doorstep of the capital, reddening the London skies.

And as it happened, radio reporters were standing by below with open microphones, increasing the propaganda fallout by bringing the mass raid directly and for the first time into American living rooms.

Earlier in the week, Eckersley, with fingers crossed, had been back to the MOI: The Americans wanted to relay eyewitness accounts of "aerial combats around London." Could they explore the possibility?

It was a daring request. Wartime remotes were strictly off-limits to aliens, even friendly ones. And then, the security problem . . .

Eckersley hastened to provide assurances: They would broadcast from several vantage points, making it harder for enemy planes homing in on radio beams to pick up the relay; reports would go through the BBC of course, subject to the usual censor at the switch. Murrow and Bate were well experienced, would adhere to security requirements. Now, if ever, was the time to show the Americans "that we are, for once, in earnest when we say we want to do all in our power to help them."[12]

The request went through in exactly three days; the date set was August 24.

That Saturday night, eleven-thirty London time, Ed Murrow stood before the Church of St. Martin's-in-the-Fields, microphone in hand, looking out toward Nelson's Column; at the curb, a BBC van packed with equipment. "This—is Trafalgar Square." Positioned elsewhere around the city, awaiting their cues, were Larry LeSueur at an air-raid precautions station, Eric Sevareid at a dance palace, Vincent Sheean in Piccadilly and in Whitehall, author-broadcaster J. B. Priestley for wrap-up commentary. The program was *London After Dark*, produced in cooperation with the BBC, starring the citizenry of London and the better part of 1,000 un-invited guests.

The fires from the smashed oil dumps had already started up as Murrow began, the glow lighting the sky to the east. "The noise that you hear at this moment is the sound of the air-raid siren. . . . People are walking along very quietly. We're just at the entrance of an air-raid shelter here, and I must move the cable over just a bit, so people can walk in." As 30 million Americans listened, he let the open microphone pick up the howling of sirens, the hollow clang of the shelter door, the anti-aircraft guns in counterpoint to the chugging of busses as the lights changed from Stop to Go. He crouched down on the sidewalk to pick up the sounds of passersby walking unhurriedly to the shelter, their footsteps audible, their bodies invisible in the murk, "like ghosts shod with steel shoes."

It was not a new technique—prewar broadcasts had caught the sound of bat and ball at cricket matches; German radio reporters picked up the massive tread of soldiers on parade—but it was a new use of sound, conveying an attitude, a point in history. The Londoners' calm footsteps— plus Murrow's brief ad lib—were more eloquent than any broadcast essay.

The sporadic bombing begun on Friday night continued that week, hitting North-Central and East London. Fires started in the City, once the old walled town, racing through the crooked lanes, leaving several blocks of charred wreckage. At the Church of St. Giles, where John Milton lay buried, a hole gaped through one wall; outside, the poet's statue lay in the gutter, toppled from its plinth.

In the meantime, some eighty RAF bombers were sent to bomb Berlin, few getting through, the damage negligible; yet shocking to a population told its capital was bombproof.

The following Wednesday, with the air war closing in on London, the

Americans were back at the Liaison Office, requesting an agreement "in principle" to broadcast eyewitness accounts from, say, the roof of Broadcasting House or, for that matter, any point where facilities could be given. The subject of request had been changed from "aerial combat" to "air raids in progress."[13]

The Luftwaffe was by now a nightly presence, the raids still, however, comparatively light. In the north the cities and towns of Merseyside were taking a pounding, fires set in the heart of Liverpool. In Berlin the Nazi hierarchy, its credibility at stake, was switching its main priorities in bombing from military targets to civilian, claiming reprisal. At the *Sportpalast*, an infuriated Hitler vowed before a cheering audience to raze Britain's cities to the ground.

It was a grim group of men who assembled at the Ministry of Information in London on September 4 to consider the Americans' proposal—representatives from MOI, Air Ministry, Home Security and Censorship, American Division. The military were in no mood for arguments. The thousand-plane attacks against the RAF were continuing without letup: over 400 fighters lost in the past two weeks, over 100 pilots killed, more pilots seriously wounded, a quarter of the fighting force; forward airfields had been damaged, key sector stations so badly hit that the entire communications system was in danger.

"It is evidently not going to be easy to obtain permission," wrote Lindsay Wellington, the capable former BBC official who had stepped in for the MOI, together with Frank Darvall, to argue the Americans' case. Objections had been raised at once: Such broadcasts would give information to the enemy, would lower morale; the public was certain to resent their sufferings "being made the subject of broadcasts to America."

A heated debate had followed, the MOI men insisting that it no longer *mattered* whether the public liked or didn't like it. The question now was, What effect would the broadcasts have "in persuading America to give more help to this country?"

And what about censorship? the airmen countered. The problem of security? Bring back some sample records, they insisted, something Intelligence could evaluate. Then, maybe, they'd talk.[14]

Two days later, a weary Lindsay Wellington reported to the BBC. The Air Council was adamant: no samples; no action.

He would suggest, therefore, a night record, a day record, a remote from Broadcasting House perhaps "and one from one of the places . . . which is more likely at present to be within range of active bombing."

The message was clear: Someone was going to have to risk his neck, with no guarantee of final results. "I hope you will be able to persuade Ed, in particular, to take pains with this and produce a really effective record. It is obviously our chief hope."[15]

It was Friday, September 6. On the Continent, preparations were being made for Day One of the new German air offensive, shifting the onus of attack to the cities and changing the context of everything: the Anglo-German war, Nazi strategy, American broadcasting from overseas, and the swing of American public opinion.

In London, Ed Murrow talked with Roger Eckersley, then made his plans for the weekend. After days of overwork, he was taking time out with two friends on the lower Thames, a sort of working holiday: View the damage; watch for aerial dogfights; enjoy the warm September sunshine.

For the rest, he would get to it on Monday.

The morning of Saturday, September 7, engineers at CBS master control, New York, setting up the feed as usual for the morning news roundup, failed to get Berlin. They tried repeatedly; nothing was coming through, no reason evident, no explanation. For some, it would be the first indication of things gone wrong.

Sometime later, the news flashes began coming in off the wires: London under air attack, great fleets of bombers with fighter escorts, hundreds and hundreds of them, pounding the city. Further reports were expected momentarily, no details as yet, though it seemed undoubtedly the worst bombing of the war.

Twenty-four hours later, Ed Murrow faced the microphone in London, red-eyed and light-headed with lack of sleep. He had spent the night of September 7 variously in a ditch, under a haystack, and sprawled, exhausted, in a waterfront inn. Acres of London had been reduced to ruin, the dockside districts a mass of smoldering wreckage, every railway line to the south, and its defenses, blocked off. Hundreds were dead, thousands wounded or trapped in the rubble, more thousands homeless. And it all had happened in a matter of hours, with more due to come.

"Yesterday afternoon," he began, "it seems days ago now, I drove down to the East End of London. . . . the East India Dock Road, Commercial Road through Silvertown, down to the mouth of the Thames Estuary. It was a quiet and almost pleasant trip. . . ."

The warm Saturday weather—the finest in a generation—had brightened slums unrivaled in the Western world for poverty or congestion. Murrow, edging his convertible through the teeming streets, drove past docks crowded with householders buying meat and cabbage for the weekend or just lured outdoors by the clear and cloudless skies.

Vincent Sheean sat beside him; in the back seat, Ben Robertson of *PM*, a big, likable, round-faced boy from South Carolina. Three inseparables, though Murrow and Sheean still fought as much as ever, joined in the debate by Robertson, to the amused perplexity of English friends (*Americans—just like big children!*).

They followed the riverbank eastward, the top down, then, as September 7 stretched into the late afternoon, parked the car on a small plateau of the Thames estuary, facing London. So far the day had been uneventful.

Rooms for the night were reserved for them at a riverside inn; in London, Sevareid was taking over the Saturday night broadcast.

At a farm near the river, they filled their tin hats with apples, paid the farmer two shillings apiece, then stretched out at the edge of a turnip field. Farther up the Thames, smoke was rising from two oil tank fires set by the German raiders the night before. Out on the river, seven big ships steamed slowly inland toward the capital, its skyline just visible on the horizon.

Suddenly the wail of a siren shattered the afternoon stillness. They looked up to see a small group of enemy bombers above their heads, flying inland. From a nearby airfield, British fighters rose to meet them, antiaircraft guns swinging into action. The air battle moved westward out of sight, and briefly there was quiet.

Then came the main onslaught. From the east, huge waves of bombers in V formation—they counted twenty to twenty-five in each—roared in and swept upriver toward London, RAF fighters rising again to meet them, trying vainly to turn them back.

The three reporters, pinpointed in the bright sunlight, ran for cover to a haystack. Above them shrapnel exploded in mid-air, releasing a deadly hail of shell fragments. Minutes later they heard the first explosions as the bombers began leveling the estuary ports, thick black columns of petroleum smoke billowing upward into the September sky.

A nearby ditch seemed to offer better cover; they ran again, scrambled down, protected their ears against the deafening cacophony of airplane motors, antiaircraft fire, and the chatter of machine guns. As each successive wave swept overhead, they flattened themselves against the earth wall, crawling back to the edge once the planes had passed. At one point Murrow tried the haystack again, without success; it had begun dwindling almost at once, and he was soon back in the ditch, shouting that he had felt like an elephant cowering behind a peanut.

It was to keep up for twelve hours.

In London, at 84 Hallam Street, Janet Murrow struggled with the roof door of her apartment building. She was trapped. Earlier, a friend had telephoned news of the attack, sending her upstairs, like other Londoners, to have a look.

Everything had seemed so far away at first, quite unreal—those little silvery planes in the distance, so pretty, like birds wheeling over London, she thought, impossible to think they were sowing destruction. *I'll bet Ed is right down there in the middle of it, the silly man.* Then, all at once, the planes seemed to be moving farther upriver, bigger, no longer birdlike.

She headed for the stairway door; it was locked, snapped shut from inside. The motors grew louder; shrapnel drummed on the roof. She ran to the edge, threw herself flat, and tried to signal for help to the pedestrians running for shelter in the street below. No one looked up.

Finally, after what seemed like hours, a lone passerby caught the rooftop signal, ran up the six flights, and released her. By that time Janet Murrow had started wondering which side of the chimney would offer the best protection for the night.

Out on the estuary the sound of the all clear rose in the sunset, as fires raged the length of the Thames and oily smoke obscured the sky. The three reporters climbed out of the ditch, brushed off the dirt, found a pub for dinner, and decided to stay, convinced the Germans would be back. So far they had no way of knowing fully what had happened, the view upriver blocked by the smoke and glare.

Ten minutes after eight, the siren sounded again. Murrow, Sheean, and Robertson returned to the haystack—now sufficient cover in the darkness—and saw, for the first time, the terrible truth, blazing in high relief on the horizon.

The earlier waves of planes had smashed at the East End, creating lakes of fire in the teeming districts that Murrow and his friends had driven through that morning: East India Dock Road; the Commercial Road through Silvertown. Factories; warehouses crammed with flammables; the arsenal at Woolwich—all had become sheets of flame, the fires serving as beacons to successive waves of bombers dropping high explosives onto the nearby rows of flimsy tenements where London's working poor lived cheek by jowl, in a too-dense concentration of humanity.

Now the raiders were back, flying in pairs, following the river and the trail of oil fires set that afternoon—a blazing corridor of light leading directly to London.

Out on the flatlands, Ed Murrow and his two companions looked on, weeping, swept by nausea as the flames of the burning boroughs filled the western sky. They stared at the horizon—"like people bewitched," said Robertson later[16]—frightened, sick to their stomachs, wondering aloud about their homes and the fate of those on the other side of that wall of fire.

A huge cloud billowed above the city, spreading a pall of black as far as the North Sea. The London they had known seemed to be going up in smoke,[17] in a nightlong ordeal Murrow was to remember all his life: "The fires up the river had turned the moon blood red. . . . Huge pear-shaped bursts of flame would rise up into the smoke and disappear. The world was upside down. Vincent Sheean lay on one side of me and cursed in five languages; he'd talk about the war in Spain. Ben Robertson . . . lay on the other side and kept saying over and over in that slow South Carolina drawl, 'London is burning, London is burning.' "[18]

CHAPTER VII

At 3:00 A.M. they were still watching by the haystack, chilled to the bone, dazed by the pounding and the flashing lights and the drone of planes flying above the inky smoke. "The searchlights bored into that black roof, but couldn't penetrate it. They looked like long pillars supporting a black canopy. Suddenly all the lights dashed off, and a blackness fell right to the ground. It grew cold. We covered ourselves with hay. The shrapnel clicked as it hit the concrete road nearby. And still the German bombers came."

There was no longer any point in staying. They picked themselves up, dazed and stiff, and drove through the exploding countryside to the inn at Gravesend. Sometime later, in rooms lit by the glare of burning gasoline, they fell into bed and slept unmoving in their clothes, as the walls shook and gunfire rattled the windows.

Now, on Sunday night, Murrow sat at the microphone, telling his tale of September 7 and its aftermath: the slow, tortuous return through blocked and rubble-strewn streets, now unrecognizable, the fires still smoldering; red busses lined up to take away the homeless and the hopeless—"men with white scarves around their necks instead of collars . . . dull-eyed empty-faced women. . . . Most of them carried little cheap cardboard suitcases and sometimes bulging paper shopping bags. That was all they had left. . . ."

Six hundred and twenty-five bombers, supported by over six hundred fighter planes, had pounded the city. At seven-thirty Sunday night they were back, leaving almost 1,000 dead for the first two nights, more than 2,000 injured. It was to continue without letup into the fall and winter, even when all military or strategic reasons to keep it up no longer existed.

In the meantime, the comfortable, civilized city of a week ago had turned into the front line—the nighttime streets deserted, given over to the antiaircraft batteries, the ambulances, and the constant clang of fire engines.

"There are no words to describe the thing that is happening," Murrow told his listeners—and then proceeded to describe it: "A row of automobiles, with stretchers racked on the roofs like skis, standing outside of bombed buildings. A man pinned under wreckage where a broken gas main sears his arms and face . . . the courage of the people; the flash and roar of the guns rolling down streets . . . the stench of air-raid shelters in the poor districts."

He talked with cockneys queued up before a public shelter:

They'd been waiting in line for an hour or more. . . . They had no private shelters of their own, but they carried blankets. . . . Of course they don't like the situation, but most of them feel that even this underground existence is preferable to what they'd get under German domination.

We are told today that the Germans believe Londoners, after a while, will rise up and demand a new government, one that will make peace with Germany. It's more probable that they'll rise up and murder a few German pilots who came down by parachute. The life of a parachutist would not be worth much in the East End of London tonight. . . .

In a few days, however, the bombers had equalized the war, the raids spreading to the fashionable West End, the payloads dumped on rich, poor, and middle class, even a few on Buckingham Palace, imposing a sense of community where none had been before. "The politicians who called this a 'people's war' were right," Murrow observed after four nights, "probably more right than they knew at the time. I've seen some horrible sights in this city . . . but not once have I heard man, woman or child suggest that Britain should throw in her hand."

The question was, Where was it leading? Night bombing, however sensational, didn't win wars. "Where then does this new phase of the air war fit? What happens next?"

After the fall of France, it had been assumed that landings would be attempted on England. Indeed, some days in July and August, the RAF embattled, defenses almost nil, it had seemed only a matter of timing. In the north, on a strip of beach, Murrow interviewed a youngster commanding two ancient naval guns and 27 rounds of ammunition, to be carefully apportioned once the German landings had begun. With the air battle raging over London, the latest estimate was sometime in September.

In the capital, Jimmy Sheean, his writings banned in Germany, joked bleakly about a magazine offer from America—25,000 words, an eyewitness account of the upcoming German entry into London. Where the hell did the publisher think *he'd* be when Hitler entered London?

But he was staying. So were the others. Among the British, Murrow found and reported what seemed to many an almost quixotic determination to resist. Among his acquaintances, the aged and redoubtable Lady Milner, widow of one statesman, aunt to another,[19] had vowed personally to defend her home in Kent. Relatives had finally persuaded her westward, though Murrow smiled at the thought of the determined dowager facing the invaders with a shotgun.

As for the Murrows, they had no contingency plans.

In early July, following her decision not to go home, he had confessed— though only afterward—that he wanted her to stay. Then, with the bombs falling, he announced one day that he had booked her passage after all. Ships were still leaving, wives and children returning. Almost all the wives in their circle had gone home, and so was she; he wanted her out of danger, and that was that.

It wasn't. They *had* no children, she countered, meeting every argument with one of her own, quietly and firmly; he canceled the booking.

But she knew what she was facing in sharing his commitment not to leave, whatever happened. Embassy evacuation plans, they knew, did not include them; they were nonofficial, hence expendable. Such were the realities, even without their knowing the savage outlines of Nazi plans for Britain, taking shape in those same weeks under the name Operation Sea Lion.[20]

They turned their minds elsewhere, Janet busying herself with the evacuation of children to America, her husband still insisting Britain would hold out—"one of the few," she recalled later, "who felt that somehow by some miracle they were going to win." Nonetheless, as a practical New Englander, she took the payment forced out of an unwilling insurance company following the robbery and bought a pin set with small diamonds. "You see, if we suddenly had to flee somewhere," she told her family with sweet logic, "I could stick a diamond in my pocket, whereas anything larger would be a nuisance."

At 84 Hallam Street they were almost alone now, the other tenants fled but for a minister living downstairs and a neighboring masseuse, a big, cheerful north country woman who had introduced herself and who relieved Murrow's tension with ultraviolet treatments at special blitz rates, her high-priced clients having taken off.

Otherwise, the building was deserted, the empty windows and corridors reverberating to the thud of explosives dropped outside as the Luftwaffe tried repeatedly to knock out Broadcasting House, just four blocks away. Hallam Street itself, so small and charming in prewar days, so conveniently close to work, had become a potential deathtrap, just one of a warren of tight little arteries, no wider than two small cars abreast, honeycombing the area, leading nowhere; shallow sidewalks overhung with pseudo-Georgian gingerbread that shuddered with each vibration of the bomb blasts, peeling off in slow motion to come hurtling downward in an avalanche of bricks and masonry.

Across the bottom ran Langham Street, the narrow lane abutting the back wall of the BBC, a single unseen curve leading to the open air of Langham Place—the only escape route and a prescription for disaster should fire and bombardment ever trigger off a mass scramble to escape.

At night Hallam Street was a blacked-out canyon, lit fitfully by bursts of antiaircraft fire that turned the black to blue-white daylight and back again, the short walk to the studio a literal gauntlet as bombs hit the small blocks of flats and the little bandbox Georgian houses, sending shock waves down the street, blowing out the windows, shattering glass in all directions. A synagogue two blocks down from 84 had soon been hit, the blackened hull gaping as though a target of some special wrath.

Murrow, making his way nightly, learned to negotiate the stretch as needed—groping, striding, running, throwing himself flat as recommended when a bomb went off, arriving finally at the bronze doors of Broadcasting House, often out of breath, occasionally dusty, very occasionally on all fours.[21]

Behind the bronze doors, the last traces of the old upper-class aura had departed. Steel partitions and gas-tight doors chopped up the Art Deco interiors; guards with live ammunition and orders to shoot on sight if necessary, okayed passes at key entrance points. Civilian BBC volunteers patrolled the darkened, fortresslike corridors around the central studio tower, nervously on the watch; at one point the editor of the BBC's *Radio Times*, prowling the dimmed-out seventh floor, found himself turning a corner outside the system's telephone exchange, heart beating, truncheon ready, only to confront the editor of the *Listener*, brandishing a shotgun, a situation inconceivable a few short months ago.[22]

Below street level the great concert hall, its seats ripped out, had become a dormitory, mattresses laid down for employees. In a farsighted earlier move, vast quantities of shroud material, accumulated in the phony war and then discarded, had been bought up and sewn into sheets and pillowcases and makeshift sleeping bags.[23] Now sleeping bodies were strewn about nightly on the floor—men to one side, women to the other, a curtain of blankets drawn discreetly down the middle.

Farther down in the subbasement, at the blue clay level of ancient Roman London, the BBC had set up emergency news facilities—first supplementing, then virtually replacing those upstairs—gouging out what had been a vaudeville studio, desks and teletypes moved in, a machine-gun nest poised in the balcony.

Lounges, even lavatories had been carved up; delicate *trompe l'oeil* murals, once intended to soothe the claustrophobic, covered by sound-proofing. More studios and control rooms took shape down below street level, among them the little closet known as B-4, used by the Americans, the lifeline to the West. Iron-framed bunk beds served those working through the night.

In the distance, they could hear the rumble of the underground, plus all the ventilation plants, generators, boilers, and general support systems of Broadcasting House. Overhead, the drain pipes clanked their loads away, Cecilia Reeves insisting it was their tragic destiny to be drowned someday in sewage. For years afterward a story made the rounds that secret invasion plan contingencies provided for the last two men to stay behind with axes, cut the cables, and escape through a manhole.

In that driven, troglodyte community of news editors, hard-bitten journalists, most of them, with little use for radio correspondents, Murrow quickly found acceptance. Godfrey Talbot, later himself a distinguished BBC correspondent, then a big northerner brought down for his newspaper experience, recalled the scene three stories underground: the rows of desks, sub-editors dictating the six and nine o'clock bulletins to the typists sitting at their elbows, and the man everyone knew simply as Ed coming and going, the inevitable cigarette dangling—checking the tickers, updating his copy at a spare typewriter, sometimes putting whole pieces together with his unique concentration, often staying to talk when things were quiet. On heavy bombing nights he was their link with the streets—"a messenger from hell," as one man put it—filling them in as they worked their six-hour shifts bent over the wire service tapes, isolated from the world upstairs.

Yet he seemed always immaculate, unruffled, his shirt a snowy white even on those nights when one had to crawl the last few feet through shrapnel. A comfortable presence, spinning yarns, in the late hours, about the strange country he came from—"marvelous stories which you couldn't repeat, half of them, made us all laugh very much."

As professionals, they admired his copy—always accurate, Smithers recalled, generally analytical, sometimes based on information they themselves didn't have. "The fiber was very tight," said Godfrey Talbot, "no room for flanneling, it was all good, hard stuff." They admired, too, his courage, his insistence on first-hand corroboration—a shrewd reporter who "saw through pretentiousness and frills," as Talbot put it, who "enjoyed more being at the coal face than at the pit head," and liked being called a good workman.

"He had of course an inordinate admiration for what Britain was like in those days," said Talbot later, "and he was concerned, very concerned, that his own country wasn't aware of the facts of life. And that if Hitler & Co. were not stopped here, the next stop was Manhattan."

Throughout those months, Murrow worked like a man possessed. He seemed to be everywhere at once: driving through the air raids in his little Sunbeam-Talbot to check out the casualty reports, never working from handouts; talking with cockneys in the subway shelters one moment, with cabinet ministers the next; checking with sources in the offices of governments in exile; monitoring the Commons; patrolling as neighborhood fire warden, and, of course, broadcasting up to four or five times a night.

Drew Middleton would see him some nights, stopping in at a small bar at the Savoy, white with fatigue, two or three broadcasts behind him. The two men would talk shop, then go their separate ways at 3:00 or 4:00 A.M., Murrow possibly back to Broadcasting House, possibly home for a few hours' sleep before starting the cycle all over again.

He was living at the two extremes of London life: the upper-class, old-school-tie circles that still peopled much of the government and the bureaucracies, and the grimy, blasted, crime-infested streets and shelters of the East End. In contrast with the more finicky among the press corps, Murrow was comfortable in the London ghettos, with their ethnic mix, feeling a sense of kinship with those who, having the least, stood to lose the most. "These people are exceedingly brave, tough and prudent. The East End, where disaster is always just around the corner, seems to take it better than the more fashionable districts in the West End."

In fact, the West End, though hit less hard, was bearing up very well. But for the boy from the logging towns there was something familiar about the poorer districts: the women brewing tea in all emergencies; families getting out spare blankets for troubled neighbors—the memory, perhaps, of another time and place where human life was similarly cheap, disaster just around the corner.

In late September, the Germans had begun dropping land mines by parachute, landing softly and noiselessly, then going off with devastating force. The daytime raids had been abandoned following an all-out effort on the fifteenth, made expensive by RAF resistance—the Luftwaffe limping home, the bid for air supremacy abandoned, Operation Sea Lion, unknown to the British, indefinitely called off. It was a victory for the RAF and, in retrospect, a turning point.

But in London the killing continued at night, the population turned guinea pigs for the latest in bomb technology. In the city mortuaries medical students worked in teams, reassembling bodies for burial. Murrow, walking the early-morning streets, watched rescue squads tunneling through wreckage, carefully lifting out limp figures, "looking like broken, castaway, dust-covered dolls," those already out discreetly hidden under canvas. Just south of Broadcasting House, on Oxford Street, the blackened hulls of department stores gaped open to the sky. Once-fashionable Regent Street seemed to one observer like the thoroughfare of a ghost town, powdered glass frosting the sidewalk like a snowy blanket.

By day, there was a semblance of normal life. After dark, the raiders would be back, the skies exploding, a clear, bright moon turning a stage light on the neighborhood. In the midst of it Broadcasting House loomed above the surrounding rooftops, a great blue-white eight-story target.

Friday, September 20, Roger Eckersley got the official notification he had been waiting for: "As you know, no objection is being raised to the commentary by Ed. Murrow from the roof of Broadcasting House . . . tomorrow night."[24] It was the final go-ahead to the request made in late August before the blitz, during light air raids that now seemed, in retrospect, like a harmless practice drill.

By that time, however, the broadcaster himself had had ample practice—possibly more than he cared for.

Following the cataclysm of September 7–8, he had somehow managed to work in the sample records as promised—long, noisy sessions on the topmost tier of Broadcasting House, made after clambering through dust and flying soot, the air raids in progress, past the exhaust fans, past the roofwatcher's hut to a microphone installed to transmit wartime sounds downstairs, a feed set up by engineers below to a waiting turntable.

Six recordings were transcribed, sent to the Ministry of Information, and, as Murrow recalled it, promptly lost somewhere in the pipeline. There was nothing for it but to go back for another set of nights, another set of takes. His recollection of it later was philosophic ("I had a lot of time up there");[25] his reaction at the time, perhaps mercifully, unrecorded.

Finally, the third week in September, Sir Walter Monckton, one of Churchill's inner circle, Director General of the Press Bureau, MOI, and the ministry's pipeline to the cabinet, passed down official word, granting permission.

Saturday night, September 21, American radio audiences tuning in to *London After Dark* heard footsteps 3,000 miles away, the warning hoot of London police whistles just dimly audible, the whine of aircraft, and Murrow's voice: "I'm standing on a rooftop looking out over London . . . for reasons of national as well as personal security, I'm unable to tell you the exact location from which I'm speaking. . . ."

It was, of course, Broadcasting House. An air raid was going on—of small dimensions, big enough to convey the experience directly to the listeners, the sounds of air attack in counterpoint to the reporter's terse, graphic ad-libbing: "Streets fan out in all directions from here. . . . Off to my left, far away in the distance, I can see just that faint, red, angry snap of antiaircraft bursts against the steel-blue sky. . . . More searchlights spring up over on my right . . . swinging over in this general direction now: you'll hear two explosions—there they are! . . . The plane is still very high and it's quite clear that he's not coming in for his bombing run. . . ."

The next night he continued, his quiet narrative underscored by the steady crashes of antiaircraft fire as he described scarred buildings directly opposite, windows gaping blackly, the frames blown out:

> Out of one window there waves something that looks like a white bedsheet, a. . . . curtain swinging free in this night breeze. It looks as if it were being shaken by a ghost. . . . The searchlights straightaway, miles in front of me, are still scratching that sky. There's a three-quarter moon riding high. There was one burst of shellfire almost straight in the Little Dipper.

It was *The War of the Worlds* come to life, the fantasy of 1938 become the reality of 1940, the rooftop observer, reporting on the life and death of cities, no longer an actor in a studio. This was the real thing, broadcasting's first living-room war. A world was ending, and the reporters had become the chorus, playing out their roles on a stage of awesome dimensions.

Once CBS had made the breakthrough, the others followed, Bate and Arthur Mann, John Steele's assistant at Mutual, both cleared for rooftop commentaries. But it was Edward R. Murrow whom the American public had come to follow nightly, Murrow to whom they turned first for information, the Murrow broadcasts—and those of Shirer in Berlin—that were becoming a national listening habit, as essential, in millions of homes, as the evening meal.

The Overseas Press Club honored him that fall for the best foreign radio news reporting of the past year, the symbolic typewriter, presented *in absentia*, sitting in Paul White's office.

Journalists pouring into England beat a path to his door, satisfying public curiosity about the man behind the voice. He was photographed, sketched, interviewed. His broadcasts were run as newspaper columns back home under large, eye-catching headlines. He had become an authentic American hero, as much a part of the story as the blitz itself.

The result was a certain dichotomy, not uncommon to those years in broadcasting. Three thousand miles away, he was a celebrity. In England, while sought after, as were most American correspondents—then in their heyday, courted, the official atmosphere as warm now as it had been chilly under Chamberlain—he was essentially a reporter among reporters, though clearly first among his peers.

To the mass British public, however, he was largely unknown, not up to the celebrityhood of American media stars whose voices were familiar over the BBC: Dorothy Thompson;[26] Raymond Gram Swing, who had been broadcasing to England for years; and especially Quentin Reynolds— genial, gregarious, a walking symbol of the American press, his face known all over London, warming the hearts of BBC listeners with hearty gibes at "Mr. Schickelgruber."

They were in fact friends, Reynolds and Murrow, twin stars of the blitz, one in print, the other, broadcasting. They were also temperamental opposites. "Quent was very popular in a different way from Ed," said Sidney Bernstein, later founder of Granada Television, then producing films for the government, among them the Reynolds-narrated classic *London Can Take It*. "He was a good drinker and so on. Ed was a more aristocratic man, I don't mean in any snob way, but in mixing.

"Quent knew a lot of [English] newspaper people, I introduced him and they *loved* him, could tell you all kinds of stories about him. The result was, when he did his broadcasts, when he did *London Can Take It* for us, Quent got the the headlines."[27]

By contrast, Murrow's recognition level was still confined to a relatively small, though potent, circle, his daily life among the English one of comparative anonymity—a private man, as one colleague put it, doing a public job.

October 15, the first bomb hit Broadcasting House. It was a Tuesday night, the nine o'clock news under way downstairs; outside, one of the worst air assaults since the start of the blitz, single-engine fighter-bombers hitting London with every new wrinkle in the German arsenal, including the airborne time bombs known as UXBs.

One had flown in through a seventh-story window, 500 pounds of metal and explosives crashing downward through the concrete flooring, through the emptied upstairs newsroom, through the solid brick wall of the inner studio structure, and into the music library, where it lay inert.

It was still there an hour later—intact, an unknown quantity. Staffers dawdled, reluctant to leave their posts despite warnings to evacuate, no one certain whether the damage done upstairs meant the bomb had done its worst. A squad finally tried to move it.

It went off that moment, scattering bodies and debris in all directions, the library with its valuable holdings blasted; studios wrecked; the inner structure damaged. The extensive ventilation system, of which the builders had been so proud, became a conduit for flying glass, sucked up into the ducts and sprayed out elsewhere in a deadly rain.

Murrow, in the subbasement at the time, watched the stretcher parties make their way to the underground first-aid station with the wounded and the dead: four men, three women. Outside, the fires burned under a full moon, the historic Middle Temple Hall destroyed, the devastated areas reminding some of Rotterdam.

That same night in New York, Bill Dunn, an editor in the CBS newsroom, was monitoring the overseas reports for the late-evening roundup. They were trying, he knew, to spare Murrow the late broadcasts if possible; therefore, the editor, calling London on the cue channel, was surprised when a familiar voice answered, hoarse and hollow, barely recognizable: "Hello . . . London calling . . ." Dunn could hardly hear him.

"Ed?"

"Yes."

"You sound tired."

There was a brief pause at the other end. "I *am* tired, Bill. It's a tired world."

Said Dunn afterward: "I didn't know that friends of his had died."

(Broadcasting legend placed Murrow at the microphone that night, describing the corpses carried past the studio, which would have involved the ability to see through two steel doors, not to mention a security violation in disclosing damage to a strategic target. It was, in fact, some time before CBS, New York learned the details.)

Everything possible had come down: UXBs, parachute flares, high explosives with incendiaries, and the dreaded "breadbaskets"—demolition clusters that scattered fire bombs as they exploded in midair. Yet the BBC engineers were back at work next morning, restoring equipment, replacing the blackened wiring. In the upstairs newsroom, Pat Smithers found a hole in the middle of his desk where the bomb had splintered through on its downward path—one hole in the ceiling, another in the floor, and in between, the skeleton of the desk, still upright.

"High-explosive bombs are not an ideal weapon for the destruction of the human race," Murrow commented on the air, "something more devastating is required. But many of the best scientific brains of the world are engaged on that problem and presumably they'll find a solution in time."

But it was his coolness under fire—not his bitterness—that made up the legend, that the public loved to read about, with its overtones, from time to time, of locker-room bravado. The story made the rounds of how, driving through a raid with Jimmy Sheean and Quent Reynolds, he'd braked to a halt so that Reynolds, on a bet (Sheean's), could get out and read a paper by the light of burning buildings.

Dick Marriott, suppering with Murrow one night at a hotel opposite the BBC, choked on his food as a crashing upper-story hit sent shock waves through the dining room. The room's two-story pillars seemed to stagger in place. Marriott worked to get a grip on himself. Murrow looked under the table—"I think I've dropped my watch"—and went on eating.

He seemed at times to court disaster, almost nerveless, seeking out the action at its thickest. A death wish, said some. To colleagues of the working press, it seemed no more than a cut-and-dried professional ignoring of the risks. And the fact was, reporters who didn't take risks, who stayed in shelters, also didn't get the story.

Besides, basic survival instincts had set in, like an automatic pilot. LeSueur later recalled walking by Murrow's side once, when a rain of bombs caught them in the open. Murrow threw himself flat. LeSueur, fascinated by the fireworks, stayed upright until an earsplitting, "Get down, you goddamn fool!" sent him, too, diving for the gutter.

As CBS bureau chief, he worked himself hard, worked his staff, perpetually short-handed, his temper growing shorter still, under the strain. In place of the old patience with mistakes, there was flaming anger— "Listen here, buster!"—then self-conscious mildness, indicating he was sorry. Bill Henry had been recalled the first winter of the war. In mid-October 1940, Eric Sevareid, ill and worn down from that summer's ordeal, went home. They were sad, but no one blamed him. He had broadcast heroically amid the French defeat, and who among them could control what the decibel level of an air raid did to nerves already stretched to the limit?

Murrow had wanted to hire Helen Kirkpatrick of the Chicago *Daily News*, part of the inner circle that included Stoneman, Beattie, Middleton, and himself. Like most, she had had little radio experience—"Girl, you are the *worst* broadcaster I have *ever* heard!" he said once—but Ida Lou Anderson's pupil offered to coach her.[28] Kirkpatrick's voice was low-pitched and decisive; more important, she was one of the best correspondents in London.

Columbia turned thumbs down. No more women; Klauber was inflexible. Murrow accordingly went after someone he could train: Charles Collingwood, a young UP correspondent, not yet available, with only a year's experience and nothing like Kirkpatrick's stature, but more acceptable to New York.

The office was hit repeatedly, the first time in September—no one hurt, the staff coming in next day to find the windows gone, plaster everywhere, Bill Paley's photo portrait dangling by a single wire. They went through it three more times, perpetual gypsies, once even setting up headquarters in the Murrow apartment when office space in the badly bombed neighborhood could simply not be found.

For Ed and Janet Murrow, it was the final phaseout of the young-couple era. Janet Murrow accepted her loneliness as the blitz forced their lives to opposite ends of the day and night. She filled her days with work, understanding as her husband courted danger; understanding, too, his need for the long, solitary nighttime walks, no encumbrances; knew essentially that he liked being alone.

They were concentrating on survival, grateful, she later said, just to be alive another morning. At one point she had told him of her rescue, the first night of the blitz—and the subsequent reversion to convention as her rescuer, an officer and a gentleman, had walked her back downstairs: Should she invite him in? Would he think it improper? In the end she hadn't. And felt like a fool.

Ed had laughed uproariously: "Only a girl born in Middletown, Connecticut, who went to Mount Holyoke, would think twice about inviting in the man who saved her life!"

Underneath, he worried for her safety, talked of her returning home. "I'd go if I really thought he'd be much happier," she wrote her family, "but I'm afraid of his being ill again."

She agreed, finally, to a short stay in the country, acutely weary by now and disenchanted with evacuation work which had become an escape valve for the children of the rich. Once away, however, she chafed at the separation, the isolation, unable to enjoy the quiet or the pretty seaside town enfolded in the western hills.

He wrote constantly. She didn't know how much it helped, he said, to have her in the same country with him. But he was glad she wasn't in London: "This is something no one should go through. . . ."

As for himself, he was, if anything, a fatalist, resigned in his letters home to Washington—aware, as he wrote his parents, of the razor-thin margin between life and death.

In late September, he came out briefly to West Somerset and the tiny village at the end of the world where she was staying. The little inn had room for seven, laid on a tea with scones, thick cream, and honey, a country idyll untouched by war, with the promise of absolute quiet. He spent nonetheless an insomnia-ridden night, getting to sleep in the early morning, when a German bomber passed within yards of the hotel and crashed in the bay.

Janet Murrow was wide awake. She couldn't believe Ed had slept through it; he looked so thin and white, lying there beside her.

Later that day, they sat in the lee of a breakwater and watched the rising tide cover the wreckage of the bomber. The survivors, rounded up, had been trooped off by the Home Guard. The pilot, dead, was still inside the plane, below the water line.

All that fall, the voice of Edward R. Murrow was a living link between North America and the besieged island, bringing a new definition to the concept of war reporting, focusing not on soldiers but on civilians, his "unsung heroes. . . . Those black-faced men with bloodshot eyes . . . fighting fires. . . . The girls who cradled the steering wheel of a heavy ambulance in their arms, the policeman who stands guard over that unexploded bomb. . . ."

"These things must be seen," he kept insisting, and the audience saw them in vivid word pictures that needed no TV cameras. A night bomber's exhaust trail was "a pale ribbon stretched straight across the sky." The glasses of an antiaircraft spotter resembled "the eyes of an overgrown owl"; antiaircraft barrages "seemed to splash blobs of daylight down the streets."

Listeners stood beside him on windswept rooftops, watching fire spotters phone in bombing locations as high explosives fell nearby:

> The first two looked like some giant had thrown a huge basket of flaming golden oranges high in the air. The third was just a balloon of fire.
> A shower of incendiaries came down in the far distance. . . . It looked like flashes from an electric train on a wet night, only the engineer was drunk and driving his train in circles through the streets. . . . Our observer reported laconically, "Breadbasket at 90—covers a couple of miles."

His main job was, of course, to cover all fronts, the midnight broadcasts—timed for the early-evening news in New York—focusing largely on the political scene, London a prime listening post on the latest developments from the Balkans to Eritrea. In the midst of the savage pounding of October 14–15, Murrow's main newscast had concentrated on oil-rich Rumania's slide into the Axis camp and growing tensions between Berlin, Belgrade, and Ankara.

It was in the early hours of the morning, London time—with Europe asleep, the news tickers relatively quiet—that he walked the city's streets, a solitary observer, gathering material for the later broadcasts ordered by the network. Stories were needed, nothing much happening, the result, the reflective, impressionistic pieces that captured the public imagination and established his image as the poet of the blitz.

There were the sharp late-night fragments—"the things the mind retains": a rainbow bending over the battered East End as the all clear sounded; a flower shop intact among the ruins, a funeral wreath in the window, price tag legible in the moonlight; the silence of a devastated street during a bombing pause, broken by a solitary drip-drip from inside a smashed grocery shop—"two cans of peaches had been drilled clean through by flying glass and the juice was dripping down onto the floor."

He spoke of individuals—an East End woman, her house gutted by incendiaries, clutching a dirty pillow snatched up while fleeing from the flames; a British bomber pilot just back from over Germany, walking through an air raid with the broadcaster, stopping midway, horrified: "I've seen enough of this; I hope we haven't been doing the same thing in the Ruhr and the Rhineland for the last three months!"

In graphic images, Murrow conveyed the impersonal nature of the new technology of killing—"three or four high school boys with some special training. . .flying around over London in about one hundred thousand dollars worth of special machinery. One of them had pressed a button; the fire and a number of casualties was the result." Below in the rubble, he watched soldiers digging for victims with their hands, their backs bent. "All the modern instruments seem to be overhead."

He walked quietly at 3:00 A.M. among the sleeping shelterers in a London tube station—"London's new underworld"—feeling out of place, an intruder among the rows of limp, silent bodies. His sense of social injustice flared constantly—the ever-present awareness that "the kind of protection you get from the bombs. . .depends on how much money you have."

In a Mayfair hotel lobby, he saw dowagers and retired officers facing the raids from overstuffed settees. Not the best protection from a half-ton bomb, he said, "but if you were a retired colonel and his lady, you might feel that the risk was worth it because you would at least be bombed with the right sort of people, and you could always get a drink."

In a park two blocks away, he visited a trench dug from a stretch of lawn: "Inside were half a hundred people, some of them stretched out on the hard wooden benches. The rest huddled over in their overcoats and blankets. . . .[The] reverberation of the big stuff the Germans were dropping rattled the dust boards under foot. . . .You couldn't buy a drink there."

At the deluxe underground shelter of the Dorchester he found "a cosmopolitan crowd. But there wasn't any sparkling cosmopolitan conversation. They sat, some of them with their mouths open. One of them snored. . . ."

Word had it that he had gone around the BBC concert hall with open microphone, picking up the sound of snoring. By now, however, Broadcasting House itself was one large dormitory. In Studio B-4, Murrow made his way past recumbent forms on mattresses, lowering his voice ostentatiously one night—speaking "rather softly," he told listeners, so as not to awaken his colleagues. Down on the floor, Cecilia Reeves and the others laughed quietly: Who could sleep, with all that going on?

In fact, it made no difference; the engineers took care of loud and soft. "Kay Campbell was shocked," said Reeves, "but it was good propaganda."

Said BBC correspondent Robin Duff, then their youngest reporter, "I don't think anybody other than Ed could have got away with that."

By now, too, his real home was the embattled news community living below ground—a cross-section of urban society, from Oxford graduates to working class. Most would remember him as outgoing, easy-mannered, almost self-effacing—working on his own, then emerging during breaks in the routine to chat with editors, ask a question or two of the typists, over a shared cup of tea: How were they coping with the blitz, how were things at home, was it hard getting to the office? Said a staffer later, "I think some of his summary of the British reaction to the war came from those conversations."[29]

The editors, he questioned about their work—the day's news, their approach to a given story, a constant interplay between the BBC staff and the still-young reporter honing his skills. A competent two-finger typist, he had nonetheless taken on the newsroom's practice of dictating broadcasts directly into the typewriter; the resulting copy took on more distinctly the natural rhythm of spoken English.

Emerging was a symbiosis, a classic compatibility between the BBC Home News, reputedly the most trusted voice in Europe, and the American visitor—a shared "professional astringency," as one man put it. "We were giving in full the bad news, the hellish communiqués, and this meshed with Ed's desire to tell the truth even if it was a hard and nasty truth. There was a complete meeting of the minds on that."[30]

There was also a complete meeting of minds with the man responsible for that policy—Home News Editor R. T. Clark, former editorial writer for the Manchester *Guardian*, military historian and classics scholar, whose self-effacing manner hid the toughness of spirit that had landed him on the Nazi blacklist.

Stooped, perpetually smiling, dressed always in dark, shiny three-piece suits, cigarette butt pursed tightly between his lips, he ran the newsroom with the lightest of touches, father figure to the staff and role model.

"I think R. T., as we called him, had a great influence on Ed," recalled Michael Balkwill, later a news official, then a young duty editor come down from Oxford in the prewar days. "Not, perhaps, for the handling of a story—Ed had very much a style of his own. But for the wisdom and historical comparisons, and the larger context of presenting the news."

Through the long, disturbing nights, the two men, Clark and Murrow, would sit talking in the underground cubicle that doubled as Clark's office and sleeping quarters. R. T. and his wife had a flat nearby, but the great editor preferred to camp out at the BBC, in what was known as R. T.'s dungeon—"Very small," Balkwill remembered, "with a bed and a desk, and lots of paper all over the place. Ed would be sitting on the bed, R. T. in the only chair, sitting there until you couldn't see across the place for the tobacco smoke, leaning forward, old pals having a chat."[31]

"They would talk about everything," another recalled, "life, backgrounds, their philosophy. I sometimes wondered if Ed ever *did* sleep."[32]

It was a warm and rewarding relationship, the younger man sometimes bringing in small items he had picked up in his daytime forays—turfs of grass for the tabby cat the Clarks kept back at their apartment, or a couple of eggs, produced during a peak shortage. One editor recalled Clark's stooped figure that particular night, groping cautiously out into the blackout, feeling his way with his walking stick, the precious eggs clutched to his bosom.

After midnight, R.T.'s cramped dungeon would become still more cramped, staffers from the newsroom and elsewhere, forgoing sleep, joining the discussion. "A symposium," Balkwill called it, everyone very hyper, talking away or listening to Clark draw parallels from history—from Shakespeare's England and Thucydides' Greece, the Spanish Armada and the Athenian fleet besieging ancient Syracuse, as the blitz reverberated upstairs: "Remember the Athenians in the Great Harbor, brothers."

It was a unique mixture of bravery and erudition, appealing especially to the boy from Washington State College, who evidently held his own in the late-night symposiums.

It was also a special kind of companionship, a special time—something he would miss later, everything reduced to a few essentials. The issues were simple, as one man put it: Life or death, they would win, or the enemy would win; and you either lived another day, or you didn't.

At three in the morning, Clark would coax orders of tea and bacon sandwiches out of the waitresses in the canteen, the whole party often moving on to 84 Hallam Street, walking over broken glass, past burning, unidentifiable things. At the flat, discussions continued while Murrow poured American bourbon and did devastating imitations of the British army brass. Or, as dawn came up, read Thurber stories to the guests, the newsmen settled back, mellowed over bourbon, listening to tales of small-town Ohio and of "The Night the Bed Fell."

"He was a good reader, very good," said Balkwill later, "and of course, it was very nice to hear Thurber read in American."

New worries arose that winter with the added fear of epidemics, in a city where coal heating and congestion produced one of the highest TB rates in the world. Murrow, in late-night broadcasts, spoke of the "cold, choking fog" taking command of the street: "It seeps down into the shelters and subways. After a visit to one of those shelters, one climbs the stairs into the damp darkness of the night, pursued by the sound of coughing. . . ."

His own pulmonary problems, despite brief illness in November, seemed packed in for the duration. The convalescent of early 1940 had become the iron man of the blitz, living on adrenaline, black coffee, and cigarettes, heedless of weight loss and insomnnia, his six-foot-two frame down to 150 pounds of sleepless, relentless energy.

He had, of course, no choice—what with no supporting forces; no army of assistants, cameras, even tape; and live broadcasting throughout. At times, his temper frayed, he fought with White over the non-admission of recordings, taboo by network fiat. Once you let them in, went New York's reasoning, you wouldn't need a network—which meant, in practice, missing out on action scoops that didn't happen punctually at 12:03 A.M.

When he managed to get away, the tension followed. Ronald Tree, a friend and Member of Parliament, invited the Murrows to Ditchley, one of the great English country houses and his home. Guests later recalled Murrow, oblivious to everything, stalking through the stubble fields all day, nervously, febriley tired.

At night, he lay awake in country guest rooms, listening to the rustle of straw turn into the crackle of falling incendiaries; the tattoo of horses' hoofbeats on the road, into bursts of gunfire; the swish of gravel, into the distant tumble of bricks and mortar. His mind grasped the realities, but sleep patterns thus disrupted never did return to normal, with the onset, from that time on, of nocturnal teeth grinding and chronic insomnia.

His smoking had intensified, a chemical means of keeping down the pressure. The cigarettes were now a necessary adjunct—just how much, Lindsay Wellington came to realize on an overnight trip when the two of them shared a room. Waking in the early-morning hours, Wellington had looked over just in time to see Murrow beginning to stir, reaching almost in his sleep for the pack beside his bed. "It was the first thing he did," the BBC man remembered, "barely awake, just an automatic movement."

He was borrowing heavily against the future, in a world where few thought further than making it from day to day. Any thoughts about the future were moreover focused elsewhere, as the winter's hardships heightened calls for social justice.

Throughout the battle, he had sounded one consistent note: the war as an instrument of change. In midsummer, as others focused on the air war, he had quoted the writer-broadcaster J. B. Priestley on "the revolt against too-long rule by old men"; spoke of the need for an alternative "more workable than that presented by European democracies of the last twenty years"; cited the millions of voices now rising even as the bombs fell, asking: What were the war aims of the country—the shape of the victory to come?

Half a century before in Greensboro, Josh Murrow had stood up to support organized labor's call for "bread and roses." In the mid-October chill of London, 1940, on the cataclysmic night of the fifteenth, his grandson, stepping past the sleepers in the subway, suddenly recalled the line, "God gave us memory that we might have roses in December." It stayed with him as he climbed back up into the blacked-out, fiery streets. "These people have their roses and will have them in December, their memories of Britain's past glories, their belief that the Germans can't beat them. . . . The question is, will they see the roses reappear in the spring?"

It was still with him two hours later at the microphone at five in the morning, the moon still up, the guns still working, the fires dying:

> This country is undergoing a revolution, a revolution by consent but a revolution none the less. This long range pounding from the air . . . should not blind one to the fundamentals of this business.
>
> It is a struggle between two ways of life, two systems of governing a people. . . . The amount of damage done is only incidental. There is no way for the average man to hit back in this kind of war. In many ways [it] is a race . . . to see which can produce the most fanatics, and which can evolve a relationship between the State and the individual sufficiently attractive to cause him to be willing to be bombed indefinitely. . . . [But] there must be equality under the bombs. He must be convinced that after he has suffered, a better world will emerge. His memory will give him "roses in December," but there must be at least the promise that the Spring will bring better roses for all.

The painful year of 1940 was drawing to a close. Janet Murrow organized the London office of Bundles for Britain, becoming friends in the process with its honorary chairman, Clementine Churchill. She was also continuing her broadcasts for CBS, learning the discipline of condensing to a minute and a half, wincing as Ed blue-pencilled her copy, a cruel and demanding editor.

Their lives overlapped at the odd hours when guests came back to the flat, from colleagues to party leaders. R. T. Clark was now a regular, as was Allan Wells, Foreign Editor for the BBC Home Service, a student of history and a favorite of Ed's. The Wellses lived across the street from the Murrows, the two young couples conspiring to coax R. T. out of his hidey-hole. Jan Masaryk, roly-poly, irrepressible, came by for dinner and after broadcasts, pounding away on Janet's piano while Ed let off steam by singing folk songs—the hour notwithstanding—at the top of his voice, Janet quietly retiring while the walls reverberated to "Joe Hill."[33]

Kay Campbell had become a part of both their lives—tiny, organized, a heavy smoker like her boss; "a splendid person," a colleague recalled, "and Ed's other self in Europe."[34]

The tension potential notwithstanding, the two women got along, a strong, subtle bond forged between wife and secretary, each discerning the qualities in the other. The American woman would be consistently amazed at the other's cool, carry-on competence under fire—such as the night of a heavy raid when Campbell, working in the next room, had knocked softly on their door, opened it and, standing diffidently on the threshold, announced with typical British imperturbability, "I'm sorry to disturb you, Mr. Murrow, but there's a fire bomb on the roof."

A third woman completed the picture. Ida Lou Anderson, at Murrow's request, had been giving him feedback on his broadcasts, comments on technique. She had stopped teaching—nearly blind, her frail health fading, but still the searching critic, advising on pacing, suggesting the pause in the opening "This—is London," now Murrow's wartime signature; as vigorous mentally as when she had sat in the corner of the classroom at WSC. Janet Murrow saw her letters come in, with their large, assertive handwriting in green ink, postmarked "Colfax, Washington," but didn't see the contents.

On the more public side, they were both frequent guests at Downing Street, generally at Mrs. Churchill's invitation. Murrow's access to the PM was known to be good, though so was that of Reynolds, Swing, just about any major U.S. correspondent. Winston Churchill, half American and a former journalist himself, knew the importance of cultivating American reporters, plumbing American opinion.

Downstairs among the Churchill staff, the broadcaster was well liked— one of the small group, they knew, that could get appointments with anyone, without much waiting; a comforting presence in that winter of anxiety about American intentions, a neutral with no pretense of neutrality.[35]

As for relations with the great man himself, they remained primarily professional, reporter to politician, despite suppers in the private dining room at No. 10—a wives' occasion, the two men talking briefly over dinner or afterward, Murrow perhaps sounded out for American reactions on some matter, deferential always, no presumptions of press power, influence, or friendship. "Churchill was too bound up in himself," said Janet Murrow later, "to be seeking out the advice of an American journalist. He was fond of Ed, and Ed, of course, worshipped him." And there, essentially, it stayed, though contacts were to grow after Pearl Harbor.

Bill Shirer was going home after years as an expatriate, sick and bitter at the fate of the Continent, wife and child sent ahead. December 8, Murrow flew to neutral Portugal to say good-bye. "He's not very keen to go," Janet noted, "and wouldn't, but that he wants so much to see Bill."

It was an emotionally charged reunion—the last perhaps, they both felt, given the fortunes of war. A booking had been obtained with difficulty aboard one of the small boats sailing weekly from Lisbon, where anxious refugees jammed shipping offices, seeking passage and escape.

They spent almost a week together, sunning on the beaches, talking through the nights, making up for the year apart, losing at roulette in the casinos, trying for one last broadcast together: Murrow and Shirer, inseparable, the Dioscuri of the airwaves.

"He wasn't just a friend," said Shirer. "We had built up radio news from nothing. . . . had been so close."[36] He promised to return to take Murrow's place in London should the other go home for a spell.[37]

The evening of Friday the 13th, they were at the dock, both depressed, drinking until sailing time, downing shot after shot of the rotgut brandy poured out at the little dockside bar. Six drinks later they were still coldly, deadeningly sober. Murrow had begun crying. It was not until the gangway was literally being pulled in that Shirer finally hurried aboard, watching from the deck as the other turned and walked away into the dark.

Back in London, Murrow found Langham Place a disaster area, hit by a parachute mine, Columbia's third office wrecked, no injuries—they had cabled him in Lisbon—parts of Broadcasting House a waterlogged, fire-charred ruin.

The mine had set off a ton of high explosives, ripping the BBC and the hotel opposite. Down in Studio B-4 Larry LeSueur, caught in mid-broadcast, had been forced to the door by a rising cascade of water and sewage. At the shattered NBC offices just opposite in Portland Place, the frightened women had been helped out, blackened with soot and bleeding from multiple cuts. Fred Bate, caught in the open, had managed to stagger into Broadcasting House, in shock, still clutching his script, trying to reach the studio, unaware that one of his ears was nearly severed, both legs cut and burned. He was now in the hospital and would need further months of convalescence in the States.

Through it all, the newsroom staff under Michael Balkwill had calmly filed to a waiting armored car and finished the night's news writing in a converted skating rink in Northwest London. Next day, they were back in Broadcasting House, work continuing in the scarred, once-elegant building that now stank of fire and mildew.

December 29, Ed Murrow, at the microphone, reviewed 1940—a year of "blasted hopes, futile ambitions, false confidence, small men, and a wreckage of proud and pleasant nations."

In America, Roosevelt was addressing the radio public on lend-lease—like lending one's neighbor a garden hose, he said easily, when his house caught fire. It was more than a metaphor in England that night, as bombers, in a year-end present, hit London in a mass arson raid. The historic City burned: walls collapsing; ancient steeples crashing with a clang of bells as the conflagration consumed national treasures, warehouses and slums alike.

Murrow, his broadcast ended, had started walking eastward, then picked up Ed Beattie of the UP and Bob Post of The New York *Times*, both headed for the glow around St. Paul's. Near the river they ran into Bill Stoneman and Drew Middleton, who had come out of the Savoy to see the eastern sky ablaze.

At the site the streets had been roped off. The heat was intense, the reporters walking gingerly around, unable to get too close, apprehensively aware that the Germans could see all from two miles up, maybe make another try.

Because it was a business district, the loss of life would probably be negligible; rather, it was the symbolism of the act—hundreds of years of history going up in smoke, the financial capital, the heart of the empire and to some extent, the Western world. Down one block, another warehouse flared, sending up a soft, distinct aroma. One man sniffed the air. "There must be sugar in there." No one commented as they made their notes, watching the roaring furnace consume Samuel Pepys' London, in their nostrils, the sweet smell of burning sugar.[38]

The flames were still going, sizzling and smoking in a thin dawn rain, as the Americans walked up Ludgate Hill, disheartened—this was somehow the worst yet—then separated; the newspapermen to file their stories, Murrow back to Langham Place, walking west, the rain falling, the windows along his path red with reflected fire, the drops like blood upon the panes—an image etched forever in his mind.

In those same hours, another figure had left the furnace-hot streets: Arthur Harris, future chief of RAF Bomber Command, soon to be known as Bomber Harris; ahead were the raids on Hamburg, Dresden, and Cologne. That night he, too, had been watching helplessly as the fire storm consumed the City's heart, then turned away, tight-lipped: *They have sown the wind.*

2.

In the late afternoon of January 9, 1941, the gaunt figure of Presidential envoy Harry L. Hopkins, right-hand man to FDR, alighted unobtrusively from a seaplane at a small site in southern England, his task, to lay the groundwork for the anticipated lend-lease plan coming up next day before Congress. In his pocket were greetings to Churchill and the official itinerary including, for day one, morning meetings with Foreign Secretary Anthony Eden, lunch with the Prime Minister, and dinner with "Mr. Edward R. Murrow, Columbia Broadcasting Service [sic]."[1]

Whether Murrow knew he was on the itinerary seems doubtful. Press conferences had of course been scheduled for Friday with the British and American news media, drawing just about every reporter within hailing distance of London. When Murrow suddenly found himself asked to dinner, therefore, he thought he was being handed an exclusive.

Instead, it was a brain-picking session on the situation in Britain, the reporter the one answering the questions, supplementing first-night briefings by the American chargé d'affaires; Ambassador Kennedy had gone home, unwept and unregretted.

There was also evidently some urging from the President's man for Murrow to go home himself and "talk with a few people," as the broadcaster wrote a brother afterward, but he had no intention of doing so, he added. He had no political ambition and didn't propose to go home and do propaganda.

It would be the first, though by no means the last, of various attempts to get him on the team, the broadcaster's basic agreement on Rooseveltian policies at odds with his concern as a reporter, not to become an adjunct of the administration.

Bill Shirer wrote from Chappaqua, acclimatizing after sixteen years away, lecturing and putting his book together. Their friends were well, he wrote, Jimmy Sheean due back soon in London. Eric Sevareid was in Washington, none too happy, he gathered. Scotty Reston was there, too, "trying to wake up the country—which God knows it needs—to produce a few implements of war."

> This country is still fantastic and still asleep and still listening to quacks and still living in a fool's paradise but there are signs that it is waking up and its core, I think, is very sound. You are doing more than you probably realize to wake it up, even if you do sometimes shock our execs at the office whose thoughts are still on the time they sell. But I suppose if they weren't, you and I would starve.
>
> . . . I feel bound to tell you, Edward, that in my long trips up and down this sprawling land I have ascertained beyond doubt, you are now the #1 man on the air. No one here touches you, or has your following. . . . Everywhere I go old dowagers and young things ask if I know you and whether you really are as handsome as your photographs and what you eat for breakfast and when you are coming home. . . . If and when you come home next fall, ponder well, my friend, the wisdom of doing a lecture tour. You will be mobbed.

Raymond Swing was "definitely tops at home—a fact admitted everywhere except at 485 Madison."

His own plans were uncertain, except he refused to turn expatriate again as Paul White wanted, hoping instead to broadcast from New York provided he could sell management on the idea. "The ignorance of this country about its enemy is titanic and there is much good work to be done." In the meantime, Washington was calling on an unnamed "very important project."

"Actually Butcher told me on the phone today that Washington very much wanted you for the job. The point is that after being an unofficial and unimportant observer all my life, I would very much like for once to be of some direct use to this country in a struggle that for once I believe in and where, for once, I have a little expert knowledge."

He promised again to come over in the fall as planned, to take Murrow's place. "I know it depends upon events not predictable now. But I want very much to do it."[2]

With the passage of lend-lease that March, Americans began arriving in Britain. Educators, businessmen, White House advisers poured into London, all seeking out the CBS European Director, known to be the best-informed American in England, effecting virtually overnight a transformation in Murrow's status from a lone journalistic outpost to vanguard of the growing American presence.

Many of the faces were familiar from IIE days. For Murrow, however, the most important was to be a tall, brooding New Englander, a friend from the early thirties and Murrow's favorite candidate for the opening left by Joe Kennedy: John Gilbert Winant, Washington's new Ambassador to the Court of St. James.

He was in the tradition of the Murrows, a progressive Republican: three-term Governor of New Hampshire, pioneer in labor legislation and social reforms, advocate of the four-day workweek, first Chairman of the Social Security Board, until recently Director of the International Labor Organization, a New Deal loyalist who had turned down a GOP nominating bid in 1936, still spoken of as possible presidential timber in 1944.

"Ed had enormous regard for him," recalled an English colleague. Indeed, the affinity between the two men, the twenty-year disparity in their ages notwithstanding, was obvious to those who knew them: two brooding Lincolnesque figures, alike in their introspection and intermittent depressions. "Both rather inward-looking," as a friend put it, "both absolutely dedicated, on the same wavelength."[3]

At the other end of the scale, among the unofficial newcomers was a small creature showing up one day at the naval public relations office. "Excuse me, I've got to write columns."

Heads turned to see "a funny little man with an enormous great hat and a tiny little face."[4]

"Name, please?"

"Ernie Pyle."

Pyle, sitting in on a Murrow broadcast, wrote up Studio B-4 for the hometown readers: the censor with one hand on the switch, the green felt-covered table at the center holding the square microphone, a glass of water, and an ashtray (the BBC's no smoking rule had been unofficially waived in Murrow's case).

The newspaperman had found himself fascinated as he watched the broadcaster pace himself, one eye on the clock, timing the manuscript in his head as he talked. That night, as it happened, Murrow's timing sense told him that the piece was going to be too long, that he had overwritten. As a nervous censor and 30 million Americans listened, he rewrote in his head, wound up the prepared copy and ad-libbed through the remaining minutes, walking a fine line between dead air and uncensored material.

His voice betrayed no hint of effort. But when it was over, he sagged back, beads of sweat standing on his forehead and upper lip.

By now, however, even a routine broadcast on any night would produce rivulets of nervous sweating—the result of tension, awareness of responsibility, and above all, of mike fright.

Others came through London, notably Alexander Woollcott, the massive, crusty critic and fellow broadcaster for CBS, cashiered once by a sponsor, though not the network, following an on-air slap at Hitler. From

Studio B-4 the fat man spoke to America, with Murrow as a sort of unofficial host for CBS, the acid-tongued guest from New York an una-bashed admirer of the Murrow broadcasts. With Helen Kirkpatrick, they toured the makeshift shelter communities of the East End, enjoying each other's joshing, the broadcaster answering to "Repulsive," Woollcott to "Uncle Winsome."

Murrow had also started a new series for the BBC, *Meet Uncle Sam*, a cram course on the American experience for British listeners, intro-ducing and reading continuity for guest commentators—Alistair Cooke, the historians D. W. Brogan and Allan Nevins—and leading off himself with a scathing overview articulating the viewpoint of a Depression Kid, as he spoke of the "motley crew" who had once "poured" westward:

> They were ahead of the law, ahead of education and established in-stitutions. They made their own. . . . There grew up a tradition of violence and lawlessness. . . . They fought a four-year civil war. And the status of the Negro . . . is still one of the greatest problems facing the nation. I believe we lynched only three or four of our black fellow-citizens last year, which is some improvement. . . .
>
> We . . . engineered a frontier incident with Mexico. We took that huge territory of Texas, and what is now California. . . . Later on, we were to land marines in Nicaragua and Haiti, narrowly avoid war with Germany over Venezuela, and create a heritage of mistrust amongst the South American peoples as a result of high-handed methods and dollar diplomacy. Cuba and the Philippines came into our *Lebens-raum.* . . .
>
> And all the time we were despoiling a continent. We cut the top off it, and sent the timber floating down the rivers. We ploughed the prairies, wasted our oil. . . . Later on in this series you will hear all about the New Deal, our racial problems, and how we came to be a nation of which one-third is ill-clothed, ill-housed and ill-fed. You will also hear something of our achievements. . . .[5]

He also put British listeners on notice of the national debate now rising back home, among Americans "in lumber camps in Oregon, on the cattle ranches of Montana, down along the bayous of Louisiana . . . in the steel mills of Pittsburgh and the lobbies in Washington. . . ."

"Many of them will be thinking for the first time of America's respon-sibility as a nation; that is something rather new for us. We have heretofore been too busy building a nation, exploiting its resources, and then won-dering what hit us. . . ."[5]

The BBC, jarred at first by Murrow's tone, ran the piece, noting "his vigorous criticisms of some things American, which would come ill from an Englishman."[6]

It was a bleak spring. In the Balkans, the Norway debacle was being repeated as the British Expeditionary Force, sent to aid Greece against

German attack, retreated before the Wehrmacht. On the high seas, convoys and U-boats fought for mastery of the North Atlantic.

In London, Murrow added to the staff, relieving the desperately short-handed situation with two UP reporters: Paul Manning and a youngster whose name would be invariably linked with Murrow's but who seemed an odd choice to BBC personnel on his first stop at the newsroom.

"I don't know what we'd expected," said Pat Smithers later, "but what appeared . . . was a chap who looked exactly like the dummy out of a rather good tailor shop window: impeccably dressed, with a collar too high for him, so that he looked as if he were about to choke. Very broad shoulders; crimpy, curly hair. A very strange chap, we thought, to be a war correspondent.

"How wrong we were—how wrong we were. He vanished into the blue and we began getting back his dispatches and were filled with admiration for the man's courage, guts. He always seemed to be right up at the center of things. In due course, months later, he reappeared in the newsroom, still looking just like a tailor's dummy."

It was Charles Collingwood, whose sartorial style had almost caused Murrow at first to reconsider. A Rhodes Scholar, Collingwood had left off reading Jurisprudence at Oxford in 1939 to turn reporter, joining UP the same day as Howard K. Smith, also down from Oxford, another Rhodes Scholar, and soon to start working for CBS in Berlin. Both men would pursue somewhat parallel careers, winding up as card-carrying members of the inner circle known as the Murrow Boys.

The young man had expected a training period, a few weeks of research for Mr. Murrow, perhaps, studying the radio scripts, learning how it was done. Instead, there was a dry run or two, nothing much. Suddenly he was thrown in at the deep end when Murrow telephoned one day: He had a dinner date with the Prime Minister of the Netherlands; would he, Collingwood, do the show tonight?

Nervously, Collingwood went through the agency wires. He'd been shown the layout of the BBC, had seen Murrow broadcast, knew the routine. He wrote and rewrote his copy, then headed for the studio. No Murrow. He passed the script to the censors, put on the headphones. It was well after twelve by now; still no Murrow. New York came in on the cue channel, and they talked. Finally, at one minute to airtime, "Ed slid into the seat opposite me," and Collingwood picked up on cue.

It went without a hitch until the final sign-off, forgotten by the neophyte in the relief at ending his first newscast. Without missing a beat, Murrow, who had sat smoking, leaned into the microphone: "This is Charles Collingwood in London; now back to Robert Trout in New York."[7]

The young reporter expected a full-scale critique. There wasn't any. A few nights later, going on again, he asked the boss outright: Weren't there any tips or something? Well, said Murrow, these mikes were pretty sensitive—"You don't have to shout as though you were at the end of a long-distance telephone." As time went on, he would toss him more hints: how to write a story, construct a sentence.

Years later Collingwood, then a veteran himself, asked Murrow about those times; after all, signing him on as a raw young correspondent, no instructions, hadn't he taken a chance?

"I suppose I was," the other man replied. "But I wanted you to sound like yourself and not like me."

There was a full moon on Friday, April 11. Over the late winter, with its heavier cloud cover, the bombing had let up. The thirteenth was Easter Sunday; CBS was arranging a roundup from locations scattered throughout the island, with Collingwood and LeSueur, Manning, Ben Robertson taking time out from *PM*. At Westminster Abbey, Ed and Janet Murrow reported on the services, Janet proud to be adding her minute-and-a-half.

The weather was still fine that Wednesday night, April 16, as the Murrows dined at l'Étoile, a favorite neighborhood restaurant, where the Continental owners worked wonders with the purveyings of wartime rationing.

Going home, they passed Broadcasting House and, behind it, the small two-abreast known as Duchess Street. At No. 1, behind blackout curtains, Kay Campbell was working late in CBS's fourth office since the start of the blitz. Sounds of talk and fiddle scraping emerged from the Devonshire, the corner pub whose owner had kept up customers' spirits all winter, playing his violin for BBC personnel stopping in for a pie and a pint.

There were hours to go before airtime, Murrow's newscast set for 12:50, the material already pulled together, focusing on the bad news from the Balkans—Greek and British forces in retreat; Yugoslavia under German attack; Belgrade leveled from the air, 17,000 civilians dead.

Possibly it was the news from Belgrade, more likely the relative quiet of the past months, that made Janet Murrow suddenly aware of the whine of aircraft to the southeast, the muffled sounds of distant explosions, drawing nearer.

They were right at the corner now, before the Devonshire; Ed suggested a brief stopover.

The sky seemed to hum and throb above them; for the first time in her life Janet Murrow felt a sense of dread. She faced her husband. "I'm really scared tonight. I'd be grateful if you'd walk home with me."[8]

Somewhat scornfully, he agreed, and bypassed the pub.

By the time they reached 84 Hallam Street, the guns had started working. "Let's go to the roof and watch!" he said. She followed automatically.

For a brief time, six stories up, all action seemed suspended—a cloudless night; bright stars; red flares suspended above the housetops. *Like lanterns in the sky*, Janet Murrow thought.

A moment later the angry *whooosssh* of a bomb sent them running for the stairwell, there to huddle in the dark, arms wrapped about their heads to protect the eardrums as the thing approached with the noise of an oncoming freight train. The blast shook the building. Then silence.

"Are you all right?"

It was her voice, but they both were unhurt. The bomb had narrowly missed Number 84.

Shakily, they edged back onto the roof and saw a scene from hell.

The neighborhood was on fire, the back-wall canyon of the BBC lit up like a stage set as one by one, the houses along Duchess and Langham Streets popped into flame, the planes bombing directly into the fires to spread them.

Murrow looked in the direction of the explosions. "It's the office!" He grabbed his tin hat, rushed back downstairs, and began running toward the inferno that was Duchess Street. Janet Murrow, transfixed, looked toward the Devonshire. It was gone, the result of a direct hit, the flames already spreading to the hotel next door. In its place, a great balloon of black smoke, shot through with gold sparks, mushroomed into the night sky.

She ran downstairs, got some things together, told their young maid Betty to pack a bag in case they had to evacuate, then sat down to wait as the fires outside lit the flat with an unsteady orange glare.

Over at the BBC, in the underground newsroom, there had been at first a sickening jolt, then total darkness as the power went. The staff groped their way about sixty feet below ground level, almost afraid to move, a disembodied voice, recognized as the engineer's, raised plaintively in the inky blackness:

"Has anybody got a fucking match?"

A staffer flicked a cigarette lighter and groped his way to the voice. "Thanks, pal." Holding its sputtering light ahead, the engineer crawled gingerly to a wall switch and activated the reserve diesel generators, which, throbbing into life, restored light and broadcasting.

Meanwhile in Duchess Street, Murrow had found Kay Campbell where the blast had blown her through an open doorway—badly frightened, hair coated with plaster, but unhurt; the building, though battered, had not burned. He left her in the care of an air-raid warden, then ran to the NBC offices on another floor. Fred Bate's assistants were scratched and sooty but alive. The pub was a lost cause.

At Broadcasting House, he went to the rooftop and looked out. Pat Smithers, who came along, later remembered him silhouetted against the flames rising from the street, rising into a clear yet smoky sky, charred building remnants eddying in the updraft created by the fires. "Just dust and muck," he recalled, "sparks and dust and muck."

They came back downstairs, covered with grime. Someone had lent

Murrow an old mackintosh. He was dirty and disheveled and shaken. In B-4 he gave his broadcast somehow, then stumbled back to retrieve what he could of the office, the bombs still dropping.

At 84 Hallam, Janet Murrow had been waiting in an enforced calm that was getting progressively harder to keep up: *The fires are worse, and Ed's there.* Then suddenly he was standing in the doorway, unmoving, tin hat pushed to the back of his head, in his eyes a dazed reflection of the horrors in the street; under one arm he held a typewriter, under the other a bottle of scotch. Kay was all right, he said. For the rest there was nothing to say.

The telephone began jangling at 9:00 A.M.—anxious friends with the unspoken question, Were they alive? Overhead, blue April skies contended with palls of gray smoke; underfoot, Janet Murrow noted in her diary, "glass, glass and more glass." All over the city, sleepless firemen were hosing down the steaming skeletons of buildings. Murrow saw them behind Broadcasting House, hollow-eyed and coal-faced, training streams of water on the charred rubble that had been Duchess Street. "A considerable number of people were down there somewhere. . . . Some of them were friends of mine; perhaps they will be dug out some time next week."[9]

Everywhere there was the sickly sweet smell of death. At a corner near the BBC, a mound of rubbish marked the site of the Devonshire, where thirty had died when the bomb and incendiaries came through the ceiling. Earlier in the day a boy of seventeen, the owners' son, had been seen picking his way through the debris, unearthing suddenly the broken, dust-covered box section of a violin. Wiping it with his sleeve, he had climbed down silently and walked away, crying.

At Broadcasting House, Smithers told Murrow about it. The reporter's carefully controlled features began to twist: "God, how sad."

"For a moment," said Smithers afterward, "I thought *he* would cry, but he didn't."

Some 500 tons of high explosives had been dropped on the city, a revenge raid for minor damage inflicted on Berlin, with the threat of more to come as the weather cleared.

That same night Jimmy Sheean, back from America, met at the Claridge with Murrow, Robertson, and Stoneman. He was shocked at their appearance; all three looked haggard, and Murrow had aged visibly.

The epic days were over, they told him, public morale near rock bottom. Rationing and food shortages probably had a lot to do with it, they guessed; everyone was a little undernourished.

Sheean had written Murrow that winter, following a coast-to-coast speaking tour, warning of the climate in his native Middle West—"a sort of chilly disbelief." His first audience had been in Minneapolis, he said, "and boy, was it cold."

The whole press from one end of the country to the other is dominated by wishful thinking which misleads the public horribly. I have actually seen an hour-and-a-half or two-hour alarm over Berlin treated as more important than a ten-hour full-fledged bombing of London. It isn't deliberate policy of course . . . just an unfortunate journalistic trick common to all our colleagues.

Murrow, replying, had found the news "discouraging, but very much what I had expected.

"When the American papers come in, or when I listen to American broadcasts, I am almost overcome with the desire to be ill. I suppose there's nothing to be done . . . they won't listen to what you say, what I say, or what anyone else says."

Two nights after their reunion, the raiders were back; chalked slogans proliferating on blackened walls in the smoking aftermath, all variations on a single theme: BOMB BERLIN. But the focus of international attention had shifted to the Balkans; the German drive for Suez; the Japanese drive on Singapore. The bombings were old news, no longer hot. The British were hanging on by their fingernails, lend-lease notwithstanding, grimly, because they had to.

Murrow, writing his friend Chet Williams that spring, was convinced that America would not long survive a British defeat, "that if this country goes down we at home will tear ourselves apart within five years, probably less."[10] He was changing his mind about coming home—"thinking perhaps I could do more good there than here"—but not before the fall.

At the same time his closeness to American officialdom in London was proving problematic; aspects of his job as reporter, he told Williams, getting harder to sort out. "I know in my own mind that I have more and better information than ever before. But it's exceedingly difficult to know just what to do with it. I have no desire to use the studio as a privileged pulpit, but am convinced that some very plain talking is required in the immediate future, even if it be at the price of being labelled a warmonger."

Williams, filling him in on the scene at home, wrote of a growing credibility gap:

The people as a whole simply do not understand that a Hitler control of Europe, Asia, Africa and the high seas would put us at the mercy of the Nazis for about 25 essential resources. . . . Facts like that have not been explained. . . .

The very fact that the word "interventionist" is so widely used in describing those of us who insist on preparing national defense . . . is indicative of a public misunderstanding. . . . The average man still does not see that the Nazis are the interventionists who have been working like ants . . . since 1933. . . . There is a good deal of resentment against the tendency of the Administration to creep up on the public. [And] while this procedure appears to work, I think it is very dangerous.

Morale is the product of an understanding cooperation and that cannot be induced by superficial methods. . . .[11]

Murrow found the report "disquieting"—"but it's about what I would have expected to happen."

In early May, Elmer Davis of the New York office came to London, a wry, gray-haired, gray-suited presence and for Murrow, a much-needed shot in the arm. "Elmer," said a mutual friend later, "was a sort of father figure to Ed."

The two men had met briefly just before the war, during Murrow's last visit to the States, the Davis nightly commentaries over CBS—concise, biting, witheringly accurate—striking instant rapport in his younger colleague. A former New York *Times* man, Rhodes Scholar, and student of American politics, Davis had moved into the number one analysis spot at CBS with Kaltenborn's departure to NBC; living testimony to the impact of the unschooled voice, his flat, no-nonsense, Midwestern delivery—once the bane of White's existence—now the trademark of the 8:55 P.M. spot, the highlight of the network's news analysis as the Murrow broadcasts were those of straight reporting.

They complemented each other, Murrow admiring the veteran journalist, the intellectual and hardheaded Hoosier wit. Davis had just completed the editing of a Murrow broadcast collection for CBS, scheduled for fall publication, paying tribute in the foreword to Murrow's "excellence as a reporter of pure news," while admitting to being "faintly scandalized that such good reporting can be done by a man who never worked on a newspaper in his life."[12]

They were inseparable over those weeks, Davis broadcasting from the BBC subbasement, driving around London in the Sunbeam-Talbot, Murrow at the wheel. Their first day out, the visiting American had taken one look of disbelief at the tiny two-door roadster, then snorted in a voice that was pure southern Indiana: "This isn't a car you get into—you put it on!" Enough days of speeding around London and environs, wheels screeching, corners cut, were to leave him with the comment that he'd heard of the horrors of war but hadn't known they included Ed Murrow's driving.

They planned a trip to the badly hit western ports, Davis anxious to see the damage in the Bristol area. A former opponent of U.S. involvement in the conflict—Trout could remember vehement confrontations in the newsroom—he was now fully committed: turned, like so many, by the bombing of the mother country and the fall of Paris. On a Friday morning, they packed a few items and departed by car; the weather was clammy, an unseasonable cold turning spring into late winter. It was May 10, 1941.

The news coming into Bristol that night seemed to dwarf anything that had gone before: The Luftwaffe was finally burning London in an incendiary attack unprecedented in the past weeks or the worst nights of the blitz—a fire raid, unequaled in its ferocity, on residential areas.

Back in the capital, some 2,000 fires were spreading, raging out of control throughout the city, iron streetlamps wilting and bending under temperatures soaring to 2,000 degrees, water pressures falling as fire fighters drew on the Thames and the river level sank, leaving fire hoses dry and useless, citizens in bypassed areas throwing themselves before fire trucks rushing to other priorities, while the bombs kept raining down.

In Portland Place, John MacVane, an NBC reporter and a neighbor of the Murrows, had been called to the street, where three inert figures lay as if flung on the sidewalk, like heaps of rags. One was the building porter; one a woman, skirt blown up, white legs sprawled grotesquely in the flickering light. A man lay nearby, breathing with loud, ripping sounds, his long hair wet with clumps of blood soaking through the toweling provided by a rescue worker. The NBC man recognized Claire and Allan Wells.

At dawn the departing planes left the city reeling: 700 acres blackened, communications disrupted; almost 3,500 dead and injured.

Murrow, returning from Bristol, was told about the Wellses: Claire had been killed instantly; Allan was in the hospital unconscious, not expected to live. They had been patrolling as fire wardens, trying to deal with an incendiary when the bomb hit. Murrow could picture them in his mind, going out with their small sand buckets as the high explosives came down. "What a rotten world!" Janet noted in her diary.

London's past lay in ruins, the result of air strikes that included Westminster Abbey, the RAF Church of St. Clement Danes, Big Ben, and the British Museum. At Westminster, the House of Commons had been gutted, the chamber of Gladstone and Disraeli gone, in its place a calcined shell, gaping open to the sky, the Members' lobby choked by twisted girders, staircases still intact leading to empty air and blue, sudden daylight.

In a small neighborhood church, the Murrows attended last rites for the Wellses, listening in dismay as the tired minister rattled through the perfunctory sermon. Ed, who had kept his feelings bottled up, came home furious—"As though he were reading a laundry list!" It added to his growing low regard for organized religion.

There were too many funerals, everyone slightly numb, Londoners digging out again, rising unsteadily for the count, not sure if this time they could take it. But the May 10 fire storm, it would turn out, had been a diversion.

June 22, the guns along the German-Russian border roared into life as Germany, driving eastward into the Soviet Union, launched Operation Barbarossa.

That evening the BBC news staff stood by anxiously as Churchill prepared to broadcast, wondering what the old anti-Bolshevik would say.

Many had been pro-Soviet in the great days before the Hitler-Stalin pact, when they all had been seemingly on the side of the angels. Said Reeves, "There was agony in the newsroom." Out of the corner of her eye she could see Murrow standing among the news staff, sharing their apprehension.

The relief, therefore, was almost palpable as Churchill, going on the air, launched into a violent denunciation of the invasion and pledged all-out support to the Soviets.

Murrow, later that night, called the declaration "a combination of humanitarian principle and national self-interest.

"The Prime Minister brought all his oratorical power to the appeal for aid to the Soviet Union, which he has always hated—and still does. . . .

"What he implied was that the Russians, after all, are human but the Germans aren't. Russia's danger, he said, is our danger. . . . Any man or state who fights Nazidom will have our help, he said."

Nevertheless, as Soviet forces fell back in those early months, the broadcaster accepted predictions current among the military of a quick, even imminent Russian collapse, differing with friends who thought otherwise. Williams' insistence that Hitler like Napoleon would "bog down in Russia" left him unconvinced. He responded: "Maybe you are right . . . but I am still inclined to think that the German estimate of ten weeks for the whole operation is about right."[13]

It was a military, not ideological, assessment, shared at the newsroom by R. T. Clark, who believed initial German inroads into Russia to be simply too sweeping, both men gloomily aware that if the Soviets went down, Britain would be next. To a friend at the Rockefeller Foundation, Murrow wrote of being "profoundly discouraged. The results of a Russian collapse are not altogether appreciated here, and apparently scarcely understood at all at home."

The assessment grew less gloomy as Moscow held; indeed, the broadcaster would in time become one of the staunchest admirers of the fighting abilities of the Red Army in World War II.

But right now he was tired—supersaturated, ready at last to go home and do some talking after all.

Janet was going on ahead, a speaking tour arranged through Sue White on behalf of Bundles for Britain—something of a disappointment since she had hoped to talk to more than the converted. Gil Winant, ever helpful, managed to obtain a precious booking aboard the Atlantic Clipper departing Lisbon in early October. Ed, to follow a month later, had had to settle for slow passage on the *Excambion*, Bob Trout to fill in for him in London. Shirer wasn't coming after all.

The Battle of Britain was already a year in the past, London no longer the front line. LeSueur was on his way to Murmansk with a convoy of tanks and trucks for the Soviet Union. Harry Hopkins, stopping off in England en route to Moscow, lunched with Murrow. At the drab new

CBS offices, the staff settled in for the grueling, workaday reporting of what looked to be a long, drawn-out war.

But one more blow was to fall before they left—one that had nothing to do with the conflict or the world situation. In the past months Ida Lou Anderson had started writing to Janet Murrow, bridging the old gap as her health declined, her resentment softened, culminating in a recent letter admitting in effect that she'd been wrong: that she, Janet, had been really good for Ed.

They probably sensed that she was dying, the frail, crippled body, at forty-one, no longer capable of sustaining the determined spirit. Her eyesight had finally gone; Ed had arranged for a radio to be sent her at her new home near the Oregon coast. "FEELING LIKE CINDERELLA," she cabled from Corvallis, "IMAGINE ME BESIDE BEAUTIFUL NEW RADIO YOUR GIFT MY GREATEST COMFORT."

Janet Murrow was home alone the night of September 16, when a cable arrived not from Corvallis but from Pullman: Ida Lou Anderson had died three days ago. Her funeral was to be next Sunday.

Ed was at Broadcasting House. She took the cable in her hand and waited; but when the front door opened, she saw that he was not alone, R. T. Clark along as usual, the two men settling down for one of their marathon sessions.

She sat down too, marking time, unwilling to break the news with others present. Still the conversation continued. She waited. They kept talking. Finally, she went to bed.

Next morning, she broke it to him gently, then drew back, startled, as the tears came in a rush, streaming down his face through a string of reproaches: Why had she waited? How could she not have told him? The obvious explanations, so reasonable, so logical in context, seemed inadequate as he stumbled down the long corridor, his back to her. From behind the closed bedroom door she could hear him weeping, but did not go in—one of those times, she knew, when he was best left alone.[14]

In time he would pay tribute to Anderson as teacher, the "tolerant skeptic," the woman who had set his course, embodiment of what he had tried for, or hoped to be: "She believed nothing and reverenced all."

November 10, from a hotel room in Bristol, he penned a quick farewell note to Gil Winant: "Leaving this country is not easy. It is, in fact, more difficult than I had expected."

There were several hours to go before his departure for Lisbon and ultimately, home. On the Continent, Hitler held sway from the Arctic to the Balkans, the Nazi armies at last count forty miles from Moscow, the Soviet ministries evacuated east; and, despite lend-lease, U-boat confrontations on the Atlantic, or the Roosevelt-Churchill meeting off Newfoundland, there seemed little likelihood of direct action by the United States.

For the first time in his career, the broadcaster seriously considered leaving radio to turn activist. "If some time in the unpredictable future," he wrote Winant that night, "you decide to go home and seek political power, I may be one of the 'goodly company' to travel with you."[15]

In the meantime, he was going back to the country he had not seen since Christmas 1938, grim, reluctant to leave—he left an affectionate, almost homesick thank-you message for the BBC engineers[16]—yet impelled to go; convinced, as he told friends, "that the hour is much later than most people at home appreciate."

VIII

Total War

The first weeks back were strange ones—at once euphoric and unsettling, pleasure at being home at odds with culture shock. In New York Harbor there had been a hero's welcome, and he'd enjoyed it to the full, posing exuberantly for press photographers—framed against the Manhattan skyline, gloved hand raised in greeting, one foot crossed breezily over the other à la Groucho Marx.

In London there had often been a sense of remoteness, even isolation, as he broadcast at night to an unseen audience 3,000 miles away and more. Like leaving letters in a hollow log, was how he put it, or talking to yourself in a darkened room.

The sudden rush of adulation, therefore, the awareness of a living, massive listenership at the other end of the circuit, were almost overwhelming, the broadcaster thrust abruptly into the limelight in a sudden change of roles—from a private man doing a public job into a walking symbol in the nationwide debate peaking that winter of 1941, amid encounters between U-boats and supply convoys that were now American. Only a week before, with one destroyer sunk, Congress had agreed to arm U.S. merchantmen carrying supplies to Britain.

In New York—the communications center, responding to each new development with the sensitivity of a tuning fork—America First rallies were virtually alternating with antifascist rallies at Madison Square Garden. The war of words was escalating on radio, uniting old opponents like Burton Wheeler, insisting Germany could not be defeated, with old friends like Norman Thomas, warning against a war "that no man may win unless perhaps Stalin picks up the pieces,"[1] while Colonel Lindbergh assured audiences this was just another European family fight and not a war in which our civilization was defending itself against some Asian intruder.

It was a supercharged atmosphere, in which the London broadcasts had played their part, that Murrow had come back to: public sentiments divided, sympathetic generally to Britain, little love lost for the Nazis—even in the Midwest, Polish- and Czech-American communities had a personal stake in what happened on the Continent—yet stopping short of commitment as a cobelligerent, the watchword at best: All aid short of war.

But there was no ambivalence about Ed Murrow.

He was feted, celebrated, interviewed, spending most of his time, he wrote Laski after ten days in New York and Washington, trying to keep his temper in check.

> It was a shock to see so many well-dressed, well-fed, complacent-looking people—shop windows crowded with luxury goods—the chamber maid in the hotel wearing silk stockings—a big formal Bundles for Britain ball . . . fat chorus boys with marcelled hair dressed in sailor uniforms singing nautical songs—little boxes in expensive night clubs marked "Tin Foil for Britain"—wealthy friends moaning about ruinous taxation. . . . My mind would not work—still have a curious feeling of being suspended between a skyscraper and a bomb crater. . . .
>
> Have seen Felix Frankfurter, Ferdie Kuhn, Marvin McIntyre, Mrs. Roosevelt and . . . Harry Hopkins. . . . Felix somewhat worried about you. . . . I tried to explain but found it completely impossible to make one who is as intelligent as Felix understand what is happening to sensitive, thoughtful people in Britain. . . . why you will not leave England now. . . . Words mean something entirely different over here. . . . Maybe it was a mistake for me to come. . . .

At 485, the news floor was almost unrecognizable, transformed wholly from the small setup he remembered into the hub of a global news operation, with correspondents in Europe, North Africa, and the Middle East; Moscow and Chungking; the Philippines and the Dutch East Indies.[2] In Southeast Asia, Bill Dunn, now Chief Pacific Correspondent, was setting up new broadcast links.

Ed Klauber's reconstruction orders had been carried out meticulously, replacing the improvisation of the thirties, when technicians had had to bring in portable sound equipment to do a broadcast. Old hands like Trout could still remember the time of the Anschluss, the engineer setting up facilities "as though he were doing a dance band." Even in the Munich crisis some features had originated from audition rooms lacking permanent speech-input equipment or from Talks studios at the topmost building levels, far away from the news department.[3]

By 1941 and well before, however, all that had given way to a carefully designed broadcast setup, a radial affair centering on the newsroom, easily overseen by Paul White—the old Studio 9, with its heavy acoustical curtain and primitive resources, updated; the smaller Studio 12, listening rooms for monitoring shortwave broadcasts (and later, tape replay); a bullpen for writers and editors, plus adequate office space for White himself, for his assistant, Wells "Ted" Church, and the busier newscasters. Murrow, when necessary, simply used whatever was available.

Next door, a traffic department handled arrangements for network use of telephone lines, ensuring optimum coordination in setting up overseas broadcast circuits.[4]

There were the familiar faces and the inevitable reunions. Alexander Woollcott, slowed by a near-fatal coronary, wrote from a Syracuse hospital that he expected to be "bedridden and very, very frail for a week or eight days and then go to New York in a tantrum." Murrow wrote "Uncle Winsome" to let him know of his arrival and "where and when to report."[5] As soon as he was up to traveling, the fat man promised, he'd come back to London—"and we'll do some *real* broadcasts."

Bill Shirer was continuing his career from New York with a Sunday news analysis spot over the CBS network, sixty-seven stations, and his name on the best-seller list. Murrow had plugged *Berlin Diary* on his London newscasts, ordering several armloads from the British publisher just before leaving England, for distribution to his private mailing list.

At 485, the two friends took up where they had left off as company photographers posed and shot still after still of Columbia's twin news stars. Away from the office there were the endless conversations and the usual horseplay. Shirer seemed unchanged, his fringe a little grayer, the classic pipe-smoking, battered-hat image of the veteran correspondent. The battered hat was real, and Murrow had always hated it. Returning from lunch one afternoon, he had finally, without warning, plucked it off Shirer's head and sent it spinning out into traffic, where a passing bus finished the job.

"*Now* will you let me buy you a new hat?"[6]

December 2, at New York's Waldorf-Astoria, CBS tossed a formal banquet honoring the "Chief of the European Staff, Columbia Broadcasting System," with a guest list drawn from the front ranks of the networks, wire agencies, business and labor, education and government—the movers and shakers, who had clamored for weeks for a coveted invitation. On the dais, bending over their filet mignon *forestière*, were notables of the city, the news media, and the Archdiocese of New York. Down the table, Hugh Baillie of the United Press talked with Lindsay Wellington of the BBC.

At the center sat William Paley, together with Elmer Davis and the guest of honor; to their left, the poet Archibald MacLeish, Librarian of Congress, past playwright for the Columbia Workshop, now head of the newly organized Office of Facts and Figures, forerunner to the Office of War Information, the U.S. propaganda arm in World War II. At the poet's elbow, Ed Klauber, seated with Bill Shirer and Paul White, glowered just a touch less than usual. At the far end, overhead lights reflected off the eyeglasses of FCC Chairman James Fly, an unremitting critic of commercial broadcasting but tonight beaming approval. A question-and-answer period had been provided for, with Kate Smith to end the evening's festivities.

It was a scene distinctive of the time and place, government and radio journalism at one in the cause, in a way that would be impossible in future years or even, to a certain extent, in the latter stages of the war to come. It was also emblematic of a subtle change in emphasis going hand in hand with the new developments, a gravitational shift in communications: radio was the undisputed star of the evening, the minions of print, there largely in a working capacity, consigned to two tables at the back, in the section marked "Press."[7]

In the meantime, microphones were open on a national hookup, Elmer Davis a genial emcee, laudatory speeches by Shirer and the President of CBS, in among his reporters, never closer than in this, their common moment of affirmation. At a rear table Stephen and Sarah Duggan, invited at Murrow's insistence, beamed like proud parents.

In words that were to become classic, the poet MacLeish paid tribute not only to Murrow but to radio itself, to the qualitative change in mass perception brought about by the mass medium: "You burned the city of London in our houses and we felt the flames that burned it. You laid the dead of London at our doors and we knew that the dead were our dead . . . were mankind's dead . . . without rhetoric, without dramatics, without more emotion than needed be . . . you have destroyed . . . the superstition that what is done beyond 3,000 miles of water is not really done at all."

There were cables from the BBC Director-General, the Secretary of State, Harry Hopkins; and the Oval Office: "You of the Columbia Broadcasting System who gather tonight to honor Ed Murrow repay but a tiny fraction of the debt owed him by millions of Americans. . . . He is to be congratulated in receiving this tribute. I wish I could be with you."

Originally it was Columbia that was to be congratulated, the prepared draft changed by FDR himself, careful as always not to play favorites or stress too overtly the network connection.[8]

As Murrow stepped finally to the rostrum, some 1,100 VIPs rose to their feet in a roar of acclamation that took him visibly aback—a man of thirty-three, standing skinny and bewildered in his London tailcoat. To Janet Murrow, sitting at a forward table with Dorothy Paley and Mrs. Elmer Davis, he seemed "stunned by the whole thing—it was so out of our whole experience; he had absolutely no idea of the effect he had had on his audience; the home office never let you know. . . ."[9]

Recovering, he got down to business, tight-lipped and serious, as he stated openly that American decisions were now the ones that counted, his record for telling it straight underlining his credibility not only with those present but with the general public, his obvious sympathies notwithstanding.

"Murrow's distinction," commented *Time* magazine, no invariable supporter of administration policy, "was that he did more than his job. . . ."

No bunk, no journalese, no sentimentality. When Dorothy Thompson
was telling the British that the poets of the world were on their side,
he spoke for the sweating people who doubted the poets' effectiveness.
At a time when the official British were still egg-walking on the subject
of the U.S., he reported the truth in plain words: "They want us in
this war."[10]

He spoke plainly. Therefore, he was believed, and in diametric opposition—a symbol whether he liked it or not—to the leadership of America First. MacLeish had touched on the symbolism indirectly in his address: "There were some in this country, Murrow, who did not want the
people of America to hear the things you had to say . . . who did not
wish to remember that . . . freedom of speech . . . is freedom also to
hear. . . . to assure people a chance to hear the truth, the unpleasant
truth as well as the reassuring truth, the dangerous truth as well as the
comforting truth. . . ."

The reference, though oblique, was clear. In a sense Murrow, as a
spokesman for involvement, had locked horns with another popular idol,
the Lone Eagle Charles Lindbergh, who, sent to Germany on a fact-
finding mission in the late thirties, had come back with a Nazi decoration,
a certain admiration for the efficiency of the new order, and the conviction—transmitted to the British and American governments—that the
Luftwaffe was invincible.

It was a fascinating contrast: two American heroes, each a symbol of
courage in his time, their paths never crossing directly yet juxtaposed in
glaring opposition in the public arena.

Murrow himself was generally noncommittal, in public and in private,
about the man who had been the idol of every red-blooded kid in western
Washington. Just once, however, walking with Sidney Bernstein in rural
Kent, he had stopped at a country house lent years back to the young
Lindberghs, taking refuge from the press following the tragic kidnapping
of their child. It had been taken over now by the Royal Society for the
Prevention of Cruelty to Children, housing young evacuees from the
devastated inner cities, small cots crammed into every corner.

Just that once, his bitterness had boiled over as he referred to "the
house which gave refuge to Charles Lindbergh—now giving refuge to
children who had to leave London because of the bombing by Lindbergh's
friends!"[11] It was an isolated instance, atypical of the man who by nature
preferred to deal in issues rather than in personalities.

"Archy MacLeish talked for five minutes," Murrow wrote Laski, describing the banquet, "copy attached—refrain from sending you a copy

of my speech because was definitely undistinguished altho' they tell me it jarred a few people."

It was Saturday, December 6. The following morning Paul White, instead of sleeping late, came into the office at eight o'clock, drawn by a feeling for which he had no explanation. In Washington, Ed and Janet Murrow were getting ready for a day of golf at Burning Tree, to end with dinner at the White House and a private briefing for the President. The news of Pearl Harbor broke in midafternoon.

Murrow hurried to the CBS offices for confirmation and talked with Paul White in New York. Janet Murrow, calling the White House, was told dinner was still on.

They ate Mrs. Roosevelt's scrambled eggs that evening, in a ghostly replay of victory night, 1936, at Hyde Park. Outside in the corridor, a steady stream of officials went past to the Oval Office. Murrow had been asked to wait, and he did, long after Janet had gone back to the hotel, the lights turned down in the family dining room. He sat on a bench in the hall, chain smoking, a witness on order, observing top figures from the cabinet, Congress, and the military coming and going, sometimes exchanging a few words as they passed by. "There was ample opportunity," he wrote in postwar years, as the first charges of foreknowledge began to be leveled at the Roosevelt administration, "to observe at close range the bearing and expression of Mr. Stimson, Colonel Knox, and Secretary Hull."[12]

> If they were *not* surprised by the news from Pearl Harbor, then that group of elderly men were putting on a performance which would have excited the admiration of any experienced actor. . . . It may be that the degree of the disaster had appalled them and that they had known for some time. . . . But I could not believe it then and I cannot do so now. There was amazement and anger written large on most of the faces.[13]

Harry Hopkins, looking even gaunter than usual, emerged from the inner sanctum. "What the hell are you doing here?"

"He told me to wait."

Briefly, they chatted in Hopkins' room, two doors down from the Oval Office, joined by Secretary of Commerce Jesse Jones, Hopkins preparing for bed as they talked. "His body was frail," Murrow recalled afterward, "and he looked like a death's-head. He groaned, 'Oh God, if I only had more strength.' "[14]

In the flood of that night's images, the memory of December 7 would be inextricably intertwined with that of Harry Hopkins' wasted frame and a pair of striped pajamas.

Shortly after midnight[15] Murrow stepped into the Oval Office. He was later to describe Roosevelt as "calm and steady," though gray-faced, asking about morale and friends in England as beer and sandwiches were brought in, then outlining in detail the losses at Pearl Harbor: the death count; ships sunk at the dockside; planes knocked out—"On the ground, by God, on the ground!"

"The idea," said Murrow afterward, "seemed to hurt him."

Years later in an interview, he mentioned that Colonel William "Wild Bill" Donovan had come in partway in the discussion, the talk then veering to the Philippines; Donovan, soon to be director of the OSS, was already in the process of setting up a government intelligence organization, to be separate from the armed services. The historian Anthony Cave Brown, however, citing the usher's diary at the White House, with the presumed backup of the Donovan papers, revealed in the 1980s that Murrow and Donovan went in together and that it had been a three-way conversation;[15] that Roosevelt sensed this would change the balance of American opinion; that he seemed a slight degree less surprised than the men around him; that the casualties—the element of surprise, being caught like sitting ducks, the magnitude of death and destruction—were what appalled him; and that the attack itself was somehow not unwelcome.

Churchill had telephoned with news of Japanese attacks on British bases; was there perhaps a joint Axis plan? Donovan had no evidence, but there seemed a good likelihood of it. Both visitors, queried by the President, thought the country would now support a declaration of war.[16]

After thirty-five minutes, Murrow was back out in the cold of Lafayette Square with his burden of knowledge—nothing had been put off the record—and the memory of Roosevelt's remark, as vivid in later recollection as it was that night: "Did this surprise you?"

"Yes, Mr. President."

"Maybe you think it didn't surprise us!"

Said Murrow later: "I believed him."[17]

To the end, whether the three-way meeting was intentional or merely an expedient would remain unknown, but Roosevelt did few things by chance.

In the meantime, Murrow was sitting on the scoop of the decade. At the CBS office he stopped off, saw the anxious faces turned to him, all with the same unspoken question.

"It's pretty bad," he said.

Sevareid was working through the night. To both men, the crowds now thronging the White House fence had the look they remembered from London and Paris in September 1939.[18]

He left the office, the story still unfiled. Janet Murrow watched him pace the hotel room for the rest of the night. The biggest story of his life, he said, and he didn't know if it was his duty to tell it or forget it![19]

In the end he passed it up, decided it was off the record. An AP colleague was leaked a few details, scoring a minor beat. His own voice, however, didn't join the chorus of reporters.

But he couldn't forget it either, blaming himself at times thereafter for not going with the story, never determining to his satisfaction where his duties lay that night or what had been in the subtle mind of FDR.

Four years later, when the first accusations of White House complicity were raised, he did a brief, narrow-focus commentary on that night, feeling perhaps he had been kept as witness. More details came out piecemeal, but never the entire picture. When long after the war John Gunther, over lunch, asked about Pearl Harbor night, Murrow responded with a long look. That story was going to send his son through college, he said, "and if you think I'm going to give it to you, you're out of your mind." In the end the big story stayed unwritten.

The morning of December 8, the President, appearing before Congress, asked for a declaration of war against Japan and had it within hours. Three days later Germany and Italy declared war on the United States.

It was a small, subdued group that gathered a few nights later at the Scarsdale home of James and Ina Seward of CBS, the shock waves of December 7 hanging like a pall over what was to have been a dinner party for Ina Seward's birthday.

Murrow was more than usually quiet. There had been rushed meetings and consultations at the office. Before him loomed a coast-to-coast lecture tour for the CBS affiliates, lined up sometime back.

The two little girls—Gwyn, four, and Emily, born that March—were brought in to say good night. Murrow held the baby in his lap awhile and, as Ina Seward remembered, "showed her her toes," then went upstairs with Gwyn to view the hobby horse bought recently for Christmas. When sometime later his chair was still empty, the hostess went upstairs to rescue him—those children!—only to find him seated on the nursery floor, deep in conversation with the dark-eyed, serious four-year-old, the company downstairs forgotten in the intensity of the ongoing discussion.

The weeks that followed found both Murrows on the road—Janet for the second time—in a country at war and a population on the move: a shifting kaleidoscope of crowded trains, strange towns, audiences, copies of *This Is London* stacked in local bookstore windows, endless posing for local papers with the city fathers and the junior league. He wanted to be working; she was exhausted, falling ill along the way, then catching up.

He himself fell ill in New York, marooned for a time in his hotel room at the New Weston. They set constantly the date of their return to England, then changed it. Sometimes they wondered *if* they'd return. The International Silver Company wanted to sponsor a fifteen-minute Sunday commentary, contract details discussed with Paul White; Murrow told Klauber he wouldn't sign if it interfered with his duties for Columbia and the news department.[20]

Alone in Virginia, he wrote Janet from en route:

Darling—Not so good here tonight—now two A.M. leave for Columbus at 5:00. I'm lonesome for you. Much time with Klauber on the phone about do I—or rather *we* go back to London. . . . Wherever you are I shall be happy. This business is hell—whoever gets this money ought to appreciate it! I love you—

In Chicago, as everywhere, the crowds were gigantic, a reporter recording the sentiments heard all along the tour as the public matched voice and appearance: "Everyone who sees Ed Murrow says, 'I'd no idea he was such a young chap!' "[21]

In Cleveland, 3,000 crammed the auditorium for his joint appearance with Bill Shirer. At Pullman, Washington, some 7,000 turned out to welcome WSC's most famous alumnus, a smaller group from the class of 1930 retiring for lunch to the local Kiwanis Club. A Pullman reporter, viewing the visiting celebrity in close-up, saw "a tired-appearing, thin-faced young man" in a collar grown too large for his neck, a trifle abstracted and smoking incessantly, nervously wiping his mouth in the pauses in an endless chain of cigarettes.

Frank Graham, the distinguished President of the University of North Carolina and a friend from IIE days, cabled the broadcaster, requesting that he address June commencement at Chapel Hill. It was impossible to accept due to scheduling, but the ultimate gratification for the grandson of North Carolina dirt farmers.

At the women's UNC campus in Greensboro, all Guilford County flocked to see the local boy who had made good. In the audience was a heavy, dark-eyed woman in a Quaker shawl; Roella Murrow, now eighty-five, had insisted that Edgar Murrow take her to hear her grandson.

The preliminaries were appropriately fulsome, the welcome thunderous. As the broadcaster stepped to the rostrum, Edgar Murrow, in a flash of recognition, saw the image of Ethel's brother, the younger Van Buren Lamb, and indeed the Captain himself, dead these many years, reproduced as though in a dark negative.

He nudged his aunt. "That's Boone Lamb standin' up there!"

The ancient woman repressed a low laugh. "Never noticed it before, but Lord, he looks just like him."

Yet the voice, with its earnestness, its deep gravity, was that of Josh Murrow, off the train in 1898 ("*This* is what they're using to kill colored folks in Wilmington!").

How much did they really understand? How much was the welcome for the radio star? Neither Ed nor Janet Murrow had the answer. At parties a casual "What's it like to be in a bombing?" would be followed by wandering attention. "Happens in all wars," said Janet Murrow, from the perspective of the seventies.

In Los Angeles, they arrived to no rooms when the hotel lost their reservations, settling for two cots in the anteroom of a guest cottage, Janet

Murrow inquiring timidly at intervals about a change until at length the desk clerk drew himself up stiffly, exuding rectitude from every pore. "Mrs. Murrow, you *must* remember—there's a *war* on."

She stared at him, speechless, then turned, fled back to the cottage, threw herself on the bed, and had hysterics. A friend who came upon her there, shaken and tear-stained, took in the scene without comment. "Come on, fix yourself up. I'll buy you a drink."[22]

At the same time, Murrow was under renewed pressure from Washington. Playwright Robert E. Sherwood, author of the moving *There Shall Be No Night*, speech writer for FDR, and future biographer of Harry Hopkins, had begun setting up the propaganda effort known as the Office of War Information (OWI). For the radio side, he wanted Ed Murrow. Murrow said no.

Sherwood, undeterred, appealed to Hopkins. There was an enormous audience out there in Europe; many understood English, now listened to the BBC. They would be broadcasting, of course, in many languages, but for "the voice of America," they wanted, indeed were "most anxious to get," Ed Murrow, to use his broadcasts all over the world; however— "Murrow is reluctant to do this job for the government because he feels it is more important for him to return to his old job in London. . . . It seems to me he could do far more important work here."[23]

In short, a word from Hopkins or even the President would be helpful. Next day, Murrow received a White House telegram over Hopkins' name, urging him not to return to England ("IT SEEMS TO ME YOU SHOULD BE RELATED TO THE GOVERNMENT...").[24] A second cable had gone to Sherwood in New York: "HAVE WIRED MURROW RECOMMENDING HE WORK WITH YOU."

In the context of January 1942, it was not an easy decision—a time of national emergency, the country trooping to the colors, a personal appeal, if not from the commander-in-chief, then from his right-hand man.

It was more than a week before Murrow answered: "AFTER MUCH SOUL SEARCHING AM CONVINCED MY DUTY IS TO GO BACK TO LONDON." He foresaw "troublous times" ahead for the alliance, he said; "BELIEVE FIVE YEARS TRAINING THERE PLUS OPPORTUNITY DO SOME BROADCASTING FOR BBC MAKE SERVICES IN COMMON CAUSE MORE VALUABLE THERE THAN HERE AND THATS THE ONLY THING INTERESTS ME. . . ."[25]

They wanted to be away, trying repeatedly for a Clipper booking for early spring. Murrow substituted, for some weeks, in the 8:55 P.M. commentary spot for Elmer Davis ("torture," he called it) and traveled to Washington to talk Gil Winant, now in the U.S., out of his opposition to a proposed American press and information office in London. It was in part the brainchild of Chet Williams, now with the Office of Education, and Frank Darvall of the MOI, but if it materialized, Murrow wrote a friend, he wanted "a few Americans who will represent something other than Washington and New York."

The Clipper booking came through in early April. Newspapers announced that Edward R. Murrow would begin a Sunday commentary series from London, starting on the twenty-sixth at 6:00 P.M., Eastern War Time.

They didn't leave, however, without one last consideration. The proceeds for the speaking tour had gone to British War Relief and related charities. The question remained: Would the IRS want its cut? Jim Seward, handling matters, received assurances that the broadcaster wouldn't have to pay taxes on money he had given away.

It would be remembered as the sour year: Allied defeats in the Pacific and North Africa; blood, sweat, and tears on the Russian front; London drab as ever, though a nerve center now for Allied planning in the West. Murrow, arriving just before Easter Sunday, found the British capital abloom with American uniforms, news sources in the U.S. offices, military and otherwise, that seemed to have sprung up overnight around the green island facing the U.S. Embassy—known on London maps as Grosvenor Square and popularly as Little America, Jeepside, or Eisenhowerplatz.

More often Murrow was a source himself as denizens of Grosvenor Square sought practical advice: whom to see, what channels to use, how to go about the day-to-day business of living. He saw Harry Butcher, once CBS's Washington vice-president, who had once cleared his path to Hyde Park, now in London as Naval Aide and general factotum to General Dwight Eisenhower.

The BBC wanted more commentaries. In early March, Murrow had broadcast from New York via shortwave, *Questions America Is Asking*, and in the time elapsing, the British were asking back—notably about the unknown lieutenant general with the German name who as Commander-in-Chief, U.S. Army, European theater of operations, topped the pyramid of power at Grosvenor Square.

Over the BBC Home Service, Murrow characterized Eisenhower as "a 'good hand' . . . a normal middle-class American soldier . . . an officer with great singleness of purpose. He has the ability to soak up information in a surprisingly short time. . . . His light brown hair is fast disappearing and when his grin disappears his face can look as bleak as a Kansas cornfield in mid-winter."[26]

His private assessment was that of a good committeeman, getting others to pull together in a loaded situation.[27] A situation which he himself regarded with a certain skepticism. At the BBC, a staffer made a comment to the effect that "Now that the United States has entered the war—"

He got no further. "The United States did not *enter* the war," Murrow interrupted, glaring at the speaker, "it was *bombed* into it at Pearl Harbor."

In August 1942, Bill Paley arrived in the British capital. The CBS chief had his own pipeline to Churchill and Eisenhower, yet couldn't help being impressed as his European Director, escorting the boss around

London, opened the doors to one cabinet minister after the other. "He was number one American in London," Paley recalled afterward, "firmly established as the person who was best posted on what was happening in England and in Europe generally."

They met further with Eisenhower, saw each other daily in those weeks, discussed everything. The London correspondent had "a wealth of knowledge and good intuition about situations. . . . He was greatly admired, completely trusted . . . probably the most important American there."[28]

And an asset to the company. Though there had been London contacts in prewar years, it was the 1942 visit that cemented the Murrow-Paley friendship, the older man confirmed in his regard for the younger, though in this case the "older man" was barely forty-one.

The radio scene in London had itself changed radically—the final metamorphosis of what had once been a broadcasting backwater, a prewar appendage of network offices in New York, into a front seat at the working end of the Western war effort; site of radio news bureaus and coordinating point for transmissions from Europe, North Africa, and the Middle East. Staffs were bigger, the stakes higher. At CBS Trout, Manning, and Collingwood were joined by Bill Downs, a chunky, sensitive young man from UP. By winter Downs would be in Moscow, LeSueur moved to Cairo, Collingwood in North Africa, with more and more correspondents coming into London from the New York office, eager to be on the scene.

At NBC Fred Bate was out, sidetracked back at New York headquarters, a victim of the growing competitiveness in overseas coverage; the biggest thing in wartime radio was news, and sponsors were rushing in to underwrite it. Bate had had his jealousies, but he had also been a good friend, gallant competitor, and selfless newsman; it had taken him half a year to recover from the injuries sustained in the blitz. His replacement, Stanley Richardson, was a two-fisted AP veteran, out to restore the balance between the networks.

For Murrow, Bate's departure spelled the end to an era—that of the small radio community that had survived between Munich and the blitz, the all-for-one spirit of 1939–41, when overseas broadcasting had been almost a cottage industry, the end of the old days of Ed and Fred.

Yet battles with the military continued. British commando raids had been launched on the Continent—the press invited along, radio excluded.[29] Murrow threatened to take his fight for parity to Washington—to Grosvenor Square—to the bloody *Commons* if he had to.[30] Eckersley dissuaded him, i.e., wait for improvement. But access continued to be problematic, the networks when admitted forced to rotate, their turns decided on the tossing of a coin.

Norman Corwin—good-natured, idealistic, effervescent, with the dapper mustache and corrugated hairdo that lent him a faint resemblance to a younger Lowell Thomas—came over that summer. With him was a slight, sandy-haired young actor named Joseph Julian, whose gravelly average-guy voice had landed him the role of narrator in the new eight-week series, *An American In England*, written and directed by Norman Corwin, produced by Edward R. Murrow in cooperation with the BBC, and broadcast Monday nights, live, over CBS.

Like others of its kind, it was OWI-inspired, overt domestic propaganda of the sort proliferating on the air, celebrating antifascist One World liberalism, the common people in a common cause—embodying the themes, sometimes the very phrases, of the Murrow broadcasts.

For the two men it was a collaboration of kindred spirits. Technically, it was almost unprecedented, involving the live transmission, via short-wave, of a full-scale documentary-dramatic series involving cast, sixty-piece orchestra, and specially commissioned score by the youthful Benjamin Britten; the most ambitious transatlantic project to date.

And the most problematic. Just how much, they discovered after opening night—or rather morning, the broadcasts done in the predawn hours to correspond to prime time in New York, weekly buses conveying the company, director, and producer through the blackout, to the converted roller rink in Maida Vale; sometimes, said Julian afterward, through minor bombing.

That first night, everything went off on cue: no fluffs; a perfect run from beginning to end; one hundred people jubilant and high as the last note died away on Britten's tuneful score. Only Murrow, emerging from the control room, seemed restrained.

Once the buses had returned to central London, he took Corwin for a walk. Then and only then did he tell him the truth: Nothing had gone out; there had been a mix-up at the other end in New York. He hadn't wanted to tell the others—not at that point, not right away; better to let them sleep a night on it. Corwin, once recovered, was grateful.

After that the programs went through, a vivifying team effort. When they ran short of Americans to cast, Collingwood stepped into a dramatic role. Murrow played himself once, firing off pet lines on changing societies, the cloudiness of Allied war aims, and the virtue of those with dirt under their fingernails.

For the broadcaster, the programs were almost an extension of another project taken up those same weeks for the BBC—*Freedom Forum*, a panel show featuring no-holds-barred debates on controversial issues of the day, Murrow as American panelist, talking, sometimes tangling with his old socialist friend Harold Laski and others, discussing hotly such topics as "The Future of Imperialism," "Can We Achieve a Classless Society?" "Is National Sovereignty Compatible with World Peace?"— a labor of love that took on even greater meaning as the war progressed.

By summer's end *An American in England* had to pack up, due to atmospheric problems, the final programs to be done from New York. It had had considerable acclaim and a small devoted public despite Monday night competition from Bob Hope. Murrow said good-bye to Corwin and his American, both homeward-bound, having done their bit for democracy from England. Murrow's path and Julian's would cross again in the coming decade, when the actor would be blacklisted and barred from working in the broadcast industry.

In the meantime, Kay Campbell was trying to locate their composer after CBS's check for Mr. Britten's score had come back in the mail, addressee unknown. The young man, it turned out, had been evicted from his rooms for nonpayment of rent.

One day in late August, the Corwin series still running, the feminist "Women of Britain" segment just completed, Murrow wrote to Lanham Titchener, producer for the BBC of *Freedom Forum*. He was bowing out, for reasons shared with no one—not his friend Norman Corwin, not Bill Paley, sitting smiling at the broadcast sessions—until now: "For several weeks I have been fighting a rearguard action with the Doctors and I have lost."

It was more than two years since the pneumonia contracted in Paris, with its drawn-out aftermath, easily forgotten in the heroic days that followed, days which in themselves had not been entirely free of small illnesses. What was coming through now, in the relative quiet of that summer, was a possible indication that he had spent beyond his means, the body suddenly pressing its demands, a creditor presenting a bill long overdue for debts incurred.

They were allowing him to finish the Corwin series, he wrote Titchener; after that he was to leave London for several weeks, with permission to come in only on Sundays. "I am terribly sorry about all this but it can't be helped."[31]

The Englishman, replying, swore to hold out against all medical advice "even to the extent of endangering your life permanently,"[32] refusing to take no for an answer. Murrow continued with the program.

That fall, church bells rang all over England for General Bernard Montgomery's victory at El Alamein; the Japanese Navy had been stopped at Midway, the German Sixth Army at Stalingrad. They were the first victories, followed by the first political storms as American forces, landing in Algeria, struck a deal with the fascist French authorities—Admiral Jean Darlan, the Vichy secretary of state for foreign affairs, interior, and the navy, a noted Anglophobe and pro-Nazi collaborator, placed in charge as the price of cooperation and nonresistance.

The shock waves of the so-called Darlan deal reverberated in the free Western capitals. In London an appalled Ed Murrow, breaking openly with administration policy, reviewed the record of the newest Allied appointee:

One of his first acts was to turn over political refugees to the Germans. . . . His government was responsible for the sending of foreigners, mostly Spanish Republicans . . . to slave-gang labor on the Trans-Sahara Railway. He intensified anti-Semitic measures. His police force helped the Germans round up Alsatian refugees. . . . In July, his government practically turned over Indo-China to the Japanese. . . . And now this man is given political dominion over North Africa, with American support.

The British press and radio, acting under guidance, take the line that for the time being military considerations dominate. One can only wonder if this answer would impress the Fighting French who died trying to stop Rommel's advance at Bir Hacheim. . . .

At Broadcasting House, the overseas service was in a state of shock. Cecilia Reeves, now with the French desk, and her future husband, Darsie Gillie, were approached by the Free French broadcasters, still reeling: Could they have it suppressed somehow? It was just too appalling. Numbly, Gillie rang up the Home Service. "Can you do anything?"

"Sorry, chum, this is news."

A party was being held for Ambassador Winant. Anxiously, Murrow corralled Reeves: Come along and *tell* him. The three of them spent the evening sequestered in a corner, talking at length as Janet Murrow marked time, but they were simply preaching to the converted. (Days later the Ambassador himself fell into line: What did mothers in Ohio know about Charles de Gaulle or Darlan, and did it not save lives?—a hard argument.)

It was Murrow's most serious, though not his first, confrontation with the Rooseveltian policy of snubbing De Gaulle while treating the Vichy puppet regime as the heir to the Third Republic. Sometime earlier there had been a run-in over Murrow's inclusion of the French leader in a collective broadcast by the exiled European heads of state. This time the British objected: De Gaulle was not a head of state; Murrow would therefore have to drop him. The broadcaster refused, whereupon the MOI had itself informed the General that he was out.

Murrow's stance had nothing to do with hero worship or even liking. Charles de Gaulle seemed to him vain, overbearing, possibly dictatorial, and the only viable alternative to Vichy. He was not acceptable to the fascists in Algeria, of course, though Murrow felt they would go with the winners in any case, warning that "wherever American forces go they will carry . . . food and money and power, and the quislings will rally to our side if we permit it."

The decision, however, had been made. In North Africa, the labor camps and racial laws continued under a hands-off agreement—hundreds of Free French arrested, Vichy control restored, with the newly appointed Governor-General of Algeria emerging as the same minister who had signed De Gaulle's *in absentia* death warrant. In streets and shops, people told American reporters they had been had by the fascists.[33]

Murrow, scanning news photos, saw the Admiral smiling between an unsmiling Eisenhower and General Mark Clark. Eisenhower as overall commander took responsibility, but Murrow, on radio, called it a political decision—scoring certain unnamed U.S. political advisers as "consistently sympathetic with the Vichy regime." It was a guarded reference to the smiling figure at the crop-edge of the photograph: Robert Murphy, formerly American chargé d'affaires in Vichy, now Eisenhower's chief adviser, architect of the Darlan deal, praised by officialdom, distrusted by the press for what seemed an overly high degree of intimacy—albeit under orders—with the pro-Hitler officials of the Pétain regime. Said Murrow: "We have made a choice in North Africa. It may or may not have been dictated by military necessity. But there is nothing in the strategic position of the allies to indicate that we are either so strong or so weak that we can afford to ignore the principles for which this war is being fought."

The reaction wasn't long in coming, either in a divided Washington or in New York. At the White House, a critical Henry Morgenthau pressed a transcript of the broadcast on a stung Henry Stimson, the administration muting its praise of the new appointee. From 485, Paul White rushed a cable furiously to Murrow: Why couldn't he wait until all evidence was in before becoming prosecuting attorney, judge, and jury?

One listener, calling the broadcast "definitely dangerous," begged Murrow not to attack his country's policy before knowing the whole story.

Murrow assured the listener courteously that he did indeed know the whole story. "Certainly I did not knowingly engage in an irresponsible or emotional attack upon my own Government, but I believe that all Governments are capable of making mistakes just as are all broadcasters."

"As you will imagine, I have encountered headwinds," he wrote to Ted Church that December, "due in part to the fact that for weeks it was impossible to quote . . . and therefore necessary to say things on one's own responsibility which might have been confirmed from a dozen different sources. This whole development has produced a revulsion in this country like nothing that has happened since the Hoare-Laval deal, and you can imagine what it has done to the exiles who came here."

But the screws were on. To Alfred Cohn, who had cabled his thanks for speaking out, he hinted wryly at possible "interesting consequences" in the offing; "but I am fortified by the knowledge that the sentiments I tried to express were those with which you have sympathy. Indeed, you are in no small measure responsible for what I say on many occasions, for I learned much from you." (The cable, he added, "warmed my heart. As you can imagine, the response was by no means one of unanimous approval.")

Darlan's assassination hours before Christmas Eve and the rush to judgment of his killer amid heavy Allied censorship made the matter a moot point, leaving in its wake a further poisoning of relations between Washington and the Free French.

For Murrow the pressures were off. "For a while it looked as though they might be serious," he wrote home, "but events have demonstrated that I was not entirely wrong. God knows I have been more wrong over more important issues."

In their place, however, was a growing misgiving that saw the whole affair as possibly symptomatic. To Cohn, in January, he voiced his concern "that Allied policy may be no more than to achieve Fascism which will favor us instead of favoring Germany."

"Developments in North Africa," he told Ted Church, "would be heart-breaking for anyone who had any hope of a decent post-war world. . . . The fact that the British don't like what's going on . . . isn't as important as the fact that the Russians don't like it. The censorship is, as you know, appalling. . . ."

To another friend in New York, he wrote of "a great fear, not only in this country but amongst the Governments in exile, of the use that America will make of its predominant power once this war is ended. That is just one way of saying that the British fear that America will do what Britain did in the 19th century. . . ."

> Our policy, as it has been displayed in North Africa, looks like a sort of amateur imperialism, which aims at making the Continent safe for the National City Bank. That policy is not going to work, and the only people who believe it will appear to reside in Washington. . . .
>
> The thing that impressed me at home, and even more since I came back over here, is that the little men on both sides of the ocean want the same thing; the thing that we call for lack of a better phrase "more economic democracy. . . . [And] there is another . . . aspect of this whole thing, and that is the belief in the States that Britain being unable to go with the angels must go with us. . . . In Britain today Russia is more popular than the United States, and this country if faced with a choice would certainly plump for Russia. . . . There is after all such a thing as communal suffering, and the middle class in America, from which we both come, will know damned little of suffering when this war is over. . . .
>
> So far as [the] news is concerned, one of the most vicious developments is the tendency to stretch military censorship in order that it may cover political machinations. There are times when I am almost as much afraid of the American Army as of any other. . . .[34]

On another front that same winter, reports had begun filtering in from the Continent about a different kind of warfare. Murrow had checked it out, incredulous at first, then went with it: "One is almost stunned into silence by some of the information. . . . But it's eye-witness stuff supported by a wealth of detail and vouched for by responsible governments. What is happening is this: Millions of human beings, most of them Jews, are being gathered up with ruthless efficiency and murdered."

It had come through clandestine radio transmitters and the intelligence networks of the European underground—"a picture of mass murder and moral depravity unequaled in the history of the world." He went through a detailed listing, some of it based on his own close questioning of eye-witnesses: "Information coming out of Holland proves that each week four thousand Dutchman are being sent to Poland and that is no guess. It is based upon one of the best secret service organizations in Europe. . . . At Falstad [Norway] concentration camp, Russian prisoners of war were made to dig an open grave . . . stripped naked and shot. . . ."

Worst of all were the reports from the Warsaw Ghetto, where since midsummer tens of thousands had been shipped off in freight cars:

> The floors were covered with quicklime and chlorine. Those who survived the journey were dumped out at one of three camps, where they were killed. At a place called Treblinka, a huge bulldozer is used to bury the bodies. . . . The Jews are being systematically exterminated. . . . Nobody knows how many have committed suicide; nor does anyone know how many have gone mad. Some of the victims ask their guards to shoot them. . . .
>
> All this information and much more is contained in an official report issued by the Polish Government. And few people who have talked as I have with people who have escaped . . . will doubt its accuracy. The phrase "concentration camps" is obsolete. . . . It is now possible to speak only of extermination camps. . . .
>
> . . . newspapers, individuals and spokesmen of the Church in this country are demanding that the government make a solemn statement that retribution will be dealt out to those responsible . . . not only for those who gave the orders, but also for the underlings who seem to be gladly carrying them out.

The statement was never made forcefully, the Nazis never put on notice. The gas chambers and rail lines servicing the camps would all be spared by the bombers that leveled nearby population centers, even factories within the camps, the calls for disruption of the death machinery ignored by Western governments until the very end.

In March of 1943, Ed Murrow returned to frontline reporting, covering the fighting in Tunisia after months of chafing at the bit in London and coping with an inability, he told Church, "to adjust to the inactivity of this place as compared with what it used to be. . . . I want to see some action again."

He had been frankly skeptical about the African campaign, the time coming, he wrote home, "when people will debate whether we diverted the Germans or diverted ourselves by that operation."

Beyond the lure of gunpowder, moreover, lay the need, as the tide turned toward the Allies, to sort out the increasingly confusing skeins in French-American relations, a nagging concern over the continuing quarrels between De Gaulle and Churchill and, even more so, between De Gaulle and Franklin Roosevelt.

In Algiers the Hotel St.-Georges, perched high on a hill overlooking the harbor, now housed the Allied Force Headquarters, a jumble of Anglo-American offices representing the joint drive in North Africa known as Operation Torch. At the bottom near the port, along the sweep of the Boulevard Boudin, loomed the Maison Agricole, formerly the agricultural ministry, now headquarters for the army's Mediterranean news desk, feeding bulletins to the press in the liberated territories and broadcasting to the French resistance. Murrow, shown around the frenzied newsroom, saw a short, compact young man with thinning hair and mustache at the center of the operation, directing the activity, throwing out material to the writers, bawling out someone for a time-consuming error. The young man, looking around, saw the broadcaster standing at the back of the room, arms folded, chuckling. Introductions followed.

Hours later Murrow, returning, found the same officer in the studio, broadcasting in flawless French.

"How many jobs do you do around here?" he asked when it was over.

"Come back after everybody goes home," came the answer. "I also sweep the floor."

His name was David Schoenbrun, a teacher of modern languages in peacetime, now serving with army intelligence, chief editor of the news desk, assigned to Eisenhower headquarters for French affairs; one of the very few at headquarters who—army or no army—remained persistently and openly critical of Washington vis-à-vis De Gaulle.

They talked in the deserted newsroom, the visitor closely, nervously questioning, conscious of his lack of background: What truth was there to Roosevelt's view of De Gaulle as budding dictator? What was the overall picture? He'd talked with Eisenhower, he said, who wasn't altogether sure. (Not surprising, said Schoenbrun later, given the dictatorial aspects of De Gaulle's personality, let alone the stance of Ike's political advisers.) He was therefore going around Algiers, seeing everybody else. They talked on, intensively, Murrow's earnest need for answers clearly evident. "He knew that French politics were very complex, that he wasn't close enough to understand them; he didn't like the Free French in London at all—nobody did—De Gaulle was an impossible man, which was irrelevant as to whether or not we should support him. And Ed, with his good mind, understood that. But Roosevelt's charge that he was an apprentice dictator, a man on a white horse, did—correctly—trouble him."[35]

Schoenbrun swept the idea aside: It was the right of the French to pick their own leaders—not our business. As for General Henri Giraud, urged by Washington as counterweight to De Gaulle, he was a fine soldier and a total idiot. Lots of people were calling Roosevelt a dictator, and to some extent they were correct. And Murrow knew damn well that Churchill was something of a dictator, bent arms when he had to. Every strong leader of government was open to that charge, and De Gaulle, with his stubborn, obstreperous nature, more than most. But the charge itself was damn plain nonsense, and France was not going to become a dictatorship!

It was confirmation. Murrow told the young man to look him up next time he came to London.

Charlie Collingwood, now broadcasting from Algiers, agreed totally. "It seemed to me clear, and I communicated this to Ed, that De Gaulle, whom we had both known in England since 1940—not terribly well, but we knew him—that he and his movement represented what was going to be the future of France, and not these remodeled Vichyites or these rather stupid generals. Both of us felt that."[36]

And Murphy? A charming guy, they told him, and a good soldier: bright, affable, charm the pants off you; don't be seduced.

The rest of the story was up at the front, three hours away by plane, where Allied armies fought for the corner of Tunisia still held by the Axis: stark mountains, biting cold.

Supplies were being funneled with difficulty into the hotly contested mountain pocket—a small front, as Murrow put it, with a large behind. Arrived, he made his way by jeep and on foot past lines of army mules hauling gasoline cans over trackless lunar slopes; walked through minefields; wrote under fire—cryptic entries jotted in a small black loose-leaf folder with a pencil stub, through a veil of acrid smoke that seared the eyelids and impaired vision:

> *Shelling—bursts in town like giant walking on puff balls—cold country with a hot sun—faces like smoldering holes in a gray blanket—it's cold—Arabs with 6 white oxen ploughing—red soil—bells on monastery—planes going out—pray god they all come back—prisoners— looks—wish they were Hitler and Rommell [sic]—What town is this?— Don't know—Dead here more peacefull [sic] than in London for they had arms in their hands. . . .*

His pencil stub traced rough topographic maps of hills, wadis, troop positions, using techniques he had learned as a young surveyor in western Washington. At roadsides he talked with officers and enlisted men (*U.S. troops—over equipped and undertrained—living like animals—holes in ground—8 tanks—position and WASTE*). The statistics of warfare were noted in quick strokes. Then, on a facing page:

> *Marigolds*
> *Morning-glory (blue)*
> *Blue jintzen*[37]
> *wild geranium*
> *wild orchids*
> *U.S., British flowers came from here X*

On the air the brief notes, expanded, became unglamorized and un-compromising views of a bitterly contested war:

> Everything is covered with that white, tired dust; men's red-rimmed eyes look like smoldering holes in a gray blanket. . . .
> Where the road cuts down to meet the stream there is a knocked-out tank, two dead men beside it and two more digging a grave. A little farther along a German soldier sits smiling against the bank. He is covered with dust and he is dead. On the rising ground beyond a young British lieutenant lies with his head on his arm as though shielding himself from the wind. He is dead too. . . .

Back in Algiers, he said good-bye to Collingwood and stopped off at the newsroom in the Maison Agricole to thank Schoenbrun: "Keep in touch with me, buster."

It was evidently then, on returning to London, that he encountered a potential twist in a hitherto ordered existence, one of those rogue episodes capable of changing lives and careers overnight, presented unexpectedly in the restless, redheaded figure of Brendan Bracken, Minister of Information and right-hand man to Winston Churchill.

It was a matter, he was given to understand, of the utmost confidentiality, coming in the midst of—perhaps prompted by—the precarious state of Anglo-American relations, so private that later references to it would be kept off the official record.

What had touched it off, it seemed, was the state of affairs, by mid-1943, at Broadcasting House, where the longtime rule of Sir John Reith had given way to a series of short-term successors. Of the two director-generals now working there in tandem—one handling programming, the other finances—the former was ill, his resignation imminent; the latter, onetime manager of a utility concern, unable to run a broadcast operation on his own.

They needed, in short, an editor-in-chief, a sort of deputy director-general to take charge of programming, responsible for everything relating to the content of what went out, worldwide, over the BBC.

Churchill wanted to know: Would Murrow take the job?

It was an extraordinary offer to make to an American; nor was it, evidently, a pipe dream born of the glow of after-dinner brandy. Bracken assured Murrow that the Prime Minister had given the matter "full consideration" before authorizing the approach.[38]

The broadcaster didn't know what to say. He would have to go home, he told Churchill's man, and consult with several people first. And who were they? Murrow named them. Bracken approved.

He flew home that month. In New York there were planning sessions with White and Klauber, plus the usual company luncheon, himself as centerpiece, sharing off-the-record observations on the war with invited business and civic leaders; in the background, making the arrangements, smoothing the way and totally unobtrusive, the slight blond figure of Frank Stanton, moved up from Director of Research. They didn't talk much; there were too many demands on Murrow's time.

"Everyone at the office very nice," he wrote Janet from the New Weston, "haven't been sleeping too well but that's just the excitement of New York. . . ."

> People still remarkably well dressed . . . surprising number who think the war is won . . Have a feeling I am not going to be too happy on this trip. . . . Going out to see the Paleys this afternoon. . . . The Silver show has been cancelled. . . . They are returning to a half hour entertainment show . . in many ways I am glad. . . . Bill Shirer will be bringing this . . he is the same old William . . be sure and give a party or two for him. . . . Am sitting here looking out the window at the trees around st patricks and I am very lonesome. . . . Please dont worry about my working too hard on this trip . . I am perfectly relaxed . . not drinking too much and more sure of myself than ever before. . . . This is an inadequate letter . . but you know I cant write good letters . . I have discovered one fundamental fact of great and overwhelming international significance . . and it is that I love you even more than I thought I did . . Nothing would please me more right now than to climb on a plane and start for London. . . .

In Washington he called at the White House. The reporter had sent the sea-loving President a cigarette box of nautical design; an appreciative FDR assured him that the sloop on the cover was "more Dutch than English" and that the man at the tiller looked like a Roosevelt.[39]

At the same time there were other stops that only he and Brendan Bracken knew of.

"Ed Murrow came to see me after dinner," Supreme Court Justice Felix Frankfurter noted in his diary the night of Wednesday, June 16. Frankfurter, an old associate of Alfred Cohn and Stephen Duggan, had been a valued adviser since IIE Days, when Murrow was Duggan's assistant and the Justice was Professor Frankfurter of the Harvard School of Law.

Frankfurter urged him to take the job. It was a step in the right direction, he argued. Any decent world order presupposed cooperation; if the British and Americans couldn't work together, what hope was there, in terms of world peace, for "collaborative relations" with the Russians or Chinese?

Murrow, for his part, had misgivings—among others, that postwar differences between America and Britain would leave him in "an awkward position." The offer, he added, had its amusing aspects, though.

Why amusing? the other asked.

"Well, can you imagine an American broadcasting company asking an Englishman to take charge of it?"[40]

Other aspects of the Washington trip were decidedly less amusing, the cozy visit with FDR notwithstanding. To Frankfurter, Murrow complained of the "awful reactionary feeling" he sensed this time around, following the 1942 congressional elections. Summoned to the State Department, sat down in a closed-door session, he found himself subjected to a torrent of abuse by the Secretary of State, an infuriated Cordell Hull tearing into him over the Darlan broadcast and his alleged undermining of the war effort.

Murrow, surprised and incapable of response, sat speechless as the old Tennessee politician known as The Good Gray Judge poured forth a nonstop stream of icy invective.

"It seemed to me," he recalled later, "that this was Captain Hull of Company H, 4th Tennessee infantry, and I was a recruit in the Spanish American War who had just dropped his rifle and made a rude remark to the Captain. . . . He never raised his voice . . . made no gesture, but every word cut and stung. . . ."[41]

Out of the blue the Secretary, switching tacks, suddenly asked him where he was born. North Carolina, said Murrow, and his grandfather had fought under Stonewall Jackson. Hull seemed to relax. Well . . . go back to Europe and try to do better. Murrow told the story to a perplexed and saddened Alfred Cohn.

A final stop had nothing to do with politics, the BBC, or the war. He had been uncomfortable since North Africa, with its biting cold, brought almost to the edge of quitting by constant fatigue. Cohn had been urging him for some time to enter a hospital, arranging now for a stay and tests before Murrow's departure, plus consultations with a specialist in pulmonary problems, who by one of those ironies of fate would be the attending physician twenty-one years later, in the broadcaster's final illness.

The tests indicated no pathology. He was of course overworked, Cohn wrote a mutual friend, and would perhaps return to England with "a better comprehension of the limits of his physical abilities."

But he continued to feel something was basically amiss. "Ed had what he described to me, in the English vernacular, as a sort of constitutionally 'weak chest,' " Collingwood recalled. "How far back in his youth this went, this respiratory difficulty, I don't know, but I rather got the impression from him that this had been a long-standing thing."

Nor were matters helped by his continued daily consumption, the doctors notwithstanding, of three packs of Camels.

In early July the *Queen Elizabeth*, now a troopship, slipped away from its berth in New York Harbor, headed east; among the 15,000 men aboard, a radio reporter who had decided he didn't want to be a director-general of the BBC. His final reasons would remain unknown, but he never spoke of it again, respecting Churchill's and his minister's confidence to the last.

There was a respite that summer, better news coming in from the fronts. Elmer Davis, drafted from CBS to head the Office of War Information, was briefly in London, calling up on the night of July 15, midway through a supper party, with the news that Mussolini had resigned. Jan Masaryk, jumping to the piano, began playing "Believe Me If All Those Endearing Young Charms."[42]

Then, on August 6, the Murrows felt a shock wave when without warning, CBS announced the retirement, at fifty-six, of Edward Klauber. The reason given was ill health. CBS President William Paley, in a release, expressed "deep appreciation" for Mr. Klauber's outstanding contributions and many years of service.[43]

The abrupt departure of one of broadcasting's most powerful figures rated only two inches in The New York *Times* of 1943, sandwiched between a divorce notice and an OPA ruling on home-canned salmon.

Some saw it as inevitable. Indeed, Paley's lawyer, Ralph Colin, outside counsel to CBS and longtime member of the board, had long urged that the abrasive Klauber be fired: "a genius but unfortunately a sonuvabitch— a very able man but a destroyer of morale.

"When he created CBS's broadcast news," said Colin later, "he created *all* of broadcast news, everything was modeled on CBS; and to his eternal credit, he *did* it. . . . The trouble was that he was a cruel person; if he was going to criticize someone, he'd call in the whole staff and criticize the guy in front of them. Which made me finally go to Paley and tell him time and time again, 'You've got to get rid of Klauber.' " (Colin, a forthright puritan, would thereupon tell Klauber he had done so; Klauber, another puritan, would retain Colin as his lawyer in the postwar years.)[44]

But to the newsroom, accustomed to the ways of the city desk, the boss's bark was worse than his bite. Klauber had been a staunch ally, always there in times of crisis and an unfailing backup, a newsman first and last, with the will and authority to preempt commercial programming—"Let's tear the network wide open!"—where White could not ("Paul would have been cautious, hesitated").[45] Some had grown fond of the old curmudgeon.

The point was, he had made enemies, whether for reasons of personality, the usual power shifts, or both. Paley and the corporation continued to cite health factors, and in fact, the older man, a heavy smoker, had been troubled sufficiently to be collecting disability on his retirement. From Klauber himself there was no comment. To his closest friends he seemed bitter, despairing, near-suicidal—"It wouldn't have surprised me," said one of them later, "if he had turned on the gas"—buoyed up at last when his *Times* friend Elmer Davis asked him to Washington as associate director and administrator at the OWI, replacing the departing Milton Eisenhower. Paley himself arranged for continuation of the disability payments, the new job notwithstanding, allowing him to take the lower-paying job without financial hardship. Klauber ran the agency throughout the war, unslowed evidently by the ill health that officially forced his departure from broadcasting.

At 485, Paul Kesten moved into the number two slot as Executive Vice-President—a post, said others, he hadn't really wanted despite the long-standing rivalry with Klauber—Frank Stanton under him, on his way to becoming General Manager. Whatever the reasons, the old newspaper-man was gone. A new constellation was forming at the top, rooted in sales promotion and market research—a pivotal change, its long-term effects delayed for the duration, while Paley himself was called to Eisenhower headquarters in Algiers, to head Allied broadcasting facilities in North Africa and Italy.

Murrow, in London, was shocked and unhappy; Klauber had been the rock, one of the few he had consulted about the BBC job. The shock, however, was muffled by distance and the difficulty of communication. To all appearances he took it in stride, as did Paul White in New York. Radio was big business; these things happened. Both young men were immersed in their work: running offices, expanding staff, keeping up with the latest from the Roosevelt-Churchill summit at Quebec, the Allied landings in Sicily—first things first.

Besides, there was the reassuring figure of William Paley, walking among his men—understanding, intelligent, young enough to relate to their generation; the living embodiment of CBS's continuing commitment to news and information.

But four weeks later, the network itself was enveloped in controversy as one of its news stars resigned, charging censorship.

Cecil Brown, hired by Murrow himself in 1940 to cover Rome, had come home in 1942 by way of Asia—a passionate antifascist, who had run afoul of the Mussolini government in Italy and the British colonial government in Singapore, been bombed in Sarajevo, and had a battleship sunk out from under him in the South China Sea, returning a media hero and heir to Elmer Davis' 8:55 spot.

The eruption had occurred when Brown, criticizing the present trend of Allied leadership, stated over the air that "a good deal of enthusiasm for this war" was evaporating.

White had flared up—it was editorializing, defeatist—touching off arguments about the expression of opinion on the air, at least unpopular opinion. Brown, charging he was being gagged, left CBS.

From London Murrow asked repeatedly, What happened? But the mails took forever, and the flow of New York scuttlebutt, usually so plentiful over the cue channel, had seemingly dried up.

In New York, Hans von Kaltenborn, guiding spirit of the Association of Radio News Analysts, was charging CBS with stifling the discussion of controversial issues. White, appearing with Frank Stanton at an ARNA lunch meeting, read a statement urging radio news to "remain simon-pure, honestly objective and utterly non-editorial."[46] Most of the members thought it poppycock, Shirer alone defending CBS, saying he would "resent"—just as Ed Murrow or Elmer Davis would—Brown's implication that Columbia had "clamped down" on the broadcasters' freedom of expression.

Little Cesar Saerchinger, pouring oil on the waters, noting Shirer seemed "anxious that this should not become an attack on Columbia," assured him this was nothing of the sort.[47]

In the meantime, CBS was taking out full-page ads in the *Times* and the *Tribune*, disavowing "opinionated" statements by its correspondents. In a volatile free-for-all at the Overseas Press Club over "Freedom of the Air," Shirer was speaking up for CBS against Drew Pearson, Walter Winchell, and Brown himself, countering, he said, "the impression that our network is the particular villain" and denying censorship down the line.[48] Of course pressures existed—they were part of the scene; so what else was new?

He sent Murrow a copy of the CBS ad—a mistake, he thought, because readers would now think they were being gagged; and what both of them and Elmer had been saying for the last three years on radio spoke for itself.

Cecil Brown was out, he added, and might try to make plenty of trouble. Though he was puzzled, he said, by the whole question of whether a guy should be allowed to shoot off his personal prejudices on the air. Case in point: Hans had been labor-baiting for the last two years. As for Paul's memo, he didn't see where it had prevented gents like himself and Ed from expressing themselves about the Free French, the State Department, or anything else.[49]

Murrow was grateful for the enclosure and the news; he'd been requesting it for weeks, he said. "One of the many things I like about you is that you are puzzled and unsure about such important matters." Yes, he was puzzled too—"but I am sure that we should not permit the Kaltenborns and Fulton Lewises to have the field all to themselves."

The trouble, he thought, lay rather with the company's permitting advertisers to select their commentators—"somebody [with] a rather dramatic delivery, or an emotional throb in his voice. . . . We ought to hire the best half-dozen people in the business, and then say to any sponsor who comes along: 'O.K. you can have one of our men, but you can't choose some nitwit who will follow your party line.' "[50]

It was a question, overshadowed in 1943, that would return to haunt not only both men but the industry itself, with the coming shift in postwar radio and the breakdown of the national consensus.

Shirer had been similarly troubled, though philosophical, over the temporary loss of his Sunday time slot, forced for the nonce onto the sustaining schedule, with a resultant lowering of income; he didn't see why CBS couldn't "allocate some good commercial time" for news analysis. Murrow, more casual about such matters, wished him another sponsor—"if you want one. It seems to me that the only advantage in being sponsored now is that it's the only way we can be assured of a network, and therefore an audience."

In fact, a new sponsor had picked up for International Silver; fewer bucks, said the agency, but plenty all the same.

Shirer congratulated Murrow on a dedication in Harold Laski's latest book, *Reflections on the Revolution of Our Time.* Yes, he was right proud of that, said Ed, "and it has freed me from the pressure of some Tory dinner invitations!"

Nevertheless, the Cecil Brown episode had left a bad aftertaste. "Seemed very stupid of White and a very weak position for him to take," Janet Murrow noted. "It won't do broadcasting any good in the long run."[51]

For Murrow these were the good years, the peak of his career as working reporter, bureau chief, and, increasingly, spokesman for the American news community in London; one of the first to realize and utilize its potential clout, along with AP chief Bob Bunnelle and Geoffrey Parsons of the *Herald-Tribune*.

There was, of course, nothing new about the Correspondents Association. As Drew Middleton later pointed out, "It was just that Ed was smart enough to see that with all these new people, we'd get greater leverage. A lot of us had the idea but [weren't] bureau chiefs. So it was the responsibility of people like Murrow and Parsons and Bunnelle to make the Army realize what [we] represented in terms of readers. . . . And Eisenhower always had a pretty sure eye for public relations."[52]

They played it to the hilt, the arguments often vehement between reporters and Anglo-American officialdom on anything from censorship of war stories to coverage of the ugly racial incidents erupting with the arrival of segregated GI units. Murrow served on the complaint board, the executive board, working to keep Army PR distinct from the military censorship function, helping ensure among other things—and at Eisenhower's say-so—the continued reporting on race problems among American GIs. Eventually he would take over from Parsons as president of the association, heading the group that had denied him membership seven years before.

Harrison Salisbury, arriving in late 1942 to head the UP's London bureau, was later to recall Murrow at the numerous joint meetings between official spokesmen and the press, both men representing their organizations in the confrontations over censorship and access. To the wire agency chief, his CBS counterpart came across as "a good solid newsman, technically.

"Ed probably moved in wider circles than any of us. He was not only the senior American in London, he was a sort of international figure. . . England was at his disposal; anything he wanted. But I will say this: that although he had this really exalted status—we all sort of bowed to him—he didn't put *on*. . . . Just because he'd done all these things, he didn't think that he'd been knighted. And he never lost touch with the fact that this was a news operation."[53]

Rivalries, in fact, were fierce at the operational level. The CBS chief made it a point to know practically all the bright young Americans funneling into the wire agencies—gifted, ambitious, underpaid—monitoring their performance and skimming the cream.

UP raids were something of a CBS tradition, as old as Paul White's defection to radio in 1930. But even the amiable Salisbury drew the line when Murrow went after "the two best men we had." One was William Dickinson, later Editor of the Philadelphia *Evening Bulletin*; the other, a go-getting, ginger-haired youngster named Walter Cronkite, who covered the Eighth Air Force for United Press.

"Walter," Salisbury recalled, "was without doubt the best operating hard news man in London. And like everybody, he was ambitious and eager, and Ed very quickly spotted his abilities and in the spring or early summer of 1943, he made Walter a big offer—big money. . . ."

I can't remember what it was, I think it was maybe a hundred and twenty dollars a week, to come right over. Now Walter was then getting, I think, sixty dollars or sixty-five dollars a week from the UP . . . and although the UP was extraordinarily chintzy on money, I went to bat for him and got him a twenty-five-dollar-a-week raise, which was unprecedented—so unprecedented that Walter, taking it as an enormous vote of confidence by the UP, gave up the offer which Murrow made to him. And I thereby did Walter a very profound disservice because he could have been with CBS in 1943, which would have been helpful since those who came in early had the inside track.

Murrow, who had Cronkite's agreement at the time, didn't hold it against him. On the other hand, he didn't forget it either.

A raise also came through for Dickinson. "I succeeded in doing *him* in too," said Salisbury afterward. As for the rival bureau chiefs, they did not discuss it. "I'm sure Ed was a little bit sore at me, and I was a little bit sore at him on that occasion."

Dealings for the press corps vis-à-vis authority, however, were another matter, the CBS man a "prime mover," as Salisbury put it, in the detail-loaded haggling over coverage, getting the best arrangements possible, both for himself and for the others:

"Unlike some agency and broadcast men, he didn't try to carve out special advantages for CBS, and he could have, easily, with his influence. This doesn't mean that he wouldn't use his own influence to get a special interview or a special position for himself or one of his men. But in the overall negotiations he couldn't have been more fair."

It was the heyday of the war correspondent—the great story, the great personalities. Weekly correspondents' luncheons at the Savoy, straight-from-the-shoulder addresses by the newsworthy, questions and answers reverberating in dining rooms bearing names out of Gilbert and Sullivan operas. Thick carpets, high windows overlooking the Thames, Allied uniforms, London-cut suits, with here and there a dress still fashionable.

In that world Ed Murrow had become the centerpiece—more than a reporter or bureau chief, of near-official standing; the intimate of government ministers, a welcome guest upstairs at Downing Street, dining with the Churchills when Mrs. Roosevelt or Harry Hopkins came to England. It was an elegant, high-level balancing act, straining—possibly threatening at times—the reportorial ethic as laid down by Ed Klauber, making earlier efforts to enlist him on the team seem crude and simple by comparison.

After the war, he would have some words of advice for Leonard Miall, an English colleague off to Washington as correspondent for the BBC. Beware of having your mouth shut for you, he warned, of too much information too freely given—the eager beavers anxious to tell you the *whole* story, off the record, those delicate negotiations that might just come apart if you talk; those offers to tell the situation as it really is, and then you'll see, of course, why it's simply *impossible* to do a broadcast about it at this time. . . .

Don't get conned, he said; don't bother about Anglo-American relations; "Just report on what's going on." He spoke with the authority, the finality of one who'd known the scene, been through it all.[54]

By the latter part of 1943, the CBS London bureau had expanded to nearly ten full-time reporters[55]—some in from New York, some new additions to the payroll, including Richard Hottelet, a young German-American with a background in wire agency reporting, a stretch in a Gestapo jail, and broadcasting for the OWI into the Reich. Some were outright Murrow choices; others moved quickly into his orbit, joining those earlier acquisitions—Shirer, Sevareid, Collingwood, Downs, LeSueur—who were already household words in the public consciousness.

Through it all, Murrow continued to turn to print rather than the ranks of radio, in the search for talent, almost anti-voice, his own controlled tones notwithstanding.

He was to write in later years:

> In putting together our crew in Europe, I tried to concentrate on finding people who were young and who knew what they were talking about, without bothering too much about diction, phrasing and manner of speaking. There were occasional complaints from the home office on this score, which were generally answered by saying that we were trying to collect a group of reporters who would be steady, reliable

and restrained, even though they might not win any elocution contests.[56]

Acute observers in the press would note one more, perhaps essential element in his criteria for those he took aboard. Said Harrison Salisbury, remembering: "He had an extremely good sense of personality. What he looked for first was somebody who was a very good newsman. And then a person who was not only a good reporter but had some sense of drama of what he was doing, so that he could project it over the air. And I must say, he made marvelous choices.

"There's no doubt that the staff he built up, on the eve of World War Two and certainly by the end of World War Two, was the finest news staff anybody had ever put together in Europe. They were all professionals, every single one of them. It was a magnificent achievement."

Sometime late that year, the phone rang on Pat Smithers' desk at the newsroom in the BBC. Murrow's voice was at the other end. His appearances had grown more sporadic, in common with those of other correspondents, often off for foreign fronts or flying combat.

He'd been briefly back to Washington, he said, returned that day in the belly of a scooped-out Liberator aircraft, known familiarly in the trade as "no seating, no heating," arrived in England very cold, very uncomfortable. Would the BBC crowd by any chance care to join him in a little party at the Connaught?

The five-star Connaught in Mayfair? The editors, survivors of a dreary wartme diet—followed, so far as they knew, by Murrow himself—gulped and yes, they certainly would. Arrangements were made for a crosstown dash by taxi once the early-evening news was off the air, leaving a few sub-editors to hold the fort, with instructions on how to reach them, just in case. The air raid started up as they drove off.

At the Connaught they were met by a sight that was truly dazzling, "such as we had forgotten and had never expected to see again." Smithers takes it from there:

> A long buffet table was laden with all the good things—roast turkeys, spiced Virginia ham, lobster, crab, rare beef, all the trimmings, wines galore, spirits aplenty. Ed, shaking hands with us all, said, "Tuck in, friends," and we tucked in. Suddenly somebody said, "Christ, it's half past eight." Our main news bulletin of the day was at nine o'clock. We rushed for the doors, found that Ed had ordered taxis for the return trip, and anxiously counted the minutes till we were back in Broadcasting House and hurtling downstairs to the newsroom.
>
> Fortunately nothing important had happened. But if students care to look back at the nine o'clock news script for that night, they *will* find that it bears a striking similarity to the bulletin that went out at six o'clock, three hours before.[57]

Elsewhere, the ranks were thinning. Ben Robertson had died in February on returning to Europe after a series of hard-hitting reports on India, killed when his Clipper flight ditched and broke up in Lisbon Bay. "Out of War into Peace. There never was a night so black Ben couldn't see the stars. . . ." Of all the losses, it was one to which Murrow could least reconcile himself. "He was the least hard-boiled newspaperman I have ever known. He didn't need to be, for his roots were deep in the red soil of Carolina, and he had a faith that is denied to many of us."[58]

Alec Woollcott had never made it back to London—dead the month before of a final heart attack and too many speaking tours through the isolationist towns of his native Middle West. "Many people here will mourn him, for there is none to take his place."[59]

Bob Post of the old gang of 1940 had disappeared in those same weeks, lost over Wilhelmshaven while out with the Flying Fortresses. A couple of chutes were seen opening beneath the smoking bomber, but The New York *Times* reporter was never heard from again.

That December the big RAF Lancasters had begun the nightly pounding of Berlin, the climax to a year of massive step-ups in Allied air attacks: Hamburg was a tornado of flame, 30,000 dead, the fire raids of 1940–41 paid back with dreadful interest; Cologne, in ruins. In London, Murrow, Steele, and Richardson kept tossing the coin.

The correspondents' corps had few illusions. There was no press immunity in the sky, the German capital's air defenses known to have been beefed up since Hamburg, concentric rings of antiaircraft fire, searchlights, and night fighters that were to cost the RAF 1,000 planes with their crews. Murrow himself had never been a partisan of the theory prevailing at bomber command, that six months of bombing would destroy the will to fight; he'd seen bombing do precisely the opposite. But it was the overriding story, and in early December 1943 Ed Murrow departed for an unnamed airfield.

Janet Murrow tried gamely to inure herself, particularly after an earlier false alarm, under similar circumstances: a quick good-bye; the departure for an unknown destination; then security blackout. One day had passed, no word; a second day, again no word. The third day the BBC reported the raid and the losses; still no word from Murrow. Unable to stand it, she telephoned Kay Campbell, heard the relief in the voice at the other end—"I've been waiting for *someone* to call!"—then waited as the secretary dialed the secret number left with the office.

He'd never gone.

Said Janet Murrow: "I took to my bed for three days."

"Well, I knew I was all right," he told the wife who looked up at him with semiglazed eyes, "but it never occurred to me that you'd think I wasn't."

December 2, at sunset, he was with the Lancasters as they took off.

Some twelve or thirteen hours later, in the predawn darkness of Hallam Street, Janet Murrow was jangled awake by the telephone. It was 4:00 A.M.; at the other end of the line, skipping the preliminaries, an oddly young-sounding, frightened voice blurted into the receiver, "*I'm all right!*"

"By that time," she said, "I was more hardened."[60]

He returned to London, wrote his report, and, still without sleep, broadcast that afternoon. At the BBC LeSueur saw him come in, a red-eyed, unshaven apparition, sit down in the studio and begin on cue: "Last night some young men took me to Berlin. . . ."

It was to become a classic of wartime journalism: the terrors of aerial warfare. First the prologue—the briefing, the black Lancaster, "D for Dog"—the takeoff at sunset, clouds piling up to form "cities tinged with red"; the flight over the sea, the German coast, and the first flak sparks crackling above the cloud tops—"Like a cigarette lighter in a dark room"—the searchlights below, turning the cloud cover from gray to white, highlighting the plane, "like a black bug on a white sheet." He was flying with the wing commander in the third wave.

Where others would dramatize, he gave the purely subjective impressions as they approached the outer defenses, the sense at first of unreality—"no one seemed to be shooting at *us*, but it was getting lighter all the time"—and of the night sky as they moved in on the target at 20,000 feet up, a psychedelic nightmare of lights and lurches: blobs of green and yellow; red flares like rows of stoplights; the "great, golden slow-moving meteor" that was a British fighter going down—"but we kept going in."

To the right of them, two Lancasters were caught by the searchlights. One broke out; the other didn't. "The lights seemed to be supporting it." Tracer bullets drove at it from two sides. "The German fighters were at him."

Then, suddenly:

D-Dog was filled with an unhealthy white light. . . .

I was standing just behind Jock and could see all the seams on the wings. His quiet Scots voice beat into my ears, "Steady, lads, we've been coned." His slender body lifted half out of his seat as he jammed the control column forward. . . . We were going down.

Jock was wearing woolen gloves with the fingers cut off. I could see his fingernails turn white as he gripped the wheel. And then I was on my knees, flat on the deck, for he had whipped the Dog back into a climbing turn. The knees should have been strong enough to support me, but they weren't, and the stomach seemed in some danger of letting me down, too. . . .

As we rolled on the other side, I began to see what was happening to Berlin. . . .

Below them was a mad landscape, unrecognizable. Incendiaries from preceding waves were going down, "like a fistful of white rice . . . on black velvet," the high explosives, cynically dubbed cookies, bursting below "like great sunflowers gone mad." At one point, caught in the searchlight that seemed mounted on their wing tip instead of 20,000 feet down, he remembered the explosives in the belly of the plane. "And the lights still held us. And I was very frightened."

They finally broke free, and he looked out the window again. "The white fires had turned red. They were beginning to merge and spread, just like butter does on a hot plate." He thought he could make out city streets, but the bomb aimer didn't agree, "and he ought to know."

Before dawn—after more battles, more searchlights, more twisting out, and a near collision with another bomber—they departed. "I looked on the port beam at the target area. There was a sullen, obscene glare. The fires seemed to have found each other—and *we* were heading home."

Crossing the coast jarred loose a memory of 1938, another flight back to England, and a couple sitting just ahead of him—"two refugees from Vienna, an old man and his wife. The co-pilot came back and told them that we were outside German territory. The old man reached out and grasped his wife's hand. . . ."

He called the raid "a massive blow of retaliation." Yet his ambivalence was manifest—no triumph in his voice, no attempt to gloss ("Men die in the sky while others are roasted alive in their cellars"). The colleagues who had crowded the studio barely breathed as he finished: "Berlin was a kind of orchestrated hell. . . . In about thirty-five minutes it was hit with about three times the amount of stuff that ever came down on London in a night-long Blitz. This is a calculated, remorseless campaign of destruction. . . ."

The action, they learned later, had been particularly rough both on the ground and in the air, even in the context of a savagely contested war. Of the four reporters gone along that night, two had been shot down in the exploding skies. Murrow was still shaken up in retrospect when Drew Middleton encountered him several evenings later over drinks.

Yet he continued going back, repeatedly, indeed compulsively; before the war was over, he totaled some twenty-five combat missions—parachute drops, reconnaissance, etc.—over the specific protests of Paul White and the news department, interested less in broadcast classics, even if they *were* picked up by the press nationwide, than the obvious risks in having the linchpin of the CBS news operation spending his time getting shot at in midair.

Bill Paley, in from North Africa, hit the ceiling. "*Goddammit!* You're going off on these missions every second or third night. I can understand, as a good reporter, your wanting to go up to see how it felt, get this sense of fear, this sense of suspense, whatever you get—but you do it four or five times, you oughta *get* it by this time!"

It seemed to make a dent. Murrow was suddenly thoughtful. "I think you're right. Think you're right. Shouldn't go up anymore, and I'm *not* going to."

"Two days later," said Paley, recalling the incident, "he was out over Berlin."[61]

His BBC friends were appalled. The war was not going to be won, Reeves told him acidly, because he'd been over Berlin. No, he said, but it was going to be lost "if people doing our sort of job haven't the guts to go." There was no arguing; at dinner parties Paley would appeal to the others. Wasn't this all foolishness? Wasn't Ed more valuable here in London? Murrow cut abruptly across the argument: No one was indispensable; no one was that important. "I don't go for that stuff."[62]

"I think he deeply wanted to face danger," said the CBS chief afterward. "I used to say it myself, I thought he had a death wish. I don't know what it was, but danger to him was an exhilarating experience. . . . I wouldn't drive a car with him after a while, the most reckless driver I've ever known."

Whether it was the lure of danger, the *macho* component so much a factor in his psychic makeup, the companionship of men in battle, a sense of guilt at not being in the fighting, the need to prove he could measure up or was still a member of the working press—all would remain a matter of conjecture. To fellow reporters who shared the danger, it was no more than the mark of a pro—different in any case from the doomed fatalism of young Bob Post, the Harvard *summa* who, racked by guilt at not being in uniform, seemed to seek death in each assignment, staring bleakly into his drink the night before Wilhelmshaven: "I'm not coming back."[63]

Murrow's courage—or compulsion, as some saw it—was of another nature; very possibly he simply knew his number wasn't up, the poker player and quintessential gambler sensing somehow that the cards were running in his favor. Airmen had it that Murrow's presence on a plane was "lucky."

Whatever the tangled motivations, he continued going up through two wars, for reasons he couldn't explain to himself, much less to others.

It was the end of a year in which the Big Three met for half a week at Teheran, the long-awaited, much-debated invasion in the west now imminent, the war moving into its latter phase, bringing long-gestating problems to the fore.

Months earlier, Murrow had heard his friend, MP Harold Nicolson, formerly of the Foreign Office, talk of coming strains in the U.S.-Soviet alliance over postwar territorial demands by the Soviets on their smaller neighbors, anticipating not only heightened tensions—"America's missionary spirit will resent this"—but the recriminations that would fuel the postwar witch-hunts.

"Ed Murrow refers to my 'soul-satisfying pessimism,' " Nicolson had noted, "but agrees with what I say."[64]

Over the BBC, Murrow had tagged those elements in America ready to take up the cudgel—"those who hate Roosevelt more than they hate Hitler. . . who would be prepared to see us win this war if somehow the Russians could lose it."[65]

He himself had come full circle since 1941, whole-hearted in his admiration for the Red Army, the sacrifices on the eastern front; firmly discounting rumors, in the worst days, of a separate peace, and lending his voice as narrator to the Anglo-Soviet propaganda film, *The Siege of Leningrad*.

Politically, he was ambivalent, a native American suspicion of a Communist state—the two systems, he thought, were "bound to compete"— concomittant with a gut-level sense of urgency for the two great powers to resolve their differences while there was time—on the future government of Poland, on the Balkans, on Russo-Polish security needs in Eastern Europe versus the rights of those in the disputed areas—"East Prussia and Danzig; a pretty strong case has been made for their transfer to Poland."[66] (In fact, Danzig would become Gdansk, East Prussia divided between Poland and the Soviet Union, their German inhabitants fled or expelled.)

Like others, he had feared unpublicized concessions by the West, a breakup of the Continent back into spheres of influence, bringing backlash and the breakdown, once again, of collective security—the only guarantee, he felt, against another war.

That fall's sweeping declaration, therefore, by the foreign ministers meeting in Moscow, calling for a united nations setup, and assuring unanimity without a mention of agreement on the thorny issues, had left him apprehensive—skeptical amid the general euphoria, convinced that nothing had been settled; and that if nothing was ever settled, there would be no peace.

Elmer Davis wrote him angrily and unexpectedly from Washington— for heaven's sake, why must he rain on the parade, sound like "the McCormick-Patterson [newspaper] axis"? Of *course* they were all for telling the truth but there was room here, surely, for interpretation; and wasn't the patient more likely to recover if told he had a chance, rather than being told that only a miracle could pull him through?[67]

Murrow was devastated. The letter, he replied, had "distressed me more than anything that I have seen on paper in a long time." He had reread his broadcasts, he said, and "so help me God, if I were to do them over again, I would try to put the points more forcefully." As for the patient, he insisted, it would take not one miracle, but several. "I refuse to believe that three or even four Heads of State can sit down and make an agreement that will ensure that it never rains on Sunday or that a pint tankard will always be full. . . . The whole history of the world between the wars is littered with 'complete agreement conferences. . . .' "

It may be that I have been too long in this country, or it may be that certain of the financial and political powers in this country speak too frankly to me about their aims and aspirations. Whatever the reason may be, I am more than half persuaded that the pigs are in fact going to inherit the earth. . . . It is easy enough to confess that I know none of the answers [but] the refusal to face unpleasant facts was the primary reason for this war happening as it did and it will also be the reason why a vast number of the boys who are fighting . . . will feel within three years of its end that they have been betrayed.

It is time for me to shut up. I wish that we might sit and talk for an evening and believe me this is not only a big war, it is also a lonesome war.[68]

To Alfred Cohn, he wrote at length of a deeper despair, of his desire to stop broadcasting, feeling acutely a lack of leadership among the politicians, and his own loss of faith. Funny, he said—once he'd been one of the few optimists in London, back when it was life or death. Now it seemed that everything had turned around: "Decisions simply are not being made. . .deferred by the employment of wisecracks. . . . Much of the community of interest, the willingness to sacrifice, the determination to demand change. . .has disappeared. The defenders of the Old Order have come out from wherever such defenders hide. . . . People seem to want to be misled, want to believe that things are going to be easy. . . . Any slight effort at realism is immediately labelled weariness, cynicism and pessimism. . . ."

There was a time when I believed that out of this war there would come some sort of spiritual revival, some increase in dignity and decency. . . . none of that has happened. One hears, here and at home, the rising chorus of the brittle voiced businessmen who have done very well out of this whole thing, and who are at heart not in the least appalled at the prospect of a repetition in a few years time.

In more rational moments I am amused at the childlike belief displayed by some British and more American officials, that when we arrive on the Continent people who have suffered and been tormented will be very glad, and indeed willing, to take their instructions from us. There is no disposition to learn from what has happened in the resistance movement in France, in Yugoslavia or in Greece. There is no appreciation of the great community of suffering that is being created . . . and that these people will be remote from us . . .[69]

He was caught—between his distrust of Wall Street and the City on one hand, his wariness of Stalin on the other; between memories of the Darlan deal in North Africa, and what he privately called "a policy of appeasement toward Russia."[70] The problems of peace, he wrote a friend at home, were already dimly foreshadowed by what he called "the Polish-Russian business. . . . and that's a damn dim shadow compared to what the reality will look like.

"Some German, I think it was Engelbrecht, went home from Paris after the last war and said, 'It's all right. They're beginning to quarrel among themselves already.' "[71]

The sessions on *Freedom Forum* were therefore increasingly important to him—a way of listening to himself, to others; a standard recording date whenever possible, Mondays at 6:30 for BBC transmission overseas.

They were a close-knit debating club by now: Laski for Labour, Conservative historian G. M. Young, Sir Frederick Whyte as chairman, Murrow chairing in his absence. Guests ranged from the radical Labourite Aneurin Bevan to British industrialists to Jan Masaryk, the disagreements lively, the American often isolated, made to see the world through others' eyes.

It was Laski, as star of the proceedings, who had first talked of another war arising out of failure to reach an understanding. It was Laski, too, who now voiced his fear of what he called "private industrial empires" challenging the state—his fear of "American imperialism."

Murrow picked right up on it: Did he, Laski, really think that such empires now challenged the authority of the state?

He did indeed.

In both America and Britain?

In both America and Britain.

Young, the Tory, jumped in with English fears of not being allowed a free hand in the postwar world.

Well, what would prevent them?

Their business elements, the Conservative replied, and "their friends and allies in your country, Murrow."

"Where," the chairman interjected, "they are much stronger."

Murrow couldn't let it go: In other words, if the U.S. returned to a domination of big business interests, then it would force the rest of the world, even Britain, to unite against it.

Exactly so.

The American drew a long, bleak breath. "All right. We understand that."

The chairman broke in once again. "Murrow, do you agree with what he says?"

"Yes, I do. Entirely."[72]

The series, above all, cemented his longstanding friendship with Harold Laski, philosopher of the Labour left, a friendship replete with differences yet rich in affection and mutual esteem. And in marked contrast with the newsman's friendships in the Conservative Party, to which he seemed at first glance much more instinctively attuned.

Said Collingwood, remembering, the Labourites were simply livelier; certainly their social commitment found an echo in the man who wrote letters home about "economic democracy," still bore traces of the New Dealer. "There was Laski, who threw off ideas and opinions like sparks, with which Ed at least as often as not disagreed—he loved disagreeing with people. But Laski *fascinated* him, simply because of the quickness and virtuosity of his mind, a sort of intellectual swordsmanship, the matching of ideas. Churchill he saw as a great man, with all his flaws, of which Ed was *perfectly* aware; whereas he saw Laski as a fascinating individual."

There were other favorites among the party intelligentsia, including Kingsley Martin, editor of the *New Statesman and Nation*—"another fellow that Ed *loved* to argue with and talk with, and try ideas out on, and let them try their ideas out on *him*."[73]

But it was Laski in particular—the friend of Alfred Cohn and Stephen Duggan, who had once sent one hundred dollars to the strapped Assistant Secretary of the Emergency Committee—who was in many ways the dominating factor: chiding "Ed" on the air for not reading his Hobbes ("the defects of an American education!"); lecturing his fellow panelists on the obligations of the richer nations to raise the living standards of the poorer; warning Murrow, the American, of the necessity for laying the foundations of "a really enduring peace," that they could not afford again another age of disillusion: "The young of this generation . . . [must] know that they are fighting to live, and not fighting to die."

> MURROW: And you think this may be the last chance—that history is now knocking for the second time?
>
> LASKI: . . . history never knocks more than twice. This is one of the great crises of civilization. Like 1789. Like the Reformation. Like the fall of the Roman Empire. And if we don't seize the opportunity now, those living are not going to see a similar opportunity again in their lives. . . .
>
> MURROW: Then we're agreed that . . . unless we take advantage of the present, the future will take its revenge. . . .[74]

The professor certainly never made a socialist of Murrow or succeeded in urging an enthusiasm for the Soviet Union that the newsman never shared. Yet early and later broadcasts would attest to Laski's influence on Murrow's wartime view of the world and the shaping, to some extent, of the postwar liberal—to the point at which the newsman would stand before a Town Hall audience in the fall of 1945, urging Americans to give up their national sovereignty in favor of a world community, to seize the moment before it was too late.

Monday evening, June 5, 1944, Paul White talked with Ed Murrow on the cue channel—the usual exchange before airtime, with a little extra thrown in, the Fifth Army having just reached Rome. White, however, had other things on his mind, thanks to a War Department tip-off that

Murrow had been selected for the on-the-air reading of the text of Eisenhower's proclamation to the troops on D-day. And after months of preparation, clogged with internetwork conferences, consultations, and waiting for the go-ahead, the suspense was killing. A special microphone sat waiting, locked away in a pine cabinet in Studio 9, ready to take over the network at the flick of a switch. A signaling device had been installed on White's desk that spring—"Paul's piano" they called it—a push-button affair of lights and special circuits that enabled the CBS news chief or editor on duty to evaluate the incoming signal, connect with the studio and control room, listen in on transatlantic facilities, and talk with his reporters overseas.[75]

All they needed was the date.

"I suppose I may be talking with you later tonight."

No, said Murrow. He was tired and planned to turn in early.

Six hours later the AP ticker in the newsroom clattered into life with the first, unconfirmed report of the Allied invasion, picked up off the enemy wires.

Six hours was the precise difference between London and New York. As White slapped down button after button on the "piano," trying to contact London, Murrow and his colleagues, roused from their sleep, were being briefed on Operation Overlord.

The calls had gone out between four and five in the morning, telephones ringing all over London, sending reporters out into the already daylit streets and over to the big white building in Bloomsbury that had once housed the administration of London University and was now headquarters for the MOI.

It was the result of careful planning, in counterpoint to the military buildup for D-day, a special committee set up by Eisenhower to work out coverage of the landings, representatives of the American, British, and Canadian armed forces sitting down with the designated representatives of the American news media: Bob Bunnelle for the wire agencies, Joe Evans of *Newsweek* for the magazines, Helen Kirkpatrick for the newspapers, and Ed Murrow for radio.

All through the early months of 1944, from January through May, there had been regular meetings in a small committee room upstairs at the ministry, working out logistics—how many correspondents could go in and when, with what groups, by what routes, what facilities would be needed, how to get the copy back—threshing out the nuts-and-bolts aspects of covering a complex, fast-moving, and in all likelihood hard-fought invasion involving air, sea, and ground forces on an unprecedented scale, an anticipated 130,000 men expected ashore the first day alone.[76]

For Murrow, it had been obvious from the start that he wouldn't get to go, that on the critical day of the western war, the long-awaited opening of the second front, his duties to radio would tie him down to the role of supervisor, directing combined operations for the American networks from the broadcasting center to be set up in the basement of the ministry.

It was at once a necessary job and a bitter disappointment. As the likely time approached, in fact, the suspense growing, so did his irritability, his obvious mounting resentment and frustration evident as he prowled the apartment, hating the idea of "that hole in the ground," muttering discontentedly or sitting hunched, staring gloomily ahead of him, chewing on his nails: "*Mmmmmmmfffff. . . . dammit!*"[77]

At Malet Street the scene was one of organized chaos, the whole of the British and American press, it seemed, milling excitedly about in the lofty entrance hall. Behind the closed doors of the auditorium, military spokesmen briefed them on what was happening. The session over, reporters dashed for the exits, the print and wire correspondents off to file their stories, Murrow and those working with him, downstairs to the studios.

It was overseas radio's biggest operation—a pooled effort by the four networks, including the new American Broadcasting Company, set to feed the hoped-for incoming information to the public as part of a stream of continuous coverage, the usual London–New York circuits supplemented by a special Signal Corps circuit passing through all four network offices in New York, ready to go into business at H-hour.

Recorded messages were ready for beaming to the Continent and replay over the American airwaves: Eisenhower to the peoples of Europe; Allied leaders to their countries—piles of records cut under the supervision of Colonel William Paley, now chief of radio broadcasing within the psychological warfare division of SHAEF, the acronym for Supreme Headquarters, Allied Expeditionary Force. Assisting Paley was Dave Taylor, formerly of CBS programming, now in uniform, far removed from that evening in Ed Murrow's living room in 1938 ("There's going to be a war, isn't there?").

At 3:07 A.M., eastern war time, the War Department hot line rang in network newsrooms in New York with a standby order followed, a tense twenty-five minutes later, by the official SHAEF announcement of the invasion, the next voice from overseas, that of Ed Murrow reading the Supreme Commander's order of the day ("Soldiers, Sailors and Airmen of the Allied Expeditionary Force . . .").

It was an honor conferred by common consent—one the broadcaster would have gladly traded in for a few minutes over France. Instead, his role that first day, barring a short report and brief appearances, was to be behind the scenes, in charge of the pool: coordinating the reports, testing the quality of recordings in from the field (the network ban was giving way to necessity); reading off at times eyewitness stories sent back by other channels—the gritty yet essential role of traffic manager, keeping up a smooth, steady flow of accounts, live and recorded, to the greatest radio audience in history.

Headed for France were those he had hired over the years. Not all were at Normandy: Shirer was in New York; Sevareid, on the hard-fought Italian front. Charles Shaw had been assigned to London, covering British reactions.

Of the rest, Downs, LeSueur, and Collingwood were in landing craft, headed for the beaches. Correspondent Willard Shadell was with the U.S. naval forces on the Channel; Dick Hottelet, with the Ninth Air Force, flying with the first wave over Utah Beach.

At midmorning, London time, the first eyewitness stories went over the air—reporters returning with the planes, led off by Wright Bryan for NBC, describing the first parachute drop over France. Dick Hottelet stumbled in, his face a pale pea green after a stomach-wrenching mission in a Marauder bomber, twisting and bucking under the low cloud cover over Utah Beach, capped upon return by a final dash to London by car, winding giddily along the twisty, turning country lanes. He went on following James Wellard of ABC, with insides heaving and a bucket at his side.[78] On the ground at Utah, Collingwood struggled in the wet sea wind to get a bulky recording machine, with its primitive celluloid band and stylus, into gear and working.

Much would not get back in that first day. The material that did was a triumph of ingenuity as even the best-laid plans failed to percolate downward: mobile transmitters not yet set up; equipment already antiquated; the obvious priorities in the first crucial hours those of gaining ground and staying alive.

Nevertheless, twenty-nine overseas broadcasts, both live and recorded, would be transmitted from London in those sixteen hours of reporting as the public listened into the night—hours studded with news flashes, agency reports, a prayer by the President, commentaries from New York, Washington, and London, special features, much of it filler material for an audience waiting for the intermittent pooled reports that were at the heart of radio's coverage of The Longest Day.

Then, an hour before midnight, eastern war time, Murrow told White over the cue channel of a recording made at daybreak just off the French coast, sent back by small boat: "I think you'll like this." He put it on; the New York–London circuit had become impossible. They waited awhile, tried it out again, and agreed to use it. The reporter was George Hicks of ABC, perched aboard a tower of the Allied flagship *Ancon* three miles offshore, viewing the full array of the invading forces, the exchanges between the German batteries and the offshore guns. His broadcast, cutting through the static and punctuated by the sounds of battle, became the classic account of the D-day landings in the early morning of June 6, 1944.

As the invasion moved inland, so did the correspondents, broadcasting from truckborne transmitters. From London, Murrow coordinated a widening news network, himself as a sort of working foreman, the core of the operation, his handpicked staff, known ever after as "the Murrow boys"; an extended family and the professional incarnation of the traditional Murrow brotherhood, the most satisfying period of the broadcaster's life. "There were no editors or re-write men," he wrote in later years. "We had no budget; nobody gave orders. New York asked us only to find the news, try to report it, and keep our heads."[79]

On the surface the London office seemed almost casual. Assignments were handed out with no explicit instructions; they were experienced journalists and expected to know their business. Ideas cutting across another's territory were referred back to Murrow, the answer a prompt and unequivocal yes or no. They were on their own, yet the occasional failure to get after a story fast enough—no matter where in Europe—would bring on a sudden call or cable from London; "an interesting combination," as one Murrow boy put it, "of close but nonexistent supervision."[80]

Between assignments they checked in at flat 71 in Hallam Street, where Kay Campbell reigned as den mother and an extra desk and typewriter were always available. A few blocks away, the white Art Deco exterior of Broadcasting House had fallen victim to the times, a wartime coat of greenish brown cloaking its scars. But at Columbia, location and decor aside, the office boy gone off to join the army, things were basically much as they had been in September 1939: Murrow, Campbell as his assistant, two typists as supporting staff, the full extent of the CBS wartime office in London.

With the liberation of Paris Murrow flew over, found little changed from his memories of January 1940 ("those familiar, well-fed but still empty-looking faces around the fashionable bars . . .")[81]; noted malnutrition in working-class districts, a few newspapers showing signs of independence, high-priced luxury goods, and the striking lack of physical damage in contrast with battered London. He wasn't interested in hearing who had collaborated, how much and with whom. After forty-eight hours in "the most civilized city in Europe," he decided there wasn't much to say.

While there, however, he had met a young Southerner who, like Collingwood, had left Oxford in 1939 to join UP, later broadcasting for CBS in Berlin and Berne. In the past weeks Howard K. Smith with his young Danish wife had made his way to southern France, then northward through the Maquis lines to Paris, assigned from there to cover the U.S. Ninth Army.

A socialist and former student activist who had been a leader in the prewar campus Labour Party at Oxford, Smith had escaped Germany on the last train out in 1941, found himself trapped by the war in Switzerland, and stayed to cover underground movements for CBS. The meeting with Murrow in Paris produced, he recalled, "instant attraction." For the time being, though, Smith's work would keep him at the front; it was not until well after cessation of hostilities that he would get the ritual summons: "Come see me in London."[82]

To Murrow, back in the British capital, Paris seemed even farther off in the general anxiety over Allied parachutists dropped "a bridge too far" over the Dutch town of Arnhem—he had gone with the drop the week before—in a vain and costly attempt to secure a bridgehead on the lower Rhine. Even worse was a new agony of bombardment as the era of the long-range missile exploded over London and into modern warfare.

The V-1's had started coming down about a week after D-day—pilotless planes carrying a ton of explosives, followed by the rocket bombs known as V-2's—robot weapons, striking without warning: a motor cut; no sound; then the explosion. A vivid imagination, as Murrow put it, was now a definite liability in London.

The Germans called them *Vergeltungswaffen*—weapons of revenge, challenging traditional concepts of warfare and boundaries. "It serves to make more appalling," said Murrow on the air, "the prospect or the possibility of another war, and may thereby inject an added note of urgency into the rather casual conversations that have been going on between the Allied nations."

Ten thousand had been hurt and killed the first week alone, the overall toll to rise to more than 33,000 by the time the launching pads in Holland were overrun by Allied troops. To a friend, Murrow would later speak of people he knew, staunch throughout the war, suddenly ready to throw in the towel.

The friend was shocked: How could they when they had endured so much, were so close to winning? The answer was revealing: "Look. . . . The first time someone hits you over the head with a hammer, it hurts. The second time, it's worse. The third time, you can't *stand* it!"[83]

The Guards Chapel in Whitehall had come down on 200 people taking cover; apartment blocks were pulverized. As the deadly thuds reverberated around Regents Park, Janet Murrow, working in Bloomsbury, would ring the CBS office, waiting for someone—anyone—just to pick up the phone.

As the war went on, she had been living, increasingly, a life of her own; broadcasting for CBS and over the BBC's School Service. Though an accredited war correspondent, she had instead answered Gil Winant's plea to serve on the British-American Liaison Board, helping smooth over Anglo-American problems at the grass-roots level.

She had her own friends, her own circles, her friendship with Clementine Churchill. In the past it had been part of being the wife of a journalist and public figure. Now other factors were entering the picture in the bomb-ridden summer of 1944, when death was again imminent, living for the moment a matter of increasing urgency as the war turned ingrained values on their head.

* * *

She was the former Pamela Digby, wife of Randolph Churchill, the prime minister's daughter-in-law and a great favorite of the old man—in her twenties, auburn-haired, aristocratic, a society beauty experienced in the ways of the world, separated from her husband and a general favorite in the Anglo-American colony, keeping company with the prominent, among them Averell Harriman and, in 1944, Ed Murrow.

"There was an aura about her because of Churchill," a family friend remembered. "It was just a group, and she was available. . . . Of course, he loved Janet very, very much. But he wanted Pam. Really thought he wanted her. Of all the men, she had to pick this puritan. . . ."

It was a relationship entirely in the open and a radical departure for a man who formerly wouldn't so much as be photographed without his wedding ring. Janet Murrow, looking back on it, was to cite it wryly as "quite an experience for Ed. . . . She was a great beauty."

The two women had little contact. Once or twice Janet had come along with him to Mrs. Churchill's salon, where men of power congregated. Though few or no women. Feeling like a fish out of water and unwelcome, she did not go back.[84]

Their separate circles, separate hours made it somehow feasible. Rumors started up to the effect that he had asked—was asking—would ask for a divorce. Women friends in particular felt for the wife: "Janet was not glamorous. She was enchanting, a superb wife, but not glamorous." He never spoke about it, the message clear to even Murrow's closest friends—Paley included—that it was not a topic for discussion.

Janet Murrow had been planning a visit to the States for the past year, to see her family. She departed that September, sending Gil Winant her resignation from the Liaison Board. She had had disturbing news about her parents' health, she said, and it was "quite possible" that she would be away for six months.

Originally Murrow had had no plans to follow or if so, briefly. Instead he now wrote of coming over in November, writing and cabling constantly, from the moment she left:

September Twenty-six

Dearest Cook . . . Eating at the Etoile, feeling blue, and missing you very much . . . Plan to go Hollandward tomorrow. . . . I must try to do better broadcasts now account you will be listening . . . or will you?. . . .

Betty's father has come up and is now sleeping in your room . . he's a nice fellow but I prefer you as the occupant. . . . Our friends have been kind, Colfax, Bernsteins, Milner, R.T. and others inviting me to dinner but I go to the Etoile or to the club. . . . Wonder what you are making of America, to me it seems far far away . . You are the only thing over there that I want to see. . . Twill be nice to go back to Holland . . . will be very careful . . Have even bought me a heavy pair of shoes today AND will wear my winter underwear . . . . I love you very much.

Sept. 29

Dearest Cook . . . here am I still in London . . the big Holland trip was as usual scrubbed. . . . My temper is not improved by your absence . .

This morning while shaving I was thinking of our last ten years . . think we have missed too much . . and what we have secured hasn't been worth the price we have paid . . How long is it since we went walking together . . or fishing . . or just loafed . . If we have any sense the best years of our lives should be ahead of us . . I am more and more tempted to suggest that we should take our sabbatical year as soon as this war is over . . . . take a slow boat around the world, or just vegitate [*sic*] in Mexico, or sit on a high mountain somewhere in the Cascades . . My mind is weary and people sicken me . . . maybe we cant get away from this life and this way of making a living but it seems to me we ought to try. Otherwise we shall soon be the sucesfull [*sic*] people who are pitied by the young because we have missed so much. . . .

Behind his concern were the pressures from Paley to take over the news department and reports of what was happening at 485 under the new regime. "Have been thinking a little about that business of going back to NY," he wrote her, "and right now am convinced I could not stand it . . Maybe its just fatigue and maybe I dont really want power. . . . have definitely decided to stall brother Paley till we have had our holiday . . if he objects he can withdraw his offer. . . ."

In the meantime, most of "the boys" were in London, weary, often ill. LeSueur had been hospitalized at least once. Downs was back from the western front, vomiting bile and resting up at the Murrow apartment. Tempers were short, everyone pushed to the limit; Murrow had blown up at Janet for discussing money matters over the cue channel, then wrote, contrite. Paul Kesten, due in from New York for talks with Ed, postponed from week to week, keeping him trapped in London.

Oct Seven. . . .

Dearest . . I am lonesome and harrassed . . Right now Shirer, Sevareid Downs Leseuer [*sic*] and Shaw are all here . . . They are all unhappy, feel they havent enough air time . . Shirer says the six forty five show has gone to hell . . which is probably true . . he also reports that the row with Kesten had pretty serious repercussions . . that gentleman is due over here next week . . dont know why he is coming . . Afraid our whole European organisation is going to hell. . . most of the boys are getting offers of better paying jobs . . . I dont much care what they do but this is now the best group of reporters in Europe and I hate to see it collapse . . they just feel that there is no chance for them to get a hearing . . and I dont blame them much for feeling like that. . . . . Shirers report of the money mad attitude of American radio rather frightens me, as do the things he tells me about the way Kesten is running the organisation. . . Right now I can only concentrate on trying to get things outstraightened so I can get away from here. . . .

Instead, he was kept waiting through October, increasingly disquieted about the news department and indeed, CBS.

"I have an idea," he wrote Janet, "that Kesten is going to try to sell me the NY job. If he does I shall say that I will do it if he will keep hands off otherwise not." The last word from New York, he told her, was that they MIGHT have more time for war coverage when the football season was over—"those fools should have sense enough not to put that sort of thing in writing."

It was almost the time of their tenth anniversary, coming up in this, their longest separation, Murrow's letters from London growing ever more insistent.

Darling Janet. . . .Have had only two letters from you and I am oh so lonesome . . sometimes I think this separation isnt a bad thing . . maybe I had begun to take your love and kindness and tolerance too much for granted . . maybe it's a good thing but I dont like it. . . .

Darling. . . .Tis getting cold over here. . . .Have had but one letter from you . .think the army has messed it up. . . .Hottelets baby has arrived . .nice girl. . . .we shall have one of those, only twill be a boy. . . .I long to see you and be with you . .each night I look at your pictures in my bedroom. . . .

He'd been at a dinner party thrown by "little P," he wrote her finally, and left early. Much of the talk had been of her, Janet, with the lion of the evening, the reknowned Chief of the Air Staff, Sir Charles Portal, "particularly enthusiastic . . didn't go so well with the hostess . . think probably the saturnine flyer is marked down as next victim. . . ."

Afraid have been a failure at cutting the wide swathe [sic] while the wife is away. It might be that I am still in love with you . . tomorrow is our uniwoisity . .and I remembered it all on my own . .lets renew the contract . .and I should like an indefinite option.

It was their private language: the annual contract renewal. "LETTER JOYFULLY RECEIVED," she cabled him, "COUNTING ON REUNION."

He cabled back: "SUGGEST TEN YEARS EXPERIMENTATION SUFFICIENT LETS MAKE IT PERMANENT STOP SEE YOU END NOVEMBER."

She booked a dude ranch holiday for two near San Antonio, and let him know she would await him in New York—"24TH NOVEMBER LONGING FOR YOUR ARRIVAL."

* * *

He arrived in New York as the Allied drive, after bloody battles, found itself stalemated in the soggy winter snows of northern Europe, his reunion with Janet cut into by the usual public demands. On a wintry Tuesday in early December, addressing representatives of the newspapers, magazines, and press associations, he warned that frontline troops resented reported celebration plans for V-day and spoke of the concern abroad over the future of U.S. policy, its influence on the internal affairs of liberated areas.

Europe, he told his audience—whether "going Communist" or not— was moving toward the left, with nationalism on the rise and greater calls for government control. American policy was "obscure," British policy, "a paradox," increasingly liberal domestically, its foreign policy, Churchill-based, supportive of reaction on the Continent; an implicit reference to the civil war in Greece, where British outside forces were shoring up the royalist regime.

Fundamental cleavages, he warned, were now making themselves felt, "and it is going to be impossible to say that America will not exert its influence on one side or the other."

The question was, Which side?

The triumph of Allied arms, he had written back in 1943, referring to both Eastern and Western Europe, would bring not peace but revolutions; the outcome determined "by whose armies are where." Confusion and conflict, he said, would color politics, competing factions vying for power, occupation armies in control of food and services. Governments in exile, he said, might seek to ride back into power on Allied food trains.[85]

America itself, according to his friends in England, had stirred up expectations among the liberated peoples, "thereby creating a tendency toward revolution." Instead, he now noted "a tendency to freeze in power those groups or individuals who would deny the free flow of thought." And he posed the question troubling many with whom he had talked: "whether or not Britain and America propose to build a crust over a revolutionary condition in an effort to maintain the traditional systems in Europe."[86]

December 16, news of the Battle of the Bulge made strategy once more uppermost. "Poor Ed was going crazy," Janet Murrow remembered, "because he wasn't *there*."

But for once they kept to themselves, already departed for San Antonio and sending Christmas greetings from the ranch to the "grand crew" in London. "YOUR OFFICE MESS," Sevareid cabled back, "CHAMPAGNE CORKS POPCORN STOP WE ALL SEND WARMEST GREETINGS GOOD WISHES YOU JANET STOP RIDE EM COWBOY."

They began heading back in late February. Before departing, however, Murrow had asked Jap Gude, now turned agent, to represent him, resisting thus far the pressures from the CBS hierarchy to come aboard.

They arrived in London as the western offensive, recovered from the counterattack in the Ardennes, moved toward the Rhine; in the east the Soviets had penetrated the borders of the Reich. The beginning of the end.

March 24, Ed Murrow was back over Germany, recording aboard a Halifax bomber towing a glider at the end of 120 feet of rope—part of the massive airborne assault by British and American divisions on the far side of the Rhine. The night before, the British Second and the U.S. Ninth Armies had spilled across the river to the north. Half a continent away, the Red Army was driving westward past Danzig through eastern Germany, toward the Oder River.

Sitting around in the commissary at the RAF base in Essex, waiting for the Rhine lift, Murrow had started talking with a colleague from *Time*, Wilmott Ragsdale, a friendly pink-cheeked Northwesterner, the two men discussing not the coming operation but going home. Ragsdale was going back to Tacoma to write a novel. Murrow fantasized about running a regional chain of radio stations, somewhere out there.

"They want me to go to New York and be a vice-president," he began, "but . . . really I'd like . . ."[87] His voice trailed off.

That spring he went back into the field, one of a small group of correspondents based at General Omar Bradley's headquarters near the front. Frank Gillard of the BBC later remembered him there, bent over the typewriter, with cigarette dangling, a meticulous craftsman polishing his copy word by word, oblivious of the madhouse of activity around him.

He joined up with General George Patton's Third Army, moving eastward into the heart of Germany. Collingwood, then also with the press contingent, recalled vividly what was to follow.

The night of April 11 there had been an uproarious poker game among the correspondents, the stakes astronomic, Murrow's luck running high. "He was a terrible poker player," said Collingwood, "but stayed in every hand. . . . bet on inside straights, things which experienced or serious players don't do. But every now and then these long shots all hit. That night, they all hit. Ed's uniform was *stuffed*—with occupation currency, greenbacks; it was almost as though he couldn't lose."

The uniform was still stuffed as they left the base next morning, eased through military checkpoints by accompanying officers with orders to take them where they wanted, impelled by British reports to the north of a barbed-wire enclosure called Bergen-Belsen. Another camp was said to be in their immediate area. Being more or less on their own, the reporters headed toward Weimar, home of Goethe, Schiller, and the short-lived republic; next-door neighbor to one of Hitler's deepest cesspits.

They found it on a hill, four miles outside the comfortable town—"one of the largest concentration camps in Germany," as Murrow described it three days later, in what would be his most harrowing report. "The first broadcast from Warsaw," he had once said, "will test the man who does it." His own testing came now, at Buchenwald.

They had stopped first outside the camp, made inquiries, then entered through the main gate to a scene seared permanently into the broad-caster's consciousness:

> There surged around me an evil-smelling horde. Men and boys reached out to touch me; they were in rags and the remnants of uniforms. Death had already marked many of them, but they were smiling with their eyes. I looked out over that mass of men to the green fields beyond where well-fed Germans were ploughing. . . .[88]

He had wandered off like the others, the accompanying officers, stunned, making no attempt to follow.

Dr. Paul Heller, a young Czech Jew, a veteran of both Auschwitz and Buchenwald, was in the X-ray room of a small Gestapo hospital just outside the gate, once reserved for the Nazi guards, now taken over by those inmates still capable of functioning—the walking wounded, trying to care for the others.

Their guards had fled as the Americans advanced, leaving a camp filled with the dead and half dead, trying to organize as best they could, isolated, uncertain of their fate. To the young doctor, tending to the sick and dying, ill himself, the immaculate figure that suddenly materialized in the door-way—"a very handsome man, tall," he remembered,[89] in a well-pressed Allied uniform, overseas cap folded neatly under one shoulder band—seemed like a being from another planet.

Their conversation was halting, hampered by a language barrier and Heller's awe of the towering stranger, on one hand ("I thought it was an inspection tour by some higher-up"), and Murrow's reticence on the other. Yet somehow they managed—a little English, a little French.

"Take me around?"

"Sure."

Their first stop was a barrack occupied by inmates from Czechoslovakia. Murrow described it later: "When I entered, men crowded around, tried to lift me to their shoulders. They were too weak." Scattered applause arose from those unable to get up from the tiered wooden shelves: "It sounded like the hand clapping of babies. . . .

"I was told that this building had once stabled eighty horses. There were twelve hundred men in it, five to a bunk. The stink was beyond all description."

In the center of the barrack one of the pajama'd figures tottered up to the broadcaster. "You remember me. I'm Peter Zenkl, onetime Mayor of Prague." They had last met in 1938; the broadcaster remembered him but did not recognize him.

On Murrow's asking how many had died there in the past month, Heller located a camp doctor's records. "There were only names in the little black book, nothing more—nothing of who these men were, what they had done, or hoped. Behind the names of those who had died there was a cross. . . . They totalled 242. Two hundred and forty-two out of twelve hundred in one month." As they walked back out into the courtyard, a man fell dead. "Two others—they must have been over sixty—were *crawling* toward the latrine. I saw it—but will not describe it."

At the camp kitchen, the inmate in charge showed him the rations: "One piece of brown bread about as thick as your thumb, on top of it a piece of margarine as big as three sticks of chewing gum.

"That, and a little stew, was what they received every twenty-four hours. He had a chart on the wall; very complicated it was. There were little red tabs . . . to indicate each ten men who died. He had to account for the rations, and he added, 'We're very efficient here.' "

On a folded piece of paper, the broadcaster began making notes: Six thousand dead in March. Nine hundred Poles a day in 1939. *"Need for haste. 200 died day we got there—& people outside are so well fed."*

In another part of the camp they showed him the children—"hundreds of them. Some were only six. One rolled up his sleeve, showed me his number. It was *tattooed* on his arm. D-6030, it was. The others showed me their numbers; they will carry them till they die."

An elderly man standing beside me said, "The children, enemies of the state." I could see their ribs through their thin shirts. The old man said, "I am Professor Charles Richet of the Sorbonne." The children clung to my hands and stared.

Dr. Heller later remembered the odd picture—the gaunt Frenchman and the tall, uniformed American, the small skeletal figures crowding around the two men, following as they walked on. Somewhere along the way, on the by now well-worn slip of paper, Murrow scratched a note: *"Oh how treat kids?"*

The professor spoke excellent English, his easy politeness a macabre contrast to his emaciated state. He apologized for his appearance as they walked along: And how was Paris? Yes, of course, he knew Alfred Cohn of the Rockefeller Institute; they had met at some conference—'36, he thought it was. . . .[90]

Others had begun emerging as word of Murrow's presence got around. "Men kept coming up to speak to me," he said later, "and to touch me, professors from Poland, doctors from Vienna, men from all Europe. Men from the countries that made America."

Was he thinking of the Emergency Committee, those who hadn't made it over, the failed projects, the grudging acceptance of a handful, the fear of accepting more (*"The decision was an unfavorable one . . . keenly regret the disappointment . . . a latent anti-Semitism . . ."*)? Certainly Collingwood, linking up with Murrow at intervals throughout the day, realized as never before the emotional baggage he was carrying to the task, the fundamental difference in their perspectives and, indeed, their very presence there. "People would remember him, and they'd seek him out, at which point, just out of human decency, I would leave and go look around myself. . . .

"Ed had a special thing, you see, he'd been in Austria and Germany. He had known some of these people in conditions of freedom. I'd been appalled by the jackbooted Germans in the streets of Berlin in '38 or '39. But Ed had real experience with them; he'd covered it, he *knew*. He had done his best to help those who needed help or were threatened. And to get them into [the United States] through the web of bureaucracy. So that when we went into Buchenwald, he came in with a different mindset. To *me*, it was a mere spectacle of horror. To *him*, it had personal implications."[91]

But there was worse yet ahead. Would he care to see the crematorium? the doctor asked. Of course the Germans, having run out of coke, had no longer burned the bodies but dumped them nearby. Murrow said yes. The French professor, turning, told the children to go back.

They entered a small courtyard—walled, floored with concrete. Murrow looked and felt his insides begin to heave. "I knew then," he told a friend afterward, "that I was going to be sick."[92]

He swallowed hard, forced it down, and slowly, steadily began counting:

There were two rows of bodies stacked up like cordwood. They were thin and very white. Some of the bodies were terribly bruised, though there seemed to be little flesh to bruise.

. . . All except two were naked. I tried to count them as best I could and arrived at the conclusion that all that was mortal of more than five hundred men and boys lay there in two neat piles.

Another fifty or so bodies spilled out of a nearby trailer, the clothing piled in a heap against the wall.

The broadcaster stood, dazed, shaking his head slowly. "The Germans have to see this." He had been saying it all afternoon, his careful composure close to cracking as he spoke about it:

God alone knows how many men and boys have died there during the last twelve years. . . . I was told that there were more than 20,000 in the camp. There had been as many as 60,000. Where are they now?

Collingwood remembered him going through the camp, pulling greenbacks and occupation currency out of the stuffed money belt, passing it around as best he could—to Zenkl, to anyone. "Ed just emptied his pockets." He felt inadequate, defeated by his inability to handle the rest of what they saw: the torture chambers; lampshades of human skin; the piles of clothing, gold teeth, human hair, children's shoes in the thousands—the indescribable. One pair, several pairs of shoes, he said after-ward, *that* he could describe. But *thousands?*

A French newsman, imprisoned there throughout the war, had summed it up: "To write about this, you must have been here at least two years. And after that—you don't want to write any more."

Elsewhere they stopped at a slave labor camp, just liberated. A Russian woman, overcome, clutched at his hand until the feeling went out of it.

"*Thursday* P.M.," he noted later that night, ". . . *hand still sore from grip of Russian woman and heart sore from sights of Buchenwald.*"

He waited until the Sunday broadcast, letting others score the beat, needing time to get himself together. But he was trembling when he went on.

I pray you to believe what I have said about Buchenwald.

I have reported what I saw and heard, but only part of it. For most of it, I *have* no words. Dead men are plentiful in war, but the living dead. . . . And the country round about was pleasing to the eye. . . . American trucks were rolling toward the rear filled with prisoners. Soon they would be eating American rations, as much for a meal as the men at Buchenwald received in four days.

If I've offended you by this rather mild account of Buchenwald—I'm not in the least sorry. . . .

Geoffrey Bridson, a BBC friend sitting in on the broadcast, had never seen him "so cut up." Said Bridson: "He was shaking with rage by the time he finished. . . . What he had seen, he wanted the world to know. Something which he would get across to the starry-eyed listener who thought, *Oh, well, that's a long way away, doesn't really have anything to do with us.*

"Well, Ed was just in a mood to kick them right in the teeth."[93]

It was by no means the most horrendous or most graphic of the reports coming back with the opening of the camps. Richard Dimbleby's account of Bergen-Belsen had been a good deal more hard-hitting, not run at first by a management perhaps unduly squeamish—the excuse was the ex-perience of World War I propaganda—about "atrocity stories," to the point of not going public with the information on the death camps that had first begun emerging in 1942; indeed, the newsroom editors could later not recall such information being made available to them. In the end, though the Dimbleby report and others went through, even were reprinted in the *Listener*, it was the Murrow Buchenwald report that got the play in the press, the lower shock level evidently deemed more acceptable to the English public.

Even then, recorded and replayed by the BBC, it made many weep.

A Bucks County friend wrote Murrow about it, having to assume, he supposed, "that the facts are wholly unknown to the German people in the mass."

"I do not believe that the facts were wholly unknown to the German people in the mass," Murrow replied. "Certainly many people in Weimar knew not only where Buchenwald was but what it was. The civilians were most reluctant to visit it. The Nazis have succeeded in doing a much more thorough job of brutalizing than I would have believed possible."

In Allied-controlled areas of Germany, the broadcast was translated into German and carried over radio some six to eight times a day. At the camp fellow inmates came running up to Heller: Had he heard the broadcast? What broadcast? Didn't he know—the American who was here, the guy he showed around the camp . . . ?

It was only then that Heller grasped the meaning of the mysterious strip of lettering on the Allied uniform that had spelled the words *War Correspondent*.

For Murrow, Buchenwald would remain a benchmark, a permanent reminder of man's capability. "Those *scenes* . . ." said Collingwood in 1981. "They remained with Ed and *haunted* him. It was something which affected him, I would guess, for the rest of his life. And it deeply colored his attitude toward Israel."

At the edge of his jottings of that April day, on the slip of paper carried all day through the camp, there had been one last note, just before the final tallies of the dead: "*After few hours I shall remember.*"

Later that month he was back on the front lines, in the final drive eastward: Nuremberg, Leipzig, through bloody street fighting. In the west he had stopped off at Bayreuth. The Wagner family mansion, where Hitler had so often been an honored guest, was now deserted, the house a shambles. Downstairs a bottle of champagne, half-empty, stood atop the piano.

Freed slave laborers were foraging for food, groups of tanks rolling along the concrete roads—"like a huge sausage machine"—with tiny scraping noises in between, "of wooden-soled shoes and of small iron tires. . . . The power moves forward while the people, the slaves, walk back, pulling their small belongings. . . ." The devastation all around, he wrote, made Coventry and Plymouth look like the damage done by a petulant child, "but bombed houses have a way of looking alike wherever you see them."

He returned to Buchenwald with an armload of messages for Paul Heller, sent in response to the broadcast; the young man had given him the name of an elder brother teaching at the University of London.[94] He dropped the letters off and waited while Heller penned a reply. Peter Zenkl's wife, also in England, had learned in the same way of her husband's survival. (Zenkl had already left, following a tip from Murrow the first day, when some Communist inmates confided to the broadcaster that the ex-mayor and former member of the Beneš government was marked for "liquidation" once the Soviet armies, as expected, had control of the area. It was an indirect warning, perhaps, but also an indication of emerging fissures in the wartime front.)

In the meantime, Vienna had fallen, Munich was in Allied hands. From the west, Allied armies were pushing into Czechoslovakia and Central Europe; the Russians were at the gates of Berlin, the Führer trapped in his bunker. The afternoon of April 25, seventy-five miles south of Berlin, American and Russian forward units met and embraced on the banks of the Elbe River.

It was an elated group of correspondents that clustered in late April around the bar of the Hôtel Scribe in Paris, site of radio and press facilities since the SHAEF headquarters' move to the French capital. Victory was in the air. Robert Lewis Shayon, a CBS producer back from a tour of the battlefronts, sat quietly, very young, very humble, watching the excited gathering.

They were all there: Murrow, Collingwood, all the "boys," the wartime news stars, still young; national figures, supporters of a world order, a global community of equals; who had made the antifascist cause their own, buoyed by a sense of unity at home—the broad support of the mass listening public—and the determination not to repeat the mistakes of 1918, that this time things would be different.

Shayon later remembered the mood of euphoria, the spring night, 1945, the reporters' exuberance, Murrow at the center of the group: "We've seen what radio can do for the nation in war. Now let's go back to show what we can do in *peace!*"[95]

For the Murrows there was another reason for euphoria. After years of trying, hoping, and disappointment, and deciding finally on adoption, the doctor told Janet Murrow that at thirty-five, she was going to have a child. To both of them, she recalled afterward, it seemed like a miracle.

Ed, once recovered, insisted he wanted the child—son or daughter—named Casey, gender notwithstanding. Janet achieved a minor compromise: Thinking of Charles Brewster, they agreed to Charles Casey if a boy, Charlotte Casey if a girl. Thereafter every letter from en route was addressed to Cook and Casey.

V-E Day came on May 8. Radio moved from one city to another, picking up the sounds of rejoicing. London, Murrow reported, was "a city of celebration and song and thanksgiving. . . . The organized killing has ended in Europe. . . ."

In crowded Piccadilly Circus he sought refuge for his microphone atop a London cab, sitting with Ann Hottelet and Kingsley Martin above the surging, singing crowds. For once he was unable to keep to his usual role of sober observer, joining in with the laughter of the celebrants who tossed confetti at the serious young man with the microphone.

Later he made a pilgrimage along Hallam Street. "Your best friend was killed on the next corner. You pass a water tank and recall, almost with a start, that there used to be a pub, hit with a two-thousand pounder one night, thirty people killed. . . ."

The seven-year momentum had ended, too suddenly. "Tonight, trying to realize what has happened, one's mind takes refuge in the past. The war that was seems more real than the peace that has come."

In a newspaper column, speaking of the general public, he had likened the effect to that of coming out from under an anesthetic; he felt that way now.

Change was moving forward with dizzying speed. The day of the Buchenwald liberation, news had come of the death of Roosevelt. Murrow had nearly wept, reporting it. The ultimate father figure to his generation was gone; the end of an era.

Churchill had been the next to go—politically at least, Murrow's early estimate of a Conservative squeaker in the national elections changed when it became obvious to him it would be Labour's day. Frank Gervasi, his old Rome contact, now in London for *Collier's*, thought the socialists' edge would be small. Murrow by then disagreed. Said Gervasi afterward: "He saw it as a sweeping victory."[96]

At the same time the East-West alliance, never stable, was straining at the seams amid new reports of boxcars headed east in Soviet-occupied Europe and the arrest in Moscow of the fifteen-member Polish government in exile, flown in from London to negotiate a postwar government for Poland. Murrow, while quoting British comments characterizing the action as "abrupt," "unmannerly," and "secretive," was generally cautious, fearful of tearing at the fragile peace in Europe:

> One difficulty arises from the difference in the definition of the word Democracy. . . . In America and Britain Democracy is taken to mean a government chosen by the people, responsible to the people, where people are free to oppose, criticize. . . . For Russia Democracy means a system where economic security and the right to education . . . are guaranteed by the State. . . . Criticism must be confined to the mechanics of government. . . . How much freedom . . . exists east of [the Elbe] or west of it, depends on your definition of Democracy.
>
> There are stories circulating in London of mass arrests and deportations east of the Elbe. It is impossible to assess the accuracy of these reports, since the Russians continue to deny correspondents other than their own access to these areas. The reports, however, are believed in responsible circles here. . . .[97]

That July, weary and played out, he returned to Berlin, his first visit back since the thirties. The Big Three were meeting over the ruins in the mosquito-ridden heat; the war in the west was over; he dreaded going to the Pacific.

There was no satisfaction in his return, or feeling of victory.

"The devastation is terrible," he wrote Janet, "and the small children are hungry. . they scavenge in the GI garbage cans . .the conference is a mess. . everyone and everyone [*sic*] behind barbed wire. . absolutely no reporting of any kind. . Came up here yesterday afternoon after spending three days with Paley and his boys. . I was depressed . .no answers to any problems. . and more than ever sure that the time is drawing near for us to depart Europe. . I crave . .some stability. . . ."

They had put him up in a German house with other correspondents, its owner moved to the basement. One day, without a word, the woman had gathered his dirty clothes and taken them to wash. The dam broke, spilling over in his revulsion against the situation, the forced posture of master and vanquished: "I am sick of tired people and bombed towns and misery and hate. There just doesn't seem to be any emotion left."

Some three weeks later, on August 6, the first A-bomb turned Hiroshima into a radioactive inferno, followed by a cremated Nagasaki and the Japanese surrender.

"Seldom, if ever," Murrow reported from London, "has a war ended leaving the victors with such a sense of uncertainty and fear, with such a realization that the future is obscure."

He found Truman's statement that the U.S. and Britain would keep the secret of the bomb until means were found for its control, not particularly reassuring. "It does for the moment alter the balance of power, but such a solution is only temporary."

At the same time the uncertainties about his own future persisted. Janet Murrow, early on, had made it clear she wanted to go home; she had had it with the expatriate life, belonging neither here nor there.

That fall he began the uncomfortable long-distance shuttling between London and New York. He was filing weekly copy for Ted Thackeray at the New York *Post;* the column, besides added income, gave him a sense of satisfaction. "The Atlantic Monthly wants me to file twenty five hundred words a month for them on Britain," he wrote Janet, "offer five hundred a shot. . Would like to try it but there is a limit . .If only I could write with some speed then maybe we could make some money. . . ."

Jap Gude and his partner Tom Stix, negotiating since early May[98] with the agency for Campbell Soup, a wartime sponsor, had come up with what Gude later described as "a fantastic contract" for a nightly news spot—$2,500 a week, with an ample budget. The offer was remarkable at a time when sponsors were pulling out of news, but in this case agency and sponsor were eager to provide the proper context for Edward R. Murrow's return to America.

The final steps, however, were put off from month to month. Murrow talked of signing the contract, wanting to sign it but holding off. No problem, the Wheelock agency assured him, they understood his position fully and would await the result of his meeting with Paley.[99]

In New York that September he broadcast his impressions of America over CBS; then, teaming up with Raymond Swing on ABC's *Town Meeting of the Air*, he argued for international control of the A-bomb, an end to superpower vetoes in the UN Security Council, and a yielding of national sovereignty to the world body—"we must give up our freedom of action when it comes to making war." Harold Laski's disciple, calling on the public to seize "the fleeting moment," as he called it, the historic opportunity: "This is a great nation. I have seen its power thrown round the world. But we must *live* with the world. We cannot dominate it!"[100]

Meeting with Stix and Gude, he was assured all was well on the Wheelock deal. He passed the news on to Janet, though adding that he was going out to Paley's, "at which time he Kesten and I are to have a session. . . . Seems to me the office is full of intrigue and I am more than ever determined to stay out of it. . . ."

To Gude he confided that he'd been under "tremendous pressure" from Paley to take over the news department.

October 1, with Bill Shirer, he boarded the *Queen Mary* for England, controlled, keeping his options open, but the contending pressures were perhaps stronger than he realized. Shirer in any case was to remember a strange occurrence, inexplicable and troubling. There would be two accounts of that night: one, rather uneventful, in *End of a Berlin Diary*, the sequel to his best seller and published at the time; the other, recalled twenty years later, told in the words of the only other person present—himself.

It happened after they both had disembarked, Shirer said, following an uneventful voyage. They had stopped first at a local radio facility so that Shirer could make a scheduled broadcast, followed by a long, liquid dinner, with a car brought around afterward to take them to London. The rest is told as Shirer recalled it: "Ed was drunk, but we often got drunk together. We were young, drank hard, the pressures. . . ." It was later in the car, said Shirer, that "he attacked me," turning "belligerent," cursing and punching away, taking swings at his friend in the close confines of the back seat. Shirer backed away from the bigger man. "Ed, you're drunk!" It seemed to help; besides, there wasn't that much room to swing in.

Recollection had Shirer dropping off hurriedly at the CBS apartment, with Murrow at the door next morning, contrite: couldn't understand what had come over him. (In the published account they had walked the streets for hours, talking, after reaching London.)

Was it, in fact, the booze? Murrow was rarely belligerent when in his cups, more apt to go into what one friend called "a cheerfully dreamy state."

Was it jealousy, the other wondered, *Berlin Diary* a best seller whereas *This Is London* was not? But that was back in 1941, and Murrow had never taken the book seriously, felt it was more the CBS editor's than his.

Had Murrow perhaps resented Shirer's not returning to Europe to take his place as promised or not resuming the old partnership? There had been no such indication, and he had his own career to think of, after all. "I'd made a modest name with *Berlin Diary* and the Sunday broadcasts."

Or had the pent-up anger, the tension of the past weeks and months or longer, come spilling out, triggered by the drinks? Had there been a reversion to childhood patterns, so long in close constraint, Egbert Murrow lashing out against the brother figure in a burst of fury and depression that Lacey or Dewey Murrow would have recognized?

As for Shirer, "I'm still trying to figure it out."[101]

What remained for the other man would be the memory of momentary shock, the unsettling glimpse of violence and emotions out of control in the friend he thought he knew, roiling beneath the surface calm, a turbulence of the soul that he simply couldn't deal with.

November 6, 1945, Charles Casey Murrow, tiny and wrinkled, with the hairlessness common to blond infants, was born in a lying-in facility in West London. By the bedside stood a huge bunch of roses, sent by Gil Winant. Murrow cabled home: "WONDERFUL SON NORMAL BIRTH JANET FINE." Photographers snapped pictures of the family group: the gowned and booted infant; the beaming mother; the pleased father holding a CBS microphone.

He slipped easily into the role of adoring parent, primed, moreover, by a preview encounter with the newborn when he had visited Dick Hottelet's wife and infant daughter, squalling in her crib throughout the visit. Ann Hottelet would recall him staring, perplexed and fascinated, at the loud red bundle. "This was before someone discovered that all babies looked like Churchill!"[102]

The big decision could no longer be delayed. Some four weeks later Murrow took off again for New York, arriving in the newsroom straight off the plane, disheveled and unshaven after twenty-three hours in a bucket seat, asking anxiously over the cue channel about his wife.

The conversations were urgent now. CBS wanted him and even more, needed him.

Paley, for one, was anxious to see Murrow go up the corporate ladder: "I saw in him a top executive. [He] had more than just good technical skill about news. I thought he had a deep insight into what was happening in various parts of the world, particularly in Europe. . . and that he would give us very good leadership and the kind of depth of knowledge about some of the important issues. . . that maybe very few other people would be able to produce."[103]

But why not Paul White, in line for the top job, who had performed brilliantly throughout the war years? Together he and Murrow, the two surrogate sons of Edward Klauber, had built up the small-scale operation into a worldwide information network. Each man had his partisans, though Paley later stood up for his choice: "Paul was a very experienced newsman. I don't think he was a deep thinker, but he knew how to *run* people who were responsible for organizing the news. . . . No, I had great respect for Paul White. But there was something special about Ed. And I wanted CBS to get the benefit of it."

On the other side, there were the problems that had begun emerging in late 1944, the new look of American radio, less news airtime in the football season, the flight of sponsors. For four years, news had been the most salable commodity, as Jap Gude later pointed out, speaking as an agent; the big sponsors, not having much in the way of consumer goods, just wanted their names up there before the public. "Then, after the war, everybody got out. During the war, anything that was sponsored, you got a bonus payment. Now you were paid a basic guaranteed salary but making nothing on top of that."

The cream of the staff might well be skimmed, the best and the brightest siphoned off by better-paying high-class print jobs, as Murrow had feared in 1944. Howard K. Smith had been on the point of going with *Life* when Murrow called him to London—"You don't want to work for Luce"—and held out a CBS contract. Smith signed it.

What they needed, in short, was a centripetal force, commanding loyalty in a time of squeeze and leaner budgets, White's roughhouse, occasionally brutal *modus operandi,* hardly the answer; word was also coming back that Paul's drinking was getting the better of him.

For Murrow himself, the choices seemed clear. He didn't want the overseas staff to go to hell? Was Kesten really moving in? Well, here was his chance to do something about it. As for Kesten, it was agreed: hands off, or he wouldn't take the job.

Except he loved being a reporter. "Don't tell the home office," he had told Janet once, "but I'd do this for nothing." Maybe, as he said, he didn't really want power.

Yet Paley's arguments were strong ones. CBS needed him. But also the mass audiences were gone now; the action was at the policy level. Come home and shape policy—as an officer of CBS: a hard line to resist. "I think it was also flattering to Ed," said a close friend afterward, "that Mr. Paley should want him for the job."[104]

To the end he put it off. With Stix and Gude, he went to dinner; the Campbell contract was drawn up, awaiting his signature. Together the three men went back to the Stix apartment for the signing—or what should have been. Years later Jap Gude could still visualize the scene in Tom Stix's living room: Murrow on his feet, the two agents seated, watching, contract in hand.

Ed was pacing up and down. I had the feeling he wanted us to make up his mind for him. Finally I said, "Ed, it's your decision."

He smoked. And paced some more. Then stopped in the middle of the room. "Look, if they really mean what they say, I've got to do it."

I tore up the contract; we shook hands and parted. We were still friends after that, but there was nothing more to say.[105]

Christmas Day, he cabled Kay Campbell that he had taken the job. The news media carried the announcement that Edward R. Murrow would be returning to America as Vice-President and Director of Public Affairs for CBS. *Newsweek,* carrying the item, summed up the common reaction: "A brilliant broadcasting career is over."

It was a long, dreary stay: detailed arrangements; lengthy conversations with glum officials in Washington. In London, Janet Murrow waited. Pamela Churchill's divorce had come through. She was in the States; so was Ed. She wondered at times if the old fascination was still there, too.

Back in London, on a Friday in early March, he finished up his last nightly news report. The BBC engineers, whose favorite he had always been, thereupon clipped the wires of the old square microphone and gave it to him. At the bottom they had set up an engraving:

THIS MICROPHONE, TAKEN FROM STUDIO B4 OF
BROADCASTING HOUSE, LONDON, IS PRESENTED TO
EDWARD R. MURROW
WHO USED IT THERE WITH SUCH DISTINCTION FOR
SO MANY BROADCASTS TO C.B.S. NEW YORK
DURING THE WAR YEARS 1939 TO 1945
MARCH 8TH 1946

Over the BBC he thanked the British people, who had, he said, lived "a life, not an apology." Then, on March 10, the last of the Sunday series, he made his last broadcast to America. Churchill's "iron curtain" speech at Fulton, Missouri, had sounded the tocsin. Murrow in passing pointed out that Churchill himself had been voted out of office and ventured that Britain, like much of the Continent, was choosing a middle ground between "the conservatism of Mr. Churchill and the suppressive collectivism of Mr. Stalin."

But in the main that night he spoke of the past, the days under fire, and, above all, Britain's preservation of civil liberties: "[They] feared Nazism but did not choose to imitate it."

Howard Smith, in from Nuremberg, had watched him dictate the piece: pacing the room, editing silently in his head, bringing out a few phrases here, a few there—the typewriter clicking steadily under Kay Campbell's fingers—changing the phrases and creating them again as the broadcast took slow, satisfying shape. Said Smith, "It was simply a beautiful thing to listen to."

There had been the matter of his successor. Eric Sevareid, heading the London office in his absence, wanted to go home.

Murrow told Smith that he wanted him to take his place as European Director in London, that he had gone over the heads of "many people with seniority" to do so. Smith was surprised, unprepared; he didn't even have a wardrobe, he said, outside of his war correspondent's uniforms. "That's all right, I'll leave you three suits," said Murrow. And he did, though the pants had to be cut down. "I'd forgotten," said Smith afterward, "how long his legs were."

There was a farewell party at the Savoy, a snowy day, CBS as host, hundreds in attendance from government, journalism, the crest of public life—Gil Winant present, a speech by Foreign Minister Ernest Bevin—

plus those who were simply friends. Dr. Paul Heller, brought to England, stood in the crowd with Howard Smith and Janet Murrow.

Then, abruptly, it was over. They packed nine years away, the flat on Hallam Street vacated to the Smiths. Those last few days, Murrow, on his best behavior, had put up wife and child at Claridge's, five-star, the top hotel in London. And for their departure, a Rolls-Royce was to take them to the airfield at Bournemouth, flight reservations, obtained with difficulty, still handled by the military.

The last day, in a heavy rain, they loaded the Rolls with their remaining luggage, bundled Casey inside, and headed confidently for the south of England.

Around Bournemouth it was pouring. At a local farmhouse the owner, responding to a heavy rapping at the door, opened to a tall, distraught man with a strange American accent, out of breath—he had obviously been running—rain dripping from his hatbrim: Their car had broken down; he was trying to catch a plane; they had a small child with them; could he get them to the airport? Could he use his telephone?

The farmer went to get his keys. In the background he could hear the American on the phone with the airport authorities, begging them to hold the plane.

The Rolls was sitting in the mud just up the road, bogged down in the driving rain; in its recesses, like a backseat madonna, a fair-haired young-ish woman, holding a tiny infant.

They arrived at the airfield, careening to a stop at the fence as they watched their plane take off.

A miserable two days followed in cramped, makeshift accommodations at a motel of sorts nearby, Janet quieting Casey, the weather foul, Murrow scrambling for another set of bookings. The factor of a small child helped, and forty-eight hours after leaving London, they finally boarded a west-bound plane, wet and weary but headed for New York.

They were returning to a country they hadn't lived in for a decade, a life together that had to be rebuilt, an industry changing gears, and a job Ed Murrow didn't want.

They had left as a young couple at the start of the Second New Deal. They were coming back in the first year of the Truman presidency, in a postwar world overshadowed by the A-bomb, and in a congressional election year that would see a sharp swing to the right, including the election, as freshman senator, of an obscure Wisconsin judge who was to give his name to the coming era.

Ed, sitting in the plane, was gloomy, haunted by his recollections. They were going back, he told her, to fight the same damn stuff they had been fighting all these years. "It could happen here." She thought it an ominous thing to say.[106]

IX

Decompression

"I am not taking this job with the idea of getting rid of anybody!"

He was upset all over again, just talking about it years later, reliving it over drinks as Bill Dunn listened in the quiet darkness of the early morning in a Tokyo club, the first summer of the Korean War. Ed Murrow was recalling his homecoming in 1946, the dislocation of New York, his first management meeting, and two things "they" told him he was going to have to do: First, fire Bob Wood, news director at WTOP in Washington, and eventually, of course, get rid of Paul White.

His reaction had been explosive. Under no circumstances, he shot back. "You hired 'em, you worked with 'em, you want to get rid of them, it's up to you. But you're not gonna tack it on *me*—I won't do it!"[1]

Such was his reentry.

He had come back in early March, took two months off to see the country, then tried to fit back into the setting he had left nine years before—behind a desk again, one story up from the news floor, in a suite shared with Dave Taylor, similarly back from Europe and in charge of programs. Both men were key vice-presidential figures on the organizational chart, with one line of command running to the President of CBS, another to the Chairman of the Board.

Murrow's appointment had been part of the new company alignment— Paley moved up to Chairman, and in his place as President, Paul Kesten's protégé Frank Stanton, onetime Director of Research, who had moved up through administrative echelons, the former newcomer from Ohio who had once sat tongue-tied and diffident while Ed Murrow and his guest talked about their days in the NSFA. Kesten himself, racked by illness, had recommended for the top spot the able young executive who had run Columbia's day-to-day affairs so well in Paley's absence.

CBS had changed. So had broadcasting, responding to a booming post-war economy rapidly shifting to the output of consumer goods, with radio the place to sell them—and television waiting in the wings. The Columbia program books, published quarterly or monthly for the network's advertising clients, had been traditionally stark, two-tone affairs: high-minded; earnest; heavy on news, as was proper to the times. The fall issue for 1945, by contrast, kicked off with a chorus line in living color, splashed across the front—a sampling of a television image transmitted that September from New York.

Not that news would be neglected. Murrow's appointment was supposedly proof of its importance; indeed, CBS was spending well-publicized amounts for new sustaining shows. But news was no longer center stage, pushed back slowly to the edges of the schedule. The big story was over, and the mass audiences that hung on to every word in wartime had flipped the dials, to the sound of departing sponsors and the plop of falling ratings.

Murrow, taking over in a fanfare of publicity, was doing so at a time when the network, gearing up for television, was shifting prime-time emphasis away from news—the bedrock of its wartime reputation—to big-name entertainment.

On top of that he had his personal problems to contend with: the inevitable postwar letdown complicated by culture shock and a too-abrupt change of life-styles, from London to New York, austerity to affluence, broadcasting to paper work. (Never stay away too long, he told Howard Smith in 1949, and watch out for the adjustment on reentry; "I haven't entirely made it after three years.")[2]

Another worry was Paul White, whom he had superseded, who sat downstairs as news director, the last rung of the ladder permanently, terminatively beyond his reach.

"Paul went to pieces when the war ended," said Lee Otis, later of the TV news division, then a young Ohio news editor brought in by White during the war; who, like many on the staff, had admired, feared, and, in his own way, loved him. "I guess he felt there wasn't anything more for him to *do* now that the war was over. I know we all used to sit around and say, 'Well, what do we—what do we put on the air when . . .'

"And that's when he got really bad. On uppers and downers. Pills as well as his drinking. And his health wasn't good."

"Paul was a tragic character," said Dunn, another White recruit and a friend from the old days at UP. "He was a genius—absolutely a genius. One of the greatest newsmen I've ever seen and *no* morals whatever. I mean he'd have made a pass at Bill Paley's wife if the situation had arisen, and they knew it. Plus the fact that his alcoholism was increasing and increasing . . ."

Nonetheless, there was a hard-nosed questioning, on 17, of corporate motives in passing over White. Said Dunn: "The hierarchy just didn't consider him anybody they wanted in their organization—not enough veneer; Paul could be awfully crude."

> Of course, White knew that Ed was on the way up. We all knew it. He had everything that they wanted on the twentieth floor. Number one, he had the basic ability. He had good judgment. He was a gentleman. And Paul was—well, he was liable to show up tight at any time; he was liable to make a pass at anybody. But he used to sit there, "All right, now we're going to cover this, we'll have a mike here, now NBC will have a man *here*, they'll also put one over *there*," and it'd all work out. I mean, he'd sit there and tell what the opposition was gonna do and how we'd beat 'em! And he *beat* 'em, there's no question about it!

But by 1946 arthritis and hard drinking were making inroads. All too often, when the phone rang in the glassed-in office of the news director, it was Lee Otis who picked up.

White's old ebullience, which had always masked a basic shyness, had gone off-key—forced, overlain by constant pain. Jim Seward recalled the worst days, when he ran over to the White apartment on Fifty-fourth Street to see the news director lying immobile, looking up with tortured eyes, trying hard to cut down on the booze, to keep from killing the pain in his joints with the bottle.

Said a staffer later: "Not getting the executive news job finished him off."

Murrow, sitting upstairs in the job he didn't want, looked on disquieted, watching the other self-destruct.

The irony was that beneath the surface brashness, it was White who as administrator had always been the good soldier, with Murrow, beneath the smooth exterior, much more the maverick.

Nothing helped—not the comradely lunches, not the earnest appeals to White to pull himself together. Dave Taylor, another of the old gang from 1935, lent a sympathetic ear whenever Murrow crossed the secretaries' outer office to get a sounding from him—"What do we *do* about this?"—but there wasn't much he could say. (It was a situation Murrow knew from close up; his oldest brother, after a brilliant early start as innovative engineer and military officer, was similarly undergoing postwar burnout and having problems with the bottle.)

In the end the decision forced itself.

The News Till Now was to be the showcase of the news department, a nightly roundup underwritten to the tune of a million plus by Campbell Soup—the sponsors who had wanted Ed Murrow—with Bob Trout as anchorman, the kickoff set for April 1946.

White, no stranger to the microphone in wartime, decided he would introduce the premiere broadcast, bolstering his courage hours before airtime with repeated visits to the watering hole downstairs at street level.

"He did it because he was scared," Trout recalled, "the old mike fright. He had all afternoon to think about it, and he kept popping down to the bar, getting worse and worse. . . ."

The program staff, Trout at its head, appealed to Murrow: Talk to Paul. *Please*. They didn't want him to go on.

Murrow came downstairs, stepped into White's office—they saw the two men talking—then emerged shortly afterward. "It's all right."

At 6:45 that evening, Dave Taylor, in his office on the eighteenth floor, turned on the evening news . . . "And there was Paul." The Vice-President of Programming listened, his heart sinking, to the man who had brought him into CBS, talking away in thick, slurred tones, unmistakably, blatantly drunk.

The next minute he saw Murrow in the doorway. The two men regarded each other, the voice rambling on over the loudspeaker, as backdrop. Murrow spoke up first. "I'm afraid that tears it."

Said Taylor later: "I felt terrible."[3]

Next day's scuttlebutt had it that Murrow had gone thundering downstairs to Studio 9, but White was off the microphone in any case.

In the studio everything was a blur as Trout and a horrified staff struggled to get the new show back on track. Said Trout: "They'd advertised it *enormously*, as they always do, that I'd discovered a new way to do the news, and so on. Whether Paul left the studio, I don't remember; I had my own problems. But we were very upset about Paul. It was just the end. There was no turning back after that."[4]

May 7, 1946, CBS announced the resignation of Paul White, Supervisor of News and Public Affairs Broadcasts, Director of the News Division.

Former Assistant Director Wells Church, ran the announcement, would be taking his place.

The severance terms were generous, the parting, amicable. White, after a brief fling with ABC and a stay in Colorado, went on to what seemed a new lease on life in San Diego as editorial writer, radio commentator, and news director for the CBS affiliate. Contacts with Murrow continued to be close—more so, probably, than when they were under one roof. There were no recriminations, the thing had happened. But for Murrow, there was no way around the given: All other factors notwithstanding, he had fired Paul White after all.

If he had his doubts before, the White incident intensified them in a way that was impossible to conceal. The younger Stephen Duggan stopped by one day to sell him on a youth center project in lower Harlem. A building was available, the money raised; the trustee board was to include Joe Louis, the champ himself—would Murrow be chairman? Wouldn't have to do anything, just be the head, lend his name to it.

Duggan would recall the sight of Murrow's fingers curling, as though grasping at something unseen: "Oh, this appeals to me, it's so . . . *manageable*."

"He'd like to take the job," Duggan told his wife that night, "but he's not going to take it, and I don't think he likes what he's doing now."[5]

Bill Shirer, too, thought the new job was a bad idea. "Ed, you're much too *good* to be a company man."[6] Murrow made it freezingly clear that it was not a topic for discussion. Quite the contrary. He wanted Shirer to join him in administration. Television would be coming, new developments in broadcast news, and the two of them, working together again, just like in the old days. This time it was Shirer's turn to demur.

The rapid souring of the peace, a process Murrow followed closely and anxiously, depressed him further. He had left a Europe—his home for almost ten years—that was obsessed by fears of renewed warfare, starved and splitting into new enemy camps, the continuing Soviet occupation of Eastern Europe on the one hand, the Anglo-American atomic monopoly on the other. Stalin, over Soviet radio, hadn't ruled out the possibility of a military confrontation; and then there was Churchill's iron curtain speech at Fulton, Missouri. The Soviets had already rejected the U.S. loan offered to help ease the blow to U.S.-Soviet relations brought on by Truman's abrupt ending of lend-lease.

Murrow, no admirer of the rhetoric or policies of postwar Secretary of State James Byrnes, wrote an English friend that the situation in New York and Washington filled him with foreboding:

"It isn't so much that the men who are conducting our affairs are vicious or irresponsible; they simply fail to appreciate the importance of issues that they are deciding in an altogether offhand manner. Their knowledge of the dynamics of history is altogether inadequate, and I am fearful lest my country in the near future become what Professor [R.H.] Tawney described as 'merely a great straggling island off the coast of Kamchatka.' "[7]

Howard Smith thought he leaned to excessive pessimism (and himself, to excessive optimism), but from Murrow's perspective, it seemed a dreadful confirmation of his fears of 1943, that the two giant powers had indeed been talking past each other.

"The Russians are our allies, aren't they?" he had shot at Smith in Paris once, without warning, not long before his departure for New York. Why, yes, the other said, surprised.

"Well"—his tone was bitter—"in a couple of years we're going to be *begging* the Germans to take up arms. Oh, we're punishing them now, but . . . I wonder if it'll be one or two years before we'll be begging them."

It was a bad time all around. New York was disconcerting, its frenetic pace a brash contrast with the battered dignity of London. Murrow had always sworn he'd never go back, but as Janet Murrow observed, "the job was there." They had tried to cushion the fall by going away together for a time, Casey after some deliberation left with a nurse found by Dorothy Paley; the Paley marriage, like so many others in their wartime circle, had broken up. They kept up contacts with both sides.

In the meantime, it was an uphill climb: two homesick puritans in a strange house. They missed England, their old life, the old friends. Murrow was ill at ease both at work and in the golden rectangle of the Upper East Side, where a house had been found for them: a world of sleek, undamaged streets; sunlight spanking off the manicured dividers on Park Avenue; well-fed children sporting the uniforms of the fashionable prep schools.

He felt himself an anomaly: a network vice-president, showered with all the perks, to whom a stocked grocery shelf was a thing of wonder, who was startled by the free cakes of soap in hotel rooms and planes with comfortable seating and attendants serving food.

Like many returning veterans, he was having profound problems, manifested in the overt symptoms of clinical depression. Dorothy Paley, after their first meeting, sensed a terrible weariness that was obviously more than physical. "I think he was so deeply, deeply distressed—by the war, everything about it—and the things in his own life [that] were disturbing. Though it was *some* rough time for Janet."

Mary Warburg, socially connected, the sister of a wartime friend in England who had taken up the Murrows in New York, remembered "deep depressions." Discreet, empathetic, she lent a sympathetic ear when both husband and wife began talking frankly, separately with her, neither aware the other was doing so, each intent on saving the marriage. She found herself admiring the "fortitude," as she later called it, of the troubled couple (and becoming, along the way, another of the women drafted by Murrow into the role of mother confessor. "You're rather like an old aunt," he told her once, with unconscious gaucherie; she took it as the compliment intended. Besides, he was older than she was).

Nor was the new home very helpful: a tall, mansard-roofed tombstone of a place in the East Seventies, steep-staired, ill-lit.

There were, of course, familiar faces, from the Shirers and the Davidson Taylors to the Emergency Committee friends and, of course, "the boys." Much of their new circle, however, tended to be from the upper economic levels: the Edward Warburgs; Ruth and Marshall Field. There was entertaining to be done, whether they wanted or not, as suited a corporate executive.

The IIE, still in the old loft building on Forty-fifth Street, proved itself a sanctuary of sorts. Murrow had retained his affiliation with the board, taking over as chairman shortly after his return and presiding over the retirement of the elder Stephen Duggan. The founding father was stepping down, and Murrow was holding out for Duggan's son Laurence to fill the professor's shoes.

Larry Duggan, unhappy with the atmosphere in Washington,[8] resigned from the State Department sometime after the departure of his mentor Sumner Welles, wanted to return to New York; Murrow, from his position, put through the appointment over other front-runners for the job. Brother Stephen threw a party welcoming the new director.

"Ed came," he recalled, "went to put his coat away in the children's room, found my son—he was eight or nine—and spent the entire time playing with him. Then came out and said good-bye, smoking. 'Good night, Stephen, great party, great time,' et cetera. He didn't really like cocktail parties, probably didn't want to come. But he didn't want to say no to Larry."

At the management level there were new relationships to be worked out in the wake of the reshuffling—above all, with Stanton, the new, still insecure President of CBS.

Stanton would later discount reports of his alleged jealousy of the closeness between Murrow and Paley—a great wartime friendship, after all; a "given," and quite justly so, obviously superseding whatever relationship that *he* might have with Bill. Why he, Stanton, had never even had a one-on-one meeting with Paley until the day he'd motored out to the Paley estate on Long Island, one September day in '45, to be offered his appointment: an employee discussing company matters with the boss down by the pool, while Mr. Paley's friends—Ed Murrow among them— were socializing up at the house. Who was he, therefore, to be saying anything?

The same prevailed when Paley remarried in late July 1947, to socialite Barbara ("Babe") Mortimer Cushing, three days after the divorce from Dorothy became final. The wedding, Paley gave out, was to be a small one—family only. Stanton, giving a final scrutiny to the home movies developed afterward by CBS, looked at the screen and saw Ed Murrow. Both Stanton and Ralph Colin—similarly uninvited after having provided the marrying judge—would deny there'd been resentment. (Said Colin, they'd made something of a joke of it, toasting the newlyweds in champagne.)

But Murrow's position in itself as Paley's favorite had created ambivalences all along. "Mr. Paley," Dorothy Paley Hirshon would recall, "had always made it a rule never to have a social relationship with anybody who worked for CBS. *I* had a relationship with certain people, but he did not. He did not. Ed was the exception.

"Well, that created a certain feeling, I think. Not a good feeling, as far as CBS was concerned. Because there were other people there who had in a way as much claim to a social relationship as perhaps Ed did. But that was not the case. . . . There were enough reasons to be envious of him anyway. He was such an unusual person, really overshadowed everybody. So that that feeling would have been natural under any circumstances, and this only exaggerated and aggravated it."

At the office employees found him unfailingly polite and helpful, yet remote, a silk screen, as one later put it,[9] seemingly between him and the world. Sometimes, briefly, there would be a lowering of the screen, an easing of the magisterial manner that served increasingly as armor plate. Rosalind Downs, Bill Downs's very young, very pretty, also very smart, new wife, a former desk assistant in the newsroom, was brought around one day to the great man and received with a stately, "I approve."

Who cares? thought Roz Downs, a member in good standing of the underground clique on 17 known as the Murrow-Isn't-God Club.

Not long afterward she found herself attending a reception at the Murrow town house—crowded, noisy, full of smoke and heated faces. Exits blocked. Stairways leading to nowhere, lined by pots of geraniums wilting in the heat. Roz Downs, twenty-one, hated the noise, the crush, and "the dumb, dried-out geraniums" and made for the exit.

Instead, a press of bodies shoved her into the library. Empty. Fine. She hauled down a copy of *A Shropshire Lad*, A. E. Housman's bleakly romantic lyrics of youth and death, and was settling in when a voice boomed behind her. "What are you doing in here?"

She looked up into the famous face.

"What are you doing with *my* book?"

"But—but—it's *my* book," she stammered charmingly, bubblingly artless. "What are *you* doing with *A Shropshire Lad?*"

"He writes the way I feel."

She shut the volume and began reciting:

> *Terence, this is stupid stuff;*
> *You eat your victuals fast enough;*

He shoehorned in:

> *There can't be much amiss, 'tis clear*
> *To see the rate you drink your beer—*

"From then on," said Roz Downs, "we were great pals."[10]

The turning of the seasons, 1946–47, saw a last ebbing of the postwar optimism. In London and Moscow, Paris and New York, the foreign ministers wrangled over German reparations, the future of Korea and Japan, elections in Eastern Europe, and the western boundaries of Poland, amid rising mutual invective.

Domestically, national unity was giving way to dislocation—inflation; strikes; labor warfare in the industrial heartland; a controlled economy yielding in fits and jerks to uncontrolled expansion; the flight of the poor into the cities; a veteran army looking for jobs, housing, educational opportunity; returning nonwhites, for some of the freedom they'd supposedly been fighting for.

In Murrow's native North Carolina, an older world was passing. At Polecat Creek, Roella Coltrane Murrow died at ninety-one. To the last, the boys had tried to persuade Roscoe to come see Grandma, but her son, his health already fading, had never made it. He suffered a stroke in the wake of her death—the first of a series that were to paralyze and ultimately to kill him.

They buried her down the hill from the old Center Meetinghouse, next to Joshua and the small firstborn of Roscoe and Ethel Murrow. Edgar put in a stand of pines. A gray headstone bore the verse: "*Change and decay all around I see / O Thou, who changest not, abide with me.*"

In the meantime, Roella Murrow's grandson was traveling the country, attending industry conventions and conferences, sometimes with Dave Taylor, at other times alone, quieting the restlessness that came from too many hours at a desk. He drove for the most part, seeing America the way he liked it, from behind the wheel: a country still strongly regional, not yet homogenized by telecommunications, jets, and interstate highways.

Which had its drawbacks of course. One night, as he drove through Montana, the car broke down. He nursed the limping Lincoln into Missoula, garaged it, and, at loose ends, went off to find the CBS affiliate. The station seemed deserted, but he tried the stairs, then a dim corridor where a sliver of light poked its way through an open office door.

He stepped inside. "I'm Ed Murrow."

The station manager stared coolly back. "Oh, yeah? I'm Napoleon."[11]

Personal discontents aside, the traditional picture of Murrow as executive in those months, brooding the time away, does not hold up on examination. It was, in fact, a highly active period. It had to be. As head of public affairs for CBS, he had taken on responsibility for a worldwide army of correspondents and stringers, staffs of news writers, news editors, and news directors, plus those monitoring broadcasts from overseas. A global communications empire with more reporters in the field, it was said, than the Associated Press. A staff built up through reporting on the progress of armies and the summitry of war leaders, now covered issues that were infinitely more complex.

"The testing time for radio news is now," said Murrow, writing in the columns of New York's *Herald Tribune*. A little courage, some knowledge of military science, the ability to write the language of speech, and an interest in people made for a pretty fair radio war correspondent, he wrote. However, the postwar correspondent would need a knowledge of history, economics, political philosophy, languages, and even law, interpreting an unfamiliar world to an America just coming to realize that "what happens abroad affects us directly."

Of the public, he asked for greater sophistication. ("It is surprising how many listeners will conclude that a reporter, doing his level best to explain the problems and philosophy of a Socialist or Communist state, is advocating that philosophy and recommending it to us over here.") And in ending he stated what would ring even truer in the era of instant access, videotape, and communications satellites: "It is said that we are the best-informed nation on earth. I do not know about that, but I do know that we have access to more information than any other people. There is a difference."[12]

CBS had come out of the war with permanent bureaus in the major European capitals, with full-time correspondents in Asia, Latin America, the Middle East, and the Pacific. New faces were added, among them David Schoenbrun. The story has often made the rounds of how Murrow, in London at the war's end, asked the former teacher, Did he intend returning to the classroom? And given Schoenbrun's "yes," answered: "I can offer you the biggest classroom in the world—CBS News."

The classroom, however, was some time in coming. Schoenbrun stayed on in Europe as bureau chief for the ultraliberal Overseas News Agency, sharing column space with such byliners as Harold Laski and China expert Owen Lattimore while Murrow kept in touch from London. At Murrow's request he seconded young Douglas Edwards, sent to Paris for a little seasoning, filling in on backup newscasts. Paul White had liked his work. But when the Paris posting opened up, it went to "someone from New York," much to Schoenbrun's dismay and Murrow's considerable annoyance.

"Luckily," Schoenbrun commented years later, "he turned out not to be a very good correspondent."

In the meantime, Murrow, now ensconced at 485, called from New York. "I see you haven't gone back to college."

"No, I'm still here."

"Well, we're gonna do something. You'll hear from me."

Weeks later at seven in the morning, in a freezing hotel room in Czechoslovakia, Schoenbrun and his wife, Dorothy—young, pretty, and pregnant—awoke to a rap at the door. "Telegrammsky!" Schoenbrun still remembers the moment the envelope slid beneath the door as he watched, bone-chilled and bleary-eyed.

My wife said, "What is it, what is it?"

I said, "That's my stupid editor in New York asking me why I have not yet interviewed Masaryk or something. I'm *not* getting out of this warm bed at seven o'clock to look at a goddamn telegram."

So my pregnant wife says, "Well, how do you know, maybe it's something important."

And I said, "Look, if it's important at seven o'clock in the morning, it'll be important at nine o'clock in the morning."

She says, "If you don't get out of bed, I *will*, and I'm pregnant!"

I said, "Well then, get your ass out of bed—I'm not getting up!"

She got up. Got the telegram, opened it, *screamed*, and scared me out of my wits! I had no idea what made her scream. Jumped into bed and showed me the telegram, and it said, "WOULD YOU LIKE TO BE MY PARIS BUREAU CHIEF, SIGNED EDWARD R. MURROW."[13]

In New York there were the divisions inevitable in any office and with the coming of any new boss—in this case between the Murrow people and those whose first loyalties had been to White; a pervading sense, outlasting Murrow's stewardship, that those outside his circle didn't really make the grade. Inevitably, too, there was the feeling that the new vice-president, as one observer put it, was skimming the cream off the jug, handing out the plum assignments to his "boys." Still, few could fault his appointments, with the possible exception of Eric Sevareid, an unhappy and uncomfortable bureau chief in Washington, who hadn't wanted his good fortune any more than Murrow wanted *his*.

Dissenters took refuge in the Murrow-Isn't-God Club, spearheaded by gleeful newsroom staffers clustered around Jesse Zousmer, a veteran journalist, crackerjack writer of news copy, and nobody's patsy. The edge was taken off the joke, however, when Murrow, getting wind of it, applied for membership. (Zousmer, dean of the news editors at CBS, in a further twist became one of Murrow's closest associates.)

But one important element was gone for good. Elmer Davis, his war-time service ended, had gone to ABC, the fall of 1945. Davis, writing Murrow at the time, put it down to "certain working conditions that seemed reasonable to me and did not seem reasonable to Colonel Paley." They had agreed to disagree, he said, and he would miss CBS.[14] He did not elaborate.

Jap Gude, as his agent, was to blame it on a breakdown of communications, with Paley and White both absent at negotiating time, Kesten altogether offhand in his dealings. Davis, wooed by other networks, said the hell with it and went with Robert Kintner, head of ABC, sweeping aside his agent's entreaties to wait just a little longer.

"There wasn't one of them there who could hold Elmer's *hat*," said Gude later, "*including* Ed. If Ed had been back, of course, it probably wouldn't have happened. . . ."[15]

Their friendship remained unaffected, but the loss was real.

By late 1946 some dozen new features were added to the sustaining schedule: weekly reports from Congress, the White House, and the UN; summaries from the Far East; spot checks of regional news and editorial opinion; foreign commentary on the United States; roundups from the cities of America.

Quincy Howe commented on the economic and political implications of new developments in science. On *Cross Section—USA*, Bill Downs, as roving reporter, covered the turbulent industrial scene, scoring in one case a notable beat on the attempted assassination of United Auto Workers President Walter Reuther.[16]

But two programs in particular engaged the interest and attention of the Director of Public Affairs.

One he had personally set up. *CBS Views the Press,* a journalism review, turned an uncompromising spotlight on the powerful New York City dailies. A local show, aired Saturdays at 6:15 P.M. over WCBS, it raised the hackles of the press establishment, coolly dissecting the handling of stories, not favoring right, left, or center, sparing neither the tabloids nor the good gray *Times.*

To head it, he had picked a relative newcomer to the staff: Don Hollenbeck, an ex-newspaperman from Nebraska, a veteran of wartime radio reporting, and former national affairs editor of the old *PM.* A bony, furrow-faced man, three years Murrow's senior, with a nervous stomach, a deceptively velvet voice, and the look of a tortured intellectual, Hollenbeck had the toughness born of twenty-one years as a working reporter.

The show was denounced, red-baited, applauded, developing a devoted listenership that included much of New York's working press. Publishers, for the most part, were indignant. Company scuttlebutt had it that William Randolph Hearst, whose *Journal-American* was a frequent target, had talked to Paley to *do* something about Hollenbeck and Murrow. Paley, so ran the story, said it was up to Murrow.

The news staff loved the program, coming up with leads and tidbits for Hollenbeck & Co. to chew on. "Too good to last," said listeners, but Murrow insisted the program would stay on the air. For some time, in fact, he considered a Midwestern spin-off, commissioning a trial run for the Chicago press. WBBM, their flagship station in Chicago, proved less than enthusiastic.

Nor was New York always smooth going. When Hollenbeck questioned a New York *Sun* "scoop" reporting the supposed pilferage of top secret A-bomb data from the laboratories at Oak Ridge, Tennessee—a charge denied by Truman but upheld by House Un-American Activities Committee Chairman J. Parnell Thomas, a supporter of military control over the atom and a story source—the paper demanded and got rebuttal time, the entire fifteen minutes; even though the program had covered all sides of the controversy.

It was a matter of equal time, ran the argument, of fairness. Hollenbeck protested, but Murrow insisted. Until a lanky six-footer came charging into the vice-presidential suite—Joseph Wershba, one of the program's almost fanatically devoted reporters, come up through the newsroom ranks, protesting with Brooklyn-born directness and the indignation of his twenty-six years. It was wrong, how *could* he, and what kind of newspaper would turn over the entire issue for an editorial reply?

Murrow looked up at the angry youngster with amusement and gave Hollenbeck the final thirty seconds—all the newsman needed to make mincemeat of the *Sun* publisher.

Murrow's other interest was the CBS documentary unit, staffed by young people out to change the world, fresh from the production of wartime documentaries, wearing their consciences on their sleeves, using the techniques developed in radio news and applying them to a systematic investigation of social issues.

No expense was to be spared, said CBS. The workers would be free to work exclusively on their own projects, no deadlines, the full resources of the network at their disposal. Robert Heller, the earnest, youthful unit head, proclaimed it, in the euphoric language of the time, "a virtual Utopia for craftsmen who believe in radio's usefulness as a social force."[17]

A going concern by the time Murrow came home from the wars, the unit got new impetus and prominence under the new regime. "It was Ed's idea that we should take prime time, do a one-hour show, give it extensive promotion, and devote it to important subjects," recalled Shayon, writer-producer for the unit, who had sat at the Scribe bar in May 1945, listening to Murrow talk about radio's postwar mission.

The programs carried $100,000 price tags each, plus another projected $50,000 minimum for pre-empting a commercial feature from an evening time slot. When CBS announced that Bob Shayon was taking a full six months to research a study of the roots of juvenile crime, *Time* and *Newsweek* gasped together.

Murrow, speaking for the network, projected ten to twelve documentaries a year, broadcast at peak listening hours, no commercials, no interruptions. Proof positive that CBS was ready to put its money where its mouth was. A prestige effort which, amid the rising criticism of postwar radio, cast CBS in what *Newsweek* called the "role of public benefactor."[18]

Topics included survival in the nuclear age, health care, hunger, education, the problems of labor. Only Norman Corwin enjoyed similar freedom. Murrow, as godfather to the unit, played an active role, deciding on subjects and producers and running interference with the front office. He might suggest changes, said Shayon later, but defended the creative people "very strongly" against upstairs pressures, as the network found, in the nervous winter of 1946–47, that they couldn't have it both ways.

What was prestigious was also abrasive, Paley's blessing notwithstanding. Memos bristled back and forth between 18 and the legal department as Murrow fought off continuing attempts to gut the scripts, sending back sizzling rejoinders to the constant litany of "Take it out."

They led off in early 1947 with *The Eagle's Brood*, Shayon's baby: a nationwide tour of ghettos and death rows and a shocker for its time ("The noose came down *here* and the ropes were tied . . . *there*. . . . But now we've got the most modern improvements; we're going to have a portable electric chair"). Brought in as counterweight were the words of Saul Alinsky, patron saint of community activism.

CBS, in a burst of do-good energy, hyped the show with affiliates and community groups. Murrow went back on the air with recorded spot announcements, urging the public to tune in.

It did. And it stayed tuned, riveted, in fact. The reviewers laid on adjectives like "brutally frank," "hard-hitting," "a piece of tough, clear journalism." (The series, interestingly enough, was still dramatized, utilizing such well-known talents as Joseph Cotten and Richard Widmark, with Luther Adler as Saul Alinsky's voice.)

Everything seemed to be going right. "CBS has demonstrated," said *Time* magazine, "that when radio has something to say about an important problem—and says it intelligently—people will listen."

"It demonstrated conclusively," echoed *Variety*, "that . . . vital issues can be presented without sugar-coating, cankerous sores can be exposed, national weaknesses can be aired . . . and find eager, listening audiences."

Audience feedback indicated that nonfiction radio could draw listeners in solid numbers and elicit strong responses when the elements were right.

Media critics hailed a new flowering of the sustaining schedule. Bob Heller, in the first flush of public acclaim, called it "a minor revolution."

It was, in fact, an Indian summer, not a spring, a last burst of good faith, as Shayon was to see it in retrospect, against the background of a fading national consensus and a growing reluctance to rock the boat—a tendency accelerated, at CBS at least, by Murrow's eventual departure as department head.

The warning signs were all there, had been so since 1945, when the House Committee on Un-American Activities had commandeered whole batches of radio news scripts, including those of Raymond Swing and Cecil Brown. HUAC Chairman John S. Wood had tried to get a measure through, forcing stations to display each commentator's place of birth, nationality, and political affiliation. Clearly preposterous, Elmer Davis had told Murrow, "but it's an interesting sign of the times."[19]

By early 1947 increased cold war tensions and a stepped-up schedule in HUAC subpoenas were giving the domestic climate a distinctly chilly edge. By 1950 they would all be out—the Shayons, the Corwins, the Hellers. *CBS Views the Press* would be on its way to oblivion, four of the principals of *The Eagle's Brood*, including the producer himself, red-baited in *Red Channels*.[20]

Politics, however, was only part of the problem.

Ted Berkman, a reporter friend, was sitting in Murrow's office sometime in 1946 on a visit, when a man from programming charged in, arguing for the replacement of a news segment by a folksy feature. Programming was for it, he said, the advertisers were definitely for it, and furthermore, the top brass at CBS Sales would appreciate "a little gesture of cooperation."

To the visitor, it was obvious that the two men had been through this before.

Murrow shook his head. The answer was still no.

How about splitting the time, fifty-fifty?

No. Not half the time. Not any time. The format stayed as is.

As the staffer stalked out, Murrow turned to his guest. "Every organization needs a 'heavy,' " he said, "a 'bad guy' who can say no. Around here, I'm the heavy."[21]

He was aware, however, of tides running in the other direction. In those same months he lunched with Simon Michael Bessie, later the publisher and cofounder of Atheneum Publishers, then a young newsman who had spent the latter war years working for Colonel Paley. "Paley was beguiled with me," said Bessie, "because I had run the overseas news operation for OWI, and wanted me at CBS."

Murrow spent the lunchtime persuading Bessie to stay away. "He thought it already apparent that the expansion, commercialism, and impending advent of TV were all going to make news increasingly the servant of entertainment and commerce. [And] he felt that in the battles that were shaping up, I might not be temperamentally right for that sort of thing, for that kind of fight."

Bessie, in turn, chided Murrow for turning executive. Murrow grew defensive. It was necessary. Someone had to defend the news operation. Someone with access to Paley.

"Well, the fight wasn't over," Bessie recalled afterward, "but clearly, in his mind, the odds looked formidable."[22]

The year 1947 would be one to remember. In Washington the most conservative Congress in years went into session, swept in the previous November in a massive election upset, changing the political complexion of the country.

In New York, a *New Republic* article was making the rounds, charging the removal of some two dozen broadcasters, all "left of center," from the airwaves. At the Waldorf Henry Wallace, former Vice President and Secretary of Commerce, accepting the Public Affairs Achievement Award of the New York Newspaper Guild, denounced the "elimination of liberal newspapermen and commentators."[23] At the same time a four-year independent study on freedom of the press had come up with statistics concluding that the manufacturers of food, tobacco, drugs, and soft drinks—the backbone of broadcast sponsorship—decided what Americans would or would not hear on radio.[24]

In early January Jack Gould, the respected radio critic for The New York *Times*, blasted commercial sponsorship of news and the industry's "willingness to relegate comment to the competitive market place in the same manner as a daytime serial." Among those scored was CBS, for moving Quincy Howe from his nightly news spot because the sponsors wanted Eric Sevareid, the question raised being, Who's calling the shots?

The sponsors were, of course. The shuffling about of newsmen, chessboard-style, was nothing new. Almost every broadcaster, including Murrow himself, had been through it. No one questioned it within the industry. When the ax fell, you went down to the basement of the schedule, there to wait for a return to daylight or early evening. But in the tensed-up atmosphere of early 1947, the growing scarcity of airtime made the question more acute.

Murrow, in the hot seat as Paul White had been before him, protested to the *Times*: CBS broadcasters were *paid* by CBS and *responsible* to CBS. No one else. "Under no circumstances will we permit the sponsor to select a broadcaster who is not wholly acceptable to us or to influence the content of the broadcast."[25]

Gould, replying, compared it to a newspaper advertiser's deciding which reporter would cover a story.

Back in 1943, things had seemed so clear-cut: Just hire the best people in the business, as Murrow had written Shirer, give the sponsors their pick, tell them this was the selection—not "some nitwit who will follow your party line."[26]

Now a rising tide of public controversy was carrying matters one step farther, the implication being that even under the CBS policy he who paid the piper called at least some of the tune.

At the same time Murrow was facing major disappointment within the house: the collapse of his priority effort as a news executive.

The so-called Mayflower Doctrine, laid down by the FCC in 1941, in the touchy final days of neutrality, ruled that a broadcaster could not be an advocate. The time-honored Klauber doctrine said Columbia was to help listeners weigh and judge events, not make up their minds for them. Neither of which had kept controversy from arising over what was and what was not opinion.

Murrow, returning as vice-president, had set out as a main objective the hammering out of a consistent editorial policy, ending the ambiguities of the past.

Paley, at the time, gave it the go-ahead. "There was nothing that said we couldn't," he recalled afterward, "as long as we had balance."[27] Russell Davenport, writer, editor, onetime Willkie supporter, and respected by both Paley and Murrow, was picked to do the job.

What followed was a drawn-out trial-and-error process, complete with consultations, haunted every step of the way by the specter of Mayflower and the thought of licenses possibly hanging in the balance.

Finally everything had come together, and by mid-February 1947 the drafted report was on Murrow's desk: "The talk is that CBS has been editorializing . . . for years, and every first-rate analyst or commentator knows it. What we were unable to escape in the past cannot be escaped in the future. . . . The time has come, in my opinion, to stop kidding ourselves and the public about this. . . ."[28]

Everything CBS dealt with, the report pointed out, including the voice of the announcer, was "subjective, prejudiced, one-sided, opinionated. That is why we have to be *fair* . . . give due place in the argument, due time on the air, to other opinions. . . . What, in the end, we guarantee, is *opportunity*."[29]

The plan as formulated offered the radio equivalent of an op-ed page, presenting a wide range of views on controversial issues, with input from sources as diverse as *Time/Life* and the *New Republic*. Other proposed features included airtime for letters to the editor, more depth to the nightly news, liberal and conservative commentators in debate, more on economics, and better coverage on what was really going on in Congress.

Everyone was sold, from Paley down. There was a high-level huddle at the Chairman's estate out in Manhasset, getting everything down on paper. One of the most stimulating weekends he ever spent, said Paley afterward. They were prepared to go.

Then all at once, everything came apart.

"It had been decided," Frank Stanton later recalled, "that before we launched it, there would be some informal conversations, to let the FCC know that we were about to defy the rule." They foresaw no problems, but it seemed the tactful thing to do.

Instead, Chairman Charles Denny dropped a bombshell of his own— that the FCC was about to hold hearings on a possible revision of May-flower. Said Stanton: "It took the wind out of my sails. Before we could jump into the fray, the FCC had taken the play away from us."[30]

The CBS forces retreated in confusion. The legal department made its position clear to Paley: Don't mess around, not where the wavelength might be at risk. Stanton considered it "impolitic" to force the issue. Said Paley, recalling, "We were all sick about it. Just hadda scrap the whole thing."[31]

Murrow took it hardest. The one really satisfying experience of his first year in the United States, he complained to Davenport in a bitter morning-after comment.

By the time the bureaucratic wheels turned—to little purpose, it would turn out—the CBS plan was in the dead file. Said Stanton: "It disintegrated." The problems remained.

To Murrow, it became a memory that rankled, a nagging, deeply-lying disappointment and sense of lost opportunity. When four years later Paul White, than at KFMB, San Diego, forwarded a transcript of his first radio editorial—show it to Ed, he wrote Ted Church. "I know he'll get a terrific kick out of it in view of the 'no editorializing' slogan I was forced to follow for so long"[32]—Murrow's reaction was instantaneous.

"What you are doing," he wrote White, "is in essence what I tried to do for a period of six months and considerable thousands of dollars of Mr. Paley's money. . . .

"This is . . . the open and overt editorial policy which I hoped to introduce, but for which I was kicked soundly in the teeth."[33]

What broke the camel's back, however, was not the FCC, postwar adjustment, or the failure of the best-laid plans. The final push, arriving in those same weeks, came from another, unexpected quarter.

It was billed as the Greek Crisis: Truman before Congress, March 12, 1947, calling for containment of Communist expansion, requesting massive aid to buttress the Athens regime against onslaughts by left-wing guerrillas with sanctuaries in Yugoslavia; and touching off a bitter policy dispute over the open-ended premise that American security was involved "wherever aggression, direct or indirect, threatens the peace."

In private the usual high sources were reassuring Washington reporters: All this ideological stuff about communism was just to get the Congress going—to contain old-fashioned Russian expansionism, "stabilize" U.S. and Soviet spheres of influence, and ultimately, of course, settle with the Russians as any sensible people would. (It was all our fault anyway, ran the argument. We had placed all our eggs in the atomic basket, ended lend-lease, dismantled the military, contracted our power; therefore, we had no one but ourselves to blame if another superpower had gone ahead and filled the vacuum.)

Congress and the news media bristled with arguments over the proposed aid bill, dubbed by one legislator as "nothing but an entrance fee." Howard K. Smith, at the foreign ministers' conference in Moscow, noted the lavish partying at the Greek Embassy ("the height of bad taste for a government whose people are starving . . .").[34] Joseph Harsch, CBS news analyst in Washington, said the new policy, whatever its ultimate purpose, made Greece an American protectorate, using men and institutions "which could be dressed up to look like champions of liberty only with the greatest strains on definition and credulity."[35]

In the meantime, at the UN, the U.S. delegation was assuring member nations that the world body had not been bypassed. From Moscow, Howard Smith reported the Truman speech, with its either/or position, hitting the conference "like a bombshell," the "heartfelt" appeal for unity among the powers from the old veteran Secretary of State George Marshall all but swamped by the glee among his predominantly conservative advisers, led by John Foster Dulles. Why compromise with the Russians? an observer told Smith. We've got them on the run.

Jap Gude was sitting in his office at 30 Rockefeller Plaza when a call came in from Bill Shirer, a client and a longtime friend, his voice distraught: He was losing his sponsor, as well as his time slot of the past three years. As far as the agent could ascertain over the telephone, his client had learned of it by accident—a passing remark made by "someone from the ad agency, as though Bill knew about it. He thought Ed should have told him."

The remaining details were unclear, but the upshot seemed clear enough. "He was very, very upset, and so were we."

As it happened, the contract with the sponsor—the J. B. Williams Company, manufacturer of Williams shaving cream—had been renegotiated that December with the usual thirteen-week options, the first to end on March 30, 1947, a contract admittedly negotiated not through Stix & Gude but directly between the sponsor and CBS. Versions of how the word came down would depend on who remembered what. A *PM* story, quoting Shirer, said that the Williams Company itself had telephoned the newsman March 10 to let him know of his replacement by a commercial feature; that he had then gone to Murrow who said Yes, he might be replaced, though not by a commercial feature; that he, Shirer, had then appealed to an unnamed "higher official," who declined to interfere with news decisions; and that almost two weeks later Murrow had told him the decision was final. The New York *Times* story, on the other hand, quoted Shirer as saying that he had had only short notice and could get no explanation from either the sponsor or the network. Whatever had happened, the fact remained, as Gude later pointed out, "that before Ed had called Bill in and told him about it, Bill had heard that he was losing the show."

Gude could find, he later said, no evidence of sponsor unhappiness. The Shirer-Williams relationship, dating back to December 1943,[36] had been a good one, but it seemed the manufacturer of shaving cream, one of the last holdouts of sponsored fifteen-minute commentary, wanted a change, which in 1947 meant getting out of news. For the newsman, however, the potential drop in income was substantial.

Gude, an old hand in the business, could hardly blame the sponsors for acting like sponsors. He did blame Murrow and the network, however, for what he saw as a total mishandling of the situation and the offhand treatment of a great commentator who was not uncoincidentally his client.

Shirer, for his part, charged that the reason was political. Like other CBS commentators, he had been an active and outspoken critic of the government of Greece, and of Allied policies in that divided land. Said Shirer later: "Someone at J. Walter Thompson [the agency handling the Williams account] wanted me out."[37] Madison Avenue was famous for its conservatism. The word getting back, he later said, was that he was being purged for his opposition to the Truman Doctrine—that an unnamed agency executive with connections to the fervently anti-Communist churchman and activist, Frances, Cardinal Spellman, lately Archbishop, head of the archdiocese of New York, had "got to Paley," in a move to whip the news media into line.

The third aspect to the picture was the Murrow-Shirer relationship—fine on the surface, problematic underneath, despite the socializing and the attempts, at least on Murrow's part, to return to the old days of Ed and Janet and Bill and Tess. Except there was no going back.

Shirer, though Murrow's earliest recruit, was not one of the "boys." Since 1941 he had built up his position as a national commentator of insight and importance at CBS, as a top news analyst in a department top-heavy with talent, and had gone his own way. (To Joe Harsch, a prewar newspaper friend taken on by CBS in 1943, he gave somehow the impression that he'd been hired by Paul White.)

For both men, their relationship had been unique. For Murrow it was the only true peer relationship among his CBS colleagues in his broadcast career, marked, if anything, by a certain deference. Shirer was the more sophisticated, the great newspaperman, with the legitimizing experience of print that he, Murrow, had never had. Murrow was the greater broadcaster. They had been complementary and also, at a subtle level, rivals. With Bill Shirer he could never act the boss.

There was even, and understandably, a little envy among the younger staff members, back from the wars, looking for *their* place in the scheme of things. "Ed was a hell of a lot rougher with the rest of the guys," said a staffer later, "than he was with Shirer." In any case, there had been differences.

It was known at the shop that Murrow had wanted Shirer to do more eyewitness-based reporting, that the other had held out for a more reflective, think piece-oriented program. In fall 1946 Murrow had asked Shirer to get out into the country for some pre-election observation. Shirer declined. Murrow didn't push it. Instead, he did what a good executive never does: grumbled in other directions. To Jap Gude, over lunch, he complained that Shirer was spending most of his airtime reading quotes from other news media, wasting his enormous talent. "Goddammit, Bill's getting lazy."

Gude, conscious of rumblings elsewhere to that effect, sensed his discomfort. "He was reluctant to take Bill for a drink or dinner and have it out with him. And he wasn't the type to say, 'Come into my office.' It was one reason he was reluctant to take the job."

What particularly stuck in Murrow's craw, however, was an incident in 1946, when Shirer needed surgery. An operation had been scheduled in the resort town of Lake Placid, in the beautiful Adirondacks of upstate New York. Murrow urged the newsman to take time out, accept a stand-in for a while. Instead, a news ticker was moved up to Lake Placid, and Shirer kept on broadcasting. The sponsor, he said years later, had threatened to pull out otherwise. "I nearly killed myself."

Murrow, for his part, made no secret of his irritation. "Whatever the benefits of Lake Placid might be," he wrote Harold Laski, "it is not considered the ideal place from which to report and interpret world affairs."[38]

What would be decisive, however, would be Bill Paley's attitude— dissatisfaction with performance, he insisted afterward, not politics, brought finally to a head by the sponsor's cancellation when the thirteen weeks were up.

* * *

At close to five the afternoon of March 23, William Shirer, his voice somewhat uneven, ended with the announcement that next Sunday would mark his last appearance on the program, that he had been so informed by the sponsor and by CBS.

At a news conference immediately following, the broadcaster called the move an attempt to gag him for his "liberal views."

The opening shots had already been fired, however. Shirer denied calling the press conference, but there were the reporters, waiting. Nor was CBS surprised; a rebuttal was at the ready, over Murrow's name: The change had "nothing whatever" to do with Mr. Shirer's political views; the decision was CBS's, not the sponsor's; Mr. Shirer would have a new time; no one said anything about his leaving. Shirer, talking with reporters, indicated that yes, Murrow had offered him a post-11:00 P.M. spot on sustaining, an offer "clearly unacceptable."

"To suddenly change my spot," he charged, "seems to me purely because of my editorial position. I certainly consider it a move to gag me."[39]

It was like setting a match to dry kindling. Shirer was not some local personality; he was one of the great names in broadcasting—in journalism, for that matter. When he made charges, others listened. The foreign policy debate was raging. It was two days before the launching of Executive Order 9835, authorizing the Truman loyalty program for civil service employees, and the Attorney General's list. In that atmosphere Shirer's allegations of political pressure found a ready echo.

"I worked nine years under Nazi censorship," he was quoted as saying, "and would hate to see that come to us." No one asked Murrow to comment.

Many in the news department, however, were in shock. "We weren't *used* to those kind of things," a newswoman recalled. "Usually you'd talk things over, and you'd say, 'Okay, you can't have this anymore, so how about that? If you can't have Rome, will you take Berlin?' that kind of thing, but something had happened."

Mostly, it was a matter of surprise. Shirer himself was a believer in "the great diplomatic struggle against Russia and the spread of Communism,"[40] as he called it—more flexible than some, however, more wideranging in his world view, less apt to close the doors on discourse; who moreover felt the Truman Doctrine was a rush job, ill-considered—a misgiving shared by others in those weeks at CBS. Harsch, from Washington, queried dryly about "the path to greatness" starting in "the mire of Greek politics."[41] For the younger staffers, the flaming standard-bearer of dissent was Howard Smith, outspoken in the manner permitted to those broadcasting from overseas—Murrow's handpicked successor in London, heir to his Sunday slot; who said that there had *always* been an iron curtain, one of poverty and feudalism; whose broadcasts were blatant editorials on accommodation with the East; and who peppered the government in Athens as "the worst I have seen at work anywhere. . . .The cruelty of its Nazi-trained police has forced honest men into the mountains. . . .It seems to believe it needs no policy—except when the trough of foreign funds runs low, to shout 'Communist' and President Truman will send more."[42]

Strangely enough, the Truman Doctrine, often brought up in later accounts of the Murrow-Shirer confrontation, hardly entered the debate. The issue cited was one of "liberalism"—a label fairly apt for some nine-tenths of the CBS 1947 lineup.

What was certain, however, was that the Shirer program, like other news shows, had been losing audiences steadily, less and less of a commercial venture. Respectable enough in winter, bombing half the year. Hardly a valid journalistic norm, but there it was. And as a newsroom veteran later put it, networks, like newspapers and press associations, alas, are in the business of making money. "A lot of people had stopped listening to Shirer. But suddenly this small outrage—and it really was a very small thing—was built up into a big thing. And nobody could quite figure out how, or why, or who built it. We read these articles and didn't believe what we were reading."

The pickets showed up on Monday morning—from where, no one knew—pedestrians rubbernecking at the sight of actor Sam Wanamaker and sundry show biz celebrities marching before 485. The Political Action Committee of the CIO was lodging a protest, it was said, with the FCC. The Voice of Freedom, a media monitoring group of left-liberal political persuasion, Dorothy Parker at its head, had telegrammed Paley, calling Shirer's loss of the 5:45 P.M. slot "a shocking blow to those who had faith in the freedom of the airwaves."

The signatories included actor Gregory Peck, playwright Arthur Miller, and, for Murrow, names that struck home like a personal reproach: John Gunther, Jimmy Sheean. There were telegrams of protest from Bob Sherwood and from Archibald MacLeish.

The Downses had taken over Paul White's old apartment on Fifty-fourth Street, a favored stopover for the news staff. A large sofa sat at the entrance to the living room; another, at the far end. Murrow paced between them, agitated. "Now they're saying I'm *censoring* him!"

Said Shirer afterward: "I was told that this thing burned him up more than anything else."

Appalled, evidently, was more like it. He was paying for his managerial blunder as he floundered in a middleman position for which his experience had given him no training.

On 17, the overriding reaction to the flap was one of disbelief. So one more commentator had had his time slot changed; what of it? Slots and sponsors were ephemeral and everybody knew it—including Shirer, knocked from his time slot back in '43, dropped by General Foods, his sponsor, fished from the sustaining basement by the manufacturer of shaving cream, then ping-ponged between late afternoon and evening before settling, in June of '44, into his present time. A game of musical chairs that came with the territory. There had been, certainly, no charge of censorship despite Shirer's outspoken commentaries on touchy wartime issues. In fact, he had been busy defending CBS and White, then shuffling him around the schedule, against the "gag" charge leveled by the gone but not forgotten Cecil Brown.

He had even joked about it, back then, to Murrow—about being "freed of your commercial taint,"[43] and too bad CBS didn't keep that "good commercial time" open for newscasts. Murrow, more casual about such matters in those days ("Hope you get another sponsor if you want one"), would blame himself afterward for being perhaps *too* casual, not realizing just how much that "good commercial time" had meant to Shirer.

Possibly, too, there were just some things the other would accept from Paul White but not from him.

"He used to ask Bill," Roz Downs recalled, "he was asking everybody, 'What should I *do*—what should I do? This is an old friend. And he doesn't understand. He keeps saying, 'This is *my time;* this time belongs to me.' I can't explain to him: This time does *not* belong to him.

"He was ready to quit then and there," she said.

Early that week, at the CBS Washington bureau, Joe Harsch, a favorite of Ed Klauber's, a columnist at the *Christian Science Monitor* and a thoughtful analyst for CBS, whose commentaries went out at 11:15 P.M., received a call from Murrow. Would he come to New York, please? There was something he, Murrow, wanted to discuss. Harsch caught the next train.

At 485 he found the chanting pickets massed before the doorway: "*Joseph Harsch is Murrow's choice. We want William Shirer's voice.*" Harsch, a mild-mannered, genial man and a liberal of the old school, crossed the picket line in a daze.

Inside, he made his way first of all not to Murrow, but to Shirer, a buddy since the old days in Berlin when Harsch had been bureau chief for the *Monitor*, covering for Shirer on occasion, his first broadcasts. They had been former neighbors at the Adlon, visiting each other during air raids, throwing open the French windows for a fuller view of the straggling British bombers trying to dump a few on the *Pariserplatz*. In 1943, when Paul White asked Harsch to join CBS, they had become full-time colleagues, Shirer in New York, Harsch in Washington. He had always regarded Shirer as the man who brought him into broadcasting. He knew, liked, and respected Murrow, but Bill Shirer was a friend.

He found him in his office. "Bill, just what the hell is going on?"

In virtually the next moment, said Harsch later, Freda Kirchway, editor and publisher of the *Nation*, came bursting in, fresh from leading a protest delegation. She stopped short—"You! Joe Harsch!"—surprised and none too pleased. In fact, as he recalled it, rather irritated. "You make it difficult for us to contend that there's an issue here of liberal persons."

At some point afterward, alone, Shirer told his side. The exact details, in recollection, would be blurred by the passage of over thirty years, but the burden of Shirer's account, as Harsch recalled, was twofold: that they were getting rid of him because he was a liberal, and—something that Harsch had been hearing from his friend for some time—that Murrow was in some way "out to get him."

"Bill was sure that Ed was jealous of him because *Berlin Diary* had greatly outsold Ed's book, which never did make much of a splash. That [this] was to silence the voice of liberalism, and to get rid of a rival."[44]

Up on 18, Murrow was smoking heavily as usual, but seemed in complete command. Politics had nothing to do with it, he told Harsch, and the sponsor had nothing to do with it. They were revamping the schedule, as they had with other broadcasts, and if Bill would only quiet down and be sensible, they'd find him another spot. Certainly it was not on account of his quote liberalism unquote. In the meantime, would Harsch step into the slot until they worked things out?

Harsch considered himself as much a card-carrying liberal as Shirer ("I didn't quite feel that Ed Murrow was out to destroy the voice of liberalism"). He agreed to take the spot. "I've forgotten how it all worked out," he said afterward, "but I suppose Bill never forgave me."

Harsch's own view of the vexed Truman Doctrine—which had not come up at all that week—was admittedly more favorable than Shirer's, albeit only in degree. "My own fear" he wrote a listener that month, "is that if we try to shore up the present government in Greece as a means of containing Russian expansion we will end by making ourselves the champion of a cause so narrow and so atavistic that we will discredit ourselves . . . and in the end harm our national purpose more than we will help it."[45]

"Many of us were troubled," said Harsch of that time and of his doubts raised by his friend and colleague Walter Lippmann. "He felt that it was a dangerous overcommitment of American resources and would get us unnecessarily into a lot of global concerns that were really beyond our true concern. . . . The Truman Doctrine had an appealing ring; I wasn't *against* it. But there were question marks in my mind." In the meantime, a commentator who accepted the opening arguments with undisguised trepidation, who rapped the open-ended nature of the doctrine, the risk of underwriting not freedom but a global status quo, who denounced the "ominous and hysterical note" in the new national mood and talked of "making Greece an American protectorate" was hardly likely to get a bear hug from those who had allegedly wanted Shirer out.

It would be a week to remember. Sunday evening there had been Shirer's remark about Nazi censorship. On Monday Murrow, announcing

Harsch in the 5:45 P.M. slot, said the move would "improve Columbia's news analysis in this period." Shirer, stung, said his usefulness to CBS was ended.

The Progressive Citizens of America, revving up for a Madison Square Garden rally, announced the "Shirer matter" as part of the agenda at the upcoming Wednesday board meeting. On Friday afternoon a delegation marshaled by the Voice of Freedom Committee and led by Freda Kirchway, spent forty-five minutes in Paley's office, though neither side convinced the other.

In the meantime, leads and headlines were suggesting that the newsman either had been or was already fired. (WILLIAM SHIRER, LIBERAL COMMENTATOR, GETS AXE[46]); CBS's—meaning Murrow's—insistence that he wasn't being dropped met with open skepticism. Shirer pointed to his Hooper rating—6.9 percent, well over 6 million listeners, unusually high, he said, for Sunday afternoon. "If the Columbia Broadcasting System throws me off when I have this tremendous audience," he told *PM*, "then they must not like my views."[47] The figure was accurate—for a single Sunday. The week before, it had been 3.8, and before that, 5.3,[48] the rise and fall of ratings indicative of anything from an international crisis to a sudden snowstorm keeping everyone at home.

The Shirer figures were respectable enough for the winter months, beefed up now by the debate over Greece and the sharp increase in listeners as Truman, appearing before Congress, had followed Senator Arthur Vandenberg's advice to "scare the hell out of the country." News listening had punched dramatically upward as expected. But they were not the ratings of the glory days, when the program carried anywhere between 8 and 10 million listeners. The "tremendous audiences," unhappily, were not those of the Shirers, the Sevareids, the Smiths. Those prizes Hooper gave to—or rather recorded for—such as Walter Winchell, Drew Pearson, H. V. Kaltenborn, CBS's Lowell Thomas, the newsman heroes of the periodic *Hooperade of Stars*.[49]

Certainly the Shirer program, whatever its state, meant more to the public weal than *Quick as a Flash* or *Counterspy*, its network competition in the time slot. And Shirer's conclusions were always vintage. But the argument had been raised to a different plateau, the context changed from a questioning of industry practice to dark hints of political conspiracy. Suddenly everyone was talking about Bill Shirer's 6.9 rating, cited now as proof of malice.

Drew Pearson scored Columbia's increased "timidity," citing 1943 and Cecil Brown ("He had been telling some unpleasant truths about the conduct of the war").[50] But Ben Gross, the veteran radio critic of the New York *Daily News*, recalled that on that occasion it was Shirer who had gone to bat for CBS, denying political censorship after Brown charged he had been gagged.

If Murrow thought of 1943 and Shirer's letter—Cecil Brown making trouble, and should a guy shoot off his personal prejudices—it could not have sweetened his disposition.

His stance that week veered between a public cool and a private mounting anger and frustration as the protests snowballed into a media avalanche, speckled with catch phrases about "Nazi censorship . . . conspiracy to silence American liberal voices. . . ." It was during that time, recalled Shirer, that he received an unexpected call at home—Murrow was telephoning from Seventy-fourth Street, his cool gone, in its place a stream of language straight out of the logging camps of western Washington: "You lousy son of a bitch . . . pickets . . . getting these liberals down on my back. . . ."

Against all odds they tried to backtrack—Murrow, by his account, probing acceptable alternatives, Shirer insisting on the slot, both trying to negotiate in what had become a goldfish bowl, to salvage the situation.

"I had the feeling, I suppose," said Shirer later, "that everything had got out of hand." He sensed pressures from others who he suspected wished neither of them well, including an unnamed company executive "who I'm sure was a member of the CP. Every time Ed and I came along, it was 'Well, Ed, I see you're selling out to Shirer,' trying to provoke a confrontation.

"The air was poisoned."[51]

Jap Gude, in the hot seat all that week—friend to both men, one of them a client[52]—was sitting over drinks at Shirer's Beekman Place apartment when the telephone rang. It was E. V. Hurlburt, President of the J. B. Williams Company, returned from vacation—so the agent gathered—to a stack of angry telegrams and wanting to know just what the hell was going on.

Said Gude: "I heard only Bill's end of the conversation, but I could pretty much tell that this man was upset. [Bill] was not *obsequious*, but it sounded like he was apologetic, conciliatory. 'I understand, I'm sorry that this has caused you trouble. . . . I had no control.' He *did* have control. Why, he *called* that news conference."

Shirer's recollection, on the other hand, was of the Williams executive coming to his apartment Thursday night—"he had sheafs of telegrams"—agitated and ready to renew the option. ("For Crissake, go to the telephone and get Paley immediately," Elmo Roper allegedly told him over lunch. "Tell him the sponsor wants you back on the air." Paley, said Shirer, refused.)

Certainly attitudes were hardening on 20 under the impact of protests, delegations, and Shirer's almost daily statements to the press.

Paley was openly resentful, then as later. "I don't think I thought very kindly of Mr. Shirer. . . . He knew darn well that the matter of changing him or being dissatisfied with him—let's put it that way—was very much in the air. And he was very knock-it-off about it. I don't think he paid any attention."

The decision to move Shirer, said Paley, had been a joint one. "Ed and I discussed this long before the thing blew. We were both conscious of the fact that Shirer just wasn't working at it. . . . He never went to the news; the news came to *him*. . . . It was a good period, but it didn't reflect the effort of a newsman who wanted to dig deep and get information on his own. And he was reminded, quite often, [though] *I* didn't have direct contact with him.

"But when the change was made, it was made by Murrow *and me*—nothing I shoved down Murrow's throat. Oh, Ed was very unhappy about it. He didn't like to demote, or make a change—[though] he wasn't actually demoting or firing him. . . ."

As for the agency and sponsor, "They didn't put on the heat; they just canceled the contract. I never heard any complaint about Shirer from an advertiser that they didn't like what he was saying and doing. *We* were dissatisfied. . . . It was an inside evaluation, happened to occur at about the same time the cancellation came through. And it was just unfortunate."[53]

Enter Frank Stanton, CBS President for the past year and sympathetic, probably the "unnamed official" Shirer had first appealed to: "It seemed to me that this was a great talent that had gotten caught up in some policy differences, and it seemed to me that there was a way that Bill could be—saved, if you will—and [that] we could operate within the policies that had been developed by senior management. Bill tended to go, in terms of voice and content, with an opinion. Which was in violation, if that's not too strong a word, of the [CBS] policy. [But] I wasn't directly involved, and indeed, I can't throw any light on it other than the speculation that's been around.

"The other issue that I think gave *Ed* problems was that he thought that Shirer wasn't working very hard, that he read the Sunday papers, came over to the studio late in the afternoon and gave it a lick and a promise, and that was *it*. Ed was a hell of a craftsman, a hardworking reporter. Not having been a reporter in the sense that Shirer had been, I believe he resented the knock-it-off kind of attitude that Shirer had. . . . But I was one step removed from it."[54]

Surprisingly, much of the newsroom rank and file agreed for once with management's assessment, including the young Turks who might have been expected politically to side with Shirer. The feeling in the department, as former Paul White staffers later described it, was that of a great reporter resting on his laurels ("This wasn't the Bill Shirer we knew and loved"),[55] rewriting other people's copy.

"They didn't agree that this was political," said Joe Wershba, the feisty reporter for *CBS Views the Press*, "you couldn't bullshit them."

The consensus seemed to be that the newsman, starting from an understandable position—lesser Shirer was after all still Shirer—had got himself in deep water and couldn't get out. Commentators elsewhere were regarding the whole thing as an industry flap and as "a weak 'cause célèbre,' " as *Variety* put it. "Those around New York with long memories recalled that when Cecil Brown left CBS three years ago in a clash with Paul White . . . it was Shirer who stood up at an Overseas Press Club Luncheon and defended CBS news policies and ethics. . . . Shirer finally found himself in a strange box when he himself invoked the sympathy of his colleagues and publicly rapped his bosses."[56]

Meanwhile, Paley was known to be stewing over the uproar in the press. "We were the villains and he was the hero, caused very largely by his efforts to bring about this reaction. He was out to get even with us, I guess, and I was very upset by that because I didn't think it was fair. . . . It was too rough for him, I think, to admit to *himself* even that his job, and the quality of it, had been seriously questioned. . . ."

It was late in the week when Murrow figuratively tugged at Shirer's sleeve and got them both away from 485 and its pressures. Alone and uninterrupted, said Shirer later, they hammered out a face-saving statement, to be issued jointly by Shirer and CBS, including the announcement of a new broadcast time, Saturdays at 6:45 P.M. Satisfied, they rushed back to the office, dictated the statement, and presented it to Paley.

The Chairman, said Shirer, rejected it out of hand. "He wanted me to crawl, and I wasn't crawling."

In a statement to the press he said that Paley had "shocked" him by turning thumbs-down on the agreement, insisting that he sign it alone— a request, said the statement, unbefitting his dignity "as a person, a writer, and an internationally known commentator."[57]

Jap Gude remembered making one last-ditch phone call to Murrow, reaching him in Paley's office. "Ed, tell me if I'm not minding my own business. Can I help arbitrate?"

Murrow sounded low. "Thanks, but there's nothing that can be done."

J. B. Williams had turned down Harsch as well. CBS announced that he was staying in the slot.

But something else had happened in that last day or two.

Word had leaked about the compromise, *PM*, jumping the gun, already gone to press with the announcement of a settlement. Company scuttle-butt, however, had it that Shirer, partway through negotiations, had cabled H. V. Kaltenborn, calling for protests from the Association of Radio News Analysts as in the Brown case; that Kaltenborn for unknown reasons gave the telegram to Paley, asking, couldn't something be done?; and that Paley had flashed the cable before Murrow and an embarrassed Shirer, asking, was this being fair to the network?, and ending any further dialogue. Such at least was the story making the rounds.

It had been Shirer's contention, then as later, that the protests were entirely spontaneous—that the press conference immediately following his newscast must have been reporters who happened to be listening, who called his agent or Murrow on that Sunday afternoon, and rushed down on their own: the *cri du coeur* of a shortchanged, angry public.

What had happened was that Wednesday afternoon, Hans Kaltenborn, spearhead of the censorship battle with CBS in 1943, founder and president of the Association of Radio News Analysts, known as ARNA—everyone of note was in it, Murrow, Shirer, Quincy Howe, Elmer Davis, Raymond Swing—received a cable at his town house on East Sixty-fourth Street: "ANY INTEREST IN ARNA OVER ISSUE WHETHER SOAP MAKER SHOULD DICTATE WHO SHOULD NOT BE HEARD ON AIR. INFORMATIVELY HAVE HEARD FROM HUNDREDS PROMINENT CITIZENS, MANY ORGANIZATIONS. BUT ARNA'S SILENCE GROWING ELOQUENT. REGARDS BILL SHIRER."[58]

No one had been particularly gung-ho on the matter, barring possibly John Gunther, now inactive, but if Bill wanted the matter raised, so be it. Notify the secretary, Kaltenborn wired back, include a detailed statement, and ARNA would take it up at the upcoming business meeting.

The exchange of telegrams—and could he make the meeting?—was forwarded to Murrow.

Sunday morning, said Shirer, the telephone rang again. It was Murrow, shouting in a voice from which all restraint had vanished, "You dirty bastard, if you start anything, I'm going to beat your brains out!"

Shirer had promised to take up the details of his severance on the Sunday broadcast. The flat, Midwestern voice answering was cold as steel: "Ed, I'm not going to be intimidated by your little yes-men."

Such, at least, was the survivor's recollection. The question asked in later years—wasn't this rather un-vice-presidential behavior?—would elicit a smile: "That wasn't the vice-president talking."[59]

At 5:45 P.M., March 31, 1947, William Shirer made his last report for CBS. Outside, the press was waiting; in the control room, a row of faces—"about ten people," he recalled later, empowered, he was sure, to throw the switch if necessary. Murrow was absent—"He didn't dare show up himself." (To a Chicago reporter in 1979, he would place Murrow in the control room, while another account that same year would include not only Murrow but Stanton.) An intimidating sight in any case, though it may be questioned whether any network would have thrown the switch with a roomful of reporters waiting just outside the door.

It was anticlimactic. Important issues were involved, he said on the air, but this was "not the place or the time to discuss them." The ensuing statement to the press was similarly unrevealing, in fact, surprisingly careful: In view of "certain circumstances" connected with his replacement on Sunday at 5:45 P.M., a move first communicated by the sponsor, though the final decision, he was ready to believe, was made by CBS, "I feel that the Columbia Broadcasting System has brought my usefulness on its network to a sudden end. . . . I am therefore resigning."[60]

A Murrow counterstatement denied again the charge of gagging or of sponsor pressure: "The Columbia Broadcasting System and no one else decided to place another news analyst in the period . . . and Mr. Shirer doesn't like it, and that's all there is to it!"[61]

Circumstances were to bring the two men together just once more that spring, on April 16, at the Hotel Élysée—ironically, before the Overseas Press Club, where just three-and-a-half years before, Shirer had played the heavy vis-à-vis Cecil Brown, now seated in the capacity audience of editors and correspondents jamming the oak-paneled dining room. The smell of a good fight was in the air, anticipation sharpened by the news that Shirer had just won the Peabody Award for commentary. As it happened, the topic, decided weeks before, was "Freedom of the News."

Shirer, opening, went with it, called the "affaire Shirer" a case in point, citing his Peabody citation; *some*, at least, appreciated his work as a journalist.

Murrow, putting down his copy, tendered his congratulations in a voice dangerously formal; as a matter of fact, he had won a Peabody himself, in 1944—three years *after* he had stopped doing his best work.[62]

As the fascinated crowd watched, the two former friends, who had once been so close, clashed in bitter debate, to mixed reviews.

"I think you probably missed an uninteresting, embarrassing and rather unfruitful session," Murrow wrote next day in his own defense, to a disapproving, querying Edgar Mowrer. "Bill chose to review the affair-Shirer [*sic*] and I had no alternative but to reply. . . . It seems to me entirely legitimate for Shirer, or anyone else, to question our editorial judgment in replacing him . . . but when sinister motives are implied, it seems to me that I have no choice except to state the facts."[63]

To Laski, he admitted handling the matter "without any great skill" but was prepared, he insisted, to defend the basic decision.

> Out of the whole unfortunate incident I learned one thing: that is the willingness of so-called liberals such as Freda Kirchway and Archie MacLeish, to rush into print with anguished howls of condemnation without bothering to inform themselves of a single fact. If you meet Joe Harsch, as I hope you will when he comes to London in a few months—you will, I think conclude that Bill was replaced with a man who is neither less able nor less liberal.[64]

("Our red scare continues," ran the postscript, "and will, I think, increase in intensity and irresponsibility.")

But beneath Murrow's anger there were rising doubts about other matters, bedrock practice in his industry, heretofore so easily accepted. (To Mowrer: "There are very serious problems involved in the sponsorship of news and opinions. . . . I hope that when you are in New York again you will . . . give me the benefit of your counsel.") Worse yet were the doubts about himself. Several times during the past week he had been close to coming apart, the landscape of his personal feelings become a disaster area, a yawning gulf in which his puritanic self-distrust had suddenly free play or, worse yet, was confirmed. "Murrow—my God, he was absolutely destroyed by this," a close associate recalled. "He was in horrible shape, kept saying, 'I have no business in this job, I can't *do* this kinda thing to my friends.' He felt as if he was responsible because he couldn't talk the broadcasting industry into this—this. . . ." The associate later laughed dryly at the recollection:

"Look, if Walter Cronkite were still broadcasting and his ratings went to hell, what would you say? 'We're sorry, Walter.' As a matter of fact they did replace him once in the early sixties, at the conventions. But Walter didn't say, '*That's my time*, you can't take it away from me.' "

But the hurt ran deep. That month Elmer Davis told Murrow of a small hitch in Murrow's election to the Century Club, a few days' delay because of paper work, a mere technicality, was all.

"Maybe as the result of the last few weeks," Murrow replied bitterly, "the members will conclude that I am a crypto-fascist and should not be given admission."[65]

Said Paley: "I think Ed suffered from it more than I did. He didn't go through the school of hard knocks the way *I* had to, never had a job where he had to fire anybody . . . where he might be blamed for something of this nature. Course, I've been in this business for a long time; I didn't *like* it, but at least I was sorta used to it. . . . In addition to [which], he and Shirer were very close friends. . . ."

No longer. After the OPC lunch meeting at which they shared the dais, Murrow and Shirer had left separately, without speaking to each other.

Shirer, for the moment, seemed the winner—his *Herald Tribune* column intact, a respectable rallying point, his public profile, down somewhat before March of 1947, given new prominence by the controversy, with Mutual Broadcasting and a national sponsor eager to pick up the slack from CBS with an outlet of 200 stations.

His ratings continued to drop, however, and in 1949 the Piedmont Shirt Company failed to renew its contract. He broadcast briefly over a short-lived Texas-based network trying to go national, but a great broadcasting career was over. And a great newsman was lost to CBS, a steadying voice lost to the mass media. In 1950 he would be scooped up in *Red Channels*—the result, he thought, of signing an *amicus curiae* brief for the Hollywood Ten, the beginning of a nine-year slide into the wilderness and the blacklist. He retreated back into writing books and the hard life of the lecture circuit, holding on to the farm in Connecticut, emerging from exile only in 1959, with the monumental *The Rise and Fall of the Third Reich.*

Through the bad times and the good, the seven days of March would be burned into his mind, a symbol of when things first went sour. Decades later, he would still be sorting out his feelings about it—it was political; things had gotten out of hand; you never knew with a guy like Ed; maybe he was jealous; maybe the old feeling was there. They had been so close; he had wept there on the dock in Lisbon; he wasn't just a friend. . . .

Thus the eminent writer and historian William Shirer in 1975, speaking as though it were not ten years after Murrow's death, but March 1947.

Jim Seward was sitting in his office when Murrow stopped by. Campbell's had been urging him to go back on the air, he said. It seemed like a good offer. He thought he'd talk it over with Paley.

It was as much as he would say about leaving a job that he had come to hate.

July 19, 1947, CBS announced the resignation of Edward R. Murrow as Vice-President and Director of Public Affairs. Mr. Murrow, said the release, would be returning to his former duties.

Rumors in the industry ran the gamut of reasons, from differences with Stanton to fired for incompetence. Murrow himself insisted that he had been a bad administrator, but CBS was to receive two Peabodys for shows originating in his eighteen months. New programs had been launched, the strains of postwar conversion weathered, the staff by and large intact.

"He was not a terrible executive," Jap Gude would insist, "he was excellent. Except for Shirer, everyone stayed. . . . correspondents with pretty good names—any one of them could have had a job with *Time*, *Life*, *Newsweek*, *Look*, even The New York *Times*. But they all stayed; there was not a single defection. And he organized it."

Except for Shirer. Through the years that followed, Janet Murrow would watch her husband trying to retrace his steps of the week of March 24, a mental maze with no exit: He should have realized what the time slot meant to Bill, been more gentle with him, explained things better, made it all come out right.

The past months had made it clear, however, that he lacked the one essential critical to an executive: the ability and readiness to convey bad news, especially to those he liked. Eric Sevareid, sitting in Washington, learned of the resignation as he opened up the pages of *Variety*. A reluctant bureau chief at best, he had agreed to take the job knowing Murrow would be boss—and only if Murrow was boss. He dialed New York. Was it true? he asked, then sat back stunned, near weeping, as confirmation came. Why had there been no warning? Why hadn't he been *told*?

Asked up to New York, he sat with Murrow over drinks in an uncomfortable silence. Finally, Murrow spoke up. He was sorry. He should have let him know.[66]

Publicly and privately he was closemouthed about his reasons for the switch. He didn't like In and Out baskets, he said, or firing people; who was he to be firing people, God Almighty? Differences with management were denied. "I have never enjoyed administrative work very much," he told Maurice Gorham of the BBC, "and nine years of broadcasting finally caught up with me." From Frank Stanton he extracted a verbal promise to keep up with *CBS Views the Press*.

The changeover was completed in nine days, Dave Taylor yanked from programming and installed, none too happily, as head of news, Murrow moved back down to 17, where a small corner office was commandeered— a luxury in news—two windows, a desk, two chairs, and a coatrack.

A bright young secretary was brought down from 18; a writer-editor and a researcher completed the staff, the opening broadcast set for September 29.

To Paul White he wrote, "I have been liberated."

X

"Investigate, Intimidate, and . . . Legislate"

1.

He knew he was skating on thin ice when he went with the editorial the night of October 27, 1947. He hadn't actually been there for the second Monday of the Hollywood hearings, wasn't actually present to see the caucus room turned movie set, the floodlights bouncing off the bald head of gavel-wielding HUAC Chairman J. Parnell Thomas, or the succession of hostile witnesses dragged bodily away by uniformed guards in full view of the newsreel cameras.

In a way, though, he felt he had: "This reporter approaches the matter with rather fresh memories of friends in Austria, Germany and Italy who either died or went into exile because they refused to admit the right of their government to determine what they should say, read, write or think." It was enough for him to throw away his promise not to engage in editorial opinion, made just four weeks back, on his opening broadcast.

"Movies should be judged by what appears on the screen, newspapers by what appears in print and radio by what comes out of the loudspeaker. The personal beliefs of the individuals involved would not seem to be a legitimate field for inquiry, either by government or by individuals. When bankers, or oil or railroad men, are haled before a congressional committee, it is not customary to question them about their beliefs. . . ."

For the past five months, he had been tracking the resurgence of the old Dies committee, new blooded through the 1946 elections, its spring offensive in Los Angeles rife with attacks on pro-Soviet wartime films and the Screen Writers Guild, and promises of juicy revelations in the fall.

In June he had had an exchange with Joseph Davies, former ambassador to the Soviet Union, whose best-selling *Mission to Moscow*, filmed (simplistically, most thought) by Warner's, was being held up as Exhibit No.

1. Davies sent along a copy of his protest to the committee ("It was vital to civilization and to ourselves that Russia should be kept fighting . . . that anything that could be done to sustain their morale, their courage and their fighting, was a service to the war effort and deserved support").[1]

Murrow, replying, called Davies' letter "a magnificent statement of recent history that most people have forgotten"[2] and tried, the night of October 27, two years after the war, to jar public memory: "There was heavy fighting at Cassino and Anzio . . . heavy fighting in the Solomons and New Guinea. . . . Stalin said the opening of the Second Front was near. . . .

"If these pictures, at that time and in that climate, were subversive, then what comes next under the scrutiny of a congressional committee? Correspondents who wrote and broadcast that the Russians were fighting well and suffering appalling losses?"

He worried, too, about the chilling effect on an industry "not renowned in the past for its boldness in portraying the . . . social, economic and political problems confronting this nation."

Congressional committees had the right to investigate—deeds, not thoughts. Certain government agencies, the State Department and the Atomic Energy Commission, for example, faced the dilemma of maintaining security without violating the "essential liberties" of those who worked for them. Granted.

> But no such problem arises with instruments of mass communication. Either we believe in the intelligence, good judgment, balance and native shrewdness of the American people, or we believe that government should investigate, intimidate and finally legislate. The choice is as simple as that.
>
> The right of dissent, or if you prefer, the right to be wrong, is surely fundamental to the existence of a democratic society. That's the right that went first in every nation that stumbled down the trail toward totalitarianism.

The reaction, by that fall, was already predictable. *The Screenwriter*, official organ of the guild, hailed the broadcast, highlighted his comments in a special section—"Freedom Vs. Fear"—in company with nineteen others, including Senator Claude Pepper of Florida and playwright Lillian Hellman. In other quarters it was Darlan all over again.

"Surely a reporter has resources for discriminating," a colleague wrote angrily, "rather than by implication taking these bastards under his wing like a mother hen."[3]

"I'm sorry you didn't like the editorial," Murrow replied. "So far as the individuals in the Hollywood hearings are concerned, I hold that it is no part of my responsibility to pick out the sheep from the goat. . . . I just don't think legislation exists which permits that a congressional committee of inquiry should inquire into what people believe."

As for the films themselves, "I ain't a movie critic."[4]

But the role of gadfly was clearly more congenial to him than that of shuffling correspondents and programs around the schedule, even in the claustrophobic atmosphere of 1947–48. When a New York City congressman, Leo Isaacson, a Henry Wallace supporter, and one of two American Labor Party members of the House—the other was Harlem's peppery Vito Marcantonio—was denied a passport to prevent his attendance at a Paris conference including supporters of the left-wing Greek guerrillas, Murrow stepped into the breach, scoring not only the State Department for the decision but The New York *Times* for supporting it: "For the act itself endangers the freedom of all of us. Probably the most significant and serious aspect of the affair . . . is that it has produced so little controversy in Congress and in the country. . . ." Reporting on the progress of the controversial Subversive Activities Control Act, otherwise known as the Mundt-Nixon bill, he ended with Lincoln's warning that those forging chains for other people "should see to it that in tying it around the neck of one, they don't have the other end around their own."

Finding it less than congenial were the sponsors, who had signed what they thought of as a consensus figure, but who now, it seemed, was controversial.

The trouble was, the consensus had long since broken down, given way to polarization, wartime comrades-in-arms finding themselves suddenly on opposite sides of the fence. Paul White, returned from a stay with Charles Collingwood, now broadcasting out of KNX, Los Angeles, wrote Murrow of the "bitter argument" that had erupted:

> I said that Communism represented a menace to this country just as it would to Russia if it were tried there . . . that persons who were loyal to Communistic principles would probably be disloyal to this country in event of war between the United States and Russia . . . that Communists and fellow travelers were a potential enemy within the gates and would very likely do us no service should the war thaw from a cold to a red hot stage.
>
> Charles looked at me as though I had advocated the theory of the divine right of kings. I talked, he sneered, like a Hearst editorial. He was never more upset, he added. The one person of balance in whom he had always had faith was I. . . .[5]

By the weekend the Collingwoods were back to see the Whites in Chula Vista. But it was nonetheless, as Elmer Davis said in 1945, "a sign of the times."

In November 1947, Ed and Janet Murrow returned to England for the wedding of the twenty-one-year-old Princess Elizabeth, whom Murrow remembered as a child broadcasting to English schoolchildren in the blitz.

They traveled separately nowadays as a precaution, Casey—a self-contained two-year-old with a startling sagacity that helped assuage his parents' guilts—deposited with his Brewster grandparents in Middletown.

Janet Murrow, going first, often did the preliminaries through her English contacts, in this case gathering the details on the royal gown, Murrow following amid publicity, Kay Campbell, his well-known assistant, on his arm, a scene that had Janet Murrow smiling wryly in recollection: "I'd go ahead alone, and she'd come down the red carpet, dripping orchids, with *my husband!* But—I loved doing it."[6]

They saw old friends, the Churchills foremost, all recipients of food parcels from New York. Murrow visited with R. T. Clark. It was a sentimental journey back, keynoted by a poem sent to Murrow by Professor Duggan ("Goodbye America! I am going home. . . .").

He broadcast from Westminster Abbey, did a late-night wrap-up, and attended the wedding ball, an uncomfortable guest in a tightened tailcoat, unworn since the lean war years, and threatening to come unstitched.

But even in London there were reminders of the scene back home. The day before the royal wedding there was a memorial service, quite unpublicized. Gil Winant, retired as ambassador, ill and weary, had been working on his wartime memoirs. The depressions had been getting worse, made more acute by the untimely death of a son. Then, in the closing days of fall, had come a subpoena from the House Committee on Un-American Activities. The morning of November 3, John Gilbert Winant, fifty-eight, whom many had once thought of as Roosevelt's possible successor, took a gun and blew his head off.

They read the lesson at St. Paul's: "The souls of the righteous are in the hand of God, and there shall no torment touch them. . . ."

Murrow, when he heard the news, sat dazed, shaking his head. "What a waste—what a waste."

The celebrations were a bright spot in a city pockmarked and partly leveled by five years of bombing. Britain was on strict rationing, nutrition levels at the borderline. Much of the Continent was near starvation, its economy in ruins, the past freezing winter succeeded by a famine summer with another hard winter coming on. Western hopes were pinned on the Marshall Plan, but the front lines of the cold war were freezing into place.

Historians would later argue over who cast the first stone; certainly rhetoric, action-backed, was mounting rapidly on both sides, as Western occupiers in Germany consolidated their zones over Soviet protests, with moves and countermoves leading to fresh confrontations and, in the coming months, the Soviet blockade of West Berlin.

In Prague the Czech government, strongly dissuaded by its Soviet neighbor from accepting Marshall Plan aid, looked nervously to both sides. Beneš, presiding over a coalition balanced precariously between East and West, aligned of necessity with Moscow, expressed Czech fears of "a second Munich," calling on both sides to draw back from the brink of isolation.

Jan Masaryk, now a nonpartisan foreign minister in a cabinet dominated increasingly by its Communist faction, was seeing fewer people on his visits to New York. To the Murrows, on his rare visits to Seventy-fourth Street, he seemed like a man who had undergone a personality change, the old buoyant optimism given way to a kind of depressed futility. He had stopped playing the piano, he told Janet Murrow wearily; it was so much easier listening to records. Worried queries about emigration came up against a blunt "Do you think I enjoy what I'm doing?"

He had to do what he could, he told them; stay with his people. Maybe a corpse but not a refugee.

Murrow's own position in that pivotal time was typical of many postwar liberals: disenchanted with the Russians, yet hardly champing at the bit to join the new crusade.

"Ed," recalled a friend, "was a liberal, reasonable man. He had seen the valor of the Russian people. He *knew* that they had paid in this war with twenty million lives. And he just wasn't about to switch around and regard them as the new Hitlerites."[7]

But an ingrained pessimism was at work, made more acute by the firsthand experience of the disastrous bungles of the thirties and early forties, the letdown now of postwar hopes, and fears of a repetition.

"You can't imagine the *euphoria*," Collingwood remembered, "which possessed most people, but particularly those who had been intimately involved with the war—this idea that having got rid of Hitler, we would now open up into a new world of peace and prosperity and—you know, humanity was gonna have a chance! Then, as these became progressively disappointed, it seems to me that it was *then* that Ed became more disillusioned. . . . There's no question that he possessed, or pretended to possess, a profound pessimism about the future, based on his experience of man's inhumanity to man and of the lack of communications between Americans and those with whom they were thrown into contact."

Even in the war, there was the side to Murrow that had distrusted Soviet leadership, right through his love affair with the fighting Russian people—all the more reason, he had thought, for the Big Three to engage each other frankly while the front was still united; hence his near despair with wartime conferences whose leaders, he suspected, were merely talking past each other.

The fissures now widening, therefore, seemed to him a realization of his own worst fears of 1943.

Undeniably, however, he had undergone a sea change, a shifting away from the one-worlder who had called in 1945 for a unilateral abdication of sovereignty, to a supporter of the Kennan doctrine of "firmness" through containment—a change prompted to a large extent by what he, in common with many others, saw as Soviet violations of the agreements made at Yalta.

The process, characteristically, had been gradual. "You must throw yourself back into that period," a correspondent recalled.

"We used to sing Red Army songs—we *loved* them. They were fighting so valiantly, they were killing these goddamn Nazis. When we met 'em on the Elbe, we embraced, we kissed, it was—you know, it was great! Then came Yalta, and then came Stalin's moves in Eastern Europe and, you know, getting the stardust out of your eyes. . . ."

In his own way Murrow had been a believer, more apt to criticize the U.S. in his wartime broadcasts, to a point at which Paul White had felt compelled to admonish him that "not everything we do is bad."

But by 1947 there was no more talk of learning from resistance movements in Yugoslavia and Greece, or of Britain and America building crusts over revolutionary conditions—the Greek situation, with Soviet-backed neighbors in the mix unlike 1944, seen less as a revolution than as a power grab, a try at consolidating Soviet influence in the Balkans.

On the Truman Doctrine, therefore—that litmus test of "standing up to the Russians"—he came down finally, if guardedly, on the side of the proponents, the wise men of his youth, sainted names from the Council on Foreign Relations. These weren't the Martin Dieses, the Owen Brewsters, or the Homer Fergusons. They were the men he most admired, figures such as George Marshall, Averell Harriman, with—despite some prominent minority voices—no considerable pro-Soviet establishment, no Laski figure of the loyal opposition to argue with until the small hours of the morning.

"I think he did come around," said Collingwood, as close to Murrow as anyone in that time, "to the idea that the interests as seen on each side, of the Soviet Union and the United States, were not compatible, that while we would have to do everything to avoid a war, we needn't expect any favors from them or expect them to put our interests above theirs. He did *not* come to feel that the Russians—bled white as they were—constituted on immediate menace to this country. [But] he may well have felt that we were in for a long run of incompatibility."

At work, however, the disciple of Kennan and man of the establishment backed his reporters when they fell afoul of that establishment.

The 7:45 program, with Murrow at the helm, was essentially a joint venture, drawing on the resources of the CBS organization, utilizing the cables, voice reports, and off-the-record backgrounding of the full range of correspondents. (And outside as well; Paul White, among others, furnished cables for the standard fifty-dollar fee.)

Small, even minute by later network standards, it packed an amazing amount of hard information into its twelve minutes of news, including headlines, commentary, and eyewitness reports, live or taped, relating to the top story of the day. The veteran Jesse Zousmer wrote the hard news, John Aaron completed the staff. It was the mid-evening showcase, favored by reporters over the network shows. Being sponsored, it had

Janet Murrow with Eileen Shirer.
(Courtesy of Janet Murrow)

Amsterdam, 1940, left to right:
William L. Shirer, unidentified,
Murrow, Mary Marvin Breckinridge.
(Courtesy of the Murrow Collection)

1941: Reunion in New York. (Courtesy of Janet Murrow)

1941: With Ethel and Roscoe Murrow. (Courtesy of Janet Murrow)

1941: With Shirer at CBS. (Courtesy of CBS)

Flying combat, probably 1944. On assignment, left to right: Lt. M. P. Royston, Murrow, unidentified, probably Col. Joe Kelly. (Courtesy of Janet Murrow)

In the CBS wartime office, left to right: Richard C. Hottelet, Charles Shaw, Larry LeSueur, Murrow; seated: Janet Murrow. (Courtesy of CBS)

September, 1945, left to right: Paul Kesten, Col. William S. Paley, Frank Stanton, at CBS reception for William S. Paley. (Courtesy of CBS)

George Polk, Athens, 1946: press card. (Courtesy of CBS)

From the CBS series, *Reports on the Murder of George Polk*, left to right: Winston Burdett, Murrow, General William ("Wild Bill") Donovan. (Photograph by Al Canido, courtesy of CBS)

1948: At the Governors'
Conference. (Photograph
by Janet Murrow, courtesy
of Janet Murrow)

With Casey. (Photograph
by Janet Murrow, courtesy
of Janet Murrow)

the bigger budget, constituting at times a mini-news department. Scoops cabled in, targeted for the Murrow program, effectively bypassed the network, raising the hackles of successive news directors from Ted Church onward.

For the correspondents, it was a prestige linkup, offering maximum impact for their stories and, most of all, sufficient airtime, with assured cooperation at the top. (At one point, Murrow, overburdened, asked Howard Smith about returning to New York, possibly dividing the week with him. Alex Kendrick, then CBS's man in Southeastern Europe, talked to Smith—if Howard only knew what working with Ed, sending him their cables, *meant* to the staff; it was their only source of genuine journalistic satisfaction, the only thing that made the job worthwhile. Smith finally declined the offer, convinced that only one man could head the show.)[8]

It also offered support. When David Schoenbrun, broadcasting from Paris, began calling the Americans "the new Romans" and U.S. policy "an imperial policy"—dealing with the Europeans, he said, like a subject people—the State Department got its back up. Accusations flew, the trail leading back, it would turn out, to the U.S. Embassy in Paris: Schoenbrun had written for the Communist press. Well, his byline *had* appeared there, he *had* worked after all for a news agency; if the centrists and Gaullists could buy his articles, so could the Communists.

Then, too, he went "frequently" to Communist headquarters, it was charged. "Of course I did!" said Schoenbrun later. "I interviewed [Communist Party Secretary] Maurice Thorez, I interviewed [Party Chairman] Jacques Duclos. Got a congratulatory cable from Murrow, was the only man who was able to do it."

A supporter of the Marshall Plan, Schoenbrun questioned nonetheless how far down the reconstruction funds were trickling in France—"too many sticky fingers at the top."

State was not exactly thrilled. There was suddenly a call for Murrow from the sponsor's agency in Philadelphia: Who was this pro-Communist Schoenbrun?

The CBS correspondent in Paris, Murrow replied, whom he had personally hired, and he would continue to use him when he thought it advisable.

Schoenbrun knew nothing of it at the time. "He didn't want to make me anxious, took care of it himself; absolutely typical." It was not until clearance problems started turning up in Joe McCarthy's heyday that Murrow told him: it wasn't the first time this had happened.

Like others, Schoenbrun was kept insulated by the man at the top. "He never ever said to me, 'You're going a little far, why don't you ease up?'; never said, 'Hey, watch it, it's getting a little rough.' In fact, he kept saying, 'Dave, that was a great, great broadcast.' The only stricture was, you better damn well *prove* what you think. If you say there were too many sticky fingers, you better name the sticky fingers and say how much money and how the money disappears. You hadda have the research; you hadda prove your case."

But it was another, more public dispute that would set the CBS news department and the State Department on a collision course, in one of the more bizarre episodes involving foreign policy and broadcast journalism.

If any of the postwar crop of correspondents seemed to symbolize the future, it was George Polk, CBS's new Mideast reporter and a Murrow recruit, a driven, meticulous newspaper veteran—"in love with his work," a friend remembered, "not his byline"[9]—and genuine war hero, wounded in the Solomons, commended for bravery; the classic tall Texan, lean and sandy-haired, with the good looks of a film-style college quarterback.

"He was what we call in America an awfully swell guy," said I.F. Stone, who had known him in the Middle East, "unpretentious, considerate, honorable, no radical, but a good reporter, with an instinctive sympathy for the underdog and a healthy disrespect for stuffed shirts."[10]

Polk had first sought out Murrow in London, in the fall of 1945, joining the staff a few months later—"a kind of pet appointee," said Ted Berkman who, hired for the same Mideast job by the peripatetic Doug Edwards, would later recall reporting for his first day in the Cairo studio, when "this tall blond guy came in."

Edwards seemed to know him. "George—Ted Berkman. He's the new CBS guy here in the Middle East."

"But *I'm* the new CBS guy in the Middle East."

Polk, it seemed, had his mandate directly from Murrow in New York. Berkman, reading the signals, stepped aside, eventually working alongside Polk as friend and correspondent for ABC.[11] The assignment covered Cairo, Athens, and just about anywhere else in the eastern Mediterranean.

Like most of the younger correspondents, Polk had patterned himself on Murrow. "George admired him and spoke about him," recalled John Donovan, then NBC's knowledgeable stringer in the Middle East, a close friend to Polk and sometime roommate. "He and Murrow were the same kind of people in a way. That's why I think there was a kind of bond there."

A decorated war veteran, Polk had begun as a favorite among the Anglo-American community in Cairo. Said Donovan, "Almost everyone in Egypt thought he was the cat's whiskers—this tall, good-looking young Texan, a hundred percent true blue American. There may have been supreme confidence that he would cooperate. . . ."[12]

By the winter of 1947–48, however, everybody's golden boy, the onetime favorite among the brass hats and diplomatic set, was causing reverberations from Athens to Washington with his hard-hitting reports on divided Greece, sparing neither side, though raising howls of protest from the U.S. Aid Mission and the Athens regime. Over the CBS network, he described the cabinet strong man, Populist Party leader Constantine Tsaldaris, and his fellows as "semi-Fascists." In the December 1947 *Harper's*, Polk called the economic system "rotten to the core," called for a definition of U.S. aims in Greece, and warned that the "treadmill of Balkan affairs" was easier to board than to abandon. He was known to have his own sources in the Greek community, giving him, as a colleague put it, "a window onto the machinations, the corruption, everything that was going on." He used material from the Greek press, little being used and translated effectively by Americans. All of it fueled the controversial *Harper's* piece and bulletins that he had started sending back—"and a lot of it was really shocking stuff," Donovan recalled, "and the Greek ambassador raised hell."[13]

In New York, complaints to Stanton were forwarded to Murrow and returned, hands down: ". . . I have watched Polk's stuff very carefully and have frequently queried him, either by cable or phone, on material for my own show. I have come to regard him as one of the most careful, able correspondents in the whole CBS organization."[14]

In Athens, Murrow's backing, and that of Howard Smith in London, were evidently no secret. Ted Berkman had known of "a kind of private file to Murrow—personal letters; private reports; talking over the cue channels before and after broadcasts; an inside pipeline that was almost separate from and more important than, if possible, the network."

There was even talk that Murrow was saving the reports, waiting for the correspondent to come home, put it all together, and blow the whistle, a double-edged potential, although, as Donovan observed, "everybody dreamed of tying the can to Tsaldaris."

There were ugly incidents. In his private notes and backgrounders, Polk told Murrow of midnight telephone threats and backstage efforts to undermine troublemakers in the American press: "Lacking official guts to attack us openly, the Greek officials are working behind the scenes. . . . I've never been reproached by the numerous . . . press ministry officials. Yet the . . . ministry has been actively seeking to discredit me. . . ."[15] Denunciations of Polk as a Communist were growing in segments of the Athens press and echoing back to Washington.

Ironically, these were not reporters who opposed the U.S. basic policy in Greece. Even Polk believed it "sound," serving American and, ideally, Greek self-interest—the question not one of basic policy but of backing the wrong horse, not an espousal of the Far Left, but a repugnance at getting into bed with the Right.

In the meantime, the Athens government, protesting to the State Department, demanded equal time from CBS and got it. In those same weeks Polk informed Murrow of "vague hints" passed on to him, to the effect that "someone was likely to get hurt." He figured at worst a black-market frame-up and expulsion.

Friends in the area worried. Said Donovan: "He made terrible enemies. And there were a lot of cowboys around, ready to kill for a pair of shoes."

New Year's, 1948, was unpleasant in New York, an icebound city digging out from the aftermath of the worst winter storm since 1888—a fit opening to what Ed and Janet Murrow always referred back to as "that awful year."

The Czech coup came in February. A badly shaken Howard Smith, back from Prague, described the Communist coup forestalling new elections—the take-over of public and private institutions; silencing of the opposition press; militiamen marching through the streets of Prague; troops and police manning submachine guns on corners, in the center of the city. At the radio station, a porter told Smith he would have to wait: Everyone else was locked up with the new action committee; the purge had started. Next day, in an eerily quiet capital, he was told he could no longer broadcast. "The spectacular part [is] over. The ugly, quiet part [has] begun."[16]

Masaryk had stayed on in the new government, bitter at the failure of the superpowers to let his country steer a middle course. "America must offer the world a position program," he had stated in an interview arranged by Murrow the past winter, "not such negative nonsense as the Truman Doctrine. It must never accept as a final fact the division between East and West. . . ."[17]

Murrow, trying repeatedly to reach him by telephone in the final days of the crisis, had finally succeeded, only to find the voluble Masaryk oddly reticent. They spoke briefly; Murrow, sensing the other man's constraint, did not call again.

March 10, the pajama-clad body was found on the flagstones of the courtyard beneath the window of the Masaryk apartment. It was two weeks after the coup and nearly ten years after Munich.

The atmosphere was close in Studio 9 that night: "They say he committed suicide. I don't know. Jan Masaryk was a man of great faith and great courage. . . ."

Decades later, the feeling of the tension in the studio still lingered somewhere in the mental makeup of those who had been there, watching Murrow, his voice barely controlled, hands gripping the script, raking over memories of the death watch of September 1938, late nights at the piano in the blitz, a flash of humor as the bombs fell:

Somehow this reporter finds it difficult to imagine him flinging himself from a third-floor window. . . . A gun, perhaps poison, or a leap from a greater height would have been more convincing. . . .

Did he make a mistake in this last crisis? I do not know. He stayed with Beneš. . . .

Czechoslovakia was, if anything, a watershed. Said a friend: "It was a turning point for Murrow, for the others. This country, which had been so victimized by the Nazis . . ." This had been no backward semifascist state with the usual extremes of wealth and poverty such as abounded in Eastern Europe; they were all shocked. Murrow couldn't accept what had happened to Masaryk, dwelling on it constantly, uncharacteristically: Such a kind and brilliant man, wouldn't hurt a fly; why'd they have to kill him, what kind of *people* were these?

More than anything else, the events of late February and early March in Prague, 1948, marked a hardening of the broadcaster's attitudes toward the Soviet Union, toward those calling themselves Communists, a heightened suspicion of Soviet motivation, and a lessened flexibility in dealing with the cold war.

In the meantime, he was having problems with the cold war at home, caught in the prototypical dilemma of the postwar liberal whose anticommunism was not of the traditional bred-in-the-bone variety but rather a gut repugnance for authoritarianism whether of the left or right—more fearful, in the prevailing climate, of the pressures from the right, and wary of the siege mentality intensifying since Truman's call to Congress. "It seems the only way to induce action in this country is through the creation of fear and hysteria," he wrote to Lady Milner that April. "There is probably a greater willingness to go to war with Russia than there was to take action against Germany in December of '41."[18]

Certainly there was no lack of pressure, either subtle or overt. Dave Taylor came back disturbed from two grueling sessions in Washington, where Secretary of Defense James Forrestal, complaining of security leaks on technical military data, exhorted representatives of the news media to refrain "voluntarily" from disclosing information detrimental to the national security.[19]

To those present, veterans themselves of wartime reporting, as security-conscious as any, the secretary's complaints seemed without substance, a hard sell for a return to wartime self-censorship, and they weren't buying. A follow-up resolution firmly rejected peacetime censorship as not "workable or desirable in the public interest."[20] But the olive branch had to be there, too, and a so-called Security Advisory Council, whether cosmetic or not, was proposed as liaison between Defense and representatives of the press, radio, and motion pictures.[21]

Closer to home, Murrow had received an urgent memo from Larry Duggan, calling a meeting of the IIE executive committee regarding a request by the State Department for CIA access to the files of the institute. The normally quiet, understated Duggan was upset and agitated. It would be prejudicial, he wrote Murrow, for the institute to become party to the gathering of government intelligence except in time of national emergency, and he didn't think things had yet come that far.

Murrow himself was feeling the heat, both as a prominent voice over the radio, one well believed, and in the wake of his continued lambasting of the Un-American Activities Committee—the latest in the case of Edward Condon, Director of the National Bureau of Standards, who had caused a furor by advocating closer working relationships with Soviet science. Murrow for his part had drawn fire after backing Dr. Condon ("In a society where the individual is not free to pursue the truth . . . there is neither progress, stability nor security").[22]

His own sense of security, in fact, was faring none too well. Harold Laski, whom Chairman Thomas had called "the red Fascist leader of England," wrote early in the year that he was coming over for a while, provided Parnell Thomas, HUAC, and the FBI didn't mind.

Stay with us, Murrow wrote back, and they all can watch you together. "I suspect they are currently informed on my own activities and particularly the guests who stop with us."[23]

As it happened, the FBI *was* running a check on him in those months— primarily in *Who's Who*; J. Edgar Hoover had been asked for an interview on the Murrow program. The request was denied. But also, unknown to Murrow at the time, Jim Forrestal, the new boss at the Pentagon and hard-line powerhouse of the administration, wanted him in Washington, a comment on the broadcaster's cold war credentials and a dichotomy fairly common to the times. Forrestal, out to shape up the six-month-old Defense Department, build up the national military establishment, whip the news media into line, wanted Edward Murrow on his team.

Essentially a ninety-day posting, it was nonetheless considerable in context—a time when government, with America the leading power in the world, was still seen as something of a higher calling; and to be up there with the power figures in those years—the Marshalls, the Forrestals, the Achesons—was pretty heady stuff.

Murrow obviously passed. Just how familiar the Secretary was with Murrow's daily broadcasts was unknown and no doubt immaterial. It was as much the *idea* of Murrow, the prestige, the nonpartisan war hero image, that was needed and wanted. It was above all an image still so strong in 1948, three years after the war, so all-American, that the offer had been made, evidently, with little or no security check, even though the job meant access to all secret communications and the handling of all information regarding the Defense Department.[24]

This man—at least the concept of this man—was above suspicion. But there was a wide gap between that concept and how Murrow viewed himself, a yawning gulf, in fact, between his self-image of embattled newsman and the pedestal on which the establishment had placed him.

The Bureau, however, was not the only body, public or private, to have watchers in the field. To his friend David Lilienthal, once Roosevelt's TVA Director, now the embattled Chairman of the Atomic Energy Commission, Murrow confessed his despair of remaining on the air much longer. All "they" wanted was "hate Russia," and if you didn't talk that, then you were a quote dirty Communist. There had to be another way of making a living, and he was making plans for getting out.[25]

In fact, indications were that Madison Avenue was running well ahead of Washington; that while Forrestal sought to have him at his side, he was already too far left for certain listeners in the changing, claustrophobic atmosphere of the late forties. Further down Madison, not too far from CBS, three former FBI men had built up a booming business with a mail-order bulletin known as *Counterattack: The Newsletter of Facts On Communism*, fingering alleged Communists or sympathizers in the mass media. The growing subscriber list included radio stations, networks, ad agencies, and government offices. "Clearance" was available for a fee; those who wouldn't play, attacked beneath the black and orange banner. They called themselves American Business Consultants, Inc. CBS, a favored target, kept a full set of the bulletins in its files.

By 1948, the sponsor who had signed Murrow up so eagerly the year before, was having second thoughts. And no sponsor meant no evening time.

"It was not a happy relationship," recalled Dorothy McDonough, a tall, attractive brunette who, two years out of high school, had been Murrow's secretary in the vice-presidential suite, asked down to 17 when he returned to broadcasting. (Kay Campbell, brought over to assist Ted Church, came down the hall at five o'clock to type the broadcasts and accompanied Murrow on his jaunts, later becoming his executive assistant.)

As far as Campbell Soup was concerned, it hadn't taken long to learn the obvious—that sponsors, not surprisingly, were in the business of selling products, not of making enemies in airtime they had paid for. That paying a broadcaster's huge salary, moreover, they expected to call the shots or expected their beneficiary, as they saw it, to take guidance.

One effect of selling minutes in the later world of television would be to diffuse the single sponsor's clout, a hallmark in the cheaper world of radio, where the advertiser often owned the time slot and a piece—or so he thought—of the performer, whether newscaster or entertainer.

"It is the policy of the Campbell Soup Company," a corporate statement read, "to permit Mr. Murrow to be available for as many meetings as practicable in connection with his radio broadcasts."[26] The company meant it, too: dealer meetings; chamber of commerce appearances; ribbon cutting in the boondocks; invitations to the Murrows' summer home in Pawling. Render unto Caesar. The problems arose with attempts to cross the fine line into program content, when the conviviality would suddenly stop, to be replaced by confrontation.

The differences had started peaking in the spring of 1948. Murrow, broadcasting from Italy during that nation's first postwar elections, did a close-focus piece on Anzio, with its World War II associations: the Communist mayor, the local priest, and a voter of the town ("a gray, tired little man") who produced a letter from a brother in America, telling him not to vote Communist "because that would mean loss of freedom and loss of American aid," and no, he would not vote Communist.

The voter was described as living in "the one room that's left of a house—"

> cardboard over the windows, no running water, no carpets, one chair, a small wardrobe with a ragged piece of cloth instead of a door and a small battered chest. . . . He scrabbled around in that little chest . . . and came up with a picture of his brother, a fine, healthy-looking man, well dressed, obviously a successful American businessman. The little brother in Anzio is a night watchman, when he's working. Did that letter really change the vote of the little brother in Anzio? I don't know. That's his business. . . .[27]

The lid blew off at Campbell headquarters in Camden, New Jersey, the sudden target of a flood of irate letters and telephone calls. From Philadelphia, the Wheelock agency wrote Murrow of "violent protests." The sponsors panicked at the dismaying prospect of unsold cans of soup and spaghetti. When a Bretton Woods housewife, incensed over the sentence, "The mayor is a Catholic as well as a Communist," threatened to organize a boycott—enclosing a Heinz label as proof that she meant business—alarmed executives insisted Murrow write a letter to be personally delivered by a company representative who, they assured the outraged citizen, would be glad to answer any questions, and they were completely confident that Mr. Murrow was not a Communist.[28]

The agency head, funneling Camden's continued apprehensions, sent Murrow a friendly warning: Hadn't he better change his approach, be more clear-cut, get on the soapbox now and then about the United States versus communism? That Isaacson piece, for example—not really that important, too subject to misinterpretation by the folks out there, too much like defending a Communist. Of *course*, Murrow was right; *they* knew he was right; it was just not good for business. What the program needed was a good "Americana background"—i.e., never mind these lefties from the Bronx.

Then abruptly the smiling mask had slipped. "There are comments— not all from the nuts (who are always with us)—that you are pink.

"And I think there are enough to rate careful thought as to what to do about it."[29]

May opened in a whirlwind. Murrow, called suddenly to Washington, spent several days in meetings, then a week later wrote to Forrestal that he wasn't taking the job. Turning back to his calendar, he reset a lunch date at the Century with Prince Peter of Greece—a maverick member of the royal family and critic of his cousin, King Paul I, arrived in town with a letter of introduction from George Polk, certain the two men would find a meeting "mutually interesting." In Greece the Parliament had been suspended for a month.

Polk himself was due to come home in three weeks to a Nieman fellowship at Harvard and the start of work on his projected book, *Middle East Mosaic*. A final backgrounder was in the mail to Murrow. In the past months Polk had become an angry man, obsessed, shooting off thick, closely typed reports on the Balkans to Murrow, Drew Pearson, all the opinion makers, clashing with members of the Greek establishment press in Athens, his temper aggravated by the flare-up of injuries sustained months before in a plane crash, which had left him facially disfigured. To John Donovan he disclosed that he had concrete proof that the Greek diplomatic pouch was being used to move drugs—the evidence, he said, to destroy Tsaldaris.[30]

Robert Skedgell, the pink-cheeked young day editor, the kid home from the wars, was on duty the morning of Thursday, May 6, talking with the correspondents over the cue channel before the morning news roundup—lining up the spots, taking messages, the usual. Polk, readying his spot from Athens, said he was on to something; couldn't say more about it just now, but it was a pretty good story, probably an interview, and he'd be going off after the show. "I'll see you in a couple of days, Bob." His infectious laugh rang through the static.

Monday, May 17, was a heavy workday in the newsroom, beginning with Stalin's positive reaction to a recent open letter by Henry Wallace calling for mutual reduction in armaments and easing of East-West tensions. The Stalin comments over Radio Moscow were preceded by the announcement that the Soviet Union had recognized the new state of Israel.

In the Middle East, amid heightened fighting, Egyptian warplanes were strafing and dive-bombing Tel Aviv for the third straight day. Arab sources were claiming, unverified as yet, the surrender of the Jews of Old Jerusalem, with claims and counterclaims flying on both sides on the progress of the invading armies of Egypt, Syria, and Transjordan.

For the CBS news staff, however, attention was riveted not on Jerusalem or Moscow but on northern Greece, where less than twenty-four hours before, a boatman in the harbor of Salonika had come across a trussed figure in the shallows, not far from the wide sweep of hotels and waterfront cafés, bobbing gently in the decomposing folds of a camel hair jacket and U.S. Army trousers. It was George Polk, last seen May 8 and missing for the past week.

His hands and feet were tied; a bullet hole gaped behind one ear. In Athens an unnamed government official called it the "work of the Communists."

Word had gotten out that Polk had come north on the trail of an interview with the guerrilla general Markos Vafiades through hoped-for intermediaries in Salonika. By May 8, a CIA cable was to reveal, he had developed those leads, telling an American diplomat over drinks that final Saturday, that he hoped to meet the general "fairly soon."[31]

Rea, his young Greek wife, come to join him four days later, found a chaotic room, empty for more than half a week, and raised the alarm.

The AP reported the questioning of "twenty or more Communists."

"The record does not show that any *non*-Communists have been questioned," Murrow seethed over the air as incoming details of the murder rocked not only CBS but the entire news community and much of the public.

Valuables—cash, a watch stopped at twelve-twenty, identity cards, a leather wallet, a silver identification bracelet—all had been left untouched, notwithstanding the area's desperate poverty. A press card from the Greek War Department had been dropped into a mailbox, in a crudely lettered, unstamped envelope, addressed to the police station near where the body was found floating. Missing were Polk's notebook and a small black address book with names and appointments, both of which he always carried on him. In Athens the CBS files had been rifled.

Polk, like other good correspondents, was "not popular with the Greek Government," said Murrow on that Monday night.

"Such men as Raymond Daniell of The New York *Times* . . . Seymour Freidin of the New York *Herald Tribune* . . . Homer Bigart of the *Herald Tribune*, Constantine Hadjiargyris of the *Christian Science Monitor*,[32] have all been attacked either openly or by indirection as Communists or 'pinks.' This is a device that is frequently used in Europe and is not altogether unknown in this country. . . ."

A call made earlier in the day to Ray Daniell, now in London, had confirmed Murrow's own feelings that an assassination team of the paramilitary royalist "Xists" had more likely liquidated the independent-minded Polk than any Communist conducting group. There was therefore little chance, so the *Times* man said, of anything coming of a government investigation.[33]

Forensic evidence reaching the press indicated an execution-style slaying. Polk had gone out for the evening, eaten a big dinner, evidently with people he trusted, rushed back to his hotel and then out again, and was most likely dead within the hour: shot in the back of the head, bound hand and foot, and tipped, still living, into the filthy waters of the bay. The coroner concluded death by drowning.

Sitting on a desk back in his hotel room, in envelopes not yet sealed, were two letters typed that afternoon—one to his mother; the other to Ed Murrow, with the latest on his efforts: "With a contact through a contact I'd like to get to the people who count," and indicating such a contact had been made.[34]

Murrow had rarely sounded more bitter: "Since this reporter returned to broadcasting . . . much of the material about the Middle East, and particularly about Greece, carried on this program came from Polk. Invariably it was clean, hard copy, well documented. And his stories stood up—*every last one of them.* . . ."

Then, in a radical departure, he read off sections of the murdered correspondent's off-the-record last dispatch from Athens, never intended for reading on the air, giving a nod to the cold war, the Truman Doctrine, a situation that was "neither all black nor all white":

> Yet Greece is in the grip of politicians who are amazingly unwilling to serve anybody except themselves. . . .
>
> My humble opinion is, it's time the United States got honest internationally. We are not supporting Greece because of brotherly love or democracy. We are engaged in a battle of wits with Russia for grim stakes. Greece is important strategically, so the United States is providing funds to the Greek Government, in order to prevent its collapse tomorrow. . . .

The normally jaded control room personnel sat up, startled, as the former vice-president in charge of news read off, in essence, what William Shirer had said in the *Herald Tribune* months before: If this was to America's advantage, then why not call it as it was "and not mention the gobblegook about Greek democracy"? The alternative was to stop automatically getting into bed with the Right. "Certainly, American policy in Greece is not fooling the Greeks. . . . Certainly likewise, American policy in Greece is not fooling the Russians. Certainly, American policy in Greece is not fooling American reporters. That leaves only the American people to be fooled. . . . I think it is time that the nonsense of fooling Americans ceased.

"One thing is clear—where there's so much smoke, fanned by so many reporters, there's hot fire."[35]

The dispatch ended, Murrow paused for a moment. "George Polk probably knew more about Greece than any other American reporter there. He was coming home; he was murdered; it may be that he knew too much. . . ."

(In an accident of timing, Jim Forrestal had written Murrow earlier in the day, expressing regret at his declining and rest assured, he would be back to him again. After that night, on the evidence available, the Secretary of Defense issued no more invitations.)

At first all was fervor. CBS rushed Rome correspondent Winston Burdett to Salonika to make an independent finding and report back. Polk's mother was rushed to Athens by the network, with the personal condolences of Paley and Stanton. The news department launched a report series on the case; it would continue into 1949. A group of news associations spearheaded by the New York Newspaper Guild, among them Polk's old colleague Ted Berkman, set up the Newsmen's Commission to Investigate the Murder of George Polk, an independent inquiry of the working press.

In Murrow's office a dark-haired, pugnacious young man in his late twenties had become a familiar sight. John Donovan, back in New York and working with the Newsmen's Commission, had picked up his courage one day, marched into the Murrow corner at 485, and somehow found himself sitting on the edge of the broadcaster's desk, talking about Greece as the other listened, and continuing as a source of private information not only on the Polk case but on his own dealings with Greek officialdom.

Murrow, talking on the air with Hollenbeck and Howard Smith, called the murder "a cold, political demonstration . . . planned to be spectacular . . . planned to intimidate." Smith charged that Polk had walked into a trap, "organized and directed from . . . where [his] advance movements were known, in short, from Athens."[36]

Next day's *Times* picked it up (POLK MURDER HELD TO BE INTIMIDATION. MURROW, IN CBS BROADCAST, CHARGES THAT KILLING WAS "POLITICAL DEMONSTRATION").

Then, slowly, came the lid. Mrs. A. R. Polk of Fort Worth, Texas, returned from Athens complaining of "the atmosphere of fear" surrounding the investigation of her son's murder.[37] Burdett complained the police were working the assumed Communist angle "to the almost total exclusion of every other possibility."[38] In Athens John Donovan had found his sources dried up, people to whom he'd once been close, terrified at the sight of him, walking quickly past. "They'd been warned off," he later said. "It was so obvious that there was a cover-up."

In the States, the Newsmen's Commission found its inquiry suddenly pre-empted—through what arrangements would not be disclosed for years— by a blue-ribbon committee of Washington journalists, including such luminaries as James Reston and Marquis Childs, chaired by Walter Lippmann, that eminent critic of the Truman Doctrine. Who could fault it? However, it took as counsel General Wild Bill Donovan, the near-legendary former OSS leader, a trusted wartime name—certainly Murrow and the CBS staff thought so—but whose ties to officialdom made him seem to others "a rather dubious champion," as Berkman later put it, for a dead reporter who had nettled the establishment.[39]

In the meantime, CIA cables from abroad were raising the question of an adverse public reaction, possibly endangering continuation of U.S. military and economic aid, due to lapse June 30, the end of the fiscal year, unless renewed by Congress; and was that the intention of the killing? At a time, added a confidential cable, when the chief of the U.S. Aid Mission was attempting to present "the best possible case at home"?[40]

The moves, once made, were made fast.

At CBS all relevant material was gathered together in the name of the company investigation—very little of those long Polk reports would be left in Ed Murrow's files—and cooperation with the "official" committee, everything siphoned off and funneled upward through management levels. Justice would be done, matters handled by the proper people, the members of the club, the 485 news staff effectively insulated from the mainstream of the inquiry, Howard Smith, abroad, kept off the case. At NBC John Donovan, told to resign from the Newsmen's Commission—"They're only trying to prove the Greek government killed George Polk"—refused and found his services terminated.[41]

Murrow, feeling itchy, queried Burdett, back in town: What news of the investigation?

Oh, the General was on top of it, dissatisfied with the politically lopsided police work, would see to it that the scope was widened, every avenue explored no matter what.[42]

In fact—and unknown at the time—General Donovan, in Athens, had already seen a worked-up list of suspects that explicitly included members of the Greek government, eliminating all the names but that of a small-time Salonika ex-Communist, promptly referred to the police. The fact would be revealed years later by the General's assistant, a Greek-American OSS veteran with a brilliant war record of behind-the-lines work with the resistance under the Nazi occupation, who had taken on the present job reluctantly, intent on fairness. He would complain afterward to his superiors of harassment in his work, of "direct and indirect sabotage by [deleted] certain members of the American Embassy," and of open hostility from the American chargé d'affaires, asking, Why was he "killing himself" over George Polk?[43]

In the trial that followed, two fingered Communists would be condemned *in absentia* as the killers, the suspect plucked from the list—a news stringer who had played all sides of the political spectrum—convicted for complicity on the basis of a confession retracted in the seventies as being obtained under torture. Alex Kendrick, following the proceedings for CBS, remarking on the atmosphere of hate and right-wing press attacks, wondered if it was the alleged killers or Polk himself who was on trial.[44]

Murrow, like most, had his doubts about the outcome—too many "unsolved questions"—and was to say so on the air. Burdett, similarly, found too many "gaps" in the official story.[45] Should not American policy makers, asked Kendrick, ask themselves why they and the Greeks should be afraid of American correspondents, and were not honesty and integrity also laudable war aims—no matter what kind of war was being fought?[46]

The ripples of the Polk case would be wide, a litmus test among the professional red hunters. A loose end and potentially explosive issue bobbing always to the surface, government agencies ever on the alert for signs of its reappearance, year after year,[47] and keeping an eye sometimes on its participants. Polk himself, described forthrightly in early CIA reports as anti-Communist, would by 1955 be re-examined for "indications of possible Communist involvement."[48]

At CBS the story faded gradually into the background, the figure of Polk into memory. John Donovan, persisting on his own, found his assignments drying up. Arrangements made to file with Murrow as a stringer foundered on a sudden inability to obtain a number to transmit his cables. A Hollywood studio decided on a movie on the case. Working as consultant, he found himself called in one day by the producer: The picture was out—scrapped. There had been a call from Washington, it seemed. They didn't want a movie about Polk.[49]

The final, inconclusive report by the Lippmann committee would make no impact in the atmosphere of 1952: a nation deep into presidential elections and the Korean War. Polk would be memorialized, awards established in his name, papers declassified, new facts unearthed, new theories forwarded—on the possible involvement of British intelligence, of the Xists, of a KKE assassination to embarrass the Greek government, of a rightist with an itchy trigger finger.

In the end, nothing changed essentially, as John Donovan looked back on that time from the viewpoint of the 1980s:

> I was naïve and I know *George* was. I mean *now*—in retrospect, hindsight being what it is. . . . You step into an area where the government, in one way or another, is maybe spending a hundred and fifty or two hundred million bucks trying to back some regime. And if some guy wanders in and starts filing stories that are contrary to their likes, I mean for God's sake, they're not gonna change policy for a three-hundred-dollar-a-week employee—that's a joke![50]

2.

Working the convention floor at Philadelphia, 1948, was like reporting, fully dressed, from a steambath. The mercury was soaring, humidity at an all-time high, no air conditioning in the aging hall. But Philadelphia was wired into a grid bringing first-time live TV convention coverage to eighteen cities on the Eastern Seaboard and that was what the major parties wanted.

Radio was still king; for most of the country it was still an audio convention—with TV wrap-ups and commentary broadcast from a tiny enclosure where Doug Edwards sat by a camera, reached by going through the radio room where the main action was. But for the correspondents, working both sight and sound, the new medium was a fact. So was the early technology, which could only be described as brutal.

"I can remember Ed and a couple of other reporters," a news editor said later, "had to go out on this hot, hot floor wearing these packs, that carried the voice transmitters—batteries, power, audio. The cameras were stationed, one or two, around the hall, to pick them up and get the picture. But you had to transmit the sound by this backpack. And I can remember Ed coming off that floor, just absolutely soaked in perspiration. Oh, my God, he looked terrible."

The long-winded proceedings on this, TV's political shakedown cruise, had little other than the novelty of live images to recommend them. (The undoubted highlight of the Republicans' first day was not a politician but the daughter of bandleader Meyer Davis, modeling a dress bearing likenesses of the leading candidates, then hitching up her skirt before the camera to display, reportedly well up on one thigh, a portrait of Harold Stassen.)

John Crosby, the literate critic of the *Herald Tribune*, described Murrow and two colleagues, slouched before the cameras at the tag end of the day, just before midnight, looking bored and wilted. It had to be the heat, the newsman said. "We've been here ten minutes and all we've said is that nothing much happened today, or if it did, we don't know about it."[1]

It was perhaps the first and last completely open statement about the true nature of convention reporting.

After some practice they got their act together, The New York *Times* commending "the CBS trio of Ed Murrow, Quincy Howe and Douglas Edwards" for "straight adult reporting, seasoned with real humor . . . in a class by itself," with Murrow singled out for "ad lib quips [that] were far and away the most amusing words heard all week in Philadelphia, reflecting . . . a good-natured yet perceptive sense of detachment that was truly mature journalism."[2]

In June, they watched Thomas E. Dewey accept the GOP call with the certitude of a man who'd just won the election, as a thunderstorm raged outside and the dankness inside approached a steamy, junglelike consistency. "It must have been somewhere between ninety-five and one hundred degrees on the floor," Bob Skedgell remembered, "just awful. The humidity was about a hundred and twenty-nine percent. I've always remembered Ed, and I've forgotten who else, coming back just drenched; they must have lost six or eight pounds in liquid." It certainly helped kill any enthusiasm the reporters might have had for television.

Three weeks later, in a different scene, they watched Harry Truman's nomination and a spell-it-out civil rights plank rammed through, over Southern objections, in a roaring voice vote; watched Hubert Humphrey, the fiery young Mayor of Minneapolis, carried shoulder-high following his plea to "get out of the shadow of states' rights and . . . [into] the bright sunshine of human rights"; saw the Mississippi delegation and half that of Alabama, spearheading the bolting of the South, walk down the center aisle and out into the pouring rain.

(There was also some coverage of the Wallace-led, third-stream convention of the Progressive Party. At one point in those proceedings, as the singing started up, one of the young CBS staffers began mouthing the text along, automatically, under his breath. Ted Church turned around sharply. "How come *you* know the words?")

Truman's victory that fall, heading a truncated party, surprised CBS as much as anyone. At 4:00 or 5:00 A.M., a staffer recalled, Dewey seemed to have it wrapped up, or at least seemed sufficiently ahead to send everyone home. Then the later returns started coming in, Ted Church calling hotel rooms all over town, reassembling the staff, sleepy-eyed correspondents pulling on their pants and staggering back to work. "It was our version of the Chicago *Tribune*."

Murrow, delighted with the black eye given the poll takers that November—"those who tell us what we think, believe and will do, without consulting us"—asked, had the press "abdicated reporting . . . in favor of Messrs. Roper and Gallup?" While radio, he pointed out, had simply sold the most time to the party with the most money—"and that may not be the best way of conducting a national debate over the air."[3]

He had put his time in with the candidates, an average-to-middling campaign reporter with little flair for party politics, some colleagues thought, unless he was reporting from the spot. (Back in the spring he had called Truman "a dead duck" and fingered Vandenberg to take the GOP nomination, possibly with Stassen as a running mate. "The latter," he wrote a friend, "scuffered Mr. Dewey in the Wisconsin primaries, for which he deserves well of his country."[4]) Like most reporters, he complained about the level of political debate by candidates spending "most of their time telling us what to do about Russia instead of . . . what they propose to do about *this* country."

In Alabama he had linked up with the Wallace campaign, then fresh from a tomato- and egg-pelting gauntlet in the cities of North Carolina and shouts of "Sell your junk in Moscow, Henry!" Before sundown in Birmingham ("a hot, shirt sleeve sort of afternoon"), he watched Police Commissioner Eugene "Bull" Connor tell the good folks on the courthouse lawn—blacks to one side, whites to the other, a barrier between them—to give Mr. Wallace a respectful hearing, a stark contrast with the violence greeting Wallace's running mate when a major media figure wasn't present.

Egg throwers heaving away at Alabama Progressive party Chairman J. P. Mooney were collared and led away, everything carefully controlled. "Most of the colored people . . . remained expressionless during the whole proceedings." The candidate himself did not appear to the divided crowd, due instead to make a broadcast; "there is no segregation in radio."[5]

Murrow himself had feared a backlash, possibly adding clout to the States' Rights party, the fourth group, the bolted so-called Dixiecrats. But his own coverage, his own reaction, ranged from ambivalent to overtly hostile—i.e., where did this outsider, his mouth full of strawberry shortcake over dinner afterward, talking loftily of this dreadful place, where did *he* come off making judgments? He felt resentful, choosing to see a bid for Northern sympathies in the seemingly quixotic Southern tour; with an unspoken challenge to his Yankee audience not to feel so damn superior.

Conversely, he gave Wallace a forum on his program, as part of a presidential candidates series, to expound his party platform, answer listener questions, and blast "international big business, which . . . dominates our foreign policy and controls governments abroad." Asked by Murrow whom he would appoint to head State and Defense, the candidate declined to name names, "[but] I can say that my Secretary of State would not be a general or Wall Street lawyer."[6]

It was just six weeks after the warning from the Wheelock agency, and possibly intended as reply. More likely it was simple news judgment— i.e., if Robert Taft could be included in the series, so could Henry Wallace or, conversely, Norman Thomas. But the perimeters within which that judgment could be exercised were tightening perceptibly, public opinion hardening, in months that saw the indictment for conspiracy of twelve Communist Party leaders (eleven were tried), Alger Hiss facing Whittaker Chambers, and, concomitantly, the rise to prominence of Representative Richard Nixon of California, guiding spirit of the so-called Hiss case, the bright new star and best legal mind on the House Un-American Activities Committee, pursuing the theme of Communist infiltration of the New Deal.

Alger Hiss. The classic State Department success story. President of the prestigious Carnegie Endowment for International Peace, fingered suddenly as an alleged prewar Communist operative, and focus of a shift in the investigative function—from the fringe to the respectables, driving home the message, magnified through well-timed leaks to the news media, that no one was above suspicion.

"The general climate of opinion here has grown worse," Murrow wrote a friend in those months. "The witch-hunting has increased, so has the inflation. We're in for a merry time."[7] Earlier he had shocked a British visitor by talking of possibly going back to England as a political refugee.

On radio, he was openly skeptical of the published revelations in the Hiss case, commenting dryly on "purple-faced congressmen reaching for headlines," and on microfilmed alleged evidence stashed away in pumpkins, noting that "the documents so far released haven't contained much information that wasn't generally known to any able reporter of the time."[8]

December 15, Hiss, denying Chambers' charge about his past, was indicted for perjury by a federal grand jury. Five days later, on a dark and rainy evening in mid-Manhattan, police cleared the crowds away from the sidewalk in front of 2 West 45 Street, where a body lay on the wet pavement, next to a smashed pair of glasses. White male Caucasian, ran the police report, early forties, fully dressed, overshoe on one foot. The other was found sixteen floors above the street, just inside the office window from which he had fallen to his death. The victim was identified as Laurence Duggan, Director of the Institute of International Education.

That night in Washington, Acting HUAC Chairman Karl Mundt, with the concurrence of his colleague Richard Nixon, told waiting reporters in a hastily convened meeting that Duggan, a State Department friend of Alger Hiss, had been identified in closed-session hearings as one of six former officials passing documents back in the thirties, purportedly to Whittaker Chambers, then in his red phase.

And the other five? Mundt promised to name them "as they jump out of windows."

At his home in Falls Church, Virginia, Joe Wershba, now working out of Washington, D.C., ran to where his phone was jangling off the hook; it was Murrow, calling from New York. He wanted a statement from Sumner Welles—fast. The reporter dialed the number of Roosevelt's former undersecretary of state and longtime mentor to Larry Duggan.

The valet answered. Mr. Welles was in the bathtub. Wershba left a message. Thirty minutes later Murrow was on the phone again: *Where was that statement?*

Wershba routed the former undersecretary out of the tub and got an official statement calling Duggan "one of the most brilliant, most devoted and most patriotic public servants"—he emphasized the last—whom Welles had ever known.

The next day was a nightmare of contradictions and confusion. The FBI said, yes, it had questioned Duggan in connection with the Hiss investigation; it had questioned lots of people. Besides, it hadn't turned up anything. Chambers categorically denied receiving papers from Duggan. Of course, he *did* remember telling a Roosevelt adviser that in his opinion Laurence Duggan was a member of a "pro-Soviet bloc" in the State Department back in 1939, though again he'd never really *met* Mr. Duggan. . . .[9] The committee's original informer, who had cited Chambers, was out of town, his office said, and would not be back for two weeks.

Back at the scene, there had been no witnesses, no note or sign of struggle in the office. The police said the IIE Director either "jumped or fell."

The younger Stephen Duggan was at home, confined to bed with bleeding ulcers when Murrow's call came in. His voice was shaking: "I'm doing a special broadcast on Larry tonight." He sounded "totally distraught," said Duggan later, like someone who could not quite believe what was happening.

It was that night's lead story and editorial. A dead man's character was being destroyed: "Some of the headlines that I have seen might as well read: 'Spy Takes Life.' " He reviewed the case, then ended on a personal note: He had known Laurence Duggan for eighteen years, he said.

I was Chairman of the Board of the Institute of International Education when he was selected as Director. . . . [He] did not seek the post, but was rather persuaded to give up a lucrative career. . . . his ability as an administrator . . . the high esteem in which he was held by leaders in business, government and the academic community . . . his experience in international affairs. . . .

And tonight the headlines are shouting: "Duggan named in Spy Case." Who named him? Isaac Don Levine, who said he was quoting Whittaker Chambers. And who denies it? Whittaker Chambers. . . .

The members of the committee who have done this thing . . . may now consult their actions and their consciences.[10]

The uproar that followed caused the men of HUAC temporarily to backtrack. Mundt declared the case "a closed book." Nixon regretted "misunderstandings." But accusations made would not be laid to rest—not in the atmosphere of 1948.

It was a week before Murrow could bring himself to write the aged man who had opened the doors of his home to him, back in 1932. Sarah Duggan had died some years before, the Fifty-fifth Street apartment long since vacated, the Professor living in semi-retirement, alone.

Dear Chief:
I have tried a half a dozen times to write this letter. . . . My sense of personal loss is probably as great as that felt by anyone outside your family. My contempt for the instruments for public information [sic]—particularly the press, is unlimited. . . .

The old man was grateful—"Dear Ed, you knew Laurence so well"—expressing his indebtedness, as he put it, "for the manly and courageous manner in which you at once sprang to the defense of his honor. . . and also for your indignant condemnation for [sic] the mean-spirited little men who undertook to destroy his character."

The interests of "Justice and the national welfare," he suggested pitifully, would best be served by the abolition of the Un-American Activities Committee.

As for Stephen Pierce Duggan, intimate of statesmen, apostle of education, and believer in the betterment of man, he was to die in less than two years. Murrow, though keeping his own counsel for the most part, never again regarded young Mr. Nixon as just another politician out for headlines.

In the meantime, there was thunder along Madison Avenue. Ward Wheelock called up the day after the broadcast to give fair notice: The president of the Campbell Soup Company objected to the piece. It was engaging in personal defense, editorializing. There was to be a meeting between the client and the agency on Tuesday of next week to discuss the matter.

Coldly, Murrow informed the adman that the conditions for the broadcast were spelled out in his contract, that he did not propose to discuss his news judgment with either him or the client, and that the client, if sufficiently dissatisfied, could always, he assumed, fail to pick up the option.[11]

A load of listener letters followed, with Murrow's suggestion that the sponsor perhaps might like to eat them.

The agency, after a sampling, backed down: Fine, fine; they'd send them on: "I think we can now bury the body, eh?"[12]

Murrow's reaction went unrecorded.

In another memo, this time to Paley, he proposed—"urgently"—a thirty-minute documentary on the case. He'd take care of production—no cost to CBS, without billing if the network wanted. There were no results.

There were strong editorials in the *Times* and the *Herald Tribune*; defenses of Duggan by such people as Elmer Davis, Joe Harsch, Martin Agronsky, Eleanor Roosevelt, Raymond Moley; tributes from the State Department and the do-gooders. The Hispanic press mourned Duggan as a much-needed friend of Latin America. But the argument wouldn't die, revivified whenever the events of 1948 were raked over, a permanent cloud about the evening of December 20 and the mark of controversy about the tragic figure of Laurence Duggan. Even at the IIE, in the splendid reception area of its post-sixties incarnation opposite the UN, there would be a large oil painting of the Professor, another of Kenneth Holland, Duggan's capable successor, but none to mark the tenure of the quiet, scholarly man who had guided the institute through the turbulent years of the early witch-hunts.

"The trouble is," Murrow mourned to a mutual friend, "that a lie can go around the world while truth is getting his pants on."[13]

3.

He was young, huge, heavy, and a little nearsighted, a six-foot-four package of whirling energy, whose very presence could exhaust; who, bounding into Murrow's life the year before, was there to stay.

The story goes that when Ferdinand Friendly Wachenheimer turned up for his first day's work at WEAN in Providence, Rhode Island, the station manager took in his name, then said, "Okay, from here on in, you're Fred Friendly."

It was as Fred Friendly that he made it through the war as correspondent for the *CBI Roundup*, the Pacific Theater version of *Stars and Stripes*; winding up ultimately in postwar New York City with a tiny bank account, big plans, and fresh ideas about the use of sound—based on wartime work with tape and, back in Providence, the production of modest minidocumentaries for radio.[1] They were small efforts, forgotten until 1942 and a musicians' strike that left the recording companies hungry for material.

Young Sergeant Friendly got a phone call in the middle of the war from Decca: Were there recordings of his programs? Why yes, he said; his mother had them somewhere. Well, could they be bought for, say, twenty-five a piece? Friendly figured twenty-five cents per record, did some calculating on his fingers, gave his mother's phone number in Providence, and nearly fell over when sometime later he received a check for thousands of dollars—1942 dollars.

It was still a warming memory in 1947 as Friendly, long out of uniform, sat over drinks, knocking ideas around with Jap Gude, a top-drawer contact who knew a comer when he saw one. James Petrillo, the feisty little Napoleonic leader of the AFL musicians, had called the troops out once again. Friendly told the Decca story. No reason why it couldn't work a second time, with something made to order; think what you could do now with magnetic tape. . . .

They were both, it turned out, reading *Only Yesterday*, Frederick Lewis Allen's popular social history of the twenties. It was Friendly who actually broached the concept of a history in sound. These things had *happened* after all; a good deal must have been recorded, sitting out there somewhere on shellac or whatever, waiting to be transferred onto tape. After that, all you needed to pull things together was a good ear, some Scotch tape, and a razor. Done, said Gude; they'd get Allen to research it, obtain his imprimatur, and call it *Only Yesterday*.

Allen, though intrigued, proved unavailable.

They were back to square one. Then, said Gude later, Friendly had a brainstorm: "We need a good name to narrate—someone like Edward R. Murrow."

"Why not Edward R. Murrow?"

"Do you know him?"[2]

They met over lunch. Gude made the introductions, then let the young unknown speak for himself. "He was most persuasive."

Murrow didn't need persuasion ("I've *done* some of this"), falling in with stories of his own use of tape recorders in the war. "Look, I'm with you. It sounds like a good idea—a terrific idea!"

They drew a blank at Decca. Columbia Records, with expensive new LP equipment standing idle, proved more receptive, with Goddard Lieberson, head of the classical music division, deciding on the go-ahead against prevailing wisdom that said talking records didn't sell.

No one stood to make a dime, they thought. But Friendly was getting married. Gude, setting up the three-way contract, asked Lieberson about "a small advance? We'll be doing a lot of research. . . ." Lieberson authorized $1,000.

"Make it out to Fred." Some while later they got Columbia to come up with another thousand, also "to Fred."

I Can Hear It Now, 1933–45, released in the winter of 1948, was an instant hit, selling a quarter of a million albums in its first year, a classic, and a staple of the LP catalog. It also launched an historic partnership in communications.

For Murrow and Friendly it was a first experience at working together. While one put in the major portion of the work, full time, the other proved considerably more than a good name to narrate. For in Murrow, Friendly had linked up with one of the great editors, who had spent the war years guinea-pigging audio technology.

"Ed was always interested in new developments in sound," said Joel Tall, formerly of CBS master control, the pioneering editor of Norman Corwin's *One World Flight*, who cut and pieced the fought-over selections on his splicing block[3] as the new partnership distilled 30,000 recorded minutes into the time span of an LP disc.

The "scrapbook for the ear," as its creators called it, differed radically from the old norm in sound documentaries. There were no actors, no music or effects other than the indigenous sound. The narrative was restrained, in Murrow's understated style. And the voices—Roosevelt, Hitler, Churchill, Huey Long, Will Rogers, Edward VIII, et al.—were edited into a skillful, fast-paced mix, new to the medium, of the epic and the purely human: Neville Chamberlain commenting on Munich, juxtaposed with sportscaster Clem McCarthy reporting from ringside on the Louis-Schmeling fight; the death of Roosevelt and House Speaker Sam Rayburn, about to introduce a nervous new President, unaware of open microphones: "Just a moment, lemme present you, willya—Harry?"

Two more volumes would follow, one on the immediate postwar period (the vast BBC library provided recorded material, R. T. Clark did the selecting), and the third on the twenties, using actors in the absence of transcriptions ("That was a mistake," said Friendly later). When the partnership moved into television, features from the TV sound tracks would make lucrative Columbia releases under the Murrow-Friendly imprimatur, though none would match the impact and endurance of that first recording.

The major share of royalties went to Friendly; it was, after all, his idea, as Jap Gude pointed out. For Murrow, it meant outside earnings added to a broadcasting salary of $125,000 yearly, which by the height of his TV career, would total up to a quarter million, making him one of the highest-paid men in America.

He had never lived lavishly, but he liked to live well—a good address, good schools, good clothes, fast cars, dinner parties at Voisin and Le Pavillon (where he was known to order scrambled eggs, partly through a nicotine-induced indifference to food, partly for the sheer pleasure of watching the waiter's reaction).

It was the ad executive Ward Wheelock who in the late forties had opened Murrow's eyes to the magic world of trust funds and tax shelters on a big scale[4]—all arcane and wondrous to someone totally unable to keep money in his pocket. To a friend, he put himself down once as "a peasant. When I get cash money, I spend it."[5] One associate, going further, guessed that had it not been for Seward's care at home, Murrow would probably have come back broke from London.

It accounted in part for his continued personal connection with the adman—an association that others would have found hard to understand but for his manifest attraction to men who radiated power, whose abilities out there in the "real" world of corporate and financial dealings seemed so greatly to outstrip his own. It marked his frequent preference for the company of conservatives and his close, if troubled, ties with corporate sponsors. Politicians he could see through as reporter, but the self-made country boy would always be impressed by the captains of industry, the man's men who *really* made things run.

Typically, all this coexisted with a puritanical embarrassment at the money and the high-toned friends, finding outlets in dinner party litanies about his poverty-stricken youth, the tough times, in embroidered detail that left the impression that the Murrows had lived in total squalor. Marietta Tree, Ronald Tree's second wife and a wartime friend, had had enough on one occasion: "Ed, that's the forty-fifth time you've talked about it. Just why are you *boasting* so much?"

"He pretended he hadn't heard me," she recalled afterward. "It was all a little bit childlike—the rest of us were soft and he'd made it up the hard way. [There was a kind of] innocence . . . refreshing . . . thank goodness he kept it.

"But he wasn't absolutely straight with himself; neurotic people don't really know themselves and inverted snobbery is basically neurotic. I think he was interested in power but didn't *think* he was. He thought he wanted the simple life, had this fantasy of seeing himself as a simple farmer or English squire. But he was really part of the urban scene, the excitement; he couldn't have stayed away from it."[6]

It was somehow characteristic, therefore, that Murrow, his name synonymous with liberalism, choosing a summer place in the latter forties, would pass up the intellectual (and largely liberal) watering holes of Cape Cod and Martha's Vineyard—he couldn't swim anyway—in favor of Pawling, New York: the country seat of Thomas Dewey, Lowell Thomas, and Dr. Norman Vincent Peale. Specifically, he chose the select community dotting the long ridge known as Quaker Hill, on the New York–Connecticut border: low-key, high-prestige, quietly moneyed.

A seventy-five-mile drive from New York City, the Hill was decidedly upstate—staid, expensively rural, centered on golf, hunting, riding, teetotaling family nights at the clubhouse led by its *grand seigneur* and promoter Lowell Thomas, then with CBS. Murrow, invited up by Thomas in the last nervous weeks before his return to broadcasting in 1947, had found the green hills restful and the golfing good.

For a while in 1948, it seemed as though the Dewey place would be the summer White House, and indeed, many on the Hill saw Hyde Park, on the other side of Dutchess County, as enemy territory; back during the New Deal a team of Roosevelt aides regularly squared off for softball against a Pawling lineup known as the Nine Old Men.

"Surrounded by reactionary Republicans," Murrow quipped to a colleague at CBS.[7] But he liked being there. The foursquare community addressed something foursquare in him. He was top-drawer, they were top-drawer; no controversy on the golf tee or at the dinner table. "Though Dewey and I are friends and neighbors," Murrow wrote David Schoenbrun, "we have a strictly arms'-length relationship when it comes to politics."[8]

For Democrats, they could always visit Mrs. Roosevelt at Hyde Park, an hour and a quarter's drive away; less if Ed was driving.

For housing, they settled on a long, low structure, with its own fourteen acres, perched precipitously on a high ridge looking out across a broad expanse of fields and woodlands. "It's built of pealed [sic] cedar logs," Murrow wrote Ken Merredith, his old supervisor back in western Washington, "split-cedar shaker roof; the whole thing hand-axed; the only house in the eastern part of this country I ever wanted. . . ."[9]

A huge stone fireplace dominated the living area. Just inside the door, nailed to the wall, was a slab of hemlock chopped from a tree on the Olympic Peninsula, in western Washington, where as a twenty-one-year-old compassman he had marked off a section corner in the summer of 1929; a gift sent by Merredith from Clallam County. Outside, on a clear day, they could see sixty miles westward to the Hudson and out toward the round gray outlines that were the rim of the Catskill Mountains.

In the early days they entertained, Murrow very much the lord of the manor, playing host to "the boys," also the weighty VIP types invited up from the city; and disclosing, conversely, a considerably earthier side when on his home turf. Weekend visitors were startled by the sight of the normally fastidious Murrow appearing stubble-chinned at breakfast, unshowered in an ancient bathrobe that had seen better days; or going through the weekend unshaved in a work shirt and dungarees, at a time when blue jeans were still bought over the counter for five dollars at Army-Navy stores. (One guest recalled an evening on the Hill, an odd jumble of screening Churchill footage delivered by a slavey up from 485 on one hand and of imbibing on the other or, as simply stated, "The men had had a lot to drink." When physical needs became acute, Murrow, impatient with the lineup for the bathroom, led the male company out to the porch, a line of power figures trooping to where the house faced an eighteen-foot drop, where they turned their backs and, in the darkness, peed out over Dutchess County.)

But in general, Pawling, with its hunting and fishing, its privacy and slow country pace, was another world, a needed escape hatch, a weekend and summer ritual kept to in all but the severest weather. Janet Murrow, battling outgoing Friday night traffic with Casey, Murrow following on Saturday, later admitted she would just as soon have stayed at times in town.

It was around Murrow's needs, however, that the household revolved. Though just past forty, he was tiring more rapidly, hard put to deliver five newscasts a week when he had once delivered up to that many in a single night, drawing with ever greater effort on dwindling reserves, relying increasingly on that second wind, on extra bursts of febrile energy. His youth was gone. The "doctors" were back in the picture, dictating periods of rest, controlling what he could and could not do on his own.[10]

The times in Pawling, in that context, emerged as more than a country idyll; rather, they were an absolute necessity, which, if not held to, could bring results proving both physically and professionally disastrous.

Throughout 1949, the horizon closed in. At CBS, heads were rolling in the wake of declining first-quarter earnings, under the impact of escalating TV costs. Paley warned the stockholders of "sizable" anticipated losses before the equally expected upturn.[11]

In the meantime, cutbacks on 17 were ending associations dating back to World War II. Murrow wrote to Farnsworth Fowle, who had covered the landings at Salerno and the march on Naples for CBS, speculating bleakly on the future of the news department. "I hope you don't feel that because your team is being broken up, you ought to leave too," Fowle replied. "That would be the wrong kind of solidarity. More than ever, CBS will need you more than you will need them."[12]

In one case—that of Alex Kendrick, Vienna-based, a veteran newsman and expert on Eastern Europe—he managed to keep down the body count, putting Kendrick on his program payroll, a move, the correspondent later said, that ensured his being in place when upheavals in the Soviet bloc and the death of Stalin suddenly made Vienna the best dateline in Europe.[13]

But Murrow's feelings on the cutbacks were no secret—nor, possibly, was the offer made by David Sarnoff, long desirous of luring Paley's top news property to NBC. Just state your terms, said the master of RCA; write your own contract.

"I replied that I was quite happy where I was," Murrow later wrote to Howard Smith, "and there was no point in pursuing the matter. Neither Paley nor anyone else in this shop was aware of the offer and they still aren't; this is for your information alone. . . ."[14]

Word had got around, however. That spring the broadcaster, somewhat dazed, announced to Joe Harsch: "A guy named Murrow—much to his surprise—was elected a member of the Board of Directors of Columbia, where his counsel won't be listened to."[15] NBC London was whispering that the move had been made to forestall his possible departure from CBS.

Whatever the ultimate reasons, the fact stood that Murrow, almost two years after leaving management, was suddenly invited back—a newscaster sitting in with the mix of Paley in-laws, CBS officials, outside corporation heads, and Wall Street lawyers directing the finances of a major broadcasting complex.

April 20, 1949, he became officially a company director, a position that proved to be controversial. Richard Salant, a distinguished news head who himself began in upper management, thought that it was a mistake—"someone from news shouldn't be on the board of directors"—that no one in the sensitive news area should come in direct contact with boardroom concerns, which, given the nature of things, would largely be financial.[16]

Murrow himself, the sheer cachet of his directorship aside, admitted at the outset to ambivalence—"I had [sic] very much of two minds in taking it," he told Howard Smith—feeling in the upshot, as did most on 17, that his new access to the boardroom, coming when it did, would give the abraded news department a needed friend at court; "that at least once each quarter," as he explained it, "I would have a chance to say something about the big over-all budget and might be able to exercise a little influence and support for about the only aspect of broadcasting that I know or care about."[17]

Instead, it drew him into gray areas and many complications as outside events translated into new pressures on the broadcast industry.

And events moved quickly in those months: the announcement of the Soviet A-bomb ("The Russians not only exploded an atomic weapon, they exploded an American myth . . . that we had, and could maintain, the secret of the bomb's construction"[18]); the final stages of the civil war in China ("It is an old lesson of war that an army cannot operate successfully against guerrilla tactics unless it has the support of the local population. Clearly . . . in vast areas of China, Chiang Kai-shek's armies do not enjoy that support"[19]). The Senate ratified the North Atlantic Treaty Pact in a historic reversal of U.S. policy—"the tradition against foreign commitments that is as old as this nation."[20]

By all indications Murrow was in firm agreement on administration policy—at least in Europe: proud of what his country had accomplished militarily in wartime, proud of the Marshall Plan, which, at that stage and for all its flaws, was helping Western Europe to its feet in an aid move unprecedented by a major power. In broadcasts he labeled Secretary of State Dean Acheson as "intellectually arrogant" but backed the Secretary's policies in general and privately considered him, as he told R. T. Clark, "the ablest man in the administration."[21]

Conversely—and there was always a "conversely"—he spent as much time looking critically at the details of plans and policies that he supported on essentials. A NATO backer, he questioned the siting of NATO bases at Russia's doorstep, asking listeners how *they* would feel about Soviet cannon staring down at them from Canada—a prospect likely, he suggested, to raise apprehension levels "and reduce the possibility of our reaching a peaceful settlement with the Soviet Union";[22] in which case, one could not quite blame the Soviets. It kept Washington from counting too firmly on his unqualified support.

And while East and West were seemingly bunching themselves into fists, he commented ("Each . . . labeling that fist as purely defensive"), not everyone was lining up: "There is a third force of great wealth and potential power: India, Pakistan, the countries of Southeast Asia, Indonesia, the richest archipelago in the world, and the Arab countries—all hoping to stand aloof, to occupy the middle ground. It seems reasonable to expect that the forces contending in Europe will use their fists— economic, political and propaganda-wise—to drive those areas into one camp or the other."[23]

His program, moreover, showcasing top-line correspondents and outspoken bureau chiefs, continually went one further in challenging prevailing political orthodoxies, indicating a world more complicated than that reflected in the Hearst press or the slogans of domestic politicians. Correspondent Bill Costello, in from Tokyo, spoke of "a tremendous social revolution in every part of Asia" and of the split in ideology between Stalin and the emerging Chinese leadership—"one of the new and highly important political factors in the world." The United States might be powerful enough to dictate some form of alliance in the West Pacific, he said, "but it wouldn't be worth the paper it was written on. . . . It doesn't much matter whether Communism or nationalism is on top, the White man is no longer a demi-god in Asia. He can no longer lord it over subject people."[24]

From Shanghai, awaiting the Communist advance, CBS stringer Robert Martin's voice reports detailed collapse, arrests, and curfews, Black Marias screaming through deserted streets, on the hunt for suspects, the business community dickering quietly with the Communists to hold off until it paid the other side to clear out. "This is Shanghai—which welcomes, rather than fears, the coming occupation."[25]

Free-lancers with firsthand information were invited to the microphone. Back in 1948, speaking from Kansas City, Walter Cronkite, introduced as "an old friend and fellow reporter," fresh from closing up the Moscow UP bureau—"hog-tied by Soviet censorship," as he called it, and "worried for fear the lessons of Eastern Europe weren't sinking in back here at home"—worried now that "the pendulum has swung too far the other way.

"It does seem to me, Ed, that we Americans have gone hysterical over the Russian situation, and over the prospects of war. . . . Russia is *not* ready for a war right now. That is perfectly obvious to anyone sitting in Moscow."[26]

But the more reasoned voices were being drowned out by cries of "Who lost China?" and charges that traitors were to blame for Soviet possession of the A-bomb. In Washington, Senate Bill 595, introduced by Pat McCarran of Nevada, red of face, dyspeptic of disposition, known unofficially as the Senator from Kennecott Copper, proposed easing wiretap restrictions and facilitating the seizure of telegrams and cables without official court subpoenas. The House Appropriations Committee voted the FBI another 8 million following Director J. Edgar Hoover's appeal for added forces to meet what he called "the persistent threat of Communism."[27]

At the federal courthouse in New York's Foley Square, Alger Hiss was on trial for perjury on one floor, eleven CP leaders on another, the two proceedings, though separate, melded together in the headlines. Murrow, following the Hiss case, had noted early on "the tendency to convict Alger Hiss before he has been tried."[28]

Toward the Communist eleven, he was notably cooler, his on-the-air tone of moderation notwithstanding. (And in contrast with views privately expressed. "I regard communism," he said once in 1950, "the way I do a virus.")[29] He contested the prevailing view of the CP as a serious threat to national security—"the fact is that the climate for the development of Communism in this country is less salubrious than any other in the world"—[30] yet didn't question the catchall advocacy-of-change-through-violence charge on which the government had based its case, and which many legal minds at both ends of the spectrum considered constitutionally doubtful. Instead he had relied on "due process of law" as protection, with insufficient attention paid, perhaps, to economic sanctions, and the fortunes of due process under the Vinson Court.

At the same time a distinct section of the listenership was angered by his insistence that Communists had any rights whatever, that CP membership was not illegal, and that advocating change was not illegal either; that Justice Oliver Wendell Holmes had called wiretapping "a dirty business," and that espionage, whatever the headlines, had been "employed by every tribe and state since the beginning of history."

By the end of the forties, however, there were no two ways about The Enemy, as the charge of "soft on communism" reached out to embrace the very authors of containment. The times demanded total commitment. Like others in his position, trying to hold a steadily eroding center, Murrow was finding himself increasingly on the left as the country marched to the right.

Ironically, his career had never been in better shape. The prestigious Alfred I. du Pont Awards of the Columbia School of Journalism commended him that year for "aggressive consistently excellent and accurate . . . reporting of news by radio"; the *Motion Picture Daily* poll showed him in first place as best news commentator for the second year running; there were new awards from the OPC and the National Headliner's Club;

the Peabody Committee, honoring *CBS Views the Press* and Don Hollenbeck, cited also "the courage of Edward R. Murrow, who conceived the program."

On and off the mike, he seemed untouchable, supremely assured, using his considerable clout to chip away at the McCarran bill or the expansion of FBI surveillance, an unassailable figure, enveloped by his wartime reputation as by armor plate, and a catchall for information on the state-level clones of HUAC, then carrying the witch-hunts to the grass roots.

From California, Paul White, somewhat subdued nowadays, forwarded clippings on the local Tenney committee, the granddaddy of them all, writing glumly to Ed about "trial by headline travelling from Congress to the States."[31] In Murrow's own Washington State, the local Canwell committee was riding herd on the University of Washington, hunting for Communists on the faculty, with overtones of the glory days of A. Mitchell Palmer.

"Many have learned about small fear," wrote a colleague from Tacoma, "the fears in which they only half believe and of which they are half ashamed." Wilmott Ragsdale, the former *Time* correspondent who had talked about the Northwest with Murrow, the night before the Rhine drop back in '45, had returned home, unlike Murrow, to find you can't go home again.

"I believe you really would like to live in this region of mountains and deep forests," he wrote Ed. "But you are obliged not to. I learned why by living here."[32]

Ragsdale, trying to spearhead a citizens' opposition to the Canwell committee, had found himself a stranger in his own home town—isolated, stigmatized, attacked in the local press.[33] "There is a kind of intimidation toward any who openly oppose 'persecutions,' " he wrote Murrow, "effective because of the general ill-information. . . . That is why you must know that you and a few others are listened to far more intently out here than in the big cities."

At the Canwell hearings, he had seen his old professors in the dock.

It has to be seen for one to feel the shamefulness of the proceedings. . . . [They were] more dramatic than any murder trial I ever covered for it was not men's lives that were at stake but their honor and their reputations. And when the hearing is over the effect goes on. . . .

And my own mean fear to visit a professor I had known and respected, because he was accused of communism. Might not someone see me entering his house? Would I be followed, questioned? It was a moral triumph when I finally called. Imagine so trifling an act assuming such proportions?[34]

So you can't come home, Murrow read off the sheet, "however much you might like to escape . . .

"Now I know how necessary it is to have people like you and Collingwood and Elmer Davis on our national networks. You are far out-quantified by the Fulton Lewis's, the Winchells. It is the rampant commentators who goad up the small fear and the distrust, and it is the good ones who give people the courage to take their small stands. You are obliged to do as you are doing. . . ."[35]

Murrow, responding, had to play it straight, admitting his own fear—"I have never known a time when it was more difficult to know what to say"—unable to live up to Rags Ragsdale's billing:

> Your account of the local Un-American Activities Committee doesn't surprise me. The situation that confronts everyone who writes or talks under a byline in mass communications is more desperate than most people realize. I don't know a half dozen people in the business who haven't got tucked away in the back of their mind each time they sit down to write, the fear that if they lay it on the line as it seems, they will come under severe and sustained attack.[36]

It was also his instinctive reaction to the despoiling of their Eden—to the message coming through in the letter, saying in effect, as Ragsdale later put it: "This is your homeplace too, Ed, *your* home I'm talking about. It's not New York City. This is your place and it's *bad* now—not good!"[37]

The opening of 1950 saw the Murrows in London. At home, the government had announced the go-ahead for the building of a thermonuclear bomb to top the Russians, despite known Soviet capability—a move Murrow regarded with dismay: "It may be that this two-power world is so utterly and irrevocably divided that the two great powers must continue to prepare to destroy each other, and perhaps the rest of the planet with them. . . . But if we and the Russians proceed . . . without further effort to call a halt, then diplomacy, statesmanship and reason stand defeated, and we are consigned to a hair-trigger existence."[38]

In Britain, a German-born physicist named Klaus Fuchs had confessed to passing atomic secrets to Soviet agents in London, New York, Boston, and Los Alamos, with talk of a connecting spy ring in North America.

Murrow, in London to report on the British elections, stopped off at the old Bow Street Police Station to see Fuchs, white-faced, trotted out before the press in a small courtroom usually reserved for traffic violators. He met with R. T. Clark, troubled lately about divisions among the Western powers, and about France's attempts to retain its crumbling Indochinese empire, trying to hold back the tide of nationalism, he said, through "three puppet governments kept in power solely by French rifles." The veteran newsman, discussing an upcoming series of articles, expressed concern at Paris' efforts to enlist Western backing and help in an area "where it is not only likely to be wasted but where the effects of waste, not to say defeat, will have highly undesirable consequences. . . ."[39]

Back home, America's own election politics were heating up to the steady drumbeat of "Traitors in Our Midst." In New York Alger Hiss, convicted of perjury on the second go-round, drew five years at Lewisburg. Family friend Dean Acheson, answering reporter queries, said he would not "turn his back" on Hiss. Amid the uproar from the right, an obscure Wisconsin Senator asked, Did this mean the Secretary wouldn't turn his back on the *other* Communists in the State Department?

Murrow, readying the copy for the night, noted a marked silence among congressional Democrats, then penciled in, in afterthought, that "a vicious controversy is just beginning."[40]

The morning of Monday, March 13, back one week from Europe, he sat in the press section of the Senate caucus room, nursing the remnants of a gastric flu persisting from London, sweating beneath his jacket as the heavy warmth of a Washington spring floated to the high ceiling and seeped into the crimson carpet.

The big room, though chosen for its size, was a hotbox—wall-to-wall people steaming under the klieg lights, VIPs edging against reporters at the long press tables. It was the first full week of the Tydings committee hearings investigating the charges raised by Senator Joseph Raymond McCarthy, Republican of Wisconsin, alleging Communist influence in the State Department. At the front, directly in his line of vision, were the panel of committee members and the burly, energetic figure of McCarthy—a man not much younger than himself, an overnight sensation, playing to a capacity audience and the newsreel cameras; shuffling through a bulging briefcase, swinging treason charges like a sledgehammer, hitting out in all directions as Democrats parried defensively and Republicans waited for another Hiss case.

"After a week in Washington," Murrow wrote to Clark, "I am prepared to refugee back to London. The whole McCarthy business is squalid beyond words."[41]

XI

1950

That spring, he lost his sponsor.

He was broadcasting out of Washington, reporting on what had become a media bonanza for a freshman senator whose name, until four weeks ago, had meant a couple of datelines in the boondocks and a phantom list on which the numbers kept changing—election year stuff, nothing Murrow had paid more than passing attention to.

Five days of hearings and the political fallout, and he'd revised his estimate. "Acheson," he wrote R.T., "is in serious trouble."[1]

The show began the same way every morning: spectators milling about; next the well-timed entrance of McCarthy, to the pop of flashbulbs and the click of camera shutters; then, at ten-thirty precisely, Chairman Millard Tydings (D.-Md.) gaveled the hearing to order.

Up front, congressmen and witnesses squared off at the T-shaped committee table, virtually eyeball to eyeball across a few feet of polished mahogany, with McCarthy generally the focus of attention—naming alleged traitors, beating back rearguard action by committee Democrats, or sitting back uneasily in the section reserved for distinguished visitors, his large head framed by the wall map that dominated the hearing room.

For Murrow, much of the shock of the attacks was personal. These were people he *knew*, institutions he had dealt with, people who'd sat with him on the Emergency Committee,[2] the whole do-good network of his formative years in New York.

The Hearst chain aside, there had been at first no monolithic press rush for the McCarthy bandwagon. Numerous influential columnists, broadcasters, news magazines—not necessarily liberal; Henry Luce's *Life* magazine warned against joining "McCarthy's lynching bee"[3]—were skeptical or downright hostile.

Murrow was therefore in good, indeed substantial company when that spring he took a stand of unequivocal opposition to McCarthy, pointing out over the air that the Senator, whatever noises made, had not produced one shred of evidence to back his claims.

To a listener accusing him of "bias and hypocrisy," Murrow replied that he reported both sides "as adequately as time permitted. . . . If the weight of the public testimony has tended to show that so far, Senator McCarthy's charges are unproven, that is not my responsibility."[4]

True enough. The reports were generally straightforward, carefully detailed, often setting straight a public record mangled in the tabloids, free of the incendiary catchwords marking much of the print and some of the radio coverage; a cooling process that took the heat—and often the wind—out of McCarthy's allegations. Murrow could say with some accuracy, as he did to another listener, that he had "engaged in no editorializing." Yet given the writing, the selection of material, the reading, almost every broadcast was an editorial; it was the standard end run around company restraints on opinion—editorializing through the report itself.

China expert John Stewart Service, hauled before his fourth loyalty board hearing after being fingered by McCarthy, was answering "dead, discredited *and* disproven charges." The words were the State Department's; the emphasis was the broadcaster's.

When Dorothy Kenyon, another target, a scrappy gray-haired New York City judge and former delegate to the UN Commission on the Status of Women, called McCarthy "an unmitigated liar" and flew down to confront her accusers, Murrow described the encounter in words needing no commentary:

" 'Had she advocated lifting the arms embargo in shipments to the Spanish Government?' She had, and she saw nothing wrong with it. . . . 'Had she joined with others in sending greetings to Russian women in 1943?' She had indeed, thought it a good and proper thing to do, and reminded the Senators that . . . Russia was an *ally*, and fighting a great battle at a place near Stalingrad. . . ."[5]

The stress was on vindication. These fine and loyal people couldn't possibly be Communists, the whole emphasis centering on the nastiness of McCarthy and the uprightness of his victims. The man was even *helping* Communists by tearing down the founding fathers of NATO, clearly no way to proceed. "What we are getting, is all the danger and damage of a witch-hunt, without much chance of catching a witch."[6]

Did the witches exist? Murrow believed they did, yet in the next broadcast he could infuriate half his listenership by maintaining that even witches—or alleged witches—were still covered by the Bill of Rights.

The Administration seemed paralyzed, as Murrow found out for himself in those weeks, attending a meeting one night at the home of his friend, the Washington columnist Marquis Childs. Other friends were there as well, among them Walter Lippmann as prime mover, Elmer Davis, Charlie Collingwood, Joe Harsch—plus the embattled Secretary of State, Dean

Acheson. In later years, Lippmann's biographer Ronald Steel was to reveal the details of that evening, of the newsmen's attempts to talk the Secretary into taking on the China Lobby—Chiang Kai-Shek's U.S. supporters, well financed, powerfully connected with the Congressional Right and now fueling McCarthy's drive on the State Department.

The Treasury had the goods on these guys, they told Acheson: the money they made off the drug trade, Congressional appropriations for Chiang funnelled back for PR and political payoffs. It was all there in the Treasury files—the secret operations, the shoddy details. Use it, they argued; discredit the bastards and stop McCarthy in his tracks.

Acheson seemed strangely reluctant, wasn't picking up. Too many prominent Democrats involved, Lippmann later noted.

In the midst of everything came the news of the sudden death in London of Harold Laski, at fifty-six, of bronchial pneumonia, another link severed to the past. Over the air, Murrow mourned the death of the friend who had taken him to task over the BBC for not reading his Hobbes: "Laski was a Socialist. . . . He was a man who believed, with Heywood Broun, that no body-politic is healthy until it begins to itch. . . . His allegiances were fierce, and neutrality was not known to him. . . . More than most professors or pamphleteers, he caused people to think furiously, because he believed that it was only through the exercise of the mind that men could remain free. . . ."[7]

But in Washington, the McCarthy phenomenon and its related tensions continued, all-consuming, attention-grabbing, pervading the atmosphere—just how much so, Murrow learned one afternoon in a crowded elevator, with his family; Janet and Casey had come to Washington for the duration.

A well-meaning grandmotherly type bent down to the little boy, all blond curls and blue-eyed innocence, to ask, Had he been to the playground?

Casey Murrow drew himself up with the dignity of his four-and-a-half years. "I have not," his startled parents heard him reply. "I have spent the day investigating Washington."[8]

The effect on family aside, Murrow worried, on the evening news, about the "McCarthy business" distracting public and media attention from the more important stories, a sort of tunnel-vision setting in that spring. Ambassador-at-Large Philip Jessup, denounced by McCarthy for so-called Communist affinities, had just returned, ironically, from making U.S. commitments to French-backed Emperor Bao Dai of Vietnam. Acheson was announcing the assumption of military aid to the French in Indochina. General Ike Eisenhower, appearing before a Senate panel, voiced "concern" over the extent of U.S. disarmament and urged military and economic assistance "to countries resisting Communism in Asia."[9]

"And now, preposterously," wrote a friend of Murrow's—Harold Isaacs, one of the great Asia correspondents—"the United States Navy is going to fly 80 planes over Viet Nam in order to show the local benighteds that Bao Dai is good for them or else. Or else precisely what? That the next time the bombs will drop? How, precisely, is this going to serve any useful American purpose?"

No one seemed to realize "the full significance of what's been done," Isaacs wrote him. "The McCarthy headlines over the security risks in the State Department make pretty mordant reading when the fact is that the security of the United States is being actually threatened infinitely more by the makers of these policies."[10]

As Acheson, speaking in San Francisco, talked of supporting the "aspirations of the people of Asia for independence," U.S. warships were showing the flag in Saigon Harbor, the ensuing protests leaving three dead and thirty injured. The action was denounced by Murrow, echoing the Isaacs letter, as a high-handed exercise in gunboat diplomacy, redolent of "the colonial struttings of the great powers in the nineteenth century. . . .

"Saigon is a place of which we know little, but it seems to me reasonable to believe, that what we *do* there may have more effect upon opinion in Asia than what we *say* in San Francisco."[11]

Though impressed by arguments of the area's importance ("twenty-five million people. . . . one of the most literate areas in Asia. . . . the rice bowl of that part of the world, [with] coal, iron, tungsten, manganese"), he was by no means convinced that the issues were as clear-cut as State Department spokesmen made them out to be:

> The French have been fighting Ho [Chi Minh], without too much success, for three years. They've got better than a hundred and fifty thousand troops tied up there. . . . Bao Dai, [their] candidate for power, surrendered to, and collaborated with, the Japanese. On the other side is Ho Chi Minh, now recognized by Russia and Mao Tse-tung, communist-trained in Moscow, who led the underground resistance against the Japs during the war. The French admit that the majority of his followers are Nationalists, not Communists, who want to drive out the Europeans. . . .
>   The political and economic stakes are high in this Asiatic contest. . . . And it is a conflict that will *not* be decided by *bombs*. . . .[12]

Speaking off the mike before an educator's group that spring, he called the new commitments "a policy of doubtful wisdom" which "may lead us into a disastrous situation."[13]

In general, however, there was little or no feedback from a public mesmerized by the spectacle of Joe McCarthy.

It was in late April that Murrow received the packet with the photostats with a Charlotte, North Carolina postmark and a desperate appeal from the campaign headquarters of Senator Frank Graham of North Carolina, an old IIE friend, the revered former President of Chapel Hill, a Southern liberal seeking renomination in the teeth of a primary challenge, amply funded, combining red-baiting and racism, and focusing national attention on Murrow's native state.

He recognized the photostats—the cover of the flyer announcing the 1935 summer session of the Moscow State University, "Anglo-American Section," and the inside page listing the National Advisory Council.

"Graham's name appears on the list," ran the covering letter, "as does also yours."[14] Copies were circulating throughout North Carolina in leaflet form as evidence that Graham was a Communist. Would Murrow, they asked, help by going public with the facts of the summer school? "If this group succeeds in defeating Graham by these means in North Carolina, it will show them that they can do likewise in other states. . . ."

Murrow, furious at what was happening, replied that while he refrained as a rule from personal participation in political campaigns, he was "both willing and anxious" to demolish the charges against "my friend Dr. Graham."

He gave them the particulars on the Moscow summer school, authorizing the Graham forces to use his letter "by all means."

Nevertheless, Graham was to go down to defeat that spring, victim of an unholy alliance between prejudice and red-baiting, harbinger of a national trend that would further change the face of Congress in the fall.

Murrow took a week out, in those months, for a flying trip to the West Coast, getting an update on local issues and testing the climate of opinion with regard to "the hysteria" in Washington, as he put it.

Canwell and John Tenney notwithstanding, the answers indicated a calm verging on remoteness. These were the great, healthy, open spaces, editors and reporters assured him, people were into bread-and-butter issues, none of this East Coast stuff. Only in Los Angeles, talking over KNX with Chet Huntley and Nelson Pringle ("two of the best-known news broadcasters on the Coast . . . old friends of mine"), was there any sign of concern, triggered by the current battle over an imposed campus loyalty oath, with protests at Berkeley pitting the faculty against the regents of the University of California.

(The trip also developed its sideshow when Murrow, traveling with a heavy cold, was put finally to bed by Zousmer, given a sleeping pill, the hotel phone put on hold. Awaking the following midday, he recalled, too late, a breakfast meeting set up with Campbell's representatives, unaware of their frantic calls to the hotel. Returned to Washington, he would find his first day back divided between covering the McCarthy hearings and drafting an apology to the infuriated representatives of Campbell Soup.)

Matters started coming to a head that April with the case of Owen Lattimore, Asia scholar, wartime adviser to the government, a former mover in the IPR, now director of the Walter Hines Page School of International Relations at Johns Hopkins University—linchpin of McCarthy's theory of treason and alleged chief architect of the policy that "lost" China.

Murrow, using a more tempered description ("an acknowledged expert on Far Eastern affairs [who] . . . served as President Roosevelt's political contact with Chiang Kai-shek"), read off, in covering the hearings, a Lattimore memorandum that formed the crux of McCarthy's accusations:

> It said, among other things, that we should avoid premature or excessive strategic deployment in the Far East. It said [that] if there is to be a war it can only be won by defeating Russia . . . not Northern Korea, or Vietnam, or China. It urged abandoning further support of Chiang Kai-shek . . . said we should not try to bring trade pressure on the Chinese Communists . . . urged us to withdraw as soon as possible from "entanglements" in South Korea.
>
> Lattimore said and proved that the Senator had not produced a single act or document to support his charges. . . that instead of being the architect of our Asian policy he had been the least consulted of our Far Eastern consultants. . . .
>
> Mr. Lattimore said there already exists in Washington and throughout the country, an atmosphere of intimidation which is rapidly lowering the quality of research work. . . . that charges such as those to which he has been subjected endanger freedom of inquiry; limit the frankness with which scholars and writers would state their own conclusions; damage our own intelligence service.[15]

Lattimore himself later acknowledged his "special debt" to Murrow: "Even when the hysteria was at its height . . . he kept the record straight."[16] The result for Murrow, however, was a step-up in an already heated letter-writing campaign directed at his sponsor.

Enough was happening in those same days, in fact, to show up McCarthy as the heightened agent of the mother virus. The Supreme Court had refused to review the contempt convictions of the Hollywood Ten, leaving standing the lower court decision. Murrow regarded the decision as an abridgment of the First Amendment. ("The [Court] finds itself in disagreement with Justice Holmes who said if there is any principle of the Constitution that more imperatively calls for attachment than any other, it is the principle of free thought.")[17]

Three weeks before, in a first testing of loyalty procedures, the federal appeals court had ruled against Dorothy Bailey, a black government worker who had taken the loyalty board to court following her dismissal on anonymous charges of alleged CP membership.

"She was fired for THINKING *supposed* disloyal thoughts," Murrow bristled. "A Constitution that forbids speech control does not permit *thought* control."[18]

By now the listener mail was pouring into Camden, a virtual explosion from the usual 20 to 30 per week, to upward of 200 a day. ("In his attack on the courts and laws of our country to defend two convicted Hollywood writers, Mr. Morrow [*sic*] not only revealed his own Communistic leanings, but also he showed that his sponsor was putting his money on Un-Americanism.")

The tone was generally the same throughout, likewise the sentiment, as expressed by one listener who wrote that Senator McCarthy was "rendering the country a distinguished service."

Tempers in New York and Camden were stretched to the breaking point, complaint letters forwarded to Murrow with the brusque directive to provide a carbon of his answers "for our guidance in future correspondence."[19]

"I do not regard your replies to these people as exactly a vigorous . . . defense of myself," Murrow responded, "or of the program. You say that the charge [of bias] . . . 'is a serious charge.' What, precisely, is serious about it? We are living in highly emotional and contentious times and such accusations must be expected."[20]

The subtext to the growing clash, however, was the knowledge of what had been happening behind his back, "*the representations,*" as he called them in a rough draft, "*by the Campbell Soup Company to my employers regarding broadcasts I did. . . . I have been apprised of these conversations and I cannot but regard them as coming very near to a withdrawal of confidence. . . . If that should prove to be the case, it would be a matter of minor regret to me. . . .*" The issues were now strictly between New York and Camden, as the ad agency ran for cover. "*I have never regarded my news judgment as infallible, but I am not accustomed to having it questioned in a framework that . . . causes my loyalty and objectivity to be called into question. . . .*"

A good deal of his reaction went into the wastebasket or the dead file, a spilling of his fury till the adrenaline ran out. Reporting on McCarthy took on, if possible, an added edge ("*The Fine Art of Reviling . . .* by an unknown Chinese Scholar. . . . Select a person at least slightly superior to yourself. . . ."[21]; "Senator McCarthy is telling a group of newspaper editors tonight that . . . he knew there would be 'vilification, smear and falsehoods, peddled by the reds, their minions and the egg sucking phoney liberals who litter Washington with their persons and clutter American thinking with their simple-minded arguments.' What would . . . be required before *anyone* can make up his mind, is not argument, profound or simple-minded, but a few *facts!*")[22]

May 2, the taped voice of Owen Lattimore, addressing the Tydings committee, was heard on the program, calling for the rights of American authors "to think, talk and write, freely and honestly" and charging "that the processes of the Senate of the United States have been debased by this man McCarthy . . . that he has lied, distorted and vilified . . . that he has used discreditable and disreputable sources of false information; that he has disgraced his Party and the people of the State and Nation; and that he has grievously prejudiced the interests of our country."

The following week there was a call for Murrow from corporate headquarters in Camden, indicating the sponsor's intention to terminate as of Friday, June 30.

A brief, noncommittal letter followed from the agency, confirming both the phone call and the intention to go off the air. They were sorry "in more ways than one," they said, but were sure Ed understood the problem.

The story given out was ratings. In fact, there had been a poor West Coast showing back in 1949, resulting in huddles that centered on style, not on substance, all aboveboard. By mid-'50, in fact, the Murrow program was outdrawing the competition in the time period, with the exception of *The Lone Ranger*.[23]

There was, however, an extended acrimonious epilogue as Campbell's tried to get the time slot for a music feature. In contrast with the Shirer case, CBS reserved the slot not only for news broadcasts but for the broadcaster—namely, Murrow. Camden threatened to cancel a second show on CBS; Paley still said no.

In one sense, CBS could afford to; the Murrow program was no sinking ship. Quite the contrary, it was doing rather well, one of the highest-rated news shows on the air.[24] But they were also standing up to pressure without a sponsor waiting in the wings.

Frank Stanton, master of statistics, got to work with facts and figures, telling prospective buyers among his corporate contacts how they could reach almost half the radio homes in the country for a mere $7,500 a week. Regional sponsors were lined up in place of the coast-to-coast arrangement, a financial plus for CBS, sparing the discount given to a single sponsor. But it was a slow and complicated process, the last piece falling into place only in the second month of the Korean War. *Edward R. Murrow with the News* never enjoyed national sponsorship again.

For the East Coast, Amoco, a wartime advertiser, had been quickest to pick up the slack, hopping in the weekend after termination. The pressures were to lessen notably, despite Murrow's periodic potshots at the oil depletion allowance. Relations with the agency were better, arrangements more to the newsman's liking. "I am told," he wrote Elmer Davis, "that high octane gas with a dash of soda makes a better drink than soup similarly treated."[25]

On a Monday in mid-June he broadcast on the economy. With two weeks to go, it seemed like easy coasting to July 7, end of the broadcast year and, beyond that, Pawling. The economic picture looked rosy, prospects seen by the experts as pretty good. Just before airtime he gave the script a once-over, then, as often, penciled in a last-minute thought: "If nothing unexpected happens."

Things started happening that Thursday, with the appearance of *Red Channels*, 200 pages thick, the brainchild of American Business Consultants, Inc., now moved to bigger quarters on the land rush success of *Counterattack*. Friday morning, the Hearst papers jumped in (RED INFILTRATION OF TV, RADIO BARED) as *Counterattack* kept up a steady drumbeat—"A copy of *Red Channels* should be in every American home . . . next to the radio or TV set." Among those listed inside, beneath the cover with the red hand clutching at the microphone, were no fewer than six current employees of CBS, including Bob Heller, Alex Kendrick, and Howard K. Smith.

(The *Red Channels* mentality had already penetrated CBS. Bob Shayon, listed in the book, had been abruptly fired the year before, no explanation. A studio director, Betty Todd, had been let go in May after being subpoenaed by HUAC and refusing to answer questions about alleged CP membership. As the story made the papers, a clipping sent anonymously to Frank Stanton, *Counterattack* jumped in with a broadside. Todd was quietly fired in two weeks. The network was evidently ready to back a news star who stood up to McCarthy-generated pressure, but not a middle-level employee who took the Fifth Amendment.)

Then, on Saturday, June 24, 1950, industry reaction was swamped suddenly by other matters as a UP dispatch with a Seoul dateline confirmed the movement southward by the North Korean Army across the thirty-eighth parallel.

All bets were off in the confusing days that followed, amid a hailstorm of agency bulletins punctuating the rush of events that ended with the dispatching of American ground troops to Korea.

Reactions from Europe registered alarm and mixed emotions. Howard Smith in London reported backing by the Labour government "with mental reservations," even the *New Statesman* calling the North Korean action "aggression," the one word *Munich* heard on all sides.

The Murrows had been up at Pawling, entertaining Drew and Estelle Middleton, in from Germany, the two couples making a weekend of it when the news came in.

"We sat and listened to Dulles on the blower," said Middleton later, "and I remember saying to Ed, 'Do you want to go?' And he said, 'No, but I guess I'll have to.' "

Did *he* want to go? Murrow asked him.

No, said the other, but he would if they told him to.

"Then you're all right."

How so?

"Well . . . if this is really what they think it is, then Germany'll be next."[26]

It was indicative of the official thinking of the time—Asia, 1950, viewed through the lenses of Europe, 1938—and of a generation, South Korea seen as a sort of Asian Czechoslovakia, commitments made in the name of collective security seemingly put to the test. Murrow commented: "We were caught in a position where we had to shoot or put down the gun. If we had put it down, our friends and allies would have done likewise, until in due course they would have been awakened in the dark of night by Communist gun butts hammering on the door. . . ."[27]

Aggression had to be checked at the outset, small nations defended. Just as "No more Vietnams" would be the watchword of a later era, the slogan now was, "No more Munichs," the watchword of a generation that had paid for the blunders of its elders, as determined as that of a later time not to repeat the mistakes of the past.

Only a month before, ironically, Murrow had been urging U.S.-Soviet relations to get back on track ("Lost, strayed or stolen/ quantity of goodwill/ last seen vicinity Elbe River, Germany, May 1945/ Reward, no questions asked".)[28] What had happened, at least as viewed on information given, seemed a betrayal, a seeming indication that one couldn't trust the Kremlin, and the broadcasts began their steady drumbeat as the nation mobilized:

> We have reversed our Far Eastern policy, drawn a line, risked a war and committed ourselves beyond the possibility of turning back. . . . This action . . . commits us to much more than the defense of the southern half of the Korean peninsula. We have commitments quite as binding, obligations quite as great, to Indo-China, Iran and Turkey as we have to Korea. We have drawn a line, not across the peninsula, but across the world. We have concluded that Communism has passed beyond the use of subversion to conquer independent nations. . . . And we, for our part, have demonstrated that we are prepared to calculate the risks and face the prospect of war rather than let that happen.[29]

It kept up as U.S. troops were flown to the peninsula—"If southern Korea falls, it is only reasonable to expect . . . that there will be other and bolder ventures"—and as he prepared to leave: "Ten years ago the allies stood in need of our weapons and resources. Now *we* stand in need . . . of their political and moral support. . . ."

Eleven days later the brakes began applying to his personal crusade as he stepped onto a blistering Tokyo runway with William Lawrence of The New York *Times*, to see a dirty, bearded apparition flapping toward them, shouting, arms waving wildly, "Go back, go back, you silly bastards. This ain't our kind of war. This one is for the birds."

It was Bill Downs, transferred to Korea sometime earlier, with what Murrow was to call the best piece of advice he ever ignored.[30]

MacArthur's headquarters, an air-conditioned island in steaming Tokyo, seemed unreal, mimeograph machines grinding out communiqués, the sounds of combat planes taking off for the mainland mixed with those of a dance band, floating over from the nearby officers' club.

In Korea, by contrast, all was confusion, the ill-equipped, ill-trained American and South Korean forces pushed back by the North Koreans to a toehold in the south around Pusan. There was no front line; communications ranged from primitive to nonexistent.

A press camp had been set up at Taegu, some seven to fifteen miles from the shallow, yellow Naktong River, the fallback position, where the outnumbered Americans had been ordered to stand or die. Journalists from twenty-four countries, mostly American, had descended on the small space, from agency reporters in their early twenties to the World War II group who called themselves the Retreads and promised to level anyone threatening to rehash old memories. Murrow made a foursome with Bill Lawrence, Hal Boyle of AP, and Bill Dunn, the big, burly, breezy onetime chief Pacific correspondent for CBS, now covering the action for NBC, "much to Ed's digust," said Dunn afterward.

Army cots, ten to a room, were set up on the second floor of what had been a schoolhouse, the air heavy with the ancient smells of country, DDT, and hole-in-the-ground toilets. A single telephone line linked the correspondents with Tokyo, resulting in a waiting line for connections which, when they functioned, could take up to an hour to get through.

The first days, they were half-sick with heat, dust, and dousings of DDT, the natty newcomers with their pressed uniforms soon worn down to facsimile editions of the earlier arrivals—"the hardest working, dirtiest and most flea-bitten gang of press correspondents," as Walter Simmons of the Chicago *Tribune* put it, "assembled anywhere in recorded history." Radio reporters in addition shouldered twelve-pound battery-operated tape recorders, held in place by straps that itched, stained, and dug in as the day wore on.

For the veterans Korea came like an ax blade between the eyebrows. "It was not like the other wars," said Dunn, himself a veteran of the Pacific. "In other wars you had a pretty good idea of where the enemy was and where *you* were. In Korea you didn't. You just went somewhere and hoped they weren't there."[31] By week two of August 1950, twelve correspondents, ten of them Americans, had been reported killed, wounded, or missing.

They were unprepared, too, for the savagery of what was essentially a civil war, Korean against Korean—"just butchered each other," one man recalled—and by the scorched-earth tactics of the forces retreating before the North Korean advance, villages leveled in the path of retreat to keep the other side from using abandoned buildings as cover.

With Dunn and Lawrence, Murrow watched the rail center of Kumchon evacuated, refugees fleeing what was now fighting ground, pouring southward in a steady stream: "The old women, small children, the blind and the crippled with huge packs carried on their heads. . . . whole villages in the countryside were burning. . . . On the far side of the river, about 500 yards of red fire capped by black smoke rises up to the sky, and hangs a thin curtain in front of a blood-red sun that is dying in the west. We see muzzle flash from a gun in the center of the town. . . ."[32]

The reporters stood on the high ground as the endless columns of refugees snaked past, faces expressionless. Dunn nudged Murrow. "I wonder what in hell they're thinking behind that . . . . . mask."

"You're lucky you don't *know*," Murrow replied. "You don't *wanna* know what they're thinking."[33]

At Pohang he saw the one U.S. operational airstrip abandoned, the result of Army disregard of warnings of an enemy attack, a reinforcement column, breaking through with appalling loss of life, arriving too late.

Murrow watched them come, the weary remnants of a black platoon. "Their helmets and their clothing were pearl grey from the mud of the rice paddies. . . . They had fought, crawled, and scrambled nine miles across country, but they were there. . . ."[34]

It wasn't their kind of war, and it wasn't 1940. He was older, more scared, bolstering his nerve with a mixture of whiskey and water, kept in his canteen and passed around on those occasions when, at forty-two, things were hitting harder than they had at age thirty.

The near-turmoil, however, meant they could go where they wanted when they wanted. The four correspondents, with the combined clout of CBS, NBC, AP, and The New York *Times* behind them, easily commandeered transportation, drivers, even pilots, from commanders eager to accommodate, with the resultant escalation on the odds of getting killed and, as they later agreed, "a very idiotic thing to do."

Driving one day along the Naktong, they found they had driven right past enemy lines when they arrived to a chewing out by the area commander, who called them a bunch of damn fools and they were lucky no one had shot them. Moving, they thought, to safer ground, they ran smack into an oncoming column of Asians carrying red banners. No place to run to. They stopped the jeep. If this was it, so be it. The armed men, approaching, turned out to be members of a South Korean youth movement. They'd adopted the red banner, said Dunn later, because they liked the color. "We had no trouble after that. I'll never forget *that* one, though. Thank God for the youth movement!"

The danger, when it finally arose, turned out to be from their own side.

Hal Boyle was not along the day they set out to meet the 1st Division Marine Brigade, newly arrived and camped northwest of Pusan. A fourth was made by James Hicks, later the distinguished editor of the *Amsterdam News*, then reporting for the Afro-American Press, appearing on the runway as they were boarding a twin-engine Beechcraft. Were they going to meet the marines, and could he come along?

"And Jim'll tell you," Dunn commented later, "that was one of the big mistakes of his life."

Hicks watched bemused as they flew first to Japan to stock up on scotch shipments for the colleagues at the schoolhouse, only then flying back to get themselves a jeep from a local Korean commander. "By this time poor Jim didn't know *what* was going on. All he knew was he'd been to Japan when he wasn't expecting to go to Japan, he wasn't quite sure what was going to happen now. Neither were we."

They started north at twilight with a jeep and driver, plus an armed escort of South Korean troops trundling behind in a flatbed weapons carrier, the two vehicles following the road as night fell, past Korean checkpoints assuring them the marines were just ahead.

They drove blindly until halted suddenly by voices in the darkness. They had found their marines—a nest of kids, demanding to know the password, just off the boat, scared to death by infiltration briefings "that anybody who didn't look like an American was probably a North Korean infiltrator. Of course, our drivers were Koreans; so were the guys in the weapons carrier."

That was only natural, considering they were in Korea, but reason wasn't working very well.

No one knew the password. The reporters offered their credentials. Instead, they were ordered out onto the ink-black road, lined up a yard apart, their hands extended in front of their bodies, an occasional flashlight trained on them. In the dark they heard the unmistakable click of rifle bolts.

A few minutes of rigidity, and a plaintive voice came up from the group of four: "Listen, I'm an old man, I need a smoke."

Permission was given. Then, as the reporter's hand went to his pocket: "Drop that!"

"What's going on here?"

"Shuddup!"

One young voice—apparently the sergeant's—seemed to be running the show. "Don't *anybody* move." No one had.

Murrow made a try. "Son, I'm Edward R. Mur—"

"Shuddup!"

He shut up.

They continued motionless for what seemed like hours, the guns trained on them—three whites and a black who had materialized out of the darkness with a bunch of Asians. Said Lawrence later, "They would not buy the idea that we were Americans."[35] No one spoke. The Koreans watched, silent and no doubt puzzled by the strange behavior of Occidentals.

The feeling among the newsmen was, Any minute now. Just one move.

Somehow Murrow managed to get out a request to talk to their commanding officer. A hurried conference, and a seventeen-year-old stepped forward, informed Murrow shakily that he was his prisoner, and marched him off with a gun in his back. The other three, watching them go, prayed the rifle wouldn't go off in the nervous boy's hands.

Some time and a few false starts later they were reunited at the command post, where the captain, who had recognized Murrow's radio voice, explained that the whole area was on Condition Red and suggested they stay for the night. They assured him that he couldn't get them out at the point of a bayonet.

They camped out on the ground as the mosquitoes buzzed and the camp rang with the sound of "friendly fire," resulting in two deaths, several wounded, and bullet holes made through the tent of the marine commander. "These kids were shooting each other up," said Dunn. "Anything that moved they took a shot at. I was disgusted. *Jesus*, I thought, *if these guys are gonna fight our war for us, we might as well quit now.* Do you know, they went into combat in a matter of days . . . and the minute they were in combat, they became terrific; they knew what they were doing. But I'll tell you: That night, I wouldn't have given you ten cents for the whole United States Marine Corps."[36]

As it happened, their overriding problem in Korea wasn't trigger-happy troops. It wasn't access. Rather, it was getting the story out. The single phone line at Taegu seemed too much a coincidence. Mobile transmitters, so plentiful in World War II, just didn't seem to be forthcoming, making the home folks more dependent for their information on the "communiqué commandos" back in Tokyo, who took their cue from Army briefers.[37]

The problems between the high command and the press had been there from the start—less basic than in Vietnam's later stages, more bitter than in World War II, differences focused largely on tactics, in a war the mainstream press approved in principle. The question was not of policy but how to carry it out.

Even then, complaints emerged from the Army Public Information Office. The press wasn't getting on the team, asked too many questions, interviewed the shell-shocked, followed reports of firing on human decoys—complaints that often touched top correspondents. Scuttlebutt had it that General Douglas MacArthur had gone after CBS to get Murrow out of Korea—unconfirmed, though indicative of the existing atmosphere. Reporters found themselves caught up in a Catch-22, between the Army's denial of formal censorship and its ruling that "unwarranted criticism" of command decisions would not be tolerated. Translated, it meant a one-way ticket back to Tokyo and had correspondents, on pain of expulsion, guessing as to what was or was not "unwarranted." (Within weeks, the 700-member Overseas Press Club would find itself in the anomalous position of actually requesting formal censorship, as preferable to working in the dark under a set of rules known only to God and to the high command.)

In mid-August Murrow left for Japan, en route home for the upcoming broadcast season, due to start in three weeks. The certitudes of June were gone, replaced by the sights and sounds of Korea. At the Correspondents' Club in Tokyo, a colleague stopping at his room retreated quickly when he saw Murrow through the door slightly ajar, slumped at the edge of his cot, his head in his hands; the sound of grinding teeth filled the room.

Early Tuesday morning, in a Tokyo studio, he made his last report from the Far East.

The broadcast was made in an atmosphere of growing friction. Two wire reporters had been expelled from Korea. The Sunday before, Bill Lawrence had delivered a blistering challenge to the Army criticism ruling on page one of The New York *Times*. Sharing front-page space was a report on the President's Voice of America message to the Associated States of Indochina, offering economic aid and military aid "to provide the internal security for a vigorous, healthy and prosperous life in Vietnam, Laos and Cambodia."[38]

The Lawrence story got through; the *Times* wasn't licensed by the government. The Murrow story did not; the public never heard it.

In New York it was still Monday, August 14, late afternoon. The broadcast was being recorded for playback on the 7:45 P.M. news.

"This is a most difficult broadcast to do," he began. He had never believed, he said, in correspondents' engaging in criticism while a battle was in progress, but "the question now arises whether serious mistakes have been made."

It began as a military comment—an indictment of the top command decisions that had decreed a meaningless offensive in the south, starved vital defenses, cost innumerable lives. "Experienced officers . . . called it folly. . . . This was not a decision that was forced upon us by the enemy. Our high command took it because, in the words of one officer who was in a position to know—'We decided we needed a victory.' "

Commanders he had talked to predicted another six months of hard fighting, given greater troop strength and "assuming that the Chinese Communist troops and Russian air do not join the battle."

> And yet correspondents here have received cables from their home offices indicating that air-conditioned sources in Washington think the thing can be wound up this fall. To paraphrase the GIs in Korea—that ain't the way it looks from here.
> So far as this reporter is concerned, he doesn't see where or when this conflict will end. For this is not an isolated war, except in the purely geographical sense. It is isolated only for the men who are fighting it. . . .[39]

In the newsroom at 485, Ted Church took one look at the Murrow transcript, just in off the teletype, and rushed the copy to the office of Ed Chester, Director of News for CBS.

"I am aware," the transcript continued, "that some of the things I have said may have violated directives from general headquarters, particularly in quoting officers who believe that we paid too high a price for that southern offensive. I have not identified them because no reporter knowingly embarrasses generals or sergeants with their superiors. It is my personal opinion, for what it is worth, that we shall stay on that peninsula. The stuff is there, and the troops have the heart."

> But when we start moving up through dead valleys, through villages to which we have put the torch by retreating, what then of the people who live there? They have lived on the knife edge of despair and disaster for centuries. Their pitiful possessions have been consumed in the flames of war. Will our reoccupation of that flea-bitten land lessen, or increase, the attraction of Communism?

Chester gathered up the copy. He was taking it upstairs, he said; there might be "legal aspects" to this.[40]

Within minutes the transcript was on its way to 20 for a top-level conference that included the CBS President and the Chairman of the Board. Sometime later Chester came back to the waiting Murrow staff: "It's killed." The reasons: The piece gave comfort to the enemy, could be used as propaganda by Radio Moscow; Murrow's sources might be unreliable; it was "unfair" to criticize those quoted as being in air-conditioned offices. Ed was probably tired, probably wouldn't even have written that piece if he had been home to reflect. . . .

Zousmer and LeSueur, sitting in for Murrow, protested: Ed knew, out there, who was reliable and talking sense. Besides, how could the piece help the enemy? *They* knew what was going on. As for the quote legal aspects, who was going to sue—the North Koreans?

By now it was an hour and a half before airtime. The kill order would gouge an eight-minute hole in the newscast. Would they reconsider—make some cuts? The answer was no. Chester went upstairs again and promptly came down: "The kill order stands." No one was to contact Murrow in the time remaining or, for that matter, anyone else in Tokyo.

That still left the eight-minute gap. Could they substitute a cable from Costello, they asked, dealing with intelligence reports? Chester scanned the first line. "No, it's killed."

Who would be the one to tell Murrow? Paley told Chester to do it. Chester said Paley ought to do it. The Murrow people finally said *they'd* do it. No one objected.[41]

Murrow, returning, learned that he'd been blacked out on his own show.

As late as 1981, the recollection of the blowup that followed would still be an emotional sore spot for William Paley, a highly charged personal collision that he didn't like discussing. Murrow, getting the background from his staff, learned that in addition to his broadcast, three cables had been killed altogether, including one by Bill Downs dealing, ironically, with MacArthur's censorship. According to one colleague, Murrow thought seriously of resigning.

He did not, of course, resign; he did not go public. The incident, however, had no problem leaking out. As the 700 correspondents of the Overseas Press Club cabled their protests to MacArthur, *Newsweek* broke the CBS story, stating: "Murrow's stormy objections brought the censorship problem to a head in the network's newsroom and for other Americans trying to report the war in Korea." The accompanying photo showed the broadcaster, suitably grim, below it the dramatic caption *"Murrow: Censorship started at home."*[42]

It was in the same period that there occurred a meeting later recalled only faintly by a few, not at all by Paley, vividly by Joe Wershba, who had wondered at the time why he was there.

The scene, said Wershba later, was the Waldorf—a private dining room, a correspondents' luncheon, all the big names at CBS, the news stars. Wershba was there with his boss, Ted Church.

The lunch consumed, said Wershba, Paley got up. "He began to chatter about these being difficult times, we had to be careful of what we say et cetera. Murrow was just glowering. He turned black—his face was black. Paley sat down. No one said anything."

The young Washington reporter, mellow with food and drink, got to his feet, thanked for the meal, in effect called the Chairman to account— these people were the soul of the corporation; you couldn't order them around, propitiate everybody—then sat down, figuring he'd lost his job. Instead, there was seconding from around the room.

Next day, the company grapevine had it that the meeting had been called for Murrow's benefit. "He was in trouble with MacArthur; you know the technique of these meetings—begin everything couched in pleasantries, then lead up to 'Don't make waves.' This was autumn 1950. The loyalty oath was coming up. The meeting had been called to rebuke Murrow, we heard, and let everyone else know: 'Fellas, don't make trouble for us.' "[43]

Murrow's feelings about Korea would remain divided. In a return broadcast that startled many for its candor, he told the audience flat-out that the Communists had "captured and channelled the surging desire for change, the resentment of foreign domination" among Asia's miserable millions; "they talk the language of Asia's aspirations." He explained why East and West spoke different languages, in telling of the propaganda fallout in the bombing of a factory ("The people of Asia regard [it] as something which lightens their load just a little. . . . It has taken decades to build. . . . They feel a sort of part ownership. . . . In Asia there is no greater crime than to destroy a man's rice bowl, and the factory is regarded as a kind of big community rice bowl").[44] Unusual language for network listeners in 1950, though not necessarily espousal of the other side. It was simply up to us to learn the language, the better to win friends and keep the Russians from dominating them. At the same time it was indicative of the push given by Korea to the political pendulum: that anything explaining why any masses might be drawn to Communism—no matter what the context—was now seen as the height of flaming liberalism, if not downright espousal of the Moscow line.

For Murrow, one thing was certain: The experience in Asia, brief as it was, had sent him back to the caution of early 1950 and a permanent ambivalence about the feasibility, if not the motive, of drawing a line across the world—a dichotomy between the idea, as he saw it, of helping the little guy out there in Asia against the Communist "enemy," and the horsesense which told him that the U.S. had bitten off more than it could chew; that even America had not the strength for global policing.

For this country to become involved in a land war in Asia was "unthinkable," he told an interviewer that winter as UN troops raced to the Yalu River and the Chinese made their first appearance. "If we decide, as we did three years ago, that Europe is our primary interest, and that militarily Korea is of no importance, then there is no reason why we should not pull out of Korea lock, stock and barrel."[45]

Speaking in Birmingham that winter as UN troops retreated before the Chinese, he urged that the United States not be led into a war with China, that the U.S. Navy do a Dunkirk: Line up everybody at the narrow waist of Korea, get out the ships, and take them home.

The atmosphere had changed, the hostilities in Asia no longer a "police action." Murrow himself was suddenly, infinitely tired. "Korea," he wrote a colleague, "was just plain hell and convinced me that I have become an old man."[46]

In the past ten months he had been fighting McCarthy, fighting the Korean War, fighting MacArthur, and—most painful—fighting Paley. He had jumped from the cauldron of Korea back to the pressure cooker of the new broadcast year without a break, without vacation, and he was exhausted.

The country was at war. House Speaker Joseph Martin (R-Mass) was calling for tougher antisubversion measures, arguing that there was no logic in waging war in Korea while allowing Communists "free rein" at home. Joe McCarthy's speaking schedule had made a quantum jump. New battles were heating up, and Murrow was worn down.

Ironically, the war had sent his value up, with another quantum jump in the size of audiences for news and a new element in the mix: television. Little figures on a little screen showed newsreel footage, talked about the war with maps and pointers, unable to compete as yet with radio. *Newsweek* called the medium "a backward country cousin."

But the tiny screen had moving pictures. The year before, the 7:30 TV evening news with Douglas Edwards had received the ultimate industry imprimatur: commercial sponsorship. For CBS the future was taking shape in the maze of cables, corridors, and studios set up above Grand Central Terminal—the 700,000-cubic-foot complex described to the stockholders as "the nation's largest television studio plant."[47]

It was a haunt that Murrow avoided and had no wish to know.

That winter he heard from a staff man in Washington, the CBS correspondent Gunnar Back, writing of his decision to stay with radio, and a new program he was starting. Murrow, sending his congratulations, wished him luck, hoped his sponsors would be rich and tolerant, and ended with a fervent wish for the year ahead: "that neither one of us has to try to make a living in television."[48]

XII

See It Now

1.

"He was our leader—the boss—we was all his camp followers!" Thus Charles Mack in the summer of 1973, dean of the first generation of CBS cameramen, big, blunt, and barrel-chested with white, tightly curling hair, talking of the 1950s over coffee in the Howard Johnson's at the Washington-Bethesda district line.

He had been in his late forties, a savvy newsreel veteran, when CBS contracted for camera and production personnel from Hearst Metrotone for the new Murrow show. Charlie Mack remembered being not at all impressed, not after half a lifetime filming in Washington, going back to the days of the fireside chats and FDR chatting in the breaks as cameramen reloaded, practicing insiders' jargon, swiveling invariably in his direction—"Shift and mix, eh, Charlie?"

His new boss, at first meeting, came across as "uppity," standing taciturnly, chin down, hardly speaking, in that fancy double-breasted suit that made him look like some British MP, not a newsman. Mack didn't think they would get along, and he wasn't too crazy about this television thing either.[1]

On New York's Ninth Avenue, Mili Lerner, later Mili Bonsignori, an editor of feature films, had been eking out a dry spell cutting segments for a Betty Crocker program when a little man sharing her coffee in the corridor, one August day in 1951, turned out to be the near-legendary Gene Milford, editor of *Lost Horizons*, scouting talent. Was she interested in work at CBS—a half-hour show, just a pilot, but good for six weeks at least. She figured it was worth a try.[2]

At Barbetta's in the theater district, then a favored parmigiana emporium for film folk, Palmer Williams, an independent producer who had

351

worked with Pare Lorentz and Frank Capra, marched up to the front table where Bill Montague of Hearst held daily court.

"What's going on in town, Bill?"

"We-ell, we got this crazy deal with CBS. . . ."

Murrow and a fellow named Friendly were starting up a television program, he explained, "and they need somebody like you 'cause these guys don't know from left field about *film*. Why'ncha go see them?"

Williams, a former Greenwich Village neighbor of Jap Gude, had had some contact with Friendly over an idea he had to convert *I Can Hear It Now* to television. (The stuff obviously came from newsreel sound tracks; why not use the film, do a picture history? Nothing happened.)

Why not indeed? thought Williams.[3]

They assembled in September 1951: newsreel crews; feature film editors unlearning habits made in Hollywood; two CBS reporters—Joe Wershba and Edmund "Ed" Scott—who had never worked with cameras; and two producers who knew sound tape but not film. ("Well, what can you *do* for me?" Friendly had asked of Williams, who proceeded to explain why film production needed a production manager.)

To the new staffers, their two bosses seemed the odd couple: the younger one, a breezy giant, excited and voluble; the elder, tall and gaunt, seemingly detached, drawing audibly on a cigarette while the other did the talking. "Mr. Murrow would like to be called Ed," Bonsignori remembered being told afterward, "because we'll all be working together."[4] It was some time before she could get herself to do it.

As far as CBS was concerned, it was all set; releases confidently promised "personal interviews, overseas reports, biographical features, human interest stories, documentary features. . . . [*See It Now*] projects into the medium of sight and sound the Murrow-Friendly technique of presenting the news. . . ."[5] Fine. But first they had to get it on the tube. In Friendly, however, they had one of the fastest learners in the business.

By 1950, Fred W. Friendly had parlayed a nose for news, unerring sense of showmanship, energy, ideas, and, of course, the Murrow linkup into a thriving career as a packager and producer for NBC Radio (billed in its publicity as "the writer and editor of *I Can Hear It Now*")[6] and one of its most versatile commodities. He was creator at once of the acclaimed four-part series on nuclear weaponry *The Quick and the Dead*, released the first summer of Korea, and of the breezy panel show *Who Said That?*, where news personalities identified quotes from the week's top stories— a commercial success, pushed by both NBC and the critics as the thinking listener's entertainment.

He posed the perfect combination, therefore—adroit at handling both cosmic issues and the demands of show biz, with just the right touch of what NBC called "class appeal."[7] Enough to enable his NBC superiors to look past a cheekiness bordering at times on nail-file abrasive.

"It was my idea to bring Friendly to CBS," said Jap Gude later. "Fred

and I had talked about it. He and Murrow by this time were good friends."
As it happened, Volume II of *I Can Hear It Now* had just followed the
best-selling Volume I. What more natural thing than to extend the partnership to radio? Gude hied himself to Sig Mickelson, Public Affairs
Director at 485, and suggested that the successful young producer join
the payroll. "He knew by then about Fred's reputation."[8]

As Mickelson told the story, Stanton and Paley, dissatisfied with the
traditional radio-drama treatment of the CBS documentaries, had asked
him in those months for suggestions on upgrading, in response to which
he wrote a memorandum recommending "taped actualities" in lieu of the
old "fictionalized" approach, and was promptly asked to 20.

"So I went up to see them, and they said, 'Well, of course, this is the
right direction to go, but who's going to produce?' I had to think very
quickly."

Well, he recalled saying, there was this young fellow over at NBC
named Fred Friendly, who had parlayed both Bob Hope and William L.
Laurence of The New York *Times* into a team in that series on the atom.
Judging by the success of that series, they ought to go get Friendly.

But *The Quick and the Dead* was largely in the old style. "Taped
actualities" really meant the format of *I Can Hear It Now*, a big earner
for Columbia and one that made Friendly, or rather Murrow-Friendly,
a known quantity and a most attractive prospect now that the folks out
there had started listening to news again.

Murrow was in Korea. Mickelson called Friendly on his own; over a
Chinese meal on Fifty-first Street they "decided that this was an entirely
workable solution," and sealed the deal with a nightcap at the old Ritz
bar. Friendly said he wanted to do a *Life* magazine of the air. "But we
obviously weren't ready for that yet, so we agreed that what we ought to
do, to start, was a season of one-hour radio documentaries on a weekly
basis—sort of a newsreel by tape." *I Can Hear It Now*, said Mickelson,
was shortened to *Hear It Now*, "and in the meantime, Ed came back
from Korea."[9]

A pilot of sorts was sitting in the mothballs. *Sunday with Murrow*, a
weekly news review using "taped actualities," had been auditioned back
in 1948, then shelved for lack of takers at the time. Unlike the projected
radio newsreel, however, *Sunday with Murrow* had included a long commentary on the prevailing fearful atmosphere and the trend toward guilt
by association.

They took the air for six months over radio, beginning late December
1950, and did well as expected. Unlike its TV successor, the program
included radio columnists: Red Barber on sports; Abe Burrows on the
entertainment world; Don Hollenbeck on the press. Virgil Thomson's
original score set the stamp on the series' image as a class act. "Of course
Fred was getting ready to produce the television version," said Mickelson.[10] Murrow was writing Gunnar Back of his fervent hope not to have

to make a living in TV. But that was where the power was, a fact obvious as far back as prewar London, when he had turned on his BBC set, with the little green screen, for Sevareid: "That's television—that's the future, my friend."

Wary or not, he knew as a communicator that it was the way to go, his wariness stemming not from disdain but from distrust. Far from underestimating television, he recognized its power all too clearly and had, in fact, sketched out an article for the *Atlantic Monthly* in early 1949, after the elections—never completed, despite editor Edward Weeks's entreaties—posing basic questions:

> Will people turn to television rather than to print to find out what is going on in the world? . . . This is a visual medium . . where editorial judgment has been largely pictorial. . . . Problem of mobility. . . . Editorial control . . who decides . . need for marriage between newsman and director . . Instance Alabama delegation at convention . . . Problems of privacy . . . Editorializing by pictorial selection. What lends self to pictorial treatment when most news is made up of what happens in mens [*sic*] minds as reflected in what comes out of their mouths. And how do you put that in pictures? . . . Need for television to recognize limitation of medium . . . danger of ad lib camera . . need for sifting and sorting through mind to avert distortion . . . .

At the end, under "Prediction," he asked, "Will TV regard news as anything more than a saleable commodity? . . . Will they control it or abdicate like AM [radio]? . . . Financial pressures may induce servility by operators . . . need to argue this out before patterns become set and we all begin to see pictures of our country and the world that just aren't true."[11]

At 3:30 on a Sunday afternoon, November 18, 1951, it was his turn before the cameras.

From the opening seconds, it was clear that *See It Now* would be more than televised newsreels or radio with pictures. Images and voices came at the viewers in a shifting kaleidoscope of sight and sound; cue channel talk let the audience in on preparations—San Francisco calling in; Murrow talking with San Francisco—music up again, and they were on.

Murrow looked into the camera, no longer a disembodied voice: "This is an old team, trying to learn a new trade." He was speaking, as the announcer said, from the control room of Studio 41; behind him, in full view of the camera, were the very tools of telecasting—the controls; monitors; cameras one and two.

He was genial, informal, a little nervous at first, a little anxious to please. Then he settled gradually into the pace as though it were second nature—"My purpose will be not to get into your light any more than I

354

have to, to lean over the cameraman's shoulder occasionally and say a word"[12]—a cool host suited to a cool medium.

Of that first half hour, which included footage from London, Paris, and Korea, the moment that remained enshrined in TV history, immortalized in countless kinescopes run in countless communications schools, would be Murrow looking at two TV monitors, each carrying respectively a live transmission from New York Harbor and the Golden Gate, the on-site cameras panning the eastern and western skylines at his instruction. It was the first time two coasts could see each other simultaneously, thanks to the microwave relay system set up that October, which made possible the instantaneous transmittal of images, both ways, across the country. Suddenly viewers could look into the small glass rectangle and see what was actually happening 3,000 miles away, even if what was happening was an ocean lying there, doing nothing. No matter; it was real, not a movie, and to audiences of the time, near-miraculous. "Three thousand miles," one critic wrote, "compressed to the vanishing point. . . . This was television."[13]

The rest of the show was fast-paced, alternately irreverent and serious, filmed and live. Howard Smith, in Paris, talked of UN disarmament proposals and a brief "peace scare." Winston Churchill spoke at London's Guildhall. Eric Sevareid answered questions from Washington. At a Republican fund-raiser candidate Robert Taft sat through a fulsome introduction by his colleague Everett Dirksen, the camera fixed not on the speaker but on Taft's enraptured face.

It closed with the Korea footage, totally unlike the combat shots that provided the standard fare of the evening news strips. "We wanted to see the faces, hear the voices. . . ."

The cameras spent a day and night with Fox Company, 19th Regiment, 24th Infantry Division. The daily round, the talk, the waiting, Murrow's scattered comments on the voice-over ("Yesterday it was hot, today it's cold . . . the water is treated by Halizone tablets; it's supposed to chase the bugs away. . . . The food is plentiful but as mixed up as the negotiators . . . a quiet sector of the line but a guy *could* get killed . . .").

It marked a sharp break with the newsreel tradition, the war in close focus, shot to the dimensions of the little screen. ("If I was *you*," a dogface told correspondent Robert Pierpoint at an advance position, "I'd get the hell out and start diggin' me a hole.")

At the end the soldiers gave their names and hometowns, then moved out as orders filtered down to take a hill and a pin was moved on a map. Murrow, back on camera, listed the casualties taken since. "They may need some blood. Can you spare a pint?"

"The first Korea picture report that actually brought the war home to us," wrote one critic next day, part of the virtual flood of accolades greeting the Murrow-Friendly TV debut.

"Sunday was a milestone in history," Elmer Davis wrote Murrow, "the first time I voluntarily turned on a television program. . . . I imagine you are going to have to scrabble around pretty hard to find material to keep it up to that level. . . ." Joseph Barnes, the talented former foreign editor of the *Herald Tribune* and a wartime friend, called it "the best job of reporting I have ever seen in my life." Norman Corwin, off in Hollywood, said he couldn't remember a half hour "that has made the belly of the cathode tube so powerfully absorbing every second of the way."[14]

Murrow gratefully acknowledged the master's letter and asked for comments—if it wasn't too much trouble. "They will be most carefully studied, not only by me, but by my colleagues."[15]

Critics praised the program's honesty, pace, informativeness, innovation. The television critic Merrill Panitt, then reviewing for the Philadelphia *Inquirer*, recalled TV ads promising "the world at your fingertips."

"It's been a long time a-comin', but we're beginning to See It Now."[16]

Miraculously, the results had shown, and not the effort. The control-room-as-studio idea meant extra heat and overcrowding—a producer's nightmare, yet undeniably effective on the tube. In one later version, it was Don Hewitt, the boy genius producer-director of the Douglas Edwards news, who had first suggested it when asked by Friendly: Where would *he* do the broadcast? ("Friendly may deny it was my idea," says Hewitt today, "but I tell you it *was*.") He became their director.

The camera angle was wrong, said Mili after the opening, made Murrow look short and squat. Hewitt got a frantic call from CBS maintenance: Fred wanted to dismantle the announce booth in the control room. Friendly, dialed hastily, confirmed; he wanted the precise angle on Murrow, he said. But they could get ninety-nine percent of it right now! Hewitt insisted. Was there a *one* percent difference? asked Friendly. Well, yes. "Then I want it down." Hewitt, entering the control room that afternoon, found a workman with a sledgehammer, demolishing the booth.

Murrow hated everything about television. The mike fright that beset him in radio intensified before the camera. The hot lamps exacerbated his nervous sweats, and the head-on lighting made him want to squint. His makeup ran. He needed coaching and the nonstop chain of cigarettes to get him past the nervous gesticulation that didn't matter on the radio, and the machine-gun jogging of his right knee.

"It's God's truth," he replied to a *Variety* request for copy that December, "that I don't know enough about TV reporting to write a piece on it. . . . In six months or a year I may learn enough about this medium to commit something to print on the subject. But right now I find that half the time I don't know what I'm doing, and the other half the thing doesn't come out the way I expected it to."[17]

It was a crazy quilt of improvisation—live TV and film, sound film and quarter-inch tape, film flown in from God knew where, impossible deadlines, no backup copies, no precedent, everything done virtually down to the last minute. That first evening no one had known if it even worked. Janet Murrow, watching at home, had thought it all a big mistake. The two partners suspected the same. Palmer Williams had dashed home to watch the opening shot on his TV set, looked at the two oceans, and thought, *So what?* He staggered to bed that evening in a state of near collapse. Next morning he told his wife he'd have to start looking for another job.

"But I thought this was supposed to come out weekly," she said.

Well, yes, but now they'd see how tough it was—those endless hours, around the clock. My God, this couldn't last. Why, it would *kill* a person to keep this up week after week.

"And of course," Williams later recalled, "we kept on killing ourselves and kept on doing it. And I think it was a year, or a year and a half later, when I was in the can one time, and Murrow comes in and parks in the next urinal, and he looks over at me with a baleful eye and says, 'And *you*, you son of a bitch, *you* knew how hard this was gonna be. Goddammit! I suppose if you'd ever told us, we never woulda gone ahead with it.'"

Says Williams: "I always treasured that conversation."[18]

The first *See It Now* was on sustaining, a purely temporary situation thanks to an embattled corporation's need for good PR. The Aluminum Company of America, emerging from a lost antitrust suit, wanted an image brightener, and a Murrow news show seemed to fill the bill.

According to one of many stories, the series was still in the planning stage, a meeting arranged between producers and sponsors, when one of the ALCOA executives supposedly spoke up: "Mr. Murrow, just what *are* your politics?"

"Gentlemen," the broadcaster supposedly replied, "that is none of your business."

In any case, the agreement was, hands off program content; you do the programs, we'll make the aluminum. ALCOA needed Murrow more than Murrow needed ALCOA. He was a national figure, almost a national emblem. He was also presumably safe. Indeed, there was little in Murrow's "politics," the fall of 1951, that would have troubled any major corporation. The fact was, his entry into television had coincided with a low point in his life, his health, his outlook and output.

The battles of 1950 had been followed by a marked winding down that saw outspokenness replaced by caution, skepticism by rigidity. The summer in Korea had been succeeded by a disastrous fall and winter, and in January, he had to stop broadcasting. Whatever the reasons—his health, a cold war turned hot, four years nightly on the barricades—the fighter of 1950 seemed to have lost his will to fight.

There were no more comments on McCarthy, his allies in the House and Senate, or the new rounds of hearings multiplying in the wartime atmosphere of 1951. On those cases that would be among the bench marks of the times—the new Hollywood hearings, the Remington case, the Rosenberg case—he remained the straight, detached reporter; there were no more commentaries or questionings of justice. Indeed, on the Rosenbergs, he would go so far as to approve the final refusal of presidential clemency, convinced, despite initial reservations, that the government had proved its case, and if there was a penalty, so be it.

By the spring of 1951 the war had formed the background to everything else: If U.S. armed strength was inadequate, then the answer was a buildup—if not for global policing, then for one's allies; if not for Asia, then for Europe. As with so many of his generation, the Korean war had swept away the final traces of nostalgia for the "gallant Russian ally."

It was the mood of the country. In Washington, both the Senate Foreign Relations and the Senate Armed Services Committees, recommending seven-and-a-half billion dollars to arm America's allies, declared the public and the Congress "almost unanimous" in feeling that "Soviet communism" was the principal threat to world peace. Four leading Senate Democrats on the Foreign Relations Committee—Brien McMahon, William Green, John Sparkman, and William Fulbright—were quoted as saying it was more important to balance the Kremlin's power and win, than balance the budget and lose; and they would fight for the full eight-and-a-half billion requested by the Truman administration.

That spring Murrow broke his long-standing rule against lending his name to organizations, when he joined the Committee on the Present Danger—billed as private and nonpartisan, but composed of men prominent in the revolving-door dynamic between government and the private sector, headed jointly by James Conant, President of Harvard, and Tracy Vorhees, Undersecretary of the Army. The roster ran the gamut from Rooseveltian liberals to the more strident anticommunism of Father Edmund Walsh of Georgetown University, though it was weighted heavily with college presidents, writers, scientists, liberal lawyers—names like those of Conant, Samuel Rosenman, Vannevar Bush, apostles of preparedness, old allies from the lend-lease days in London, 1941, who, like Murrow, considered Europe America's area of primary concern.

The group, while rejecting calls for "preventive war," advocated a further arms buildup against "the Soviet menace,"[19] universal military service, support of the United Nations, and unilateral presidential authority to commit troops overseas. The decision to join was in itself symptomatic of Murrow's new position, for in 1947, he had declined to lend his name and prestige to a similar organization. (Or to lend airtime; Conant and Bush both appeared as spokesmen for the CPD with Murrow over CBS. Despite disclaimers over using the microphone as a "privileged pulpit," it was, in fact, being so used already, pushing a consensus point of view.)

At the same time, Murrow was active in a local group to keep the left-wing magazine, the *Nation* from being pulled off library shelves in New York City public schools, a contradiction increasingly endemic to the times: fighting the cold war abroad while coping with its side effects at home. Inevitably, too, the contradictions surfaced on the air in those months, the split between skeptic and Manichaean frequently manifested on the same broadcast, sometimes in the same piece. One night he had started with a hard-nosed defense of the administration and the joint chiefs for holding out against a rising chorus of "Bomb China" in the wake of the MacArthur firing: "It *could* be that they were all wrong in declining to take action that might lead to unlimited war in Asia. . . . Maybe the Russians *wouldn't* have moved if we had bombed . . and landed Chiang Kai-shek's troops (if they were *willing* to land). . . . Not even General MacArthur has always been right . . . because he didn't believe the Chinese Communists would intervene when he sent his columns driving up toward the Yalu with their flanks hanging in the air. . . ."

It was then the skeptic abdicated, suddenly in mid-script, and the crusader took over, going on about "the shadow of the malignant force that threatens to determine the fate and future of all of us. To meet and hold that force in check is our duty and our destiny. . . ."[20]

The broadcast over, at what prompting none could guess, he took a pencil and printed at the bottom: "Sir you sounded like an ass."[21]

At the same time he continued, in the face of overt U.S.-Chinese hostilities, to push for normalization of relations between Washington and Peking, pinning the confrontation at the Yalu on the lack of diplomatic contact and concomitant misreading of Chinese objections. In February 1951, as Americans retreated southward before Chinese troops in Korea and large portions of the press drummed on about the "yellow peril," he gave his commentary over to that day's New York *Times* story by British journalist Arthur Moore, returned from the Chinese mainland:

"He says, 'For the first time . . . prices are stable. For the first time, public opinion regards the "squeeze" as morally wrong. For the first time, soldiers learn that they are protectors and servants of the public, and *not* masters. . . .' This is not the usual picture we get about conditions in China. . . ."[22]

He criticized the U.S. government for refusing exploratory talks with the Chinese and gave broad play to Indian Prime Minister Jawaharlal Nehru's stricture's on American efforts at a UN vote naming China the aggressor. "Mr. Nehru says, 'There is still an attempt to treat the great nations of Asia in the old way.' He thinks the crossing of the 38th Parallel in Korea was a major mistake. . . .

"We may eventually be able to get the necessary votes. . . . But surely we have now had enough experience to realize that votes at the United Nations do not change the realities of power, or position."[23]

Similarly, he continued to speak out on the tightening national security lid, and when in late 1951, an executive order decreed security officers for every government department, with absolute power to start classifying documents, he went after it in broadcast after broadcast.

> Mr. Truman "hopes" that this . . . will "increase" the "flow of news." Every precedent indicates that it will do exactly the opposite. . . . This executive order makes possible—indeed, it invites—the extension of secrecy into vast areas where, by no stretch of the imagination would legitimate security interests be involved.
>
> Loss of freedom and the suppression of information generally come gradually. . . . And it is my personal view that if those who purvey and those who receive information about our government do not protest, . . . we will have lost—without battle—something that we have heretofore regarded as rather important.[24]

He contested House Speaker Sam Rayburn's ban on microphones and cameras at open committee hearings and blasted the announced House investigations into alleged "crime and immorality in the media": "There is material on radio, television and in print that is an offense to both the eye and ear. . . . But . . . when Congress attempts to legislate on matters of taste . . . then it is only another short step to increasing controls over what the individual may say. . . . What is required is more information, more widely spread, regarding what our *government* is doing, and that is the thing that is in danger."[25]

With Richard Salant, then a bright young lawyer from Ralph Colin's firm, soon to join CBS, he dreamed up a scheme for sneaking a small mike into committee hearings, concealed in a briefcase. "We had fun working it out," said Salant later, "then the more conservative lawyers discouraged it."[26]

But Murrow's performance was erratic, his schedule spotty, with every indication, despite a deceptively busy public appearance schedule, of incipient burnout.

The physical symptoms had started showing up the first winter of the 1950s, the familiar pattern of sporadic illness—shortness of breath, general debility, and heavy coughing made worse by heavy smoking; and by the refusal, possibly the inability, to know when to stop. David Lilienthal, stopping by Murrow's office in early January 1951, found Sevareid midway through delivering a lecture over what he called Ed's "show must go on" attitude and didn't he know how this was worrying his friends?[27]

Roz and Bill Downs stopped off at the Murrows' new Park Avenue apartment, moved into just that fall. Janet and Casey were off on a brief trip, and Roz Downs saw something that gave her pause; she had reared three children after all.

"You've got a fever."

Nonsense, Murrow insisted.

She made him take his temperature. It was 103 degrees.

When forced, he took breaks, unwillingly, restless at his grounding.

Marietta Tree recalled him at her place in Barbados, an uncomfortable, asocial guest, "standing in the water up to his knees—he couldn't swim—throwing a ball to his little boy," then disappearing to his room, throwing himself on the bed—"feeling perfectly ghastly," she remembered—remaining secluded with an Agatha Christie thriller until suppertime.

Too much of the radio program routine was being followed almost by rote, pointing up among other factors the fallacy of trying to cover, in twelve minutes, a world growing daily more complex, and of being the studio commentator expected to display expertise on every conceivable subject—the war, financial scandals in the Truman administration, inflation, congressional wrangling over wage and price controls, committing troops to Europe, and containing the fighting; not to mention Britain and Egypt tangling over Suez, France hanging on to its empire in North Africa and Southeast Asia, hostilities in the Middle East, and Iran trying to kick out the British oil companies.

A friend wrote from Paris, scouting talent for UNESCO. Could Murrow recommend "a good liberal English journalist"?

"The way I feel right now," came the answer, "I am tempted to ask if you would settle for a confused American broadcaster."

But it was precisely in those months—particularly the weeks before his departure from the air—that the fifties began taking shape at the network.

In late December 1950, CBS instituted the in-house questionnaire soon known in the business as the loyalty oath—i.e., Are you now or have you ever been? If so, explain and sign. The Attorney General's list was attached for reference. Cynics saw it as a PR ploy for *Counterattack*'s favorite target in the media. Civil liberties groups were horrified. The Authors' League protested.

Mike Bessie, by then an editor at Harper Brothers (and cousin of the Hollywood Ten writer Alvah Bessie), remembered a grueling session at the apartment of his father-in-law, lawyer Morris Ernst, a session lasting into the night as both men worked on Murrow to oppose the move. Said Bessie: "Morris and I tried to persuade Ed that if *he* signed the loyalty oath, the lesser people would have to do so."

There were no two ways about the argument: This was preposterous—the CBS people weren't involved with national security secrets—it was "inappropriate" for CBS to be asking these kinds of questions. It was up to Ed to exercise his leadership position, and if he didn't speak up, who would?

They didn't seem to be connecting. Murrow sat listlessly, his responses limited to halfhearted rejoinders about the war, CBS's position in Washington; Bessie and Ernst had no idea what CBS was up against, this was just window dressing, he had to keep his access, hold the line for the news department. . . .

"My recollection," said Bessie later, "is that Ed was beaten down on the subject, that he had been persuaded to go along. Morris felt strongly that something had knocked the stuffing out of him. . . . All I recall is the sense that he wasn't fighting."

The corporate decision made, Murrow had obviously given up on changing it. "My guess at the time," Bessie added, "was that he would fight a losing battle. It's become increasingly difficult in retrospect to recapture the moods and the pressures of the McCarthy time, and it's become increasingly easy to take a position now that we know how it came out. . . . I was not on the firing line; my hesitation is against that background. I think it was wrong of CBS to yield on the loyalty oath thing and wrong of Ed, but I have more sympathy for his state of mind then."[28]

The dynamics of the situation, however, would turn out to be somewhat more convoluted.

The questionnaire had gone out just before Christmas week, 1950, against a background of widened conflict in Korea, a hemorrhaging of the northern front, and the specter of all-out war with China. "The President of the United States has declared a national emergency,"[29] began the covering memo bearing the name of Joseph Ream, Executive Vice-President of CBS.

Crisis and a shooting war against a Communist power. In Washington the network was being depicted in FBI files as the harborer of a "group . . . believed to be communistically inclined or fellow travelers."[30] *Counterattack*, beating the drum in a wartime atmosphere, was saying the same thing out loud every other week. Ream, a conservative former Wall Street lawyer, one of the company's most respected and able legal minds, dean of the twentieth-floor group, the arbiter on matters of policy and law, decided something must be done—a gesture to take off the heat. "It is difficult," says Ream today, "to envision now the atmosphere and circumstances existing in 1950. What seemed right to me then would today be an unwarranted invasion of one's right of privacy."[31]

Despite its sweep and impact, however, it was considered an administrative move—never, to the recollection of Paley, Stanton, or Ream himself, actually submitted to the board for comment or discussion. Instead, evidently, Ream had taken the idea first not to a fellow executive but to Murrow, who had consistently challenged the "Are you now or have you ever been" as an infringement on the First Amendment. Who was, moreover, notoriously impatient with forms and administrative questions.

Why Murrow, therefore? Not, evidently, because of his position on the board; the board didn't see the questionnaire. No, Murrow was approached, recalled Ream, "as a friend and fellow employee and as one whose reactions would have great, although not controlling weight with me."[32] Murrow, he said, did not object, though the details of the matter, recollected in letters twenty-five years later, unclarified by records, would be somewhat hazy:

The questionnaire and my accompanying memo were shown to Murrow prior to their promulgation. I do not now recall whether he "acquiesced" in a positive sense or merely took the position that this was a matter for my decision—more likely, I think, the latter. I do not recall any particular discussion or even if we met, or simply used the inter-office telephone. It is true that he made no strong objection, and as I look back I think I would have gone ahead even if he had. . . . I am quite sure that I had no conversation with Murrow concerning the questionnaire subsequent to its promulgation, although I can readily believe that he had doubts about it not expressed to me.

Reading over the foregoing, I realize it falls short of a neat button-up. . . .[33]

Next, Ream had gone to Stanton with the word that Murrow had seen the questionnaire already, the presumable implication, that he had not objected. Stanton, unwilling in later years to Monday-morning-quarterback his own view of the questionnaire, did recall seeing it and that "Joe told me that he had shown it to Ed."[34] The President of CBS, that being said, presumably made no objection either. The form went out.

To a few, however, Murrow was known to have expressed his doubts, at least once the questionnaire was out. There was no way the thing could even work, he told a colleague; a genuine four-carat subversive would hardly come out and say so on a form. It could only backfire. Speaking with William Fineshriber, one of the prewar Paley crowd at CBS, he called the loyalty oath "a very stupid thing." In earlier months, says Fineshriber, they had discussed the *Red Channels* phenomenon. Fineshriber was trying to get up an ad hoc industry committee to fight the blacklisters; Murrow, he said later, had been "a moral help," his feeling over the red book one of "absolute outrage. . . . He would have no part of it."[35]

He was part of it now. Whatever the circumstances of his first entanglement with the so-called CBS loyalty oath, this much was on the books: In one way or another, he had seen it first and hadn't stopped it, the possibility always present of someone from the inner circle saying, "Well, *Murrow* approved it."

The newsmen protested. Downs came to Murrow, furious: there was no way he was going to sign this thing.

Murrow looked at him somberly: "You have no choice." Neither, by now, had he.

The questionnaire itself had been patterned on the Truman loyalty program for the civil service, "with such changes," said Joe Ream later, "as were appropriate for corporate rather than government use."[36] And with the same rationale of self-defense. "A very small step," Paley called it, "compared to what most corporations were doing by way of protecting themselves against the onslaught of McCarthy and people of that kind."[37]

Instituted, like the Truman program, allegedly to stop the sniping, it would end, similarly, by feeding on itself.

In the meantime amid the rising controversy, one voice conspicuously missing, the former Dorothy Paley wondered what had happened to her friend Ed Murrow—it was just not in the *nature* of the man not to put up a fight—and sensed something bad had happened: "The only place that I ever felt let down by Ed. I don't know what it cost him. I think a great deal. Of his own self-respect."[38]

That January, there was an agitated note marked "Personal" from Morris Ernst, more and more uptight over growing controls in the media. ("Morris was a strong anti-Communist," said Mike Bessie later, "but that didn't mitigate his belief in the rights involved.")

CBS, Ernst had heard, was hiring a former FBI man to screen its files. Which if true, certainly didn't indicate to him "that CBS is thinking in terms of high vision." Murrow referred the note to Ream and was dissatisfied with the response. He had agreed to say nothing on this "vexed subject," he complained, "and I take it that means *write* too," but this was no reply; Ernst deserved a better answer.[39]

It was not, in short, his kind of setup, a writer of the time soon noting it "no secret that Murrow is something less than enthusiastic about his network's 'screening policies.' "[40]

There was more to come.

Daniel T. O'Shea—Harvard Law, 1930; short, florid-faced, articulate, with a beguiling command of the English language—had been a film-industry attorney, a former right-hand man to David Selznick when Paley asked him to CBS as a general executive in the fall of 1950. He had been hired for business affairs, he liked to point out, in a company about to divisionalize, engaged to be consultant to all CBS divisions and especially on matters touching real estate (including early negotiations for the site of the later CBS corporate headquarters known as Black Rock).

"It was an assignment," said O'Shea later, recalling Joe Ream coming to him one day, requesting that he take over screening procedures for the network. Said O'Shea: "There was a backlash because of the loyalty oath, and I think he wanted to get out of it."[41] The questionnaire was proving the tar baby many thought it would. Some had lied, causing red faces back at CBS after admissions were wrung out of subpoenaed employees in committee hearings, and after sponsors and agencies, "tipped off" by outsiders, rejected the talent offered them by the network.

"It was beginning to heat up at that time," O'Shea recalled, "[and] Ream asked me if I would kind of shepherd and watch these areas."

Shepherding the areas meant making sure the wrong people didn't represent Columbia in the marketplace. He was to run checks, therefore, on employees grown controversial and, if possible, on those who were about to be, but handle it within the house; in short, check out who could or could not work at CBS. Of the ultimate source of the mandate there were no indications and no questions were asked. Paley didn't give out assignments, said O'Shea later; Ream did. "[He] asked me if I would do it, [and] in keeping with the policy of doing what they asked me, I did." He'd do it if they wanted, he told them, but he'd have to do it *his* way.

"I was given no guidelines, no rules; what rules there were, were formulated by myself, in trying to be fair and decent in the thing." The ex-FBI man, Alfred Berry, a patent attorney with an engineering degree from Purdue who had been working with Ream, was assigned to assist— i.e., "Berry will help you."

"So off I went."

As is well known today, CBS, developing its own resources since the early lean years, unlike other networks, had likewise attracted offbeat talent and wound up with more uncomfortable people—"a nest of Commies," in the pungent words of one observer; society's rebels, according to another. The network was a direct employer, not a conduit for packaged programs, therefore—in the fifties' sense—vulnerable.

There were some on staff, O'Shea insisted, actually subject to the Smith Act, which in effect made CP membership a crime—"who were more than dilettantes," as he put it, "who had to take flight because of certain federal statutes that were on the books, later declared unconstitutional." He did stress that most were simply caught in the middle—the popular fronters, do-gooders. "There *were* injustices. People *were* hurt.

"These weren't bomb throwers, plotters. The public was against them; McCarthy didn't create it." What with the climate created by the Vinson Court, the expense of TV, and the importance of big sponsors, the ultimate yardstick, said O'Shea in retrospect, was one of economics:

> They didn't do the blacklisting because of what people had done; they did it because of business. Shows were beginning to cost more. A client would say, "Listen, we can't have this. We're spending forty or fifty thousand dollars for goodwill. We don't want to be identified with this. . . ."
>
> I kept some people off the air. Never deliberately unjustly. It wasn't that I felt myself in the middle of ridding the world of Communists— rather of some group or other who were affecting CBS's business.

They worked from notes kept by Berry—"working cards" O'Shea called them, including those on employees who "were complained of or were recently identified. One of the investigators from the committee staff would come and tell us who they would call. I had a digest from the FBI, just to justify me in what I was doing."

The digest was kept for reference, to be checked against information coming in on individuals, "sometimes anonymously." As for other "information," as he termed it, "Mostly the guys on the congressional committees would come and tell us, get us to cooperate with them."

At no time, he insisted, did they have a formal list, use informers, or trade names. "We could have had a list; people were coming to us all the time, wanting to be put on retainer. We didn't have a list at any time.

"We handled things on an individual basis, whether news department or programming department or whatever. . . . We were largely consultative for the divisions . . . weren't set upon to go into the corners and ferret out people. I'm sure that a lot of these guys, when they didn't want to hire a guy, could always say, 'Upstairs.' "

Decisions were not "irrevocable." A decision made, however, was he speaking for the company? "Sure was."

Since some of the areas most "vulnerable" were news and, even more so, public affairs, said O'Shea, "I ran into Murrow."

He had no animus toward Murrow. Quite the contrary. He liked him, admired his style, his broadcasts from London—"one of the building blocks of CBS," he called them, in recognition of their value to Paley. They just had different jobs.

"I wasn't the same kind of fellow. . . . Murrow had come through the war, was a pretty big, stalwart kind of hero right out of a book. His concerns were different from mine; he had the long-term view that I couldn't. . . ."

Their encounters were infrequent. "On things that came up, he would talk to me. . debate about 'victims.' " Murrow he remembered as "direct . . . a man of strong convictions," defensive about the news staff.[42]

There was no friction, O'Shea noted, no personalizing; each came from a different place. There seemed little doubt, however, that news needed defending, even before the screening procedure was in place.

Fred Friendly later told a colleague about Bob Heller—who had once called CBS "a virtual utopia for craftsmen who believe in radio's usefulness as a social force"[43]—appearing in tears in Murrow's office with the news that he'd been told to leave, following his listing in *Red Channels*. Bob Shayon of *The Eagle's Brood* was long since gone.

Red Channels had also reached into the hard news area, tagging, at CBS, Howard Smith, its radical in residence, and Alex Kendrick, the expert on Southeastern Europe and skeptic on the Polk case. Bill Fineshriber recalled Murrow's "going to bat"[44] for the two reporters. Joe Ream, for his part, could recall "no knowledge of any relationship among Murrow, Kendrick and Howard K. Smith as may have been affected by *Red Channels*."[45]

Whatever the circumstances, both correspondents stayed at CBS, and *someone*, Howard Smith later insisted, had to be running interference. "I'm absolutely sure that Ed Murrow was the wall that kept anybody from approaching me—because his anger was so manifest. And because I knew of specific cases in which they had reproached reporters and he had defended them against people inside the corporation. So that when *my* name appeared in *Red Channels*, and I got *absolutely no flak* from the most sensitive people, who would *certainly* have complained in some way, I knew that he had done it."

(Murrow, said Smith, was responsible for others being kept at CBS as well, "who had been either attacked by McCarthy or were mentioned in some House Un-American Activities session in a derogatory way. I was not the only one; I shan't list the others. But I know several people, some of them not reporters, whom he protected against the doubters in the hierarchy.")[46]

"If you're in trouble, we're all in trouble," Kendrick recalled Murrow telling him.[47]

Apparently it didn't work for Heller, who had to take the now-familiar route of Mexico, then England, starting a second career in Britain with Murrow's old friend Sidney Bernstein, at Granada TV, one of the growing pool of Americans in exile, the talent drain that had become a by-product of the blacklist.

For Murrow, who had set up both the contact and financial help for Heller, it was piecemeal stuff, treating the symptom, not the cause.

In those same months, his friend Harold Isaacs, the old Asia hand and dissident on Indochina, found his passport renewal held up indefinitely— no explanation, limbo. It was standard government operating procedure by now, thanks to the tireless Ruth Shipley, head of the Passport Division and a friend of Joe McCarthy. Isaacs, seeking help, got lots of sympathy, no action, not that many, as he later put it, ready to throw pitches for you.

Murrow began pressuring Shipley. "He really went to bat," Isaacs recalled, "my heavens—wrote letters, did the telephoning."[48] A cabled threat to "start asking questions publicly,"[49] finally dislodged the passport from its pigeonhole. Isaacs, a hardened veteran of many tough assignments, could still recollect, years later, his relief: "I felt as though I'd been reinstated in the human race."

But unlike 1948, the broadcaster had not gone public. Nor was Ruth Shipley about to forget the incident.

From every viewpoint, 1951, after the *Sturm und Drang* of the past years, was a letdown. He no longer felt capable. "Ed was increasingly glum over the mounting police state mentality take-over in America," said John Henry Faulk, then a relative newcomer to CBS, hosting an afternoon talk show, a cracker-barrel philosopher and frequent lunch companion. "It disturbed him deeply."[50]

Faulk, from Texas, active in the Wallace campaign of 1948, whose hiring—unknown to him—had been opposed by Dan O'Shea, had come to New York with regards for Murrow from a mutual friend, the Texas writer and folkorist Frank Dobie. ("Look up Ed Murrow," said Dobie as the country boy left for the big city, "he's the kind of man you need to know.") Their interests, it turned out, were "mutual"; the rapport was instant.

Over drinks they discussed the state of the nation. "I remember McCarthy was riding high," Faulk recalled, "the country capitulating." Television must stand up for the Bill of Rights, he had argued, not fall down. The inroads on the Constitution were enveloping the media. The First Amendment was a *mandate*—not a suggestion. People were being rounded up, deprived of their rights, Communists or not.

Murrow agreed, but what happened when you said it out loud? The public wasn't buying. Just center on the First Amendment; keep it up; keep it general; bring them around.

By hindsight, Faulk said later, he could see his point. "When you're dealing with hysteria, you have to get hold of it. When you're dealing with a madman, you can't just tell him he's mad; you have to deal with his fears."

Then, late that year, just before the start of *See It Now*, Murrow had a shocking glimpse of just how far the mass mood could penetrate.

They called it PREVIEW OF THE WAR WE DO NOT WANT, the title spread across the cover of *Collier's* magazine: a special issue depicting a hypothetical World War III, touched off by Tito's assassination, won after much travail by the United States, over the Soviet Union. More than thirty distinguished writers, among them great journalistic names, relived the war years, depicting collectively another global conflict only six years after the last one. The participants included Quentin Reynolds, John Gunther, Joseph Barnes, John Hersey, Robert Sherwood, Hanson Baldwin—and Edward R. Murrow, who had flown so many combat missions, describing in a two-page article the dropping of a retaliatory atom bomb on Moscow.

The horrified reaction to the issue's appearance on October 27 echoed through the State Department, the UN General Assembly meeting in Paris, U.S. embassies, Eastern and Western European governments—a sellout on the newsstands and a first-magnitude diplomatic disaster. The contributors, as Murrow stated afterward, had possibly no concept of the collective impact of their pieces; the thinking public, however, was left stunned by the easy postulation of an atomic war in which there could be winners, let alone a war waged so cavalierly in the pages of a magazine. In Murrow's case, it was particularly jarring, coming from one who had opposed the building of the H-bomb and the stockpiling of nuclear weapons.

He had been abroad when the piece appeared, covering elections in Britain, the General Assembly, and developments at Supreme Headquarters, Allied Powers, Europe (SHAPE). After the recycled opinions of New York and Washington, his reports from overseas had always the effect of a window pushed open. In London's poorer districts, he visited local Labour clubs with his friend Herbert Morrison, now Foreign Secretary, and talked with the elderly women sitting around coal fires, stuffing envelopes. ("I asked for the dominant issue in the campaign and everywhere got the same answer: 'Poverty and peace.' No going back to the poverty they knew in the early '30's and no more war. . . .")[51]

From the Continent he reported growing apprehensions about U.S. policy, "a real and abiding fear about the future" among America's friends in Western Europe, seeing the U.S. as trigger-happy, "the suspicion that we may use our strength . . . in such fashion that the destruction of their nations will be insured. . . .

"Every bellicose speech in Washington, every reference to a policy based solely upon power, every reference to an eventual ultimatum to Russia, serves to increase the fear that once we get that military might we would demand a showdown. . . ."[52]

Collier's World War III was already on the newsstands. That weekend he returned to piles of mail from outraged listeners, asking, Would the real Ed Murrow please stand up? "It may interest you to know that I was in Paris when the Collier's issue was published," he answered one letter, "and the reaction and criticism of my French friends both in journalism and in government was considerably less restrained than was yours. . . ."[53]

He hadn't known the full content of the issue, he wrote a friend, but that was no excuse; he should have. It was a case, he suspected, where reasonably responsible people had been sold individually on a collectively irresponsible project; a cold war booby trap for liberals, as one writer later saw it, and a costly bit of self-revelation.

He acknowledged his critics as best he could—they were, he told Chet Williams, "entirely justified"—then gathered the rest into a pile, a note set at the top: "Colliers/ no answer/ There isn't one!"

The ghost of George Polk stalked CBS in early 1952. That February, Long Island University's School of Journalism notified Murrow that he and *See It Now* had won the memorial award set up in the name of the late correspondent. The announcement and presentation would not be for some time. Eight days later, somehow, *Counterattack* opened fire on George Polk, the awards, the school, Howard Smith, and, for the first time, Edward R. Murrow ("defends those involved in Communist causes").[54] It was three months after the start of *See It Now* and, perhaps more to the point, nine weeks after the airing of a short but devastating segment on McCarthy.

The Senator himself, gearing up for the elections, was in fine fettle in those months. In Cudahy, Wisconsin, he attributed MacArthur's firing to "a many headed . . . monster conceived in the Kremlin, born to Dean Acheson, with Atlee and Morrison as midwives." On the Senate floor, as two more China experts went flying, he denounced "the prancing pink punks who have taken over our government."

Truman, without naming McCarthy, inveighed against "slandermongers [who] are trying to get us so hysterical that no one will stand up to them," only to be denounced by *Time* magazine—itself a leading critic of McCarthy—for allegedly discounting what it called "the red afterglow of Communists in and around the Government. . . . 'McCarthyism' is not going to be stopped by Truman speeches or by the witch-hunting of witch-hunters, or by proving that McCarthy is a slippery character and no gentleman. 'McCarthyism' is going to be around until Harry Truman, the President of the U.S., eliminates from U.S. foreign policy the tendency to appease Communism."[55]

The *See It Now* piece, aired in mid-December 1951, had shown the Wisconsin Senator complaining tearfully of a purported smear campaign ("when we've been kicked around and bullwhipped"), followed by Murrow live on camera, recalling "*another* McCarthy, on other days," leading into a rapid-fire film sequence of McCarthy as accuser: "The planks in Mr. Lattimore's platform are *identical* to the planks in the platform of the *Communist Party*" [cut]; "The law firm that was on record as the agent of Communist Poland was the law firm of Dean Gooderham Acheson" [cut]; "The almost criminal folly of the disastrous Marshall mission to China. . . ."[56]

The brief closing needed little more than Murrow's wry observation that the difference between smearing and straightforward attack depended, evidently, on whose reputation was being gored. The editing said it all, or seemed to—an early indication of TV's power, at least for those who watched. But the four-minute segment, tough as it was, made hardly a ripple in those months of McCarthy ascendant. Many more would feel the impact when the footage became part of the so-called McCarthy show of 1954. Television, with small audiences, was not yet that important.

For those who did watch, however, it was simply what they had come to expect in a very short time: a program with a point of view, topical, irreverent, fast-moving; the kind of program that could kid the pants off Joe McCarthy, Robert Taft, or, for that matter, Truman, Stevenson, and Eisenhower. Especially the unfortunate Taft. Their second week—they never did it again, admittedly—the announced coverage of the Taft campaign in the South turned into a sequence of fund-raising dinners, with the emphasis on dinner: shot after shot of steak hacking, jingle singing, then the candidate. It was at first amusing, then hilarious in its cumulative effect. For icing, Taft, live on camera at his home, had been asked to watch.

The film sequence ended, they switched back to Taft. The candidate was smiling—barely.

Geoffrey Bridson of the BBC was in the studio that night, watching the telecast, convulsed, and just a bit appalled. He'd never, he said, seen anyone pull a gag like that. "Brother," Murrow replied, "you saw nothing.

I was watching Taft on my monitor when he was watching the film. You should have seen him then!"[57]

(Throughout, Friendly was his happy collaborator. Unknown to many, the producer had already shown a taste for controversy back at NBC, where the comments of outspoken guests on *Who Said That?* riled the sponsors and a vocal segment of the public. Friendly, still running the program during his first year at CBS, wouldn't clamp the lid down. NBC, wanting to have its cake and eat it too, finally decided in July 1951 to keep the show but buy out Gude and the talented but uncontrollable Friendly.)[58]

There was also, in a curious episode, the show they didn't do, which, though never broadcast, left a residue of irritation in powerful places. In early 1951, Morris Ernst had sold Murrow on the idea of a *Hear It Now* show on the FBI—the real story, he said, not the cops-and-robbers stuff, clarifying the Bureau's function.

Murrow was reported "enthusiastic."[59] This was stuff he hadn't known before. An exuberant Friendly flew to Washington in late June, met with Hoover's deputy Louis Nichols, got the full tour and a backgrounder— i.e., what the Director had done for the Bureau, for the country, their training program, their deep concern for civil rights. Friendly was ready to go: The program would clarify public thinking on the FBI's role, tell the Bureau's real story, "who its agents are, the extensive training they receive, and why the FBI is not a Gestapo."[60] He promised a preliminary proposal after the weekend.

The Bureau hierarchy was all for it: a "real objective job"[61] could be done, they thought; Murrow was "one of the great voices on the air" and if through this program they could bring him into "intimate contact" with Bureau operations, they might profit in the years to come. It was, they agreed, definitely in the Bureau's interest. J. Edgar Hoover gave the project his blessing.[62]

It never came off. *Hear It Now* became *See It Now*, negotiations lapsed. Murrow, getting back to them in '52, wanted another kind of story—anti-Klan action, or possibly telecasting, live, from FBI headquarters, the great documentary somehow put out of mind. The FBI itself seemed wary—of the medium and, to some extent, of *See It Now*; Murrow wasn't raising quite the same feelings of confidence, the newsman's repeated attempts to follow up met with distant politeness tinged with a faint resentment at the earlier failure to deliver; a lingering memory, at upper Bureau levels, of Murrow-Friendly having given them the brushoff.

In the meantime, the foibles of the 1952 campaign provided ample grist for the mill. *See It Now* filmed a bumbling advance man warming up the crowds for Ike; Senator Estes Kefauver trying and failing to plant his famous coonskin cap on a symbolic donkey; Stevenson and Eisenhower, intercut, pitching to the locals ("My grandfather . . . spoke here in Richmond" [Cut]; "My son, who was *also* educated in Connecticut" [Cut]; "My Mamie is an Iowa girl . . .").

At other times the laugh was on Murrow and Friendly—generally because the technical problems in those early days were horrendous and because the two producers, as old radio men, were used to working with quarter-inch sound tape, the show building on the audio technology already in place in 1951. Besides, there wasn't time for extensive synchronization procedures à la Hollywood.

Murrow's narrated segments were recorded at 485, separated by leader tape, piped to the *See It Now* screening room on Fifth Avenue and dovetailed with the film sound track, the Murrow sound and film sound then piped to a second tape machine back at 485. It was part of the program's Rube Goldberg invent-it-as-you-go amalgam of film, sound tape, and live TV, concocted in the pressure cooker of the Sunday deadline. "Murrow's narration came down on the telephone line to us," said Palmer Williams later. "Meanwhile, the sound that was on the film was going to that second tape machine."

> Now on the picture, we're looking at the frames go by, watching for an X mark in grease pencil, going on about oh, three, four frames. As it comes by on the screen, Friendly, holding a telephone to the tape room which has the Murrow sound, yells, "Hit it!" Up comes Murrow's narration and plays over the film on our screen. The resultant output— Murrow's tape, film sound—goes back on that second tape; *that* was our mixed sound track. Eventually the tape and picture were taken to Vanderbilt Avenue to telecine, to a tape machine and a projection machine, now asked to run in synchronous lock and put the thing out on the air. Which generally worked. Except when it misfired. So that in 1952, once, we had Eisenhower doing something, and up came Adlai Stevenson, started to speak, and a ten- or twenty-piece orchestra came out of his mouth.[63]

They were dogged by blackouts, loss of picture on remotes, technical failures of all kinds, and in one case, a complete breakdown that left Murrow ad-libbing on camera, without a show. They took it in stride; in some ways, it kept the program human, non-omniscient. The focus of reporting was kept likewise to a human scale—what Murrow and Friendly called the "little picture," as opposed to the large-screen newsreel footage that was still the staple of the nightly newscasts. *See It Now* cameras went underground with coal miners in West Virginia, rode school buses in the upheavals following court-ordered desegregation, reported on housing problems in the Shreveport ghetto and in Harlem, and on a Chinese immigrant barred by neighbors from buying into a San Francisco suburb. They went back to the East and West Coast shots for that one, panning, at the end, to the poem at the base of the Statue of Liberty, *very* slowly. And incidentally, ran Murrow's concluding copy, last week on both coasts

was known as Brotherhood Week. Fade-out. "He might have editorialized," said Palmer Williams, "but examine the words. He just finished
the piece, and all he did was turn back to the camera, and look at you
with those eyes and say, 'And may I remind you . . .' Bam!"

TV clichés? Decades later, perhaps, when innovation would be replaced
by imitation. In the early fifties, however, it showed the first real capabilities of reporting on the tube, close-focus real life at a time when the
director of the tiny new network operation was trying to convince the
CBS management that the evening newscast could be more than just a
fifteen-minute fill-in before Perry Como.[64]

But it was the kind of programming, obviously, that needed a certain
degree of independence, more in keeping with the freewheeling traditions
of radio than the centralized control of network television—an independence closely guarded by Murrow and one that would from the outset
start the television news operation on a two-track course, with all the
attendant and inevitable tensions.

Siegfried "Sig" Mickelson was a hard worker, five years Murrow's junior, a serious radio newsman and onetime journalism teacher in his native
Minnesota. He was an able and articulate organizer, light on policy decisions, brilliant on detail, with the professional drive that had gained
him Frank Stanton's confidence and brought him in two years from the
public affairs department at WCCO, Minneapolis—one of the top CBS
farm teams, where he had built a solid local reputation—to head of the
nascent network news operation at Grand Central: still very much the
younger sibling of tradition-proud radio, totalling thirteen persons plus
its boss, dependent for its film on outside newsreel contractors and, in
1951, trailing NBC.

The incoming Director of CBS-TV News and Public Affairs, with two
years at 485 under his belt, had naturally taken it for granted that his
supervisory function would include See It Now. After all, he had brought
Friendly over from NBC, worked with him in the tape room on Hear It
Now, sat in on that first short test run of See It Now on a sweltering
Friday in early August 1951, when ALCOA had decided to buy in. The
show on the road, obviously successful, he sent a memo down the hall:
Now, about a budget meeting . . .

Murrow, no stranger to the corporate life, sat up. Meeting? What
meeting? No one had said anything about a meeting. Mickelson, deeming
discretion the better part of valor, not about to tangle with the big boss's
pal and a board member at that, decided he had too much to do anyway
and concentrated his attentions elsewhere. But short months later, they
were almost head to head again when the energetic Mickelson, having
finally convinced the management to set up a worldwide network news
film operation of its own (said Mickelson later: "they didn't think there
was any reason for having your own camera crews [when] you could buy

a newsreel service"),[65] cast covetous eyes in the direction of the Murrow-Friendly talent pool.

The idea, quite logical, was to set up a single source of news film in the company, get everybody under one umbrella—amalgamate the budgets and production personnel, transfer the *See It Now* camera crews to an umbrella corporation, and in effect fold in the Murrow-Friendly production operation like a well-prepared meringue. It also meant the transfer elsewhere of Palmer Williams, linchpin of the day-to-day operation of *See It Now*.[66]

Then, suddenly, the *See It Now* part of the deal was out. The Murrow-Friendly unit stayed intact. For Mickelson it was back to square one.[67] "We had to go on our own and set it up entirely separately. With a lot less money."

The irony was that Murrow, for all his arm's length treatment, respected the other as a newsman. They had worked the 1948 conventions back in Mickelson's WCCO days; his reports were used on the 7:45 P.M. news. "Ed had a high regard for Sig," said a staffer later. "It was only when the two were placed in this juxtaposition that hostilities arose."

Mickelson, for now, threw in the towel. "They kept in touch with me from time to time. I knew what they were doing. But in no way was I ever directly in charge." The ground was set for the two separate entities, developing side by side: one workaday, under network control, soon to be cloning new departments and managerial levels; the other remaining small and lean, attention-getting, with direct lines of command, answerable to Paley and maddeningly unassimilable.

In one of those industry paradoxes, it was in many ways the wave of the future, granddaddy to the documentaries and TV news magazines, incubator of TV techniques which, cross-fertilizing, would influence not only CBS but all three networks, network news and documentaries alike. The problem of the time was money—news wasn't making any. News was, in fact, a loss leader, budgets tight, with too many feeders at the trough, as one management figure put it, resentments quick to rise.

Budgets were a sticking point even for *See It Now*, a symbol of corporate myopia, its seeming human embodiment, Frank Stanton, the President of CBS.

The Murrow-Stanton differences were, of course, an open secret. They were, after all, said Stanton, "two very different people."

Both men were devoted to CBS, to Paley, and, in the long run, to the news department, Murrow as newsman, Stanton as the chief operating officer of CBS, responsible for the fiscal health of the corporation. But more than that, as Stanton himself later pointed out, they simply came from different directions, with resulting differences in perspective and especially on the question of market research in broadcasting. Said Stanton: "Ed came in with the idea that a journalist was a much more reliable reporter of public opinion than Gallup or Roper or—Stanton if you will, because I was doing polling. His opinion didn't vary much from the opinions of Scotty Reston and others of that generation, who didn't welcome the intrusion of the pollster into the business of reporting the mood of the country. Ed was more articulate, had a little more decibel, and didn't much like the idea of having any polling touch news and public affairs."

> I also think that Ed had inherited, or had gotten by osmosis, the strong antipathy of *anyone* in programming for anything approaching a measure of public acceptance of the broadcasts. In other words, he was opposed to ratings. . . . I came from a hundred and eighty degrees away from him because that was my whole entrance into the *business*: How do you begin to measure the impact. And if you're gonna measure the impact, you gotta find out who is listening and you've got to get the demographics and all of that. This was a mumbo jumbo area as far as the news people were concerned, and Ed was their disciple.[68]

It began with small matters at first, snowballing as time went on, despite efforts on both sides to maintain cordiality. "We did a program," Stanton recalled; "Lyman Bryson was the moderator. A serious effort to bring two or three people with strong, informed backgrounds to talk about a particular issue. I suggested that Lyman might include Elmo Roper as a public opinion analyst who could, at the conclusion of the broadcast, say, 'Here's how the public feels on that particular issue. . . .' [Well], Ed took strong exception to that. He felt that that was cheapening the program and belittling the participants."

In 1948, Murrow's gleeful judgment on the pollsters following the Dewey debacle had provoked an angry memo from Stanton. There were reported disagreements over the pre-empting of commercial programs in favor of news coverage, arguments over ratings as a basis for programming. Many of the tales making the rounds were no doubt apocryphal, but the fundamental lack of chemistry between the two men seemed increasingly evident as Stanton's position firmed up within the company—nothing the others could put their finger on, just occasional spurts as might show on an electrocardiogram. "A sort of running thing," as Ralph Colin, a longtime associate of both men, put it, "[with] periods of greater or lesser irritation.

"Frank and Ed were simply people who were not made for each other— that's all. There are people like that. There were long periods when nothing happened, they'd reach joint conclusions about things, it wasn't a constant war at all. Then something would happen, and they'd spit at each other. . . ."[69]

Bill Fineshriber remembered Murrow in the latter forties, returning from upstairs meetings, muttering, brows knit blackly: "Goddamn place . . . money-mad . . ."[70] Dan O'Shea, by contrast, recalled scenes up on the executive floor in the fifties, himself sitting with a colleague and

Stanton stalking in: "He's at it again"[71]—the kind of verbal shorthand they had come to read as indicating some sort of unpleasantness with Murrow. It was impossible, most agreed, to separate policy differences from personality differences.

"There was a little bit of jealousy," opined O'Shea. "Murrow was so handsome, a mannish-looking man, widely applauded, friend of Paley's. Stanton was also a good-looking man, [though] a little on the vain side, a fussbudget. When, as I did early in the game, we'd go together to see Paley, Stanton always fixed his hair, fixed his tie. To me it was probative that these guys weren't as friendly with one another as they ought to be."

Conversely, Murrow's access to the Chairman—and his liberal use of it—was known within the company to be a sore spot, an unwanted anachronism from the old days. "Ed was the only one other than me," said Colin, "who disregarded all organization setups and when he had a gripe, went directly to Paley. And that's something that irritated Frank because it was violating the rules of command. Ed should have gone to the head of news, he should have gone to Stanton. . . .

"Of course, Ed went to Paley because Paley was his friend, and he thought that was the fastest way to get something done. And it *was*."[72]

But neither was Frank Stanton anymore the diffident young outsider of 1946, who had waited humbly by the pool for his first one-on-one meeting with Mr. Paley out at Kiluna Farm while Ed Murrow and the wartime crowd regaled themselves up at the house. There was a sense of jealousies in both directions and of vying for attention.

In the meantime, *See It Now* itself personified the leapfrogging of chains of command, its budget a constant source of friction, with frictions easily personalized. Murrow, returning one time from grueling day-and-night coverage of the flooding Missouri River, found his expense account likewise returned, with a deletion. "1 pr. mud boots." Disallowed.

Bypassing middle management, he went directly up to 20 and, as he later told the story, into Stanton's office.

Was he still wearing the boots? asked the President of CBS.

Murrow allowed as how he was.

"Then don't expect Columbia to buy your boots."

He departed, wordless, reappearing next day without warning and with two size elevens—filthy, worn, caked with the mud of the Missouri, slammed them down onto Stanton's desk, cleats grinding into the immaculate veneer. "Take your fucking boots!"

Altercations, however, were kept in the higher spheres, away from the staff—as protected, insulated, and envied a group as any working in broadcasting; the Band of Brothers, Murrow called them in conscious or unconscious imitation of Henry V at Agincourt. Mickelson at the outset had urged two names on them: young Av Westin and Irving Gitlin, who had worked on *Hear It Now*. But Gitlin, a talented producer developing as counterpole to Friendly, wanted out of Friendly's orbit ("didn't want to be errand boy to another genius," said Mickelson, "and, of course, became one of the great stars of the business"). Nothing came of either proposal, and in any case Murrow and Friendly were hiring their own, reaching into radio news, where Mickelson had no control.

Accordingly, the staff emerged as a creative, beautifully messy hodgepodge of disparate elements, beginning with the two staff reporters Ed Scott and Joe Wershba from *Hear It Now* and *CBS Views the Press*, now dead, canceled in the month that produced *Red Channels*, an act for which Murrow had never quite forgiven management. Both were superb investigative journalists. Scott, a PM graduate, had made his name in wartime, working undercover as a stevedore for a story proving sabotage in the sinking of the liner *Normandie*. Of course, both *PM* and the old Hollenbeck show were now suspect in the prevailing *Red Channels* atmosphere. The outspoken Wershba, working out of Washington, on Murrow's payroll for additional jobs done, had been "under a bit of a cloud at that time," or so Mickelson recalled from his vantage point in middle management. "The blacklisters were after him. And of course, Murrow was doubly interested in getting anybody who was in any kind of trouble with the blacklisters. . . . It was a relatively safe haven at that point, or seemed to be. And of course, Joe was one of the best that Murrow and Friendly had." Whether the young reporter himself had been aware, he couldn't tell.[73]

For camera crews, they ran the gamut from *News of the Day* personnel leased perforce from Hearst thanks to restrictive and Byzantine craft union jurisdictions, including Charlie Mack and Leo Rossi, a camera artist who could remember punching sprockets in film as a youngster back when Fort Lee, New Jersey, was the film capital, to Bill McClure, later a star producer, then their cameraman in Europe, working with the correspondents, the one and only on the payroll.

"The birth of *See It Now*," says McClure today, "was the beginning of television for CBS overseas."

A stocky, energetic filmmaker shooting newsreels for Pathé in 1951, he had begun on documentaries with the Signal Corps in Europe and the Pacific, one of "a sort of *Nouvelle vague*," as he called it, of American documentarians who had come out of World War II, very young, trained in the war. Unlike the shoe-leather newsreelers, he was primarily interested in documentaries. "And in fact, what my interest was, was precisely what Murrow offered."

(Referred originally by Dick Hottelet, he simply stopped by one day on his lunch hour while in New York, saw Friendly, was taken in to see Murrow, then out again, and hired on the spot. How much? said Friendly. McClure figured his salary and added fifty more. "I should have put five *hundred* dollars on top"—he laughed later—"because the money in broadcasting was so incredible. But he didn't blink an eye. He said, 'Fine.' "

When could he leave? asked Friendly. When did they want him to? Tomorrow. For London. Impossible, he said. You have to, said Friendly. McClure walked back to Pathé, told his boss he wanted his two weeks' vacation money and he wasn't coming back. He can't remember if they paid him.)

With that, television descended on the European fiefdoms of CBS, on the modest radio bureaus, making for a sink-or-swim situation which, if not harmonious or comfortable, was at least productive. "The most incredible marriage," McClure was to call it, "between very sophisticated and highly trained correspondents, the best journalists in the country I think, or at least at CBS at the time. And these characters who came out of *News of the Day*. With ideas far to the right. And yet they were joining up with a guy who was a liberal's liberal, had to adapt to the Schoenbruns and the Collingwoods and all these people. An incredible marriage."[74]

But the marriage had its strains from the outset. Schoenbrun later remembered sitting in the BBC basement in the weeks before the show's opening, with Howard Smith and Murrow. Murrow introduced McClure, explained how the show was going to work, and how they'd work with Bill. And just who'd be in charge? asked Smith. No one, said Murrow, they'd be a team. That wouldn't work, said Smith. Yes, it would, said Murrow, very quietly: "And that's the way it's gonna be." Schoenbrun and Smith left with misgivings. Somebody had to call the shots, and they had a feeling that it wouldn't be the correspondent.[75]

Back in New York, at the gray-walled cutting room at 501 Fifth Avenue, the three editors worked around the clock: Bonsignori, Bill Thompson, Bucky O'Neill. The cutting room complex was Friendly's turf—three tables holding Movieolas, a couple of desks, a few rats, a few old theater seats, a screening room next door—and it stayed that way. "Ed was kept away from us," a staffer said, "because that was Fred's department." If a problem developed in Murrow's presence, it was put on hold for later.

Friendly drove them, stretched their horizons, and learned in turn to write to film. "We made him a film person; he made us journalists."

Adept at producing "Murrow" copy, Friendly turned out the first draft of the narrative, the product of close interplay between the writing and the cutting. Said Bonsignori:

> As the pages came out of the typewriter, we would grab it. We knew how long it took Murrow to say a line, so we'd read and cut the film to coincide with Murrow's timing. When it didn't go with the film, we'd go back and have him rewrite. Then, when we finished cutting, the script would be typed up, and Natalie, Fred's assistant, would take the first draft to Murrow. There was constant contact between them on the phone, too, even in the first stages. But you always [had to] cut the film, structure it, *then* write. You can't proceed from written script. Its dead, mechanical.[76]

The copy, thus prepared, then went through numerous reworkings, nonstop, Friday into Sunday, with input from both the producers, repeated drafts drawn up by the infinitely patient Natalie Foster, expert in decoding scribbles, unfailing backup, and unruffled soother whenever things got manic. Sunday morning on Park Avenue, she took down Murrow's closing piece on the little Royal portable that was his present from the OPC—the copy boiled down quickly into notes, transcribed on the block-letter typewriter at the CBS-TV newsroom at 15 Vanderbilt, and stashed at Murrow's feet for ready reference in the broadcast. Teleprompters were taboo.[77]

They throve on jangled nerves and sheer adrenaline, producing foreign and domestic coverage in an age before jet transport, videotape, communications satellites, or logistical supports. There was no traffic department, all arrangements for airlines, hotels, ground facilities, customs, film shipments, pickups, and lab negotiations juggled by the invaluable Williams and his assistant.

Friendly, with Murrow's authority behind him, did the elbowing to get them what they needed, uncaring as he drove up the budget, unashamedly demanding. They were not intimates, much as Friendly would have liked it, in some ways not close friends at all; said Gude, "Fred could never get beyond that barrier." Professionally, however, they worked as one, the perfect pairing. "Fred had the *chutzpah*," as a staffer put it, "Ed had the prestige."

Everything fought its way onto the show. Pieces of a report might be blocked out and cut, then dumped for better footage. Nineteen out of every twenty thousand feet of film wound up on the cutting room floor. A story breaking before the airtime might dictate a last-minute change, knocking the whole Rube Goldberg apparatus out of whack. Fights over cuts bordered on the manic, spilling over into outright violence. Friendly was known to throw pencils—points first. Once, in a fury, he put his fist through a loudspeaker; they left it there as a reminder. Editors recalled him vaulting onto a desktop, his 200-odd-pound bulk looming against the loft ceiling, arms extended: *"You're killing me!"*

Murrow, if present, never interfered—at least not before the others. Once, though, as they were leaving for the night, the two partners going off together, a staffer saw them stop partway down the block, heard Murrow's voice, more in sorrow than in anger: "Fritzl, don't be such a *maniac*."[78]

But Friendly was a loyal boss, commanding loyalty in turn. He didn't shoot, he didn't edit, and he didn't sit long nights over the Movieola as the write-ups claimed; that, after all, was what one had film cutters for. But he had taste and style and knew what he wanted, a perfectionist, constantly in from the screening room—"How long until we see it?"— tearing through the latest cut, only to send it back, and back again. He put in long, hard hours, was on call day and night. (What's wrong? he asked Bonsignori as she telephoned a query in through chattering teeth one wintry midnight. "I'm freezing." The heat was down. He turned up an hour later, arms piled high with outsize woolen sweaters, socks and mittens, looking like a one-man garage sale.)

If Friendly was the presence, Murrow was the gray eminence, the editor-in-chief and buffer vis-à-vis the management, the guy on the bridge, as Williams later saw it, setting the course for the stokers in the engine room. He also acted as a brake for the exuberant Friendly, maintaining the balance of information versus showmanship.

Mike Bessie would recall sitting in Murrow's office one day when Friendly came in with word about advance preparations for an upcoming program—"something they were going to do in the South, maybe on school desegregation." The producer laid out the handling, the approach; a sharp disagreement followed, ending with Murrow telling his partner they couldn't set things up the way *they* wanted them to go.

> Friendly said, "Well, maybe nothing will happen." And Murrow said—I thought rather sententiously—"But Fred, that's the sort of thing we can't *do*." After he had left, I said to Ed, "That was an impressive exhibition—was that for my sake?"
>
> "No," he said, "this television thing is terribly tricky. Maybe nothing *will* happen. It's a very troubling question." I know it disturbed him.[79]

Edward Bliss, a talented newswriter soon to replace Jesse Zousmer on the 7:45 news, watched an interchange over a bridge passage that Friendly had just written—and that sounded just a little too good to Murrow: "That *exactly* what happened?"

"Well, it's the gist of what happened."

They checked back. "What happened," Bliss recalled, "was not quite as dramatic as what Fred had written."[80]

"Sometimes artistry can get in the way of reportorial fact," said a staffer later. "And Murrow was the guy who kept the record straight."

He saw himself as a text, not a picture man, listening to the sound track during screenings. Actually, it was out of radio, his highly individualized brand of journalism, that *See It Now* derived the concept of "the little picture," a concept as old as the blitz broadcasts, with their striking, easily graspable vignettes. By the same token, the horrors of Buchenwald had defeated him by their sheer vastness—"when we found thousands of well-worn children's shoes, the children's bodies having been consumed in the ovens. I think the impact would have been greater, had we found one or two well-worn but eloquent pairs of shoes."

"Symbols, if they are to be understood, must be small," he wrote in January of 1952. "It must be possible to isolate them from the mass, whose faces or names cannot be recognized or remembered."[81]

"The little picture" may have begun in radio, but it was perfect for the little screen, and the film staff felt he understood the medium.

Of the two partners, he was the more aloof, more comfortable in the field with the blue-collar bonhomie of the camera crews, relaxing over scotch and a few hands of poker. For the rest, and for a long time, there was deference on one hand, shyness on the other.

One time, Wershba, kept in New York, accepted Murrow's invitation to stay over. In the library at 580 Park Avenue, Murrow had shown him a small, worn book, the title faded on the plain wartime binding—*Red Hills and Cotton*, Ben Robertson's memoir of his Carolina boyhood. "He was my best friend," said Murrow.

He pressed the book into Wershba's hands. Read it, he said; only please, be sure to give it back. Obviously, it meant a lot to him.

Wershba returned to Washington, bemused, unable to grasp the tentative effort to reach out. After a decent interval, he returned the book, unread.[82]

Their real contacts were on the road, or in the screening room, when the chief came down to view the all but final cut—in boots and blue jeans if he came from Pawling, rounding off the screening with a mumbled "helluva job," occasionally flipping round silver dollars to the editors.

Sunday afternoons, the star, three TV cameras, and sundry personnel squeezed into the cockpit that was the control room of Studio 41—Murrow seated before the monitors; Friendly, crouched at his feet, cuing him from out of camera range; Don Hewitt, controlling video and audio output via hand signals or by breathing instructions via a chest mike to the technicians sitting inches away, wearing earphones. The open microphones picked up everything, absolute stillness essential.

Hewitt, later the top producer in TV news, creator of the popular *60 Minutes*, was an outsider; not really on the Murrow team and made to feel it; the boy wonder of TV news until Friendly had come along to nudge him out of first place. But, said Hewitt later, "I learned a lot in that control room—about pauses, and emphasis. Working with Murrow and Friendly, I learned that it is your ear, as much as your eye, that keeps you at a television set. It's what you hear, as much as what you see." It was one reason, he said later, for the success of the post-sixties show.

He also studied Friendly—commenting on Murrow's reading in the run-through before airtime, a critical listener, then settling on the floor for the telecast, prompting the newsman with a tug at his pants leg, or a poke with a pencil:

And I remember once—right on the air—Fred jabbed a little *too* hard. And Ed, in the middle of his piece—he couldn't see him because it was out of camera range—just kicked Fred right in the face, and went on doing his piece. What he was saying was, "Stop poking me with that fucking pencil."[83]

The producer emerged, happily, with his glasses intact and no missing teeth.

2.

Joseph McCarthy, gearing up for reelection, was barnstorming across the country, with the media as usual in tow—San Francisco to Appleton, Wisconsin; Laramie, Wyoming, to Northampton, Massachusetts and the ivied walls of Smith College, with a return engagement back in Wheeling for the Lincoln Day Address before the Republican Women's Club.[1] A tireless campaigner, moving in an aureole of popping flashbulbs and klieg lights, each pronouncement given wide dissemination by the gaggle of reporters in his wake.

See It Now had practically begun its TV run with Joe McCarthy; there was in fact no guarantee that the first *Counterattack* citation hadn't been a trophy of the broadcast. Following the December piece, they had tried to interview the Senator himself, live from Chicago, in an ill-advised three minutes. The idea initially was to question McCarthy one week, then his Senate nemesis, William Benton of Connecticut. But McCarthy, no gentleman on camera, had walked all over Murrow and, in the process, Bill Benton, a personal friend of Murrow's, waging in those months a lonely, courageous fight in Congress for the Wisconsin Senator's expulsion.

Sidestepping Murrow's polite, persistent queries about the rights of citizens before congressional committees, McCarthy used his time to accuse Benton falsely of hiding behind congressional immunity—McCarthy's favored tack—before he made his charges, deliberately misquoting, as he did so, the man he called, over the air, "a mental midget."

Benton, two days later, overtly waived immunity, thereby inviting a $2 million libel suit from, of all people, Joe McCarthy.

Murrow—polite, even affable in his appearance with McCarthy—was a study in tight-lipped fury when, the following Sunday, he virtually called the Wisconsin Senator a liar, reading back the program transcript in an icy voice, deliberately pointing out where McCarthy had falsified. "When we began this series of reports, we said that we would try to be the first to correct any errors. . . . That applies likewise to our *guests!*"[2]

Bill Benton—the urbane, enlightened publisher of the *Encyclopedia Britannica*, the living antithesis of "Jumping Joe"—appearing live in follow-up, denounced the runaway investigations and discussed his resolution for expulsion, which would in fact lay the groundwork for McCarthy's censure two years hence.[3]

A gentleman to his fingertips, Benton had absolved Murrow on the

Senate floor that week, praising him as "one of the . . . most eminent commentators in the history of broadcasting . . . I suspect that he is more embarrassed and distressed about this abuse of his broadcast than anyone else can possibly be."[4]

(In a curious twist McCarthy withdrew his suit in 1954, claiming no one believed Benton's charges. An answering torrent of public response proved that a good many folks believed them. The suit was never reinstated. "I'm encouraged by the fact that your program played such a part in the whole episode," Benton was to write to Murrow. "I'm positive there wouldn't have been a suit except for what happened. . . . It would never have occurred to me to waive immunity.")[5]

But they had been used, outmaneuvered by a master of the medium who didn't play by the rules. It wasn't going to be easy, handling Joe McCarthy on television.

At the outset Murrow had placed his hopes, like so many others, in the Republican mainstream—the old true-blue party conservatives, self-proclaimed upholders of the old values, who would surely consider a Joe McCarthy beyond the pale. There was one whom he respected above all, their differences notwithstanding: Mr. Republican. One man could do it, he had told Johnny Faulk. Senator Taft. An honest man.

Shortly thereafter, the AP was quoting Robert Taft to the effect that he had personally told Joe to keep it up, and if one case didn't pan out, try another.

Murrow, sitting next day in post-mortem, was appropriately sheepish, angry and embarrassed at having called it so bloody wrong.[6] For all his image as a liberal, an underlying old-American conservatism drew him emotionally to the long-term pros in Congress, the men of the old rural America, *his* America, no flaming liberals but the embodiments of decency, fairness. It was more than a political sellout, therefore; it was a breach of faith, sparking a lingering resentment that ran through his chilly relationship with the Ohio Senator.

After that he placed his bets on Eisenhower, gearing up for a triumphant return from SHAPE, convinced, with the Democrats on the defensive as "the party of treason," divided and almost paralyzed—Bill Benton was complaining he couldn't get the time of day from party chiefs[7]—that it would take McCarthy's party to put the curbs on Joe McCarthy.

Despite his Democratic ties, therefore, and reservations about the General's apparent lack of sophistication in economics and politics—the Darlan episode still rankled—Murrow initially liked Ike. The war hero was an internationalist and, like himself, a Europe-first man, a believer in firmness with the Russians yet no saber rattler, committed to peace in private off-the-record conversations; who, unencumbered by an unpopular Asian war, was obviously the man to end it, and whose victory might just assuage the White House fever that had led the Republican main-stream down the McCarthyite track[8] and capture control for the moderates now that Taft had sold out.

See It Now features kept the General, while still abroad, safely in the public eye, Murrow's one concern, as he wrote a friend at WEEI in Boston, "that if he returns too soon without a solid record of achievement behind him, the Taft boys will beat his brains out before the nomination."[9]

As an old Europe hand, he was well versed in Ike's ability to charm the press, perfectly willing to let himself be charmed. To David Lilienthal once, he had described the Eisenhower manner as essentially one of "Ed, I've been sitting here for months just waiting till I could have a good long talk about all this with just *you*."[10]

Eisenhower having once declared, there was an eight-minute, down-home preconvention segment shot in his in-laws' garden, sunshine stream-ing down, the General and Murrow in their shirt sleeves, talking and sipping Mamie Eisenhower's iced tea. (Of necessity, perhaps, the piece was balanced off by a live at-home with Taft, all apparently forgiven. The Tennesseean Kefauver, campaigning on a shoestring, Murrow's personal choice among the contenders, also got a TV visit. "It's wonderful to see how friends come to your help," he wrote to Murrow afterward, without a blush.)[11]

But Ike as candidate posed problems from the start, beginning with the kickoff hometown press conference at the movie house in Abilene, where an attempted ban on cameras by the Eisenhower people threatened to leave TV outside in the Kansas mud. Paley, the New Dealer turned Eisenhower supporter, had had CBS run a cable in from Chicago for a live feed, but the press objected; besides, the later TV candidate *par excellence* just didn't like TV. Dave Schoenbrun, earlier, had written in despair from Europe about the frustrations of getting Ike to let himself be televised. (Schoenbrun himself was now in Abilene.) What happened subsequently would be subject to varying accounts.

Murrow's recollection—he was covering for radio and *See It Now*—was that the cameras had been installed the day before, when word went out about the morning meeting with the press. He hadn't spoken with the candidate, didn't know if Paley had. Next thing they knew, representatives from the Republican National Committee were telling them to get the cameras out. They refused.

The wrangling began, culminating in a heated late-night exchange aboard the campaign train with the Eisenhower coterie led by Press Secretary James Hagerty. CBS stood firm, Murrow pointing out with quiet emphasis that the cameras, as he put it, were both expensive and delicate. And if anyone other than the CBS technicians moved them, the Republicans would be liable for a considerable sum of money.[12] The cameras stayed in place.

As the standoff continued into next morning, the Eisenhower people threatened to remove the equipment themselves, then evidently thought the better of it. The meeting went ahead, televised—both live and filmed for later dissemination over the network, the press conference as a media event and the baptism by camera of the first television candidate for president.

When, therefore, that July, the Taft old guard—controlling the party machinery, plumping for a closed convention—moved to ban the cameras from committee hearings on contested delegations, the broadcasters had the Eisenhower forces on their side—"not," as Murrow observed in his nightly radio sum-up from Chicago, "because of any great fondness for [the] gadgets, but rather because . . . a full airing of the proceedings would advantage their candidate."[13]

The lights and cameras, it was alleged, would make the participants look like monkeys in a cage, a development Murrow called impossible "because the camera . . . has not yet been invented that can transform statesmen into monkeys, or monkeys into statesmen. . . ."

> Full visual and oral reporting of the proceedings . . . might of course tend to persuade the citizen, be he Democrat or Republican, that he really doesn't have very much to say about the selection of his candidate. . . . I do not pretend to know what the public reaction would be . . . but it would at least be interesting, and my guess would be that the public could stand it. Whether some of the politicians could survive it is another question.

At Chicago's International Arena, wafted by the rich midsummer aroma of the Union Stockyards, Republicans clashed over Eisenhower versus Taft, cameras versus no cameras. At one point, all cameras were banned from the convention site, then just as abruptly allowed back. "Maybe something matured out there near the stockyards," said Murrow dryly.

As in 1948, he worked both radio and television, but with a difference. In the four short years elapsing, the tilt had gone to TV, from Doug Edwards in the back room at Philadelphia to a major media event, broadcast coast to coast. For the first time more Americans were watching than listening in the prime evening hours, the technical strides, as Bob Skedgell recalled, "enormous [and] by the time we went to Chicago, it was all turned around, all turned around. Radio had become a rather small part of the television broadcast, like two ships passing in the night."[14]

Murrow himself had a low opinion of conventions as a vehicle for nomination ("a political shell-game. . . . rigged, traded, bought and bargained for. . . . There is more freedom of choice . . . at a track, where the horses run"). As one who had cut his professional teeth in the first tense encounters between the parties and the networks, he was concerned with the volatile mix of politics and the temptations of a raw, powerful medium, the heightened prospects of manipulation. He wondered if the parties would now substitute "a carefully timed, smooth-flowing chunk of entertainment" for what was really happening; if the broadcasters would cross the line between reporting the event and influencing it; if directors would be tempted to "engage in a little sleight-of-hand" by editorializing through camera cutaways, deliberately determining impact by what was or what was not put on the screen.[15]

As always, he preferred floor work to analysis, using his contacts, always able to finger a delegation chairman, suggest a drink or two, to get what he was after. He therefore had no feelings, one way or the other, about the new setup which had Walter Cronkite—arrived at CBS on his own, now in his second year—as one-man anchor, unlike 1948.

At forty-four, a veteran of the first big radio conventions, Murrow was now assistant at the birth of the first big TV conventions, the excitement of those earlier times as ancient as the photomikes of 1936. Of that first CBS team, he and Bob Trout were the only survivors. Hans von Kaltenborn was on for NBC. Paul White had turned up for KFMB, desperately ill, his wit still razor-sharp, his face emaciated, the big body bloated from the waist down. "Don't get scared when you see him," Ted Church had warned the others.[16]

The second week of July, the convention was opened up. TV won; so did Eisenhower, the strains of the fight, however, leaving a sediment of antimedia resentment that persisted long after party divisions had been healed.

For the broadcast personnel, working both conventions, the work was harder, the hours longer, the strain greater than it had ever been in radio. "I don't see how you stood the pace," Murrow heard from Walter White, Executive Secretary of the NAACP, following the Democratic meeting. "The longest rest I got . . . was three and one-half hours. But that was loafing compared to what you underwent."[17]

"Already I am dreading the thought of more conventions four years from now," Murrow told him.[18]

He wasn't exaggerating. Nothing, evidently, had shown up in the tests in early January, but in late March, continuing fatigue, weight loss, and sleeplessness had caused the doctors to send him off for two weeks to Florida. Eleven days after his return, however, he was climbing a mountain of mud and clay to interview the pilot of an earthmover, in a cold, driving rain, reporting on the Missouri floods that had made a brown sea of much of the Midwest—crawling over rain-soaked sandbags, holding the microphone to volunteers in civil defense uniforms at 4:00 A.M. on the Douglas Street Bridge between Omaha and Council Bluffs, the picture jumping under the thuds of the dark floodwaters cresting just below. It wasn't stunting; it was part of the scene. Cameraman Martin Barnett would shoot, drag the heavy, wet equipment back to the hotel, dry it off with towels, dry himself, don his sopping trousers, and go back out into the cold night for more filming. The bottom line was, TV reporting made rugged demands, and one either accepted them on their own terms or forgot about working in television.

There was also nightly radio, dropping precipitously in mass audience appeal, but still Murrow's favored news medium—where he could handle topics not addressed on *See It Now*, such as the case of Owen Lattimore, resurfacing in those months and raising questions of surveillance as the State Department barred the eminent Sinologist from leaving the country. Lattimore, exhausted by new grillings before the Senate Internal Security Subcommittee, protested he wasn't going anywhere. The action turned out to be triggered by a tip-off from the CIA, an agency, Murrow pointedly remarked, whose job supposedly began at the water's edge, and which had no domestic—he stressed the word *domestic*—powers.

Over the telephone, an agency spokesman insisted everything was fourteen-carat, Lattimore was going to skip, they had it from a reliable source. Murrow commented: "The CIA could have done two things: either thrown this information in the wastebasket; or pass it on, without either evaluation or proof to the State Department and the FBI. They passed it on. It would appear on the evidence available so far, that the State Department went off half-cocked, and not for the first time."[19]

Similarly troubling him and overshadowed by Korea was the other war in the Far East, which he'd been warned about by such diverse men as Isaacs and R. T. Clark, not paid much heed in 1952 ("Something like 30,000 French soldiers have died in Indo-China . . . "), yet persistingly worrisome, like an itching hidden boil about to break:

> The French have been fighting this war for five years. They have spent more money on it than they have received in Marshall Plan and military aid from this country. They have lost the cream of their younger officer corps. . . . This effort has wrecked, to a large extent, French economic recovery. . . .
>
> American officials are likewise inconsistent. We are supplying arms and munitions to the French, urging them to hold onto Indo-China, to keep Communism from overrunning all Asia. And yet these American officials recoil from the prospect of sending our best troops to fight on the mainland of Asia, where they might well be involved in an Asiatic war, on an even bigger scale than the one in Korea.
>
> It is instructive to remember that in 1947 the British came to us and said of the situation in Greece: "It is beyond our economic and military capacity—you Yanks take over." We did. We now confront the possibility that the French may say the same thing to us about Indo-China. . . .
>
> Of course, I do not know whether these things will happen, but they are possibilities that should be considered and debated lest we improvise our way, without due deliberation, into another minor or major war.[20]

* * *

He was the political reporter that fall, following the Eisenhower mo-
torcade working the New York suburbs, jostled in the crowds turned out
for Stevenson in mid-Manhattan. Personally, he had shown few leanings
toward the top of either ticket, his "friendship" with Eisenhower notwithstanding; besides, the Murrows were instinctive Democrats—enough
so to be startled when Casey, 6, came home from his prep school sporting
a button saying he liked Ike.

Howard Smith thought Murrow "enthusiastic" about Stevenson; others
would recall a slightly macho disdain for the Illinois Governor's tendency
to agonize over decisions, though in style, the newsman inclined less to
the General than to the articulate former lawyer who had presided back
in 1938 when Murrow came to Chicago, to speak on war and peace. In
any case, on foreign policy at least, neither candidate seemed in his view
likely to deviate much from the outlines set by Truman and Acheson.

He had nothing to say publicly regarding Eisenhower's choice of young
Senator Nixon as his running mate. In fact, he rarely expressed himself
these days on the controversial Californian, and then only in closed circles.
His reporting, hence, remained deliberately judicious, nonjudgmental
even after disclosure of the so-called Nixon "slush fund," his comments
restrained after the so-called Checkers Speech and Ike's endorsement
following the public response to "this amazing performance," as Murrow
later put it, "which caused many to weep and only a few to laugh."[21]

The disenchantment, when it came, would not be over Nixon.

No one had written more extensively, indeed more understandingly
than Murrow on the intraparty problems facing Eisenhower, or better
recognized the General's "extraordinary ability to reconcile and compromise divergent views." A talent now needed, after the bruises of Chicago,
to conciliate the party right.

The question loomed large that October, as the Eisenhower campaign
train headed for Wisconsin in the wake of a stunning victory in the September primaries for McCarthy, Tail Gunner Joe outdrawing easily all
other candidates combined—Republicans and Democrats—in an unprecedented voter turnout that confounded the demographers and mowed
down the opposition of the top newspapers and organized labor.

"A clear-cut McCarthy sweep," David Lawrence's conservative *U.S.
News and World Report* termed it, "leaving no room for argument about
the power of his appeal to the voters. McCarthyism . . . emerges as a
political force to be reckoned with, not just in Wisconsin, but in other
states where others in politics will be tempted to exploit its vote-getting
possibilities. . . ."[22]

The question remained: Would the GOP standard-bearer, out to re-
unite the party, bring the Junior Wisconsin Senator under the tent; in
other words, would Ike back Joe?

The signals were mixed. In late August Eisenhower had hedged on
supporting McCarthy, intimated he would not support the *ism*, defended

George Marshall, his wartime mentor—called "a living lie" by William Jenner of the Senate Internal Security Subcommittee, scourge of the State Department's China desk—and accused by McCarthy of "a conspiracy so monstrous" as to dwarf any in history.

Two weeks later, in Indiana, Ike was calling for support of the entire statewide ticket headed by Jenner, a decision, Murrow commented on radio, "in the tradition of the political game. . . . In politics, as in war, there is no substitute for victory."[23]

Next question: How would the General do on the Wisconsin Senator's home ground? The issue came down to a single paragraph in Ike's announced Milwaukee speech. Bill Lawrence of The New York *Times*, with the Eisenhower forces in Wisconsin, learned from inside sources that the candidate planned a ringing defense of Marshall, to best McCarthy on his turf.

It never happened. At the Arena in Milwaukee, Eisenhower, speaking over a coast-to-coast hookup, assailed the poisoning of "two whole decades of our national life" by "a tolerance of communism," charging further the "contamination in some degree of virtually every department, every agency, every bureau, every section of our government. . . . a government by men whose very brains were confused by the opiate of this deceit. . . . advisers in a foreign policy that . . . weakly bowed before the triumph in China of Communists . . .condoned the surrender of whole nations. . . . It meant—in its most ugly triumph—treason itself."[24]

The candidate then called for fairness, the rights of fellow citizens to disagree, and election of the statewide ticket. The Marshall paragraph was out. McCarthy took the credit. Eisenhower aides later denied it, but that was how the *Times* story appeared on October 4.[25]

In Green Bay, Ike told the voters that McCarthy and he had differences but he wanted "to make one thing very clear": that the "purposes" they both had "of ridding the government of the incompetent, the dishonest and above all the subversive and disloyal" were "one and the same" and that they differed only over methods.

Murrow, screening the footage in New York, was livid. Like most news veterans, he took his politics with a grain of salt. No candidate was a white knight on a charger; the name of the game was compromise; Eisenhower couldn't win, presumably, without "the Taft boys." But this was Marshall. His hero. Ike's hero. London. For Chrissake, Marshall had *made* this man's career. . . .

"He was terribly upset about that speech," said Janet Murrow later. "It was a real betrayal."[26]

That Sunday *See It Now* departed briefly from its usual stance of showcasing the candidates, stringing out instead a series of film portraits: Eisenhower wooing the party Right ("Either they have joined him or he has joined them"), Murrow on the voice-over, narrating as though through clenched teeth—"We bring you now some of the new Eisenhower themes":

Ike with Taft, who had made McCarthy ranking Republican on key committees; Ike with James Byrnes; Ike with Jenner; Ike telling Green Bay voters that his and McCarthy's purposes were one and the same; Ike endorsing the Wisconsin slate, including "your junior Senator," the rapid succession of frames highlighted by an overly familiar, jowly figure with a nervous giggle: *"Joseph McCarthy—of Wisconsin."*[27]

Memories differ. It was then, said Bonsignori, that Murrow told them to start laying in McCarthy footage, to compile a film dossier. Not so, say Friendly and Palmer Williams. The order came sometime in 1953. Whatever the timing, something had been radically altered those last weeks of the presidential contest, a corner rounded.

Election night in the newsroom, they watched the Eisenhower-GOP landslide bulldoze the twenty-year-old Democratic coalition. Ted Church was crying. The rock-ribbed Republican conservative was standing and looking at the numbers, tears running down his cheeks. Funny thing, though: he didn't *look* happy. Did their news chief and sometime worker for the party national committee know something they didn't?[28]

Murrow saw the Eisenhower victory as a personal one, the General running well ahead of his party, the Rooseveltian formula unstuck, the Democratic candidate—"a man who spoke often in the accents of greatness"—defeated because "too many people liked Ike." As for the winner, "He will have great freedom and great power, if he chooses to use it. . . . He can unite and lead, or he can be captured. . . . Only time will tell. . . ."[29]

Bill Benton had been unseated in the Senate sweep. He was taking his children to Paris for Christmas, he wrote Murrow; "when they enjoy their knowledge of French, they can always say, 'We owe this to Daddy's defeat.' "[30]

The way was open for the big change in committee chairmanships, determined now by Robert Taft, who in 1951 had handed McCarthy his first appointments to the sensitive appropriation bodies that had given him his forum as the State Department's Grand Inquisitor (in a double act with the red-baiting Democratic Chairman of the Senate Internal Security Subcommittee, Pat McCarran of Nevada). Scuttlebutt now had it that the Wisconsin Senator would be handed the powerful Government Operations Committee—which, incidentally, had a permanent investigating subcommittee—once the transfer of power was completed, the lame-duck liberals retired to lick their wounds. Brought to mind were the warnings of Adlai Stevenson, himself bearing the clawmarks of McCarthy, speaking out against "the fantasy of fear" earlier that fall before the Murrow-Friendly cameras and sounding a note of caution about "the big guns, the not-so-secret weapons of . . . the Republican Campaign[31]— the Junior Senator from Wisconsin. Will *he* be enlightened and chastened by the heady wine of triumph?"[32]

* * *

November 23, fewer than three weeks after the elections, *See It Now* for the first time left its normal beat of party politics, local color, foreign affairs, and the military, to plunge headlong into McCarthy's America.

Scott and Wershba were busy, so it had been left to Palmer Williams to get the cameras to Harrison, New York, population 17,000, bitterly divided over a proposed loyalty oath for all organizations using local schoolbuildings: the national malaise in microcosm. "I don't know where the information came from, how we knew it," Williams recalled. "But we knew there was a story out there, that there was a battle over the thing."[33]

The battle raged at the public hearing in a local high school, and *See It Now* filmed it. For the first time, the angers and frustrations of the domestic cold war spilled out onto the television screen—not from the perspective of a Washington hearing room but from the grass roots, small-town America in 1952, and it wasn't *The Adventures of Ozzie and Harriet*.

For the first time, too, *See It Now* took sides, making small pretense at evenhandedness while filming the debate ("Must you go 'round signing oaths to prove you're a good American?" as a woman speaker put it, plaintively).

It was fascinating sociology and, in a grim way, good theater; not a television playhouse but the real thing. The cameras and sound had caught Americans figuratively at each other's throats ("*You're* the ones that are creating the dissension . . ."); the clash of raised voices; the pandemonium touched off by the tirade of a witch-hunter imported from out of state; and, saved for the closing shot, rising in effect above the clamor, the words of a local minister, quoting the jurist Learned Hand: "That community is already in the process of dissolution, where each man begins to eye his neighbor as a possible enemy. Where nonconformity with the accepted creed is a mark of disaffection; where denunciation takes the place of evidence; where orthodoxy chokes freedom of dissent. . . . Those who begin coercive elimination of dissent, soon find themselves exterminating dissenters. Compulsory unification of opinion, achieves only the unanimity of the graveyard."[34]

There was a further twist, however, a first-time effect of TV on the event itself. Williams, looking for the story, chasing around the building with a *News of the Day* operator, had come across the school board, meeting upstairs in the library, voting on the proposal that was ostensibly to be debated. "So that when they came out to go down to the auditorium," he said later, "they had already made the decision—before they held the public hearings. But the people in the hall apparently didn't know that the fix was in.

"Well, I came back and sat down with Fred when we ran the film and said, 'You know, the whacky thing here is that these guys held this goddamn meeting up in the library and made their decision right then and there; and *then* went down to sort of ameliorate the public.' And that's what we said on the air. And then, of course, the people in Harrison were ten times as mad."[35]

Amazingly, the school board, in that earlier, more naïve time, less practiced in TV, had let themselves be filmed taking the loyalty oath. It made an odd scene, distinctly unedifying: the assorted members lined up like automatons, swearing in chorus that they were not now nor had they ever been . . . "Now sign this—"

To the denizens of CBS it must have seemed even odder—the choice alone of subject; the edited-in voice of the wheedler at the meeting ("Ladies and gentlemen, don't make a *problem* of it . . ."); Murrow on the voice-over—"They *signed* the oath"—his own voice expressive of his obvious feelings not only about loyalty oaths but those who signed them.

When the President-elect went to Korea that December, in fulfillment of his campaign promise, the Murrow-Friendly cameras followed, filming GI reactions ("Hasn't made any promises on how he's gonna get us out"). One young soldier, out of earshot of his officers, summed up the general mood of the program: "I'm over here in this [blip] place here. . . . Don't want to stay here longer . . . don't think I can cut it."[36]

A week later Murrow himself was headed for the war for the first time since 1950, filming "Christmas in Korea," a projected one-hour special, the most ambitious undertaking yet of TV news, involving almost the entire *See It Now* pool of camera and sound personnel, the two staff reporters, and CBS correspondents Bill Downs, Larry LeSueur, Robert Pierpoint, and Lou Cioffi: five camera crews, filming on the front line in the depths of the Siberian winter. "A risky undertaking," said Downs on his departure, "especially for Murrow, who still has to answer to my wife for ruining the family holiday."[37]

They worked in near-zero temperatures, snow, rain, and sleet reported along most of the front. Murrow doubled as reporter and executive field producer, with responsibility for assignments and for army arrangements in moving the camera crews in and around the strip of no-man's-land where both sides exchanged artillery fire or fought battles for a few yards of hilltop. They filmed on windswept ridges, air bases, a hospital ship; watched the wounded being unloaded from the helicopters; sat with nurses at the 8055 Mobile Army Surgical Hospital, better known under the acronym of MASH; panned ruined villages, the streets of Seoul, field services on Christmas morning; and rode a C-47 dumping leaflets over North Korea. The footage plus each reporter's "dope sheets"—the descriptive notes and information accompanying the rolls of film and audio—went to Tokyo in batches, and from there to Friendly in New York.

It was a seat-of-the-pants procedure, eclectic, no scenario other than the basic concept, i.e., the Korean war in closeup. "The least usable picture we could get," Friendly had written, "would be twenty bombers flying in formation . . . or a correspondent interviewing a general about strategy. . . .") They had a collective list of ideas, expanded on during ad hoc huddles in the field or at the day's end. Mornings before 8 A.M., they departed for the front by air from an abandoned racetrack near Seoul. Murrow decided which units would be where; thereafter they were on their own. There were no armies of assistants, no directors, just the basic trio of reporter, camera and sound, plus the heavy thirty-five-millimeter equipment that left the camera operators with a legacy of back problems and kidney ailments.

Mack remembered being dumped on mountaintops within firing range between the bursts—just himself, Murrow, and the sound engineer— with scant minutes to grab up the equipment and scramble for cover. Mack, with the automatic reflex of the card-carrying IATSE member,[38] would react with horror to the sight of Murrow reaching for the stuff— "Ed, don't pick it up; you're not used to it; you'll only hurt yourself"— answered with a mumbled, cigarette-obstructed "yeah, yeah."

"And of course," said Mack later, "he'd go right ahead, humping the equipment."[39]

Charlie Mack was to work more closely than anyone in the field with Murrow: two good old boys with shared blue-collar origins and an instinctive understanding, based partly, one suspects, on Murrow's willingness to admit there was a lot he didn't know. Film people, therefore, found him easy to work with, open to what would be "a helluva picture," and a thoroughgoing pro, ready to go through innumerable takes without a tantrum. He might suggest a shot, but it was as a word-man talking to the experts.

"He could think of vignettes to shoot," said the cameraman, recalling, "the focusing on people." Often he didn't think much of Murrow's suggestions pictorially at first; "when I got the idea behind them, I understood. . . . But you had to be quick to grasp what he wanted, divine the thoughts behind his request."

(It was a request from Friendly, however, that led to the program's most memorable shot. Everyone had been told to send back a shot of a foxhole being dug. Actually, said Palmer Williams later, World War II was the big foxhole war, more so than wintertime Korea, but Fred wanted that old front line symbol. Up on a ridge, Murrow found a sergeant from Nebraska hacking away with a shovel. "This was his 24th birthday," the newsman noted for Friendly, "[a] possible opening for show . . . . boots boots boots."

Charlie Mack shot the boots, the hands holding the shovel, the shovel fighting the frozen earth. Friendly made it the opening: a cooperative effort and a wartime TV classic.)

They shot for nearly a week, Murrow filming the closing sequence on Thursday, Christmas morning. He had been working through a severe cold, apologizing in his notes for some of the narration. He'd also kept up his radio reports, on call constantly, the man in charge, his film notes for Friendly evincing growing signs of weariness:

> Opening shot Xmas tree. . .battalion hquarters 1st tank battalion. . . interviews general conversation. . . .Roll Two Eyemo are cut ins for Sound roll No. One. . . .PANMUNJOM. . . .Comparison of DELE-GATES LATRINES. . .THIS is real cleavage. . . .NOTE . . the mortar and 155 stuff could be plainly heard. . . .Roll #4—EYEMO—cut in scene. . . .
>
> Cheers boy. . .I am too old. . . .Having wonderfull time. . .you should be glad you arent here. . .sorry but thats the way it is. . . .Mack is shooting too much of me . . this is NOT a piece to make a hot shot of Murrow. . . .
>
> Third day. . .i think. . .Fourth Interceptor group . . tough day . . notes would be better but am bushed . . . will try open and close for show Pusan cemetery tomorrow . . also will try some method fast shot all camera men who sure as hell deserve visual credit. . . God bless. . . .[40]

The neutral zone at Panmunjom came as a shock—a surrealistic scene where the anonymous fighting forces on both sides became teenagers with heavy weapons, Americans moving freely within the magic circle 3,000 yards inside enemy lines: "Their buddies are up on those dirty brown hills, killing and being killed, and then they walk up the road . . . and meet Chinese and North Koreans whose buddies are also up on those hills, killing and being killed."[41] Yet in a lasting dichotomy he could still broadcast, on Christmas Eve, an open letter to his son employing the starkest cold war language, reminiscent of the bitterest days of 1951.

Nonetheless, the cold, harsh Christmas week of 1952 sent him back somewhat chastened, the images of Panmunjom lingering in his mind, and of "American and North Korean boys, exchanging mortar fire"[42]— part of a qualitative change beginning in those weeks and soon to accelerate with the death of Joseph Stalin.

Friday, December 26, they began the long journey back via Tokyo to Seattle—the last of the film sent to New York the day before, for the Sunday broadcast—the mood good, if somewhat bleary, following a late-night windup celebration. Wershba, after staggering back with a comatose Ed Scott slung over his shoulder, saw next morning where they had narrowly skirted a sheer drop. Murrow had been up at six, making the rounds of command posts by helicopter, thanking individual officers for their cooperation. He had been in the field more than anyone that week.

A story later went the rounds, confirmed by Charlie Mack, that they spent the hours over the Pacific playing poker, using Life Savers as chips, Mack absentmindedly nibbling at the pile before him before realizing with a shock that he was eating his winnings. The grinning faces around him gave nothing away.

"Why didn't somebody stop me?"

"From what, Charlie?"

In desperation he turned to Murrow. "Ed, you're an honest man—*tell* them."

Murrow looked up, straight-faced. "I didn't see a thing, Charlie."

As they neared the West Coast, Murrow began to complain of feeling ill. Probably just his stomach, the others assured him, but he felt worse by the time they had landed.

At the Seattle-Renton Airport, they made their way in little groups to the VIP room. Wershba later remembered watching Murrow come in— "very pallid, very weak, no strength. So worn out, he hadn't even had a drink. And this was someone who'd always given me the impression of resilience, of physicality. I suddenly saw how frail-looking he was."

Inside the room, Murrow dropped onto a bench and stretched out. He'd rest a while, he told Mack, until they cleared their cameras through customs. It seemed reasonable enough.

At the customs counter the official gaped at 125 pieces of photo and sound equipment—"If you think I'm gonna go through all that, you're crazy! Get those things the hell outa here!" Chortling, the cameramen headed back to the lounge with a good story, they thought, for Ed.

He lay unmoving on the bench, the others crowded around him.

Someone had rounded up a doctor. "This man has to go to the hospital." The *See It Now* people stood stunned while arrangements were made. Wershba would remember bending down to Murrow, asking, Should they let him know how the show turned out? It sounded so obvious, said Wershba later, so downright silly even as he asked it of Murrow—"and with his last strength, he gave me one of those looks and said: 'That wouldn't be a bad idea.' "[43]

Shortly thereafter, still dazed, they boarded the New York flight while an ambulance rushed Murrow to the General Hospital in Renton.

"Christmas in Korea," aired December 28, was a smash. Jack Gould in next day's New York *Times*[44] called it "one of the finest programs ever seen on TV. . . . a unified mosaic that gave the persons sitting thousands of miles away at home a sensation of participating in the ordeal. . . ."

Filmed at the height of the cold war, the program reflected the consensus supporting the American presence or at least U.S. motives in getting in; but it reflected just as clearly the sacrifices and frustrations of what the Army itself, in a summary total released that Sunday, called "a bloody stalemate."[45] And in that connection, amid the greetings home and stock answers to the stock question ("Well, soldier, what do you think of this war?"), there was some footage—previously unthinkable in wartime broadcasting—of soldiers replying that they thought it was a bunch of nonsense.

The overall effect was nonjudgmental, kaleidoscopic. At the end, Murrow, the icebound hills at his back, told the audience, "There is no conclusion to this report from Korea because there is no end to the war."

Almost benign in retrospect, it was nonetheless a giant step ahead of standard TV and newsreel fare. As two TV historians were to put it, summing up the impact in the 1980s, with the perspective of three decades:

> For two and one-half years, most of the day-to-day television coverage of the Korean war had consisted of Washington-based battle reports or mild combat footage, often supplied by the government itself. . . . Seeing the war portrayed in . . . human terms came as almost a shock to viewers. . . .
>
> The program ignored the usual topics of why the war was being fought, how the fighting was going, and what political games of one-upmanship were transpiring at the truce talks. Murrow focused instead on average people and how they reacted. . . . A French officer who kept shrugging his shoulders as he noted that nobody really knew how to end the war. . . . a weary patrol being given its orders and then trudging off to face the enemy. . . . For many, Ed Murrow's Christmas documentary served as their only real glimpse of the confusion, frustration and personal dedication of the forces stationed halfway around the world.[46]

It was a quality caught up at once in the contemporary press. "No artillery barrages, no platitudes," wrote one critic, "the most graphic and yet sensitive pictures of war we have ever seen."[47] What Eisenhower saw on his trip was still a secret, noted *Variety*, remarking on the first true intrusion of the war into the living room. "What Murrow & Co. saw, the American people saw." Gould of the *Times*, not often given to effusion, called it "a visual poem. [It was] a masterpiece of reportorial artistry, a document that in its sensitiveness caught at the heartstrings of the viewers. . . . For Mr. Murrow and his colleagues were only incidentally concerned with armaments, airplanes and guns; their interest was people and what these people did under the grim realities. . . ."

That same day's edition of the *Times* announced that Senator McCarthy had been awarded the Distinguished Flying Cross plus sundry medals for purported "heroism" in World War II.

Murrow didn't see the program. He was out cold that weekend, behind a closed door marked "POSITIVELY NO VISITORS," sleeping like a dead man through the better part of thirty-six hours, the physician's considered diagnosis: flu and nervous exhaustion.

The calls and telegrams accumulated in the interim—well wishes and congratulations from friends in the press, Frank Stanton, CBS Programming VP Hubbell Robinson, Friendly and Zousmer, Paul White, telling him: "STAY THERE UNTIL YOURE REALLY WELL YESTERDAY WAS A NOBLE OPUS FRIEND."[48]

He woke up to the news that the press was waiting; it wasn't every day a celebrity crashed in Renton, let alone a native son who'd made good. Finally, on Tuesday morning, what began as melodrama ended in a Marx Brothers scene as the hospital room distended with photographers, newspaper people, TV reporters, and a delegation from city hall. Murrow, still in his pajamas, sat up amiably in bed as Mayor Joe R. Baxter went into his welcoming speech, climaxed with the presentation of a steel-headed fishing rod and reel, compliments of the city fathers as photographers clambered for shots and an overflow crowd rubbernecked from the corridor.[49]

Asked by reporters about Korea, Murrow said he'd found no sense of purpose, no one knew the answer; Americans couldn't see any end to the war, "only an end to their part of it."

"TAKE YOUR TIME AND REST DARLING," Janet Murrow pleaded in a cable. Late Tuesday night, however, less than sixty hours following his cave-in at the airport, he was aboard a Northwest Airlines' Stratocruiser headed for New York, a Wednesday night appearance on the evening news, and the correspondents' round table to be emceed on Thursday, New Year's Day. The warning lights might be blinking at the man who, as a friend put it, wanted life to be faster than it was, but he seemed determined to ignore them.

3.

"I am gradually getting back on an even keel," he wrote to Dr. Keigwin back at Renton General in early January, but the prognosis was premature. In fact, the feelings of exhaustion persisted through those opening weeks of 1953, leaving him continually irritable. Wershba recalled a heated argument in the lobby of Murrow's Washington, D.C., hotel over a fruitless attempt to get drinks at eight in the morning following a night's work preparing for the Eisenhower inaugural—Murrow edgy and unshaven, insisting on service; the manager adamant in his refusal; Wershba and Murrow's radio assistant Johnny Aaron looking on uncomfortably.

Defeated, Murrow led the way upstairs in a wordless fury to his quarters, the others following—just why, they didn't know. Their confusion was compounded as he stormed into the room, bringing the three of them abruptly face-to-face with Janet Murrow sitting bolt upright in bed, the blankets pulled around her, looking wide-eyed at the door.

Inauguration Day, he was again the public man, less reporter than visiting dignitary in dark homburg and London-cut overcoat, smiling for photographers with Mr. and Mrs. William Paley, at the height of his career and, for the last time, a national consensus figure.

The next day, he signed himself back into the hospital, again for testing and again with no palpable results,[1] the third confinement inside of a year.

What had altered, evidently, was his outlook: the last stage in the sea change beginning in the fall of 1952 and synthesizing under what had been the massive impact of Korea—the cold dark days, the human cost, the lack of answers—followed by his collapse; events and images tumbling over themselves in too-rapid succession like frames in a projector speeded up, ending in the sleep of exhaustion in a strange room in the middle of nowhere, back in childhood surroundings. It was the beginning of one period and the end of another.

Of the waning winter's events, moreover, two in particular were to hit a raw nerve, propelling him further in new directions or, more accurately, old ones. McCarthy, sporting his new medals and new chairman's gavel, announced that one of his first activities would be the investigation of subversive influence in the nation's colleges; "an awfully unpleasant task," he told reporters regretfully, but someone had to do it.[2] Elsewhere Bill Jenner, trading off SISS chairmanship with Pat McCarran, announced the call-up of New York City schoolteachers. HUAC, getting in on the act, announced its own investigation.

The schools. 1933. Germany.

On a Thursday morning, after a virtual two-year silence, delivering the convocation address at the City College of New York, with the press in attendance, radio microphones open, TV and newsreel cameras present, Murrow suddenly tore into "the pompous, posturing, practitioners of terror, those nightriders who would ride down those who are searching for truth."

It was unplanned, evidently, the result of a last-minute plea to stand in for the indisposed Bernard Baruch, first turned down graciously by Murrow—no, he wasn't making speeches nowadays—then suddenly acceded to, thanks in part to the persistence of the City College president, who had simply stationed himself by the Studio 41 door and buttonholed Murrow as he emerged from the control room.[3]

In retrospect it would seem singularly apt that his reemergence, in effect, should have taken place in a university setting, the neo-Gothic stage set of the Great Hall at City College—soaring arches, stone pillars, the draped flags of the great universities—telling the audience he addressed as "fellow students" that great nations were not killed by outside attack:

They commit suicide.
Many of us are inclined to think that we have found the ideal answer to the relationship between the individual and the state. Many of our friends have doubts. . . . We have no need to persuade them that we can produce tanks and aircraft. They have seen them over their cities and rumbling through their streets. The thing we need to convince them of is that freedom is safe here; that we practice it; that we expand

it; that there is not going to be a repetition of what has happened in other countries. . . .

We are so much bigger than we realize. Our potential both for good and evil is so much greater than those of us who have lived . . . in this generation and in this capacious land can possibly appreciate. I would suggest that in matters of politics and public affairs we put our trust not in Mr. Eisenhower or Mr. Stevenson but rather in the essentials of the Bill of Rights because if that goes, all goes.[4]

His comments went out over CBS Radio at 11:30 in the night. TV ignored them altogether, newspapers carried excerpts on the education page; media stars away from their familiar context did not make news in 1953. By that time, however, both the Murrow radio news and *See It Now* had started on a different track, the latter at first cautiously, eye dropper style, then with growing confidence and impact in an upward line that would lead directly to the history-making programs of the fall.

In early February, amid powerful congressional voices raised for the "unleashing" of Chiang Kai-shek—Senator William Fulbright suggested planes for Chiang to bomb the Chinese mainland since the Russians, so went the reasoning, supplied planes for attacks on allied forces in Korea[5]—*See It Now* raised the hackles of the China lobby with a devastating report from Chiang's base on Taiwan, then called Formosa, and on the fate of American military hardware. ("This is a warehouse of spare parts which have been wasting away. . . . Airplane engines worth tens of millions. . . . Vital equipment has deteriorated into scrap. . . .") Troops in training shots were described as liking it on Formosa: "Few of them have ever lived so well before."

But it was the tailpiece that made the difference, breaking, for the first time, with the circumspection of the past. Friendly's drafted ending had been low-key, judiciously dubious of any Chiang invasion of the mainland, of his "navy," and the impact of his American-advised marines: "To most of them and even to their leaders, the 'shame' will not be erased until they have landed on the coast of China. But even if all the troops on Formosa were as good as the marines, six destroyer escorts and a half dozen LSMs does not a landing force make. . . ."[6]

Murrow, pencil in hand, rewrote the copy:

But even if all the troops on Formosa were as good as the marines— and they aren't—Chiang has not the ships, nor the air, nor the supplies, for an assault against the mainland. One U.S. advisor . . . says they *might* manage a landing. But—it would be the *shortest* landing in history. Our Seventh Fleet could *conceivably* put them ashore. But this would involve the United States in a major war with China and possibly the Soviet Union. . . . One military fact is clear: If Chiang's forces go ashore, in strength, *we* will have to put them there. *We* would have to supply them. Give them air cover. And face the prospect of a major land war on the mainland of Asia.[7]

Weeks later, with the Korean War still raging, *See It Now* presented the case for normalization of U.S.-Chinese relations and recognition of Peking, the British parliamentarian Walter Eliot debating and easily besting California's William Knowland, of the Senate right and mainstay of the Chiang supporters. The program filmed debates on censorship among the Arkansas state legislators, in down-home accents that went Frank Capra one better—"members don't have any business goin' over there in Crittenden County and investigatin' a *thing* that they do"—life imitating art. Murrow-Friendly covered the Klan in North Carolina, hunger as a fact of life and politics in southern Italy, and racially motivated busing as a fact of life in Louisiana ("At 5:30 in the morning [School Bus No 34] begins its sixty-mile ride. . . . It will pass . . . five high schools but they are for whites").[8]

But it was the third pass at McCarthy, a full year after the Benton fiasco, that raised eyebrows among those who caught it. They had run two features, back to back, the two Joes, CBS wags noted: Stalin dead; McCarthy live and at his most obnoxious—engaged in relentless inquisition of one Reed Harris, a State Department aide, for opinions held and published as a college radical in 1932, the badgered witness turning at last on his tormentor: "It is my neck, my public neck, that you are, I think very skillfully, trying to wring. . . ."[9]

See It Now called it, dryly, "an example of investigatory technique."

Also caught on camera, seconding the Republican bullyboy, was Democratic Senator John McClellan, who in 1935 had denounced CBS for treason when Murrow put Earl Browder on the air.

The bellwether, however, was radio—quicker than TV, better at picking up the ball as the atmosphere thickened in those early months of 1953 under the new administration. McCarthy, running his committee as a personal fiefdom, hunted alleged reds in the Voice of America;[10] forced the resignation of the head of the International Information Agency (IIA), forerunner of the U.S. Information Agency; and renewed the attack on surviving China experts in the State Department. The newly ensconced Secretary of State, John Foster Dulles, called for "positive loyalty to the nation's policies." Murrow, on radio, differentiated between "loyalty to one's country and blind loyalty to the policy that a particular administration happens to be carrying out,"[11] a distinction not much noted by the Hill or Foggy Bottom.

Instead, the exodus begun under Acheson was accelerating under Dulles. "[George] Kennan made a speech last Friday saying that if we tried to promote the internal disintegration of Soviet power, we would be breaking our international obligations. This appears to bring Kennan, our foremost

Russian expert, into conflict with the Dulles foreign policy. Mr. Dulles said today he had not yet 'gone into the Kennan matter.' "[12]

John Carter Vincent, former chief of the Far Eastern bureau at State and a favorite McCarthy target, had resigned. "Vincent suggests that the Eisenhower Administration re-study the idea that we 'lost China.' He says this is a phony idea, peddled by the China lobby."[13] A new government loyalty program upped the ante of the old one, with one Scott McLeod, an ex-FBI agent and avowed admirer of Joe McCarthy, installed at State as security chief. "Foreign Service personnel are scared to death," Murrow reported, quoting a senior officer who had requested anonymity. "They are afraid of Senator McCarthy, of the committee staff. . . ."[14]

His old friend Raymond Swing, working at the besieged Voice of America for the past three years, phoned in the casualty figures. Murrow offered him the microphone: Say anything about McCarthy you want. Swing declined but kept the information coming. In Europe, McCarthy aides Roy Cohn and David Schine were making the rounds of IIA libraries, knocking suspect titles off shelves. In Washington the State Department pledged cooperation with the ongoing hearings.

"So far as Senator McCarthy's investigations are concerned," said Murrow, "the record merely indicates that neither President Eisenhower nor Secretary Dulles are [sic] prepared to criticize or condemn, either his objectives or his tactics."[15]

By the same token he was re-examining other articles of faith, including the arms buildup he had so vigorously supported, against the backdrop of a changing set of international realities: a possible truce in Korea; the death of Stalin, his last months marked by calls for a summit with the President-elect, cold-shouldered by Dulles as a PR move.

What was changing for Murrow was less his view of the Soviets than his view of the United States. Indeed, he publicly distrusted the initiatives going out from Stalin's successors ("They'll always settle for the world" was his favorite assessment; Soviet tactics might change, he would say, but not long-range objectives, "for unless they are willing to deny their doctrine and their dogma, . . . to reverse their revolution . . . they must go on down that road that Stalin charted.")[16]

Yet he was too close to Western Europe and its leaders not to be aware of growing sentiment—though he didn't believe it himself—that the US, not the USSR, was the main obstacle to a thaw in East-West relations, "that we, the United States, are a greater threat to peace than the Soviet Union."[17]

"A nation's capacity for compromise decreases as its re-armament increases," he broadcast weeks before the death of Stalin. "In seeking to create the will to fight, do we not thereby destroy our ability to negotiate?" It was a borrowed notion,[18] somewhat heretical for network radio in 1952, as was the observation that there was "no reason to think that the Russian people, who have had a lot more first-hand experience with war than we have, do not dread and fear the prospect of another one, as much or more than we do."[19] He went on:

> The term negotiation implies compromise; painful concessions on the part of both parties. But the only alternative to diplomatic negotiation is eventual war. . . .
>
> Assuming the improbable, if Stalin should announce tomorrow that he is sincerely ready to negotiate a world-wide settlement of our differences, what would we say? What are we prepared to give up? And if we confess the inability of our own statesmen to compromise on these vital issues, we must also recognize the difficulties facing the Kremlin.[20]

Hardly a radical position, but it was coming from a centrist, the most prestigious broadcaster, possibly, over the mass media, the absolutes of the past two years ("We will win this struggle for the world")[21] fading as a point of reference.

"Back in '40 and '41," he told an interviewer, "I was sure about what we had to do. They called me a warmonger but that didn't bother me, for I knew I was right. Now we have two opposing forces equipped with the most devastating weapons ever known to man. What do we do? I just don't know. And it's that uncertainty that makes me feel absolutely helpless."[22]

To the public at large, the Murrow of 1953 was no crusader, no ax-grinder beyond a mild Americans for Democratic Action (ADA)–certified liberalism on the standard domestic issues. ("Civil rights," as he once put it, "social and economic equality of opportunity, conservation of our natural resources, housing, public health, inflation; the whole vast complex set of problems [to] be solved if this country is to remain stable.") Within the cold war consensus he was considered a moderate. His slow reassessment of that late winter and spring, therefore, responding to the tides of change, couldn't help having an impact on a broad-based public that was weary of the shooting war and, increasingly, of the cold war.

The result, accordingly, rubbed off not only on radio but on television.

"Ed wants . . ." It was Friendly's favorite opener inside and outside the *See It Now* organization. Did Ed really? Often, no one knew. It was Friendly they saw from day to day, Friendly who gave the orders.[23] "For a couple of years," said Palmer Williams, "I thought, *Jesus, this guy Friendly's a bloody genius.* I used to *hear* Ed whenever I could but quite often missed him because we were working."

In fact, later comparisons of *See It Now* with *Edward R. Murrow with the News* would reveal that the former often took its cues and viewpoint from the latter; and that the more controversial the topic, as *See It Now* grew more venturesome, the more was it likely to do so.

Increasingly in those months, radio launched the trial balloons for television, whether on McCarthy, the chances for a U.S.-Soviet thaw, or U.S.-Chinese relations. Occasional rare memos would also land on Friendly's desk (the phone was favored), laying down precise directions—"Subject: Lancashire/. . . should be shot in relatively small textile town. . . ./Unemployment in a textile town and what it means . . ./How do the people feel about . . . trade with the Soviet Union? /Do they feel that American policy against trade between the Communist and non-Communist world is justifiable and workable (Anything we can get here on the fear of American policy leading to war or economic collapse would be useful)."[24]

Editorially, therefore, *See It Now* was Murrow's instrument, the more so as it moved away from its two-year diet of official spokesmen, Americana and the military, into adversary programming.

It was the spring of the book burnings, of frightened IIA staffs in Europe making autos-da-fé of objectionable titles, concomitant to an East German purge of books allegedly containing "pacifist tendencies," including *All Quiet on the Western Front*. They were merely catching up with the Americans, as Murrow saw it: "The sense of superiority which we had when the Nazis were burning books can scarcely sustain us now."[25]

The atmosphere in Washington, between the hearings and the expanded loyalty review dragnet, was near-manic. Bill Downs, reporting for CBS-TV, finding himself screaming and drinking too many martinis, begged Murrow's help: "Ed, just get me out of here!"

"Nobody at the State Department would talk to him anymore," Roz Downs said later, "nobody at the Defense Department would talk to him anymore, nobody in government would talk to anybody—they weren't even talking to their own friends anymore, the things that were happening were so awful. It had just reached the point where everybody in Washington seemed stark, raving *mad*. Everybody was crazy—and frightened."[26]

Downs, one of the media's angry men, kept after Murrow, one of a rising chorus intoning, *Do* something about McCarthy. Not one of these clever let-the-audience-decide numbers. Hit him head-on. Hard. Forget radio; everybody bitched about McCarthy on radio. It had to be TV, and only he, Murrow, had the access.

It was getting to be a leitmotif. Roz Downs later remembered an evening at the Murrow apartment, following their sitting in on the 7:45 news. Janet was out. Murrow was fixing drinks, fumbling unhappily with the ice bucket.

He said, "My God, don't we have any ice?"

I didn't know if he knew how to get ice out of the refrigerator, so I said, "I'll get the ice," and Bill said, "Oh, for cryin' out loud, *I'll* get the ice."

So Bill starts out to the kitchen, and Murrow turns around to me and breathes this great sigh of relief because he could see Bill was just *ready.* "Make you a bet that it's gonna be two minutes before he mentions McCarthy to me and he's gonna say, 'Okay, Ed, when are you gonna take on McCarthy?' "

I looked at him and said, "Ed, you are completely wrong. I'm surprised he went to get the ice out first. He's going to walk back through the door with the ice, and he's gonna say, 'Okay, Ed, when are you—' " and just then Bill walked back through the door.

Ed looked, said, "You won."

And Bill said, *"Okay, Ed, now I've gotten the ice. When are you going to stand up to McCarthy?"*[27]

They broke up. "It's not funny, goddammit! Do you know what that man is doing to the country?" Murrow grew serious. He knew Bill was covering this every day, he said, that he was close to the story. But Friendly just didn't feel it was time yet.

What did he mean, Friendly didn't think so? It was *his,* Murrow's, decision. Though obviously there were problems, they agreed, and yes, timing *was* important. Eisenhower had endorsed McCarthy only a few months ago. How did you attack McCarthy over something as powerful as nationwide TV when the President of the United States, the war hero, the landslide incumbent, had made him respectable?

"If you had not had elections in 1952 . . . ." as one reporter put it, "because remember, Eisenhower came in, in January of '53, having been with McCarthy in the '52 campaign. You've had the President side by side with this man, calling for his re-election. Are you going to say this man is undermining the country?"

Newspapers and radio were saying just that. Over TV, just possibly, where images counted for more than words, there might have to be some daylight between McCarthy and the President. Draw a bead, without seeming to take in the White House or the Republicans at large.

It raised another problem. "On radio," said a reporter who made the switch to TV, "you could report some things McCarthy said and leave it that way. But on television you also had to have film. *And then you were advertising for him.* You suddenly made him a big hero on television."

It would be heard to recall, in the 1980s, the fact that there had been as yet no TV news exposés, that TV news itself was just out of its infancy, the mystique of government concomitantly stronger than in later, more disenchanted times. "It was a touchy thing to do" said a correspondent, "to attack a U.S. Senator. It could go one way or the other. Had it been done before? Not on TV. They were breaking new ground, Ed and Fred, and everybody was a little afraid. The only way they could do it was by using the man himself, which was finally the way they did do it."

There were, however, other elements in the mix, which Murrow understandably did not discuss, either then or later.

"Were you aware that some persons have been spreading accusations against you?" a colleague wrote from Little Rock. There had apparently been a flare-up at a local TV station where a representative of Facts Forum—the Dallas-based media operation funded by the food processor and oilman H. L. Hunt, bankroller of McCarthy—went into a fury at the mention of Murrow's name ("that fellow traveler!"), promising to provide proof of the broadcaster's "tainted leanings."

"The 'proof' has not yet arrived and I doubt it will," Murrow's informant wrote, "but the man can do a great deal of harm. . . ."[28]

At the same time a "guest" radio commentator surfacing in Houston was heard launching an attack on HUAC's critics, from Drew Pearson to William Shirer, but singling out for special attention "the case of the fellow traveller Edward R. Murrow . . .

"Now mind you only a few people know that he was one of the directors of the Moscow Summer School."[29]

"This is not exactly news to me," Murrow wrote an informant. "I know these things are said. . . . I do not propose to worry over them. One just has to learn to live with a situation of this kind."[30]

He was candid in that it was not exactly news, less so in his philosophical stance; truth to tell, he had known about the "situation" for some time.

It was Chet Williams who first talked about it openly some twenty-five years later, recalling those years when his own government career had fallen victim to the McCarthy onslaught.

Williams, a quarter century after the fact, could no longer pin down exactly where the first warning had come from. There were numerous informal networks, individuals, organizations, monitoring McCarthy by means overt and occasionally covert, all trying to spot his next move and Williams knew them all: State Department colleagues out to protect Dean Acheson in the backwash of the Hiss case; private groups concerned with McCarthy's links to the radical right[31]; an ex-newspaperman trained in intelligence, ingenious at effecting infiltration of McCarthy's staff, right-wing groups, and right-wing files, using McCarthy's own techniques against McCarthy.

Williams would object to calling it a network: "It was defensive; there were people under attack, colleagues in danger. They were concerned with [McCarthy's] dishonesty, the threat to the country."[32] And it was somewhere in the mix, evidently, that word came down the pike that his friend Ed Murrow was in for serious trouble—something along the lines of a major investigation into Murrow's alleged Communist ties in the thirties. An exposé of America's top broadcast journalist. Juicy stuff. Not for some time yet, though; a few more heads had yet to roll. Said Williams later, only half-jokingly, "Why pick on Murrow until you had enough of his cronies practically locked up? But McCarthy made a considerable mistake in picking on the Army."

The time frame, he recalled, was, at the latest, early 1953, possibly earlier.

Why Murrow, with others—notably Elmer Davis—much more unrelenting, some denounced on the Senate floor? The word was simply, he was vulnerable and prominent, the classic headline-getting combination. The Alger Hiss case of broadcasting, maybe? Said Williams later: "They thought he would be a very good victim, easy to pin to the cross. They knew very well what his connections and friendships were, so when it all came out in the open, they had no difficulty pulling the things out of their file.

"It wasn't Murrow pursuing McCarthy; it was that McCarthy didn't like Murrow."[33]

The major participants mostly deceased, there would be frankly little documentation to substantiate Williams' early-warning account. The network did exist, its existence documented in memos and reports. Murrow, outwardly and publicly, seemed aware of something in the works—"This is not exactly news to me . . ."—almost deadline-conscious. And it was to Williams, with his access to the network, that CBS turned when Murrow, in effect, forced the issue.

Chances are, therefore, that the broadcaster, by early 1953, was probably aware he was on some sort of hit list, in which case timing would be crucial in terms of effectiveness and sheer self-preservation, knowing that on TV especially, you got only one chance to go for the jugular. That in the flattened landscape of the early 1950s, there would be no second try. And that to be caught in the open, drawing McCarthy's undivided, undistracted fire, could well mean having the Senator come down on *See It Now* like a ton of bricks and possibly consign the program to the scrap heap of the gallant gesture.

McCarthy, quoted in a *Newsweek* interview that spring, was saying he wished all commentators were as "fair" as Murrow. Murrow himself made no comment beyond a certain gallows humor over lunches with Chet Williams, who had now joined the ranks of the New York self-employed.

May 11, Winston Churchill set off a furor by his support of new Soviet initiatives, and his call for a summit. Murrow seized it with both hands; no one could accuse the old anti-Bolshevik of being soft on the Russians. "He believes that there does exist a real chance to negotiate. . . . And he is fearful that the inflexibility of our policy may prevent it. He is concerned that our hatred and hysteria may prevent our administration engaging in secret and unpublicized conversations with the Russians. And he is worried lest our intransigence cause our allies in Europe to come to believe that we don't really *want* to ease the tension, or achieve an agreement. Many of them already feel that way. . . ."[34]

When, two days later, a State Department reply insisted on "concrete evidence" that such talks would bring results, Murrow compared it to "a fighter who says he will enter the ring provided one or the other wins a clear-cut decision. . . . If we are going to refuse to sit down and talk with the Russians, we had better find a better answer than the one so far advanced."[35]

At South Bend, Indiana, George Kennan, severed from the State Department, dragged down by the momentum he had helped create, attacked those marching "under the banner of an alarmed and exercised anti-Communism . . . of a quite special variety, bearing an air of . . . proprietorship. . . . the excited accusers [who] exclude everything and everybody not embraced in the profession of denunciation." Murrow gave it the major portion of that same night's newscast, reading passages from the released transcript—scoring those who "sow timidity where there should be boldness, fear where there should be serenity," assailing the prevailing "semi-religious cult [made] out of emotional political currents of the moment." He quoted the onetime ambassador ("Mr. Kennan") as saying that he had lived more than ten years in totalitarian countries and that "I know where this sort of thing leads. I know it to be the most shocking and cynical disservice one can do to . . . the spiritual equilibrium of one's fellow men."

Then, proceeding with the rest, Murrow removed all distinction between himself and the news source, identifying completely with words that obviously touched his deepest consciousness:

> What is it that causes us to huddle together, herdlike, in tastes and enthusiasms that represent only the common denominator of popular acquiescence. . . . Is it that we are forgetful of the true sources of our moral strength? Afraid of ourselves, afraid to look into the chaos of our own breasts? Afraid of the bright, penetrating light of the great teachers? This fear of the untypical, this quest for security within the walls of secular uniformity—these are the traits of our national character we would do well to beware of and examine for their origins. . . .

During the war, he wound up, back in character, there was a sign reading YOU HAVE BEEN WARNED. "Mr. Kennan has done, what *one* man can do, to warn us."[36]

The networks, however, were more absorbed in the transatlantic competition to cover the coronation of the young Elizabeth II, a great picture story and technological free-for-all involving massive expenditures, live radio coverage, and—in a time before communications satellites or videotape—a race between the two broadcasting giants to get the film back first for televising. CBS turned a BOAC Stratocruiser into a processing lab and cutting room, readying footage for transmission as the film was ferried westward.[37]

See It Now cameras shot footage in the streets of pre-coronation London and aboard the press flight, Pan Am No. 100, flying from New York via Newfoundland. Murrow, Mack, and Palmer Williams, working with Murrow for the first time,[38] wandered among the media-name passengers, filming small interviews. At one point, shooting the bar scene at the plane's lower level, Murrow learned of the presence upstairs of the radio personality Mary Margaret McBride. Could they get the camera back upstairs? he asked Williams. No problem, said the other; they'd just knock off here and go back up. "But"—Murrow looked suddenly concerned— "how would it go *together?*"

Williams realized he meant a transition. The producer explained that you didn't *need* one, that all you needed was a cutaway shot—the pilot flying the plane alone, whatever. Murrow took it in. "Oh. Okay, fine!"

It was a cutting room problem, said Williams later, and he wasn't normally concerned with it, which explained why, after one and a half years, he was still innocent of the basic devices of film editing.

However the coronation film race went, the ratings race went to CBS, featuring as it did the one reporter that Alistair Cooke, in the Manchester *Guardian,* called its secret weapon. Said Howard Smith, rarely one for superlatives: "He shone like a gem on that occasion."

Originally he was to have had the choice reporting spot inside Westminster Abbey, just above the Queen's throne, but he insisted the spot go to Howard Smith as CBS's London bureau chief. Smith said he didn't want it. "You're gonna take it, by God!"[39] The film race made it unfeasible anyway, Murrow reporting instead from along the coronation route, in a drenching London downpour. Then, his stint completed, he rushed for the flying film lab and, without a change of clothes, knocked out his narration for the CBS coronation special, to be telecast virtually on touchdown.

On television all was pageantry and continuity. The radio Murrow followed a dual agenda, commenting, of course, on the festivities, sharing the microphone, as in earlier times, with "my colleague Janet Murrow," but at the same time using the broadcasts as a springboard—sounding out friends in politics and the press, reporting over the air his findings that the British were viewing American policies and pronouncements with "bewilderment and alarm:

"When our spokesmen talk about rolling back the Iron Curtain or liberating the satellite nations, the average Londoner is inclined to say, 'Oh, wait a minute, how do you do that without a war?' And no one from the other side of the Atlantic has told him how that is to be done. And the Londoner looks at the scars from the last war and he says, 'Thank you very much, we just had one, and we would prefer not to have another.' "[40]

A round table linking the CBS correspondents in the major European capitals confirmed growing misgivings on the Continent. "This is not the traditional anti-Americanism, based upon the belief that we are an uncultured, mechanized, money-mad society. This present apprehension is based upon the knowledge that it is *their* lives, *their* institutions, *their* survival that our spokesmen are talking about. . . ."

Both from London and after his return there was one repeated note in his broadcasts—the damage done to U.S.-Allied relations by Mc-Carthyism, a shift in the ancient European concept of America as a haven of freedom, change, experimentation, as he put it. "Every statement about going it alone, every hearing or accusation which destroys a man's live-lihood and terrorizes his colleagues, is regarded as a [further] sign that we have lost our balance."

But beyond that, he said, was "another factor . . . a subtle one . . . a matter of individual liberty in relation to the state; the toleration of the minority view; the right to be wrong; to be non-conformist."

> The British spilled a lot of blood winning those rights, and they pro-tected them even during the darkest days of the war. . . . They believe they see those ancient rights now abused and endangered in America by spokesmen and representatives of the party in power, with no substantial protest or disciplinary action by the Administration. . . .
>
> This state of affairs gives the British furiously to think, and it causes them to wonder, occasionally out loud, about the true nature and intention of the great nation to which they have mortgaged so much of their future.

In early June, John Royal, the grand old man of NBC programming, congratulated Murrow on a *See It Now* interview with George Marshall, driven out of public life with McCarthy's accusations still echoing through the news media. The General, wrote Royal, had had a raw deal from the press. "It would seem that 'freedom of the press' means frequently just a license to be plain, unadulterated bastards."[41]

Murrow thanked him for the note: Yes, Marshall was one of the greatest public servants he had ever known, a view he thought historians would share. "I think, too, that the press and radio have a great deal to answer for since they, more than anyone else, have created McCarthy."[42]

But in radio as in TV, McCarthyism reigned—at least at the two big networks, even, ironically, as CBS correspondents assailed McCarthy over nightly radio. Early in 1953, Ted Church, with an open news slot to fill and given the names of two distinguished journalists—John Van-dercook and Raymond Swing, the latter still with the Voice of America—rejected the two men out of hand, though both were friends of Murrow's. They were "unacceptable to CBS," industry code for blacklisted.[43]

By June, Swing himself, hauled before McCarthy, had left the Voice, calling the State Department "spineless." His listing in *Counterattack*, two years before, ruled out any possible return to commercial broad-casting, in fact shut doors everywhere. What was he going to do? asked Murrow when Swing called him. I don't know, said the other.[44]

Well, would he be interested, asked Murrow, in editing a radio series on CBS for which he, Murrow, did the introductions—something inspi-rational called *This I Believe*, Ward Wheelock picked up the tab. Also, perhaps he, Raymond, could rough out a couple of commentary scripts a week for him, for the evening news, thus freeing him on some nights for TV. And maybe they could "dream up" a few other income-producing ideas between them, and could he tell everyone they'd be working in the same vineyard?[45]

An "ad hoc" arrangement, Murrow called it, which the other man could terminate at any time; a stopgap meant to keep Swing, now sixty-six, afloat. They didn't think much more about it for the moment; at least Murrow didn't.

In the meantime, Bill Leonard, later President of CBS News, then hosting the program, *This Is New York,* found Dan O'Shea's assistant Al Berry vetoing his plans to invite the journalist Theodore H. White, under attack then for his dissenting views on China, onto the show. Murrow, a friend and admirer of Teddy White, dashed off a bristling memo to Mr. Paley and "Mr." Stanton—i.e., who was this individual to be prohibiting a Book-of-the-Month Club author from appearing over CBS, and was he, too, expected in the future to clear guests with this person? "If you have not had an opportunity to read White's [latest] book, I commend it to you. . . ."[46]

June 14, *See It Now* signed off with a student debate on academic freedom and the announcement that the show was going into prime time in the fall, after two years on the screen—"time enough to graduate from kindergarten," as Murrow put it, and trusted its postgraduate programming would be worthy of the public's attention. It was as far as Murrow-Friendly would go in reference to their plans.

In the past months they'd acquired a point of view, worked the bugs out, gotten a headstart on laying by McCarthy footage. Accounting queried the film costs. Mili Bonsignori would remember Friendly replying vaguely about a projected program on investigating committees. As for transmitting on the air, said Williams, "We were pretty trouble-free by then."

It was a serious consideration; they couldn't afford a fluff midway through an attack on Joe McCarthy.

The whole thing, in fact, was problematic. Murrow on radio, talking about McCarthy's tactics, would have to be different from Murrow hosting a half-hour TV program. Murrow as one of a mounting chorus of radio McCarthy critics—even Kaltenborn was tempering his earlier support—differed from Murrow as a lone voice on television. And would the message, given the new evening time slot, draw more attention than the first two shorter McCarthy segments, which had escaped not only viewers but their colleagues?

Finally, there was the context. The radio broadcasts of such as Sevareid, Downs, even Murrow notwithstanding, the leading anti-McCarthy voices—

Elmer Davis, Martin Agronsky, and until recently Drew Pearson—came from the smaller networks that were conduits, essentially, for differing opinions; from commentators who were often under pressure, but were backed to the hilt. At ABC, Robert Kintner, the ex-newsman network president who had wooed over Elmer Davis and who would take the lead in televising the Army-McCarthy hearings, had won a Peabody for refusing to cave in to the blacklist.

At CBS the situation was ambiguous, a certain liberalism permitted—within limits. Murrow was supposedly autonomous, a board member, but nonetheless a member of the news staff operating under a set editorial policy, however much he bent that policy. The public called him a commentator; to CBS he was a news analyst, working under a double standard that viewed a pro-government perspective as objective reporting and damned dissent as editorializing. *See It Now*, pushing the arms buildup, was a news feature; *See It Now* criticizing Chiang Kai-shek, opinion.

The question now was: How much further could he venture without losing the backing essential to professional survival? And how much was he willing to give up in exchange—the basic dilemma of the broadcast journalist, in the 1950's in particular, operating within an industry framework that offered few, if any, alternatives.

Was he really autonomous, therefore, or just at the end of a very long leash?

A small incident, unpublicized, occurring in those same days of mid-June 1953, may have hinted—at least in part—at the answer.

The Ford Fiftieth Anniversary Show remains to this day one of the great all-time TV spectaculars, the night Ethel Merman and Mary Martin sat on stools, sang nonstop, and held the country entranced. In its day it was unprecedented—a two-hour telecast carried live over NBC and CBS, a purported fifty-year overview of U.S. history in song, dance, news clips, no commercial interruptions, bankrolled by the Ford Motor Company at a reported quarter of a million 1953 dollars. The agency handling the show was the Madison Avenue giant Kenyon & Eckhardt; the executive in charge, Wilbur B. ("Bill") Lewis, the former innovative head and virtual creator in the thirties of CBS programming.

It was the show's writer, Howard Teichmann—author of *The Solid Gold Cadillac*, a mild ribbing of corporate capitalism and McCarthyism, a former writer for CBS and graduate of the old John Houseman–Orson Welles Mercury Theater—who first suggested bringing Murrow in to narrate. Here was a man who told the truth, he told the powers, a familiar face, a man whose word could be trusted, who had the credibility to tell America's story in the last fifty years.

The Broadway producer Leland Hayward, mounting the show for Ford, accepted the proposition after some resistance. Says Teichmann, "Leland was for Oscar Hammerstein; he wanted Rodgers and Hammerstein's next show. Oscar was a darling man, very sweet, I didn't know what he was doing. But this was Leland's wheeling and dealing thing." Hammerstein, in compromise, co-hosted.[47]

Murrow once again proved to be more than a "name to narrate," Hayward later acknowledging his "unfailing help creatively [and] editorially,"[48] which had included suggestions for cuts and changes fed to Teichmann in the course of preparation. The projected ending, however, was strictly Murrow's own, and he intended it to be a strong one, a somber closing note to "fifty years of fun and folly": "Right now we are fat while the rest of the world is either lean or hungry. . . ."

The editorial, knocked out in private, misspellings and all, was an unmistakable appeal, to be aimed at that big audience out there, the folks who didn't tune in *See It Now;* a shopping list of national priorities as seen by Edward R. Murrow: negotiations with the Russians, cautions about "indefinitely piling up armaments," warnings that "we are unlikely to solve our problems with dollars or with bombs," and, finally, a plea against the prevailing atmosphere of 1953.

> If we confuse dissent with disloyalty—if we deny the right of the individual to be wrong, unpopular, eccentric, or unorthodox—if we deny the essense of ratial equality [sic] then hundreds of millions in Asia and Africa who are shopping about for a new allegiance will conclude that we are concerned to defend a myth and our present privileged status. Every act that denies or limits the freedom of the individual in this country costs us the . . . confidence of men and women who aspire only to that freedom and independence of which we speak and for which our ancestors fought.[49]

Hayward, by his account, loved it. It was brilliant, he said, something that needed saying. Then he told Murrow to put it in his pocket. "Don't show it to anyone else, please, Ed."[50]

No way, said Teichmann later. "Everything that goes out on the air via network has to be cleared by the commercial editors—that's a fancy word for censors. Each network has its own. It never would have gone out."

Besides, Teichmann knew all about the speech, had budgeted the time; dammit, that was the whole *point* of the show. (His interest was more than academic; he had been red-baited in the local press, his very presence on the show "suspect," as he later described it: "They wanted to make sure I didn't slip in any anti-government gook.")

The agency and sponsors evidently didn't think so.

The confrontation, as Hayward recalled, came short days before the telecast, in the dim recesses of the Center Theater at Rockefeller Center and Forty-ninth Street, nerve endings frayed, rehearsals dragging on into the small hours. "At two or three in the morning," wrote Hayward twelve years later, "Bill Lewis . . . came up to me white-faced, and said Ed had shown him what he proposed to say, and that obviously it could not go on the air—it was anti-McCarthy—anti-government—it would cost the agency the Ford Account, etc."[51]

Teichmann, from his perspective, guessed the censorship came from the networks: "The commercial editor probably saw it, sent it to Bill Lewis, and said, 'No way, José, can this go out.' "

An incredible reaction in retrospect. Certainly there was nothing particularly radical about the speech, nothing Murrow hadn't said on radio, nothing the *Times*, the *Tribune*, the *Washington Post*, or any centrist liberals weren't saying every day of the week. In fact, it could be argued, it had a certain cold war context—i.e., being good enough to win the hearts and minds of the oppressed.

But then, Murrow hadn't worked in commercial television.

He knew Bill Lewis as a friend from the old, pioneering days of *The Fall of the City* and the antifascist poetry of Archibald MacLeish, the nurturer of offbeat talents such as Norman Corwin. But Lewis, Kenyon & Eckhardt, and Ford had learned their collective lesson back in 1950, sponsoring the Ed Sullivan program, when protests against a red-baited guest—the dancer Paul Draper—had brought sponsor and agency under pressure from the right, resulting in their total cave-in and fixing the blacklist firmly in place on Madison Avenue. By June 1953, the last thing Kenyon & Eckhardt wanted was another controversy.

Recollections later differed as to what happened next at the Ford show. Leland Hayward remembered a tussle lasting almost up to airtime, with Murrow apologetic and himself in the role of Murrow's champion, standing up to Lewis, declaring he would go to Henry Ford if necessary.

Teichmann remembered Hayward as the heavy and Murrow not at all apologetic. Just angry. And ready to walk, as arguments moved down to the finish line and Hayward, under pressure from above, made it final. "Leland just said, 'Take the pages out.' "

Teichmann was furious. "My closing was gonna be Murrow. . . . This show had been built for him to do his pitch." Then, in a final twist, Henry Ford decided *he* would close the show. "So he went on. And there was nothing you could do about it 'cause time-time-time was happening and if the powers that be say it's gonna be *this* way . . ."

It was the day before the show. Murrow saw no reason to stay on. "He was ready to leave. And of course, it was Leland's charm; Leland was a man of infinite charm—he could just sell you anything. If I had tried, he'd have walked; but Leland doing it . . ."

The show went on, a smash hit and a classic forever, still effective in the kinescopes decades later, the one enduring image in the public recollection, that of Merman and Martin singing their hearts out. The Murrow speech became a harmless closing dialogue, its message diffused, its impact lost.

He had missed his chance. From here on in, he would play his cards closer to the vest.

XIII

"The Fault, Dear Brutus . . ."

1.

Joe Wershba was the first to see the photostats; though he would never be quite sure in his own mind whether their disclosure had been intended from the start, or whether they had been flashed before his eyes in a fit of pique like an X-rated postcard.

The man who held them out was Donald A. Surine, a Washington acquaintance and McCarthy's top investigator. The press had always thought Surine handsome in a sleazy sort of way—mid-thirtyish, jowls coming on, with the dark, close-cropped widow's peak that gave him a slightly Mephistophelian air. He could be pleasant, however, and his relations with Wershba over the past two years had been cordial. In contrast with the publicized Roy Cohn, he was Mr. Inside, directing an informer network from the basement of the Senate Office Building; a onetime FBI agent cashiered for reportedly maintaining a hooker in a Baltimore hotel at the Bureau's expense[1] and picked up two weeks later by McCarthy; a quick mover whose extralegal commandeering of the IPR dead files from a New England barn had brought down Owen Lattimore and fueled afresh the China controversy; the accused doctorer of photographs whose expert assistance had helped defeat Senator Millard Tydings of Maryland in an election year vendetta. Charges of dirty tricks and strong-arm tactics, laid to his door repeatedly, just somehow never stuck.

The encounter had begun in the corridor outside the Senate Caucus Room on a Tuesday morning, November 17, 1953. Inside, Eisenhower's Attorney General, Herbert Brownell, and FBI Director J. Edgar Hoover were testifying before the Jenner subcommittee, the news media, and a record audience, to the effect that Truman while in office had knowingly promoted a purported Soviet spy in government employ—the late Harry

Dexter White, a New Deal Treasury official—despite FBI reports supposedly proving culpability, and the Director's warning that White was "unfit." The case was a bombshell, dropped some days before by Brownell himself, in a speech reportedly cleared with the White House staff.

White, fit or unfit back in 1946, was dead, his story never concluded, exhumed now in the last weeks of 1953, before the start of an election year. In the meantime, the press and public followed the spectacle of a Republican Attorney General accusing a Democratic former President of consciously harboring a spy.

HUAC had rushed in—unsuccessfully—to subpoena Truman, Eisenhower fast distancing himself from the impugning of a fellow President, while the feisty Truman, over TV and radio, accused the new administration of embracing McCarthyism "for political advantage."

The climax—Tuesday's doubleheader—had therefore been awaited eagerly. Wershba, shooting for that night's *See It Now*, had an air charter readied to fly the film to New York, in no mood to dawdle as partway through Brownell's testimony he rushed from the hearing room into the corridor, looking for his sound technician.

Instead, there was Surine, blocking his path.

"Hey, Joe, what's this Radwich junk you been putting out?"[2]

Wershba tried to sidestep. Surine obviously meant the *See It Now* of a month before which had produced a minor bombshell of its own, the case history of one Milo Radulovich, an Air Force reserve officer facing dismissal because of his family's alleged political sympathies, an indictment not only of security procedures in the armed forces but by implication, the entire context of the national security mania that was at the heart of McCarthyism and indeed predated Joe McCarthy. The response had been tremendous.

"What's Murrow trying to do?" The investigator's eyes were long and wide, with whites that seemed to grow overlarge when he was agitated.

"No time now, Don—"

The other grabbed his arm. "What would you say if I could prove to you *right now* that Murrow was on the Soviet payroll in '35?"

The stunned look on the reporter's face must have told the other that he had struck home.

"Follow me."

Upstairs in the fourth-floor corridor, Wershba waited in a daze of disbelief as Surine disappeared into one of the office doors lining the endless hall—was it McCarthy's? Probably. Alexander Wiley, Wisconsin's "other" Senator, had his office just across the way, though maybe not. By now Wershba wasn't thinking clearly anymore.

Surine emerged again, in his hand two photostats—pages 1 and 6 of the old Hearst Pittsburgh *Sun-Telegraph*, dated February 18, 1935, the headline, AMERICAN PROFESSORS, TRAINED BY SOVIET, TEACH IN U.S. SCHOOLS. The Hearst denunciation of the Moscow Summer School, complete with pictures of the 1935 prospectus, the words *Moscow/USSR* unmistakable beneath the subhead: "Linked to Moscow—American 'Advisors' to Communist Propaganda School." Wershba, scanning the list, stopped dead at "Edward R. Murrow, Assistant Director, Institute of International Education."

Surine ran his finger down the page, "identifying" for the reporter's benefit: Communist, Communist fronter, pro-Communist, relation of suspected Communist. Of course, it didn't mean that *Murrow* was a Communist; however . . .

The ensuing diatribe went on for twenty minutes as Surine railed against the Radulovich program—ridiculing loyalty board procedures, that's what it was, *Daily Worker* stuff; of course, they didn't suspect Murrow but for God's sake, couldn't he understand the issues? The implication was that if Murrow kept quiet, McCarthy would keep quiet. "Mind you, Joe, I'm not saying Murrow is a Commie himself, but he's one of those goddamn anti-anti-Communists, and they're just as dangerous!"

They walked back down the stairs. Wershba paused. Could he show the photostats to Murrow? Sure. But in that yes, the reporter thought he saw a moment's hesitation, the flicker of something undefined in Surine's face, uncertainty, perhaps—enough to make him wonder whether all this had been planned. Or had McCarthy's man let something slip in a fit of bravado?

They parted company, Wershba to pick up the sound man and return to the hearing room. The investigator left behind an extra jab: It was a terrible shame, wasn't it, what with Murrow's brother being a general in the Air Force?

That afternoon, the shooting completed, the film dispatched, Wershba showed the photostats to Charlie Mack. The cameraman peered over his glasses: "uh-oh."

McCarthy's instincts, as usual, were deadly accurate. The "Radwich junk" had indeed been aimed directly at him; Murrow had privately called it "a small footnote in the fight against the Senator,"[4] and he had deliberately picked television as the main arena. Radio, in a historic role reversal, took a back seat with a single paragraph with a Michigan dateline, just the bare facts about a lieutenant discharged for maintaining "too close and continuing" relationships with his father and his sister. "The father is said to [be] a reader of radical publications, and the sister is said to have participated on a Communist picket line."[3]

With that, the action moved to TV. "It may be our case history," Murrow had told Friendly, handing him a wrinkled clipping from the Detroit *News* (AIR FORCE TRIES TO OUST VET; LINKS FAMILY TO REDS).

The hunch paid off. Milo Radulovich, filmed at his home in Dexter, Michigan, was articulate, impassioned, with no self-pity, and a good communicator. In TV terms, moreover—youthful, attractive, a family man, white ethnic working his way through college—he was perfect.

The hearing board had offered him a choice, he said: Break with the family or resign as a security risk—which translated, he explained, meant unemployable. "The implications seemed . . . to be that if I had said, I will cut the blood ties, et cetera, everything would have been beautiful with the Air Force. Well, I simply cannot see that type of reasoning."[4]

Why, they had asked him, did he not denounce his sister's views?

"If I am being judged on my relatives, are my children going to be asked to denounce *me?*"

Wershba, filming with Mack, had sensed right off that this was going to be "a helluva story," as he later put it. "Murrow and Friendly had a big feel for getting out into the country, they felt the better stories were out there."

The townsfolk were indignant—at the authorities—and stated so in no uncertain terms, openly, unafraid to talk, not at all camera-conscious. ("The people in the cities were scared to death to open their mouths.")[5] Here was no effete eastern radicalism, just the unselfconscious decency of Main Street America, the perfect note for a mass audience, crowned with the image of a local Archie Bunker, who, tapped for a minority opinion, replied with Capra-esque eloquence that if "they" could purge this one man, "they" could "do it to *anybody.* You—or me—or anybody else!"

In Detroit, Radulovich's lawyer gave a chillingly Orwellian account of the hearing, involving his client's confrontation with a sealed envelope— the "allegations."

"We were not told who the accusers were. We had no right to confront them or cross-examine them. . . . In all the thirty-two years that I have been a practicing attorney . . . I have never witnessed such a farce."

More than the *See It Now* case history, the affair posed numerous questions—not only about "McCarthyism," but the institutionalized obsession that had produced a Joe McCarthy. Murrow decided on the full half hour.

The momentum started, one step led invariably to another.

The Air Force out at Selfridge Air Base wasn't talking. Friendly, trying for a statement from the Pentagon, got a hostile "Does Murrow know about this?"

It was a fair question, given Murrow's continuing close ties with the military, especially the Air Force—the many hours of *See It Now* coverage; Murrow narration of Defense Department films (a fairly widespread practice then among newsmen); the whole network of personal relationships sustained at the highest levels and deeply rooted in the common experience of World War II.

When the phone call came in to the Pentagon, therefore—i.e., *See It*

Now on the line, proposing to question security procedures in the armed services over nationwide TV—the public information officer on duty must have wondered if he was hearing right.

"Does Murrow know about this?"

Friendly came in on cue. "It was his idea."

Friendly in his classic account of his TV years, *Due to Circumstances Beyond Our Control*, described the scene ensuing forty-eight hours later in Murrow's office, as a general and a lieutenant colonel, rushed up from Washington, tried to talk him out of it. Reasonably, of course; they were all friends after all. It was a matter of national security . . . the cold war . . . one couldn't be too careful . . . these were difficult times. . . .

Murrow just as politely stuck to his guns: no statement, no case for the Air Force.

It was then that the tactics switched. The general didn't think the program would get on the air. He reminded Murrow of the old days, his decoration for "Distinguished Service to Air Power," then ended on the punch line, "You have always gotten complete cooperation from us, and we know you won't do anything to alter that."[6] With that, he faced an adversary.

They watched the visitors file out, then went ahead anyway. To do otherwise would mean censorship by omission. But it also meant no balanced show.

The program aired October 20 pulled no punches, homing in at the outset on Air Force Regulation 35-62 and opening a sustained inquiry not only on a blanket regulation—AF 35-62 had branded Radulovich a security risk for "close and continuing association with Communists or people believed to have Communist sympathies"—but the mentality embodied in its sweeping application, the McCarthy Era in one stark example.

It was commercial television, 1953, handling, suddenly, the hottest political potato of the time—not in euphemisms, not through debates or surrogates but directly; not in retrospect but at the height of the national obsession and over a medium dependent for its license on a government that had partly caved in to, and partly fanned the hysteria. A half hour of undiluted controversy thrown like a jagged rock into the placid surface of the so-called golden age of television.

It was also the first time the victim was provided with a forum over the mass media—heretofore the prerogative of the accusers—spelling out what it all meant, financially, socially, in terms anyone could understand: "Are [my children] going to be judged on what their father was labelled? Are they going to have to explain to their friends . . . why their father's a security risk? . . . I see a chain reaction that has no end. . . ."

("The guy has a fire in his belly," said Murrow when the film first came in.)

Backing it all up were the good folk of Dexter, Norman Rockwell's America rising in its wrath. Murrow, on camera for the windup, read first from the transcript of the hearings, then from the typescript of his commentary in a final change of ground rules: no pretext of impartiality, no quick concluding jab ad-libbed from Natalie Foster's notes. The tailpiece was a precise, straightforward Murrow editorial, carefully drafted, the product of successive rewrites, and ending on the note that "whatever happens in this whole area of the relationship between the individual and the state, we will do it ourselves—it cannot be blamed upon [Soviet Premier Georgi] Malenkov, or Mao Tse-tung, or even our allies. And it seems to us that—that is, to Fred Friendly and myself—that this is a subject that should be argued about endlessly."

It was the individualist assertion of the radio commentator on TV, the single focus of responsibility, in contrast with the composite, more diffuse image already characterizing network television.

Reply time was extended to the Air Force, finer points drawn on the question of due process in the military, the respective differences between so-called security risks and loyalty risks. But the program was unquestionably loaded; nothing could compete with those images. Nor was there anything about the rights of Communists or just plain radicals, the father a political innocent, the sister's interview judiciously brief. It was an undisguised attack on guilt by association that stopped short of the nature of the "guilt," the focus kept deliberately narrow, set by a communicator who understood instinctively the temper of the public, homing in on one simple biblical, overriding message—that " 'The son shall not bear the iniquity of the father,' " that any country requiring otherwise was headed in a pretty frightening direction, and the time had come to get it in the open.

Public reaction was swift and outraged, the Radulovich affair transmuted from local issue to national test case inside half an hour, via television.

"In a sense, you are his Zola," wrote columnist Harriet Van Horne in a private note to Murrow. "And thus we are all in your debt. . . . Your 'J'accuse' was quiet and cool, and therefore the more effective. Considering the climate of opinion we live in these days, you are an extraordinarily brave man."[7]

There was no question about the program's cathartic effect. Thirteen years later Friendly recalled the studio technicians thronging Murrow at the show's conclusion, some with tears in their eyes. "I've just left my TV screen," Laura Z. Hobson, author of *Gentlemen's Agreement*, wrote that Tuesday night, "so moved, so profoundly grateful. . . . During the last minutes when you were speaking from the screen, I actually said out loud, 'Bless you, damn it, bless you.' "[8]

Jack Gould in next day's New York *Times* called it "a superb and fighting documentary. . . .a long step forward in television journalism," commending both network and sponsor for permitting "a vigorous editorial stand in a matter of national importance and controversy."[9] That the network had consented—in the sense that it had not said no—was indisputable; some middle-management shock, says Friendly, but no interference. But neither, the program ended, was there any feedback. CBS had also drawn the line at advertising, leaving the partners to purchase ad space on their own in Tuesday morning's *Times*, minus the CBS logo, putting up $1,500 cash up front when the network refused to advance the money to the *Times* on its regular account.[10]

By contrast, sponsor feedback was favorable. Although likewise declining to run an ad, ALCOA had agreed beforehand to drop the middle commercial. Meeting for his annual luncheon with the two producers, ALCOA's president, Irving Wilson, with whom they dealt directly, praised the program while hoping they would not concentrate exclusively, as he put it, on "civil liberty broadcasts."[11] For now, however, "Chief" Wilson, the heart and soul of ALCOA, known in the industry as Mr. Aluminum, was solidly in their camp.

It was the CBS affiliates, rather, that seemed restive; in addition, said Friendly later, unease emanated from the top at having been presented with an eye-popping *fait accompli* (though not wholly: Middle management, offered a peek at the footage, opted out). Hostile columns, too, began appearing for the first time, amid the choruses of praise from the establishment and the left.

Radulovich himself, in one of those ironies of network broadcasting, didn't get to see the program. Three weeks before, the CBS Detroit affiliate, WJBK-TV, had dropped *See It Now* for something more salable. (Nor, for that matter, did old John Radulovich, a retired auto worker who, feeding the camera crew their last night on the case, gave his real opinion as they trooped out the door, logy with Serbian salami. "You know why they do this to my boy Milo? They *jealous*—because *he* a *lieutenant!*")[12]

The final scene would be written on a late November morning, with a call to Murrow's home from Washington. It was 8:00 A.M.; the caller, Air Force Secretary Harold Talbott—Murrow had met with him a month before, with no result; the Secretary wanted Charlie Mack over at the Pentagon by 9:00 to film a statement.

Hours later in the screening room, they got the word that the Air Force had backed down. A cheer went up. It was still before noon, but Murrow broke out the scotch. They lifted their glasses: "To Milo!"

"Ed was more pleased about this than anything else," said Wershba, thinking back on that day. "It was clean. No rough edges. It was a victory."[13]

"So that's what they've got."[14]

Murrow looked down at the photostats, the headlines and layout different from those in the New York *American* of February 18, 1935, but the story the same: the screaming boldfaced catchwords, advisers' list,

I. V. Sollins' pamphlet in facsimile, wreathed in a jumble of display ads for Washington's Birthday and Cherry Week at McCann's Shopping Court.

Wershba, describing his encounter with Surine, told of McCarthy's investigator running down the adviser list to stop at "Edward R. Murrow" (*Graham's name appears on the list, as does yours*).

Wershba saw his boss glance up at him with an oddly sheepish smile, almost embarrassed. He had not been looking good that night when the reporter sought him out after the evening news: rather pallid, obviously going through another of his heavy colds. For a few minutes he talked, not about the photostats but about McCarthy, his effect on the country, the news media, himself. He asked Wershba to write up the incident, then went off down the corridor. To the other man he seemed tired and defeated; Wershba had intentionally omitted the threat against his brother. Watching Murrow's retreating back, with its familiar hunch, the young reporter felt suddenly sorry for him.

Next morning at the water cooler, it was obvious that the Senator—or someone at his office—had made the same miscalculation as the Air Force the month before. Murrow was in a fury, his cold gone, along with his usual low-key manner, lips drawn back so tightly that his teeth showed: "The question now is, *When* do I go against these guys?" Wershba was reminded of the deadly boxer who before the main event asked the referee, "Which corner do I go to *after* I've knocked him out?" Murrow, said Wershba, seemed mad enough to chomp a live bear. For a fleeting moment the reporter transferred his feelings of pity to Joe McCarthy.

As it happened, another round was already in the offing. Alan Reitman, later Associate Executive Director of the American Civil Liberties Union, then handling ACLU publicity, was on the phone with Friendly about a lockout in Indianapolis, where they had been prevented from hiring a hall.

"We were organizing affiliates throughout the country," said Reitman later, "ironically prompted because of the McCarthy movement."[15]

The start-up meeting, scheduled at the Indianapolis War Memorial Building, nearly wound up scuttled when local officials, under pressure from the American Legion and the Minute Women, canceled the reservation. Suddenly every place in town was booked. Then, in a dramatic turn, a local priest offered his parish hall, turning a near rout into a PR bonanza—"particularly from the image point of view," as the ACLU official put it, "since it wasn't often [then] that a Roman Catholic priest was allied with the Civil Liberties Union; there was sometimes much difference of opinion. But he saw the dangers of McCarthyism."

It was not the sort of thing TV had handled, but now there was Radulovich, and besides, Murrow off-screen was a friend of the house, "one of those people," said Reitman, "who understood what civil liberties really were.

"We didn't have a close working relationship, but we knew the general thrust of Murrow's programs and his attitude. [So] we just literally seized on the opportunity, and knowing Ed and his colleagues understood the issue—and it was just a marvelous story—we simply called them up. There was no problem of quote selling the story. I mean, they saw it immediately: 'Quick, where is the meeting to be held?' I told them and they said, 'We'll have someone on the plane.' "[16]

It was two days after the confrontation in Washington, one day after delivery of the photostats. Said Ed Scott later, "We went ahead, even after the Surine warning."[17]

The following Tuesday, November 24, See It Now ran "An Argument in Indianapolis," preceded by a short: three minutes and nine seconds of Secretary Talbott reinstating Lieutenant Milo Radulovich.

Then came the argument: crosscut footage from the ACLU meeting and an American Legion meeting, held three blocks away in protest; the Legion, asked for a statement, had decided on a meeting of its own. As a result, two camera teams were working full time in the two locales, an early indication of TV, by its very presence, shaping the outline of the event.

The content, it could be argued, was diffuse—less a debate than two sides talking past each other more or less in generalities ("Controversy is as American as the . . . Fourth of July"), lacking the sharp focus of Radulovich, both sets of speakers tending, if anything, to ramble in their TV incarnation. The point was more strongly made by the camera odyssey tracing the ACLU's earlier room hunting amid the landmarks of the downtown Midwest of the 1950s, the prevailing mindset caught in chilling interviews ranging from determined opposition to the more common desire simply not to get involved. This wasn't Dexter, no solid phalanx of citizens standing up for the Bill of Rights, but the program sounded, once again, a simple centrist theme: *If it can happen to these nice people, it can happen to you.* Or as Father Victor Goosens of St. Mary's put it, everyone sooner or later wound up in a minority group of some kind.

And as at Harrison, now one year past, the valedictory was with the decent clergyman: "When the climate is such that so many people are so quick to take the law into their own hands, or rather . . . to ignore the law and to deny to others the right to peaceful assembly and free speech— then somebody certainly has to take a stand. . ."[18]

Contrary to appearances, it was totally ad-libbed (prepared speeches were taboo on *See It Now*), resulting from a query as reporters chatted with the priest before the meeting, i.e., How'd you get into this? Father Goosens had started in about how there was something more basic here than just a meeting place, when they cut in—"Hold it, Father!"—and waved the cameras over.[19]

The message got through; critics and civil libertarians were ecstatic. Norman Thomas complained afterward to Murrow that the ACLU speakers had not stressed sufficiently their anticommunism,[20] though what gave the show its timelessness was precisely its rejection of the usual disclaimers, the focus, rather, on the Bill of Rights.

The ultimate impact, of course, resulted from its being televised at all, in that winter of 1953–54, when the very term *civil liberties* had come to be equated somehow with subversion in the public mind. Reitman, looking back, saw Murrow's role in those months as one of "public education," getting the viewers back on track, the ACLU program part of an uphill series, in which McCarthy would be but the icing on the cake. "What he was talking about," said Reitman, "was the moral question and the fundamental concepts of this country. Not just as a newsman looking at a story which was interesting, but as someone fighting to get the public to understand the intrinsic value of free speech, and free association, and due process of law, as the fabric—the central fabric of the whole American democracy."[21]

As for the Indianapolis show, it was also a clear-cut private message to McCarthy, telling him what he could do with his photostats.

Leaving Vanderbilt Avenue the night of November 24, Murrow asked his partner, How much McCarthy footage did they have in the vault? Friendly figured about 50,000 feet. Was there a film of the Wheeling speech? When Friendly expressed doubt about it, he asked him to hunt up an audiotape.[22]

That winter *See It Now* brought Truman and Brownell before the cameras, in filmed debate over the Harry Dexter White case. The program ran debates on the admission of wiretaps as evidence in the federal courts, requested in those months by Attorney General Brownell, Murrow warning listeners over radio that "he who listens once may listen twice."[23] *See It Now* had planned another full half hour on the topic, ostensibly giving both sides, Friendly calling Lou Nichols at the FBI, and with perfect earnestness asking to film two agents doing a demonstration wiretap.

The horrified official said no way, and surely they wouldn't want their program teaching people how to tap a telephone!

Friendly was audibly taken aback at the other's unexpected vehemence; he understood, he said. Still, they thought a demonstration would be good "pictorially."

Oh, he was *sure* it would be good pictorially, Hoover's deputy spluttered, but it was not particularly in the public interest to furnish the wrong people with a TV manual on wiretapping.

"I hope to live long enough to have you say yes to something," sighed the producer. Nichols pointedly reminded him that the Bureau had said yes once upon a time and nothing had ever come of it. Besides, the FBI was not about to be "kissed off" the way Murrow had kissed off the Director in his coverage of the White hearings, with a "mere" one-line sum-up of his testimony. The statute of limitations, Nichols announced, had run out.[24]

(Their talk, it happened, coincided with another call from CBS, requesting current wiretap statistics and replied to with "no comment." Both incidents were duly recorded for the Director's information and commended for the handling, this being a matter, said Hoover, on which they must remain "meticulously silent.")[25]

Murrow and Friendly nonetheless went on with the debates. They aired programs on citizens' rights under the Fifth Amendment, the uses and abuses of congressional investigative powers, and the merits and demerits of congressional proposals to blockade the Chinese mainland. They reported once again from Shreveport ("Thanks for the magnificent exposition . . . of what 'separate but equal facilities' are," wrote NAACP leader Walter White),[26] from Harlem, and from Lawrence, Massachusetts, once a center of IWW organizing. They probed links between redbaiting and anti-Semitism in California and attempts by the Veterans of Foreign Wars of Norwalk, Connecticut, to start a campaign of informing, with directives to the citizenry to forward reports, on "suspected Communists or subversive activities" to VFW national headquarters, for "relay to the FBI."[27]

(That was the one where Eddy Scott called in from a pay phone, after being held by the police: Oh yes, the film was fine, he was coming in, some angry busybodies got the cops out—disturbing the peace, it seemed—but then they turned around and let him go. Send the film, they shrieked into the phone, but see if you can't go back and get yourself arrested! In New Jersey, at a right-wing women's meeting, suspicious members blocked the door as a film crew tried to move in: Who *were* they? "*News of the Day*," said Charlie Mack smoothly, pointing to his camera cases, which, of course, were courtesy of Hearst. Tensions subsided. "Well, as long as it isn't those goddamn Ed Murrow people.")[28]

But it was also the first winter of another kind of Murrow program.

In the spring, evidently, the concept had been pristine, a new idea— he thought it was a lovely one, was how he put it to a friend over lunch— TV broadcasts by people no one had ever heard of, but whose quality and character would come through on the screen, a teacher maybe, a farmer, anybody. The essential thing was, *they'd have to be unknown*. None of this fame stuff; let's hear the philosophy of the extraordinary "ordinary" man.

The listener, Charles Siepmann, once of the BBC, a longtime friend and close associate, professor of communications, and unremitting critic of the media, thought the idea "splendid."[29] At the time.

By fall, of course, *Person to Person* had evolved into live camera visits with the rich and famous, the quintessential home tour of celebrities, Murrow in an armchair in the studio making small talk with the big-name guests appearing on the monitor. The word was, self-styled network experts said no one wanted ordinary people.

The public loved the show. Most of Murrow's friends hated it. Some claimed Murrow hated it as well; others, that he enjoyed it at the outset, showing the public he was more than "just a newsman."

The known facts were that Zousmer and Aaron, following Murrow onto *See It Now*, had clashed with Friendly, found themselves off the show and consequently out of television. Murrow didn't intervene; if Fred had *See It Now*'s headaches, he also had authority. But when the two longtime aides approached him with the idea—one needing the Murrow name and presence to make it viable—he agreed. A private corporation was set up, Zousmer and Aaron as producers, Murrow on camera, the program owned and packaged by the three men, the ownership divided 30–30–40, the series bought by CBS for Friday nights.

Almost everyone he knew opposed it.

"You know, you don't have to do this," Roz Downs remembered telling him.

"I promised Jesse and Johnny."[30]

Friendly understandably resented the claims on Murrow's time, and the use of the electronic visit, developed first on *See It Now*.[31]

Charlie Mack summed up, inimitably, the staff position: "Aw, Ed, whaddaya need that for?"

"Wait, you'll see, Charlie," Murrow assured him, "it'll be something."[32]

As ratings went, it was most surely "something," despite reviews that were mixed at best and the inescapable fact that Murrow wasn't very good at chitchat. In addition, the technology was new and cumbersome, the guests often uncomfortable. The Humphrey Bogarts, as both actors and friends of Murrow, were relaxed before the cameras. But the graceful newlywed John Kennedys, televised from the Senator's former bachelor apartment in Boston, came across as shy and stilted, the bride nearly inaudible behind a glassy smile, the Senator just happening to find a book with his favorite passage within reach—it was by Alan Seeger, author of "I Have a Rendezvous with Death"—and reading in a Boston monotone while an abstracted Murrow struggled with a cigarette that wasn't pulling.

Never mind. The newness and the mix of news star, glamour, and the public's love of rubbernecking were enough to scoot the program to the top ten, where it stayed, enriching its owners and CBS in the course of its long run, a fixed star in the fifties firmament.

It also gained its host instant acceptance among a huge viewership, making Murrow as much a celebrity as his guests, his face familiar in millions of households that didn't follow *See It Now*, and providing, as things would turn out, large-scale credibility when it was needed. (Some thought it no coincidence that the lightweight mass-appeal show premiered fewer than three weeks before Radulovich, though this may have been pushing cause and effect. But the program, undeniably, was worth its weight in leverage. When a friend ragged Murrow once in afteryears about "hamming it up on *Person to Person*—don't say you don't enjoy it," he turned on the man in sudden anger: "Listen, do you know what I can get *away* with because *Person to Person* is a big hit?")[33]

The winter of 1953–54 would be remembered by many as the depth of the McCarthy Era, turning at times into a theater of the absurd. Those were the months in which a textbook commissioner of the state of Indiana called Robin Hood a Communist, the state superintendent of education subsequently promising to reread the Robin Hood literature, presumably for its subversive Soviet implications. In which case, Murrow pointed out on radio, he would come across the versions by Shakespeare's contemporary Ben Jonson, the Victorian Lord Tennyson, and the now-aging Alfred Noyes. "If these writers themselves should now come under suspicion, it *can* be said at least for Ben Jonson and Tennyson [who] predated the rise of modern communism . . . that any communist propaganda in their writings about Robin Hood is purely coincidental. But Alfred Noyes would not be able to shelter behind the calendar in this way, and would have to find some other defense." Also recommended was a purge of textbook references to the Society of Friends, since Quakers didn't believe in fighting wars. The ending to a remarkable week, said Murrow, "notable for the dedication of a new, historic . . . gallery of 'Red rogues of the past.'

"And it is fitting that nominated to it, should be such differing servants of Communism, as Robin Hood, and William Penn."[34]

Even mighty Joe McCarthy had overstepped himself in a bid to hunt for Communists within the establishment clergy and the CIA. In his attack on the Army, however, begun the previous September, he was hanging on with furious bulldog tenacity, stymying peace efforts by the new Army Secretary, Robert Stevens, urged at all costs to get along with Joe.

However self-defeating it may have seemed in retrospect, the smart money at the opening of 1954 was on McCarthy, sporting a rising, broad-based popularity, if Gallup Polls were any indication, plus his clout among the party leadership: a "bulwark"—so said *Life* that winter, toting up McCarthy's chances—rooted in "conviction that anti-Communism is a good vote-getting issue, unwillingness to split the party, and . . . respect for his great strength."[35]

A CBS incident, some three years before, would best illustrate the attitude among the military, already prevailing in the Truman era, in the matter of McCarthy.

David Schoenbrun remembered Murrow calling him in one day in 1951. Army Intelligence had been on the phone, he said. "They won't clear you to cover Ike's headquarters at NATO. And of course, if they don't, you can't cover the beat."

I said, "Well, that's great news. What'll I do about it?"

"Well," he says, "you've got a great friend, Omar Bradley, and number one, you're going to see Omar."

Bradley, says Schoenbrun, "threw a fit" and called Army Intelligence, "who told Omar Bradley, Chairman of the Joint Chiefs of Staff, to go to hell.

"So I went back and told Ed. And he says, 'Uuuuuuuooh, it's a lot more serious.' He says, 'Look, you're a close friend of Morris Ernst, aren't you?' I said, 'That's right.' 'Well,' he says, 'Morris is a good friend of Hoover's deputy. Go see Morris.' "

Army Intelligence had based its decision on an FBI file. Ernst called Washington, Schoenbrun went down to read his file: "absolute drivel . . . the most chilling experience of my life." Advised to submit counterbalancing information, he detailed his wartime record in intelligence, top-level clearances, confidential work for Eisenhower, endorsements by leading American ambassadors. Army Intelligence said no again.

"So Omar took the case to George Marshall, who as Secretary of Defense had the authority to issue my creditation card, but he didn't want to compromise his high office." In the end, recalled Schoenbrun, Marshall got a newspaper friend to sign the cards for him *pro forma*—there were twenty-two such "cases"—because, he said, he didn't want a subpoena from McCarthy. ("And that was the end of it. Murrow had kind of saved my life, what with steering me, though the man who really saved my life was Morris Ernst." It was also then that Murrow told him about the denunciations of 1948: "This isn't the first time it's happened.")[36]

From Europe, the correspondents were reporting fears of an American slide into fascism.[37] From Princeton, Albert Einstein warned in an open letter of "the far-reaching analogy" between his native country and "the U.S.A. of 1954:

"I must think of the Germany of 1932, whose democratic community, through similar means, was so deeply undermined that Hitler could quite easily deal it a deathblow. . . . I am firmly convinced that the same thing will happen here if those who are clear-sighted and capable of self-sacrifice do not resist."[38]

But those resisting in the news media weren't getting much encouragement. On February 2, as *See It Now* probed vigilantism in Norwalk, the Senate voted the McCarthy committee another year's worth of appropriations by a vote of 85 to 1. Fulbright alone dissented, others were simply absent, with a divided administration, for all its backstage jockeying, conspicuously silent.

It was at Colbee's, off the CBS lobby, that Murrow saw the slight figure approaching, familiar mostly from twelve years ago in London—Joe Julian, Norman Corwin's lead for *An American in England* back in '42, more recently seen now and then at Colbee's, though there hadn't been much contact.

"Ed, I'm suing *Red Channels* for libel. Will you be a witness for me?"

To Julian, it sounded wacky even as he said it. But almost four years on the blacklist had made him a little desperate—that, and a case which, taken up in 1950, was about to go to trial without a single industry witness for the plaintiff.

As for Murrow, it was three years since he had refused to debate the publisher of *Red Channels*.

"Just say where and when, Joe."[39]

February, at the federal courthouse in Foley Square, scene of so many cold war confrontations, McCarthy was publicly ripping into a local base commander, General Ralph Zwicker, a decorated war hero, over the automatic promotion of a drafted army dentist who had taken the Fifth, raising the cry among his press allies of "Who promoted Peress?" In a tasteless follow-up, the Senator had done a gleeful reenactment for the Washington's Birthday celebration of the Sons of the American Revolution, a bad PR move for once, alienating further the soldier in the White House; but McCarthy, as anyone knew from the past four years, was a survivor, facing down momentary bumblings, corruption charges and expulsion resolutions ("I don't answer charges, I make them"). The January Gallup Poll figures indicated 50 percent approval for the Senator's performance, only 29 percent opposed, all others uncommitted. He had openly challenged administration nominees, said "communism" would be an issue in the 1954 elections, though Ike had said that it would not—thus publicly contradicting the President and nominal leader of his party—and looked to be changing his "twenty years of treason" theme to twenty-one.

Tuesday, February 23, Murrow pored over the Zwicker hearing transcripts, published verbatim in a sensational disclosure by The New York *Times*, then added his evening commentary to the chorus of criticism in the press and radio—i.e., how long was McCarthy to "delve into departmental matters, goad subordinates into criticism of their superiors, taint them with insinuations of Communist sympathies and impugn their judgment and integrity to the demoralization of the department."[40]

At the cutting room he had Friendly rack up their entire backlog of McCarthy film and run it for review. In a nice bit of irony, Palmer Williams fished around in the well-stocked Hearst film library of *News of the Day* and came up with a choice tidbit for the show. Things had started gelling, evidently, well before the Zwicker hearing. To Bob Heller, passing through New York in early February on his way to Britain, Murrow had revealed his plans for the upcoming program. The former CBS producer, symbol of so much gone wrong and off to London with Murrow's introductions, wished him "Good gunning, Godspeed, and victory!"[41]

That week of February 22, events were seesawing back and forth. A bold stance by Army Secretary Stevens on Sunday, was shattered on Wednesday, following a forced peace lunch with McCarthy, in which the

1950: The first annual CBS correspondents' round table was broadcast over radio; left to right: Murrow, Larry LeSueur, Bill Costello, Winston Burdett, David Schoenbrun, Bill Downs, Eric Sevareid, Howard K. Smith. (Courtesy of CBS)

Korea, summer 1950, after a dive in the dirt: With Bill Dunn. (Courtesy of Bill Dunn)

Working the 1952 conventions: an off the tube shot; left to right: Murrow, Walter Cronkite, Eric Sevareid. (Courtesy of CBS)

See It Now: In the control room.

Korea: winter 1952. (Courtesy of CBS)

With the camera crews for "Christmas in Korea." Cameras, back row, left to right: Charles "Charlie" Mack, John "Bocky" Bockhurst, Leo Rossi, Martin "Marty" Barnett, Norman Alley. Sound, front row, left to right: Andrew Willoner, Robert Huttenloch, Chick Peden, Donald Geis, Herbert Tice. (Courtesy of CBS)

Hubbell Robinson (left) and Fred Friendly.

Relaxing in the office. (Courtesy of CBS)

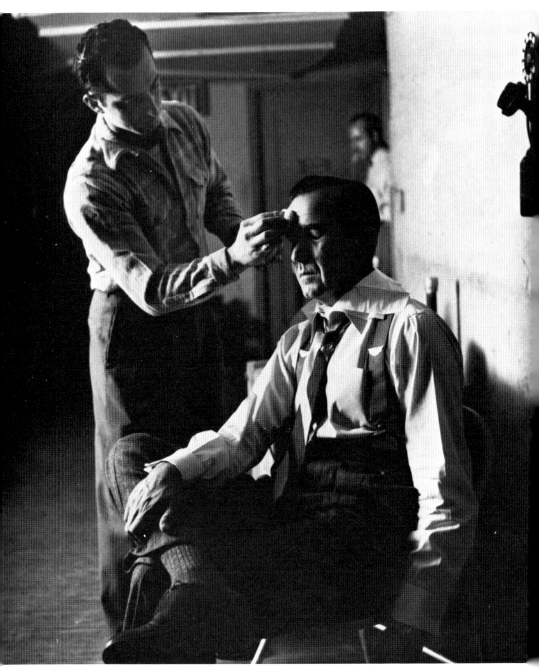

Getting ready for air. (Photograph by Peter Martin, courtesy of Janet Murrow)

Army had backed down. "Loser and Winner" ran the *Life* caption underlining the double shot of the Secretary and the Senator. The press was in an uproar. James Hagerty, White House Press Secretary, was telling reporters that the executive had nothing to do with it, while Vice President Nixon in a not-for-attribution leak told NBC's Earl Godwin that he himself had urged that the GOP's dirty linen not be aired in public and a private meeting *must* be held.[42] ("Let's not pussyfoot on this story," ran a desperate news desk memo, echoing public reaction. "The administration has backed down to McCarthy. That is the simple fact of the story.")[43]

Then, late Thursday, in a sudden switch of signals, Stevens told the press he would not "accede to the abuse of Army personnel," and yes, said Hagerty, the President endorsed it—touching off what newsroom memos were calling "the hottest political story in years,"[44] a red-hot intraparty fight, the future anybody's guess, Jim Hagerty recording in his diary: "Everybody jittery."[45]

That same week at 501 Fifth Avenue, Mili Bonsignori recalls, Murrow said to the staff, in effect, "We go."[46]

The next broadcast, half a week away, was in the works. They targeted the Tuesday afterward.

"I've decided to go ahead with it. The date will be March 9." Janet Murrow later admitted to an involuntary cold shiver running down her spine at the statement, followed by immense relief. It was rather like when the first bombs had started falling, the waiting over.[47]

The timing was, of course, essential, though not without its later controversy: Why had they not done it sooner? From the perspective of TV history—certainly of image—a program done in 1953 would have redounded more to Murrow's reputation. Whether it would have been as effective in another time frame is another question. Indeed, Murrow asked it of himself. (In retrospect, in fact, there would be little dispute on that score among his colleagues. "He had a great sense of timing," as one put it, "knew when to pause and when to speak. And he knew the time was coming for McCarthy to be vulnerable—and he hit!")[48]

Each week's delay thus far had increased the risk, the possibility of McCarthy's striking first. But now the big fish had other matters in his line of vision, the chances lessened of being lunged at with undivided attention, of McCarthy's being free to come down on them with total tonnage, brandishing his research.

More than anyone on staff or indeed at CBS, Murrow was uncomfortably aware of what that research was, or might be—of the whole complex of pre-CBS relationships of which the Moscow Summer School was but a part: the old American-Russian Institute; the whole network promoting New Deal–Soviet rapprochement; the close contacts of the early thirties, doing the world's work with prominent young fellow travelers; the IPR connection, a fact of which the FBI, unknown to him, was long aware. Taken together, it was a prospective incendiary bomb, with damage potential not only for himself and his associates but also implicitly for the IIE and CBS, plus possibly the thought of any further time bombs, forgotten matters, conceivably ticking away at the Institute.

It meant, therefore, deciding on the show in full knowledge of what might well be waiting. He spoke a good deal of Larry Duggan nowadays, in a voice that "smoldered anger," as a crony put it, speaking of 1948 in one breath, 1954 the next, "forecasting—he knew what they would dredge up."[49]

The March 2 broadcast ended with a reference to the "retreat into unreasoning fear" and a promise to "deal with one aspect of that fear next week." They were committed. Strangely, no one picked it up.

The timing, as it turned out, was dazzling. That Saturday, March 6, in the first of a series of events that no one could have foreseen, Adlai Stevenson, addressing Southeastern Democrats, charged over TV and radio that "a political party divided against itself, half McCarthy and half Eisenhower," could not produce national unity, thus beginning the Ten Days That Shook McCarthy.

A stung Republican National Committee asked for reply time and got it, McCarthy, demanding airtime for himself, refused for once.

That Sunday in the cutting room, the *See It Now* team reviewed the next-to-final edit of the McCarthy footage, assembled in a six-day cut-and-splice marathon, everyone pressed into service—from their gofer Ed Jones, fact-checking through mounds of back-number newsprint, to Jack Beck, their West Coast reporter-producer. The dapper L.A. news official who worked for both Murrow shows west of the Rockies, had breezed into town with 20,000 feet of Navaho footage, to be greeted by Friendly with a mock-up of a New York *Times* ad slated for that Tuesday on McCarthy. Again there was no reference to CBS; again the two producers paid the bill.

It bothered Murrow more than he was willing to say. Sidney Bernstein, in town that week, was asked up to the office. "I've got a McCarthy program going out in two days; can you come over?" Over a monitor, Bernstein viewed some of the footage—"still a bit rough," said Murrow. Bernstein was impressed with the sequence of material. A film and TV veteran, he could fill in the gaps; an important program, he told Ed. But something was obviously eating Murrow.

"I want to advertise it in The New York *Times*, make sure people look at it."

"Fine," said the Englishman.

Murrow paused a moment: "Well, the trouble is, Sidney, CBS won't put the money up for it."

"And of course," said Bernstein later, "he and Friendly had to put the money up. But you could see how things were closing in on him a bit."[50]

Years later, William Paley, by then retired from CBS, was to tell Don Hewitt that he hadn't been in favor of the show and yes, he'd said as much to Ed—in private.[51]

As for the corporation, it had turned, to all appearances, a blind eye—no ads, no promos. No one asked to view the final edit, however late in the day, or for whatever reason, would take up the offer. The show would go out, therefore, with the CBS hierarchy wholly innocent of its contents. At the same time CBS Television Press Information cabled the FBI on Monday afternoon, notifying J. Edgar Hoover about the program.[52]

The atmosphere in the screening room on Sunday, March 7, was unusually grim and thoughtful, the flexibility of the past days and weeks freezing into the hard, final decisions of a Sunday night, any bandwagon effect dissipated. Quite the reverse. The signals coming out of the administration seemed to be switching again in an evident backoff, an anticipated strong presidential statement emerging as watered-down sweet reason at Wednesday's press conference, leaving a disappointed, angry press, columnist Joe Alsop overheard commenting audibly, "The yellow son of a bitch!"

"Isn't the White House going to do something about McCarthy?" asked Bonsignori at one point in the screening.

"The White House," said Murrow evenly, "is not going to do, and not going to say, one goddamned thing."[53] His face was red.

That long Sunday session would often be depicted in later accounts by those who were there. The informality, everyone in work clothes, Murrow in blue jeans and suspenders, wearing the red hunting shirt that staffers thought singularly appropriate. The tugs over cuts, shifts of sequences—some of the best clips came from the older shows—and the comments on the film itself: thin stuff; just Joe doing his thing; what was the point? Murrow, indicating the darkened screen, saying, "The terror is right here in this room," that it was *their* fears they were projecting, that the film was neutral; that the context—i.e., the narration—would make the difference.

Asked what he would say, he replied, "No one man can terrorize a whole nation unless we are all his accomplices," elaborating somewhat.

"Mr. Murrow, it's been a privilege to have worked for you," a voice piped up.

"What do you mean—to *have* worked?" roared Friendly.

Nervous laughter. "We were really tense," one man recalled.[54]

It was on what happened afterward that accounts would differ, in what would be a lingering source of controversy.

One of the many ironies of the time was the fact that the McCarthy program ended the insulation of those on *See It Now*. Attacking McCarthy, they became themselves fair game, with Murrow, a buffer in the past, soon to turn target, no longer inviolable, therefore unable to vouch. (The one fear among the staffers, Scott recalled, was, Is Ed too vulnerable?)

Which meant ultimately, under the doctrine of guilt by association: everyone under the microscope.

Bonsignori remembered Murrow's meeting with the film editors earlier that week. None of them, he said, could have lived to this age in this atmosphere without the possibility of *something* in their backgrounds. If there was anything they thought worrisome—"Don't tell me; I don't want to know. But if your credits appear on this show, you might be investigated."

He gave them the choice of bowing out, if they wanted, and starting in on next week's show.[55] No one took him up, doubts notwithstanding ("I wanted to do the show"), and there the matter stayed. "Murrow had a great sense of personal privacy," was Bonsignori's recollection; "he didn't want to go into our backgrounds."[56]

But that Sunday evening, recalled Friendly, the staff in fact was encouraged to speak up. Was there any reason, he had asked, why they should not do the broadcast?

"I said, 'Look, this program is going to have impact beyond anything ever done. And the one who's gonna be attacked is gonna be Murrow. . . . Is there anyone in this room who, in their past, has done anything that could be used to hurt Ed?' "[57]

That being said, he later wrote, they took turns unbosoming, resulting in only minor reservations, no one taking himself or herself out of the line of fire, an action criticized in later, admittedly safer times.[58] There was no question, Friendly insisted later, of jobs threatened or of not going ahead, just a matter of knowing what they could be hit with: "*Nothing was going to keep that program off the air.*"[59]

Said Jack Beck: "He didn't imply that anyone would be fired; it was just so we'd know what's coming—better know now than later."[60]

Others, however—Palmer Williams, Mili Bonsignori—had no such recollection of inquiry or collective self-examination in the cutting room that night. Wershba recalled Friendly bringing up the question of past associations, then quickly cutting off response—i.e., "And if anybody tells me, I'll break his head," or words to that effect. To the newsman it seemed clear that Friendly didn't want to compromise the broadcast. When twice after that, said Wershba, some seemed to feel the need to talk, he cut them off. CBS had had it with the blacklist mentality, he said, and Paley was agreed: They weren't going to play these games anymore.[61]

Monday, March 8, Joe McCarthy came roaring into town, demanding airtime now that the Republicans had designated Nixon, not McCarthy, to reply to Stevenson. The networks would grant him time, he threatened, "or know what the law is." An opening attack was scheduled for Tuesday with an address before the Dutch Treat Club, some of whose members had resigned in protest.

At Forty-fifth Street and Fifth Avenue, the cutting room was alive with activity, Murrow openly in charge, working directly with the staff, Friendly at his side, no intermediary, no "Ed wants." Rarely seen in the cutting room two days in a row, this time he kept on top of things, giving the orders. Bonsignori later remembered his constant, restless presence— "looking at this, looking at that.

"He kept saying, 'This is *mine*'; he wanted it to be exactly right, exactly *his* way, *his* concept; said he wanted McCarthy to convict himself out of his own mouth."[62]

The same held true for the narration, heretofore Friendly's in the first draft, dictated this time, word after word, by Murrow, taking over "completely," then working through the script with the producer, Wershba recalled, in an atmosphere "incredibly tense," the communal atmosphere of Sunday night replaced by a professional absorption, the public man in action:

> . . . cold, reserved, seemingly even bored as he methodically reached for the relentless words that would hammer nails into McCarthy's political coffin. At one point he directed me to excerpt key lines from the editorials of the nation's newspapers. . . . "Give me the short, active words," he ordered. . . .[63]

It might have helped account for the McCarthy program's special quality, although dramatically it was not up to the others. More than any other, it was a "Murrow" program. But there was another aspect to the matter, one that disturbed Murrow deeply.

The title notwithstanding, "A Report on Senator Joseph R. McCarthy" was no report; it was a virtual half-hour editorial ending in a call to action,[64] the final step from TV news purveyor to TV activist, with all that that implied.

It was a paradox that the very memories of the thirties that impelled the broadcast—memories sharpened by McCarthy's lavish funding by the corporate right wing, his sub rosa ties with the hate groups of the radical right, his use of anti-Bolshevism as a steppingstone[65]—also caused Murrow to have second thoughts, based on his own experience of the media manipulation of Fascism in its heyday; the concerns he himself had raised at Chatham House in 1937, concerns subsequently proved so painfully valid; above all, his recollections of the Austrian ex-corporal whose rise, oratory, and skillful use of the airwaves reminded him of the man some still persisted, somehow, in seeing as a clown (or would do so later, with the benefit of hindsight).

"He felt," as an associate put it, "that we were in the presence of a man who could turn America around, who had so much power just in terms of being a destroyer. He feared the beginning of a Nazi-like mass movement."[66]

Nonetheless, he questioned his own use, or possible abuse, of the mass media, the power of TV and his proved ability to sway the masses. Colleagues said he was wary of it; Bill Downs later claimed he feared it. Certainly it was the one quality which, run amok, he recognized and hated in a Joe McCarthy.

He was too experienced a newsman not to be aware of the consequence of throwing out the rulebook after sixteen years to mount, openly, a thirty-minute attack on another individual. He worried about the possible example set: Was it a question of two wrongs making a right?

To Ed Scott over drinks, he confessed he'd been walking the streets until all hours, trying to sort it out. "Eddy," he asked, "do you think I'm doing the right thing?"[67]

Of course McCarthy, it could be argued, had amply had his day in court (still did, in fact, via televised subcommittee hearings weekdays at 11:00 A.M.), with little such consideration given to his victims.

"Ed would never hurt anyone," said Janet Murrow with conviction, "but he felt McCarthy was hurting the country."[68] She had left that week unwillingly for Jamaica, fulfilling a long-standing invitation, Murrow adamant that the McCarthy business have no bearing *whatsoever* on family plans. Better to leave than argue, she figured. The Brewsters moved in from Middletown to look after Casey. Jenny Brewster, waking nights, could hear her son-in-law pacing the living room.

"The McCarthy program bothered the *hell* out of him," said a friend from CBS. "The question was, Did he or anyone else have the right to use this tremendous power to attack one man?"

The question never was completely answered. Despite the program's overwhelming success, Murrow was always uneasy about it, almost anxious at times to disown it. When, in 1955, the producers published a hardcover *See It Now* collection with the New York firm of Simon & Schuster, "A Report on Senator Joseph R. McCarthy" was not included.

If the choice of that week—March 8—was astute, the convergence of events March 9 was near-uncanny. In midtown at the Park Lane Hotel, Joe McCarthy, before the Dutch Treat Club and a record audience, parried the barbed queries of Hans Kaltenborn, a onetime supporter turned opponent, and renewed his demands for air. Dick Nixon was an excellent choice to answer for the party, he told reporters, "but Stevenson's main attack was against me." The Senator appeared ruffled for one of the few times in his career.

In Washington another former backer, Ralph Flanders of Vermont, accused McCarthy on the Senate floor of setting out to wreck the GOP and set up a one-man party. At 485 Madison, Murrow, working on his script, worked in Flanders' description, hot off the wires, of the Junior Senator ("He dons his war paint. He goes into his war dance. . . . He goes forth to battle and proudly returns with the scalp of a pink Army dentist").

In the morning there had been a call from Paley: He'd be with Ed tonight and tomorrow as well—a personal gesture for which Murrow was understandably grateful.

Paley also urged Murrow to offer McCarthy reply time on the air. "Beat him to the punch," he said.

"Of course McCarthy would have insisted on it anyway," he recalled later, "but it put Murrow in a much better position. Put *us* in a much better position, for having invited him to."[69]

The program was "an exceptional case," said Paley after three decades, a one-time suspension of the company dicta. "We gave him carte blanche . . . to develop an editorial opinion. . . . We changed our policies in connection with certain matters that we thought were of vital importance to the future and health and security of the country."

How much carte blanche? No one, evidently, cared to know, beginning with the Chairman, who declined to see the film. "I said no, I'd rather not. I'll look at it tonight." And so it went, right down the line.

Thirty years later it would be almost impossible to find a CBS executive who, knowing of the program—fair knowledge following the vetoed ad request—would admit to even the slightest trepidation (a typical comment: "Oh, I was all for it, thought it was great"). Yet Friendly recalled having a hard time finding a middle-management exec willing to discuss the show either before or after airing.

Rumors which circulated of Murrow's being called upstairs for urgent last-minute conferences, were discounted afterward by Friendly: "I think Ed was maybe up there once." But then, he added, he himself was at the cutting room, not 485. The actual extent of 20's backing would remain a matter of debate. "Paley felt he had a tiger by the tail," said a personal friend to both men, who declined to be identified. "No one stood up to McCarthy like Murrow did. Bill was in the corner going oh, gee, oh, gee. [He] would be calling up, raising hell. . . . no one will talk on that subject. They were all busy climbing up the ladder themselves."

Nonetheless, the bottom line, when all was said and done, was that CBS aired the show, where the rest of the TV industry was silent.

"Murrow," said Dorothy Paley Hirshon, the knowledgeable outsider, "obviously deserved the fullest credit—because I'm sure he carried the day against people who were far more timid than he would ever be. But just from knowing how it operates . . . he couldn't have done it alone. Because you've got to have the final authority."[70]

That being so, the program, its explosive implications notwithstanding, was virtually slipped out the side door—carried over network facilities, unpromoted, unseen by a single member of the working management, released under a set of bet-hedging priorities that refused to alert the viewing public, yet made sure to alert the FBI.

At 7:45 P.M. Murrow read the evening news as usual: a tax bill pigeonholed, McCarthy labeling the networks "dishonest and arrogant,"

GM record sales, Flanders in the Senate. The French commander in Indochina said his forces would soon take the offensive; in Washington Defense Secretary Charles Wilson refused to comment when asked about possible U.S. troop commitments.

At Vanderbilt Avenue last-minute snags caused the run-through to run late. During a break Wershba saw Murrow standing outside the control room, wiping his face: "It's awful hot in there."

"Gonna be a lot hotter in the country when this goes on the air."[73]

Security guards stood by the elevators, posted in response to crank calls coming in since the morning's *Times* ad. In the newsroom at 485 editors found their attention divided between readying copy for the late news and awaiting the scuttlebutt from Grand Central, the tension palpable, as one said later, "as though someone close to you were on the operating table,"[71] a devastating comment on industry morale.

The makeup went on and ran almost immediately; it always did under the lights, pointing up again the qualitative difference between what Murrow was about to do and comparable efforts in print or even over radio. It was a reminder that impact depended not only on program content but on voice and demeanor, the lifting of an eyebrow or the angle of a tie, on sustaining tension and interest over almost thirty minutes; that in going after McCarthy over live TV—no room for fluffs or retakes— he was giving the performance of his life.

Ten-thirty. The titles came on, opening announcements, opening commercial. Murrow looked into the camera—"Good evening."

> *Tonight* See It Now *devotes its entire half hour to a report on Senator Joseph R. McCarthy, told mainly in his own words and pictures. Because a report on Senator McCarthy is by definition controversial, we want to say exactly what we mean to say; and I request your permission to read from script whatever remarks Murrow and Friendly may make. If the Senator feels that we have done violence to his words or pictures, and desires, so to speak, to answer himself, an opportunity will be afforded him on this program.*

Every now and then they had typed in "LOOK UP," but he kept his eyes fixed on the pages, his total absorption more convincing than any pitch to the camera.

Essentially, the program followed the technique of their first McCarthy feature: catching the Senator in his own contradictions, on film, or audiotape when film was unavailable, followed by Murrow as corrective, live or on the voice-over.

There was McCarthy on film, warning statesmanlike that if "this fight against Communism" became a fight between America's two parties, one party would be destroyed—"and the Republic cannot endure very long under a one-party system."

"*But on February 4,1954, the Senator spoke of one party's treason.*"

Murrow, back on camera, flicked a tape switch, and out came McCarthy's voice charging "those who wear the label 'Democrat' " with "the stain of a historic betrayal."

There was McCarthy brandishing alleged secret evidence, "never supposed to have seen the light of day." Murrow coldly identified it as a committee hearing transcript, readily available: "Anyone can buy it for two dollars."

There was McCarthy questioning a witness—"You know the Civil Liberties Union has been listed as a front for . . . the Communist Party?"—with Murrow right behind him: *The Attorney General's List does not and never has listed the A.C.L.U. as subversive. Nor does the F.B.I. or any other federal government agency.*

It was the first time McCarthy's allegations had been systematically dissected in the full glare of the mass media.

They re-ran the Milwaukee banquet of December 1951, a choked McCarthy sniffling of being "smeared and bullwhipped," playing on audience sympathies ("My cup and my heart are so full, I can't *talk* to you").

"But in Philadelphia . . . his heart was so full, he could *talk. . . ."* The footage rolled on the Senator's gleeful Washington's Birthday reenactment of his bullwhipping of General Zwicker, to gales of laughter and applause.

They showed McCarthy putting down his press opposition as "extreme leftwing," then cut to Murrow reading from a stack of papers, beginning with the Chicago *Tribune*, infuriated by the attack on the Army (though no less furious, it would turn out, at its inclusion on the program), reading off the "active words" he had asked for: *The unwarranted interference of a demagogue . . .*"; *"The line must be drawn or McCarthy will become the Government. . . ."*

They showed McCarthy defying the administration, vowing to call the shots as he saw them "regardless of who happens to be President," quoting Shakespeare as he mocked the battered Army Secretary, "Upon what meat does this our Caesar feed?"

"And upon what meat does Senator McCarthy feed?" In quick response Murrow pointed up "two staples of his diet . . . the investigations, protected by immunity, and the half-truth," and ran the Reed Harris footage of the year before, but still effective: "I resent the tone of this inquiry, Mr. Chairman. . . ." (*See It Now* never did come up with the Wheeling speech, location efforts all dead-ended; a station said to have a tape told them it had been "accidentally" wiped.)

Despite the fear of bugs or breakdown, it went smoothly, the bits and pieces coalescing through the teamwork of the sweating men in the control room, as though the last two and a half years had been a practice drill for this half hour. An effort so successful that in the easier times of film and videotape it would be hard to remember that the so-called McCarthy program was actually a kinescope of what was in large measure a live show.

Some of the specifics later seemed remote, dealing as they did with day-to-day events, aimed at a newspaper-reading public not yet dependent on TV as a primary news source, therefore expected to bring its own context to the viewing. But even when the names and headlines had receded in the public consciousness, two overriding elements would still emerge from the old kinescopes, as powerful as ever: the damning portrait, for better or worse, of Joe McCarthy, and Ed Murrow as electronic adversary.

The program rounded off with a brief update, including the latest on McCarthy versus Benton. Then, reading from the script again, Murrow doubled back to McCarthy's sneering "Upon what meat does this our Caesar feed?" and began the windup on the Senator:

"Had he looked three lines earlier in Shakespeare's *Caesar*, he would have found this line, which is not altogether inappropriate: 'The fault, dear Brutus, is not in our stars, but in ourselves.' "

His eyes glued to the paper, he attacked not, as McCarthy was to claim, the Senate's investigative power, but its abuse, to the effect that "the line between investigation and persecuting is a very fine one, and the Junior Senator from Wisconsin has stepped over it repeatedly." (Indeed, memories of the crossing of the line would come back to haunt the Senate decades later in the Watergate investigation, as charges of "McCarthyism" emanated from the Senator's former associate, now in the White House.)

But the true virtue of the Murrow sum-up would be that it put McCarthy in his place, treating him as a symptom rather than a cause, picking up on Kennan's earlier challenge to the society that had produced McCarthyism and the witch-hunts ("What causes us to huddle, herdlike . . .").

Looking straight into the camera—no Teleprompter, direct eye contact—Murrow stepped out of the role of newsman, into the leadership vacuum:

> We will not walk in fear, one of another. We will not be driven by fear into an age of unreason, if we dig deep in our history and our doctrine; and remember that we are not descended from fearful men. Not from men who feared to write, to speak, to associate, and to defend causes that were for the moment unpopular.
>
> This is no time for men who oppose Senator McCarthy's methods to keep silent—or for those who approve. We *can* deny our heritage and our history but we cannot escape responsibility for the result. There is no way for a citizen of a republic to abdicate his responsibility. . . .
>
> The actions of the Junior Senator from Wisconsin have caused alarm and dismay amongst our allies abroad and given considerable comfort to our enemies. And whose fault is that? Not really his. He didn't create this situation of fear, he merely exploited it; and rather successfully.

Cassius was right. "The fault, dear Brutus, is not in our stars, but in ourselves."

Good night, and good luck.

The announcer came on with the incongruous commercial; the credits went up; the tension snapped. Friendly saw Murrow slump in his seat.

Looking at the monitors, they saw Don Hollenbeck on with the eleven o'clock news, his gaunt, harrowed features aglow, announcing his total agreement with "what Ed Murrow has just said." The calls were pouring in at a rate that made the Radulovich response look stillborn.

Down the hall, the *See It Now* staff, friends, and dependents spilled out of the studio where they'd been following on the monitors. Shirley Wershba, herself a former news staff member, taking time out for a family and nine months pregnant, was among the viewers, later recalling the sober group that filed toward them out of the control room—descending the iron steps to the floor of the narrow corridor, Murrow as usual surrounded by the others, a camel hair overcoat slung about his shoulders.

She ran up and grabbed his hand. "Ed, if it's a boy, I'm gonna name him after you!"

Murrow, usually shy and constrained, held on, unsmiling. "Do you think it was worth it?"

He seemed like a man, she said, "facing his complete defeat.

"He was tense, still living it. And I knew what he meant—were we just whistling in the dark?"[72]

They were not. By 1:30 that morning, CBS, New York had received more than 1,000 telegrams, almost all of them approving, with Western Union reporting a huge backlog of the same. More than 2,000 calls had made it past the overloaded switchboards, hundreds more backed up, with similar responses reported by the CBS stations and affiliates throughout the country—the first surge of a tidal wave reaction running between two- and ten-to-one against McCarthy in the greatest mass response ever generated by a network TV program (the highest figures since the Checkers Speech, said KPIX in San Francisco). CBS in New York reported the switchboard swamped with calls, nineteen hours after *See It Now* had gone off the air.[73]

Whatever was out there, waiting, the show had touched it off—more than the politicians' speeches of the past week, however headlined in the press, or the rumored maneuvers of a party coping with a former asset turned embarrassment. For the general public one thing alone was tangible: A nationally known figure, nonpartisan and no polemicist, with a high factor of trust, had spoken up on national TV to say he didn't like McCarthy. And tens of thousands were suddenly replying, in letters, calls, and cables, that they didn't like him either.

It might have explained the theme running through most of the letters—i.e., "Thank God somebody said something," cold comfort to the legions that had fought the good fight in the wilderness years and stark proof that for many, even in 1954, what didn't happen on television wasn't happening.

What the program had done, of course, was provide a flash point. It had served as a catalytic agent, mobilizing and coalescing opinion, hitherto fragmented, into a nationwide expression of popular sentiment, a fact not lost on the White House, itself the recipient of anti-McCarthy telegrams, more than a few reading "LISTEN TO MURROW TOMORROW," the sign-off of the 7:45 radio show. The usual unnamed sources indicated considerable interest in the statistics coming out of CBS.

More than that, there was a palpable relief in the communications, now totaling well over 100,000, complete with names and addresses, predicated for the most part on one supposition: *If a big-time commentator could say it out loud on television, it must be okay*.

The major liberal TV critics were ecstatic. Jack Gould called the program "crusading journalism of high responsibility and genuine courage." True, it was "strongly one-sided," conceded the *Times* writer, "But the alternative to not handling the story in this manner was not to do the story at all, by far the greater danger. The Senator seldom has shown relish for letting others do the cross-examination."[74]

"He [Murrow] put his finger squarely on the root of the true evil of McCarthyism," wrote John Crosby in the New York *Herald Tribune*, "which is its corrosive effect on the souls of hitherto honest men. . . .

"Now it takes great courage to attack Sen. McCarthy in the first place (though why every one is so afraid of that bumbler I can't imagine), but it takes far greater courage to look you and me in the face and say it's our fault."[75]

But strangely, it was the New York City pro-McCarthy press that gave the program its first headlines, in one case by mistake. The giant *Daily News*, thinking it a backhanded CBS response to McCarthy's roar for airtime, gave the show next morning's front page in the three-star late edition (MCCARTHY GETS TV TIME OFFER. MURROW BLASTS SENATOR, MAKES BID). The afternoon *Journal-American*, solid-gold Hearst, whose peppery critic, Jack O'Brian, had detested the show, more accurately and simply ran a massive head: TELECAST RIP AT MCCARTHY STIRS STORM.

The program had indeed set off a press reaction, from the New York *Post* to the San Francisco *Chronicle*, though upstaged temporarily by the Flanders speech; a Senator outweighed a mere news show by the press standards of 1954 (also as an A.M. story, in contrast with the late-closing *See It Now*), an outlook that was to change radically in the next forty-eight hours.

In the meantime, all was euphoria, especially on 17; "like V-J day," said a staffer, "the war was over." Murrow, walking back from lunch the day after the broadcast, found himself mobbed on the street as word of his presence got around, the crush of pedestrians jamming traffic on Fifth

Avenue. "We had to get a taxi to get Ed out of it," remembered Frank Gillard, then visiting from the BBC. *Variety* was calling Murrow "practically . . . a national hero."[76]

At the Waldorf that month 1,500 men and women attending the annual OPC dinner rose in a spontaneous standing ovation as Murrow entered the room. Wershba, returned to Washington, felt the atmosphere there as though a boil had been lanced (also the occasional dig: "Hey, Joe, Ed gonna run for President?").[77]

Alistair Cooke, writing for the British *Guardian Weekly,* called the overall response "a stunning endorsement of Murrow's courage.

"Hence the surprising rally of candour in public men who have stayed astutely silent for 5 years. Hence President Eisenhower's relieved approval of Senator Flanders. Hence a morning chorus of . . . newspaper columnists praising Murrow for 'laying it on the line.' Hence the confident laughter in yesterday's [McCarthy] subcommittee hearing. . . .

"Mr. Murrow may yet make bravery fashionable."[78]

The praise was not unqualified. *Variety* on one page dubbed March 9 " 'Good Tuesday' . . . when 'See It Now' took its stand for television, the networks and the people," and on another, called the program "an expedient of great interest, and some belated courage, but basically . . . a footnote to history rather than a definitive answer to McCarthyism." The distinguished critic Gilbert Seldes, once of CBS, an avid fan and personal friend—in a roasting disputed by his colleagues on the *Saturday Review*— accused Murrow of stacking the deck and setting a dangerous example, best not to have done the show; reflecting Murrow's concerns, if not his conclusions. Dorothy Schiff, whose New York *Post* had been in the forefront from the start:

"This is no time for men who oppose Senator McCarthy's methods to keep silent, said Ed as he leaped gracefully aboard the crowded bandwagon."

(A few days later, Murrow, coming on Seldes at the Century Club, fixed him with a glare: "You sonuvabitch! You've made me think about a lot of things I thought I'd settled—but God bless you.")[79]

Yet overall, the highest praise came generally from those who had been in the fight the longest, from *I. F. Stone's Weekly* ("Hats off to Ed Murrow") to the editorial writers of the St. Louis *Post-Dispatch,* to cartoonist Walt Kelly, to Joe Alsop, who had immediately sent a cable (ONE OF THE GREAT ACTS OF POLITICAL COURAGE OF OUR TIME).

The reaction abroad, after word of the program hit the news wires, was "phenomenal," as a correspondent put it. "The European newspapers went crazy, they were delighted; it was like America coming into its own again."

The BBC ran a kinescope. In Rome Bill Downs, now bureau chief for CBS, ran nightly screenings at his home to packed houses and standing ovations, mostly from Americans in Rome. (His own reaction: "About time!") Said Roz Downs: "We were getting calls from the embassy, from the USIA, saying, 'We are desperate, we want to *see* this thing.' The State Department was overjoyed; they were terrified of what was going on. And the military attachés—after all, the Army was being attacked.

"The effect was sudden—overnight. Murrow was a hero in Europe. CBS could do no wrong. But it was more than that. Everybody suddenly felt as if there was a chance that the country would start thinking again, instead of this terror, this being frightened of each other. Because that's what it really came down to."[80]

"I can tell you—you were unquestionably the man of the hour," Lauren Bacall wrote him from Europe, where the Bogarts had heard about the program. "Thanks for starting the ball rolling. God knows we're all affected by what's been going on."[81]

At the office, add-on staff coped with the snowstorm of mail while Murrow told Joan Walker of *Newsweek* magazine that he hadn't said anything about McCarthy over TV that he hadn't said on radio and denied that the program marked, as so many claimed, TV's coming of age: "No single show can change the whole medium."[82]

Variety reported the industry virtually galvanized into a chorus of praise for Murrow and for CBS, led by NBC in what the trade paper called "the biggest Macy's Loves Gimbel's Week in the history of the medium." Sarnoff himself—the grand old man of RCA—appeared over *Person to Person* (or rather, being scheduled, didn't cancel out), interviewed back to back with Secretary of the Treasury George Humphry: a double imprimatur, proving the usefulness of the mass appeal show.

Telegrams and letters were still pouring in: from Chief Justice Earl Warren, from Clark Clifford, from Fred Bate; a hand-delivered note from Albert Einstein, asking to see him again, in the modest, courtly tone Murrow knew so well from 1934; messages from Adam Clayton Powell, Jr., and Hazel Scott, the artist William Walton, Walter White of the NAACP; from Sig and Maybelle Mickelson; and from his old adversary Burton Wheeler. John Gunther, who had criticized him in the Shirer matter, cabled him on Friday: "BROTHER BROTHER AM PROUD TO CALL YOU FRIEND."

More revealing, however, were the many messages from colleagues in broadcasting and the press. John Scali at the AP cabled as "a fellow reporter," thanking Murrow outright for the show: "It speaks for scores of us who must stifle our opinion even when it hurts."

"When you sailed into McCarthy," wrote the newsroom personnel at an affiliate, "we in this business who are arbitrarily confined to straight reporting must as a man have raised our voices to shout, 'at last.' "

From the various departments at CBS, and the other networks, came an outpouring of sentiment: mass signings and individual notes of gratitude from secretaries, makeup artists, reporters, publicists, producers; from the mail room to programming, across the board. At the other end were fervent thanks from small-town editors, writing of years of isolation.

In fact, far from being an East Coast or liberal-elitist phenomenon, as often later claimed, the show's success was based in large part on strong grass-roots support ("We midwesterners look to you for leadership," wrote the mayor of Chillicothe, Ohio), proving once again that Murrow knew his audience and the trap, to be avoided, of preaching to the converted. Indeed, some of the strongest reactions were to come from that undefined entity later known as Middle America, where the Walter Lippmanns didn't penetrate but many still remembered "this . . . is London" and where, in a rare salute from one medium to another, a cartoonist for the Cleveland *Plain Dealer* depicted a jowly McCarthy staggering in defeat, an object labeled "Murrow's mike" wrapped lethally around his neck.

As press praise turned to hyperbole, however, he grew restive and embarrassed, especially when talking with a bloodied veteran of the McCarthy wars: "I ain't exactly a pioneer in this thing, you know."[83]

Thursday evening, March 11, after a puzzling two-day silence, McCarthy struck back, appearing on the Fulton Lewis, Jr., program over Mutual, the wire services alerted, photographers snapping the Senator with Roy Cohn, waiting for the elevator in the corridor outside the studio. It was billed as a partial reply to Stevenson, but as the AP reported next day, "some of McCarthy's strongest words were devoted to Murrow."

2.

"If I may say, Fulton, that I have a little difficulty answering the specific attacks . . . because I never listened to the extreme left-wing bleeding-heart elements of radio or television. However, after you invited me to come over here . . ."

It had been vintage McCarthy all the way: "I have in my hand a copy of the Pittsburgh *Sun-Telegram* [sic]; it's dated February 18, 1935. . . . The Moscow University taught, if I may quote from [the story], the violent overthrow of the entire traditional social order. . . ."[1]

To Murrow, half an hour later, fell the unpleasant task of broadcasting the story as it came in off the wires, reading with as much self-control as he could muster, reserving, he said, "personal reaction and perhaps correction" for another time; meaning nothing further overnight.

This time it was McCarthy who had scored the beat—a lesson to CBS in real publicity—getting the story and alleged documentation on the wires in time for the Friday morning editions, while Murrow's point-for-point reply on Friday night would be swamped in the avalanche of weekend news. Who said the Senator had lost his sense of timing?

The appropriate headlines erupted accordingly on page one, Friday, in the pro-McCarthy press: MCCARTHY ON RADIO RAPS MURROW, ADLAI (San Francisco *Examiner*); MCCARTHY CALLS ADLAI CHARGE UNTRUE . . . STRIKES BACK AT EDWARD MURROW (Chicago *Tribune*). The Dallas *Morning News* ran a three-column head: MCCARTHY CLAIMS MURROW TAINTED. The Hearst evening paper in L.A. carried the full transcript of McCarthy's comments.[2]

Had it remained there, the damage might have nonetheless been minor because the big story that Friday morning was the administration bombshell—the Army report detailing months of strong-arming by the Senator, released on Thursday night and ushering in the final chapter in the rise and fall of Joe McCarthy.

Events were moving fast. Thursday's subcommittee sessions had seen open rebellion among committee Democrats, rallying to the defense of a badgered witness, the questioning gone sour, the Senator departing early, ostensibly to ready himself for Fulton Lewis, the Murrow-Friendly cameras covering his exit.

Eisenhower, meeting with the press, commended Senator Flanders for "doing a service," simply citing dangers of a party split but never mind, it was a slap, with transcripts released by the White House just in case anybody had missed it.

The winds had changed since Tuesday. There had been applause and laughter from the galleries at Thursday's subcommittee session—the laughter noted by Alistair Cooke. There had been laughter in the public reaction to Murrow's broadcast comment at McCarthy's labeling him "extreme left-wing"—to wit, "if the Senator means that I am somewhat to the left of his position and of Louis XIV, he is correct."[3]

That Sunday, March 14, the New York *Times Week in Review* front-paged the developments in an eight-column story (TURN OF THE TIDE? MCCARTHY ON THE DEFENSIVE) and for the first time gave a TV newscast the imprimatur of a news event, with a portrait gallery spread across the page—A WEEK OF CHARGES AND COUNTER-CHARGES ON THE POLITICAL FRONT—SIX OF THE HIGHLIGHTS: Murrow was top-row center, his TV address quoted in the caption, McCarthy to one side, Flanders to the other, the grouping rounded off by Roy Cohn, Secretary Stevens, and a grim-faced Eisenhower.

A new Gallup Poll showed a plunge in the Wisconsin Senator's approval rating from its all-time January high.

Those were the weeks when Murrow was given his standing ovation by his working colleagues of the OPC. At the correspondents' dinner in Washington, Joe Alsop saw Eisenhower come up behind Murrow and place one hand upon his back. The reporter turned to see Ike, grinning from ear to ear. "Just feeling to see if there were any knives sticking in it," said the President of the United States. Hearty laughter on both sides. "From hereon in," Murrow reportedly responded, "it's up to you, Mr. President."[4]

McCarthy's own subcommittee had voted to dethrone its chairman pending investigation of the Army charges and McCarthy's countercharges. "We should have preferred," commented The New York *Times*, "to see the present crackdown on McCarthy based on moral indignation over his whole philosophy—if one can call it that.

". . . in any case the Senator and his friends have now been truly hoist with their own petard [though] the harm they have done will live after them."[5]

Indeed, the long-awaited Republican TV reply to Stevenson had just proved to be more of the same—Nixon, on as spokesman, administering a light tap on the wrist to unnamed men who had "done effective work exposing Communists" but been a wee bit overzealous: "When you go out to shoot rats, you have to shoot straight. . . ."[6]

"We couldn't believe it," said a Murrow staffer, "that cop-out metaphor, when they should have been going after McCarthy and everything he stood for."

Friendly, arriving at the Murrow apartment partway through the speech, found his partner on his hands and knees before the TV set, Nixon talking on the tube, an open bottle by the set, Murrow pounding the floor with his fists: "The sonuvabitch! The sonuvabitch! The sonuvabitch! . . ."

The week after the broadcast, Janet Murrow returned from Jamaica. Out of touch and worried despite Ed's cable, she had paced the deck of the ferry to the mainland, foraging with her eyes for an old Miami paper, anything at all, trying not to draw attention.

Murrow, still on his high from the broadcast as he met her at the plane, turned serious in the car. Casey, he said, must never, never, *never* be left alone.[7]

It was the first she knew of the threats and hate mail that were the underside to the McCarthy controversy—not the usual complaints but an effluvium reflective of the paranoia that was the underpinning of McCarthyism and fed locally by the right-wing press. The thundering of syndicated columnists was backed up daily by small gratuitous nastinesses, from the sportswriter who blasted Dodger owner Branch Rickey for inviting Murrow to the clubhouse (obviously polluting the Great American Game) to the poetry of the *Daily Mirror's* Nick Kenny, whose ode "The Commy-tator," making the rounds, named no names and left little to the imagination:

> *He glosses quickly over news*
> *That sounds Red, White and Blue,*
> *And saves his drooling, pear-shaped tones*
> *For Communistic goo.*

You wonder how he still goes on,
Polluting Freedom's air,
This worm whose body's over here
But whose heart is over there.[8]

Publicly Murrow toughed it out (to an interviewer: "I never pay attention to that stuff").[9] Privately he winced, in the classic reaction of the
covertly shy and thin-skinned, less equipped than most suspected for a
public battle of personalities. The Murrow home address being no secret,
threatening postcards were finding their way to the apartment and even
to the hideaway at Pawling, some perversely creative in their ugliness,
a cram course in what others had been undergoing for years. Wershba,
running into Janet Murrow at the office, asked how they were coping.
She smiled. "We were under worse in London."[10]

CBS offered protection for the family. Murrow said they didn't want
a bodyguard, but for the first time, publicity made reference to his Pawling
gun collection, if not specifically to the two licensed handguns kept at
580 Park Avenue.[11]

Casey Murrow was watched constantly, though unobtrusively—he was
used to being chaperoned—his parents anxious, however, to strike a
balance between imprudence and fear-inducing panic. He had known the
McCarthy program was coming and recalled in adulthood the tension in
the household at the time: his parents' concern over the show, he thought—
or was led to believe. "I realize now that they were concerned about my
safety."[12]

On one point, however, they were powerless.

Fifty years after Edgar Murrow had been taunted by schoolmates for
his father's being a supposed "nigger lover," Casey Murrow was taunted
at school for his father's being a supposed "red"—a comment on the extent
of McCarthy support among the school's ostensibly elite parent body.
The bright, popular eight-year-old was unequipped and unprepared for
the sudden reversal, confused by hostile questions—"about whether Dad
was a Communist and so forth. Of course, I didn't know what that was
all about—*I* didn't know if he was a Communist or not."[13]

The Murrows didn't hold it against Buckley. The school authorities,
though sympathetic, could do classically little in the face of trial by peer
group. In later years the time would be blacked out almost totally in
Casey Murrow's recollection, "quite successfully," as he would put it
wryly, bits and pieces of unpleasantness remaining barbed in the
conscious.

It was the one consequence, endemic to the time, that Murrow couldn't
deal with. Sitting with colleagues after broadcasts, he would complain
bitterly, "How'd you like to have your kid called a dirty Communist when
he's eight years old?" The cold war had come home.

"He felt helpless," said a staffer. "He felt Casey was taking it on account of him."[14]

In the meantime, cables flew back and forth between New York and Washington. Murrow renewed the airtime bid, offered March 16. It was refused, indirectly. McCarthy designated young William F. Buckley, Jr., to answer in his place; Murrow said the invitation was "not subject to transfer." The Senator finally took up the challenge in a two-page cable rehashing the charges made over Mutual and released to the press: "NORMALLY I WOULD NOT WASTE THE TIME TO MERELY PROVE THAT A RADIO AND TV COMMENTATOR WHO ATTACKS ME IS LYING. HOWEVER, IF I AM CORRECT IN MY POSITION THAT YOU HAVE CONSCIOUSLY SERVED THE COMMUNIST CAUSE THEN IT IS VERY IMPORTANT FOR YOUR LISTENERS TO HAVE THE CLEAR-CUT DOCUMENTED FACTS. . . ."

He asked for April 6 ("In view of the fact that your sponsorship of Moscow State University which was co-sponsored by VOKS which was a Russian intelligence agency dates back more than twenty years, it will take considerable time to put together all the pertinent facts in your record").[15]

Murrow, agreeing to the date, denied the charges in a similarly publicized response, and as for his serving the Communists, the facts, he wrote, would soon determine who had done so—"You or I."[16] Things were getting personal.

Through much of that week, McCarthy tore through the Midwest on the all-expenses-paid after-dinner circuit—a New York *Times* report noted ample free radio time and TV coverage—ramming, at every opportunity, at Edward Murrow. During one appearance Ed Scott, present with the cameras, felt suddenly the full heat of McCarthy's glare: "I want those CBS people to stop filming everything I say!"[17] They left but later got a duplicate.

See It Now, for its part, ran a second McCarthy program for the second Tuesday running, in the time slot turned down by the Senator: the subcommittee mutiny of March 11, scene of McCarthy's hasty exit—the so-called Annie Lee Moss hearing, focusing on a low-level Pentagon clerk subpoenaed on an informant's tip-off. The cameras focused especially on John McClellan, the old Southern conservative—who had accused CBS of treason back in 1936 for putting on Earl Browder and had badgered the hapless Reed Harris—stepping now to the aid of a small black woman with a ringing denunciation against "convicting people by rumor and hearsay and innuendo."[18] Applause rang in the background as the camera panned repeatedly to McCarthy's empty chair.

At the same time, arrangements for April 6 were firmed up. The deal was: the full half hour minus the usuals for opening and closing and no wisecracks. McCarthy paid a call on Stanton—"licking his chops," Stanton recalled, "just eager to get at the screen." It had not been a meeting the CBS President looked forward to or one he would recall, said Stanton, "with any sense of pleasure. He was *not* an attractive person.

"He thought he had a lot of evidence. . . . I suppose like all politicians, he felt that he had the right on his side, and he was eager to be heard."[19]

As it would turn out, the Senator was getting undercover help from a powerful, unpublicized quarter in amassing the supposed "evidence."

FBI papers released twenty years later would reveal that the State Department—specifically its Passport and Security Offices—was covertly cooperating with the Senator, leaking materials from its files, with the knowledge of the FBI, for the preparation of McCarthy's TV case against Murrow. The centerpiece of that operation would be Scott McLeod, security chief, McCarthy's man, manager of the new purges at State, scourge of what was left of the China hands, and the object of adverse Murrow commentaries for the past year.

Murrow in his radio response of March 12 said he hadn't accompanied the summer session group to Moscow. March 31, a week before McCarthy's scheduled TV appearance, a Passport Office employee informed a contact at the FBI that McLeod's office had called, requesting a summary of Murrow's passport file. The requested summary had been thereupon provided that same day over the telephone, a written memo with the information promised in follow-up, said information to be handed over to Don Surine.

The report, telexed to the Director, reminded the Bureau of Murrow's recent broadcast on McCarthy and of McCarthy's upcoming appearance on that same program; reminded them, too, that McCarthy had recently unearthed the information about the Moscow summer session.

In the meantime, the file already disclosed that one of Murrow's passport applications in the thirties had indeed included proposed travel to the Soviet Union, for "business."

"It is requested," the report specified in closing, "that this information not be furnished outside the Bureau because the Bureau's source will be obviously identified and this could result in grave embarrassment to the Passport Office and thereby to the Bureau."[20]

McCarthy's reply, to be filmed on a hired Fox Movietone sound stage, was obviously to be more than the simple live rebuttal at first anticipated. Quite the contrary. The Senator was going about it methodically and professionally, using the medium to the maximum with his enemy's help. And that of others: Newspapers reported the gratis services of columnist George Sokolsky, among others, and the veteran PR man Carl Byoir, the latter name of some embarrassment to NBC, where Byoir served as consultant, and of irony to Murrow recalling the early thirties, when Byoir Associates had been briefly under contract to the Reich.[21]

In the meantime, McCarthy wanted a kinescope of the March 9 program, scripts of specific radio broadcasts, exact timings. Murrow provided them (even more, CBS offered them in the name of fairness) down to detailed timing instructions—i.e., twenty-two minutes exactly, without interruption.[22] It was more than McCarthy's victims ever got.

"This . . . leaves us with only one minute thirty seconds for my opening and close," Murrow informed Paley none too happily.[23]

McCarthy's people agreed to a one-time run-through the day of the broadcast, in the presence of both staffs, just to check for timing, the condition of the print, anything possibly actionable by third parties, etc. For the rest, the Murrow people steeled themselves and waited.

A day or two before the show, Palmer Williams got an unexpected phone call from the expeditor at Hearst's *News of the Day*. Relations had always been good with the working stiffs at Hearst, unaffected by the bitterness upstairs. This time they went one better. For one hundred dollars, the Hearst man told Williams, he could get them a copy of the sound track of the McCarthy film.

The track? Oh, Jesus. Williams ran to Friendly, then to the appropriate vice-president—"I need a hundred dollars, cash, don't ask why"—then to the CBS cashier. Inside an hour, he had the three rolls of track constituting the McCarthy answer.

They ran it through a Movieola, Vera Marsh, the *See It Now* librarian, taking down the words in stenotype, Friendly on the phone with Murrow: "They accuse you of this, that, the other thing . . . the Moscow Summer School . . . and oh, yeah, he hit you on Harold Laski. . . ." The finished transcripts were rushed to Murrow, sitting with the lawyers.

McCarthy's people, viewing the print together with the Murrow people as agreed on the day of the broadcast, couldn't understand that Murrow wasn't there to see it.

The morning after April 6, the liberal consensus was: McCarthy had done himself in. The man was a caricature. And the makeup—terrible. Why, that film was the most damaging thing of the whole exchange, thought Paley. So did Stanton. Just proved Murrow's point, wrote Jack Gould in followup: "Mr. Murrow only reported as best he could on the use of innuendo, insinuation, the half-truth and the frantic smear. The Senator, on the other hand, gave the expert's own authorized version. It may take a little time before the Senator realizes he was had."[24]

But Drew Pearson, a battle-scarred McCarthy fighter with no love for Murrow—a feeling strictly mutual—dubbed it "a savage and effective job."[25]

It was, in fact, a virtuoso performance, a twenty-two-minute workout of every trick in the McCarthy arsenal. First, the low-key opening: McCarthy at a desk, cloaked with the dignity of office, quietly, deliberately describing Murrow as "a symbol, the leader and the cleverest of the jackal pack which is always found at the throat of anyone who dares to expose individual Communists and traitors." From there he worked up to his familiar ranting style, playing on old fears like a piano, tossing out code words that had never failed of impact: "China . . . delivered to Communist slave masters by the jackal pack of . . . propagandists, including the friends of *Mr.-Edward-R.-Murrow.* . . . In every country they of course had to find glib, clever men like *Edward-R.-Murrow.* . . . *Mr.-Murrow* by his own admission was a member of the I.W.W. . . . a terrorist organization. . . . The Institute of International Education . . . was chosen to act as a representative of a Soviet agency to do a job which would normally be done by *the Russian secret police.* . . ."

(They laughed in the control room. Who'd believe it? But who at one time would believe Dean Acheson to be a Communist, or that the name-sake of the Marshall Plan had sold out to the Russians?)

"Documents" were waved aloft, with large block-letter labels sporting the word *Communist* or *Moscow* somewhere in the copy; tributes were hauled out of the woodwork—Lattimore's grateful acknowledgment for support in 1950; the *Daily Worker* citing *See It Now* among its "Best Bets" listing for TV; Harold Laski's co-dedication to Murrow of *Reflections on the Revolution of Our Time,* that memento of 1943 and *Freedom Forum,* McCarthy now denouncing Laski as "admittedly the greatest Communist of our time in England" and lingering lovingly over the title.

Then, in a classic ploy, he shifted focus, charging that Communists in government had fatally held up research on the H-bomb, and "our nation may well die." (Next day's headlines would spotlight presidential denials of delay. Thursday's headlines: IKE OK'S H-BOMB SPEEDUP. The cover was blown on the heretofore closed-door investigation of atomic physicist J. Robert Oppenheimer. Who said McCarthy had lost his touch?)

Shifting gears again, McCarthy defended his record of "exposing" mal-efactors and, holding the March 9 *Daily Worker,* came down with deadly calm on Murrow's statement about giving comfort to the enemy: that if such were the case, he, McCarthy, ought not to be in the Senate. "If on the other hand Mr. Murrow is giving comfort to our enemies, he ought not to be brought into the homes—of millions of Americans—by the Columbia Broadcasting System."

He ended quietly—the concerned statesman once again—referring to "the shadow of the most horrible, destructive weapons that man has ever devised," calling on Americans to follow him, vowing not to be deterred by "the Murrows, the Lattimores, the [William Z.] Fosters, *The Daily Worker,* or the Communist Party itself."

His voice was low; his manner, warm. He was ingratiating, strangely youthful, desperately sincere, offering up "all that I have and all that I am . . . join with me. . . ."

Fade-out. Murrow, back on camera, did the thirty-second closing, jaw set—"That was a film of Senator Joseph R. McCarthy"—making no com-ment, as agreed, though reserving the right to do so "subsequently."[26]

"I just want to do this without any emotion," he had told Friendly before going back on, but, Friendly said afterward, "You could sense the emotion."[27]

By now reporters were swarming in the corridors outside, in preparation for the announced news conference, called for after the show; a second conference, before the cameras, was to follow at the Hotel Commodore. Palmer Williams remembered filing with the others into a rehearsal room where chairs had been laid out, everybody handed, as they entered, a CBS release containing Murrow's point-for-point rebuttal to the program that had just gone off the air.

Williams took a seat, a little apprehensive. Murrow, at the front, took questions.

"Of course," said Williams later, "I was anticipating what would happen—i.e., how come he's never seen the program, yet here are detailed answers to everything that's *in* the program? And inevitably a reporter, I think from the *Daily Mirror*, got up and said to Murrow exactly that— I mean, 'You never saw the program and yet here is a detailed answer and we understand that you people never saw this program until noon of this day.'

"And Murrow said, 'That's absolutely true.'

"And the guy said, 'Well then, how did you do that?'

"And Murrow looked at him evenly and said, 'Does Macy's tell Gimbel's?' And the room broke up in laughter, and it was passed over. A lovely incident."[28]

The pendulum, McCarthy's partisans were learning, could swing in both directions; when the press turned, it did so inexorably.

Murrow seemed in complete control; Friendly even saw him laugh once during the running of the film when McCarthy touched on the Summer School: "I never even got to *go* to Russia!"[29] Of course, he was angry. Who wouldn't be after twenty-two minutes of that on nationwide TV? The footage from the Commodore would show an unusually emotional response. But it was still a public, measured anger. His private reactions he kept as always to himself; the fact was, the experience—particularly McCarthy's twisting of the memory of Harold Laski ("a friend of mine; he is dead," said Murrow in the aftersession)—had gone deeper than anyone realized at the time. Or almost anyone.

Sam McSeveny, later professor of history at Vanderbilt University, then a graduate student finishing a stint with the Army and still in uniform, was walking up Park Avenue at lunchtime when he saw Murrow emerging from a doorway. Emboldened, he approached, apologized for invading the great man's privacy, complimented him on the March 9 show, viewed down on base at Camp Gordon, Georgia.

Camp Gordon? Fine! Fine! Murrow switched from polite thanks to rapt attention. He'd like to keep talking, he said, but had to get back to the office; had he time to share a cab uptown?

They discussed Army reactions to the program, to McCarthy, as the taxi inched through midtown traffic, Murrow firing off questions—about the response among the draftees, among the career people. (Camp Gordon was of course G. David Schine's hangout; Murrow waved the reference aside: Schine wasn't worth talking about.) Murrow in the cab, the young man noted, was just like Murrow on the air, the private conversation echoing the public presentation.

It was in the midst of it that McSeveny brought up Laski: He'd just read *Reflections on the Revolution of Our Time*—a little utopian, but never mind, he admired the man and what he stood for. And here was McCarthy, the defender of the SS perpetrators of the Malmedy massacre, attacking Murrow because he and Laski were on the same side in World War II. It was so patently unfair, to both of them, using Laski this way.

"That brought on an outburst," said McSeveny later, "controlled, but emotional."

The Laski angle, from the public's view, had been a minor item. Conversely, in the taxi with a stranger, the bitterness came pouring out. Said McSeveny, "I saw him reveal himself, i.e., it was despicable, hitting below the belt, one more indication 'why this man must be dealt with.'

"*He* knew why Laski had dedicated the book to him, and I felt everyone should have known, which might have made him feel he was talking to a kindred spirit."

He noticed, too, how Murrow spoke McCarthy's name with loathing, "as if it were something sleazy that had to be named; you could tell by the tone of his voice, a sense of the man's evil. You certainly didn't feel he went after him because he thought it would be safe to do so."

Earlier in the conversation Murrow had been the detached reporter, getting at the "facts," though obviously with strong feelings on the matter. "But the business about Laski—it hurt very much."

Come see me when you get out of the army, Murrow told him as they shook hands; there might be a job. "Our various vice-presidents will probably make obstacles, but that's what they're there for."[30]

At first everyone rallied 'round, even in the face of headlines that made the publicity of March look like a tea party and without an Army report to draw the fire; a devil's mix of McCarthy's Murrow charges and H-bomb allegations, backed by an editorial barrage, Hearst and Colonel Robert McCormick of the Chicago *Tribune* leading the pack: REDS GET MURROW "AID AND COMFORT" SAYS McCARTHY (New York *Journal-American*); CHARGES MURROW APED COMMUNISTS (Chicago *Tribune*); McCARTHY CHARGES MURROW HEWS TO REDS' LINE (New York *Daily Mirror*).

Even papers friendly to Murrow and inimical to McCarthy spotlighted the charges on the grounds that they were "news"—the familiar split-personality phenomenon, between front page and editorial page, one New York paper, a consistent McCarthy foe, backing Murrow in the center section, the two-column front-page story: McCARTHY ATTACKS MURROW

AS "LEADER OF THE JACKAL PACK." Viewer response indicated Murrow still out front, but the odds had shrunk.

Muddying the picture further was the disparity between the audiences for March 9 and April 6 respectively, thanks to advance publicity bringing about a quantum jump in viewership. Many, therefore, viewed the rebuttal to a program they had never seen. (Pulse pollings reported McCarthy's appearance more than doubled *See It Now* ratings in the New York area.) In Detroit, where *See It Now* was blacked out, irate callers swamped the switchboards of the local Hearst sheet and CBS affiliate WJBK-TV, demanding to know why the hell they couldn't see McCarthy. At WFBM-TV in Indianapolis, the films for both shows were flown in for telecasting back to back in a special Sunday night showing, pre-empting the *Colgate Comedy Hour*.[31] (Both shows or none, said CBS; altruism had its limits.) In the end it was McCarthy himself who added to the program's ripple effect through his dogged insistence on overkill.

For the moment, however, the center held. The New York *Times* of April 7 announced E. R. Murrow leading the recipients of the New York Newspaper Guild's prestigious Page One awards, with the prize in public affairs—"for distinguished contributions to the adult and responsible use of broadcasting as a medium of information and enlightenment"—heading an honoree list that included E. B. White and James Reston.

At the White House Wednesday news conference, Joe Harsch, now with NBC, asked pointedly for comment on "the loyalty and patriotism of Edward R. Murrow," the President declining specific comment on things of which he "knew nothing," but he had known this man for many years and considered him a friend.[32] The afternoon New York *Post* made the most of it in huge black letters: IKE BACKS MURROW. CALLS JOE'S TARGET "HIS FRIEND" (a double whammy against the Senator, in stark contrast with the Marshall deletion back in 1952, when the politicians had needed him. No matter; Murrow was relieved and grateful).

CBS issued a statement listing his honors, expressing confidence in the broadcaster but silent on *the* broadcast.

ALCOA, despite McCarthy rumblings about IRS audits and spending tax dollars to finance the reds, wasn't canceling, keeping up an impassive public stance in the face of a campaign geared to embarrass. In a well-publicized move, McCarthy sent ALCOA his production bill from Fox Movietone—$6,436.99—since it had after all, he purred, used his answer to advertise its product and "paid for the cost of Murrow's attack." And oh yes, there was another $1,900 for "expenses."[33]

Irving Wilson—white-haired, handsome Mr. Aluminum—whose personal support of Murrow was the backbone of *See It Now*–ALCOA relations, returned the invoice, said his company had had no prior knowledge of either program, paid CBS a fixed sum, had no say in the manner of production, and in effect told the Senator to buzz off, "1 cc" to Dr. Stanton. CBS finally paid the bill. (A few skeptics in the press noted

McCarthy's top-dollar lecture fees, liberal free radio and TV time, and the reported free expert assistance on the film from Louis B. Mayer, among others.)[34]

The press laughed at the tempest in a teapot; to Murrow, CBS and ALCOA, it wasn't funny, Chief Wilson admitting before a stockholders' meeting in those same weeks that the position of their management had not been "a favorable one."[35]

In fact, there was considerable unease.

CBS board member Adrian Murphy later recalled the nervousness—not entirely unwarranted under the circumstances—in the boardroom, particularly among the so-called outside directors, the Wall Street people, as he called them. They were after all concerned with the bottom line, men of substance who represented the large holders of stock, though in theory the whole board did, and who were in a position to throw 100,000 shares on the market if they saw fit to do so.[36]

There was talk, too, of incipient boycott, CBS's economic rear guard, the big soapmakers, for the moment standing fast—"not through morality, but self-interest," Murphy said, "they didn't want to yank the business because they might not get back on the same time period later. [There was] no waiting to find out how the land lies."

NBC, all raves at first, had fallen notably silent. The past weeks had seen confusion and dismay at Rockefeller Center as the press, in the wake of the McCarthy program, asked hard questions on the nature of the medium and "fairness," a hot issue now that it was McCarthy's turn. The NBC high brass had groped and sweated, scrambling to come up with something suitably formatted for the March 29 *Newsweek* cover story.[37] On top of that had come McCarthy's counterpunch, the few viewer letters sent next day to Sarnoff—when would they, too, take a stand?—routed to NBC head Sylvester "Pat" Weaver with the notation "No answer required."[38]

"Macy's Loves Gimbel's Week" was over; CBS and Murrow were on their own.[39]

Overshadowing everything, however, was the backwash of the Mc-Carthy response—a countercampaign unparalleled even in a career of rejoinders to critics that had included subpoenas, attacks from the Senate floor, sponsor and advertiser intimidation, and physical violence.

"For mousetrapping the Senator," Jack Gould had written of Murrow after April 6, "the commentator is bound to pay the price temporarily. When as much mud is thrown at an individual as Senator McCarthy threw at Mr. Murrow, it is futile to expect that all the debris can be wiped from the public mind."[40]

In fact, the TV rebuttal, like its radio counterpart, was just the tip of the iceberg, the real damage inflicted below the waterline. The counter-offensive was actually proceeding on two levels: one, highly visible, over the tube; the other, through the older medium of print and mailings, a systematic leaking of the contents of McCarthy's files—using *Counterattack* and the nationally syndicated columnist Westbrook Pegler as the pipeline—to local newspapers, libraries, broadcast media, and, finally, the federal bureaucracy. It was a well-planned, sustained, expertly coordinated grass-roots campaign, of which the McCarthy appearances had been only the spearhead, less an exercise in mud spattering than a river of sludge—slow-moving, less spectacular, and in the end, quite effective.

In mid-March Pegler's column, acknowledging McCarthy's help, had started breaking the alleged details of the Moscow Summer School and Murrow's IIE connections, deliberately forging links in a chain of alleged guilt by association, from the IIE to Stephen Duggan ("father of . . . Lawrence [*sic*] Duggan")[41] and from there in stages to Whittaker Chambers and Alger Hiss.

The column also caught out Murrow's first mistake about the school, in answering McCarthy—mentioning the Russian cancellation back in 1935, but not the session held in 1934. (Ironically, McCarthy's investigators had confused the IIE program with an obscure travel and study tour group, long since forgotten, to which Murrow had once lent his name, their glowing reports of seminars in Russia cited now as Murrow's copy and proof of a deliberate cover-up.)

Two days later *Counterattack* jumped in, sounding the same notes plus a few extra riffs, devoting the entire issue to the broadcaster (WHY DOES THE COMMUNIST PRESS PRAISE EDWARD R. MURROW SO HIGHLY?) and indicating in the process the obvious monitoring of his radio newscasts of the past year.

"Murrow preaches dangerous doctrine." [42] It was a detailed denunciation, disseminated through *Counterattack*'s powerful mailing list, surfacing in editorials and lead articles around the country, an act with competition in the eastern urban centers but playing very well in Peoria. (In fact, a major news chain paper in Peoria quoted *Counterattack* in a full-length editorial ["The Case of Edward Murrow"], referring readers to the public library for the entire issue—"an essential statement for those who want to see things clearly in these troubled days.")[43]

In New Hampshire, the powerful Manchester *Union-Leader*, whose right-wing voice rang through the state and northern New England, ran the contents in a two-part series, quoting Murrow's alleged copy ("provoking experiences . . . unforgettable memories. . . . Russia . . . offers to the world a new challenge. . . .")[44]

Needless to say, 485 was getting the feedback—from New Hampshire and Illinois, from Iowa and Southern California, and from almost anyplace reached by Hearst or the Chicago *Tribune*. Stanton later recalled his mail "flooded with editorials and news stories . . . some of them sent by our affiliates—not necessarily condemning the broadcast but simply wanting us to know. . . .the grass-roots reaction. . . . I believe that McCarthy was totally convinced in his own mind that he [had] mortally wounded Murrow."[45]

The affiliates wanted goodwill, not grief, and their share of a growing market, where the competition was fierce. New York *Times* applause for Murrow, even local applause, meant little if some of the home folks disapproved—unhappy people didn't buy—or if a newspaper of standing in the marketing area virtually leveled treason charges at the newsman who was synonymous with CBS.

That April, Stanton, returned from a Chicago business meeting, asked Friendly to his office—Friendly had been there only once before—and pulled out the figures of a Roper Poll commissioned by CBS the weekend after April 6. The results, "neatly bound and annotated in Stanton's hand-writing,"[46] indicated that fifty-nine percent of the adult population had either "seen or heard of" McCarthy's TV reply and that of these, thirty-three percent—answering a purely negative question and including people going admittedly by hearsay—thought the Senator had proved Murrow a "pro-Communist" or at least had raised doubts about him. The thirty-three percent was marked with thick orange brackets.

Friendly, by his account, protested: It only proved how necessary the show had been.

Stanton, however, was upset, said Friendly later, disturbed by the comments in Chicago, Midwestern executives telling him that Murrow's "attack" might just cost the company the network. In his mind such controversy was "harmful to the company's business relationships."[47]

There was no doubt in Friendly's mind that Stanton, unhappy with the figures, regretted having done the show—a position Stanton himself later contested as "editorial emphasis": "If he thinks I was upset, that's his judgment."

The survey, Stanton later insisted, was not at all extraordinary, just one of CBS's "polls of public attitudes toward specific broadcasts and programming in general"; one could see where Ed and Fred themselves, but for their prejudices, might be interested in the public reaction, though of course, this didn't "deny the validity of what they had done, or the decision of the management to do it."

> I can report that I wasn't upset. . . . [I]t was simply a matter of courtesy and interest that I wanted to share it with Fred. . . .
> You have to turn the clock back to the period when McCarthy was riding roughshod over the country. . . . And with the leadership of the government cowering, in a sense, before McCarthy, it's not sur-prising to me that there was concern among the affiliates; certainly there was deep concern in the business community. . . .[48]

What was the point of it all? McCarthy's position was eroding; the spotlight had long since shifted to the upcoming Army hearings, sides lining up. The Senator had more than enough to keep him busy, however much the odds takers were betting on his emerging with a whole skin. Yet reports kept filtering in on efforts by his staff to dig up more dirt on Murrow, in what now seemed pure vendetta, or as an observer put it at the time, preferring to remain anonymous, "McCarthy knows he's on the way down, and he's determined to take Murrow with him."

Finally, there was one consequence that would manifest itself more subtly, an invisible momentum, keeping pace henceforth with Murrow's career.

Friday, March 12, even as an officer of the Eisenhower cabinet and the Chairman of RCA bestowed the blessings of the establishment on Murrow over *Person to Person*, the FBI was taking a long, hard look at the broadcaster's dossier.

The day after the McCarthy show, Director J. Edgar Hoover, whose friendship with McCarthy was common knowledge along the Potomac, had sent down the query: What do the files show on Edward Murrow?[49]

A sixteen-page review began the turnaround. New items were unearthed; old items long on the books, re-examined—the repeated surfacing of Murrow's name in the IPR files commandeered in connection with the espionage investigation of the Institute of Pacific Relations; the Polk case; Murrow's wartime associations; his stance on the Hollywood Ten and the House Committee on Un-American Activities; citations in *Counterattack*, specifically regarding Theodore White and Owen Lattimore.

Associations with those farther to the left went back under the lens: known to have corresponded with . . . named as reference on passport application of. . . . "a good friend" of . . . . reported to have arranged appointments for . . .[50] The McCarthy and Radulovich programs became, of course, a matter of record.

Six days later the Pegler "exposé" hit the streets with the Moscow Summer School details, causing red faces at the Bureau. Pegler, noted the Director crisply, seemed to have come up with a lot more on Murrow than the FBI had.[51]

There arose one of those awkward situations common to any organization, that of explaining to the boss: Pegler had blown up one phase; the Bureau went after many; the IIE was never cited; besides, Pegler had missed "several choice bits," whereas they themselves had linked Murrow to the following—see below—in the past five years alone. . . .[52]

From that time on nothing was left to chance, with Murrow, though not precisely under surveillance, a watched man. His activities, including, at times, his movements abroad, were monitored, field offices keeping tabs, private communications on his activities encouraged.

As recently as the previous February, FBI memos had described contacts with the broadcaster as "cordial," give or take a certain distancing on the Bureau's part, even a little lingering pique over Murrow-Friendly's failure to deliver back in 1951.

The feeling now seemed to be: they had been had. The gears reversed, the mindset switching from cordiality to innate suspicion. "I will never have anything to do with anything with which Murrow is connected," the Director noted in the firm, inimitable hand that laid down the law at the Bureau.[53]

Agents following up on McCarthy's televised charges contacted the IIE to find out if Murrow had indeed "selected" for the Moscow Summer School a prominent Communist currently under observation under the 1950 Internal Security Act and named by McCarthy over the air.[54] The broadcaster's dossier went from a balanced, sober profile drawn from public and private sources to one reflected increasingly through the fun house mirrors of *Counterattack* and Pegler, plumping up with every controversial broadcast and circulated through the government bureaucracy as requests for name checks suddenly cloned in the wake of the controversy. It was a file in which *See It Now* programming would be filtered less through The New York *Times* than the output of *The Daily Worker* and American Business Consultants. The Radulovich program would be gauged not through the Republican *Herald Tribune* but through an obscure Serbo-Croatian-language periodical currently under an Internal Security Investigation. It was a file that would omit Eisenhower's backing vis-à-vis McCarthy—the friendship protestations which had specifically avoided comment on Murrow's loyalty—but would perpetuate the endorsements (also, in all fairness, the rebukes) of the publications of the Communist Party.

On the surface, nothing seemed changed; underneath, a new dynamic had been set in motion, the beginning of a new sensitivity and an object lesson in the climate of the time. The morning after April 6 the U.S. Military Academy contacted the Bureau in a virtual panic: What did the files show on Murrow and they needed the information, please, by 1:00 P.M. Murrow, it seemed, was due to lecture the cadets on April 25, but what with the controversy and McCarthy last night on TV, West Point didn't know if it should go ahead or cancel.

Sorry, came the answer, there's no time, you should have thought of it before inviting him. The Point, reluctantly, let matters lie, advised by its own people that the Army would in any case be "damned if they do and damned if they don't."[55]

But Murrow had also asked to film a TV segment on the grounds—old grads returning to the Point—leaving sufficient time to make a check, and it was therefore recommended that a summary memorandum be prepared "containing background, as well as derogatory data for dissemination to G-2."[56] The Director gave it his approval. It would form the basis for the subsequent summaries in Murrow's file.

Outside, the liberal and trade press was acclaiming Murrow's lecture at the Point as proof of the establishment's support.

The *See It Now* cameras were at last deemed safe to film old grad reunions—hardly at issue—but there was no question which way the wind was blowing. In 1948 a James Forrestal could call Murrow to the Pentagon for a sensitive position involving access to top military information[57] without so much as a prior check. By 1956 the Office of the Secretary of Defense would require an FBI check for "subversive derogatory information" before issuing accreditation to attend a press conference.[58]

What was happening was the onset of an almost schizoid attitude in the government bureaucracy regarding Murrow—a bureaucratic paradox allowing for uninterrupted access to the military at the highest levels, taking place now in an unseen context of calls to the FBI, file searches, and file updates. A strange new duality, in which awards from the armed services and warm invitations to War College seminars, requests to narrate army films, *See It Now* entrée at all installations, would alternate with CIA reports and repeated requests by military intelligence for checks on subversive references. More than for some journalists, less than for others; unthinkable the far side of the great divide that was the spat with Joe McCarthy.

In 1951, in high FBI circles, Murrow had been "one of the great voices on the air."[59] After March 1954 he became, for purposes of description, simply a figure tied in to various "cited"—read "subversive"—groups, recipient of "both favorable and unfavorable comments by the Communist press."[60] In 1951 the total report on Murrow took up no more than two-thirds of a sheet of paper; by 1954 the reports went on for page after page. A brief summary prepared for the White House in 1955 was to depict him as "connected"—no specifics—with such "cited" organizations as the IWW and the American Student Union, as someone in contact with several individuals "known to belong to the Communist Party or Communist fronts," both praised and knocked in the Communist press, and criticized by the editors of *Counterattack*—whose opinion, evidently, merited White House attention—for "presentation and defense of individuals of questionable loyalty."[61]

At the Passport Office, Director Ruth Shipley received a query from the Honorable Carroll Reece, Republican of Tennessee, Chairman of the special House committee investigating foundations and wanting to know more about the Moscow Summer School. Did Murrow hold a passport for the years in question, and had he asked for, and received, a visa from the Russians?

Shipley, replying, confirmed that Murrow's passport application, back in 1935, had specified a business trip to several countries, including the USSR. The expired passport not being in department files, however, it was impossible to ascertain whether said passport was subsequently visaed for a trip to Russia.

Five days later, a refusal was placed in Murrow's file at the Office regarding renewal of his passport, on the grounds of "alleged Communist affiliations," and signed, R. B. Shipley, Director.

March 9, just before the start of the McCarthy program, in the thirty-second interval before going on the air, the so-called blackout period, Friendly had turned to Murrow—"This is going to be a tough one"— remembering afterward Murrow's reply, delivered in those final seconds:

"After this one, they're all going to be tough."[62]

Meanwhile, a team of outside lawyers had moved into the twelfth floor at CBS.

From the outset it was obvious that McCarthy had done his homework as he saw it and that Columbia would have to do the same, a view confirmed by the subsequent blasts from Pegler, *Counterattack*, and others, catching Murrow in his omission of the 1934 Moscow Summer School—a potential source of erosion of public credibility, possibly perjury had it been said under oath. (The possibility wasn't too remote; Chet Williams' sources in Washington leaked word back of planned Murrow hearings should McCarthy come through the latest round intact, probably with Joe Kennedy's son Bobby as counsel in place of the controversial Roy Cohn.)[63]

Murrow, said Stanton later, was obviously going to be subject to enormous counterattack, and not just by McCarthy. "Toward that end I joined in insisting that we get the best outside counsel we could get to work with him."[64] CBS accordingly engaged a legal team from the blue-ribbon Wall Street firm of Cravath, Swaine & Moore, headed by Bruce Bromley, a prominent New York Republican, formerly on the bench of the New York State Court of Appeals; a close associate of Tom Dewey, who had appointed him, and about to throw in the name of Joseph Welch, a Boston lawyer of his acquaintance, for the job of special counsel to the Army.

The lawyers went in, scoured the files, collected information on Murrow, McCarthy, CBS, but especially on Murrow—a detailed investigation of a past about which, it turned out, CBS actually knew little, as surprised as any by the revelations of the Moscow Summer School. What else was there in the dead files of the IIE? And how about the student movement? Alarm bells had gone off when Pegler began quoting the veteran red identifier J. B. Matthews, director of research for the old Dies committee, the old ex-Communist of alleged encyclopedic memory, expert on student movement infiltration, close to McCarthy, and oh yes, he remembered Murrow very well. No Communist but . . .[65]

From out of the woodwork came the discussion sessions held so many years ago at the home of James Shotwell, the old President of the Carnegie Endowment, surfacing via the IPR files and a tip to Pegler—just the professor arguing with a bunch of young Marxist ideologues, it was said, potential traitors; and Murrow was among them. The information coming back to CBS was that attempts would be made to get Shotwell to swear to it under oath. The lawyers got his quick denial in a two-page letter.

But the IPR example haunted them, summoning up visions of potential bombshells in some undiscovered barn.

Chet Williams, brought in to help and also to research the student days, hunted for the missing papers of the long-defunct NSFA, the few surviving files indicating vast opportunities for distortion, a potential field day for McCarthy.[66] A twisting, turning trail led through New York and Washington, D.C., dead-ending on a windswept corner in downtown Manhattan, where a garage was last reputed to have stored the archives in a backroom at twenty dollars the quarter: the final resting place of the records of Ed Murrow's early years and what had once been America's biggest student organization. Except the garage was gone, a new building on the site. *But the files—what of the files?* No one knew until a local bartender finally remembered that the garage went out of business sometime, kids breaking into the padlocked backroom with all those stacked-up boxes no one wanted, playing with the papers, and lighting bonfires on the vacant lot.

Such was the climate of the time that the only reaction to the news was one of relief and gratitude.

But compared to the IIE files on Moscow, now made available to CBS, the NSFA was a sideshow, the lawyers shaking their heads over Murrow's active role in organizing and negotiating with the Russians back in the early thirties. He hadn't chosen the courses, but his participation was still very worrying, couldn't be "played down too much."[67] Indeed, the twenty-year-old announcements were a headline hunter's delight, laced with promotion copy probably from the pen of the forgotten I. V. Sollins, now ascribed to Murrow: "The spirit of the Anglo-American Institute is that of the true Soviet school. . . ."[68] So were items of the 1934 curriculum, preserved intact ("*Sociology 2:* Social background to Communist society. . . . a brief history of the development of communist theory in a study of the social factors of revolutionary movements through the history of civilization").[69] Try that one on the Jenner subcommittee.

Nor would some of the faculty listings fall easily upon the ear: Professor Mintz, of the Institute of Red Professors; Lukatch, of the Marx-Engels Institute on Dialectical Materialism; Lifshitz of the Communist Academy; a talk on "Soviet Law" by Assistant Prosecutor Andrei Vishinsky.[70]

Then, of course, there was the student list, studded with a trail of citations from HUAC, SISS, notations of Party affiliations and the like, even a reference, admittedly ambiguous, to Ring Lardner, Jr., later of the Hollywood Ten, defended so vigorously by Murrow in the latter forties.

As for Murrow himself, there were the optimistic letters of the twenty-six-year-old, outweighing doubts, advising Duggan that "development of our relations with Russia should play a fairly important role in the Institute's program during the next few years."[71]

The facts were: They *had* lost control; Sollins *had* boasted that he had used the IIE; they had had no say in student or course selection. It was still a long way from McCarthy's spy school, but nonetheless the kind of breeding ground for half-truths that the press and politicians thrived on, any attempted explanations certain to get lost in the shuffle—the post-thaw eagerness that had gotten Murrow, who was not on the Soviet payroll, entangled with Sollins, who probably was;[72] the slow disenchant-ment that they might be dupes; the months-long wrangling, the struggle to regain control, followed by the Russian cancellation. Would it sound like anything except a cop-out, ineffective against anticipated cries of "Joe was right"?

The Senator hadn't tossed in a red herring; he had opened up a can of worms, with the potential for destroying Murrow, regardless of the po-litical survival of Joe McCarthy.

The records, reduced to abstracts and kept under lock and key with other material in a small two-drawer cabinet, delineated Murrow as some-one who needed defending, dependent for the first time on others, in a dramatic role reversal. It made him, in a subtle way, beholden.

He was of course grateful for support under fire, for contacts with Paley, then showing his concern in small, meaningful ways. To Adrian Murphy just before a meeting he spoke suddenly of being "a little bit terrified," thinking of all those people, he said, who had no backing, just went it alone.[73] But inevitably there was more to it than personal friendship or the protection of a star and prestige symbol whose discrediting might reflect disastrously on CBS. Morris Ernst, with a private inside track on McCarthy's moves—funneling information in those weeks, it would turn out, to the Army[74]—had got wind of an incipient attack on CBS and Paley, probably to be spearheaded by the Hearst Corporation.[75] The elaborate, wallet-consuming procedures at 485, therefore (including even checks on Paley's Army past), were also very much a case of self-protection, closing ranks against the common enemy.

On another front, McCarthy was still very much in the picture. Wesley Price of *The Saturday Evening Post*, who had done a piece on Murrow five years back, called in to say that Don Surine had been around, hot on the trail of an IWW reference in the story: What was the source? Had he the notes? The writer had tried to back off tactfully: He didn't know; it was old stuff, probably up in the attic somewhere, if at all. "Please go get it." Well, um, it was dark and dirty there, his clothes—"We'll pay for them." But what if—ha-ha—he broke a leg? "We'll pay the ex-penses."[76] Nothing had come up, of course, said Price, but he felt CBS should know.

In the meantime, the legal team combed through Murrow's broadcasts, through letters written, letters received, all critically read, digested for opinion safely anti-Communist or dangerously pro: a full-scale invasion of privacy in the name of self-defense. Magnifying the impossible, they called it; to do otherwise was to ignore recent history.[77] Murrow shut up and let the lawyers get on with it. There were interrogation sessions behind closed doors; better a dry run, went the thinking, than surprises in the hearing room. Once on the stand, forget about the Fifth Amendment, not if one wanted credibility; which meant opening the floodgates to the certainty of minute questioning on any aspect of one's life. Charlie Mack, the old conservative, recalled the whole episode with distaste; Murrow at the time accepted it as one accepted bad-tasting medicine. From the Deep Throats in Washington came bulletins on what to do if and when called.

How much was really necessary; how much security-inspired overkill? Impossible to forecast or to assess in retrospect. Certainly the company was coming to know more about Murrow than it ever had, possibly, about any single employee.[78]

There was just one area in which, if it came to it, he didn't want to be found wanting—namely, the pressure to talk about others under questioning. Chet Williams asked a Washington contact, Had he any pointers, were there matters to be wary of, should the situation arise? "Frankly, this is the thing that Ed is apprehensive about as he does not want to hurt anybody."[79]

Queried early about his staff—they had a tip, the lawyers said, about a McCarthy informant on the inside and had he some idea?—Murrow had declined to speculate, serving notice that it was not a topic for discussion. "He (ERM) has avoided inquiring into the political antecedents of his staff," ran the *aide-mémoire*, "having in mind that he might some day be interrogated under oath . . . and wishing to remain in a position where he could say with honesty that he did not know."[80]

But personnel had a file on the political affiliations of some employees, duly gone into and containing, evidently, nothing pertinent. It marked yet another step, as Murrow's associates, past and present, came under scrutiny, the *See It Now* staff, once the most insulated at CBS, now on the spot precisely because they worked for Murrow. A sudden, chilling change of climate.

Palmer Williams' twinkly manner cloaked the disposition of a maverick. He had once faced down an FBI man while undergoing clearance for a State Department job, admitting to membership in the old American Labor Party back in 1948—then as the agent objected ("That's a *front*"), reminded him about a faction fight within the party: "*I* signed up so that I could get into the primary. What *you* don't know is which side I was for. And I ain't gonna tell ya!"[81]

Worst yet, his ex, now seven years divorced, was a bona fide card-carrying member of the Party ("which didn't mean much to me, except that it was a pain in the ass when they held meetings at the house").

He was struck, therefore, by some sober conversation one night after work, sitting at the bar: just a few staff men, Murrow, and Friendly, and a little advice over the drinks. McCarthy would be out for an Achilles' heel, so if anybody had a problem, well, there was this battery of lawyers—i.e., if you think you're an Achilles' heel, avail yourself; that's what they're there for. Said Williams later: "Both Fred and Ed were very serious about the fact that the company had hired Bromley and so forth, to protect us all in this affair. . . . [And] I think it was after I went home that night that I thought, *Jesus Christ, I better talk to these guys*."

Past was past—he wasn't his wife's keeper—but best not to hand the Senator a club. Still, it was seven years ago—no big deal really.

The lawyer, told next day, wasn't so sure. "Wait a minute—did they hold meetings at your house?"

Sure they held meetings; he'd even fought with the members.

"We'll have to take this up."

The following evening he was called up to the office of Daniel T. O'Shea. "And there was the judge, and there was that lawyer and these other guys, and they said, 'We want to take down your statement.' " A secretary began taking it down.

O'Shea flashed something before him: "You signed this."

Williams recognized the loyalty questionnaire. He'd seen dozens like it, in government service ("it seemed like another piece of paper at the time"). Yes, he said, he'd signed it—and honestly. So what?

The men disappeared into the next room, emerging sometime later with the directive that he resign "for the good of the organization"—and right now.

Williams, his head reeling, asked for and got permission to call Friendly. He explained what had happened. "They say I gotta resign. Look, I *told* these guys—"

Friendly, says Williams, broke in: "*I don't want to* hear *what you told these guys*. Don't do anything. Lemme get ahold of Ed. Put O'Shea on the phone."

O'Shea finished the call as Williams sat in a state of shock. "I was sort of saying to myself, 'Why aren't *I* sort of like the Radulovich case?' "

Moments later, the phone rang. The producer saw O'Shea pick up, talk, put on Bromley, then: "He wants to talk to you."

Glumly, Williams took the receiver. "Yeah, Ed."

The line fairly crackled. "Fred just called me. This is *preposterous!* Don't you sign *anything*. You ain't resigning! Goddammit, I'll be there in ten minutes!"

It was closer to half an hour, said Williams later. "I don't know where Fred reached him, whether he had gone home, or what. But in any event, he marched in and said, 'No, no, no, no, no, he can't resign, we won't let him resign, we won't accept his resignation,' and so on, while I walked around in a sort of a daze. I didn't know what the hell was going on. Well, there was a flurry of talk in the other room, and finally they came out and said, 'Well, at least finish the statement,' which I did, and Ed went home, and finally *I* went home. And I think got quietly drunk. I don't remember."[82]

It was the last he heard of it. But Murrow himself was skirting the edge, holding down a full radio and TV schedule, coping with McCarthy-related incidents, taking questions *in camera* from the lawyers ("[In] 1931 . . . you issued a statement appealing for . . . the withdrawal of American military forces from China . . .")[83], while dealing on the nightly newscasts with major stories running the gamut from the Supreme Court decision on school desegregation to the question of armed intervention in Indochina. But it was an effort sustained by nicotine and nervous energy. Answering McCarthy's charges for the third time on the air one night, the newsman's voice had faltered briefly in the closing, the flawless diction giving way to a slight yet noticeable stammer.

See It Now was, moreover, carrying a full load, from programs on the Fifth Amendment and the abuse of congressional investigative powers to a TV assist to Senator Margaret Chase Smith (R.-Maine), fighting off a McCarthyite primary challenge, to the impact of *Brown* v. *Board of Education of Topeka*, to events in Europe and in Southeast Asia. Indeed, Murrow's editorial focus by late spring was less the McCarthy story, now entering its final phase, than the mounting debate over Vietnam in the wake of French military disaster.

The public, in the meantime, wanted its hero. So did the news organizations. *Variety* noted Murrow's sixth OPC Award (not McCarthy-related), his fifth Peabody, and his second from the Newspaper Guild; the Russwurm Award from the American Newspaper Publishers Association; the earlier awarding of the Sidney Hillman Foundation Prize for Radulovich (shared offstage with Wershba and carrying a cash prize of $500. The cash or the plaque? Friendly had asked him, adding that expenses were kind of high right now. Wershba took the hint).

Paley shared the dais as Murrow accepted the annual Freedom House Award, the citation reading: "Free men were heartened by his courage in exposing those who would divide us by exploiting our fears."

The award joined a crowded list that was making *See It Now* the most honored program of its time, Murrow the most honored newsman. *Variety* saw in *See It Now* "a new type of TV programming . . . that may in time make the 'pure' entertainment stanzas as oldhat as the local opera house. . . . 'reality' that [gives] television its golden opportunity . . . entertainment of the sort that can't be concocted and whose sole basis for being is its up-to-the-minute values."[84]

Murrow himself never seemed to know what to do with awards once he had won them. The office walls were plaqueless. Jim Seward wound up with a drawerful of medals, plunked on his desk the morning after. Often the newsman's graciousness at the festivities contrasted oddly with his haste to beat a retreat once they were over. Bonsignori recalled the aftermath of a Peabody dinner—both Murrows present, staffers sharing in the glory, passing the precious medallion from hand to hand. Suddenly, "Where's Ed?" Bonsignori looked around, then ran in the direction of his fast-disappearing back, shouting at the top of her lungs.

He turned, somewhat put out.

"You forgot this."

He shoved the medal in his pocket. Turned again.

"You forgot something else."

"What?"

"You forgot Janet."

"Oh, my God!"[85]

In late May he took the stand as witness for the plaintiff in *Joseph Julian* v. *American Business Consultants*, the long-awaited *Red Channels* libel suit.

It was day four of the trial, held in the old State Supreme Courthouse in Foley Square. His entry had shaken the tree somewhat, resulting in a small string of witnesses for the plaintiff. Murrow himself brought in Collingwood, the two newsmen scheduled back to back, beginning at 2:00 P.M. "I need hardly tell you the importance of these cases to the general cause," wrote Arthur Garfield Hays, ACLU counsel and attorney for the plaintiff, working on consignment. "If we can get a substantial judgment against these people, we will put them out of business."[86]

Called as character witnesses, they had been nonetheless prepared, said Collingwood, to talk about *Red Channels* under questioning. For Murrow, that meant testifying on the hiring practices of the employers defending him against McCarthy.

It never got that far, however. The trial was a disaster, the presiding Judge Irving Saypol, onetime prosecutor in the Rosenberg case, making no pretense of impartiality—to a suggestion that damage might be done by a *Red Channels* listing, he replied: "That's your insinuation"[87]—narrowing admissibility to zero levels, sustaining objections so as virtually to gag testimony on the blacklist, taking over cross-examination, like a prosecutor, from the bench, in tandem, at times, with the defense.

Murrow, barely able to get the title of *An American in England* through the objection barrier, under Hays's questioning, sensed the climate soon enough.

"What is the standing of Joe Julian as an actor. . . ?"

"So far as I know, it is good."

"Is he a man that one would ordinarily hire for radio or television shows, in your judgment?"

"Objection!"

The Court: "Are you an expert on actors, Mr. Murrow?"[88]

For the most part, however, he simply sat silent in the witness box— uncomfortable, conspicuous—as the case bogged down in a morass of objections and legal nit-picking, shutting off his answers, or forcing him in unwanted directions, rendering him useless. A mounting irritation grew in him at being put on cold, unbriefed and unprepared for opposition tactics. He was not competent to judge the qualifications of actors, he burst out at one point. "Hey!" Julian remembered thinking, "you're not on my side now."[89]

Said Collingwood afterward: "We both felt *frustrated* at not getting to the heart of the matter; we wanted to."[90]

It was in any case all over in a few minutes, the big question—concerning *Red Channels* itself—detoured by the bench with help from the defense attorneys, the ruling being that the witness didn't personally do the type of hiring under discussion, therefore could testify only to hearsay.

Hays, defeated, dropped the questioning. The defense waived its right to cross-examine. Said Julian: "They just wanted him off the stand—fast."

"All right, Mr. Murrow," came the voice from the bench, "I think that constitutes the extent of your appearance."[91]

He stepped down, thanking His Honor, always polite, then, passing the table where Julian sat with his counsel, paused briefly and, in full view of both bench and jury, shook the plaintiff's hand.

He had almost reached the door—Collingwood had already been sworn in, his address given—when the voice from the bench stopped the proceedings: "Mr. Murrow, would you answer this question for me right from where you are. . . ."

The newsman turned, uncertain, waiting.

He, Murrow, had testified to some acquaintance with the plaintiff. Yes, sir.

That extended to mutual acquaintances? Yes. Acquaintances in common? Yes.

Could he say, as a matter of knowledge, that as a direct and well-connected result of the publication of the plaintiff's name in *Red Channels* that he had been avoided and shunned by former friends and acquaintances?

Murrow's face was a study. The question was well calculated. What would he know of it on the basis of a few drinks at Colbee's? The point was obviously *Red Channels*, the ultimate bum rap. Julian, watching the newsman caught off-balance, knew he was being paid back for his gesture of support.

"I have no knowledge that has happened, Your Honor."

Saypol, triumphant, turned to the counsel for the plaintiff. Did he wish to follow up?

The decent Hays, worn down by these games, had had enough. No, it was quite all right.

Saypol wouldn't let up: "I beg your pardon?"

It was all right, he was satisfied.

The judge looked around. "Nobody else?" The defense was silent. "Very well."

They had done with him.

Julian v. *American Business Consultants* was dismissed without the calling of a single witness for the defense. From Collingwood, Julian heard of Murrow's deep disappointment at not being more helpful; so were the others. Even so, a juror encountered after the trial told him angrily they had been set to bring in a libel verdict. Just possibly, said Julian, the judge knew it, too.

Short weeks later Murrow was back on the stand, on behalf of his old friend Quentin Reynolds, testifying in what would be the landmark libel suit against Westbrook Pegler and the Hearst Corporation. With no hostile judge this time, the result was a verdict for the plaintiff and unprecedented damages. "When you fight the Hearst Empire," wrote his buddy of the blitz, "the dice are usually loaded against you. But you helped unload them. . . . I'll never forget what you did, Ed."[92]

There was also, no doubt, a small bonus in seeing Pegler on the receiving end, although Murrow was now certain, if he hadn't been before, of that columnist's undying attention. Above all, however, he came away indelibly impressed with the brilliant legal footwork of the counsel for the plaintiff, Louis Nizer.

The tumultuous year seemed finally to be winding down. McCarthy was visibly flailing in the Army hearings, televised daily over ABC,[93] the Senator coming up increasingly a loser, in what seemed less a matter of Joe versus the Army than Joe versus Ike. Murrow for his part had performed a final service for the administration as McCarthy shrilled first for subpoena of the President's personal advisers, then tried for the Army files, and finally, in a burst of hubris, appealed to workers of the civil service—over the head of the President—for more inside information on "graft, corruption, communists, treason,"[94] bringing down, at last the presidential foot.

Hagerty, in a statement sanctioned by Eisenhower and the Attorney General, cited the separate functions of the three branches of government, blasting by implication a certain unnamed "individual" seeking to "usurp" executive responsibility, "to set himself above the laws of our land . . . to override orders of the President of the United States."[95]

A constitutional issue, was how Hagerty put it, making quiet calls that day, in a round of secret conversations unbeknownst to anyone but Ike and certain figures in the media. Listen especially to Murrow, Hagerty told the President.

Murrow had hardly needed urging:

> The issue . . . has finally been joined. It is constitutional and therefore fundamental. . . .clearly defined by the President of the United States on one hand and the Junior Senator from Wisconsin on the other. It can be simply stated. Who is going to run the government of this country? . . .
>
> There have been times in our history when the executive . . . has attempted to dominate the legislature. . . . There have been times when the Congress has made inroads on the prerogative of the executive. What is here involved is whether a single senator shall publicly recruit and legalize what might be called a private Gestapo within the ranks of those employed by the federal government.[96]

"Many thanks," read Hagerty's note next day, on White House letterhead, "you were wonderful!"[97]

Triumph; end of story; fade-out; commercial. Except the McCarthy show was not family drama.

It should have been a good time: late June, two weeks after the Boston lawyer Joseph Welch, recommended by Bruce Bromley, had administered the coup de grâce in the Army hearings, demolishing McCarthy live on camera: "At long last, Sir, have you no sense of decency?"

See It Now was assembling footage for Tuesday night: Eisenhower and Stevenson on the witch-hunts. Elsewhere at CBS, Don Hollenbeck was calling in to say he wouldn't be doing the late news on Monday night. Ill and harassed lately, he had been barely able to make it through his newscast the day before, but no one thought further about it.

Tuesday morning, June 22, a building manager on East Forty-eighth Street, checking a gas leak, forced the door of Hollenbeck's small efficiency apartment. He found the newsman in the kitchen, slumped on a hassock, doors and windows shut, the jets wide open. He had been dead for two hours.

In the background were a failed marriage, a recent hospital stay for bleeding ulcers, bouts of heavy drinking, and severe depression—all aggravated by attacks in Jack O'Brian's column in the Hearst *Journal-American,* starting in the morning after Hollenbeck's on-the-air salute to the McCarthy show and keeping up all through the weeks that followed.

The notices, swiping at Murrow but even more at his "*PM* protégé," did double duty, rehashing Hearst bitterness over *CBS Views the Press* and hitting at one man through the other—the "graduate of the demised pinko publication" and "the pompous portsider," to quote O'Brian's favorite sobriquets.

Certainly the Murrow-Hollenbeck connection was no secret, what with the latter's appearances on *Hear It Now* and *See It Now*; the times he had taken over for Murrow at 7:45 P.M.; the times the two men would wind up the show together in the commentary period, parodying sports reporters or reading in turns from *The Decline and Fall of Practically Everybody* until the announcer cracked up.

They weren't friends socially, though Murrow undoubtedly felt a sense of kinship with the brooding, complex loner, three years his senior, who wore his nerve endings close to the surface. Expert at covering his own thin skin, he had told Hollenbeck to ignore it when the other came to him after a full-column broadside. Don't answer, he said; ride it out.[98]

But there had also been for Hollenbeck, as there was not for Murrow, a sense of isolation; CBS, said Mickelson later, had been maintaining a more or less arm's length relationship with the newsman, still nervous about *CBS Views the Press* and his old *PM* affiliation. Hollenbeck, bitter at the lack of support, at the company and colleagues, strung out physically and emotionally, could not ignore it. "If you saw my *mail*," he had brimmed over to a friend, just days before.[99]

They were at 501 Fifth Avenue, Bonsignori recalled, going over that night's final edit when the door opened, casting a sliver of light into the darkened screening room—"Ed, telephone." Friendly remembered Murrow stepping outside, then returning after a few minutes, taking his seat without a word, hunched over while the film continued rolling.

As the lights went up, they saw his face. Memories of his reaction were to vary. "Controlled anger," said Friendly. Said Bonsignori: "He was crying."

"You might as well know about it now—Don Hollenbeck killed himself."[100]

To Mili Bonsignori he seemed to be saying, "They killed him."

It was a stricken group that gathered in the bar across the street that night. Murrow was in agony, nearly inarticulate: "The Jews and Catholics, it's not in their religion to do it, so why did it have to happen to this sweet—lovely—Protestant?"[101]

Said Friendly: "He felt Hollenbeck was the surrogate for him."[102]

As in most such cases, they all felt responsible after the fact, that somehow more might have been done, someone might have kept an eye on Hollenbeck.

That night's *See It Now* ended with a tribute to the dead newsman and to *CBS Views the Press*—"a great many people liked it; some didn't. No one ever said it was anything but honest"—Murrow looking directly into the camera as he closed, as though speaking directly to Hollenbeck's accuser.[103] On a more personal note, over the radio microphone they had shared so often, Murrow called Hollenbeck "a friend of truth, an enemy of injustice and intolerance. . . .

"He was a gentle man with a well-disciplined mind. . . . There was no arrogance in him . . . but there was considerable steel. . . . His language had a cutting edge, but I never heard him employ it against an individual. . . ."[104]

Next day's O'Brian column continued with business as usual: "Hollenbeck was one of the most prominent members of the CBS lefties. . . . He drew assignments which paid him lush fees, pink-painting his news items and analysis always with a steady left hand. . . ."[105]

Said Murrow to the others: "We gotta get the hell out of that Hearst setup."

That December, the U.S. Senate voted 67–20 to censure Joseph R. McCarthy for conduct "contemptuous, contumacious, denunciatory, unworthy, inexcusable and reprehensible." To the end he had run true to form, antagonizing colleagues, senatorial patience finally snapping when he had labelled the select committee studying the censure charges— headed by Republican Utah conservative Arthur Watkins, a staunch Taft man and a pillar of SISS—as the "unwitting handmaiden of the Communist Party." Indeed, the censure adjectives had referred not to his abuse of civil liberties but to his abuse of other senators.

Only a few traced history back to William Benton's censure resolution. Benton himself, trying for a 1954 comeback, had been warned away by Connecticut Democrats fearing a pro-McCarthy backlash among white ethnics.

Missing from the resolution, moreover, was anything about McCarthyism itself or the Senate's own role in its flowering.

Murrow, disavowing his part in McCarthy's political demise, summed him up years later as "a politically unsophisticated man with a flair for publicity," whose weapon was fear:

[He was] in a real sense the creature of the mass media. They made him. They gave nationwide circulation to his mouthings. They defended their actions on the grounds that what he said was news, when they knew he lied. . . . He polluted the channels of communication, and every radio and television network, every newspaper and magazine publisher who did not speak out against him, contributed to his evil work and must share part of the responsibility for what he did, not only to our fellow citizens but to our self-respect. . . .

It has been said repeatedly that television caused his downfall. This is not precisely true. His prolonged exposure during the so-called Army-McCarthy hearings certainly did something to diminish his stature. He became something of a bore. But his downfall really stemmed from the fact that he broke the rules of the club, the United States Senate. When he began attacking the integrity, the loyalty of fellow Senators, he was censured by that body, and was finished.[106]

As for Murrow's own troubles, they had just begun.

XIV

Upright on the Treadmill

1.

At first all was rectitude and righteous indignation. *See It Now*, in those first blistering weeks of summer 1954, was the glory of the network, of all television; CBS, the guardian of the First Amendment. In the aftermath of the Hollenbeck suicide, Paley had agreed to sever relations with Hearst and damn the cost, though most likely the Hearst role in the McCarthy counteroffensive had helped bring the long-standing CBS-Hearst feud to the boiling point.

In making the break, however, the network was putting its money where its mouth was—a massive shift in operating procedures since, thanks to the wondrous ways of 1954 craft union rulings, their own film personnel couldn't work for them directly; not in the USA at least. In its three years, *See It Now* had never owned a single piece of hardware, leasing everything—editors, camera operators, cameras, the cutting room itself. Somehow, it had worked. CBS paid Hearst; Hearst paid the staff— Murrow's staff.

July 1, by contrast, found them with exactly one camera operator on the payroll, Bill McClure, in Europe with rented equipment; European coverage that fall was amazingly heavy on *See It Now*.

New arrangements had to be worked out with a new, more neutral production company, taking over the custodial and paymaster role of *News of the Day*. Gratifyingly, no bodies were lost, even the Hearst camera veterans leaving pension-heavy jobs to join the exodus. (The newsreel was dying in any case, said Leo Rossi afterward; it didn't take much to read the handwriting on the wall.)

Equipment was another problem. Mack, asked by Murrow for a quick estimate, did some figuring and made a guess; the numbers would come to almost double the amount, totaling eventually some $120,000 in 1954 dollars.[1] "That's how much *you* know," Murrow told him balefully.[2]

Palmer Williams, giving up his vacation, took Friendly camera shopping in a heroic eight-week buying spree. Mack and Rossi preferred the thirty-five-millimeter Akeleys. Akeley had stopped making the cameras. Williams talked them into building new ones from the parts available. For sound systems, they marched into Western Electric in lower Manhattan and ordered two new systems, complete. Fine, said the salesman, but they happened to cost $20,000 apiece. ("Or whatever the hell they were," said Williams later; "they were quite expensive.") Friendly grandly whipped out a checkbook and signed forthwith.

Outside he turned white. "Holy Jesus Christ, wait'll they find out that's no good. I gotta get to CBS quick and get some money and put it in the bank."[3]

But underneath the fun and games were the rumbles of a new order, a step-up of the erosion process begun that spring with the ordeal of Palmer Williams, and now targeting Joe Wershba, ironically weeks after the McCarthy flap had died down, McCarthy himself long since flayed and hung out to dry.

It had begun with a poison postcard, common to the times: no name, no address, a Brooklyn postmark, and the unsigned tip that Joe Wershba, while in college in the thirties, had been a member of the following leftwing organizations. Wershba, called upstairs to Dan O'Shea on 20, verified the information and was told he could no longer work for CBS.

A short time later, O'Shea received a call from Murrow: Just what was going on? He'd be glad to tell him, said the lawyer; should he come down? No, said Murrow, he'd come up.

He arrived, O'Shea would later recall, "in a debating mood"—polite; controlled; ready to listen but tensed for an argument. O'Shea was ready too. "Murrow was a kind of direct, forthright fellow; you weren't with him long before you knew what his position was.[4]

"Murrow thought the whole area, of course, was wrong. . . . He let me know he thought *we* were wrong. I explained to him that I couldn't sit in judgment on a guy like that—I was a lawyer—I could determine that he'd be subject to criticism. We debated it. . . ."

It was the one time O'Shea would recall their actually quarreling "because Wershba was an apparent one of my 'victims.' In that context his case took on more warmth."

> It wasn't till later that I saw what these issues were. I handled it instinctively. Not as an issue as such of right or wrong, [but] of unfair economic criticism that would be levelled at us if it were true—"had been" was as bad as "being." Murrow's big concern was the heinous conduct involved in the McCarthy maneuvers; I'm sure his concern for the Wershba case was akin to that—the thing that McCarthy was doing. . . .

Returned downstairs, Murrow sat with Wershba, in an agonized closed-door session.

"Why didn't you *tell* me?"

"Why didn't you ask?"

Easing up, they talked of the postcard, of the thirties, Murrow, of dissenting friends in England who had vowed not to fight for King and country; and of the present atmosphere, including that at CBS. Including especially the loyalty oath. "The company had my loyalty until they *asked* for it," said the younger man.

Hauled upstairs again, Wershba was asked to name names; he refused. In the meantime, CBS put him on hold—the first time the Murrow staff had been directly interfered with. Friendly kept him busy auditing tapes. Murrow, furious and frustrated, sensed the power slipping from him, watching his own personnel ordered off the job and unable to take action, glowering each time he went upstairs for another round. O'Shea was sorry, very sorry.

"He placed a great deal in Wershba. I don't know what his personal affections were. Wershba was a likable fellow." But the whole matter was in overdrive by now, and O'Shea sensed the other side was tiring. "He came back three times to give me the same arguments, to see if there was anything new." The lawyer had learned, however, a fundamental lesson over the years—namely, "in dealing with Murrow and in talking about Murrow, the guy to go to was Paley, who was his friend and great pal."

The corporate arguments, therefore, remained immovable: This was a matter not of right and wrong but of economics. He, Murrow, had of course a right to go to Paley. But he would be asking Paley to suffer the economic consequences.

They had reached the bottom line, the balance shifted, the old threat of "Get yourselves another boy," quite without meaning, gone up in smoke the night of March 9. Said Friendly: "We felt we had no options."

Fred was in a state of high emotion, Wershba recalled. "If you leave— *I* leave." Nice, but colleagues said that sort of thing, especially if they were close; it didn't change the realities.

The standoff dragged on for some time further, but the adage that each battle fought made one a little less anxious for the next, was coming true. O'Shea offered a cushion—after all, he liked the guy, nothing personal—he'd arrange a position with his good friend David Selznick on the up-coming TV electric industry spectacular, the *Diamond Jubilee of Light*, scheduled for the fall. Wershba, carrying his past up front this time, saw the job wash out before it started. O'Shea was furious. Couldn't he just have *lied*, Hollywood-style?

It was the point of no return. In a hotel lobby in London, Friendly, called to the phone, found Wershba on the line from New York, saying he had decided to resign, that it would help in the battle. They felt he shouldn't, said Friendly later, but then, Joe was a stubborn guy, had his principles.

Separation wasn't easy, Wershba recalled, Friendly overwrought: "You're through—finished—you'll never work in news again." (Said Wershba: "Fred had this thing about exit lines.") Ten years later, Friendly would be his boss, as President of CBS News, Wershba as staff producer.

But that summer, everything seemed to have come to an end. "Paley says this is the hardest thing he's ever done," he remembered Murrow telling him.

"Never mind Paley. What will *you* do?"

Murrow colored, silent, volunteering nothing of the "debates" on 20— not to Friendly, not to Wershba.

"I feel we should have fought harder," said Friendly in later years, "and that the company shouldn't have accepted his resignation. That we let the best producer-reporter at CBS go—it's something I'll always live with."

"Me today—you tomorrow," Wershba told Murrow at their parting. It wasn't said in anger; they both knew the reference, i.e., *first they came for the radicals, then they came for the Jews, then....* Murrow nodded, slowly, despondently, agreeing.

He said nothing further, then or later, feeling the words *I tried* inadequate, when the end result was failure. Wershba left CBS without knowing that anyone had stood up for him. "Take good care of Brother Ed," he wrote their mutual friend Carl Sandburg. "He's good for the country."[5]

It was late July 1954; the next phase was already in the offing.

August 16, the Columbia Broadcasting System, Inc. announced the formation of CBS News and Public Affairs as a separate staff department under the parent company of CBS. It was a step long overdue, far-reaching, and coordinating under one umbrella the often warring factions of radio and TV news, bringing order out of chaos and bestowing corporate status on the news operation with the appointment of a corporate vice-president, who would sit in council with top department heads; given complete charge—so went the announcement—of all news and public affairs broadcasts on both radio and television.[6]

The plum, significantly, went not to radio but to TV; not to the veteran Ted Church but to Sig Mickelson, the hardworking, hard-driving, broad-featured Midwesterner, the onetime journalism teacher who, barely five years out of a Minneapolis radio newsroom, had set up the TV network news operation and got it going; Frank Stanton's man, with a direct pipeline to the upper levels at CBS.

From the start, the new corporate entity was Stanton's baby and he went about its inception methodically, meticulously, beginning that August with a twelve-point list of directives for the new vice-president— from the new designation of CBS News to the formation of an editorial review board, including, among others, Paley, Stanton, and Salant and, of course, Mickelson himself.[7]

Toward the end of the memo was something called *"Script Review."* CBS, said the memo, had been subject to increasing complaints of bias. It was therefore proposed that an outside committee of experts review a six-month sampling of broadcasts by "key news personalities" for indications of said bias, noting any possible infractions of the editorial policy of CBS. Should any "cases" come up, Mickelson would be able to "treat" with such individuals on the basis of these expert opinions.[8]

It became a priority item, said Mickelson later, once he and Stanton sat down to discuss the new setup—"and he suggested to me, in a sort of a half-diffident way, [that] one of the first things we ought to do, was run a study on the objectivity of news broadcasts."[9]

Mickelson suggested Ralph Nafziger, the respected Director of the University of Wisconsin's School of Journalism, a pioneer in polling techniques, with the resources to do a fair and expert job. Stanton specified, to begin with, two radio broadcasts. "By this time Allen Jackson was doing one of the fifteen minutes; Ed was doing one. And he [Stanton] wanted Ed in it, and he wanted Jackson, and then we threw in Doug Edwards."

Far from being "key news personalities," Jackson and Edwards weren't much more than readers for the radio and TV network evening news strips.

A meeting was set up for mid-September in Stanton's office, the project discussed with a faculty representative, plans finalized. Nine days later fifty-two scripts of *Edward R. Murrow with the News*—a year's sampling, September 1953 through August 1954—were on their way to the Midwest for a sentence-by-sentence analysis to determine whether Murrow had violated editorial policy or, as the formal statement put it, to consider to what extent the program content "conformed to or deviated from expressed CBS policy statements and other reasonable standards of fair and balanced news presentation."[10]

The scripts were all on file at CBS; getting hold of them had posed no problem. Said Mickelson: "All I had to do was pick them up and send them."

The results came back through the mails—two reports on Murrow, one with Murrow as yardstick for the others, sent in over the course of eleven months to Mickelson's attention. Graduate students were put to work combing through press morgues, matching the selection of news items on the Murrow program with that of the major newspapers, on the lookout for differences: were they present, systematic, and, if so, reasonably explained? (The answer: Murrow's news judgment coincided with that of some of the best editors in the country; it raised no echoes at 485.)

Did Murrow and the others know? Says Mickelson: "There was no reason for them to know. Once they'd finished the script, it went into the files, and that was the end of it. They were members of our organization; they were not individuals."

Likewise Bob Skedgell, radio news director in those years, with overall responsibility for implementing the CBS policy in radio, was later unable to recall the study's ever being mentioned in his presence. No meeting notes, no memorandums of agreement survived; check requests sent to Joe Oleske in accounting referred simply to "a study being made for CBS News at the University of Wisconsin."[11]

That January the returns had started coming in with the first report—dealing, so ran the lead, "with the problems of agreement between CBS policy and the content of 'Edward R. Murrow with the News,' "[12]—and continuing through 1955. The final conclusion, summarized in a fifty-seven-page analysis marked "Confidential," gave the judgment: All three men, and Murrow in particular, had indeed violated the editorial policy of CBS. Murrow had evaluated, he had pointed up what he thought significant, given free rein to guest correspondents. Here, in neat columns and percentages, was where he, sandwiched by the two others, had crossed the line, and here was how he did it—though granted, if these be taboos, "one might reasonably wonder how [news] analysis would be possible under such circumstances."[13]

At which point, what had been ostensibly a three-man report suddenly narrowed down. Yes, Murrow had crossed the line but only in his commentaries, clearly labeled. Yes, he gave his opinions, let correspondents give theirs, had been clever about inserting opinion without seeming to, though how could he do otherwise, given the policy? And what opinions! In every case his fairness and integrity came shining through; let him but speak out on civil rights, and every word added up to a defeat for the forces of evil. This was no Fulton Lewis of the moderate left, for heaven's sake; this was an honest, intelligent pacesetter for the industry. Of course if you insisted on the question, Did Murrow's opinions underlie his treatment of news analysis, the answer must be yes. But if such a policy could hamstring an Edward R. Murrow, perhaps it was the policy that needed reexamination. Also, what would lesser men do with that freedom? In any case, they looked forward to continuing the study for the rest of the department.

It went upstairs to Stanton from Mickelson's office, with a three-page confidential summary: It seemed they were finally beginning to reach paydirt, said the Vice-President of CBS News. Edwards and Jackson had drawn even in the number of violations, but the Murrow tailpieces were "guilty of a considerable number of transgressions"; therefore, the Murrow scripts didn't stack up as well as the other two. Murrow's foreign correspondents were "especially guilty in the use of proscribed material."

Mickelson suggested further research on possible evidence of departmental leanings, toward the right or left, and asked to talk with Stanton on steps to be taken, or on what use they might wish to make of this material.[14]

Stanton, said Mickelson later, made no overt response to the report. "I had a strong feeling that his antagonism toward Murrow was a major factor in setting this up. But of course, they were *so* enthusiastic about Murrow that I think they lost all sense of objectivity themselves. That's the trouble with so many people around the university campuses. . . .

"I tried on a number of occasions to get Stanton to react to it. He wouldn't react. . . . He wanted nothing further to do with it; that's *my* reaction."[15] Whatever might have happened beyond that, was beyond the ken of the CBS News chief. A final bill was met, the message sent to the academics that their services would no longer be required.

But it was also part of a pattern emerging in the wake of the storms of 1954. "Post-McCarthy stuff" a news executive later called it, asking, however, not to be identified. "It was that very delicate, sensitive time. Great pressure was put on Sig by the top management to be very careful about what we did on the air. In other words, 'Don't say anything or do anything that's going to get us into another kind of McCarthy situation.' "

By contrast, Murrow, on radio and with Friendly on TV, was operating in a counter-momentum, as though new directives, corporate bodies, and vice-presidents were virtually nonexistent. *See It Now* interviewed J. Robert Oppenheimer following withdrawal of the noted physicist's security clearance by the Atomic Energy Commission. They presented college debates on recognition of the government of mainland China and exposed political attempts to stifle the debates. They ran a two-part inquiry on the possible linkage between lung cancer and cigarettes, an advertising pillar of the broadcasting industry. (Murrow for once didn't smoke on camera; Barbara Scott, sitting at his feet, kept the Camel going between film segments.) They challenged the restrictive McCarran-Walter Immigration Act, reported on anti-integration violence in Delaware, apartheid in South Africa, and book banning in Southern California.

They ran afoul of the Pentagon while shooting footage on American bombers based in England, McClure's camera capturing a giant B-36 as it lumbered onto the tarmac, the crew alighting to be gone over with a Geiger counter. Can't use it, said the military censor. What did he mean, can't use it? Means it proves the U.S. has atomic weapons in England. Can't run it.

It was the Saturday before the show. Murrow entered the fray: But everybody in England knew about it; they were debating the damn thing in the House of Commons; what was the big deal? Out. At length Murrow called a halt, quietly. "I've got a way to solve that."

Tuesday night audiences saw the B-36 approaching: *"You never hear anyone refer to bombs, not the atomic bomb or the hydrogen bomb."* The screen went white—leader tape spliced in for the censored footage—

as Murrow, continuing the narration, referred to the unseen scene as "standard operating procedure."

> *It is known to many people in this country and in Britain. The Russians have talked about it. It has been debated in the British House of Commons, but the Defense Department, editing by telephone from Washington, told us to cut it out. We still don't know why, but that's why the screen has been blank for the past 25 seconds.*[16]

Within minutes the switchboard was jammed with calls from viewers asking exactly what was going on. The reaction in Washington was swift and furious. Murrow, taking bristling calls from the Air Force, said "too bad," opposition as usual bringing out the side of his personality which, as a colleague noted once, loved rubbing the noses of authority—especially, surprisingly, military authority—in the dirt.[17]

Opposition was undoubtedly an element in his ramming through of the Oppenheimer program in the teeth of misgivings from the network and Oppenheimer himself, traumatized by his ordeal of the past months. An FBI informant had, in fact, been watching as Murrow drove out in late November 1954 to the Institute for Advanced Studies in Princeton, where Oppenheimer was Director; their preliminary conversations stayed private. The program itself earned another entry in Murrow's growing FBI dossier.[18]

It was overtly sympathetic, right from the opening frames, shot through a haze of tobacco smoke as the two men lit up amiably together, the interview as portraiture, not inquisition. Murrow, said Friendly afterward, had done his homework and the two-and-three-quarter-hour conversation—cut eventually to twenty-five minutes for air time—flowed without a break, two cameras filming in tandem, the talk interrupted only once when Oppenheimer excused himself to go to the bathroom.[19]

"A Conversation with J. Robert Oppenheimer," was exactly that; a layout of the so-called Oppenheimer case was missing but nonetheless a presence, manifest in the comments on the relationship between the scientist and the state; on the McCarran-Walter restrictions on travel and immigration ("We are rightly shamed by the contempt that the Europeans have for us, and we are rightly embarrassed that we can't hold congresses in this country"), on what the interviewee called the integrity of communication:

> The trouble with secrecy is that it denies to the government itself the wisdom and resources of the whole community, of the whole country. . . .
>
> You have to have a free and uncorrupted communication. And this is—this is so the heart of living in a complicated technological world—it is so the heart of freedom, that that is why we are all the time saying, "Does this really have to be secret? . . . Are we really acting in a wise

way?" Not because we enjoy chattering, not because we are not aware of the dangers of the world we live in, but because these dangers cannot be met in any other way.

Had humanity, Murrow asked at one point, at last found a way to destroy itself? Not quite, came the answer. However, "You can certainly destroy enough of humanity so that only the greatest act of faith can persuade you—that what's left—will be human."[20]

Murrow and Friendly took out another ad. Paley, in private, liked the film. A report of O'Shea's stiff opposition was making the rounds, a factor O'Shea himself would later neither deny nor confirm. The film was run, the reaction predictable in liberal and conservative camps; but then a longer version, including certain outtakes and distributed by the liberal Ford Foundation-backed Fund for the Republic, added fuel to the controversy—one that flared hotter when the American Legion went to court to prevent a showing at a schoolhouse in the New York area. The name of Oppenheimer was added to those "individuals of questionable loyalty," "defended" by Murrow on his programs.

In the meantime, the screws were being applied in other ways.

On a Tuesday morning at the U.S. passport agency in Rockefeller Center, Murrow, stopping by to pick up the passport he had left for renewal, was informed of a slight hitch: just a formality, no problem; his passport had been renewed. But first . . .

The clerk shoved over the counter, for his signature, a one-page affidavit attesting that he was not now, nor had he ever been, a member of the Communist Party or indeed of any organization seeking to overthrow the government by force and violence.

Murrow's stunned questions came up against a blank bureaucratic wall: Was this now standard procedure? No. Or standard for journalists? No. Was there any special regulation or consideration which had prompted the State Department to take this action? No answer.[21]

He left without signing and without the passport.

It was eight months since the "refusal" had been entered in his file in Washington, a year since Scott McLeod had sanctioned the file's opening for McCarthy, almost four years since Murrow had strong-armed Ruth Shipley into releasing Harold Isaacs' passport.

A query went off that same day to Washington, "respectfully" requesting Shipley to apprise him of the situation.[22] She was not to be reached. A form letter came back instead, over the signature of the Deputy Director: Murrow was hereby informed that the State Department had instructed the agency to request the affidavit "as to whether or not you are or ever had been a communist" by reason of "certain derogatory information" received since the issue of his last passport in 1953. Prompt consideration would be given to his application on receipt of said affidavit;

for reference please use the affixed dossier number: 130-Murrow, Edward Roscoe.[23]

By now it was Monday morning. Murrow, calling Washington, had nailed down the Deputy Director by midafternoon and obtained a tentative appointment for Thursday, 3:00 P.M. The official took the CBS number and promised to call back.

Thursday morning, Murrow was still waiting. His office tried again. In Washington a secretary took the call: Oh yes, the appointment was on, but Mr. Murrow was to see the Assistant Director instead. No reason was given for the change or failure to confirm.

The Assistant Director received him courteously, almost benignly, in a manner more like a bureaucratic time server than a prosecutor.

He asked Murrow to take a seat. The closed dossier lay between them, on the table.

What followed, as Murrow recorded it, was straight charade: twenty questions as scripted by Franz Kafka:

> I asked if I might know the nature of the derogatory information.
>
> He replied in the negative as I knew he would.
>
> I then asked if there was any machinery by which or through which I might make a reply to this information.
>
> He said there was none.
>
> I asked if it was a raw file or whether it had been evaluated.
>
> He replied, a raw file, that it had come in from various sources.
>
> I asked if it contained annonymous [sic], casual information without proof or substantiation.
>
> He said it did. In this connection he mentioned one piece in "Counter-Attack" [sic] but did not further identify it.[24]

Murrow, at one point, asked politely, Did the file include his Defense Department clearance, the job offer from the late James Forrestal, his designation as the voice broadcasting news over special frequencies in case of enemy attack? No, said the other man, surprised, but if he wanted to *submit* that information . . .

The official seemed embarrassed. The information wasn't serious, of course, but the directive under which he worked was clear, and there were no exceptions; it was so difficult nowadays, reaching equitable judgments, especially on actions and associations of so many years ago. It was the closest he would come to mention of the Moscow Summer School. Of course, he added eagerly, there were no doubts about Murrow's *loyalty*. Otherwise, the application would have been refused altogether.

Murrow had offered at the outset to answer any and all questions. No questions were raised. It was like a broken record:. Produce the affidavit, and we'll send the passport.

It was that or a court battle, stretching into years.

He sent in the affidavit under protest: "I cannot, of course, reply to the 'derogatory information' now in the file because I do not know what it is."[25] Never mind, they had what they wanted.

At the time of Radulovich he had talked often and earnestly about the things that supposedly counted, of being able to face one's image in the mirror every morning. Obviously a top network news star—let alone a working reporter—could hardly be expected to remain indefinitely confined to the country, waiting for the wheels to turn, unlike lesser folk without dependent staffs, long-range news budgets, network commitments, hostages to fortune and the system.

"I will have trouble shaving for a while," he wisecracked bleakly to Paley, "but there was no alternative."[26]

That same week came the first indications that the three-year marriage with ALCOA was winding down.

The aluminum giant had renewed its contract as recently as November 1954, just before the reported Murrow trip to Princeton, with a ringing affirmation for the press that sponsorship of *See It Now* had "benefited the company, its stockholders and the general public."[27] The affirmation included continuation of the hands-off policy regarding program content.

By the spring of 1955, however, mixed signals were coming out of Pittsburgh.

It had been a mutually beneficial relationship; Murrow and Friendly had made the programs, ALCOA the aluminum, the slain dragon of the 1951 trustbusters, become the corporate guardian of the First Amendment in the view of the public and the media. ALCOA stockholder reports from as late as 1978 still showed Murrow and Irving Wilson, captioned side by side. But the Murrow-Wilson connection, like the Murrow-Paley connection, had its limits.

The breakup started in the warm weeks of April, weeks including various features but particularly the piece on book banning around Los Angeles—interviewing list compilers, buck-passing school officials, librarians speaking with faces averted from the camera. The show was monitored, it would turn out, by the FBI and was run, ironically, the day of Murrow's first jolt at the passport office.

The letter from the sponsor bore a new signature—one Arthur Hall, in charge of advertising and PR, a level Murrow-Friendly hadn't dealt with at ALCOA. In fact, it was Hall's signature that appeared regularly under company rejoinders to complaints about Murrow, leading most recently to a personal attack in one of Pegler's periodic forays, targeting the hapless PR man as "Egbert's friend."

There had been some discussion at headquarters, it seemed, about *See*

It Now, the conclusion, that there had been "a little too much talk" in some of the programs lately. Now that piece on the Air Force—far preferable, so much more typical of "what we, as the sponsor, feel is the type of program that does us the most good."[28]

Ironically, the handwriting on the wall, if such it was, came hard on the heels of the latest round of goodwill back in Pittsburgh: Murrow as honored guest, pressing the flesh at the Chamber of Commerce, addressing the ALCOA engineers, receiving the warm thanks of Chief Wilson, gracious as ever—a day of hearty fellowship among the "man's man" entrepreneurial types, the ostensible doers of the world, who could somehow transform Murrow, the intimate of presidents and prime ministers, back into the country boy from Polecat Creek. "What a pleasure it is to work for such a group of men and to be accepted as one of you," he was to write a friend in Pittsburgh, just a week before the ax fell.[29]

May 3, *See It Now* ran "The Power of the Press," about a land scandal in Texas, attempts by state officials to defraud veterans—mostly Black and Hispanic—out of state-awarded land grants, and a tiny newspaper that fought the establishment and won. Scott and Rossi, staying with the story, caught the moment the young editor learned he had also won a Pulitzer Prize. Thirty-eight hundred wasn't much of a circulation, Murrow noted in the tailpiece, but then, courage and power don't always come in the same package. "There are newspapers and radio and television networks with much greater circulations and much more potential power than the *Cuero Record*. The Pulitzer committee merely called attention to courage, perhaps with the hope that it might be contagious."[30]

Two days later ALCOA dropped *See It Now*.

Their friend the advertising and PR head had called the day after the broadcast, asking to see Murrow. Thursday, over lunch, they got the word: termination as of the end of season, July 5. Eight weeks away.

Ostensibly some fairly big names had gotten their fingers burned in the scandal, and ALCOA, currently enlarging installations down in Texas, reportedly trembled before Austin's wrath. A whole complex of reasons could, of course be cited—growing TV audiences; the war's end and a shift of emphasis in marketing; from fighter plane bodies to Wear-Ever pots and pans, to food wrap, consumer advertising, and high-rated entertainment shows with mass appeal.

Good-bye and no hard feelings. At least ALCOA had stuck it out through the McCarthy time. "We made them smell sweet, and then they dropped us," as a staffer put it; "that's the way it goes."[31] The New York *Times* paid passing tribute to a courageous sponsor. A few, Salant among them, continued to regard the fallout from the McCarthy affair as the real reason "that ALCOA ultimately dropped out."[32]

Some time afterward, Murrow confided to Charlie Mack that he had heard from Irving Wilson. The ALCOA chief executive was saddened and apologetic. The pressure from the stockholders, he said, had been just too much.[33]

McCarthy ascendant had cost Murrow one sponsor; McCarthy defeated, another. There the resemblance to 1950 ended.

At first, the smoke cleared, little seemed essentially changed. A modest presentation was drawn up for prospective new institutional sponsors, offering the weekly program in the 10:30 P.M. time slot. Murrow and Friendly went ahead with their plans, including a thirty-minute feature on the painter Grandma Moses, their first in color, to be telecast that fall.

Four weeks after the first shock, however, the next wave hit, swamping not only *See It Now* but all of television.

On a Tuesday night in early June, Murrow looked up at the control room monitor, saw a new CBS show called *The $64,000 Question* shoved into the time slot just preceding theirs, and knew the game was up. (To Friendly: "Any bets on how long we keep this time period now?")[34]

It was a new ball game: big audiences, big bucks. TV was hot, partly because the events of 1954 had made it so. The public had grown television-conscious, *See It Now* in a sense the victim of its own effectiveness.

But the number of TV homes had also more than tripled since *See It Now* first went on the air, affiliates more than doubled, gross billings up by fifty percent over the previous year. CBS-TV was now accounted the biggest single advertising medium in the world.[35] And the quiz show phenomenon, taking fire, was about to send those costs skyrocketing, with the pressure on for a return on the advertising dollar.

The Murrow program, sitting athwart fifty-seven choice outlets in prime time—eighty-five percent of total U.S. television homes, said Sales[36]—had become the pauper in the penthouse.

Paley's proposal, laid on in early July, therefore made sense from a number of viewpoints. It was the end of the season, Murrow about to take his family to the Northwest, when the two partners were summoned to the big, ornate office up on 20 and informed that *See It Now* was going off the weekly schedule. Paley offered instead an all-film series—specials, essentially—one hour apiece or even longer, bigger budgets, more time for preparation, full-length documentaries. CBS would schedule eight or ten a season, in prime time. Murrow asked about the weekly time slot, said Friendly, but it was evidently no longer a topic for discussion.

The plan had its attractions—one-hour instead of half-hour programs, bigger per-program budgets. Palmer Williams, rung up on the West Coast by Friendly, thought, *yeah, why not?* With no sponsor, no big ratings, they needed that format, that prop; said Williams later, "I could see the sanity of it."

But Bill Downs, cabled in Rome, found the news "troubling."

"Does this mean," he wrote Murrow, "that any honest attempt to present timely and controversial documentaries will fail to find sponsorship or what?" He offered to work free of charge if necessary.[37]

Either way it meant an essential and, as it turned out, decisive change in the ground rules. The 1954 setup had made the news department—and the Murrow-Friendly show was on the payroll—a packager, selling programs to the network, all budgeted and price-tagged. Which meant *See It Now* was now a package to be sold, involving discussions from the idea stage on, decisions on air time made by network management and sales, with copies of all communications going to Mr. Mickelson, Dr. Stanton, and the President of the CBS Television Network.

The Murrow-Friendly operation had always moved quickly, without questions or paper work; which had made possible the fast-paced coverage that had ranged from ghetto streets in South Africa to U.S. college campuses, from anti-Communist immigration laws to the clampdown on public debate over the China policy. They had aired debates on constitutional protection and congressional investigative powers that went past the question of McCarthy to those first raised by Martin Dies (spotlighted on one occasion when Murrow, cutting in on a speaker's remark that the Fifth Amendment was "not a form of employment insurance," asked pointedly, Did he mean the Fifth was designed to save a man's neck but not his job or reputation?).[38]

The program had projected the concerns of black Americans into the all-white world of prime-time TV: an all-night vigil with a family sending a child off on a school bus amid threats of violence in the wake of court-ordered integration; a black PTA mother venting, in 1954, the anger that was waiting to erupt ("We don't want to be in the homes and sleeping and doing with the white people. . . . We want schools like they have. We wants streets like they have. We want homes like they have. . . . We don't want like a heap of them think we want. . . . I just burns within me sometimes . . .").[39]

Shots were often crude by later standards, cameras big and cumbersome, subjects often uncomfortable, awkward in the presence of a new technology. What had come through, however, was a basic honesty, a lack of pretension and omniscience that gave the program lasting credibility, both with those whom it covered and with the viewing public.

Not all the programs, of course, had been controversial, probably not even half. The Murrow-Friendly crews had covered Las Vegas, the Stock Exchange, the Goldwyn studios. They had visited with the poet Carl Sandburg at his goat farm in North Carolina and sounded out reflections on U.S.-British relations on the part of J. B. Priestley, Rebecca West, and Bertrand Russell. But like it or not, it was controversy that had become the hallmark of *See It Now*, that had made the program, as a critic put it, "the most widely discussed, most electric, most admired and most rabidly condemned program on television." Murrow, Paley's assurances notwithstanding, wrote a colleague gloomily that he didn't know just what would be happening to *See It Now*, come fall.[40]

Indeed, acquisition by midsummer of a new sponsor—the GM Pontiac division, agreed to take on six, maybe eight programs in the coming season—did little to dispel a sense of unmistakable foreboding. An ALCOA friend, one of Murrow's former boosters, sent his congratulations at the news. Murrow thanked him, "but it won't be like the old days."[41]

That July, the Murrow family visited Ed's parents in Bellingham—a trip that nearly turned fatal when Flight 610, lighting down for a stopover in Yakima, was blown off the runway by a sudden tailwind, and sent tearing through the countryside with motors cut, over roads and under power lines. They had been midway through lunch, Casey Murrow later remembered, the jouncing sending food flying in all directions, plastering the cabin with salad and sticky dressing as a house whizzed by outside the windows. The DC-3 plowed through a pasture and several barbed-wire fences before skidding to a stop almost a mile from the runway, the shaky passengers alighting amid soft brown cow cakes to find the right wing sheared off just short of the fuel tank.

The crowning touch came as a civilian ran toward them from a pulled-up station wagon, brandishing a fire extinguisher, behind him, the crash trucks from the airport, bogged down in mud and cow manure.

It had been a short trip, but there was time for Murrow to stop off in Blanchard, bypassed by time and traffic. "Almost a ghost town," he wrote to a classmate who had studied with him at the little schoolhouse, which now stood empty. "The old sawmills have just plain collapsed into the water, and the hill behind the town is somehow much smaller than I remember it as being."[42] The interurban trolley was long since abandoned, logging operations ended. Further up the coast, pulp mills discharged their wastes into the bay where the Murrow boys had once dug for clams and speared salmon.

The one thing that hadn't changed was Ethel Murrow—feisty, self-willed, tenderly caring for the husband two years her junior and now totally disabled. She had come to be known in the area, a good neighbor and known buyer of regional Indian art long before such became the fashion, with a keen judgment and practiced eye that traders somehow never expected in the small, frail-looking countrywoman with the quaint, old-fashioned English; a shrewd trader herself, who could wear opponents down to a few dollars' asking price, less from love of bargaining than from the stubborn conviction that it was all she could afford.

Through the years the two younger sons had watched over the parents, seeing tactfully to their needs, though it was Ethel who stayed firmly in the driver's seat, possessive even from afar, a difficult woman whose sons worshiped her but couldn't take her in more than small doses. Casey retained a mental picture, long afterward, of his father and his uncles sitting awkwardly around the family dinner table: three middle-aged men dumbly confronting their overflowing plates, the old woman hovering in the background with pot and ladle, urging second helpings.

Murrow had always talked of buying property in the Northwest, getting back to his roots perhaps, and, in fact, had made several passes in that direction. An important purchase made in those months, however, tied him once and for all to the East.

As Mary Warburg recalled, they had all gone for a drive one day when the Warburgs came to visit, and there it was, sitting in the sun, just off Route 22 a few miles from Pawling—"this divine farm with the white house; I said, 'Ed, you have to buy this for Janet.' " Sometime later he told her with a grin that it was done, and "It's your fault I bought the damn thing!"[43]

In fact, it was the happiest choice made in those years. Murrow's letters brimmed over to friends as varied as Frank Graham, Agnes Meyer of the *Washington Post,* and the Chief Air Marshal of the RAF, with the information that he had acquired a hay baler and a bulldozer.

It was also the lost patrimony regained with interest, an anchor for his rootlessness, and a much-needed outlet for the nervous energy that found satisfaction in manual labor. "I have become a farmer in my spare time," he wrote an English friend that August, "and having great fun with it; 280 acres, milking 42 head of Line Bred Holstein and banging the type-writer to pay the deficit."[44]

It wasn't exactly one's average upstate dirt farm. Wrought-iron gates opened to a sweeping treelined drive leading to the four-bedroom Colonial clapboard house with its tall windows overlooking the sloping lawn and shady oaks; a guest cottage out in back was where General Philip Schuyler had been court-martialed during the Revolutionary War. Their private domain, complete with barn, pens, and pastureland.

The Jaynses, a no-nonsense tenant farming couple, worked the property year-round, the master of the manor pitching in weekends and summers, in worn denims, with the same intense drive that he brought to broad-casting. "This is a working farm," he told a visitor somewhat defiantly. "No swimming pools, no tennis courts."

Manhattan friends smiled at the farmer persona perched on an annual income of almost a quarter million, thanks to the fabulously successful *Person to Person*. But Glen Arden Farm became increasingly important over the years, a private hideaway and escape valve, clung to with the deep-seated attachment of his peasant stock, the almost mystic need of ownership: the land hunger that had skipped a generation and marked him as Josh Murrow's grandson.

A world was phasing out that summer—ten years since the ending of World War II. A silver plaque, suitably engraved, was to go up at Broadcasting House, contributed by the American correspondents who had shared Britain's finest hour. Murrow, tapped to write the text, found nothing coming, responding with a half-completed stab, forced out after repeated prodding and sent off with apologies for what he knew was a lackluster performance: "Sorry, but I am just in no mood to compose."[45]

In Geneva, Dwight Eisenhower, Anthony Eden, Nikita Khrushchev, and Edgar Faure, meeting in the first East-West summit since Potsdam, smiled at one another in the sunshine across a green stretch of lawn while *Life* shutters clicked, the news media hyping the so-called Spirit of Geneva, despite a rearmed West Germany's entrance into NATO and Eastern Europe bunching up in the Warsaw Pact.

In Murrow's private world the ranks were thinning. Ed Klauber had died months before. Murrow, as promised, spoke at the memorial service for the father of CBS News.

Paul White had finally succumbed in a San Diego hospital, attended only by his wife and a few station people. Write him, a West Coast CBS friend had asked Murrow in the final weeks; he's so alone. Murrow tried, but the letter was groping: What could one say? Over in Grand Central on a list of news directors for the CBS-TV affiliates, an asterisk was entered opposite White's name; alongside it, jotted in ball-point, the word "July."[46]

In Indonesia, the first Afro-Asian summit had convened at the tidy Dutch-style resort town of Bandung, ignored by U.S. officialdom and the news management of CBS. Murrow had sent Raymond Swing on his own initiative to make daily voice reports, an arrangement worked out accordingly: Murrow paid the costs of sending Swing around the world, plus living expenses; CBS paid Swing twenty-five dollars per broadcast.

"Maybe the year-end show," wrote Bill Downs from Rome, "should change its name to YEARS OF CONFUSION, or WHAT THE HELL IS GOING ON?"[47]

Early in the year, Eisenhower had requested and received a virtual blank check on the commitment of American troops abroad, in the joint congressional resolution empowering the President to employ U.S. armed forces as he deemed necessary for "securing and protecting" areas now in the hands of Chiang Kai-shek.

In Southeast Asia, the new South Vietnamese state set up with assurances of aid from the administration floundered amid flare-ups between the absentee Emperor, Bao Dai, and the new Prime Minister, Ngo Dinh Diem—a bit autocratic, but whom Secretary Dulles, Murrow noted in passing, was "apparently still determined to keep . . . in office."[48]

He still felt as he had five years back, but what he had called "the Policy of Doubtful Wisdom" was going down a little more easily without the French colonials behind it; the U.S., after all, no colonizer, was coming in untainted. He had no problems, therefore, with the Eisenhower policy enunciated in those months—i.e., we couldn't be the world's policemen but did have interests, among them the mineral-rich, populous literate lands of the Mekong, rice bowl of Southeast Asia.

Withal he remained gun-shy, ambivalent, never seeing Indochina as the clear-cut issue that Korea had seemed five years before, wary, as in 1952, of the U.S. "improvising" itself into another war. When Nixon, therefore, at the height of the Dienbienphu debacle in 1954, set off an uproar with a remark favoring the dispatching of GIs to Vietnam in case of a French pullout, Murrow had quickly found it "significant" that one who sat on the National Security Council had "such strong views on keeping Indochina from falling to the Communists.

"Obviously no decision has been made to send American troops. . . . But neither has a decision been made *not* to send troops under any circumstances. And the second statement may prove to be even more important than the first."[49]

He argued in broadcasts that were an odd mixture of the time-bound and the prescient, using the confident vocabulary of the cold war. He was a believer in the domino theory, who called Dienbienphu "a catastrophe," yet warned the public away; who shared Eisenhower's doubts on military involvement yet, again like Ike, did not preclude political involvement; and who warned during the drumbeating in 1954 that while "some form of intervention may appear inescapable," such talk was "premature and even unrealistic. For one thing intervention by itself might not save Indochina. . . . And advocates of intervention are unrealistic if they assume that the problem . . . is primarily military."[50]

Only if the people of Indochina, he had argued, believed that "the fight against Communism" was the fight for their freedom would they "turn the present tide of conflict.

"At present the Communists are succeeding . . . largely because they have convinced villagers and peasants that they are liberators. . . . This is the situation, despite the promise of independence within the French Union, made by France to Bao Dai. . . . But for Bao Dai to receive such assurances in Paris, and for the village elders in Vietnam to hear about them and *believe* them, is something else."

The "victory," he said, was not to be won by more foreign troops or guns, French or American. It was not to be won by the capture of strongpoints; the Vietminh *had* no strongpoints. It was to be won in the realm of convictions, the so-called hearts-and-minds approach that would get successive administrations into trouble and that he seemed ready to follow all the way, only to draw back invariably at the ultimate step, with traces of doubt instilled in 1950 by R. T. Clark on one hand, and by Harold Isaacs on the other.

Above all, he was a pragmatist who had opposed providing either men or air support because he knew it wouldn't work; that the United States, if it entered, would be no more successful than the French. He had pointed out at the height of Dienbienphu that the French were militarily much stronger than their adversaries ("They have planes and tanks, which the Vietminh lack altogether, and they have a virtual blank check on the United States for military supplies"). He had thus far found the South Vietnamese successor state a weak reed and in 1955 told American radio audiences, flat-out, "*We* will inherit the mess."[51]

(Interestingly in a later account of the 1954 Dienbienphu broadcast, a proofreader's error would change the phrase on the original news script from "some form of intervention may *appear* inescapable" to "may *prove* inescapable"—perpetuated thereafter in other writings and cited, out of context, as evidence of Murrow's alleged early espousal of armed intervention.)

During the spring of 1954, as the administration weighed its options, and continuing thereafter, *See It Now* had kept the question of Vietnam before the TV public. David Schoenbrun's filmed straw poll of French opinion, an eerie harbinger of the American experience to come, projected the image of a country divided and drained by the conflict, with ex-premier Paul Reynaud, evoking the fellowship of World War II, proving no match for the French mom ("Madame, you have a son in Indochina?"), reading, in a trembling voice, a letter from the front: "Dearest Mother, the only thing we want is peace. . . ."[52]

At other levels, transatlantic debates aired the matter of Indochina as a bargaining chip in French decisions on the European front; American underwriting of the fighting in Asia ("but the blood is ours");[53] and what price victory, if any? All of which had found a ready echo among a war-weary U.S. public in a midterm election year replete with slogans of "no more Koreas," when young Senator John Kennedy of Massachusetts inveighed against pouring more weapons into the jungles of Indochina.

Amazingly, in retrospect, the debates included not a single Vietnamese or even Asian; not a Harold Isaacs or a Teddy White, the latter, like most dissenters, anathema to the networks. It was Vietnam as seen through the prism of Europe, Saigon perceived from Paris, London, and Washington.

Yet for all that, it was probably the only prime-time TV outlet on which Vietnam, with all its unanswered questions, came up for regular debate, moreover at a time when the larger public was still mesmerized by Joe McCarthy; and on which a French dissenter, the journalist Jean-Jacques Servan-Schreiber, could close out a program by looking the camera and the viewers in the eye and telling the American public it was "a great tragedy" the day the U.S. changed its mind on Indochina in the years after the war:

"You wanted the French Army to leave Indochina and give that to a national and independent government. You were absolutely right. That was what the British did in India, what you did yourself in the Philippines. . . . It is the only sensible course, if we want to keep friends in Asia.

Instead of that, *our* government finally convinced *you* that you had to support our fight against the Indochinese people, or so-called rebels. It was a tragically wrong policy. . . ."[54]

The *Daily Worker* labeled the program "an unabashed war-whoop for American intervention,"[55] while irate citizens wrote the FBI, denouncing Murrow for handing Indochina over to the Communists.

See It Now began the fall, 1955 season by losing its new sponsor.

General Motors had come aboard in July. In August, Murrow and Friendly announced Program No. 1, on the vice-presidency, subtitled "The Great American Lottery" ("At best it's a compromise and at worst, it's a game of roulette").[56] Detroit seemed to have no problem with it.

September 24, Eisenhower suffered a heart attack, the oldest President ever in office. The vice-presidency had become a hot topic. The following Tuesday, Murrow, commenting on the historic lack of guidelines in the case of presidential disability, mildly questioned Nixon's calling of the cabinet and NSC, implying—nay, stating—that anything further, pending legislation, might just well be out of line, in fact, might stir up "a constitutional hornet's nest."[57]

General Motors walked out on its contract, the ostensible explanation: someone had heard the upcoming show was to be a hatchet job on Nixon. Another leak was that old "Boss" Charles Kettering, the builder of GM, did not want the Murrow connection.

If anything, the program had been fairly gentle with Nixon, describing him on the voice-over as "busy" and "useful . . . to the President," the film footage including Ike before the press, explaining why Nixon made a sterling running mate. Nixon himself, invited onto the program, had reportedly refused.

Breach of contract; cancellation because of an unseen show. CBS didn't contest it. Murrow, Friendly, and staff, with four weeks to go to air time, couldn't believe it. "The worst blow we ever had" was how one recalled the disaster. Sales scrambled around and came up with spots from two other CBS divisions plus a maker of mascara. What had gone down the drain was the last hope for a replacement blue-chip sponsor or, for that matter, any steady sponsorship in prime time.

What was also a fact, unknown at the time, was that someone in the administration had had the unflattering 1955 FBI summary on Murrow in hand since early summer, requested by Jim Hagerty for purposes and parties unspecified in an administration that saw GM well represented— notably in the top Defense job, held down by Charles E. Wilson, "Engine Charlie," the former GM president, who thought that what was good for GM was good for the country. But was Murrow in September 1955 necessarily good for GM?

It would seem in any case a long coincidence that the affair should have blown up while administration members had in their hands the brief report ending with *Counterattack*'s characterization of Murrow as one whose programs defended "individuals of questionable loyalty."[58]

The questions persisted: Why was the report asked for, blind, that summer? Was it circulated, contrary to standard FBI instructions? Had its contents anything to do with GM's finding a program acceptable in August, but not in September? Did it help spur GM to renege on its contract?

It caught Murrow and Friendly at the worst possible time. They were entering an era of competition for budgets and air time with the rising documentary talents of CBS News. *See It Now* was an expensive show; it needed underwriting, was vulnerable without it, as a budget eater, a money loser and maker of waves. The GM cancellation, as it turned out, was a body blow from which it would never recover.

There were seven shows that season, Sales picking up the pieces, with subjects ranging from Egypt and Israel, to paying the education tab for the baby boom.

But it was only eight hours of exposure, as against the twenty-two hours of the preceding season—a reduction of almost two-thirds in total air time, with irregular scheduling in place of the old Tuesday night slot.

It was also their last season in prime time, Paley's promises notwithstanding. By the following October, *See It Now* would be shunted back to Sunday afternoon where it had started, back in 1951.

At the same time, a new sensitivity was developing between Murrow-Friendly and the twentieth floor.

In January, Murrow and Friendly ran a program on the vanishing small farmer, squeezed out between high costs and high-volume agribusiness, with Ezra Taft Benson, Ike's controversial Secretary of Agriculture, invited to sit in and comment. Benson read "Crisis of Abundance" as an attack on administration farm policy, glared into the camera, and called it "demagoguery at its worst." The Republican National Committee demanded equal time; CBS acceded.

Murrow and Friendly were shocked. Did this mean the government got free time anytime it didn't like the handling of an issue?

Said Friendly: "Murrow felt we had really gone out of our way. Benson was at his home; we kept on coming back to him; he seemed to like the show; then back to him at the end. He was critical. That was his right. But we did everything we could—why the half hour?"[59]

Mickelson, too, thought Benton wrong; but it was "understood," he later recalled, "that the administration was behind the whole thing."[60] Murrow learned of the decision while filming for the next show in the Middle East, handed the cable on returning to his Tel Aviv hotel, tired and grimy after an all-night working session with the cameras in the field. Friendly, arriving with him, had never seen him so angry: "He drafted a telegram, resigning; I didn't send it. Mrs. Murrow and I thought he should wait until we got back to New York."[61]

Six months later, Jim Hagerty admitted to Murrow his party's frank surprise at getting what it had asked for.

Time magazine attacked the program. Des Moines loved it, CBS affiliate KRNT wanted a print for a rerun, Clark Mollenhoff of the Des Moines *Register* offered a drawerful of backup stuff in case Murrow-Friendly needed it.

One sequence, it seemed, drew fire because a farmer leaving his land hadn't sold it. But the producers were more arguably on shaky ground in that a few minutes of off-the-cuff comment, answering a skillful one-hour film weeks or months in preparation, hardly constituted adequate response time; ironically, things could have been worked out in the old weekly format, now discarded.

"Brother Benson will get his chance to lacerate me on the 23rd," Murrow wrote a friend bitterly that February, "which will not be a new experience"[62]—strong language to use about the Secretary, who signed "Ezra" on his yearly Christmas cards to 485, but an indication of the scars left by the McCarthy affair.

The outcome was pure anticlimax—a thirty-minute election-year plug, hooted down by much of the Farm Belt press; but for *See It Now*, the controversy left a sour aftertaste.

Time, moreover, wasn't standing still at the network. By the mid- to latter fifties CBS News, under the nurturing eye of Dr. Stanton, was well on its way, organizing new departments and services to meet the escalating demands on TV, with facilities in Grand Central and the Graybar Building, since 1953 a generator and successful syndicator of newsfilm. It was the start of an age that saw the news operation not only as information gatherer and disseminator, but as potential corporate profit center—a division, as of 1957, selling goods and services to other divisions, under no big obligation to bring in huge earnings but expected to pay its way, anticipate costs, tote them up so that the books would balance and thus help keep CBS firmly in the black.[63]

It was a world in which, with its talk of projected profit figures and "news product," Murrow felt less and less at home.

At the same time *See It Now* continued as the highest cost-per-program, highest prestige item in public affairs at CBS, the crown jewel of the news schedule, lodestone for the Peabodys and Emmys, publicly identified with Paley himself.

Rumbles of discontent were known to come from less favored units, often in Jack Gould's direction—i.e., they too could have a *See It Now* if they were the boss's friend, had that budget. *See It Now*'s shooting ratio of twenty feet shot per each foot used was a perpetual sore point, as much as Friendly's heavy hand in getting the bucks. It didn't so much affect the nightly news producers. Theirs was a different kind of shooting, no competition there; in fact, said Howard Kany, the longtime manager of the newsfilm operation, they were rather proud of *See It Now*.

Rather, it was the new generation of documentary talent coming up in TV news and public affairs who felt shortchanged, kept on tighter financial reins, mindful of the budget each time they set out to shoot or simply assemble film. *Air Power*, under the gifted Perry Wolff from Mickelson's staff, including World War II footage, original score and all, came in at an estimated $35,000 a copy, and there was still "a hell of a fight" getting it on the air.[64] The weekly half hour *Sunday News Special* came in at $30,000. An hourlong *See It Now*, by contrast, could run through $100,000 and upward.

But shooting ratios and budgets, said Mickelson himself, weren't the whole story: "There was a certain element of show business and an intellectual quality [on *See It Now*] which you couldn't get simply by the number of feet of film you exposed. And Fred, of course, certainly was a real genius; there's no doubt about it."

Jealousies, however, ran in all directions, Irv Gitlin in public affairs competing for the documentary dollar with John Day, the roughhouse red-headed new director of the network news, both men battling for supremacy, Mickelson recalled, "and neither one of them . . . very enthusiastic about *See It Now*."

In the background—coming to the fore—was nightly news, struggling to define itself, with components scattered all over midtown and bottlenecks in the chain of command, the News Director literally strong-armed by his chief into leaving 485 for the Graybar Building near Grand Central, to go down to where his troops were. Another executive would turn out to have a taste for long liquid lunches, learned of too late and to his regret, said his boss later, "because I was too busy going to meetings at 485."

The head of CBS News, prodded by upstairs, called innumerable huddles on bettering the product, scoring "lack of cooperation . . . of quality . . . of [a] clear sense of direction as to what television news is and what it should be."[65] Growing pains.

Stanton, from 20, exhorted his news chief to higher efforts: to more craftsmanship on the newsfilm, more careful processing, editing. Money helped but could not "buy these things overnight."[66] Ironically, they were qualities that *See It Now* had in abundance—lean, surefooted, fast-moving—even as it was being cut back.

The process was gradual. There were still the one-on-one consultations with Paley, and the honors kept rolling in, to a continuing chorus of critical acclaim that made news execs at NBC explode periodically in frustration.

It was still a phenomenon, the only series of its kind on television, less of an anomaly, in retrospect, than a prototype of the freewheeling actuality programs of the future, pointed to with seeming pride by the front office and, indeed, the industry.

A small, brisk, no-nonsense Englishwoman passing through New York in that time—the TV news pioneer Grace Wyndham Goldie, mother figure to a generation of British documentarians, then a senior producer for BBC Television—later recalled sitting in on working sessions in the cutting room, watching the programs taking shape and the dynamic between Murrow and Friendly: "They worked together in such a remarkable way because Ed never relinquished the personal view of any film material they had got, while Fred was the practical down-to-earth man who could decide in detail how everything could be put together."

> What was clear to me about the pair of them—and one had to think of them as a pair—was that they seemed to be completely as one in their understanding of the relationship in television between editorial judgment and the technological basis upon which any television communication must be based.
>
> Now whether Ed and Fred discussed all this, I very much doubt. But what they did was to have an understanding of their unity on this front, almost as an instinct. As I saw it, this was crucial to the success of their communications. And they set a pattern which we all envied. Because it's very rare.[67]

She had asked Ed in passing about negotiating for film, some outtakes, perhaps, for showing back on the BBC, which was short of funds. But my dear girl, he answered expansively, there were thousands of cans in the basement, never opened. And she could have the lot.

Mrs. Goldie was "flabbergasted." Why didn't *they* use it?

Said Murrow: "We can't afford to catalog it."

She laughed. "If *you* can't afford it, how can *we?*" But it was a jarring glimpse of budgeting priorities at a rich American TV network.

Nor were matters totally harmonious at *See It Now*. Its success had brought the great radio correspondents into television. At the same time, the problems forecast in the first 1951 encounter, in the BBC basement, between producer and correspondent, had grown as the program went to the all-film format, and the cry intensified of "Who's in charge?"

The TV people, struggling with the logistics of early television, saw the correspondents as prima donnas. The correspondents, coping with the politics and complexities of the areas they covered, often saw the on-site producer as the proverbial bull in the china shop. They chafed over TV's voracious appetite for pictures, the sometime staging of events to provide an effective piece of film, the danger of creating an event for television.

"In a decade of work," Schoenbrun wrote Murrow, "I never had any such trouble. . . . I sent you my cables with confidence in the way you would use them and with pride in the fact that you were using them. We are now working not directly with each other but through intermediaries."[68]

An equally frustrated McClure, assured by Friendly that *he* was in charge, would go off abroad and find he wasn't.

Murrow, caught between his Boys and the new production generation, did not resolve the issue. Wouldn't, because he needed Friendly, said Schoenbrun; just wanted to avoid personalities, said Howard Smith. ("With people he respected working together, he didn't want to tell one, 'You're in charge, the others will obey you.' ")[69]

Ironically, the strongest comments were coming from those who had taken most readily to TV. Far from being hostile to the medium, a leading critic such as Schoenbrun was considered by network news officials to be "the most effective radio man on our behalf," a reporter who "thinks television."[70]

Murrow assured them he'd control the editing, and for the most part, he did. For all their differences, the Boys stayed with it; *See It Now* was still the greatest exposure they got, Schoenbrun told Friendly in New York, and well worth the bloodying.[71]

But the questions regarding television news coverage and the editorial balance of power, weren't going away, the weight swinging away from the correspondents, toward the producers.

The networks were pouring everything they had into the 1956 conventions: huge staffs; the new hand-held TV cameras; transistorized receivers; long-range camera lenses permitting exclusive coverage for the individual networks, supplementing the camera pool. Total sponsor revenue for the big three, inclusive of election night, was expected to top $14 million. Murrow, with weeks of floor work looming ahead, went for a physical examination prior to packing for a quick Minnesota fishing trip with a former colleague, Cedric Adams. The doctors said, forget it.

"[They] tell me I've got to take it easy," he wired Adams unhappily, "and I am until the conventions actually begin. I am deeply disappointed but have no choice." Maybe in September, he said, but then he might have to go to Yugoslavia. "I have really been looking forward to this outing and can't tell you how sorry I am."[72] The trade-offs were becoming mandatory as his health declined and his smoking approached three packs a day.

"As you know, I would do anything for you," he told a worried Bill Benton, "but I cannot give up cigarettes."[73]

He was pushing fifty, his system going on overload under the pressure of the demands placed on it, the stress of public controversy too often finding resolution in some Park Avenue examining room. He worried about the country, the direction of TV, things he could essentially do nothing about. A remark by a high industry spokesman the winter of the Oppenheimer program, to the effect that broadcasting was simply a conduit up for hire, had set him pacing the floor late at night at Glen Arden as David Lilienthal looked on, waving his hands in the air, talking nonstop about "power without responsibility. . . . They call us pipes, conduits, ready to carry anything for a fee . . . they might better say sewers."[74] There had been chronic headaches in the aftermath of Oppenheimer, so severe that the doctors ordered X rays of the skull, which came up negative.

Given the circumstances, it was probably fanciful to expect Murrow to give up what he himself described as an addiction, and what, by now, he couldn't do without.

The job-related pressures were intense. His shyness had grown worse. Salant watched him backstage at the Philadelphia Academy of Music, revving up for a special showing of the year-end correspondents' roundup before the local World Affairs Council: "I remember how extremely tense he was—hands, legs shaking, sweat coming down. I attributed it at the time to exhaustion."[75] Edward Warburg, sharing the dais with him at a United Jewish Appeal dinner noted Murrow smiling and confident—from the waist up, his legs trembling beneath the table. McClure, shooting with him in Europe, often had literally to prod to get him to an interview.

The cigarette, mood modifier that it was, meant control. "It's not a prop," he told a magazine reporter, "I really need it."

Evidently he did: sixty to ninety a day, his long history of congenital lung problems notwithstanding. And he smoked Camels, the harshest cigarette on the market, no filters, inhaling deeply with every drag. Eddy Bliss later remembered being horrified, watching him light up without pausing for the flame to die down—"just *drank* it in, phosphates, everything."[76] (Going for help to Zousmer, Bliss was told, "You don't tell Ed Murrow how to light up a cigarette.") Murrow had smoked his way through the two *See It Now* programs on lung cancer, watching footage on tar accumulation in a smoker's lungs, lesions on the backs of cancerous mice. Sporadic attempts to stop brought on withdrawal, "the shakes," and a quick return.

Casey Murrow, now entering his teens, had come actively to hate the weed and everything about it—the lighting up before breakfast, the smell of cigarettes, the butts and ashes—in the apartment, in the family cars; aware from his earliest years that the cigarettes had something to do with "when Dad felt crummy," the times when his big, active father was suddenly sequestered behind the bedroom door, as pallid as his pillow, and voices were lowered.

"I really detested them," he recalled later. "Mom used to worry, obviously, that he smoked too much; he would talk about it sometimes, too. But then he had that ridiculous line that he would use periodically, that they would have a cure before he got cancer.

"I mean, it was flip—it's a good way to end a conversation, isn't it?"[77]

H. V. Kaltenborn gave it a try one January night over *Person to Person*, displaying his collection of "worry stones"—for handling under pressure, he told Murrow, while lecturing or broadcasting. "You know I don't smoke. You probably smoke too much, Ed. . . ."

Murrow allowed as how he probably did. "I must try that sometime instead of smoking."

Kaltenborn looked straight at the camera. "I think you'll find it much healthier, Ed, in every way."

Murrow switched abruptly to the next question: "Hans, you're often called the Dean of Commentators. . . ."

The old newsman switched right back. Nothing to it, he clipped in the inimitable Kaltenborn style; it just meant he was the oldest.

"You'll be the dean someday. All you've got to do is live long enough. Stop smoking, Ed."[78]

NBC went to the conventions hungry and came home, if not champions, then several notches up, having given CBS something to think about with its aggressive floor reporting, successful preconvention hype, its special train service for the critics, its cushy prefab communications center, and streamlined technological efficiency. But above all, there had been the wild card—the two-man surprise combination emerging from the projected three-man anchor team, the old-timer Bill Henry fading before the hosting of Chet Huntley, once of CBS, meshing with the sprightly running commentary of a salaried thirteen-year Washington bureau veteran, long familiar from the nightly John Cameron Swayze news strip. David Brinkley, known for his Washington smarts and relaxed, innovative filmed reports; who had scored a coup in 1952 with his back seat interview of Richard Nixon, shot en route to the inauguration, the camera shooting from the front seat of the limo, a sound technician crouched by the Vice President's feet.

"A quiet Southerner with a dry wit and a heaven-sent appreciation of brevity has stolen the television limelight," Jack Gould announced in The New York Times of August 17, hailing the Huntley-Brinkley combination as "the first real change in the network news situation" and Brinkley himself as the possible forerunner of a new breed.

For years NBC had been under the gun to "get a Murrow." Once, in exasperation, Dave Taylor had burst out that he wouldn't want one if he could get one; Murrow had a messianic streak, and he distrusted messiahs—even if Murrow was his daughter's godfather.[79]

Nonetheless, Murrow had been the yardstick by which the others measured themselves, in a competition grown personal over the years, focused inevitably on the front-runner. A prize snatched from under the nose of See It Now was a double victory;[80] a second-best review, galling defeat. ("This worshiping at the shrine of Murrow burns the hell out of me," snapped NBC News Operations Manager Joe Meyers to his superiors upstairs.)[81] By the same token, Jack Gould's rare negatives on Murrow made the rounds amid murmurs of satisfaction, treasured like some hoped-for sign of spring.

Repeatedly, Dave Taylor had petitioned NBC top management to undo the money clip, to back the news talent as CBS did theirs—Murrows didn't emerge full-blown; they were developed, and when NBC learned that, they'd get somewhere.[82]

Now the picture had changed, with a coming shift in NBC management about to shake up the old order even further, altering traditional equations and impacting ultimately on both networks.

CBS, its usual first place in the ratings notwithstanding, had come across somehow as second-best, humorless, Gould in the *Times* singling out Murrow and Sevareid in the analysis spot, sitting with heads bowed "in unrelieved earnestness."[83]

But if the CBS performance was lackluster, so were the conventions—long, grinding, predictable. Murrow suggested in follow-up that gavel-to-gavel coverage be dispensed with in 1960, given a commensurate level of technological development.

He wrote to Mickelson:

> The first two days could have been compressed into a couple of half-hour reports without missing the guts of a single story. Also I had the feeling that . . . we were inclined to neglect news occurring in the rest of the world. . . . I think probably we were over-staffed. . . some of the cut-away shots during principal speeches came dangerously close to visual editorializing; why not stay on the speaker and let him bore them all by himself?[84]

The election results for 1956 were a foregone conclusion virtually from the time Eisenhower had declared for a second term. Nevertheless, and in a radical departure from his usual practice, Murrow had agreed to help the Democrats.

The actress Vanessa Brown, then working on the Stevenson campaign, later remembered meeting Murrow that spring on the West Coast, three months before the conventions, in a rendezvous brokered by Marietta Tree, head of Volunteers for Stevenson, and Polly Cowan, the activist wife of the former quiz-show packager and CBS executive Louis Cowan. "Polly," Brown recalled, "had sent me a wire asking me to contact Murrow on his arrival in L.A. She had some sort of official position in the campaign, and Mrs. Tree had gotten in touch quietly with Murrow and convinced him to help out." (Tree herself later pleaded bad memory, but if Brown said it was so, it was so. Of course, she added with a twinkle, the situation was not at all unusual. "Newsmen often do what they can, behind the scenes.")[85]

They met and talked for two hours at the spiffy Beverly Hills Hotel. "I was very nervous, of course," Brown said later, "but he was very gallant—terribly good-looking—listening to my outpourings about Stevenson." Janet Murrow, in the next room, had a platter of hors d'oeuvres sent in.

The idea had been to effect a liaison between the broadcaster and the candidate, to discuss the use of TV in the forthcoming campaign. "There had been one rather unproductive meeting between them earlier that year, and Marietta wanted me to keep Murrow's interest alive."

After the session, she remembered, he walked her to the car, held the door as she got in. "You know, you're batting your head against a stone wall," he said.

"We have to try."

"Well, I'll do what I can."[86]

The connection was kept under wraps, Murrow's identity concealed in Brown and the candidate's references, in their correspondence, to "my friend." "My idea," Brown said, "he never asked for secrecy." The understanding was, he was acting as a private citizen, the matter kept quiet, obviously, because of the CBS affiliation.

Just why did he do it, breaking a long-standing rule? He wouldn't say; friends, knowing his detestation of Foster Dulles, were not surprised.

In any case, it never came to much. Stevenson, wrote Murrow later, simply resented television: "the tyranny of the clock, the bright lights . . . everything about it."[87] In a West Side film studio in late June, the newsman sweated over the candidate, trying to inculcate the finer points of speaking to the camera. Stevenson barely endured it, chiding campaign manager George Ball about the money this was costing the Democrats.[88]

Murrow himself dictated a few ideas for issue-oriented TV spots, never put to use—remarkably akin, however, to later political advertising.

They tried to arrange a campaign documentary on atomic fallout, following the candidate's controversial proposal, in late October, for a halt to atmospheric testing of atomic weapons. The only topic in the whole campaign, said Murrow on radio, bearing even remotely on disarmament. "At a time when mankind is able to destroy itself, no subject would seem more appropriate for discussion. . . .Americans who are able to face the facts of life presumably are adult enough to face the facts of death."[89]

But the Stevenson campaign itself was doomed; too many people, as Murrow had said in 1952, "liked Ike," the contrast between the candidates pointed up by TV, with Eisenhower the easy winner on the tube as in the ballot box.

"There was no doubt about his personality," said Murrow sometime afterward:

He was a friendly, good, kind, paternal, successful General who stood above familiar political considerations, and could be trusted because he was not complicated. . . . Stevenson, on the other hand, gave the impression that things were pretty complicated and would require some hard thinking and difficult decisions.

I am not saying that Stevenson would have won if there had been no modern communications. But his gifts of oratory and political analysis, his ability to improvise sentences that would parse, his mastery of debate and the wealth of his ideas would have counted more in ... newsprint and radio than they do on the television screen.

All of which, he thought, posed troubling questions for the coming age of media politics: "Simplicity communicates itself more easily than complexity. . . . This is by no means a boon. It surely is essential to have abstruse and complex ideas simplified, so that many can understand them. But we live in an age in which intelligence may not be able to simplify truthfully. . . ."[90]

It was during the week in Chicago that Vanessa Brown, stopping in at Murrow's suite at the Ambassador Hotel one afternoon, found the atmosphere changed. Usually things were humming—phones ringing, Kay Campbell organizing, Sevareid stopping by—but now it was quiet, the five-thirty lull between the end of the long day on the floor and the start of the evening session.

The room was empty except for Murrow, sitting over a drink. She sensed something wrong. "Ed was depressed. He started talking about the situation at CBS—somehow we just got into it—the earlier days of television, the satisfaction. I knew his program was being switched around to different hours. He talked about his first job, how happy he was then, bringing teachers over; about soldiers he had met in North Africa during the war, who mentioned studying with some professor he had brought over, what it meant to them.

"He was thinking about quitting the board of directors: 'I'm just not cut out for that.' I remember he felt hemmed in, couldn't move. He didn't criticize Paley though he hated Stanton, but mostly it was just a general critique—about the timidity of people, not having the freedom to do what he knew was best, having to submit ideas in advance to the company. . . ."

She had sat listening to the sudden outpouring, trying to think of something to say. ("I was really amazed—there had never seemed anything Ed Murrow couldn't do.") Wasn't there . . . some *way*? she asked a little tentatively.

He shook his somewhat overlarge head. "I have tried; they won't do it the way I think it must be done."

"Well, if you're so discouraged, why don't you *quit*?"[91]

That fall, October 1, he ended his seven-year association with the board of directors of CBS.

Far from providing a forum for his views, it had proved a snare, entangling him in policies deemed at the very least, ambiguous. "Access to senior management cuts both ways," says Dick Salant, who sat in as

Stanton's assistant and was to ask why, if Murrow was so troubled, did he not raise the questions at the very highest level?[92]

But Adrian Murphy, who also sat on the board, later pointed out that the meetings were concerned not with policy but with the bottom line. Indeed, even the so-called loyalty oath of 1950 was not, evidently, deemed a matter for discussion. "Ninety-five percent of those board meetings," said Murphy, "were routine—reports from the divisions, of no interest to anybody except to the divisional managers and the Wall Street people. Everything was covered, then questioned—i.e., why is this better or worse than last month's report? And *they* always came from the outside directors, who really represented the large holders of stock . . . making sure that the borrowings . . . made on behalf of the company were going to good purpose."[93]

In any case, it was not Murrow's world and not his forum; "I'm just not cut out for that." His own holdings in CBS were minimal, some $3,000 or $4,000 in the aggregate. Whatever leverage may have been involved in a directorship, the experience as a whole had fulfilled the misgivings of 1949, when he had confessed to being "of two minds" in taking the appointment.

At the same time, stepping down in a company now divisionalized, meant putting even more distance between himself and the CBS management.

His resignation, beginning "Dear Bill" and marked "Personal," was mailed to Paley on a Monday morning and accepted by Wednesday of the same week. Murrow gave as his reason the fact that his contract was up for renewal; it seemed inappropriate, therefore, that he should remain a board member while negotiations were in progress; he was leaving with deep personal regret, and with increased respect for him, Paley, and indeed affection.[94]

Paley, answering, accepted "with the deepest regret imaginable," hoped he might still call on Ed from time to time for advice. Ed's presence on the board would in no way influence negotiations, but there was always, of course, the possibility of some contention that his presence on the board had influenced the judgment of the company, and therefore, he appreciated Ed's desire to eliminate the basis of this contention. He hoped that negotiations for his continued services were going well and that they would soon have the pleasure of knowing that they would have the benefits of them for many years to come.[95] He signed the letter "Sincerely, Bill."

There were divided feelings in the newsroom. "We thought it was a right decision," said Lou Cioffi, then one of the younger correspondents, come up through the ranks. "We felt it was a voluntary thing, that he wanted to do it, and for reasons which we all applauded. The only disadvantage was, he was a powerful voice in our favor, and once off the board of directors, we wondered . . . It was the one concern we had. Lessening of influence: how's that going to affect us?"[96]

But enough had happened, evidently, to bring to a head Murrow's doubts concerning his effectiveness within the corporate structure, and to reinforce the conviction that the drawbacks of directorship outweighed the perks.

Four months previously, John Henry Faulk had begun the landmark lawsuit that would take blacklisting out of the closet and onto the front page. Murrow's financial help in the case would be a matter of common knowledge; his early role, less publicized.

Given the events of the past years and more specifically, the past months, there was ample reason for Murrow to feel as he did about the blacklist; not to mention another reason having no connection with TV.

The ad hoc arrangement with Raymond Swing had become permanent. Back in 1953 The New York *Times* had praised him for standing up to McCarthy, but it didn't offer him a job; nor would anyone else. What had begun as a catchall to fill in for a blacklist situation had wound up with Swing writing more and more of Murrow's commentaries—particularly after Wheelock's death had ended *This I Believe* and much of the rationale for keeping Swing on the budget, leading both men into a pleasant, convenient trap.

They were friends of more than twenty years, who shared a common outlook, trusted each other's judgment. That, said Swing later, made the situation palatable.[97] And there were always the daily consultations, on subject, approach, points to be covered, with Murrow using the scripts intact, or making changes, or very occasionally calling in Kay Campbell for a redo. But that didn't change the fact of Swing as author of many of the putative "Murrow" commentaries—a fact known to the industry but not to the public, leaving Murrow himself open to the charge of fronting. ("He's exploiting you," Shirer would urge the other man repeatedly over lunch.)[98]

Occasionally, as at Bandung, CBS unbent to the point of letting Swing do voice reports under Murrow's auspices, paying the standard stringer's fee. For the rest, the feeler put out to Ted Church on Swing's behalf in early 1953 told the whole story: unacceptable to CBS; hence unacceptable elsewhere. The litmus test in broadcasting.

McCarthy was in the past tense nowadays, a lonely figure who had come up unsteadily to Murrow at a Washington party, slapped a heavy arm across his shoulder and breathed bourbon vapors in his face—"No hard feelings, Ed?" McCarthy, politically, was dead; the blacklist lived.

John Henry Faulk remembered first mentioning his plans to Murrow in late 1955, a time of factional fights within the American Federation of Television and Radio Artists (AFTRA), internal purges, and rank-and-file rebellion against a problacklist leadership.

"I had this idea of running in the union," said Faulk. "I don't think Ed was yet a member; he was also an employer, so he couldn't run for office and he abided by the rules; Ed Sullivan had no such compunctions."[99]

He laid out his plans: mount an antiblacklist slate, and throw the rascals out. "Ed thought it was a splendid idea."

Next, Collingwood stopped in to say Faulk had asked him to head the ticket. He didn't know much about AFTRA, hadn't been a member that long, but Johnny Faulk said AFTRA had become a nest of blacklisters and he needed a big name as running mate.

"Ed said, 'You ought to run.' So I became president of AFTRA. Well, the heavens descended. . . ."[100]

"Two weeks after we took office," Faulk recalled, "HUAC attacked our slate, put out a letter saying reds had reinfiltrated the New York local of AFTRA. I was outraged when I read this thing. Here was a committee of Congress, with *our* tax money, smearing us, interfering with union affairs! I wanted to write a letter. Ed stopped me. 'Let Charlie write it.' Charlie, of course, wrote a magnificent repudiation, which was reprinted in The New York *Times*. Then AWARE put out a bulletin. . . ."[101]

AWARE, a tidy pressure operation that "cleared" people for a fee, was the brainchild of one Vincent Hartnett, compiler of *Red Channels*. It was joined by Lawrence Johnson, the Syracuse supermarket owner who specialized in consumer boycotts. O'Shea himself had quailed before Johnson, a dyspeptic personality calling incessantly from upstate to lay down the law to the network, brooking no interruptions from a mere CBS vice-president. ("*I'm* making this call! You want to talk to me, *you* spend the money!")[102]

By early February AWARE and Johnson were blitzing Madison Avenue by leaflet and telephone on alleged Communist connections in the AFTRA slate. Collingwood was untouchable; the blacklisters accordingly went after Faulk, whose TV career, building on the afternoon talk show, was beginning to take off. "Ed was greatly concerned," said Faulk. "We kept up a running dialogue—not necessarily every day, but we were in constant contact. Quite frankly at the time, I felt that Ed was too glum; I took a more sanguine view of people, I thought he'd lived too closely to the board of directors and Madison Avenue. I had never been blacklisted. Ed, though, understood the case better than anyone beside me and Frank Dobie. . . . He knew I was enjoyin' it like hell."[103]

One notable factor had changed: Daniel T. O'Shea, anxious to get back to Hollywood, had left in 1955. Which left Collingwood in a stronger position when, with Murrow at his side, he went to Arthur Hull Hayes, President of CBS Radio, to inform him that the union would take a very dim view indeed if Faulk lost his employment at WCBS.

But sponsors were dropping away from *Johnny's Front Porch*, and the TV jobs evaporated. Faulk brought suit. "Through Harriet Van Horne," he recalled, "I had met a lawyer from the Louis Nizer firm. When the ax dropped on me, Ed said, 'That's the man!' "

Murrow saw it as a matter of not only justice but enlightened self-interest, the strategy of the failed Julian case—i.e., put those people out of business; and thereby take the heat off the broadcast industry.

The corporation, evidently, didn't see the logic. The suit filed, Faulk recalled, there was a telephone call from Murrow with a message from a mutual friend, Carl Sandburg; the men would often get together when "Mr. Carl" was in town, and maybe Frank Dobie, too—just four country boys swapping stories over a glass.

Faulk, dispirited, told Murrow he didn't have the money for the follow-through. Nizer was asking a $10,000 retainer, he had raised about $2,500, and people who had promised help had, as Faulk called it, "taken off for the bushes."

"Ed was surprised. 'Isn't CBS helping you?' He understood it was in the company's interest if the suit won. I said no. He said, 'Give me twenty-four hours.' "

Murrow spent that evening on the telephone, with a final call put in to Seward. He didn't go into details. Johnny Faulk was in some kind of trouble, he said; would he, Seward, please make out a $7,500 check payable to Louis Nizer, and was there enough in the account to cover? Seward said there was; should he enter it under "gift" or "loan"?

A pause.

"Gee. . . . . I don't know."

Seward entered it in the "gift" column, where the loans usually wound up.[104]

The next day Faulk went up to 17 and into Murrow's office. He found the newsman sitting, looking gloomily out over Madison Avenue, "like a dark cloud was hanging over him."

> He told me he called a couple of men on the board who hated AWARE as much as he did and gotten very negative responses: "Johnny, they're not gonna help."
>
> I said, "Ed, I could've told you that."
>
> He smiled. "I was a damn fool to have ever thought so, Johnny, you were right."

Faulk said he'd be candid with Nizer, say he had only so much in the kitty. Murrow shook his head: You couldn't say that with Nizer. Besides, he'd already done some checking ("with his lawyers, or Jim Seward, or someone," Faulk recalled), and the money would be there.

The short scene that followed became part of broadcast legend: the Texan's reluctance to accept a loan that size, Murrow's insistence that he was "investing the money in America":

"I've got a son to raise here. You owe me nothing. You're fighting a very important issue—Nizer *must* take it. Don't disturb it. Let me explain something to you. . . ."

It was the closest he had come in their nine-year friendship to making a speech: He, Faulk, had to think seriously about what he was taking on. "You're not just personally taking it on—you're the catalyst here. Your union won't support you; that's why they're in the shape they're in. But remember, my office door will be open to you anytime."[105]

For a time the center seemed to hold for Faulk, reduced income notwithstanding. The radio show continued, his contract renewed at the year's end. Indeed, some inside CBS would argue that Collingwood's and Murrow's backing kept him on the air when the afternoon show ratings took a dip. Then, in September 1957, WCBS, pleading falling Nielsens, dropped *Johnny's Front Porch.*

At the trial, Nizer would convince a jury that the radio schedule had suffered across the board and that the Faulk program had done better than most. What was undeniable was that following cancellation, John Henry Faulk couldn't find work anywhere in radio or TV. Murrow, Collingwood, and a few others, he says, helped keep him going through the hungry years that followed.

In 1962, a New York jury was to award Faulk a record libel judgment of $3 million plus, whittled down on appeal, nearly swamped by court costs, with the final judgment delivered only in 1964. Faulk got on the phone to Murrow about repaying the loan. Murrow, then in retirement, told him to forget it.[106]

The basic issue in the end was libel, not the *Red Channels* rationale or the thorny question of whether political associations, past or present, should have a bearing on employment in the mass media. What the case did—a full twelve years after *Red Channels*—was to make the institutionalized blacklist a matter of public record, with the blacklist organizations finally brought on the carpet, less so the networks, stations, sponsors, and agencies for giving in to them.

Christmas week of 1956, Murrow interviewed Premier Zhou Enlai of China, flying to Rangoon for a meeting negotiated by Premier U Nu of Burma. It was a first-time exclusive for CBS and a breakthrough for American TV. It was also a political hot potato, filmed without so much as a by-your-leave, a *fait accompli* dumped in the network's lap. CBS ran it after 11:15 P.M. on New Year's Eve, followed, to Murrow's dismay, by a rebuttal panel. The newsman's attempt to suggest participants, including the knowledgeable Teddy White, met with a thumbs-down. An interview with Marshal Tito of Yugoslavia filmed six months later, was also followed by a panel, less hostile than in the case of the Chinese Premier.

The news department was coming up with its own firsts by the latter fifties. Stanton himself had negotiated a controversial freewheeling Khrushchev interview over *Face the Nation* in June 1957 with Daniel Schorr—filmed inside the Kremlin—and defended the broadcast against criticism from Washington. *Variety* was hailing CBS as "the undisputed strongman of television journalism. . . . Within the past year the web has had a lineup . . . comprising Khrushchev, Nehru, Tito, China's Chou-En-lai, Egypt's Nasser, Israel's Ben-Gurion, and Burma's U Nu, all in interviews either with U.S. newsmen or with Ed Murrow via *See It Now* . . . . Having built a demonstrably superior spot-newsgathering organization. . .under John Day. . .the network is developing on a new front."[107]

It all seemed mutually beneficial, for the greater glory of the network. Stanton, defending the landmark Khrushchev interview, stood up for the Tito piece as well. The fact remained, however, that all but one of the cited pieces had come out of the one unit totally beyond the control of the news department. To John Day the interviews with Middle Eastern leaders loomed less important than the fact that Murrow, who had flown out at the time to cover the Suez War, had thereby missed work on election night.

To Murrow, the praised and damned Zhou Enlai piece was a disappointment—stilted, superformal, based on submitted questions and filtered through an interpreter. "He repulsed all my efforts at private conversation, even though . . . he speaks and understands English perfectly,"[108] he wrote Pearl Buck afterward. "Like listening to a worn and familiar phonograph record" was how he later characterized the interview.[109] At one point in the filming, the Premier, a hand over each microphone, corrected his interpreter in impeccable English, then sat back as the mediated session continued. When the film magazines were changed, he left the room.

In retrospect, both the Zhou and Tito footage pointed toward the seventies and eighties and the emerging world fermenting between the superpowers. The Chinese leader, answering Murrow's question, Did he believe the United States was against "those nations . . . struggling for freedom," strongly criticized U.S. policy in Latin America. At the same time, despite a denial of Sino-Soviet differences, the old mandarin expressed hope for resumed U.S.-China relations and even a "collective peace pact" for Asia and the Pacific, to include the United States.

Six months later, on an island in the Adriatic, Tito of Yugoslavia talked with Murrow of differences in "socialist systems," Mao Zedong, events in Hungary and the Middle East, the arms race, and coexistence as the only alternative, so said the Marshal, to annihilation. "But we should abandon the idea of intervening, of mixing in the internal affairs of each other. . . . If a majority of the people of a country decide to have a socialist system, then nobody has the right to try and impose another system on that people. . . ."[110]

In contrast with the Zhou piece, the Tito interview was relaxed, far-ranging; Murrow and the old ex-partisan got on well together, the state photographers snapping stills of the two men in their shirt sleeves, strolling the grounds around the presidential residence. The visit, in fact, left "satisfaction" in Yugoslav high circles, as Murrow's go-between informed him—"that you were first, that you demanded such respect a 'deuniforming' took place, that you were able to extract such spontaneity from the Boss, that Mme. Broz was also at your disposal—all in all the whole atmosphere is a new and healthy one."[111]

The interviews, like most Murrow pieces, were forums of opinion. He disagreed badly on camera, rarely went in for close questioning, his intent, rather, to expose the public to views not generally aired over American TV in the latter fifties.

In those same months he made return visits with David Ben-Gurion, Prime Minister of Israel, and Abdul Gamal Nasser, President of Egypt.

His first encounters with the Middle East had come only in early 1956, filming the Egypt-Israel show. The program, though tilting in its use of Murrow as reporter for the Israeli segment, had tried nonetheless for balance. Howard Smith, on the Egyptian side, talked not only with Egyptians but with Palestinians, in a first-time TV exposure, both segments plumbing the depths of passions in the region. "There is the smell of war out there," ran the conclusion, "and if it comes, then free men everywhere will have cause to examine their actions and their conscience as to whether it could have been avoided."[112]

"I don't expect anybody to agree with all of it," Murrow wrote a friend in Jordan, "but at least the Arabs and Jews get a better opportunity than they had . . . to express their views."[113]

His pro-Israeli sympathies ran deep, rooted in the old IIE contacts with such as Judah Magnes and the Friends of the Hebrew University, reinforced by bitter memories of the doors closed to escaping Jews in the 1930s, the resistance to the Emergency Committee's efforts to admit a few thousand "non-Aryans." "I had the impression . . . that the Jews qualify as one of the 'native peoples of the Middle East,' " he answered a letter once after the war, with a trace of private sarcasm that only he could understand.

On the sidelines at first over the UN vote on Palestine and partition, he had made a painful break with his beloved Britain in 1948, as the new state of Israel came under attack from three sides. For once he had agreed with the Soviets in the UN calling Britain belligerent, and censured one of his wartime heroes:

Today Mr. Ernest Bevin said . . . "Civil war as an instrument for foreign policy, or any outside power, is a dastardly thing to do. I appeal to them to stop it." But Mr. Bevin was speaking not of the war in Palestine, but of the war in Greece. . . .

There is no doubt that the British are providing arms and supplies to Transjordan and to other members of the Arab League. The provisions are there in the Treatys [sic] and the British admit it. So far as we know, Abdullah's Legion is still commanded by Glubb Pasha, a major in the British Reserve. Whether the other British officers attached to the Legion are commanding in the field is not known, but there has been no statement that they are not.

British "reluctance" in the Security Council to recognize a state of war or a threat to peace he labeled "legalistic double talk. . . ."

> If bombs on Tel Aviv do not represent an act of war, then the bombs on Pearl Harbor didn't produce a state of war. (The fact that the bombs on Tel Aviv were smaller has nothing whatever to do with the case.) . . . . Last month a responsible and honest spokesman of the British Foreign Office said that Abdullah's Legion could not be committed without the consent of the British Government. They are now in action.
> It may be that the British have a better case than they have so far presented; but on the basis of the open record, their policy ill becomes a nation which fought with such gallant determination, and so recently, in defense of the right.[114]

As a reporter, however, he could still write a viewer in the mid-fifties that there was "no question . . . that Israel's neighbors have genuine and legitimate grievances; particularly in the matter of the Arab refugees."[115]

For Murrow personally, the welcome in Israel, not yet hooked up to TV, had been more than the obvious red-carpet treatment for a powerful American journalist; this was Murrow of the London blitz, the antifascist, the man who had stood up to McCarthy. Murrow in turn was drawn to what was still an agricultural society, to the leonine Ben-Gurion, Moshe Dayan, Teddy Kollek, later Mayor of Jerusalem, and others of the then-dominant Labor Party.

Israeli officials for their part were impressed with the newsman's insistence on verisimilitude. Filming a fisherman's cooperative working at night upon the Sea of Galilee, raked by fire in those years from Syrian guns stationed opposite on the Golan Heights, Murrow had turned down suggestions to work close to the shoreline. Wouldn't be "kosher," he said, insisting on the fishing site. The guns were quiet; the choppy seas, however, nearly swamped the whole affair.

At a small house in the desert kibbutz of Sde Boker he talked frankly with Ben-Gurion, partway between the Suez invasion and a failed Israeli opening to Nasser before the Bandung Conference, asking that their two nations not be made pawns in an East-West power struggle.

Charlie Mack remembered filming until well past 1:00 A.M., Murrow growing aware of Paula Ben-Gurion shooting anxious looks at her elderly husband. They stopped to leave her an opening: "Don't you think—" The Old Fox laid it on: "Now, Mama, how often do I get a chance to talk with such a nice, interesting man as Mr. Murrow?"

Back in the car, Mack recalled, Murrow suddenly remembered they hadn't thanked them for the hospitality. He sprinted back to the house, then returned quickly, laughing in the dark.

He'd gone to the lit kitchen door, he said, and opened it carefully when no one responded to his knock. Inside, he saw the Prime Minister of

Israel, his back to the door, the water running, standing at the sink with an apron around his waist, washing out the coffee cups.

His first instinct had been to go get the cameras. Instead, he quickly shut the door; no one, he said, would ever believe they hadn't set it up.[116]

At the same time, Murrow and Friendly were trying to get themselves and their cameras into the Soviet Union—the third try for Murrow since 1951—for a program tentatively titled "Main Street: USSR," about daily life in a medium-size Russian city, a sort of Soviet Middletown, as Murrow put it.

"We would hope to portray this Russian city in depth and detail," he wrote Soviet Ambassador Georgi N. Zarubin, "the local newspaper editor, the educational system, sports, Palace of culture, a meeting of the local comsomol, nursery schools, community entertainment. . . . We would try to transport our audience to a . . . Russian town and show them what they would see and hear if they were granted . . . a visit. . . ."[117]

Requested were visas for himself, Friendly, and the technicians, plus facilities for their small group, to include Daniel Schorr, permanent correspondent for CBS News in Moscow.

The Soviets were definitely interested, provided the film was processed and edited in Moscow, with the cooperation of the Ministry of Culture. Murrow, privately doubtful about that condition, nonetheless conferred with the Soviet Ambassador, offering to fly to Moscow for further talks with ministry officials. By late summer 1956 the deputy minister of culture, visiting New York, was proposing a reciprocal arrangement for a Soviet camera team in the United States. Murrow laid the request before the State Department, sounding out the possibility of visas for the Russians.

For a time it seemed as though *See It Now* might be instrumental in an East-West breakthrough. "It [is] heartening," wrote Friendly to Moscow after eight weeks of negotiation, "to hear that we are reaching the stage where a cultural exchange in the field of television information is reaching fulfillment."[118]

In the end it fell apart. Friendly, looking back, thought it was most likely the question of the final edit. By autumn 1956, moreover, the climate had changed: war in the Middle East; revolution in Hungary. The Soviet visas were never granted; there is no record of State Department reactions. "Main Street: USSR" was dropped, an idea whose time had evidently not yet come.

It wasn't U.S.-Soviet relations, however, but U.S.-Chinese relations, or the lack of them, that were about to propel Murrow into a new confrontation with the powers upstairs.

William Worthy, free-lance journalist and columnist for the *Baltimore Afro-American*, seemed the very antithesis of the rebel stereotype: soft-spoken, with something of a choirboy look about him, the son of a black

Boston physician and an anomaly in the WASP world of network news.

He had first met Murrow in late 1955 on returning from the USSR and a string of broadcasts for CBS just prior to the reopening of the Moscow bureau, a lucky break effected through a chance confrontation with Khrushchev, Worthy recalled, after initial refusals. "Khrushchev finally said *pazhawlstoi* [please] and I got on the air a couple of days later. It was sort of a sensational beginning."[119] When the CBS bureau opened, he had worked briefly with Dan Schorr.

In New York there was talk from John Day about possible staff status—there were "complex reasons" said Worthy, why he couldn't take it—and a budding acquaintance with Murrow, ripening quickly into long discussions over drinks at Colbee's. Murrow was sufficiently impressed to cable his friend Louis Lyons, Curator of the Nieman Foundation at Harvard, backing a fellowship for the enterprising young newsman. (The interviewing committee, says Worthy, made discreet reference to the cable; the following Monday, Lyons called to let him know he was among the lucky dozen.)[120]

The bad news started when Worthy, his Russian successes behind him, went to string for CBS and others in China—forbidden ground by State Department fiat—shooting newsfilm and making voice reports from Peking and Shanghai.

Returning home, he was denied renewal of his passport.

The incident dovetailed with other developments, as eighteen American journalists, invited to China by the Peking government, were placed on notice by the State Department that acceptance would mean loss of their passports and possible prosecution.[121]

Sevareid, who had rushed Worthy to a studio on his return from China, questioned the State Department ruling. Murrow called it a curb on the American right to know. Both broadcasts were disavowed by CBS. Murrow was formally reprimanded, the Sevareid piece killed outright; Day, embarrassed and troubled, took upon himself the responsibility for its removal from the air.

In fact, high-level pressures had been present from day one of the China broadcasts, withstood by the network but resulting in a soft-pedaling of the CBS affiliation. "Those who listened in the States," said Worthy later, "said it sounded like they had picked me off the airwaves."[122] (In Peking there had been a cable from New York, asking that he refer to the Chinese capital as "Peiping," as in Chiang Kai-shek's day. A Reuters colleague suggested that he sign off next time with "This is Bill Worthy in Peiping, now back to CBS in New Amsterdam.")[123] Murrow, down at Colbee's, said he was "ashamed" of how the newscasts had been handled by the company.

By March the currents of controversy had merged, and Congress wanted to know what was going on between State and the news media. House and Senate subcommittee staffs contacted Murrow for broadcast transcripts, asking for additional information, if available, for upcoming hearings on "the seemingly unending barriers . . . against the flow of information [on] passport practices [that] interfere with constitutional rights."[124]

Worthy, down in Washington to testify, identified the pressure source as Robert Murphy, onetime architect of the Darlan deal, currently Undersecretary of State for Political Affairs. "I had it from John Day that Murphy had called Paley directly," said the newsman later, "so without revealing my source, I said so."[125] Returned to New York, he says, he caught a memorandum in the newsroom: "There will be no comment— repeat no comment—on Bill Worthy's testimony."

A few days later Murphy himself, upholding the State Department ban before the Senate Foreign Relations Committee, specifically denied applying pressure to keep CBS from using the China broadcasts: He had made "a simple inquiry" of his "old friend" Mr. Paley, just to determine the relationship of CBS to Worthy, nothing more.[126] Stanton, wiring the committee, confirmed the statement, denying pressure brought to bear on CBS. Murrow reported it verbatim—on paper. "I didn't hear the broadcast," Worthy recalled, "but people told me he had made it clear he didn't believe one word of this." In the newsroom the next day, Murrow admitted to Worthy he had editorialized with his voice, in conscious violation of house policy. In a brief digression, he spoke bitterly of the war years, of Murphy's role in dealing with "the Fascist Vichy regime," as he called it, implying that the State Department man "was on somewhat the same wavelength."[127]

Murrow was among those—Morris Ernst of the ACLU was another— who were to back Worthy through the years of confinement to the country while *Worthy* vs. *Dulles* inched through the judicial system. He maintained contact, at times curbed the young man's impatience, wrote fellowship recommendations to help tide him over, and attempted to file a friend of the court brief drafted for him by Ernst's office along lines laid down at a lunch meeting: "The right to information is not an abstract right. . . . Democratic government cannot survive unless the electorate has at its disposal all available information on which to reach intelligent conclusions....A leadership responsible only to an uninformed or partially informed electorate can bring nothing but disaster to our world."[128]

Instead, Justice Department lawyers went into a panic, threatening to fight in court, if necessary, to keep Murrow from filing, the motion for permission therefore denied.[129]

In the meantime, while political high drama played the boards in Washington, a network farce was bubbling behind the scenes.

John Secondari, Washington ABC news chief and a friend of Murrow's, a deft writer of light fiction on the side and author of the popular *Three Coins in a Fountain*, had come up with a teleplay uncomfortably close to life.

Originally sold to NBC, "The Commentator" took up the question of opinions on the air, turning on a clash of wills between a television news star and his closest friend, the owner of the network, following the star's TV broadside against a demagogic congressman. When producer Herbert Brodkin switched networks, it had wound up at CBS, to be taken from the desk drawer when the contretemps of early 1957 made it timely.

Too timely perhaps. ("Don't you people have any *control* over him? We're paying for a news show, not a political hassle.")[130] In the end the company boss fires his friend despite a loyal public because, he says, "I can't trust you." Fade-out as the night janitor, cleaning the empty office, retrieves the two protagonists' first friendship token from the wastebasket.

The TV drama, announced by *Studio One* for April 1957, was canceled four weeks later with a terse statement from Hubbell Robinson, Executive Vice-President in charge of programs for CBS-TV; it was the week of Bill Worthy's appearance before the Senate subcommittee, seven weeks after the killing of the Sevareid piece and Murrow's reprimand. The scrappy Brodkin, producer of *Judgment at Nuremberg* and later of *Holocaust*, was fairly sure that pressure had oozed down from the D.C.-oriented specialists on 20.

Jack Gould, fuming in the Sunday *Times* about Big Brother, blasted Washington and "censorship . . . behind the tiny screen."

But it was also true that the references throughout were just a bit close for comfort in the small broadcast world of 1957. So were the sharp, ambivalent exchanges between the main protagonist-antagonists, barely disguised by the slight change in names and titles:

> "I have to live with my point of view. Tom, we've worked together twenty years."
> "You don't have to remind me. . . . Are you quitting?"
> "No, if you want me out of here, you'll have to fire me."
> "Don't dare me."[131]

"The Commentator" ultimately wound up at the BBC, its cancellation a brisk but transient embarrassment to CBS. As for Murrow, evidence at least suggests that he was privately relieved to see the televised *roman à clef* pulled from the schedule.

Joe McCarthy was dead, alone and unattended in a tower room at Bethesda Naval Hospital at age forty-nine, ignored by the great world that had first made, then broken him, his last years a downward spiral into debt and alcoholism.

Ed Bliss, seeing the news come in off the wires, went to tell Murrow before proceeding with the write-up. "Just the simple facts," he was told, "cause of death, age, et cetera," the first and last time he ever had a lead suggested for a hard news story.

Bliss followed directions: age, cause, and time of death, survived by wife and adopted infant daughter, Republican Senator from Wisconsin since 1946. No matter. Listener mail, Murrow told McCarthy biographer Richard Rovere sometime later, either attacked him for mourning hypocritically or for dancing on McCarthy's grave.[132]

The BBC asked permission to run the kinescope of the old MCarthy program of March 9, 1954. Murrow declined: "He's dead now, and can't answer."[133]

But the news also marked a high tide in the steady flow of threats and hate mail ("YOU CRUCIFIED HIM/GOD FORGIVE YOU!") that had become a year-in, year-out phenomenon, the detritis of the tangle with McCarthy and a steady reminder that a substantial minority out there hated Murrow's guts. A reporter talking over drinks one night with the newsman at a bar near Madison Avenue watched with interest as an unsmiling hardhat type broke in on them, watched as the broadcaster tensed up in an instinctive fight-or-flight reaction.

Just a fan, it turned out.

The fan having departed, Murrow grinned as though found out, said he had a recurring dream: "that someday one of these guys is gonna walk up to me and he's gonna weigh about two hundred and sixty pounds and he's gonna *flatten* me!"

By 1957, he was riding the crest of his public career, a culture hero, his face on the cover of *Time*, a high-profile figure in the leadership circles of government and the media. An array of first-magnitude acquaintances ranged from David Rockefeller to John Kenneth Galbraith to Joe Welch. Senators Humphrey, Johnson, Kennedy, and Fulbright, were Hubert, Lyndon, Jack, and Bill.

His social calendar was a black-spaghetti thicket of dinners and speaking engagements, often double-booked in a miasma of forgetfulness that was the despair of his office staff. A system was finally worked out whereby at the press of a button, a secretary would listen in on calls, check the red appointment book and more often than not, go charging to his door, making frantic hand signals.[134]

He played poker with Philip Graham of the *Washington Post*, exchanged social notes with NATO commanders, traded jokes with James Thurber, and let producer Mike Todd talk him into a rare screen appearance, as himself, in the movie, *Around the World in 80 Days*. (Seward, told to make the arrangements, asked Murrow how much he'd be paid; Ed hadn't the least idea.) Even the rift with Shirer seemed patched up nowadays, the two men seen chatting comfortably at the Century bar, in company with Doubleday editor Kenneth McCormick.

"Spread thin by three TV shows," ran the *Time* cover story in September 1957, "Murrow has become more and more a performer and editor . . .his forays to the news fronts. . .spurred by a strongly felt need to replenish his credentials with the raw facts."

The story found the newsman's lead in TV justified—a man, after all,

of "social conscience and sense of mission about keeping people informed," who could make "serious matters" appeal to large audiences.
"Beyond that, as solid a reason as any for Murrow's edge is simply that
he is a fine reporter." But the publication also found Murrow's success
"by its lopsided domination. . .a reflection of the state of TV journalism
as a whole. For all the earnest thought and energy devoted to it, electronic
journalism has been illuminated with bright flashes but few steady beams
of light. Which is one reason why Murrow, living in a swirl of hero
worship, is obliged to recall the Murrow-Ain't-God Club."[135]

There were at the same time less welcome aspects to celebrityhood—
among them a re-emergence of the infidelities, beyond the periodic reappearance in New York of Pamela Churchill. Murrow was now seen openly
and often in the company of the actress Marlene Dietrich, and with other,
less familiar faces. Ed Scott, walking up Third Avenue one night, was
startled to see his boss coming the other way, a lady friend on each arm—
one he recognized as the divine Marlene—Murrow skipping between
them, obviously feeling no pain. "Women threw themselves at him," said
Scott later, "and he was flattered."

Janet, forthright as always, told a persistent columnist that she didn't
mind as long as the ladies were old. "Ed has always been attractive to
women; I try not to think about it."

Celebrityhood also ended the last vestige of his privacy. A month before
the *Time* story, he had gone fishing in the Northwest with a college
friend—a fathers-and-sons trip to the Olympic Peninsula, ending suddenly in tragedy when his old classmate lay down for a nap and died.

Murrow drove the dead man's stricken son home to Seattle—a hard
trip made harder by persistent fans, recognizing the newsman on the
ferry, driving him to seek refuge in his locked car below deck, with the
windows rolled up.

Even then they came around, maddeningly well intentioned, rapping at the window, Excuse us, we were sitting in our car and aren't
you. . . ?

Murrow's young passenger, drawn momentarily out of his troubles,
finally burst out, "Ed, how can you *stand* it?"[136]

Conversely, the man whom *Time* described as "living in a swirl of hero
worship" had been also quoted as saying that he had no friends and, if
he got into trouble, wouldn't know where to turn. It provoked a storm
of protests from appalled friends around the country, but the quote was
never totally disowned.

His office door was always open, yet he was near-impossible to reach
by phone, guarded by a three-deep secretarial defense perimeter. He
liked important people but would pass up returning Clay Felker's call at
Esquire to put his feet up with a grizzled logging buddy from the old
days who had simply wandered in off the street. At the annual *See It
Now* bash at Toots Shor's restaurant, bulging with VIP gray flannel and

military brass, Mili Bonsignori, awaiting her turn to speak, hissed at him, sotto voce: Couldn't he get Friendly to pass her by? All these important people . . . .

Those "important people," he assured her, all wore the same underwear—"and they all look ridiculous in it."[137]

He put himself down constantly, with crisp references to "my tinfoil reputation," but though uncomfortable with praise, missed it when it wasn't there—surprisingly susceptible to flattery, in need of assurance, a near-compulsive bestower of gifts and little kindnesses, rarely seen in the corridors without his entourage. ("When are you going to get rid of all those people hanging onto your hind tit?" Downs yelled at him once in sheer exasperation.) Beneath the puritan's self-deprecation, in fact, was the performer's hunger for approval, the need to know that he was needed, that he was liked; and proving surprisingly thin-skinned when others, even in fun, ventured to take him down a peg. "So few people," he wrote an elderly acquaintance in a low mood, "appreciate the potency of abuse or praise, particularly when it is aimed at friends who love them."[138]

Concomitant with the thin skin was a constant seeming need to prove his masculinity. One associate who knew both Murrow and Hemingway would remember being struck by their similarity in that respect, a trait he found puzzling, "since they were both such virile men." A family friend was later to recall Murrow's acute distress when Casey, then still small, was presented with a doll. It took Janet's persuasion, said the friend, to convince Ed that the present wouldn't turn the boy into "a sissy."

Almost excessively praised, he could be excessively thankful, writing people of no particular importance, in the midst of public adulation, of his "grateful appreciation for the notes and telegrams received from you. You know how much your encouragement means. . . . This I think is a rare quality. . . ."

Leland Hayward, constantly complimenting him on shows, found himself sounding repetitious: "This is getting very embarrassing and very difficult for me. . . ."[139]

"Dear Leland," read the answer, "Be not inhibited by your difficulties. . . ."[140]

Inevitably, he wound up laughing at himself, conscious of his tendency to dramatize and provided the putdowns came from the proper source—such as Eleanor Roosevelt, encountered one evening in the lobby of the fashionable Hôtel Crillon in Paris, come "tripping and laughing down the stairs," as he later put it, ready for a night out. Murrow himself had just arrived, fatigued after a long, bumpy plane ride.

Wouldn't he join her and her friends for dinner? she asked. He pleaded a previous engagement. Afterward perhaps? He managed something else. She persisted. Perhaps a short one after midnight, at the Montmartre.

"Mrs. Roosevelt," he pleaded, "I am just in off an overnight flight from New York and I'm exhausted."

The seventy-three-year-old former First Lady beamed her familiar large-toothed Eleanor Roosevelt smile. "How unfortunate. I am just in from Teheran and I feel fine."[141]

But the force that had made him a superstar was not the great world or the relatively small news audience; rather, it was the growing viewer masses that knew little of *See It Now* but regarded *Person to Person* as a Friday night ritual, a runaway success story posing problems both inside and outside CBS.

Friends deplored the use of Murrow's talent; critics observed that even the great newsman was not above chasing the almighty buck. In the house, Friendly resented the inroads on Murrow's time and energies, not to mention the Zousmer-Aaron appropriation of the electronic visit idea originally birthed on *See It Now*—which had, moreover, enriched its owners, in contrast with Friendly's continuing position as a $40,000-a-year producer with no additional commercial fees or royalties.[142] A hefty income, which had enabled Friendly to trade in his modest apartment for a substantial home in the posh Fieldston section of Riverdale, but hardly the quantum jump in earnings wrought by the commercial show. (Murrow, as a star and as talent, was receiving well upward of $100,000 a year for *Person to Person*, exclusive of *See It Now* and the nightly radio news.)

Accordingly, Murrow and Friendly approached the network regularly with proposals for owned-and-packaged news shows, in which Friendly might share the admittedly smaller profits.

In 1954, with *Person to Person* launched, Murrow had tried to sell Paley on a *See It Now* spin-off dubbed variously as *Mid-Atlantic Parliament* and *Mid-Ocean Parliament*, enlarging on the international two- and three-way filmed discussions over *See It Now*, linking speakers in various capitals. Unlike the more commercial *Person to Person*, it didn't fly. Besides, *See It Now*, then in high gear, needed every hand, utilizing the full resources of its production unit.[143]

In 1957 the idea was resurrected and expanded under the title *Small World*, a pilot made with Sevareid as moderator, the packaging by Murrow's company, Jefferson Productions, Murrow and Friendly to divide the profit after CBS had taken its fifty percent.[144] It still didn't fly. Syndication was suggested; Merle Jones, President of the TV Stations Division, gave the idea his blessing. Murrow, not unreceptive, asked Paley's advice, but Friendly bridled, in a stiff note to his partner: He wanted his work on CBS air, not a hundred assorted stations tied together by four deodorants, a brewery, and a loan company, and if it wasn't good enough for CBS, let it "rest in peace."[145] Back into the mothballs.

Person to Person, too, had its currents of underground discontent. Murrow had sold the program for a reputed record amount—his only way of getting out eventually from under, close friends insisted—but Zousmer and Aaron resented the program's sale to CBS following Murrow's purchase of their shares, though all three continued to do well by the show and by each other, through the disagreements. Johnny Aaron had been furious with Murrow back in 1954 for jeopardizing their operation with the McCarthy show, cornering Joe Wershba in the men's room one day, a living embodiment of *See It Now*, which was threatening to upset the applecart: "You take up with shit, and you'll wind up with your hands full of shit!"[146] Wershba thought the locale singularly appropriate.

At 485 the two Murrow staffs, both on 17, were constantly at loggerheads. *See It Now* felt the boss was neglecting the screening room except on programs of special interest to him, and said he was growing celebrity-conscious.

TV critics wrote about Higher and Lower Murrow. The years-long friendship with Gilbert Seldes, going back to prewar days, was almost ended as the upshot of published comments on the show which Murrow felt impugned him personally. In vain Seldes protested his loyalty and admiration; there was no recourse and no appeal. Murrow requested that they end this correspondence in which, as he put it, the historians would take little interest.

"On the contrary, Ed," ran the brief reply, "my biographer is fascinated. As yours will be. In time."[147]

It was some time before they spoke again.

"Sometimes I wonder if the man understands himself," a *New Yorker* critic commented.

Ironically, the one person with whom Murrow most extensively discussed the program was the one who most roundly condemned it.

If Murrow had an *éminence grise*, it was not the ebullient Friendly but an aristocratic, English-born, naturalized American teaching communications at New York University, a pioneer broadcaster and media gadfly, a true believer and author of books with titles such as *The Radio Listener's Bill of Rights*; whose heresies concerning broadcasting's role in society would become the current coin of later times and whose influence on Murrow went back twenty years and more.

Charles Siepmann had pioneered BBC news in the early thirties, lectured at Harvard, served with the OWI, and in 1945 turned Congress and commercial broadcasting on their collective ears with the *FCC Blue Book*, reminding the public that stations that didn't live up to promises to serve the public interest should by law have their licenses revoked. He had clashed with the BBC Board of Governors, the U.S. broadcast industry, assorted senators and representatives, and been denounced variously as an alien and a tool of the reds.

They had begun meeting for lunch in prewar London, and picked up after the war in New York, Siepmann evolving as the years went on into a sort of confessor figure for an increasingly depressed Murrow, depressed because "he was fighting harder and harder to get those damn documentaries on the air. . . ."

For Charles Siepmann, the transformation of *Person to Person*—"that *awful* program"—from the concept of early 1953, at least as Murrow saw it, was symptomatic of the deadening hand of commercial television: "Within three months it had turned into this vulgar—these interviews with rich and famous people, so called—walks around their furniture. He was never so embarrassed, absolutely ashamed of that program."

Why did he keep it up then?

"To keep his place in CBS," Siepmann insisted later, "to allow him to do at least *some* of the things he was wanting to do, paying a price all the way in terms of adjustment to the vulgarity and commercial mindedness. And it was a losing battle."[148]

"I think Ed had some misgivings," said Don Hewitt, who recalled flying home from Paris after producing the CBS coverage of the Grace Kelly wedding, Murrow in the next seat, on the last lap of a flight from Algiers. "And after he had had his second or third martini, he turned to me and said, 'What the hell were you doing, wasting your time at the Grace Kelly wedding?' "

Well, Hewitt figured, here was where he either got thrown off the plane or got respect from Murrow that he'd never had before.

"The same thing you were doing looking in Marilyn Monroe's closet on *Person to Person*."

Murrow's voice was low. "You got me. I got no answer."[149]

The format hardly allowed for scintillating conversation, the questions serving generally as cues for the TV cameras, lumbering from room to room. At times, however, the chemistry was right, some spark set off between Murrow and the guests: Teddy White, just moved into his home, conversing easily among the packing cases; Hans Kaltenborn, talking of his long career; Ethel Waters, singing, "His Eye Is on the Sparrow"; the spikey Krishna Menon; Duke Ellington with his young son Mercer, speaking from his sister's Harlem apartment.

Stilted though the format was, it left a kinescopic record of an era, with a guest list ranging from Fred Astaire to Stewart Alsop, from Ralph Bunche to Carol Burnett, from Al Capp to Fidel Castro, from Ella Fitzgerald to Jane Fonda, from Drew Pearson to Dr. Norman Vincent Peale, from Henry Wallace to Orson Welles.

It also offered the unusual sight of Murrow smiling, seated in an armchair in the studio, peering at a large screen, the guests brought in by remote, with a two-way conversation over the audio. Herbert Bayard Swope, dean of New York journalists, former editor of the old New York *World* and adviser to the networks, wrote Murrow, distressed at the familiarity of the guests who addressed him as "Ed." Would not "Mr. Murrow" be more appropriate?[150]

Murrow replied that he could hardly object to what he was called when he visited someone else's home. "I occasionally receive mail addressed to me as Edward R. Moron, but I guess I cannot do anything about that either."[151]

Participation got to be a status symbol, a call from *Person To Person* often sending prospective guests rushing out to rent a painting. The singer Georgia Gibbs—later Mrs. Frank Gervasi—remembered Murrow's plea to her before a slated Friday night appearance: "Georgia, please—don't show me paintings!"

When the show came on, she referred him to an empty frame with a card inserted, reading, *"Reserved for Vlaminck."* Said Gibbs, "He laughed like hell."

The program, however, almost didn't make air. Said Gibbs, they had brought up all the cameras, run huge cables to the roof. At 6:30, they had a run-through—i.e., they'd pick her up *here*, she'd talk to Ed *there*, show him the gold records—everything fast, extemporaneous. "When we finished," she later recalled, "there were the longest faces. Everyone was running around like crazy."

There was, it seemed, no picture. It turned out that a jealous neighbor had hacked at the exposed cables with a pair of garden shears.

> She could have been electrocuted! And we were going on, and there was *nothing*. There was gonna be fifteen minutes of flat—nothing—black air!
>
> Anyway, what they did was unbelievable. They had to get all new cables, run them from the basement to the roof again, it was really panicsville time, but we finally got our picture at nine-fifteen; we knew we were okay by then. They told me this had never happened. In five hundred shows. My luck! it had to happen when they did mine.[152]

He was sitting in a Paris studio, a cold, rainy Thursday night in late December 1957, when the coughing started up. It was the final day of the four-day, fifteen-nation NATO summit ending with the agreement in principle to stockpile nuclear warheads and intermediate-range missiles— subject to agreement of the member countries—in Western Europe.

The cue channel was open to New York, their Paris man Schoenbrun standing by, Dan Schorr flown in from Moscow for a prognosis on probable Soviet reactions. Murrow had been readying his sum-up of the final NATO communiqué calling for closer consultation between the member countries. Instead, everything was held up, the others looking on, concerned, as the coughing spasms shook his frame.

He had been out weeks before with a high fever—the doctors called it a bronchial condition—and returned to work in early November, the Paris trip undertaken over the misgivings of friends and colleagues, concerned about his visibly declining health.

"Ed was getting older," Schoenbrun recalled, "and ill. He was tired—tired of the fighting and tired of the intriguing and letting himself, *I* think, be pulled around by the nose." Schoenbrun, whose view of Friendly was a low one, felt the producer was taking over. "Fred was sending him all around the world. Ed permitted that to happen because he was ambitious to do great work. And meantime, what was happening was that Fred was sitting in the studio cutting film, and Ed was literally killing himself."[153]

But he traveled because he wanted to, indeed needed to, the more so as New York became more claustrophobic. Bernard Kalb would always recall Christmas week in Rangoon, Murrow's elated entrance in the Strand Hotel lobby well after midnight, returned from interviewing Chou Enlai, still on his high after "talking to a piece of history," as Kalb later put it. Kalb, in Burma for The New York *Times*, did the listening as Murrow did the talking. Imagine, getting paid every week for this! "He was very happy—happy, I think, for among other reasons the sheer sensation of being back in the field again, far away from a desk."

People back in New York, he said, had urged him not to go. Set it up, sure, but why not send someone else, why exhaust himself? He paused a moment, then smiled. "Poor guys, they miss the whole point."[154]

He seemed at times to have an inexhaustible supply of nervous energy. Killing time between a late-night change of planes at Fiumicino Airport once in 1956, he had snapped his jaded cohorts to—"Okay! Let's talk about TV; what impact do you think TV is going to have on politics?"— moderating a sixty-minute impromptu seminar complete with wrap-up, in the deserted waiting area at one o'clock in the morning.[155]

But it was an energy that fed on itself, the superwakefulness that was the corollary to the periods of depression—the times when he would simply tune out, silent and seemingly oblivious to his surroundings. His friends, as one later put it, would "leave him be till he came out of it." Increasingly, the upbeat times were offset by fatigue and weight loss. In the screening room once, pleased with the cutting, he gave his favorite editor a hug. Bonsignori remembered her sense of shock. "There was nothing there but bone."[156]

Ed Scott would recall shooting with Murrow in Tripoli, both men scheduled to go on to Rome together. Instead, Scott, summoned to Murrow's hotel room, found him packing, his face set. "Eddy, I'm going home, I feel awful. You tell anybody about this and I'll kill you."[157]

The 1957 correspondents' roundup reviewed the year of the power shift marked by *Sputnik*, ending American illusions over Soviet science and rocket capability, putting Soviet missile power out front. The reports from Paris and New York on the December meetings of the Western powers had spotlighted the new controversy over the introduction of nuclear weapons into the NATO alliance. Dan Schorr had foreseen Soviet lobbying among the member nations to head off the missile bases which offset their lead, as he put it, in ICBMs. Murrow noted the welcome given by Continental leaders to the dramatic call from George Kennan, onetime author of the containment policy, for the withdrawal of all foreign troops from Europe, East and West, and for no NATO missiles. Schorr felt the Soviets, caught in an economic squeeze, to be anxious for an agreement reducing the arms burden, but reported millions of Soviet reservists given premobilization instructions—simultaneous with calls to the West for armaments reductions and a nuclear-free zone in Central Europe—for the first time since the death of Stalin. "We have said in NATO—talks and nuclear weapons both. They will say, you can't have the two. And the one establishes a poor atmosphere for the other. . . ."[158]

Murrow himself, eager at first on catching up in weaponry, had found the brakes put on his eagerness in Paris, learning that:

> . . . our allies deplore, regret and resent what they regard as the American practice of dismissing all Russian suggestions for parleys as mere propaganda. . . .
>
> It has to be remembered that every head of Government here is faced with the Parliamentary opposition at home. . . . The British for example went along with the proposition to talk some more with the Russians, partly because British public opinion has recently [indistinct] by the knowledge that our strategic bombers, based on British airfields, had been flying about over their heads loaded with hydrogen bombs. There will be plenty of room for disagreement.[159]

But his attitudes, shifting as the decade tilted toward its close, remained nonetheless within the framework of the liberal centrist position of the time; he might complain of Dulles' brinkmanship, the Two Chinas policy, the Eisenhower Doctrine in the Middle East, or public statements about rolling back the iron curtain. Yet he supported the main thrust of the bipartisan foreign policy as it had evolved under both Truman and Eisenhower.

He voiced no objection to the SEATO string of military alliances in Southeast Asia, saw the 1954 Geneva Treaty on Indochina as a Western defeat, made no comment when the stipulated elections failed to materialize, sharing the common centrist perspective on Vietnam evolving in the latter fifties—i.e., an authoritarian Communist North against a nascently democratic South, freed of the colonialist taint. He had come around as well on Diem, to the point of membership, unlisted, in a public group known as the American Friends of Vietnam, along with Mike Mansfield, Francis B. Sayre, William O. Douglas, and Adam Clayton Powell, Jr.[160]

Yet he continued to harp on the dual themes of nonalignment and the rising importance of the Third World, believed the United States was taking India for granted, and neglecting the rising nations of Africa. He cited "Free Asia" as a "huge arsenal [of] natural resources," yet, adding his usual caveat in a list of statements of principle for a projected speech on foreign policy, cautioned:

If trying to buy friendship and gratitude, better save our money—
If trying to build military alliances through economic aid, also futile
endeavor—but if goal is to help underdeveloped countries to become
self-sufficient, independent, democratic societies then worth the effort.

The debate had not yet come up, however, on what was to be considered
a democratic society.

And though supporting his country's foreign policy in its essentials, he
scored its top three weaknesses as: "1) nuclear stalemate, 2) enthusiasm
for military pacts, and 3) split personality in regard to colonialism."[161]

He accused the U.S., on camera and off, of "self-righteous inflexibility"
and ended the 1957 year-end round table with this warning: "If we persist
. . . match bomb with bomb, missile with missile while refusing to talk—
no matter how slim the chance of success—then within measurable time
we may find ourselves a large continental island off the coast of Siberia
with the rest of the world either united against us or indifferent to our
fate."[162]

But at the moment American indifference, the pervasive apathy of the
later fifties, seemed to be the bigger problem. A study had determined
that in New York City, the communications capital, the TV station carrying
the greatest amount of hard news averaged barely more than an hour a
day. CBS News, honored as the 1957 leader with a Peabody, was still
dependent for in-depth coverage largely on the occasional *See It Now*
and the half-hour low-cost *Sunday News Special*, with occasional highlights such as the Khrushchev *Face the Nation* interview or the rare news
documentary "specials," slid quickly into the schedule as the occasion
arose.

"For a medium with the exciting possibility of taking the viewers directly to the scene as news is being made," wrote a critic in *Redbook*
magazine that year, "there is actually very little news on television."[163]

By contrast the CBS network, dominating the popular programming
schedule—of the Nielsen top ten ending 1956, nine had been CBS
shows[164]—was into its fourth consecutive year as the world's largest single
advertising medium. While for all three networks, the quiz craze was
taking over to the point where there were fourteen quiz and game shows
in the daytime hours and another twelve at night.

Murrow, addressing a university audience that year, had for the first
time openly criticized "those who control television and radio," in a speech
not much noticed at the time, but in which Charles Siepmann had had
some input. "There is a disposition to take us for *what* we are, and that
in turn is likely to keep us *where* we are. If these devices are to be used
in an effort to entertain all of the people all of the time, then we have
come perilously close to discovering the real opiate of the people. If in
dealing with events we concentrate on what and how, and ignore the
why, then we are not really searching for anything."[165]

He was accepting the Albert Einstein Award in the humanities, talking of his days in the Emergency Committee, fundraising for victims of Nazi persecution. "All but an insignificant portion of the money we raised came from Jewish sources. . . . In presenting applications . . . I was never once asked: 'Is this man a Jew?' . . . Almost half of those we financed were pure Aryans even under Hitler's definition. They were men who like their Jewish colleagues refused to bend."

Concluding, he said he was sending his award check to the author Alan Paton, facing trial in South Africa: "As most of you probably know, one hundred and fifty men and women were arrested in South Africa . . . and charged with treason for their outspoken, complete, but non-violent opposition to their government's apartheid program. . . . Mr. Paton himself is currently a defendant . . . on a charge that he took part in a public meeting at which native Africans were present. . . . In other words, the 'crime' with which Mr. Paton is charged is that he attended and spoke at a meeting not unlike the meeting at which we are here gathered tonight."

Funds were needed for the legal defense, he told the audience, "and I venture to think that Professor Einstein would have approved the use of this fund for that purpose."

Over the years, he had monitored the growth of apartheid, first with radio reports from opposition friends in South Africa, then over *See It Now*, making film privately available to anti-apartheid spokesmen in the U.S. Similarly, his programs had tracked the unfolding civil rights story at home.

Like many, Murrow had welcomed the landmark 1954 ruling of the Warren Court on *Brown v. Topeka*—a decision, he felt, which had kept the U.S. from going the way of South Africa. "The country can consider itself fortunate," he wrote a friend that year, "to have the Governor [Warren] as its chief justice."[166]

But it was the court battles and their consequences that absorbed *See It Now*, not the story in the streets. The Montgomery bus boycotts, led by a rising young Atlanta minister, had erupted in the closing weeks of 1955, but the Murrow-Friendly program, usually well ahead of the news, and in the three years remaining, never did cover the activities of Martin Luther King.

Just why, remained an open question. Murrow was known to have an aversion to mass movements, nonviolent or not. Once, talking with Joe Wershba, he confessed to a visceral unease at the sudden social changes taking place—self-conscious, fifties-style, about his Southern roots. "You guys got it all in one chunk," he said. "I had to learn it."

Ed Bliss, as Murrow's news writer, could recall no commentaries on King. Fred Friendly, questioned about the matter later, had no answer, no recollection of the subject ever coming up—"That's a hole."[167]

But even problems like "Clinton and the Law," probing anti-integration violence in a Tennessee town, created problems with the network. Tennessee's Governor praised the show, but CBS officials in New York had reportedly insisted on a prior screening for Southern affiliates. They could run it all they liked, said Murrow, but he wasn't making changes.

None refused the show; eight non-CBS stations asked for a print.[168] But relations were further strained with management. *See It Now*'s financial problems continued. Once, when sales department efforts bogged down, Friendly himself went out and got a sponsor. Pan Am stayed a season, then bowed out.

Somehow, they managed to keep going, with programs on the Puerto Ricans, on the pauperization of the older cities, on workers' jobs versus automation, and the effects of nuclear fallout. But it was afternoon viewing, away from the limelight.

There was also, by now, a pendulum effect, as the network news operation coalesced at the decade's closing. In January 1957, videotape had made its first appearance, revolutionizing TV methodology. The news specials emerging from John Day's and Irv Gitlin's bailiwicks were drawing the attention of the Peabody Committee, however much the honors still included *See It Now*.

It wasn't *See It Now*, however, but the annual *Where We Stand*, conceived not by Murrow-Friendly but by Stanton, that was being pushed as the network model—a yearly balance sheet on the U.S. vis-à-vis the USSR on rockets and missiles, economies, civil defenses, and education; and mobilizing the resources of the entire News Division. A concluding house editorial, read by Howard Smith, called Americans "overcomplacent, overaddicted to comfort, and indifferent to good government."[169]

Under the new regime, the think piece had been first researched by the production unit, then sent to the foreign correspondents and Washington staff for input, the resulting copy run past Stanton, Paley, corporate vice-presidents in programming and government relations, the Presidents of CBS Radio and CBS-TV, and the Vice-President and General Manager of CBS News. A final version was of course teletyped to the affiliates well ahead of air time.

Now *that*, Mickelson told a lunch meeting of the Radio and Television Executives Society, was how things should be done, and, in fact, *would* be done from here on in at CBS.[170] It was the very antithesis of Murrow on camera, speaking for "Fred Friendly and myself." The corporate process, it turned out, also included the deletion of an eight-minute sequence showing Robert Oppenheimer in interview with Howard K. Smith. Smith, protesting the action, asked Mickelson to release him from the program. Oppenheimer finally ended the flap by withdrawing his permission to run the interview. ". . . snivelling, weasel-worded," Murrow called the whole matter, writing to an angry Smith in the wake of the controversy.

Relations between Murrow and the news management hadn't exactly improved over the years, relations with Mickelson, once their functions had threatened to start overlapping, strictly business—polite, never warm. No one, the CBS news chief learned, could be colder than Murrow protecting his turf—"I was the enemy"—the wagons always in a circle.[171]

In the case of John Day, the clash of personalities was even more marked, the short-tempered News Director running afoul constantly of the time-honored arrangements between the correspondents and *Edward R. Murrow with the News*. "It was the showcase," explained Bob Skedgell, the assistant director for radio in those days, "*the* program; like our evening news today. So everyone did all they could to get on, and some of the correspondents would cut corners here and there to do it. And Ed *liked* to bring the correspondents in, especially Kendrick, who was a great storyteller, who was in Vienna for a time, on a bad shortwave signal: a lot of the time you couldn't understand him. So Alex would telex or cable the stories in to us, and Ed would quote them—at length."[172]

All very *gemütlich* and homey and thoroughly irritating if you were news director and supposedly in charge. When Schoenbrun and Clark tagged a NATO summit exclusive for the 7:45 P.M. show, Day scooped up the cable slated for Murrow and went with it on the next outgoing newscast. Which promptly gummed up a release agreement worked out by Schoenbrun with *Times* and AP colleagues, impinging on the breaking of the story over the Murrow program. Day regretted greatly but reminded Clark and Schoenbrun that they were working for the CBS News organization, and not just one show.[173]

In principle, Murrow agreed. Skedgell would recall an afternoon of crisis in the latter fifties—a major breaking story, CBS staying on the air with it. Murrow had joined the little group in the listening room abutting Studio 9, where the incoming reports were taped. Someone was filing a piece for his show that night. It was three in the afternoon. Skedgell was running short, filling airtime. He turned beseeching blue eyes in Murrow's direction: "Ed, I'd dearly love to use that piece." Murrow handed it over. You can't sit on news, he agreed. "It's too perishable."[174]

But Bobby Skedgell was family, Day, the quintessential outsider—a rough-spoken, often foul-spoken, two-fisted Kentuckian with a temper to match his hair. A onetime labor reporter and Nieman Fellow, former managing editor of the Louisville *Courier-Journal*, he had been brought in to manage, newspaper style, and found things didn't necessarily work that way among the correspondents, his frustrations often focussing on Murrow, symbol of the lack of organizational control. The feeling, evidently, was mutual.

"He sent Murrow some memos," Howard Smith recalled, "though at one point there was only seventy yards' distance between their rooms. Murrow penciled at the bottom of one of them: 'I wouldn't want this in my files. Perhaps you want it in yours.' And sent it back."[175]

(Accepting an award for *See It Now* once, Day suggested a new category, for a newsman who was *not* Edward R. Murrow. NBC producer Reuven

Frank, writing Ed next day, called it "an outstanding experience in taste-lessness."[176] Murrow, replying, said he hoped Frank and his other friends in the news business would appreciate "that Mr. Day's opinions were necessarily not my own.")[177]

To the newsroom youngsters, however, Murrow was a legendary figure, a talent spotter and a source of backing, his word given extra clout by his consultant's contract with CBS. Marvin Kalb, fresh from the State Department and Russian studies at Columbia and Harvard, was referred onward as "our kind of guy."[178] Nancy Hanschman, later Nancy Dickerson, remembered his help in breaking the gender barrier.

"He pushed us all," said Lou Cioffi, who had come up from copyboy to Far Eastern correspondent and would remember bringing back a bride from Japan in the early fifties, past immigration hurdles and company admonitions not to ruin his career. Returned to New York, the young couple received a dinner invitation to 580 Park Avenue, privately *à quatre*, just the Murrows and the Cioffis: a welcome for the new wife of a correspondent. Said Cioffi, "We both appreciated it."[179]

Charles Kuralt, then a young news writer pounding a typewriter in the bullpen, would remember Murrow's entrances in the newsroom, in late afternoon:

> "Well," he would say. . ."we have done as much damage as we can do. How about a drink?" The invitation was for everybody within the sound of his voice. And we would all go down to Colbee's. . .and pass an hour, the well-known correspondents and the seasoned editors and the young kids, all together, all drawn together by Murrow.

It always ended in a journalism seminar, said Kuralt, and it helped him survive in New York on $135 a week. He also remembered notes from the older newsman, after he had turned broadcaster, "complimenting me on something I had done, or quarreling with something I had said. . .or the way I said it. He did the same for many others. . .and he did it even after he had left the network."[180]

Cronkite stayed outside the Murrow circle, a sense of rivalry discernable between the two men, despite their disparate power positions. Roz Downs recalled a dinner party at her Bethesda home outside Washington during the fifties, both Murrow and Cronkite among the guests. Cronkite was after all a wartime UP buddy of Bill's, and the Downses loved both men.

Somehow, after dinner, attention got drawn to a pair of antique dueling pistols, mounted on the mantelpiece. For reasons too obscure for later recollection, a great deal having been imbibed beforehand, Cronkite and Murrow wound up going bang-bang at each other with the pistols, at point-blank range: high noon in Bethesda.

Roz Downs shot a look at her husband. "I think they're serious," she said.[181]

There was undoubtedly, at CBS, a feeling of the ins and outs. Ned Calmer was to describe Murrow as "cliquey." To J. G. Gude, it was simply the garden-variety factionalism one found in any organization, rather than Murrow consciously trying to swing his weight. Just an underground feeling, he said, of those who'd made it with Ed, and those who hadn't; a feeling ever present, like something that itched.[182]

For the World War II club, "the boys," the CBS elite, the sky was the limit. Ed Bliss would remember Sevareid and others flying in from Washington or wherever else, when they had a bone to pick with management. "He always represented us to the company," said Howard Smith. "When we needed vacations, he made sure we got them. He stood up for me on occasions when I got into controversies; he would do anything for his boys." Schoenbrun virtually apologized once for hesitating before asking a favor—"[not] because I thought you'd say no but because I knew you'd say yes."[183]

But the boys were middle-aged by now, into their own careers, their separate tracks, some brought home to be groomed for network stardom or, in the language of internal memos, to be developed as a television personality.[184] When *Where We Stand* was mounted, it was Howard Smith, highly regarded by Mickelson, who spoke for CBS.

Mickelson had had his problems with the Murrow fiefdom, but by 1958, he had reason to be satisfied as the division grew inversely to the downplay of the Murrow-Friendly operation. Forced to start from zero level, he had assembled a TV news structure complete with editors, camera personnel, specialized departments, reporters who knew how to cover for the picture medium. He would have his critics—subordinates who saw him as a "soft leader," a patient builder, brilliant on pure detail; but a committeeman, soft-core on policy, loathe to commit himself. Yet by the late fifties, he was widely respected as the architect of network news at CBS.

It was also Mickelson who had the backing of Stanton, increasingly in the public eye now as godfather to the News Division—negotiating the Khrushchev interview, recipient of the Paul White Memorial Award of the Radio-Television News Directors Association, honored for distinguished service by the venerable Journalism School of the University of Missouri.

In late November 1957, Murrow had asked Paley about turning the annual correspondents' year-end luncheon into "a sort of family round table to discuss plans and objectives for CBS News." Paley, replying, begged off; he was going away with Babe for Christmas, he said, and would not, therefore, be holding the luncheon after all.[185]

It was a truism of the time that Murrow had a pipeline to the top. But increasingly, on matters of substance, it was others who now controlled the pipeline, the natural evolution of the forces set in motion August 1954.

2.

The shock, when it came, was all the greater for being unexpected.

Admittedly, *See It Now* had had its problems, largely financial. Sponsorship, when obtainable, was covering hardly more than airtime, most of the thin profit going to the stations, the residuum hardly adequate for the high production costs. Murrow and Friendly had been holding long conversations on the program's future. For their December offering—the great black contralto Marian Anderson touring Asia—Murrow himself had sold his old friend the President of ITT on buying an hour of evening time.

But in January their luck had seemed to change, thanks, ironically, to a former blacklistee from CBS—Bob Shayon, now the respected and influential broadcast columnist for the *Saturday Review*, who praised not only the program but ITT for backing it.

It was a made-to-order promotion piece, straight from the source; bankrolling quality programming could be good for business. Sales was ecstatic, running off copies for the network salesmen, agencies, and advertisers: You, too, could polish your image with a show like this on CBS. Instructions went down the line to put out the word on Madison Avenue that this kind of programming was available from time to time[1]—i.e., attach your name to quality instead of schlock.

Paley sent words of praise to Murrow and a print to ITT for corporate screening in case anybody had missed the show. The Urban League bought sixteen-millimeter prints for nationwide rallies called for April 1. The happy sponsor was basking in the afterglow; response had been "substantial," wrote ITT President Edmond Leavey; Columbia had "scored a home run," and ITT was proud and happy to have been associated with Murrow and with CBS.[2]

A little over a month later, Murrow and Friendly, up in Paley's office, were told the show was going off the air.

It seemed the final irony that after the many planned controversies of *See It Now*, the trip wire should have been a balanced show. Certainly the March 2 program on statehood for Alaska and Hawaii—a move backed by the President, the two major parties, and most U.S. voters—was deemed at the outset no more controversial than their coverage of the Post Office.

If anything, *See It Now* had bent over backward in presenting the viewpoint of a small minority, mostly old-line diehards in the House and Senate opposing statehood on grounds of race and supposed ideology, centering in Hawaii's case on the person of Harry Bridges, the controversial, charismatic Marxist leader of the longshoremen's union and boss of thousands of dockworkers in California and the islands; Moscow's putative pipeline to Honolulu and, heaven forbid, Washington. A direct route to the Senate floor for "the rising tide of Asiatic communism," said

John Stennis of Mississippi, playing on the mixed population of the islands. Senator James Eastland of Mississippi claimed the CP controlled Hawaii and hotly denied, in answer to Murrow's pointed queries, that race was a factor in his opposition. Senator George Malone of Nevada, an old McCarthy supporter, warned against changing the "complexion" of the United States, needled Murrow on his facts, and warned that New York's day of reckoning was coming. ("Trounced New York and this reporter a little bit," Murrow had jotted in his interview notes. "Maybe we should throw New York out of the Union?")[3]

As in any balanced show, the head count evened out, though the opposition included three U.S. senators and two congressmen. (Speakers for Hawaii included the decorated World War II veteran Daniel Inouye, then of the Hawaii House of Representatives, later of the U.S. Senate Watergate Committee.) The controversial Bridges had his day in court, sandwiched between two opponents. The whimsy-mannered little man with the Australian accent took Arthur Morse's questions at the dockside in Honolulu (off to a late start when some jets buzzed by; NBC sabotage, said Bridges).

Morse quoted a statement by a congressman from upstate New York, one John Pillion, to the effect that statehood would guarantee Harry Bridges two seats respectively in the U.S. House and Senate. The little man laughed. The congressman was crazy, and he only wished it were true, but seriously, this happened to give nonwhite people the right to register and vote, maybe even send nonwhites to Washington, where they could vote on civil rights. Which was why that white supremacist Eastland and his bloc didn't want it. The rest was all smoke screen and baloney. (Showed how much *he* knew about Hawaii, said Bridges in an unused segment, this guy from New York he had never heard of, this— this—Killion? Pillion.[4]) It was maybe one minute out of fifty-nine.

But Pillion demanded reply time of CBS. Murrow thought it was ridiculous. The news department thought it ridiculous. Friendly thought if anyone deserved reply time, it was the Hawaiians, considering the Klan language thrown around in some of the interviews and quotes.

Pillion got the time.

Mickelson, who had gone along on the Benson affair, later remembered arguing against the decision for some two hours up on 20, before the editorial board, and coming up against Paley. "It just didn't make sense. In the first place, the program was reasonably well balanced, you couldn't carry objectivity to unreasonable lengths, which [this] would have. And secondly, there was no particular reason. . . ."

The Benson affair had been another matter, administration pressure, but why go through this for some ineffectual, inconsequential congressman from Lackawanna when no answer was even called for? "[But] Paley was absolutely adamant on it. The answer was going to be *given*. So I had to go down and tell Murrow and Friendly."[5]

The meeting had been called for five in the afternoon, Murrow and Friendly sitting below, awaiting the outcome, not part of the debate.

He found them in Murrow's office, the newscast over. "They were still sitting there, waiting, knowing that an editorial board meeting was in progress. I told them that the decision was firm and irrevocable and that was it: Pillion was going to get the time.

"Ed, of course, never reacted with any violence; he just took it. You had to look at him very carefully to see that there was any anger involved because he never blew completely. I'm sure I recognized an unhappiness there, but the *depth* of it I couldn't possibly perceive."[6]

For Murrow himself, it was déjà vu. "Now I'm going to have to prove I'm not a Communist," he told Joe Wershba, by then back in touch as a writer for the New York *Post.*

A date was set for mid-April. William Egan, Senator-elect from Alaska, wired Murrow a copy of his protest to Paley and Stanton: "I cannot comprehend the reasoning behind your decision. . . . See It Now gave fair time to opponents of statehood. . . ."[7]

Murrow thanked him dryly for his "courtesy" in sharing "your telegram to Messrs. Paley and Stanton. I should like you to know that I did not participate in the decision. . . ."[8]

He also wrote a letter to the management. A strong letter. "Perhaps too strong," said Friendly; an understatement if there ever was one.

(Twenty-three years later, a fingered photocopy, volunteered by Paley, was offered for examination by one of Paley's assistants, on the top floor of Black Rock. Only the "gist" might be noted. No verbatim copying. Mr. Paley—so went the explanation—didn't want to violate the privacy of his friend Ed Murrow.)[9]

It was the kind of letter written for the wastebasket or shoved into the desk drawer, unsent. It was not merely injudicious, did not merely state that the future of *See It Now* was doubtful. It said: I want out—now— effective end of the present year. It was Murrow himself, saying he didn't want things to go on. In the final scene, described by Friendly in *Circumstances* and not denied by the Chairman, Paley could look the newsman in the eye and say openly, "But I thought you and Fred didn't want to do *See It Now* anymore."

"They had *resigned,*" Paley later insisted, referring to the program, "in writing. It said they were *through* with *See It Now.* Didn't want to do it any longer. . . . People do not resign, whether in a temper or not, unless they *mean* it. And whereas they are entitled to be hurt . . . *I'm* entitled to be hurt, too. I thought it was a *misguided* letter and an *unfair* letter, and if they felt that way about it—okay!"[10]

The last act unfolded in Paley's office: just the three of them, alone.

Murrow, said Friendly, was talking about the Pillion matter, suggesting procedures that would let them in on future deliberations over equal time, when the Chairman dropped the bomb: He thought they didn't want to do *See It Now* anymore.

Murrow was thunderstruck. "It took Ed's breath away," Friendly recalled. "He just couldn't believe it—this was the most prestigious program around. . . .

"I remember Paley [behind] a small desk, sort of French—though I'm not sure; he had always had it. Murrow was sitting to his left, me to the right. Murrow was in shirt sleeves, neck open. Paley was in a blue shirt; I remember all the mikes from CBS were lined up behind him. . . ."

Murrow was by now out of his chair. Of *course* he wanted the show to continue. To Friendly, watching the other two talk past each other, it was like witnessing an unexpected request for a divorce—i.e., "I don't want to live with you anymore"; "Wait, let's talk about it reasonably"; "I'll have a lawyer draw up the papers. . . ."[11]

In an often-cited bit of dialogue, Murrow pleaded with "Bill": Did he really want to destroy all this; didn't he want something that he, Paley, had put so much into, to continue? Yes, said Paley, but he didn't want these stomach aches every time they did a controversial broadcast. Said Murrow: "It comes with the job."[12]

Friendly, watching the two giants go at each other, found himself perforce a spectator. "It was the first time I'd really seen them arguing hard. Voices were raised. Nobody was shouting but there was that intensity. Murrow was pacing up and down. Paley hit himself in the stomach when he talked of stomach aches. I didn't hear the end of it. I left early. Hoped it would help. But it didn't."[13]

The cancellation announcement came as *See It Now* won another Emmy. The official reason for the termination: it cost too much.

It had been TV's most honored program—three Peabodys, four Emmys, assorted awards from the New York Newspaper Guild, *Look* magazine, *Saturday Review*, the OPC; the Alfred I. Du Pont Award from Columbia Journalism; The Robert Flaherty Award for creative achievement in films for television—the list was endless.

"Though the need for forthright and independent reporting is greater than ever," Gould thundered in The New York *Times*, "the TV industry is virtually confessing that its structure is economically so unsound and politically so insecure that it cannot present programs of genuine substance at hours when most people can see them." The *Times* critic decried the move at a time when "the loss of urgency in international relations and decay in integrity in Washington . . . cry out for the *See It Now* type of probing. . . ."[14]

Economics were undoubtedly part of the picture, the rising importance of what Friendly calls "the cost per minute factor. The stomach aches wouldn't have done it alone. Once you had the business people saying so many dollars per week, that if you didn't have the show, you could get so and so much added revenue, then the pain in the belly becomes important."[15]

In the background was a downswing in the economy, CBS profits down from their all-time 1957 high, with cutbacks in the News Division—the big bloodletting, as a news executive later called it, following corporate orders to eliminate bodies. "They were letting people go so fast," recalled Lee Otis, "that they couldn't keep up with the paper work." Only John Day, keeping his head, resisted mandated cuts that threatened the basic structure.[16] Weeks before *See It Now*'s termination, Dan Karasik of CBS News, Vienna, had taken the drastic step of offering his bureau, kit and kaboodle, to Murrow: they were being axed, *in toto*, all their good Eastern European contacts, everything. Could *See It Now* possibly pick up the whole works? It seemed such a complete waste to let it all go down the drain.[17]

Murrow, at the time, could only sympathize—"I am as disturbed as anybody else over the recent developments here"—but *See It Now* had not enough programs per year, he said, not enough in their area, therefore could not justify the expense. The expense. It was a never-ending refrain rising to a crescendo in the early winter of 1958, adding to a mounting sense of frustration capped by the demise of *See It Now*.

Autonomous or not, it had been the centerpiece of the CBS news effort, the only continuing issue-oriented series. Murrow, brooding over the end of his program, was doing so in a landscape that would be virtually un-recognizable to a viewer of the eighties.

Badgered endlessly by TV columnists that spring, he had no comment. The show had cost too much. Period. *See It Now* finished its final season as though nothing had happened, ending with the Germany program "Watch on the Ruhr." March 30 they had had their final brush with controversy, with a ninety-minute feature on radioactive fallout, run within weeks of Albert Schweitzer's anticipated appeal for a halt to nuclear testing[18] and including a clip of Linus Pauling discussing strontium 90 and genetic mutations.

Run as usual on Sunday afternoon, it was refused by most affiliates because it didn't have a sponsor. "Yet this was a subject," Murrow told a *TV Guide* reporter, "that should have been on the full network at a peak viewing time."[19]

Two weeks later came the letter from Bill Garry, asking him to address the forthcoming meeting of the Radio-Television News Directors Association that fall in Chicago.

As luck would have it, it arrived on Murrow's desk within a few days of Senator Egan's protest cable about the Alaska-Hawaii aftermath. April 22, he sat down to reply to both—to Egan the bitter, "I did not participate in the decision"; to the RTNDA, "I would love to try my hand at a piece . . . a speech . . . which would outrage all of our employers."[20]

Strangely, no one at CBS had been paying much attention when, accepting the Einstein Award in 1957, he had attacked the "manipulation" of the ratings sytem—the sacred cow of commercial broadcasting and, incidentally, Frank Stanton's preserve—as a phenomenon that turned "persons into people—a statistic on a chart . . . symbolized by curves neatly drawn on graphs. . . ."

> All too often in radio and television, audiences are conceived and treated as people, not as persons. Quantitative response is consequently made the measure of quality. There is a willingness and indeed eagerness to answer the questions, "What?" and "How?" But not enough attention is paid to the "Why?" . . . If in dealing with events we concentrate on What and How and ignore the Why, then we are not really searching for anything.[21]

Still, answering Bill Garry that April, he had left himself an opening, not yet fully committed.

May 28, Murrow and Friendly, meeting with Mickelson and Lou Cowan, President since mid-March of the CBS Television Network, learned the new rules, going about the grim business of dismantling *See It Now*.

Management had gentled it somewhat with a consolation prize: *Small World*, taken out of the mothballs months before on the authorization of Mickelson, of Cowan's predecessor, and Paley himself; Murrow had once called him its "principal parent."[22] In mid-April, at the height of the Pillion controversy, a new pilot had been made, with Murrow replacing Sevareid as moderator, an agreement finalized May 28 to place the new program on the fall schedule, no matter what—twenty-six programs, beginning in October, at 6:00 P.M. Sundays, with or without sponsorship. Ed would have his show, keep a working nucleus of the *See It Now* staff; could hardly complain, therefore, of a lack of exposure, what with two weekly programs on the TV schedule. He'd been taken care of.

From Murrow's perspective, the present negotiations were over the corpse of *See It Now*, the Chairman and his top broadcaster—the two old friends—now following increasingly divergent paths.

The late May meeting laid down the new order: The *See It Now* production forces would be stripped down to the minimum level necessary to produce *Small World*. The unit would produce, additionally, perhaps three or four documentaries a season, Murrow, Friendly, *and* Mickelson determining the programs to be recommended to the network, such programs to be then proposed to Mr. Cowan for the obtaining of the necessary budget and airtime.

The Murrow-Friendly unit would also produce programs on order, those orders to come from the corporation, the CBS Television Network, or the CBS News Division.

See It Now would cease to exist, either as a program title or as the unit designation.

One figure, heretofore present at discussions concerning *See It Now*, was noticeably absent. Instead, the "understanding," as the management called it, was conveyed immediately and separately to Paley at the proceedings' close. The Chairman, so read the internal memo, expressed his full agreement.[23]

They were leashed—under the tent, finally, of the News Division. Operationally, they were still free-floating, but with others controlling the money tap and their access to the air; reduced to doing a selling job on management for every program that got on. Or didn't.

Cowan, an old OWI man and longtime admirer of Murrow, was reachable, sympathetic, encouraging; but it was a new ball game.

And Murrow? Wearing out, said Charles Siepmann, later recalling "Ed's confession periods" taking on an ever-darker tone, shot through with anger not at Paley but at Stanton.

"It was a losing battle. He'd spill every crisis, we'd talk it over, and I'd back him and force him and push him. God, he needed moral support. He felt absolutely alone in that shop!"[24]

Bob Shayon had gotten a phone call one day after the Anderson show, suggesting lunch. The meeting was constrained, Murrow striking him as "very troubled," with repeated trips back to the bar.

He had been pleased with the review, seemed to enjoy the company. "Let's do this again." Shayon, following up, got no reply.[25] Perhaps, he reasoned later, the other man had just wanted to touch base on what might have been.[26]

Only once, months afterward, the bitterness flared publicly, following a cheery note from *Look* magazine: *See It Now* was once again Best Public Affairs Series in its annual poll of TV editors and critics, and wouldn't he appear for the award?

Murrow thanked *Look* for the "gracious invitation," found it "very pleasant" to know that the memory of *See It Now* lingered a little. He was, however, "not very good at disinterring either memories or bodies. . . . Why don't you ask Frank Stanton if he would like to accept it on behalf of the Company?"[27]

It was a bad summer. In the old *See It Now* offices on 17, in the cutting room on Ninth Avenue, they waited anxiously for word of funding, in shock. "We had always been *special*," said Mili Bonsignori, "walked off with all the prizes. Now we were beggars."[28]

Ed Scott was let go.[29] Arthur Morse, Wershba's successor, who had covered desegregation and the New York barrios, was in limbo; so was Marty Barnett. "I have always felt proud of *See It Now*," the cameraman wrote Murrow, "because I knew what you and Fred were trying to do. . . .This is what hurts more than anything else."[30]

Murrow promised to put in a word for him with Mickelson. "I fear that

. . . our kind of TV reporting is going down and down—although it appears that NBC is going to have a real try at it. I wish them luck."[31]

In fact, there had been the discreetest of nibbles from Rockefeller Center, specifically the newly ensconced NBC President, Robert Kintner—the nearsighted, hard-driving ex-newshound, once of ABC, moved up from the number two spot at NBC, out to make his news department number one; who had taken the rubber band off the billfold, and who, with Huntley-Brinkley sponsorless—not yet commercial—evidently meant to start his reign with a coup.

The go-between was the ubiquitous Morris Ernst, passing a Murrow program idea to Kintner and reporting back that the talk had turned to "a 'property' called Edward R. Murrow," and he meant to talk to Ed about handling Casey's interest in the event NBC bought the property.[32]

For the first time Murrow didn't back off—no assurances of being quite happy where he was. He would be back in the shop, he replied, "and hope we can discuss matters shortly thereafter."[33] Nothing, apparently, resulted. But it was an indication of how far things had come.

Kintner had also proved a steadfast friend to Elmer Davis,[34] dead that spring, of the illness that had first ended his career, then snuffed him out in stages. The simple service was at the Washington National Cathedral. Murrow mourned deeply, grief mixed with relief. The great communicator had spent his last days hooked up to machines, a living corpse sustained by tubes, unable to communicate; an image that was to haunt Murrow from that time on.

He meant to take Casey fishing in Norway that summer. But Roscoe Murrow had died the year before in Bellingham, and Ethel, now over eighty, alone after tending her husband faithfully through ten years of paralysis, had to be visited.

Janet's father was ill in Middletown, Ed and Casey going alone to the Northwest—first to Bellingham, then to Oregon's Rogue River, where they shot the famous rapids in a flat-bottomed boat, camping out with another WSC classmate, Tom Stoddard of Portland, and a gaggle of Kappa Sigs. It rained; the fish bit; Murrow grew a beard. For a week it was as though CBS, New York, and broadcasting didn't exist. The party, on breaking up, agreed to meet again in 1959 for salmon fishing in Alaska.

"Casey and I," he wrote Stoddard from Pawling, "reminisce about the trip like two old men."[35] A week later he wrote to Bill Small in Louisville, confirming his appearance at the RTNDA convention in Chicago.

It was late August, and other things were happening, the quiz show empire beginning to crack amid the growing whiff of fraud. The CBS quiz show *Dotto* had been abruptly canceled, no explanation, in-house suspicions papered over, it would turn out later, with FCC compliance. *Twenty-one*, the NBC front-runner, was a center of controversy amid contestant charges of coaching and payoffs to take dives.

There had been no lack of early warnings. *Time* magazine had asked back in 1957, "THE SIXTY MILLION DOLLAR QUESTION—*are the quiz shows rigged?*"[36] indicting among others *The $64,000 Question* and producers who were apparently able to control everything, *Time* charged, except their fears of losing an audience.

It was in that time, wrote Friendly later, that an old CBS hand approached them about an in-house exposé of the quiz shows—i.e., wouldn't CBS be better off doing its own housecleaning? Murrow and Friendly said fine, but they'd do their own investigation, not a whitewash job. They heard no more about it. The lawyers, they later learned, had vetoed the idea.[37]

Small World was a hit that fall. TV columnists might write of Murrow's loss of power at the network; over the tube—with two shows a week, one in prime time—he was more visible than ever.

The program specialized in unlikely combinations, Murrow sitting in less as participant than prod and devil's advocate, stepping back as the sparks struck or, as sometimes happened, the fur flew. The conversations were filmed, the cameras running simultaneously at points of origin, the guests connected via shortwave radio to Murrow and each other.

The subject could be anything—from verbal combat between British Labourite maverick Aneuran Bevan, NATO's Alfred Gruenther, and the Bavarian CDU conservative Franz Josef Strauss, to Ingrid Bergman, Darryl Zanuck, and film critic Bosley Crowther talking of the movies. Robert Graves, Arnold Toynbee, and Philip Wylie conversed for the cameras, as did Edward Teller and Leo Szilard; James Hagerty, Gaullist Jacques Soustelle, and Malcolm Muggeridge; James Eastland, historian Denis Brogan, and Herblock. David Ben-Gurion and U Nu discussed Buddhism and Judaism and developing countries; author Han Suyin, Joseph Alsop, and Robert Boothby discussed China; John F. Kennedy, Boothby, and Krishna Menon discussed U.S.-Soviet relations and the cold war. Maria Callas, Victor Borge, and Sir Thomas Beecham took opera to pieces. Agnes De Mille and Hedda Hopper went at each other with all guns firing, over civil liberties, raising ghosts of the Hollywood witch-hunts as a bemused Simone Signoret looked on.

"I am so glad you enjoy *Small World*," Murrow replied to a note from Helen Sioussat. "As a matter of fact, I enjoy it too!"[38]

The show premiered on Sunday, October 12. The following Monday morning, the transcripts of Murrow's RTNDA speech—slated for delivery in two days in Chicago—began going out to selected recipients, with release time and date.

There was no overt anger, no fury such as that of the past spring. Rather, it was a deliberate act, carefully planned over weeks and maybe months, coolly and meticulously executed. In the background the quiz show bubble was finally bursting, engulfing the industry in a sudden hemorrhage of charges and countercharges, bulldozing toward a grand jury investigation by the office of the Manhattan DA. The six-figure money contests, with their elaborate paraphernalia of isolation booths and bank officials, which had skyrocketed the cost of airtime and, concomitantly, network profits, which had helped drive *See It Now* and other programs from the air (*Playhouse 90* was to hold out for another year), were shown up as a high-priced scam, a complicated joke on a public that had bought it hook, line, and sinker.[39]

In the meantime, cynics were betting that the public was simply surfeited, that ratings had been falling even before the summer scandals. The quiz shows, cheap to produce, quickly mounted, could be just as quickly killed off, the smart money now on Westerns, filmed in Hollywood and flooding the market.

Few had known Murrow's intentions in those weeks. RTNDA leadership did, of course; Siepmann knew about the speech; so did Friendly; neither saw the contents. Nor, characteristically, did Murrow discuss his reasons for becoming a whistle blower, going against habits ingrained over decades—of waiting, compromising when need be, keeping problems inside the house, calculating the chances of success or failure, the greater good to be salvaged from the matter. Just possibly, for once, he saw no greater good.

Instead, he went about it with the painstaking deliberation of a man laying dynamite, in a manner that seemed almost calculated to bring down the wrath of his superiors: a carefully devised exercise in bridge burning, right down to the drafts sent CBS department heads—"what I am saying at the meeting . . . tonight."[40]

Only two names had been left off the list of recipients: William Paley and Frank Stanton.

"We have a debt to pay," wrote Joe Wershba to Carl Sandburg the summer of 1954, "this air we breathe does not come free. For every breath, there is the pay-off."[41] One thing Murrow had never talked about was just where the axing of *See It Now* had left the sacrifice of Wershba.

There were chores up to the last minute: recording a narration in Philadelphia for the Liberty Bell; New York Governor W. Averell Harriman's Monday night reception for AFL-CIO President George Meany. Bill Worthy had lost round one in District Court, still had no passport, needed a quick fellowship recommendation to keep himself afloat. There was the nightly radio news, Ed Bliss readying the Wednesday edition, to be broadcast from WBBM, with time left over to make the reception in the French Room of the Sheraton-Blackstone.

The news media had been alerted, personal covering letters accompanying the transcripts in a few cases—John Crosby; George Rosen of *Variety*; Elmo Roper; John Aspinwall at AP. And CBS had been alerted.

Murrow, on the plane to Chicago, was therefore fully aware of the dynamics he had set in motion.

At the Sheraton-Blackstone that night, it was the shortest twenty minutes on record.

MURROW SAYS TV IGNORES NATION'S PERIL, read the headline in the Chicago *Sun-Times* of Thursday.

Television is failing to play its part in informing the people that "this nation is in mortal danger," Edward R. Murrow declared here Wednesday night. "Surely we shall pay for using this most powerful instrument of communication to insulate the citizenry from the hard and demanding realities which are to be faced if we are to survive. I mean the word 'survive' literally. . . ."

Murrow pointed out that when President Eisenhower addressed the nation recently on the crisis with the Soviet Union and Communist China, CBS and NBC delayed the broadcast for an hour 15 minutes— "About twice the time required for an ICBM to travel from the Soviet Union to major targets in the United States."

"It is difficult to believe," Murrow added, "that this decision was made by men who love, respect and understand news."[42]

It did not sit well at Fifty-second Street.

He had hit at the CBS layoffs of that year: "My memory . . . goes back to the time when the fear of a slight reduction in business did not result in an immediate cutback. . .in the news and public affairs department at a time when network profits had just reached an all-time high. . . ." He spoke, from his own experience, of the occasional "clash between the public interest and the corporate interest.

"A telephone call or a letter from the proper quarter in Washington is treated rather more seriously than a communication from an irate but not politically potent viewer. It is tempting enough to give away a little air time for frequently irresponsible and unwarranted utterances in an effort to temper the wind of criticism."

The problems of radio—"that most satisfying and rewarding instrument"—were easy. "In order to progress, it need only go backward. To the time when radio was . . . proud, alert and fast. I recently asked a network official, 'Why this great rash of five-minute news reports (including three commercials) on weekends?' He replied, 'Because that seems to be the only thing we can sell.' . . .

"If radio news is to be regarded as a commodity, only acceptable when saleable, then I don't care what you call it—I say it isn't news. . . ."

The centerpiece, actually, had been a plan for the financing and presentation of informational programming. Since a small group of corporations, he had said back in May 1957, paid for, therefore decided what was seen and heard over TV and radio—thereby "greatly influencing the course of our civilization"—were said corporations justified in spending money exclusively to sell goods and services? Wasn't there in fact something downright dangerous and frightening about it, this imbalance, this searching for the greatest audiences at the lowest cost?

The answer he proposed was within the existing framework: that the twenty or thirty big companies dominating network sponsorship turn over a little of their profits—"a tiny tithe"—by pooling airtime to allow for public affairs programming. The sponsors were to get name credit only, and keep hands off content; they were to pay the time costs; the networks, the production costs, while the affiliates would be obliged to carry the paid-for hour. It was a plan considered quixotic at the time but not far removed in concept from the corporate and network underwriting of public television.

"Just once in a while," he had appealed, "let us exalt the importance of ideas and information. Let us dream to the extent of saying that on a given Sunday night the time . . . occupied by Ed Sullivan is given over to a . . . survey of the state of American education [or] the time normally used by Steve Allen is devoted to a thoroughgoing study of American policy in the Middle East.

> Would the corporate image . . . be damaged? Would the stockholders rise up in their wrath and complain? Would anything happen other than that a few million people would have received a little illumination on subjects that may well determine the future of this country and therefore of corporations? . . .
>
> For if the premise upon which our pluralistic society rests . . . that if people are given sufficient undiluted information, they will then somehow . . . reach the right decision—if that premise is wrong, then not only the corporate image but the corporations are done for. . . .
>
> To those who say people wouldn't look; they wouldn't be interested; they're too complacent, indifferent . . . I can only reply: There is, in one reporter's opinion, considerable evidence against that contention. But even if they are right, what have they got to lose? Because if they are right, and this instrument is good for nothing but to enter-tain . . . and insulate, then the tube is flickering now and we will soon see that the whole struggle is lost.
>
> This instrument can teach, it can illuminate; yes, and it can even inspire. But it can do so only to the extent that humans are determined to use it to those ends. Otherwise it is merely wires and lights in a box. There is a great and perhaps decisive battle to be fought against ignorance, intolerance and indifference. This weapon of television could be useful.
>
> Stonewall Jackson, who knew something about the use of weapons . . . said, 'When war comes, you must draw the sword and throw away the scabbard.' The trouble with television is that it is rusting in the scabbard during a battle for survival.

Not everyone joined in the praise or agreed with Murrow that respon-sibility—"In spite of all the mouthings about giving the public what it wants"—rested on "big business. . .big television and. . .at the top." Yes, that was quite a piece, wrote Bill Benton. "But do you really make a case for the fact that General Motors should pay for the time? After all . . . this time was allocated by the FCC in the name of the voters."[43]

J. K. Galbraith had found the speech "effective and fascinating" but added: "Must everything . . . be sponsored by a corporation? Must we always have this image in the background?"[44]

Jack Gould, in a surprise censure, hit out at the speech for ostensibly placing the load on the sponsors, absolving the industry; and called the newsman "the newest convert" to the philosophy that TV's customers, not the broadcasters, carried primary responsibility for the medium's well-being.[45] Murrow thought his views had been misconstrued.[46]

In the other camp were those who thought him overoptimistic in his evident belief that one could recall these captains of industry to some better self, that the Chief Wilsons, the Edmond Leaveys, and by extension, the William Paleys, really wanted what he wanted and would surely do the right, obviously reasonable thing if the advertising agency types would only get out of the way.

"What Ed didn't realize," said Dick Salant, "was that this *is* the system. This was an adherent part of what *everybody* was in. The fundamental issue of what is a news organization doing in a free enterprise system. And there's still no answer."[47]

Conversely, Lester Markel, czar of the Sunday New York *Times*, had written Murrow, calling the speech "true talk if ever there was true talk and . . . moreover, courageous and stimulating."[48] Lawrence Spivak, the grand inquisitor of *Meet the Press*, thought the talk "exactly right and of great importance."[49] Edward Barrett, Dean of the Columbia School of Journalism, thought the proposal "highly optimistic . . . but I haven't perfected any better plan. . . ."[50]

Irene Mayer, borrowing an offprint from Jean Kintner, summed up the gist of many messages received: "You're crazy—but I am grateful."[51]

Jack Beck sent cheers from California. Murrow thanked him—"Your sentiments are not universally shared in this shop."[52] It was the usual pattern: rank-and-file approval, "the guys who do the work," as Murrow put it, a certain distancing, however, involving upper and middle management. "He wasn't exactly snubbed," said a colleague afterward, "but there was a definite cooling."

Said Mickelson: "I think there was considerable feeling that Murrow was striking a blow against CBS, and *particularly* against Bill Paley, and I think Paley took it personally."[53] The situation was complicated by Murrow's special relationship with CBS, the semi-incestuous closeness common to company people. His oldest friends were his company friends, Ralph Colin's law firm handled his will. Unlike a John Day or a Mickelson, whether in favor or out, he was family; decades later Dick Salant would still hold to the belief widely held among the inner circle, that Ed would still be one of them, if only Friendly hadn't "egged him on."[54]

And Paley?

Chicago was the one decision never brought to him by Ed, who never—but never—made a move without him. Not one. They had had their disagreements in the past, severe arguments, strictly in private. This was different. Twenty-three years after the fact, the voice of the Chairman of the Board, sitting in his corner suite on top of Black Rock, would turn low and distant, answering the question, Did it hurt?

"Did. It did. No conversation before it, or none after. Never referred to it either."

Why, did he think, had he not been asked?

"I think it would have embarrassed him. He must have known how I would react. *Couldn't* have been a secret to him. And yet he was of a mind to want to say it.

"I don't think he wanted to take the chance of being dissuaded. Or else didn't want to have anything blow up between us *before* the fact. *I* think he expected me to react *after* the fact, which I refused to do.

> He was a, you know, grown man, with good sense and some—good judgment. And if he saw fit to attack us—and I thought he was attacking *me personally*, after all of that—well, listen, I *was* CBS to a large extent! He was talking about things that he didn't *like*, which were under my control. So it was very much of a personal attack. Which I resented very deeply. For that reason I just didn't want to bring it up.
>
> *I* think he was waiting for a so-called showdown with me; you know, a big argument with me. And the thing had been *done*, and I—I saw nothing to be gained by having a big fight with him. If he felt that way and expressed himself, it was okay. He certainly had every right in the world of doing it—to do it. I was *surprised* he did, disappointed that he did. But—he did.

Family fallouts are the worst; the younger brother was declaring his independence. "It was a very—well, I've had—no relationship quite like it. And I think he had—I had *terrific* respect for him. And fondness and *love* for him, really. I think he felt the same way about me. Ed didn't have many close friends, you know. . . ."[55]

They knew how to hurt each other.

Election night, things were smooth on the screen, tense in the studio—Cronkite anchoring as usual; Murrow pulled from the analyst's desk, replaced by Sevareid, and put to work on one of the boards, reporting regional returns. Outsiders put it down to the Chicago speech; actually the assignments dated from September, an intended move and extension of the past spring's momentum toward control.

The assignments came as usual from John Day,[56] massively irritated by Murrow's self-elected absence on the 1956 election night; the decision, however, recalled Lee Otis, then administrator for TV news, would have had to come from higher up—a "signal," as he put it, the overall impression in the studio, that Ed was being taken down a peg or two.[57]

Mickelson himself did not recall it ("*Murrow* didn't work a board, did he?")[58] or remember why. He thought Day had no doubt good reason for turning over the analysis to, after all, Sevareid, and then, of course, Murrow had never really been enough of an organization man for their news director.

The new arrangements—other faces in charge, Murrow on the cat-walk—were lost on no one. Said Otis: "People thought, what a comedown for Ed," but then, that was the nature of the business. You shrugged your shoulders and went on, as Murrow did and was expected to: a "good soldier."

"It was a horror," said Ed Bliss afterward, "hand-moved digits; everything went wrong. He went through the paces like a thoroughbred. Messengers brought in reports; we sorted them out, brought them to Murrow; he ad-libbed from that and what was on the board. He was ill, it went past midnight, he was on his feet the whole time. It was disgraceful that they did it."[59]

Howard Smith was handling the Southern board. "I think it hurt—I think it hurt. He'd been number one for so long that that was quite a blow. I mean here he was given the Eastern board, and Cronkite was assembling it all and was the grand master. Murrow never *said* it, but you could tell, he did not like that at all."[60]

(In fact, Cronkite almost didn't make it. Early on, Mickelson had told Smith he'd be anchoring instead—Cronkite had a sore throat; they were phoning him now, to tell him he could take it easy. Fifteen minutes later, says Smith, Cronkite was in the studio.)[61]

It turned out to be a long night, Murrow leading off with the Eastern returns, beginning after nine and closing out at almost two in the morning, rattling off districts, parties, percentages, and estimates as though he'd been doing it all his life, like ammunition rounds aimed at an unseen set of targets. He was not, it was true, feeling well, and left exhausted.

The reviewers read retaliation into the assignment. "Demoted to a minor chore," said the Chicago *Daily News*, but he wasn't. A New York daily likened it to "sending a crack reporter to cover the courthouse in Bay Ridge." Jack Gould, noting Murrow as "far from happy and relaxed in being on his feet," called it "an odd bit of casting," a little startling to viewers at home, "unfamiliar with all the factors that apparently govern life at CBS News. . . ."[62]

It was a final paradox of his public versus his in-house position that he himself might have been in the race on that election night. Earlier that year, a strong faction among New York State Democrats and the local Liberal Party had seen in him the next standard-bearer in the U.S. Senate and had put considerable pressure on him, quietly and via the press, to run for the upcoming New York seat. Paley, at the time, was all for it. In some doubt, Murrow turned to the pros. "If anyone knows politics, you do, Ed," Sam Rayburn told him.[63] Truman, by contrast, told him to stay away, that he'd be more useful *on* camera than *in* camera. In the end he had gone with Truman's advice, telling reporters he'd rather watch politicians than be one.

He had made no appointments for the day after elections, his staff under orders to turn down all lunch dates,[64] to give him a breather. Four weeks after election night he was up at the Columbia Presbyterian Medical Center, undergoing testing at the Cardio-pulmonary Laboratory for signs of pulmonary emphysema.

His cough was by now out of control, waking him at night, with the added onset of pain and breathing difficulty in the late afternoon. He could be flip about it. To a manufacturer of cigarette filters who had forwarded a test sample with high-flown claims, he promised that "if it does in fact eliminate my cigarette cough, extend my life by 10 years and eliminate the usual morning hangover, I shall quit this job and go and sell them on street corners."[65]

The truth was, he needed help and, in reaching for it, found himself led into a strange, brief episode in his life.

The Doctor was prominent, a specialist in chronic pulmonary diseases, professor emeritus at a top medical school, a published essayist, widely read, who moved easily in the smart circles and talked colorfully about his patients among the New York intelligentsia. He wouldn't treat Woollcott and Gershwin because he didn't like them; was proud of his appellation of "court physician" to Herbert Bayard Swope.

Murrow had met him indirectly, through the dinner party circuit. The Doctor was a good conversationalist, given to the apt quote.

The usual tests were run—heart; lungs; abdomen; pulmonary function. The diagnosis: chronic bronchitis made worse by smoking. There was no sign, to The Doctor's later recollection, of pulmonary emphysema, and anything turning up would have been "slight." There might have been a predisposition inherited from an asthmatic mother, but the bronchitis itself was not necessarily the preamble to the more serious condition.

There seemed, in any case, no cause for alarm: There seemed no undue shortness of breath; the lungs were not overinflated. True, the tests had turned up the presence of bronchospasm—a constriction of the walls of the bronchi, accounting, no doubt, for the late-afternoon pain and breathing difficulty, but antiasthmatics, taken orally, would relieve the problem.

It was what Murrow wanted to hear. He and The Doctor got on well, met from time to time outside the office, discussed the world in general. Murrow, far from being a fatigued patient at the end of his tether, came across as the very essence of vigor: "It was a pleasure talking to him, and I think he enjoyed talking to me; you get a transfer to somebody. . . ."

Murrow enjoyed it, too. The Doctor didn't tell him to change his lifestyle. He removed his guilt with quotes from Isaiah and Thomas Carlyle—not the type of doctor, he said, to be penalizing his patients with don'ts. A student and sometime practitioner of psychosomatic medicine—ah, yes, it had certainly helped with Eugene O'Neill—he felt it wouldn't help in

Murrow's case. "He would have had to stop for ten years to obviate cancer.

"Ed had an obsession with smoking, as if taking it away from him would be an intolerable burden; the kind of person to whom smoking meant not only pleasure but a relief from some subtle impoverishment, some lack.

"A man doesn't smoke like that on TV, and you remember, he would take deep puffs, drag it right down—there's a profound satisfaction there, not just the nicotine. These very obsessive smokers, it's obvious, have strong oral trends, impulses, drives. . . . I felt that this man had such a *strong* drive—if you took away smoking, you had to substitute something in its place; you can't just say it's because you miss your mother's breasts. All you can say is, here is a man with great talent, energy, vitality, who had some unsolved problem of desiring an addition to his life, something more, some lack—and that something was made up by smoking."

Accordingly, he dealt with the symptoms. For the spasm he ordered bronchial dilator tablets, taken once a day.

For the cough, however, he ordered heavy, intensive doses of tranquilizers and narcotics: Miltown, 400 milligrams, up to six a day for ten days at a time; Demerol, 50 milligrams, twenty-five tablets for a four-day period. Prescriptions open-ended.

Why Demerol, a powerful painkiller?

"A four-day course. We often prescribe that for a cough."[66]

Murrow, from where he sat, was most uneasy. Never mind the nicotine, he did not like pills, often put up with insomnia, snorting righteously when Janet went to the occasional sedative. The small prescription slips with the Park Avenue address went at first into the file drawer. After some weeks, however, he informed his friend Agnes Meyer that he had "finished eating the first handful of pills my doctors have prescribed."[67]

"He may have been puritanical about taking soporifics," The Doctor later conceded.

It was not a happy situation.

As the year turned, matters turned from bad to worse, though at first there had seemed a glint of hope for the Murrow-Friendly unit. Lou Cowan had come up with money and airtime to send Arthur Morse and Marty Barnett to Virginia, to report on the shutdown of the Norfolk school system, thus preventing the enrollment of seventeen black teenagers, under the policy of massive resistance to court-ordered integration.

"The Lost Class of '59" was to win a special Peabody; a leading Southern paper, the Richmond *Times-Dispatch* was to call the show "a valuable contribution to the nation's understanding."

"A climate of intolerance now exists in the South which, in my opinion, far exceeds, both in intensity and danger to our country, the type of intolerance which came to be known as McCarthyism," warned Murrow's old NSFA friend and later Supreme Court Justice Lewis Powell, then practicing law in Richmond, in a private letter to the newsman:

You made a major contribution in . . . the latter situation and I hope your forthcoming program can help to some extent to solve the present, and much more acute, problem. . . . to bring out the truth and dispel the illusion that the Court decision can be circumvented. . . . to restore reason to the point where we do not in effect abandon public education for most, if not all, of our children.[68]

A date was set for January 21. Two days before airtime, however, the show was almost swamped by other, unconnected events in a flare-up further muddying the waters and bringing Murrow-CBS relations to a new low.

CBS Radio's Unit One was in effect a resuscitation of the old documentary unit. Its producers were talented, enterprising; investigative reporters like Jay McMullen and George Vicas, who were to make their mark in television journalism, going now into areas where TV still lagged: Central America; racial tension in the changing Northern cities; women's rights. Irv Gitlin, then Director of Public Affairs for the division, had talked Murrow into narrating.

It was a favor; he lent his name, hence drew listeners. He walked in, read the scripts, walked out. And occasionally prodded Arthur Hull Hayes for a little promotion money, where the young producers couldn't.

He wasn't always happy he had done it, the controversy getting scratchy now and then, involving Murrow as the front man. The hassles generally smoothed out, however; the research on the whole stood up. But there was nothing in the scripts to indicate that these were not Murrow productions; indeed, the omnipresent editorial "we" led the public to presume precisely the opposite.

In mid-January he had taped *The Business of Sex,* charging the use of call girls by corporations to clinch deals, as a routine part of business transactions, with tax write-offs for the expense involved. Producer George Vicas had recorded interviews with the hookers, the madams, with judges, psychiatrists, and sociologists, even a few whither-are-we-going reflections by Margaret Mead.

"He [Murrow] probably didn't see the script until the taping," said Charlie Mack, "but once he said yes to something, he wouldn't back out. Vicas was young, talented. It was an explosive subject, but he had confidence that Vicas knew what he was talking about."[69]

It went out over CBS Radio on Monday night, January 19 of the new year. Murrow probably wasn't even listening. A decision that day by the Supreme Court of Virginia, outlawing massive resistance, had sent "The Lost Class"—due for airing in two days—back to the cutting room amid the usual frantic flurry of last-minute revisions. Absorbed in all the attendant problems, Murrow got off at 17 on Tuesday morning, to find himself mobbed by waiting reporters, firing off questions about *The Business of Sex.* Murrow, his back to the elevators, stared at them, dumbfounded.

The call-girl program, as it was already known, had made the early editions across the country, praise and—more often—damnation seething forth in editorials and headlines: Murrow had smeared American business.

The National Association of Manufacturers, in a blistering denunciation, attacked him as "a past master of innuendo, smear, snide implication, and unsupported accusation—tactics which he alleged were used by the late Senator Joseph R. McCarthy, a man whom he pilloried unmercifully and unfairly."[70]

CBS, too, was on the carpet, Frank Stanton, up on 20, trying to field the corporate protests, deflect the anger of such as the president of Du Pont, and the chairman of the board of Young & Rubicam.

The public cry went up for names—the proof. It couldn't be produced; Vicas, to get his sources to talk, had promised anonymity.

"It was a difficult time," Friendly recalled. "The program was somewhat prophetic but not terribly well documented. Criticism was coming in from Senator Barry Goldwater, company heads, et cetera. Ed felt he should have known who the accusers were, have been more involved. The program had not been under his control; that made it hard for him to fight back."[71]

The voices of George Vicas and Irv Gitlin were drowned out in the clamor, while Murrow's statement that he had only narrated was pounced on by Pegler and Sokolsky as an effective admission that he was merely a performer after all.

In a further twist, New York Police Department officials beat a path to Murrow's door about the allegations that more than 3,000 call girls were going in for corporate entertainment in the city. Under TV lights, with flashbulbs popping, Police Commissioner Stephen P. Kennedy asked Murrow for names. Murrow, with the cameras closing in for his statement, replied politely that he didn't know and, if he did, would not disclose them. The Commissioner departed, making noises about a contempt citation.

"The CBS commentator," ran the wire story, "said he himself did not do the research but . . . that he has implicit trust in the persons who did. . . . He agrees with the policy set down by TV columnist Marie Torre, who recently spent ten days in jail for refusing to divulge a news source."[72]

Nothing more was heard of it, but for a few days reporters had fun speculating about Ed Murrow marched off to the Tombs in handcuffs. "Anyhow," one wrote him afterward, "I'm glad Commissioner Kennedy doesn't want to lock you up."[73]

The *Journal-American* put a reporter full time on his tail—a small, unrelenting presence who, denied an interview, parked herself on 17 and stayed there, determined on a statement. At one point, seeing him emerge from his office, headed in the direction of the stairs, she threw herself resolutely in his path. He stopped abruptly, looked down from his height with an odd sort of smile, and meekly asked her permission to go to the men's room.

Publicly he played it cool. ("I think to sue the NAM for $1.02," he wrote Joe Ream. "Would you be willing to act as my counsel?")[74] To a Pawling neighbor who had found the whole thing quite "distasteful. . . . Leave the sex business to the pulp magazines, Ed, and get back to the easy chair of *See It Now*," he answered, "No chair is 'easy' in this business, and, for my own part, I would not have it otherwise. Sorry if the program cost you . . . embarrassment . . . with your children. My own thirteen-year-old was inclined to agree with those critics who said I was dealing with an old story."[75]

But he had been left in the unenviable position of a broadcaster held to account for charges he could not personally substantiate, waiting for the corporation to own up to the show as CBS's, a creation of the network. After a full three weeks had gone by, Arthur Hull Hayes sent an explanation to the NAM, backed by CBS Radio, but nothing came from 20. Said Friendly later, "Ed felt very much alone and almost naked."[76]

"The last couple of weeks around here would have amused you," Murrow wrote a colleague that February.

> The National Association of Manufacturers uttered a classic blast, including an announcement of their belated support of McCarthy. The *Journal-American* headlined the sex show as a hoax, whereupon the Company assembled all its well-calloused consciences, debated for a full day about issuing a statement, and finally decided to keep silent. Big sponsors were moaning that I had destroyed their reputation in the community, and I have just informed Miss Campbell and Miss Hogg that the collective wisdom of this corporation is not capable of running even a moderately successful whorehouse.[77]

The friend, replying, said he was surprised at Murrow's comments on the whorehouse: "I thought that was what we had been doing all along."

"The Lost Class" was having repercussions of its own. Another friend reported on a barbershop encounter: An oil company salesman, known to him, plopped down in the next chair, exploding about the turmoil back at the office—"Boy, did Murrow fuck us up!" It seemed "The Lost Class" had mentioned his company's being segregated, and now blacks were picketing all over Virginia. "That bastard Murrow must have it in for us. I cover Newark . . . and we do a lot of business with the niggers there." But what had that to do with Virginia? "Are you kidding? If that picketing ever hits us here we stand to lose plenty. . . . Boy, Murrow hasn't heard the last of this!"[78]

For an establishment figure, he was making an awful lot of enemies' lists.

The newest flap notwithstanding, however, his overall position seemed rock-solid to the industry. "The King of the Schedule," *Variety* dubbed him—the right shows, the right people, the right timing; the best fare on TV. The 1959 *Radio Television Daily* poll showed him in first place as Commentator of the Year for both radio and TV.

Underneath, he was flailing, a newsman without a news job, caught in a downward spiral of frustration and eroding health, the one feeding on the other. The nightly radio news had become a burden, Swing saddled with more and more of the commentaries. "Anything fifteen minutes live every night is a strain," said Howard Smith later. Up from Washington, sitting in, he had found himself thinking of 1946 in London, Murrow creating that last broadcast to America—brisk, in full command, coming up with those perfect phrases that made one want to throw one's typewriter out the window. It was like watching two different men. "He was tired of it, felt ill-treated."[79]

His office door, heretofore always open, was now shut at given times of the day: doctor's orders. Kay Campbell's renovation—finally—of the littered corner office had left room for a leather couch, and he lay down on it faithfully every afternoon, eyes wide open. His aides looked at the shut door and worried. Ed Bliss remembered, in those months, a long, dreary drive to Maine in Murrow's Thunderbird, and a waiting honorary doctorate from Colby College, an ill-timed trip—endless rain, not enough highway, not enough markers. Murrow, silent even by his laconic standards, was feeling ill; Bliss, at the wheel, had lost his way, driving aimlessly and trying not to panic.

As though through a fog, he heard Murrow's voice: "Where are we?" Bliss, the gentle, earnest, minister's son, tried to wing it with a feeble crack, then froze as the voice turned Humphrey Bogart icy: "Don't—get—smart, Buster." It was the first and only time the father figure had ever used that tone on him.

Their hotel reached, the management, they found, had set a huge bouquet in Murrow's room (with a scaled-down model, accordingly, for his lieutenant), the scent filling the place. "The next morning," said Bliss, "I went to Murrow's room. He looked awful. He told me he hadn't slept more than an hour all night."[80]

Marietta Tree was jarred by his unprecedented bursts of anger at dinner parties—Murrow, always so "repressed," so cautious, so much the reasoned debater, unless, of course, one justified McCarthy. "I can remember his eyes," she recalled, "how black they were, the black fire that came out." She felt he was drinking more heavily and sensed despair—with himself, the world, their society, a conflict of the spirit—behind the anger.[81]

The Doctor, still treating Murrow then, remembered sudden phone calls at odd hours from the newsman's friends: Had he seen Ed? "Quite distraught," he remembered, "people from CBS, people he was working with—'We haven't heard from him, we don't know where he spent the night.' They couldn't find him. When they did, they'd never find out where he'd been. He was away for twenty-four, thirty-six hours. This happened several times."[82]

Then, early in the year, Ed Bliss saw something that made his stomach tighten.

It was mid-evening, almost 7:45, the offices mostly emptied, only the newsroom and studios active. Murrow, script in hand, had gone down the corridor to Studio 9, visible through a glass panel facing the hallway, and sat down to read. Ten years after Murrow's death, Bliss would record what happened next:

"It was three or four minutes before the radio broadcast. . . . His face was unusually pale. He held the script with both hands, which rested on the table; still the script trembled."

Through the glass, the young news writer saw Murrow say something to announcer George Bryan, then suddenly rise and cross the corridor to the cubicle where Blair Clark was preparing *The World Tonight*. "Blair, can you read for me?" he asked.

> It was an emergency. Only seconds remained before Murrow was due on the air. Clark took Murrow's script and went into the studio. Bryan read the amended introduction: "And now, substituting for Edward R. Murrow, here is Blair Clark." I looked to see how Murrow was. He was walking, a bowed figure, toward his office. Some green filing cabinets, holding old scripts, stood against the wall outside. . . . There he stopped. I did not realize until then that he was crying. He folded his arms over the top of one of the cabinets and put his head down on them. He was sobbing like a child.[83]

February 11, 1959, he requested a leave of absence.

The letter, addressed to Stanton and beginning "Dear Frank," simply called the company's attention to a contractual clause permitting a year's sabbatical, applied for herewith, effective July 1. The tone was friendly, casual, no mention of recent events: "any reporter or analyst should take a year off somewhere around the age of fifty. . . . I am fifty and that is what I should like to do."[84]

He proposed to travel, filming *Small World* en route, maybe do some reporting, returning to full-time duty on July 1, 1960, and signed the letter "As ever yours." Stanton, replying, was "happy" to grant his request; Ed's suggestions were "completely satisfactory and much appreciated"; they all looked forward to his return and hoped his sabbatical would be the rewarding experience he so well deserved, signed "Warm personal regards."

The exchange of letters, released to the press in an evident attempt to defuse the controversy, only revived it, fueling speculation about whether Murrow's sabbatical was, in fact, an ouster. The newsman, in countless interviews, denied management problems, said he had an increasing feeling of being spread too thin, of working from memory, of too little firsthand knowledge of people and places. A first-class diagnosis, in fact, of where things were at, the decision strictly his, to cut the Gordian knot, take himself out of the running.

The announcement caught almost everyone by surprise, The Doctor included. Skeptical columnists ascribed the move to Murrow's losing out in what was widely interpreted as a power struggle. "The likelihood is that the winner of the battle was CBS," wrote Janet Kern in the Chicago *American*. "For fundamentally the battle was not really between Murrow and the President of CBS but between the era of autonomous, news broadcast personalities and corporate news-gathering and reporting departments."[85]

In any case, it called forth a flood tide of communications, including those from McCarthy diehards ("Your turn has come") and from a single Shirer fan from 1947, voicing satisfaction at the turn of events. Logging buddies asked him back to Clallam County, old Emergency Committee scholars offered campus retreats, Puerto Rico Governor Luis Muñoz Marín offered a guest cottage and renewed thanks for *See It Now*'s "The Puerto Ricans": TV had suffered "a great loss. . .and so have the people who . . . benefit from independent social-minded programs. . . ."[86]

"Does an old admirer have to tell you what an enduring ally you have been all these tough years?" wrote Roger Baldwin of the ACLU.[87] Walter Lippmann had heard the news "without surprise," as he wrote Murrow: "First class creative work like yours cannot be done as an endless routine. It demands time to lie fallow and become renewed. So I congratulate you and rejoice over you."[88]

Groucho Marx, on the other hand, protested: "You may or may not know what a severe loss your voice will be to liberty, democracy, the American flag and prostitution on radio. Anybody that's worth a damn is going to miss you. . . .

"I can't send you my love because I understand you're not a female. However, if you should happen to journey through Denmark on your travels, and get fixed, we would certainly have a common meeting ground."[89]

Editorials blossomed in tribute around the country. I. F. Stone feared the worst, as did McCarthy's Wisconsin nemesis, William Evjue. Altogether, Murrow told Thomas Finletter, so many kind things were being said "that I feel as though I had been reading my own obituary."[90]

Herblock was in touch; so was Joe Alsop. Julian Huxley wanted an essay for a humanities symposium, E. P. Dutton, a book-length enlargement of the Chicago speech (Murrow did promise to keep it in mind). The *Saturday Review* offered him his own page; he protested in reply at being "elevated far beyond my stature. Please forgive the delay in answering . . . but it takes a little while to get over the shock."[91]

Jack Gould wished him godspeed in the Sunday *Times*; *Time* magazine was betting he wouldn't be back; Westbrook Pegler kept up a steady brimstone-larded drumbeat. ("I really don't know what Pegler will do for copy during my year off," said Murrow, the public reaction significantly raising his spirits and his energies.)

And the reaction at CBS? asked a well-wisher at Armed Forces Network.

"So far as I can tell," he replied, "my departure on July 1 has left the corporation eye entirely dry."[92]

In fact, to all appearances the corporate eye was fairly red by now, the latest flap impacting with dismaying force on a company already reeling under a hailstorm of adverse publicity.

Mickelson, first excluded from discussions on the sabbatical, then sworn to secrecy, felt the Division had been caught with its pants down when the story broke. He had never, he told Stanton, been so concerned about the PR of CBS News. Here they had just about pulled back into position following NBC's inroads among the eggheads when bam! the *See It Now* cancellation story, that Chicago speech, the Murrow election assignment story, "The Business of Sex," and now this sabbatical story. Obviously someone on the inside was fanning the flames, the impression making the rounds that CBS News was leaderless, that its only spark came from Murrow, that it was run by committee, and that without Murrow there was nothing. No one was writing about their many news specials, or *Where We Stand*, or *The Twentieth Century*, or all their straight newscasts, none of which had anything to do with Murrow.

He called for an upgrading of CBS News to bona fide divisional status, with the title of president for its leading officer (and if not, why, he was ready to step down), wondered how much longer CBS wanted Friendly on the payroll, and hoped the company would somehow get back to stability before the damage done by the sniping became irreparable.[93]

But CBS itself was helping to fan the flames.

The Stanton letter had gone out on Monday, February 16, the story breaking amid in-house confusion, with John Day kept in the dark by orders from above until 5:30 in the afternoon. As everything fell apart, Mickelson had called Kidder Meade, the vice-president who was Paley's right hand for corporate PR, suggesting that he step into the situation.[94]

In the meantime, Murrow had agreed to an interview with Daniel Schorr about the sabbatical, plus another with Harry Reasoner for the Douglas Edwards program: an interview before the cameras, taken on with misgivings, and filmed for playback Tuesday night. Reasoner, a former newspaperman in his mid-thirties and onetime writer for WCCO, a three-year veteran of the CBS newsroom, hired by Mickelson, his former journalism teacher, had offered to disclose his line of questioning. Murrow declined.

The edited clip run that night followed at first the familiar pattern, the stock questions and answers relating to the sabbatical—i.e., everything was fine, he just wanted a year off, disagreements were the norm in this business, relations with management had "nothing whatever" to do with his leave request, and yes, he'd be back.

Then Reasoner went off on another tack: He, Murrow, had been critical of television, called for more prime-time airing of controversial subjects. Why, then, didn't his prime-time Friday night show do just that, schedule people who could shed light on these matters, instead of sports and entertainment figures?

Murrow clearly hadn't been expecting it. Did he, Reasoner, think all their guests had been in sports and entertainment?

Reasoner thought it "fair" to say that yes, either they were, or in most cases didn't go in for discussing the critical issues Murrow had been talking about.

Murrow agreed: Yes, that was true, to a considerable extent.

The other man persisted: Why, then, hadn't the show been used for the kind of programming which he thought was so important?

Murrow looked his interlocutor in the eye: Partly because it wasn't set up for that kind of program, and secondly, because it was done in the home—"and when you go into someone's home, at least *I* was brought up to believe that you do not start by asking a penetrating and embarrassing question."[95]

Word traveled fast. Reasoner came home that night to a furious call from a CBS colleague: Had he been ordered to put those questions to Murrow? The newsman's protestations that he hadn't brought on the accusation of an apparent sellout.[96]

Next day, the columnists were reading the tea leaves, wondering in print about the CBS correspondent who had "roughed up" Murrow on the air. Zousmer and Aaron prepared a breakdown on the *Person to Person* guest list for Murrow's files—224 in show biz, 26 sports figures, 231 with no connection to the entertainment world—just in case the issue came up again, they said.

There was also a "Dear Ed" memo from Harry Reasoner, telling of the phone call and disclaiming ill intent. The questions, he "assumed," had been intended to elicit a reply to those who wanted nothing more than to see a rift between him and CBS. He hated to see the organization, for which Ed had done so much, divided into "cabalistic groups," preferred believing Ed was "completely ingenuous" in his comments about disagreements being natural in this kind of setup. But in case the caller represented a large number of people or Murrow felt the questions were unfair, he wanted to restate his "assumption" and thanked him again for cooperating on something about which he admittedly had doubts.[97]

Two days later Murrow answered with a "Dear Harry" memo: Anybody agreeing to sit before a camera for a freewheeling interview "must expect to take what comes.

"I was mildly surprised by your line of questioning, but sure as hell do not question your motives, harbor no resentment, have complained to no-one and was due no explanation from you. I hope that, in future, you will have more promising and responsive material with which to work."[98]

At the same time he got off a cryptic one-liner to John Day: "I trust the Reasoner interview was satisfactory?"

That February, a special five-man committee, including Kidder Meade and Dick Salant, right-hand men to Paley and Stanton respectively, met in closed session to outline a massive PR campaign among the general public and opinion makers. The aims were to restore CBS's battered image and, most of all, to make friends among the so-called special publics whose goodwill was essential to the company's growth and survival— figures in government and the major parties; the critics; the intellectual community; the print communicators. A campaign to counteract, as the committee put it—to overcome, if possible—the impression that the CBS management didn't care enough about any of its responsibilities, other than that of making a profit.[99]

The resultant proposals, drawn up in a sweeping seventy-one-page document marked "Confidential," ran the gamut from broad statements of philosophy to programming suggestions to talk of seminars wooing the academic world, on the model of the rehabilitation of Standard Oil—once the object of contempt among the eggheads but now at the point, the report noted, where the oil giant's "strongest non-business friends" were in the academic community. *Public relations*, the report underlined for its high-level readers, *was everybody's business.*

CBS—let's face it—had a public opinion problem, said the committee, understandable in view of public "confusion" about TV or advertising, but never mind: Unfavorable impressions could no longer be ignored. CBS had to bite the bullet, take the leadership in reexamining the sources of trouble in its customs and practices, take a new, hard look at itself, its policies, its philosophy, its behavior. The PR campaign could succeed only if "based on sound, substantive policy and program content." (Ten months later, the first name on the special committee roster—the listing went alphabetically—James T. Aubrey, Jr., was to preside as network head over a virtual doubling of CBS profits and a lowest-common-denominator program schedule epitomized by *The Beverly Hillbillies*.)

The committee now proposed a sustained year-in, year-out effort of programs, seminars, publications, general fence mending, with a projected PR budget of about $992,000 to reduce "the number and effect of ill-informed or distorted criticisms of television," to convince the public that CBS, while a profit-oriented operation, was concerned not just with the bottom line but with the commonweal.

"Not the least of the misunderstanding," however, was focused right inside their own shop, the committee noted, the ideas formed by many critics about CBS based in part on conversations with, or statements or speeches by, their newsmen (as well as some producers and directors). "Unquestionably," the attitudes, public and private, of these "groups of CBS personnel" were at the root of some of the difficulties the company had been having. The committee proposed, therefore, internal seminars to talk things out, defuse dissension, the "antagonisms," explain the problems of the business to the staff.

They also recommended a weekly half-hour on TV itself, explaining CBS Television to the public. A program which would not avoid the hard questions once the public made it clear it wanted answers—for example, What happened to *See It Now*? Or, Is Mr. Murrow really taking a sabbatical because he's tired?

Central to the report, however, was the proposal involving the News Division, "one of CBS's most valuable public relations assets," an asset which could accordingly be "capitalized on" by instituting a regularly scheduled "news special" presented midweek in prime time beginning once a month. The idea was quickly taken up and quietly discussed in those same weeks in which Murrow had applied for, and quickly received, his leave of absence.

"A flagship program," they called it, providing "a continuing all-purpose and highly visibly showcase for CBS News Correspondents," designed to prove CBS meant what it said about the importance of electronic journalism. Such a program, noted the report, would be "powerful ammunition" against criticism that the serious uses of TV were being shunted into second-class time slots, that the Sunday afternoon "ghetto" was presumed "evidence" that TV schedules were at the mercy of commercial considerations.

They were virtually paraphrasing Murrow's pointed language in Chicago.

To be sure, the committee concluded, the network had pre-empted more than twelve programs in 1958—fifteen, in fact—to present prime-time news specials. Such broadcasts not being part of the regular schedule, however, "exploitation measures" had been "only partially effective"; indeed, there was "little awareness" of their number even at CBS. It was a tacit admission that the sporadic specials, however meritorious, had been no substitute for the demised Murrow program, that to restore prestige, the network was forced now into what was called "a new form of news program," but was actually *See It Now* resuscitated, under new management.

May 6, Frank Stanton, addressing the Ohio State University Institute of Radio and Television at his alma mater in Columbus, officially announced the bold new series, in a speech widely hailed for its vision, outlining the scheduling, starting that fall, of regular hourlong broadcasts once a month in prime time; then biweekly; then once a week; the network "determined," he said, "to press the medium to its fullest development."

Friendly, rereading the text in later years, was deeply moved, thinking of Murrow, saddened that he and Stanton couldn't get together. The phrases sounded so much alike, "Stanton's plan" so much the resurrection of *See It Now*. . . .

It was a dream assignment, with airtime tight and a stableful of producers champing at the bit. Actually, said Mickelson later, the idea had been knocking about for some time in the News Division, both the Day unit and the Gitlin unit turning out the long-form takeouts—everyone loathed the word *documentaries*—and darn good ones at that. "I had been proposing to Frank Stanton that we formalize the whole thing, produce on a fairly regular basis, alternating between the two. Finally Stanton called me in one day and said he had an idea about somebody who might buy it, what would it cost to do it, and I gave him the price, and he said, 'What could you do with half of that?' I said, 'Provided the Television Network would accept it, we'd do very well.'

"He said, 'All right, go on down to Philadelphia Monday morning, to the Sheraton Hotel, and sell it to Chuck Percy of Bell and Howell,' which I did."[100]

It was mid-April. By the time Stanton made his announcement at Ohio State, the deal was long since confirmed: six programs, underwritten by Bell & Howell, the other six finally picked up by B. F. Goodrich.

Murrow and Friendly considered themselves out of the running. In April they had besieged Mickelson and Cowan with proposals, from the population explosion to "Iran: Brittle Ally" to the U.S. economic domination of Canada to Northern and Southern Rhodesia ("7 million blacks to ¼ million whites . . . perched on the edge of violence") to Washington, D.C. ("larger in population than 18 states, but where no one votes . . . the ghetto on the Potomac"), to the biography of a missile from blueprint to launch pad.[101]

They could do the programs on low budgets, they pleaded, maybe $35,000 to $45,000 per, turn them out between now and September. "We could fill any time that was made available," Murrow told *Newsweek*.

Out of some eleven topics, one—the missile story—got the go-ahead, the Iran project conditionally approved. For the rest they drew a blank. As for "The Population Explosion," sorry, it had already gone to the news department for production within the new six-hour nighttime series.[102]

By late May, in spite of Stanton's announcement, the outlook was chilly. Murrow himself, in a flash trip to London, had filmed a one-hour piece with Field Marshal Montgomery. They had permission to proceed with Cape Canaveral. Otherwise, the old *See It Now* team, but for the *Small World* nucleus, was slowly drifting apart, dying of attrition. "I share your hope," Murrow wrote to Marty Barnett, at the point of departure after a failed appeal to Gitlin for employment, "that someday . . . we may be able to pick up where we left off, and go on."[103]

Then, in mid-June, Fred Friendly, up from Cape Canaveral and Hunts-ville, Alabama, was called into Mickelson's office and offered the job of executive producer for the entire nighttime series. Bringing up Murrow's participation, he was told there would be "problems."[104]

A "compromise candidacy" was how Mickelson later described the offer, his own suggestion to get around dividing authority between the contending Gitlin-Day forces. But it was also more than eight weeks since the Bell & Howell deal, six since Ohio, not much movement in sight. And here they were—mid-June, a superhyped series on the books for the fall and nothing happening—or not enough. In the background, ed-itorials such as the Washington *Post*'s, lamented that nothing yet had "filled the void left by *See It Now*."[105]

As Stanton told the story, Gitlin, originally tapped for the job, wasn't providing the spark, nothing very exciting turning up in the planning: "I didn't see enough action. [And] my neck was out because there were a lot of people saying that this was just a sort of a gesture that the network was making. . . .

"I was dissatisfied, as was Sig, with the lack of progress; and sometime during the summer, I got Sig and I think Lou Cowan, maybe Dick Salant, I'm not sure, and a couple of others up to my office and said, 'We're not making enough progress. And I want to consider moving it away from where it is, to Fred and to Ed.' "[106]

The man recalling those weeks, in 1981, would be twenty-two years older, not the presider over a commercial network called to account by the public and press, but a retired icon of broadcast journalism. A man honored in his time as the buffer, through the Vietnam years and Wa-tergate, between the News Division and successive administrations, who had personally faced down threatened congressional contempt citations, sat on the outtakes of "The Selling of the Pentagon," and dared a bellicose House committee chairman and a hostile attorney general to do their worst. A man proud of the chair in the First Amendment endowed in his name by CBS at Harvard, an official who was to leave CBS with the loyalty and gratitude of the News Division, who without denying "real differences," was to see Murrow as a brother-in-arms and who couldn't imagine in retrospect why what became *CBS Reports* couldn't have been offered to both Murrow and Friendly as the logical choices once the first choice had been, so to speak, disqualified.

"There was only one way I could move—because Ed and Fred had built up, in *See It Now*, a strong unit, and that was to bring them in and turn the thing over to *them*. And that's what happened. . . . And because Ed was leaving for sabbatical, and the team was not going to be working the way they had worked up to that point, it seemed to me that Fred was free."

Said Stanton, it was a matter of some eight to ten programs, no more— "no one knew where the series was gonna go after that"—and Murrow, after all, was leaving; there was no way for him to be a coproducer. But they had talked it over, the offer made right in his office, with Ed sitting there; he, Stanton, had asked Mickelson to write up a memo of understanding, the question specifically raised "about Ed's participation. And to the extent that Ed was going to be available, sure he was the *guy*.

"I was asking Fred to bail us out. We hadn't gotten what we wanted, and I wanted to see the programs get into the series and into the schedule as soon as possible. So that this wasn't an offer as much as it was, Here's a challenge and we're in trouble and, you know, help us."[107]

Indeed, it was the last thing Friendly had expected, the summons to Mickelson's office at first setting him to hunting for his contract, for a last glum look to find out when the next option date was up: October 1960.

His instincts, in fact, were sounder than he knew. Back in February Mickelson had asked Stanton, How much longer did they want to keep Fred on the staff? A brilliant producer, but did not his divisiveness outweigh the advantages? His contract, by the way, was up October 1960. A note appeared shortly thereafter, opposite the query: "Okay after *Small World*."[108]

Contrary to later assumptions, therefore, it was Murrow who was still being retained, Friendly, his outlet to TV, on the point of being canned—i.e., keep Moses; fire Aaron.

Instead, in instant role reversal, Friendly had gone from virtual *persona non grata* to the point at which he had the News Division by the short hairs. They needed his drive; he didn't have to do it permanently, they assured him, just get it started. Then if he wanted, the job was his for good: the series, the budget, the call on every news producer, every production unit in the place; the full resources of CBS News, with the ultimate dazzling prospect of fifty-two shows a year—and, of course, the immediate renegotiation of his contract pending his decision to go forward.[109] (At the same time Mickelson, with Stanton's approval, was quietly laying long-range plans, including the development of young Av Westin from John Day's unit as "permanent producer" for the series in the coming years.)[110]

And Ed? Going away, after all, hardly part of the full picture for the foreseeable months. Hard to tell what his work load would be in 1960, said Mickelson; presumably he'd still have *Small World*, could work as reporter or narrator on its share of the prime-time series, whatever that might be—"if he so desired." The top producer's job, however, was another matter, and it was Friendly, not Murrow-Friendly, whom the company wanted to see in place.[111]

In fact, said Mickelson years later, he had gone into negotiations "assuming" that Stanton—and he had, he said, a lot of evidence to back it—did not want Murrow to participate.

"There was a long-standing animosity between the two, from the time

I got there. I felt the two were incompatible . . . that any time the Murrow name came forward, that Stanton was going to fight it. And I just didn't believe that he was going to permit it to happen.

"I think, too, that what Stanton wanted was an all-CBS type of production. And if Murrow were a producer, it would *not* be. . . ."[112]

Friendly, shocked, knocked off dead center, had essentially no answer. Think about it, Mickelson told him.

The producer spent the weekend on a detailed memo, not at all reluctant to take up the "enormous challenge," but coming down to the essential question, Where did this leave Murrow? And, by derivation, Friendly? What would happen next year, the big one, with the twenty-six programs and Ed returning? What, in fact, did CBS expect of Murrow and Friendly, then and in the years ahead, both as a team and as individuals, and what about their people?[113]

The haggling began, Murrow suddenly aware of what he had done by opting to remove himself back in the time when everything seemed at a standstill, the series still a boardroom secret, his bid for a sabbatical so readily accepted. The "celerity" for which he had publicly thanked Paley and Stanton was now setting a deadline for his departure from the scene.

He had been busy in the past weeks, with both the missile story and tying up loose ends: filming in Huntsville and Cape Canaveral; tidying the final radio broadcasts and blasting the latest adverse decision on the Worthy passport case; enlisting Scotty Reston's help in starting up an annual lecture series in memory of Elmer Davis; exploring job openings for Raymond Swing; lining up *Small Worlds*; writing Han Suyin of his "overwhelming appetite to spend some time in China,"[114] to get a camera team inside and would she mention Rangoon 1956 to Zhou Enlai, remind him of his invitation and say he was both eager and willing?

He had lunched with Paley in March and Stanton in May, all apparently forgiven, Stanton obtaining Murrow's promise to show him the copy, in advance, of his final sign-off on *Person to Person* and the evening news.

At the Waldorf, he had emceed the testimonial dinner for the educator Harold Taylor, a graceful and witty toastmaster, introducing Robert Oppenheimer, Archibald MacLeish, and Mrs. Roosevelt before an audience of kindred spirits that included Agnes De Mille, Roger Wilkins, Alexander Meiklejohn, a last hurrah of fifties liberalism.

He was addressing Casey's graduating class at Buckley and handling snags on *Person to Person*, Arthur Godfrey having dropped out as replacement (Collingwood took over). He was fending off phone calls, interview bids, offers to set up contacts on his travels, taking invitations from a chosen few, running faster to keep in place, his constant refrain "If I can keep upright on this treadmill until July . . ."

Now suddenly, with the abruptness of a rug retracted from underfoot, everything had changed. His leave was timed to start officially July 1, two weeks away, the boat sailing for Sweden in August, the start of a projected one-year absence. Instead of preparing for the long vacation, that time for reflection and recharging of batteries, he found himself involved in protracted negotiations over his future, locked into a departure date with the clock ticking away as he bargained for a toehold, some measure of input, to keep the parade from passing him by, a fifty-year-old company man with no place to go.

Mickelson, a meticulous keeper of records, would record everything in detailed file memos—a confidential diary and, as it turned out, running account of the day-to-day negotiations; the evolving relations, in that watershed period, between Murrow and Friendly, and CBS.

Friendly had asked for "a long-range plan" into which they could be integrated, their responsibility within CBS defined—not so much for 1959–60 but from 1960 onward. Regardless of who was executive producer, he argued, Murrow could then carry much of the load, as could their unit, an "essential ingredient" which had stood the test of time. Certainly these issues should be "explored and charted for the future," and it was in this sense *only* that he spoke for his senior colleague as well as himself and they both were prepared to assist in any way.[115]

It was to Friendly alone, however, that Mickelson turned in reply: Yes, he assumed Fred would be working with Murrow on the contributions of the *Small World* unit, certainly their old unit could be *a* component but not *the* component, and no, the series could not be a Murrow-Friendly property. Murrow could be "one of the reporters," and would he be satisfied with an advance commitment of, say, one-third of the total?

But that was only four programs out of twelve, Friendly protested; Murrow was a star, a drawing card for viewers and advertisers, essential to the series' success! And what about Murrow himself—would he be asked back for the year-end show, would he continue with the evening news on radio, how about *Person to Person* or arrangements to utilize his services in the course of his sabbatical? Wasn't it time somebody talked to him, gave him some assurances?

Should not Murrow, asked Mickelson, rather come to them?[116]

Earlier, reading Friendly's memo, he had sensed the producer's using the offer as a "platform" to bargain for a new "status" for the Murrow-Friendly team, seeking possibly more freedom.[117]

Now he was getting the distinct feeling, he noted for his private file, that Friendly was trying to use the negotiations as a bargaining chip to "re-establish a position for Murrow."[118]

Obviously, Fred's future status was no problem, once he understood what was expected of him. Murrow's future, by contrast, was "something quite different," dependent on next year's schedule, whatever that might be.

Certainly they could be integrated as requested, the CBS News head noted—provided they were willing, but also provided that it was not "essential" that they be integrated as a team.[119]

The following Monday, Murrow flew to Cape Canaveral. He returned briefly late in the week, to close out *Person to Person* and the evening news, arriving in a hot and overcast New York, thunderheads rolling in for an oppressive weekend of rain, fog, and drizzle.

That Thursday, he met for ninety minutes, one on one, with Mickelson, the first time—a day before his departure from the air—that anyone from the management had sat down to discuss his future.

It was a rushed day, a final commentary turned out for the evening news: his own, not Raymond Swing's, blasting State for denying Justice William O. Douglas the right to go to China. The promised valedictory for Friday night had gone upstairs to Stanton as agreed ("I haven't been fired, haven't quit, my health is all right. . . ."), smoothing things over. Warm handwritten notes had passed back and forth between the two men. Stanton had won; Murrow was negotiating for a toehold, tired of fighting and glad of a respite. So, possibly, was CBS.

In Mickelson's office, as the rain began outside, Murrow and the news chief started talking, skirting around the central issue, Murrow a constrained advocate on his behalf. "He let Friendly carry the ball; Friendly was the aggressive pleader of the Murrow cause. It was part of Ed's personality. I don't think he ever pushed himself forward; I think it was done more skillfully than that. I think if Ed wanted to do something, he had a more effective method of getting it done. And in this case he had Friendly to do it for him."

Friendly, said Mickelson, had hitched his wagon to a star. "I think he felt that Murrow was an important part of it and that he, Friendly, needed Murrow to make the thing work. And in this sense he was right because Murrow was the biggest star of the period."[120]

Except the biggest star had no leverage but for his influence, in a dramatic role reversal, on the one who had it. "He felt humiliated," said Friendly later. "Imagine the position he's in where his junior partner—me—is arguing with his peers. He didn't say anything; he didn't have to; you just *knew*."[121]

Accordingly, that Thursday, Murrow discussed the number of programs he might "appear in," possibly the eight or nine discussed, more likely six. He worried about *Small World*; should Friendly take on the bigger assignment? Wouldn't it be too much for him? Mickelson suggested an assistant executive producer to help out.

They discussed details for post-July 1960: Murrow wanted no more nightly radio news. Mickelson suggested a weekly roundup with the correspondents; Murrow liked it. They took up the next year's conventions, Murrow's feelings against the quick news specials and narrator-only jobs à la The Business of Sex. They covered everything, it seemed, except the big question: Would Murrow coproduce, the number one issue at a time when control was passing—thanks in part, ironically, to *See It Now*—from the correspondent to the producer. It wasn't Murrow's participation that was at stake now; it was his role, Murrow himself too proud, or simply unable, to urge his case.

The question of the year-end show came up. Mickelson sensed the other man's eagerness to be asked back to moderate. Mickelson had no intention of doing so. Would Murrow be available, he asked instead, to take part in the program in case he toured an area that might "justify" his inclusion?

Murrow said he would, given enough warning. Did this mean, he asked, that they were ruling out his appearance as emcee?

Mickelson simply repeated what he had said.

On one point only was there a flash of the old determination—just in case, said Murrow, Fred took the assignment and their unit came in on it: They wanted access to the top. They wanted, once a topic was duly cleared, the freedom to go ahead and produce in their own way. They didn't want "a freer hand than anyone else," he argued, but they needed that access to the people making the decisions.

And argue those decisions with the editorial board, thought Mickelson.

He made the policy decisions, he told Murrow; he might consult with "experts within the Company" on certain questions, be guided by their opinions, but ultimately the decisions were his. He foresaw, of course, no problem in getting go-aheads for "product," in which case "supervision" would be limited as before. If the Murrow-Friendly team were willing to cooperate, they could no doubt establish a satisfactory working relationship—provided they understood that he, Mickelson, must be the final judge on policy.

Not sure they'd arrived at an understanding, the news chief confided to the file, "But at least Murrow dropped the subject."[122]

However, it was also clear by now that Friendly would make no commitment—Murrow had said so right out—without a three-way meeting. A date was therefore set for a week from Thursday, when the two men would be back again from Huntsville.

July 2, hot, gusty winds lashed the tarmac at Idlewild Airport as inside the terminal Murrow and Friendly, returned from filming, sat over lunch with Mickelson, pleading with CBS not to break up the partnership: They realized *See It Now* was dead; they had no hope of reviving it. But together they had something to contribute, were more effective as a team, they argued, than as individuals. Titles and credits were immaterial. If the company was afraid specifically of perpetuating Murrow-Friendly, they'd work in the background, but they would work only as a team.

Mickelson, impressed, realized just how much they wanted to proceed, was convinced of the genuineness of their enthusiasm—Friendly perhaps more committed emotionally, but Murrow, too, caught up. No doubt they wanted the vindication of the team, thought the executive, but more important, they obviously wanted to get on with the project simply because of its importance, its challenge.

Over the table, they laid down a plan of operation involving all the CBS News production units, Murrow and Friendly as executive coproducers dealing jointly, they said, with basic subject, treatment, and policy decisions, the execution to be left to the different units, including their own, its share to be decided by a Murrow-Mickelson-Friendly committee. The plan excluded no one and gave the reporter an equal voice (with Murrow, no doubt, preponderant) in overall production, for which precedent existed not only in the old *See It Now* but in the News Division.

They did need that access to the top, they said, but were sure it could be worked out to everyone's satisfaction. A successful series, Murrow argued, was bound to deal with topics causing "squeamishness" within the company. It was better to get procedures set ahead of time, avoid the situations of the past. Mickelson, not all that convinced, didn't press the point, noting simply for the record the two basic conditions set down "very firmly" by the partners, contingent to their proceeding with the series—consultation with the decision makers and executive production to be in the hands of the team of Murrow and Friendly.

A single sour note broke into the discussion. Mickelson, recalled Friendly, had asked him initially to think about using Howard Smith as "reporter." The program was, after all, a showcase, so conceived by the parent confidential CBS committee: revolving talents, not just one news star. Such at least was the argument originally put forward to Murrow and Friendly.

Now, over lunch, Mickelson sprang the news that the Bell & Howell order letter specified Howard Smith.

Murrow, down from the clouds, drew his head up sharply. What could Smith possibly do?

Mickelson hastened to add that the order letter hadn't been as yet accepted, no arrangements made with Smith. But it seemed there was now "a feeling among everyone concerned" that there be only one "continuing personality" for the entire series.[123]

But otherwise, the mood was upbeat. The talks were defined by Mickelson, back in his office, as "amicable and enthusiastic," the Murrow-Friendly stipulations notwithstanding, conditions for a working triumvirate largely met. The CBS News chief seemed almost won over; and for once, for whatever reason, the usual up-front objections to the team concept, to Murrow as coequal, had not been raised.

Records are silent about the long weekend that followed, with no further feedback to Murrow or Friendly, separately or together. Every move, of course, had been discussed upstairs, the CBS President kept abreast on each step, with Paley "in the background," as Mickelson later put it— never conferring with him directly but known on 20, he said, to be "even more opposed" to Murrow's becoming coproducer. ("Quite disillusioned with him," said the news chief, "after that speech in Chicago.")

Stanton, by contrast, had shown unexpected moderation from what had seemed a hard-line position. "I had felt he was not going to subscribe to

Murrow being involved in any way," said Mickelson, "[and] I was surprised every time he made an additional concession."[124] But they were coming from different directions.

Friday, July 3, came and went. Monday came and went. On Tuesday Friendly met alone with Mickelson.

The timing had been bad for their session with Murrow, he began. They should have acted before the Huntsville trip. Murrow, he thought, would have been quite agreeable to his, Friendly's, going ahead with the project. Now he had had time to think about it and had evidently decided—so Mickelson gathered, listening to the producer—to "project himself into the pattern." Friendly was sure, however, that a satisfactory arrangement could still be worked out and that Murrow's wish to project himself into it was a good deal less "substantial" than it had seemed last week.

He had three suggestions, therefore, points to be solved before they could arrive at a working arrangement:

First, he wanted a meeting with Stanton on overall policy and objectives.

Secondly, he would want access, as executive producer, to the top decision-making personnel—and attendance at meetings dealing with broadcast policy.

Finally, he agreed to be executive producer for the non-Murrow-Friendly programs. Of course he wanted still to consult "frequently" with Murrow on the entire schedule. It was in the interests of getting the best possible programs, making "maximum use" of Murrow's considerable resources. He could not function without this contact.

He wanted it understood, he said further, that Mickelson, Murrow, and Friendly would meet often to discuss the direction of the series, the topics, possible approaches, and "other problems in conjunction with the production."

Mickelson immediately offered to set up a meeting with Stanton—very soon, he was reasonably sure. As for access, no problem; the precedent existed. In fact, he would encourage it on major questions, but there was to be no abuse of the privilege and no end runs, understood?

As for the Murrow partnership, it was back to square one. The executive producer offer was to Fred Friendly. Period. Mickelson realized, of course, that their "contribution" would be jointly produced, had no objection to Friendly's consulting with Murrow or to meeting with them both, informally and frequently as requested. In fact, for those summit meetings on policy, if their joint productions were involved, joint discussions necessary, why, Murrow would certainly "go along with Fred."[125]

At one o'clock the following afternoon, at Friendly's request, Mickelson went over what he had said, this time in Murrow's presence. A meeting had been arranged with Stanton for 10:00 P.M.

For Murrow's benefit, Mickelson stated once and for all that the executive producer offer was to Friendly, not Murrow-Friendly. He agreed, however, to those frequent meetings, promised they would be held; was not only "willing," he said, to accept Murrow's counsel for Fred and himself but would encourage such counsel. All other points were similarly restated.

As he spoke, he felt an unease in the room. Friendly seemed a lot less firm about the willingness to go it alone now that he was in Murrow's presence. Possibly he was still eager to start, just didn't want to show it in front of the other man. He had hinted as much to Mickelson a few times.

More disturbing, however, was Murrow's statement that he couldn't do eight or nine shows a year and still do *Small World*. Did he think his duties would expand when they moved to the longer schedule?

Then there was Fred, seemingly doing a flip-flop, saying you couldn't separate the Murrow-Friendly shows from the rest of the series, meaning presumably that their influence would have to be pronounced throughout. If that meant Murrow's regarding himself, and Friendly's regarding him, as "an anonymous producer," they might have some problems.[126]

Concessions or no concessions, the line had been drawn. Said Mickelson later: "I still felt that Stanton was going to oppose it."[127]

But Stanton seemed quite flexible that night as all four men met in his office for discussions that ran well after midnight, the CBS President, in Mickelson's view and despite all expectations, actually leaving a back door open for Murrow. Even Friendly, as they concluded the long session— everyone weary, Mickelson worrying about the trains back to Greens Farms, Connecticut—had felt encouraged.

Indeed, the draft summary drawn up after the meeting seemed to hold out the beckoning promise of Murrow's sabbatical becoming a springboard for his increased role in the twenty-six-program season coinciding with his return.

The agreement contained, among other clauses, the points covered earlier with Mickelson—access to the top, the promise of eight to ten programs for the Murrow-Friendly unit in the second year, the "frequent" informal consultations with Murrow across the board. Mickelson even specified Murrow and Friendly as a "consultative group" to confer with on program plans for the entire series.

But they had specified further, definitely leaving the back door—to some extent, even the front door—well ajar: Murrow, it was agreed, would be "encouraged," during his travels, to begin preliminary planning on next year's programs, 1960–61. Specific reference was made to "the production team of Murrow-Friendly and their related support units," and to Murrow's proposal of a possible third production, this year, if circumstances permitted, by the Murrow-Friendly team in addition to the two on the boards.

Further, decisions on the next season would be deferred to May 1960, when it was to be decided if Friendly would stay on as executive producer, but in the meantime, they agreed, the Murrow-Friendly team could make plans and even start production on the *Small World* unit's share of the 1960–61 schedule.

Murrow, in concluding, said that he would do whatever the company wanted, that he preferred, however, a weekly radio news program to the five a week, and that his work on the new series would preclude continuing with *Person to Person*, that he wished to "abandon" the show.[128]

It took a week to type up the minutes. The final draft approved for release emerged after nine days, the product of successive rewrites and virtually another document; like most *aides-mémoire*, wrote Friendly in later years, "noteworthy for what it did not contain."[129]

Gone was the agreement encouraging Murrow's preliminary planning on his sabbatical; deleted, the go-ahead for the Murrow-Friendly long-range planning and production, the head start on the schedule for 1960–61, the references to the proposed third program, all specific mention of the Murrow-Friendly team.

Friendly's continuation, it stated still, would be decided in May 1960, until which, went the addition inserted by Friendly himself, he would "serve as Executive Producer, making whatever editorial and production decisions are required to put the project on a permanent basis with continuity for future seasons."[130]

July 20, CBS News announced the appointment of Fred W. Friendly as Executive Producer of *CBS Reports*—"the most important programming project ever undertaken by CBS News," according to Sig Mickelson, CBS Vice-President and General Manager, citing "the plan announced recently by Dr. Frank Stanton, President of the Columbia Broadcasting System." Mr. Friendly, said the chief executive of CBS News, would supervise the various production units in his new capacity. Fred Friendly, he commented, had made major contributions to TV with such distinguished programming as *See It Now* and *Small World*. In his new assignment, he would find a broader scope than ever for his creativity, energy, and skill.[131]

It went out as usual from Information Services, CBS News Division, a copy per routine left in Murrow's hopper.

In private, a grim, uncomfortable Friendly faced an uncomfortable Howard Smith, who hadn't asked for the assignment. "You're going to do some of these," Smith would recall him saying. "Murrow is not doing them all. But I want you to know: I will *not*—be—a party—to the downgrading of Edward R. Murrow!"

Smith assured him he wouldn't be part of it either. "He thought that was what they were trying to do—by bringing me and the others in. And *they* felt they were downgrading Murrow. I think he felt so, too."[132]

The star stable he had built up, and protected in the bad times, was now precisely the reason he could be replaced.

August 26 was a scorcher, the mercury almost at ninety, a sweltering, humid glow beating down on the confusion of the transatlantic docks on New York's West Side, a madhouse of departure: The *Gripsholm*, Swedish-America Line, sailing for Göteborg. In the crush was Murrow, with wife and child in tow—the start of their trip around the world and the tail end of an ungodly rush in those last days that had included a quick flight to Bellingham to see his mother, then a half week in New York filming links for *Small World*: a constant assignment on his travels, plus filming taken on for the Iran program. And China, he hoped. And anything he could get his hands on.

Edward and Mary Warburg had seen them just before departure. To Mary he seemed like someone abandoned—"a very disappointed man.

"He was disappointed with Friendly; he hadn't been a good friend. I think he thought he had let him down, that Paley had let him down—[though] he never *said* anything about Bill Paley—he had too much pride.

"There was just this tremendous disappointment—he could have been used in so many directions. I think he must have wondered where he was going. . . ."[133]

XV

"... To Love the News"

If *CBS Reports* could be said to have had a social center, it was the screening room on Ninth Avenue—the place where everyone gathered, exchanged gossip, and watched incoming rushes while the producers sweated as the rough copy flashed across the screen.

They were a competitive bunch, the pick of the lot—self-enclosed, as one of them later put it, self-protective, with a little of the corps feeling of the old *See It Now.* Usually, therefore, there was an undertow of apprehension when new film came in and Friendly asked to see what you'd done, with everybody sitting in.

But the stuff from Florida on the migrants was good. They knew it from the first frames on, and every editor in the place wanted a crack at it; especially John Schultz, a slight, quiet-spoken newcomer, the son of an itinerant logger and field worker, who'd picked potatoes in his childhood back in eastern Washington and knew the real article when he saw it.

"What do you think?" It was Friendly talking to him; which was funny because he didn't usually ask opinions on rough copy.

"I like it. I did migrant work in Washington State—"

"Washington State? Ed's from Washington State. Hey, Ed, come over here!"

It was April 1960, and Murrow was back from sabbatical.

Schultz had seen him in the screening room by Friendly's side, watching the screen, unsmiling, uncommunicative beyond the low, laconic comments murmured now and then to Friendly; a gaunt, sunburned figure with a tight cough: diffident in manner, self-effacing, almost, it seemed to the young editor, apologetic.

John Schultz, revved up for the past weeks by the general excitement—

"Ed" was coming back—expecting he didn't know what, felt let down. *This* was Edward R. Murrow?[1]

From the start, things had gone wrong with the sabbatical: the late arrival in Sweden, the truncated tour, speeding the 300-odd miles to Stockholm in the Thunderbird brought with them, and foregoing Janet's longed-for look at the region where her grandparents had lived; the overall rush to make official welcomes, meetings, military reviews for the distinguished guests—all the things they'd promised themselves to avoid. Even so, they enjoyed the beauty of the Swedish capital.

The plan had been to go from there to London, where Murrow was to deliver a talk on TV and politics, first dropping off Casey for a short term at a Swiss *pensionnat*—the condition of the thirteen-year-old's acceptance at the prestigious Milton Academy, and makeup for the year of missed school—then picking him up in December. Instead, it was Janet who bundled Casey off to the mountaintop at Villars while Ed, in a last-minute change of schedule, flew to Teheran to interview the Shah for the Iran show.

It was an unlucky trip. Murrow wasn't well, troubled by stomach spasms that had beset him since his last stay in Cairo. McClure, now producing for *CBS Reports*, joined him in Teheran with a camera team. Later McClure recalled what happened: "It was at the palace outside of town—a huge, monumental structure. We had the interview scheduled for the next day, Murrow thought he'd go along with us when we set up the cameras in the ballroom. Well, we spent about two hours getting the gear in because they had to go through all the boxes. There was enormous security around the Shah; he'd sent all of his best sort of FBI types to the States, and they'd studied under the White House Secret Service, so they sort of tried to be more correct and more investigative than the average Iranian officer."

The equipment cleared at last, the crew went about setting up lights, positioning cameras, stringing cables. His Serene Majesty and guests were playing cards in the garden house. It had begun raining. McClure and crew were halfway finished when "suddenly everybody started scurrying around—you know, a bustling, a feeling, and you get a little bit nervous."

Next thing they knew, the security men, well-muscled types in business suits, were ordering them out. The Shah, it seemed, wanted drier quarters for his card game, and they were therefore to vacate—at once.

I said, "Well, all right, though I don't know why the Shah would want the ballroom; he has lots of apartments." They said no, they wanted the *ballroom* to play cards in. Murrow said, "We aren't finished," but they kept insisting we had to leave. Murrow said, "I won't leave—that's all! My men are not finished." He was very parental, as you know, towards the people that worked for him; that's why he was so popular with all of us. But they just said, "You *have* to go."

It was getting nowhere; they could hardly stay on their own authority, McClure told Murrow. They turned to go and were stopped instantly. Oh no, they'd have to take all their equipment, too.

By now the rain had turned to a downpour. Murrow hit the ceiling. "He started arguing, objected so much that they nearly picked him up— I wouldn't say exactly *picking* him up, but they got two men on either side, and he was ushered, without very much ceremony, down the steps and out of the palace. He said he wasn't about to be in the rain without his car, so they *forced* him to walk, about five hundred yards—at least the length of a football field—to our car, so that he got terribly wet."

The Americans drove back to town, drenched to the skin, their streaming clothes plastered against them, Murrow silent and miserable, his once-crisp Savile Row suit a sodden, shapeless bag, making rivulets on the floor of the rented auto. "He lost a lot of his usual savoir faire. . . .

"And so he was virtually thrown out of the palace—a man who was a friend of Churchill and who had, by this time, been in the company of practically every great of the twentieth century. [And] the Shah had him— just tossed out."

Next day's encounter with the Shah was polite; Murrow never mentioned the incident. Said McClure, "He did a superb interview, was able to ask tough questions without being nasty; I think that was one of his great skills."[2]

Still, a coolness, to the point of stiffness, came across on the screen.

In early October, worn out and trailing a heavy cold, he arrived in London. The womb. Where everything was as it should be: old friends, the waiting suite at the Connaught, Janet back from Switzerland, Kay Campbell in from New York. There was an invitation to Chartwell from Sir Winston and Lady Churchill; the ritual meeting at the club with R. T. Clark; a lunch appointment with Hugh Carleton Greene, Director of News and Current Affairs for the BBC, soon to take over as Director-General. Pat Smithers from the wartime newsroom was now head of television news; Michael Balkwill, his top assistant.

BBC Television had planned for Murrow to open the series *After the Battle*, featuring correspondents who had covered the war, looking back over the years since 1945.

He also gave a talk over the Home Service, and began filming *Small Worlds*: one with Jack Kennedy, Bob Boothby, and Krishna Menon, another with Jackie Gleason, the critic John Mason Brown, and the poet Brendan Behan—the last-named arriving before the cameras gloriously inebriated, roaring his way through a brilliant, wild performance.

For Murrow, however, the main event was the talk to be delivered October 19 at the Guildhall (the part that had survived the blitz), the second in the inaugural season of the prestigious lecture series cosponsored by Granada TV and the British Association for the Advancement of Science. The invitation had come at the prompting of Murrow's old friend Sidney Bernstein, who recalled: "We had a number of Americans through the years. Ed was one of the early ones. We tried to make it easier for him to come over, pay him fees and and so on, because he had no *big* money, wasn't a wealthy man despite the things that he had done."[3]

It was a nostalgic occasion. In the great Gothic hall, the statues of Gog and Magog looking down, Murrow spoke in opening of "the wounded walls of this venerable building" and the city "where this reporter left all of his youth and much of his heart."

The theme was television and politics; the gathering, distinguished. It was just twenty-two years less one month since he had stepped before the audience at Chatham House on the eve of World War II, a twenty-nine-year-old just beginning his career.

He still had hope, but fewer illusions.

"Television by itself," he told his audience, "does not usher in the democratic millennium, and its inability to do so is not its own peculiar fault. It is due to the unwillingness of men and women . . . to take more trouble to govern themselves better."

Public affairs, he said, was a form of specialization, not recreation, and the public, he said, wanted its fun. "By the time most people turn on the television set the work of the day is over. There is a welcome break in drudgery. Most people, after working hours, prefer to be called away from reality, not made to face it. . . ."

And while TV and politics, combined, might yet produce a more informed electorate, he saw potential danger in the mix:

> The politician in my country seeks votes, affection and respect, in that order. . . . Most of them are men of undoubted charm, ability and incredible energy, and yet too often they lack purpose or appetite for anything beyond their own careers. With few notable exceptions, they are simply men who want to be loved. . . . But when it comes to television, the politician is severely handicapped. He is trained in the art of inexactitude. His words tend to be blunt or rounded, because if they have a cutting edge they may later return to wound him. . . . [He] must choose between talking at length and precisely, and probably boring [his] audience; or talking briefly and misleading the audience. . . .

He worried about "the editing of informational film for television," about politicians being "unduly fascinated" by the mechanics of TV, "a little too inclined to make political television a competition between film cutters and producers, rather than a competition of ideas and convictions.

"There is, I suggest, no substitute for the man who has at least a mild fire in his belly, and is able to pierce that screen with his own conviction."

Television, he felt, could yet serve as a marketplace for the competition of ideas, but the instrument was no wiser than those who watched it:

"The voter may elect to purchase the second-rate, shopworn or shoddy idea. . . . He may vote for Profile rather than for Principle. An unruly lock of hair may be more effective than a disciplined mind. There is no way to guarantee that television will prevent [him] from being as wrong as he has been so often in the past. Television offers no guarantees that demagogues can be kept from political power. It merely provides them with wider and more intimate, more immediate circulation. . . ."

He doubted that Lincoln or Jefferson could have been either nominated or elected given TV:

> Jefferson had a most abrasive voice and did not suffer fools gladly. . . . He might have told a particularly obnoxious [interviewer] just what he thought of him, and that, of course, would have been fatal. Mr. Lincoln did not move gracefully, was not a handsome man, had a wife who was not a political asset, and . . . was a solitary man.
>
> In our present society, he probably would have been examined at an early age by a psychiatrist, received an unfavorable report . . . and advised to enter a trade school if he could gain admittance.

Above all, Murrow feared TV's ability "to magnify the components of personality," defects as well as merits, weaknesses brought to light, "which is all to the good. But that is not all that happens, because a public leader in the age of television must be popular as well as sincere . . . A politician to be popular must not be too complicated. . . . [must] not appear to be too subtle. He must be accessible, must be able to avoid the difficult question without appearing to do so."

He spoke of McCarthy, Nixon's Checkers Speech, Ike versus Adlai, and living in the age in which intelligence perhaps couldn't simplify truthfully:

> The frontiers of knowledge have been pushed back, and the more that comes to be known, the less is understood . . . . The art of self-government is not going to be perfected by the process of simplification alone. Indeed, looking ahead to the time when human destinies are to be determined by the uses or abuses of new sources of almost unlimited physical power, one may well ask if democracy will be able to develop the competence to deal with these complexities. If so, it must be through a broadening of education and a use of communications not yet realized, or perhaps even conceived.

It was a year since Chicago, and he was still in there pitching, calling TV "a tool. . .not being used to finish the job of education. . . ."

> Both radio and television started as novelties. . . . They cost a great deal of money to develop. The pioneers in what Americans call "the industry" were businessmen and financiers, not scholars, statesmen or politicians. They still do not put public service first, for the simple reason that in my country it must pay its way. Business success has to come first. . . .

But now our societies must take on a new and more conscious development and television must rise to a more constructive task. We must rid ourselves of our allergy to unpleasant and disturbing information.

Returning to his images of 1937, he called it the duty of the politician "to see to it that the controls imposed on television do not prevent it from being a medium where ideas may compete for the allegiance of the viewer. And it is the duty of those who control television to use it as a sound mirror to reflect conditions as they are. If what is reflected on the end of that tube is bigotry, poverty, discrimination or prejudice, that is good and wholesome so long as the picture be true. . . ."

Television must find a little time to remind us of our inheritance, and it must find more than a little time for the dissenters, the heretics, the minority spokesmen who may be tomorrow's majority. . . . Politicians, whoever they are, should not be permitted to control television. Let them use it; let them be as persuasive as they may be. *But do not permit them to use this instrument to prevent today's minority from becoming tomorrow's majority.*

In closing, he called for a regular transatlantic exchange of views, the TV parliament he had tried to sell CBS on:

We need to argue more. . . . when you are reluctant to have American intermediate range missiles on British soil, or are somewhat less than enthusiastic about American bombers flying about over your heads with a bellyful of nuclear weapons, let's argue about that. . . . Controversy makes good television. . . . and we might just possibly learn something. The right to disagree, indeed to revile each other . . . is one of the many things that makes us different from totalitarian states. . . . If this alliance of ours flinches or falters—it will be because we have failed to communicate with each other. . . .

The audience response was warm, as expected, superlatives making the rounds over champagne at reception time: Never had Murrow been more eloquent. Then a quick drive north to Euston Station and the late-night train to Manchester, where Murrow was to film the address for Granada TV, plus another *Small World*, Manchester facilities having been put at his disposal. It was there, the next day, that developments 3,000 miles away engulfed him without warning, the capstone to a week of peaking controversy in New York.

Variety had called it TV's sorriest hour—the quiz show boil erupting in a welter of grand jury findings of perjury and a Manhattan DA's announcement of the exposure of "a national fraud." In Washington, a House subcommittee, fresh from probing the coziness between broadcasters and the FCC, had started in on a parade of witnesses—contestants, producers—testifying to deliberate rigging, coaching, payoffs, and widespread patterns of deceit.

Overnight idols were toppling, the eggheads revealed as actors pursuing easy bucks, and no doubt perjurers to boot. The nice young college instructor from *Twenty-one*, who had won the nation's heart, a hundred thou', and an NBC job, who had told the DA he had not been coached and assured *Today* Show audiences that not to believe in the honesty of the quiz shows was somehow not to believe in the American Way, had been subpoenaed by the Harris subcommittee. Then disappeared. Then just as suddenly resurfaced on Monday, October 12, promising to tell all in Washington. The hearings, now recessed, were to resume November 2, as the press ran down any lead it could.

A judge had allowed the subcommittee access to the closed grand jury minutes. In the meantime, the dam was breaking on *The $64,000 Question* amid surfacing admissions of fixing, the Harris panel announcing its intention to take up the now-defunct CBS show and its clone, *The $64,000 Challenge*.

On Friday, October 16, Frank Stanton, addressing the RTNDA in New Orleans, announced the cancellation by CBS of its three remaining big-money quizzes. "Whoever" might produce the programs, he said, in a clear reference to the independent producers who had presumably led everyone down the primrose path, "whoever" might be to blame in the whole "tawdry business," it was now hurting all of broadcasting. Regardless of this "who," it was now "crystal-clear" that the American people held the networks responsible for what appeared on their schedules. They had failed in their duty, should—given the benefit of hindsight—have been more critical, faced up to the "broader implications" of programs based on human greed, and there would be no more of this. No policing, he said, could "plug up the possibilities for hanky-panky."

He promised, too, "a fresh, hard look" at everything appearing over CBS, an assurance to the American public that what they saw would be "exactly what it purports to be."[4]

The speech, a front-page item in that Saturday's New York *Times*, had gone over with a leaden thump as regulatory fever rose in Washington over the weekend. The *Times* story virtually dismissed the announcement as made "to forestall regulatory action," noted officials as "skeptical" about the CBS move and efforts at self-policing, the implication, that of policing looming from the top. An Illinois Democrat on the subcommittee was calling on Congress to "plug up loopholes, regardless," to probe tie-ins between "contestants, networks, producers, and advertisers,"[5] and to question big winners, "particularly on *The $64,000 Question*."

More worrisome, however, was the threatened turning of the friendlies on the FCC and the Federal Trade Commission—now under fire for not being better watchdogs—in the face of congressional clamor for the licensing of not just the stations, but the networks themselves. A form of more direct control, traditionally opposed by broadcasters and their congressional allies: a front that now showed signs of crumbling.

By Sunday, October 18, FCC Chairman John Doerfer—close to the industry, CBS's good friend on the commission, the houseguest of Murrow himself in better days—announced that he had "modified his former opposition to licensing the networks," and was now ready, however reluctantly, to consider such a move.[6]

What happened next, would become a matter of considerable controversy.

"Following my talk in New Orleans," says Stanton today, "it was a luncheon address—I received a call from Jack Gould. About what I had said. Jack had received the copy of my text before I went to New Orleans. It was *he* who asked me whether the rules that I had announced publicly would apply to news and public affairs, the answer being 'yes.' Did they apply to entertainment programs across the board? 'Yes.' And did they apply to *Person to Person*?

"*My* recollection is that Jack asked the question and I said yes. A wholly understandable thing from Jack's point of view, and certainly *I* was, you know, quoting the—the New Testament, in my answer."[7]

The "moral problem," Stanton had assured his caller, was "far broader than just the quizzes." CBS was going to houseclean down the line, the start of "a policy to curb real or possible falsifications" jeopardizing TV's "integrity," and in earnest of its intentions Stanton cited *Person to Person*, on which guests, he said, knew the questions in advance.

He cited, too, a bit of froth called *The Big Party; The UN in Action*, a minor Sunday morning show; and the overall practice—without naming names—of canned laughter and applause.[8]

"We were trying to make sure," Stanton said later, "that nothing had seeped into the news and public affairs areas that came out of the bad practices of some of the entertainment productions. There was at that time an incident—not on CBS but on another network—where in a Nixon trip to Germany as Vice President, the producer or someone in the organization had dubbed in some applause. . . .This. . .on CBS would have violated our policy about things [having] to be what they *purported* to be."[9]

Jack Gould for his part would recall a phone call on Monday afternoon from Kidder Meade—a familiar voice, courtly, soft-spoken, with the information that Stanton was ready to amplify on the speech made in New Orleans: the one written up two days before on the weekend with not a little skepticism—the implication now, that there was more to be heard.

Gould knew the CBS man not only as a company spokesman, but from a brief, unhappy stint of his own on 20, working for Stanton in a corporate PR capacity, before fleeing back to the arms of Turner Catledge. (Said *The New York Times* man later, "I knew Meade very well; he succeeded to the job which I quit.")

The advance text, said Gould, had given him "the first hint that Stanton was thinking of news and interviews in addition to canned laughter. Kidder encouraged me along those lines and had Stanton's phone number right at hand." It was an exchange in Texas.

"So I got on the phone and got Stanton. And that's when he said that he included, in his general cleanup sweep, the Murrow show, because it used rehearsed questions. And he wanted to clean up TV entirely so there'd be no question about *any* program. And we printed the story on page one. And it raised a hell of a stink."[10]

The story went out Tuesday morning, October 20, under a two-column head: C.B.S. REVISES TV POLICY TO END PROGRAM "DECEITS," in which production practices on *Person to Person* were listed under the "deceits" to be "weeded out of the schedule of the Columbia Broadcasting System."[11]

Gould didn't think much about it at the time. His high esteem for Murrow the journalist was a matter of record, his low opinion of the Friday night show likewise a matter of record, and well, there were times when Ed would have to take his lumps like all the rest. At least it seemed so that week in October.

"I could see Stanton's point then because the pressure was pretty great and he wanted to really tidy up his place. It was unfortunate that he had to include Murrow. But *Person to Person was* rehearsed; it was not spontaneous." Admittedly, though, few could conceive the ponderous machinery of *Person to Person* house tours, in those antediluvian days, as anything suggesting spontaneity. "It wasn't a serious show. You could tell, as you kept on listening, that obviously it was rehearsed and Murrow was following the questions. Sometimes Ed would get a provocative answer and then not follow through on it. I think from that standpoint I could see how Stanton was upset about it. He didn't like Murrow. They never got along.

"I remember calling him about, oh, I don't know, three or four o'clock in the afternoon, my time. And Frank was conveniently waiting in his bedroom. I mean, I imagine Frank wanted to get it out. And he knew we were pretty hot on this whole quiz show. . . ."

The exact details, said Gould, would turn fuzzy with the passage of twenty-five years, but then—"Kidder Meade wouldn't have called me on a blind goose chase. I mean, he couldn't have tipped me off that Stanton was panting down in New Orleans, or Texas, with all that he could talk . . . I don't think that out of a clear blue sky I would have thought to drag in Murrow and *Person to Person*. Because that was pretty far removed from the quiz scandal. . . . Somehow I had reason to ask Frank that. And then I got the 'yes' and we were off to the races.

"Stanton is probably technically correct when he says I did the asking, but he was obviously prepared for such a question. He went into the details without any pushing. You can be sure there were hours of preparatory discussion in New York before Stanton took the plunge in Texas."

"A peripheral matter" was how the *Times* man put it, in the context of those weeks, "and Murrow got swept up in the claw Stanton was putting out. . . . I mean, CBS took it a hell of a lot more seriously than we did at the *Times*. I mean, it was just a good story and that was *it*. It wasn't any, you know, exposé of Ed or anything. . . ."

In retrospect, however, he termed it "unfortunate that Ed should have become tarred by the quiz scandal, and it's easy to understand his indignation."[12]

Unfortunately, there were no indications that anyone had gone to Murrow or, failing that, Zousmer and Aaron, before the story went to press. Murrow himself had learned of it that Tuesday afternoon in Manchester, caught between astounded fury and shocked disbelief as his office read him the article over the transatlantic phone.

Returned to London, he held off a flood of queries, his crowded schedule leaving no time to think. Instead, he waited for a sign of life from CBS management, with whom he'd parted on such cordial terms, reflecting with grim irony on the call to reform from the official who had once called the quiz shows "in the public interest" because they interested the public; and the sudden posture of the 20 group. "After all, they put Mr. Cowan, who thought up *The $64,000 Question*, in his position as President of CBS TV!!" Janet Murrow wrote home. "Isn't it a crazy world?"[13]

In New York, Zousmer and Aaron, in a stormy session with Stanton, demanded a retraction of the "slur." No slur intended, replied the CBS President in a stiffly worded letter; he had merely asked that they inform the viewing public of the production practices on *Person to Person* so that the program could be "exactly what it purports to be."[14] A carbon went to Murrow, his only communiqué thus far from 20. By Friday the producers had resigned.

The show had never been *intended* as a "spot news interview," they told Jack Gould in a daze, just reflected the way people lived, general interests. How could a run-through for live TV, going over topics to be covered in the twelve to thirteen minutes involve "unethical practices"? No viewer could be so *naïve* as to think that all that TV equipment could be just planted in somebody's home without planning. Sure the show was prepared—it had to be—but how did you go about calling that deceit, linking it publicly with the quiz frauds?[15]

It was true, of course, that the questions were largely camera cues, gone over in the run-through ("Now he'll ask you this. . . . Then you'll show him your gold records . . ."), then expanded when they went on live, the results quite unpredictable.

In the meantime, industry insiders smiled over Stanton's upright insistence that guests be either denied advance questions ("Is that a golf trophy you have there?") or notice given that the program was "rehearsed." Chuckles were making the rounds in the news department over the proposed new guidelines in news, Stanton talking not of the pitfalls of Teleprompters, setups, tricky editing, or questions filmed after answers, but that the dinky little Sunday morning show didn't mention that UN diplomats cleared questions in advance.

Meanwhile, Murrow, pursued by the press in London said "No comment" and waited for a phone call.

"It shouldn't have happened that way," said Stanton later, pleading the heat of important events, of people central to them assuming that other people were "doing what they should be doing. I was trying to hold the ship together, and I—I certainly didn't call Ed." There were others, after all; Jack Benny was mad over the imputation about the laugh tracks, couldn't call him either. "Ed *did* have a short fuse in some areas. . . . But in the end, like most men of ability, he was reasonable and you could sit down and discuss it. [But] he was away at the time, so there was no opportunity. . . ."[16]

By the weekend, *Person to Person* was inextricably entangled in the quiz show story, now breaking in one great mess. Eisenhower, calling the scandals "a terrible thing to do to the American people," asked Attorney General William Rogers to look into the matter. The FTC was getting into the act, huge disclaimer ads run by quiz show sponsors, two big money winners admitting they had lied to the grand jury, and Manhattan DA Frank Hogan talking perjury indictment. It was a day-to-day front-page serial as the media and public revved up for November 2, invariably including a paragraph or two on *Person to Person* as Zousmer and Aaron implored Murrow from New York—for God's sake, clear our names.

At the Connaught, Ed and Janet Murrow, finally alone, considered what to do.

"I sat still for three days," Murrow later wrote to Seward. "The telephones rang night and day, particularly with calls, both local and transatlantic, from the newspapers and wire services. No one from CBS management even bothered to call me or send me a cable, I finally decided something had to be said. . . ."[17]

Saturday he came to Sidney Bernstein with a cable draft, addressed to the head of CBS News, for release to the press. "What do you think of this?"

Bernstein, who thought the pairing of *Person to Person* with the quiz shows absolutely ludicrous ("one was cheating; the other was taking the cameras into a house—entirely different story"), nonetheless advised against it. "If I were you, I'd cool it a bit, Ed."

Murrow bridled. "No! That's what I mean! If you can find better words, okay. But—that's it!"[18]

"They had touched him," commented another friend, "where no one dared touch him, and he was outraged—that Stanton had had the gall to smear him with the crap that he managed to get all over himself. It's a good thing there were three thousand miles between them."[19]

What the outcome would be, Janet Murrow wrote their family, no one knew. "But I am so glad that Ed has spoken out at last."[20]

Hours later in Burlington, Vermont, Sig Mickelson, on a busman's holiday, scrambled out of a duck blind with the local CBS station manager to find the shortwave radio in their parked car going crazy with messages from the station: Call Frank Stanton in New York.

Murrow's cable had come in, was evidently intercepted by Stanton, who had been in that Saturday, probably received a copy, and, judging by what he said on the phone, had taken "a good deal of action."[21]

Sunday morning, there was a new two-column CBS story on The New York *Times*'s front page: MURROW SAYS STANTON CRITICISM SHOWS IG-NORANCE OF TV METHOD.

Dr. Stanton, the text read, had "finally shown his ignorance" of both news and TV production.

He has discovered suddenly that not all diplomats at the United Nations will answer all . . . questions. He suggests that *Person to Person*, a program with which I was associated for six years, was not what it purports to be.

Surely Stanton must know that cameras, lights and microphones do not just wander around a home. Producers must know who is going where and when and for how long. . . . The alternative . . . would be chaos. I am sorry Dr. Stanton feels that I have participated in per-petrating a fraud upon the public. My conscience is clear. His seems to be bothering him.

More than a response, it was a long-delayed cry of pain, an eruption of the pent-up emotions of the past year.

CBS, by contrast, kept its cool—at least on the surface, getting in a statement before the story went to press, responding with a measured dignity that threw Murrow's fury into high relief: CBS hadn't the slightest objection to how *Person to Person* was produced; Dr. Stanton had tried to make that clear. Indeed, they were very proud of it. CBS just wanted the procedures revealed up front so that the program would be "exactly what it seems to be."[22] The story ended with an update on the quiz show scandals.

It was so logical, so reasonable. Even in the News Division, mostly on Murrow's side, there were some reservations: Wasn't Ed after all over-reacting, goaded possibly by Jesse and Johnny, being somewhat—*blunt* about it?

The day after, Murrow, still seething, wrote to Jim Seward, explaining his action: "I am sorry this whole thing arose, but I had nothing to do with it."

He was calling off a quick trip home to help out with a *CBS Reports*, he said, just in case a congressional committee decided to subpoena him. Not that he was reluctant about answering questions, but they might range beyond *Person to Person*, involving answers under oath which could further destroy the credibility of television. "This I want to avoid and I am sure the Company would feel likewise."

"If Stanton and co. choose to have a thorough-going public row, I am of course quite willing. But it seems to me the better part of wisdom to quietly disappear into the countryside. . . .

"The last three weeks here have been plain hell, and the last four days have not been pleasant. Had it not been for Miss Campbell's presence I probably would by now be teetering on the parapet of a bridge over the Thames!"[23]

That same afternoon in New York, Paley, Stanton, and Ralph Colin, outside counsel to the corporation, met in the chairman's office, the purpose: to discuss a *modus operandi* for procuring a retraction, or whatever might be necessary, from Murrow.[24]

Ruffled feelings aside, from the perspective of the company, about to don the hairshirt before the Harris subcommittee, the spectacle of one of their biggest stars going public with unfriendly comments couldn't have come at a more awkward time.

Said Colin, recalling the mood of the two top CBS officers: "I would say pissed-off was the word."[25]

Someone would have to fly to London. Not Frank, not with their history of differences; no way those two strong-minded men, said Colin later, could have worked it out. "It would have been a bad job." No, this called for a mediator.

Colin himself, fond of both Stanton and Murrow and a long-time friend to both men—it was he who in late 1945 had ferried Janet Murrow to the hospital when false labor pains had started up—volunteered to go, to be helpful if he could. "I said I didn't know whether I could *get* a retraction from Murrow, or *what* I could get from him; but I was willing to try to get oil on the waters."

It was agreed, quickly and quietly, nothing leaking belowstairs, Sig Mickelson informed only afterward (and delighted, as he said later, to be a bystander off in the distance): "This was tough corporate infighting at the very highest levels."[26]

Colin in the meantime caught the 9:00 P.M. flight to London. He arrived Tuesday morning and went straight to the Connaught, where Ed and Janet Murrow were waiting, alerted by an advance cable.

They breakfasted together, with Murrow, he would recall, "perfectly willing to talk to me, to see whether we could work something out—without abandoning his guns."

It was their twenty-fifth wedding anniversary, Murrow told him, and would he join them for lunch? Actually it was the day they had planned to "quietly disappear into the countryside."

Colin had had no idea. But he had a job to do, and Ed, he noticed, wasn't asking him to put it off.

Far from posing a "sign or resign" situation, Colin insisted later—"it had not reached that crucial stage"—the idea was simply to get out a joint statement if possible, "a public relations document . . . to get the public to feel that the fences had been mended and there was a united front." Accordingly, he says, he urged diplomacy, some softening of language, to resolve "a mess" in which he was not assigning blame.

Murrow, for his part, seemed as little inclined as CBS to prolong an open rift, ready to consider, said Colin, "whether we could reach a statement that would not make him look like a fool in having issued his first statement, but would still try to mollify the New York people, and issue something which would be helpful.

"We battled throughout the day—not battled—we juggled words. [We] scribbled and tried to first reach a concept and then put it down. . . . Murrow was willing to try; he was willing to elaborate. But as it turned out, he was unwilling to withdraw or apologize."[27]

Lunch arrived, complete with champagne; toasts were drunk, little jokes traded across the table, much good humor. Colin, light-headed with jet lag and lack of sleep, felt the bubbles rising to his head ("by this time I was gaga"). "This is a hell of a way to celebrate our anniversary," someone was saying. The three of them laughed; yes, a hell of a way to celebrate; cheers. In midafternoon Janet Murrow left, still smiling, for an appointment; outside the suite she struggled for composure.

The streetlamps were on—nearly 6:00 P.M.—by the time they hammered out a draft that seemed acceptable to Murrow; Colin had a feeling that it wasn't what they wanted in New York. Murrow didn't seem too pleased about it either, having gone further than he cared to:

> . . . no suggestion was intended that either Mr. Murrow or his associates had been lacking in integrity in the past production of Person to Person. Mr. Murrow's comments . . . were made in London without a full realization of the background facts and in the mistaken belief that his integrity and that of his colleagues as producers had been attacked. In those circumstances his remarks were, perhaps, unduly vitriolic. Mr. Murrow not only applauds and vigorously supports, but has previously advocated, the CBS basic policy of assuming responsibility for what appears on the network . . . and for seeing to it that in the future its programs will be exactly what they purport to be. Mr. Murrow will conform to that policy by continuing to produce his own programs in full accordance with the principles.
>
> Mr. Murrow, still on leave in London, authorized the comment that "If this policy is carried out—is generally supported by the industry, by sponsors and the public—television will become, as a result of CBS leadership, a more reliable and responsible medium."[28]

In New York it was 1:00 P.M. The lawyer placed a call and telephoned the one-and-a-half-page statement to 485. It was the best he could come up with, and likely to please no one, a fact sensed by both him and Murrow. "We both realized—because I started out aiming for something and he started out not willing to give it—that this was a compromise. And we didn't know whether it would meet the purpose they had in mind. But he was unwilling to go as far as I *hoped* he would go, and they weren't satisfied with what they got."[29]

Alone that evening, Colin called New York again. At 485, the CBS President and the Chairman were waiting, along with an officer of a leading public relations firm. ". . . *had another long talk with Paley, Stanton and Newsom*," Colin noted in his diary, "*in which they voiced their objections to the procedure*."[30]

"What *they* wanted in New York, really," Colin summed up later, "was a withdrawal or an apology. But the best I was able to get out of Ed was really an explanation. . . . They didn't feel it went far enough. I think Ed was just as happy not to have it used."[31]

Colin missed his plane and, collapsing in a servant's room at Claridge's, slept for twelve hours.

Returned to New York next day, the lawyer cabbed straight to 485 for a six-and-a-half-hour session with Paley, Stanton, and the PR man, trying, he later noted in his diary, "to revise method of handling Murrow's statement." Stanton, calling London, talked twice with Murrow as Colin and the others looked on. "Result inconclusive, matter held in abeyance pending Stanton's return from Pebble Beach."[32]

And there it remained. In fact, Murrow, putting down the phone in London in the early hours of the morning, wasn't sure whether or not he still had a job.

Colin, recollecting, could imagine no reason, carried away no "impression that there was ever a point at which it was said to Murrow, 'Do it or else.' "[33]

"If Ed had that feeling," said Stanton years later, "it was not reflected or matched by any feeling that *I* had. I don't believe—and I think I can say this with reasonable authority—I don't think it was matched by any feeling that *Bill* had. And the two of us were the critical members of the triangle. . . ."

It was a policy difference that exploded across the Atlantic. Ed wasn't here when the policy was established. Had he been here, who knows, maybe it would have been softened or maybe it would have been different—I doubt it. In *Person to Person* Ed walked into the home, by camera . . . there was no *way* that couldn't be prearranged. And all that I was suggesting was . . . that that point be made. Ed felt that it demeaned the program and his integrity, to insist on that kind of a disclaimer. It was a—it was an emotional difference. . . .

Look, we disagreed: there's no question *about it*. . . . but I don't recall having fired Ed Murrow. . . . There was never any doubt in my mind that he would come back.[34]

But it was the personality clash that had given this last controversy a particularly bitter edge, the climax of differences—the phrase was Colin's, based on twenty-four years' observation—"which had developed and were under the skin for a long time. This broke it out into the open." It was the terminus of the relationship begun over a lunch table in the fall of 1935, when the Director of Talks led the conversation and the number three man in market research was too shy to speak up.

"Ed and Frank never hit it off," said Colin. "I don't think there's any question that each had a regard for the other's abilities. . . . But it's one of those things where some people get along and some don't."[35]

It had been late evening in New York, still later in London. Both men were under pressure. Paley, ostensibly present, did not come to the phone. After that night of October 28–29, communications with 20 dried up altogether.

"The last word I had from him," Murrow wrote Seward, "was . . . when he said, 'We haven't been able to solve this matter and I must leave for the coast.' He had earlier indicated that the decision to fire me had been shelved. That was the last word I had from him."[36]

And so it would be, for the rest of his sabbatical.

Murrow wrote, just once, to Ralph Colin, about a possible declaration of his own, he said, on radio and TV practices, dealing with the dangers "inherent in increased government control"—to make a contribution regardless of his relationship with CBS.

Colin promptly advised against any more statements, more "open breaks" with the industry, or lending "aid and comfort" to the enemies of television.[37]

At 1:00 A.M. Thursday morning, the telephone began shrilling again. Ed and Janet Murrow packed up and headed for the Cotswolds, hiding out in the little villages until the weekend was over. "Chances are," Janet wrote home, "that nothing more will be done, except that CBS will keep feeding to the press the fact that it is terribly sad that Murrow spoke out against [them] just when everything was so tough. But that's life in a big corporation. They have a great deal of power. . . ."[37]

Mike Bessie, in London on business, on notice from Morris Ernst, found Murrow at the hotel, by himself, dejected. Ernst, also in town, had seen Murrow. The newsman asked about starting a libel suit; the lawyer advised him not to.[38]

Said Bessie later: "He was sort of holed up at the Connaught, sitting in the living room of that suite he had at the back."

Bessie's wife, Connie, was back in New York undergoing surgery, door to door with Lou Cowan, laid low and on his way out of CBS. He had been a friend to Murrow and the News Division, but his name was still associated with the quiz shows.

"Lou had been assassinated," said Bessie, "and my understanding was that they wanted something of Murrow that he was loath to do."

> He was sitting, drinking a certain amount, but then he always did, and of course smoking endlessly. He was very bitter. He felt that people besides him had been made scapegoats. I think he felt real separation from the top management, that little or nothing had happened that they were not aware of and that their attempt to unload this onto the operating and creative people was unjust and not admirable—he *disliked* the whole thing. Oh, he was cynical and skeptical by this time, but I think it was in part a defensive pose; idealistic people often put on a cynical front.
>
> He didn't know if he could work in this thing anymore—not because of the quiz scandals but because he felt it was increasingly in the hands of the entertainment and financial people. . . . He gave off very little of the sense of life and appetite that one hopes for; and I didn't have any of the sense, on his part, of either elation or comfort at being in London, which after all meant a lot to him. . . .[39]

In the meantime, Overseas Talks and Features, BBC, was after him to join a *London Forum* panel on the mass media, particularly television, appealing for assistance to another in-house friend of Murrow's, J. B. Clark, Director of External Broadcasting: Could he help them "land" Murrow? Clark, acting as go-between, reported Murrow perfectly ready to "do something"—on politics, though, not radio or television. "At the moment his conflict with CBS is front-page news and he doesn't know if they are still his employers or prospective re-employers."[40]

He had promised Murrow to call back, to let him know, as he put it, whether they had a proposition to make.

The BBC officials had already decided, however, in view of the matters Murrow would not discuss, that there wasn't anything he could do for them after all.[41]

The Murrows' London stay had eight days to go. There was nothing for it but to continue with their tour around the world—and find out, sometime or other, whether or not the leave was permanent.

In one of those ironies of timing, The New York *Times* of October 28 had hailed the Murrow-Friendly "Biography of a Missile," kicking off the first season of *CBS Reports*, as being "in the best traditions" of *See It Now*. The study of a ballistic missile from concept to launching, it was intended for telecasting—so the partners had announced at the outset— regardless of success or failure.

In fact, the launching was a failure. "The missile," ran the review, "plunged grotesquely to the ground in five and one-half seconds, a $5,000,000 casualty. . . . This was a realistic documentary that reflected great credit on the integrity of those who produced it. . . . Mr. Friendly, Mr. Murrow and their associates on 'CBS Reports' have started a new television series with distinction."[42]

The last week in November, Ed and Janet Murrow crossed to France with their Ford Thunderbird, beginning the long tour set up for them through Europe and the Middle East, India and Southeast Asia, Hong Kong and Japan, returning via Hawaii.

Back in Washington, in the climax of the Harris subcommittee hearings, a parade of witnesses was confessing to rigging and lying under oath, including an executive testifying that CBS had "backed away" from investigations of *The $64,000 Question* and its twin when suspicions had been raised a year before.

Stanton and Kintner, appearing for their networks, denied knowing anything before August 1958. Stanton, a convincing witness, had offered no alibis for "the mess," said he would scrap the remaining quizzes—on their way out in any case—and, steady in the face of stern questioning, vowed to clean up CBS's act. No doubt new formats were needed, he told the panel, but the problem wasn't willingness to put on different types of programs; it was finding them.

He denied that ratings invariably ruled the schedule, cited "Biography of a Missile" as example, and said the public could make its wishes known to the industry by means "as simple as a four-cent stamp and a letter."[43]

He was complimented on the program and commended for his forthrightness.

Meanwhile at Villars, high in the Alps, the Murrows picked up Casey—taller, thinner, his exams completed, with an acquired expert French pronunciation and the French-English patois of his expatriate classmates.

Once again, however, they were nearly late. Landing at Calais two weeks before, they had started on a long-planned auto tour of France—leisurely, their first time alone—driving westward through old cathedral towns, then south, not minding the November fog and rain obscuring the French countryside. At the Chartres Cathedral, an organist picked at a Bach chorale while they strolled around below, the only tourists. Hotels and restaurants were emptied, silent, all theirs, with meals for two laid before a roaring fire.[44]

Then on Thanksgiving evening, six days into their trip, they had called Casey in Villars, and Kay in London—only to find that New York had been frantically trying to reach Ed about the Iran program. It seemed Winston Burdett, narrator for the show, was being pulled to help cover Ike in Europe. The program was going on the air in three weeks. Could

Murrow get himself to their Geneva facility and complete the job—fast?

Their trip was ended. Murrow turned the car, and headed across central France, for Geneva.

"I wish Ed could have told them that he couldn't do the job either," Janet wrote from en route, "but he'd never let Fred Friendly down to that extent."[45]

Returned to Geneva after Villars, he faced more work, filming a *Small World* with Senator Mike Mansfield, Eisenhower speech writer Emmet Hughes, and the French journalist Jean-Jacques Servan-Schreiber. The assignments—filmed all along his route, an anchor in the uncertainty—cut nonetheless into what should have been a time of rest, the need for even more, unplanned, arising constantly, never enough segments in the bank.

In Zurich with McClure, he screened the Iran show: a disappointment. "Must try to write Fred a critique soon," he wrote Jim Seward.[46]

In countless letters home he claimed he was "completely relaxed," yet letter after letter attested to a growing mental turmoil as the unresolved controversy ate away at him, leaving him arguing with an adversary *in absentia*, a mental shadowboxing continuing around the world.

As if to match his mood, there was the cold, sleety weather of midwinter Europe, pursuing the Murrows through Switzerland and Italy. Driving south from Florence through the rain and snow, they blew a front tire; the Thunderbird, fortunately, held the road.

Janet struggled with bronchitis; Murrow's depressions had become more frequent and severe, the cough grown worse. He worried about money. Seward kept them up-to-date with packages of clippings ("they help us to keep in touch with the strange land of TV at home," said Murrow in a thank-you note.)[47] He read up on the sequence of events and drew his own conclusions. "They panicked over the quiz show business," he wrote his mother, "and thought to throw me to the lions. I wasn't standing still for that, and said so. . . .

"Over the years I have become what is known as a controversial individual. This means I must expect to be attacked, and when that happens, I must answer. Please don't let it bother you. It doesn't bother me at all."[48]

By contrast, he told Seward of feeling "rather like Clive in the House of Commons when he said to the Speaker, 'by God, Sir, in retrospect I am amazed at my restraint.' "[49]

He had still heard nothing, he wrote, in the inimitable two-finger typing that dispensed with capitals or punctuation: "agree with you that the next move is up to them, although i suspect that they are merely waiting to get Congress out of their hair before dealing with me . . i am still determined that if there is a break they must fire me . . after all they hired my services . . not my silence . . ."[50]

In St. Moritz, uncomfortable among the jet set (to Seward: "didn't care much for those high altitude parasites"),[51] he tried writing something on the future of TV—what was "wrong," what might be done, realistically— then threw it away, dissatisfied; "probably just as well."[52]

From Washington he heard from Raymond Swing, returned to the Voice of America and unhappy at his job: Could he come back to work for him? Murrow "cherished" the hope, adding that "my own status so far as CBS is concerned remains obscure, and that's all right with me."

Some opportunities, however, might come up by spring, he said, inside and outside the existing framework. As for the present agitation, he saw nothing coming of it. Barring "a real reversal of attitude" by sponsors and networks, he wrote, "the only thing people like us can do is to attempt to destroy the system or at least create an alternative."[53]

But however much he tried to get his thoughts on paper, they wouldn't come. And as always, the underlying turmoil notwithstanding, his demeanor still presented to the world a surface smoothed, unruffled, willed to be picture-perfect. Years later Janet Murrow, with a sense of wonder unabated after all their time together, remembered arrivals at hotels after long, hard hours on the road, Ed emerging from the car immaculate, crisp, not a hair out of place, she and Casey bundling out after him, weary and bedraggled, bringing up the rear like servants, in the wake of the splendid creature.

Rome the Eternal greeted them with thunderstorms and sleet. The leave just wasn't working out, Murrow wrote Seward in mid-January: "i can neither sleep nor relax . . the complete exhaustion is worse now than when we left. . . . this strictly between us. . . . have heard nothing from powers that be at cbs and am well content. . . . take care of yourself . . . dont work too hard . . or take anything too seriously. it can become a habit. . . ."[54]

It wasn't really a vacation either. He filmed four *Small Worlds* in Rome, following up on the filming in Milan and St. Moritz. Over the cue channel he talked with Mickelson about the weekly half-hour radio correspondents' roundup discussed before his departure, to be done, presumably, on his return. "i see it as a real backgrounder," he wrote Seward, "something that is not now heard on radio or television. . . . assume he had checked this with you but now am not certain. . . ."[55]

In fact, nothing seemed quite certain, the discussion evidently failing to lay to rest the question of his overall status or convey any word from higher quarters on the matters left in abeyance the night of October 28, before Stanton left for Pebble Beach.

Mickelson, not knowing, he said, of Colin's mission and its aftermath, had made the assumption that they were going on despite "these interludes."[56] But Casey Murrow, out with the *Small World* crews, enjoying himself tremendously, later recalled a certain tension at the edges in that time in Rome, a bustle of activity connected somehow with New York, the corporation—his father talked constantly of how good it was to be away—and with problems never brought up in his presence, though vaguely indicated in his mother's letters to him at school.

But developments at 485 had been moving forward steadily in Murrow's absence, beginning weeks before his blowup with Frank Stanton.

Murrow had in fact barely landed in Sweden when in New York, Friendly came to Robert Lang, Mickelson's administrative deputy, unhappy at that day's publicity release naming Howard Smith the "key figure"—as indeed, he was—for *CBS Reports*. Lang, however, passed on the word to Mickelson that it was in the long run, "swallowed and accepted."[57]

Then, one day in late November over lunch, Friendly informed Mickelson that he thought *Small World* had run its course. It was taking too much of the unit's time away from *CBS Reports*; the staff might lose interest, moreover, in doing a good job of it. They were, of course, under contract for the season, but might it not be possible, he asked, to transfer the sponsor over to *CBS Reports*?

He brought up again the *Mid-Atlantic Parliament* idea, suggested a test run; Ed had after all mentioned it in his speech in London. It was the predecessor, really, of *Small World*—indeed, the *Small World* sponsor might be "a prospect." And they could run it once a month, as part of *CBS Reports*.

He asked, too, about the upgrading of his contract, in negotiation since July.[58]

Eight days later, November 27, Friendly informed Mickelson of his intent to fly to Geneva in about a week's time, to put the last touches on the Iran show with Ed.

The news chief rushed a memo to Stanton, urging a private meeting with him before Friendly left, since Fred, he said, was planning to discuss with Ed his future role in *CBS Reports*.

Fred, Mickelson added, felt Ed's "full participation" essential to the future of the series and hoped to bring about a reconciliation.

The implications of the Geneva meeting, said Mickelson, were obvious, Fred's importance to the future of *CBS Reports* was equally obvious, and he wanted him under contract before he left; though now, he guessed, he'd probably delay until after his return.[59]

For one reason or another, Friendly never made it to Geneva.

January 25, the three Murrows left Naples for Israel and on the twenty-eighth arrived in Haifa with a boatload of Jews from Morocco. Murrow did a *Small World* in Jerusalem, interviewed Golda Meir, and with Casey drove the black Thunderbird, getting a final workout before being shipped back, from northern Israel down to Elath on the Red Sea. "Real frontier town," he wrote Seward, "some fine desert scenery on the way . . much like arizona . . [Casey] writing like mad in his diary and behaving very well. . . . Am quite sure that it was a wise move to bring him. . . ."[60]

McCarthy replies to his critics. (Courtesy of CBS)

CBS publicity photo, 1953. (Courtesy of CBS)

Murrow, Friendly, Carl Sandburg. (Courtesy of CBS)

Discussing *Person to Person*; facing the camera: John Aaron (left), Jesse Zousmer. (Courtesy of CBS)

At home in Pawling, New York: Glen Arden Farm. (Courtesy of Janet Murrow)
(Courtesy of CBS)

With Harry Truman in Key West, Florida, for *See It Now*. (Courtesy of the Murrow Collection)

With Field Marshall Sir Bernard Montgomery. (Courtesy of CBS)

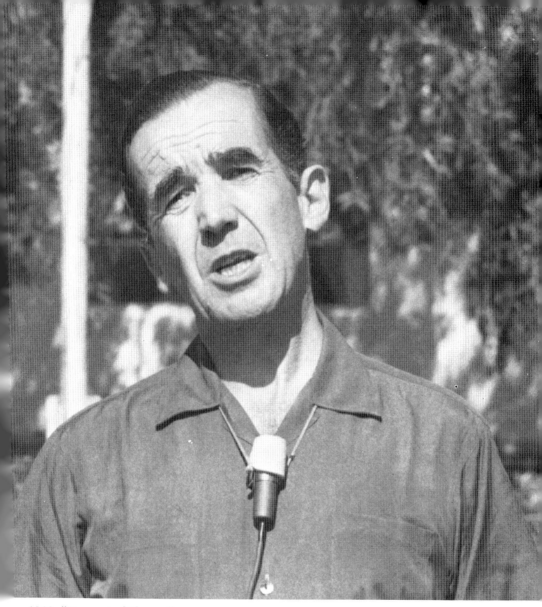

1960: "Harvest of Shame."

At the USIA: left to right: Reed Harris, unidentified, Donald M. Wilson, Murrow, Thomas C. Sorensen (back to camera). (Photo by Ed Clark, courtesy of Life Photos)

Back in Italy the bouncy youngster, out from under the constraints of boarding school, had started out by reacclimatizing with a vengeance, to the point at which his father told him flatly he could either join in with their plans as a family or go home, and he'd be glad to give him his ticket. (Dad was admittedly "exasperating to be around" at times, said Casey later, quite clear on any matter, never leaving you in the dark about what he was saying or what the choices were. Which was all to the good, unless of course, you were a kid wanting it your own way and hoping for just a trace of ambiguity.)

Over the months, however, the somewhat chubby preadolescent had changed into a lean, attractive young man, though with a mind decidedly his own. Recalled Casey Murrow, "They included me when they might have expected to have a hard time with me, but it worked out incredibly; I had a wonderful time—well, *almost* all the time."[61]

In fact, it was the first time all three were constantly together, other than the intervals at Pawling, with Murrow freed of deadlines and for once a full-time parent. He wrote Friendly that he had come to realize more than ever just how much his family meant to him.[62]

They had hoped to visit at least one Arab country, possibly Egypt, but for reasons of time or visa complications, it did not come off.

In Israel, at one point, father and son had visited a border post looking up toward the Golan Heights and Syria—a hillside perch reached in army trucks climbing steep switchback roads and located by an ancient Roman bath, all tiled, incongruous up in the mountains. Casey grabbed his field glasses to look over into Syria only to have the glasses knocked abruptly from his hands by an Israeli officer, anxious about reflections making a target and getting his visitors back in one piece.[63]

Their many friends from 1957 were attentive, Teddy Kollek met them at the boat, everything arranged, the red carpet out, but public attention was too much, and Janet Murrow's health had taken a turn for the worse— "in bed since we arrived here," Murrow wrote Seward, "bursitis and rheumatism. . . have good doctor. . . . ought to know future plans in week or ten days. . . .am being driven mad by well meaning hebrews who want lectures, interviews, articles etc. . .so far my lips are sealed . . but after reading Stantons testimony which reached me today. . .i am tempted to utter . . but i wont. . . ."[64]

Getting away, however, driving to Elath with Casey, he seemed relaxed and happy, speeding along the single-track desert road, the two of them stopping at collective farms, the kibbutzim, along the way, the son recalled: green patches in the waste ("Seeing that desert land and then— bang!—the irrigation; far more advanced than it was in this country").[65]

They saw the Dead Sea and visited Masada with the archaeologist Yigal Yadin, who was working up a possible Bible-as-history series on locale in modern dress, at Murrow's suggestion, an idea taken up years later by the BBC. An outline was going back to Friendly; Murrow thought it "sure fire."[66] For the first time in a long while he felt enthusiasm.

Janet's health, however, continued to deteriorate. "She must remain in bed another week," he wrote home, "then recuperate in Tiberius . . doctor doubts wisdom of her going India because of weather.[67]

In the meantime, he flew briefly back to Rome for more *Small World* filming and made a pilot for the proposed *Mid-Atlantic Parliament*.

By late February Janet Murrow, somewhat better, said she would continue. They decided to try the India leg of the trip, traveling via Iran, but Murrow, notifying Seward, could not commit himself beyond that point: "all will depend on janets health."[68]

At the same time his own health was declining rapidly again, his letters home a litany of deadly fatigue and depression: "please say nothing about janet's illness. . .casey is well and seems to be absorbing much. . .as for me. . .i am tired beyond endurance and wish myself in some far place but know not where. . . ."[69]

In New Delhi, all three came down with the local intestinal bug, but Janet and Casey Murrow managed to see the Taj Mahal while, as Murrow later wrote, "the old man writhed in bed with a fair case of delhi belly," looked up at the huge luxury suite—the agent, he figured, must have thought he was still on expense account—and wondered how he was going to pay for it. ". . may have to cable for money to bail us out . . but very pleasant. . .this country sort of bowls you over the first few days."[70]

He met with government officials, saw Nehru and Menon, and tried to arrange for entry into China—without the State Department's blessing if need be, Friendly quietly put on standby for a camera team. Nehru tried being go-between, but the two nations were momentarily at odds over the recent Chinese invasion of northeastern India and it was clearly not the time. Nothing came of the attempt.

All that was happening, he wrote Seward, was "a great sense of frustration and loss of time. . . maybe it is because it is hard to break with habit. . . and i am sure that part of it is that i suffer from a curious sense of guilt when not working. . [and] i haven't found a place where i am not recognized. too many american and British tourists. . . ."[71]

The family flew to Thailand and Cambodia, saw the ruins at Angkor Wat, and, the last week of March 1960, arrived in a cloudy, rainy Hong Kong, where they spent much of their time dodging old friends and reporters asking about CBS.[72]

". . unless i hear from someone in authority," he wrote to Seward, "i am likely to say that. . . .they sent a man to London to tell me i was fired . . and later I was told on the phone that they couldn't quite figure out a way to do it . .and thats where it stands . . as you know i am in basic agreement with what stanton is trying to do . .but his last speech made me want to vomit. . . ."[73]

His wife was better, but he was "simply too tired to breathe properly . . there seems to be no way to get away from people . . . it will be worse in tokio [sic]." The "whole expedition," he said, just hadn't worked out. "sorry to moan like this . . but you are the only one to whom i can talk with any candour. . . ."[74]

Seward, concerned, suggested a statement for the press on Stanton, something conciliatory; Murrow would have none of it.

> please remember that the last word i had from him was on the phone in London. . . .
> now . .i have no desire to prolong a controversy with him. but under no circumstances will i say that my belated comment was extreme or unwarranted. . . . i think i am an old enough hand not to be provoked into indiscretions by reporters. . . .i think i know what corporate loyalty is. . . i shall come back to work with good will . . . but. . . .if my conscience. . .wherever it resides. . .summons me to make public comment on the state of tv and radio. . .i shall certainly do so. . .and be prepared to suffer the consequences. . . this sounds pompous as hell, but you will know what I mean. . . right now the whole bloody business seems too juvenile to bother with. . . .[75]

The signature beneath was shaky, without its familiar flourish.

By late May, after stopovers in Honolulu, Seattle, and Bellingham, the Murrows were back in New York, well ahead of schedule. To Janet Murrow, her husband seemed calmed down, almost resigned, as they approached home, "prepared," she said, "to accept almost anything that happened."[76]

But Jack Beck, their former West Coast man, now working full time for *CBS Reports* and producing Murrow's opening assignment, did a double take at their first meeting and said later, "I was shocked at his appearance."[77]

It was Friendly who had met him at Idlewild, bubbling over with news of the shop—the program on the migrant workers that they'd always wanted to do, a new producer, shooting nearly completed; a hard-hitting piece on the criminal justice system, Murrow would be working once again with Jay McMullen from the old Unit One. . . .[78]

Friendly dropped him off at the Ambassador Hotel in midtown. The apartment was still closed, wife and son staying over briefly with his mother on the West Coast. Outside, the lights on Park Avenue led to Grand Central and the old studio complex. The year's sabbatical had lasted less than eight months.

Reentry was unheralded. He threw himself into his work for *CBS Reports*: two programs that same May and June; four more on the books for telecasting by the end of December; another four scheduled through May 1961.[79] Ample work, supposedly.

But not all of it was full time. More to the point, the power had passed; *CBS Reports* reflected the new center of gravity, in which the old, admittedly problematic give-and-take between producer and correspondent had swung permanently toward the producer. It had been the nub of Murrow's negotiations in the summer of 1959—negotiations which, in the cold light of 1960, turned out to have netted him absolutely nothing in terms of his official status. However his old partner might consult with him, assure him nothing had changed, the fact remained that Murrow was no longer editor-in-chief and was instead, in company eyes, a member of the staff he once had headed.

And though the cutting room was a familiar scene, the welcome warm, there was no getting away from the reality that the operation had been humming along quite nicely without him.

Johnny Schultz, as a newcomer, had hung back the first day, watching the near-pandemonium among the Murrow people and observing Murrow himself—an obviously shy man, at once pleased with his reception and flustered in dealing with it.

But the vibes were off, as Mili Bonsignori put it: "It was like going back to an old love; it didn't feel right.

"Everything had meshed in his absence. There was no place for him."[80]

To newcomers, Friendly seemed the boss. Friendly had always given the orders in the cutting room, but even the old-timers sensed a qualitative difference. To Schultz, the returned man seemed "a little like a beaten dog," who didn't *act* like someone of importance, entering always hesitantly, like a guest asking if he was in the right room. "He was like someone semi-retired—not asked to give his all, nor expected to. Fred tried to bolster him, tried to use him wherever possible, encouraged him; but he seemed disillusioned. . . .almost as if he didn't belong there."[81]

For those on the outside, at 485, the change was marked. To young hero worshippers like Jim Lavenstein, the kid who had handled their budgets, the hero had simply not come back. "Fred was always making like Ed was his puppet," said Dick Salant, "[and] by then Ed really *was* Fred's puppet."[82]

To Mili Bonsignori, disturbed by what was happening, Murrow seemed like someone who "belonged nowhere and everywhere at the same time. You always felt he'd be more comfortable next door—somewhere else. He was good on the camera or the mike—but only when he was working. There was no feeling that this was *his*. When he sat on a chair, it didn't seem to be his. Everything had closed up while he was away, and he was like a displaced person. There was a feeling, too, that Fred didn't fight for him, though we couldn't prove it."[83]

Part of the problem was his declining health, so obvious to Jack Beck on their first meeting for "The Year of the Polaris." But a good deal had undoubtedly to do with his consciousness of being tolerated, the rift created the preceding fall left permanently open. Despite the failure to communicate, the company had clearly been expecting his return, but the door to 20 was now shut—or nearly so.

In those first weeks, he had weighed the chances of reopening the pipeline to Paley, then gave it up. He saw the Chairman, even lunched with him, but the free-and-easy camaraderie of the past was gone, contact made through memos, scheduled appointments, everything correct and in its place. "The association wasn't what it had been," said a colleague, "and he didn't try to use it."[84]

His TV appearances, however, had been drastically cut back; for on returning to New York, he learned that *Small World*, his one remaining program, had been canceled. The sponsor was switching to *CBS Reports*, as Friendly had suggested when telling Mickelson he no longer wanted to continue with the smaller show.

Ironically, the program had had its partisans among the hierarchy of the News Division. Indeed, the editorial board itself had given it the go-ahead for another year, while turning thumbs down on *Mid-Atlantic Parliament*. There were even thoughts of moving *Small World* into prime time, Mondays at 10:30 P.M. on a two- out of three-week basis, amid confidence that the sponsor would put up the extra money.

Robert Lang, Mickelson's vice-president for administration, liked the show, found it useful for divisional accounting, suggested going to video-tape, and pointed up its "profit potential." By moreover absorbing certain costs now charged to *CBS Reports*, he had urged Sales, it could even reduce the budget of the bigger series, thus proving itself further "helpful to network finance."[85] He had argued against giving the Monday spot to *Face the Nation*, as some proposed, or switching *Small World*'s sponsor over to *CBS Reports*—both of which, however, happened.

Small World undoubtedly had served its purpose in preserving the core of the *See It Now* staff in lean times; even Murrow had once worried about keeping it up in the event of an expanded role for him on *CBS Reports*. Friendly was overworked (and possibly underpaid, drawing about $1,000 per *Small World* and about $7,500 per *CBS Reports*, a bargain, executives agreed, and decided on a future increment).[86]

But its demise also cut off Murrow from his last steady means of access to the tube.

Suddenly the corner on 17 known as the Murrow area—the hub, a year before, of two TV shows, nightly radio news, and a television documentary unit—had grown quiet, haunted by the ghosts of dead programs (*Person to Person*, hosted by Collingwood, was fitfully surviving), at the perimeter, not the center of the action.

In the cutting room Friendly deferred to him, "as did we all," a staffer said. (John Schultz, still under the impression, years afterward, of Murrow as some kind of coproducer, would be horrified when told he wasn't: "You mean, *just Friendly?*")[87]

But the News Division charts reflected the realities. For years, for all the diagrams and little boxes fixing everything in place, the Murrow operation had been independent, not at all accountable to division officers. Then, in 1958, the traditional operating components—news, public affairs, sports, film syndication—listed a fifth category, "Edward R. Murrow Programs," Murrow's name run in the space given the department head.[88]

By December 1959, Murrow's name had disappeared. So had the Murrow programs, in their place in the component lineup, the designation: "CBS Reports/ Exec. Producer/ Fred Friendly."[89]

Paradoxically, Murrow was doing some of his best fieldwork—no celebrity treadmill to distract, no demands from *Person to Person*, a fresh perspective gained from eight months of knocking about the world; looking forward to the opening of the sixties, and convinced, he told a radio audience on his return, that "the big story is right here in this country."[90]

Jack Beck, beginning work with him on the Polaris missile story, sensed his commitment, whatever his relations with the company, the old air of authority, missing at 485, still evident out on the road. Said Beck: "He was still Ed; they couldn't carve *that* off of him."[91]

(He also noted, smiling, that Murrow was still at his old bend-over-backward game of playing the obedient, cooperative reporter anxious to do the producer's bidding. "He didn't want to seem fatheaded, but you had to watch two things: Better not give him a false direction, and don't push it too far." The producers accordingly had to latch on fast to the rules of the game: "Do it right, do it professionally, and you had his respect. Get slipshod, goof off, and you wouldn't be giving him instructions much longer.")[92]

Charlie Mack, back as cameraman, was delighted to find him still quick on the uptake, the perfect team player. Sent out to film a sequence for "The Great Holiday Massacre," a projected Christmas week *CBS Reports* on traffic fatalities, they had staked out by a tollbooth doing a rushing business. The lined-up cars reminded the cameraman of horses at the starting gate—"Must be three hundred fifty horsepower behind each one," he ventured. Murrow, going with the metaphor, improvised an ad lib for the camera, ending with a warning about the horsepower that killed.[93]

But in contrast with the late fifties, he was now a fairly frequent presence in the Ninth Avenue cutting room—constant, in fact, when the migrant footage was on the screen.

"Harvest of Shame"—the title was Friendly's—had begun as an idea back in 1959. Edward P. Morgan had been handling the migrant problem on radio; Murrow and Friendly wanted to do it on TV. The matter was still open when Murrow left on sabbatical, the stumbling block, grower cooperation.

Enter David Lowe, a plump teddy bear of a man with an open, ingenuous manner that belied his legal training, master of the naïve opening,[94] a filmmaker with little or no documentary experience, who appeared once a week at CBS, looking for work. No way, said Friendly, they were knee-deep in producers.

Just one project then?

Friendly put him on the migrant story, with a small retainer—"maybe $1,000"[95]—and a month's time, then went ahead when, four weeks later, Lowe informed him he had gotten the growers to cooperate.

"Harvest of Shame" was first and foremost the creation of David Lowe and Marty Barnett, a labor of love emerging out of months of following the migrants up and down the eastern seaboard with car and camera. Murrow had come on the scene only after months of shooting.

His emotional involvement was evident, however, from the time of his return. Schultz, editing the film, got used to the sight of Murrow in the screening room, day after day, "looking just rapt at the footage."[96] (Someone years before had asked him, Why was he so invariably pro-union? "Because I hoed corn in a blazing sun," he shot back.)[97]

He wanted to see the camps for himself. Lowe took him down, two or three times, to the Okeechobee labor camp, a dust-blown shantytown not far from Palm Beach, where he talked with agricultural workers and the missionaries who worked among them in the camps.

Friendly, troubled by Murrow's worsening cough, had had misgivings about his going, but "he wanted to. . . . The subject was exceedingly close to him. [These were] people who worked with their hands; he identified with them. Don't forget, Ed had been poorer than anyone who worked on that program."[98]

Almost anyone. Johnny Schultz had come to realize that at least some of Murrow's quiet was a sort of "inwardness," a sense of understanding growing in the cutting room between the logging engineer's son who had hoed corn and seen his parents go hungry, and the migrant logger's son, with his childhood memories of picking potatoes.

July 3, he began *Background* over CBS Radio.

However small the personal return on his eight months abroad, the fact was the professional benefits had been enormous, clearing the debris of half a decade, sending him back with more of a global outlook and less inclined to view the world from the perspective of the Western capitals. He told his listeners:

Vast areas of the world would like to contract out of the current power struggle between the United States and the Soviet Union. They reason this way: If these two great giants decide to destroy each other . . . we too may perish, but not earlier than if we tie ourselves to the tail of this rather erratic American kite. . . . For the time being, the West Europeans have no alternative. . . . But there is discernible and not far beneath the surface the desire to become a spectator. . . .

In the so-called backward or emerging countries we encounter a special problem. We expect them either to imitate us or to obey. They are going to do neither, and no amount of economic aid will change that. . . . There is here not a competition for men's minds, but for their bellies. . . . Below a certain caloric intake the words we cherish—freedom, independence, human dignity, the right of dissent—are quite simply without meaning. . . .[99]

The program went out on Sundays at 12:05, midday, the CBS correspondents participating, Ed Bliss as producer. That first broadcast before the Fourth—taking up world reaction to the U-2 incident, the destroyed summit conference, Tokyo demonstrations ending Eisenhower's plans to visit Japan—brought in Alexander Kendrick from London, David Schoenbrun from Paris, Peter Kalischer from Tokyo, Winston Burdett from the Congo, and Richard Kallsen from Havana.

It was Murrow's kind of show. News aficionados welcomed it and his return. But news radio in 1960 seemed a dying medium, the great mass audiences turned to television.

Late June saw him filming interviews at the Governors' Conference at Glacier National Park, Montana. CBS publicity was playing up his return from sabbatical as part of its preconvention hype. In fact, he had been busy filming *CBS Reports*, only peripherally concerned with politics, "shooting a lot of the time," said one producer, "when he might otherwise have been hacking around the campaign."

To Beck, however, shooting with Murrow, there seemed almost a note of desperation in the voice on the telephone telling them of arrangements in Los Angeles ("We've got to have his face on the screen!").[100]

The year before, Murrow had suggested to Mickelson that his convention role be limited to specifics on foreign policy—platform deliberations, stances of the candidates, and such—on grounds that a year away would hardly qualify him to comment on American politics.[101] He had asked, too, that instructions, please, be more explicit than at past conventions and that adequate time be allowed for proper coverage.

None of which panned out. Arriving in L.A. for the Democratic convention the first week of July, he found himself down for roving reporter on the convention floor, nothing further. He'd offered to do substantial interviewing, again touching foreign policy. Nothing about that either. To an AP reporter he described his role as "a sort of free spirit," free to rove about and speak whenever he felt like saying something. "That's all right with me, I might not utter a damn word during the whole convention."[102]

In fact, not that much got back from the floor, what with constant switches to the anchor booth. Beck, stopping by at the Chateau Marmont after the first session's closing, found Murrow depressed; he wasn't looking forward to the rest of the week.[103]

Broadcasting, on the ropes six months earlier, was out to show its public spirit, the convention top-heavy with high brass, from Stanton and James Aubrey to Bob Kintner, lobbying among the pols amid an outlay of some $18 million, for an expected audience of 90 million viewers.

But it was NBC's year to cash in the chips, the Kintner forces rolling home and leaving CBS News for the first time in second place. Total trauma.

"The H&B magic," as Les Brown called it in *Variety*, had captured both critics and public, the Huntley-Brinkley anchor team supported by the aggressive floor work of Frank McGee, Merrill Mueller, Herb Kaplow, and Martin Agronsky; and by down-the-line follow-through under the firm direction of convention producer Reuven Frank and Elmer Lower, the latter formerly with CBS, now convention operations manager for the enemy camp.

Above all, there was David Brinkley, whose irreverent, knowledgeable quips on the political "fertility rites" set a new tone in TV reporting.

By contrast, the CBS lineup, top-heavy with serious-miened analytic talent, set loose on a dull and predictable story, seemed like a battleship out to sink a rowboat.

"A convention," says Dick Salant today, "is a peculiar thing. . . . You have to cover something which isn't happening. And what Huntley and Brinkley did to fill in those long lulls had wit and style and was better than trying to cover the rostrum or chasing stories that didn't pan out."[104]

In the meantime, Murrow, dour over the air about the Kennedy campaign—"a combination of hard work, a driving and unlimited ambition, and unlimited money"—hadn't been winning any popularity contests in the Kennedy camp, infuriating, as it turned out, the usually urbane Abraham Ribicoff, Governor of Connecticut and manager of the Kennedy forces on the convention floor.

"Murrow had made a broadcast in the preconvention week," recalled Roz Downs, who had flown out to L.A. to join her husband, "a comparison of the past history of the candidates. And Kennedy's did not show up very well. Of course, he had been a McCarthy man, which was not Murrow's favorite kind of person. His voting record was atrocious; there were several other things; it was pretty strong.

"Now this was before the opening of the convention, when the stuff really happens, the gathering of the forces, everybody choosing up sides, the platform written, deals on votes—in those days the parties were a lot stronger. In any case, the broadcast Murrow made had impact."

The morning after, she and Bill Downs entered the lobby of the Biltmore—headquarters for Kennedy, Lyndon Johnson, and also CBS. "It was a mob scene absolutely! There must have been eight million people, coming from the side rooms, all these gatherings. And out of nowhere this *man* showed up—whom I didn't know frankly.

> I have never seen such anger. He *grabbed* Bill, and I thought he was going to attack him. Then he started trying to shake him. Bill said, you know, sort of—"What the hell?" And *I* was about to kick him. I didn't know who it was—I didn't know why this man was grabbing Bill. And Bill keeps saying, "Governor! Governor! This is—please—"
> And I'm saying, "Governor? Governor? Who is this maniac who is attacking my husband?"
> Then suddenly he realized what he was doing, and he stood back and said, "You tell your—boy—Murrow to just stop attacking our guy." Bill says, "You want *me* to tell Ed Murrow what to say or what not to say?"
> And he says, "No, but goddammit, that wasn't fair, what he did last night."
> And so Bill says, "I'll tell him you said so, Governor, and thank you very much for your opinion"—you know, We appreciate your opinion, that kind of thing.
> And I'm standing there—I had my mouth open, I didn't say a fucking word, I was flabbergasted; I didn't believe this. I kept saying, "Who is that maniac? Who *is* that man?"
> Bill says, "It's Ribicoff."
> I said, "Oh, my God!"

The day had only begun. At around noontime the Downses met with Murrow upstairs at CBS and prepared to go to lunch. Everyone else in the building had the same idea, resulting in interminable waiting as one jam-packed elevator after another passed their floor without stopping. "And finally one stops and the doors open, and who's standing there right in front—whom I *do* recognize because he was not red in the face or furious or anything else—but Bobby Kennedy. And there are the three of us. And Bobby Kennedy looks at Murrow and Murrow looks at Bobby Kennedy, and there's this thing going back and forth, and there *was* room for one or two people on that elevator. And nobody moves, and Bobby Kennedy goes 'Nya-a-a-a-a-a-h!'—and sticks out his tongue. Which is one of the funniest things I have ever seen in my life. And all I can think is, *Oh, my God, I'm going back to Washington.*"[105]

Floor reporting, with its long, unremitting hours and emphasis on legwork, is essentially a young reporter's game, but the fact remained that Murrow—despite middle age and leaky lungs—preferred it to playing oracle: circulating among the pols, most of whom he knew by first name, grabbing here and there an elbow, suggesting perhaps a small drink at the bar when a story might be breaking; using senses sharpened since 1936 and coming out with barbed one-liners such as that describing the Kennedy-Johnson donnybrook before the Texas delegation as "a magnificent demonstration of the gentle art of political in-fighting, conducted by two experts."[106]

"Murrow's new convention role is a good one," said *Variety*, two days into the convention, "and ought to pay off."[107]

But CBS was lagging in the ratings. He was ordered to the anchor booth, in one of the all-time bloopers of miscasting. "*I* take the rap for that," recalled Don Hewitt, who as producer had come up with the idea.

"When Huntley and Brinkley came along," says Hewitt today, "I thought, *Holy shit! We've been king of the hill for all these years—where did these guys come from?* It was like a steamroller coming down the street. So I panicked. I went to Mickelson. I said, 'We gotta team Murrow with Cronkite.' Boy, was *that* a disaster! I mean, if there were two chemistries, two personalities that didn't blend, it was Murrow and Cronkite."

Worse, there was no opportunity to sound them out, no night-before arrangement. "No, that morning I came in, I found out about the ratings and I said to Mickelson, 'We gotta do *something*,' he said, 'You got it.' Poor Sig. He believed me."[108]

In fact, Mickelson thought, *Why not?* Murrow was after all the biggest star in the business. Why not make better use of him? Just don't seat him next to Cronkite; they wouldn't mesh.

The idea, Mickelson insisted later, was to keep Murrow in a separate corner of the booth, cutting away to him for commentary. Murrow, against the whole plan to begin with, as was Cronkite, was not about to be sat somewhere off in a corner. "He moved to sit with Cronkite," said Mickelson, "there wasn't much of anything to do with him . . . it was easier to let the thing roll that way than it was to argue with him to get over on the other side of the studio . . . [and] it seemed a lot more reasonable. It was hard to argue the artificiality of separate chairs and separate corners of the studio, for a conversation between two people."[109]

Cronkite, for his part, had evidently learned of the change when he arrived in the booth to find technicians ripping out wiring to make room for a second anchor. "He had arranged his anchor area just the way he wanted it," recalled Howard Smith, who had been perched up on a catwalk high above the hall, "and they made him tear out his machines and make place for Murrow. . . . Murrow was miserable because he was there as an extra thumb; Cronkite was miserable. . . . Then, to compound it, at the end of each day they would bring me down from my perch and get one or two of the floor correspondents in and force us all together—five of us packed into this area, knees jammed against knees, discussing for an hour. A pitiful case of CBS's panic."[110]

It was, as Hewitt rightly called it, a disaster—Murrow, stripped of his self-assurance, demoralized, not at all sure what he was doing there; Cronkite, trying to improvise: two solo stars forced into an awkward duet ("The big story of today and I think you'd agree, Ed . . . ").[111]

Whatever could go wrong, did. The draft-Stevenson demonstration seemed endless; the Governor was being coy again, said Murrow, could have stopped it had he wanted—and reminded Cronkite of 1952, when Stevenson as nominee had "almost prayed that this political cup would pass from his lips." Politically speaking, the Governor seemed to have become a secret drinker.[112]

The correspondents chuckled up and down the line, but within minutes the switchboard lit up with complaints that Murrow had accused Stevenson of boozing it up in private.

It was after midnight by the time the Kennedy steamroller had pushed through the roll-call votes to nomination, both newsmen dour and hungry.

"Well, Ed, that's it." They were released: Murrow, voice raw, self-deprecating to the point of embarrassment; Cronkite, gone from resentment to open empathy—a tough night.

Murrow didn't want to go back to the hotel, where everybody knew him. Instead, with the Downses, he found refuge at an all-night hamburger joint, neon-lit, Hollywood style. They took a table out of the way, but people kept coming up, asking for autographs.

He couldn't handle it. "For God's sake," he burst out across the table, "I can't even eat in public with my friends, or with my kid. . . . Why do they *do* it? I'm not a film star!"

"He couldn't understand," said Roz Downs. "I felt sorry for him that night."[113]

Adjustment was coming hard. He didn't like the new look anywhere, including the new breed of pol come to power back at the Sports Arena: "the men with the gray suits, the organizers . . . who believe in market research, and polls, and fast communications."[114]

Much of the spare time, he was floating around the edges. Lee Otis of the news department was stepping out for dinner after a late session one night with Kay Campbell and a few others when Campbell came up to him quietly: Ed said he'd like to come along—she hoped none of them would mind. Mind? Hardly!

Murrow was bitter all through dinner: Stanton had knifed him, hadn't lived up to his commitments. It turned out he was talking about 1947, about promises made to keep *CBS Views the Press*. They let him go on; it brought back memories. Former old radio hands like Otis had been proud of the show, made small contributions in their time, missed it when it was gone; and thought suddenly of Hollenbeck, now six years dead.[115]

Nielsen and Arbitron confirmed the public judgment: NBC had not only trounced CBS in the ratings, but walked off at times with as much as CBS and ABC combined.

To *Variety*, the Huntley-Brinkley combination suggested "the new era and spirit of youthfulness which . . . permeated the Kennedy win itself."[116]

"It wasn't only the political old guard that perished in Los Angeles," wrote Jack Gould; "the pontificating commentators of television also succumbed." An era was declared over: "the older school of oracles, so meticulously solicitous of their rounded deliveries. . . outdated. . . the stuffy, old-fashioned concept of ponderous reportage on the home screen. . . . The pre-eminence of CBS . . . no longer exists."[117]

By late July and the Republican convention in Chicago, the Murrow-Cronkite shotgun marriage had gotten its act together; but the patterns had been set. There was no use in Jack Gould's backtracking about "the 'new' Edward R. Murrow" or the broadcaster's "increasing zest and wit."[118] It was the turn of the new kids on the block.

"The honors again had to fall to NBC," wrote Les Brown, ". . . no major scoops to be had. . . . And the incisive Edward R. Murrow, with his analytical gifts and extensive background in world and national affairs was largely wasted at a convention in which only the expected happened."[119]

To Murrow, the same gray-suited men seemed to be taking over in Chicago as in L.A.

Watching Eisenhower's helicopter arrive, he and Cronkite had drawn briefly on their memories of World War II. The crowds made Cronkite think of the liberation route in Holland. Murrow recalled his BBC broadcast about Ike and the followup phone call from the General, saying the war wasn't being fought to make a hotshot out of Ike Eisenhower. "And he hasn't tried to make a hotshot out of himself as President either."[120]

He had often been critical of Eisenhower as President. Now, watching the helicopter, he described the man in it as "heavy with honors, with responsibility and with disappointment. Because he . . . wanted his place in history to be that of the architect of peace and tranquillity in the world; and in that he has failed." But the old magic was still there, he thought, and if it weren't for the Twenty-second Amendment, "they'd probably nominate him again tomorrow."[121]

Nixon, he said, had "taken over the party with a firm hand, but he hasn't yet taken over the *country*."[122] Murrow's voice had an odd sound.

Actually, he had found little essential difference between the two party platforms, give or take a bit more flexibility on China from the Democrats. But then Howard Smith brought up rank-and-file reaction to the Republican keynote speech, with its foreign policy section, both men agreed, straight out of 1952—not to mention the audience response, sounding just like the old cry of "Twenty Years of Treason," passions that were to haunt a minority presidency.

And indeed, the party platform, as presented by Charles Percy of Illinois—the part-time benefactor of *CBS Reports*—included a huge map depicting "Communist expansion up to the year 1952."[123]

Otherwise, they just watched the proceedings unfold smoothly—Congressman Gerald R. Ford of Michigan seconding the vice-presidential nomination; Richard Kleindienst of Arizona moving to make the Nixon nomination unanimous; Henry Cabot Lodge nominated for second place under the banner, KHRUSHCHEV CAN'T DODGE NIXON AND LODGE; the keynote speaker telling the cheering delegates, "You know what you are getting when you vote for Nixon."[124]

To the newsmen, the forty-seven-year-old nominee seemed affable and accessible, much more so than Kennedy; "a friendly political soul," said Cronkite. Murrow, in a preconvention at-home with the Nixons, *Person to Person* style, had conducted a most amiable interview, the candidate on nomination night passing up questions from other reporters to talk with "Walter and Ed."

CBS ran a remote from the Nixon family suite at the Blackstone, a group portrait with the party nominee. The piece was marred, however, by the persistent sound of coughing—dry and tight, from somewhere off camera—punctuating Nixon's comments on his boyhood, the cough of someone who couldn't get away, ending in a choking spasm as the owner tried to suppress it.

The conventions over, Murrow was glad to get back to *Background* and *CBS Reports*. "They sic'd him onto Lowe," Jack Beck remembered. "I was snatching Ed back from Lowe—needed him for the studio shots. The rest of the time he was chasing around with Lowe and Mack."[125]

It was also a time for something much more fundamental.

Come 1961, Murrow's contract would be up for renewal. But contract terms needed a base of some kind, and the fact remained that but for an occasional *CBS Reports*, Murrow—unlike Smith, Sevareid, and others on the series—had nothing else to do on television, a matter of considerable concern to Mickelson, who would be doing the negotiating.

They had had their differences in the past, been on opposite sides in the power struggle. But Murrow was a star, still the biggest name in the house, and the most underutilized, who, if he were lucky, would make perhaps four appearances on TV between now and the end of the year.

Mickelson, accordingly, began casting about for a vehicle—"using all kinds of approaches," he recalled, "to try to find *some* way to bring Murrow—and Seward, who was operating more or less as his agent, even though he was a vice-president, to come up with some kind of terms Paley would agree to; struggling to find almost anything that would bring them together. And it just wasn't working."[126]

Face the Nation was getting an overhaul, part of a hard look at the news schedule that was about to cost Doug Edwards the *Evening News*; CBS was not as yet convinced that Cronkite was the right replacement.[127]

Murrow's name had been put forward for *Face the Nation*. A lunch meeting was called. Murrow and Friendly outlined the conditions Murrow needed to work on the program; Mickelson knew it was no go and warned them. Later that afternoon, he called Murrow to tell him that the terms could not be met.[128]

Upstairs, Paley was kept abreast of developments, as he had been since removing himself from direct negotiations back in 1958. The Chairman was staying in the background, debriefed by his executives and in meetings of the editorial board—generally attended by Paley—where "the substance," as Mickelson later called it, of dealings with Murrow, or Murrow and Friendly, "would have been reported."

"I don't know," says Mickelson today, "how much additionally Frank Stanton would have reported in personal conversation, but I should think Paley would have known exactly what was going on the whole time."[129]

In late August Mickelson, in Stanton's absence, met alone with the Chairman for an update on the News Division. Had Murrow been offered *Face the Nation*? Paley wanted to know. Mickelson told him yes but that the deal was off, outlining what had happened. The Chairman registered the fact, then went on to the question of bonuses for the correspondents during the past conventions.[130]

It was a bad autumn. Jack Beck, weekending at Pawling, asked Murrow, How was the atmosphere in the shop? "No better," he replied. Said Beck later: "He was pretty depressed about it."

Murrow needed to talk. He was seeing the work of a professional lifetime swept aside, he complained, and it was hard, watching everything he had contributed being "lightly held by those in authority," who hadn't even the guts to stand up when the chips were down. He was tired—tired of being the one to do the standing up lest everything cave in, the closest he had ever come to the unspoken "Why me?"

To Shirer, over drinks at the Century, he said he was "all washed up" at CBS.

He stayed away from the campaign trail that fall. "As far as our elections are concerned," he wrote a friend in Britain, "I have never had less difficulty with . . . personal or emotional involvement. At this point I am inclined to agree with those who say neither man can win. . . . Both candidates will be packaged, processed and polished by the Madison Avenue boys, and I have no doubt we shall get what we deserve."[131]

In his work alone, it seemed, on the road and in the cutting room, he was finding the commitment that he failed to find elsewhere.

"Harvest of Shame" was in final editing. A monster compilation at the outset of filmed interviews, it was being hammered into shape, the draft narrative roughed out by Friendly and the producer in Lowe's first stab at "Murrow copy"—then reworked repeatedly, said Friendly later, by Murrow himself.

(The copy was always turned out first, said Schultz, in what he called "the *CBS Reports* Murrow-Friendly dogma," text and editing tailored till they fitted each other like a glove, involving close work by all concerned, in contrast with a unit like *Twentieth Century*, where "there was very little communication between people: The researcher got up a research packet; gave it to the director; the director would go out and shoot; the film and research packet would go to a writer; then Cronkite would be brought in to narrate.")

A show like "Harvest," on the other hand, was more of a cooperative venture. "David would appear with the copy he had written; Murrow wrote the tailpiece; all the rest was close consultation between Murrow and Friendly."[132]

The tailpiece had been Friendly's idea. "Ed, you've got to do an ending just like the McCarthy program," he told him one day. Murrow wrote it out one Tuesday morning, with perhaps a rewrite.[133]

Lowe had gotten his subjects to open up, the interviews following one another in a drumfire momentum, the pace of the cutting quickening under Friendly's constant admonition to "Tighten it up! Keep it going!"—a filmed continuum of American faces crossing the screen: black members of picking crews; rural whites straight out of Dorothea Lange's Depression photographs. Murrow's people. They screened a clip from Waycross, Georgia, a stranded picker down to his last $1.45. "Say, looks like your father, doesn't he, Ed?" Friendly boomed out.[134]

To Schultz, Murrow, hunched over, saying little, seemed to exude "a sixth sense about human beings—these kind of human beings." At one point, with most of the end copy in hand, Schultz had decided on the final sequence: a girl singing a plaintive song, the camera panning all those faces. The screening room was awash in tears and compliments. Murrow told him, "You don't need it."

Schultz was in shock. But he threw it out.

"He was right," said the editor. "He wanted anger, indignation, not this sort of 'tsk, tsk, those poor people' "; no release in a good cry.[135]

It was clear-cut advocacy journalism, and Murrow's skillful narration, ranging from understated irony to flaming anger, carried along Lowe and Barnett's portrait gallery of pickers, farmers, lobbyists, missionaries, and politicians, from the introductory voice-over juxtaposed against the early-morning "shape-up" for the hired help ("This . . . has nothing to do with Johannesburg or Capetown. . . . This is Florida. . . . These are citizens of the United States") to the closing appeal for action in the muckraking tradition of Ida Tarbell and Lincoln Steffens. It was a new, impassioned style for Murrow, contrasting with the coolly committed, Olympian TV persona of the fifties, marking him as a man of the new decade.

He watched the Nixon-Kennedy debates from afar that fall—Stanton's brainchild, for which the CBS President received his second Peabody in two years.

"After last night's debate," he wrote a friend, following the opening round, "the reputation of Messrs. Lincoln and Douglas is secure."[136]

On *Background* he charged both party platforms with "perpetrating a fraud upon the American people," a voice in the media wilderness: "There is not the slightest chance that any government can supply security from womb to tomb, solve the problem of civil rights, expand our economy, compete with the Russians economically and militarily, nourish the underprivileged nations and continue with business as usual. . . . [There is no way] that we as a people can stand in line for a second helping of automobiles, refrigerators and television sets and all the rest while more than half the world goes to bed hungry at night."[137]

His feelings about Nixon, going back to HUAC and the Duggan affair, had never changed, though on foreign affairs, the China issue aside, the Republican candidate's views weren't far from his own: a preparedness man, internationalist, and supporter of NATO.

His views on Kennedy were ambivalent. The Senator was intelligent, charming, articulate, mildly liberal, a good spokesman, appearing repeatedly on *Small World*. Murrow and Friendly had once wanted to send him abroad, interviewing with a camera crew as they had with Margaret Chase Smith, but then Kennedy's back gave out. It was even said that Murrow himself had suggested Kennedy as keynote speaker for the 1956 convention.

On the other hand, there was his absentee record, access to and use of vast amounts of money in his four-year drive—Murrow in his convention commentary used the term *traveling salesman*—and wishy-washy stance toward his father's old friend Joe McCarthy. And then, of course, there was Joe Kennedy himself.

He argued about it with Walter Lippmann shortly after the election, over lunch at the Century, as Friendly and Howard Smith looked on.

"Murrow had said something to the effect," Smith recalled, "that this nation had never been in greater *danger* than it was with the election of this boy to the presidency. And Friendly kind of looked out the window, I whistled softly to myself while looking downwards—I knew Murrow had this thing about Kennedy. And Walter Lippmann stared Murrow straight in the face and said, 'What, specifically, are you talking about?'

Well, they had an argument and I'm afraid Murrow didn't come off too well in it, because his facts weren't marshaled for the great peril we were in due to Kennedy."[138]

Throughout the campaign he had worried over what seemed to him a preoccupation with foreign affairs, neglecting "our . . . racial and social problems," said both parties were "running against Khrushchev," and saw the televised foreign policy debates—on Cuba, Quemoy and Matsu, the alleged missile gap—as wild swings before an audience, especially on Nixon's part ("playing with dynamite. . . . mortgaging future policy under the glare of lights in a television studio").[139]

There might have been just a touch of the sour grape in his comments on the hottest TV event of the campaign, from which he, as newsman, had been excluded, but it extended to the campaign as a whole. A tearing piece, ten days before elections—over the debate on American "prestige"—was pulled before airtime by a worried management, with Murrow called on the carpet afterward by John Day ("prestige was once defined as 'a conjuror's trick' . . . presumably neither candidate means to employ the word in that sense"). There had been particular distress over the line about the candidates' "shooting craps with destiny in the eye of a television camera."[140]

He hardly seemed to care, a gaunt and harrowed figure with a consistent anger to him, speaking the language of the outsider:

> Last winter I lunched with the editors of the *Züricher Zeitung* . . . and one of them said to me, "It has just been announced that your great President is going to cuddle up to Franco, while he has also appointed a committee to examine into the reasons for anti-American sentiment in Latin America." He suggested that one step or the other was not necessary.
>
> Our enemies and our friends were looking when the President went to Formosa, accompanied by the Seventh Fleet with five hundred jets flying cover about a hundred miles off the mainland of China. The visit perpetuated the myth that Chiang Kai-Shek's government represents six hundred million Chinese, when there is no assurance that it represents the majority of the Formosans. It is a fair question to ask what our reaction would be if Khrushchev should arrive in Cuba accompanied by such a display of military might.[141]

But he was speaking to a minority audience from what had become a communications backwater.

When a State Department spokesman telephoned the networks to suggest soft-pedaling the Khrushchev visit, Murrow commended ABC and Mutual for standing up and blasted "the others" for their silence:

> I am not saying that [their] news judgment was influenced. . . but they should have risen as one man and said: "Thank you very much. We are in the news business, think we are competent to make our own decisions . . . and require no editorial assistance from the State Department." They might also, with just a little intestinal fortitude, have reminded the Department that a man named Adolf Hitler once said: "The great strength of the totalitarian state is that it will force those who fear it to imitate it." . . .
>
> The danger, I suggest, lies not in Khrushchev's propaganda, or in the fact that the State Department improperly sought to bring pressure to bear upon the networks, but rather that the networks did not seize the opportunity to defend not only their limited independence, but one of the basic principles of a free society.
>
> I should like to make it clear that what I have just said does not necessarily represent the opinion of this network. . . .[142]

It was picked up by the old New York *Post*—through the good offices of Joe Wershba, by 1960 one of the paper's most valued columnists and feature writers. The former CBS man sent his regards and his regrets that the piece hadn't been on TV, where people might have seen it.

Murrow sent his fervent thanks in a letter marked "Personal": "I . . . heard about your midwifery on the State Department piece and say gratefully that had not some reference been made to it in the *Post*, my superiors would not have been aware that it had fouled up their air. As it is, I have had an unusual number of requests for my deathless prose from the boys upstairs."[143]

Middle management, however, was paying close attention—thanks, said Bob Skedgell, then heading radio, to a stepped-up vigilance ordered from the top, going beyond the old Klauber-White policy of automatic review for facts and fairness. Howard Smith, who had gotten *CBS Reports* off to a distinguished start on television, was stirring up the animals with his radio persona in his outspoken Sunday commentaries. And broadcasting, back in the politicians' good graces thanks to the conventions and debates, was not about to ruffle feathers.

"The News Division," Skedgell recalled, "was under great pressure from upstairs—meaning Mr. Paley and Dr. Stanton—about the CBS news policy, that no one should be allowed to go beyond it. And there was a constant furor about Howard Smith. And we were told by our chiefs, John Day and Mickelson, to watch the copy *very*, very carefully—the editors knew what the policy was—and to report or call attention to the bosses if anybody went beyond it, no matter who.

"Well, this was early Friday evening, and I went in and read the copy. Ed had done a piece—I can't remember what the story was, something to do with State Department policy—and it was apparent to me that he had gone beyond the line my bosses had drawn, and I was beholden to tell them."

He called Day at the Graybar Building and read him the copy. "Go bring it to Sig's attention," Day instructed him.

Mickelson had his coat on, ready to leave. He had to catch a train, he said; why didn't he just go back to Murrow and see what he could work out? Skedgell, a gentle man, never forgave him.

The Assistant Director for Radio walked to the end of the corridor, the upcoming scenario tying knots in his solar plexus: Bobby Skedgell telling Ed Murrow that he couldn't use a piece of copy.

Bliss was in the office with him. Skedgell started in: "Ed, I've got to talk to you about this—section here."

Murrow, sizing up the situation, smiled, pulled a scotch bottle from a desk drawer, and poured him a stiff one. When Skedgell had finished with the story, he agreed to drop the copy. Not change it. He was leaving him, Skedgell, with dead air, and it was up to him to fill it. And they'd leave it at that.

Skedgell, relieved and grateful, sprinted off to line up replacements. "He knew I was just a little middleman, and he was treating me with great human decency. I have never forgotten how compassionate Ed was when I had to go through that business. . . ."[144]

But the situation overall was growing more untenable. On top of it he became ill, in his worst pulmonary attack since 1940.

"Harvest of Shame" was almost done, moving down to the wire in a last push to get it on the screen the day after Thanksgiving. Murrow, laid up with bronchial trouble following a brief trip to London, insisted on completing the shooting on site as planned, overriding Friendly's misgivings about the dust and heat of the migrant camps. He spoke his last on-camera lines in Florida through a lungful of congestion coming through audibly on the sound track—the critics would put it down to emotion—and came back to New York with high fever, chills, and a diagnosis of pneumonia.

This time he was out on election night—"the first time in twenty-five years that I missed a major news story," he told a friend unhappily[145]— and for almost the rest of the month. But there was nothing he could do.

It was also the first weekend the Murrows were to visit Casey, in his first year at Milton Academy and a little lonely. Ed insisted that one of them go. Janet, rather than wear him out with arguments, gave in reluctantly, driving to Boston with a divided mind, stopping at almost every highway phone to call the apartment.

In late November he was back in the office and *Background*—"shakily," he admitted to Sevareid,[146] allowed a few hours a day by strict permission. Five weeks after the attack he could write to Walter Reuther that he was almost fully recovered. But the doctors had forbidden him to fly for the next few weeks, to give the abused lungs time to recover. He was confined, the tide of his usual activity receded, leaving him stranded on the high ground. His physical equipment was giving out; but so were the motivation and momentum that had kept him going in the past.

That December was a time of reassessment: coming to terms with powerlessness, chasing his thoughts continually around the track in a deepening bitterness unrelieved by his old humor.

To a friend that winter, questioning the workings of the press, he said he had "never shared the view that we have the best news coverage in the world. It is true that we throw at the public more unassorted, more undigested, more unevaluated information than. . .in other countries, but that doesn't necessarily mean that the public is well informed."[147]

In answer to another, he favored a proposed study of columnists and commentators ("something in the nature of an examination of the credentials of those of us who regurgitate our prejudices under the title of news analysis might be useful. . . . In short, I am for full disclosure not only so far as the news is concerned, but so far as those who manipulate it").[148]

Lou Cowan was in touch: How was his health bearing up? "My health," he replied with unaccustomed savagery, "is as good as my surroundings permit."[149]

In the meantime, it was Armageddon up on 20. Paley, back from Europe to find profits down and CBS knocked from its Nielsen perch by long-despised ABC, was reported "on the warpath" by *Variety*, industry watchers advised to look for changes in the News Division.[150]

The first weekend of December, Sig Mickelson, in Stanton's office, read a release announcing the formation of a news executive committee to be set up over the division, in charge of policy, with Mickelson reporting not to Stanton as in the past, but to the new committee chairman, Richard Salant—Stanton's right hand, described by the trade press as "most active in political and legislative areas. . .finely attuned to the Washington angles insofar as they reflect on news and pubaffairs. . . ."[151]

Mickelson, offering to step down, was assured he'd have a tough time finding a good position elsewhere, but should the new arrangement prove not to his satisfaction, rest assured, they'd make a niche for him until something better opened up.

Asked for his input, the CBS News President had then worked out a compromise—startled when the final release, the following Friday, bore little resemblance to their supposed agreement. The committee had been given charge of policy *and* operations, meaning, in effect, Salant.[152]

It was now, his position eroding, the ground shaking under the News Division hierarchy, that Mickelson, presiding over a demoralized department, was told to get down to brass tacks on negotiating Murrow's contract and ran consistently, he said later, "into nothing but a blank wall." A five-year renewal plus five-year exclusive, quite standard. Murrow, even then, was willing. That, says Mickelson, was not the problem. "I wasn't getting any response from Paley. I was submitting not only contract terms but ideas—you know, places where we might use Murrow—additional ways to use him. But I was getting no response. And I should have read that to mean that Paley didn't care whether Murrow stayed or not."[153]

At the same time Friendly, by his account, still trying to salvage the shreds of the putative agreement of the summer of 1959, dealing this time with Salant, was coming up against the same blank wall. (Salant later pleaded vagueness on the details, adding, with a smile, "But it *was* a period of hard feeling between Murrow and Paley.")[154]

TV Network President James Aubrey, a member of the news executive committee, was moving *CBS Reports* into a biweekly spot on Thursday nights, the sacrificial lamb opposite ABC's Eliot Ness, but never mind, it was a steady spot. For alternate weeks, Friendly suggested the political debate format, so successful in the fall, cheap and easy to produce. (Actually, said Stanton years later, it bombed when they tried it.) The high brass, meeting on the issue, liked the idea. Then Friendly said he wanted

Murrow in on it "as anchor man," he later wrote, "and co-editor of the entire Thursday night series."[155]

As in 1959, it was a matter not of shutting out the other reporters, but of placing Murrow in a decision-making role. The answer was still no. Said Friendly: "I couldn't win those arguments."

It seemed clear to him that the corporate argument of 1959—making Murrow first among equals for the greater good—had undergone a twist: "It wasn't that they wanted to use the other correspondents so much as lower the impact of his visibility."[156]

To the producer it was maddening, even self-defeating. "He was *so* good and had such presence. It's always a problem finding a correspondent willing to go full time on documentaries—Ed *wanted* to do them. He would have filled the vacuum."

In fact, Jack Gould, praising the first raft of *CBS Reports*, including a Peabody winner and Howard Smith's classic interviews with Walter Lippmann, had taken to wondering: With all the emphasis on corporate entity, not individuals with whom the viewer felt rapport, wasn't some of the "excitement and distinctive character of C.B.S. News" being slightly blurred?[157]

Said Friendly in recent years: "It didn't seem to me to be fair to Murrow or the public. And documentaries haven't had that impact since. Because of that one personality. When people think of them today, they think of "Harvest of Shame," "McCarthy," "Indianapolis," "Radulovich." Even "The Selling of the Pentagon" is remembered mostly because of the criticism against it.

"Now, I may understand this better than anybody, and I haven't said this before, but I think it's important: The question of identification. People believed the shows; people could identify. This was the great lesson of my life. And if we fought for the principle of identification, it was because we knew this—not because Murrow wanted to be the big cheese."[158]

But the network, it seemed, didn't want its biggest drawing card out front.

Friendly's point had seemed proved in late November, as "Harvest of Shame" burst upon the public, an updated *Grapes of Wrath*; a black-and-white document of protest ushering in the sixties on TV, combining Lowe's vision, Barnett's camera eye, Friendly's overall whip hand, and the editorial punch of Murrow—standing among the crop rows, tieless and in shirt sleeves, a lavaliere microphone around his neck, looking like a combination of Henry Fonda and Woody Guthrie.

For Murrow, despite other programs in the works, it was effectively the last hurrah—the final round of *Times* editorials, the praises and damnation in the press and Congress, the anger of the interest groups, the squirming by the sponsors (two executives dispatched to Florida had virtually apologized),[159] as well as the public calls to action that would probably fizzle.

But TV, he always said, could only hold the mirror; the idea was to hold it until something happened: a seven-day-a-week job, defending the Republic and pointing up the warts.

The program also, as things turned out, laid a time bomb.

In company terms he had by now become the extra thumb. Moreover, it was getting crowded at the top. The relationship with Cronkite, the man who had made it in CBS on his own, had never been a good one, a subtle vying for power noticeable even when the balance was in Murrow's favor. It was the classic problem, as a CBS friend observed, of the front-runner: "There's Eric Sevareid in London, sitting in the wings; there's Smith, you had three stars, you had four stars, *you had a whole goddamn galaxy out there!* All sort of champing at the bit."[160]

Why was he staying? The counterquestion was: Where would he go—having never worked for a newspaper, rarely written for print; leaving a department which was in part his creation and the associates of twenty-five years, breaking the semi-incestuous, many-layered ties of the long-term employee and company man.

His recklessness had always coexisted with a strong security drive—the milltown-bred dread of being jobless, the ethic that you didn't quit a job unless you had a job to go to; the hard proletarian conditioning which, his large back salary notwithstanding, had him visualizing income—even the six-figure variety—in terms of a pay envelope.

Bill Downs had thought of quitting CBS to write a book, asked Murrow's advice: How did he think Roz would bear up? "She'll bear up," he answered, "until the second paycheck doesn't come in."[161]

Above all, leaving CBS, still the only place for him, in an industry and time without alternatives, meant leaving broadcasting and therefore journalism. Professional upheaval. At fifty-two, he looked around for a way to spend the rest of his life.

The morning of December 15, Frank Stanton came to the Georgetown home of the President-elect. There had been speculation throughout the campaign of a possible government appointment for the president of CBS, in the event of a Democratic victory and the accession to Vice-President of his good friend Lyndon Johnson. But it was Kennedy who had summoned him to Washington.

They talked, said Stanton later, on "a wide variety of subjects," leading to Kennedy's question, Would he, Stanton, take over the U.S. Information Agency, the USIA? And if he couldn't, would he recommend someone?

Stanton said, "Ed Murrow."

Kennedy asked that Stanton discuss it further with Dean Rusk, newly appointed Secretary of State. The CBS president agreed, and a private meeting was set up at Foggy Bottom for December 29.[162]

At the CBS office in Washington, Howard K. Smith picked up the ringing telephone. "Is Mr. Clark there?" Blair Clark, socially connected and a Harvard friend of JFK, was sitting with him. Smith handed him the phone, heard the words, "Mr. President," and beat a quiet retreat.

Sometime later Clark emerged from the office: The President had been asking about three possibilities for USIA Director.

"I hope you don't mind. I suggested Murrow."

On the contrary, said Smith. He'd have insisted on Murrow, had he been in the other's shoes.[163]

Friday, January 6, was Epiphany in London, and darkness fell early. Hugh Carleton Greene, for the past year Director-General of the BBC, was preparing to go off for the weekend following a five o'clock meeting with Ed Murrow, in town for a short visit, ostensibly to do a program for the BBC.

The newsman came quickly to the point: "I'd like to come and help you over Pilkington." Greene immediately realized he was looking for a job.[164]

The Pilkington Committee—so called for Sir Harry, the Lancashire glass magnate heading it—was one of those independent commissions appointed periodically to conduct the mandatory inquiry preceding each renewal of the BBC charter, a public review, determining in effect the course of British broadcasting for the next fifteen years.

"How much I'd like to come and help you over Pilkington." The phrase would stick in Hugh Greene's memory: "I thought that was a nice way of putting it, though I didn't know exactly how Ed would help with *Pilkington*. But to have him working for us, would be good public relations."[165]

They weren't intimates or even friends, though both men liked and respected each other, with intermittent postwar contact. Both careers had been forged in journalism and the crucible of World War II, Murrow at Broadcasting House; Greene, a former correspondent, over at Oxford Street, directing the BBC German Service beaming into the Reich; later becoming Controller of Overseas Services, then Director of News and Current Affairs before taking over as Director-General.

An independent, innovative, nearsighted giant of a man, from one of those gifted British dynasties (his two brothers were the writer Graham and the distinguished physician Raymond), a later influence in global telecommunications, he would do as much as anyone to bring the still-tradition-bound BBC into the second half of the twentieth century.

As they talked, it had occurred to Greene that Murrow could be helpful after all with Pilkington. Lusty, up-and-coming commercial Independent

Television—ITV—was vying with the Gray Old Lady, the BBC, for control of a third television channel; a Murrow series might be most "attractive" in drawing that larger audience needed in the new Battle of the Channel, a battle of which Murrow was fully aware, in making his offer.

"So I suggested to him, as a production possibility," recalled Green, "that we might have a series called *Ed Murrow's England*, that we would give him a camera team and just let him do his own picture of England. Well, he *seemed* to me, at any rate, to be very much tempted by this idea, and keeping out of the United States for a while, which I think he was quite keen on. You know, ease the break with CBS.

"This was something that he liked—that he was leaping at. . . . I really thought, I'd probably got him."[166]

Returned home, Murrow was caught up in a sudden burst of activity, every inch the busy, sought-after news celebrity: chairing the CBS correspondents' roundup before the National Press Club in D.C.; the star attraction at the gargantuan WBBM-TV luncheon in Chicago; addressing the Radio and Television Executives Society Newsmakers luncheon in New York; chasing around in a heated, hectic schedule that contrasted strangely with his crumbling career.

Speaking before the Radio and Television Executives Society in what the news reports would call "an abrasive voice," he made one last slap at the industry—"bloated with statistics, concerned about our underarms and the middle colon. . . . indifferent to what our words and pictures are doing to the mind of America"—calling for an independent public interest group, drawn from many sectors, to study the news media, to awaken and educate the public in the workings of the media themselves ("information about information"), and to guard against "threats to the public welfare that take the form of assaults on freedom of the press."

It was a last look back to *CBS Views the Press*, to Chatham House, 1938, the controversies of 1935 and 1936, and the plain principles he still believed in:

> There can be no real. . .democracy unless the people understand the basic political, social and economic issues upon which their welfare depends. . . .
>
> If a deceived or confused public is betrayed into creating or allowing to be created an America in which it loses faith, democracy will not survive. . . . If the people finally come to believe either that they cannot grasp or they cannot cope with America's problems, or that those who inform. . .and those who act are inept or malign or both, then distrust, dissatisfaction, fear and laziness can combine to turn them in desperation to that "strong man" who can take them only to destruction. . . .
>
> There are many faint-hearted students of the American scene. . . . The more the pattern of information contrives to be confused, distorted and manipulated, the more likely are these prophets to be right.

Ending, he had evoked the main author of the plan, a name unspoken for years in the industry: "Ed Klauber, one-time Executive Vice President of CBS—a great editor, committed to the pursuit of truth. . . ."[167]

It was to be his last speech as a broadcaster. Three days before, in Washington, he had met privately with Chester Bowles of Connecticut, about to become Deputy Undersecretary of State, acting now as go-between on the USIA offer from the new administration.

Bowles, an acquaintance through their mutual friend Bill Benton, the ultraliberal in the Kennedy campaign and standard-bearer of the "third way" in foreign policy, urged Murrow to take the job. Murrow in turn asked about policy input, going on the advice of Sidney Bernstein, consulted as one who had, after all, worked for the Ministry of Information.

Bernstein had seemed open to the idea. He had met Kennedy, he said, didn't really know him, of course; seemed a bright enough man—Granada had covered him in the primaries—capable of learning, fairly decent record. Of course, he *loathed* the old man, "a nasty piece of work," but as for the son—"he's your President, Ed."

But state your terms, he warned: Brendan Bracken had succeeded with the wartime Ministry of Information because he could walk into Church-ill's bedroom and get his yes or no on matters, no time wasted. Now, he didn't know about walking into Kennedy's bedroom, but Ed could certainly ask about attending meetings of the cabinet. "If they agree—you'll be there."[168]

Accordingly, Murrow asked about being in on the decision-making processes—being in on the takeoffs, as he called it, as well as the crash landings, playing a formative role in policies the USIA would be called upon to justify.

Bowles was to pass it on to higher quarters, urging, however, a meeting with Dean Rusk.

The job itself was no great plum—taking charge of propaganda for a country that didn't believe in propaganda, at least not by the government; and an agency plagued by problems of identity, bureaucracy, and politics from the time of its inception; ravaged by McCarthy; suspected by the left for its identity with ideological cold warfare and by the right as an alleged nest of egghead-liberal pinkos. Unknown to him, he hadn't even been the new President's first choice.

By now, however, the pressures were considerable: He was *needed*; the strongest argument one could use with him. Chet Bowles wrote him late that week, "encouraged" by their visit. He was taking a long weekend, he said, but hoped Ed would get in touch with Dean Rusk even before he returned to Washington: "You are in a position to make an enormous contribution to our foreign policy in these next few years."[169]

Still, Murrow waited for a sign from Kennedy, not yet ready to commit himself.

* * *

January 20, Inauguration Day, he stood in the snow with the other reporters in the record cold, the end of three killing weeks and he was beginning to feel it. Another *Background* was still to be taped for Sunday, on the inaugural address and a speech he would find even more arresting—the outgoing President's warning against the military-industrial complex.

He had a two-minute spot to fill following Kennedy's address, his commentary based on an advance text. The ceremony itself he would follow over TV in the warmth of a small enclosure, smelling of sawed pine, that was his temporary office, part of the broadcasting complex thrown up in the basement of the Capitol. He had also promised Bob Skedgell a piece for radio.

Ed Bliss, there when he entered, was alarmed by his obvious fatigue.

"I knew he had been suffering cruelly from insomnia," Bliss later wrote.

He watched Murrow, the text of the inaugural address before him, put paper in his typewriter and start typing—slowly, thoughtfully. Once a word was down on paper, Bliss later wrote, it was there to stay. The new President, read the last line, appeared to recognize "that difficulty is the excuse history never accepts."

They followed the ceremony on the monitor. Murrow turned back to the typewriter: "It was a speech full of confidence, without arrogance."

He finished the two-minute spot, took his copy to the studio, came back shortly afterward, and reached wearily for his overcoat. Reluctantly Bliss reminded him of his radio commitment.

"Do I have to do it?" he asked.

"You said you would."[170]

The radio booth was an enclosed platform two stories above the inaugural site—a kind of fire tower arrangement accessible only by an outside ladder, whipped in the wind that had blown up in the wake of the previous night's snowstorm.

Murrow was coughing badly; Skedgell followed his two-story climb, hand over hand, with apprehension. "Gee"—he heard Kay Campbell's voice beside him—"I hope he gets up the ladder all right." They both breathed more easily when it was over.[171]

In the meantime, word of the USIA offer had gotten out. Roz and Bill Downs, running into Murrow at an inaugural ball that night asked, Was it true? Was he really considering?

Well, yes, he replied, he thought it was confidential, but it was obviously making the rounds and he'd appreciate their not saying anything.[172]

To the end, however, he was torn.

That Monday he sat in a motel room in downtown Birmingham, waiting for David Lowe to show up with a visitor.

"Who Speaks for Birmingham?" had really started with Harrison Salisbury's New York *Times* series months before, on racial violence in that city. David Lowe, finishing "Harvest," had called the *Times* man to say that Ed.Murrow was contemplating going down and doing a story of that type for television.[173] Suitably briefed, Lowe then went down, did the usual legwork, made the contacts, gathered material, Murrow joining him after the inaugural, with the intention of staying through the rest of January. It was a new undertaking for the team of Lowe, Murrow, and Barnett.

So far it was a schizophrenic stay, nice people saying all was well; others—mostly blacks, some whites—talking of fear, coercion, killings. Appearances were set up for Murrow: the all-white Kiwanis Club on one hand, a Tuesday luncheon, no more than thirty minutes of talk, please, and could they have two glossies;[174] on the other hand, a nighttime meeting at the black First Congregational Church—a small biracial group of hardy souls known as the Greater Birmingham Council on Human Relations, gathered regularly in defiance of the segregation laws and Bull Connor's police, taking down license numbers in the parking lot outside, for transmittal to the Ku Klux Klan.[175] Both were scheduled for Tuesday.

For the rest, he had been following Lowe, going after contacts undercover, a situation suddenly recalling Berlin, 1935: the furtive phone calls, the street corner meetings after dark or indoors behind closed blinds, the furtive "Don't call, just come."

Lowe, telephoning Salisbury, had called the situation even worse than he'd described it and oh, yes, Ed had said he hadn't seen an atmosphere like that since Nazi Germany.[176]

The Reverend C. Herbert Oliver, the young president of the Council on Human Relations, was on his way to the motel, shepherded by Lowe. A black Birmingham-born activist and ordained minister, Oliver had been in the forefront of the local and statewide civil rights movement, a cottage industry so far, documenting human rights violations in the teeth of numerous arrests and threats against his family, hoping for media exposure to help keep him alive.

The *Times* series notwithstanding, it had been a local story, sporadically covered in the mass media, blank-screened on local TV and in the press. For Herb Oliver, returned from the North, fighting, it seemed at times, in utter isolation, Murrow's imminent arrival was like a helping hand from the outside.

"The word was out publicly," he remembered. "Everyone knew that Ed Murrow was coming to Birmingham. He was coming to Birmingham to show what it was like. And it gave joy to black citizens and to those white citizens who were working along with blacks. And it put consternation into the hearts of those who wanted everything to be kept down.

"We'd been saying it for all our lives, and it hadn't been listened to. But here was someone of his stature, who could come and say, 'Let's look at Birmingham.' Believe me, that was a wonderful thing to happen."[177]

It was a different scene from thirteen years back, when he had covered the Henry Wallace campaign with the blessings of Bull Connor. Instead, in spite of the Kiwanis invitation and the excitement of local educational TV, there was a nervousness, even resentment in some quarters, anger at "The Lost Class of '59," open discussion of what Murrow should or shouldn't do. Said Oliver, recalling, "I think they were afraid of the documentary. They just didn't like it; he was *meddling*."

At the motel the minister felt immediately at ease; the newsman struck him as "very calm—at least outwardly, in possession of himself," though consuming cigarette after cigarette.

"Just a plain, calm, dignified man," he remembered, "down-to-earth, no airs, just talked with me the same as he would with anybody. A warm man, not a crusader. Just someone who was interested in . . . *people*."

They began preliminaries. Oliver wished him well on the documentary, expressed his pleasure that it was being done. Murrow had undoubtedly seen some of the depositions and was asking about them. The phone rang. Someone picked it up, answered, then handed it to Murrow. There was a brief conversation—hardly seemed to last a minute, thought the Reverend.

Murrow put down the receiver. Well, that was a call from Kennedy, he said, asking him to become head of the USIA.

It just emerged, like that, matter-of-fact, as though noting the arrival of a takeout dinner. Said Oliver: "He didn't explode with enthusiasm."[178]

Nonetheless, everything had changed. The visit was soon wound up, appearances cancelled, including the gathering at First Congregational— though Murrow's name, Oliver wrote him afterward, ensured a record turnout at the usually poorly attended meeting. More of the substantial citizenry had come, he said, who usually couldn't care less, and it was heartening to know they could be motivated. At any rate, there was new interest in the council:

"The news of your presence reached every nook and cranny, and stirred up the dregs of many hardened consciences. Our appeals so often go unheard, but somehow your coming brought to the forefront that fear of the light which haunts creatures of darkness."[179]

He looked forward, he wrote, to Murrow's return to Birmingham. The letter arrived moments before Murrow's departure from CBS.[180]

In Washington, Howard K. Smith received an unexpected phone call from Murrow—in town, as it turned out: "Can you come and see me?"

He found him at the Sheraton-Carlton, two blocks from the White House, in a small bed-sitter, obviously gotten on short notice.

"That boy has offered me a job."

Smith allowed as to how he'd heard rumors to that effect. "I'd take it."

Murrow looked sheepish. "I'd have to eat a lot of words."

The other man started laughing: Not to worry. It was the common diet in this town—topped every menu in Washington, and he might as well get started.

One more thing, said Murrow—Birmingham; would he take it over? Smith agreed to do so. They didn't go into it, he said later; "he didn't have to—we both felt the same way."

They left the hotel together—Murrow had an appointment—walking down the street talking shop, then parting ways, Murrow off to his meeting, Smith back to CBS.[181]

Friendly, called en route to New York, met Murrow at the train. They went for drinks. The producer was flat against the whole idea: "Is that what you want to do—become a PR man for the government?"

"We could have ironed it out if he had stayed," Friendly kept insisting in later years, "he was so good. . .they would have used him more of the time. . . .I wanted him to stay. . . .In a year he would have been doing most of them. . . ."[182]

Paley, however, in a three-way meeting requested by Murrow, told him it was *his* decision. "I said to him at the outset, 'Ed, you're free to stay here as long as you want to—this is a decision you have to make, I'm not gonna tell you to take it or not take it.' "

But if he *did* take it, he said, then insist on participation in decision making. "But I made it perfectly clear to him there was nothing in *my* mind that suggested that we didn't want him to stay."[183]

Stanton, sitting in, kept silent for the most part. "I didn't say I had—after all, I'd seen JFK—*seen* Kennedy. I didn't want to tell Ed. It had to be his decision; he had to do what was best for the country."[184]

For Murrow himself, the choice now seemed to lie between going into the government or going into exile.

The appointment was announced that Thursday, January 27. *Background* was yet to be taped. He asked Blair Clark to take it over. "But what should I tell the audience?" asked Clark.

"Tell them I've gone to serve my country," Murrow replied in a cold fury.[185]

CBS threw a farewell party.

"Everyone was there," said Friendly, "Paley, Stanton—as though nothing had happened."[186] Tears were shed; everyone was family again. The correspondents presented Murrow with a bust of FDR by Jo Davidson.

"You owe your country a summer," he told Bonsignori at a lull in the festivities. "I'll contact you."

"But he never did," she recalled. "Maybe he knew. . . ."[187]

They taped his farewell speech for piping January 31—following Kennedy's announcement—to the network and affiliates over closed-circuit TV. Friendly made the introductions.

But what was intended as a graceful, paper-it-over farewell became an ordeal as he choked on the phrase, "some part of my heart will stay with CBS" and the transparent clichés of gratitude to the management for "releasing" him, voice breaking uncontrollably and face distorted, held in the eye of the camera like an insect impaled under glass. He recovered with one last swipe at the affiliates that had so often bridled at his programs before the final "good luck . . . and good night."

For his public of twenty-two years, there was no leave-taking, just a fitful phasing out, according to the *CBS Reports* still in the can or in progress. As for *Background*, one week he was on, the next he wasn't.

A listener—or viewer—wrote in, asking for a copy of "Mr. Murrow's farewell." A secretary, replying, assumed she meant the "farewell" made on the closed circuit. They were sorry, but they had no copies in the office.[188]

Hugh Greene, in London, heard the announcement and realized he hadn't gotten Murrow after all. The newsman had never gotten back to him—the rush of events, perhaps, or the old habit of overlooking things he did not like to do.

The announcement, he wrote Ed, came as "a great surprise," though a very welcome one. "I hope that I am right to congratulate you. I have no doubt that I should be right to congratulate President Kennedy." Everyone here was delighted, he added, looked forward to all kinds of cooperation with him, and hoped soon to see him again.[189]

Privately, he would confess to being "very disappointed."[190]

Why had Murrow turned down the attractive offer? A whole complex of reasons, no doubt—not the least, perhaps, a basic insecurity about working within a strange TV setup, without Friendly as the ultimate production arbiter; a hesitation, on reflection, about being in effect on his own in a medium in which, unlike radio and for all his expertise, he had never felt wholly at home. Perhaps he was satisfied to let his record— the Murrow-Friendly record—speak for itself.

Then, too, he had to be at the center of the action. And that center was in Washington, not the English countryside; not when the torch, as the new President had put it so eloquently in his inaugural address, was being passed on to a new generation. He was after all attuned, generationally and temperamentally, to the call of "Ask what you can do for your country. . . ." The puritanical tradition of the Murrows, leading him possibly to turn down a dream assignment for a tough one: explaining the America now shaping up—of violence, abrupt change, racial confrontation, and social upheaval.

Above all, there was power. He'd always criticized these guys, he told reporters; maybe now it was time to try their shoes on. And here was Chester Bowles, seemingly so close to Kennedy, with all his credibility, assuring him personally of his potential "enormous contribution to our foreign policy." A cabinet position. Input, not the runaround.

Finally, and unknown to anyone at the time—unknown, in fact, until the opening of official papers twenty-three years later—there was Kennedy's promise to agree to Murrow's terms in writing, naming him his "principal advisor on psychological factors dealing with foreign affairs"; to participate—"when appropriate"—in the development of foreign policies.[191]

He was going into the government, armed ostensibly with the promises never before given a Director of the USIA, assured that those pledges would be held to by the forthcoming administration.

At CBS, his departure was regarded with ambivalence. Jim Lavenstein, the young guy in budgets who had worshiped Murrow and withered under Friendly's screaming, was "heartbroken": "It was the end—a premature ending to an era. I remember how bitterly I felt, as did many: writers, producers, creative people. The feeling was that he got axed, that his resignation was accepted with phony regrets, though for everyone who hated Friendly, it was New Year's Eve."[192]

"Nothing took over," said Lou Cioffi, then one of the younger correspondents. "That was the problem; there was a void left. And that's what disturbed a lot of people. Murrow was not *replaced* by anyone—until much, much later. And a lot of people were unhappy for purely selfish reasons. We felt that Edward R. Murrow was there to protect us; as long as he was there, everything was gonna be all right. The minute he left, then we were thrown to our own devices, we didn't know *where* the hell we were going, and we didn't know what was gonna happen to us. There was that great drop in morale because we felt *now* we're at the mercy of the money men. And it took a long while, quite frankly, for CBS to get back to number one."[193]

He was leaving, as it turned out, at the nadir of the fortunes of the News Division, buffeted by the Huntley-Brinkley phenomenon and the overall problems of the network. That Thursday, the luckless Mickelson, called into Stanton's office, was presented with a release announcing his resignation, effective immediately.[194]

John Day had finally resigned under pressure. To trade papers he said he had no plans but had asked Edward R. Murrow about an opening at the USIA.[195]

Lou Cioffi, in from Paris, asked to see his immediate superior. Resigned, said the secretary. Well, whom should he see? Don't know.[196]

The great department, knee-deep in talent, was floundering like a whale in shallow waters, with upheaval at the top, sagging ratings, *CBS Reports* under attack and network president James Aubrey making noises about its million-dollar losses. The start of an uphill era for the News Division and a long climb back. *Variety* was talking about "an unprecedented public relations rap" for the network, the departure of their biggest news star, and "CBS top command's. . .readiness to push the panic button."[197]

Dick Salant was sitting in his office. The news executive committee strategy had been more or less to ease him into the top News Division spot—getting his feet wet, as he called it—and ease Mickelson out. The dogged man from Minnesota had never been corporate family in quite the same sense.

Like his boss Frank Stanton, Salant had long been fascinated with the News Division, had sat on the five-man special committee which had drawn up the blueprint for *CBS Reports.* He was also frightened.

Murrow came in to say good-bye. The two men, acquaintances of ten years or more, sat and talked, Salant about his worries in the new position. "I was scared to death," he recalled:

> And I remember, Ed moved his chair up closer—he was always a warm, sympathetic guy—put one hand on my knee and said, "Dick, you're just where I was when I started. I wasn't a journalist either; but you love it, and that's it. All you have to do is love the news."[198]

The break wasn't total; he could still be seen at times in the old cubicle over the weeks, commuting in from Washington, answering mail, tying up loose ends. The Park Avenue apartment had gone on the market, his salary of more than $200,000 traded in for a civil servant's income of $21,000, his move financed in effect by deferred back pay. "Resolving his displeasures with CBS the hard way," *Variety* had called it.[199]

But for all intents and purposes he was the government's, his work begun at once. February 1, not yet confirmed, he had sat in on the National Security Council, by invitation of the President, a gesture widely publicized.

All the same, there were few illusions about the toughness of the job, none at all about the problems landsliding on the government of which he was now a part. January 8, on *Background,* he had dealt at length on the outgoing administration's good-bye present to Kennedy: severing relations with Havana, closing the large U.S. Embassy, revoking diplomatic recognition—a response, it said, to Fidel Castro's orders to cut the staff to eleven, including clerks and janitors. In forty-eight hours.

"President-elect Kennedy was 'informed' of Mr. Eisenhower's decision . . . he was not consulted."[200]

Well, Castro had provoked, we had responded; the United States had shown that it would not be "pushed around." Castro, Murrow suspected, might even be pleased. "One is entitled to observe, however, that breaking off relations is not a cure."

A final paragraph was to have finished off the broadcast—to the effect that the boat carrying the embassy personnel home from Havana had landed at West Palm Beach, "a place which Mr. Kennedy is wont, from time to time, to make his headquarters."

It was deleted before airtime, whether over opinion differences or simple timing considerations would not be known.

"The problem—literally—now lies ticking in his lap. . . ."[201]

XVI

Washington

Sufferers from a creeping illness who know their days
are counted may say aloud: "I am in a hurry." Under
their breath, they whisper, "I am pursued."
—COLETTE

Donald M. Wilson, Deputy Director, USIA, did not as a habit go charging
into the Director's office. Nor would he ever forget Murrow's face when
he told him about the Bay of Pigs, that morning in mid-April, following
an early breakfast with Tad Szulc of The New York *Times*, a news friend
since the time they had dodged rocks and bottles, covering Nixon's tour
through Latin America.

What Szulc had heard, was of a planned landing in Cuba sometime
soon, the next few days probably, U.S.-supported; he was going down to
Florida, try to get to the island from there. In the meantime, wouldn't
the reporters covering the thing be needing some kind of press office in
the area? Wilson sat listening, thunderstruck.

It was eight A.M. Wilson rushed to 1776 Pennsylvania Avenue and
sought out Murrow in his office: "I gotta see you on an urgent matter."
Inside, he spilled out the story.

Murrow nodded his head throughout the recital, Wilson recalled later.
"But as he nodded, his face clouded up. He was clearly getting madder
and madder. He looked me up and down. Then he pushed the buzzer.
'Get me Allen Dulles.' "

A short time later, they stood in the office of the CIA chief—"Tell him
what you told me." Wilson went through it a second time. Dulles pulled
at his pipe and kept his comments noncommittal.[1]

Back at 1776, says Wilson, there was a phone call from Special Presidential Assistant McGeorge Bundy, asking Murrow over to the White
House where, once arrived, he received confirmation and objected: It
was wrong, unworthy of a great power, and probably wouldn't work.
Besides which, the last opinion poll from Cuba had given Castro high
marks among Cubans generally, precluding any thought of a disaffected
populace rising as one to join with the invaders.

(In fact, wrote Chester Bowles years afterward, it was the timing that had caught most of them off balance, less so the plan itself—an Eisenhower Era legacy, hotly debated in those past weeks. Bowles would recall arguments in meetings that included Bundy, with Bowles himself, backed by Murrow, vigorously protesting "the Cuban adventure," as he called it.)[2]

In any case, the message in mid-April seemed to be: too late.

The following morning, Henry Loomis, Director of the Voice of America, was driving in to work when news of the invasion flashed over the car radio. He slammed the accelerator, exceeded several speed limits, arriving with brakes shrieking at the Voice to find that no one knew anything. Dialing and reaching Murrow, he held the receiver at arm's length as a stream of expletives exploded out of the earpiece, ending in "Dammit, if they want me in on the crash landings, I'd better damned well be in on the takeoffs!"[3]

They'd have to start round-the-clock broadcasting in Spanish, Loomis told Murrow; it was going to cost them a bundle and he needed his approval. The broadcasts begun, they found reliable information almost impossible to come by. In the meantime, three Cuban exile stations in Miami and the CIA radio operation for the area, Radio Swan, were each broadcasting contradictory reports. The VOA, unprepared, was encountering problems controlling its own Spanish language staff, many of them Cubans. In New York, Adlai Stevenson as UN Ambassador, kept in the dark like so many others, was hooted down as he spoke.

Murrow, in the backwash of the failed operation, said nothing of his opposition, his only public role, that of presiding over the exchange of prisoners in return for tractors for Castro.

Two months into his job, it looked as though his written assurances on input into foreign policy decisions weren't amounting to the proverbial hill of beans.

From the outset, Murrow's long experience of Washington notwithstanding, it had been a little like learning to walk all over again.

Arrived with Janet at Union Station on a gray day in February, he had been taken in hand by Don Wilson—his deputy, purely provisional, of course—thirty-five, on leave from *Time*, formerly Washington bureau chief; a close friend of Bobby Kennedy who for the past weeks along with outgoing Acting Director Abbott Washburn, the PR man who had put in eight years for Eisenhower, literally ran the Agency.

It was Wilson who would suggest the No. 3 spot for Tom Sorensen— a USIA career officer, brother to Kennedy aide Ted Sorensen and, like Wilson, part of the transition team. Two capable, ambitious young men in their mid-thirties, going places, whose connections to the White House and the Kennedy circle far outstripped Murrow's. And whose recommendations had already helped shape the direction of Kennedy's USIA.

"I was imposed on him," says Wilson today. But Murrow just as surely needed them—particularly Sorensen—in mastering a government warren of 12,000 with worldwide functions and variegated departmental layers. Sizing up the situation, he made the provisional appointments permanent.

Wilson, at the outset, had been just a bit star-struck, greeting his new chief at Union Station, but Murrow, he said later, was "gracious and welcoming . . . we hit it off immediately."

At the hotel, Wilson unloaded the books and documents brought along to start the Director's education. Murrow seemed "somewhat bemused" by it all but immersed himself in the mounds of paper "like an eighth-grade honor student."[4]

Unlike others arrived for the great transition, he had come to Washington without a staff. Not even Kay Campbell, left in New York after some painful talking. There was nothing worthy of her, he insisted, she was executive level, not some steno girl; he could never get for her the GS standing she so rightfully deserved.[5]

There had been great kindness and concern of course, arrangements made with Sidney Bernstein, for Campbell to head the new Granada office in New York. Personal contacts continued, warm as ever. But for Kay Campbell, the door had closed on an era.[6]

Others whom he wanted hadn't come. Marvin Kalb, the Soviet scholar and one-time foreign service officer, now in Moscow for CBS, thought it over, then declined. Over the telephone, Murrow assured him explanations weren't needed, that their friendship would remain untouched; that Kalb's career was at the "take-off point." The younger man nevertheless felt it incumbent upon him to explain that he wanted to stay a reporter. "You set an example not only for me but for every journalist in radio and television. . . . You embodied radio-TV news with a dignity that is awesome—and you gave CBS News life, and the Murrow tradition. I want to follow that tradition. . . ."[7]

The letter, Murrow replied, was "one of the few letters that I shall keep. It will serve to warm me when the chill winds of criticism begin to blow.

"I thank you for the kind words about myself and I cannot but agree with your decision. . . ."[8]

It was April 3. By that time, the winds had started blowing with tornado force.

At first the only problem seemed the holdup on his nomination—a result partly of White House lateness in ordering the requisite security check for a sensitive position, partly the FBI's determination this time to know all there was to know.

By 1961, Murrow's profile at the Bureau was that of one who was or had been "a member of, associated with, or sympathetic to, or on the mailing list" of "cited organizations"; who had associated with individuals subject to security investigations; who had served on the Advisory Council of the Moscow University Summer Session; who had been placed at arm's length by personal order of the Director himself.[9]

This time they would not be hoodwinked. "The derogatory information available concerning Murrow" required "a thorough and penetrative investigation," involving "extensive field reviews at the seat of Government and in the field. . . .

"This case," ran the directive, "will be closely supervised and followed."[10]

A month after starting work, Murrow seemed no closer to nomination—in the limbo of the uncleared appointee—as the Bureau ran down every conceivable lead, sifting through the detritis of McCarthy's accusations in a massive nationwide investigation reaching back into his childhood, going into every aspect of his personal and public life, from checks on his wife, parents, son, and in-laws, to running down every allegation in every pamphlet, every leaflet cranked out in the post-McCarthy days. Citizens whose hand-scrawled letters to the Bureau over the years, complaining of Murrow's broadcasts—this man should be watched, was no friend of America, "slam-bammed the Republicans," was obviously paid by the liberals—had never gotten more than a polite thank you, were now themselves visited by agents asking if they had proof or personal knowledge of wrongdoing.

College officials who had spent an evening at the most with Murrow, stopping by at commencement for the honorary doctorate, were pumped in the eventuality of "adverse information." A political science professor at a small Pennsylvania school was questioned about Murrow's conversation the weekend he'd been a houseguest, back in 1947.[11]

Suspect connections discounted by the Bureau itself back in the fifties were re-opened, informants queried in far-flung cities as to whether Murrow was a member of the local CP cell, to their knowledge, or on the rolls of the Socialist Workers Party. Days were spent, streams of ink spilled, trying to pin down an alleged Castro-Cuban connection. West Coast agents scoured the old logging areas of Clallam County, looking for hard evidence of an IWW connection, hunting for old-timers who might recall if Murrow, in those college summers, had indeed carried the red card. Even the *Saturday Evening Post* writer gone after by Surine was sent back to his notes to find his source in linking Murrow and the Wobblies.

The post-McCarthy *Counterattack* charges of March 19, 1954 were gone into. The information, it turned out, had come from a source connected with the House Committee on Un-American Activities and yes, he'd been keeping a file for years on Murrow. Get after it, went the directive, "verify or disprove,"[12] with a p.s. from the Director: "Yes, nail it down."[13]

By late February, Attorney General Robert F. Kennedy was inquiring nervously into the status of the new administration's most publicized appointment. Granted, there'd been sloppy desk work at their end, but couldn't they do something in this case? The pressure was simply "tremendous."[14]

The Bureau assured the Attorney General they'd do their best. There were, however, "allegations" which needed checking out.

Of course they'd expedite the matter, Hoover noted in the house, but thoroughness was paramount, "particularly as to such a character as Murrow."[15]

In the meantime, an embarrassed administration fended off queries from the press about the holdup—yes, the nomination was still "in the works" and no, they couldn't say when Murrow's name would go up to the Hill.[16] The AP, fed by leaks from unnamed "Congressional and other sources," let it be known that the FBI was holding up the process.

But in the end the Bureau played it straight, misgivings about Murrow notwithstanding. He was a newsman, they were cops, the job, within the given limits, solid and professional. Guidelines had been observed, sources evaluated, personal knowledge separated from hearsay, and if it didn't hold up, so be it, the reams of reports dotted with the final judgments: "not pertinent" or "no derogatory loyalty information developed." The allegations hadn't stood up under the tests and they accepted it.

Hoover did not like Murrow. Did not trust Murrow. Didn't want him in the job. With a marked lack of enthusiasm showing through the formal language, the FBI nonetheless turned over the summaried reports—the few who thought Murrow a menace and the many who thought him the greatest thing since the founding fathers—and let the Kennedys decide.

March 14, Murrow went before the Fulbright committee—the most nervous witness of the season, according to one columnist, despite the goodwill radiating from a senatorial VIP lineup including the Chairman, Majority Leader Mansfield, Humphrey, Symington, Javits, Aiken, and Scoop Jackson. Murrow, by contrast, sat tensed at the edge of his red-leather seat, peering up at the panel like a condemned man—without a cigarette.

Finding no ashtrays at the witness table, he'd assumed a ban on smoking, going through the hearing with hands tightly clasped, fingers interlocked, feet shaking between the legs of the chair; going through questions and answers for an hour and fifty-six minutes, answering in his familiar low, unhurried accents as his system screamed for nicotine. To one observer watching the proceedings, he had the look of a tired, sad basset hound.

His opening statement promised an Agency voice "firm but not belli-cose," operating "on the basis of truth," the message, "that we as a nation are not allergic to change and have no desire to sanctify the status quo."

Answering questions, however, he assured the Senators dryly that USIA would try to make U.S. policy "everywhere intelligible and wherever possible, palatable."[17]

There were a few scratchy moments—e.g., Homer Capehart, the pho-nograph magnate from Indiana, offering an old sales manager's advice, as he called it: after all, wasn't promoting the U.S. abroad pretty much like selling a Buick, i.e., you didn't go around pointing out weaknesses in the product. McCarthy's old committee partisan, Bourke Hickenlooper of Iowa, bringing up *Crisis of Abundance*, the appointee's history of emphasizing the less attractive side of things, asked, why couldn't we be more like the Soviets, keep our propaganda upbeat?

Because ours was an open, pluralistic society, said Murrow, visibly restraining himself. And no, you couldn't tell "the American story" ef-fectively if you talked only in superlatives.

The hearing over, a Washington reporter watched Murrow return to his seat among the spectators, tear through a beat-up cigarette pack, retrieve a weed, and light up, calming visibly with a long, deep draught.

The confirmation came through by unanimous vote, first in Committee then in the full Senate. Confirmed at the same time were Don Wilson, new ambassadorial appointments to Sweden and Ceylon,[18] and the ap-pointment of Frederick A. Nolting, Jr. as Ambassador to the Republic of Vietnam.

A rumored nomination fight on Murrow had not materialized, his ap-pointment sailing through smoothly without a single dissent. Perhaps, given the events that followed, just a bit too smoothly.

Exactly why he tried to stop "Harvest of Shame" from being televised over the BBC would remain complicated and to some extent obscure—at least upon the written record. The word went out, when it was over, that the White House had requested it. But Murrow himself had been jolted by the sale to England of the program—a muckraking effort, as he'd conceived it, to move Americans to action, not for merchandising abroad to turn a buck, a view he would retain long after the incident itself was past.

But word had also gone down the line, in the days before the hearing, of a possible holdout on the Senate Foreign Relations Committee. Spes-sard Holland, Democrat of Florida, with reputed close ties to the citrus growers, had threatened allegedly to vote no if Murrow didn't try to kill the televising abroad of the broadcast libeling the Great Sunshine State. There had been talk of an organized opposition coalescing on the right—not enough to block, perhaps, but sufficient to cause delays and embar-rassment to a minority presidency that had squeaked into office on the narrowest of margins, and to an ex-broadcaster going on fifty-three, who had burned his bridges behind him.

Concomitantly, there was the prospective spectacle of Kennedy's USIA Director hosting a devastating exposé of the American scene over European television, beamed into British parlors and what would our friends and adversaries make of that? Henry Loomis came into Murrow's office to find him in the midst of phone calls, totally distraught: "Oh my God! and there I was *in* this thing—"

He put the receiver down, aware of the other's presence. He wished he'd never *made* the film, he went on, it was going to be harmful to the U.S. abroad, here he'd meant to build up the USIA and now this happens—this was it! How was he going to stop it?

Loomis, an old hand in these matters, laughed—"You *can't*, Ed, you can't."

"He knew it himself," said Loomis later, "deep down; he'd just never worked for the government. Well, it took him a day or two to settle down; he had no choice."[19]

Don Wilson stood by as Murrow, in early March, rang up the BBC. "He was afraid of embarrassment to the Kennedy administration and to him," was Wilson's recollection, "still wearing his old hat where he could do anything he damn well pleased; so he didn't think anything about calling Carleton Greene."[20]

To Hugh Carleton Greene, however, Murrow sounded distinctly uncomfortable as he opened the transatlantic conversation—"I've got an awkward request to make."

"I can remember him sounding rather embarrassed over the telephone," Hugh Greene remembers. "It was not long before 'Harvest of Shame' was due to be shown. The *Radio Times* had already gone to press with the announcement—it goes to press about a fortnight in advance. Well, Ed asked, in a rather embarrassed way, whether it would be possible for me to consider canceling the showing. And explained something about the political difficulties he was in—told me exactly what they were. I remember it was something to do with the Senate, or the House. And that there was a fuss being made about this program made by the man who was now in charge of the U.S. Information Agency. And which showed part of the United States in such an *extremely* bad light. Being shown abroad. That was the political background."[21]

Murrow by now showed visible signs of being pressured, the final FBI report still pending, his status still in limbo. The Hearst-owned New York *Mirror* was reporting the American Legion as "girding its loins for an all-out fight, having never forgotten "Argument in Indianapolis," to be joined presumably by "conservatives of both parties" who had never forgiven Murrow's "assassination" of McCarthy. New Hampshire conservative Styles Bridges, an old McCarthy ally, was expected to lead the battle on the Senate floor.[22]

Meanwhile, the anger over "Harvest of Shame," now almost three months past, flared up afresh. On the Senate floor, legislators clashed bitterly over the program. The UPI reported a New Jersey Farm Bureau spokesman attacking Murrow as "unfit" for his new office, addressing that organization's annual breakfast meeting with the state congressional delegation.[23]

Passions raised over the years of controversy were coming home to roost.

Hugh Greene was no innocent. A multifaceted personality who had run so-called "white" radio propaganda in the war against the Nazis, the author of respected papers on psychological warfare that were still on file at the Special Warfare School at Fort Bragg and elsewhere, he knew perhaps better than Murrow the pitfalls of the corridors of power, the fine line to be observed.

"I remember thinking to myself during the conversation," he says today, "that Ed had been caught in an intentional trap.

> Because if I didn't say yes, his enemies would say: How powerless he is, he can't even persuade his friend Hugh Greene not to put this program out, he's blackening the name of America. If I had said, Oh of *course* Ed, we won't put it out, he would *then* have been attacked for exercising censorship.
> So that he'd really put his foot in it, as badly as it was possible to put your foot in it.

Not unkindly, the Director-General replied that "Harvest of Shame" was already on the schedule. "I explained to Ed that though I hated to make difficulties for him or leave him in a difficult situation, that *he* would understand that if a program already announced was canceled, there would certainly be a terrific brouhaha in the press. And that this, too, would do him a great deal of harm. And he—sadly, as I remember it— saw my point and that was that."[24]

In Washington, Don Wilson saw Murrow put down the phone: "I gotta watch myself. Of *course* they have every right to put on that show."[25]

But Hugh Greene had guessed rightly. Short days after the uncontested nomination, the story hit the press. Spessard Holland—friend of the citrus lobby, formerly of the coterie gathered for smart weekends at the horse farm of D.C. publisher Ruth McCormick (Bazy) Miller, where the star guest was often Joe McCarthy—took credit for the leak.

The liberal establishment which had hailed Murrow's appointment only days before, descended on him with the outrage of a lover betrayed, echoes reverberating as far as Fleet Street. The Washington *Post* called the action "foolish and futile." Murrow, wrote Jack Gould in The New York *Times*, "should have resigned after twenty-four hours in office rather than concur in an incredible intrusion on the free informational medium of an ally. If [he] acted on his own responsibility, his action constitutes an inexplicable refutation of a principle he has enunciated for years. . . . Mr. Murrow is off to a dismaying start as Director of the United States Information Agency."[26]

The Baltimore *Sun* in its editorial columns called it "an attempt at censorship and suppression of facts and opinions which Mr. Murrow, in his private capacity, had believed to be true and proper." The ACLU, registering "shock," sent an open telegram calling on Murrow to reaffirm the principle of freedom of communication enunciated so eloquently at his Senate hearing.

The *Times* of London, carrying Jack Gould's blast calling Murrow's action "as indefensible as it is futile," said it would be interesting to see "if this great reporter's gift (the gift of candor) survives officialdom."[27] The program by contrast, run in late March, got raves, the two Ed Murrows in a strange competition, the whole affair reaching up into the BBC Board of Management, the minutes noting ever so briefly, "Press support for D.G.'s action in resisting Ed Murrow's attempt to stop the BBC showing of Mr. Ed. Murrow's 'Harvest of Shame.' "[28]

But in the U.S. media, there was a certain undertow, a slightly gleeful note in catching the Great Man in a contradiction. "Sort of like, God had stubbed his toe," a producer at CBS remembered.[29]

"The sound you hear in the background," ran a typical quip, "is an embarrassed cigarette cough."

In early April, taking questions from assembled radio and TV executives at a State Department–sponsored briefing, he took full responsibility, denied that pressure had been brought to bear and agreed, he said, with the "foolish and futile" label applied by his critics. Press leaks seemed to indicate pressure from the White House after all, however. Gould suggested that the administration shoulder some of the responsibility; Mr. Murrow, he said, should not be left holding the bag.

Murrow himself, deeply depressed over the whole matter, had in private offered Kennedy his resignation. This was it; he had failed, the office compromised. Only one thing to do. The young President, as an old politician, assured him it wasn't that serious.[30]

Speaking before USIA employees—he had forgotten, he said, which hat he was wearing but hoped he still had a place to hang it—Murrow did his best to pick himself up from his first stumble over the New Frontier.

For an active, restless man, however, kept too long without sufficient outlet for his energies, the demanding, multifaceted job with its ultimate responsibility for worldwide USIA operations had more than its compensations, at least at the outset. Having turned his back publicly on the old life, working in an office bare of all mementos of his broadcasting career— the one exception was the old mike from the BBC—he threw himself into administration with a vengeance, surprising many who had never known the old Ed Murrow of the early thirties. Somewhat ostentatiously, almost defiantly, he called himself a bureaucrat and as always, dressed the part, working shirtsleeved, tie loosened, but sporting now the dark-rimmed glasses that previously he had worn only for reading, in deliberate repudiation of the trenchcoat image—a sober-suited, bespectacled figure accentuating in dress and manner the anonymity he continually talked about but never really managed.

Press attention had followed him into office, with ample encouragement from the administration, a certain glamour rubbing off on a slighted, little-known agency with a stepchild history. An agency now in the foreground because Ed Murrow was taking charge. His old friend Scotty Reston, heading The New York *Times* Washington bureau, had put two of his best talents on the story—Tom Wicker covering the confirmation hearings; David Halberstam interviewing the new Director in his office, noting the absence of CBS memorabilia.

Letters poured in by the hundreds from intellectuals and professional communicators volunteering their services, from the Editor-in-Chief of the *Encyclopaedia Britannica* to Bob Shayon of *Saturday Review*. Hollywood liberals, set aflame by the combination of Ed Murrow and Jack Kennedy, asked what they could do for their country, an advisory film committee set up on the Coast, headed by the producer Fred Zinnemann.

The smooth stream of good relations was momentarily rippled when Murrow, appearing in Hollywood, took the industry to task for the Dodge City image of America purveyed in its high-volume B-grade exports, not to mention films about Africa which, he charged, were downright racist. The film community yelled censorship, Eric Johnson as industry spokesman administered a stiff public rebuke, and the whole affair made a story for several days. It soon blew over, numerous Hollywood figures agreeing with Murrow under the table: yes, the films were mostly perfectly awful, just a shame Ed had to say so as head of USIA. Murrow and Johnson were soon back to "Dear Ed" and "Dear Eric," their brief encounter the only aspect of the otherwise close USIA-Hollywood relations to receive much attention from the news media.

But all in all, it was an era of good feeling, the first heady burst of New Frontierdom. Agency retirees would later remember the procession of celebrities paying calls on the Director—living, glittering proof of how the USIA had come up in the world; whisperings of Pearl Buck in the outer office; young secretaries rushing to the corridor as word got around that Marlon Brando was out there, large as life, waiting for the elevator.

To younger administration members, Murrow was an object of veneration, a legendary figure. One story had it that Bill Moyers, the Peace Corps' youthful Assistant Director for Public Affairs, ventured to ask the great man about his time in broadcasting.

"It was a great life," Murrow supposedly answered, "but they'll break your heart."

Stories in the press stressed the ugprading of the Agency's status, Murrow's hotline to the Oval Office, symbol of USIA input and presumed closeness to the White House. The President had made it clear—the Agency was to tell it like it is; no hard sell, no Dulles bombast. The new themes: a nuclear test ban treaty, an effective United Nations, a free West Berlin, "free choice" for developing countries, consonant with their traditions and aspirations. . . .[31]

American propaganda was to be turned around, operations to be lean and efficient, objectives defined, with accountability directly to the top—not the boys at State who had left the Agency, in its earlier incarnations, to sink or swim under McCarthy's onslaughts.

As a sign of the fresh new climate, the White House felt it appropriate to reinstate Reed Harris, the steadfast IIA official who had stood up to the Wisconsin Senator in that striking film sequence on the McCarthy show. Ed Murrow and McCarthy's victim, united on the New Frontier: the perfect symbol. Murrow would get the credit, but the idea had first filtered down through channels. Murrow went in on it immediately, the connection quickly made, the ensuing scene depicted in the later recollections of those present—the officers assembled, Murrow announcing, in his best understated style: "Gentlemen, I want to welcome back Reed Harris after an absence of eight years."

It made its impression. "These men around the table," one of them recalled, "they were old hands. They remembered. The tears started running down their faces; the McCarthy Era was over."[32]

(Raymond Swing was still at the VOA. Bill Robson, formerly of CBS before *Red Channels*, applied to Murrow for a job and joined the Voice, making the Agency something of a haven for the blacklisted.)

Harris, installed by Murrow as his personal executive assistant, proved more than a sentimental choice; the former IIA man's expertise, experience of the Agency, understanding of the workings of the system proved invaluable to someone coming from the outside.

The move also helped dispel the lingering suspicions about John Kennedy, Murrow's first weeks at the Agency having been marked by offhand references to "that young man" or "the young man in the White House."[33] His attitude, however, had started changing in the backwash of the Bay of Pigs fiasco, with Kennedy's readiness to shoulder the blame. "That's some young man," he told his counsel. Not passing the buck—it was the right thing, the manly thing to do.

From the start, Murrow had made it clear that his was not to be a figurehead directorship. Two days before his confirmation hearing, a memo had gone out from Wilson to all heads of elements within the Agency: Mr. Murrow wished to be up to date when he attended Secretary Rusk's Monday-Wednesday-Friday staff meetings; a special assistant would therefore be available for early briefings from the staff on those mornings, ready to pass any and all important matters on to Mr. Murrow. A nighttime number was available if necessary. Mr. Murrow needed to be kept abreast first of major developments within the Agency, and on matters "particularly germane to the State Department."[34]

Murrow himself, contacting all Agency elements, laid down the lines of direct responsiveness to the policy needs of the President—a major shift for the Agency, in accordance with recommendations drawn up by the transition teams that had included Wilson, Sorensen, and George Ball, now with State as Undersecretary in the new administration, Murrow's two deputies-to-be, Don Wilson and Tom Sorensen, and including recommendations made in the last year of the Eisenhower presidency.

In practice it meant moving away from the bread-cast-on-waters philosophy of Murrow's predecessor, George V. Allen, to the honed-down approach of carefully targeted objectives. From information to "persuasion," to furthering "climates of opinion" favorable to U.S. objectives[35]— the result, actually, of recommendations by Tom Sorensen in early January to the President-elect in a meeting at his home in Georgetown. Murrow, coming in cold and given the President's instructions, was therefore working within the framework of an approach outlined by his own deputy, now in charge of Policy and Research: Thomas Sorensen, the ten-year Agency veteran to whom he turned of necessity for expertise on program operations; the one responsible for effecting the new, close policy-product relationship.[36]

The emphasis under Eisenhower had been ostensibly cultural and informational, though in Southeast Asia agency functions had become more politicized. Under the Kennedy administration, the political aspect was now stepped up, with so-called Country Teams, Objectives, regularly drafted Country Plans, and a direct and immediate tie-in with Agency product going out via radio, TV, films, and publications.

Murrow, at the outset, had no problems with an activist role. He shared Kennedy's view of the world—the U.S. in competition with an expansionist Sino-Soviet bloc—though again like Kennedy, more flexible on the "Sino" aspect than implied by public rhetoric. He accepted the administration view of the Agency job as that of psychological warfare, political not military battles, words instead of weapons, though not excluding the happy possibility of dialogue. A stance puzzling to some who knew him as a newsman, but not to those who knew him as one who like Jean Anouilh's Becket, having taken on a job, would pursue it all the way, with puritanical consistency. Therefore he could as easily testify against legislation threatening a cut-off of mail service between the U.S. and Eastern Europe, on the grounds that the flow of information went both ways;[37] or urge that "Red China" not be barred from access to American-developed communications satellites.

Still, there had been a noticeable change at USIA, the cultural long-term approach, as a later analyst would write, subordinate to "a more directly political short-term approach. . . . conveying broad understanding of American culture and life, subordinated to giving specific understanding of and favorable responses to American foreign policy initiatives."[38]

To some extent, there had always been that dichotomy within the Agency. Hans Tuch, then deputy director of the Soviet Branch, formerly cultural attaché in Moscow and a believer in the long-term view, would later speak of the tug of war between the two camps—the quick-results advocates, as he put it, and the long-term programmers. Now, in Kennedy's USIA, the balance was swinging in the other direction, keynoting the Murrow administration. Burnett Anderson, Sorensen's second-in-command who worked with the Director on policy questions, was later to recall Murrow as "totally responsive to the White House," differing little from Sorensen in "perception, outlook, objectives."[39] By contrast, Hans Tuch, who worked with Murrow on Soviet-related matters and often found himself opposing Sorensen ("more intent on promoting the Kennedy administration," he felt, "than the USIA should be involved with"), would remember the Director as being responsive to political realities, yet no ideologue; as a Kennedy appointee who was not conspicuously beholden to the White House. Tuch would remain convinced that the pendulum would have swung even further without Murrow at the top.[40]

At the same time the new Director was learning about the supposed real world, the government within a government; learning there was more to Telling America's Story than met the eye.

The day after the Bay of Pigs, and in the wake of the shadowboxing with Allen Dulles, Murrow moved to regularize their relations with the CIA—chaotic, evidently, in the past—making any future operational use of his employees or anyone "currently of interest" to that agency subject to clearance at the top by USIA.[41]

Dulles was agreeable; certainly there was no animosity. Quite the contrary, the two men knew and respected each other, part of the long history of good relations between the CIA and the news media in those years, particularly with CBS, marked by annual briefing sessions. There were freewheeling discussions with the correspondents, delightful evenings at Dulles' club or at his home in Washington—the Director set a good table—top newsmen, top agency men, good talk and cigars, each side out for what it could get but then, said one who was there, they were all adults; you took the point of view into consideration as you would anybody else's. And the fact was, some of these guys had the best information going and you were free to check it out. (The fact also was, said Sig Mickelson later, that anyone newsgathering abroad who *didn't* check in with a station chief as part of his rounds would have been remiss in the performance of his duty.)[42]

Murrow, as newsman, had known pressure in the past, had slapped back when he felt it warranted, both on and off the air. But in a case of Us versus Them, they were our side, the good guys.

Now, running the USIA, he found himself sitting on the same councils, in the NSC and elsewhere, with the CIA Director as with other top administration notables, called to the same interagency task forces pondering national security decisions, the inevitable overlap of the inner government. Within the USIA, the Chief of Training was a CIA officer on a two-year detail, just as their security head was a former special agent of the FBI.

But when it came to the use of their personnel by the so-called "other agency," said an official of the time, who declined to be identified, USIA leadership had never been particularly happy. Said the official, they all had more to lose than to gain.

For obvious reasons, therefore, they preferred to avoid it when possible, didn't want the agencies synonymous in image or in fact, complying rarely, the official insisted, and with great reluctance; ruled out anything clandestine for their own people, refused featherbedding for the others; conscious above all of the problem of credibility and the position of the thousands in their employ who had neither connection with or knowledge of CIA operations.

Murrow himself, said Wilson later, was "absolutely against it" in principle. "We felt strongly that if any USIA men were caught helping the CIA in any country, it would ruin the program."[43]

Meeting with Dulles, Murrow laid down lines of demarcation, taking the unprecedented step of recording the agreement on paper and keeping a copy in his files. Sorensen, who had been the CIA's point of contact for policy, themes, and operations discussions, was to continue to work chiefly with the two designated officers (one of them the later CIA Director Richard Helms). Sorensen and USIA's chief of security would, however, determine the Agency's position on individual requests for "operational use" or "cover interest," with Murrow brought in on borderline or unusual cases. The agreement precluded, finally, all individual approaches by the CIA to USIA personnel, with each instance to be decided separately. Even then, weeks later, Murrow, obviously uneasy, still wanted a memo sent around stating specifically that no prospects were to be undertaken "with or on behalf of the CIA" without the necessary clearance.[44]

There was also something called the Business Council for International Understanding, a legacy of the Eisenhower years, one of the public sector groups cooperating with the Agency under Section 1005 of PL-402, directing the USIA to "utilize to the maximum extent practicable, the services and facilities of private agencies";[45] put through by the Republican Congress of 1953, 1005 had specifically linked the newborn underfunded agency and the well-endowed business community in the attainment of presumably common goals.

Kicked off in the wake of Nixon's violent reception in Latin America in the latter fifties, the BCIU was made up of the senior executives of leading U.S. corporations doing business abroad, with a policy board that included the presidents of Standard Oil of California, the Bechtel Corporation, ITT, and Time, Inc., as well as the chairman of the board of RCA and the president of CBS. Secretary to the board and go-between for the private sector was Abbott Washburn, Acting Director of the USIA in early '61, now working out of a PR office in the National Press Building. The point of contact in the government was Undersecretary of State George Ball.[46]

After all, as one official put it, American business had for many years carried on projects which assisted in the accomplishment of mutual objectives.[47] The Council sponsored executive training courses for life abroad, underwrote worthy international programs. They were also, Washburn told his successors at the agency, "carrying on various efforts to counter Castro-Communism in Latin America."[48] When the time came, therefore, it was only right that the Council be kept up to date on Kennedy's Alliance for Progress, being in close contact as they were with influential groups in Latin America who could make or break the *Alianza*.

Because without business support the Alianza was nowhere, requiring as it did the cooperation of the private sector: a joint drive to remedy the many ills afflicting the region and just possibly, the area director told Murrow, the U.S.'s "last chance" in Latin America.[49]

Murrow believed in the Alianza; so did the devoted souls at USIA. It was the right way, the good way: the middle way; evolution, not revolution. No more northern Big Brother laying down the law, just helping the Latin Americans help themselves.

They were limited, however, by their context. Some of the strongest opposition to the Alliance for Progress, Murrow wrote a friend at the Carnegie Corporation, was coming from "certain members of the U.S. business community in Latin America."[50] From Central America, country officers reported their biggest stumbling blocks to be the landowning oligarchs who liked things just the way they were. Following the Inter-American Economic and Social Conference at Punta del Este, Uruguay, Murrow was informed of the "unhappiness of the business community."[51]

There were of course those business groups from whom they'd expected problems, who thought the USIA insufficiently aggressive vis-à-vis the reds, that there was nothing wrong in Latin America, Castro aside, that a little restored investor confidence couldn't cure. But now it seemed the so-called "progressives" were uneasy. Discussions with Walter Wriston of First National City Bank and Peter Grimes of Chase Manhattan had turned up "suspicions," Murrow was told, regarding the motives behind some of the proposals for reform. Not that they objected to the proposals themselves, of course, just wanted to be sure that people in the administration hadn't formulated them out of some theoretical belief in a "semi-socialist society" for Latin America.[52]

Meeting with the Business Council's Joint Latin American Committee, sitting with representatives of government and industry, Murrow listened to arguments over semantics from the private sector. Of *course* they supported the principles of the Alliance. But what exactly did the U.S. government mean with its statements favoring "tax reform" or "agrarian reform"? And did they know the very word, "reform," had fallen into disrepute down there as representing "Castroism"? Murrow pointed out that even the word "revolution" was subject to varying interpretations.[53]

Taking questions from the standing Committee on the Immediate Communist Danger in Latin America, representing 125 American firms operating in the region, he listened to demands that the air be cleared "as to the attitude of the United States Government toward private enterprise."[54]

Murrow, briefed by his staff, assured them the USIA welcomed their input, supported the Alliance for Progress, and of course, combated international communism—please see your folders, gentlemen—but that propaganda itself had a point of diminishing returns, particularly when not matched by deeds, and maybe U.S. business had best make sure its own house was in order down there in Latin America.[55]

It was a split-personality arrangement for the Agency, kept chronically on short rations and expected to produce; calling for a new order while relying on the old arrangements; pushing social progress on one hand while continuing the covert financing of anti-Communist propaganda, privately funded, unattributed, begun under the Eisenhower administration. Pepsi-Cola had paid for over a million anti-Castro cartoon books for dissemination in Mexico, the USIA's Office of Private Cooperation wrote Murrow, and it looked as though others might be interested. They didn't like bringing him into these matters but could he sign the drafted letter requesting an appointment for their representative?[56]

It was another world, without the familiar moorings. Early on, Jack Fischer of *Harper's* had warned him that the job "might well turn out to be the worst meatgrinder in Washington. . . . As a citizen I am delighted you have accepted . . . as a friend, I can't help having some forebodings."[57]

But there was one aspect that friends in the news media didn't see, therefore couldn't comprehend, welcoming as balm to a man who'd been too long at the bottom of the totem pole. At the beehive on Pennsylvania Avenue, on junkets abroad, he was The Director, with willing hands around to do his bidding. Did the new head of Television Services have the support he needed? The appropriate officer would see to it. The Director was finding the delays in elevator service quite intolerable; underlings moved to light a fire under General Services to speed things up. The Director was requesting that his home and office be tied into the hot line conference telephone system serving top State Department officials. It was done.[58]

Three mornings a week, and many afternoons, he sat with power figures from State, CIA, the Pentagon. ("I don't think it matters," Sidney Bernstein once commented, "as long as you don't inhale.")[59] When he corresponded with the brass at the networks, it was as an equal and more.

Though the habits of a lifetime, it turned out, were a little hard to break. At his first NSC meeting, he had started off by taking notes as each member spoke, working up a head of steam until he suddenly realized he didn't have to do a broadcast. He was still laughing about it when he returned to his office.

But the doors had by no means closed on the broadcast world; the VOA alone precluded that. Quite the contrary, there were constant contacts— complicated now by years of friendship and memories of battles fought on the same side of the barricades.

There was embarrassment in New York *Times* publisher Orvil Dryfoos' refusal to allow two staff members to appear over the Voice, wary of a possible perceived link—even a fallacious one—between his reporters and the U.S. government. As Ed would no doubt understand, he wrote, and maybe they could discuss it over lunch.[60]

Murrow, replying, conceded the matter to be "troublesome," and he wasn't too sure about it either.[61]

(VOA records in fact disclosed more cooperation between the *Times* and the Voice than Dryfoos was apparently aware of. Besides, the Agency complained, *Times* correspondents got help from USIS posts around the world, and names like Marquis Childs, Elie Abel, Pauline Frederick, managed to appear over the Voice without feeling compromised.[62] The decision, however, stood.)[63]

CBS on the other hand had reversed itself early on, even before Murrow officially took up the reins. "IN THE EVENT A CERTAIN NETWORK ABAN-DONED AN HISTORIC POLICY AND MADE BROADCASTS AVAILABLE TO A CERTAIN GOVERNMENT FOR TRANSMISSION ABROAD," cabled Blair Clark, CBS News Director and Harvard friend of JFK, "TO WHOM SHOULD WORD BE SENT, SINCE MURROW WAS CLEARLY OUT OF CHANNELS?"[64]

They indicated Abbott Washburn, still Acting Director at the time. Dick Salant accordingly reviewed and changed a 1959 decision denying the excerpting of broadcasts "involving the voices of CBS news correspondents."[65]

Welcome news, Washburn told Wilson, and he thought he detected ERM's hand.[66]

For better or worse, Murrow was out to get things moving, his determination on behalf of the Agency as strong as it had been at CBS. Though conceivably there were now other elements in the mix: the badly shattered self-confidence that needed to prove it could still swing weight. And the altered perspective of what John Morgan of the BBC and Alexander Kendrick were to term "the poacher turned gamekeeper." Now that he was in it, he was in it all the way, ready to take direction though impatient at the same time to take the initiative again, to set loose the energies so long on semi-tether. And getting his fingers continually burned in the process.

David Sarnoff, an early congratulator, had wanted to resurrect a pet project—tying the words "For Freedom and Peace" onto the Voice of America—disappointed that this splendid idea somehow hadn't caught on at USIA and would Ed set matters right. Murrow, not overoptimistic, promised a look at it and ventured a query of his own to Sarnoff—strictly informally, he stressed, just wanted his opinion.

The letter, labeled "Personal and Confidential," boiled down essentially to this: there was a "vast export of television films and programs abroad." The Agency hadn't the money or capacity to turn out anything like what the networks were producing. Whenever the national purpose could be served "through established commercial channels," it seemed to him, that method should be used. At least things seemed set up that way in the Agency as he had inherited it.

He had no desire, he said, to influence exports, but if the Agency could define its needs more clearly than in the past on what was useful for showing abroad, perhaps the networks might be persuaded to produce them for initial screening in the U.S., with the USIA making "secondary use of them abroad." Once they got priorities straight, perhaps they could have informal talks with the news directors of the networks, with maybe "you, Bill Paley and someone from ABC" down for lunch to discuss it with the President.[67]

On the surface, it wasn't as far-fetched as it seemed. There was a long tradition of cooperation, going back to World War II, between the USIA, its predecessors, and the networks. Both NBC and CBS had produced for the VOA until 1948 and the gradual takeover by State of the programming function. CBS Television had furnished the Agency with programs for foreign broadcasts, also supplying film material.[68] They had done lab work in processing prints of programs owned by the Agency. Contracts existed granting the USIA rights to rebroadcast the Nixon-Kennedy debates as well as lighter fare; in addition, the Agency had authorization from CBS to rebroadcast on audio, under given conditions, its public affairs and discussion programs.

Both networks, of course, had been operating shortwave stations for the Agency and its forerunners, with Columbia Records moreover under contract to the government for the furnishing of all sound recording and transcription services.[69] A fine interweaving of interests.

But this was another matter, touching TV news departments, and Murrow trod carefully, uncertain, still part newsman. "A purely personal and informational query to an old friend," he called it as he asked Sarnoff for feedback. "I would value your counsel greatly."[70]

Instead, Sarnoff turned it over to Bob Kintner, who turned it over to Bill McAndrew, resulting in an open rap on the knuckles from Kintner for the attempted planting of documentaries and another bawling out for the attempted suppression of "Harvest of Shame": "I think you were absolutely wrong. . . ." As though Murrow needed reminding.

To rub it in, a copy of Kintner's open memo to McAndrew was enclosed, a proud statement that Murrow himself, under other circumstances, might have penned, that "such a procedure would involve a direct Government influence on. . .network programming. . . .The Government could justifiably be charged with using the U.S. networks as domestic propaganda instruments, possibly in violation of the spirit establishing the USIA. . . ."[71]

But whatever the merits of the argument, and they were indisputable, the bristling letter conveyed, perhaps, just a shade of self-righteousness—Kintner had been among the first to privately offer the new Director his services "in any way possible"[72]—of the NBC man talking to the CBS man, the industry spokesman giving the perennial critic a taste of his own medicine.

Murrow, replying, noted only that "My letter to General Sarnoff . . .was slugged 'Personal and Confidential,' " that he had been "thinking out loud to an old friend," hadn't the slightest desire to interfere with or influence domestic programming, indeed hoped some of the excellent NBC documentaries could be acquired for use in areas where commercial sales didn't seem likely. And he certainly intended calling Friendly and Irv Gitlin, at NBC, with ideas that might just have merit.[73]

Friendly in fact was perfectly open to suggestions, resulting in input on at least one *CBS Reports,* on fallout shelters.[74] Murrow also suggested "the progress of the American Negro." "No departure from the old technique," he wrote his old partner. "In other words, I am not suggesting that for our purposes the piece ought to say that all is lovely in the garden." Time and events were soon to swamp the whole idea.

NBC having said its say, the three network heads went ahead and lunched with the President. Nothing much happened.[75] The Agency's real constituency was out in the country, among the individual stations, not with the broadcast chains based in New York.

In the fall of 1961, Howard Smith came and told him he was at liberty, fired by CBS over the issue of editorializing.

"Why don't you sue the bastards?" Murrow told him. "I'll go to court and testify you never broke any rules at all."[76]

The bitterness was undissipated; and his feelings about the industry remained unchanged. When the new FCC Chairman Newton Minow had gone after television as "a vast wasteland" before the National Association of Broadcasters that spring, Murrow had sent him his immediate endorsement: "I doubt not that certain vice-presidents of networks will remain in a state of shock for weeks to come. The counter-attack will of course develop in due course, and it will be skillfully mounted and directed. If I can be of any help, you need only command me. In due course I purpose to have a bang at the boys. . . ."[77]

Yet his own position vis-à-vis his former employers was a strange one, with contractual ties still in effect on the long-term basis negotiated back in '56–'57, no longer for broadcasting but under legal constraints unbreakable—so went the stipulation—by either party.

Loyalties to colleagues persisted. His last assignment, "Crossroads Africa: Pilot for a Peace Corps," overlapping with Howard Smith, was actually completed, its producer would recall, after he had gone to USIA, though officially of course the word went out that it was done prior to departure.

Salant, by his account, wanted Murrow back at the network, hoping for Stanton and Paley to "calm down—I wanted to smooth all that over; I wanted Ed."[78] But normalization, apparent on the surface, hadn't yet set in. (The height of the ritual dance had perhaps set in when Murrow, entering his job in Washington, received a telegram from Stanton: "WE AT CBS ARE PROUD OF YOU.")

Nor had the problems contributing to his departure gone away. Quite the contrary, Smith's cashiering, ten months after his own departure, seemed clearly to indicate that things had gotten worse instead of better. There had been months of wrangling with management over Smith's outspoken Sunday commentaries, but it was the Birmingham show that did it—the one he had inherited from Murrow, stepping in as the covert violence turned overt and bloody, as the freedom riders bussed into town.

"I saw what happened," the newsman would recall, "Klansmen, without their hoods, attacking them in broad daylight. The police had disappeared. I saw men with blood running down their faces; one was beaten so badly— I saw him years later, in a wheelchair, partially paralyzed. He cried when he saw me. I knew it was the KKK."[79]

At the show's conclusion, he had quoted Edmund Burke: "The only thing necessary for the triumph of evil is for good men to do nothing." Management wanted it out, citing likely Southern affiliate reactions. Howard K. Smith, the boy from Ferraday, Louisiana, objected. ("Remember, this was early. It wasn't until two years later that support for civil rights became fashionable; then everyone wanted to get in on it. This was earlier and they were scared.")[80]

Personality battles and other confrontations were as always part of the mix, but at the heart of the issue was the old stumbling block: The Policy, at least as interpreted by the high brass. In October, Smith had lost first his commentary spot, a week later, his job. A CBS source told Bob Shayon of *Saturday Review* that his departure left "an icy cold feeling in the News Division"; part of a progression of events, wrote the critic, "undermining the once high image of the network."[81]

It was in that time of unemployment that Smith came to Murrow for advice, and came away wondering about Murrow himself.

Ed had had no problem in talking of the USIA. A whole new world, he said, and he was enjoying it. You got a new perspective on things, being on the other side—the official side. He was glad he'd taken the job.

Then one day Smith was offered an official post:

Assistant Secretary of State for Public Affairs, which is really a PR job for the State Department. And I went to see him, to ask if I should take it.

He said, "Oh, please do! I'd *love* to have someone to work with whom I know." And he said, "And don't worry about this business of 'if you're off the air, you're forgotten in three months.' I think you can go back and be just as effective after a period in government.

Smith was still doubtful. Murrow advised further:

Why don't you go to talk to Walter Lippmann, why don't you go to talk to Robert Kennedy. You have the thinker and you have the doer; they both know more about politics than anybody in the world.

Both Lippmann and Kennedy advised against it; a short time later, Smith went to ABC.

But he kept coming back to Murrow's remark, that old saw about television, i.e., three months away and you were a forgotten quantity, and not to believe it. Was he simply being reassuring, or was he thinking of eventually going back himself?[82]

In one area, certainly, Murrow had found himself at odds with the psywar aspect of the job and therefore, by derivation, his mandate from Kennedy.

An adequate and effective government news service, he had declared back in '53, had to be staffed by "competent newsmen, adequately paid. It cannot be the plaything of advertising men or 'psychological warriors.' "[83]

He had been testifying on the Voice of America, at Bill Fulbright's invitation, before a Senate subcommittee. News broadcasts, he told the Senators, should not be slanted; there were too many alternate sources of information in the world. The ideal, he said at the time, was credibility—"for the measure of our success will be the degree to which we are believed."

His own ideal was the BBC—or rather its External Services: quiet, autonomous, believed—and he had often talked about it with Hugh Greene. Said Greene, "He very much envied its independence."[84]

On taking over the USIA, Murrow had commissioned outside appraisals of the Voice and in-house studies, both urging a toning down of the rhetoric, warning against underestimating the patriotism and just plain smarts of listeners in Eastern Europe. Russian audiences wanted news and not denunciations.[85]

The Voice itself was uneven, ranging from the stridently simplistic to the thoughtful, balanced commentaries of a Raymond Swing. It broadcast in thirty-six languages,[86] considered itself, under its director, Henry Loomis, an entity apart—news professionals, not subject to the dicta of a particular administration line. The administration, despite its rhetoric, wanted an instrument. Murrow, his instincts working one way, the policy pressures from his deputy Sorensen the other, was often caught in the middle. To the Voice people, the Agency continually threatened censorship. To the policy officers, the Voice was getting away with murder, refusing to take guidance.

Murrow generally sided with the Voice—inclined, said Burnett Anderson later, to "come down with the people actually doing the work, rather than with Sorensen's judgment."[87] Loomis was glad of the support. But it remained a continual balancing act, the two sides hacking it out in Murrow's office until it seemed to one or the other that the Director was thoroughly sick of both of them.

In late 1961, Hugh Greene came to Washington, meeting with Kennedy and Murrow on broadcast matters. Relations between the two men seemed easy and friendly, Greene noted. They sat alone, just the three of them, talking in the oval office. At one point in the conversation, Greene remembered, Kennedy turned to Murrow: "Ed, would you like the Voice of America to be more like the BBC?" Murrow sat bolt upright. "My *God*, I would, Mr. President!"[88]

Murrow was in Berlin watching the wall go up, the summer of 1961, partway through a bleak year for the Kennedy administration—beginning with the Bay of Pigs and to include a new escalation in the arms race, the disastrous Kennedy-Khrushchev meeting in Vienna, growing incidents in Berlin, mounting tensions in Laos, and Soviet resumption of atmospheric nuclear testing.

The young President had come back from his first meeting with Khrushchev, shaken by the verbal explosions and threats over Berlin, his overtures rejected, convinced that America would have to stand tall and that Vietnam—the only place with "a real challenge," he told columnist James Reston—looked like the place to make their power credible.

But for the USIA, the focus of attention mandated thus far had been Laos (hold on there at all costs, Ike warned Kennedy on leaving office, even if you have to go to war for it), along with Cuba and Latin America, the nuclear testing issue, and perennially, Berlin.

Murrow had just happened to be in the old capital that Sunday in August, as East German workers threw up the wall while the other side gaped, caught off guard. Returned to Washington, he had raged about the lack of response: a bunch of workers with trowels and shovels—anyone could have stopped them, nipped it in the bud. Dammit, a little girl with a *lollypop* could have stopped them! Well, the West had lost its nerve and they would pay for it.[89] Friends listening to him weren't so sure.

He was quite as ready, therefore, as any New Frontiersman for that firm but steady response that would presumably get the Russian Bear to back down and be reasonable; reassure our Allies by a worldwide stance of firmness. Including Southeast Asia. It was eleven years since his misgivings about the Policy of Doubtful Wisdom, six since his warnings about inheriting the "mess," his path in some ways a parallel of Jack Kennedy's— from wariness of a French colonial involvement to ultimate support of Ngo Dinh Diem. Both men were members of the American Friends of Viet Nam, the pro-Diem group that counted Kennedy among its founders. Both men had come full circle to view the struggle in Vietnam—particularly in the wake of Khrushchev's January declaration of support for so-called national wars of liberation—in strictly cold war terms: Soviet flood waters leaking through the dike.

If there were any doubts or recollections of R. T. Clark's misgivings of the early fifties, or Harold Isaacs', or his own, they seemed resolved or pushed to the back of his mind by the rush of events in the administration, early 1961.

Like others of the press and public, Murrow had been unaware of the cable in September 1960 from Eisenhower's Saigon ambassador, recommending continued support of Diem as the current best bet, but already hinting that Diem himself could be replaced if his position should continue to deteriorate among the Vietnamese.[90]

Murrow had been confirmed exactly four weeks when Walt W. Rostow, senior White House specialist on Southeast Asia and deputy to Mac Bundy, recommended "gearing up the whole Viet-Nam operation." He had been in office five weeks when JFK ordered a review of the Vietnam situation, to "prevent Communist domination of that country"; and six weeks as an interdepartmental task force made its recommendations, including assistance by Saigon USIS to the government of South Vietnam—the purpose, building "public confidence in the GVN's determination and ability to deal with the Communist threat."[91]

It was an almost immeasurable leap from migrant farm workers and civil rights in Birmingham, even the dispassionate analysis of *Background*. It was an almost equal distance from the ostensible job of "telling America's story to the world."

He had come in a believer, like his friend and recruiter Chester Bowles.

"He had this faith [about] the power of words," said Eric Sevareid, "even among enemy countries, or enemy ideologies, this 'winning the hearts and minds of people' idea. . . .And by that time I'd come down to the deepest doubts."

Sevareid had written a column calling world opinion an abstraction with "no meaning in a moralistic sense." Murrow, angered, said he was sorry to see Sevareid abandon his principles. Sevareid said it was a matter of strategies, not principles, that he'd been talking about:

645

This was a much tougher game than that. People wanted to be on the winning side, not necessarily on the righteous side. . . . And this upset Ed. But I think I was basically right.[92]

In the meantime, Murrow was in a situation that was also a tough game, demanding fast decisions, a corresponding toughness, and if you couldn't stand the heat, get out. A situation for which his life's experience as newsman had left him unprepared—agreed, presumably with those around him but dependent, for the first time, on the expertise of others.

It was a situation that would prevail as he sat in the NSC meetings that laid down for the President's approval those decisions that were to escalate American involvement in Southeast Asia, start the USIA on the track of working in support of incumbent governments in host countries, and leave open-ended the possible commitment of U.S. forces to Vietnam—an option as yet resisted by the President.[93] And an ironic position for Murrow, nine years after his call for a public debate on Indochina, "lest we improvise our way into another minor or major war."[94]

But for the USIA as for the others, the ground had been laid by predecessors—the other side of the cultural activities that were the Agency's supposed hallmark under Ike.

John Anspacher, Public Affairs Officer in Saigon since the Eisenhower days, wasn't going back for a second tour of duty. He had created "opponents" in the Vietnamese hierarchy, the Agency report noted, "fighting for U.S. aims," and it had been therefore Ambassador Nolting's and Don Wilson's view that it was time to put in a fresh face.[95]

Returned home, Anspacher had been installed as in-house expert and advisor to the Director on counterinsurgency, "the best qualified person"—so ran the Agency's evaluation—thanks to his Saigon experience.[96]

Counterinsurgency: the new watchword on the New Frontier and ostensible answer to Khrushchev's challenge; fighting guerrillas with guerrillas; countering insurgency with its own weapons, the guidelines laid out in a multipaged memo by General Maxwell Taylor, with mimeographed copies marked "Confidential" distributed among the agencies.[97]

As the psychological warfare branch, the USIA had been called on by the White House to develop training for Agency personnel "designed to provide background in the nature of insurgency movements in various parts of the world as they have arisen or may arise in the future, and the manner in which the U.S. Government may react."[98]

Indeed, the Agency was in the forefront, sending Anspacher to advise on setting up the new counterinsurgency course at the Foreign Service Institute, now requisite for higher officers;[99] called upon for lecturers at the war colleges and for a liaison instructor at the U.S. Army Special Warfare School at Fort Bragg, North Carolina, with its homegrown guerilla training, where Walt Rostow himself had lectured on counter-insurgency.

Murrow as USIA Director sat on the Special Group recommending to the President that the Foreign Service Institute "offer training in new techniques, notably counterinsurgency," and that the Institute be accordingly revamped and expanded.[100]

There was no way they could not be in the middle of it. In Southeast Asia, in the field, USIS was now the principal source of PR supporting counterinsurgency efforts in Northeast Thailand and the new GVN strategic hamlet program in Vietnam; turning out a stream of propaganda support services via film, leaflets, pamphlets, radio, even proposed TV mobile units with large-screen projection capability for viewing in the countryside among the villages.[101]

They were taking on an important role—the words were those of the Far East Area Director[102]—in the coordination of "psywar" programs in several Far Eastern countries, and in Vietnam and Laos, chairing the country team's so-called Psychological Coordinating Committee.

In Washington, high-level officers from the appropriate Area Director's office attended the weekly staff meetings of Averell Harriman, Assistant Secretary of State, since late '61, for Far Eastern Affairs. An interagency task force had advised even more of an activist stepup in the field, proposing among other options participation in the "rehabilitation of Vietcong prisoners" and the broadcasting of defectors' testimony to "Communist-held areas, including North Vietnam."[103]

At the Director's level, there was the pressure to produce—from above and from within; urging by the experts citing the seriousness of the situation, the lateness of the hour; and pushing with the familiar drive of career personnel not wanting to miss out on the action, getting the Agency up there with the people who counted.

Sorensen came back from a session of Maxwell Taylor's Counterinsurgency Committee—the High Command of counterinsurgency, "the inner sanctum," Anspacher called it. The Agency should be regularly in on that, he told Murrow.[104] Murrow spoke to Wilson. August 13, National Security Action Memorandum No. 124 was modified to admit the Director, USIA to regular membership in the Special Group, with notification going to the Secretaries of State and Defense, the Attorney General, the Chairman of the Joint Chiefs, the CIA Director, the Administrator of AID, and the President's Military Representative.[105]

Defense, an aide learned, was planning to discuss the counterinsurgency (CI) plan for Thailand and the strategic hamlet program in Vietnam at its upcoming Honolulu meeting. Shouldn't USIA be in on that?[106]

Was it not time, urged John Anspacher, to "crystallize" Agency doctrine on counterinsurgency, for Murrow to prepare an advisory memo to all Agency personnel on why counterinsurgency programs must be considered now a part of "the total USIA mission." To be effective, it should be an Edward R. Murrow concept, writ in his own hand—though of course he might consider going over it "with several of us" before crystallizing his own ideas.[107]

Would it not be appropriate that the Director pay a personal call on the FSI Seminar in "Problems of Internal Defense (CI)," representing the Agency in the footsteps of such notables as Taylor, Rostow, the Attorney General himself—just fifteen minutes, maybe, on the Agency's role in CI programs.[108]

He was generally agreeable—why not?—briefing "students" at the National War College with generalities, introducing speakers and letting the experts get underway. The appropriate letters were drafted as usual by the appropriate officers, submitted for approval and signature—same with all directors—though drafters found he paid more attention than most to what went out over his name, a rare, triumphant day when copy emerged intact.

Burnett Anderson, a veteran career officer and Tom Sorensen's deputy, who prepared the Director for the CI meetings and went along as briefcase carrier, would remember Murrow as being "faithful about his participation" in the special group.

Discussions, says Anderson, covered "where governments were in trouble, whether that particular government should be assisted, and if so, how." Not "kneejerk" sessions, he insisted, more like a sober effort to discover, define, and deal with specific situations. USIA was assisting in research, was occasionally involved in "actions which had to do with publicizing, information activities." Early in the game, they'd come up with a study, drawing on the experience of the British in Malaya (successful), the French in North Africa (unsuccessful), and the civil war in Greece, implying lessons to be learned in Vietnam. Unfortunately, said Anderson, they didn't follow their own advice.

Anderson himself would later label counterinsurgency a narrow way of looking at a major problem.

> It's got to begin long before you recognize the elements. I think at the time it was probably needed—we were *not* watching what was happening. . . .As a permanent way to run the government, I don't think it would be a good thing. . . .
>
> Bobby Kennedy chaired the meetings and we did deal with a lot of Southeast Asian questions; the domino theory was at least nascent at the time. It was the place to take up these questions—evaluations brought up constantly where insurgency problems might arise as well as Bobby using it as an action forum and swinging the whip. He was *merciless* in these sessions. Suppose a shipment of equipment for the municipal police of Bangkok was late, was tangled up in the bureaucracy somewhere. Well, the person from AID in that room was likely to get a verbal horsewhipping for not getting that stuff out there on time.

And embarrassingly personalized, if you will. Bobby was not—not a fun person to be around much of the time.[109]

Murrow himself, respectful of Max Taylor, could seem oddly equivocal at times, not quite serious about the thing. Once, Anderson recalled, he dropped a problem on the meeting "in considerable detail, in his characteristically studious and thorough fashion," and having nothing whatever to do with the deliberations or, for that matter, counterinsurgency.

Kennedy didn't seem to know how to react: Well, uh, he could see Ed had a problem there, obviously was looking for answers. "But why did you bring it *here*?"

Murrow shrugged. "Didn't know where else to take it."

"So we looked at it a little bit," said Anderson later, "and then we tried to give him some help. Whatever it was."

Anderson's recollection had Murrow giving the CI program reasonably good marks. Don Wilson, on the other hand, would recall a growing disenchantment, Murrow sending him increasingly to sit in his stead in the inner sanctum. Said Wilson, "It wasn't his bag."[110] The Agency in any case had never gotten to play the role that some there had hoped for. Lost somewhere in the shuffle, wrote Tom Sorensen years later, were the causes of insurgency.[111]

At the same time, the Vietnam experience, with its new emphasis and new techniques, was coloring the Agency. Other countries were considered "critical," so designated by the Special Group.[112] Area directors for various regions—Africa, the Near East, Latin America—were asking what this meant for them, in terms of budgets, priorities; how much more emphasis would they now put on supporting a local government rather than on simply "reflecting Americana per se?"[113] Taking the USIA onto new, uncharted paths.

(In counterpoint to the frenzied can-do, came a plaintive note from Sorensen, passed on from the Foreign Service Institute, to the effect that not a single USIA officer—in fact, no one from any agency at all—had signed up for the language course in Vietnamese. Given the problems now faced in Vietnam, he asked, wasn't this being a little shortsighted?)[114]

Even early on, however, some doubts had begun showing, piecemeal at first, in the context of the policy. But where Murrow felt himself on firmer ground.

November, 1961, debates had started in the administration over the first proposals to use defoliants in Vietnam—just the Vietcong, of course: hideouts, ambush places, food supplies. Murrow had immediately opposed it across the board, putting his arguments in the manner of the counsels of the great—not right or wrong but practicability, the problem as seen by the administration's public opinion expert, with all the prerequisite options. The language of the cold war, letting understatement do the rest, in a secret two-page memo to the President anticipating "a major propaganda attack" if defoliant operations were undertaken in Vietnam.

They might be able to cope with repercussions arising from defoliation of hideout areas, he said, along roads. *"But chemical attacks on crops would, in my opinion, put us in an altogether different position with respect to world opinion, especially in the newly developing countries where food has been a perennial problem. There would appear to be a strong possibility that destruction of food crops would be interpreted largely as an effort to suppress a disaffected Viet-Nam population."*

He raised the prospect of a campaign comparing "the new dimension of chemical food-killing with the American use of atomic weapons against Asians in Japan—[tying] us, in effect, to another 'first' in warfare."

> I fear we would be deluding ourselves if we hoped to escape blame for these actions by having them carried out by Vietnamese planes and pilots. Leaflets to loyal inhabitants of affected areas would be helpful locally but would make little difference in our world-opinion problem.

There was as always the required other option, i.e., if the President decided to proceed anyway, he concurred about getting the "non-toxicity-to-humans" across—which would read strangely in the light of later knowledge, down the road—and keeping the emphasis on what the insurgents were trying to do.[115] But the six out of seven paragraphs had made the point.

In the end, defoliants sneaked in the back door—just at roadsides, in ambush areas, proponents argued; and argued successfully.

Murrow was a good deal blunter and grimmer about the whole matter when Bob Pierpoint, for the past five years CBS White House correspondent, called him sometime afterward, asking urgently to see him.

Their relationship was easy. Pierpoint had been one of the charmed circle, the kid from Southern California who had begun in broadcasting by stringing as a student, which was enough for Murrow; a friendship kept up when Murrow came to Washington—relaxed, big-brotherly rather than newsman to news source.

Pierpoint, a veteran of the CBS Far Eastern Bureau, had asked Bobby Kennedy in late 1960, Did he think the domino theory was accurate? "Because I didn't," he recalled later, "and I got the impression that he *did*. That he, Bobby, felt that if Vietnam fell, then it was only a question of time until Thailand and Indonesia would go. Well, that troubled me. . . ."

Pierpoint came to Murrow with his burden, handed him by someone he knew at the Pentagon in arms research; a guy they both owed, said Pierpoint afterward, a marine captain back in Korea who'd criticized the brass. *See It Now* had filmed it. And used it. And it had hurt him for a time.

The former captain had asked Pierpoint to meet him at a restaurant. Arrived, the reporter found a manila envelope shoved at him, the top page inside stamped "Secret" right across the front. "What in hell is this—!" Never mind, said the other, read it and talk to Ed Murrow about it. At home, eyes popping, he read over a secret plan for defoliation operations in Vietnam.

In his office on Pennsylvania Avenue, Murrow took a quick look— "Someone must really trust you."

"Well, yeah, he's got a reason to."

"Why is that?"

"Because you and I got him in real trouble."

Pierpoint refreshed his memory; he wouldn't have done it except that they owed the guy. All he had wanted was that Murrow read it over. "Yeah, okay—I remember."

He agreed to take a look, then added, with sharp dislike: "I've *seen* this plan. I know what it is."

A day or two later, says Pierpoint, Murrow called to ask him back:

"Well," he said, "I've read it. I am opposed to it and Harriman is opposed to it." I said, "Well, this guy wants you and Harriman to back him." He said, "I don't think we can do it," and he explained why basically he didn't believe in warfare, where you wiped out other people's food supplies, starved innocent people.

Good enough, said the reporter, they'd done their duty and he'd just return it. Though in retrospect, says Pierpoint today, he made one mistake—"and that is that I never did a story on it until much later, when the defoliation came out and I knew much more about it. I probably should have done a story at the time."[116]

The fact of warfare itself, the underlying rationale, hadn't yet become an issue—just the implementation. But for Murrow it was possibly the first crack in the structure of his beliefs over the course set in Southeast Asia, growing wider with the stepped-up pace of militarization throughout 1962 and increased commitment.

"He was troubled," says Pierpoint, recalling the "pretty close contact" between them at the time, "and I was troubled. By what was going on— the increasing involvement in Vietnam. And a sense that we were drifting into a situation that might not be a very healthy one.

"It would be inaccurate for me to claim that I was opposed to the administration's policy—that wasn't until about early '65. I was troubled by what was happening but I wasn't quite sure that we were going to get as deeply involved as we later did. And I think Ed was probably in about the same place; at least that's my recollection. He was troubled by the drift of events. But not exactly sure what we should do, or how we should do it."

Nonetheless, Vietnam was still only a small desk at the Agency, weightier issues expected to absorb the Director's attention. Another problem was that there were too many, and too many details. Notwithstanding the tireless Reed Harris and the deputies Murrow called his two right hands, who were almost, in effect, the co-Directors, the fact remained that everything of importance had to pass across his desk—from negotiations over a transmitter in Turkey or Thailand or Liberia, to hosting for the U.S. government at the Washington meeting of the European Broadcasting Union; from arranging with Defense for the no-cost shipping of mobile transmitters, thus saving the Agency a few dollars, to following up on pet legislation for Bill Benton and the U.S. publishers, to breaking the traditional color line among the higher echelons of USIA, up until then lily-white and an anomalous situation for an Agency speaking to a largely non-white world; something that had to be done because, Murrow told Sorensen, it was "right."[117]

Beginning in November 1961, they had begun enforcing Equal Employment Opportunity standards with the express intent of seeking out and encouraging the move upward of black officers, and appointing watchdogs to ensure enforcement. New directives guaranteed that all employees were kept informed of all training opportunities within the Agency. Murrow, assembling heads of Agency elements and their administrative officers, emphasized the importance of the steps taken, calling particular attention to what he termed "the possibility of abuses arising from certain aspects of the merit promotion system."[118] At the same time, the Director of Personnel had begun visiting black colleges, building contacts for the recruitment of junior officers. It was also a time that saw the first appointment of a woman—Barbara White—to the top senior post in the field, as Chief of USIS, Santiago, Chile.

There were in addition the many fact-finding junkets expected of a conscientious agency head—Latin America, Africa, neglected in previous administrations, to which Murrow and the Kennedys attached particular importance; where national leaders, remembering his television days, received him as a friend. En route home, he rendezvoused in Paris with Pierre Salinger, ostensibly for consultations with embassy press officers, in fact to meet with an emissary from Moscow—Mikhail Kharlamov, head of Soviet radio and television—to work out a prospective exchange of TV appearances by Khrushchev and Kennedy, addressing each other's publics. The PAOs in Bonn and London had been ordered to Paris as backup for the cover story, USIS/Leopoldville briefed by the White House just in case questions arose, ensuring complete secrecy and enabling the representatives, Soviet and American, to communicate in private without encumbrance.[119]

There was some scratchiness to begin with. Kharlamov led off with a bristling offensive about the Voice and tagged Murrow "a master propagandist." Murrow, nursing a January cold unmitigated by the fleecy Lanvin sweaters stocked up in the course of the Paris trip, countered that he wished Kharlamov could repeat that before a congressional committee: with that kind of testimonial, they'd probably double his appropriation. Getting down to business, they discussed, as two professionals, an exchange of TV programs between their countries, although the USIA would meet with small success in hawking the Soviet product outside educational TV, the networks being unreceptive, not on the ground of ideology, but the technical quality of the Soviet offerings. The Khrushchev-Kennedy exchange was canceled in mid-March.

At first he seemed to thrive on returning to a stepped-up schedule, the sweet adrenalin-laden flow of a packed twelve- or fourteen-hour day, Saturdays and Sundays thrown in, more work brought home for nighttime reading. Jetting off to Latin America, then back to Washington, then to Europe, then back again and off to West Africa.

When the doctors registered an eight-pound weight loss, it was put down to overwork. Was his cough worse? Well, the new pressures hadn't exactly made him cut down. When a rumor made the rounds that Murrow had gone cold turkey, someone called the Director's office. "Tell them the ashtrays are still full," came the answer.

At the Agency, he was well liked—unfailingly courteous, considerate under pressure, yet a demanding boss, expecting top-line performance in his lieutenants. Hans Tuch, in a staff meeting, once commended the Director for a suggestion. "*You're* paid to have the ideas," Murrow shot back, "not I."

"He could be really tough on you," said one official, "needle you unmercifully. But never in front of others, strictly in private." Anderson would rate him "an absolutely top-flight administrator," who worked hard at the job, delegated well, and was good at picking people—with the single exception, he recalled, of one "spectacularly bad appointment," the mistake acknowledged afterward with the laid-back humor that contrasted so startlingly with his intensity: "When I blow one, I blow it *real* good!"

Anderson also recalled sitting in the Director's office watching a televised presidential news conference. Or trying to, as Murrow fidgeted with the remote control device, trying to get up the sound. Kennedy's mouth opened and closed: no audio. Anderson finally walked over to the TV set and turned up the volume. Murrow looked at him gratefully. "You know, I never *could* run one of those damn things."

It was a different life, living as a bureaucrat, as he called himself, and as a citizen of Washington, with a blue slate–roofed house in the expensive Foxhall section: a square white box set into a green, hilly rise, back to back with the McGeorge Bundys, perched one level up. More guarded—though not invariably—with his old friends from the news media, he was nevertheless still capable of kicking over the traces and going off for a toot with the boys as in the old days. Bernard Eiseman, then with CBS and a boon companion of that earlier time not always with Janet's approval—would recall a deep-drinking White House correspondents dinner and a bunch of them piling afterward into the Agency limo, topping the night off in one of the strip joints in Baltimore, then rolling back in the early hours of the morning to go pounding on the door of columnist Mary McGrory, getting "Mother Mary" up at 5:00 A.M.[120] Times when he would chuck The Director and play at being one of the guys.

Bill Downs, whom he had always called "a bit of conscience," had finally left CBS to write that novel about labor history that was gestating in him. Roz didn't give a damn about the missing paycheck, figured they could type until the money ran out. They were the perfect outsiders, their home a port of call, as in the old days, a place to unwind, Roz Downs keeping an eye out for the Agency limo in the late afternoon—"Ed's here"—pulling up, long and black at the curbside.

As Director, he found himself appearing with old colleagues on TV: on the screen with Howard Smith on ABC (he was thrilled "as some teenager in the presence of a star" at being on the same program again with him, Smith wrote afterward);[121] reminiscing with Harry Reasoner over CBS, relaxed and genial; talking with Martin Agronsky on the *Today* Show; holding his own on *Meet the Press* (don't expect special treatment, Larry Spivak had warned him; it was the all-time understatement). Public affairs producers lined up for air dates, with urging on the other side to get out there and sell the Agency (might come in handy at appropriations time).

Members of Congress sought his presence alongside them in TV tapings to be broadcast for the folks back home—gladly assented to, smoothing as it did USIA relations with the Hill. Modest offerings, videotaped at a small facility on the Hill set up for use by the members, but Murrow had lost none of his camera fright. Their first time out, his young congressional liaison and general counsel Stanley Plesent, sharing the company car, sat astounded, watching his chief break out in a cold sweat, his visible wretchedness increasing, the closer they came to the Capitol.

"You! With all those years in television?"

Murrow managed a lopsided grin. "Now you know my terrible secret, Stanley—I *die* every time I go before a camera!"[122]

Plesent, a young New York lawyer and reform Democrat recruited by Wilson, who had left a job at Young & Rubicam and a fat offer from CBS to work, as he put it, for Jack Kennedy and Ed Murrow, was there essentially to run interference with the so-called Irish Mafia at the White House under Kenny O'Donnell and with members of Congress, a function he would describe as partly a matter of getting his back lacerated in Murrow's place, and partly "like being the agent for Marilyn Monroe."

It was easy to get appointments. I could call up the administrative assistant to Margaret Chase Smith, for instance—that was a professional love affair, from the McCarthy days—and get the response: What day do you want, Monday, Tuesday, Wednesday, Thursday? I had that advantage over other legal counsels because of Murrow's standing. Even those who disagreed with his politics regarded him as "a man of character." I could trade on pro-Murrow sentiments, i.e., calling up troublesome congressmen around appropriations time when he first came into the job, like—"Now you don't want to do this to Murrow just as he's getting started, do you? How about waiting a year?" And they'd wait a year.[123]

But there was no romancing their congressional watchdog, John J. Rooney, the long-term Brooklyn conservative who chaired the House Appropriations Subcommittee on the State Department and the USIA, and hadn't much use for either—tough but well versed in his facts and figures, who believed in a short tether and ate USIA witnesses for lunch.

They were wearing, abrasive sessions, nickel and diming, haggling over budget cuts, arguing for restorations, justifying salaries, programs, and general expenses in the face of vocalized dislike. Murrow called it his "exercise in self-restraint" as leadoff witness in the ritual parade of Agency self-justification, running through the area directors, the directors of the publication, motion picture, information center, broadcasting, television, and research and reference services; and going into technical as well as financial testimony. Murrow sometimes stayed through the entire proceedings to back up his personnel, even stepping in, to Rooney's considerable annoyance. (The whole lineup would then of course be repeated for a Senate subcommittee.)

Rooney, no budget-cutter when it came to the military, got a certain well-publicized mileage out of tightening the pursestrings of the meager Agency budget (about $158,000,000 by 1962; less than the cost of one missile, Murrow would comment). "This narrow little man," Murrow called him. Privately, they were on a first-name basis, but either way were not each other's kind of people. (The VOA's job, said Rooney once, objecting to its airing of dissenters, was to "promote our way of thinking.")[124]

At times, inevitably, restraint wore thin at hearings, briefly replaced by verbal tilting between the chair and the witness table.

"As a taxpayer and, I take it, a substantial one—" the congressman began on one occasion, about to loose a peroration.

"Not any more, Mr. Chairman," Murrow shot back.

Washington was to have meant more time with his family, but the job kept eating into his personal life. "When Casey turned sixteen," Janet Murrow would recall, "he got his first license."

Well, Ed decided it was time for him to learn responsibility, that a car was not just something to show off or go speeding in. So they drove across the country, with Casey driving. But at Salt Lake City, I think it was, Ed was called back for a hearing before Rooney. So I flew out, and came back with Casey.

It was a nerve-wracking trip—the anxious mother alongside the fledgling driver—"I kept saying 'watch out' at every corner, while Ed let him learn from his own mistakes."

"Gee Mom," said her offspring, dragging their bags into a motel that night, "with Dad I was never tired, but one day with you and I'm *exhausted*."[125]

Christmas, 1961, the Murrows all reunioned in Arizona, Lacey Murrow's home following a pneumectomy. The years had not been kind to the eldest brother—struggles with alcoholism, and the blown promise of his early successes, though he was reasonably stable now as partner with a Washington-based engineering firm. A heavy smoker, he had developed lung cancer and undergone surgery for the removal of a lung; the doctors nonetheless gave him even chances for recovery. Dewey alone had stayed out of the big time, living the quiet life of a successful Spokane contractor, tartly articulate at pulling the two hotshots down a peg but all in all the quintessential middle sibling, steady and obliging and there when needed. They met out in Arizona with their families—the two dark brothers and the blond middle brother—all with gray beginning now in their heavy brows.

Ethel, however, had come unwillingly. She'd never taken planes. Also, she wasn't feeling well, blinded in these last years, the eighty-five-year-old heart giving out, dictating terms to the strong-minded, long-lived woman whose father had fought with Stonewall Jackson and whose last-born was in John Kennedy's cabinet.

Lacey insisted that she come: Dewey would bring her down, Ed take her back. But she felt ill all through the holiday, with just one last resurgence of her energies as first the Tucson–L.A. flight, then the connecting Seattle flight almost didn't take off because Ethel Murrow wouldn't fasten her seat belt. If something happened, she told the stewardesses, she wanted to be able to get off.

Casey Murrow watched with amusement as the flight crews argued fruitlessly with the old woman, who remained immovable: these things were a bunch of foolishness, she knew what was right and wrong and seat belts were *wrong*. Murrow, scrunched down in his seat, tried to make himself invisible. Threats of non-takeoff finally worked where other arguments could not.

It was the final effort of the imperious will that had so often determined the lives of those around her. By the time they landed, an ambulance had to be called, taking her the rest of the way. They stayed several days, Murrow fearful that she might not pull out of it. But she seemed to feel better; Dewey and his wife Donny were coming from Spokane. Reassured, Ed returned East with his family. In the middle of the night, they got the news that she had died.[126]

Murrow, distraught, got dressed and caught the next plane back, needing to be alone with his grief—the breaking of the special bond between mother and youngest son, and the passing of the strongest influence in his life, a presence felt even at a 3,000-mile distance, now suddenly no longer there.

Nor was there time to mourn properly, because he had to go to West Africa that week.

From the start, he'd been aware, as no director before him, that African policy especially began at home. In small ways, through Adam Clayton Powell, Jr. of the House, he had tried for legislative input into local laws. Before the National Press Club, in his first major speech as USIA Director, he complained that African diplomats found it "near-impossible" to live in Washington: "Landlords will not rent to them, schools refuse their children; stores will not let them try on clothes, beaches bar their families." And if U.S.-African relations were damaged, remember, this was one we couldn't pin on the Communists. "We do it ourselves in our own capital."[127]

Talking with NASA Administrator James Webb about the lack of black astronauts, he got a negative response to the effect that candidates must be qualified test pilots and, sorry, there weren't any blacks among them. If this "qualification" was indeed essential—which there seemed reason to doubt, Murrow wrote Kennedy—hadn't they better start training "Negro" test pilots? "The first colored man to enter outer space," as he put it, "will, in the eyes of the world, be the *first* man ever to have done so. I see no reason why our efforts in outer space should reflect with such fidelity the discrimination that exists on this minor planet."[128]

The Progress of the American Negro idea was a washout, swamped by the pictures over the tube every night. Alone with Bill Worthy, speaking not for attribution, Murrow voiced his fears of what lay ahead for the country. He was quoted simply as "a very high Kennedy Administration official" by Worthy, writing for *Midstream* in the spring of 1962, predicting in paraphrase that Birmingham would eventually ignite "nationwide racial fuses that will drown State Department and Voice of America propaganda in a sea of bloody embarrassment."

"The despairing official," Worthy continued, "compares Birmingham's police-state atmosphere to that of prewar Nazi Germany, which he knew so well."[129]

There were other discontents, unvoiced at Pennsylvania Avenue. Telstar, the pioneering communications satellite developed for the government by AT&T, at public expense, was being turned over to the private sector with the backing of the administration. There had been a high degree of USIA involvement in setting up the opening supershow, an exchange of transmissions between Europe and America with all three networks participating, a project on which Murrow had worked closely with Friendly, producer at the American end of it. USIA had programming suggestions; the networks had their own ideas.

None of which mattered much, except for the role Murrow was called upon to play in followup, appearing before the Senate Foreign Relations Committee, an unconvincing administration witness endorsing the bill containing the proposed turnover to a private corporation dominated by AT&T. To panel members, he seemed to be listing all the reasons not to—citing soaring commercial rates after a national investment, and at the very least, USIA should get a rate break as "partial repayment" for what the government had laid out.

Would he nonetheless, the panel asked, support the bill as is?

A pause from the witness table.

"Yes, sir."

Albert Gore of Tennessee, a liberal opponent of the measure, expressed surprise: Would the witness care to expound on that reply?

Cabell Phillips of The New York *Times* watched Murrow draw himself together with a pained grin: "I'm a little surprised myself, Senator, at the way I answered that question, and I don't propose to compound the difficulty by answering yours."[130]

The Downses were at home as usual that afternoon, knee-deep in the crises of 1919. The Agency limo pulled up, preamble to a surrealistic scene. Says Roz Downs:

> Here Bill was worried over President Wilson's madness and Mrs. Wilson running the country, I was worried, would Eugene Debs go to jail, and Ed was sitting there, rambling on and on over his testimony over the sale of Telstar to AT&T—that it was wrong, a giveaway, went against every principle he believed in. Personally, I think they purposely wanted *him* in on it.
>
> Bill said, "Listen, this is *always* happening. We develop something, then we give it away to private industry; look what happened after the splitting of the atom. Ed, it's not such a big *deal*."
>
> "But the taxpayers have *paid* for this," he said. He was bothered by it, both before and after the testimony. He wanted us to tell him to be ashamed of himself.[131]

It was one of the few times they had known him to be furious with Kennedy. A short time later, he told them there had been a one-on-one confrontation in the Oval Office, that he had made it clear that he never expected to be called upon for anything like that again.

His feelings about the Kennedy brothers would remain ambivalent. John Kennedy, he felt, had grown in office, shown himself capable of further growth. Said colleagues, he took his relationship with the President, his junior by some ten years, very seriously, admired Kennedy's intellectual curiosity, his capacity for the almost instantaneous absorption of information. Burnett Anderson would remember him returning from sessions at the White House, full of admiration: "Golly, that guy—he'll look at a piece of paper for about thirty seconds—it's *remarkable* how quickly he can absorb and play back at you, almost verbatim."

In the case of Bobby Kennedy, matters were more complicated.

He admired the doer, as he had described him to Howard Smith; the drive to cut through bureaucratic red tape, the grasp of realities, the no-nonsense give-and-take of the rap sessions at his home in Virginia, his readiness in the rough arena of student debate on his Third World jaunts where resentment of the U.S. ran high.

On the other hand, there had been his closeness to Joe McCarthy, the closest of any of the Kennedy children. Also, said a friend later, he was disturbed by RFK's politicizing of the office of Attorney General—though he, too, it could be argued, had politicized the USIA—and by the known bugging of the rest of the administration. A feeling worked to a higher pitch when, stopping at his office unexpectedly one day, he found a stranger going through his desk.

He knew by instinct how to move quickly and quietly. Before the other knew what was up, and with the full force of his logging-country temper, he propelled himself into the room toward the desk, slamming the center drawer shut on the intruder's hand, with every intention of breaking it, thrusting his face into that of the stranger who writhed in unarticulated pain as he struggled to free himself—"Now I don't know who the fuck you are but . . ." He whipped the drawer open. "Now you get your fucking hand out of my desk and move your fucking ass out of here and tell Bobby if he wants to know something, he can ASK JACK!"

At the Downses, he threw himself into a chair and poured it all out. Said Roz, recalling, "He was still steaming about it."[132]

"What do you want to do, resign?" It was a question they had asked at times, most notably during the Telstar giveaway. Well no, he said, he thought he could still do some good in other places. And indeed, in those areas where he knew his ground, he could be effective. The shrillest rhetoric had been eliminated, winnowed out of the Agency offerings, notably the film, "Operation Abolition," lauding the House Committee on Un-American Activities. In contrast to the activity in South Vietnam, the output of product praising Chiang Kai-shek was abruptly halted. There was to be no more "distribution of material glorifying the Taipei regime," Murrow wrote in a brisk note to the Far East Area Director. "This is not a proper function for the Agency. Please see that it is stopped immediately."[133]

In mid-1961, as the Soviets broke the informal 1958 moratorium on atmospheric nuclear testing, his was the voice listened to, as against that of the faction urging Kennedy to follow Khrushchev.

"Worldwide protests now directed against Soviet nuclear tests," he had warned the President, would be turned on the U.S. if they followed suit; indeed, some would interpret it as an admission of weakness, of American non-confidence in its nuclear capabilities.

His private reaction to the Soviet announcement had been one of un-mitigated fury. Hans Tuch, part of a group called into the Director's office, found him "incensed. He felt it was a real setback to the U.S.-Soviet relationship. And starting up massive nuclear testing again—it was just a crime against humanity."

He was massing all transmitters broadcasting to the USSR, he told them, protesting the resumption, and would go on the air himself with a commentary, and he was writing it. The decision, evidently, had been made unilaterally, without the usual staff work. "I really didn't feel that his broadcasting or his action was going to really change matters any," said Tuch later, "but he took it so very personally."[134]

In the NSC and in successive memorandums to the President, he argued against the voices raised in Congress and in the administration—the Joint Chiefs, the CIA, and the Atomic Energy Commission among them—calling for immediate American resumption of nuclear testing.

"What is required is *time*," he wrote Kennedy the day after the Soviet announcement. "Those who urge you to resume testing immediately will tomorrow contend that the decision to do so was merely another belated reaction to Soviet action."[135]

The tests moreover seemed to serve "no useful or important military purposes," and surely, the world being mad at the Soviets, the President wouldn't want to throw away such a propaganda coup, a chance to isolate the Soviet bloc, maybe induce a little sanity, as he put it, into the SANE nuclear policy group. They could of course resume testing at a later date, let the rest of the world down easily, minimize the damage among the "strongly-committed" countries aware that free world security must be protected. However,

> acknowledgment of that need would be reluctant. . .and the general public throughout the world would give little consideration to this point. The unaligned and neutral countries tend to view all nuclear testing as an unmitigated evil.[136]

His view, for the moment, won out over that of the Rusk group, standing by with a draft statement announcing resumption. The statement was cut back to vague "preparations," reluctance to pursue such a course, the options left open. Eight months later, the U.S. resumed on its own. He considered it bought time.

(In a postscript, Research came up with public opinion surveys indi-cating widespread support for the move in Western Europe. He was surprised— "my *viscera* tell me this isn't right"—but signed the report, trusting the close work of his staff. Actually, said Burnett Anderson, they'd been as surprised as Murrow, but subsequent feedback proved them right.[137] It was one case he'd have preferred being wrong; "viscera," however, were never an acceptable criterion in policy discussions.)

In early spring of 1962, they celebrated Raymond Swing's seventy-fifth birthday. The veteran newsman was retiring from the Voice, arrangements made for his part-time employment, with Murrow assured that all financial arrangements would be "fair and suitable."[138]

They had seen little of each other since Murrow's coming to Washington as USIA Director; Swing accepted it as excess baggage of the new position but somehow the inverted father-son relationship still held, the younger man still feeling responsible for the older. Murrow let his administrative officers know that he expected to be filled in on just what those "fair and suitable" arrangements were to be.[139]

It was a small but close-knit group, some twenty altogether, that gathered for dinner at the Hay-Adams on a Wednesday night in late March—Murrow and John Gunther co-hosting, Henry Loomis present for the Voice, and old friends: Walter and Helen Lippmann, Sally and Scotty Reston, Mr. and Mrs. Marquis Childs; Ferdie Kuhn of the Washington *Post* and a well-known face since the mid-thirties; Marcel Fodor from the time of the Anschluss, lately of the Voice, who had had to run for it that night in 1938 with his beautiful wife Martha when the Nazis were coming. But Martha had been dead for years and Mike Fodor, ailing and just out of the hospital, had to leave the dinner early.

Toasts were drunk, tributes offered by the hosts, a suitable reply from the guest of honor. They were all, in a way, survivors.

At the same time there was the reminder of a more recent past, John Henry Faulk's lawsuit against AWARE coming finally to trial. Murrow had kept in touch with Nizer, had even discussed, it would turn out, a possible appearance as witness for the plaintiff. From New York, Nizer sent him the conversation notes—subject entirely, he stressed, to Ed's deletions and additions—plus a folder with detailed preparations for cross-examination, and suggesting three alternate dates in May.[140]

In the end, Murrow didn't appear; possibly on advice. But the Director was also needed to inaugurate the counterinsurgency courses in Washington in late May. Due to scheduling problems, he told Nizer, he saw no possibility of getting to New York in the foreseeable future.[141]

Nevertheless, the finding some weeks later for the plaintiff and heavy judgment against the blacklisters left him "delighted," he told a friend, answering the flood of mail pouring in following columnist Murray Kempton's reference to "the distinguished CBS commentator" who had aided Faulk. He could not, however, he wrote Frank Kelly of the Fund for the Republic, "help thinking that other organizations and individuals should have been added to the list of defendants. . . ."[142]

He did get to New York in time to open the first public television channel there, answering the call of Richard Heffner, the broadcaster and recently assistant to Frank Stanton, now General Manager for WNDT, soon better known as Channel 13.

The signs were not auspicious. Murrow was for some reason in a great deal of pain, Heffner remembered, dragging one foot and limping badly,[143] the broadcast complicated by an AFTRA strike that left them dependent on a skeleton supervisory crew. But the visitor helped keep the long, live broadcast going, the public seeing Ed Murrow over the tube again as host, in his familiar role, cigarette smoke curling, saying he'd been asked back because he still owned one blue shirt.

When asked, he spoke always of his satisfaction with the job—never so happy, hadn't known such fulfillment since the blitz. To John Schultz, listening to him in the course of a flying visit at CBS, he seemed almost *too* enthusiastic—though, granted, maybe they were being egocentric, unable to visualize the broadcaster actually liking a desk job.

Stan Plesent had asked him once, midway through one of those periodic diplomatic crises building up in some far-off hot spot—how about it? Was he really *happy* at the Agency?

Murrow, as usual, didn't answer right away; instead he paused, looked out the window.

"To tell you the truth, Stanley, I'd rather be out *there*—covering it."[144]

Something, however, was bothering him, manifesting itself as in the past by a steep increase in the consumption of alcohol. Not the old-boy jollity but a steady, grim imbibing. Katie Louchheim, a New York friend and prominent Democrat, then with State as Deputy Assistant Secretary for Public Affairs, was sitting up with him one night on a long flight overseas, the two of them talking through the hours. Murrow, she noticed after a while, was also drinking through the hours; then, as orders for breakfast were taken, asked instead for a double brandy. Louchheim would later recall being somewhat surprised and just a little worried.[145]

Back in Washington, Defense was trying once again for defoliation in Vietnam, 2,500 acres, Phu Yen province—a military necessity, they argued, to get at Viet Cong food supplies, force the Cong into the open. Murrow, with Sorensen drafting, warned against the implications: "We have a tradition in this country of not using food as a weapon of war." Rachel Carson's *New Yorker* series, he warned, soon to be published in book form, set forth "with devastating impact the consequences of insecticides on insect-plant life balance and human health. . . .If we launch a defoliation program in Viet-Nam our enemies and many of our friends will use this book against us."

Were there no alternatives, he asked, whatever the military arguments? Had all else been tried and failed? "No matter how reasonable our case may be, I am convinced that we cannot persuade the world—particularly that large part of it which does not get enough to eat—that defoliation is "good for you."

September 26, 1962, he took off for a five-week trip to the Near East and South Asia. USIS/Teheran looked forward to his presence at dedication ceremonies for their new bi-national center, described in reports as "impressive," obviously to be "a landmark in Teheran for some years to come."[146] After which Murrow had planned to fly to India.

The agenda had simply read "South Asia" as his final objective—whether India alone, or whether with a stopoff in Vientiane or Saigon, where USIS problems had been peaking, would be left unspecified. In any case, he never made it past Iran.

The pattern was the old one—a bad cold ignored, then collapse; Teheran had never been a lucky city for him. He was rushed to the hospital, given a diagnosis of pleurisy, discharged after only a week, and sent back to the States. Janet, meeting the plane, wanted another hospital for him but Murrow, with a desperate homing instinct, insisted on going to Pawling. If he could get back there, he'd be all right.

They went back to Pawling. It was October 12. Two days later, a U.S. spy plane photographed the launching sites for intermediate-range missiles in Cuba, crystallizing the tensions growing since the installation that August of Soviet surface-to-air missiles on the island, and putting the two superpowers on a collision course.

At the farm, Murrow's condition grew worse, hospitalization now deemed essential. He decided on Washington, D.C., to be near enough for consultation, but it wasn't needed. Don Wilson, Acting Director by mutual agreement in Murrow's absences, was already sitting in on the group known as Ex Com, dealing with the crisis, beginning the so-called "eyeball to eyeball" confrontation that would end with ostensible Soviet withdrawal of the missiles and their sites. At 1776 Pennsylvania, a duty officer sat night and day in Wilson's office, by the phone, the Agency's full media mobilized to put out the administration view of the crisis.

The Agency itself, however, had been brought early into the decision-making virtually over the President's objections.

The developments also exacerbated the tensions inside USIA as Policy took over the Voice for the duration. And as Loomis said later, "Murrow wasn't there for me to appeal to."

Burnett Anderson, himself a former newsman, plucked suddenly from a group working that week under Walt Rostow, felt distinctly awkward when Wilson ordered him down to VOA to vet the scripts, with the disquieting news that he was henceforth personally responsible for every word said on the air. They wanted someone there with a pipeline to Ex Com. Henry knew all about it and was completely *d'accord*. "Well," said Anderson later, "Henry was *far* from *d'accord*."

At the Voice the two men, personal friends who respected each other, worked in an atmosphere of intense unease. Over lunch, the VOA director thought aloud about resigning. "I did my best to persuade him that he shouldn't," said Anderson, "and happily he didn't. We remained friends, but the same set of underlying tensions eventually led to his resignation under Carl Rowan."

"Bernie is a very able guy," said Loomis afterward. "I believe he was uncomfortable in that mission. But we did have a series of disagreements and when Murrow got back, I told him I thought that was the wrong way to do things."

(Raymond Swing, still broadcasting part-time, came up to Anderson after a few days, with his usual tact. His first reaction, he said, had been to leave on hearing of the "takeover." Then, watching the officer at work, he'd decided to wait, give the thing a chance. But now he had decided, however reluctantly, that he'd have to leave after all. "And he did, so far as I know," Anderson remembered, "until the crisis was over.")

This time there were no discordant voices, the message uniform on all outgoing channels—the USIA media, the commercial stations talked into assisting. A one-note crisis-oriented operation painted a doomsday scenario and, unlike the Bay of Pigs effort, was effective. The administration got its point across.

Throughout the crisis, Murrow, out of touch, had fidgeted restlessly in one of the VIP tower rooms at Bethesda Naval Hospital where five years before, Joe McCarthy—out of his head, his liver spongy—had died a lonely death. Stateside doctors had changed Murrow's diagnosis to pneumonia and explained away the shadows appearing on the chest X ray: scar tissue, they assured him, just scar tissue from the past pneumonias. (A year later when the diagnosis was cancer, the shadows were still there, just larger. "I often wonder," said Janet Murrow, "what would have happened if they'd operated earlier.")[147]

He was still there the second week in November—convalescing, said his office, answering inquiries. But he made it that month to the funeral of Eleanor Roosevelt: the passing of the great mother figure, a second loss. He did not approach the grave edge with the others but stood away at some distance in the late fall murk, under a drippy sky, photographed on that day, pale and tall, a group gathered around him as though propping him up.

He had not in fact regained his full strength; something had changed radically in that last attack, as though sapping his powers of recuperation. Don Wilson would recall this as the onset of a period "dotted with illnesses," others standing in for him increasingly in what would be his final months as Director.

It coincided with a period of growing problems for the Agency. Henry Loomis, not much liking what had happened to the Voice, was asking for a high-level meeting in the wake of the missile crisis to determine where the VOA went from there. They had been through it months before, Murrow sitting down with Loomis and Sorensen, each pushing his view on the Director, Sorensen urging a stronger hand for the Office of Policy. The resulting memorandum had had something for everyone—for the Voice, the key phrase saying news programming should be "accurate, objective and comprehensive," for the policy people, the recognition that treatment of stories was "properly a matter for post-audit and long-term guidance. . . ."[148]

That November, the questions, newly reopened, awaited Murrow on his return as he came in for a few hours a day, the arguments starting up again. Certainly they wanted "credibility" for the VOA, Sorensen argued, but there was credibility and there was credibility, and VOA credibility referred to the credibility of the U.S. Government. Like it or not, VOA *was* the Voice of America, overtly controlled, operated and financed by the American Government, regarded therefore as the voice of the government, and carefully monitored abroad for nuance. Bound, therefore, not to mislead either enemies or allies as to official U.S. intentions with heavily speculative commentaries and "on-the-other-hands." VOA credibility could not, therefore, be placed in the same context as that of an Eric Sevareid on CBS or a Howard K. Smith on ABC.

The Voice, the memo argued, had no patent on truth; our government, with some "notorious slippages," had generally gone on the basis of "self-evident" truths. If we believed, therefore, that its foreign policies were honest and enlightened, then making policy considerations pre-eminent would enhance, not damage, VOA's credibility and effectiveness.[149]

A new compromise was again thrashed out in discussion, reaffirming the principles of "accuracy, objectivity and comprehensiveness," in a new declaration over Murrow's signature, but actually giving the Office of Policy more control, in language reflecting the Sorensen memo.[150] Loosely applied under Murrow—"Most of the time our decision held," said Loomis, "after he left, most of the time it didn't"—it would lead to a situation in which, by 1965, every commentary would need clearing before broadcasting, with OP.[151]

It was to seem a minor matter, however, compared to the ballooning of their problems in South Vietnam, where a back-burner issue, simmering for the past year, was turning red-hot, and where the Diem Government looked like an ever frailer reed.

The "fresh face" arrived so confidently in May of 1962 as Anspacher's successor belonged to John Mecklin, on leave for the past months from *Time* magazine, plucked from a NATO posting for a situation which, as Murrow wrote in an explanatory note drafted by Wilson, was "probably more pressing for USIA than any other in the world."[152]

Mecklin was the perfect choice, they assured Murrow—*Time* bureau chief in Southeast Asia, 1954–55, relations with Diem excellent, a respected correspondent and no-nonsense reporter with old friendships among other veterans of the Saigon scene such as Stanley Karnow; commended in the mid-fifties by the American Saigon Military Mission for cutting through "French propaganda" to give an objective account of events in Vietnam.[153]

Mecklin had been eager for the job, Murrow himself telephoning him in Paris to discuss the posting. The new Public Affairs Officer, however, had been soon caught in the crossfire between the Saigon government, the U.S. Mission for which he was spokesman, and the small, determined U.S. press corps trying against odds and official curbs to report on some 4,000 American advisors now in South Vietnam.

Earlier, Homer Bigart, now in Saigon for The New York Times, had telexed Murrow on the efforts of USIS officials to improve "the information situation," hoped Ed would back them "against snipers."[154] Murrow thanked him, wished him luck. Three weeks later he got the news of Bigart's imminent expulsion from the country, along with Newsweek stringer Francois Sully, on the orders of the Diem Government. Shortly afterward, a secret memo assured him the order was rescinded for both men following the protests of the U.S. ambassador, warning of adverse reactions in Congress and the news media.[155]

The controversy, however, had boomeranged back to New York and Washington as the gap widened between what was happening in Southeast Asia and what the administration would admit to.

"The United States is now involved in an undeclared war in South Vietnam," wrote Scotty Reston in his New York Times column that February, putting hard questions about the Geneva Accords and calling on the government to level with the public. The Times editorial page noted thousands of uniformed Americans training and ferrying Vietnamese troops under combat conditions, raising "the possibility that what we are doing in South Vietnam may escalate into a major conflict. . . .a situation . . .about which American officials ought to be candid."[156]

The question, however, remained not so much the policy as the secrecy involved; and just how far should the U.S. go to keep the South from being "overrun"?

If Murrow had any feelings on the issues thus far raised, he wasn't saying, at least not in private. Taciturn by nature, he was even more so now that his position made him part of the national security apparatus. Official records later available on those months would be similarly unrevealing.

Nor were his friends of the Washington press corps raising any questions in private. Murrow was still "something of a folk hero," as Scotty Reston put it, an entity apart, the image of the USIA, one of the least covered of agencies, somehow separate from the growing question mark in Southeast Asia. Reston, years later, could not recall "a single conversation that I had with him about it. It's rather dumb of me not to have thought of it, but I don't remember perceiving the connection."(Then too, he added, they were a lot less critical in those days.)[157]

The USIA now had a representative sitting on the interdepartmental Vietnam task force, umbrella'd in turn under a new Southeast Asia task force chaired by Averell Harriman himself. Undersecretary George Ball informed Murrow in followup that he, Ball, had specifically requested the new task force to assume responsibility for keeping the counter-insurgency group up to date on "matters falling within its particular competence."[158]

That summer a *Newsweek* story by Francois Sully labeling the war "a losing proposition" had finally gotten its author expelled. *Newsweek* stubbornly put Sully on its Washington beat, covering the visit of Diem's Defense Minister and State Secretary Nguyen Dinh Thuan. Sully was claiming he had written the article on the orders of his editor.[159]

At the USIA, the Area Director for the Far East, just returned from a meeting at State of the Special Vietnam task force, approached Murrow urgently. Task force director Sterling J. Cottrell had called the current *Newsweek* stance virtually a declaration of war, poison against the government of Vietnam. State was trying to set up a lunch between Graham, as owner of *Newsweek*, and Mr. Thuan, but in the meantime, they wanted to know, wasn't there anything he could do with his old friend Phil Graham? There was thus far no visible objection on his part, in State's effort to manage the news.

Throughout 1962, at the Agency as in the rest of the administration, the controversy had been seen as one of image: a public relations problem, presumably resolvable in Saigon at least through a really good PAO: one who could, they hoped, possibly mediate between a mandarin government and the foreign press in this undramatic, nasty little war of self-defense, which unfortunately had to be fought.

Mecklin had arrived at the outset, full of hope and projects: a weekly bulletin going back to Washington which, under the upbeat title of *Hi-Lites*, reported on the steady uphill progress of USIS/Saigon. A talent search for an American speech writer for President Diem to suitably couch the mandarin's phrases, drum up press interest in his pronouncements (the plan, though ostensibly having Murrow's concurrence, eventually petered out).[160] At the same time, of course, a new leaf was to be turned over with the press.

Back at the Agency, the tide of official news for months told only of successes—cables from the U.S. Mission, Saigon, passed on by State to Murrow, lauding military gains, the village democracy of the strategic hamlets, the rooting out of corruption, the alleged success of the "information" program carried out in cooperation with the Vietnamese on behalf of the Saigon government,[161] which along the way had shifted the traditional USIS function, from making propaganda for America to making propaganda for a host government on grounds, presumably, of mutual policy objectives. (Admittedly not a normal role for USIS, as one American ambassador to Saigon put it at the time, possibly even a unique role for the Agency, but vital to the success of the war against the Vietcong, he assured them, and the desired objective, therefore, of their main effort.)[162]

Within 1776 Pennsylvania, the Far East Area Director repeatedly called the "effectiveness" of the operation to the USIA Director's attention. "Your cabled report," wrote Murrow in the drafted letter of commendation presented for his signature in late '62, "is fascinating reading. It makes it apparent that you are now tooled up and organized to operate with good effect. . . . Keep up the good work."[163]

Mecklin himself had come up with the idea of the Field Support Operations and sold the Saigon government on the plan, briskly staffing and equipping teams carrying out anti-Vietcong propaganda in the countryside with movie and megaphone,[164] followed by glowing cables back to Washington of happy receptiveness among the population.

Doubts were clearly to be rejected, both in Saigon and Washington, about the viability of the administration's course, even sporadic skepticism to be faced down. In June, Averell Harriman, now heading Far Eastern matters at State, wrote Murrow of his concern at what he called the " 'no win' theme," the importance, he stressed, "of hitting it before it gets too wide acceptance."[165] (Though a trial run before the Council on Foreign Relations had come off rather well, it seemed, ensuring the continued backing of the foreign policy establishment and their rejecting of the "no-win nonsense.")[166]

But the problems with the press weren't going away. Don Wilson, talking that September in Washington with Secretary Thuan, a top Saigon official—for reasons undisclosed, it was Wilson who met with the minister rather than Murrow—found the visitor remote, overly quick to agree when he used expressions such as "image," "briefings," "credibility,"[167] the Agency seeing itself increasingly in the position of defending a government that was at the very least—such were the latest reports—inept and heavy-handed.[168]

In another time, another context, it was Murrow who had cautioned others against attempts to shut out the news media. *Reporters must write*, he had warned Dean Rusk, speaking from personal experience. Not given the facts up front, they'd speculate; denied information, they'd turn elsewhere, making reticence in the long run self-defeating.[169]

In October, a week before the missile crisis, Mecklin warned them of a threatened ban in South Vietnam on U.S. publications. Reporters in Saigon were calling it "direct intimidation," and just when the military picture was improving. . . .[170]

Then, on a Monday morning in December, four weeks after his return from the hospital, Murrow came in to find a thick sheaf of papers, together with a memo from his Far East people, calling his attention to the recent

Hi-Lites report from Mecklin, specifically the section on press relations; it painted, they said, a grim picture.[171]

Underneath was a copy of an eight-page memo to the U.S. Saigon ambassador from a disenchanted Mecklin, plus the text of a furious letter, also addressed to the ambassador, from David Halberstam, Homer Bigart's capable young replacement from The New York *Times*. The newsman had composed it hastily in Mecklin's office, wrote the PAO, then thrown it on the desk in disgust, telling the USIA man he could "do any damn thing you want with it."[172]

Halberstam, wrote Mecklin, had arrived in Saigon determined to be detached and fair to the local government—his output proved it—but events weren't making things any easier.

The memo to Ambassador Nolting lay uppermost, a bleak litany as Murrow read it through, outlining for the first time just how far things had gone: a "deliberate new campaign of harassment" against *all* resident reporters, critical or not, "in a spirit of bitter contempt for their protests.

"American newsmen in Saigon believe they are regularly tailed," the memo read. "They are threatened with reprisals if they fail to be properly 'objective.' . . . There have been continued public and private recriminations."

Talking to Diem's strongman brother, Ngo Dinh Nhu was evidently useless, the last session producing a tirade against America for ostensibly not understanding communism and "cold war realities." "He capped all this," the PAO reported, "with the reckless (and psychotic?) remark that the U.S. should now mount an atomic attack on Peking."

The expulsions of reporters—Sully, James Robinson of NBC—were obviously no longer isolated incidents but part of a deliberate policy and there seemed grounds to doubt whether "newsmen of the U.S. mission" could live with this; whether in fact USIA could live with it.

But it was last week's helicopter operation, Mecklin complained, that did it, brought matters almost to the breaking point—American copters with American advisors in combat conditions, no press; a massive ferrying operation and a massive clampdown on coverage, backed by the U.S. Military Assistance Command, Vietnam (MACV). "The newsmen felt that the ban on reporting this to American readers was an outrage. Inevitably many of them found their own sources . . . notably Neil Sheehan of UPI, whose story led to a MACV investigation."

Then on Sunday, Murrow read, Halberstam, out with the Vietnamese junk forces, had gotten an excellent briefing from a U.S. Navy advisor, only to have the same officer come back later, saying he'd been rebuked by the Vietnamese commander and he'd have to ask him not to use it. Returned to Saigon, said Mecklin, Halberstam had been "literally shaking with anger."[173]

The newsman's letter, attached to the correspondence, called the press ban and its security rationale "stupid, naive, and indeed insulting to the patriotism and intelligence of every American newspaperman," and he was cabling his office to make "the strongest possible protest in Washington."

> American reporters have been barred from American helicopters, and our people have gone along with this. It is, I think, that simple. . . . forty-five American helicopters (one of the greatest number of helicopters ever used in a single military operation . . .) flew into operation and two hundred Americans risked their lives. Yet we were not allowed to cover. . . .
> Let me point out that we, as our predecessors, in time of conflict have been, are fully prepared to observe the problems of security, to withhold printing classified information; and that in this running conflict the government has never raised the charge of giving out military information. . . .
> Let me also point out that from the moment [the] helicopters landed . . . certain aspects of the operation lost all classified status. You can bet the VC knew what was happening; you can bet Hanoi knew what was happening. Only American reporters and American readers were kept ignorant . . . a precedent has been set. . . .[174]

Mecklin, lending his voice, was appealing to the ambassador, to MACV, to stop the suppression of news, open up to the press, tell American advisors to ignore efforts to muzzle them, start releasing limited classified information to "reputable Western newsmen," and give them "a true picture of what is going on.

"This is not in any way meant to invoke the weary argument that we're spending millions here and that the U.S. has a 'right' to special treatment by the GVN. . . . The point is rather that the GVN is infringing on a root *American* right; the right of the American people to be informed of the facts on which the policies of their government are based, and on the activities of U.S. military personnel committed to combat."[175]

Murrow's spoken remarks in response remain unrecorded, speculation useless on conjectural reactions to Halberstam's inadvertent echo of George Polk's last report from Greece.

He gathered up the correspondence and had fifteen copies run off, the topmost set but one dispatched to Harriman with a covering memo backing the newsmen, saying that he, Murrow, felt the recommendations to be sound, and that resentment of the Saigon government was apparently rubbing off on the U.S.[176]

Another set, with a carbon of his remarks, went to Pierre Salinger at the White House.

But the problems and questions continued. Harriman, writing Fritz Nolting that January, cautioned against over-optimistic public statements on what would be at best, he said, "a long, dirty war."[177]

At the Agency, the dichotomy went on: two levels of communication—

one official, self-congratulatory, the other confidential, introspective, and uncertain; commendations on one hand, on the other, the unmistakable message: we're in trouble.

Yet for all the questions, Murrow hadn't gotten to Vietnam. Plans had been made that spring for a one-month midsummer Far East tour to include a twelve-day swing through Southeast Asia (excepting Cambodia, a deliberately low-key USIS operation). Four days each for Bangkok, Vientiane, Saigon.[178] Not much time, low-profile—in contrast to the publicized visits of other administration figures—the plan, to take off from Seattle partway through a West Coast family trip, Janet to return home while Murrow himself went on to Saigon via Honolulu and Manila.

But there were always other matters. The administration needed him for the hearings on Telstar in early August. Laotian Prime Minister Souvanna Phouma would be visiting Washington in late July. There was concern over the political direction of the new Laotian minister of information, the looming prospect of aid offered by Peking and Hanoi. The end result was that of the many fact-finding missions sent to Vietnam in those decisive years, the one individual not sent was the one in charge of propaganda on behalf of U.S. policy in Southeast Asia, and the only cabinet-level member of the administration with the trained eye of a journalist.

Conversely, he was also still a suspect figure to a sector of the public that was theoretically looking over the administration's shoulder—the FBI was still receiving denunciations about this red in government, still maintained a clip file on his movements—his judgments, therefore, potentially open to challenge as coming from one who might just be soft on communism.

The December pressures, coming so soon after his illness, had left him badly worn down. Guesting that month on Howard Smith's program in New York, he took an ill-advised walk through a snowstorm to get to the studio, cabs being unavailable. Smith saw him arrive at ABC, out of breath and wracked by coughing. They held off the taping while he recovered, quieting the hack with swigs from a small brown bottle with the label of a D.C. pharmacy. Smith remembered being torn between gratitude and frustration: he shouldn't have *come*.

To Burnett Anderson, who carried Murrow's briefcase to meetings, the Director seemed as much in command as ever. Others, New York *Times* columnist Arthur Krock among them, saw Murrow's control slipping away.

The doctors had given him a clean bill of health: No worry, he was recovered. But at Manning Place, the bronchial cough persisted through the nights, even while the problems mounting in the spring of 1963 demanded ever longer hours.

It wasn't all frustration. He worked with Harriman and a State Department legal team to liberalize travel controls, in a proposal calling the existing regulations "an inroad and a hindrance to the free exchange of information upon which our domestic society depends."[179] (Burnett Anderson, reading the draft, detected Murrow's hand.) Recommended was the wholesale removal of almost all countries from the proscribed list, including North Vietnam, China, Albania, and North Korea. Cuba, barring special cases and "all bona fide newsmen," remained the one exception, the overall proposal, they felt, about as far as the administration could conceivably go in the present climate.[180]

On Cuba, however, regulations had tightened, if anything. At VOA, even before the missile crisis, the "underlying policy" as reflected in internal area office memorandums was to "expose, weaken and isolate the present government there with a view to its eventual elimination and replacement by one friendly to the United States."[181] Castro, read Agency communiqués, had "betrayed a legitimate national revolution," demonstrated his intention to "subvert existing governments," and created thousands of refugees; had begun by saying "our revolution is as native as our palms" and ended with something "as native as Russian missiles and troops."[182] (Though for all the programming aimed at Cuba, the Voice kept to a set policy of not jamming Radio Havana—or any other radio, for that matter.)[183]

Murrow agreed on the administration's anti-Castro stance, though occasionally if not fundamentally going off on a separate track. The broaching of assassination plots in secret sessions, even as supposedly theoretical options, drew a furious response from him and earned him something of a backhanded reputation as a Boy Scout. Christmas, 1962, he had gotten off an oh-for-heavens-sake memo to Dean Rusk over the prohibition of student travel to the island, and the world was not going to come to an end if a bunch of kids wanted to go chop cane.

"The right to travel," he wrote the Secretary, requesting the validation of as many student passports as possible, "is part of our own law and tradition, was restated in the Universal Declaration of Human Rights . . . is generally looked on as a basic right in the non-Communist world." He asked, too, that the government "exercise great restraint in prosecuting any who go illegally."[184]

Some time before, he had come unexpectedly on Bill Worthy—in hot water again following non-sanctioned travel to Cuba and facing prosecution—their encounter unavoidable, Worthy later recalled, the two of them emerging from respective stalls in the men's room of the House Office Building. They had talked briefly—the newsman wasn't sure in retrospect if he asked specifically for help; obviously the situation posed embarrassment potential for USIA. Murrow removed himself as quickly as politeness permitted. The other tried to be philosophical; people's roles changed when they went into the government, he figured. As for Murrow, who had been following the case, he wasn't talking, even at the cost of personal misunderstanding.

He was also working to anticipate possible opposition, PR loopholes, to the limited nuclear test ban treaty draft emerging in stop-start negotiating sessions between the U.S. and the USSR, emerging in those post-missile crisis months as both superpowers drew back from the brink.

Unsympathetic to the Ban the Bomb movement, Murrow with his policy people had nonetheless spearheaded, within the administration, the USIA drive to link nuclear testing with both disarmament (an Agency paper termed the one "a first essential step" to the other), and halting "the development and spread of nuclear weapons."[185] In fact, it had occupied much of his efforts, by presidential order, over his past two years as Director.

In early 1963, with the threatened blocking of a prospective treaty in the Senate, their work had gone into overtime forestalling overseas image problems that opponents could turn into arguments.

"We know from polls and from common sense that most people think a test ban would be a good thing," Murrow wrote that March to Assistant Secretary of Defense Paul Nitze. "It seems likely that most have not considered this in relation to its possible effect on U.S. strength. . . . The medicine for this is a well-marshaled argument on why the test ban is better for our military security than no test ban."[186] The resultant treaty, signed that summer in Moscow, would pass the Senate by the requisite two-thirds, a major victory for Kennedy and a source of satisfaction for USIA. Though, characteristically, Murrow worried at once about public euphoria perceiving the treaty as an end, not the beginning, of a long, maybe tough haul.

"This treaty," he wrote Ted Sorensen, for pass-on to the President, "will not feed the hungry, educate the illiterate, shelter the homeless or offer hope to the hopeless. It provides only that those nations possessing this awesome power will no longer experiment with it in such a fashion as to endanger the future well-being of all who live on this planet."

U.S.-Soviet relations seemed to be thawing—even as U.S.-Cuban relations were hardening—in the wake of the missile crisis. Back in 1962, two months before the crisis, Murrow, meeting with Soviet Ambassador Anatoly Dobrynin over lunch, had suggested that *Ameryka* and *USSR*, their two respective slick propaganda publications, swap editors for an issue or so; the ambassador was noncommittal. At the Agency it was even suggested that Dobrynin himself be invited onto the Voice for a broadcast to the folks back home.[187]

But Vietnam wasn't going away.

The trouble had been mounting from the opening of the new year, with the failed military operation at Ap Bac near Saigon, which a disgusted American advisor, before newsmen, called "a miserable damn performance," and MACV called a victory. In Saigon, Mecklin, pressured to turn out a report blasting the correspondents, cursed himself afterward. Arrived in Washington for a throat operation—the diagnosis would be cancer—he was rushed to the President to plead, hoarsely, for more candor with the press.

Defoliant operations were up for appraisal. As early as a year ago, a secret memo had informed Murrow of the Defense survey team which, visiting Vietnam, had come away finding the project not only oversold but improperly planned, a review reportedly then underway to decide whether it was wise operationally to continue.[188] That March, Michael Forrestal, Senior Staff Member, NSC, asked to take another look, returned from a fact-finding mission to Vietnam with grave doubts about the whole situation.

State, still leery of herbicide operations, was settling for limited continuation, heavily controlled; they wanted Murrow's comments on their answer.[189]

Until mid-1962, his "viscera" had had the backing of his top Far East officer, who hated the whole idea, cited chapter and verse on why not to do it, a perspective not shared by his successor. Besides, Defense wanted it, said they needed it, the pressures taking on a life of their own.

Murrow responded: "little if any" military advantage had been gained, arguments for continuation "based more on speculative hopes . . . than past experience." Then, as though guessing the outcome, he proposed even tighter controls, also a prerequisite finding before any operation, determining a "clear military advantage." Under those conditions, he concurred—"if reluctantly"—in the recommendation that operations be continued.[190]

Yet they were still nervous, strung it round with buts, decisions on future use put on hold in midsummer pending evaluation.

(The final chapter would be written in October, Murrow no longer in full command at the Agency, the Far East Area Director stating the departmental position on requests from Task Force Saigon for a stepup and referring to that earlier message: the one "bearing Mr. Murrow's concurrence"—which placed such stringent restrictions on defoliation. On the evidence, however, of the new reports of its effectiveness against the Vietcong, he was supporting Saigon's request that the controls be "liberalized" and that Saigon be authorized to expand operations on their own without prior approval from Washington.)[191]

That May, the Diem government began its crackdown against Buddhist opposition, ending once and for all the comforting official certitudes that things were getting better.

For some time, the Agency had been asking itself a basic question. They were mostly ex-journalists after all, not the suppressing sort by training or by inclination. At a PAO meeting, country officers had tried to reason out the contradictions of helping undemocratic regimes in the name of protecting democracy—or at least warding off something presumably worse—the "dilemma" of being identified with "an unpopular superstructure."[192] A point given particular emphasis back home now as fiery protest suicides and mass demonstrations began showing up on the nightly news, bringing TV audience opinion into the mix.

By the spring of 1963, the Agency itself was caught up in the divisions splitting the administration as arguments ping-ponged in the NSC: military context versus political context, pro-Diem versus anti-Diem, the unspoken or half-spoken question underneath: was the situation really viable?

At the USIA, the divisions were graphic, the VOA beaming uncensored American press accounts over its Vietnamese service, directly to Vietnamese listeners. Standard, said Loomis later: U.S. editorial opinion was turning; they reflected it, identified it. "Then we would try to find out what the U.S. policy was, and that was very difficult. Because no one was in a position to say."

Murrow, though sharing the general ambivalence, had long been wary of the increasing militarization of the U.S. commitment, above all to a seemingly doubtful government that his agency was expected to peddle as a bastion of lofty values. ("This is no democrat we're nurturing," he allegedly told an aide once, "any way of making him look like one?")

The open record on his overall perspective would be sparse at best, close Agency associates—Loomis, Anderson—unable to recall in retrospect a single privately expressed opinion.

"Murrow's view of Vietnam was no damned different from Kennedy's or anybody else's," said Don Wilson. "We thought we were doing what we had to do." But Kennedy himself had grown uncertain, cautiously weighing the option of a pullout, according to at least one survivor of the warfare in the NSC, one of a faction of doubters coalescing that spring and summer around Harriman—now moved up to Undersecretary, less disdainful, evidently, of the "no-win thesis."

Roger Hilsman was close to Harriman. As the new Assistant Secretary, Far Eastern Affairs, formerly head of the State Department's Bureau of Intelligence and Research and early exponent of counterinsurgency, he had come back from Saigon with Mike Forrestal after the New Year, profoundly pessimistic. The reports from his office on Vietnam—hardnosed, downbeat, challenging Pentagon appraisals and the win-the-war optimism of the Saigon Mission—had gotten themselves a select mailing list as word went round in Washington, and a sympathetic reading, via Bundy, from the President. (Understandably: Hilsman, while at the Legislative Reference Service, Library of Congress, had worked long and hard getting reports up for the young Senator from Massachusetts, knew what Jack Kennedy wanted in a paper.)

Murrow, added to the mailing list, would call Hilsman at times or drop a note of commendation, i.e., "good thinking," "right on target," "useful to the Agency." Personal ties developed, feelings of sharing a wavelength on a number of issues including a turnaround on China, Hilsman seeing to it that the USIA Director got documents and items that normally wouldn't come his way via the chain of command. Murrow for his part was grateful.

Hilsman in turn would recall him as "a staunch ally," however second-string, associated in his mind with the high-level lineup trying to turn U.S. policy in new directions, including generally Harriman, Forrestal, Ball, Mac Bundy, Bobby Kennedy, and the President himself—"that was the group." A group, he recalled, probing however cautiously the prospect of disengagement in Vietnam; "looking for ways," he later claimed, "to get out."[193]

The USIA Director was not of course a first-team player, rarely if ever seen at policy-originating sessions—the government just didn't work that way.

He sat, however, on the NSC; the President respected him. A needed voice, therefore, when it came to a head count—important in the infighting, as Hilsman put it, and in coalition building, as horns locked over policy in Southeast Asia.

But deep divisions meant drift. At home, Murrow was expressing doubts about the course they had adopted—not necessarily the cause itself, i.e., preventing a Communist takeover of the South—but its sheer unworkability, remembering the French.

In the cabinet room, in working groups, he heard the arguments rehashed, adding little, having little, he felt, to contribute: a quiet figure, speaking when asked, surrounded by the men to whom he had always deferred, the professors from Harvard and MIT, the captains of industry—Bundy, Rostow, McNamara, the men who *knew*—more, certainly, than a half-educated guy from a Western cow college.

In Saigon, the Nhus complained to Nolting about the Voice of America, with charges of trying to provoke a coup. Loomis denied it then and later: "I'm not saying that our broadcasts may not have had that impact, but it certainly was not deliberate. It showed that the U.S. didn't know what it was doing, that it was flapping around. Which it was."

"Indeed there was no strong policy," said Burnett Anderson, "because decisions hadn't been made. . . . Sometimes you simply can't get guidance."

At the Agency, Tom Sorensen came up with a snippet from Shakespeare's *Henry VI*, which seemed bleakly appropriate:

> *Among the soldiers this is muttered,*
> *That here you maintain several factions,*
> *And whilst a field should be dispatched and fought,*
> *You are disputing of your generals:*
> *One would have lingering wars with little cost;*
> *Another would fly swift, but wanteth wings;*

A third thinks, without expense at all,
By guileful fair words peace may be obtained. . . .

Janet by now was getting used to seeing him come home, depressed, after a day of meetings: "I don't think they know what they're doing."[194]

For various reasons, there seemed enough feeding the rumors circulating in New York and Washington by early '63, that Murrow was thinking of leaving the administration.

As far as the Agency was concerned—the talented men and women of the various services—there was no question of his loyalty. He felt that his country, despite all, had a contribution to make; there was another kind of war out there, he was to tell the staff before his departure, combatting "ignorance and fear, suspicion and prejudice."[195]

Indeed, there seemed signs of a new, hopeful phase in the administration, with Kennedy, speaking at American University that June, trying to point a way past the antagonisms of eighteen years of cold war. Murrow had had input in what was referred to in the corridors as "the President's peace speech." In the new atmosphere evolving in the wind-down toward the partial test ban treaty, Moscow was no longer jamming the Voice of America, the USIA stressing for the first time the common interests of the two superpowers. (Murrow suggested further openings: a daily hour-long program exchange between Radio Moscow and the Voice; reciprocal broadcast time on Soviet and American TV; reciprocal low-budget travel; a joint U.S.-Soviet peace corps project in a country to be agreed upon; the list went on.)[196]

Domestically, the planned filming of the Martin Luther King march on Washington that summer was similarly a source of satisfaction; a counterweight, they hoped, to the prevailing images of racial confrontation. Though, not surprisingly, *The March* was already drawing fire.

But it was only part of the story. Kenneth Adam, an old BBC friend of Murrow's visiting the USIA, found him looking ill, visibly not happy. "I'm not an officer," he told the Englishman. "I want all the time to be *there*, not here."[197]

It had also become clear by mid-1963 that he'd never made it into the inner circles of the administration, for all the committees and task forces or his own seat on the NSC; it wasn't the NSC where Kennedy's policies were formulated. Even during the missile crisis, with its heavy USIA involvement, it was Bobby Kennedy who had brought the Agency into their inner group, to the President's initial annoyance. Nor had Stevenson been on the Ex Com list. In another era, said Murrow sadly, this man would have had some function in which his talents would be the glory of the world; now he sat around evenings, waiting for old friends to stop in for a drink.

At his own end, there were communications problems with other agencies. There was the duality of Kennedy himself, the problem for the Agency of mixed signals. Hans Tuch had been in Moscow with Harriman for the partial test ban treaty negotiations when JFK, in Berlin, carried away with his "Ich bin ein Berliner" speech to the throngs, stated words to the effect that, Anyone who thinks we can work with the Communists, let him come to Berlin. The next day, says Tuch, there was a reproachful nudge from their Soviet counterparts: "Look—your President!"[198]

Above all, the crash landings were outnumbering the takeoffs, Kennedy's guarantees of March, 1961, notwithstanding: the presidential invitation to participate ("when appropriate") in the development of foreign policy; the vaunted designation of principal psychological advisor.[199]

In June of 1963, not for the first time, Murrow stated his case to McGeorge Bundy, a channel when necessary to the White House. He debriefed his deputies after the meeting:

> I opened by saying I did not believe the Agency could operate effectively or efficiently unless we were able to plan by participating in policy-making decisions. . . .
> I instanced troop reduction in western Europe, arms aid to India and Pakistan, and our lack of information regarding planning in connection with Haiti, as example. . . .He urged me not to be reluctant to bother him, again insisting that he recognized the importance of our job, its difficulties, and the skill with which it was being done.[200]

Interestingly enough, one man to whom he openly vented his feelings was William Paley, their relationship, with the passage of time, back on something of the old footing. Even Stanton had been asked to stand in for Murrow, sometime back, at the dedication of a transmitter.

To Paley, visiting Washington and listening over lunch, Ed seemed a deeply disappointed man; and even more, personally disappointed. Says Paley, "I think one of the worst hurts that certainly he ever suffered was that after a while Kennedy forgot about his promise. Little by little, you know, when you get into very touchy situations where you have to make quick decisions, when you have a small group of people who are your principal advisors, you forget about those people who are supposed to be observers.

"And Ed told me all this, and he said he didn't know what to do about it. He was very, very hurt. And his last days there were days he did not enjoy at all."[201]

There was talk at the time, even at 485, of Murrow's possible return to CBS. But at no time did Paley, reminiscing about those meetings in Washington, mention asking Murrow to come back.

* * *

Dick Heffner, formerly of Channel 13, was at liberty, power-played out of his job at WNDT. Murrow called him from Washington: "I have designs on your body."

They lunched across the street from USIA. Murrow had come with his two deputies. Heffner finished the lunch, knowing he wouldn't take the job. "They treated him with contempt—made it so clear that *they* were in charge. Cut him off when he spoke, talked across him, talked directly to me as though he weren't there. I didn't know about the job but it was so clear they were in charge, and I wouldn't have worked for them for anything." As the two others got up to leave, Murrow, momentarily alone with Heffner, said he'd never been so happy. "I couldn't see it."[202]

In May, the Murrows had gone to Europe for what would be the last time—a pleasurable trip, visiting USIS posts, stopping in England for an international conference at Ditchley, the great country house where they had so often guested in the war years, now turned over to the nation.

At the BBC, Pat Smithers got a call from a secretary—the Murrows were in London, hoped to see a few old friends, hoped he and his wife Olive were free for drinks with them at the ambassador's residence. To their surprise, there were only about six others present, an easy, happy reunion as Smithers recalled it, Ed about the same, the same ready smile, same gentle wisecrack, same insight. Smithers would remember "one sad remark" made on that last occasion, with a slight shrug of the shoulders: "The trouble is," said Murrow, "America is going Right and the rest of the world is going Left."[203]

He thought he detected, moreover, a subtle difference in Ed, a change from the time he had last seen him a year or two before in Washington. "There was something a bit shadowy about what had been substance. Physically, not intellectually or mentally. We'd seen many people in our time who were, shall we say, on the way down. And you think you see telltale signs of it—a certain transparency, as if some nasty old man were pointing a little finger at you. You know the kind of thing I mean?"

The late August heat in Washington was made hotter by the bulletins out of Saigon following new moves against the Buddhists, the midnight raids on the pagodas by Nhu's private army—martial law declared, 1,400 arrests made as the surprised Kennedy administration, its options running out, tried to deal with what was happening. Fritz Nolting had gone home, the ARVN generals, weighing a coup, probed prospects of support through the new American ambassador (Henry Cabot Lodge, Nixon's erstwhile running mate and the incumbent unseated in the 1952 Massachusetts Senate race by young John Kennedy).

USIS/Saigon was reporting harassment by the Vietnamese authorities, cooperation replaced by confrontation, field representatives shadowed, the rural program nearly at a halt, pro-Diem propaganda long since phased out. Hamlet dwellers, Murrow wrote the President, weren't believing their government radio on the Buddhist crisis, preferring the uncensored VOA reports, and accounts traveling by word of mouth.

At 1776, frantic new recommendations were streaming in from Mecklin, now wholly turned around—Vietnam needed new leadership (with a face-saving solution of course for Diem), the U.S. should send in combat troops, the U.S. commitment should be unlimited.[204] In contrast to his earlier communications, they went unadorned to State, leaving behind a terse note from Murrow: "Passed on without comment."

The reporter Marguerite Higgins, an old friend and supporter of military policy in Southeast Asia, was in town, back from a month in Vietnam, a dissenter from the prevailing anti-Diem view among the Saigon-based press corps and asking urgently to talk to Murrow.

Higgins was "distressed," Murrow's office informed him, about the VOA's alleged reliance on the dispatches of Sheehan, Halberstam, and Peter Arnett of AP—"a cabal of young men," she charged, dedicated to pulling down Diem, and whose reporting was "synchronized distortion." The note further added:

> While she esteems Halberstam, except for his political judgment, she pointed out that Sheehan has been a newspaperman for only eighteen months....Hardly ever do any of them check with the Embassy. . . .[205]

At the VOA, they assured her they used many sources, official stuff: look at the transcripts. Maybe so, said Higgins, but the fact was that the Voice, by feeding anti-Diem copy back to Saigon, was exacerbating an already difficult situation; they should depend more on State and CIA reporting and she meant to talk to Ed about it.

In the meantime, messages were flying back and forth between Saigon and Washington, a reply cabled to Lodge in the wake of the pagoda bust, over George Ball's name as Acting Secretary—drawn up by Harriman and Hilsman with input from Ball and Rusk, all bases touched, including the President—instructing the Ambassador to assure the generals support, promising to "back" him to the "hilt." Followed by a confirming head count among the lead players and cold feet, evidently, among the generals.

In another NSC head-to-head on August 31, Hilsman cited world opinion, i.e., the problem was moving to a political and diplomatic plane, and others in Asia were watching to see how much repression we'd tolerate before withdrawing aid. Murrow, sitting in, said press condemnation was now worldwide.

It was the meeting at which Paul Kattenberg of Hilsman's staff, the Asia-wise head of the interdepartmental working group on Vietnam, first floated the possibility of "honorable" withdrawal. It was quickly talked down by the so-called hawks, the final note sounded by Rusk, i.e., no coup, likewise no pullout till the war was won. With agreement from Secretary McNamara and Vice-President Johnson.[206]

In Saigon, the coup seemed at any rate collapsed, the war of nerves continuing, another presidential mission sent from Washington, its findings inconclusive.

In a divided NSC, arguments escalated—fixated, said Murrow afterward, on the Diem-must-go versus Diem-must-stay schools, the processes of reason, he said, no longer functioning.[207]

Murrow's own friends on the outside found him looking drawn, coughing incessantly. The sessions dragged out, acrimonious, dead-ended. He felt lousy.

At one point, another expert was going into another *spiel*, as Murrow would later tell it, about Diem's unpopularity, i.e., army officers allegedly going civilian to drop off food parcels with young relatives detained after student demonstrations. Obviously this meant the army was growing disaffected.

The news editor in him had finally rebelled. The man who rarely talked, spoke up: *How do you know*? What's your source? Who knew *what* was in that officer's head, maybe he was telling his little brother to straighten up and fly right. Had anyone bothered to check it out? It turned out to be hearsay, a story from a *Paris-Match* photographer, unchecked and unevaluated.

"Now I ask you," Murrow told Maggie Higgins long afterward, when events had run their course, "is that the kind of evidence on which to base decisions?"[208]

But when, that September, expert USIA opinion was sought, it was Mecklin, just back from Vietnam, who spoke in the NSC, urging a U.S. troop commitment, quickly discounted as unthinkable. In any case, USIS/Saigon was already primed—part of the Country Team—for its stance in a coup, virtually, by all evidence, an agency to itself.

"We are launched on a course," Lodge had cabled Rusk that summer, "from which there is no respectable turning back."[209] But now the coup seemed dead, the decision taken not to "run" one, the President's men back to the first square. Later opinions on Kennedy's possible directions would remain divided. Hilsman insisted the President wanted to get out—"because he made it clear to me so many times." Burnett Anderson—admittedly operational, not top level—who sat weekly with Mac Bundy, would stay "strongly convinced that nobody knows what Kennedy would have done in regard to the Vietnam war."

One fact, though, was certain, unknown at the time: Murrow was ready to leave. Because by early fall of 1963, he had a date to talk with Elmer Lower, the newly ensconced president of ABC News, about a job.

Murrow's discontent with his role in the administration, said Lower, had been an open secret for some time in the broadcast industry, prompting the ABC news chief to pick up the telephone that September and ask for an appointment.

Fewer than a handful knew of it at the network—Jesse Zousmer, now Lower's assistant; ABC head Leonard Goldenson who encouraged him to go ahead. "He's going to ask a lot of money," Lower warned. ("ABC," he said later, "was very poor in those days.") Never mind, came the answer, if he could get Murrow, it'd be worth every penny. Lower called Washington. "I'd like to come down and see you."

"What about?"

"We-ell, I'd like to see if we have any mutuality of interest that would bring you to ABC."

"Well, come on down."[210]

Salant, at CBS, had been floating the idea of bringing Murrow back to do the documentaries. "I stayed in touch, and he got tired of the USIA; by that time Paley and Stanton had calmed down."[211] There was, of course, the question of the second, ostensibly unbreakable, half of his CBS contract, though the larger question was, could anyone go back, having known the secrets? Murrow seemed to feel he could. (And in fact Carl Rowan, his successor at the USIA, and John Chancellor, heading the VOA in the mid-sixties, as Scotty Reston pointed out, later seemed able to manage the reentry into journalism.)[212] Murrow's feelings about CBS, however, might have been more complicated than evidenced in the comradely lunches with Paley.

Dave Schoenbrun had been in touch with him that June about a proposed article for *Esquire* ("Whatever Happened to Ed Murrow?"), exploring the history of his relations with CBS, the circumstances and seeming paradox of his entering the government, his position there; also how long he expected to stay in the job and what, if any, were his future plans?[213]

Murrow at the time had thought it over, then declined, saying, "I just don't think I could talk with sufficient candor about either the past or the present as long as I am in this job."[214]

He talked again with Lower in New York. "I didn't know what he was going to ask," the newsman recalls, "I didn't even know whether he would be interested. ABC's thinking was of a senior commentator spot. But he was mad at CBS and he was through with USIA in his own mind. He knew the subject of my wanting to come down and said he was willing to listen."[215]

The night before their meeting, a secretary called ABC from Washington: Mr. Murrow would be unable to keep the appointment, as he was going to the hospital.

Stan Plesent would remember that last Thursday in September as being on planes a lot and rushing a lot, a day packed with appearances: a luncheon; a dinner; an interview on afternoon TV over the local CBS affiliate. In Washington the President's inner circle was jockeying with Diem in a last-ditch attempt to retrieve a crumbling situation, and Murrow was flying to Philadelphia to address civic groups: an indication in itself, possibly—an India-Pakistan trip was on for that October—that his presence in the high councils was harldy indispensable.

It was during the luncheon address before the Federal Bar Association that he was hit by a hemorrhage and loss of voice, the familiar baritone changed to a harsh rasp. He apologized and finished, answering critics of USIA who didn't want, he said, America's race problems exposed to the rest of the world. Well, those problems were perfectly obvious to the rest of the world, a domestic fact; and facts would determine America's position. "At the end of the day, it's what we *are* that matters."[216]

They went for a rest to the suite provided at the Bellevue-Stratford. Once inside the door, he sagged. Let's go home, urged Plesent. Murrow waved him off: No, no, he'd just nap awhile and would he, Stanley, please come for him at four, in time for the interview.

At four o'clock the young man, returning, was frightened by Murrow's appearance. He offered to stand in for him. Murrow acceded but insisted in seeing their evening engagement through.

He made it through the black-tie dinner, speaking off the cuff, regaling the audience with stories of his early days at the IIE and the Emergency Committee, in good spirits, seemingly oblivious of the rasp that had replaced his speaking voice.

On the plane, the counsel felt a sense of foreboding: "My bones told me that this was more than just a cold," he said later.

His misgivings increased as, the drinks arriving, he watched Murrow, a habitual sipper, bolt down two scotch-and-waters nonstop, then lean back.

"I've got some pain, Stanley."

"Where?"

He indicated an area around his throat, then, in answer to the other's question about a doctor, admitted he had a doctor's appointment for the next day.

It was late when they arrived in Washington, the Agency limo waiting. Where was his car? Murrow asked Plesent. Just a few blocks away, the other man replied, he'd walk it. Nonsense, they'd drive him over.

At the lot the Director waited as the young man found his car, started it up, and drove off. Stan Plesent's last memory of that night was the rearview mirror image of Murrow, standing in the deserted parking lot, looking after the departing car.[217]

Ten days later a medical team removed his left lung in a three-hour operation and confirmed the presence of lung cancer.

Get-well wishes poured in from friends, colleagues, strangers; from columnists and newspaper editorials. The doctors sounded reasonably optimistic; so did his visitors. One, however, knew better. Dr. Paul

Heller, the Buchenwald survivor from 1945, who had kept in touch over the years, stopped in for a short visit, their respective positions now strangely reversed: Heller upright and healthy; Murrow horizontal in the high bed, drug-ridden and nauseous. Said Heller later, "I just said a few encouraging words; I knew how sick he was."[218]

It was just the beginning, as post-operative sessions of cobalt radiation brought further debilitation and turned the chest skin to brown, dessicated leather.

Outside, events ran their course. That same week of early October, coup momentum had started up again in Saigon, leading in early November to the toppling of the Diem government and the murder of the Ngo brothers, leaving dismay and shock in Washington, with lingering questions at the highest levels about the cables of the past weeks, the possible complicity.

Don Wilson, by mutual agreement, had taken over as Acting Director though Murrow, when possible, tried to make it into the office for an hour at a time. He showed up at his first meeting "looking like the wrath of God," an employee recalled, a wool vest added for extra warmth, easing himself slowly into his chair and speaking in gasps, uncomfortably aware of the silent attention of his officers.

"Whoever said talk is cheap," he said, "had two lungs."[219]

Then came November 22.

Murrow had been home all that day, weakened and ill with radiation sickness. It was Janet who told him of the President's being wounded in Dallas, making him get back under the covers before breaking the news. He tried to reassure her, two people in a private nightmare, caught up in the national nightmare. When the word from Dallas changed to *assassinated*, he grew silent and wondered about Johnson.

Don Wilson, on the other hand, remembered him as "devastated" when he telephoned later that afternoon, after the full impact had sunk in. Said Wilson, "He was in bad shape, tears in his voice, enormously shaken; it was a combination of the enormity of the crime and his physical weakness."[220]

That Saturday he pulled himself together, to pay his last respects, with others of the government, before the bier set up in the East Room of the White House.

Press and TV cameras were lined up at the portico, with many, keeping their grief private, using the back entrance where an elevator usually carried visitors one floor up to the Pennsylvania Avenue level. Arriving, they had found the elevator, hand-operated, standing idle and the visitors using the stairs, a sad, silent flow of mourners proceeding up toward the East Room or down away from it. Murrow, with his horror of exceptions, decided cautiously to give the stairs a try, stumbled as he nearly blacked out, revived with the aid of smelling salts, and continued upward. Wilson came upon him there—"three-quarters of the way up," he recalled, "looking awful, a grayish-green, terrified that he was going to pass out. He made it up those stairs, but it just took a gigantic bite out of him."

Later that week, however, he was climbing stairs again.

The USIA had a job to do, explaining to the rest of the world that the government of the United States would continue, an orderly transition, that the assassination, as Sorensen put it, was not the beginning of World War III.[221]

But as Stan Plesent was to point out, that cost money—"We needed a budget for this."

And Murrow was recuperating from this devastating operation, still terribly weak; could hardly talk, still adjusting after having one lung removed. Nevertheless, he used his time in the office to call key members of the Senate who would vote on the budget. And I had to watch him sitting there at the telephone, gasping for breath—literally—calling one senator after another. Well, the Senate vote was okay, but the House vote was less, and the measure went to conference. We wanted nine million, but the House said five.

Murrow decided to see John Rooney. His General Counsel tried to talk him out of it—he was in no condition to face down Rooney. "Let *me* go!" Murrow insisted, and they made the appointment.

At the House Office Building, they faced steps. Murrow, one hand on the railing, pulled himself up with almost savage determination, Plesent, following behind, not daring to offer help.

We saw Rooney. Murrow of course had to be careful how he talked— he ran easily out of breath, so he'd have to plan his phrases in such a way as to have enough breath left to finish. And when you thought of what this man's voice had been. . . .

But for once, Murrow had Rooney at a disadvantage. How could you argue with a sick man? Rooney gave in a *little*; he still withheld something—i.e., 8 million instead of 9 million. But I'm sure it was damaging to Ed in the long run. It was stupid! Three million! What is that? One missile or bomber cost more than our whole operation! But it was important to Murrow. It was for the Agency.[222]

There was also undeniably that flair for the dramatic, the urge to self-sacrifice in a time of crisis, that had him throwing his infirmity onto the scale—Plesent could conceivably have made those phone calls, though not half so effectively—not to mention the satisfaction of watching John Rooney squirm for a change.

Thanksgiving at Pawling later that week was a somber affair. Dewey Murrow had flown in to join them, helping his younger brother and his sister-in-law get up to New York by train. The Sewards were waiting at Penn Station; Murrow was wrung out, apprehensive: What was going to happen to the *country?*

Jim Seward, covering all contingencies as always, had arranged for a wheelchair. Ed wasn't at all sure he needed it, but, said Seward later, "he was still very frail and it was a kind of a long platform and why, he decided he'd take advantage of it."

It was a gray time. That December, he managed a note of approval to young Hilsman, then urging recognition of the government of China, in an address cleared with Kennedy just before his death. The speech had gone almost unnoticed. Hilsman himself, along with other doubters, was on his way out.

Six days later, he submitted his resignation to the new President, for reasons of health, effective mid-January. He had told President Kennedy, before his death, of such a possibility, he wrote; his present inability to continue, therefore, was "deeply disappointing."[223]

Johnson, summoning him to the White House, sympathetic but trying to keep the cabinet together for the nonce, asked him to stay on for the good of the country, an argument he could not refuse, except to remind the President that the choice might not be his to make. They agreed finally on a quick resignation in case of "medical emergency."

That January, he took a turn for the worse. Get out of Washington, said the doctors, go someplace warm, someplace dry. He made plans for California, called the White House and found no one to take his resignation.

There had been all along a disquieting subtext to the Murrow-Johnson relationship—productive during LBJ's Senate years, turning prickly under Kennedy.

They had never been, personally, each other's kind of people, the LBJ style grating on Murrow like a fingernail run across a blackboard, the lack of chemistry exacerbated by the Vice-President's restiveness in the restrictions of his role under Jack Kennedy. Agency people came back with complaints about the vice-presidential missions abroad, his demanding behavior on tour, the grousing when the VIP treatment wasn't up to par.

Both men, to do them justice, had tried on their own, endeavoring to keep relations even between USIA and the office of Vice-President—not easy with the boxed-in power figure, the great parliamentarian who for three years had been suffering the frustrations of being the extra thumb. But Murrow was still "Ed," the USIA doing its best to keep LBJ happy on his appointed rounds, right down to the leather-bound photo albums prepared by the overworked Agency as mementos for distinguished visitors and junketing VIPs.

The final irritant, evidently, had been Johnson's request for the exclusive services of USIA's top photographer, the master artist Yoichi Okamoto. Murrow said no, and found LBJ was not easily said no to, keeping up a constant needling that didn't let up even during their common attendance at the memorial service for Sam Rayburn—Mr. Sam, Murrow's idol among the politicos, and Johnson's mentor.

The USIA Director dug in his heels: "Okie" was their best talent; the

Agency needed him. Case closed. But it was also a case of two Old Americans—two Old Southerners—stubbornness breeding resistant stubbornness; the rock and the hard place.

After November 22, "Okie's" transfer was a foregone conclusion. But the tug of war had left a bitter aftertaste, undissipated in those weeks of early January, as an overburdened new President trying to hold the pieces together, not wanting it said, possibly, that Edward R. Murrow was leaving the administration, made himself unavailable.

Murrow tried to arrange an appointment and got nowhere. He tried calling the President; LBJ wasn't in to him. He left messages; the calls were never returned. Wilson tried a contact through young Bill Moyers, once of the Peace Corps, now working for LBJ; Moyers, though sympathetic, couldn't manage it.[224]

Finally, no one would take his calls. Murrow decided to leave.

The day of departure, there was a call from LBJ—hours before the California flight, by one account; paged at the airport, by another—reading off the White House statement to be made public shortly, accepting Murrow's resignation, with the assurance that he was leaving "with the thanks of a grateful President and a grateful nation."

Some time before, he had said goodbye to his people at the USIA. The maverick Henry Loomis, who was to resign in a little over a year, would recall his words:

> Communications systems are neutral. They have neither conscience nor morality; only a history. They will broadcast truth or falsehood with equal facility. Man communicating with man poses not a problem of how to say it, but, more fundamentally, what is he to say.[225]

The doctors had assured him there was a chance; Lacey seemed to be beating the odds. Given a quiet life and no smoking, he might do the same. He went with the prognosis, even cheering up his younger aides from the Agency to the effect that much as he relished danger, he'd as soon have faced it "some other way."[226]

They'd see.

XVII

Twilight

The house was in La Jolla, not far from the Salk Institute for Biological Studies, the arrangements made by Jonas Salk himself, discoverer of the polio vaccine. Murrow had befriended Salk in the 1950's, the favor returned now with the eminent physician's invitation to the Murrows to come out West, for what would obviously be a lengthy convalescence. The circumstances seemed ideal: the whitewashed California house, open spaces, soft golden cliffs with gently graded paths leading down to the beach and the Pacific, and the gentle, eternal sun of Southern California.

Instead, it rained incessantly, the skies dark, Murrow's efforts at regaining his strength halted by bouts of pneumonia in his remaining right lung, itself scarred and impaired by the years of illness and cigarette abuse, not up to the demands placed on it by the big body. His spirits low, he coped with the adjustments of the hyperactive man finding himself by one stroke a pulmonary cripple.

At home in his apartment in New York, Dick Heffner was sitting down to dinner, just off the plane from Los Angeles and a meeting of his new employers, the American Association for the Advancement of Science, when his wife called him to the telephone.

It was his boss, the chairman of the AAAS board, whom he had seen that afternoon in L.A.—the mathematician Warren Weaver, calling from his home in La Jolla and putting on the line his friend and neighbor Jonas Salk asking, Could he take the next plane back to California?

"He explained to me," said Heffner later, "that he owed a great deal to Ed Murrow, a debt of gratitude for the help that Ed had given him when the Salk vaccine was announced, that he had sort of taken Jonas under his wing, protected him from what could have been media difficulties. Well, he had asked Ed to La Jolla, he said, for recuperation so that he, Jonas, could keep an eye on him. Though what he really wanted to do was help him overcome the depression and despondency that he knew Ed would feel."

The problem, said Salk over the telephone, was that nothing seemed to be working. "Ed was depressed. Instead of Janet's being able to get him interested in things and people, he just sat in the house all day. Well, Warren had told Jonas, I guess, that Ed knew *me* and that maybe I could do something—a flight of fancy, but I guess they were grasping at straws."

Arrived next day in La Jolla, the young man was driven to the Murrow house.

> And I'll always remember this. You know this scene from *Citizen Kane* in which you enter this huge room. And you see this great brooding giant of a man seated at the far end, and everything about the scene is dark. Sense of foreboding. Well, I remember walking into that room—a long living room—and Ed seated at the far end of it, just sitting there, looking out the window, withdrawn from the world. Now you think of anything in San Diego or La Jolla as bright and sunlight. I don't know if it was raining or not; maybe it was. But it was *dark*. And Ed's mood was dark. And he was gracious and kind. But he wasn't going to be drawn out of his shell.
>
> I don't remember what we discussed, just of failing at the task. The only thing I recall, really, is that he talked of coming back to New York, to go up to the farm. Warren Weaver told me what the doctors had told *him*: that the removal of a lung—I'll always remember this expression—is the greatest insult that the body can take, because of what it does to the rest of you. And that *he* felt that Ed's doctors had not adequately prepared him for an understanding of how he would feel, how totally debilitated he would feel.[1]

Yet slowly, he fought his way back and by February was two-finger typing letters to New York. " 'tis a slow business," he wrote Seward, forwarding the stream of doctor bills and Blue Cross forms. "am seeing practically no one . . . many calls from old friends in the area, but haven't the energy to see people."[2]

Bill Paley, down from L.A. in early March, was one of the exceptions, arriving in time for lunch and surprised to see Ed waiting behind the wheel of a car, intent on showing him the sights. But the try at mastery was transparent; it wasn't the old Ed Murrow driving, controlling his speeding with fingertip lightness in a dangerous, casual grace. The effort showed as Murrow's hands clutched tightly at the wheel, never relaxing their grip.[3]

Janet was waiting at the house. They talked about CBS, laughed over the couple's mounds of unanswered correspondence. Paley left the phone number of a social secretary—his treat. Salk came by to show Paley around the institute, still under construction. Underneath the sunny afternoon, the easy hospitality, lay the realization that Murrow wasn't getting better.

It was kind of Bill to come, wrote Murrow after Paley had departed.

Friendly's impending visit, however, was another matter. Try to discourage him, Murrow had pleaded with Seward: He couldn't hold Fred's hand again, hadn't the strength; couldn't stand up to the exhaustion of his presence, Murrow's tone for the first and only time taking on the querulousness of the very ill.[4] But he didn't tell Friendly and no one else did and Friendly came anyway, never suspecting he was anything but highly welcome, exuberant in his new dignity as President of CBS News.

The times had not been good to CBS News, in for a long siege of trailing Huntley-Brinkley, which might have helped start up the rumors that spring of Murrow's always-imminent return. "i hear from friends in wash. that stanton is passing the word that i am definitely coming back to cbs," he wrote Seward, "right now i feel i aint going anywhere."[5]

As with *CBS Reports*, it was Friendly's spark that the network leadership had turned to for warmth and fire; so in early 1964 Salant had stepped down, and Fred Friendly—brought in fourteen years back as Murrow's junior partner, who had so closely skirted getting sacked but for the one fact, then as now, that he was needed—had been made head of the CBS News Division.

"I am *appalled*," Murrow wrote Seward, on hearing the news.[6] The greatest producer, bar none, but overall news chief? It might have been as much a reaction to putting the top job in any producer's hands. But one of Friendly's first acts met with his overwhelming approval.

"I want to get Joe Wershba back," he said over the telephone from New York. "What do you think?" Friendly had talked to Wershba, but not to Jap Gude.

The relief over the line from La Jolla was almost palpable. "I think it's the best idea you ever had."[7]

Blair Clark came out to see him; publishers were writing, asking for a book ("many, if not all," he complained to a friend); Bobby Kennedy wanted him to do interviews for an oral history of JFK. He had made no commitments, he told Jesse Zousmer, now at ABC, and wouldn't until May or June. "I am, however, going to talk to the educational television boys sometime during April. That might turn out to be a home for both of us. . . ."[8]

Back in 1962, he had set down guidelines that would later be followed by public television, had declined at the time an offer made through Morris Ernst to run an educational TV network, leaving matters open-ended. The offer was renewed in 1964. He wondered about his CBS contract, yet seemed to want to pursue it.

But the signs of progress in his recovery kept crumbling away like the sides of a sand pit. Back at golfing, he had attacked it in "rather too vigorous a fashion," he told Chet Bowles,[9] and had to stop. This is a slow, slow business, he intoned again to Seward. In April, instead of meeting with the "television boys," he was felled again by pneumonia. They had hoped to return to the farm; instead, Janet Murrow told friends, she was trying to get Ed well enough to get back to Washington. The Manning Place house had been sold, which meant they had to vacate before Memorial Day.

Robert Evans, formerly of CBS and Murrow's aide and speech writer at the USIA, came out for a visit. Janet served him lunch alone on the patio while Murrow lay inside the house. She hoped he would understand, she wrote him later, but Ed had been running a high fever that day.

Letters kept flooding in to him, from Washington, from USIS posts around the world. "We felt sheltered by your courage," wrote Henry Loomis, already tangling with the new administration over Vietnam, ". . .but above all we knew you cared—about the world, about our government, about the agency—even about us as individuals. . . ."[10]

Bill King, Area Director, Near East and South Asia, had felt tears come on, he wrote, while reading of Ed's resignation: "I find I have wept a great deal lately, and felt like weeping even more often. . . ."[11]

Vietnam, wrote Don Wilson, was preoccupying them, "although we don't know yet whither we goest in that one." The USIA was having a much rougher time in being heard in committee—a direct result, he wrote, of Murrow's departure.

The March, barely grazed past the old-boy unfriendlies on the Foreign Relations Committee, had run into setbacks from unexpected sources: "Averell doesn't like it, Bobby Kennedy doesn't like it, Dean Rusk doesn't like it, nor do many others." The bottom line, said Wilson, was, "the 'expectables' like Hickenlooper . . . hate it and our friends aren't with us. They don't feel that it presents a 'balanced picture.' "[12]

"I am unrepentant about *The March*," Murrow replied. "It is a good film and anyone, including Bob Kennedy and Rusk, who believes that every individual film must present a 'balanced' picture, knows nothing about either balance or pictures."[13]

John Mecklin was going back to *Time*. He had signed with Doubleday, he wrote Ed, for a book about the Saigon years and one of the "monumental squeezes" of a lifetime.[14] Murrow wished him well, bypassing Mecklin's offer to send him the outline for comment.

A bound album of tributes arrived in the mail, with letters from former administration colleagues, his office staff, the President, the widow of John Kennedy. He had left a lot of his friends wiser than he found them, wrote Mac Bundy, "grateful for advice they took and woeful over some they didn't."

"Even when many of us were. . .pontificating around the table in the Cabinet Room," wrote George Ball, one of The Group, "you were always the barrister with a brief for sanity. And, greatly to your credit, you were always against letting America act out of character."

"The subject of our deliberations was not a pretty one," wrote Mike Forrestal, another doubter on Vietnam, "but. . . .I shall never forget the quietly humorous way you kept us from forgetting that we were talking about people who had hopes and fears as well as guns and grenades.

"You are sorely missed. . . ."[15]

Returned to the wet heat of late-spring Washington, Janet Murrow worked at clearing the house before the deadline, and keeping an eye on Ed.

When possible, they saw old friends. A car and driver took them to the Howard Smiths in suburban Washington. Benedicte Smith was in the driveway when the car stopped partway up the hill, Murrow getting out to join her, managing the steep incline with difficulty.

Smith, watching from the terrace, suddenly saw him listing as he approached—a balance problem, obviously—leaning ever further, lopsided, until he seemed ready to pitch over onto the tarmac.

The newsman started up. "I'd better help him," he told Janet, who had reached the house.

"Don't. He'll right himself. Leave him alone."

Smith stayed where he was. Murrow made it on his own. *Such a waste,* thought Benedicte Smith, *of a human being.*[16]

The Warburgs stopped by, en route to Virginia, inquiring about Ed's health. "He was incredibly thin and beautiful," Mary Warburg recalled, "like a poet, iridescent; or a handsome Abe Lincoln."[17]

(Was there something they could bring? they had asked beforehand. Well, he wasn't eating, said Janet Murrow, and he did miss those New York soups from the deli. They brought a quantity down on the air shuttle, in what must have set a new record in long-distance takeout orders, carefully balancing the sloshing containers between New York and Washington.)

The farm finally reached, the Murrows found the midsummer climate almost as oppressive as Washington, as Dutchess County sweltered in a heat wave. The move from Washington, Janet wrote Sidney Bernstein, had nearly finished her. Ed, though reasonably cheerful and looking better, was suffering from pulmonary hypertension, the remaining lung unable to accommodate the flow of blood from the left side of the heart, causing severe discomfort. She had wanted an air conditioner installed in Ed's bedroom, and ran into the Murrow stubbornness ("In Pawling, definitely *not*").[18]

The weather eased, however, and so did the illness. Though it was hard for Murrow to go cold turkey; the sudden cutoff of the lifetime nicotine habit brought on shaking, sweats, and the range of withdrawal symptoms that were tough to go through, tough to witness. "But he never wanted sympathy," Jim Seward recalled.

The habit licked, he acquired the reform zeal of the born again. "Who knows," he wrote his Washington M.D., still among the unsaved, "maybe my powers of persuasion have improved to the point where I can persuade you to stop smoking."[19] But he felt he had been kept alive a year, and was grateful.

He began answering letters again. CBS, he told Bernstein, wanted him to do a documentary on the British elections, but he doubted it was possible.

His three years in government—on which he had asked Bernstein's advice—he called the most interesting and rewarding of his entire experience. "I now think I really understand the process of decision making in this governmental structure of ours, and I am sure I did not understand it at all before I got involved in it."[20]

He wrote similarly to Chet Bowles, who hadn't been sure, he told Ed, that he'd done him an unmitigated favor in recruiting him in 1961. Not at all, said Murrow, he'd learned a lot; wouldn't have missed it for all the backbiting.[21] Bowles, long banished from the upper circles, now out in India as ambassador, thought Murrow had made "an enormous contribution, particularly in giving our overseas information a sense of integrity and direction which I am earnestly hopeful will not be lost or compromised in the future."[22]

(When, on the other hand, Johnson asked Friendly to come to work for him and Friendly asked Murrow's advice, Murrow said it was the worst idea he had ever heard of and they'd cut his balls off in four weeks.)[23]

In New York, he visited CBS News, bringing work almost to a halt, all goodwill and smiles. Stanton, closeted with a visitor, saw him poke his head in at the office door and wave hello. At *CBS Reports*, he seemed to take special pleasure in talking with Joe Wershba, following up as producer on a *CBS Reports* suggested by Murrow—"Gideon's Trumpet," based on the landmark *Gideon* case dealing with the right of the accused to representation by legal counsel.

Their relationship had mellowed, Murrow almost paternal, as he had never been in their younger years on *See It Now*. He asked Wershba to come up to Pawling.

It was a summer of warmth and good friends and good feeling. He played golf again with Jim Seward, just nine holes, but winning as so often in the past; Seward was never so happy to be beaten at golf. Alfred and Blanche Knopf came by, bringing their own refreshments in a picnic basket, not wanting to trouble the Murrows, they said. Teddy Kollek came up, in the course of a visit to the States. If he could just get this licked, Murrow told him, he'd want to be ambassador to Israel. There was a lot he could do, he felt. Israel wasn't out of the woods yet, he warned Kollek; there were tough times ahead, and they'd need friends.[24]

As from a distance, he watched the Johnson versus Goldwater campaign. "A lot of nonsense," it seemed to him, was being written about it in England, he told Bernstein. "The trouble with the so-called Liberals over here is that they tend to panic whenever they face a real collision. The Goldwater boys will collect a fair number of people who are frustrated, who seek easy and quick solutions, but we have not yet reached the point where the country is prepared to turn over power to such a group."[25]

Joe and Shirley Wershba, taking up Murrow's invitation, had a jeep tour of Quaker Hill, their host at the wheel. They passed a steepled little building. "That's a church," Murrow commented dryly, "for them as needs it."

They drove around the farm, Murrow pointing out repeatedly that it was paid up, no mortgages, no debts, owned free and clear; his family would always have a home. The producer suddenly realized—the hearty company, wry talk, bumpy, macho jeep ride, and general high spirits notwithstanding—that Murrow knew he was going to die.

But there was something obviously tugging, as they talked, on the sick man's mind—Vietnam, and the premonition that Americans were headed for disaster.[26]

There had been great regard for John Kennedy, also doubts. He had "great difficulty" he wrote Oppenheimer in those months, reaching some judgment regarding "that young man's relation to his time. I saw him at fairly close range under a variety of circumstances, and there remains for me a considerable element of mystery—and maybe that is good. I always knew where his mind was, but I was not always sure where his heart was."

(Though in Johnson's case, he added, there was never any doubt where his heart was, "as he was generally beating me over the head with it.")[27]

Misgivings had been escalating all through 1964 on many fronts. Chet Bowles, writing in the spring from India, worried about the new administration—"off to a good start in domestic affairs" but not abroad—concerned, he told Murrow, about "our continuing insensitivity to forces which are shaping events in Africa, Asia and Latin America. We still persist . . . in putting too high priority on military equipment and economic growth in per capita terms with too little regard for what happens to people in the process of their development. . . ."[28]

Murrow, replying, thought they would see "even less sensitivity after what is happening in Latin America.

"The Johnson Administration is in the process of creating a real record of political opportunism. . . . Domestically none of this matters very much, but I am deeply worried about our foreign policy, particularly since Rusk continues to think that if he believes anything he should not believe it too hard. . . ."[29]

But the so-called Gulf of Tonkin incident that night in early August—Johnson on national television announcing an "unprovoked attack" on American destroyers in the gulf by North Vietnamese, calling for powers to deal with it, the necessity for retaliation—sent him rushing to the phone.

CBS, unlike NBC, had given it a bare two-minute sum-up, then returned to the regular schedule. Murrow—who had sat on the NSC, had seen the national security action memorandum when the first decisions had been taken in 1961 on covert action, as unaware now as the rest of the country of the large-scale military step-up since early 1964, of the secret plan known as 34A, drafted while he himself had been trying to get out of Washington—picked up the receiver and dialed Friendly's number at CBS. A call out of the night, spurred by knowing possibly too much on one hand, not enough on the other, his fury fueled by what he couldn't or wouldn't talk about.

What did they mean by going off the air? he raged at Friendly. By what "God-given right" could they treat it this way?[30] How much did they *really* know about what had happened out there? *Why* it happened? How could he, Friendly, not have put Dan Rather and the boys on the screen, asking questions? If he meant to telegraph a message, it wasn't being picked up. In fact, Friendly would later tell David Halberstam, Rather himself had been on the phone that day, smelling a rat, his boss telling him, for God's sake don't say something like that on the air, they couldn't deal with it.[31] Friendly himself was to leave CBS in two years, a vocal opponent of the war, his departure precipitated in part over the televising of what had become by then a national debate over Vietnam.

There were good days and bad days now. With Janet, despite initial misgivings about his ability to do so, he attended Casey's graduation from Milton Academy, an honor student bound for Yale in the fall; but Ed had had to ask Howard Smith to stand in for him, delivering the commencement address.

Sevareid saw him for one last time in western Pennsylvania, driven hundreds of miles by Janet to attend the wedding of one of his twin sons, born in the midst of the fall of Paris, 1940. A day of sun and happiness, he recalled, and of old friends.[32] Chet and Elizabeth Williams came to the farm for lunch. "Janet had said that Ed would like to see me," he recalled afterward. "He seemed to be in a clearer state of mind than he had been in for some time and wanted to do some things on which I might be able to help him."

They had corresponded during Murrow's time in California about educational television, Williams being quite active in the field. "I remember how he objected to the word *educational*; he thought it wasn't feasible for that kind of broadcasting. He also feared that educational TV as it had developed to that point wasn't going places. He didn't want it classroomish, wanted it to go in the direction in which it is now."

They talked through the afternoon, the two old roommates from Thirty-eighth Street, seated on the lawn before the house under a huge oak, looking out over the valley, bathed in a late-summer glow. Williams remembered it in retrospect as "a kind of temporary opening of the clouds for him because very shortly thereafter they closed in again and he was unable to do anything more. It was as if Ed were grasping for a kind of final word on the human condition, something summarizing; I think Janet understood that."[33]

That same summer CBS, leaving 485 Madison, broadcast *Farewell to Studio Nine*, a loving tribute to the old facility and decades of reporting: a compendium of reports and reminiscences, live, taped, and on shellac, of the great CBS Radio News team. It had been anticipated as Murrow's return to broadcasting, but even before the final tape went out over the air, word had leaked that the voice was not what it had been.

Murrow himself spoke with anchorman Bob Trout from Lowell Thomas' studio in Dutchess County, talked shop about the old days and commented on his recordings from London, the confident young voice on the aging discs contrasting starkly with the flat, dry tones of the man who now labored to finish his sentences.

There was Kaltenborn on Munich; Elmer Davis; Sevareid comparing Paris in June 1940 to a dying woman with her lifeblood oozing; Murrow on a rooftop; Shirer peering into the railroad car at Compiègne, watching Hitler accept the French surrender; John Daly announcing the attack on Pearl Harbor in December 1941; Collingwood describing the German surrender in May 1945.

A few of them reminisced: Kaltenborn, still spry, Sevareid, Daly. Murrow, up in Dutchess County, said he could still visualize the studio—the leather couch, Trout's habit of swinging the mike around for a three-quarter angle. Together they talked about the Christmas party of 1936 and Murrow's unsung newscasting debut, about colleagues living and dead, and about Elmer Davis. The half hour was up much too soon. "So many broadcasts," said Trout in his valedictory, "so little time to remember them. Let us salute the words . . . as the electric current dies and the microphones grow cold, as the lights are switched off and the soundproofing comes off the walls, as Studio Nine itself passes into the history of our times. . . ."[34]

The old *See It Now* music welled up. It was Murrow's last broadcast.

Tributes continued to pour in. Irv Gitlin wrote from NBC:

> Over the years you have been in my guts, in my decision making, consciously or unconsciously. What would Ed do? What would Ed think? These questions are always with me, every time we address ourselves to a story or an issue.
>
> So you see what I am saying. I want to acknowledge my personal and professional debt to you, and to say what you probably would not permit yourself to think—that your work and standards, that what you stand for, continues through all of us who have been fortunate enough to come in contact with you. This is the intangible gift you have given this country that only the professionals can know.[35]

Jack Gould, reminding the public of 1954, saluted "the man who put a spine in the broadcasting industry"; who "risked and received the wrath of Mr. McCarthy to a degree not experienced by any other journalist. . . ."

> It was the Murrow broadcast that first made clear to a mass audience the dimensions and implications of McCarthyism. It was the beginning of the series of challenges that were to lead to the Senator's ultimate undoing. . . . His immense curiosity, his disciplined feeling for outrage and his fierce independence can continue to be an inspiration to his fellow craftsmen. Broadcasting gave fame and fortune to Mr. Murrow, but it remains in debt to the man.[36]

In September Murrow went to Washington to accept the highest civilian peacetime honor, the Presidential Medal of Freedom, from the hand of Lyndon Johnson, his movements quick as in earlier times, shoulders just slightly hunched, remembering at the last moment to crack a smile. To Don Wilson he seemed his old self again, no longer the semi-invalid of 1963.

But the bad days were outnumbering the good, the summer drawing to a close, everything changing. CBS itself had split up, 485 just another aging Manhattan office building, corporate CBS moving on to Black Rock, CBS News to a vacated milk bottling plant at the edge of the West Side, a block from the New York waterfront. Before vacating, they had taken down the door on 17 that still read "MR. MURROW" and taken it along. (They never did quite know what to do with it, though; Wershba finally took it home to New Hyde Park and stashed it in his garage.)

Mili Bonsignori was working late, cutting film, when someone came in, saying Mr. Murrow was outside, looking for his old staff. Together with another editor, she rushed out into reception.

He was seated at a desk, thinner than she remembered, and older. The thick black-brown hair was drab, clipped short, but he was in good spirits: "Where's my band of brothers?"

The office was nearly empty, almost everyone gone home. Only she and a co-worker were left, the two sides regarding each other, groping for words and not finding them. ("What could you talk about?" she said later. "How's your health? You're looking fine?")

It was like an old love affair long past. There was nothing to say.[37]

Jap Gude, entering Louis and Armand's where the Murrow-Friendly partnership had started, saw Murrow at a table, just as in the old days, bent over a drink. They talked awhile; he was in town briefly, he said, staying at a hotel, down from the farm; all very pleasant. Then, abruptly, he called for the check, paid it, and got up. Gude realized he hadn't finished his drink, then looked to the door, where Murrow was stumbling toward the open air.

He hurried after him. Could he help him get a cab? Yes, Murrow replied, he'd like that.

It was five in the afternoon, a weekday in mid-Manhattan, not an empty cab in sight. The diminutive Gude began ranging up and down Fifty-second Street. Murrow told him not to bother, he'd just start walking uptown—a patent impossibility. Gude, thinking fast, got him down the street to the Athletic Club, where taxis were likely to stop, and propped him against the building wall. Worried by now as he chased along Park Avenue, he finally flagged a taxi and helped Murrow get inside. "He was so exhausted," Gude recalled, "that he couldn't even answer when I asked him if he could make it home all right. Just managed one of his familiar grins and a weak wave of the hand. It was the last time I ever saw him."[38]

There was just one meeting, however, that he obviously wanted very badly. Janet Murrow, accordingly, called Tess and Bill Shirer at their farm in Connecticut: Could they come to spend the day in Pawling? Ed would so much like to see them.

On the surface, there seemed no great dramatic gulf; no chasm of separation over the years. Janet Murrow was after all godmother to one of the Shirer girls. And they were both aware, said Shirer, of the situation. Tess Shirer wanted very much to go—she was fond of Janet Murrow. Shirer himself was less eager: "I was afraid that if he was going, he might get sentimental." Finally, he acceded. "Why not?"

The two couples met. Murrow, Shirer recalled later, was in bad shape—"he was emaciated, heaving, breath short." They lunched together, chatted over coffee, when Murrow suggested to Shirer that they go off together; he wanted to show Bill the farm, he said. That was all right, said Shirer afterward; after all, he had a farm of his own—"but Janet was concerned about his going off alone."

They spun off in the jeep, with Shirer determined not to discuss 1947. Murrow's upper lip, he noted, was damp with perspiration. *If he brings it up*, he thought, *forget it!*

They drove a while, Murrow pointed out the sights. Then he pulled the jeep to a stop in front of a house.

Murrow was perceptibly nervous, sweating profusely by now. "I couldn't tell," said Shirer later, "was he perspiring because he knew he was doomed, or was he trying to get this off his chest before he was dead?"

They talked, Murrow evidently trying to bring the conversation around to The Topic, Shirer changing the subject whenever it threatened to emerge. "There may have been times when he was approaching it," said Shirer afterward, "and I would get him off it."

The past hung between them until it was time to go—never mentioned—still unarticulated as the guests got into their car and drove off. Murrow and Shirer never saw each other again.[39]

By late September, Murrow's energies were ebbing. He was put in the care of a specialist in pulmonary diseases—ironically, the doctor Alfred Cohn had referred him to in 1943, when he returned from North Africa: an eminent practitioner, distant in manner, who gave Murrow the feeling he was being treated as a set of organs.

"I'm afraid he finds me a rather dull and uninteresting patient," he wrote his Washington physician. "I can only agree with him."[40]

He was sitting on his farm, he added, "acquiring real skill at doing nothing, but in the course of the next few days, if the pheasant will learn to walk on level ground, I may frighten a few of them."

To Bill Benton, following Murrow's progress with the concern of a mother hen, he wrote of his plans to stay at Pawling through the rest of the year.

Early in the year, in California, there had been fears of the cancer's metastasizing, sputum tests ordered; everything had checked out. Now again, there seemed to be warning signs.

Jim Seward had called up one day to ask, did he feel up to being honored at the annual Family of Man dinner of the Protestant Council of New York? It carried with it a $5,000 award, tax-free.

Murrow figured he could. In any case, he said, "Be a good time to find out."[41]

But the brief acceptance speech didn't go as planned. Murrow's phrases were slurred; everything was off. So brave despite his infirmity, said a guest later—exactly the impression he wanted to avoid. Said Seward: "It was ghastly."

A few days later at Pawling, as he walked with a visiting Jonas Salk and the NBC reporter Sander Vanocur, his speech gave way to a sudden stream of gibberish; he knew it—that much was obvious—but could not control the word salad tumbling from his mouth.

At New York Hospital they shaved his head and removed a tumor from near the brain, but other trouble spots were noted. The cancer had metastasized and was moving toward the brain.

It was a long, drawn-out stay this time. At one point an infection of the scalp wound necessitated a return to the operating room and replacement of the plate that had been put in to cover the gap in his skull created by the surgery. But the operation had succeeded in restoring his ability to communicate, and he was discharged on Christmas Day, followed by a note from his surgeon, saying he had strangely "mixed emotions" about Murrow's leaving, since he had so thoroughly enjoyed their conversations.[42]

Jim Seward had gotten them an apartment, first on Fifth Avenue, then on the West Side at the Dakota, the great gloomy pile of neo-Gothic masonry that was the last home in later years of John Lennon.

It was the beginning of the end—the terminal, unpretty, messy stage. New radiation treatments were prescribed, making the hair fall out, sapping what energies were left after the devastating operation, but necessary, the doctors said, to relieve the symptoms as the illness closed its iron grip. Friends coming by one day had had to cut their visit short when a seizure came over him.

Janet Murrow, always in the background—"omnipresent," a friend would call her—held up through it, tending him faithfully, on the phone constantly to make sure he had visitors when his condition allowed. Friends came by to talk shop and share the one drink a day permitted by the doctors. Mary McGrory, among others, was a faithful visitor. The "boys" stopped in—Hottelet, Collingwood, others. Howard Smith, commuting between New York and Washington, would recall Murrow's head swathed in a kind of turban the evening he came over, his turning questioningly to Janet—"Can we have a drink?" The three of them sat together for a small one, said the newsman, "but I could feel the life ebbing from him."[43]

A few whom he wanted to see, didn't show; and it hurt. Others he couldn't face. "He wants you to remember him as he was," Janet Murrow told Roz Downs; they kept in touch instead by telephone.

The Warburgs came by. He wasn't beautiful anymore, nothing like a poet: a wasted figure in an old-fashioned bathrobe over a nondescript shirt and slacks, elegance sacrificed to warmth. "His hair had fallen out," Mary Warburg recalled, "and he was wearing a stocking cap; he was ashamed of it, mentioned it briefly—he was very vain, you know. I remember his hands, so thin you could almost see the bones through them."

Janet had asked her to come alone, "but I was nervous; I'd never visited anyone before who was so close to death."

It was a constrained visit. Janet Murrow for some reason had had to go out. She dashed into the kitchen to hunt up a vase for the flowers they had brought, glad of an excuse. "He was so weak he could hardly function; but he still had those beautiful manners, still the good host." Indeed, he seemed to be trying to ignore his condition. "There was still a forceful personality. He was *ashamed* of his illness."

They had wanted to leave. "Oh, no, you must have a glass of sherry." He poured it, somehow, into the tiny little glasses. She hated sherry—dusty old stuff—but drank it anyway as they managed halting three-way chitchat and he told Churchill anecdotes.

He saw them to the door and held her fur coat: It was heavy, cumbersome, made for New York winters. She thrust her arms through the sleeves and shouldered it quickly, terrified for his sake that he'd drop it, and hurried away. The image haunted them all the way home: the thin hands, with the strength gone out of them, fumbling with the coat.[44]

Bill Paley was a constant visitor, very much the concerned friend. (Back in 1964, Seward recalled later, he and the Chairman had met with Arthur Godfrey, back on the air after a successful bout with cancer, extolling cranberry juice as an anticarcinogen. Later that afternoon Seward had had a call from Murrow in Pawling, who had just heard from "the boss," his tone puzzled: "He wants me to start drinking cranberry juice. . . .")[45]

Paley, who was himself to lose a wife to cancer, would grow somberly thoughtful as he recollected those visits. "He faced death without complaining. . . . Lung cancer is terrible."[46]

The long, lagging days were now divided between home and the radiation sessions at the hospital, a long taxi ride across town. Throughout it, he fought against the spiritual devastation of the illness, fighting for the integrity of the self, using the wry humor that had served him all his life.

At the hospital one day with his wife, wheeled up in the elevator, the attending nurse's clipboard in his lap, he had found himself cornered, the unwilling object of a gush of recognition from an overeager fan.

The woman seemed totally oblivious, rattling on nonstop as the elevator rumbled too slowly upward—i.e., how well he was looking; how his public hoped he'd soon be on the air again. Janet Murrow was silent. The nurse looked at the floor and bit her lip. Finally Murrow looked up, with a ghost of his old smile, holding up the nurse's clipboard.

"As you see," he explained, "I have another profession now."[47]

At home, he tried to get around the apartment when he wasn't sitting in the big black reclining chair set up for him by the window—a marvel machine, with dials for heat control, massage, all the latest. Friends remembered him showing it off, radiant: "Look what Janet gave me for Christmas!"[48]

Fewer days were finding him on his feet, however, more in the chair, looking out at the blank brick apartment towers of West Seventy-second Street; or, if he looked at an angle, a brown wedge of late-winter Central Park, bare-twigged and transparent; a far distance from the forests of his boyhood or the rolling hills of Dutchess County.

Other days saw him in bed now, drugs dulling both the edge of pain and sensibilities. The Downses kept tabs by telephone from Washington. How was he? "Well, better today, I read to him and he followed some." "And when you thought of what this man had *been*," Roz Downs said afterward.[49]

Suicide wasn't in his credo, a vestige perhaps of his religious upbringing; but the unnamable new twist of the disease was occasionally named. "I don't want to be a vegetable," he told Casey.[50]

Somehow he still followed the news on radio, when possible, or over television when the image didn't make dancing spots of painful light before his eyes. He followed the Vietnam drama with impotent anger and dismay, watching administration spokesmen step before the TV cameras, exuding optimism, then lowering his face into his hands. "They're out of their *minds*. They're lying. How can he *say* that?" These were the men he had so often admired in the days under Kennedy.

February 1965 marked the start of the sustained bombing campaign and, as it turned out, the first dispatching of U.S. marine battalions. Dorothy Paley Hirshon was visiting with Murrow. "Janet had called," she remembered, "and asked if I'd come over, and I was only too delighted to do so. Well! We got into a whole *thing*. He thought Johnson was the end of the *world*, the biggest liar; he had just utter and complete contempt for him. He went on at length: that he'd deceived the American public inexcusably on Vietnam, he was a liar, a deceiver, the *lowest* kind of . . .

"I can see Ed sitting there in his stocking cap, the hair gone, all from those treatments, and I knew it was the last time I was probably ever going to see him and—there he was, as passionate as ever, just exactly the same."[51]

In those same weeks, dovetailing two worlds, he watched Winston Churchill's funeral. Marietta Tree, come over to watch, wondered as they followed it together, what was going on inside him, what thoughts were going around under the red ski cap. Once she had considered him the best-looking man she'd ever seen and found his quiet dealing with the savage destruction of his looks ("he had had a right to be vain of his beauty") as heroic in its way as anything he'd done.

Watching the funeral, he seemed "drained of emotion. This was the death of the great man of his life and the death of his era. I was wondering what he must be thinking because obviously he was dying, too; he must have known it. But he kept it pretty much inside himself."[52]

"*A shame you were not there,*" his English friend Alan Moorehead wrote him afterward, sending regards from Drew Middleton and Charlie Collingwood,

> *It was like a second ending of the war, all the old faces, terribly cold day, all the old places, Whitehall, Nelson's column, the Savoy, and I'm not sure that any of us were less happy then than now....So many of us over here remember you so well. Do hope you don't forget us.*[53]

In early March, he could no longer be cared for at the apartment. Readmitted to New York Hospital, he was tested, the worst confirmed: the cancer had reached the brain. He asked to go home, back to Pawling: the old reflexive instinct of his many illnesses. The doctors were against it ("couldn't admit they couldn't win," said a family member). It was too complicated, went the arguments, too many ifs involved—the proper care, the proper dosages, the question of transporting the terminally ill patient; impossible.

A battle of wits ensued, the final fight—spurred possibly by the dread of ending like Elmer Davis, hooked up to machines. Casey Murrow, seeing his father's mind made up, his mother agreed, sensed the doctors would have hard going.

The story would be told of Murrow's calling for a friend and Quaker Hill neighbor, CBS announcer Bob Dixon—big, hefty, a skilled physiotherapist who had treated him in Pawling; of Murrow clutching at Dixon on his arrival by the bedside, begging him to get him out, carry him out if he had to.

Prolonged discussions began—between the doctors, Dixon, the Murrows. Their Pawling physician was enlisted in the cause, consulting on the telephone with the attending physicians in New York, a drug sequence worked out, arrangements made for the shipping of a hospital bed, for nurses around the clock. Friends stood by, the elements finally falling into place, the situation turned around. For all their grimness, Casey Murrow would recall those weeks as a kind of affirmation: those who cared, rallying around so that his father could die with dignity.[54]

An ambulance carried him back to Pawling, a seventy-mile ride for the patient, but the homing instinct was stronger. He died a few weeks later, the end when it came, said Casey Murrow, "a massive release."

It was April 27, 1965, two days past Murrow's fifty-seventh birthday. To the end, he had refused to see a clergyman.

On just one count—publicity—they had been spared. The story later reported by Mary McGrory was that Murrow, hearing the radio in his hospital room, had also heard the bulletin of his worsened condition. By common agreement thereafter, his friends in the news media agreed on a news blackout until it was over.

"Everything proceeded as quietly as possible," Janet wrote to Sidney and Sandra Bernstein afterward, "and Ed was as brave and uncomplaining as you would expect him to have been. I never will understand why he was made to suffer so, but I suppose I'm not meant to. . . . And we all appreciated the fact that our agony was not spread over the public print. . . . I do regret that we put him through the weeks of radiation. He hated it so. Thank God, we have many happy memories."[55]

The news went out over the major media. The BBC and CBS had been laying by film, readying programs, for the past months. In New York, Joe Wershba had put together a one-hour memorial, with Collingwood and Sevareid. In London, Richard Dimbleby, himself dying of cancer, broadcast the BBC television tribute to his American colleague. He had made television news a profession a man could be *proud* of, said Walter Cronkite on the evening news, while Sevareid's voice almost broke, ending his commentary with lines from *Hamlet*.

In London, at the White Tower, a favorite journalists' hangout since the blitz days, David Buksbaum, the producer who had started as a gofer on *See It Now* and whose driving had terrified even Murrow, burst in, in tears, to pass the news on to the others.[56]

At Carnegie Hall that evening, the BBC Orchestra under Pierre Boulez added to its program the noble Beethovenian "Nimrod" segment from Edward Elgar's *Enigma Variations*, followed by a moment of silence. "His death leaves a very big gap in all our lives," Frank Gillard had written Janet Murrow. "In a very real sense we were all his pupils."[57] Over BBC Radio, Leonard Miall himself had narrated his personal tribute. It was noted in the papers that Murrow had been made a Knight Commander of the British Empire—honorary knighthood—in the last weeks of his life. *Variety* called him "a giant." Jack Gould in The New York *Times*, calling him "broadcasting's true voice," said he had "left a glowing heritage for a craft and a country."

The nondenominational funeral dispensed with speeches or sermons. Janet wasn't even sure he would have wanted a funeral, but then there had been their friends to think about. The Reverend Thomas Kinsolving, paraphrasing Kipling, said, "He reported the thing as he saw it, for the God of things as they were." The coffin, carried shoulder-high, seemed to float above the mourners. Many faces were streaked as they emerged out of the half-light of St. James into the bright sunshine of early May. A small party held back, for the long drive to the Brooklyn crematorium.

Frank Gervasi walked some blocks down Madison with Eric Sevareid, part of a small group that included Robert Kennedy, now the Junior Senator from New York. The two newsmen talked together, Gervasi recalled, about what kind of a world it was going to be without Murrows, and were there any Murrows around? Kennedy walked taciturnly, in his own world.[58]

It was April 30, 1965, twenty years almost to the day since the euphoric gathering around the Scribe bar in liberated Paris. "We've shown what radio can do in war. Now let's go home and show what we can do in peace!"

That same weekend there were 22,000 troops in Santo Domingo, the air war in Vietnam stepped up, the decisions already taken for a commitment of American ground troops, to total almost 200,000 by the year's end. To Bob Shayon, sitting in St. James, thinking of that night in 1945, it seemed as though the generation burying Murrow were burying its hopes of that younger time.

His ashes were scattered over the glen of his farm as he had wished, a plaque with his name, dates of birth, and death set on a boulder on the property. Janet got personal messages from governments and private citizens. Consular employees in India wrote of small people stopping in to offer the Americans condolences on the loss of this great man. Cronkite wrote of strangers coming up to him, a CBS face, to say how sorry they were.

On the U.S. Senate floor, Robert Kennedy, to whom Murrow had refused his 1964 endorsement because he came from Massachusetts, quoted Shakespeare's *Julius Caesar*, as Murrow had done years before in ending the McCarthy show, giving Antony's valediction over Brutus:

> His life was gentle, and the elements
> So mixed in him that Nature might stand up
> And say to all the world, "This was a man!"

In his cubicle at *CBS Reports*, Joe Wershba was going through The New York *Times*. "Gideon's Trumpet," eleven years after "Radulovich," had just been selected for the Sidney Hillman Foundation Award. It was all his this time, no sharing with the bosses; no bother about the money or the plaque. No Friendly pressuring him about running a little short lately.

He ran over the obits—the small, formal notices; the ones that didn't differentiate between the big fish and the little fish. And there was Murrow's: "Beloved husband of . . . devoted father of . . . Instead of flowers please send a donation to the Salk Institute or the Institute of International Education." He put down the paper, resigned.

"Dammit, Ed got the money again."

NOTES

A NOTE ON PRIMARY (MANUSCRIPT) SOURCES

Much of the material relating to Murrow's postwar broadcast career has been drawn from the Murrow Collection, Fletcher School of Law and Diplomacy, Tufts University, containing largely Murrow's CBS papers and broadcast scripts for the years 1947–1961. Other material relating to these and other years has been drawn from Murrow's private papers and from the papers of Mrs. Edward R. Murrow. Other sources are listed herewith.

For the years 1930–37:

The Archives of the Institute of International Education, New York, New York.

The Papers of the Emergency Committee in Aid of Refugee Scholars, 1933–37, New York Public Library, Manuscript and Archives, New York.

Franklin D. Roosevelt Presidential Papers, the Franklin D. Roosevelt Library, Hyde Park, New York.

Chester S. Williams Papers. (These relate to postwar and wartime years as well and are now at the Library, Special Collections, University of Oregon, Eugene, Oregon.)

Mary Marvin Breckinridge (Mrs. Jefferson Patterson) Papers, 1930–1941.

For the years 1937–1946:

FDR Library: Presidential Papers; also papers of Eleanor Roosevelt, Harry Hopkins, Robert E. Sherwood, Henry Wallace, John Gilbert Winant.

The BBC Written Archives Centre, Caversham Park, Reading, U.K.; Files: R 34/600/10 (Program Board Mintues & Papers—illeg. 10, 1938); R 61/3/1 (Censorship & American Liaison—American Liaison Unit—Facilities); R 34/325 (Policy—Czechoslovak Crisis; General File—1938); other folders: Monitoring Service-World War II; America—Murrow, Ed. Also *The Listener* for broadcast transcripts; transcripts are also on microfilm.

The Mass Communications History Center of the State Historical Society of Wisconsin, Madison, Wisconsin: National Broadcasting Company Papers, 1923–60, including NBC Foreign Office: Fred Bate, Max Jordan; the H. V. Kaltenborn Collection; also, papers of the following: Cecil Brown, John Charles

Daly, George Hicks, John MacVane, Edward P. Morgan, Sue Taylor (Mrs. Paul) White.

For the years 1946–1961:

Manuscripts Division, State Historical Society of Wisconsin, Madison.: William Benton Papers.

Mass Communications Center, State Historical Society of Wisconsin, Madison: National Broadcasting Company Papers; including the postwar papers of David Sarnoff, Sylvester "Pat" Weaver, Davidson Taylor, William F. Brooks, NBC News, Sidney Eiges, John F. Royal, Niles Trammell; Kaltenborn Papers, including Papers of the Association of Radio News Analysts (ARNA), Also Papers of the following:

Robert Fleming, *Milwaukee Journal*—McCarthy files, Joseph C. Harsch, Sig Mikelson—CBS News files, Howard K. Smith, Av Westin, Helen Zotos, C.E. Hooper, Incorporated, 1944–47.

The Freedom of Information Act opened areas long closed off. Requesting under FOIA is a long, involved process, lasting years, and it is only right to thank the Federal Bureau of Investigation, the Department of State and the United States Information Agency for their dispatch, cooperation and courtesy in the lengthy task of declassifying the files on Edward R. Murrow. In the case of the United States Information Agency, it was a matter not only of review and declassification, but of tracking down the files themselves, packed away after Murrow's resignation in the dark days following the Kennedy assassination, sealed and sent off to storage, and then forgotten. Declassified, the files of the Office of the Director, 1961–64, provided a first-time, first-hand account of Murrow's years at the Agency.

Other sources include: Edward R. Murrow files, 1948–64, Federal Bureau of Investigation; George Polk file, 1948–77, Central Intelligence Agency; Freedom of Information Act–related documents from the Department of State, the Department of Defense, NASA, the National Security Council, and the White House; and the John F. Kennedy Presidential Library.

Material has also been drawn from the private papers of Chester S. Williams and of Mary Marvin Breckinridge (Mrs. Jefferson Patterson), and from Joseph Wershba's unpublished memoir about the Murrow-McCarthy encounter, *The Broadcaster and the Senator*, later carried in condensed form by The New York *Times Magazine*, under the title, Murrow vs. McCarthy: *See It Now*.

Source material on Murrow's early years and family background has been provided by the Southern Historical Collection, University of North Carolina, Chapel Hill; the North Carolina Collection, University of North Carolina, Chapel Hill; the public and private records at the North Carolina State Archives, Raleigh; and the private memorabilia of Mrs. Edward R. Murrow. Information on the National Student Federation of America period has been drawn from the papers of Chester A. Williams, his unpublished memoir, "To Casey Murrow: Memories of Your Father" (1965), the NSFA 1930 Yearbook, the papers of Mary Marvin Breckinridge Patterson, and published and unpublished contemporary accounts.

The CBS archives have provided films and audio tapes for *See It Now* (1951–58), *CBS Reports* (1960–61), *Edward R. Murrow with the News* (1947–59), *Background* (1960–61); convention tapes; and miscellaneous programs. Videotapes were also provided by the Museum of Broadcasting.

Other primary sources include CBS Radio logs; Hooper ratings, network radio;

annual reports to the stockholders of the Columbia Broadcasting System; AFRA and AFTRA yearbooks; *Counterattack*, 1947–1956; Bulletin of the Overseas Press Club; the Norman Thomas archives; the Morris Ernst archives; CBS program books, 1939–1947.

I. THE HERETICS

1. North Carolina was, in fact, the reverse of the national picture; the state Democratic Party was the main ally of the large businesses, dedicated above all to the maintenance of the status quo.
2. Speaking schedule, *Greensboro North State*, October 7, 1886.
3. Report of the Republican county convention, J. S. Murrow, chairman, ibid., September 23, 1886.
4. Ibid., October 28, 1886.
5. *Greensboro Patriot*, October 1886.
6. *Greensboro North State*, November 4, 1886.
7. *North Carolina Senate Journal*, 1887.
8. *Greensboro Patriot*, February 3, 1888.

Oral material in this chapter is based on interviews with Joshua Edgar Murrow and Hazel Richardson Murrow, September 19 and 26, 1978; hereafter referred to as J. E. Murrow, interviews. Joshua Murrow's State Senate career is detailed in the *North Carolina Senate Journal* for the year 1887 and may be found in the North Carolina State Archives.

II. "EGG"

1. J. E. Murrow, interviews.
2. Edward R. Murrow, "Outline Script Murrow's Career," typescript, December 18, 1953. This is a five-page summary drawn up by the broadcaster at the request of CBS. Typescript. Hereafter referred to as ERM, outline script.
3. J. E. Murrow, interviews. Also Alexander Kendrick, *Prime Time: The Life of Edward R. Murrow* (Boston: Little, Brown, 1969).
4. ERM outline script.
5. A small guide and summary published by *Mount Vernon Herald*, September 1, 1921.
6. John B. Evans, letter to ERM, September 11, 1958.
7. Casey Murrow, interviews of July 7, 1983, and July 8, 1983, hereafter referred to as Casey Murrow, interviews.
8. Ibid.
9. Sebring, *Skagit County Illustrated* (1902, no pub.).
10. "Those Murrow Boys," typescript, undated, probably February 1944. This was a memoir written about the family, prepared by neighbors and members of their church in Bellingham, Washington.
11. Ibid. Janet Brewster Murrow, interviews of 1973–85, hereafter referred to as Janet Murrow, interviews.
12. "Those Murrow Boys," loc. cit.
13. Dewey Joshua Murrow, interviews of October 25, 1972, and November 5, 1972, hereafter referred to as Dewey Murrow, interviews.

NOTES

14. ERM to Joseph Wershba, interviews, 1973–85, hereafter referred to as Wershba, interviews.

15. Dewey Murrow, interviews.

16. Stanley Brode, superintendent, "Our School," *The Mazda*, published by the Associated Students of the Edison High School; yearbook for 1925.

17. Mazda, 1925.

18. *Mazda*, 1924.

19. *Mazda*, 1925.

20. ERM, outline script.

21. Brode, op. cit.

22. Last will and testament of Joshua S. Murrow, August 2, 1916; J. E. Murrow, interviews.

23. Kendrick, op. cit.

24. ERM, outline script.

25. W. K. Merredith, affidavit, April 9, 1954. (ERM to W. K. Merredith, May 21, 1948: "There are times when I sit here trying to figure out how to write a story when it seems to me that what you taught me about 'staying on line' is valuable training.")

26. Gwyn Seward Singer, interviews of October 28, 1978 and December 13, 1978, telephone interview March 10, 1979; hereafter referred to as Singer, interviews.

27. Robert Sandberg, speech of April 22, 1983, Washington State University Symposium: "Commemoration of the seventy-fifth birthday of Edward R. Murrow"; recollections of Ida Lou Anderson by one of her students.

28. Ibid.

29. E. R. Murrow, ". . . And Reverenced All," memorial to Ida Lou Anderson, Washington State College, 1947.

30. Thomas Russell Woolley, "A Rhetorical Study: The Radio Speaking of Edward R. Murrow," Ph.D. dissertation, Northwestern University, 1957.

31. Sinclair Lewis, *Elmer Gantry* (New York: Charles Scribner's Sons, 1927).

32. Westerman Whillock, interview, 1973, hereafter referred to as Whillock, interview.

33. Channing Pollock, *The Enemy*, playscript, undated, Theater Collection, Lincoln Center Library for the Performing Arts.

34. *Chinook*, yearbook, Washington State College, 1928–29.

35. Chester S. Williams, taped reminiscences, September 21, 1978; also letters to the author, telephone interviews of September 14, 1978, January 25, 1979, April 1, 1979, et al.; hereafter referred to as Chester Williams, interviews.

36. Ibid.

In addition to the notes listed, material for this chapter has been taken from interviews with the following: Rosalind Downs, Mrs. Jefferson Patterson, and Gwyn Seward Singer.

III. NEW YORK

1.

1. Not to be confused with the present WABC, which assumed the call letters in the mid-forties.
2. *Edward R. Murrow with the News*, November 30, 1953.
3. Chester Williams, interviews; also Joseph Cadden, interviewed in 1973 about the NSFA years.
4. Stephen P. Duggan, Jr., interview of January 23, 1979, hereafter referred to as Duggan, interview.
5. Ibid.
6. Chester Williams, interviews.
7. *Atlanta Journal*, December 31, 1930.
8. Chester S. Williams, "To Casey Murrow: Memories of Your Father," unpublished.

2.

1. Duggan, interview.
2. ERM, correspondence, June–July 1932.
3. Ibid.
4. Janet Murrow, interviews of 1973–1985; hereafter referred to as Janet Murrow, interviews. Material relating to Janet Murrow in this chapter is based on these interviews.
5. ERM to exchange students in Germany, April 4, 1933.
6. Memo to ERM, February 1, 1934.
7. American Friends Service Committee to ERM, February 21, 1935.
8. Betty Drury to ERM, undated.
9. ERM, correspondence, February 15, 1934.
10. Ibid., February 5, 1934.
11. Ibid., February 1, 1934.
12. Karl Vogt, Berlin, to ERM, December 22, 1933.
13. *New York Times*, July 11, 1934.
14. ERM, Albert Einstein Award ceremonies, May 5, 1957.
15. ERM for Emergency Committee, to James McDonald, July 5, 1934.
16. ERM, correspondence, undated, probably 1943.
17. ERM to Walter Kotschnig, April 19, 1935.
18. ERM to Horatio Krans, 1935, undated.

IV. 860 ON YOUR DIAL

1. Helen Sioussat, interviews of June 21, 1973 and December 5, 1973, hereafter referred to as Sioussat, interviews.
2. *New York Times*, October 11, 1935.
3. See Chapter III, fn. 1. In the early 1940s the CBS station began operating at 880 kilocycles.
4. Stephen Early to Marvin McIntyre, secretary to the President, Confidential, October 28, 1935.

5. Stephen Early to Harry Butcher, Columbia Broadcasting Company, Washington, D.C., September 25, 1935, with note "Above letter also sent to Mr. Carlton Smith, National Broadcasting Co., Washington, D.C.;" marked "Confidential."
6. *Of the People, By the People, For the People*, Columbia Broadcasting System, Monday, March 4, 1935, 2:30 to 4:30 P.M.
7. *New York Times*, "Radio's 1936 Finale," December 13, 1936.
8. Jerry Maulsby to J. M. Seward, December 27, 1976.
9. J. M. Seward, talk of February 1978; also J. M. Seward, letter to author on CBS news operations in 1930s.

Material in this chapter has also been based on interviews with the following:
J. G. Gude, interviews of October 9, 1973, November 18, 1973, December 17 and 20, 1976, January 31, 1977, September 14, 1982, hereafter referred to as Gude, interviews.

Adrian Murphy, interview of February 7, 1977, hereafter referred to as Murphy, interview.

Janet Murrow, interviews.

William S. Paley, interviews of July 9 and 17, 1981, hereafter referred to as Paley, interviews.

James M. Seward, interviews of 1973-1985, hereafter referred to as Seward, interviews.

Frank Stanton, interviews of July 20 and 22, 1981, hereafter referred to as Stanton, interviews.

Robert Trout, interview of January 22, 1981, hereafter referred to as Trout, interview.

V. ANSCHLUSS

1. Richard Marriott, interview of June 1, 1981, hereafter referred to as Marriott, interview.
2. Max Jordan to John F. Royal, March 23, 1937, NBC Records, Foreign Offices.
3. William L. Shirer, *The Nightmare Decade* (Boston: Little, Brown, 1985).
4. A reference to the immigrant hero of Leo Rosten's *The Education of Hyman Kaplan*, whose malapropisms were a comic byword in those years.
5. International Labor Organization.
6. ERM to Harry Butcher, October 6, 1937.
7. Max Jordan to John F. Royal, February 15, 1938, and March 7, 1938, re meeting of March 5, 1938, NBC Records, Foreign Offices.
8. Trout, interview.
9. *Columbine*, CBS, Inc., vol. 2, no. 7 (April to May 1974).
10. Frank Gervasi, interview of November 26, 1980, hereafter referred to as Gervasi, interview.
11. Cecilia Reeves Gillie, interview of June 12, 1981, hereafter referred to as Gillie, interview.
12. William L. Shirer, interviews of February 13–15, 1975, hereafter referred to as Shirer, interviews.

Material in this chapter has also been based on interviews with Helen Sioussat; and on an interview with Dorothy Paley Hirshon, November 9, 1977, hereafter referred to as Hirshon, interview.

VI. THE STEAMROLLER

1.

1. Versailles in the overall sense, specifically the Treaty of St. Germain.
2. William L. Shirer, *Berlin Diary* (New York: Alfred A. Knopf, 1941).
3. Ibid.
4. A. A. Schechter and Edward Anthony, *I Live on Air* (New York: Frederick A. Stokes Co., 1941).
5. Ibid.
6. William Dunn, later CBS Chief Pacific Correspondent but still working for Paul White as news editor in 1938, had the following recollection:

"H. V. Kaltenborn in 1938 had become a minor problem for White and CBS. The success of his broadcasts from Spain had dimmed a bit and there just didn't seem to be any place in the program to fit a man of his experience and ability. He was appearing each Sunday night on a broadcast called *Headlines and Bylines*. . . . Nothing wrong with the show but hardly worthy of H.V.'s reputation and abilities.

"In September, 1938, the Munich crisis began to develop . . . and Paul White wanted to promote a name on the U.S. end of the story. . . . He tried to sell Bob Trout on what the opportunity could mean to him. But Bob wasn't buying. He was a *Special Events* announcer (and the best in the business) and he wasn't about to read bulletins and copy that any announcer could handle. Of course, the "any announcer" was exactly what White was trying to get away from. [So] Paul turned to H.V. and Hans got the message immediately. The idea of being the No. 1 source of information on Munich and central Europe, was one he could visualize and he grabbed at the opportunity.

"The rest is history. Hans moved a cot into the studio. . . . White let the press know . . . and the publicity, pictures and stories, were terrific. When Neville Chamberlain finally returned to Downing Street with "Peace in our Time," H. V. Kaltenborn was the most discussed personality on the air, the fountainhead from which all knowledge of the crisis flowed. . . .

"From then on there was never any question of what to do with Hans. He was the number one name in broadcast news and in constant demand. I certainly do not want to give the impression that Hans, at that time, was a washed-up has-been. He was far from that. . . . Something else could well have happened to bring him back to the forefront but it was Munich that actually did just that.

"I have often wondered, but never asked, what Bob thought when he realized what he had turned down." (William Dunn, letter to the author, undated: also interviews of November 13, 1981, April 23, 1982, et al.; hereafter referred to as Dunn, interviews.)

7. William Shirer, CBS Radio, September 16, 1938.
8. "Czechoslovakian Crisis: Diary of Chief Events," BBC Written Archives, typescript, undated.
9. Ibid., under "General Notes": "Notes on the more confidential aspects of broadcasting during the crisis, e.g. the Corporation's relationships with the Government . . . cannot be dealt with here. There was no censorship by the Government of B.B.C. news bulletins or broadcast material, although the Corporation naturally kept in the closest touch with appropriate Departments, and the bulletins fell in line with Government policy."
10. The development of BBC television, though still in its early stages, was well in advance of that of the American networks.
11. Robert J. Landry, "Edward R. Murrow," *Scribner's Magazine* (December 1938).
12. Programme Board, Minutes and Papers, "Raymond Swing's American Commentary," October 15, 1938, BBC Written Archives. The BBC, in fact, had no reporters on the scene. The prevailing attitude of the era was reflected in a memo from the director of overseas services to the controller of programming (October 24, 1938) to the effect that while he was not "blindly opposed" to broadcasts from the scene of the action, "I think there are times when such broadcasts are liable to be unhelpful, misleading and purely sensational, and therefore not in accordance with the principles which guide our action as a British organization."

    Swing, by contrast, called the American effort "radio fulfilling the vital need for information."
13. The full text of the agreement would be NBC's scoop, however, by virtue of Max Jordan's access to a microphone in the Führerhaus.
14. Gillie, interview.
15. John Coatman, Memo from Northern Regional Director to Controller (Programming), "The B.B.C. and the National Defence," marked "Private and Confidential," October 5, 1938, BBC Written Archives.
16. Landry, op. cit.
17. Davidson Taylor, interview of May 1973, hereafter referred to as Taylor, interviews.
18. The actor was the talented Ray Collins of the Mercury Theater troupe, whose face became known to audiences in *Citizen Kane*, and later in the fifties as the insufferable Lieutenant Tragg in the TV *Perry Mason* series. Ed Klauber's morning-after reaction was recalled by Davidson Taylor, interviewed May, 1973.
19. William Shirer, *The Rise and Fall of the Third Reich* (New York: Simon & Schuster, 1959). Secret documents of that time also indicated plans for the occupation of Belgium and Holland, a "life and death" war with England and France, the aim, "to force England to her knees."
20. Murphy, interview.
21. Eric Sevareid, *Not So Wild A Dream* (New York: Alfred A. Knopf, 1946).
22. R. Franklin Smith, *Edward R. Murrow: The War Years* (Kalamazoo, Michigan: New Issues Press, Institute of Public Affairs, Western Michigan University, 1978).
23. Shirer, interviews.
24. Shirer, *Third Reich*, loc. cit.

2.

1. Pat Smithers, interview of June 7, 1981, hereafter referred to as Smithers, interview.
2. As distinct from the BBC Overseas Services.
3. ERM to Marvin Breckinridge, December 18, 1939.
4. S. J. de Lotbinière to Major General J. H. Beith, War Office, September 15, 1939; BBC Written Archives.
5. De Lotbinière to ERM, September 21, 1939.
6. De Lotbinière to Peter Fleming, September 21, 1939. The official in question was Geoffrey Dawson, the former powerful editor of the *Times* of London.
7. Roger Eckersley to Winston Churchill, December 14, 1939.
8. ERM, CBS Radio, April 22, 1940.
9. Gillie, interview. Also Janet Murrow, correspondence, February 1940.
10. Roger Eckersley to Director General, BBC, memo marked "Confidential," March 21, 1940.
11. BBC Memo, probably January 1940.
12. Roger Eckersley to Sir Frederick Whyte, Ministry of Information, April 18, 1940.
13. Earl de la Warr to Roger Eckersley, April 17, 1940.
14. ERM, CBS Radio, March 10, 1940.
15. Memo, Lanham Titchener to Roger Eckersley, April 15, 1940.
16. Memo, Roger Eckersley to Denis Johnston, BBC, April 13, 1940.
17. ERM, to Charles Siepmann, May 6, 1940.
18. Mary Marvin Breckinridge (Mrs. Jefferson) Patterson, interview of July 7, 1977, hereafter referred to as Patterson, interview.

VII. TRIAL BY FIRE

1.

1. Frank Darvall to Roger E. Eckersley, May 18, 1940.
2. Roger E. Eckersley, memorandum, "Broadcasts to the United States by the American Broadcasting Representatives," marked "Private and confidential," May 21, 1940.
3. Eckersley to ERM, May 30, 1940.
4. Eckersley to Duff Cooper, June 21, 1940.
5. Eckersley to Frank Darvall, July 6, 1940.
6. Ibid.
7. Darvall to Sir Walter Monckton and Colonel Neville, July 7, 1940.
8. Brigadier Turner, War Office, to Colonel Neville, M.I.7., July 8, 1940.
9. Extract from Monitoring Report No. 358, July 10–11, 1940.
10. Darvall to Eckersley, July 16, 1940.
11. Drew Middleton, interview of February 16, 1982, hereafter referred to as Middleton, interview.
12. Eckersley to Darvall, August 21, 1940.
13. Eckersley to Darvall, August 28, 1940.
14. Lindsay Wellington to Eckersley, September 6, 1940.

15. Ibid.
16. Ben Robertson, *I Saw England* (New York: Alfred A. Knopf, 1942).
17. In fact, it was principally the East End that was hit that night.
18. ERM, CBS Radio, September 8, 1940.
19. Aunt to Lord Cranborne, Secretary of State of Dominion Affairs in Churchill's wartime cabinet.
20. For details, see Shirer, *Third Reich*, loc. cit.
21. John Swift, *Adventures in Vision* (London: John Lehmann, 1950).
22. Maurice Gorham, *Sound and Fury* (London: Percival Marshall, 1948).
23. Leonard Miall, interview of June 1, 1981, hereafter referred to as Miall, interview.
24. "Mr. MacGregor, MOI to Mr. R. H. Eckersley, BBC"; September 20, 1940.
25. *Farewell to Studio Nine*, CBS Radio, July 25, 1964.
26. The pecking order of the time is pretty much reflected in a note to ERM from G. R. Barnes, Director of Talks for the BBC, confirming a BBC broadcast date with the assurance that, "Unless the Prime Minister or his Cabinet, Dorothy Thompson or Quentin Reynolds need the air, I can offer you June 7th or June 14th for your talk. . . ."
27. Lord Bernstein, interview of June 9, 1981, hereafter referred to as Bernstein, interview.
28. Helen Kirkpatrick Milbank, interview of June 15, 1983, hereafter referred to as Kirkpatrick, interview.
29. Michael Balkwill, interview of June 6, 1981, hereafter referred to as Balkwill, interview.
30. Godfrey Talbot, interview of June 11, 1981, hereafter referred to as Talbot, interview.
31. Smithers, interview.
32. Talbot, interview.
33. Janet Murrow, interviews.
34. Cecilia Reeves Gillie, interview.
35. Sir John Colville, interview of June 13, 1961, hereafter referred to as Colville, interview.
36. Shirer, interviews.
37. Shirer to Murrow, April 16, 1941.
38. Middleton, interview.

2.

1. Harry L. Hopkins, London itinerary, dated January 4, 1941; Hopkins Papers, Franklin D. Roosevelt Library, Hyde Park, N.Y.
2. Shirer to ERM, April 16, 1941.
3. Robin Duff, Cecilia Reeves Gillie, interviews.
4. Robin Duff, interview of June 20, 1981.
5. ERM, "The New World," BBC Home Service, January 13, 1941.
6. "N. G. Luker to C. (H), 10th January, 1941."
7. Charles Collingwood, interviews of July 27, 1978 and March 19, 1981, hereafter referred to as Collingwood, interviews.
8. Janet Murrow, interviews.
9. ERM, CBS Radio, April 17, 1941.

10. ERM to Chester S. Williams, May 9, 1941.
11. Williams to ERM, July 10, 1941 and August 12, 1941.
12. Edward R. Murrow, *This Is London* (New York: Simon & Schuster, 1941); foreward by Elmer Davis.
13. ERM to Chester Williams, July 24, 1941.
14. Janet Murrow, interviews.
15. ERM to John Gilbert Winant, November 10, 1941.
16. It expressed his "appreciation and gratitude for the kindness and consideration shown . . . during the years I have worked in London" and was sent to the head of the overseas and engineering information department for transmission to the engineering staff. Several days later, the senior superintendent engineer sent the department head his thanks: "As you know, Ed. Murrow was a very popular programme figure with the operational staff firstly because he was always considerate towards the Engineers and secondly because he knew exactly what he wanted and when he wanted it. When you are writing to him I sincerely hope you will thank him very much indeed from me for his kind message to the chaps; tell him that it will adorn the Control Room notice board and that the sincere good wishes of the Operations Department go with him. Put simply, we wish he had not gone." (November 17, 1941).

VIII. TOTAL WAR

1. *America's Town Meeting of the Air*, Blue Network, January 9, 1941.
2. BBC memo, December 25, 1941. Also CBS Program Book, Winter 1941.
3. Seward, interviews.
4. Murphy, interview; James M. Seward, *Network Operations for News Broadcasting*, CBS memo, August 8, 1944.
5. ERM, CBS Radio, January 24, 1943. Also Murrow-Woollcott correspondence, 1941.
6. Shirer, interviews.
7. Program, dinner in honor of Edward R. Murrow, chief of the European staff of the Columbia Broadcasting System, at the Waldorf-Astoria Grand Ballroom, on Tuesday, December 2, 1941.
8. President's Personal File, hand corrections by FDR on draft of White House telegram to William Paley, December 2, 1941, Franklin D. Roosevelt Collection.
9. Janet Murrow, interviews.
10. *Time* (December 15, 1941).
11. Bernstein, interview.
12. Secretaries of the Army, Navy, and State respectively.
13. ERM, CBS Radio, September 23, 1945.
14. Wesley Price, "Murrow Sticks to the News," *Saturday Evening Post* (December 10, 1949).
15. White House usher's diary, cited in Anthony Cave Brown, *The Last Hero: Wild Bill Donovan* (New York: Times Books, 1983).
16. Ibid.
17. ERM, CBS Radio, September 23, 1945.
18. Sevareid, op. cit.

19. Janet Murrow, interviews.
20. Murrow to Klauber, April 2, 1942.
21. *Chicago Daily News*, 1942, undated.
22. Janet Murrow, interviews.
23. Robert E. Sherwood to Harry L. Hopkins, telegram, January 9, 1942.
24. Hopkins to ERM, telegram, January 10, 1942.
25. ERM to Hopkins, telegram, January 19, 1942.
26. ERM, BBC Home Service, July 1942.
27. Janet Murrow, interviews.
28. Paley, interviews.
29. Eckersley to Cecil Graves, Director General, BBC, April 29, 1942.
30. ERM to Eckersley, June 25, 1942.
31. ERM to Lanham Titchener, August 25, 1942.
32. Titchener to ERM, August 26, 1942.
33. Two veteran correspondents differed on this point: Drew Middleton, that it was the only way of taking the territories, short of conflict with the French; John MacVane, that the Free French already held the city (Algiers) but the Allies hesitated.
34. ERM to Edward Dakin, Hill & Knowlton, January 6, 1943.
35. David Schoenbrun, interview of May 9, 1980, telephone interviews of May 19, 1973 and February 27, 1980, hereafter referred to as Schoenbrun, interviews.
36. Collingwood, interviews.
37. Actually, blue gentian; Murrow, an erratic speller, spelled it as pronounced back home.
38. Joseph Lash, ed., *Diaries of Felix Frankfurter* (New York, Norton, 1975).
39. FDR to ERM, June 24, 1942.
40. Lash, op. cit.
41. ERM, CBS Radio, October 2, 1947.
42. Janet Murrow to family, July 16, 1943.
43. *New York Times*, August 6, 1943.
44. Ralph Colin, interviews of May 17 and May 24, 1982, hereafter referred to as Colin, interviews.
45. Dunn, interviews.
46. CBS release, "Talk Delivered by Paul White, Director of News Broadcasts, CBS, Before the Association of Radio News Analysts at a Luncheon Held at the Hotel Algonquin, Thursday, September 23, 1943," dated September 23, 1943.
47. ARNA Luncheon, September 23, 1943, transcript.
48. *PM*, Thursday, September 30, 1943.
49. William Shirer to ERM, September 21, 1943.
50. ERM to Shirer, October 15, 1943.
51. Janet Murrow to family, October 29, 1943.
52. Middleton, interview.
53. Harrison Salisbury, interview of December 10, 1981, hereafter referred to as Salisbury, interview.
54. Miall, interview.
55. BBC, American Liaison Unit, American Companies' Commentators, memo, August 19, 1943.

56. CBS Radio, "We Take You Back," March 13, 1958.
57. Smithers, interview.
58. ERM, CBS Radio, February 28, 1943.
59. ERM, CBS Radio, January 24, 1943.
60. Janet Murrow, interviews.
61. Paley, interviews.
62. George Stevens, *Speak For Yourself, John: The Life of John Mason Brown* (New York: Viking, 1974).
63. Kirkpatrick, interview.
64. *The Diaries of Harold Nicolson: The War Years, 1939–1945* (New York: Atheneum, 1967).
65. ERM, BBC Home Service, June 14, 1942.
66. ERM, CBS Radio, May 24, 1943.
67. Elmer Davis to ERM, November 7, 1943.
68. ERM to Davis, December 15, 1943.
69. ERM to Alfred Cohn, December 29, 1943.
70. ERM to Edward Dakin, Hill & Knowlton, May 5, 1943.
71. Ibid.
72. BBC Overseas Service, *Freedom Forum*, "After the Armistice," August 8/9, 1942.
73. Collingwood, interviews.
74. *Freedom Forum*, "The Future of Imperialism," September 19/20, 1942.
75. Seward, *Network Operations for News Broadcasting*, August 8, 1944; Paul White, *News on the Air* (New York: Harcourt, Brace, 1947).
76. Kirkpatrick, interview.
77. Janet Murrow, op. cit.
78. Richard C. Hottelet, interview of 1973, hereafter referred to as Hottelet, interview.
79. CBS Radio, "We Take You Back," op. cit.
80. Hottelet, interview.
81. ERM, CBS Radio, September 24, 1944.
82. Howard K. Smith, interviews of June 3, 1977, July 1977, and April 3, 1985, hereafter referred to as Smith, interviews.
83. Howard Teichmann, interview of July 28, 1982, hereafter referred to as Teichmann, interview.
84. Janet Murrow, interviews.
85. Edward R. Murrow, *"After the War, What?"* 1943.
86. ERM, Ambassador Hotel, Tuesday, December 6, 1944.
87. Wilmott Ragsdale to ERM, January 18, 1949; also Ragsdale, interview of July 28, 1983, hereafter referred to as Ragsdale, interview.
88. ERM, CBS Radio, April 15, 1945.
89. Paul Heller, interview of March 12, 1977, hereafter referred to as Heller, interview.
90. ERM, Buchenwald broadcast notes.
91. Collingwood, interviews.
92. Gwyn Seward Singer, interviews.
93. R. Franklin Smith, *Edward R. Murrow: The War Years*, op. cit.
94. Who turned out to be the distinguished literary scholar, Erich Heller.

95. Robert Lewis Shayon, interview of November 1972, hereafter referred to as Shayon, interview.
96. Frank Gervasi, interview.
97. ERM, CBS Radio, May 13, 1945.
98. Earlier contractual matters had been handled for Murrow virtually within the house, through the CBS Artists Bureau, then through MCA, upon the sale of the bureau to that company following FCC divestiture orders. Dealings had been on the whole perfunctory, taking a back seat, as far as Murrow was concerned, to the exigencies of his job in London.
99. Cable: Columbia to Murrow, July 20, 1945.
100. ABC, *America's Town Meeting of the Air*, September 20, 1945.
101. Shirer, interviews.
102. Ann Hottelet to Janet Murrow, 1965.
103. Paley, interviews.
104. Seward, interviews.
105. J. G. Gude, memo to the author, October 3, 1973; also Gude, interviews.
106. Janet Murrow, interviews.

IX. DECOMPRESSION

1. Dunn, interviews.
2. ERM to Howard K. Smith, June 21, 1949.
3. Taylor, interview.
4. Trout, interview.
5. Duggan, interview.
6. Shirer, interviews.
7. ERM to Cranborne, March 1, 1946.
8. Stephen Duggan to ERM, May 9, 1944.
9. Shayon, interview.
10. Rosalind Downs, interviews of May 27, 1982, July 26, 1982, February 24, 1983, March 24, 1983, April 24, 1983, et al.; hereafter referred to as Downs, interviews.
11. James C. Cole to ERM, December 20, 1957.
12. Edward R. Murrow, "Notes on the News," *New York Herald Tribune*, September 5, 1947.
13. Schoenbrun, interviews.
14. Elmer Davis to ERM, November 25, 1945.
15. Gude, interviews.
16. The popular historical series *You Are There*, first titled *CBS Was There*, using CBS reporters, dated from this period. It auditioned on March 28, 1947, and was first broadcast on July 7, 1947, with Murrow a reluctant participant in preliminary discussions during the developmental stage with Davidson Taylor and the program's originators, Robert Shayon and staff writer Goodman Ace. Murrow said in 1954, "I opposed the use of CBS newsmen in a simulated situation and as a matter of fact, I still do" (ERM, memo to G. W. Schmidt, December 17, 1954).
17. Robert P. Heller, "The Dynamic Documentary," in Max Wylie, ed., *Radio and Television Writing* (New York: Rinehart & Co., 1949).
18. *Newsweek* (March 17, 1947).

19. Elmer Davis, op. cit.
20. Other participants listed in *Red Channels* included the performers Luther Adler and Gail Sondergaard.
21. Ted Berkman, "Nice Guys—and Good Men," *Christian Science Monitor*, September 17, 1979.
22. Simon Michael Bessie, interviews of August 14, 1978, January 23, 1980, and March 11, 1980, hereafter referred to as Bessie, interviews.
23. *New York Times*, January 7, 1947.
24. Report of the Commission on Freedom of the Press, *New York Times*, March 30, 1947.
25. ERM, "To the Radio Editor," *New York Times*, January 26, 1947.
26. ERM to William Shirer, October 15, 1943.
27. Paley, interviews.
28. Russell Davenport, Memorandum to the Board of Editors, February 1947, undated.
29. Ibid.
30. Stanton, interviews.
31. Paley, interviews.
32. Paul White to Wells Church, undated.
33. ERM to Paul White, July 11, 1951.
34. Howard K. Smith, broadcast of March 16, 1947.
35. Joseph C. Harsch, broadcast of March 7, 1947.
36. Columbia Program Book, December 15, 1943—CBS Program Supplement.
37. Shirer, interviews.
38. ERM to Harold Laski, June 5, 1947.
39. *PM* (March 24, 1947).
40. William L. Shirer, *New York Herald Tribune*, September 21, 1947.
41. Joseph Harsch, broadcast of March 7, 1947.
42. Howard K. Smith, broadcast of July 6, 1947.
43. William Shirer to ERM, September 21, 1943.
44. Joseph C. Harsch, interview of October 2, 1982, hereafter referred to as Harsch, interview.
45. Joseph Harsch to John Campbell Ausland, March 1947.
46. *PM* (March 24, 1947).
47. Ibid.
48. C. E. Hooper, Inc., 1st Evening Report/Network Hooperatings.
49. C. E. Hooper, *Hooperade of Stars*, 1946–April 1947.
50. Drew Pearson, quoted in *OPC Bulletin*, clipped, no date.
51. Shirer, interviews.
52. Gude, interviews. Some question arose later on the matter of representation. Shirer, interviewed, said that Gude was not his agent, that his agent at the time was Herbert Rosenthal of MCA. Gude cited records and receipts to back his assertion that he was Shirer's agent at the time. Rosenthal, the onetime CBS director of program operations who wound up heading Columbia Artists when it was the in-house talent agency representing CBS stars, went over to MCA in the mid-forties when CBS was forced to divest itself of the operation. (He ultimately became President of MCA Artists Inc.) Said Rosenthal later, of the years in question, "a fine fellow named Jap Gude and a personal manager named John [illegible] got together to represent

Commentators—they succeded in handling Ed—Elmer Davis and others—Not for lectures but in relationship to Network deals and other opportunities—It did not bother me as I was deeply involved in MCA in handling of talent—radio packages and fortunately successful in the Company." (Herbert I. Rosenthal, letter to the author, March 1, 1984).

53. Paley, interviews.
54. Stanton, interviews.
55. Robert Skedgell, interviews of September 21, 1983, and November 2, 1983, hereafter referred to as Skedgell, interviews.
56. *Variety*, April 9, 1947.
57. *PM* (March 31, 1947).
58. William Shirer to H. V. Kaltenborn, March 26, 1947.
59. Shirer, interviews.
60. *New York Times*, March 31, 1947.
61. Ibid.
62. *OPC Bulletin*, April 22, 1947. Also Shayon, interview, and Hottelet, interview.
63. ERM to Edgar A. Mowrer, April 17, 1947.
64. ERM to Laski, June 5, 1947.
65. ERM to Elmer Davis, undated, probably April 1947.
66. Eric Sevareid to R. Franklin Smith, R. Franklin Smith, op. cit.

X. "INVESTIGATE, AND...LEGISLATE"

1.

1. Joseph E. Davies to ERM, June 10, 1947.
2. ERM to Davies, June 1947, no date.
3. James Fleming to ERM, October 27, 1947.
4. ERM to Fleming, undated.
5. Paul White to ERM, February 7, 1948.
6. Janet Murrow, interviews.
7. Schoenbrun, interviews.
8. Howard K. Smith to ERM, May 5, 1954.
9. Ted Berkman, "George Polk's Buried Under 30 Years of Lies," *Santa Barbara News & Review*, April 1, 1982.
10. *New York Star*, August 20, 1948.
11. Ted Berkman, interview of September 7, 1982, hereafter referred to as Berkman, interview.
12. John Donovan, interviews of September 23, 1982, and October 3, 1982, hereafter referred to as Donovan, interviews.
13. Donovan, interviews.
14. ERM to Frank Stanton, February 11, 1948.
15. George Polk to ERM, undated.
16. Howard K. Smith, broadcast of February 29, 1948.
17. Interview published posthumously *New York Herald Tribune*, March 10, 1948.
18. ERM to Lady Milner, April 19, 1948.
19. William F. Brooks, NBC, to Niles Trammell, March 9, 1948; also Davidson

Taylor, CBS, letter to Justin Miller, National Association of Broadcasters, March 11, 1948.

20. Memorandum for the Press, Office of the Secretary of Defense, March 29, 1948.

21. Ibid.

22. ERM, broadcast of March 4, 1948.

23. ERM to Laski, February 18, 1948.

24. "Memorandum for Mr. Nichols Re: Edward R. Murrow, January 10, 1948, FBI File No. 62-86094, Section No. 1; Murrow to James Forrestal, May 14, 1948; ERM to Rex Budd (draft), April 18, 1950.

25. David E. Lilienthal, *Journals*, vol. 2, *The Atomic Energy Years* (New York: Harper & Row, 1964).

26. Campbell Soup Company: Statement, 1948, undated; in Murrow files.

27. ERM, broadcast of April 14, 1948.

28. James McGowan, Jr., Campbell Soup Company, to Mrs. Ruth S. Walsh, April 23, 1948.

29. Ward Wheelock to ERM, April 21, 1948.

30. Donovan, interviews.

31. Cable, File Number, IN 43811, May 26, 1948; also Winston Burdett and John Secondari, "Report to Mr. Wells and Mr. Davidson Taylor," marked "Confidential," undated; "The George Polk Case: Report of the Overseas Writers of the Special Committee to Inquire into the Murder at Salonika, Greece, May 16, 1948, of Columbia Broadcasting System Correspondent George Polk"; also "Memorandum for the Director of Central Intelligence," from the Assistant Director, May 27, 1948.

32. In a further twist, Seymour Freidin was named by Carl Bernstein, writing in *Rolling Stone* (October 20, 1977), as a CIA operative; Bernstein cited unnamed "Agency officials" quoted in the wake of hearings of the Senate Intelligence Committee.

33. Raymond Daniell to ERM, May 18, 1948.

34. ERM, *Report No. 4 on the Murder of George Polk*, CBS broadcast of April 27, 1949; also Burdett and Secondari, op. cit.

35. ERM, broadcast of May 17, 1948.

36. *New York Times*, June 20, 1948.

37. *New York Times*, June 18, 1948.

38. *Report No. 2 on Probe of George Polk's Murder*, Broadcast from Rome by Winston Burdett, CBS, August 2, 1948.

39. Berkman, interview; also Berkman, *George Polk*, op. cit.

40. Cable, File Number IN 43712, May 25, 1948; also "Memorandum for the Director of Central Intelligence, Subject: Further Information on Polk," May 26, 1948.

41. Donovan, interviews.

42. *Edward R. Murrow with the News*, broadcast of August 20, 1948.

43. James G. L. Kellis, December 3, 1952; untitled deposition, CIA files, released May 31, 1978.

44. *Report No. 4 on the Murder of George Polk*, loc. cit.

45. Ibid.

46. Ibid. In 1955 Burdett testified before the Senate Internal Security Subcommittee about his Communist membership until 1942 and the fact that he

had engaged in espionage activities for the Soviet Union in the early war years. He later quit the party and was criticized in the journalism review *More* for possible anti-Communist bias in the Polk case (May 1977). On the other hand, a CIA dispatch of September 6, 1955, cited Burdett's record as part of a two-page listing of "possible communist involvement on the part of the POLKS," though not providing "substantial evidence." The dispatch pointed out that Burdett "held the same critical views of the Greek government as POLK . . . investigated the case after the murder and showed special interest in recovering POLK's missing CBS files."

Kendrick, quoted in the May 1977 *More*, was certain the doubts he expressed at the time "helped" his being listed in *Red Channels* a year later.

47. Released documents would indicate reports continuing into the late 1950s and picking up again in the 1970s.

48. Official dispatch, CIA files, addressee and sender deleted, dated August 25, 1955, stamped September 5, 1955.

49. Donovan, interviews. Declassified FBI files on Murrow later carried a sanitized reference to an unconfirmed report in the *New York Herald Tribune* of June 21, 1948, of a projected motion picture on the Polk case, to be written by Murrow. Murrow's private records reveal nothing about a projected movie script, and the prospect seems unlikely. The FBI item, however, did include a reference to State Department files and the deleted advice of "another government agency," the standard euphemism for the CIA (Federal Bureau of Investigation; name check to: Office of the Secretary of Defense, June 7, 1956, marked "Confidential," p. 4). The Polk case was certainly closely monitored, becoming among other matters part of Murrow's permanent dossier.

50. Donovan, interviews.

2.

1. John Crosby, *Out of the Blue* (New York: Simon & Schuster, 1952).
2. *New York Times*, July 18, 1948.
3. *Edward R. Murrow with the News*, November 15, 1948.
4. ERM to Lady Milner, April 19, 1948.
5. *Edward R. Murrow with the News*, September 1948, undated.
6. Ibid., June 3, 1948.
7. ERM to Paul Wright, August 26, 1948.
8. *Edward R. Murrow with the News*, December 16, 1948.
9. Ibid., December 21, 1948; also *New York Herald Tribune*, December 22, 1948; *New York Times*, December 23, 1948.
10. *Edward R. Murrow with the News*, December 21, 1948.
11. ERM, memo for the file, December 22, 1948.
12. Ward Wheelock Co. to ERM, January 10, 1949.
13. ERM to John Rothschild, December 30, 1948.

3.

1. The series title was *Footprints in the Sands of Time*.
2. Gude, interviews.
3. The splicing block was developed by Tall to meet the requirements of the

new developments in tape, an instance of the programs themselves dictating the technology.

4. Dorothy McDonough Corbett, interview of December 1, 1982, hereafter referred to as Corbett, interview.
5. ERM to James Seward, undated.
6. Marietta Tree, interview of June 15, 1977, hereafter referred to as Tree, interview.
7. ERM to Cabell Greet, June 28, 1956.
8. ERM to David Schoenbrun, undated.
9. ERM to Ken Merredith, June 1948.
10. To Howard K. Smith, June 21, 1949: "My plans for the summer are all up in the air. I am very tired of this . . . grind and the doctors are insisting on a complete rest."
11. CBS clipping files, "TV Cost, Drop in Record Trade Hit CBS Profits," April 21, 1949.
12. Farnsworth Fowle to ERM, January 1949, undated.
13. Alexander Kendrick to T. J. Bilski, Sr.; Bilski: "A Descriptive Study: Edward R. Murrow's Contributions to Electronic Journalism," Ph.D. dissertation, Case Western Reserve University, 1971, Journalism (Ann Arbor, Mich.: University Microfilms).
14. ERM to Howard K. Smith, June 21, 1949.
15. ERM to Joseph Harsch, May 6, 1949.
16. Richard Salant, interviews of A.M. and P.M., February 16, 1977; hereafter referred to as Salant, interviews.
17. ERM to Smith, June 21, 1949.
18. *Edward R. Murrow with the News*, September 23, 1949.
19. Ibid., November 2, 1948.
20. Ibid., March 18, 1949.
21. ERM to R. T. Clark, March 21, 1950.
22. *Edward R. Murrow with the News*, broadcast of March 9, 1949. Murrow was highlighting an unexpected speech by John Foster Dulles that urged the United States not to seek military bases too close to the Soviet Union and adding that he knew of no "responsible high official, military or civilian, in this government or any government who believes that the Soviet state now plans conquest by open military aggression."
23. Ibid., March 18, 1949.
24. Ibid., September 16, 1949.
25. Ibid., April 29, 1949.
26. Ibid., August 30, 1948.
27. A Bureau report stated that the FBI was carrying out more investigations than during the peak war years: "more men, money, and effort, investigating subversive activity now than were required at the height of the war."(*Edward R. Murrow With the News*, 1949, undated.)
28. *Edward R. Murrow with the News*, broadcast of December 16, 1948.
29. ERM to U. C. Tillett, April 25, 1950.
30. ERM, broadcast of June 9, 1949.
31. Paul White to ERM, undated.
32. Wilmott Ragsdale to ERM, January 18, 1949.
33. Ragsdale, interview.

34. Ragsdale to ERM, January 18, 1949.
35. Ibid.
36. ERM to Ragsdale, February 10, 1949.
37. Ragsdale, interview.
38. *Edward R. Murrow with the News*, January 18, 1950.
39. R. T. Clark, "West Powers' Bid for Unity, France's Mistaken Devotion to Vanished Empire," newspaper unspecified, March 3, 1950.
40. *Edward R. Murrow with the News*, January 25, 1950.
41. ERM to R. T. Clark, March 21, 1950.

XI. 1950

1. ERM to R. T. Clark, March 21, 1950.
2. Above all, the Harvard astronomer Harlow Shapley.
3. *Life* (April 10, 1950).
4. ERM to E. C. Culbertson, April 24, 1950.
5. *Edward R. Murrow with the News*, March 14, 1950.
6. Ibid., April 6, 1950.
7. Ibid., March 24, 1950.
8. Ibid., March 23, 1950.
9. Ibid., March 24, 1950.
10. Harold Isaacs to ERM, March 14, 1950.
11. *Edward R. Murrow with the News*, March 15, 1950.
12. Ibid., January 31, 1950.
13. ERM, "The World Crisis—Our Way Out," address given before the annual meeting of the American Council on Education, Chicago, Illinois, May 6, 1950.
14. U. C. Tillett to ERM, April 17, 1950.
15. *Edward R. Murrow with the News*, May 2, 1950.
16. Owen Lattimore, *Ordeal by Slander* (Boston: Little, Brown, 1950).
17. *Edward R. Murrow with the News*, April 10, 1950.
18. Ibid., March 22, 1950.
19. Campbell Soup Company to ERM, April 14, 1950.
20. ERM to R. M. Budd, Campbell Soup Company, April 20, 1950.
21. *Edward R. Murrow with the News*, April 21, 1950.
22. Ibid., April 20, 1950.
23. A. C. Nielsen Co., Network Radio Programs 1949–50.
24. According to the listings, Nielsen ratings for that particular time period averaged 9.7.
25. ERM to Elmer Davis, July 6, 1950.
26. Middleton, interview.
27. *Edward R. Murrow with the News*, June 30, 1950.
28. Ibid., May 22, 1950.
29. Ibid., June 27, 1950.
30. Ibid., December 12, 1952.
31. Dunn, interviews.
32. *Edward R. Murrow with the News*, August 4, 1950, cabled to Bill Costello in Tokyo for reading over the air.
33. Dunn, interviews.

34. *Edward R. Murrow with the News*, August 11, 1950.
35. Bill [*sic*] Lawrence, *Six Presidents, Too Many Wars* (New York: Saturday Review Press, 1972).
36. Dunn, interviews; details of this incident also drawn from the *Bulletin of the Overseas Press Club*, August 12, 1950, and from William Lawrence's account in the *New York Times*, clipping undated, probably August 7 or 8, 1950.
37. Lawrence, op. cit.
38. "Truman on 'Voice' Exhorts Vietnam," *New York Times*, August 13, 1950.
39. Script, *Edward R. Murrow with the News*, August 14, 1950, not broadcast.
40. "Background to Murrow 'Kill Order,'" Murrow CBS files, no signature, possibly Jesse Zousmer, undated, probably August 1950.
41. Ibid. This was a memo addressed to Murrow, drawn up obviously at his request, detailing how his August 14 report came to be dropped from the program. It might also have been drawn up by Larry LeSueur, who was left in charge of the program when Murrow went to Korea.
42. *Newsweek* (September 25, 1950).
43. Wershba, interviews.
44. *Edward R. Murrow with the News*, September 6, 1960.
45. *Birmingham News*, December 1950, undated.
46. ERM to Steve Laird, October 5, 1950.
47. CBS annual report to the stockholders, 1947, quoted in "Television News," a short history of the development of television news at CBS, prepared under the supervision of Sig Mickelson, CBS News, in early 1955.
48. ERM to Gunnar Back, December 15, 1950.

XII. SEE IT NOW

1.

1. Charles Mack, interview of June 21, 1973, hereafter referred to as Mack, interview.
2. Mili Lerner Bonsignori, interviews of May 11, 1973, May 12, 1973, August 1973, February 19, 1976, March 17, 1976, 1977, et. al.; hereafter referred to as Bonsignori, interviews.
3. Palmer Williams, interviews of May 2, 1973, December 15, 1982, April 19, 1983, April 20, 1983, October 20, 1983, et al.; hereafter referred to as Palmer Williams, interviews.
4. Bonsignori, interviews.
5. CBS release, October 29, 1951.
6. "NBC News and Special Events Department to Central Booking Office re *The Quick and the Dead*," National Broadcasting Company, Inc., Sustaining Program Booking, June 27, 1950.
7. NBC files, draft of promotion brochure for *Who Said That?* prepared for William F. Brooks, vice-president, news and special events, undated.
8. Gude, interviews.
9. Sig Mickelson, interviews of January 13, 1984, March 5, 1984, and March 20, 1984, hereafter referred to as Mickelson, interviews.
10. Ibid.

11. ERM, draft, February 18, 1949.
12. *See It Now*, November 18, 1951.
13. Merrill Panitt, " 'See It Now' Show Proves Worth of Cable," *Philadelphia Inquirer*, November 20, 1951.
14. Letters respectively of November 20, 1951, December 12, 1951, and December 26, 1951.
15. ERM to Norman Corwin, March 27, 1952. Corwin obliged with a three-page expert critique on the spring season.
16. Panitt, op. cit.
17. ERM to Abel Green, editor, *Variety*, December 19, 1951. Recollections of the problems of broadcasting from the control room are from: Palmer Williams, interviews; Bonsignori, interviews; and Don Hewitt, interview of November 27, 1984, hereafter referred to as Hewitt, interview.
18. Palmer Williams, interviews.
19. The Committee on the Present Danger, "Objectives," two pages, April 5, 1951.
20. *Edward R. Murrow with the News*, 1951, undated, re MacArthur dismissal, typescript.
21. Ibid.
22. Ibid., February 22, 1951.
23. Ibid., January 24, 1951.
24. Ibid., September 25, 1951.
25. Ibid., May 19, 1952.
26. Salant, interviews.
27. Lilienthal, op. cit.
28. Bessie, interviews.
29. Columbia Broadcasting System, "To: The Organization; From: Mr. Ream," December 19, 1950.
30. "Confidential Memorandum from M. A. Jones to Mr. Nichols; Subject: Edward Roscoe Murrow, CBS News Analyst," FBI File No. 62-86094, April 4, 1950.
31. Joseph H. Ream, letter to the author, dated October 13, 1975.
32. Ream, letter to the author, dated December 23, 1975.
33. Ream, letter of October 13, 1975.
34. Stanton, interviews.
35. William Fineshriber, interview of November 30, 1973, hereafter referred to as Fineshriber, interview.
36. Ream, letter of October 13, 1975.
37. Paley, interviews.
38. Hirshon, interview.
39. ERM, memo to Joseph Ream, January 24, 1951.
40. John Cogley, *Report on Blacklisting: Radio-Television* (New York: Fund for the Republic, 1956).
41. Daniel T. O'Shea, interviews of October 9, 1975, January 11, 1977, February 2, 1977, and May 27, 1977, hereafter referred to as O'Shea, interviews.
42. The foregoing information is based on the interviews listed above.
43. Heller, op. cit.
44. Fineshriber, interview.
45. Ream, letter of December 23, 1975.

46. Smith, interviews.
47. Cogley, op. cit.
48. Harold Isaacs, interview of April 1975, hereafter referred to as Isaacs, interview.
49. ERM to Ruth Shipley, telegram, undated.
50. John Henry Faulk, interview of November 10, 1976, hereafter referred to as Faulk interview.
51. *Edward R. Murrow with the News*, October 23, 1951.
52. Ibid., November 1, 1951.
53. ERM to D. F. Fleming, Vanderbilt University, letter of December 18, 1951.
54. *Counterattack: Facts to Combat Communism* (February 22, 1952).
55. *Time* (August 27, 1951).
56. *See It Now*, December 16, 1951.
57. R. Franklin Smith, op. cit.
58. NBC News and Special Events, correspondence of March 21–July 13, 1951.
59. Mr. Tolson to Mr. Nichols, March 8, 1951, File No. 62-86094.
60. Mr. A. Jones to Mr. Nichols, *aide-mémoire*, June 22, 1951, "Notes on Fred Friendly's visit," op. cit.
61. Ibid.
62. Ibid.
63. Palmer Williams, interviews.
64. Mickelson, interviews.
65. Ibid.
66. CBS Television, "Mr. Mickelson to Messrs. Van Volkenburg, Jones and Harrison, cc: Mr. Robinson, re: Proposed CBS Television News Film Project," October 27, 1952. The proposal included the suggested transfer of Palmer Williams "from *See It Now* to job of foreign editor." It also projected the transfer of the *See It Now* film crews from *News of the Day* to a set-up corporation, which occurred as an interim measure two years later, though it served only *See It Now*. Another deleted item proposed moving the suggested additionally hired CBS-TV personnel in with the *See It Now* crew. Bill McClure, on the CBS payroll, did lend a hand in Europe, but all references to *See It Now* were systematically eliminated.
67. Mickelson, interviews.
68. Stanton, interviews.
69. Colin, interviews.
70. Fineshriber, interview.
71. O'Shea, interviews.
72. Colin, interviews.
73. Mickelson, interviews.
74. William McClure, interviews of February 20, 1982, and September 30, 1982, hereafter referred to as McClure, interviews.
75. Schoenbrun, Smith, interviews.
76. Bonsignori, interviews.
77. Natalie Foster Paine, telephone interview of June 21, 1984, hereafter referred to as Foster, interview.
78. Bonsignori, interviews.
79. Bessie, interviews.

80. Edward Bliss, interview of June 10, 1973, hereafter referred to as Bliss, interview.
81. *Edward R. Murrow with the News*, January 3, 1952.
82. Wershba, interviews.
83. Hewitt, interview.

2.

1. McCarthy's 1951 and 1952 speeches, from the files of Robert Fleming, *Milwaukee Journal.*
2. *See It Now*, March 23, 1952.
3. A fact confirmed the day of the censure vote against McCarthy and inserted by New York's Senator Herbert Lehman in the *Congressional Record.*
4. *Congressional Record—Senate*, March 18, 1952; also ERM to John Howe, office of William Benton, May 1, 1952.
5. Benton to ERM, March 18, 1954.
6. Faulk, interview.
7. Robert Fleming, "Anti-McCarthy Campaign," undated, probably late 1951 notes.
8. Ibid.
9. ERM to John H. Crider, WEEI, Boston, February 9, 1952.
10. Lilienthal, op. cit.; Eisenhower, Murrow told Lilienthal, was "running for the presidency as fast as all get-out." He was "unlettered," said Murrow, in economics and politics and had shocked him by remarking, in their last meeting, that when he read about "those fellows at Oak Ridge" even thinking about going on strike, "I want to reach for my gun." Murrow, startled, countered, "General, you can't say a thing like that."
11. Estes Kefauver to ERM, February 25, 1952.
12. ERM, letter of April 23, 1964.
13. *Edward R. Murrow with the News*, July 1952, no date.
14. Skedgell, interviews.
15. *Edward R. Murrow with the News*, January 16, 1952.
16. Shirley Wershba, interview of February 16, 1977, hereafter referred to as Shirley Wershba, interview.
17. Walter White to ERM, September 17, 1952.
18. ERM to White, September 12, 1952.
19. *Edward R. Murrow with the News*, June 24, 1952.
20. Ibid., January 14, 1952.
21. ERM, "Television and Politics," the British Association–Granada Lectures, delivered at the Guildhall, London, October 19, 1959.
22. "McCarthyism: Is It a Trend? Other Candidates Would Like to Find the Secret," *U.S. News & World Report* (September 19, 1952).
23. *Edward R. Murrow with the News*, September 9, 1952.
24. Quoted by William H. Lawrence, *New York Times* News Service, Milwaukee dateline; see also *New York Times* story of October 4, 1952. In his book *Who Killed Joe McCarthy?* (New York: Simon & Schuster, 1984), William Bragg Ewald, Jr., a member of the administration and historian of those years, maintains that Eisenhower yielded not to McCarthy but to the reasoning of the heavyweights on his staff and in the party, that McCarthy had

never seen the advance text of the speech and had simply lied about this role after the fact.

25. Ibid.
26. Janet Murrow, interviews.
27. *See It Now*, October 5, 1952.
28. Wershba, interviews.
29. *Edward R. Murrow with the News*, November 5, 1952.
30. William Benton to ERM, December 1, 1952.
31. According to a postconvention AP story (Phoenix, undated), picked up by the *Milwaukee Journal*, "Senator Carlson (Rep., Kas.), one of the top advisers of General Eisenhower, said Tuesday that McCarthy would be asked to play a part in the national Republican campaign. Senator Mundt (Rep., S. Dak.), chairman of the Senatorial campaign committee, said that about 20 requests for speeches by McCarthy had been received."
32. *See It Now*, November 2, 1952.
33. Palmer Williams, interviews.
34. *See It Now*, November 23, 1952.
35. Palmer Williams, interviews.
36. *See It Now*, December 2, 1952.
37. *Edward R. Murrow with the News*, December 12, 1952.
38. Mack, interview.
39. Ibid.
40. *See It Now*, "Christmas in Korea," cutting room notes.
41. *Edward R. Murrow with the News*, December 22, 1952.
42. *See It Now*, segment filmed December 1952, aired May 29, 1953.
43. Mack, interview, and Wershba, interviews.
44. *New York Times*, December 29, 1952. Even filmed programs were not previewed for review at the time.
45. *New York Journal-American*, December 28, 1952.
46. Harry Castleman and Walter J. Podrazik, *Watching TV: Four Decades of American Television* (New York: McGraw-Hill, 1982).
47. Ben Gross, *New York Daily News*, December 29, 1952.
48. Telegram, Paul White to ERM, December 29, 1952.
49. *Seattle Post-Intelligencer*, December 31, 1952.

3.

1. As of this writing, the hospital records are unavailable. In the absence of evidence to the contrary, it must be assumed that the tests were negative. The tests themselves, as indicated by Murrow's correspondence, included an electrocardiogram as well as X rays of the chest, sinuses, and shoulders.
2. Charles Collingwood, on *Edward R. Murrow with the News*, December 29, 1952.
3. *Observation Post: Undergraduate Newspaper of CCNY*, February 20, 1953.
4. Ibid.
5. *Edward R. Murrow with the News*, February 4, 1953.
6. *See It Now*, "Formosa," cutting room notes.
7. Ibid., February 1, 1953.
8. Ibid., June 7, 1953.

9. Ibid., March 8, 1953.
10. Among those ousted was Reed Harris, whose interrogation was featured on the March 8 McCarthy show. The same film clip provided the centerpiece for the more famous McCarthy show of a year later.
11. *Edward R. Murrow with the News*, January 22, 1953.
12. Ibid.
13. Ibid., April 29, 1953.
14. Ibid., February 16, 1953.
15. Ibid.
16. *See It Now*, March 8, 1953.
17. *Edward R. Murrow with the News*, November 1, 1951.
18. Ibid., February 6, 1953. The broadcast was based on an article written by S. Grover Rich for the *Antioch Review*, a common device to get around the no-editorializing policy. "I have quoted at such length this article by Professor Grover Rich of the University of Utah," Murrow said at the end, "because I agree with what he says, and he said it rather better than I could have done."
19. Ibid.
20. Ibid.
21. *Edward R. Murrow with the News*, 1951, date unclear on typescript.
22. ERM, interview, *Cue* magazine (February 21, 1953).
23. Palmer Williams, interviews.
24. ERM to Fred Friendly, April 15, 1952.
25. *Edward R. Murrow with the News*, April 29, 1953.
26. Downs, interviews.
27. Ibid.
28. William H. Hadley, Jr., to ERM, September 14, 1953.
29. Reynolds R. Kraft, Jr., to ERM, July 18, 1953.
30. ERM to Hadley, September 25, 1953.
31. Chester Williams, interviews.
32. Ibid.
33. Ibid.
34. *Edward R. Murrow with the News*, May 11, 1953.
35. Ibid., May 13, 1953.
36. Ibid., May 15, 1953.
37. Leonard Miall, letter to the author, July 10, 1981.
38. Williams debarked at Newfoundland.
39. Smith, interviews.
40. *Edward R. Murrow with the News*, May 26, 1953.
41. John F. Royal to ERM, undated.
42. ERM to Royal, June 8, 1953.
43. Wells Church to Carl Ward, CBS Radio, January 12, 1953, cc: ERM, Adrian Murphy. John Vandercook was listed in *Red Channels*, Raymond Swing was attacked in *Counterattack*, published by American Business Consultants, publisher of both *Red Channels* and *Counterattack*.
44. Raymond Swing, *Good Evening: A Professional Memoir* (New York: Harcourt, Brace & World, Inc., 1964).
45. ERM to Raymond Swing, letter of June 5, 1953.
46. "Edward R. Murrow: To Mr. Paley and Mr. Stanton, November 24." Two

months later Murrow was cited in the January 15 issue of *Counterattack* as part of a blast against Theodore White.

47. Teichmann, interview.
48. Leland Hayward to Janet Murrow, April 28, 1965.
49. ERM, Ford Show "(Conclusion)," typescript.
50. Hayward, op. cit.
51. Ibid.

XIII. ''THE FAULT, DEAR BRUTUS . . .''

1.

1. Robert Fleming, *Milwaukee Journal*, notes on Donald A. Surine, April, 1951, typescript; also depositions of April 4, 1951 and May 9, 1951.
2. Joseph Wershba, "Murrow vs. McCarthy: See It Now," *New York Times Magazine*, March 4, 1979; this is a shortened version of a longer unpublished memoir. Also Wershba, two-page report to Murrow, November 24, 1953. Also Wershba, interviews.
3. *Edward R. Murrow with the News*, October 13, 1953.
4. *See It Now*, October 20, 1953.
5. Wershba, interviews.
6. Fred W. Friendly, *Due to Circumstances Beyond Our Control* (New York: Random House, 1967); hereafter referred to as Friendly, *Circumstances*.
7. Harriet Van Horne to ERM, "Tuesday night."
8. Laura Z. Hobson to ERM, October 20, 1953.
9. *New York Times*, October 21, 1953.
10. Friendly, *Circumstances*.
11. Ibid.
12. Wershba, interviews.
13. Ibid.
14. Wershba, "Murrow vs. McCarthy," loc. cit.
15. Alan Reitman, interview of March 21, 1983, hereafter referred to as Reitman, interview.
16. Ibid.
17. Ed Scott, interview, June, 1973, hereafter referred to as Scott, interview.
18. *See It Now*, November 24, 1953.
19. Wershba, interviews; also Palmer Williams, interviews.
20. Norman Thomas to ERM, December 2, 1953.
21. Reitman, interview.
22. Friendly, *Circumstances*.
23. *Edward R. Murrow with the News*, November 18, 1953.
24. Memorandum to Mr. Tolson from L. B. Nichols, November 19, 1953.
25. Ibid., handwritten notation by the Director.
26. Walter White to ERM, December 16, 1953.
27. *See It Now*, February 2, 1954.
28. Palmer Williams, interviews.
29. Charles Siepmann, interview of September 19, 1981, hereafter referred to as Siepmann, interview.
30. Downs, interviews.

31. At various times proposals were drawn up for Murrow and Friendly-packaged programs, titled *What's New, Mid-Atlantic Parliament,* and *Small World. Small World* finally made it onto the schedule.
32. Mack, interviews.
33. Downs, interviews.
34. *Edward R. Murrow with the News,* November 13, 1953.
35. *Life* (March 8, 1958).
36. Schoenbrun, interviews.
37. ERM, correspondence, January-February, 1953.
38. Albert Einstein, open letter, March 10, 1954.
39. Joseph Julian, *This Was Radio: a personal memoir* (New York: Viking Press, a Richard Seaver Book, 1975); also Joseph Julian, interviews of November 10 and December 3, 1975, hereafter referred to as Julian, interviews.
40. *Edward R. Murrow with the News,* February 23, 1954.
41. Robert Heller to ERM, February 5, 1954.
42. NBC News, to Joseph O. Meyers from Chet Hagan, *The Nightly Report,* February 1954, probably February 24.
43. Ibid.
44. Hagan to Meyers, February 25, 1954.
45. Ewald, op. cit.
46. Bonsignori, interviews.
47. Janet Murrow, interviews.
48. Teichmann, interviews.
49. Jack Beck, interview of May 23, 1973, hereafter referred to as Beck, interview.
50. Bernstein, interview.
51. Hewitt, interview.
52. Telegram, CBS Television Press Information to the Hon. J. Edgar Hoover, March 8, 1954, 3:00 P.M. It should be pointed out that CBS occasionally cabled the Bureau to alert it to public affairs programs considered important by the network—e.g., the premiere of *See It Now* in November 1951.
53. Wershba, op. cit.
54. Wershba and Scott, interviews. Quote is from Wershba.
55. Bonsignori, interviews.
56. Ibid.
57. Fred Friendly, interview, BBC biography of Murrow, 1975.
58. Fred Friendly, interviews of October 24, 1973, November 16, 1973, and November 19, 1976, and telephone interviews of November 30, 1976, December 21, 1976, and June 1977, hereafter referred to as Friendly, interviews.
59. Ibid.
60. Beck, interview.
61. Wershba, interviews.
62. Bonsignori, interviews.
63. Wershba, op. cit.
64. According to Joe Wershba, it was an idea resisted at first by Murrow—i.e., This is no time to keep silent—as too much of a direct appeal for support. He finally agreed to it under urging, insisted on inserting the phrase *Or for*

those who approve as a sort of counterbalance. It carried little weight, however.

65. The files of Robert Fleming and other McCarthy watchers indicated ties with Gerald L. K. Smith, Merwin K. Hart, and others prominent among American neofascists.
66. Wershba, interviews.
67. Scott, interview.
68. Janet Murrow, interviews.
69. Paley, interviews.
70. Hirshon, interview.
71. Bliss, interview.
72. Shirley Wershba, interview.
73. *San Francisco Chronicle*, March 11, 1954.
74. *New York Times*, March 11, 1954.
75. *New York Herald Tribune*, March 12, 1954.
76. *Newsweek* (March 29, 1954).
77. Wershba, interviews.
78. Alistair Cooke, *Guardian Weekly* (March 18, 1954).
79. Seldes to ERM, December 20, 1962; also ERM to Seldes, January 4, 1963.
80. Downs, interviews.
81. Lauren Bacall to ERM, April 20, 1954.
82. *Newsweek* (March 29, 1954).
83. ERM to Jay Nelson Tuck, *New York Post*, clipping, no date.

2.

1. Fulton Lewis, Jr., WOR, March 11, 1954.
2. The *Dallas Morning News*, early city edition, interestingly enough, gave a bigger play to McCarthy's charges against Murrow than to the Army report on McCarthy, Cohn, and Schine.
3. *Edward R. Murrow with the News*, March 12, 1954.
4. Joseph and Stewart Alsop, "McCarthy on the Run," March 29, 1954.
5. *New York Times* editorial, March 13, 1954.
6. Richard M. Nixon, telecast, March 13, 1954.
7. Janet Murrow, interviews.
8. *New York Daily Mirror*, March, 1954.
9. *Look*, August 24, 1954.
10. Wershba, interviews.
11. NYPD, pistol license information: Make, Colt .38 and Smith & Wesson 22/32. "Reason: Protection of valuable documents used in connection with business/carry large sums of cash and jewelry." April 22, 1959.
12. Casey Murrow, interviews.
13. Ibid.
14. Scott, interview.
15. Joseph McCarthy, telegram to ERM, March 15, 1954.
16. ERM to Joseph McCarthy, March 15 or 16, 1954.
17. Scott, interview.
18. *See It Now*, March 16, 1954.
19. Stanton, interviews.

20. FBI File 162-86094, "AIR-Tel/ FBI WASH FIELD/ from Laughlin," March 31, 1954.
21. *Variety*, April 14, 1954; also *New York Times*: May 28, June 5, July 22, August 30, September 11, 1940; also the *Nation*, article by Ludwig Lore, clipping, marked "1933."
22. ERM, telegram to Joseph McCarthy, April 2, 1954.
23. ERM, memo to William Paley, April 2, 1954.
24. Jack Gould, *New York Times*, April 9, 1954.
25. Drew Pearson, *Diaries, 1949–1959*, edited by Tyler Abell (New York: Holt, Rinehart & Winston, 1974).
26. *See It Now*, April 6, 1954.
27. Friendly, interviews.
28. Palmer Williams, interviews.
29. Friendly, interviews.
30. Sam McSeveny, interview of July 11, 1979, hereafter referred to as McSeveny, interview.
31. *Detroit Times*, April 7, 1954; information on Pulse ratings from *Broadcasting and Telecasting*, April 12, 1954.
32. Memo to ERM, unsigned, April 7, 1954; the rest of Eisenhower's reply was picked up by just about every wire agency.
33. Joseph McCarthy to ALCOA, undated. The returned invoice plus ALCOA's reply went thereupon to Frank Stanton. ALCOA returned the invoice, unpaid, to McCarthy, with Wilson's covering letter on May 4, 1954.
34. *Variety*, April, 1954.
35. Murrow Collection, *See It Now* files, 1954; typed copy, marked: "*New York Times*," undated.
36. Murphy, interview.
37. NBC files; transcript of conversation between Syd Eiges and Joan Walker of *Newsweek*, 4:45 P.M., March 19, 1954; Joan Walker to Syd Eiges, letter of March 17, 1954; Joe McCurdy to Syd Eiges, March 19, 1954; Syd Eiges to Sylvester L. Weaver, Jr., March 19, 1954.
38. Handwritten notation, April 8, 1954.
39. " 'Strange Silence' " from NBC on McCarthy Imbroglio Riles CBS", *Variety*, April 14, 1954.
40. Jack Gould, *New York Times*, op. cit.
41. "As Pegler Sees It," King Features Syndicate, Inc., *New York Journal-American*, March 17, 1954.
42. *The New Counterattack: Facts to Combat Communism*, vol. 8, no. 12 (March 19, 1954).
43. *Peoria Star*, March 25, 1954.
44. *Manchester* (New Hampshire) *Union Leader*, April 8, 1954.
45. Stanton, interviews.
46. Friendly, *Circumstances*.
47. Ibid.
48. Stanton, interviews.
49. Bureau files, memorandum to Mr. Nichols, March 11, 1954. Search slips, indicating the pulling of "All References," are dated March 10, 1954, the day after the McCarthy program.
50. Ibid.

51. "Memorandum, Mr. A. Jones to Mr. Nichols," March 18, 1954.
52. Ibid.
53. Handwritten notation, October 10, 1956.
54. AIR TEL, Bureau, NY, NY, April 7, 1954, from Kelly, 3-Bureau (101-5828) (Regular).
55. "Memorandum, Mr. A. H. Belmont to Mr. V. P. Keay, Subject: Edward R. Murrow, CBS Commentator," April 14, 1954.
56. Ibid.
57. ERM to Rex Budd (draft), April 18, 1950.
58. "From L. N. Conroy to Mr. A. Rosen, Subject: Edward R. Murrow/Name Check Request" June 7, 1956.
59. "Memorandum: from Mr. A. Jones to Mr. Nichols," June 22, 1951.
60. Note to Miami SAC, April 16, 1956; also limited file check for Presidential Press Secretary Hagerty, July 8, 1955.
61. File check for Hagerty, ibid.
62. Friendly, *Circumstances*. Background to Shipley order and Shipley-Reece correspondence is from an FBI report ("To: Director, FBI, From: SAC, WFO [161–176]") dated February 21, 1961, drawn up in the course of the prerequisite background check made in connection with Murrow's appointment as USIA Director.
63. Unsigned, "CONFIDENTIAL/ Points to take up with Ed Murrow (and Ben Shute, CBS lawyer)," March 21, 1954; also Chester Williams, Confidential Notes, March 31, 1954.
64. Stanton, interviews.
65. Pegler, King Features Syndicate, Inc., *New York Journal-American*, March 19, 1954.
66. Chester Williams to Elizabeth Robertson Miller, March 30, 1954. "Many people could be hurt if they got into hostile hands," he wrote. "You cannot imagine how hysterical the situation is here. . . . Completely innocent people have been suddenly confronted with old records about which they know nothing, especially from the files of the IPR. . . . [T]he scoundrels are now re-writing history, as the Soviets have. . . ."
67. *Matter of "M" File*, Murrow Collection, Survey of IIE files—I I 3. These were the locked files relating to Murrow, McCarthy, and CBS, prepared in readiness for a possible congressional hearing.
68. Ibid; "Mimeographed publicity material re Anglo-American Institute of the First Moscow University."
69. Files of the Institute of International Education; Announcement, *Anglo-American Institute of the First Moscow University, Summer Session, 1934, July 15 . . . August 16, Moscow, USSR:* 'Courses.'
70. Ibid.
71. ERM to Stephen Duggan, June 21, 1934.
72. As stated in earlier chapters, the Anglo-American Institute was funded by Intourist.
73. Murphy, interview.
74. Ewald, op. cit.
75. Matter of "M" file, op. cit.
76. Jesse Zousmer to ERM, April 15, 1954; also Wesley Price to Zousmer, undated ("Dear Jess, Surine on the phone again . . .").

77. Memo, unsigned, possibly Chester Williams, "Things to Be Done."
78. As an example, his old logging supervisor, Ken Merredith, was called in Washington State and asked to wire a deposition to the effect that Murrow had never been a member of the IWW plus general character references from 1925 on.
79. Chester Williams, notes for Adrian Fisher and W. T. Stone, March 26–29, 1954.
80. *Matter of "M" File*; memorandum for the files, "Conference March 22, 1954, with ERM," March 23, 1954.
81. Palmer Williams, interviews.
82. Ibid.
83. *"M" File*; memo to ERM, undated.
84. *Variety*, March 17, 1954.
85. Bonsignori, interviews.
86. Arthur Garfield Hays to ERM, March 12, 1954.
87. *Julian* v. *American Business Consultants, Inc.*, transcripts.
88. Ibid.
89. Julian, interviews.
90. Collingwood, interviews.
91. Julian transcripts. The rest of the account is based verbatim on the transcripts and interviews with the plaintiff.
92. Quentin Reynolds to ERM, June 29, 1954.
93. ABC alone carried the hearings live, intact.
94. Quoted on *Edward R. Murrow with the News*, May 28, 1954.
95. Ewald, op. cit.
96. *Edward R. Murrow with the News*, May 28, 1954.
97. James Hagerty to ERM, May 29, 1954.
98. Loren Ghiglione, "Don Hollenbeck: (Broad)casting the First Stone," Perspective on the Press, *The Evening News*, Southbridge, Massachusetts, undated.
99. Elmer Lower, interview of February 29, 1984; hereafter referred to as Lower, interview.
100. Friendly and Bonsignori, interviews.
101. Wershba, interviews.
102. Friendly, interviews.
103. *See It Now*, June 22, 1954.
104. *Edward R. Murrow with the News*, June 22, 1954.
105. *New York Journal-American*, June 23, 1954.
106. ERM, "Television and Politics," Guildhall, London, October 19, 1959.

XIV. UPRIGHT ON THE TREADMILL

1.

1. Mack, interview.
2. Ibid.
3. Palmer Williams, interviews.
4. O'Shea, interviews.
5. Joseph Wershba, letter to Carl Sandburg, July 21, 1954; other sources for

this section were Friendly, interviews; Wershba, interviews; and Beck, interview.

6. Columbia Broadcasting System, Inc., "For release Monday, August 16," dated August 13, 1954.

7. Frank Stanton to Sig Mickelson, August 14, 1954. The other two board members suggested by Stanton were Jack Van Volkenburg, President of the CBS Television Network, and Adrian Murphy. The board, wrote Stanton, would be there for purposes of consultation with senior management on the development of new policies and also for the purpose of reviewing the administration of existing news and public affairs policies.

8. Ibid.

9. Mickelson, interviews.

10. School of Journalism Committee; "CBS Project," typescript, 3 pages, undated.

11. Sig Mickelson to Mr. Oleske, request for $1,640. February 3, 1956.

12. "Progress report": "Objectivity in Radio News and News Analysis," January 21, 1955.

13. "Confidential" report to CBS, November 28, 1955. "An Objectivity Study of Three CBS News Broadcasts."

14. Sig Mickelson to Frank Stanton, "Confidential," December 6, 1955.

15. Mickelson, interviews.

16. *See It Now*, April 26, 1955.

17. Wershba, interviews.

18. Bureau File No. 62-86094. The informant, who had "furnished reliable information in the past," had reported the two men meeting on November 17, 1954, but evidently couldn't make out the substance of the conversation (multiple references in file).

19. Fred Friendly, transcripts of the Columbia Broadcasting System News Clinic, New Weston Hotel, January 3–4, 1955; Monday afternoon session, January 3.

20. *See It Now*, "A Conversation with Dr. J. Robert Oppenheimer," January 4, 1955.

21. ERM, memo for the file, "Conversation with Mr. Ashley Nicholas, Assistant Director, Passport Division, State Department, 3:00 P.M. Thursday, April 28, 1955," dated April 29, 1955.

22. ERM to Ruth Shipley, April 19, 1955.

23. Form letter to ERM, April 21, 1955. Some confusion seems to exist on this point. The FBI report of February 21, 1961 (cf. Chapter XIII, fn. 62) indicates that the "adverse information" concerning Murrow was "subsequently" considered "not sufficient to warrant the taking up of his passport." ("To: Director, FBI/ From: SAC, WFO [161–176]," dated February 21, 1961). Evidently the "refusal" recorded by the Passport Office as of August 2, 1954 for "alleged Communist affiliations" was somewhat mitigated.

24. ERM, Memo for the file, April 29, 1955, loc. cit.

25. ERM to Ashley Nicholas, April 29, 1955.

26. ERM to William Paley, covering memo with conversation notes, undated.

27. *New York Times*, November 16, 1954.

28. Arthur P. Hall, ALCOA, to ERM, May 3, 1955.

29. Murrow to Pittsburgh (no addressee), April 28, 1955.

30. *See It Now*, May 3, 1955.
31. Bonsignori, interviews.
32. Salant, interview.
33. Mack, interview.
34. Friendly, *Circumstances*.
35. *Columbine*, Vol. 2, no. 7 April–May 1974, special history of CBS issue.
36. *See It Now*; prospectus, probably early June 1955.
37. Bill Downs to ERM and Friendly, July 25, 1955.
38. *See It Now*, June 1, 1954.
39. Ibid., May 25, 1955.
40. ERM to William Robson, July 5, 1955.
41. ERM to (illegible), July, 1955.
42. ERM to John B. Evans, September 26, 1958.
43. Mary Warburg, interviews of July 10 and July 14, 1977, hereafter referred to as Warburg, interviews.
44. ERM to Air Chief Marshal Sir Philip Joubert, August 23, 1955.
45. ERM to Sol Taisheff, *Broadcasting-Telecasting*, September 1955.
46. CBS, Jim Burke to news staff, "list of primary CBS Television Affiliates and names and phone numbers of their News Directors," October 7, 1955.
47. Bill Downs to ERM, December 1955
48. *Edward R. Murrow with the News*, May 4, 1955.
49. Ibid., April 20, 1954.
50. Ibid.
51. Ibid., May 4, 1955.
52. *See It Now*, March 30, 1954.
53. *See It Now*, May 11, 1954.
54. Ibid., March 30, 1954.
55. "Why 'See It Now' Gets Top Response on TV," *The Daily Worker*, April 18, 1954.
56. *See It Now*, October 26, 1955.
57. *Edward R. Murrow with the News*, September 27, 1955.
58. "Edward R. Murrow, CBS News Commentator, Limited File Check, to Presidential Press Secretary Hagerty," Bureau File 62-86094, July 8, 1955.
59. Friendly, interviews.
60. Mickelson, interviews.
61. Friendly, interviews.
62. ERM to George Dunning, February 16, 1956.
63. Mickelson, interviews; also memos, CBS News, 1954–59.
64. Mickelson, interviews.
65. Mr. Mickelson, memo to Messrs. Day, Lower, Burke, Bush, Kany, Zellmer, September 7, 1955.
66. Frank Stanton to Sig Mickelson, August, 19, 1955.
67. Grace Wyndham Goldie, interview of June 10, 1981.
68. Schoenbrun to ERM, April 4, 1956.
69. Schoenbrun, Smith, interviews.
70. Frank R. Donghi to Sig Mickelson, marked "Confidential," January 11, 1954.
71. David Schoenbrun, transcripts of the Columbia Broadcasting System News Clinic, New Weston Hotel, January 3–4, 1955; Monday afternoon session, January 3.

72. ERM, telegram to Cedric Adams, July 31, 1956.
73. ERM to William Benton, undated.
74. Lilienthal, op. cit.
75. Salant, interview.
76. Bliss, interview.
77. Casey Murrow, interviews.
78. *Person to Person*, January 13, 1956.
79. Davidson Taylor to Pat Weaver and David Sarnoff, July 28, 1954.
80. Merrill Mueller to William Fineshriber, February 4, 1954, NBC files: "Many thanks for your very thoughtful note abut the Polk Award. I am doubly happy because in the final judging we took it away from Ed Murrow's 'Christmas in Korea' show."
81. J. O. Meyers to Ted Cott, December 1, 1954.
82. Taylor to Weaver and Sarnoff, July 28, 1954.
83. *New York Times*, August 17, 1956.
84. ERM to Sig Mickelson, October 2, 1956.
85. Tree, interview.
86. Vanessa Brown, interviews of February 26, 1977, April 24, 1977, May 28, 1977; also letters to author: May 22, 1977, and May 21, 1977; also typescript, "Edward R. Murrow: A Remembrance," 1965; foregoing hereafter referred to as Brown, interviews and correspondence.
87. ERM, "Television and Politics," loc. cit.
88. Thomas H. Wolff to ERM, June 26, 1956, confirming studio availability and crew for Thursday, June 28; enclosed bill to "Stevenson for President," for production, facilities; see also George Ball, *The Past Has Another Pattern: Memoirs* (New York: Norton, 1982).
89. *Edward R. Murrow with the News*, October 16, 1956; also Brown, interviews and correspondence. Murrow, says Brown, was "very excited" at the prospect of the documentary and provided the Stevenson people with the names of a writer-director, cameraman, film editor, and nuclear physicists ready to speak out. The film was made without the scientists, however. They withdrew suddenly, says Brown, reportedly under AEC pressure; which in effect left the project gutted.
90. ERM, "Television and Politics," loc. cit.
91. Brown, interviews and correspondence.
92. Salant, interviews.
93. Murphy, interview.
94. ERM to William Paley, "Personal," October 3, 1956.
95. Paley to ERM, "Personal," October 3, 1956.
96. Lou Cioffi, interviews of March 8, 1977 and March 29, 1977, hereafter referred to as Cioffi, interviews.
97. Raymond Swing, op. cit.
98. Shirer, interviews.
99. Faulk, interview.
100. Collingwood, interviews.
101. Faulk, interview.
102. O'Shea, interviews.
103. Faulk, interview.
104. Seward, interviews.

105. Faulk, interview; for other details see also John Henry Faulk, *Fear on Trial* (New York: Simon & Schuster, 1964), and Louis Nizer, *The Jury Returns* (New York: Doubleday, 1960), also letter of Louis Nizer to ERM, 1955, undated.

106. Faulk, interview.

107. *Variety*, July 10, 1957.

108. ERM to Pearl Buck, January 9, 1957.

109. *Edward R. Murrow with the News*, June 26, 1957.

110. *See It Now*, June 30, 1957.

111. Karla Duhar, Yugoslav Films, to ERM, July 3, 1957.

112. *See It Now*, March 13, 1956.

113. ERM to Ann Hamlet, March 7, 1956.

114. *Edward R. Murrow with the News*, May 20, 1948.

115. ERM to John Gulick, December 10, 1956.

116. Mack, interview.

117. ERM, draft of letter to USSR Ambassador Georgi N, Zarubin, January 19, 1956.

118. Fred Friendly to Vladimir Surin, Deputy Minister of Culture, USSR, August 25, 1956.

119. William Worthy, interviews of March 13, 1977, May 21, 1977, et al.; hereafter referred to as Worthy, interviews.

120. William Worthy to ERM, May 29, 1956.

121. *Edward R. Murrow with the News*, February 6, 1957.

122. Worthy, interviews.

123. Ibid.

124. Paul Southwick, staff, Government Information Subcommittee of the Committee on Government Operations, House of Representatives, to ERM, March 6, 1957. Also Charles H. Slayman, chief counsel, Senate Judiciary Committee on Constitutional Rights, to ERM, March 14, 1957.

125. Worthy, interviews.

126. Foreign Relations Committee, U.S. Senate, transcript, hearings of April 2, 1957. Also *Edward R. Murrow with the News*, April 2, 1957.

127. Worthy, interviews.

128. Rough draft for ERM amicus brief, January 15, 1959.

129. Morris Ernst, January, 15, 1959, p. 186; also Alan U. Schwartz, of Greenbaum, Wolff & Ernst, to ERM, January 15, 1959.

130. John Secondari, "The Commentator," typescript.

131. Ibid.

132. Richard Rovere, *Senator Joe McCarthy* (New York: Harcourt, Brace, 1959).

133. Bliss, interview.

134. Corbett, interview.

135. *Time*, "This is Murrow," September 30, 1957.

136. Robert L. Foster, taped reminiscences, May 17, 1977.

137. Bonsignori, interviews.

138. ERM to Remsen Bird, July 9, 1951.

139. Leland Hayward to ERM, December 4, 1956.

140. ERM to Hayward, December 12, 1956.

141. ERM, introduction for Mrs. Roosevelt, Harold Taylor dinner, May 21, 1959.

142. Mr. Klinger to Sig Mickelson, "Fred Friendly," confidential memo of July 16, 1959.

143. Sig Mickelson, "presentation to FCC Study Staff, October 6, 7, 1958, VII; (b) *Small World.*"

144. J. M. Seward to ERM and Fred Friendly, memo, March 14, 1957; also JMS to ERM, cc: Mr. de Orsey, Mr. Friendly, September 23, 1957.

145. Friendly, memo to ERM re Murrow memo of October 2, 1957, to William S. Paley.

146. Wershba, "Murrow vs. McCarthy," unedited version, typescript; also Wershba, interviews.

147. Gilbert Seldes to ERM, undated.

148. Siepmann, interview.

149. Hewitt, interview.

150. Herbert Bayard Swope to ERM, February 1958.

151. ERM to Swope, March 5, 1958.

152. Georgia Gibbs, interview of November 26, 1980.

153. Schoenbrun, interviews.

154. Bernard Kalb to Janet Murrow, May, 1965.

155. Mack, interview.

156. Bonsignori, Beck, interviews.

157. Scott, interviews.

158. Daniel Schorr on *Edward R. Murrow with the News*, December 19, 1957.

159. ERM, ibid.

160. John W. O'Daniel, chairman, American Friends of Vietnam, to ERM, June 1, 1959.

161. ERM, speech notes, undated, probably 1956.

162. CBS; *Years of Crisis*, 1957.

163. William Peter, "What You Can't See on TV," *Redbook* (July 27, 1957).

164. *Time* (January 14, 1957).

165. ERM, speech of May 5, 1957, Albert Einstein Award.

166. ERM, letter of July 30, 1954.

167. Wershba, Bliss, Friendly, interviews.

168. Peter, op. cit.

169. Quoted in *Time* (January 20, 1958).

170. Sig Mickelson, speech before the Round Table Luncheon of Radio and Television Executives Society, February 26, 1958.

171. Mickelson, interviews.

172. Skedgell, interviews.

173. John F. Day to Messrs. Clark and Schoenbrun, cc: Mr. Murrow, Mr. Skedgell, December 11, 1957.

174. Skedgell, interviews.

175. Smith, interviews.

176. Reuven Frank to ERM, April, 1958.

177. ERM to Frank, April 23, 1958.

178. ERM to Irving Gitlin, Louis Cowan, June 6, 1957.

179. Cioffi, interviews.

180. Charles Kuralt, "Edward R. Murrow," *North Carolina Historical Review*, vol. XLVIII, no. 2 (April 1971).

181. Downs, interviews.

182. Gude, interviews.
183. Schoenbrun to ERM, May 24, no year, possibly 1957.
184. Av Westin to John Day, July 8, 1957.
185. ERM to William Paley, November 19, 1957; Paley to ERM, November, 1957.

2.

1. Robert Philpot to network salesmen, January 21, 1958.
2. Edmond Leavey to ERM, February 4, 1958.
3. See It Now, cutting room notes, undated, "Statehood for Alaska and Hawaii."
4. Ibid., transcript of uncut Harry Bridges interview, August 12, 1957.
5. Mickelson, interviews.
6. Ibid.
7. William A. Egan, to ERM, April 11, 1958.
8. ERM to Egan, April 22, 1958.
9. The offer to copy the "gist" was not taken up. But the anger in the letter was obvious to any reader.
10. Paley, interviews.
11. Friendly, interviews.
12. Friendly, *Circumstances*.
13. Friendly, interviews.
14. *New York Times*, July 8, 1958.
15. Friendly, interviews
16. Lee Otis, interview, December 8, 1983; hereafter referred to as Otis, interviewed.
17. Dan Karasik to ERM, February 4, 1958.
18. Norman Cousins was about to forward to him, in confidence, an early draft of the appeal (letter of April 28, 1958).
19. "Is Television Too Timid? Edward R. Murrow Gives Some Reasons Why It May Be," *TV Guide* (May 10–16, 1958). The article, marked "FYI," was immediately forwarded within the house by Bill Ackerman to Sig Mickelson's attention.
20. ERM, letters to William Egan and RTNDA, April 22, 1958.
21. ERM, speech of May 5, 1957.
22. ERM to William Paley, October 2, 1957.
23. Sig Mickelson, memo for the file, May 28, 1958.
24. Siepmann, interview.
25. Robert Lewis Shayon to ERM, February 17, 1959.
26. Shayon, interview.
27. ERM to S. O. Shapiro, Vice-President, *Look*, November 24, 1958.
28. Bonsignori, interviews. The cutting room site had been moved.
29. Scott, interviews.
30. Marty Barnett to ERM, July 29, 1958.
31. ERM to Barnett, August 13, 1958.
32. Morris Ernst to ERM, August 6, 1958.
33. ERM to Ernst, August 28, 1958.
34. Gude, interviews.
35. ERM to Tom Stoddard, August 13, 1958.
36. *Time* (April 22, 1957).
37. Friendly, *Circumstances*.

38. ERM to Helen Sioussat, October 27, 1958.
39. Terry Turner, "Why Quiz Empire Collapsed," *Chicago Daily News*, October 18, 1958.
40. ERM, FYI, cc: John Day, Sidney Garfield, Sig Mickelson, James Seward, Arthur Hull Hayes, Lou Cowan, October 14, 1958, and October 15, 1958.
41. Joseph Wershba to Carl Sandburg, July 21, 1954.
42. *Chicago Sun-Times*, October 16, 1958.
43. William Benton to ERM, November 11, 1958.
44. John Kenneth Galbraith to ERM, November 13, 1958.
45. *New York Times*, November 2, 1958.
46. ERM to Paul Russell, January 8, 1958. (Russell to Murrow, December 29, 1958: "Jack Gould saw fit to comment . . . that you excused the broadcasters of all responsibility for 'public service' programs and that you placed the entire load on the sponsors. I re-read your article . . . and, sure enough, you had pointed out that the sponsors should be willing to ante up the time costs *and* the networks, in their turn, would be expected to pay for the programming costs. . . . [You also said] that there be a modest and brief mention of the sponsor and his product—and no more!" Murrow to Russell: "I am glad you bothered to reread my small Chicago effort. You grasped the essence of it. I am afraid Jack Gould did not.")
47. Salant, interviews.
48. Lester Markel to ERM, no date.
49. Lawrence Spivak to ERM, October 25, 1958.
50. Edward Barrett to ERM, November 20, 1958.
51. Irene Mayer Selznick, November 20, 1958.
52. ERM to Jack Beck, undated.
53. Mickelson, interviews.
54. Salant, interviews.
55. Paley, interviews.
56. John F. Day, memo re "election coverage meeting for the regional experts," September 22, 1958.
57. Otis, interview.
58. Mickelson, interviews.
59. Bliss, interview.
60. Smith, interviews.
61. Ibid.
62. *Chicago Daily News*, February 18, 1959; *New York Times*, November 9, 1958.
63. Katie Louchheim, *By the Political Sea* (New York: Doubleday, 1970).
64. Secretary's note, November 5, 1958.
65. ERM to Merritt R. C. Schoenfeld, December 5, 1958.
66. Material about this episode based on interview with Dr. Alvan Barach, April 7, 1977; also prescription slips, January 15, 1958 (probably 1959), plus undated, verified by Dr. Barach.
67. ERM to Agnes Meyer, February 5, 1959.
68. Lewis F. Powell to ERM, January 9, 1959.
69. Mack, interview.
70. *NAM News* editorial, January 30, 1959.
71. Friendly, interviews.

72. Quoted in letter of Steve Banker, WNEW, to ERM, January 21, 1959.
73. Ibid.
74. ERM to Joseph Ream, February 3, 1959.
75. ERM, letter of February 3, 1959.
76. Friendly, interviews.
77. ERM to Charles Collingwood, February 4, 1959.
78. Steve Allen, account to ERM, July 27, 1959.
79. Smith, interviews.
80. Bliss, interview.
81. Tree, interview.
82. Barach, interview.
83. Edward Bliss, "Remembering Edward R. Murrow," *Saturday Review* (May 31, 1975).
84. ERM to Frank Stanton, February 11, 1959.
85. *Chicago American*, February 18, 1959.
86. Luis Muñoz Marín to ERM, March 3, 1959.
87. Roger Baldwin to ERM, February 19, 1959.
88. Walter Lippmann to ERM, February 17, 1959.
89. Groucho Marx to ERM, April 15, 1959.
90. ERM to Thomas K. Finletter, March 16, 1969.
91. ERM to William D. Patterson, associate publisher, *Saturday Review*, March 19, 1959.
92. ERM to Ken Kantor, AFN, Frankfurt, March 23, 1959.
93. Sig Mickelson to Frank Stanton, "Confidential," February 20, 1959.
94. Ibid.
95. CBS, Reasoner-Murrow interview, February 17, 1959.
96. Harry Reasoner, memo to ERM, February 18, 1959.
97. Ibid.
98. ERM, memo to Harry Reasoner, February 20, 1959.
99. "Report of the CBS Special Committee," marked "Confidential," March 3, 1959. The material that follows is drawn from the report. The five committee members were, listed in alphabetical order: James T. Aubrey, Jr., Louis Hausman, Kidder Meade, Richard S. Salant, Arthur B. Tourtellot.
100. Mickelson, interviews.
101. Murrow and Friendly to Louis Cowan, April 1959.
102. Mr. Mickelson to Messrs. Paley, Cowan, cc: Dr. Stanton, April 17, 1959.
103. ERM to Martin Barnett, May 29, 1959.
104. Friendly, *Circumstances*.
105. *Washington Post*, editorial, February 21, 1959.
106. Stanton, interviews.
107. Ibid.
108. Sig Mickelson to Frank Stanton, February 20, 1959, op. cit.
109. Stanton, interviews; also Sig Mickelson, memo for the file, June 16, 1959.
110. Sig Mickelson, file memo, "Conversation with Dr. Stanton, Confidential," July 24, 1959.
111. Sig Mickelson, memo for the file, June 16, 1959.
112. Mickelson, interviews.
113. Fred Friendly to Sig Mickelson, memo of June 15, 1959.
114. ERM to Han Suyin, April 6, 1959.

115. Friendly, to Mickelson, memo of June 15, 1959.
116. Mickelson, memo for the file, June 18, 1959, re conversation with Fred Friendly Tuesday, June 16.
117. Sig Mickelson, memo of June 16.
118. Sig Mickelson, memo of June 18.
119. Sig Mickelson, memo of June 16.
120. Sig Mickelson, interviews.
121. Friendly, interviews.
122. Sig Mickelson, memo for the file, June 29 and July 1, 1959, summary of ninety-minute conversation with ERM on Thursday, June 25.
123. Sig Mickelson, memo for the file, July 2, 1959.
124. Mickelson, interviews.
125. Sig Mickelson, memo for the file, July 8, 1959, conversation with Fred Friendly on Tuesday, July 7.
126. Sig Mickelson, memo for the file, July 8, 1959, meeting with ERM and Friendly on Wednesday, July 8, at 1:00 P.M.
127. Mickelson, interviews.
128. Sig Mickelson to Frank Stanton, Fred Friendly, and ERM, July 14, 1959, draft, record of the meeting of Stanton, Friendly, Murrow, and Mickelson at 10:00 P.M., Wednesday, July 8, in Stanton's office; also penciled notes of meeting and handwritten notations on typed draft; also subsequent draft of July 17, 1959.
129. Friendly, *Circumstances*.
130. Sig Mickelson to ERM and Fred Friendly, cc: Frank Stanton, July 17, 1959, final draft, summary of discussion, 10:00 P.M. Wednesday, July 8, in Stanton's office.
131. CBS News, announcement, July 20, 1959.
132. Smith, interviews.
133. Warburg, interviews.

XV. " . . . TO LOVE THE NEWS"

1. John Schultz, interview of July 25, 1973, hereafter referred to as Schultz, interview.
2. McClure, interviews.
3. Bernstein, interview.
4. *New York Times*, October 17, 1959.
5. Ibid.
6. Ibid., October 18, 1959.
7. Stanton, interviews.
8. *New York Times*, October 20, 1959.
9. Stanton, interviews.
10. Jack Gould, interview of September 19, 1981, hereafter referred to as Gould, interview.
11. *New York Times*, October 20, 1959.
12. Gould, interview; also Gould to author, letter of September 21, 1981.
13. Janet Murrow, letter of October 25, 1959.
14. Frank Stanton to Jesse Zousmer and John Aaron, cc: Edward R. Murrow, October 22, 1959; also *New York Times*, October 23, 1959.

15. *New York Times*, October 23, 1959.
16. Stanton, interviews.
17. ERM to James M. Seward, October 26, 1959.
18. Bernstein, interview.
19. Beck, interview.
20. Janet Murrow, letter of October 25, 1959.
21. Mickelson, interviews.
22. *New York Times*, October 25, 1959.
23. Murrow to Seward, October 26, 1959.
24. Colin, interview.
25. Ibid.
26. Mickelson, interviews.
27. Colin, interview.
28. Draft statement, October 1959, sent to J. M. Seward, FYI, November 21; also Murrow files.
29. Colin, interview.
30. Ralph Colin, datebook, 1959.
31. Colin, interview.
32. Colin, datebook.
33. Colin, interview.
34. Stanton, interviews.
35. Colin, interview.
36. ERM to J. M. Seward, undated.
37. Janet Murrow, letter of November 4, 1959.
38. Ernst, interview.
39. Bessie, interviews.
40. J. B. Clark to Controller, Overseas Services, November 12, 1959.
41. "VMS to Mr. Hodson," November 12, 1959, covering note to above.
42. *New York Times*, October 28, 1959.
43. Hearing transcript, quoted in *The New York Times*, November 7, 1959.
44. Janet Murrow, letter of December 7, 1959.
45. Ibid.
46. ERM to J. M. Seward, January 15, 1960.
47. ERM to Seward, December 12, 1959.
48. ERM to Ethel Murrow, no date.
49. ERM to Seward, December 12, 1959.
50. ERM to Seward, January 15, 1960.
51. Ibid.
52. Ibid.
53. ERM to Raymond Swing, December 5, 1959.
54. ERM to Seward, January 15, 1960.
55. ERM to Seward, March 1, 1960.
56. Mickelson, interviews.
57. Mr. Lang to Sig Mickelson, September 9, 1959.
58. Mickelson, memo for the file, November 19, 1959, "conversation with Fred Friendly at lunch, November 19."
59. Sig Mickelson to Frank Stanton, marked "Confidential," November 27, 1959.
60. ERM to James Seward, February 21, 1960.
61. Casey Murrow, interviews.

62. Friendly, interviews.
63. Casey Murrow, interviews.
64. ERM to Seward, February 2, 1960.
65. Casey Murrow, interviews.
66. ERM to Seward, February 16, 1960.
67. ERM to Seward, February 2, 1960.
68. ERM to Seward, February 21, 1960.
69. ERM to Seward, February 2, 1960
70. ERM to Seward, March 1, 1960.
71. Ibid.
72. ERM to Seward, March 20, 1960.
73. Ibid.
74. Ibid.
75. ERM to Seward, undated.
76. Janet Murrow, interviews.
77. Beck, interview.
78. Friendly, interviews.
79. A certain amount of shooting was also done abroad on a *CBS Reports* called "Rescue," in which the actor Yul Brynner participated. Murrow was not happy with the result. "We must stop trying to use Hollywood as reporters," he wrote James Seward on February 2, 1960.
80. Bonsignori, interviews.
81. Schultz, interview.
82. Salant, interviews.
83. Bonsignori, interviews.
84. Beck, interview.
85. "Lang to Hylan," undated; copy marked "S.M. FYI."
86. Sig Mickelson to Frank Stanton, marked "Confidential," November 25, 1959.
87. Schultz, interview.
88. CBS News Division, Structural Organization, draft, October 6, 1958, Reference No. 1-A.1. ("CBS Management Guide—Organization").
89. CBS News Division, "Organizational Chart, 12/9/59."
90. *Background*, August 7, 1960.
91. Beck, interview.
92. Ibid.
93. Mack, interview.
94. Schultz, interview.
95. Friendly, interviews.
96. Schultz, interviews.
97. Bliss, interviews.
98. Friendly, interviews.
99. *Background*, July 3, 1960.
100. Beck, interview.
101. Sig Mickelson, memo for the file, June 29, 1959.
102. AP, June 6, 1960.
103. Beck, interview.
104. Salant, interviews.
105. Downs, interviews.

106. Democratic Convention, Sports Arena, Los Angeles, July 12, 1960, CBS News.
107. *Variety*, July 31, 1960.
108. Hewitt, interview.
109. Mickelson, interviews.
110. Smith, interviews.
111. July 13, 1960, CBS News.
112. Ibid.
113. Downs, interviews.
114. July 13, 1960, CBS News.
115. Otis, interview.
116. *Variety*, July 20, 1960.
117. *New York Times*, July 15, 1960 and July 17, 1960.
118. *New York Times*, July 27, 1960.
119. *Variety*, August 3, 1960.
120. Republican Convention, International Amphitheater, Chicago, July 26, 1960, CBS News.
121. Ibid.
122. Ibid.
123. "Official Proceedings of the Twenty-seventh Republican National Convention," July 27, 1960.
124. Ibid., July 28, 1960.
125. Beck, interview.
126. Mickelson, interviews.
127. Sig Mickelson, memo for the files, August 29, 1960, meeting with William Paley, August 29.
128. Ibid.
129. Mickelson, interviews.
130. Mickelson, file memo, August 29, 1960.
131. ERM to Frank Darvall, September 1, 1960.
132. Schultz, interview.
133. Friendly, interviews.
134. Schultz, interview.
135. Ibid.
136. ERM, memo to Cabell Greet, September 27, 1960.
137. *Background*, August 7, 1960.
138. Smith, interviews.
139. *Background*, October 16, 1960.
140. Ibid., October 30, 1960, commentary, typescript, marked "Not used."
141. Ibid., August 7, 1960.
142. Ibid., October 2, 1960.
143. ERM to Joseph Wershba, October 10, 1960.
144. Skedgell, interviews.
145. ERM to Remsen Bird, November 23, 1960.
146. ERM to Eric Sevareid, November 23, 1960.
147. ERM to Wilmott Ragsdale, January 18, 1961.
148. ERM to Remsen Bird, November 22, 1960.
149. ERM to Louis Cowan, December 14, 1960.
150. *Variety*, November 30, 1960.

151. Ibid., February 8, 1961.
152. Sig Mickelson, memorandum to Sylvan Gotshal, Weil, Gotshal & Manges, cc: N. S. Bienstock, July 24, 1961.
153. Mickelson, interviews.
154. Salant, interviews.
155. Friendly, *Circumstances*.
156. Friendly, interviews.
157. New York *Times*, July 17, 1960.
158. Friendly, interviews.
159. The Tampa [FL] *Tribune*, clipping, no date.
160. Downs, interviews.
161. Ibid.
162. Stanton, interviews; also Stanton, letter to the author, July 22, 1981.
163. Smith, interviews.
164. Sir Hugh Greene, interview of May 28, 1981, hereafter referred to as Greene, interview.
165. Ibid.
166. Ibid.
167. ERM, speech before Newsmakers Luncheon, Radio and Television Executives Society, January 12, 1961.
168. Bernstein, interview.
169. Chester Bowles to ERM, January 11, 1961.
170. Bliss, op. cit.
171. Skedgell, interviews.
172. Downs, interviews.
173. Salisbury, interview.
174. Thad Holt to David Lowe, January 13, 1961.
175. The Reverend C. Herbert Oliver, interview of April 11, 1984.
176. Salisbury, interview.
177. Oliver, interview.
178. Ibid.
179. Oliver to ERM, January 26, 1961.
180. Kay Campbell to Herbert Oliver, February 17, 1961.
181. Smith, interviews.
182. Friendly, interviews.
183. Paley, interviews.
184. Stanton, interviews.
185. David Halberstam, *The Powers That Be* (New York: Knopf, 1979).
186. Friendly, interviews.
187. Bonsignori, interviews.
188. Rosemary Mullen to Bertha R. Schoen, February 13, 1960.
189. Hugh Greene to ERM, January 31, 1961.
190. Greene, interview.
191. John F. Kennedy to ERM, March 10, 1961: draft letter based on previous conversations defining Murrow's and USIA's role; prepared for the President's signature; draft sent by Murrow to McGeorge Bundy, White House, March 10, 1961; see also Murrow, covering memo for McGeorge Bundy, same date.
192. James Lavenstein, interview of January 20, 1977.

193. Cioffi, interviews.
194. Sig Mickelson, memo to Sylvan Gotshal, July 24, 1961.
195. "CBS News Shuffles at Top," *Broadcasting*, February 6, 1961; also *Variety*, February 1, 1961.
196. Cioffi, interviews.
197. "A Network of Incongruities," *Variety*, February 8, 1961.
198. Salant, interviews.
199. *Variety*, February 8, 1961.
200. *Background*, January 8, 1961, typescript.
201. Ibid.

XVI. WASHINGTON

1. Donald M. Wilson, interview of June 14, 1973, hereafter referred to as Wilson, interview.
2. Chester Bowles, *Promises to Keep: My Years in Public Life, 1941–1969* (New York: Harper & Row, 1971).
3. Henry Loomis, interview of April 4, 1985, hereafter referred to as Loomis, interview.
4. Wilson, interview.
5. Otis, interview.
6. Gabrielle Wachsner Levenson, interview, 1973, undated.
7. Marvin Kalb to ERM, March 24, 1961.
8. ERM to Kalb, April 3, 1961.
9. Bureau File No. 62-86094, handwritten notation, October 10, 1956.
10. Bureau File No. 161-296, Subject: Edward R. Murrow/ Special Inquiry, memo of February 8, 1961.
11. Ibid., Field Office File, No. 161-57, Philadelphia, Pennsylvania: investigations at Philadelphia, Pa., Temple University and Allentown, Pa., Muhlenberg College, report dated February 9, 1961.
12. Ibid., teletype, February 9, 1961, from SAC New York; also report of February 9, 1961, New York Office, cover page E; also AIRTEL, February 7, 1961, to Director, from SAC, Washington Field Office (161–176); also Report from Washington Field Office, February 20, 1961, memorandum of February 20, 1961.
13. Ibid., handwritten notation.
14. Ibid. C.A. Evans to Mr. Parsons. Memorandum of February 21, 1961.
15. Ibid., handwritten notation.
16. AP, March 4, 1961.
17. Before the Foreign Relations Committee, U.S. Senate, statement by Edward R. Murrow, March 14, 1961.
18. Respectively, J. Graham Parson to Sweden and Frances E. Willis to Ceylon.
19. Loomis, interview.
20. Wilson, interview.
21. Greene, interview.
22. *New York Daily Mirror*, March 9, 1961.
23. UPI, February 16, 1961.
24. Greene, interview.
25. Wilson, interview.

26. Quoted in *The Times* of London, March 26, 1961.

27. *The Times* of London, March 26, 1961.

28. BBC, Board of Management, minutes of meeting held on Monday, March 27, 1961: "Other Matters."

29. Ed Jones, interview of April 25, 1977.

30. Janet Murrow, interviews.

31. ERM, memorandum for: Heads of Elements and PAOs, December 20, 1963 re priorities for Agency output, first issued July 24, 1961; also Thomas Sorensen, *The Word War: The Story of American Propaganda* (New York: Harper & Row, 1968).

32. Stanley Plesent, interviews of June 11, 1973 and July 12, 1973, hereafter referred to as Plesent, interviews.

33. Ibid.

34. Donald M. Wilson, "Memorandum for: All Heads of Elements," March 13, 1961.

35. Sorensen, op. cit.

36. Ibid.; also Robert E. Elder, *The Information Machine: The United States Information Agency and American Foreign Policy* (Syracuse, N.Y.: Syracuse University Press, 1968).

37. Claiborne Pell to ERM, August 23, 1962.

38. Elder, op. cit.

39. Burnett Anderson, interview of April 6, 1985, hereafter referred to as Anderson, interview.

40. Hans Tuch, interview of April 2, 1985, hereafter referred to as Tuch, interview.

41. ERM to Allen Dulles, "Secret," April 18, 1961.

42. Mickelson, interviews.

43. Wilson, interview.

44. ERM, memo for IOP—Mr. Sorensen, June 17, 1961.

45. Memo from IOC—Mr. Marlow, January 26, 1962.

46. Abbott Washburn to Donald M. Wilson, August, 4, 1961.

47. IOC—Marlow, January 26, 1962.

48. Washburn to Wilson, op. cit.

49. IAL, Hewson A. Ryan, memo to ERM, February 28, 1962.

50. ERM to James A. Perkins, May 3, 1962.

51. IOC—Sanford S. Marlow to ERM, February 9, 1962.

52. Ibid.

53. IOC—Charles E. Harner, "Memorandum to Mr. Murrow, Mr. Wilson; Subject: Increased Interest of American Businessmen in Latin America," August 10, 1962.

54. *Report of Committee on Immediate Communist Danger in Latin America*, United States Inter-American Council, December 12, 1961.

55. IAL—Ryan to ERM, op. cit.

56. IOC—Marlow to ERM, December 20, 1961.

57. John Fischer to ERM, January 30, 1961.

58. Reed Harris, "Memorandum for IOA—Mr. Schmidt," June 25, 1962; Reed Harris, "Memorandum for IOA—Mr. Schmidt," June 2, 1962.

59. Bernstein, interview.

60. Orvil E. Dryfoos to ERM, May 8, 1961.

61. ERM to Dryfoos, May 10, 1961.

62. IBS—Henry Loomis to ERM, "Subject: USIA Cooperation with The New York *Times*," June 14, 1961.

63. Tillman Durdin of the *New York Times* Editorial Board broadcast for the Voice until January, 1962. Although approval for the broadcasts was originally given by the *Times*, he wrote Harold Courlander of the VOA on January 2, the publisher's office had now ruled that staff members should not engage in this activity, and he must therefore terminate his broadcasts.

64. Blair Clark to ERM, telegram, March 1, 1961.

65. Richard S. Salant to Abbott Washburn, March 6, 1961.

66. Washburn, handwritten notation to Don Wilson on cc of response to Richard Salant, March 9, 1961.

67. ERM to David Sarnoff, March 2, 1961.

68. To ERM, unsigned, draft letter describing status of ERM employment contract with CBS and nature of "the current business transactions between CBS and the Agency"; from CBS, "February, 1961."

69. Ibid.

70. ERM to Sarnoff, March 2, 1961.

71. Robert Kintner to William McAndrew, March 9, 1961.

72. Listing: *"Persons who have volunteered their services to the Director" (through Feb. 14, 1961).*

73. ERM to Kintner, *"PERSONAL AND CONFIDENTIAL,"* April 11, 1962, "Dear Bob. . . ."

74. ERM to Fred Friendly, "Personal," June 17, 1961; also Friendly to ERM, June 21, 1961.

75. ITV—Romney Wheeler, memo to Reed Harris: "Agency Relations with U.S. Television Networks," November 7, 1961.

76. Smith, interviews.

77. ERM to Newton N. Minow, May 10, 1961.

78. Salant, interviews.

79. Smith, interviews.

80. Ibid.

81. Robert Lewis Shayon, "Why Did Howard K. Smith Leave?" *Saturday Review* (November 18, 1961).

82. Smith, interviews.

83. Before the Subcommittee on Overseas Information Programs, statement by Edward R. Murrow, March 26, 1953.

84. Ibid.; also Greene, interview.

85. IRS—Oren Stephens to Mr. Murrow, subject: An Evaluation of VOA—Russian Programs, "Official Use Only," February 16, 1962.

86. Loomis, interview. To illustrate his point, Loomis cites his classic anecdote. He was in southern Tanzania in the early sixties, on safari, "close to the end of the world," stopped to rest under a tree, waiting for his transportation to arrive. "There was a guy sitting next to me—tattered white shirt, shorts, barefoot, dusty." After a try in Swahili, the "native" addressed Loomis in perfectly accented Oxford English: "By the way, why did you chaps send a rocket to the moon this morning?" They got into what Loomis called "one of the most difficult political conversations I've ever been in. He knew all *kinds* of facts—the steel production of Russia, what our steel production

was; I don't know whether his facts were right or wrong, I don't know *what* the hell our tonnage is!" Loomis gave him a lift down the road to his house: "a typical mud and wattle house; the only difference was, there was a little wire coming out of the smoke hole, going up to a palm tree. This guy listened to—Moscow, BBC, VOA, Peking. . . . I said, what else do you do? Well, there was no movie, he could read but there were no books, no newspapers. No car to drive down and visit Aunt Susie. He was the political leader of that section—he was a member of TANU, the Tanganyika African National Union—he was the single most important guy there. He didn't believe *anything* that he read; or that he heard. He compared. He tried to select out first of all what was important to *him*; secondly what was important to TANU, thirdly what was important to Tanzania, and, way down the line, Africa. And after that, all the decisions I had to make, I kept thinking of that guy—what would be the way to have *him* understand what we were saying, and care about what we said, and believe what we said. A lot of being politically active doesn't necessarily mean that you've got shoes. But it's a very clear peasant sense of smelling a phony; and that's what international broadcasting is all about."

87. Anderson, interview.
88. Greene, interview.
89. Singer, interviews; also Lilienthal, op. cit.
90. *The Pentagon Papers* (New York: Quadrangle Books, 1971).
91. Ibid.
92. R. Franklin Smith, op. cit.
93. *Pentagon Papers*, pp. 131–32.
94. *Edward R. Murrow with the News*, January 14, 1952.
95. Donald M. Wilson, "Memo for: Personnel File—John Anspacher," March 30, 1962.
96. Reed Harris: Memorandum for IOA/T—Mr. Grenoble, April 9, 1962.
97. Maxwell D. Taylor, "Memorandum for the Director, United States Information Agency, May 19, 1962."
98. ERM, "Memorandum for all office and services heads, May 10, 1962, Subject: Counter-Insurgency Training: ' "In response to a memorandum from the White House. . . ." '
99. ERM, memorandum marked "Confidential Group IV," March 26, 1962; also Wilson, Memorandum for Personnel File, John Anspacher, March 30, 1962; also ERM, Memorandum of May 10, "For all office and service heads," op. cit.
100. ERM, Memorandum of May 10, op. cit.
101. ITV—Romney Wheeler to IAF—Mr. Neilson, August 10, 1961: "TV Mobile Units for Viet Nam."
102. W.K. Bunce (IAF) to ERM, September 24, 1962.
103. *Pentagon Papers*, excerpts from "A Program of Action for South Vietnam," May 8, 1961; p. 127.
104. ERM, "Memorandum for: Mr. Wilson," July 12, 1962.
105. National Security Action Memorandum No. 180, marked *"CONFIDENTIAL,"* from McGeorge Bundy, August 13, 1962.
106. Bunce to ERM, September 24, 1962.
107. IOA/T—John M. Anspacher to ERM, September 24, 1960.

108. Anspacher to ERM, July 3, 1962.
109. Anderson, interview.
110. Wilson, interview.
111. Sorensen, op. cit.
112. Edward R. Murrow, "Memorandum for Heads of Agency Elements," July 31, 1962.
113. Anspacher to Harris, September 13, 1962.
114. Sorensen to ERM, July 31, 1962; with note from Reed Harris: "Discussed fully at 5 pm . . . meeting 8/1."
115. ERM, "Memorandum for The President," marked "SECRET—Group III," November 27, 1961.
116. Robert Pierpoint, interview of December 10, 1984.
117. Sorensen, op. cit.
118. Glenn L. Smith: for the files, "Meeting on Equal Employment Opportunity on October 31, 1961," dated November 1, 1961.
119. Cable, "for PAO Group 4, January 26, 1962; also cable, "to Murrow, EYES ONLY—USITO Leopoldville," January 16, 1962.
120. Bernard Eismann, telephone interview of August 9, 1981.
121. Howard K. Smith to ERM, December 17, 1962.
122. Plesent, interviews.
123. Ibid.
124. Sorensen, op. cit.
125. Janet Murrow, interviews.
126. Casey Murrow, interviews.
127. *The Washington Post,* June 13, 1961.
128. ERM, "Memorandum for the President," April 23, 1962.
129. William Worthy, "The Nation of Islam," *Midstream,* (Spring 1962).
130. *New York Times,* August 7, 1962.
131. Downs, interviews.
132. Ibid.
133. ERM for IAF—Mr. Neilson, "Limited Official Use," February 1, 1962.
134. Tuch, interview.
135. ERM, "Memorandum For The President, Subject: Considerations regarding Nuclear Testing," marked "Confidential," August 31, 1961.
136. Ibid.; also ERM, "Memorandum For The President," marked "Confidential," September 1, 1961; ERM, "Memorandum For The President, Subject: Reactions to Nuclear Tests," marked "Confidential—Group 3," undated.
137. Anderson, interview.
138. Reed Harris to IBS—Mr. Loomis, January 5, 1962; also IBS—Arthur V. Hummel to Mr. Harris, January 9, 1962, initialed by ERM.
139. ERM, handwritten note on Loomis memo of December 29, 1961, to ERM.
140. Louis Nizer to ERM, May 13, 1962; also secretary's notes to ERM, May 17, 1962.
141. ERM, notation on secretary's notes, May 17, 1962; also secretary's note to ERM, May 22, 1962.
142. ERM to Frank Kelly, Center for the Study of Democratic Institutions, The Fund for the Republic, July 24, 1962.
143. Richard Heffner, interviews of April 27, 1984 and May 21, 1984, hereafter referred to as Heffner, interviews.

144. Plesent, interviews.

145. Katie Louchheim Klopfer, telephone interview of February 20, 1982.

146. William B. King, Assistant Director, Near East and South Asia, to Robert Lincoln, February 8, 1962.

147. Janet Murrow, interviews.

148. Memorandum of Record, Thomas C. Sorensen, January 10, 1962.

149. Thomas C. Sorensen, "Memorandum for Mr. Murrow, Subject: Voice of America—The Policy Issue," November 9, 1962.

150. ERM, memorandum, "Voice of America Policy," December 4, 1962; also ERM, "Memorandum For: IBS—Mr. Loomis," December 4, 1962.

151. Mary McGrory, "Voice Chiefs Chafe at Curbs," Washington *Evening Star*, March 5, 1965, quoted in Sorensen, op. cit.

152. ERM to The Honorable John W. Tuthill, Alternate U.S. Representative to the OECD, April 5, 1962.

153. Edward G. Lansdale, Report of the Saigon Military Mission, excerpts, *The Pentagon Papers*, loc. cit.

154. Homer Bigart to ERM, March 3, 1962.

155. IAF—W.K. Bunce to ERM, "Subject: Threatened Expulsion of U.S. Correspondents from Viet-Nam," marked "*SECRET* (GROUP III)," March 30, 1962.

156. James Reston, *New York Times*, February 13, 1962, and *New York Times*, editorial: "The Truth About Vietnam," undated, probably same date.

157. James Reston, interview of April 3, 1985, hereafter referred to as Reston, interview.

158. George W. Ball, Acting Secretary, to "The Honorable Edward R. Murrow," marked "Confidential," June 21, 1962.

159. IAF—W.K. Bunce: "Memorandum for: Mr. Murrow, Thru: Mr. Wilson," September 19, 1962.

160. "Eyes Only For Mowinckel From Wilson," drafted by D. M. Wilson, over Murrow's name, marked "Group 3," May 22, 1962; also "Saigon USITO, Eyes Only For Mecklin From Wilson/Neilson, Priority," drafted by D. M. Wilson, over Murrow's name, May 24, 1962; Donald M. Wilson to John Mecklin, marked "Secret—Group 4," June 19, 1962; Wilson to Mecklin, marked "Secret—Group 4, Official-Informal," August 1, 1962.

161. Sterling J. Cottrell, Deputy Assistant Secretary of State, to Michael V. Forrestal, Esquire, Senior Staff Member of the National Security Council, marked "Confidential," September 11, 1962, citing "a list of recent accomplishments"; also Forrestal to Cottrell, September 13, 1962.

162. Henry Cabot Lodge to John Mecklin, marked "Limited official use," December 23, 1963.

163. ERM to John Mecklin, marked "Unclassified/ Official-Informal," December 14, 1962.

164. Lodge to Mecklin, op. cit. Compared with later, it was a modest operation. The big problem in 1962–63 was coming up with $35,000 to buy projectors.

165. W. Averell Harriman, memo to ERM, June 5, 1962.

166. George S. Franklin, Jr., Executive Director, Council on Foreign Relations, to W. Averell Harriman, June 4, 1962; thermofax copy from Harriman to ERM, June 5, 1962.

167. IAF—W.K. Bunce, "Memorandum for Mr. Wilson, Subject: Your Appoint-

ment with Secretary Thuan of Viet-Nam," September 19, 1962; also Bunce, memo to Wilson, "Talking Points with Secretary Thuan of Viet-Nam," September 20, 1962; "Memorandum of Conversation, Subject: Visit of Secretary of State for the Presidency Thuan of Viet-Nam to USIA (Mr. Wilson's office)," marked "Confidential," September 21, 1962.

168. Bunce to Wilson, September 20, 1962.

169. "Draft Memorandum from Edward R. Murrow," marked "Confidential— Group 4," December 21, 1961; also covering letter, ERM to Roger Tubby, State Department, Arthur Sylvester, Defense Department, December 21, 1961.

170. Daniel E. Moore, Deputy Assistant Director, Far East, to Donald M. Wilson, "Subject: Vietnamese Government's Press Relations," marked "Secret," October 2, 1962.

171. Moore to Murrow, "Subject: Memorandum on 'Press Relations' from John Mecklin to Ambassador Nolting," marked "Secret," December 10, 1962.

172. "John M. Mecklin/ The Ambassador/ Press Relations," memo, 8 pages, marked "Secret-Noform," November 27, 1962.

173. Ibid.

174. David Halberstam to Ambassador Nolting, copy, unsigned, undated, enclosed with memorandum to Nolting from John Mecklin, i.e., "Attached is a hastily written letter to you which Halberstam composed in my office. . . ."

175. Mecklin to Nolting, op. cit.

176. ERM to W. Averell Harriman, no date.

177. Harriman to Nolting, marked "Official-Informal/ Secret," January 25, 1963.

178. "Proposed itinerary for Mr. Edward R. Murrow," 1962 files, undated, handwritten notation by Reed Harris: "This one ok'd 4/19 by ERM."

179. Department of State, "Memorandum to: The Secretary, Subject: Regulations on Travel Control of U.S. Citizens," April, 1963, undated, semifinal draft; submitted to ERM April 18, 1963.

180. Burnett Anderson to Donald M. Wilson, May 15, 1963.

181. IAL—Richard C. Salvatierra, to IBS—Henry Loomis, marked "Limited Official Use Only," June 28, 1962.

182. Ibid.; also IAL—Hewson A. Ryan, to ERM, "Subject: Multi-Media Effort to Tell Cuban Story in Perspective," December 7, 1962.

183. Donald M. Wilson, "Memorandum to: The Honorable Edwin M. Martin, Assistant Secretary, Bureau of Inter-American Affairs, Department of State, Subject: Jamming of Cuban Broadcasts to the Dominican Republic," May 3, 1962. Wrote Wilson at the time, "USIA, as a matter of policy, does not engage in jamming any broadcasts. In fact, we criticize Communist jamming as an abridgment of freedom of information. . . . In any case, such jamming would certainly cause interference with other stations in other countries in the area, and would be a violation of the North American Broadcasting Agreement, to which the United States and the Dominican Republic are signatories."

184. ERM, "Memorandum For: The Honorable Dean Rusk, Secretary of State, Subject: U.S. Student Travel to Cuba," marked "Limited Official Use, cc: The White House—Mr. McGeorge Bundy," December 18, 1962.

185. "Inter-Agency Task Group for Public Affairs in Connection with Test Ban

Negotiations and Disarmament, Subject: USIA Comment on State's Working
Paper of July 31," marked "Confidential," August 4, 1961.

186. ERM to Nitze, March 1, 1963, requested comments re "Test Ban Recommendations." Nitze's office subsequently requested and received permission to send a copy of the memo to the U.S. Arms Control and Disarmament Agency, March 21, 1963.

187. Robert Mayer Evans, "To Reed Harris, Memorandum of Meeting, Subject: Operation of the New Soviet Branch," August 15, 1962.

188. IAF—Paul Neilson to ERM, "Subject: Another 'Look' at Defoliation in Viet-Nam," marked "Secret (Group III)," March 20, 1962.

189. ERM to Harriman, April 19, 1963; also Bunce to Wilson, "Subject: Task Force/Saigon's Evaluation of Herbicide Operations," marked "Secret—Group 3," December 15, 1963.

190. Murrow to Harriman, op. cit.

191. Bunce to Wilson, op. cit.

192. "Minutes of the Far Eastern PAO Conference," March 15 and 16, 1962.

193. Roger Hilsman, interview of August 5, 1985.

194. Janet Murrow, interviews.

195. Sorensen, op. cit.

196. ERM, memo to Richard M. Gardner, Department of State, "Subject: Proposed Presidential Speech at the United Nations," August, 1963. The proposals went under the heading of "the confrontation of ideas."

197. Kenneth Adam, "Seeing It Then," *The Listener* (March 21, 1968).

198. Tuch, interview.

199. John F. Kennedy to ERM, marked "Draft," March 10, 1961.

200. June, 1963, no date, memorandum to Wilson and Sorensen, quoted in Sorensen, op. cit.

201. Paley, interviews.

202. Heffner, interviews.

203. Smithers, interview.

204. Mecklin to ERM, September 9, 1963.

205. Lowell Bennett, Director, Office of Public Information, USIA, to ERM, September 17, 1963.

206. Memorandum by Maj. Gen. Victor H. Krulak, special assistant to the Joint Chiefs of Staff for counterinsurgency and special activities, on a meeting at the State Department, August 31, 1963, quoted in *Pentagon Papers,* loc. cit. Kattenberg's withdrawal suggestion, says Hilsman, had been raised "several times" by Robert Kennedy. Hilsman's position on the scene as described is that Kattenberg, a career Foreign Service officer FSO-3, was speaking for everyone at Far East in the State Department, drawing on departmental studies. "No FSO-3 is going to speak up in a National Security Council meeting unless he's sitting on top of a bunch of *paper.* The point of it is that none of that paper appears in *The Pentagon Papers.* Because nobody in the State Department was going to send Bob McNamara a copy of a document that could be used against us. So all the documents that were studying about getting out don't appear. *The Pentagon Papers* are only one side of the story."

207. Marguerite Higgins, *Our Vietnam Nightmare* (New York: Harper & Row, 1965).

208. Ibid.
209. Cablegram from Ambassador Lodge to Secretary Rusk, August 29, 1963.
210. Lower, interview.
211. Salant, interviews.
212. Reston, interview.
213. David Schoenbrun to ERM, June 18, 1963.
214. ERM to Schoenbrun, June 22, 1963.
215. Lower, interview.
216. ERM, speech before the Federal Bar Association, September 26, 1963.
217. Plesent, interviews.
218. Heller, interview.
219. Tuch, interview.
220. Wilson, interview.
221. Sorensen, op. cit.
222. Plesent, interviews.
223. ERM, to "The President of the United States," December 19, 1963.
224. Wilson, interview.
225. Quoted by Henry Loomis, President, Corporation for Public Broadcasting, Presentation Speech of the Edward R. Murrow Award, March 2, 1978.
226. Sorensen, op. cit.

XVII. TWILIGHT

1. Heffner, interviews.
2. ERM to J.M. Seward, no date, note: "Received Feb. 12, 1964."
3. Paley, interviews.
4. ERM to J. M. Seward, no date.
5. ERM to Seward, "saturday," no date.
6. ERM to Seward, no date.
7. Friendly, interviews.
8. ERM to Jesse Zousmer, April 1, 1964.
9. ERM to Chester Bowles, March 25, 1964.
10. Henry Loomis to ERM, January 22, 1964.
11. William King to ERM, January 23, 1964.
12. Don Wilson to ERM, March 14, 1964.
13. ERM to Wilson, March 23, 1964.
14. John Mecklin to ERM, March 16, 1964.
15. To ERM; McGeorge Bundy, George Ball, Michael Forrestal, overall date given as February 23, 1964.
16. Howard and Benedicte Smith, interviews.
17. Warburg, interviews.
18. Janet Murrow to Sidney Bernstein, July 4, 1964.
19. ERM to Dr. Worth Daniels, September 30, 1964.
20. ERM to Sidney Bernstein, August 18, 1964.
21. ERM to Chester Bowles, March 25, 1964.
22. Bowles, New Delhi, to ERM, March 13, 1964.
23. Quoted in Halberstam, *The Powers That Be*, loc. cit.
24. Teddy and Amos Kollek, *For Jerusalem: A Life by Teddy Kollek* (New York: Random House, 1978).

25. ERM to Sidney Bernstein, August 18, 1964.
26. Wershba, interviews.
27. ERM to Robert Oppenheimer,
28. Chester Bowles to ERM, March 13, 1964.
29. ERM to Bowles, March 25, 1964.
30. Halberstam, *The Powers That Be*, loc. cit.
31. Ibid.
32. Eric Sevareid, "Sevareid Recalls the Murrow Magic," column clipping, undated.
33. Chester Williams, interviews.
34. *Farewell To Studio Nine*, July 25, 1964, transcript.
35. Irving Gitlin to ERM, July 25, 1964.
36. Jack Gould, "Style and Authority: Looking Ahead with Edward R. Murrow," *New York Times*, February 2, 1964.
37. Bonsignori, interviews.
38. Gude, interviews.
39. Shirer, interviews.
40. ERM to Dr. Worth Daniels, September 30, 1964.
41. Seward, interviews.
42. Dr. Gary I. Wadler to ERM, undated.
43. Collingwood, interviews.
44. Warburg, interviews.
45. Seward, interviews.
46. Paley, interviews.
47. Janet Murrow, interviews.
48. Warburg, interviews.
49. Downs, interviews.
50. Casey Murrow, interviews.
51. Hirshon, interview.
52. Tree, interview.
53. Alan Moorehead to ERM, handwritten, "February 5."
54. Casey Murrow, interviews.
55. Janet Murrow to Sandra and Sidney Bernstein, May 10, 1965.
56. McClure, interviews.
57. Frank Gillard to Janet Murrow, April 30, 1965.
58. Gervasi, interview.

BIBLIOGRAPHY

Most of the material relating to Murrow was derived from primary manuscript sources. A complete listing of primary material appears in the introduction to the notes.

The books listed below supplemented my archival research.

AMBROSE, STEPHEN E. Vol. 1, *Eisenhower: Soldier, General of the Army, President-elect, 1890–1952,*. Vol. 2, *The President, 1952–1960*. New York: Simon & Schuster, 1983 and 1984.

ARONSON, JAMES. *The Press and the Cold War*. Indianapolis and New York: Bobbs-Merrill, 1970.

BACKER, JOHN H. *The Decision to Divide Germany: American Foreign Policy in Transition*. Durham, North Carolina: Duke University Press, 1978.

BARNOUWE, ERIK. *The Golden Web: A History of Broadcasting in the United States*. Vol. 2. *1933–1953*. New York: Oxford University Press, 1968.

———. *The Image Empire: A History of Broadcasting in the United States*, Vol. 3, *from 1953*. New York: Oxford University Press, 1970.

BOWLES, CHESTER. *Promises to Keep: My Years in Public Life, 1941–1969*. New York: Harper & Row, 1971.

BRAESTRUP, PETER. *Big Story: How the American Press and Television Reported and Interpreted the Crisis of Tet 1968 in Vietnam and Washington*. Westview Special Studies in Communication. Published in cooperation with Freedom House. Boulder, Colorado: Westview Press, 1977.

BRIGGS, ASA. *The War of Wards*. The History of Broadcasting in the United Kingdom, Vol. 3: London, New York, and Toronto: Oxford University Press, 1970.

BROWN, ANTHONY CAVE. *The Last Hero: Wild Bill Donovan*. New York: Times Books, 1983.

BROWN, LES. *Television: The Business Behind the Box*. New York: Harcourt, Brace, Jovanovich, 1974.

BURLINGAME, ROGER. *Don't Let Them Scare You: The Life and Times of Elmer Davis*. Philadelphia and New York: J. B. Lippincott, 1961.

CARTLAND, FERNANDO G. *Southern Heroes, or The Friends in Wartime*. Reprint:

originally issued in 1895. New York: Garland Publishing, Library of War and Peace, 1972.

CASTLEMAN, HARRY and PODRAZIK, WALTER J. *Watching TV: Four Decades of American Television*. New York: McGraw-Hill, 1982.

CAUTE, DAVID. *The Great Fear: The Anti-Communist Purge Under Truman and Eisenhower*. New York: Simon & Schuster, 1978.

COGLEY, JOHN. *Report on Blacklisting: Radio and Television*. New York: The Fund for the Republic, Inc., 1956.

COOK, FRED. *The Nightmare Decade*. New York: Random House, 1971.

CROSBY, JOHN. *Out of the Blue*. New York: Simon & Schuster, 1952.

DAVIS, ELMER. *But We Were Born Free*. Indianapolis and New York: Bobbs-Merrill, 1952, 1953.

DAVIS, ELMER. *By Elmer Davis*. Edited by Robert Lloyd Davis. Indianapolis and New York: Bobbs-Merrill, 1964.

EDMONDS, HELEN G. *The Negro and Fusion Politics in North Carolina, 1894–1901*. Chapel Hill: The University of North Carolina Press, 1951.

ELDER, ROBERT E. *The Information Machine: The United States Information Agency and American Foreign Policy*. Syracuse, New York: Syracuse University Press, 1968.

EWALD, WILLIAM BRAGG, JR. *Eisenhower the President: Crucial Days, 1951–60*. Englewood Cliffs, New Jersey: Prentice-Hall, 1981.

———. *Who Killed Joe McCarthy?* New York: Simon & Schuster, 1984.

FALL, BERNARD B. *Hell in a Very Small Place*. Philadelphia: Lippincott, 1966.

FAULK, JOHN HENRY. *Fear on Trial*. New York: Simon & Schuster, 1964.

FLANNERY, HARRY. *Assignment to Berlin*. New York: Alfred A. Knopf, 1942.

FRANKFURTER, FELIX. *Diaries*. Edited by Joseph P. Lash. New York: Norton, 1975.

FRIENDLY, FRED W. *Due to Circumstances Beyond Our Control*. New York: Random House, 1967.

GALBRAITH, JOHN KENNETH. *Ambassador's Journal: A Personal Account of the Kennedy Years*. Boston: Houghton, Mifflin, 1969.

GOODMAN, WALTER. *The Committee*. New York: Farrar, Straus & Giroux, 1968.

GORHAM, MAURICE. *Sound and Fury*. London: Percival Marshall, 1948.

HALBERSTAM, DAVID. *The Best and the Brightest*. New York: Random House, 1969, 1971, 1972.

———. *The Making of a Quagmire*. New York: Random House, 1965.

———. *The Powers That Be*. New York: Alfred A. Knopf, 1979.

HIGGINS, MARGUERITE. *Our Vietnam Nightmare*. New York: Harper & Row, 1965.

HILSMAN, ROGER. *To Move a Nation*. New York; Doubleday, 1967.

HARRIMAN, W. AVERELL AND ABEL, ELIE. *Special Envoy to Churchill and Stalin, 1941–46*. New York; Random House, 1975.

HOWE, QUINCEY. *Ashes of Victory: World War II and its Aftermath*. New York: Simon & Schuster, 1972.

HOYT, EDWIN P. *The Palmer Raids, 1919–1920*. New York: The Seabury Press, 1968.

JULIAN, JOSEPH. *This Was Radio: A personal memoir*. New York: Viking Press, Richard Seaver Books, 1975.

KALTENBORN, H. V. *I Broadcast the Crisis*. New York: Random House, 1938.

KENDRICK, ALEXANDER. *Prime Time: The Life of Edward R. Murrow*. Boston: Little, Brown, 1969.

KENNAN, GEORGE F. *Memoires, 1950–1963*. Boston: Atlantic-Little, Brown, 1972.

KOLLEK, TEDDY and AMOS. *For Jerusalem: A Life by Teddy Kollek*. New York: Random House, 1978.

LATTIMORE, OWEN. *Ordeal by Slander*. Boston: Little, Brown, 1950.

LAWRENCE, BILL. *Six Presidents, Too Many Wars*. New York: Saturday Review Press, 1972.

LILIENTHAL, DAVID. *Journals*. New York: Harper & Row, Vol. 2, 1964, Vol. 3, 1966.

LOUCHHEIM, KATIE. *By the Political Sea*. New York: Doubleday, 1970.

MACVANE, JOHN. *On the Air in World War II*. New York: William Morrow, 1979.

MANCHESTER, WILLIAM. *American Caesar: Douglas MacArthur, 1880–1964*. Boston: Little, Brown, 1978.

MARTIN, JOHN BARTLOW. *Adlai Stevenson of Illinois*. New York: Doubleday, 1976.

MECKLIN, JOHN. *Mission in Torment*. New York: Doubleday, 1965.

MIALL, LEONARD, ED. *Richard Dimbleby, Broadcaster*. London: BBC, 1966.

McKIEVER, CHARLES I. *Slavery and Emigration of North Carolina Friends*. Murfreesboro: Johnson Publishing Co., 1970.

Mount Vernon Herald. "Skagit County." Mount Vernon, Washington: Herald Publishing Co., September 1, 1921.

MURROW, EDWARD R. *This is London*. New York: Simon & Schuster, 1941.

———. *In Search of Light: The Broadcasts of Edward R. Murrow (1938–61)*. Edited by Edward Bliss, Jr., New York: Alfred A. Knopf, 1967. The manuscripts of Murrow's postwar broadcasts, and many wartime broadcasts, may be found in the Murrow Collection. The interested reader, however, is referred to the classic published collection listed above.

———, and Friendly, Fred W., eds. *See It Now: A Selection in Text and Pictures*. New York: Simon & Schuster, 1955.

NEAL, STEVE. *The Eisenhowers: Reluctant Dynasty*. New York: Doubleday, 1978.

NEWMAN, DAISY. *A Procession of Friends*. Garden City: Garden City, 1972.

NICHOLSON, HAROLD. *Diaries: The War Years, 1939–1945*. Edited by Nigel Nicolson. New York: Atheneum, 1967.

NIZER, LOUIS. *The Jury Returns*. New York: Doubleday, 1960.

O'KEEFE, PATRICK. *Greensboro, a Pictorial History*. Norfolk: Donning Co., 1977.

PALEY, WILLIAM S. *As It Happened: A Memoir*. New York: Doubleday, 1979.

PANTER-DOWNES, MOLLIE. *London War Notes 1939–1945*. Edited by William Shawn. London: Longman, 1972.

PEARSON, DREW. *Diaries, 1949–1959*. Edited by Tyler Abell. New York: Holt, Rinehart and Winston, 1974.

The Pentagon Papers. As Published by *The New York Times*. Written by Neil Sheehan, Hedrick Smith, E. W. Kenworthy and Fox Butterfield. New York: Quadrangle Books, 1971.

———. U.S. Department of Defense. The Senator Gravel Edition. Boston: Beacon Press, 1971.

PHILLIPS, CABELL. *From the Crash to the Blitz*. *The New York Times* Chronicle of American Life. New York: Macmillan, 1969.

REEVES, THOMAS C. *The Life and Times of Joe McCarthy*. New York: Stein & Day, 1982.

REID, ROBERT A. *Puget Sound and Western Washington*. Seattle: Robert A. Reid, 1912.

RENSHAW, PATRICK. *The Wobblies*. Garden City: Doubleday, 1967.

ROBERTSON, BEN. *I Saw England*. New York: Alfred A. Knopf, 1942.

ROVERE, RICHARD. *Senator Joe McCarthy*. New York: Harcourt, Brace & World, 1959.

ROWAN, JAMES. *The I.W.W. in the Lumber Industry*. Seattle: Shorey Publications, undated.

SALINGER, PIERRE. *With Kennedy*. New York: Doubleday, 1966.

SCHECHTER, A. A., AND ANTHONY, EDWARD. *I Live on Air*. New York: Frederick A. Stokes Co., 1941.

SCHLESINGER, ARTHUR M., JR., *A Thousand Days*. Boston: Houghton, Mifflin, 1965.

SCOTT, JOHN ANTHONY. *Hard Trials on My Way: Slavery and the Struggle Against It, 1800–1860*. The Living History Library. New York: Alfred A. Knopf, 1974.

SEBRING, AL. *Skagit County Illustrated*. Mount Vernon: (no publisher listed), 1902.

SEVAREID, ERIC. *Not So Wild a Dream*. New York: Alfred A. Knopf, 1946.

SHAPLEN, ROBERT. *The Lost Revolution: U.S. in Vietnam 1946–1966*. New York: Harper & Row, 1965.

SHERWOOD, ROBERT E. *Roosevelt and Hopkins: An Intimate History*. New York: Harper & Brothers, 1948.

SHIRER, WILLIAM L. *Berlin Diary*. New York: Alfred A. Knopf, 1941.

———. *The Nightmare Decade*. Boston: Little, Brown, 1985.

———. *The Rise and Fall of the Third Reich*. New York: Simon & Schuster, 1959.

SIOUSSAT, HELEN. *Mikes Don't Bite*. Introduction by Elmer Davis. New York: L. B. Fischer, 1943.

SMITH, GADDIS. *Dean Acheson*. New York: Cooper Square, 1972.

SMITH, R. FRANKLIN. *Edward R. Murrow: The War Years*. Kalamazoo, Michigan: New Issues Press, Institute of Public Affairs, Western Michigan University, 1978.

SMITH, RICHARD NORTON. *Thomas E. Dewey and His Time*. New York: Simon & Schuster, 1982.

SOCIETY OF FRIENDS. *The Society of Friends in North Carolina 1672–1953*. Guilford College, North Carolina: Guilford College, 1953.

SORENSEN, THEODORE C. *Kennedy*. New York: Harper & Row, 1965.

SORENSEN, THOMAS C. *The World War: The Story of American Propaganda*. New York: Harper & Row, 1968.

STEEL, RONALD. *Walter Lippmann and the American Century*. Atlantic-Little, Brown, 1980.

STEVENS, GEORGE. *Speak for Yourself, John: The Life of John Mason Brown*. New York: Viking Press, 1974.

STOCKARD, SALLIE W. *History of Guilford County, North Carolina*. Knoxville: Gaut-Ogden Co., 1902.

SWING, RAYMOND. *Good Evening: A Professional Memoir*. New York: Harcourt, Brace & World, 1964.

SWIFT, JOHN. *Adventures in Vision*. London: John Lehmann, 1950.

TEICHMANN, HOWARD. *Smart Aleck: The Wit, World and Life of Alexander Woollcott*. New York: William Morrow, 1976.

TERKEL, STUDS. *Hard Times: An Oral History of the Great Depression in America*. New York: Pantheon, 1970.

WEEKS, STEPHEN B. *Southern Quakers and Slavery: A Study in Institutional History*. Baltimore: The Johns Hopkins Press, 1896. Reprinted by the Humanities Press, Atlantic Highlands, N.J.

WHITE, PAUL. *News on the Air*. New York: Harcourt, Brace & Co., 1947.

WYLIE, MAX. *Radio Writing*. New York: Farrar & Rinehart, 1939.

———. *Radio and Television Writing*. New York: Rinehart & Co., 1949.

GENERAL SOURCES

BILSKI, SR., THEODORE J. "A Descriptive Study: Edward R. Murrow's Contribution to Electronic Journalism." Ph.D. dissertation. Case Western Reserve University, 1971. Ann Arbor, Michigan: University Microfilms.

BROWN, VANESSA. "Edward R. Murrow: A Remembrance." Unpublished memoir, undated.

COLUMBINE, CBS, INC. "The Way We've Been . . . And Are." Vol. 2, No. 7, April/May 1974. Commemorative issue of CBS house organ: 1927–1974.

GHIGLIONE, LOREN. *Don Hollenbeck: (Broad)casting the first stone*. Perspective on the Press, *The Evening News*, Southbridge, Massachusetts, undated.

KURALT, CHARLES. "Edward R. Murrow." *North Carolina Historical Review* Vol. XLVIII, no. 2, April, 1971).

LAURENCE DUGGAN. *In Memoriam*. Overbrook Press (private printing), 1949.

MURROW, CHARLES HARLAN, compiler. "The Genealogy of the Murrow Family." Typescript, undated, possibly 1948.

McLAUGHLIN, MARTIN M. "Political Processes in American National Student Organizations." Master's thesis, undated.

NEBLETT, THOMAS F. "Youth Movements in the United States." Annals of the American Academy of Political and Social Science, November 1937.

SEWARD, JAMES M. "Network Operations for News Broadcasting." CBS war coverage memorandum/booklet, August 8, 1944.

"Those Murrow Boys." A family memoir written by members of Roscoe and Ethel Murrow's church, Bellingham, Washington, undated, possibly 1944.

WERSHBA, JOSEPH. "The Broadcaster and the Senator." Memoir, manuscript, undated. Later published in condensed form in The *New York Times Magazine*, March 4, 1979, under the title, "Murrow vs. McCarthy: See It Now."

WILLIAMS, CHESTER S. "To Casey Murrow: Memories of Your Father." Manuscript, unpublished, 1965.

WOOLLEY, THOMAS RUSSELL, JR. "A Rhetorical Study: The Radio Speaking of Edward R. Murrow." Ph.D. dissertation. Northwestern University, 1957.

YAEGER, MURRAY. "An Analysis of Edward R. Murrow's Television Program." Master's thesis. State University of Iowa, 1956. (Two dissertations by contemporary observers of the Murrow programs.)

ACKNOWLEDGMENTS

Every biography is to some extent a mosaic. Over the past ten and more years, many helpful hands have assisted me in the assemblage. In numerous instances, it would take a small essay to express my true appreciation. For any that I may have inadvertently omitted, I ask indulgence. Fact-gathering was a combination of interviewing and archival research. Friends and associates of Murrow put their time, their memories, and often their private papers, at my disposal. Interviews were frequently conducted over a period of years, and I am grateful for the patience and helpfulness shown when inevitably, I came back with more questions.

First and foremost, I wish to extend my thanks to Mrs. Edward R. Murrow, for unfailing help and generosity over the years; for sustained cooperation, opening up to me her private papers, and those of her husband, as well as family memorabilia; and for permission to quote from letters and broadcast scripts. For her unquestioning kindness and encouragement, and for that of the Murrows' son, Charles Casey Murrow, the author is abidingly grateful.

I also wish to express gratitude and appreciation to the late James M. Seward, and to his family. It was Jim Seward, a longtime official of CBS and executor of the Murrow estate, who first opened the doors for me to Murrow's friends, family and associates, and who, with his wife Ina, shared with me their recollections of Murrow and the creative early days of CBS Radio. Jim Seward will be sorely missed.

Special thanks also go to Joseph and Shirley Wershba of CBS, two great newspeople, for their help and support over the years, and to Rosalind (Mrs. Bill) Downs.

The late Joshua Edgar Murrow and his wife, Hazel Richardson Murrow, provided insight into Ed Murrow's early life and family background. Edgar Murrow, interviewed in his eighty-sixth year, was an oral historian in the grand tradition, a link with a rich and vital past. The late Dewey Joshua Murrow, Ed Murrow's older brother, provided a colorful depiction of their boyhood in the Pacific Northwest.

Thanks are due also to Chester S. Williams, for sharing memories of the NSFA years and other aspects of his lifelong friendship with Murrow, and for granting access to his private papers. Thanks go also to Stephen P. Duggan, son of the IIE founder, for sharing memories of Murrow's IIE years and for arranging access to the IIE archives.

Archives are the backbone of this work and grateful acknowledgment is hereby made to Barbara Boyce, Associate Librarian at the Fletcher School of Law and Diplomacy, Tufts University, housing the Murrow Collection, with many thanks for hours of help and friendship. Thanks go as well to Eleanor G. Horan, the first Curator of the Murrow Collection.

Special thanks are due particularly to the Director of the Mass Communications History Center of the State Historical Society of Wisconsin: Janice L. O'Connell, a pearl without price and Wisconsin's gift to the journalism historian, and who guided my steps through one of the true treasure houses of the mass media.

In England, Ed Murrow's BBC friends opened their homes and gave freely of their time and their memories. BBC correspondent and later historian Leonard Miall arranged for my use of the treasured BBC Written Archives, documenting Ed Murrow's London years. One cannot do better than to paraphrase Murrow himself, in thanking the following for hospitality, information, and inspiration: Jill and Michael Balkwill, Robin Duff, Cecilia Reeves Gillie, Grace Wyndham Goldie, Sir Hugh Greene, who also granted access to his files and the diaries marking his tenure as BBC Director-General, the late Richard Marriott, Leonard and Sally Miall, Pat and Olive Smithers, Godfrey Talbot, Sir Lindsay Wellington. Thanks also go to Michael Tracey who, though midway through his own biography of Sir Hugh Greene, generously shared archival material with me.

I also wish to thank Patrick L. Ducker, Chief Assistant, Talks and Documentaries Radio, for extending the hospitality of Broadcasting House, and the BBC Library. At the BBC Written Archives Centre at Caversham Park, Reading, Mrs. Jacqueline Kavanagh, Written Archives Officer, was of unfailing assistance, guiding me through an ocean of material, acting on requests made frequently on short notice. For her help, and that of the knowledgeable staff of the BBC Written Archives, in documenting this important period of Murrow's life, the author is grateful. David Griffith, researching his own project at the Archives, was also most generous in indicating avenues of inquiry.

Grateful acknowledgment is also made to Murrow's two London friends, Lord Robert Boothby, and Lord Sidney Bernstein, for sharing their recollections and, in Lord Bernstein's case, private correspondence. The author also wishes to thank Sir John Colville, wartime Private Secretary to Winston Churchill, for sharing his recollections of Murrow at 10 Downing Street.

Many who were at CBS between 1935 and 1961 provided help and information above and beyond the call of duty. My thanks, therefore, to the following:

From the CBS news staff, wartime and postwar: Mary Marvin Breckinridge (Mrs. Jefferson Patterson), Ned Calmer, Lou Cioffi, Charles Collingwood, William J. Dunn, Bernard Eismann, Joseph C. Harsch, Richard C. Hottelet, Larry LeSueur, Edward P. Morgan, Robert Pierpoint, David Schoenbrun, William L. Shirer, Howard K. Smith, Robert Trout. Best thanks also go to Benedicte (Mrs. Howard K.) Smith.

From the staffs of *See It Now*, *CBS Reports*, and *Edward R. Murrow with the News*: Fred W. Friendly, Jack Beck, Edward Bliss, Jr., Mili Lerner Bonsignori, Dorothy McDonough Corbett, Edward Jones, Gaby Levenson, Charles Mack, William McClure, Natalie Foster Paine, Leo Rossi, John Schultz, Edmund Scott, Joseph Wershba, Palmer Williams. Thanks also go to Barbara (Mrs. Edmund) Scott.

Others who shared CBS recollections include: William S. Paley, Dr. Frank Stanton, Ralph F. Colin; Danforth Lansbury Bates, Herbert Brodkin, John Henry Faulk, William Fineshriber, Jr., Don Hewitt, Howard Kany, James U. Lavenstein, Elmer Lower, Kidder Meade, Sig Mickelson, Adrian Murphy, Edwin Newman, Daniel T. O'Shea, Lee Otis, Joseph H. Ream, Herbert I. Rosenthal, Richard S. Salant, Robert Lewis Shayon, Helen Sioussat, William J. Small, Robert Skedgell, James Davidson Taylor.

From outside CBS: Charles R. Allen, Jr., Frank Altschul, Dr. Alvan Barach, Edward O. ("Ted") Berkman, Connie Bessie, Simon Michael Bessie, Vanessa Brown, Mrs. Arthur Bunker, William J. Butler, Joseph Cadden, John Donovan of the Academy of Senior Professionals, Eckerd College, St. Petersburg, Florida, Morris Ernst, Dr. Robert Foster, Frank Gervasi, Georgia Gibbs, Jack Gould, J. G. Gude, Richard Heffner, Paul Heller, Hester Hensell, Dorothy Hart Paley (Mrs. Walter) Hirshon, Harold R. Isaacs, Joseph Julian, John MacVane, Sam McSeveny, Ann Marr, Drew Middleton, Helen Kirkpatrick Milbank, Adele Gutman Nathan, Reuben Nathan, the Reverend C. Herbert Oliver, Supreme Court Justice Lewis F. Powell, Wilmott Ragsdale, Alan Reitman, James Reston, Harrison Salisbury, Gwyn Seward Singer, Charles Siepmann, Howard Teichmann, Marietta Tree, Mary and Edward Warburg, Westerman Whillock, William Worthy, Jr.

For sharing their recollections of Murrow at the USIA, the author is grateful to the following: Burnett Anderson, McGeorge Bundy, Roger Hilsman, Katie Louchheim Klopfer, Henry Loomis, Stanley Plesent, Hans Tuch, Donald M. Wilson.

Thanks go to CBS for its generous and unconditional granting of access to program material, and use of its news library. In that connection, I'd like to thank Robert Chandler, CBS, for arranging that access. Long before there was a Museum of Broadcasting, the CBS News Reference Library under its then-Director, May Dowell, and Roberta Hadley, its Assistant Director, provided me with tapes and disc recordings of the earlier Murrow and Murrow-Friendly programs, and made contemporary archival material available to me. I also wish to thank Laura Kapnick, the present Director of the CBS News Reference Library, and Carole Parnes, Manager of Industry Information, for their invaluable assistance in the latter stages of my research. Special thanks also go to Kris Slavik of CBS Photos; to Samuel T. Suratt; to Betsy Broesamle and the late Dorothy Boyle of CBS Program Information, for access to program logs; to Paul Vanderbeck and John Buchanan in the CBS News Documentary Library for access to films and the original cutting room notes and unedited transcripts of *See It Now* and *CBS Reports*. Thanks go, too, to Ron Simon, of the Museum of Broadcasting, for providing needed videotapes.

For help in other research areas, I thank the following:

William J. Butler, of Butler, Jablow and Geller, for access to the transcripts of *Joseph Julian v. American Business Consultants, Inc.*, and Allan Adler, Legislative Counsel, Center for National Security Studies, for much-needed advice on proper requesting procedure under the Freedom of Information Act.

At The New York *Times*: Alice Klingsberg, Archivist.

At the North Carolina Collection, University of North Carolina at Chapel Hill: Jeff Hicks. At the Southern Historical Collection, University of North Carolina at Chapel Hill: Dr. Richard A. Shrader, Brenda Marks Eagles. Also thanks to the Director and staff of the North Carolina State Archives, Raleigh, North Carolina.

At the Institute of International Education: Nancy Harringon, Marjorie Beckles, Ann Gaynor. At the New York Public Library, Manuscript and Archives Division: Edith Wynner, for help with the Emergency Committee Papers.

At the Franklin D. Roosevelt Library, Hyde Park, New York: Donald B. Schewe, Assistant Director; also Mr. Parks, Ms. Raub, Mr. Ferris, Mr. Teichman, Mr. Renovich, Mr. Marshall.

At the John F. Kennedy Library, Columbia Point, Boston, Massachusetts: Suzanne K. Forbes, Archivist. Thanks also go to Judith Kaocky, Archivist, Office of Presidential Libraries, and to Susan Garrow.

I am most grateful to the USIA for access to Murrow's papers and for the Agency's hospitality during the times I was in Washington. I'd like especially to thank Vivian Light, Document Declassification Officer for her efficiency, helpfulness and unwavering good cheer in the face of a long, drawnout project. I'd also like to thank Charles Jones, Jr., FOIA/PA Access to Information Officer and Coordinator, for his many instances of help, and Martin Manning of the USIA library. Best thanks also go to William LaSalle, Chief, Executive Secretariat, and Ronald Post, Deputy Chief, Executive Secretariat.

Finally, I would like to extend personal thanks to Fabio Coen, who believed in this project from the start, to my agent Theron Raines, and to my publisher and editor, Lawrence Freundlich, for faith over the years, and unflagging encouragement.

INDEX

773

Loyalty oath
  at CBS, 361–64, 474, 502
  in Harrison, N.Y., 391–92
  at University of California, 336

Macadam, Ivison, 35, 47, 109
MacArthur, Douglas, 345, 359
McBride, Mary Margaret, 408
McCarran, Pat, 328, 390, 398
McCarran-Walter Immigration Act, 478,
  479
McCarthy, Joseph Raymond, 331–40,
  382–83
  death of, 513–14
  Eisenhower and, 388–89, 404, 415,
    428, 431, 444, 468–69, 730–31 n.24
  last years of, 503, 513
  and ERM, 406, 443, 447, 448–50
  ERM on, 331, 332–33, 370, 382, 401,
    428, 433–34, 438–39, 471
  popularity and public support for, 349,
    426, 439, 444
  reelected (1952), 388–89
  See It Now on, 369–70, 382, 390, 400,
    410, 428, 429–39, 447; McCarthy's
    reply to, 447, 448–50 (responses to,
    449, 451–56); responses to, 439–43
  Senate and, 434, 445; censure, 382,
    471
  television and, 404
  Truman and, 369–70, 414–15
McCarthyism, 426
  and foreign relations, 409, 427
  ERM on, 331, 409
  radio and, 409
  Senate and, 471
  strength of (1952), 388
  and Truman, 370, 415
  and Watergate, 438
McClellan, John, 400, 447
McClure, Bill, 377–78, 472, 496, 569–70
McCormick, Col. Robert, 452
McDonald, James G., 62–63
McDonough, Dorothy, 307
McGrory, Mary, 654, 700
Mack, Charles, 351, 377, 393, 394, 416,
  420, 424, 425, 463, 472–73, 509, 594
MacLeish, Archibald, 203, 205, 283
McLeod, Scott, 448, 480
McSeveny, Sam, 451–52
MacVane, John, 197
"Main Street: USSR" (proposed CBS TV
  program), 510

Mann, Thomas, 63
Manning, Paul, 191
March, The (film), 677, 691
Marriott, Richard, 102, 108–9, 123, 154
Marshall, George, 300, 389, 409, 427
Marshall Plan, 298, 326
Martin, Kingsley, 238, 254
Martin, Robert, 327
Masaryk, Jan, 127, 224, 237, 299
  death of, 304
  and ERM, 129–30, 184, 304–5
"Mayflower Doctrine," 277–78
Meade, Kidder, 552, 554, 575–76
Mecklin, John, 665–66, 667–69, 670,
  673–74, 680, 681, 691
Meet the Press (CBS TV series), 654
Meet Uncle Sam (BBC radio series), 190
Mickelson, Siegfried ("Sig")
  as Director of News and Public Af-
    fairs, 475–78
  as Director of Television News and
    Public Affairs, 373, 528
  fired (1961), 620
  and ERM, 374, 525–26, 528, 534, 541,
    552, 561–62, 564–65, 566, 602–3,
    609
  and See It Now, 353, 373–74, 494
Mid-Atlantic Parliament (proposed CBS
  TV series), 517, 588, 590, 593
Middleton, Drew, 161, 172, 186, 227,
  340
Migrant laborers. See "Harvest of
  Shame"
Millikan, Robert A., 52
Ministry of Information (MOI, Gt. Brit.),
  144, 150, 151
Minow, Newton, 641
Missouri River floods (1952), 386
Monckton, Sir Walter, 174
Morgenthau, Henry, 216
Morsbach, Adolf, 56
  death of, 61–62
Moscow Summer School, 58–59, 62
  FBI and, 457, 459–60, 626
  Graham and, 336
  Hearst on, 71–72
  McCarthy and, 415–16, 420–21, 429,
    443–44, 447, 448, 455
  and ERM's passport application, 481
  termination of, 76
Mowrer, Edgar Ansel, 80–81, 117, 119
Mundt, Karl, 318, 319
Munich accord (1938), 128–29